M000158498

THREE LIVES

(The Book of Three Lives)

Translated, interpreted and compiled by Martin Palmer,
Kwok Man-ho and Kerry Brown
With the assistance of Li Fung Chi and Fiona Thomas

DURHAM COUNTY LIBRARY
ACC. No. 3341618
CLASS No. 133.9

CENTURY

LONDON · MELBOURNE · AUCKLAND · JOHANNESBURG

A Rider Book published in the Century Paperback Series
in 1987 by Century Hutchinson Ltd,
Brookmount House, 62–65 Chandos Place, Covent Garden,
London WC2N 4NW

Century Hutchinson Australia (Pty) Ltd,
PO Box 496, 16–22 Church Street, Hawthorn, Victoria 3122,
Australia

Century Hutchinson New Zealand Ltd,
PO Box 40-086, Glenfield, Auckland 10,
New Zealand

Century Hutchinson South Africa (Pty) Ltd,
PO Box 337, Bergvlei 2012, South Africa

© International Consultancy on Religion, Education and Culture 1987

Set by Avocet Ltd, Bicester, Oxfordshire
Printed and bound in Great Britain by
Richard Clay Ltd, The Chaucer Press, Bungay, Suffolk

British Library Cataloguing in Publication Data

Palmer, Martin
    Three lives: discover who you were, are and will
    be with this practical Chinese guide to
    reincarnation.
    1. Divination – China
    I. Title   II. Kwok, Man-ho   III. Brown, Kerry
    133.3'0951   BF1773.2.C5

ISBN 0 7126 1630 6

Contents

Acknowledgements

At one stage in preparing this book, many of our friends and colleagues began to wonder if the title, *Three Lives*, actually referred to how long it was going to take us to compile the edition you now hold! That it has not taken three generations to complete is due to the enormous help and advice which we received from many quarters. Our thanks go first to the diviners in Hong Kong, Macau and Taiwan who opened the doors into this most revealing and yet most difficult of books. With charity, devotion and much laughter they taught us how to read the book and how to see its value. Words can never express what we owe to these wise people.

Secondly, our thanks to the inner team of Li Fung Chi and Fiona Thomas, who worked alongside us turning our Chinglish into English, hunting out data and tracking down obscure Chinese terms.

Thirdly, our thanks to the wider ICOREC team of Sarah Waldram, Barbara Cousins, Joanne O'Brien and Pallavi Mavani, who forced us to be clearer, more consistent and not to give up!

Finally, a thank you to our friends and families, to Sue Hogg and Oliver Caldecott, our editors, and to the staff of the Manchester Polytechnic and the School of African and Oriental Studies, London, who so facilitated our research and meetings.

May you reap the rewards of your kindness in your next birth – if you can!

Martin Palmer and Kwok Man-ho
Manchester
7th day of the 9th month in the Ping Yin year
10 October 1986

Introduction

Within everyone there is a natural desire to wonder what the future holds. Astrological predictions, horoscopes and all manner of divinations are to be found in every culture throughout the world. Most people are familiar with the Western horoscopes based on the stars and the twelve signs of the zodiac. Indeed, many people think that they know something about Chinese horoscopes, popular versions of which are fairly commonplace. Nothing new to be expected here, so one might imagine. This is exactly what the Western members of our team thought, when suddenly we were introduced by our Chinese colleagues to perhaps the most extraordinary book we have ever encountered – the *Three Lives*.

This book, available throughout the Chinese world, is held in tremendous respect by even the most Westernized Chinese. Chinese men will probably have had a *Three Lives* reading cast for them at birth, at the request of their parents. Many will still have tucked away somewhere a copy of their reading. Few, if any, ordinary Chinese will know how the reading was made, but all will regard it as having a special authority and status.

What is so special about the *Three Lives*? Quite simply, it claims not only to tell you in broad terms what your present life is like and how it will pan out, but also to give details of your previous life and of your next rebirth. It is the book of your current three lives – your last one, your present one and your future one.

To the best of our knowledge there is no other divination book which makes such a claim. Certainly in Chinese there is only the *Three Lives*, and a most extraordinary book it is, as we shall see. While ordinary Chinese people would be hard-pressed to name any major work on astrology or physiognomy, although they might be familiar with fortune-telling based on these systems, the *Three Lives* is very well known. It is therefore all the more surprising that we have been unable to find a single reference to this book, the beliefs contained in it or its influence in any Western work concerned with Chinese religion.

The book itself presents a wonderful insight into Chinese folk religion, with its powerful and harmonious fusion of Confucianism, Taoism and Buddhism. Most of the Chinese religious books that have become known in the West are the formal texts of one or other of the great faiths of China. Much of the material on divination and horoscopes which has become popular in the West is not drawn from actual texts but from interpretations made by particular individuals and as such has become detached from its cultural setting. Here, in the *Three Lives*, we have a folk classic which not only introduces us to a number of unique divination systems, but also captures in its language and imagery the full flavour of traditional Chinese folk religion.

WHAT IS THIS BOOK?

The *Three Lives* consists of nearly fifty charts and sets of predictions, based on the eight characters of your horoscope (see p. 23), which tell you about your past, your present and your future lives. Traditionally, a *Three Lives* reading is made for a boy shortly after birth. This reading, written on red paper in black ink, will then be kept by the family and resorted to on special occasions, milestones such as choosing a career, getting married and the like. Formerly readings were not done for girls at birth, although they could obtain one later on in life. The readings were made by someone skilled in interpreting the *Three Lives*. In the past this was usually a 'wandering' or 'wild' monk. Today it is likely to be a Taoist nun or priest, or possibly a fortune-teller with a stall in a Buddhist or Taoist-Buddhist temple. The casting of a *Three Lives* reading takes some time and may involve a number of sessions, either with the subject visiting the fortune-teller at a temple or the fortune-teller coming to the subject's home. There are only a few people skilled in casting a *Three Lives* reading outside China and Southeast Asia, but children of the Chinese diaspora can have a horoscope cast for them in Hong Kong or Taiwan. All that is required is that the fortune-teller has the relevant eight horoscope characters, two for the subject's year of birth, two for the month, two for the day and two for the hour. From these eight characters the reading can be done.

The *Three Lives* is to be found on sale throughout the Chinese world, though, rather like the Chinese Almanac – the T'ung Shu[1] – few people would be able to understand or use more than a part of it. For our version we have chosen the most commonly available Chinese edition, which is also the oldest. It was first printed in the 53rd year of the Ch'ing dynasty emperor Ch'ien Lung (1736–92 CE*), which means it dates from the Western year of 1789, and is illustrated with wonderful, vivid woodcuts in traditional Chinese style. The Chinese edition also contains various secondary bits and pieces which have attached themselves to the main text, and these we have discarded.

As we shall see, Chinese fortune-telling in general, and this system in particular, does not produce the final, ultimate version of what your life will be like. That remains in your hands. Rather, it 'forth-tells' what is likely to happen if you continue along your present lines. Chinese fate is not fatalism. As we shall discover, the fusion of Taoist belief, Confucianist ethics and Buddhist teaching has produced one of the most interesting and flexible systems of divination imaginable. *Three Lives* is without doubt one of the most unusual and interesting of the resulting books.

HOW OLD IS THE BOOK?

One of the most surprising things about the book is its age. We are used to Chinese books being of quite extraordinary antiquity. The Histories contain material which dates from before 1500 BCE. The *I Ching* dates in part from 1000 BCE. K'ung Fu-tzu (Confucius) was writing in the fourth century BCE. Much of the most beautiful poetry of China was composed during the T'ang and Sung dynasties (618–1279 CE). Even the manuals of physiognomy, such as the *Ma-i*, date from around the twelfth century CE. In addition there are books which claim to have been written or originated by great figures of the utmost antiquity. The Chinese Almanac traces itself back to the semi-historical, semi-mythological figure of Emperor Yao, who is supposed to have reigned around 2260 BCE. Whether or not the *Tao Te Ching* was written by Lao Tzu in the sixth century BCE is still hotly disputed, but other books which purport to be written by ancient masters can still lay true claim to great age. For instance, the *Hua Hu Ching*, which claims also to be written by Lao Tzu, actually dates from the T'ang dynasty (618–906 CE). Indeed the practice of claiming some great teacher or mystic as author is so common that even specific sections of the Almanac do so, such as 'Old Mr Chou's Book of Auspicious and Inauspicious Dreams'. Old Mr Chou is in fact Chou Kung, the Duke of Chou, who is reputed to have assisted in compiling the *I Ching* and to have lived *c.* 1000 BCE.

*CE = Common Era, equivalent to the Christian AD; BCE = Before Common Era, equivalent to the Christian BC.

We might expect, therefore, that the *Three Lives* would either be of similar antiquity or at least claim to have been originated by some great figure of the past – but far from it. The earliest date we can ascribe to it (by means of discussion with those who use it professionally as well as from historical research) is somewhere around 1500 CE. Indeed, most of our research points to a date during the decline of the Ming dynasty and the coming of the Ch'ing, *c.* 1550–1650 CE. The earliest specific date which is known is that of the end inscription in the edition we have used, namely 1789 CE. Nor does the book make any claims to have been written by Yellow Emperors, or Lao Tzu, Chang Tao-ling, or any other such figure from the past. The book has obviously been able to stand firmly upon its own credentials and the need has not been felt to claim either an antiquity it does not have or an originator it never knew.

So what are the origins of this book and who was its author, or authors? To this question we can only give rather patchy answers. While there is certain internal evidence which points to the book's various sections being written down around 1550–1650, it is through the actual group who are credited with composing it that we get the clearest indication of its likely date. For the authors of this book belonged to a curious group known collectively as the wandering monks. Usually composed of estranged Buddhist monks who had been expelled or had absented themselves from their monasteries and its laws, they also often contained Taoist monks and priests who toured the countryside. These wandering monks had broken away from the formal structures of their respective faiths and, either through a sense of mission, a desire for travel, rebelliousness or for other less reputable reasons, had taken to the road, earning their living from selling their religious and magical skills. Sometimes saintly, often not so, they were strange figures and crop up regularly in novels of the Ming and Ch'ing dynasties. For instance, Cao Xuequin, in *The Story of the Stone*, sums up their style well: 'One day in the midst of its lamentings, it [a magic stone] saw a monk and a Taoist approaching from a great distance, each of them remarkable for certain eccentricities of manner and appearance.'[2]

The wandering monks were often treated very warily by the orthodox monks and monasteries, and while they might get food and accommodation overnight, it was up to the monastery's guestmaster to vet each wandering monk who came to the door. Thus the wandering monk often had to make a living from the payments and gifts which he could elicit from the ordinary people of the villages and towns through which he passed. The easiest way of doing this was by performing certain religious or semi-religious acts. One of the reasons why these monks were frequently banned from the orthodox monasteries was because they practised in public certain skills or 'arts' which, although acceptable as part of a monk's private study, were not to be used either for profit or among the ordinary people. Foremost amongst these was divination.

In the rules and regulations of Chinese Buddhist monasteries it was expressly forbidden to practise divination as a means of earning a livelihood.

Certain practices that were forbidden to the sangha [the community of monks] as a livelihood could be dabbled in as an avocation: for example, medicine, divination, astrology and the 'reading' of faces. Although these practices were not considered so heterodox as communicating with spirits (in which no self-respecting Buddhist monk would engage), still they could not be carried on for gain. This was precisely what was done by 'vagabond monks', sometimes with a conscious charlatanism that brought discredit on the whole sangha.[3]

The pattern from which the *Three Lives* sprang is fairly clear to see, for it continues to this day in Hong Kong and Taiwan. A Buddhist monk, skilled in the five arts of Chinese fortune-telling (see below), magic, and so on, will have studied them for many years purely out of personal interest. He may then take an assistant to whom he imparts some of his private knowledge. If this assistant is a layman, then he might use this knowledge to earn a living as a fortune-teller. That is of no real concern to the master monk. However, if a young monk, perhaps one who has been placed in the monastery by his family and not at his own request, decides to start making use of this knowledge, then trouble brews. It would almost certainly lead to expulsion from the monastery and, of course, this would mean that, while the monk will have learned much about both Chinese Buddhist beliefs and various methods of divination, he will not have attained full mastery of either. Howbeit, to the ordinary layman seeking a divination this is of little relevance. Here, in the shape of a wandering monk, is a man who has studied in a monastery and who can read, write and use the five arts. Thus did the wandering monk live between two worlds and profit in a particular way from each. It is from this group that the *Three Lives* comes in part.

The other factor which fused with the tradition of wandering monks from a Buddhist background was folk Taoism. While the *Three Lives* draws heavily upon Buddhist imagery, concepts and language, it also relies to a lesser extent upon Taoist imagery, concepts and language, and part of the book's particular appeal lies in the interaction of the two. The groups of wandering monks contained Buddhists and Taoists. However, it is as likely that it was the folk religion of the audiences (a religion much older than Buddhism, which only arrived in China in the second to third century CE), as much as the presence of Taoist monks, which brought about this interesting fusion. Although Buddhism has come to have a profound sway over Chinese religion, it has often had to find its mode of communication through the images, deities and beliefs of the older folk religion which is best described as religious Taoism. This is not the Taoism of the Taoist philosophers who largely passed from the scene before the birth of Christ. This is the shamanistic cult of earth, heaven and man practised by the ordinary people of China. And they formed the paying audience to whom the wandering monks went to earn their rice.

To recap, there can now be seen to be a pattern emerging. The wandering monk abandons his studies, having been expelled or deciding to leave the monastery for any number of reasons. He comes away with bits and pieces of knowledge both Buddhist and divinational. To earn his living he makes use of his status as a monk and his knowledge of the five arts. However, the only audience who will treat him seriously and pay him accordingly are the ordinary people of the countryside. Thus he uses a mixture of symbols and devices drawn as much from religious Taoism as from Buddhism. The ultimate expression of his status as a Buddhist monk and fortune-teller comes when he is able to divine not just this life, but also past and future lives. For in the complex matrix which constitutes Chinese religion, only Buddhism teaches the doctine of rebirth officially as a credal belief. Obviously, only a Buddhist diviner could thus speak authoritatively about reincarnation.

THE BOOK IN ITS RELIGIOUS SETTING

Before going any further with the *Three Lives* is and what it contains, it is important to stop and to examine the setting within which it works and out of which it arose. Of greatest importance, of course, is an understanding of what the Chinese believe about life after death, rebirth, merit and so on. But let us start with the reglious matrix into which the *Three Lives* fits so perfectly and in which it has a position of authority.

The problem with Chinese religion so far as the West is concerned is that it is not mono-religious. In other words, the Chinese cannot be easily classified as belonging to just one religion. Whereas you can classify the Arab world as predominantly Moslem, or Europe as predominantly Christian, you cannot do the same with the Chinese. Furthermore, much of popular Chinese religious practice seems to many Westerners to consist of little more than plain superstition. Attempts have been made to classify the religious practices according to the three main traditions of Confucianism, Taoism and Buddhism. This works quite well when dealing with formal areas of these religions such as scriptures, priests/monks and historical traditions. It is then possible to talk, as, say, the sinologist W. E. Soothill does, of 'the three religions of China'.[4] However, the fact of the matter is that the predominant feature of Chinese religion as practised by the ordinary people is that it involves and intermeshes all three and much else as well. Less charitable definitions of the three strands of Chinese religion have often arisen from those not a little exasperated by the wicked Chinese habit of taking bits from different traditions and interweaving them. A classic of this genre is H. C. du Bose's *The Dragon, Image and Demon*.[5]

The Chinese themselves are fascinated by this phenomenon of religious pluralism. It really began when Buddhism itself made a significant impact upon Chinese folk religion in the third century CE. At various times attempts have been made to declare a new religion which acknowledged the interplay of the three traditions. Its credal statement was: 'The three religions are one.'[6]

It is perhaps important briefly to survey the three religions or traditions which have fused together to provide the backdrop to Chinese folk religion, and which emerge in *Three Lives* in such a fascinating way. In particular we have focused upon the teachings regarding death and the afterlife as they are of the greatest interest to the book's predictions, as well as being one of the clearest areas where the syncretism of folk religion operates.

Confucianism

In Chinese this is called *K'ung Chiao*, meaning the 'teachings of K'ung'. K'ung is K'ung Fu-tzu, the great ethical teacher of the fifth century BCE. He is better known in the West by his Latinized name Confucius which was given him by admiring Jesuit priests. K'ung was born in 551 BCE and died, to all appearances a failure, in 479 BCE. During his lifetime his advice on how to run a state was largely ignored, even when he was employed in an official capacity. He taught a return to the old values, and central to this was his belief in a strict but benevolent hierarchy. This went, on the male side, from filial piety of the son for the father up to the loyalty of the subject to the emperor. If everyone lived according to the demands and expectations of their station and were strict but benevolent to those below them and deferential and obedient to those above them, then society would run smoothly.

The teachings of K'ung were written down after his death by his disciples in *The Analects*. Within a remarkably short period of time K'ung's teachings were being elevated to the status of state philosophy. His hierarchical approach obviously endeared him to rulers who sought to reimpose order after periods of chaos, and his appeal to historical precedent assisted the sense of continuity which has been a hallmark of Chinese civilization, despite lengthy periods of anarchy and the actual break-up of the state of China.

Over the centuries the rationalist philosopher K'ung has undergone many changes. At one level the thinker has always persisted – respected as the teacher of ethics. At other levels K'ung has become a deity to be invoked for scholarly achievement; a state god whose temples were officially erected in every city and formed the basis of the school system; and, as one of the Three Holy Ones, along with Buddha and Lao Tzu (see below), the ultimate expression of the cosmos. This is all the more remarkable when we bear in mind that during his life K'ung refused to answer questions concerning the gods or the afterlife. Indeed, while he appears to have considered the supernatural as being useful for social purposes, there is little to show that he felt anything more than this. He was strictly a rationalist who would only deal with what he could quantify or analyse.

There are two major areas which have been shaped by Confucianism. First, the whole apparatus of Chinese rule, administration and official scholarship was modelled during the major dynasties upon K'ung's teachings. The famous examination system used only the Confucian classics as the basis of education. The codes of behaviour which underpinned Chinese bureaucracy, while often flouted, were nevertheless strict and highly ethical, and came directly from K'ung's teachings. In the same way, the practice of composing the dynastic histories springs from K'ung's view of the importance of history's lessons concerning statecraft. The list is immense. The pervasive influence of Confucian teachings on Chinese life at these levels can be seen by the frequent attacks which the present system in mainland China has launched upon K'ung, paralleled by his equally frequent rehabilitation by the very same system.

The second level at which Confucianism worked, and still works in its own particular way, is in the family, and especially at death. Filial piety is still prevalent in a way which few Westerners can understand. The respect given to the old and to parents is an essential element of Chinese family life. For instance, most young Chinese who are working, even if they have a young family of their own, will send money to their parents. This is one way in which filial piety is expressed. Another way is in terms of death rites. Confucianism holds that, in the natural order of things – the hierarchy of nature – women are inferior to, and should thus follow the dictates of, men, always remembering that, in K'ung's hierarchy, those in authority must be strict but benevolent. This means that, while a daughter was usually welcomed, a son was all important. An old Chinese saying captures this: 'The three great misfortunes in life are in youth to bury one's father; in middle age to lose one's wife; in old age to have no sons.'[7]

It is essential for a proper funeral that the dead man has a son who makes the appropriate sacrifices, attends to the rituals and ensures that his final burial place accords with the requirements of geomancy (*feng-shui*). K'ung himself made this a central tenet of his hierarchy of respect and authority: 'Parents, when alive, should be served with propriety; when dead, should be buried according to propriety.'[8]

It is at this level, the level of the family, of respect for the ancestors, that Confucianism had and still has its strongest hold on folk religion. Putting it simply, Confucianism teaches that the dead are still members of the family. They are no longer physically present, but they can have considerably more influence than before through their use of supernatural resources. At the heart of this is the simple ethical teaching that the family which respects its ancestors stays together and does well. Over the centuries this has become laden with additional meaning as the dead came to be seen to watch over the family, but only if they were properly sacrificed to. This element is highlighted by the major festivals which have ancestor worship either as their sole official purpose (such as Ch'ing Ming in the spring or Chung Yang in the autumn[9]) or as a major element (such as New Year). To ignore the ancestors or to deal with them in a slight or off-hand manner is to risk disaster and distress falling upon the family, for it breaks the order of nature, the order of society.

Thus we can see that from the Confucian side comes one particular set of teachings about death and life after death.

Taoism

Taoism is called in Chinese either 'teachings of the Way', which means religious Taoism, or 'philosophy of the Way', which refers to the main philosophers of Taoism such as Lao Tzu and Chuang Tzu. The origins of what we now know as Taoism lie way back in the mists of Chinese antiquity. Its roots are in the earliest of all major religions, shamanism, which spread from present-day Siberia possibly as long as 8000 years ago, and which, in the millenia between, moved out to North America, Indonesia, Japan and Tibet. Shamanism is so called after the shamans, priestlike figures who became possessed by the spirits of nature or the great spirits. Through this possession the shaman is empowered to heal, to deal with natural disasters, to perform magic and so on. He or she may also give messages from the dead or from the spirits. The shaman acts as an intermediary between the forces in nature, the dead and the great spirits and ordinary people. At its core is the establishing and careful control of a proper relationship with nature. This is echoed but brought to a much more sophisticated level in Tao Chia – the school of philosophical Taoism. The key figure in this is Lao Tzu. This name is an honorific title meaning 'Old Master'. Little is actually known about the man who, possibly, lies behind it. Indeed, many scholars believe that Lao Tzu never existed as such, but that a collection of writings was ascribed to this name to give it added significance. But assuming for the moment that Lao Tzu did live, then he is credited with writing the book *Tao Te Ching – The Book of the Way* – some time in the late sixth century BCE. Certainly a book containing the ideas of the *Tao Te Ching* concerning following the Way was in use by the fourth century BCE. At its most philosophical, Taoism teaches that the Way of nature, the Way of the world, is a balance of opposites which achieves a harmony. Those who are wise enough to follow the Way will find that life will carry them effortlessly. Those who struggle to impose their will upon the Way will find that they are broken or cast aside.

There is not enough space, or the necessity, to go into the deep levels of philosophical Taoism. It has always had a small but intense following in China, but in terms of our interest in the religious background to the *Three Lives*, it is religious Taoism which is of greater interest.

While we can see the shamanistic roots of religious Taoism stretching far back, it is around 100 CE that religious Taoism as an identifiable movement begins to emerge. It arose as a magical, healing, teaching community, and its very success testifies to the popular style of its methods. It is the combination of these three – magic, healing and teaching – with their accompanying rituals and orders that constitutes the bulk of contemporary religious Taoism. The Taoist priest, monk or nun has taken the place of the shaman possessed by the spirits and able to communicate between the worlds. Furthermore Taoism, as a literate faith, has developed an elaborate series of scriptures and rituals which make it possible for a greater control to be exercised over the natural world while still retaining the idea that the Way of nature must be followed.

The world of Taoism is filled with a mass of deities. Many of these are deities of particular stars, planets, diseases, places and so on. Others are deified humans, such as the famous example of Kuan Ti, who started life in the third century CE as a soldier and was finally elevated to the position of god of war in 1594. The highest aim of religious Taoism is to develop personal awareness and being to such a state that the person is able to achieve immortality, to become an immortal. However, this is for the few. For the bulk of the people Taoism offers, through its deities who can be invoked and its charms and magic which can be recited, a way through a disturbing and harsh world.

At a funeral, while Confucian ethics provide the structure, it is religious Taoism plus Buddhism which provides the ceremonial and the symbolism. In the Taoist system, the soul is usually destined for a rough ride in the afterlife. Religious Taoism knows of up to eighteen different hells where the dead expiate their sins and crimes committed in this life, before going in front of the supreme judge who decides if they are ready to be reborn and, if so, in what form. In order to assist the dead through these trials and tribulations the Taoist priests make offerings and recite charms and prayers. By these they hope to ensure for the dead as swift and painless a passage through the underworld as possible. Interestingly, while there is a lot of attention paid to getting through, there is very little preoccupation with what rebirth will be like. The main concern is to make sure that the dead ancestor does not suffer too much en route, because this could have bad repercussions on the living members of the family.

Buddhism

Buddhism reputedly reached China during the first century CE. Certainly by the third century it had become quite widespread and was attracting attention from many sectors of society. China has produced numerous schools of Buddhist thought and action which have expanded Buddhist teachings in previously unexplored ways. The most famous of these must be Ch'an, which, when it migrated to Japan (the Japanese learned their Buddhism from the Chinese during the seventh to ninth centuries), became the renowned Zen. As a formal religion Buddhism has always been more systematically organized than Taoism, and the Buddhist monasteries and sacred sites of China are many and spectacular. As we have also seen earlier, monastic life was well organized and conducted in a highly structured manner. However, when we move from the *sangha*, the community of Buddhist monks, out into the wider world of the lay Buddhists, we encounter the same developments as we saw with the other two traditions. Namely, folk Buddhism looks to the Buddha and his teachings to provide a way through the pains and perils of this life, as well as the next lives. While few Buddhist monks would ever openly practise magic, charms or fortune-telling, they recognize that mild forms of these help the lay people feel secure and perhaps a little more receptive to the deeper teachings of Buddhism. Thus in Buddhist temples fortune stick divination may be seen, as well as other types of simple fortune-telling.

However, what is central to all this is the Buddhist teaching regarding reincarnation, rebirth, the wheel of suffering, and so on. Essentially, Chinese Buddhism teaches that every action we make, be it for the good, the bad or even the indifferent, has a result which long outlasts its apparently immediate effect. This build-up of effect or result is called 'karma' and it is not extinguished at death. Indeed, it is the existence of this karma which causes and determines the next rebirth. While karma continues to exist, rebirth is inevitable. This is described by the fifth-century monk Hui-yuan in his book *The Treatise on the Three Rewards*.

The sutra says that karma has three kinds of response: first, in the present life; second, in the next life; and third, in later lives. In the second, the deeds are rewarded in the next life, while in the third, the deeds are rewarded in the second, third, 100th or 1,000th life afterwards.[10]

Along with this goes the belief that one may be reborn in non-human form. Depending upon the life you lead, you might be reborn as a human or as a lower animal. It is, therefore, of utmost concern to people to try to compensate for the not terribly good life they have led. In Chinese Buddhism this led to two interesting systems. First, a strict coding of rewards and punishments in terms of karma effects was developed. This mean that you could keep a rough tally. If you had eaten meat for a month – bad karma – you could cancel out the negative effects by giving generously to the monks on a festival day. The second system was the growth of belief in a compassionate order of semi-deities. These are the Bodhisattvas. Bodhisattvas are those who, through personal excellence, have come to the point at which their own karma is exhausted and there is nothing which holds them to this physical level of existence. They could die never to be reborn, having become an Arhat and attained Nirvana – perfect bliss beyond this physical existence. However, because they are filled with compassion when they look at the rest of the world, those who are doomed to countless rebirths due to karma, the Bodhisattvas take a vow not to achieve final release until every sentient being has also achieved release. From their store of good deeds they are able to assist in the removal of much bad karma. If a Bodhisattva such as Kuan Yin (goddess of mercy) is invoked with due reverence, then a better rebirth can be hoped for or, in certain teachings, release can be obtained from the wheel of rebirth.

Thus Buddhist monks and nuns will be invited to a Chinese funeral, but not to perform any specific burial rite as such. They will come to pray, recite the scriptures and generally to produce or pray for good karma, or compassion, to be extended to the dead person. With this assistance the dead person should be able to pass more swiftly through the ten Buddhist hells (the hells interlock with the Taoist ones) and thus achieve rebirth. (An interesting example of this idea is found in the story of Mu-lien; see pp. 20–21.)

In terms of the *Three Lives* it is predominantly the former system, of merit and demerit attached to actions, which informs the divination, though the role of the compassionate and merciful Bodhisattvas is also there.

It may seem that there are contradictory beliefs about life after death in these three traditions. How can you be an ancestor and also reborn, as well as be in hell? For the Chinese these are not problems. At times the ancestor concept is important, at other times the idea of rebirth or judgement in hell. The traditions simply fuse and whatever is helpful at any given time is taken from the resulting beliefs. This is perhaps best seen at the festival of the Hungry Ghosts. Naturally some people some die with no descendants to perform sacrifices to them, no friends to burn Taoist charms and good luck money, no family to pay for Buddhist monks to chant. These souls or ghosts are doomed to wander unhappily for ever unless someone offers them food, assistance in the underworld and prayers for a good rebirth. Every year a festival is held for which vast open-air shrines are built, complete with bamboo opera houses for sacred opera. Around the courtyard each faith sets up its stall where offerings are made to the dead according to the specific rites of each faith – ancestor tables with no names written in so that any ghost can make it his or her own; Buddhist shrines where prayers are chanted and offerings can be made to the Three Buddhas (see p. 19); Taoist and Buddhist temples which show graphic depictions of the hells as well as the cycle of rebirth or the pleasures of eventual release. Each faith is there, but there is no competition (except in terms of who can get the biggest site). It is the combined efforts of the three faiths which the organizers are looking for. Only to have one would be a slight to the integrity of the ghosts; one simply would not be enough. People happily wander from one shrine to another while, spanning all three, there tower giant figures such as the Buddhist Kuan Yan and the Taoist god of hell. It is this acceptance and utilization of the diverse traditions that are the hallmarks of Chinese folk religion which lies behind the fascinating mixture in the *Three Lives*.

WHEN WAS THE BOOK COMPOSED?

Having identified as far as possible the likely sources from which the impetus for the materials found in the *Three Lives* came, it still leaves two questions unanswered. Why did the wandering monks write it down and when did this happen? These are difficult questions to answer. With regard to the first, China has long been a highly literate society and the scale of book production following the invention of woodblock printing in the eighth century is quite phenomenal.[11] It should not surprise us therefore to find books such as the *Three Lives* appearing in print. Furthermore the complexity of many of the systems of divination within the book means that some form of written chart and table would have been necessary for the wandering monk to carry out the divination. There is also the fact that in the illiterate world of the Chinese peasant the authority of the written word was enormous. One of the most sacrilegous acts you could perform was wantonly to destroy a book or even a page of text. Therefore a wandering monk who could use a book to tell you your three lives was to be respected.

As to the second question of when did this happen, we can only make an educated guess. Until 1789 it is unlikely that the *Three Lives* existed in its present form. Up to half the original book is of little interest or value. Indeed, when we first embarked on this edition we were warned by the experts that we should ignore certain sections as these had 'clustered around the original text'. While it has proved impossible to identify an 'original text' as such, we have left out of this edition the sections which everyone agreed were of little value. This has led us to speculate that, although a basic book called the *Three Lives* first took printed form in the late Ming or early Ch'ing dynasty, it continued to grow as a book, attracting lesser systems of divination which were added to it until it was printed in its final form in 1789. Since the 1789 edition the tendency has been to cut back on the number of systems in the book, not increase them.

The reason we feel that the period 1550–1650 is the most likely time for the original *Three Lives* to have come into being is because of the social and religious upheavals of that time. It is a feature of Chinese history that, at times when the state was undergoing transformation and the old-established ways were under severe strain, 'superstitious' practices came into their own. The philosopher Hsun Tzu (third century BCE) noted this with regard to the collapse of the last remnants of the Chou in the Warring States period (475–221 BCE) and the corresponding rise of the brutal house of Ch'in. A similar pattern is found in the rise of religious Taoism in the days leading up to and following the collapse of the Han dynasty (*c.* 200 CE). In the period of the collapse of the Ming and the rise of the non-Chinese dynasty of the Ch'ing ('barbarians' from the Mongolian steppes) the same pattern seems to have been displayed. As the emperors showed their contempt for the traditions of the past by gross excesses and cruelty, the ordinary people found themselves once again at the mercy of officials who copied the corruption of the court. The burden for this fell inevitably upon the peasants through taxation, forced labour, foreign incursions into China and so on.[12] It is at times such as these that people turn most readily to systems which seem to indicate that other forces are and could be at play in their lives.

There are other factors which lead us to view this period as the time when the *Three Lives* was formed. Central to the book is the belief that a clearly demarcated system of merit and demerit exists which inevitably and inexorably determines at your death what rebirth you will have. Yet this idea of a clear relationship between certain actions (the *Three Lives* includes ones such as stealing silver, falsely dealing in grain, giving meat to monks, murdering a child, etc.) and the next rebirth was not developed in any explicit form in Chinese Buddhism until the Ming dynasty. This was done by a character who deserves a little of our time, for he captures the very essence of the society and of the interaction of thought which produced the conditions necessary for the *Three Lives* to emerge. The man concerned was Yuan Huang (also known as Yuan Liao-fan), who lived from 1533 to 1606 and wrote the standard text on merit, demerit and rebirth called the *Yin-chih-lu* (*Record of Silent Recompense*). His other influential book was called, most interestingly from our point of view, *Li-ming Pian* (*Treatise on Establishing One's Destiny*).

In *Yin-chih-lu* Yuan describes in some detail how he came to hold his views of merit, demerit, fate, fortune and the role of the individual in his or her own rebirth. Yuan was an ambitious young man who was scared of entering for the Imperial exams because he feared failure and the subsequent disgrace. He also had to continue the family medical business after the death of his father. But this all changed one day when Yuan met an elderly Taoist priest called K'ung. K'ung was a fortune-teller of great renown and he predicted that Yuan would pass the local prefectural exams and the provincial exams, but he would not achieve high enough marks to gain the top status. K'ung also gave a very detailed description of the particular rank and the posts he would be given. The only sour note in the whole thing was that K'ung predicted that Yuan would die at fifty-three and would have no son to follow or mourn him.

Yuan, emboldened by this forecast, took the plunge, and everything worked out exactly as K'ung had predicted. Naturally Yuan was delighted, but he also, understandably, became rather fatalistic and depressed by the end that K'ung had forecast. Then, when he was thirty-three, he met the Buddhist monk Yun Ku. The discussion which followed three days of silently facing each other is of such central importance to an understanding of Chinese concepts of fate and the intellectual matrix from which the *Three Lives* emerged to be worth giving in full.

Yun Ku spoke first. 'It is because man is held back by reckless thoughts that he fails to achieve the level of sage. I have noticed that you have sat for three days and not a single reckless thought has arisen within you.' Yuan replied, 'My fate has been foretold by Mr K'ung. The ups and downs as well as the length of my life have all been decreed by fate. Even if I want to indulge in reckless and wild thoughts there is nothing to get reckless or wild about.' Apparently Yun Ku burst out laughing at this and said, 'I thought you were an exceptional person. It turns out you are just an ordinary man.' Yuan, perplexed by this, asked for an explanation. Yun Ku replied, 'Because man always does things intentionally [the Chinese here says: 'cannot be unintentional'], he has been placed ultimately under the rule of the forces of yin and yang. Thus he cannot totally escape from fate. But only ordinary men are bound by fate. The supremely benevolent is not tied by fate, nor is the utterly depraved. For twenty years you have been tied down by his [K'ung's] predictions, and you have not tried to change them even one little bit. Doesn't this make you just an ordinary man?'

Yuan responds to this by asking if it is possible to change one's fate.

Yun Ku replies, ' ''My destiny I create for myself, my fortune I seek for myself.'' This claim in the *Book of Odes and Documents* [one of the Five Classics] is indeed an enlightened proclamation. Our Buddhist scriptures also say, ''Seek prestige and fame, they will be found; ask for wealth and status, they will be given; pray for descendants, they will be granted; request longevity, it will be answered.'' As it is a cardinal sin in the teachings of the Buddha to make reckless statements, the above verses cannot be a false claim made by the Buddhas and the Bodhisattvas to deceive people.'

However, Yuan was not yet convinced and quoted the sage Meng Tzu (Mencius). 'Meng Tzu says, ''Seek, and it will be obtained''; so the act of seeking here is done by the self. But this kind of seeking is only possible in regard to moral issues. How can such things as prestige, fame, wealth and status be sought?'

Yun Ku replied, 'Meng Tzu's statement is correct; the problem comes from your faulty interpretation. The Sixth Patriarch [of Ch'an Buddhism] said, ''All fortunes and rewards cannot be detached from the mind.'' From the mind awareness and consciousness are produced. This awareness and consciousness penetrate everything. So it is that the self can not only seek and find morality, benevolence and righteousness, but it can also gain fame, prestige, wealth and status.'

Finally Yun Ku made what, for us, is an excellent summary of the very basis of the *Three Lives*. He asked Yuan if he really felt that, given his inactivity and fatalism over the last twenty years, he had earned the right to the top rank and to having a male heir. Yuan agreed that he did not really deserve these rewards. Yun Ku then spelt it out for him. 'Those who have a thousand taels [weight of silver] are necessarily those who deserve that much. Likewise, those who have a hundred taels. Those who suffer death by starvation deserve death by starvation. Heaven thus dispenses fate in accordance with the worthiness of those who receive it. In no way will Heaven inject its own will into this dispensation. Now that you have realized where you went wrong in the past, you should completely reform yourself from the person who did not deserve to attain the top post and have a male heir to one who does so deserve. You should now set out to accumulate merit, to relieve famine, to lead a harmonious life and to preserve your essence and spirit. What is past may be considered to be dead and past. What will be in the future can be seen as starting today. Do this, and you will be reborn through proper, righteous principles and will be able to regulate Heaven. In the *Book of Odes and Documents* it says, ''Heaven-sent retributions can be disobeyed. Self-induced retributions cannot be avoided.'' Mr K'ung has predicted that you will not pass the highest exam. This is Heaven's retribution, which can be altered. When you develop fully your moral side, spend time and effort in meritorious actions and accumulate good karma, then these will be fortunes created by yourself and you will be able to enjoy the fruits of these labours. The *Book of Changes* [*I Ching*] says: ''The wise man draws close to the auspicious and avoids the inauspicious.'' If fate is actually fixed, how can you draw close to the auspicious and avoid the inauspicious? That is why the *Book of Changes'* opening chapter says: ''The benevolent household has an abundance of good fortune, while the wicked household has an abundance of misfortune.'' Do you believe this?''[13]

Yuan was completely convinced by Yun Ku's argument and set about not only applying it to his own life but, through books, spreading it far and wide. Within a very few years the basic ideas had filtered down to the lowest level in Chinese society and the climate had been established in which the *Three Lives* was able to grow.

We have spent some time on Yuan and Yun Ku simply because their discussion lays out all the essential beliefs which lie behind the *Three Lives*. It is hard to think of a more succinct way of expressing Chinese views on fate than that found in this famous discourse.

Having examined some of the history and a little of the thought that lie behind this book, we now turn our attention to why the *Three Lives* should have proved to be so popular and the factors which lie within and behind it.

THE POWER AND AUTHORITY OF THE BOOK

The *Three Lives* ought, by all normal conditions, to have little power and no authority. It is totally devoid of any teaching, preaching, examples of morality, ethics, religious insight or truth in the classic sense of the word. It has none of the literary grandeur of, say, the *Tao Te Ching*; none of the morality stories of the *T'ai Shang*; none of the antiquity of the *I Ching*; none of the venerability of the Almanac. Yet it has managed within a relatively short period of time to establish itself as the standard book of divination at birth and of prediction of past, present and future lives. It is still being printed in impressive numbers. Young women in the more egalitarian world of today resent the fact that their brothers had a reading while they did not, and, accordingly, the book is now being used for baby girls. So why does it have this power and this seeming authority?

Either deliberately or, more likely, purely subconsciously, the language of the *Three Lives* draws upon a host of powerful images and archetypes within Chinese religious literature, scriptures, deities and beliefs. To a great extent its position as a book of authority lies in this interaction. For instance, let us simply look at the number three. This is one of the most auspicious numbers in the whole Chinese religious system. A quick flick through any good Chinese dictionary will produce a vast number of items which start with three: e.g. the Three Principles (essence, breath and spirit); the Three Primordial Powers (Heaven, earth and water); the Three Friends of Winter (pine, bamboo and the *mei* flower); Three-Inch Golden Lilies (the bound feet of Ch'ing women); the Three Religions (Confucianism, Buddhism and Taoism); the Three Principles of the People (Sun Yat-sen's basic political stance), and so on. In the area of religion three is of enormous significance. The *Dictionary of Chinese Buddhist Terms* lists nearly 300 key terms concerned with the number three.[14]

In Taoism the number three is also of great importance, as in the Three Canons of Taoist texts, the Three August Ones of ancient history (Fu-hsi, Nu-kua and Shen-nung) and the Three Primordial Powers mentioned above. In Taoism there are also the Three Pure Ones, a sort of Taoist heavenly trinity consisting of three attributes or manifestations of the ultimate being, Lao Tzu. Most scholars agree that these three are a response to the highly developed Buddhist trinity, which has two levels of meaning within it. First, it refers to the core credal statement of the Buddhist faith, known as the Triple Gems of Buddhism. 'I take refuge in the Buddha; in the dharma [his teachings] and in the sangha [the community of monks who perpetuate his teachings].' Over the centuries a second level of meaning has arisen whereby the three concepts came to be manifested through specific divine figures. It is thus common to find in all Chinese Buddhist temples that the main altar is dominated by three vast statues. These are Sakyamuni (the historical Buddha, who lived *c.* 500 BCE), and on his left the Buddha of Medicine, Yun Shi-fo,[15] and on his right Amitabha, the Buddha of the Pure Land, where souls hope to be reborn. While this tends to be the most frequent combination, there are numerous other combinations, usually retaining Sakyamuni in the centre but ringing the changes on the Buddhas or Bodhisattvas that surround him.[16]

There is yet one further refinement to this idea of a trinity which has particular appeal to those to whom the contents of the *Three Lives* is directed. From the synthesis of the three religions, Confucianism, Buddhism and Taoism, came the Three Holy Ones, namely K'ung Fu-tzu (Confucius), Buddha and Lao Tzu.

So three has a very highly charged significance both within the specific faiths of Buddhism and Taoism and across the boundaries of these faiths.

The Chinese name for the *Three Lives* is *San-shih*. It can be translated as 'three lives', 'three worlds' or even 'three states of existence' and has a good religious pedigree. It occurs many times as a key phrase dealing with the very nature of the past, present and future in the sacred sutra *Hua-yen*, which is the Chinese translation of the Sanskrit text known as the Avatamsakasutra. In later developments the three worlds were given specific Buddhas or Bodhisattvas who looked after them. The past comes under the care of Kasyapa (a monk linked to the Theravada tradition of Buddhism), the present comes under Sakyamuni as the particular historical manifestation of ultimate Buddha nature for our era, and the future comes under Maitreya, the future Buddha whose coming will herald in an age of bliss for all. So we can see that this term *san-shih* is no ordinary word plucked out of thin air for lack of any better name for a book. Rather, it is deeply rooted and contains many layers of meaning. Nor should we consider it to be only a technical term, known perhaps mostly to monks and scholars in Buddhism. From the earliest days *san-shih* appears in popular Buddhist stories which were purposely designed to attract and communicate to the ordinary layperson. These were originally known as *pien-wen*, which means 'stories of marvellous events'. They arose from the tales told by Buddhist monks or travelling singers to the laity at the great festivals. They were designed to use language and ideas familiar to the ordinary Confucian-Taoist people of the towns and villages. Many of these stories, these *pien-wen*, were found in a wonderful store of pre-ninth-century Buddhist literature discovered on the Silk Road at the oasis town of Tun-huang in the early years of this century. One example will suffice to illustrate how, from at least the ninth century and almost certainly earlier, the term *san-shih* was known to ordinary people.

One of the most popular of the stories was that of Mu-lien. Mu-lien (then known by his pre-Arhat name of Lo-pu) was a devoted son who was heartbroken when his father died. Unfortunately Mu-lien's mother was a very unpleasant person, and although her son was devout and kind, she was grasping and mean. Mu-lien decided to travel abroad to seek his fortune and thus divided his lands and goods in three. One third was for his own needs; one third was for his mother; one third was to be given to the monks and to others in need. He asked his mother to undertake this charity for him and set off. His mother did no such thing. She kept the money for herself and swore at any monk who was bold enough to ask for alms, often setting the farm dogs on the poor unfortunates. Mu-lien returned successful and rich, and asked his mother if she had done as he had instructed. She swore that she had, even though Mu-lien knew full well from others that she had not done one charitable act. In a fury his mother said, 'May I die in seven days and descend to the deepest Avici hell [the lowest of the ten hells of Buddhism] if I do not tell the truth.'

Seven days later she dropped dead and was duly reborn in the deepest Avici hell. Mu-lien spent three years in formal mourning as a good son, but then was able to fulfil his greatest wish and join the Buddhist monks. Through the merit of his nature and the diligence with which he studied, he rose very swiftly in knowledge and wisdom. Soon he reached the position of an Arhat and acquired the name Mu-lien. This is the point of the story which is of greatest interest to us. For at this stage he is able to perform great acts. Wishing to repay his parents for the kindness they have shown him in his life, Mu-lien is described as 'rising up to scan the three worlds' (san-shih), that is, the worlds of the past, present and future. He sees his father in one of the heavens, but no sign of his mother, who is rightly having a tough time of it down in the deepest Avici hell.

The story then continues to tell how Mu-lien intervenes for his mother with the Buddha. The Buddha tells Mu-lien to prepare a vast feast for the Buddhas of the past, present and future. By doing this he is able to rescue his mother from hell. However, she has to be reborn. Because of the bad karma which she still has, even after being released from hell, she is reborn as a female dog who has to live off the dung hill. However, the ever patient and caring Mu-lien intercedes for her again and, using his store of merit, is able to change her fortune, and she is eventually reborn into one of the heavens.[17]

Here in outline are the core elements of the *Three Lives* theory. When this strand of popular Buddhist thought fused with the new perception of Yuan Huang, the *Three Lives* was ready to be born.

Any section of this book will give you insights into how Confucianism, Buddhism and Taoism fuse together to provide an overall picture of reality within which the book operates quite naturally. The section 'Treasure for This Life' (pp. 89–91) is a good example. Under the first star basic Buddhist precepts of the superior morality of being vegetarian and of worshipping the Buddha are stressed. In the next star the Confucian ethic of filial piety (do not forget that this book is primarily written to give readings for men) is urged, with a reminder that you should set a place in your home for your ancestors and this will aid your fortune. In the third star we are introduced to the Taoist god Chin Chia. He is the guardian of houses and assists the god of literature. A statue of Chin Chia in golden armour will ensure that he protects the home and assists budding scholars to achieve the highest results, thus earning both fame and fortune for their family. In other words, if you are respectful to Chin Chia he will aid your career – thinking here of career in the traditional Chinese sense of success as an official. In the sixth star we find mention of the five arts. These arts (which are practised as much by Buddhists as by Taoists, as we saw earlier) consist of divination, physiognomy, astrology (including *feng-shui*), herbal medicine and 'mountain studies' (self-disciplines which lead to being either a sage or even an immortal, including Tai Chi Ch'uan, for example). In the next star we find Kuan Yin mentioned, the most popular Bodhisattva in Chinese religion, indeed the most popular divine figure in Chinese faith. In the eleventh star we find the Three Holy Ones – K'ung Fu-tzu, Buddha and Lao Tzu.

Here, in just one section, we have a panorama of the interaction of the three religions. This is why the *Three Lives* has been and still is so powerful. It uses all the most accessible and meaningful symbols in Chinese religion and blends them in a way which is thoroughly consistent with folk religion as it is practised both at home and in the shrine. From this familiarity it can then speak directly and with authority about the fears and hopes, primarily of parents faced with the advent of a new life, but also more generally to anyone wishing to find out what might lie ahead if their present lifestyle is maintained.

The *Three Lives* is a strange book, an unusual book. It can only be fully appreciated within the cultural context from which it has arisen. Some readers will approach it from that context; others will not. In each case remember that it is not telling you how things will be. It is telling you how things may well turn out to be. As regards your past life – well, that's something you will have to take or leave on trust.

In this English edition of the *Three Lives* we have sought to capture the power of a traditional fortune-teller or wandering monk. To this end we have not just given a word-for-word translation, which would have left many readers none the wiser. Rather, we have taken the text and given a 'reading' using insights, knowledge and the style that our diviners used when explaining the text to us. Thus the reader can hear the authentic voice of the *Three Lives*.

How the System Works

Having seen something of how and why this book came to be, we must now outline how to go about using it. This chapter should be read in conjunction with the one that follows and with the introduction to the Calendar Tables on pp. 193–4.

To start the process of divination you need to work out the eight characters of your horoscope. In Chinese divination the significant details are the year, the month, the day and the time you were born. Each of these 'times' has two Chinese characters attached to it, one known as a 'Heavenly Stem' and the other called an 'Earthly Branch'. Thus, with two characters each for the year, the month, the day and the hour of your birth, you have eight characters in all made up of four pairs of Heavenly Stems and Earthly Branches.

There are ten Heavenly Stems and twelve Earthly Branches, as follows:

Heavenly Stems

Stem	Chinese character	Stem	Chinese character
Chia	甲	Chi	己
Yi	乙	Keng	庚
Ping	丙	Hsin	辛
Ting	丁	Jen	壬
Mou	戊	Kuei	癸

Earthly Branches

Branch	Chinese character	Branch	Chinese character
Tzu	子	Wu	午
Ch'ou	丑	Wei	未
Yin	寅	Shen	申
Mao	卯	Yu	酉
Ch'en	辰	Hsü	戌
Szu	巳	Hai	亥

To find out which of the Heavenly Stems and Earthly Branches apply to you is a complicated process which depends on the Chinese system of calculating time. In the Chinese calendrical system time is measured by a cycle of sixty. Thus, instead of decades (a ten-year cycle) or centuries (a 100-year cycle), years are counted in batches of sixty, the sexagenary cycle.

How is the number sixty arrived at? It is obtained by combining the ten Heavenly Stems and the twelve Earthly Branches in a sequence until the pattern of combinations begins to repeat itself. In other words, when the two lists are set side by side it requires sixty combinations to make a full cycle. The Heavenly Stems have to be repeated six times (10 × 6 = 60) and the Earthly Branches five times (12 × 5 = 60) in all. The full sequence looks like this:

The cycle always starts with Chia and Tzu, and is used to count not only the years but also the days; a variant of the cycle is used for the months and the hours.

From the cycle of sixty come the names for the years. Thus, for example, 1988 is Mou Ch'en year, a combination of Heavenly Stem and Earthly Branch which has not occurred since 1928 and will not occur again until 2048. The characters change at the start of each Chinese New Year, which falls somewhere between 21 January and 20 February of the Western calendar.

The characters for the year are of far greater importance than the animal sign for the year. So, although 1988 is the Year of the Dragon, for divination purposes it is called Mou Ch'en year. The importance of the sixty-year cycle is shown by the fact that the only major celebration of a person's birthday comes when he or she is sixty.

Having explained how the characters for the years are found, let us look at those for the months. The Chinese calendar is based on the lunar year, in contrast to the Western calendar, which is based on the solar year. The lunar and solar years do not correspond exactly: the lunar year consists of twelve moons (months), each of which lasts just over $29\frac{1}{2}$ days. In order to keep the days in each lunar month as full days, in the Chinese calendar the year is made up of a number of 'small' months of 29 days each and a number of 'big' months of 30 days each. A year with six 'big' months and six 'small' months will have a grand total of 354 days; while a year with seven 'big' months and five 'small' months will have 355 days; one with five 'big' and seven 'small' will have 353 days. Thus the lunar year falls short of the solar year by 10, 11 or 12 days. To bring the Chinese calendar into line with the seasons, and thus with the Western calendar, it is necessary to include an extra month every second or third year. This is called an intercalary month, and it comes immediately after the month it is equated with. In 1982 the extra month was month 4, and it came after the normal month 4. The next extra month came in 1984 and was number 10, following the normal month 10. The next occurrence is in 1987, the extra month being number 6. The intercalary months are printed in italic in the Calendar Tables.

Although the lunar months are numbered from 1 to 12 each year, they are also counted according to the sexagenary cycle of Heavenly Stems and Earthly Branches. The sequence is shown in the table on p. 26. The characters for each lunar month are determined by the Heavenly Stem for the year (column headings) and the number of the month in question (side headings). So in a year whose Heavenly Stem is Ping – 1986, for example – the 6th lunar month will have the

The Cycle of Heavenly Stems and Earthly Branches for the Months
(The cycle is shown in relation to the Western years 1984–93)

Heavenly Stem for the Year

Lunar Month	Chia (1984) Chi (1989)	Yi (1985) Keng (1990)	Ping (1986) Hsin (1991)	Ting (1987) Jen (1992)	Mou (1988) Kuei (1993)
1st	Ping Yin	Mou Yin	Keng Yin	Jen Yin	Chia Yin
2nd	Ting Mao	Chi Mao	Hsin Mao	Kuei Mao	Yi Mao
3rd	Mou Ch'en	Keng Ch'en	Jen Ch'en	Chia Ch'en	Ping Ch'en§
4th	Chi Szu	Hsin Szu	Kuei Szu	Yi Szu	Ting Szu
5th	Keng Wu	Jen Wu	Chia Wu‡	Ping Wu	Mou Wu
6th	Hsin Wei	Kuei Wei	Yi Wei	Ting Wei*	Chi Wei
7th	Jen Shen	Chia Shen	Ping Shen	Mou Shen	Keng Shen
8th	Kuei Yu	Yi Yu	Ting Yu	Chi Yu	Hsin Yu
9th	Chia Hsü	Ping Hsü	Mou Hsü	Keng Hsü	Jen Hsü
10th	Yi Hai†	Ting Hai	Chi Hai	Hsin Hai	Kuei Hai
11th	Ping Tzu	Mou Tzu	Keng Tzu	Jen Tzu	Chia Tzu
12th	Ting Ch'ou	Chi Ch'ou	Hsin Ch'ou	Kuei Ch'ou	Yi Ch'ou

The cycle repeats

*Extra month in 1987.   †Extra month in 1984.   ‡Extra month in 1990.
§Extra month in 1993.

characters Yi Wei. This cycle repeats every five years, so in 1991, a year whose Heavenly Stem is Hsin, the 6th lunar month will also have the characters Yi Wei.

As there are twelve lunar months and twelve Earthly Branches, their relationship in the cycle always stays the same, so the 1st lunar month always has Yin as one of its characters, the 2nd Mao, the 3rd Ch'en, and so on, while the Heavenly Stems change according to the sexagenary cycle.

The characters for the months are not used in the *Three Lives* predictions; the numbers of the months are used instead. However, for a full horoscope reading the month characters would be needed.

In the Chinese system the days are counted in exactly the same way as the years – in a cycle of sixty, starting with Chia Tzu. Thus any given day will have a Heavenly and an Earthly character, and that particular combination repeats every sixty days. So 19 February 1942 had the characters Kuei Mao, as did 21 December 1941 and 20 April 1942.

To find the first six characters of your horoscope – those for the year, the month and the day – you simply need to turn to the Calendar Tables at the back of the book and find your Western date of birth. There you will see the Heavenly Stem and Earthly Branch for your Chinese year of birth, and in the adjacent columns the numbers of the day and the lunar month, and the characters for the lunar month and for the day you are born. To simplify the tables we have used a system of codes for the Heavenly Stems and the Earthly Branches, the former being coded from A to K and the latter from 1 to 12. The codes are listed at the front of the Calendar Tables (p. 194).

The last two characters of your eight-character horoscope – those for the hour of your birth – remain to be discovered. They too are based on the sexagenary cycle, but the Chinese use a different system of calculating the hours to that used in the West. The Chinese 'hour' is equivalent to two Western hours, so there are only twelve 'hours' in the Chinese day. Each one corresponds to an Earthly Branch as follows:

Tzu	11 p.m. – 1 a.m.	Wu	11 a.m. – 1 p.m.
Ch'ou	1 a.m. – 3 a.m.	Wei	1 p.m. – 3 p.m.
Yin	3 a.m. – 5 a.m.	Shen	3 p.m. – 5 p.m.
Mao	5 a.m. – 7 a.m.	Yu	5 p.m. – 7 p.m.
Ch'en	7 a.m. – 9 a.m.	Hsü	7 p.m. – 9 p.m.
Szu	9 a.m. – 11 a.m.	Hai	9 p.m. – 11 p.m.

To find the characters for your 'hour' of birth a special table is used and it is shown in the following chapter (Table 3, p. 36). It is similar to the one for the months (see above) and works in much the same way, although in this case the coordinates are the Heavenly Stem for the day you were born (column headings) and the 'hour' of your birth (side headings). In *Three Lives* predictions only the Earthly Branch for your 'hour' of birth is used; however, for a full horoscope reading all eight characters would be needed.

In addition to the eight characters of the horoscope, the *Three Lives* also uses a number of other factors for prediction: these are your age, your constellation, the animal sign for the year of your birth, your palace and finally your element.

To take each in turn, according to the Chinese method of calculating age, you are already one year old at birth. And, as it is not common to celebrate birthdays other than a person's sixtieth birthday, everyone is reckoned to be one year older on the 7th day of each New Year. To simplify matters, however, we have adjusted the tables which use age as a coordinate so that they are based on your Western age.

In Chinese thought there are twenty-eight constellations which influence a person's life. They are known by the names of different animals, one for each day in a twenty-eight-day cycle. The constellation for the day you were born exerts a special influence throughout your life. The twenty-eight constellation animals are as follows:

Crocodile	Wolf
Dragon	Dog
Badger	Pheasant
Hare	Cock
Fox	Crow
Tiger	Monkey
Leopard	Gibbon
Griffon	Tapir
Ox	Sheep
Bat	Deer
Rat	Horse
Swallow	Stag
Pig	Serpent
Porcupine	Earthworm

A different set of animals is used to name the years. These are the

twelve animal signs for the years and they are linked with the Earthly
Branches as follows:

Tzu – Rat	Wu – Horse
Ch'ou – Ox	Wei – Ram
Yin – Tiger	Shen – Monkey
Mao – Rabbit	Yu – Cock
Ch'en – Dragon	Hsü – Dog
Szu – Snake	Hai – Pig

Each year has its own animal name corresponding to its Earthly
Branch; 1987, for example, with the Earthly Branch Mao, is the Year
of the Rabbit. The Chinese ascribe little significance to these twelve
creatures and view theories about their alleged influence as having
little value. Other than as a general title to the year, the animal has no
real function.

Just as we are all under the rule of one of the constellations, so we
are all seen to live under the influence of one of twelve palaces.
'Palace' is a general term, meaning much the same as 'house'. The
palaces are named after the twelve Earthly Branches and a person's
palace is determined by his or her lunar month and 'hour' of birth.
You can find your palace in Table 4, which appears in the next
chapter (p. 37).

Finally, in a *Three Lives* reading, you need to know your element.
There are five elements in all: Wood, Fire, Earth, Metal and Water.
Each one corresponds to two Heavenly Stems, as follows:

Chia⎫
Yi ⎬ Wood   Mou⎫
                   Chi ⎬ Earth   Jen ⎫
                                        Kuei⎬ Water

Ping⎫
Ting⎬ Fire   Keng⎫
                    Hsin⎬ Metal

It is the Heavenly Stem for your day of birth that determines which
element you were born under. For example, if you were born on 1
September 1940 your Heavenly Stem for that day would be Ting,
which means that your element is Fire.

To sum up: to find your first six characters – those for the year, the
month and the day you were born – and your constellation, simply
look up your Western date of birth in the Calendar Tables. The
characters for your 'hour' of birth, plus your palace and your element,
can be found in Tables 1–4 in the following chapter (pp. 34–7), which

tells you exactly how to work them out. It also includes four examples of horoscope details for specific times and dates of birth (see pp. 32–3).

Once you have worked out your eight characters, your palace, your constellation and your element, you will be able to turn to the various sections of the *Three Lives* and discover what the book has to tell you. There is no coherent pattern to the order in which the sections appear in the Chinese edition, so we have grouped them in what we feel is the most logical order. Each section contains an explanation of how to use that particular system. In most cases there will be a single reading for you to reflect upon. However, some tables do not give readings for certain character combinations, while yielding two or three for others. The introduction to each section will warn you when the table gives a number of readings for a particular time of birth.

Finally, to give you some idea of how a full *Three Lives* reading looks, we have included two sample horoscopes. These take you through the tables step by step, and will enable you to make your own *Three Lives* reading. They can be found on pp. 38–51.

How to Find Your Horoscope Characters

In this chapter we include all the information you will need to find your horoscope characters so that you can use the *Three Lives* predictions.

The main item is the Calendar Tables, which start on p. 195. From them you can find out your Chinese date of birth, the first six characters of your horoscope – that is, the Heavenly Stems and the Earthly Branches for the year, the month and the day you were born – and your constellation.

In the Calendar Tables we have used codes for the characters, and these can be found in Table 1 (for the Heavenly Stems) and Table 2 (for the Earthly Branches) below (pp. 34 and 35). For ease of reference, they also appear at the start of the Calendar Tables themselves.

Table 1 also lists the five elements, which correspond to the Heavenly Stems. If you want to find out which element you belong to, simply look up the Heavenly Stem for your day of birth in the Calendar Tables, then turn to Table 1.

Table 2 lists the Earthly Branches in relation to the Chinese system of 'hours' and to the animal signs for the years. Your animal sign depends on the Earthly Branch for your year of birth.

Table 3 gives the Heavenly Stems and Earthly Branches for the 'hours' (p. 36). In order to use this table you need to know the Heavenly Stem for your day of birth and also your 'hour' of birth.

Finally, Table 4 shows the palaces (p. 37). To find your palace you need to know your lunar month and your 'hour' of birth.

Prefacing each table is an introduction which explains how that table works.

So that you can easily and quickly find out where to look for what, we have compiled the following summary. To find your:

Chinese day and month of birth: see the Calendar Tables (column 2)

characters for the year: see the Calendar Tables (main heading)
characters for the month: see the Calendar Tables (column 3)
characters for the day: see the Calendar Tables (column 4)
characters for the 'hour': see Table 3
palace: see Table 4
constellation: see the Calendar Tables (column 5)
element: see Table 1
animal sign: see Table 2
'hour' of birth: see Table 2
Earthly Branch for 'hour': see Table 2

Below are four examples to show how the horoscope details will look
for different birth dates and times. Before you use the *Three Lives*
charts you could compile your own horoscope details, and we have
included a blank example (number 5) for you to fill in with your own
particulars.

Example 1

Born on 5 February 1924 at 11.15 a.m.
Chinese date and time: 1st day of the 1st month, Chia Tzu year, at
  Wu 'hour'
Year characters: Chia Tzu (A1)
Month characters: Ping Yin (C3)
Day characters: Chia Yin (A3)
'Hour' characters: Keng Wu (G7)
Palace: Yu
Constellation: Pig
Element: Wood
Animal sign: Rat

Example 2

Born on 23 April 1936 at 2.20 p.m.
Chinese date and time: 3rd day of the 3rd month,* Ping Tzu year, at
  Wei 'hour'
Year characters: Ping Tzu (C1)
Month characters: Jen Ch'en (J5)
Day characters: Yi Hai (B12)
'Hour' characters: Kuei Wei (K8)
Palace: Wu
Constellation: Tapir
Element: Wood
Animal sign: Rat

* This is an intercalary month; see p. 25.

Example 3

Born on 1 June 1949 at 4.50 p.m.
Chinese date and time: 5th day of the 5th month, Chi Ch'ou year, at
  Shen 'hour'
Year characters: Chi Ch'ou (F2)
Month characters: Keng Wu (G7)
Day characters: Jen Hsü (J11)
'Hour' characters: Mou Shen (E9)
Palace: Mao
Constellation: Gibbon
Element: Water
Animal sign: Ox

Example 4

Born on 7 October 1978 at 10.50 p.m.
Chinese date and time: 6th day of the 9th month, Mou Wu year, at
  Hai 'hour'
Year characters: Mou Wu (E7)
Month characters: Jen Hsü (J11)
Day characters: Jen Yin (J3)
'Hour' characters: Hsin Hai (H12)
Palace: Shen
Constellation: Pheasant
Element: Water
Animal sign: Horse

Example 5 (to be filled in by the reader)
Born: 1 2 . 2 46
Chinese date and time: KENG YIN
Year characters: PING HSÜ
Month characters: "   G 3 DG
Day characters:
'Hour' characters: CHOU
Palace: CHIA CHEN
Constellation: MONKEY
Element: FIRE
Animal sign: OX

Table 1

Heavenly Stems, Elements and Codes

In the Calendar Tables we have coded the Heavenly Stems from A to K, as shown below.

In Chinese thought the Heavenly Stems are linked with the elements, each element corresponding to two stems. To find your element you need the Heavenly Stem for your day of birth. For example, if you were born on a day whose Heavenly Stem is Hsin, your element will be Metal.

Code	Heavenly Stem	Element
A	Chia	Wood
B	Yi	Wood
C	Ping	Fire
D	Ting	Fire
E	Mou	Earth
F	Chi	Earth
G	Keng	Metal
H	Hsin	Metal
J	Jen	Water
K	Kuei	Water

Table 2

Earthly Branches, 'Hours', Animal Signs and Codes

In the Calendar Tables we have coded the Earthly Branches from 1 to 12, as shown below.

In Chinese thought the Earthly Branches are linked with the twelve 'hours' of the day and the twelve animal signs for the years.

Your Earthly Branch for the 'hour' of your birth depends on the time you were born. For example, someone born at 5.20 a.m. belongs to the 'hour' 5 a.m.–7 a.m. and has the Earthly Branch Mao.*

Your animal sign depends on the Earthly Branch for the year of your birth. For example, if you were born in a year whose Earthly Branch is Tzu you would be under the animal sign of the Rat.

Code	Earthly Branch	'Hour'	Animal Sign
1	Tzu	11 p.m.–1 a.m.	Rat
2	Ch'ou	1 a.m.–3 a.m.	Ox
3	Yin	3 a.m.–5 a.m.	Tiger
4	Mao	5 a.m.–7 a.m.	Rabbit
5	Ch'en	7 a.m.–9 a.m.	Dragon
6	Szu	9 a.m.–11 a.m.	Snake
7	Wu	11 a.m.–1 p.m.	Horse
8	Wei	1 p.m.–3 p.m.	Ram
9	Shen	3 p.m.–5 p.m.	Monkey
10	Yu	5 p.m.–7 p.m.	Cock
11	Hsü	7 p.m.–9 p.m.	Dog
12	Hai	9 p.m.–11 p.m.	Pig

---

* In the *Three Lives* only the Earthly Branch for the 'hour' of birth is used in the predictions. However, for a full eight-character horoscope the Heavenly Stem would also be needed and this can be found in Table 3.

Table 3

Heavenly Stems and Earthly Branches for the 'Hours' of Birth

To use this table you need the Heavenly Stem for your day of birth (see also Calendar Tables) and also your 'hour' of birth (see Table 2). Find your Heavenly Stem in the column headings; there are two stems per column, so a person with Hsin as his or her Heavenly Stem will use the same column as someone with Ping. Find your 'hour' of birth in the side headings, and where the row from your 'hour' intersects with the column from your Heavenly Stem you will find the characters for your 'hour' of birth.

'Hour' of Birth	*Heavenly Stem for Day of Birth*				
	Chia (A) *Chi (F)*	*Yi (B)* *Keng (G)*	*Ping (C)* *Hsin (H)*	*Ting (D)* *Jen (J)*	*Mou (E)* *Kuei (K)*
11 p.m. –1 a.m. (Tzu)	Chia Tzu	Ping Tzu	Mou Tzu	Keng Tzu	Jen Tzu
1 a.m. –3 a.m. (Ch'ou)	Yi Ch'ou	Ting Ch'ou	Chi Ch'ou	Hsin Ch'ou	Kuei Ch'ou
3 a.m. –5 a.m. (Yin)	Ping Yin	Mou Yin	Keng Yin	Jen Yin	Chia Yin
5 a.m. –7 a.m. (Mao)	Ting Mao	Chi Mao	Hsin Mao	Kuei Mao	Yi Mao
7 a.m. –9 a.m. (Ch'en)	Mou Ch'en	Keng Ch'en	Jen Ch'en	Chia Ch'en	Ping Ch'en
9 a.m. –11 a.m. (Szu)	Chi Szu	Hsin Szu	Kuei Szu	Yi Szu	Ting Szu
11 a.m. –1 p.m. (Wu)	Keng Wu	Jen Wu	Chia Wu	Ping Wu	Mou Wu
1 p.m. –3 p.m. (Wei)	Hsin Wei	Kuei Wei	Yi Wei	Ting Wei	Chi Wei
3 p.m. –5 p.m. (Shen)	Jen Shen	Chia Shen	Ping Shen	Mou Shen	Keng Shen
5 p.m. –7 p.m. (Yu)	Kuei Yu	Yi Yu	Ting Yu	Chi Yu	Hsin Yu
7 p.m. –9 p.m. (Hsü)	Chia Hsü	Ping Hsü	Mou Hsü	Keng Hsü	Jen Hsü
9 p.m. –11 p.m. (Hai)	Yi Hai	Ting Hai	Chi Hai	Hsin Hai	Kuei Hai

Table 4

The Palaces

The palaces are named after the Earthly Branches.

To find your palace you need your lunar month and 'hour' of birth (see the Calendar Tables and Table 2 respectively). Find your lunar month in the column headings and your 'hour' in the side headings of the table below. Where the row from your 'hour' intersects with the column of your lunar month you will find the name of your palace.

					Lunar Month of Birth							
'Hour' of Birth	*1st*	*2nd*	*3rd*	*4th*	*5th*	*6th*	*7th*	*8th*	*9th*	*10th*	*11th*	*12th*
11 p.m. – 1 a.m.	Mao	Yin	Ch'ou	Tzu	Hai	Hsü	Yu	Shen	Wei	Wu	Szu	Ch'en
1 a.m. – 3 a.m.	Yin	Ch'ou	Tzu	Hai	Hsü	Yu	Shen	Wei	Wu	Szu	Ch'en	Mao
3 a.m. – 5 a.m.	Ch'ou	Tzu	Hai	Hsü	Yu	Shen	Wei	Wu	Szu	Ch'en	Mao	Yin
5 a.m. – 7 a.m.	Tzu	Hai	Hsü	Yu	Shen	Wei	Wu	Szu	Ch'en	Mao	Yin	Ch'ou
7 a.m. – 9 a.m.	Hai	Hsü	Yu	Shen	Wei	Wu	Szu	Ch'en	Mao	Yin	Ch'ou	Tzu
9 a.m. – 11 a.m.	Hsü	Yu	Shen	Wei	Wu	Szu	Ch'en	Mao	Yin	Ch'ou	Tzu	Hai
11 a.m. – 1 p.m.	Yu	Shen	Wei	Wu	Szu	Ch'en	Mao	Yin	Ch'ou	Tzu	Hai	Hsü
1 p.m. – 3 p.m.	Shen	Wei	Wu	Szu	Ch'en	Mao	Yin	Ch'ou	Tzu	Hai	Hsü	Yu
3 p.m. – 5 p.m.	Wei	Wu	Szu	Ch'en	Mao	Yin	Ch'ou	Tzu	Hai	Hsü	Yu	Shen
5 p.m. – 7 p.m.	Wu	Szu	Ch'en	Mao	Yin	Ch'ou	Tzu	Hai	Hsü	Yu	Shen	Wei
7 p.m. – 9 p.m.	Szu	Ch'en	Mao	Yin	Ch'ou	Tzu	Hai	Hsü	Yu	Shen	Wei	Wu
9 p.m. – 11 p.m.	Ch'en	Mao	Yin	Ch'ou	Tzu	Hai	Hsü	Yu	Shen	Wei	Wu	Szu

How to Do a Reading

In this chapter we give two examples of horoscope readings using the *Three Lives*, following the order of the sections as they appear in this edition. The readings illustrate how a person's eight characters, plus the palace, element, animal sign and constellation are used to give a set of predictions which cover all the major aspects of his or her life. Each example starts with a step-by-step description of how to compile this basic information before actually using the *Three Lives* predictions. By working through the two examples you will see how to set about compiling a horoscope reading for yourself.

Horoscope Reading 1

Rachel was born on 27 November 1963 at 4 a.m.

Before using the *Three Lives* predictions she first records the following pieces of information for reference:

(i) *her solar date and time of birth:* 27 November 1963, 4 a.m.

She looks up this solar date in the Calendar Tables and reads across to the second column to find:

(ii) *her lunar date of birth:* 12.10 – 12th day, 10th month

At the beginning of the Chinese year for her lunar date of birth she finds:

(iii) *the Heavenly Stem and Earthly Branch for the year:* Kuei Mao

In the third column she finds:

(iv) *the code of the Heavenly Stem and Earthly Branch for the month:* K12

In the fourth column she finds:

(v) *the code of the Heavenly Stem and Earthly Branch for the day:* A11

In the fifth column she finds

(vi) *her constellation:* Gibbon

She turns to the front of the Calendar Tables and looks up the letter and number codes for the month (K12, see iv) and the day (A11, see v). She identifies:

(vii) *her Heavenly Stem and Earthly Branch*
(a) *for the month:* Kuei Hai (K12)
(b) *for the day:* Chia Hsü (A11)

In Table 2 she looks up her time of birth (she was born at 4 a.m.). She identifies:

(viii) *her 'hour':* 3 – 5 a.m.

In the same table she looks up:

(ix) *her Earthly Branch for the 'hour':* Yin

She can also use Table 2 to find her animal sign. Using her Earthly Branch for the year (Mao, see iii), she identifies:

(x) *her animal sign:* Rabbit

In Table 3, using her Heavenly Stem for the day (Chia, see vii (b)) and her 'hour' (3 – 5 a.m., see viii), she identifies:

(xi) *her Heavenly Stem and Earthly Branch for the 'hour':* Ping Yin

In Table 1, using her Heavenly Stem for the day (Chia, see vii (b)), she identifies:

(xii) *her element:* Wood

She turns to Table 4 and, using her 'hour' (3 – 5 a.m., see viii) and her lunar month (the 10th, see ii), she looks up:

(xiii) *her palace:* Ch'en

Rachel now has all the information she needs to use the *Three Lives* predictions and find the readings that apply to her. Here is how she does it:

THE TWENTY-EIGHT CONSTELLATIONS

Rachel already knows that her constellation is the Gibbon (see vi). She also knows that her palace is Ch'en (see xiii). She finds the Gibbon constellation in the text and below it the Ch'en Palace. Her reading is as follows:

You will receive help and comfort from your wife or husband.

YOUR PREVIOUS, PRESENT AND FUTURE LIVES

Rachel was born in the 10th month (see ii). Part of the reading which appears under the Tenth Month is as follows:

> . . . *you will have a reasonable income and be an artist. Your relationship with your parents will be poor and you will not be able to depend on your brothers. If you wish to improve your relationships, you should cultivate humility and a more yielding, giving nature.*

TREASURE FOR THIS LIFE (PURPLE MYRTLE STARS)

The Earthly Branch for Rachel's year of birth is Mao (see iii). The corresponding star in the chart is the Wu Ch'u Star, which gives the reading:

> *You will be clever and will have a large fortune and prosperity in old age.*

REWARDS FOR YOUR PREVIOUS LIFE

The Heavenly Stem for Rachel's day of birth is Chia (see vii (b)). In the table the 10th month does not appear under this stem. This means she has no key and no reward. This is neither positive nor negative.

THE FIVE ASPECTS OF THE TWELVE ANIMAL SIGNS

Rachel's animal sign is the Rabbit (see x) and her Heavenly Stem and Earthly Branch for the year are Kuei Mao (see iii). This means she belongs to the Rabbit Running In the Forest. The prediction reads:

> *You will always have plenty of money and be able to turn hardship to good. While young you will spend all you earn, but after your middle years you will meet the right people to bring you good fortune, and will live in splendour, with riches and honours. If you are a woman, you will be a good housewife.*

YOUR PALACE AND YOUR PERSONALITY STAR

Rachel's palace is the Ch'en Palace (see xiii). The corresponding star in the text is T'ien Hao.

> *You will encounter the right people a the right time. You are stable, kind, clever and quick to understand. There is no problem, however difficult, that you cannot rapidly solve. You are a talented all-rounder with a literary flair. One day you will be famous in the arts . . .*

'HOUR' OF BIRTH 1

The Earthly Branch for Rachel's 'hour' of birth is Yin (see ix).

You will be prosperous and honoured and will have many children. You may be promoted to a high position.

'HOUR' OF BIRTH 2: OVERVIEW OF YOUR LIFE

Here is another reading for the Earthly Branch for her 'hour' of birth, Yin.

You will not be in harmony with your parents, your wife or children. You will leave your home town. When young your luck will be poor, but after middle age everything will improve. You are clever and a good writer. At the age of sixty you will have some difficulty, but if you can get through this you will live to the age of eighty.

ANIMAL-BONE FORTUNE

The Earthly Branch for Rachel's 'hour' of birth is Yin (see ix) and she was born in the 10th lunar month (see ii). The chart gives the key Ram Bone.

You are uncooperative and impatient. You should work away from home. You will not inherit property so will have to buy your own. In old age you will have a great fortune.

NOBLE (GOOD FORTUNE) STARS

The Heavenly Stem for Rachel's day of birth is Chia (see vii (b)) and she was born in the 10th lunar month (see ii). The chart gives the star T'ien Yi.

. . . you will be prosperous, enjoy life peacefully and have a great fortune. You will have a farm or large property.

BALEFUL STARS

The Heavenly Stem for Rachel's day of birth is Chia (see vii (b)) and she was born in the 10th lunar month (see ii). The chart gives the star Ta Pai.

You will have bad luck and none of your endeavours will succeed. However, if a lucky star should shine on you, your life will be a little less harsh.

BAD LUCK AND FAILURE

Rachel was born in year Kuei Mao (see iii). The unlucky month for this year is the 7th month. Since she was born in the 10th month she has no need to fear severe bad luck or failure.

THE NINE STARS

This section gives an outlook for a particular year of Rachel's life. Let us assume she is finding a reading when she is twenty-two, i.e. between November 1985 and November 1986. This gives the star T'ai-yang.

Your life will be lucky and your endeavours will flourish. You will acquire property and land and there will be a new baby in your family.

THE YEARLY GOD (T'AI SUI)

When she is twenty-two the corresponding yearly god is Ghost.

This year you will spend time in mourning and have many legal problems. There will be sickness, injury, quarrels and trouble.

THE TWELVE CREATURES

The Earthly Branch for the year when Rachel was born is Mao (see iii) and she was born in the 10th month (see ii). In the chart this gives the creature Stag.

You will be prosperous, but will never feel satisfied, always yearning after greater material rewards.

MARITAL FATE

Rachel's element is Wood (see xii) and she was born in the 10th month (see ii). In the chart this gives her marital fate as Harmony.

You and your husband will love each other very much and live happily together.

MARITAL HARMONY

Her element is Wood and she was born in the 10th month. In the chart this gives her harmony key as Ch'ang Sheng.

You and your husband will live in harmony with each other and with your children. Your family will be happy and prosperous.

BROTHERS' HARMONY

Her harmony key, as in the previous section, is Ch'ang Sheng.

As long as you and your brothers do not live in the same house, you will get on. You will have two or three brothers or cousins.

CHILDREN'S BRIDGES

Rachel's element is Wood (see xii) and she was born in the 10th month. For a woman the bridge given in the chart is the First Bridge.

You will have three sons but one will die. If you cultivate kindness you will be healthy and prosperous.

EDUCATION STARS

The Earthly Branch for Rachel's 'hour' of birth is Yin (see ix) and she was born in the 10th month. The chart gives the star Hsiang.

You like academic work, especially writing and art, and study hard and well. One day you will be famous.

SCHOOLING AND CAREER SUCCESS

The Earthly Branch for Rachel's year of birth is Mao (see iii) and the Earthly Branch for her 'hour' is Yin (see ix). This gives three separate constellations in the chart: Rat, Cock 1 and Dog.

Rat
Education: up to a Master's degree.
Occupation: a senior clerical post.
In Tzu year (Year of the Rat) you will graduate with your Master's degree.
In Ch'en year (Year of the Dragon) you will secure the post of an area officer. Your career will blossom and you will reach a senior level.

Cock 1
Education: up to at least a Master's degree.
Occupation: a government minister or a managing director.
In the spring of Wei Year (Year of the Sheep) you will graduate.
In the autumn of Yu Year (Year of the Cock) you will start to build up your career and, before long, you will be well known in your field.

Dog

Education: secondary school.
Occupation: civil servant.
You will be successful but you will have to work hard.

THE FIVE ELEMENTS OF YOUR CAREER

Rachel's Earthly Branch for her 'hour' of birth is Yin (see ix). The 10th lunar month does not appear in the chart under Yin so there is no key. This means there is no reading.

CAREER STARS

Her Heavenly Stem for the day is Chia (see vii (b)) and she is born in the 10th lunar month. The chart gives the star Tailor.

If you have no skill in tailoring you will quarrel with your brothers.

TRAVELLING STARS

Rachel's Earthly Branch for her 'hour' of birth is Yin (see ix) and she was born in the 10th lunar month. The chart gives the travelling star Nien Sha.

You will leave home to work. Your brothers will not give you a hand. You should buy a house to live in as your family will leave you nothing.

WEALTH STARS

Rachel's Earthly Branch for her 'hour' of birth is Yin (see ix) and she was born in the 10th lunar month. The chart gives the wealth star Chih Lu.

Prosperity and success will be yours. After the first twenty years you will have splendour, riches and honours. You will have 500 catties of rice, two jars of wine, 5 catties of meat, 1 catty 4 taels of oil and salt, and 200 coins.

PROPERTY STARS

Her Earthly Branch for the 'hour' of birth is Yin and she was born in the 10th lunar month. The chart gives the stars ★ ★ ★.

You are not suited to buying a house on your own. Buy with your partner or else you will have bad luck and hurt yourself.

BURIAL PALACES

Rachel's element is Wood (see xii) and her Earthly Branch for the 'hour' is Yin (see ix). The chart gives the burial palace Lin Kuan.

You will be ill for three days, then die. On the day of your funeral the weather will be changeable. You will have a fine coffin and two sons and two daughters will perform your funeral rites. It will be a splendid funeral.

Horoscope Reading 2

Paul was born on 7 June 1949 at 4 p.m. He first records the following pieces of information for reference:

(i) *his solar date and time of birth:* 7 June 1949, 4 p.m.

He looks up this solar date and time of the Calendar Tables and reads across to the second column to find:

(ii) *his lunar date of birth:* 11.5 – 11th day, 5th month

At the beginning of the Chinese Year for his lunar date of birth he finds:

(iii) *the Heavenly Stem and Earthly Branch for the year:* Chi Ch'ou

In the third column he finds:

(iv) *the code of the Heavenly Stem and Earthly Branch for the month:* G7

In the fourth column he finds:

(v) *the code of the Heavenly Stem and Earthly Branch for the day:* E5

In the fifth column he finds:

(vi) *his constellation:* Serpent

He turns to the front of the Calendar Tables and looks up the letter and number codes for the month (G7, see iv) and the day (E5, see v). He identifies:

(vii) *his Heavenly Stem and Earthly Branch:*

(a) *for the month:* Keng Wu (G7)
(b) *for the day:* Mou Ch'en (E5)

In Table 2 he looks up his time of birth (he was born at 4 p.m.). He identifies:

(viii) *his 'hour':* 3–5 p.m.

In the same table he looks up:

(ix) *his Earthly Branch for the 'hour':* Shen.

He can also use Table 2 to find his animal sign. Using his Earthly Branch for the year (Ch'ou, see iii), he identifies:

(x) *his animal sign:* Ox

In Table 3, using his Heavenly Stem for the day (Mou, see vii (b)) and his 'hour' (3–5 p.m., see viii), he finds:

(xi) *his Heavenly Stem and Earthly Branch for the 'hour':* Keng Shen

In Table 1, using his Heavenly Stem for the day (Mou, see vii (b)), he identifies:

(xii) *his element:* Earth

He turns to Table 4 and, using his 'hour' (3–5 p.m., see viii) and his lunar month (the 5th, see ii), he looks up:

(xiii) *his palace:* Mao

Paul now has all the information he needs to use the *Three Lives* predictions and find the readings that apply to him. He goes about it as follows:

THE TWENTY-EIGHT CONSTELLATIONS

Paul knows that his constellation is the Serpent (see vi). He also knows that his palace is Mao (see xiii). He finds the Serpent constellation in the text and below it the Mao Palace. The prediction states:

You will lose your home and your fortune.

YOUR PREVIOUS, PRESENT AND FUTURE LIVES

Paul was born in the 5th lunar month (see ii). Part of the reading which appears under the Fifth Month is as follows:

. . . you will be wealthy and never suffer financial trouble, but you will not be able to depend on your parents, brothers, wife or children. You will live to a great age.

TREASURE FOR THIS LIFE (PURPLE MYRTLE STARS)

The Earthly Branch for Paul's year of birth is Ch'ou (see iii). The corresponding star is Chu Men.

. . . you quarrel a lot and have many problems. You are obstinate and suffer from minor illnesses. You must set a place in your home for your ancestors.

REWARDS FOR YOUR PREVIOUS LIFE

The Heavenly Stem for Paul's day of birth is Mou (see vii (b)). The 5th month appears twice under this stem. This means there are two rewards, Hsiang Lu and Sha Lu, and therefore two readings, which will not necessarily seem compatible.

HSIANG LU

You will be prosperous and lucky. It would be best for you to work away from home. You will have a large fortune and will never need to worry about where your next meal will come from. Strengthen your resolve and everyone will respect you. You will be able to transform suffering and hardship into good fortune.

SHA LU

You are a sybarite and will travel widely, earning your living by cunning. You will end up with nothing if you do not settle down and work.

THE FIVE ASPECTS OF THE TWELVE ANIMAL SIGNS

Paul's animal sign is Ox and his Heavenly Stem and Earthly Branch for the year are Chi Ch'ou (see iii). This means he belongs to the Ox In the Gate.

You are candid and tend to speak without thinking things through. You rely on others for money, although you have plenty of work. . . . you may marry more than once.

YOUR PALACE AND YOUR PERSONALITY STAR

Paul's palace is the Mao Palace (see xiii). The corresponding star is T'ien P'o.

You will have a great fortune at first, but will eventually lose everything. You will be eager to make another fortune, but even in your last years you will not regain your former wealth. You will receive nothing from your family.

'HOUR' OF BIRTH 1

The Earthly Branch for Paul's 'hour' of birth is Shen (see ix).

You will not be in harmony with your wife and friends. If you cultivate kindness and virtue you can live peacefully.

'HOUR' OF BIRTH 2: OVERVIEW OF YOUR LIFE

A second reading for the Earthly Branch for his 'hour' of birth, Shen.

You will not be in harmony with your parents and brothers. . . . You will have enough to live on. . . . you will quarrel a lot. You will receive help from the right person at the right time. You should leave your home town to work. You will have three sons. At the age of fifty-six you will face difficulty, but then will live to eighty-three.

ANIMAL-BONE FORTUNE

The Earthly Branch for Paul's 'hour' of birth is Shen (see ix) and he was born in the 5th lunar month. The table gives the key Monkey Bone.

You have natural skill and talent. You are clever, quick-thinking and impatient. You like eating fruit. At times you act without thinking.

NOBLE (GOOD FORTUNE) STARS

The Heavenly Stem for Paul's day of birth is Mou (see vii (b)). However, in the table the 5th month does not appear under Mou. This gives no noble star and no reading.

BALEFUL STARS

The Heavenly Stem for Paul's day of birth is Mou (see vii (b)) and he was born in the 5th lunar month. The table gives two stars, Lang Chi and P'o Chia Sha, so there are two readings.

LANG CHI

You will have no fortune. It is inadvisable for you to live in any house you might inherit. You should leave your home town to work.

P'O CHIA SHA

If you leave your home town to work, prosperity and a great fortune will be yours.

BAD LUCK AND FAILURE

Paul was born in the year Chi Ch'ou (see iii). The unlucky month for this year is the 9th month. Since he was born in the 5th month he has no particular risk of bad luck or failure.

THE NINE STARS

For Paul's age of thirty-seven, i.e. between June 1986 and June 1987, the chart gives the star T'u Su.

Although this star is baleful, no disaster will happen in autumn and winter. You can rid yourself of the bad luck by cultivating kindness.

THE YEARLY GOD (T'AI SUI)

When he is thirty-seven his yearly god is the Sun.

. . . your lucky star has arrived. Everything will be successful. You will communicate well with others and will live peacefully.

THE TWELVE CREATURES

The Earthly Branch for the year when Paul was born is Ch'ou (see iii) and he was born in the 5th lunar month. The chart gives his creature as Mandarin Duck.

You will be prosperous, for you are artistically talented and lucky. You will do well if you take up a job as a civil servant.

MARITAL FATE

Paul's element is Earth (see xii) and he was born in the 5th month. In the chart this gives his marital fate as Separation.

Due to force of circumstance you and your wife will spend more time apart than together. You will both have been married before. This marriage should be better than the first.

MARITAL HARMONY

As his element is Earth (see xii) and he was born in the 5th month, his harmony key is T'ai Kung.

You and your wife will be separated from each other unless one of you has been married before. You will be a loner with no one else to talk to or go out with.

BROTHERS' HARMONY

His key, as in the previous section, is T'ai Kung.

There will be a rift between you and your brothers and you will not talk things over.

CHILDREN'S BRIDGES

Paul's element is Earth (see xii) and he was born in the 5th month. The bridge given in the chart for a man is the Second Bridge.

You will have six sons, one of whom will emigrate to work. Your last child will be a boy. Be careful of poisonous creatures and people.

EDUCATION STARS

The Earthly Branch for his 'hour' of birth is Shen (see ix) and he was born in the 5th month. The chart gives the star Ho.

You like academic work, especially writing and art, and study hard and well. One day you will be famous.

SCHOOLING AND CAREER SUCCESS

The Earthly Branch for Paul's year of birth is Ch'ou (see iii) and his Earthly Branch for his 'hour' is Shen (see ix). Shen does not appear in the row for Ch'ou in the chart, so there is no reading.

CAREER STARS

His Heavenly Stem for the day is Mou (see vii (b)) and he was born in the 5th lunar month. The table gives the career star as Official.

You will have great wealth and prosperity. You will be a capable writer with an artistic bent.

THE FIVE ELEMENTS OF YOUR CAREER

Paul's Earthly Branch for his 'hour' of birth is Shen (see ix) and he was born in the 5th lunar month. This gives his career element as Wood Trading.

You are suited to a business or occupation related to wood (e.g. carpentry, furniture making, forestry, paper making).

TRAVELLING STARS

Paul's Earthly Branch for the 'hour' of birth is Shen (see ix) and he was born in the 5th month. This gives his travelling star as Yueh Sha.

You will have a fortune, but will not be in harmony with your wife. You are not a suitable person to live in any house you might inherit. You should buy your own house and then you will be lucky.

WEALTH STARS

Paul's Earthly Branch for his 'hour' of birth is Shen (see ix) and he was born in the 5th lunar month. The chart gives his wealth star as P'o Lu.

You will not have much money and will have to work hard to earn your living. Your brothers will be unable to help you and you will not inherit any property. You would do better to work away from your home town. Your life is ordained in Heaven, it is impossible to force anything. The later stage of your life will not be so bad. You will have 100 catties of rice, one jar of wine, 1 catty 4 taels of meat, and 100 coins.

PROPERTY STARS

His Earthly Branch for the 'hour' of birth is Shen and he was born in the 5th lunar month. The chart gives the key ☆.

Beware of accidents, especially in May, July and September each year. You will have many opportunities to make money.

BURIAL PALACES

Paul's element is Earth (see xii) and his Earthly Branch for his 'hour' of birth is Shen (see ix). The chart gives his palace as Ch'ang Sheng.

At sixty-seven you will be ill for two days, then die. The day of your funeral will be sunny. Your grave clothes will be fine and the wood used for the coffin will be yellow. You will have two sons and two daughters to perform your funeral rites. It would not be advisable for those aged forty-five to attend your funeral. There will be four to six monks to carry your coffin to the cemetery. It will be a splendid funeral.

The Three Lives
Predictions

The Twenty-Eight Constellations

The Twenty-Eight Constellations are associated with twenty-eight legendary heroes who died in a civil war during the T'ang dynasty (618–906 CE) and were immortalized. The constellations are also associated with twenty-eight animals, and it is these that are used in the *Three Lives*.

The constellations change on a daily basis over twenty-eight days. In four groups of seven they are also linked to and change with the seasons. The spring, summer, autumn and winter groups correspond respectively to the four elements Wood, Fire, Metal and Water. The constellation on duty on the day of your birth will stand with you for your entire life.

To use this section, look up your constellation in the Calendar Tables and your palace in Table 4. Then turn to your constellation below, and under it find your palace. The following prediction relates to you.

CROCODILE (unstable and slow-witted)

Tzu Palace	You must be prepared for sudden troubles.
Ch'ou Palace	You will have many misfortunes in life.
Yin Palace	You will live among poor and uneducated people and fight for their rights.
Mao Palace	You are a capable and authoritative person.
Ch'en Palace	When young, you will experience many difficulties. You would be better taking a technical job rather than a clerical post.
Szu Palace	People will not cooperate with you and things will not go well.
Wu Palace	You will suffer from frequent bad luck when you try to improve your lot.
Wei Palace	Your career will blossom and one day you will be well known.
Shen Palace	Disaster may strike at any time.

Yu Palace · You will have a successful life but it would be a mistake for you to work away from home.

Hsü Palace · You will have many trials and tribulations in life.

Hai Palace · You will pursue the good life without concern for others.

DRAGON (clever and quick to understand)

Tzu Palace · You will have a successful life and good fortune.

Ch'ou Palace · You will have many troubles in life and should be particularly wary of fire.

Yin Palace · Life may not be so easy when you are young but will greatly improve in middle age.

Mao Palace · You will be unknown in your early years, but eventually you will be famous.

Ch'en Palace · You will have misfortune when young but good luck will come in middle age.

Szu Palace · Although you are hardworking, you will never be well off.

Wu Palace · Everything in life will be blighted.

Wei Palace	You will have a difficult youth but will be very rich in old age.
Shen Palace	No matter what you do to improve your circumstances, you will be dogged by bad luck.
Yu Palace	You will be well known to others through your own efforts as well as by the fortune and reputation of your family.
Hsü Palace	No matter how hard you try, money will not come easily to you.
Hai Palace	Your career or business will collapse in ruins if you have affairs with beautiful women.

BADGER (slow-witted and irreligious)

Tzu Palace	All your endeavours will succeed.
Ch'ou Palace	You will always have enough money to live on.
Yin Palace	You are full of fears and worries.
Mao Palace	It would be better for you to work away from home.

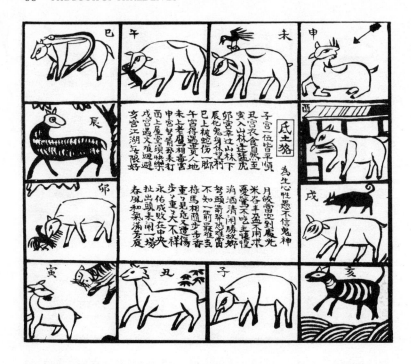

Ch'en Palace	Beware of petty people.
Szu Palace	Beware of petty people.
Wu Palace	The lucky star will bring the right people into your life to help your career.
Wei Palace	Be careful when dealing with an unscrupulous man.
Shen Palace	You will face many difficulties in life.
Yu Palace	You enjoy family life. If you live a sensible, upright life, all will go smoothly.
Hsü Palace	Beware of fire.
Hai Palace	You will receive a lot of help from friends and relatives and will fulfil your ambitions.

HARE (literary and impatient)

Tzu Palace	You greatly enjoy life.
Ch'ou Palace	You will have a successful life.

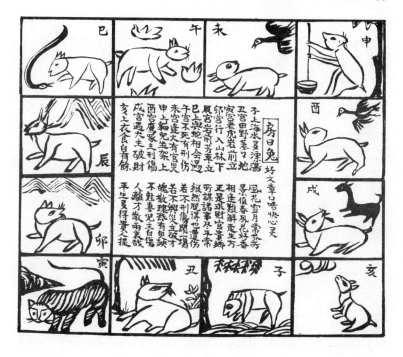

Yin Palace	It would be better for you to live and work away from home.
Mao Palace	You will be in a position to follow the career of your choice or set up your own business.
Ch'en Palace	Your career or business will enjoy moderate success.
Szu Palace	Even though you will be able to overcome your problems, the pain they leave will still trouble you.
Wu Palace	You will have a hard life and misfortune.
Wei Palace	You will suffer from many problems and may find yourself embroiled in lawsuits.
Shen Palace	Do not indulge in dangerous pursuits or you run the risk of injury.
Yu Palace	The misfortune you are destined for will also affect members of your family.
Hsü Palace	You will lose all your money and leave your family.
Hai Palace	The right people will be at hand to bring you good fortune.

FOX (loves dressing-up; lewd, but not bad at heart)

Tzu Palace   You will have a fine reputation and a large fortune.
Ch'ou Palace   Your life will run smoothly.
Yin Palace   You will experience many irresolvable difficulties.
Mao Palace   You will enjoy a peaceful life.
Ch'en Palace   You will be happy and prosperous.
Szu Palace   You will be prey to disasters and the intrigues of petty
                 people.
Wu Palace   You will suffer from many problems, including ill
                 health.
Wei Palace   Be alert for sudden disasters.
Shen Palace   You may be helped by the right person at the right
                 time. You will have a secure livelihood.
Yu Palace   You will win many hearts.
Hsü Palace   Be prepared for disasters occurring when no friends or
                 relatives can help you. There will be a time when
                 you will lose all your fortune.
Hai Palace   If you work hard you will lead a stable and settled life.

TIGER (quick to anger, quick to laugh, gluttonous, good-hearted)

Tzu Palace	Avoid legal wrangles and the intrigues of petty people.
Ch'ou Palace	The right person will be on hand to help you. Your endeavours will succeed.
Yin Palace	You will always have a roof over your head.
Mao Palace	If you avoid petty people, you will live long.
Ch'en Palace	Watch out for mean minds.
Szu Palace	You will suffer from many problems.
Wu Palace	You will receive help from the right person at the right time.
Wei Palace	Your life will be a series of happy events.
Shen Palace	Watch out for trouble caused by distant relatives. Disasters will strike.
Yu Palace	You will have many problems.
Hsü Palace	You will have very few troubles and will not need to worry about where your next meal is coming from.
Hai Palace	Throughout life you will prosper and, in later life, you will be rich.

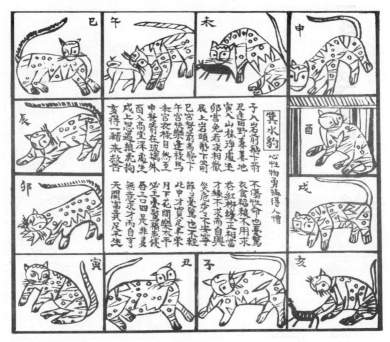

LEOPARD (brave but cruel; disliked)

Tzu Palace	Be careful of two-faced people.
Ch'ou Palace	You will always have enough to live on.
Yin Palace	You will prosper.
Mao Palace	Although you are unconcerned about it, fame will come easily to you.
Ch'en Palace	Watch out for the intrigues of petty people. Disasters will come your way.
Szu Palace	You will suffer an accident.
Wu Palace	You will be happy and prosperous.
Wei Palace	You will always have food to eat and a bed to sleep in. Life will be enjoyable and peaceful.
Shen Palace	You are a worrier, always fearing the worst.
Yu Palace	You will be plagued with troubles.
Hsü Palace	Small-minded people may cause problems for you. Although you are unconcerned about it, fame will come easily to you.
Hai Palace	The right person will be on hand to help you and you will have a rewarding life.

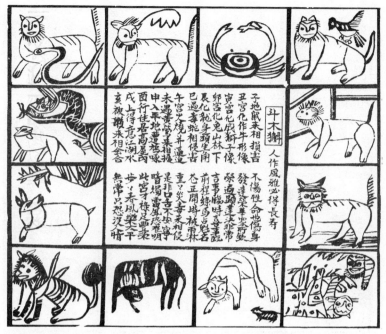

GRIFFON (refined and long-lived)

Tzu Palace	You will be prey to petty people.
Ch'ou Palace	You will be happy and prosperous.
Yin Palace	You will be well known, rich and lucky.
Mao Palace	Your life will be full of happy times.
Ch'en Palace	You will be well known and prosperous.
Szu Palace	Small-minded people will cause problems for you.
Wu Palace	Calamities will frequently befall you, causing much worry.
Wei Palace	You will be troubled by malicious gossip.
Shen Palace	You will fall foul of the intrigues of a small mind and life will be hard.
Yu Palace	You will be prosperous, with an extravagant lifestyle and a large fortune.
Hsü Palace	You will have a peaceful and successful life.
Hai Palace	No relatives or friends will sympathize with you in hard times.

OX (unstable, with a harsh life)

Tzu Palace	You will be happy and have no need to worry about your livelihood.
Ch'ou Palace	You will be a sensuous personality, delighting in eating, drinking and sex.
Yin Palace	Watch out for petty people.
Mao Palace	You will always have enough to live on.
Ch'en Palace	You will have a free and easy life.
Szu Palace	You will have many misfortunes and worries.
Wu Palace	Calamity will strike out of the blue.
Wei Palace	You will have a hard time when young but things will improve somewhat in middle age.
Shen Palace	You will be happy and very prosperous, especially in old age.
Yu Palace	You will enjoy an easy life.
Hsü Palace	Although there will be people who control you, you will be happy and well off.
Hai Palace	You will worry needlessly about your fortune which will be fine.

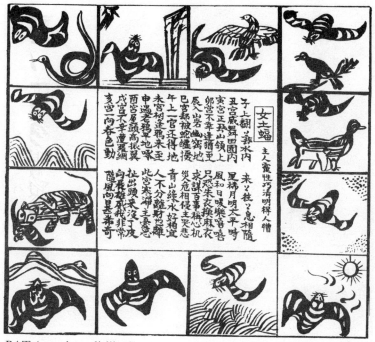

BAT (cunning; disliked)

Tzu Palace	You will have a harsh life.
Ch'ou Palace	You will always be renowned but life will be particularly good in your old age.
Yin Palace	You will enjoy a leisurely life.
Mao Palace	You may spend time in mourning.
Ch'en Palace	Your endeavours will succeed.
Szu Palace	Beware of mean minds.
Wu Palace	You will have a successful career, but you should be satisfied and not let your ambition run away with you.
Wei Palace	You could lose your fortune.
Shen Palace	There will be sad times.
Yu Palace	You will have a harsh life and nothing will go well.
Hsü Palace	Beware of being sent to prison.
Hai Palace	Beware of love affairs.

RAT (assenting with the lips, dissenting with the heart; spiteful)

Tzu Palace	You will be attractive to the opposite sex.
Ch'ou Palace	You will have good luck and happiness.
Yin Palace	You will always have a square meal.
Mao Palace	Your plans will be beset with difficulties.
Ch'en Palace	Your future will be enhanced by the right people stepping in at the right time.
Szu Palace	You will suffer from illness and calamities.
Wu Palace	You will have no trouble earning a living.
Wei Palace	Be alert for petty people and possible legal wrangles.
Shen Palace	You will have a harsh life, little money and should beware of injuries.
Yu Palace	You will have no problem finding money or building up your career.
Hsü Palace	Watch out for mean minds.
Hai Palace	You will have a balance of good and bad luck.

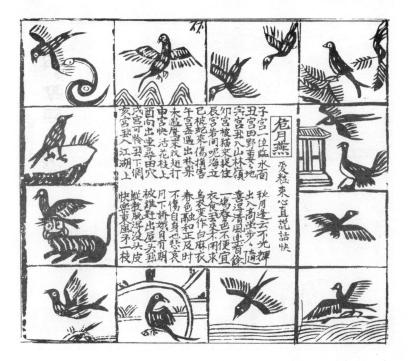

SWALLOW (loves dressing up, straightforward, quick of speech)

Tzu Palace	You will be very unlucky.
Ch'ou Palace	You will practise filial piety and be obedient.
Yin Palace	You will have a high post.
Mao Palace	Beware of affairs with beautiful women.
Ch'en Palace	You will always have a roof over your head.
Szu Palace	Beware of accidents.
Wu Palace	You will have many happy times.
Wei Palace	Beware of illness and injury.
Shen Palace	Your ventures will succeed and you will be lucky.
Yu Palace	Working away from home will bring good fortune.
Hsü Palace	Beware of lawsuits and of small-minded people.
Hai Palace	Your career will flourish.

PIG (a difficult time in spring and summer, a better time in autumn
and winter)

Tzu Palace   You will enjoy an easy life.
Ch'ou Palace   You will have a peaceful life.
Yin Palace   Beware of the machinations of a malicious person
                  who may appear to be a friend.
Mao Palace   Beware of accidents.
Ch'en Palace   You will enjoy the favours of the opposite sex.
Szu Palace   Watch out for those who secretly wish you harm.
Wu Palace   Beware of fires.
Wei Palace   You will enjoy life and avoid hard work.
Shen Palace   Be alert for accidents and disasters.
Yu Palace   It would be a mistake for you to work away from
                  home.
Hsü Palace   Beware of harm from poor and uneducated people.
Hai Palace   All your endeavours will be successful and you will
                  have good luck.

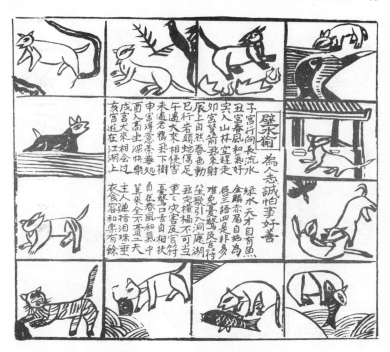

PORCUPINE (trustworthy, kind and easily frightened)

Tzu Palace	You will be talented.
Ch'ou Palace	Your relationships will be happy and easy.
Yin Palace	You will have problems.
Mao Palace	Beware of lawsuits and disasters.
Ch'en Palace	You will have a very loving marriage.
Szu Palace	Beware of accidents.
Wu Palace	Be alert for legal trouble and disasters.
Wei Palace	Beware of quarrels. You will have many worries.
Shen Palace	Your life will be happy because you will know when to compromise.
Yu Palace	Your efforts will bring a good harvest.
Hsü Palace	You will have many worries.
Hai Palace	Your daily needs will be met.

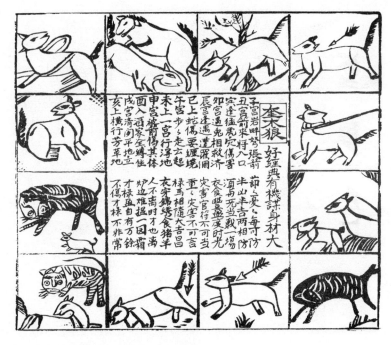

WOLF (knowledgeable; a good planner)

Tzu Palace	You will always be a worrier.
Ch'ou Palace	Beware of those who secretly wish you harm.
Yin Palace	Be alert to disasters.
Mao Palace	You will meet the right person at the right time and become rich.
Ch'en Palace	Beware of lawsuits.
Szu Palace	You will have many disasters and many worries.
Wu Place	You will be happy, peaceful and prosperous.
Wei Palace	Your livelihood will be secure.
Shen Palace	Beware of accidents and the loss of your fortune.
Yu Palace	Watch out for unhappy events.
Hsü Palace	You will enjoy life and never have to worry where your next meal is coming from.
Hai Palace	You will enjoy a peaceful life.

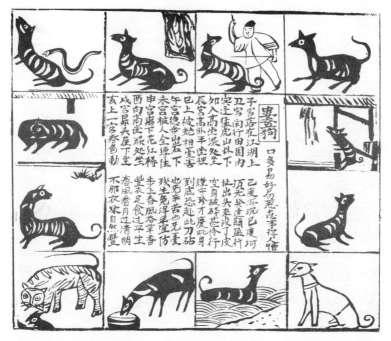

DOG (a troublemaker, loquacious, quick to laugh and quick to
  anger; disliked)

Tzu Palace   You will have a balance of good and bad luck.
Ch'ou Palace   You will have an ordinary life.
Yin Palace   Beware of accidents and disasters.
Mao Palace   You will lead a lonely life.
Ch'en Palace   You will be healthy.
Szu Palace   Watch out for small-minded people.
Wu Palace   You will have a harsh life.
Wei Palace   To ensure a long life you must always be alert.
Shen Palace   You will be very attractive to the opposite sex.
Yu Palace   You will have a hard time when young, but life will
                  greatly improve in old age.
Hsü Palace   You will watch the world from your door without
                  meddling and will have a peaceful life.
Hai Palace   Life will be good. You will never have to do without.

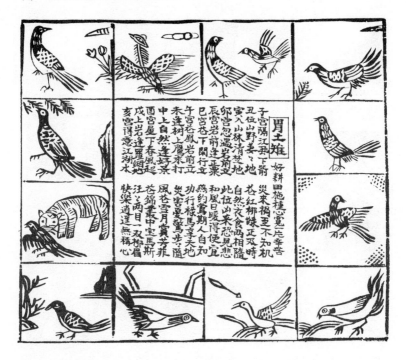

PHEASANT (generous)

Tzu Palace	Watch out for disasters.
Ch'ou Palace	You will be lucky.
Yin Palace	Daily life will run smoothly.
Mao Palace	Beware of accidents.
Ch'en Palace	Your endeavours will succeed.
Szu Palace	Many happy events will occur in life.
Wu Palace	You will have a high post and be prosperous.
Wei Palace	Beware of unscrupulous people.
Shen Palace	You will enjoy life.
Yu Palace	You will be happy, peaceful and prosperous.
Hsü Palace	Be alert to possible lawsuits.
Hai Palace	You will enjoy life and will have a secure income.

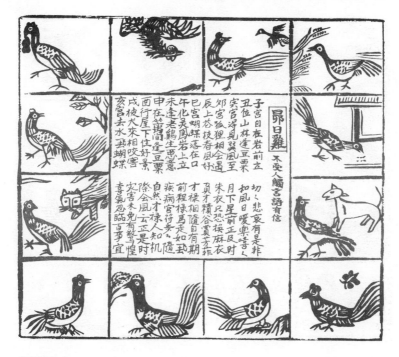

COCK (trustworthy)

Tzu Palace	You will quarrel a lot and have many worries.
Ch'ou Palace	You will enjoy life.
Yin Palace	You will have a peaceful life with much good luck.
Mao Palace	You may spend time in mourning.
Ch'en Palace	You will enjoy life.
Szu Palace	You will have a high post and a large fortune.
Wu Palace	Life will be harsh.
Wei Palace	Beware of illness and lawsuits.
Shen Palace	You will be well known.
Yu Palace	You will be very famous and enjoy great success.
Hsü Palace	Watch out for disasters.
Hai Palace	You will be able to turn bad luck into good and dangerous situations into safe ones.

CROW (enjoys leisure and fortune-telling)

Tzu Palace	You will always have enough to live on.
Ch'ou Palace	You will greatly enjoy life and have no worries.
Yin Palace	You will have a peaceful life.
Mao Palace	Beware the intrigues of malicious people.
Ch'en Palace	You will have a successful career and a large fortune.
Szu Palace	If you have patience when going through a hard time, life will eventually improve.
Wu Palace	The right person will be there at the right time to help you. Great things will happen.
Wei Palace	Be alert for disasters.
Shen Palace	You will be happy and prosperous.
Yu Palace	You will never be short of a square meal.
Hsü Palace	Be alert for possible legal trouble.
Hai Palace	You will have a steady income.

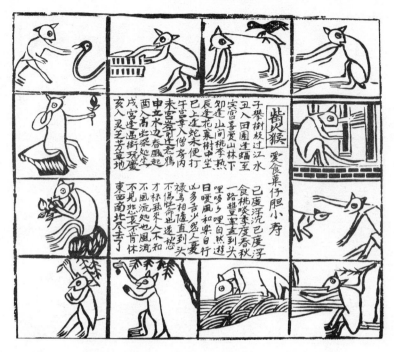

MONKEY (easily frightened, fond of fruit and long-lived)

Tzu Palace	You will have a balance of good and bad luck.
Ch'ou Palace	You will have a large fortune and good luck.
Yin Palace	Your efforts will bring a good harvest and you will be lucky.
Mao Palace	You will have good fortune.
Ch'en Palace	You will enjoy life.
Szu Palace	You will have many worries.
Wu Palace	The right person will be on hand at the right time to help you.
Wei Palace	Be alert for accidents.
Shen Palace	You will receive an unexpected fortune.
Yu Palace	A member of the opposite sex will unexpectedly come into your life and disrupt your family.
Hsü Palace	You will like being away from home and will not enjoy family life.
Hai Palace	You will enjoy travelling and will benefit from working away from home.

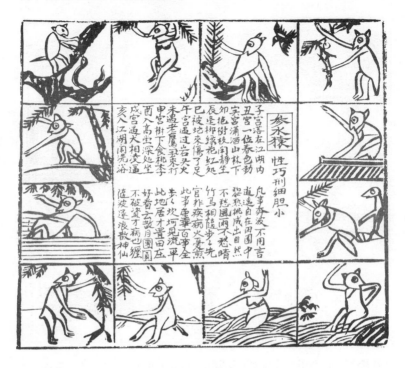

GIBBON (clever, quick-thinking, cute in appearance, cowardly)

Tzu Palace	You will have a harsh life.
Ch'ou Palace	You will enjoy life.
Yin Palace	You will enjoy life.
Mao Palace	You will have a steady income.
Ch'en Palace	You will receive help and comfort from your wife or husband.
Szu Palace	Be alert for accidents and lawsuits.
Wu Palace	You will have a hard time when young but life will improve greatly in old age.
Wei Palace	You will have a harsh life.
Shen Palace	You will be well known, happy and prosperous.
Yu Palace	You will have a hard time when young, but from middle age onwards life will be much better.
Hsü Palace	Be alert for illness and the loss of your fortune.
Hai Palace	You will enjoy life.

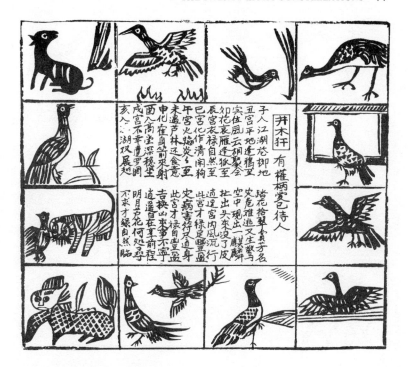

TAPIR (powerful and kind)

Tzu Palace	You will be lewd and vulgar.
Ch'ou Palace	Beware of disasters.
Yin Palace	You will have a large fortune.
Mao Palace	Although you work hard you will never have a high income.
Ch'en Palace	Your daily needs will always be met.
Szu Palace	You will have a high post and a large fortune.
Wu Palace	Beware of fires, accidents and possible illness.
Wei Palace	You will have a high post and a large fortune.
Shen Palace	Beware of sudden accidents.
Yu Palace	You will have good prospects.
Hsü Palace	Beware of ending up in prison.
Hai Palace	You will enjoy life.

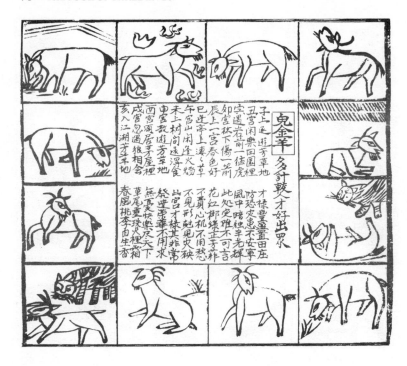

SHEEP (miserly; a show-off)

Tzu Palace   You will have a large fortune.
Ch'ou Palace   Beware of accidents.
Yin Palace   You will have a balance of good and bad luck.
Mao Palace   Beware of a possible knife injury.
Ch'en Palace   You will win hearts and have many love affairs.
Szu Palace   You will have good luck.
Wu Palace   Beware of fires.
Wei Palace   You will have a successful career and a large fortune.
Shen Palace   You will be well respected and have a large fortune.
Yu Palace   You will enjoy life.
Hsü Palace   Be alert for serious accidents.
Hai Palace   You will enjoy life.

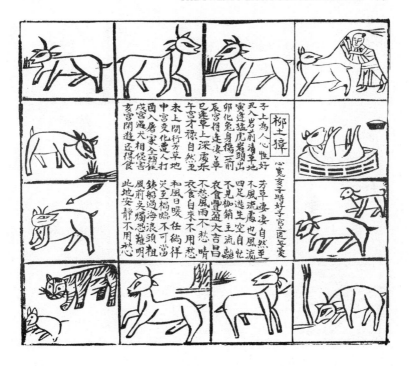

DEER (good-natured)

Tzu Palace	You are well mannered and of good character.
Ch'ou Palace	You are a womanizer.
Yin Palace	You will have many worries.
Mao Palace	You will leave home and should watch out for the intrigues of unscrupulous people.
Ch'en Palace	You will always have a steady income.
Szu Palace	You will enjoy life.
Wu Palace	You will have good luck and a large fortune.
Wei Palace	You are happy and content with a simple lifestyle.
Shen Palace	You should be alert for disasters and accidents.
Yu Palace	You will have bad luck.
Hsü Palace	Beware of petty people.
Hai Palace	You will enjoy life.

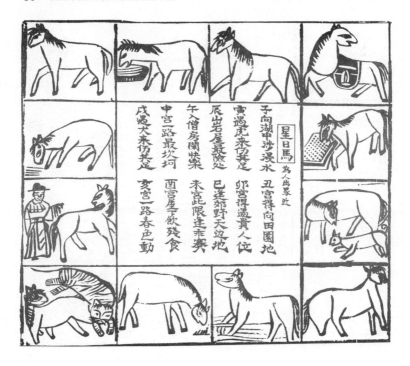

HORSE (outstanding; destined to meet the right people at the right time)

Tzu Palace	You will have a lot of troubles and difficulties throughout life.
Ch'ou Palace	You will enjoy life.
Yin Palace	Beware of unprincipled people.
Mao Palace	The right person will be there to help at the right time.
Ch'en Palace	Beware of dangerous activities.
Szu Palace	You will enjoy life.
Wu Palace	You will enjoy life.
Wei Palace	You are an odd personality.
Shen Palace	Life will be difficult.
Yu Palace	You will be poor.
Hsü Palace	Beware of malcious people.
Hai Palace	You will win favours from the opposite sex.

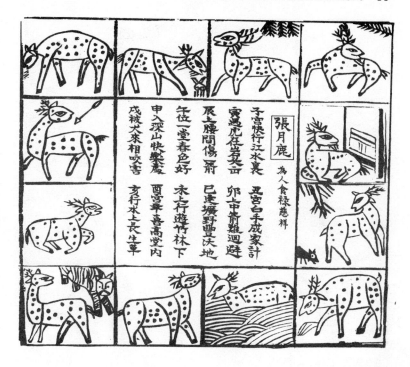

STAG (kind; enjoys eating)

Tzu Palace	You will start working early in life.
Ch'ou Palace	Through hard work you will build up a large fortune.
Yin Palace	You will be well known early in life.
Mao Palace	Be alert for possible accidents.
Ch'en Palace	Beware of small minds that wish you harm.
Szu Palace	You will be lucky.
Wu Palace	You will be a hit with the opposite sex.
Wei Palace	You will live peacefully.
Shen Palace	You will be intent on enjoying life without bothering about others.
Yu Palace	You will enjoy your home life.
Hsü Palace	Be alert for accidents.
Hai Palace	You will be very rich.

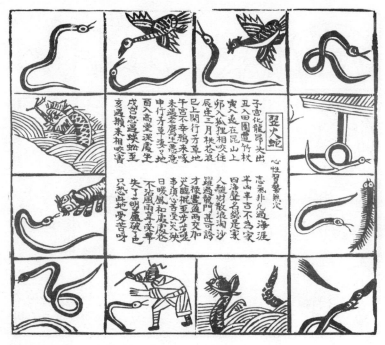

SERPENT (unskilful)

Tzu Palace   You are extremely ambitious.
Ch'ou Palace   You will have a balance of good and bad luck.
Yin Palace   You will be well known.
Mao Palace   You will lose your home and your fortune.
Ch'en Palace   You will have opportunities to succeed in your career.
Szu Palace   You will have a high post and a large fortune.
Wu Palace   Be alert for accidents and disasters.
Wei Palace   Be alert for accidents and disasters.
Shen Palace   You will have a happy life.
Yu Palace   You will be prosperous in old age.
Hsü Palace   You will suffer from disasters and lose your fortune.
Hai Palace   Beware of mean-minded people.

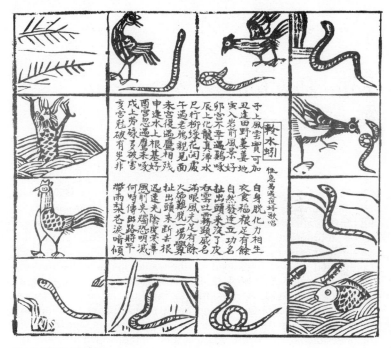

EARTHWORM (impatient; enjoys the arts)

Tzu Palace	Life will be hard when young but you will be much more successful in middle age.
Ch'ou Palace	You livelihood will be secure.
Yin Palace	You will be prosperous, with a good reputation and a large fortune.
Mao Palace	Be alert for possible injuries.
Ch'en Palace	You will be well known.
Szu Palace	You will have an enjoyable life.
Wu Palace	Beware of fires.
Wei Palace	Beware of disasters.
Shen Palace	You will be happy and prosperous.
Yu Palace	You will have a harsh life.
Hsü Palace	You will be poor and have a harsh life.
Hai Palace	You will have many troubles in life.

Your Previous, Present and Future Lives

If the *Three Lives* has a core text, this appraisal of your most recent
past life, your present life and the one to come is it. Your conduct in
one life will affect the quality of the next. Good and bad deeds will
receive appropriate rewards. Happiness and prosperity in this life
and the next can best be ensured by hard work and piety. This piety
also ensured a better livelihood for the wandering monks who drew
upon and added to this book in their role as fortune-tellers. A tight-
fisted attitude towards the monks and their needs features
prominently as a sure way to end up poor and unloved in the next
life. You will also notice that everyone's last life was in China and we
are all destined to be born there next time round, which may explain
China's one billion population.

To use this section, you need your lunar month of birth (see the
Calendar Tables). Look up the prediction for your month in the text
below. (A 'catty' is a measure of weight, approximately equal to 1
kg.)

FIRST MONTH

 You were born in the first month so you were
conceived in the fourth month of the previous year.

In your previous life you were born in Chang
Chou and your surname was Huang. You
worshipped the Buddha and donated a joss-stick urn
to the temple. You saved someone's life.

In this life you are brilliant and physically strong.
You will own many farms, but you will never be
able to depend on your children for financial support. You will not get
on with your wife so you will probably marry again.

In your next life you will be born in Chi Chou.

SECOND MONTH

You were born in the second month, so you were conceived in the fifth month of the previous year.

In your previous life you were born in Nan Kuo and your surname was Chu. You were a village elder and donated 1000 scrolls [holy scriptures] to charity.

In this life you have a noble and generous character. However, you will not be in harmony with your parents or brothers, and your son and daughter-in-law will prove unreliable. If you move away from your home town you will prosper.

In your next life you will be born into a rich family in Ts'ai Chou.

THIRD MONTH

You were born in the third month, so you were conceived in the sixth month of the previous year.

In your previous life you were born in Te Chou and your surname was Tseng. You lived in a monastery, but did not pay the fifty bowls of rice you owed as rent. You also stole clothes from an elderly person.

In this life your fortune will fluctuate, but you will always have a roof over your head, enough to eat, and keep company with the elite in both your public and your personal life. You will not be able to rely on your parents or brothers.

In your next life you will be born in Ch'ing Chou.

FOURTH MONTH

You were born in the fourth month, so you were conceived in the seventh month of the previous year.

In your previous life you were born in Szu Chou and your surname was Cheng. The malevolent fire spirit prevented you from presenting seven scrolls of T'ai Sui chanting [a traditional gift to a monastery] and you refused to guide an elderly person across a dangerous bridge.

In this life you will not get on with your parents or your first wife and you will not be able to depend on your son and daughter-in-law.

In spring and summer of each year you will have good fortune, but in autumn and winter your luck will be unremarkable. If you are a woman, you will never have to worry about where your next meal is coming from.

In your next life you will be an honourable man in Cheng Chou.

FIFTH MONTH

You were born in the fifth month, so you were conceived in the eighth month of the previous year.

In your previous life you were born in Nan Kuo and your surname was Ts'ai. You helped with the building of a Buddhist temple and gave a vegetarian meal to the monks. However, you also gave meat and drink to a Buddhist monk, causing him to break his vegetarian diet.

In this life you will be wealthy and never suffer financial trouble, but you will not be able to depend on your parents, brothers, wife or children. You will live to a great age.

In your next life you will be an honourable and wealthy man in Chao Chou.

SIXTH MONTH

You were born in the sixth month, so you were conceived in the ninth month of the previous year.

In your previous life you were born in Hua Szu Kuo and your surname was Teng. You refused to give sprays of plum blossom and ten sticks of pine to the monks. You also owed them 2 catties of rice and oil.

In this life you will have just enough to eat. You will not be on good terms with your parents, your marriage will not be in harmony and your cousin will not help you. If you are a woman, you will have minor ailments.

If you are sincere to the Buddha in this life, then in the next life you will have riches and honour in Fu Chou.

SEVENTH MONTH

You were born in the seventh month, so you were conceived in the tenth month of the previous year.

In your previous life you were born in Wei Nan and your surname was Tseng. You donated a vegetarian meal to the monks, but you owed ten bolts of cloth to the monastery.

In this life you will suffer hardship in your early years, but in later years you will have riches and honours. You will have many sons. If you are a woman, you will be on poor terms with your husband and your children will be unreliable. One of your sons will be skilled with his hands.

In the next life you will be born in Lo Chou.

EIGHTH MONTH

You were born in the eighth month, so you were conceived in the eleventh month of the previous year.

In your previous life you were born in Chiang Pei and your surname was Yang. You donated clothes to the monks and saved someone's life, but you also owed 156 copper coins to the monastery.

In this life you will not need to worry about food and clothing. You may marry more than once. Your brothers will never help you and you will have few relatives. If you are a woman, you will not be in harmony with your husband and will have few children.

In the next life you will be born in Ch'in Chou.

NINTH MONTH

You were born in the ninth month, so you were conceived in the twelfth month of the previous year.

In your previous life you were born in Yung Chou and your surname was Chu. You owed the monastery 2 catties of oil.

In this life you have an honest heart, but speak without thinking whom you may upset. You will have a roof over your head and adequate food and clothing, but this will not satisfy your greedy streak. Your relations with your parents and brothers will be poor and you will suffer from recurring illnesses.

If you cultivate virtue, in your next life you will be a happy man in Ming Chou.

TENTH MONTH

You were born in the tenth month, so you were conceived in the first month of this year.

In your previous life you were born in Huai Nan Kuo and your surname was Li. You donated 10 catties of oil and 50 coins to the monastery, but you killed a child.

In this life you will have a reasonable income and be an artist. Your relationship with your parents will be poor and you will not be able to depend on your brothers. If you wish to improve your relationships, you should cultivate humility and a more yielding, giving nature.

In your next life you will be a skilful man in Teng Chou.

ELEVENTH MONTH

You were born in the eleventh month, so you were conceived in the second month of this year.

In your previous life you were born in Sung Fo Kuo and your surname was Li. You gave a Buddhist meat and wine, breaking his vegetarian diet.

In this life you will have heart and stomach problems but you like to drink. You will always have a roof over your head and enough to eat. You will not be in harmony with your wife or your parents nor able to depend on your children. One son will be a labourer.

If you worship the Buddha in this life, then in the next you will be born in Wen Chou.

TWELFTH MONTH

You were born in the twelfth month, so you were conceived in the third month of this year.

In your previous life you were born in Fu T'ai Kuo and your surname was Ch'en. You stole a pig and killed your mother. You had the mouth of a Buddha and the heart of a snake – sweet words and evil intent. You also blew out the oil lights in front of the Buddha.

In this life you will have few children and be on poor terms with your parents. You will work with your hands and suffer from ailments in your eyes, hands and feet.

In the next life you will be born in Fu Chou.

Treasure for This Life (Purple Myrtle Stars)

The names of the stars used in this section come from a system called Purple Myrtle Flower Astrology, invented relatively recently in the Sung dynasty (960–1279 CE) by Ch'en Hsi I.

The legacy from your previous life which you bring to this one is valued in terms of money and the staples of daily life. The quantities indicate how much you will enjoy this life. (A 'catty' is a measure of weight.)

To use this section, find the Earthly Branch for your year of birth in the Calendar Tables. Then find the star that corresponds to it in the chart below and look up the relevant prediction.

Earthly Branch for Year of Birth	Purple Myrtle Star
Tzu	T'an Lang
Ch'ou	Chu Men
Yin	Lu Ts'un
Mao	Wen Ch'u
Ch'en	Lien Chen
Szu	Wu Ch'u
Wu	P'o Chun
Wei	Wu Ch'u
Shen	Lien Chen
Yu	Wen Ch'u
Hsü	Lu Ts'un
Hai	Chu Men

T'AN LANG STAR (Tzu)

From your previous life you have brought to this life 130 catties of rice and 75 copper coins. You are clever but impatient. You should eat vegetarian food and be sincere and respectful to the Buddha.

CHU MEN STAR (Ch'ou)

From your previous life you have brought to this life 170 catties of sesame oil and 100 copper coins. You quarrel a lot and have many problems. You are obstinate and suffer from minor illnesses. You must set a place in your home for your ancestors.

LU TS'UN STAR (Yin)

From your previous life you have brought to this life 250 catties of rice and 50 copper coins. You are impatient and uncooperative. You will have a dangerous encounter with water. It would be a mistake for you to work away from home. You must be sincere and respectful to the god Chin Chia, then you will be protected.

WEN CH'U STAR (Mao)

From your previous life you have brought to this life 120 catties of corn and 40,000 copper coins. You are clever and will have a large fortune and prosperity in old age.

LIEN CHEN STAR (Ch'en)

From your previous life you have brought to this life 82 catties of rice and 10 copper coins. You are petty and mean with money. If you work as a civil servant you will earn a large salary. Every spring you will have good luck, but at other times you will suffer sickness and injuries. If you are sincere and respectful to the god Chin Chia, you will avoid evil.

WU CH'U STAR (Szu)

From your previous life you have brought to this life 150 catties of haricot beans, 2 catties of corn and 40 copper coins. You are clever and enjoy playing games. You will study the five arts of divination and will use this knowledge in your work. You will suffer from illness. You must be sincere and respectful to the god Chin Chia so that you may have peace of mind.

P'O CHUN STAR (Wu)

From your previous life you have brought to this life 252 catties of rice, 2 catties of haricot beans and 9 copper coins. You are kind and know the right people. You are magnanimous but will suffer from throat problems. You must be sincere and respectful to Kuan Yin [the goddess of mercy].

WU CH'U STAR (Wei)

From your previous life you have brought to this life 32 catties of wheat, 3 catties of corn and 18 copper coins. You will have a harsh life. You should burn incense every night.

LIEN CHEN STAR (Shen)

From your previous life you have brought to this life 502 catties of sesame oil and 100 copper coins. You are straightforward and talented. You will be able to acquire a lot of money from many sources but will have a minor accident. You should be sincere and respectful to the Buddha.

WEN CH'U STAR (Yu)

From your previous life you have brought to this life 172 catties of sesame oil and 15 copper coins. You will have a fortune and need not worry about your livelihood. You must beware of a possible knife injury. You must be sincere and respectful to the Buddha.

LU TS'UN STAR (Hsü)

From your previous life you have brought to this life 202 catties of rice and 82 copper coins. You have no patience, suffer from minor illnesses and would benefit from working away from home. You should be sincere and respectful to the three holy gods.

CHU MEN STAR (Hai)

From your previous life you have brought to this life 230 catties of corn and 10 copper coins. You are proud. At first your luck will be unremarkable, but in old age you will be prosperous, have a good reputation and a fortune.

Rewards for Your Previous Life

The rewards for your behaviour in your previous life include harmonious relationships with people as well as material goods. The keys used here reflect the type of reward you will receive. For example, Pei Lu means 'back to income' – it is hard for you to make money – and Hsiang Lu means 'facing income' – it is easy for you to make money.

To use this chart, you need the Heavenly Stem for your day of birth and also your lunar month (see the Calendar Tables). Find your Heavenly Stem in the headings to the chart, and in the column immediately beneath it look for your lunar month. It may occur several times or not at all, depending on how many influences you come under. To the right are the keys to the rewards; the one(s) opposite your lunar month applies to you, and you will find the relevant prediction(s) in the text below.

Heavenly Stem for Day of Birth

Kuei	Jen	Hsin	Keng	Chi	Mou	Ting	Ping	Yi	Chia	Reward
10th	9th	8th	7th	6th	5th	4th	3rd	2nd	1st	Hsiang Lu
8th	7th	6th	5th	4th	3rd	2nd	1st	12th	11th	K'un Lu
6th	5th	4th	3rd	2nd	1st	12th	11th	10th	9th	Pei Lu
4th	3rd	2nd	1st	12th	11th	10th	9th	8th	7th	Cheng Lu
2nd	1st	12th	11th	10th	9th	8th	7th	6th	5th	An Lu
12th	11th	10th	9th	8th	7th	6th	5th	4th	3rd	Ts'ai Lu
10th	9th	8th	7th	6th	5th	4th	3rd	2nd	1st	Sha Lu
8th	7th	6th	5th	4th	3rd	2nd	1st	12th	11th	T'ien Lu
6th	5th	4th	3rd	2nd	1st	12th	11th	10th	9th	Hao Lu
4th	3rd	2nd	1st	12th	11th	10th	9th	8th	7th	Chu Lu
2nd	1st	12th	11th	10th	9th	8th	7th	6th	5th	Ping Lu
12th	11th	10th	9th	8th	7th	6th	5th	4th	3rd	Wang Lu

Lunar Month of Birth

HSIANG LU

You will be prosperous and lucky. It would be best for you to work away from home. You will have a large fortune and will never need to worry about where your next meal will come from. Strengthen your resolve and everyone will respect you. You will be able to transform suffering and hardship into good fortune.

K'UN LU

No relatives will be able to give you a hand. You will have a stable income but will face many difficulties. In middle age you will not be in harmony with others. No friends will be able to help you and your relationships with them will be poor. In old age you will have a large fortune and enjoy a peaceful time.

PEI LU

It would be best for you to work away from home. You will be separated from all your brothers. You are incapable of owning property and may lead a harsh life as a salesman. You will need to work hard and travel widely to build up your career and earn a reasonable income.

CHENG LU

Your name is unknown and you will have to work hard. You will not inherit business or property, but will set up your own business. However, you will move many times before you settle down. You will marry late, but your marriage will thrive.

AN LU

You will have a harsh life and your brothers will be unable to help you. You will not inherit a business or property and will need a partner to start a business. This partner will be the right person to help you. However, you will not be in harmony with your wife and will face many difficulties. Most of your time will be spent travelling to earn a living.

TS'AI LU

You will have a large fortune and never need to worry about your livelihood. You will be famous and prosperous and have many servants.

SHA LU

You are a sybarite and will travel widely, earning your living by cunning. You will end up with nothing if you do not settle down and work.

T'IEN LU

You will be prosperous and have a great fortune. You will have two children and you and your wife will live happily together.

HAO LU

You are a busy, efficient person. If you leave your home town you will always meet the right people and enjoy good food, and your career will flourish. You make friends easily and will receive lots of invitations to social events.

CHU LU

You are very greedy and miserly. You are never satisfied, always chasing around for something better. Although you will have children, you will not get on well with them.

PING LU

If you leave home and cultivate virtue, kindness and integrity, you will have good fortune. But if you are lazy you will have no savings in your old age. You will have no one but yourself to blame for your situation.

WANG LU

Property and a fortune will come easily to you. Your friendships will be open and understanding and you will love your friends dearly.

The Five Aspects of the Twelve Animal Signs

One of the stories lying behind the twelve animals in the yearly cycle tells of a great uproar amongst the animals over who was head of the cycle. When relations had broken down completely without the argument being resolved, the gods were asked to mediate. They suggested a race across a river to establish a heavenly order according to the order of arrival on the opposite bank. As the animals were all lining up for the event, the rat surveyed the situation and decided his chances were rather thin. He came up with a plan. Just before the animals plunged into the water the rat sprang onto the broad back of the ox, whom he had correctly identified as the strongest swimmer. As the ox approached the far bank in the lead, the rat leaped from his back and landed first, winning the title of head of the heavenly cycle. After the rat came the ox, followed by the tiger, the rabbit, the dragon, the snake, the horse, the ram, the monkey, the cock, the dog and the pig.

Each year has an animal sign, so the cycle of animals repeats every twelve years. This cycle is associated with that of the twelve Earthly Branches (see Table 2); therefore, just like the branches, within the sexagenary cycle the twelve animal signs recur five times in all, each sign combining with five different Heavenly Stems. To distinguish between the five different combinations each animal is given five aspects. For example, the Rat corresponds to the Earthly Branch Tzu, and this combines at twelve-year intervals with one of five Heavenly Stems Chia, Ping, Mou, Keng, Jen. These become respectively Rat On the Roof, Rat In the Field, Rat In the Warehouse, Rat On the Beam and Rat On the Mountain.

To use this section you need the Heavenly Stem and Earthly Branch and the corresponding animal sign for your year of birth (see the Calendar Tables and Table 2). The predictions below are arranged by animal sign. Find the one that relates to you, and under it you will see the prediction for your year characters.

RAT YEARS

Chia Tzu (1924, 1984)

Born in the year of Chia Tzu, you belong to the Rat On the Roof. You have little patience and seldom finish what you start. In youth you will suffer ill health and many accidents. To ensure a long life you should have guardians, alongside your parents, who will care for you. You will receive no help from your brothers. If you are the eldest son, you will not be in harmony with your wife. If you are the eldest daughter, you are clever and efficient and will be master of the house.

Ping Tzu (1936, 1996)

Born in the year of Ping Tzu, you belong to the Rat In the Field. You are brave and powerful, but lack education and patience. While young you will have average luck, but in middle age you will acquire splendour, riches and honours. You are a good planner, but if you are a woman, you are garrulous and annoy others.

Mou Tzu (1948, 2008)

Born in the year of Mou Tzu, you belong to the Rat In the Warehouse. You are clever and will acquire many different skills. Your children will not be in harmony with you in the early years, but there will be harmony between you and your wife. If you are a woman, you have a yielding nature and will be lucky.

Keng Tzu (1900, 1960)

Born in the year of Keng Tzu, you belong to the Rat On the Beam. You are steady, authoritative and respected. You career will be successful as you have the knack of turning ill fortune to good. You will be prosperous and on excellent terms with those around you. If you are a woman, you will be master of the house and your home will be prosperous.

Jen Tzu (1912, 1972)

Born in the year Jen Tzu, you belong to the Rat On the Mountain. While young you will face a lot of difficulties, but in middle age your prospects will improve greatly. You appear to enjoy life but your mind is always preoccupied with worries. Your brothers will not be able to help you and you will not get on with your relatives. However, you will have the opportunity to marry a good wife. If you are a woman, you have a yielding nature.

If you belong to the Rat, on the day that you die the weather will be terrible, with snow falling heavily. In the next life you will have a senior position.

OX YEARS

Yi Ch'ou (1925, 1985)
Born in the year of Yi Ch'ou, you belong to the Ox In the Sea. You will be attractive to the opposite sex. While young you will suffer from disasters and accidents. You should have guardians, alongside your parents, who will care for you. You will be a traveller and student of life. You will be in harmony with your wife and your children, but none of your relatives will be in a position to help you. If you are a woman, you have talent but no patience.

Ting Ch'ou (1937, 1997)
Born in the year of Ting Ch'ou, you belong to the Ox In the Lake. You are kind and will have plenty of money for luxuries. While young your fortune will be average, but when old you will have substantial savings. Your brothers will not be able to help you. There will be harmony between you and your wife, but you will not have children until late in life. If you are a woman, you are brilliant and gentle.

Chi Ch'ou (1949, 2009)
Born in the year of Chi Ch'ou, you belong to the Ox In the Gate. You are candid and tend to speak without thinking things through. You rely on others for money, although you have plenty of work. Whether a man or a woman, you may marry more than once. If you are a woman, you are clever and quick to understand.

Hsin Ch'ou (1901, 1961)
Born in the year of Hsin Ch'ou, you belong to the Ox On the Way. You have a gentle, giving nature. While young you will be frightened by an accident. You will always have plenty of work, but sometimes you will have a lot of money and at others very little. You will have a harsh life, receiving no help from your brothers. Your life will be long and you will have a great fortune in your later years. If you are a woman, you will have riches and live in splendour.

Kuei Ch'ou (1913, 1973)
Born in the year of Kuei Ch'ou, you belong to the Ox Outside the Gate. You will have a successful career, although in your youth you

will spend without concern for the future. You will be respected and mind your own business. You will not receive help from parents or brothers. The relationship between you and your wife will be harmonious, but you will have children late in life. If you are a woman, you are candid and sincere, with a tendency to speak before you have thought things through. You will be an excellent housewife.

If you belong to the Ox, on the day that you die the weather will be sunny. In the next life you will be a wealthy man born into a rich family.

TIGER YEARS

Ping Yin (1926, 1986)
Born in the year of Ping Yin, you belong to the Tiger In the Forest. Education will wash over you to little effect. You are impatient and inclined to speak before you think. However, you speak sincerely from an honest heart. You will have to work hard to maintain a reasonable income. The most suitable occupation for you is one connected with discipline, such as the police or the army, or otherwise an official post. You will encounter the right people at the right time. If you are a woman, you are clever and will prove a good housewife.

Mou Yin (1938, 1998)
Born in the year of Mou Yin, you belong to the Tiger Passing Through the Mountain. You are rather obstinate and as easily pleased as you are upset. While young you will work hard, although you will only have moderate success in your job. When you are older you should leave home to work, so that you may gain splendour and riches. If you are a woman, you will be neat and smart with a clever mind and a busy life.

Keng Yin (1950, 2010)
Born in the year of Keng Yin, you belong to the Tiger Going Down the Mountain. You are impatient and quick to complain, although you are also magnanimous. You are easily pleased and easily upset and unable to hide your feelings. Although your nature is forgiving, if someone greatly upsets you, you fly off the handle. While young you will be a spendthrift, but after middle age you will have splendour and riches. If you are a woman, you will be a good housewife and of great benefit to your family.

Jen Yin (1902, 1962)
Born in the year of Jen Yin, you belong to the Tiger Passing Through the Forest. You are candid, sincere and quick to speak, though thoughtful. You are incapable of keeping secrets. You will not be in harmony with your wife and will have children late in life. When young, life will be hard, but by middle age you will have a great fortune. If you are a woman, you will be lucky and prosperous.

Chia Yin (1914, 1974)
Born in the year of Chia Yin, you belong to the Tiger Standing Still. Your whole life will be spent in the company of influential people and it would be appropriate for you to be in a high post. Your family will be prosperous and you will find it easy to make money. However, you will not be in harmony with your parents and should have guardians to care for you alongside your parents. If you are a woman, you will be master of the house.

If you belong to the Tiger, it will rain on the day you die. In the next life you will be a happy man.

RABBIT YEARS

Ting Mao (1927, 1987)
Born in the year of Ting Mao, you belong to the Rabbit Looking At the Moon. You work well and hard with both your head and your hands, but find it impossible to finish projects when there are half a dozen others in your head to be started – you have a head but no tail. You will have enough work to keep you. If you are a woman, you like peace and quiet. However, although you are goodhearted you unwittingly hurt people with your abrupt candour. You love dressing up in fine clothes and have a talent for handicrafts. You will be of great benefit to your family.

Chi Mao (1939, 1999)
Born in Chi Mao year, you belong to the Rabbit Running Away From the Forest. You career will enjoy moderate success. You will not allow malicious people to hurt you. However, none of your relatives or brothers will be able to help you in times of need. If you are a woman, you will live happily with your husband.

Hsin Mao (1951, 1999)
Born in Hsin Mao year, you belong to the Rabbit In the Burrow.

You speak sincerely, but without thought for how you may upset others. You have strong resolve and natural authority and will be close to influential people. You seem to enjoy life but are constantly precoccupied with worries. You will have good luck, although none of your relatives will be able to help you. If you are a woman, you will be a successful housewife.

Kuei Mao (1903, 1963)

Born in the year of Kuei Mao, you belong to the Rabbit Running In the Forest. You will always have plenty of money and be able to turn hardship to good. While young you will spend all you earn, but after your middle years you will meet the right people to bring you good fortune, and will live in splendour, with riches and honours. If you are a woman, you will be a good housewife.

Yi Mao (1915, 1975)

Born in the year of Yi Mao, you belong to the Buddha Rabbit. You have very strong resolve. Everyone in your family will meet the right people at the right time and will be prosperous and lucky. You have literary talent and military expertise. If you are a woman, you will live to a ripe old age.

If you belong to the Rabbit, the day you die will be cloudy and dark. In the next life you will be a rich city dweller from a large family.

DRAGON YEARS

Mou Ch'en (1928, 1988)

Born in the year of Mou Ch'en, you belong to the Yielding Dragon. You are brilliant and efficient, but also gentle and kind. You will be close to high-ranking people who will help you. You will not be lonely, although you will have a poor relationship with your children. If you are a woman, you are gentle and giving, but inclined to speak without thinking. You will have a good husband.

Keng Ch'en (1940, 2000)

Born in the year of Keng Ch'en, you belong to the Angry Dragon. You are proud, always putting yourself before others. You will have a harsh life and would benefit from a military occupation. After middle age you will be well known and have more than enough to live on. If you are a woman, you are thrifty, but will have to work hard.

Jen Ch'en (1952, 2012)

Born in the year of Jen Ch'en, you belong to the Dragon In the Rain. You are diligent. While you are young your life will be hard. In middle age your fortune will come and go and there will be no savings, but by old age you will have put something aside. If you are a woman, you are elegant and will benefit your husband.

Chia Ch'en (1904, 1964)

Born in the year of Chia Ch'en, you belong to the Cheerful Dragon. You are handsome and kind, and enjoy fighting against injustice. You are respected because you keep personal and business matters separate. Generally your life will be quiet and peaceful, although in your youth there will be some hardship. When old you will own property and land. If you are a woman, you are elegant and will be of great benefit to your husband.

Ping Ch'en (1916, 1976)

Born in the year of Ping Ch'en, you belong to the Dragon Flying to Heaven. You are clever and quick-witted, with many friends throughout the world. You will not be short of money and by middle age you will have savings. If you are a woman, you will be of great benefit to your family.

If you belong to the Dragon, on the day you die there will be rain and thunder. In the next life you will be a civil servant.

SNAKE YEARS

Chi Szu (1929, 1989)

Born in the year of Chi Szu, you belong to the Prosperous Snake. You will be busy and well known, with a great fortune. You and your wife will live happily together. You will be lucky in all your dealings, and own property and land. If you are a woman, you are kind, but you will not have much money.

Hsin Szu (1941, 2001)

Born in the year of Hsin Szu, you belong to the Snake Sleeping In the Winter. You are petty and mean with money, although you have enough to live on. You have great ambitions, but are unable to stick to your own decisions. You will be in the right place at the right time for your life is ruled by the star of good fortune. In old age you will be comfortable and your marriage will be harmonious.

Kuei Szu (1953, 2013)

Born in the year of Kuei Szu, you belong to the Snake In the Forest. You are quick-witted and efficient. When young you will spend as you earn, but in old age your finances will be more stable. You will be helped by the right person at the right time. If you are a woman, when young you will quarrel a lot with your family, but you will be a good housewife as you get older.

Yi Szu (1905, 1965)

Born in the year of Yi Szu, you belong to the Snake Coming Out of Its Hole. You are respectable and enjoy a wide circle of friends. Although you work hard, show much kindness and even save another's life, you will never be praised for your actions. You will not be in harmony with your children, so it would be better to have your family late in life. If you are a woman, you will live in splendour, with riches and honours.

Ting Szu (1917, 1977)

Born in the year of Ting Szu, you belong to the Snake In the Fishpond. You will be helped by the right person and will be wealthy. You are obstinate, but if you are the eldest in your family, you are handsome and will be rich, gaining honours and living in splendour. If you are a woman, you are elegant and will benefit your family.

If you belong to the Snake, it will be cloudy on the day you die. In the next life you will be a rich man, living in a village.

HORSE YEARS

Keng Wu (1930, 1990)

Born in the year of Keng Wu, you belong to the Horse In the Hall. You are candid and sincere, but tend to speak without thinking. You will have plenty of work. If you are a man, you will be powerful and love your family. If you are a woman, you will be a great help in the lives of your husband and children.

Jen Wu (1942, 2002)

Born in the year of Jen Wu, you belong to the Horse In the Army. You are hardworking and thrifty. You will not be in harmony with your parents and when young will not have any savings. However, in old age you will live in splendour, with riches and honours. If you are a woman, you will have a great fortune.

Chia Wu (1954, 2014)

Born in the year of Chia Wu, you belong to the Horse In the Clouds. You are gentle and kind and quick to act. You will be helped by the right person and will be wealthy. You will turn suffering and hardship to good, and will enjoy a wide circle of friends. You will have only a few children, but will be prosperous in old age. If you are a woman, you tend to speak before you think how it might affect others, but you will prove a good housewife.

Ping Wu (1906, 1966)

Born in the year of Ping Wu, you belong to the Horse On the Way. When young you will have no savings. You will need to work hard and the best jobs for you are those connected with trade and crafts. In old age you will own property and be prosperous. If you are a woman, you are quiet and will be a good housewife.

Mou Wu (1918, 1978)

Born in the year of Mou Wu, you belong to the Horse Within the Gate. You are good-looking, gentle and kind and will have enough money. However, when young you will suffer from accidents and disasters, and will not be in harmony with your brothers. You will have few sisters, but will be well off in old age.

If you belong to the Horse, the day of your death will be rainy and windy. In the next life you will be a monk or a traveller.

RAM YEARS

Hsin Wei (1931, 1991)

Born in the year of Hsin Wei, you belong to the Prosperous Ram. You have great ambitions and a forgiving nature. In your youth you will suffer from disasters. If you are the eldest son, you will not be in harmony with your parents. There will be harmony between you and your wife. If you are a woman, you will be lucky and prosperous, and a good housewife.

Kuei Wei (1943, 2003)

Born in the year of Kuei Wei, you belong to the Ram In the Flock of Sheep. You are sincere and candid, sometimes too much so. You are kind, but receive no praise from others in return and will have problems in life. If you are a woman, you are elegant. In your youth you will have a harsh life, but in old age you will be prosperous.

Yi Wei (1955, 2015)
Born in the year of Yi Wei, you belong to the Ram Respected by Others. When young you will be upright, thrifty and hard-working. You will be lucky and have a great fortune in old age. You will have many children but will receive no help from your brothers. You will set up a business at your own expense. If you are a woman, you will be a good housewife.

Ting Wei (1907, 1967)
Born in the year of Ting Wei, you belong to the Lonely Ram. You are moody and enjoy argument, bringing into play your strong moral sense. You will live in splendour, with riches and honours. You will have children late in life but will not have a good relationship with them. If you are a woman, you will be fortunate in old age.

Chi Wei (1919, 1979)
Born in the year of Chi Wei, you belong to the Ram Running On the Mountain. You are straightforward and enjoy arguing. You are elegant and happy, with a promising future. You will be helped by the right person and acquire a great fortune. Whether you are a man or a woman, you will be prosperous and lucky, and will always respect your friends.

If you belong to the Ram, the day of your death will be cloudy and snowy. In your next life you will be born into a rich family and be powerful.

MONKEY YEARS

Jen Shen (1932, 1992)
Born in the year of Jen Shen, you belong to the Elegant Monkey. You are quick-witted, but petty and fickle. However, you do not mean to be unkind and will always compromise for an easy life. You will marry a good wife and be well known. Your children will be beautiful.

Chia Shen (1944, 2004)
Born in the year of Chia Shen, you belong to the Monkey Climbing the Tree. You have a gentle nature and stand out from the crowd. You will have enough money, although things will not be easy when you are young. In old age you will be lucky and wealthy. The relationship between you and your wife will be harmonious, but you

will have children late in life. If you are a woman, you are talented and will be a good housewife.

Ping Shen (1956, 2016)
Born in the year of Ping Shen, you belong to the Monkey Climbing the Mountain. If you go into trade you will make a great fortune. You will be able to buy a farm or land and, when old, you will have riches and honours and live in splendour. If you are a woman, you will be wealthy.

Mou Shen (1908, 1968)
Born in the year of Mou Shen, you belong to the Lonely Monkey. You are impatient and quick to change your mind, but hard-working and thrifty. You are elegant and will be helped by the right people. You will be wealthy, but you will not be in harmony with your children. If you are a woman, you will be a good housewife who is understanding, talented at handicrafts and loves children.

Keng Shen (1920, 1980)
Born in the year of Keng Shen, you belong to the Monkey In the Fruit Tree. Your work will be physically demanding. You are elegant and will have a great fortune. You will be helped by the right person at the right time. However, you will receive little praise for your willingness to help others, even after saving someone's life, and there will be those who wish you harm. If you are a woman, none of your relatives will help you.

If you belong to the Monkey, the day of your death will be cold. In your next life you will be a leader in your village.

COCK YEARS

Kuei Yu (1933, 1993)
Born in the year of Kuei Yu, you belong to the Cock In the Roost. You are straightforward, but incapable of keeping a secret. You have a strong sense of justice and will have plenty of money. Although none of your relatives will be able to help you, when you reach old age you will be prosperous. If you are a woman, you will build up your business successfully and have a happy family.

Yi Yu (1945, 2005)
Born in the year of Yi Yu, you belong to the Singing Cock. You are

straightforward, but at times speak your mind too quickly. You have great ambitions and will have enough money to live on. Although your family relations will be harmonious, you will receive no help from your brothers. You will live to a good age. If you are a woman, you will be a moderately good housewife.

Ting Yu (1957, 2017)

Born in the year of Ting Yu, you belong to the Lonely Cock. You are a sentimental person and love making friends. You will mix with rich and influential people. When young you will have a harsh life, but in old age you will be prosperous. If you are a woman, you are talented and elegant and will have good luck.

Chi Yu (1909, 1969)

Born in the year of Chi Yu, you belong to the Cock Announcing the Dawn. You are clever and perceptive and will have plenty of money. You will have children early in your life, but will not get on well with your relatives. If you are a woman, you are petty and fickle. There will be no disasters in your life.

Hsin Yu (1921, 1981)

Born in the year of Hsin Yu, you belong to the Cock In the Cage. You are clever, quick to understand and healthy. You will be a formidable debater and well respected. Although you will have savings, no relatives will be able to help you. If you are a woman, you are talented and will have a great fortune.

If you belong to the Cock, you will die in the spring with lots of flowers around you. In your next life you will be a steward in a large, rich family.

DOG YEARS

Chia Hsü (1934, 1994)

Born in the year of Chia Hsü, you belong to the Dog On Guard. You are someone who can never be wrong in an argument and, at times, your brusque manner in speaking your mind will offend. You appear to take life as it comes, but in fact you are naturally reflective. You are talented, and will be powerful and famous, with plenty of money to live on.

Ping Hsü (1946, 2006)

Born in the year of Ping Hsü, you belong to the Sleepy Dog. You are lucky and will be helped by the right person. You will have a great fortune and will bring up your family well. From middle age you will be prosperous. If you are a woman, you will live in splendour, with riches and honours.

Mou Hsü (1958, 2018)
Born in the year of Mou Hsü, you belong to the Dog Going Into the Mountains. You are kind but independent. When young you will have a harsh life with no savings, but in old age you will have a great fortune. You would be a suitable person to learn the skills of astrology. If you are a woman, you will be a moderately good housewife.

Keng Hsü (1910, 1970)
Born in the year of Keng Hsü, you belong to the Temple Dog. You will be happy but will suffer disasters in your youth. Your prosperity will be threatened by malicious people. If you are a woman, you will be prosperous.

Jen Hsü (1922, 1982)
Born in the year of Jen Hsü, you belong to the Family Dog. If you cultivate kindness you will have enough money to live on. However, money will come and go in your life, so you will have to work hard. If you obtain help from the right person at the right time, you will be prosperous. When young you will have a peaceful life, and in old age you will be particularly lucky. If you are a woman, you will be a good housewife.

If you belong to the Dog, the day of your death will be sunny and the scenery beautiful. In your next life you will be a noble son from a big family.

PIG YEARS

Yi Hai (1935, 1995)
Born in the year of Yi Hai, you belong to the Pig Passing By. You are kind, but have an impatient streak and are too quick to speak your mind. When young you will suffer disasters, although overall your life will be prosperous and lucky. You will not be in harmony with your parents and should therefore also have guardians to care for you. However, the relationship between you and your wife will be harmonious. You will have two sons who will both marry. If you are a woman, your life will be fortunate.

Ting Hai (1947, 2007)

Born in the year of Ting Hai, you belong to the Pig Passing Through the Mountains. You are smart. The relationship between you and your children will not be harmonious, so it would be better for you to have children late in life. You should cultivate kindness to ensure a long life, luck and prosperity. If you are a woman, you will be talented and prosperous.

Chi Hai (1959, 2019)

Born in the year of Chi Hai, you belong to the Monastery's Pig. You are smart and will have enough money to live on, although you will not receive help from your mother or other relations.

Hsin Hai (1911, 1971)

Born in the year of Hsin Hai, you belong to the Pig In the Garden. You do not worry about matters that do not concern you. When young you will have a harsh life with no savings. When old you will live in splendour, with riches and honours. If you are a woman, you will be a good housewife.

Kuei Hai (1923, 1983)

Born in the year of Kuei Hai, you belong to the Pig In the Forest. You have an obstinate nature but you will have a great fortune. However, you will not be able to rely on your relatives. When old you will be well off and lucky. If you are a woman, you will be prosperous and long-lived.

If you belong to the Pig, you will die on a hot, sunny day. In your next life you will be a woman and a concubine.

Your Palace and
Your Personality Star

There are twelve palaces, each asociated with a personality star. The palaces are named after the Earthly Branches (the meanings of the star names are given below). In Chinese the prediction for each palace consists of a four-line poem and an accompanying interpretation.

To use this section, you need the name of your palace (see Table 4). Look for it in the text below, and next to it you will see your personality star. The accompanying prediction applies to you.

TZU PALACE, T'IEN KUEI (Noble) STAR

This 'hour' of birth is the T'ien Kuei Star. You are ambitious, clever and a smart dresser. Life will be enjoyable and people will happily cooperate with you. You will be lucky and prosperous, although your great ambitions will not be wholly successful. Minor matters will be no problem. In old age you will be a rich man with a good reputation.

CH'OU PALACE, T'IEN O (Troubled) STAR

This 'hour' of birth is the T'ien O Star. Good luck comes very late. Although you will have many minor illnesses, you will have a long life which will probably be harsh. You will work hard, but you will see little result. It would be better for you to work away from home.

YIN PALACE, T'IEN CH'ÜAN (Authority) STAR

This 'hour' of birth is the T'ien Ch'üan Star. Both your family life and your career will be extremely successful. You will be very knowledgeable and a leader in society, able to maintain power and people's loyalty. You will be prosperous and have a good reputation.

MAO PALACE, T'IEN P'O (Broken) STAR

This 'hour' of birth is the T'ien P'o Star. You will have a great fortune at first, but will eventually lose everything. You will be eager to make another fortune, but even in your last years you will not regain your former wealth. You will receive nothing from your family.

CH'EN PALACE, T'IEN HAO (Good) STAR

This 'hour' of birth is the T'ien Hao Star. Your heart is spiteful in both important and trivial matters, although your face does not display your inner deceit. You may agree at first, then later refuse. You are quick-thinking and a good planner, but if you have power you will use it to benefit yourself without concern for others. No one will understand what you are up to or know what you will do next.

SZU PALACE, T'IEN WEN (Literary) STAR

This 'hour' of birth is the T'ien Wen Star. You are clever and outstanding. Whether a man or a woman, you will be lucky and happy, having both knowledge and good prospects. Your high ambitions will be fulfilled. One day you will be well known. You will encounter very few disasters. If you are a woman, you will marry a good husband. If you are a man, you will be very able.

WU PALACE, T'IEN FU (Prosperous) STAR

This 'hour' of birth is the T'ien Fu Star. Your life is built on a stable foundation and your endeavours will succeed. You are forgiving, kind and contented. You will have a great fortune and never suffer financial trouble. You will be refined and enjoy a life free of accidents and upset.

WEI PALACE, T'IEN I (Travel) STAR

This 'hour' of birth is the T'ien I Star. You will leave your home and travel for a long time until at last you find a place to stay peacefully. You are prejudiced and cool towards others and will have a harsh life. Relatives and friends will not want to stay with you or give you a hand.

SHEN PALACE, T'IEN KU (Lonely) STAR

This 'hour' of birth is the T'ien Ku Star. You will be alone and not in harmony with your brothers, sisters, sons or daughters; they will not help you. Your marriage will not be harmonious either.

YU PALACE, T'IEN JEN (Knife-bearing) STAR

This 'hour' of birth is the T'ien Jen Star. You are an outstanding and clever personality, but you are also excessively obstinate and uncontrollable. Your wife will fight you for supremacy. You have lofty aims and should be a general in the army.

HSÜ PALACE, T'IEN I (Artistic) STAR

This 'hour' of birth is T'ien I Star. You will encounter the right people at the right time. You are stable, kind, clever and quick to understand. There is no problem, however difficult, that you cannot rapidly solve. You are a talented all-rounder with a literary flair. One day you will be famous in the arts, but avoid people with the T'ien Ku Star because they can bring about your failure.

 ## HAI PALACE, T'IEN SHOU (Long Life) STAR

This 'hour' of birth is the T'ien Shou Star. You will live to a great age and will respect both your superiors and inferiors. You are kind and forgiving and fair to everyone. You never think of hurting another. You are clever and knowledgeable, and will be prosperous. Your life will be happy and this will show in your face.

'Hour' of Birth 1

This section gives a brief general forecast based on your 'hour' of birth. To use it, you need the Earthly Branch for your 'hour' (Table 2). Simply look up the corresponding prediction in the text below.

TZU

You are obstinate and will not be in harmony with your brothers and children. You will live long but will be separated from your children.

CH'OU

You are clever and talented and will have plenty to live on.

 ## YIN

You will be prosperous and honoured and will have many children. You may be promoted to a high position.

MAO

You will not be able to live in the property you inherit. You will leave your home town and trade in other places.

CH'EN

You will be separated from your brothers. If you cultivate kindness, you will have enough to live on.

SZU

You are very obstinate so the best jobs for you will be concerned with discipline. You will be well known and have a reasonable income.

WU

You will not be in harmony with the members of your family. You will be unlucky if you stay in your home town, but if you move away to work you will have good fortune.

WEI

You will have a balance of good and bad luck. If you emigrate or go as far as you can from your home town you will be more successful and prosperous.

SHEN

You will not be in harmony with your wife and friends. If you cultivate kindness and virtue you can live peacefully.

YU

You will have plenty to live on. You have both literary and military skills and talent. You should not stay in your home town. If you do your parents will only worry about you.

HSÜ

You will be lucky and powerful, with plenty to live on. You can live peacefully if you take up a job connected with discipline.

HAI

You are a very high-powered man. You can write well at home and will occupy a high post. You will have plenty to live on.

'Hour' of Birth 2: Overview of Your Life

This section gives a simple overview of your life. Like the preceding one, it is based on the 'hour' of birth. Look up the Earthly Branch for your 'hour' (see Table 2), then read the corresponding prediction in the text below. The ages are as given in the original Chinese, so each time an age is mentioned deduct one year to find the Western equivalent.

TZU

You are impatient and will not be in harmony with your relatives. You will have a lot of trouble and discord. You will not inherit anything, but will have no difficulty in acquiring a fortune, although your post is a minor one. You have three lucky stars: Noble Man, Tai Yang and Tin Fu. You should build up your family and your business by yourself. You will have three sons. At the ages of twenty-nine and sixty-nine you will face some difficulties, but if you get through these you will live to the age of eighty.

CH'OU

You will not be in harmony with your parents. You should take guardians to care for you alongside your parents, then you will prosper and be lucky. You will get help from the right people and will have plenty to live on. You are the one who can wield power. You will have three sons. At eighteen years of age you should be careful and revere the gods to ensure peace of mind.

YIN

You will not be in harmony with your parents, your wife or your children. You will leave your home town. When young your luck will be poor, but after middle age everything will improve. You are clever and a good writer. At the age of sixty you will have some difficulty, but if you can get through this you will live to the age of eighty.

MAO

You will receive no help from your brothers. At first your plans will only partly succeed, but things will eventually improve. It will be lucky for you to work away from home. You will have enough to live on. You work fast, but never finish what you start. At ages forty-nine and fifty-six you will face some difficulties, but you will then live to the age of seventy-four.

CH'EN

You will not be in harmony with those around you. You are clever but impatient. When old you will have plenty to live on. At forty-nine you will face disaster, maybe lose money, but will live to seventy-six.

SZU

You will be prosperous, lucky and well known. You will have some unexpected good luck. You will face a disaster at thirty-six or thirty-seven, and will then reach the age of ninety-four.

WU

You will receive help from the right people. It would be a mistake to live in the property you will inherit. Before the age of twenty-five things will be unremarkable, but after thirty-five you will prosper. However, you will not be in harmony with your wife. You should use the charm of Tin Tze [the Magic Master Chiang][18]. You will face difficulty at the age of fifty-nine, but will reach the age of seventy.

WEI

Your star is the Heavenly Reward Star. You will have two accidents when young. After thirty-eight you will prosper and will have splendour, riches and honours. You are clever and interested in astrology. You will live to the age of seventy-nine.

SHEN

You will not be in harmony with your parents and brothers, or with your daughter if you are a woman. You will have enough to live on. If you are a man, you will quarrel a lot. You will receive help from the right person at the right time. You should leave your home town to work. You will have three sons. At the age of fifty-six you will face difficulty, but then will live to eighty-three.

YU

You have a lonely star and will not be in harmony with your parents and brothers. However, you are dutiful and obedient towards your parents. You will leave your home town and have plenty to live on. You are an upright person and like singing, but you are very quarrelsome. If you have an illness, it will be followed by good luck. At twenty-two and forty-nine you will have some difficulties, but then you will reach the age of sixty-five.

HSÜ

When you are young your luck will be moderate, but as you grow old life will improve. You will not be in harmony with your children and parents but you will be happy. The best occupations for you would be trading, art or craft. You will face difficulty at sixty-four, then live to seventy-one.

HAI

You have a lonely star and are suited to living in the property you will inherit. You are hard-working and not fussy about food. You are respected and will have plenty to live on. You will face difficulties at forty-one, then live to seventy-five.

Animal-Bone Fortune

In the same way that the body is formed around the skeleton, so the animal bones refer to the underlying structure of your horoscope. This system is comparable in philosophy and background to the system of spiritual value and spiritual weight of your bones devised by Yuan T'ien Kang which appears in the T'ung Shu.[19] Both systems represent an approach completely unknown to Western divination.

The animals used in this section must not be confused with the twelve animal signs for the years, the twelve creatures of your horoscope or the twenty-eight animals associated with the constellations.

To use the section, you need your Earthly Branch for your 'hour' and your lunar month of birth (see the Calendar Tables). Find your Earthly Branch in the side headings to the chart, then look up your lunar month in the adjacent row. Your animal bone will be found in the heading to the column containing your lunar month. The relevant prediction will be found under this heading in the text below.

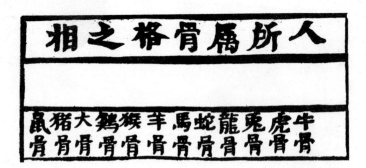

Animal Bone

												Earthly Branch for 'Hour' of Birth
Ox	Tiger	Rabbit	Dragon	Snake	Horse	Ram	Monkey	Cock	Dog	Pig	Rat	
2nd	3rd	4th	5th	6th	7th	8th	9th	10th	11th	12th	1st	*Tzu*
3rd	4th	5th	6th	7th	8th	9th	10th	11th	12th	1st	2nd	*Ch'ou*
4th	5th	6th	7th	8th	9th	10th	11th	12th	1st	2nd	3rd	*Yin*
5th	6th	7th	8th	9th	10th	11th	12th	1st	2nd	3rd	4th	*Mao*
6th	7th	8th	9th	10th	11th	12th	1st	2nd	3rd	4th	5th	*Ch'en*
7th	8th	9th	10th	11th	12th	1st	2nd	3rd	4th	5th	6th	*Szu*
8th	9th	10th	11th	12th	1st	2nd	3rd	4th	5th	6th	7th	*Wu*
9th	10th	11th	12th	1st	2nd	3rd	4th	5th	6th	7th	8th	*Wei*
10th	11th	12th	1st	2nd	3rd	4th	5th	6th	7th	8th	9th	*Shen*
11th	12th	1st	2nd	3rd	4th	5th	6th	7th	8th	9th	10th	*Yu*
12th	1st	2nd	3rd	4th	5th	6th	7th	8th	9th	10th	11th	*Hsü*
1st	2nd	3rd	4th	5th	6th	7th	8th	9th	10th	11th	12th	*Hai*

Lunar Month of Birth

RAT BONE

You are a sybarite and have many problems. You will often take your clothes to the pawnshop. You will have a harsh life with bad health. None of your relatives will be able to give you a hand.

PIG BONE

You are straightforward and trustworthy. You will be helped by the right people at the right time and will be respected. You will not like living in inherited property. You are indifferent to food and will suffer much illness.

DOG BONE

You will be lucky and the right people will be on hand when you need them. You will have fame and fortune. You are generous and will refuse money that is not rightfully yours. You will live peacefully with good health.

COCK BONE

You will be helped by the right people at the right time. You will be a renowned fortune-teller. You are scrupulously honest, refusing any part in financial jiggery-pokery. If you rise early and go to bed late, your life will be full of happiness.

MONKEY BONE

You have natural skill and talent. You are clever, quick-thinking and impatient. You like eating fruit. At times you act without thinking.

RAM BONE

You are uncooperative and impatient. You should work away from home. You will not inherit property so will have to buy your own. In old age you will have a great fortune.

HORSE BONE

You will be helped by the right person at the right time. You will always have a roof over your head. You will travel round and round like a fair-ground horse until at last you settle down. If you buy your own house you will have happiness, good health and a fortune.

SNAKE BONE

You love dressing up. You are quick and efficient but, although not particularly talkative, much of what you do say is spiteful gossip. Your health will be good.

DRAGON BONE

You will receive help from the right person and will rise to a senior post with a high salary. Spring and summer are fortuitous times for you, but autumn and winter are ill-fated. You are elegant and will be renowned and enjoy a peaceful life.

RABBIT BONE

You find it very difficult to finish what you start. In your youth you will have a great fortune and prosperity. In middle age you will have to leave your home so that you and your whole family can live peacefully and in harmony.

TIGER BONE

You will build up your own business single-handed and will encounter the right people at the right time. You are healthy, with a powerful personality that tends to unnerve people.

OX BONE

You will see and experience many things, giving you great knowledge and an open heart. Although you have a gentle nature you sometimes fly off the handle, becoming completely irrational over small things.

Noble (Good Fortune) Stars

The noble star determines how noble in character and how fortunate you will be. The Chinese also refer to their noble star as their 'noble man'. You may find that you come under the influence of more than one noble star or that there is none at all in your horoscope. Of these stars, only Yang Jen is inauspicious.

To use this chart, you need your lunar month and the Heavenly Stem for your day of birth (see the Calendar Tables). Find your Heavenly Stem in the side headings to the chart and then look for your lunar month in the adjacent row. It may occur a number of times: for example, if you were born on a day for which the Heavenly Stem is Keng in the 5th month, there are three entries in the chart. Your noble star(s) will be found in the heading(s) to the column(s) containing your lunar month. The relevant prediction (s) will be found under this (these) heading(s) in the text below.

			Noble Star				Heavenly Stem for Day of Birth
Wen Hsing	Chin Shen	Yang Jen	Ho Lu	T'ien Kuan	Fu Hsing	T'ien Yi	
8th	2nd	2nd	1st	8th	1st	{ 6th 10th }	Chia
11th	4th	3rd	2nd	{ 7th 1st }	12th	{ 10th 8th }	Yi
11th	6th	5th	4th	10th	1st	{ 10th 8th }	Ping
1st	7th	6th	5th	10th	11th	{ 8th 10th }	Ting
2nd	6th	7th	4th	2nd	7th	{ 6th 10th }	Mou
1st	7th	1st	5th	1st	6th	{ 10th 4th }	Chi
5th	9th	8th	7th	5th	5th	{ 10th 6th }	Keng
4th	10th	9th	8th	4th	4th	{ 1st 5th }	Hsin
5th	11th	10th	10th	5th	3rd	{ 3rd 4th }	Jen
4th	1st	11th	11th	4th	12th	4th	Kuei

Lunar Month of Birth

T'IEN YI

With the T'ien Yi noble man, you will be prosperous, enjoy life peacefully and have a great fortune. You will have a farm or a large property.

FU HSING

With the Fu Hsing noble man, you are in balance with yin and yang. You will have wealth, prosperity and a long life. You will be helped by an influential person and have an opportunity to be close to the Emperor.

T'IEN KUAN

With the T'ien Kuan noble man, you are not greedy or corrupt. You write with style and will have a great fortune. You will have a long, safe and peaceful life.

HO LU

With the Ho Lu noble man, you will have a great fortune and all your endeavours will succeed. No disasters will occur in your life. A large fortune, fame and longevity will be yours.

YANG JEN

With the Yang Jen noble man, none of your relatives will be able to help you. You will be injured and dogged by bad luck. You will not be in harmony with your relatives and may spend time in mourning.

CHIN SHEN

With the Chin Shen noble man, you are clever and quick-thinking. You will always have a roof over your head and adequate savings. If you are a woman, you are clever and easily understand others' instructions and actions. Your family will benefit from your generosity and will have plenty of rice and meat.

WEN HSING

With the Wen Hsing noble man, you write well. You will have a great fortune and be famous. You will always have enough to live on.

Baleful Stars

Of these stars, only Liu Ho is lucky; the rest are inauspicious.

To use the chart, you need your lunar month and your Heavenly Stem for your day of birth (see the Calendar Tables). Find your Heavenly Stem in the headings to the chart and, in the column immediately beneath it, look for your lunar month. This may appear a number of times or not at all, depending upon the number of baleful influences you come under: for example, if your Heavenly Stem is Chia and you were born in the 2nd month, there is no entry in the chart. To the right are the baleful stars; the one(s) opposite your lunar month apply to you, and you will find the relevant prediction(s) in the text below.

| *Heavenly Stem for Day of Birth* | | | | | | | | | | *Baleful* |
Kuei	*Jen*	*Hsin*	*Keng*	*Chi*	*Mou*	*Ting*	*Ping*	*Yi*	*Chia*	*Star*
1st	10th	10th	10th	10th	7th	7th	4th	4th	1st	*Ku Sh'en*
9th	6th	6th	3rd	3rd	3rd	12th	12th	12th	9th	*Kua Su*
1st	1st	7th	7th	1st	10th	4th	4th	11th	10th	*Ta Pai*
2nd	2nd	8th	2nd	11th	5th	5th	11th	11th	8th	*Lang Chi*
3rd	3rd	9th	9th	3rd	12th	6th	6th	12th	9th	*Pa Pai*
6th	6th	6th	11th	11th	6th	12th	9th	12th	12th	*Hsiao Lang Chi*
11th	11th	1st	11th	6th	2nd	2nd	6th	6th	1st	*Fei T'ien*
10th	6th	8th	1st	3rd	5th	7th	11th	3rd	5th	*P'o Chia Sha*
4th	2nd	2nd	11th	12th	9th	10th	10th	8th	9th	*San Hsing*
3rd	1st	2nd	11th	11th	9th	10th	7th	8th	5th	*Ta Hao*
2nd	3rd	4th	5th	6th	7th	8th	9th	10th	11th	*Liu Ho*
9th	10th	6th	10th	6th	7th	3rd	7th	4th	4th	*Kuan Sha*

Lunar Month of Birth

KU SH'EN

You will not be in harmony with your wife or children and will live alone. You will leave your brothers and sisters.

KUA SU

You will not be in harmony with your wife, sons or daughters and will live alone

TA PAI

You will have bad luck and none of your endeavours will succeed. However, if a lucky star shines on you, your life will be a little less harsh.

LANG CHI

You will have no fortune. It is inadvisable for you to live in any property you might inherit. You should leave your home town to work.

PA PAI

You will not have a fortune. You will be separated from your wife and children.

HSIAO LANG CHI

If you are a man, you will be a butcher. If a woman, you will not be in harmony with your relatives and will have a harsh life.

FEI T'IEN

If you are a man, you will be a butcher or have a job related to discipline. If a woman, you will not be in harmony with your relatives.

P'O CHIA SHA

If you leave your home town to work, prosperity and a great fortune will be yours.

SAN HSING

Your marriage will fail if you marry someone from your home town, but it will succeed if you look farther afield. Even though you support your brothers and sisters financially, they will not thank you.

TA HAO

You will have no money and a harsh life.

LIU HO

You will be rich and famous. Your family life will be happy and all your family will be lucky.

KUAN SHA

You will suffer from disaster and illness.

Bad Luck and Failure

This chart identifies an unlucky month in each year. If you were born in one of these months you have an 80 per cent chance of failure.

To use the chart you need the Heavenly Stem and Earthly Branch for the year you were born (see the Calendar Tables). Find your Heavenly Stem in the column headings to the chart (there are two to each column), then locate your Earthly Branch in the side headings. Where the column from your Heavenly Stem intersects with the row from your Earthly Branch you will find the unlucky month for your year. For example, in a year whose characters are Mou Yu the 9th month is unlucky; if you were born in that month you should take special care when embarking on any venture.

Heavenly Stem for Year of Birth					Earthly Branch for Year of Birth
Mou Kuei	Ting Jen	Ping Hsin	Yi Kung	Chia Chi	
6th	6th	9th	6th	6th	Tzu
9th	9th	9th	9th	9th	Ch'ou
12th	4th	10th	12th	12th	Yin
7th	12th	3rd	12th	12th	Mao
2nd	5th	6th	6th	5th	Ch'en
6th	6th	6th	1st	6th	Szu
3rd	12th	12th	12th	12th	Wu
3rd	10th	3rd	2nd	3rd	Wei
3rd	9th	9th	9th	9th	Shen
9th	9th	9th	9th	9th	Yu
3rd	3rd	3rd	3rd	3rd	Hsü
3rd	3rd	3rd	3rd	3rd	Hai

Unlucky Month

The Nine Stars

The Nine Stars correspond to the Eight Trigrams and the Central Point. The trigrams of Chinese divination are regarded as images of everything that happens in Heaven and on earth. Combined in pairs, they form the sixty-four hexagrams of the *I Ching*. The Central Point is one of the five directions of geomancy (*feng-shui*) – south, east, north, west and centre. In the *I Ching* the trigrams are sometimes arranged in a circle corresponding to the eight points of the geomancer's compass – south, southeast, east, northeast, etc. – around the Central Point.[20] Thus the Nine Stars have profound and wide-ranging associations.

In the *Three Lives* the Nine Stars appear on their own. They change each year, so you should use this chart at Chinese New Year (some time between 21 January and 20 February) to discover your situation for the coming year. Although the Chinese system of calculating a person's age is different from that used in the West (see p. 28), we have adapted the chart so that it works for your Western age.

First, find your age in the main body of the chart. Opposite, in the side headings on the right, you will find the name of your star. The prediction for your star is given in the text below.

Age											Star
90	81	72	63	54	45	36	27	18	9	0	*Lo Hou*
91	82	73	64	55	46	37	28	19	10	1	*T'u Su*
92	83	74	65	56	47	38	29	20	11	2	*Shui Hsing*
93	84	75	66	57	48	39	30	21	12	3	*Chin Hsing*
94	85	76	67	58	49	40	31	22	13	4	*T'ai-yang*
95	86	77	68	59	50	41	32	23	14	5	*Huo Hsing*
96	87	78	69	60	51	42	33	24	15	6	*Chi Tu*
97	88	79	70	61	52	43	34	25	16	7	*T'ai-yin*
98	89	80	71	62	53	44	35	26	17	8	*Mu Hsing*

LO HOU

Because you are with this star, you will suffer disasters and accidents and are likely to encounter either litigation or mourning.

T'U SU

Although this star is baleful, no disasters will happen in autumn and winter. You can rid yourself of the bad luck by cultivating kindness.

SHUI HSING

Disaster, danger and mourning await you. You must cultivate kindness and virtue.

CHIN HSING

This star is baleful. You will be injured. Mourning, disaster, an accident and many quarrels lie ahead.

T'AI-YANG

Your life will be lucky and your endeavours will flourish. You will acquire property and land and there will be a new baby in your family.

HUO HSING

You will be ill and lose money. There will also be an accident and injury.

CHI TU

In spring and summer you should beware of accidents. In autumn and winter things will generally be all right.

T'AI-YIN

This is a lucky star. You will have wealth, happiness and help from the right person. The harvest of this year will be abundant.

MU HSING

 This is a lucky star. You will have wealth and all your family will be lucky and happy. You may have a minor illness but there is nothing to fear.

The Yearly God (T'ai Sui)

The yearly god changes each Chinese New Year (on your Chinese birthday – see p. 28). The head yearly god, T'ai Sui, is the only one who is potentially both good and bad in his effects. The others fall squarely into one or other camp. As with the previous section, we have adapted this chart so that it works for your Western age.

First, find your age in the main body of the chart. Opposite, in the side headings on the right, you will find the name of your god for the year. The prediction for that god is given in the text below.

			Age				God
72	60	48	36	24	12	0	*T'ai Sui*
73	61	49	37	25	13	1	*Sun*
74	62	50	38	26	14	2	*Ill-omened*
75	63	51	39	27	15	3	*Moon*
76	64	52	40	28	16	4	*Litigation*
77	65	53	41	29	17	5	*Death*
78	66	54	42	30	18	6	*Broken Year*
79	67	55	43	31	19	7	*Dragon Virtue*
80	68	56	44	32	20	8	*White Tiger*
81	69	57	45	33	21	9	*Fortune Virtue*
82	70	58	46	34	22	10	*Ghost*
83	71	59	47	35	23	11	*Sickness*

T'AI SUI

This year you are not in harmony with T'ai Sui. Your bad luck will be very serious and other members of your family will also suffer from it.

SUN

This year your lucky star has arrived. Everything will be successful. You will communicate well with others and will live peacefully.

ILL-OMENED

This year one of your close relatives may die and you will lose some of your fortune. You may be ill or injured.

MOON

This year you meet the star of good fortune. You may have a baby and gain a fortune.

✎ LITIGATION

This year you will quarrel a lot and have many problems. There will be legal trouble and you will lose some of your fortune. Your wife's family will be in mourning.

DEATH

This year you may be in mourning. You will not be in harmony with your parents or your wife/husband.

BROKEN YEAR

This year you may lose your fortune. If you are a farmer, the year's harvest will be poor but the members of your family will be well.

DRAGON VIRTUE

This year you will win some money. Whether you stay at home or travel abroad, you will be safe from accidents.

WHITE TIGER

This year you will be injured and lose money. It will be a harsh year for you.

FORTUNE VIRTUE

This year will be a stream of happy events. You may have a baby and make some money.

GHOST

This year you will spend time in mourning and have many legal problems. There will be sickness, injury, quarrels and trouble.

SICKNESS

This year you will have to put on mourning clothes. You will not be in harmony with your parents, but worship and sacrifice to the Buddha at the beginning of the year can protect you from these troubles.

The Twelve Creatures

This system of predictions using the Twelve Creatures is unique to the *Three Lives*. Why or how this group came to be has been impossible to ascertain. The creatures used here are not to be confused with the twelve yearly animal signs, the animal bones or the twenty-eight animals of the constellations.

To use the chart you need your lunar month and your Earthly Branch for your year of birth (see the Calendar Tables). Find your Earthly Branch in the headings at the top of the chart, and in the column below look for your lunar month. Opposite, in the headings on the right, you will find the name of your creature. The prediction for that creature appears in the text below.

Earthly Branch for Year of Birth

Hai	Hsü	Yu	Shen	Wei	Wu	Szu	Ch'en	Mao	Yin	Ch'ou	Tzu	Creature
12th	11th	10th	9th	8th	7th	6th	5th	4th	3rd	2nd	1st	Phoenix
1st	12th	11th	10th	9th	8th	7th	6th	5th	4th	3rd	2nd	Lion
2nd	1st	12th	11th	10th	9th	8th	7th	6th	5th	4th	3rd	Golden Pheasant
3rd	2nd	1st	12th	11th	10th	9th	8th	7th	6th	5th	4th	Mandarin Duck
4th	3rd	2nd	1st	12th	11th	10th	9th	8th	7th	6th	5th	Swallow
5th	4th	3rd	2nd	1st	12th	11th	10th	9th	8th	7th	6th	Heron
6th	5th	4th	3rd	2nd	1st	12th	11th	10th	9th	8th	7th	Stag
7th	6th	5th	4th	3rd	2nd	1st	12th	11th	10th	9th	8th	Peacock
8th	7th	6th	5th	4th	3rd	2nd	1st	12th	11th	10th	9th	Pigeon
9th	8th	7th	6th	5th	4th	3rd	2nd	1st	12th	11th	10th	Sparrow
10th	9th	8th	7th	6th	5th	4th	3rd	2nd	1st	12th	11th	Eagle
11th	10th	9th	8th	7th	6th	5th	4th	3rd	2nd	1st	12th	White Crane

Lunar Month of Birth

PHOENIX

The phoenix is facing the sun. You are kind and will either be rich or, if you enter a profession connected with discipline such as the police, rise to a high post.

LION

You like making friends and are easy-going, but you are the subject of gossip. You like the arts. You will be lucky in all you do and will always be welcomed by influential people.

GOLDEN PHEASANT

You will be famous. You have a great literary talent and will have plenty to live on.

MANDARIN DUCK

You will be prosperous, for you are artistically talented and lucky. You will do well if you take a job as a civil servant.

SWALLOW

You are clever, quick-witted and talkative. You will enjoy good health and an easy, happy life.

HERON

You will be happy and prosperous, but not in harmony with your family.

STAG

You will be prosperous, but will never feel satisfied, always yearning after greater material rewards.

PEACOCK

You will be well known. If you work in a government department, you will hold a senior position.

PIGEON

You are kind and will have plenty to live on. When young you will have no savings, but after middle age all will go well and you will have a great fortune.

SPARROW

You will live in your home town and have a great fortune, but you will enjoy travelling and always be welcomed.

EAGLE

You are arrogant and powerful. You are fond of meat and wine and, when old, you will be well off.

WHITE CRANE

You will be well known in the arts. You should leave your home town. You will earn a good living and will be rich in old age.

Marital Fate

Each of the twelve keys used in this section describes a marital fate. This is one of the few sections in the *Three Lives* where the text traditionally applies to both women and men. There is even a reading that has specific points for women.

To use the chart, you need your element (see Table 1) and your lunar month of birth (see Calendar Tables). Find your element in the headings to the chart and look for your lunar month in the column below. Opposite your lunar month, in the side headings on the right, you will find your marital fate. The related prediction appears in the text below.

		Element			
Water	*Metal*	*Earth*	*Fire*	*Wood*	*Marital Fate*
6th	3rd	6th	12th	9th	*Hope for a Baby*
5th	2nd	5th	11th	8th	*Separation*
4th	1st	4th	10th	7th	*Suspicion*
3rd	12th	3rd	9th	6th	*Lack of Harmony with Children*
2nd	11th	2nd	8th	5th	*Second Wife*
1st	10th	1st	7th	4th	*Second Husband*
12th	9th	12th	6th	3rd	*Leaving Wife/Husband*
11th	8th	11th	5th	2nd	*Adoption (Wife's House)*
10th	7th	10th	4th	1st	*Conservatism*
9th	6th	9th	3rd	12th	*Disobedience*
8th	5th	8th	2nd	11th	*Discussion*
7th	4th	7th	1st	10th	*Harmony*

Lunar Month of Birth

HOPE FOR A BABY

You and your wife/husband will clash. You will complain about each other. For a long time you will have no children and will long for a baby.

SEPARATION

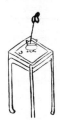

Due to force of circumstance you and your wife/husband will spend more time apart than together. You will both have been married once before. This marriage should be better than the first.

SUSPICION

There will be suspicion and jealousy between you and your wife/husband. In your previous life you did not like each other, and in this life you will not willingly marry each other. You are eccentric personalities with little common sense. You enjoy playing games.

LACK OF HARMONY WITH CHILDREN

You will not be in harmony with your children. You will have a large fortune but there will be a lot of quarrelling in the family.

SECOND WIFE

Your first marriage will be full of quarrels and suspicions. You will marry again and this time it will be much more successful.

SECOND HUSBAND

In your previous life you did not marry. In this life you will marry twice and will not be in harmony with either husband. The first marriage will end in divorce.

LEAVING WIFE/HUSBAND

You should leave your wife/husband or you will be forced to leave for reasons of illness or injury.

ADOPTION (WIFE'S HOUSE)

To ensure marital happiness you should move to the family home of your wife, otherwise you will endanger your marriage.

CONSERVATISM

You have old-fashioned values. You will be in harmony with your neighbours and kind to your children. Your marriage will be lasting.

DISOBEDIENCE

Your married life will be fairly stable but you will have two disobedient children.

DISCUSSION

You will be able to communicate well with your wife/husband. Your endeavours will succeed, but you will not be very close to your relatives and will have very few children.

HARMONY

You and your wife/husband will love each other very much and live happily together.

Marital Harmony

This section is similar to the previous one, but gives further details. Although it follows the traditional practice of being written primarily for men, we have adapted it so that it also applies to women. The twelve keys (or houses) follow a cycle from birth through death to rebirth.

To use the chart you need your element (see Table 1) and your lunar month of birth (see the Calendar Tables). Find your element in the headings to the chart and look for your lunar month in the column below. Opposite your month, in the side headings on the right, you will find the key to your marital harmony. The prediction for that key appears in the text below.

		Element			Harmony Key
Water	Metal	Earth	Fire	Wood	
7th	4th	7th	1st	10th	Ch'ang Sheng
8th	5th	8th	2nd	11th	Mu Yü
9th	6th	9th	3rd	12th	Kuan Tai
10th	7th	10th	4th	1st	Lin Kuan
11th	8th	11th	5th	2nd	Ti Wang
12th	9th	12th	6th	3rd	Shuai Kung
1st	10th	1st	7th	4th	Ping Kung
2nd	11th	2nd	8th	5th	Szu Kung
3rd	12th	3rd	9th	6th	Mu Kung
4th	1st	4th	10th	7th	Chueh Kung
5th	2nd	5th	11th	8th	T'ai Kung
6th	3rd	6th	12th	9th	Yang Kung

Lunar Month of Birth

CH'ANG SHENG (Birth)

You and your wife/husband will live in harmony with each other and with your children. Your family will be happy and prosperous.

MU YÜ (Bathing)

You and your wife/husband will not live in harmony and there will be much bickering. If you marry late, things will be a little easier.

KUAN TAI (Official Belt)

You and your wife/husband will live happily.

LIN KUAN (Entering Society)

You and your wife/husband will live in prosperity and happiness.

TI WANG (Prime)

You and your wife/husband will not live in harmony with each other. However, if only one of you is obstinate, then the marriage will be tolerable.

SHUAI KUNG (Decaying Palace)

Your marriage will not last. You and your wife/husband will have very different points of view and there will be many fights.

PING KUNG (Sickness Palace)

You and your wife/husband will not be in harmony with your son but the marriage will be all right.

SZU KUNG (Death Palace)

You and your wife/husband will either be separated for most of your lives or otherwise one of you will come to harm.

MU KUNG (Grave Palace)

As the first marriage is likely to fail, you may marry twice in your life.

CHUEH KUNG (Nothing Palace)

You and your wife/husband will be besieged by ill fortune. There will be disasters, much bickering and illness.

T'AI KUNG (Conception Palace)

You and your wife/husband will be separated from each other unless one of you has been married before. You will be a loner with no one else to talk to or go out with.

YANG KUNG (Pregnancy Palace)

If your marriage is to last, you should be at least a year older than your wife/husband.

Brothers' Harmony

The keys which relate to marital harmony also relate to harmony between brothers. Therefore the chart in this section is identical to the one in the previous section.

To use the chart you need your element (see Table 1) and your lunar month of birth (see the Calendar Tables). Find your element in the headings to the chart and look for your lunar month in the column below. Opposite your month, in the side headings on the right, you will find the key to your brothers' harmony. The prediction for that key appears in the text below.

		Element			Harmony Key
Water	Metal	Earth	Fire	Wood	
7th	4th	7th	1st	10th	Ch'ang Sheng
8th	5th	8th	2nd	11th	Mu Yü
9th	6th	9th	3rd	12th	Kuan Tai
10th	7th	10th	4th	1st	Lin Kuan
11th	8th	11th	5th	2nd	Ti Wang
12th	9th	12th	6th	3rd	Shuai Kung
1st	10th	1st	7th	4th	Ping Kung
2nd	11th	2nd	8th	5th	Szu Kung
3rd	12th	3rd	9th	6th	Mu Kung
4th	1st	4th	10th	7th	Chueh Kung
5th	2nd	5th	11th	8th	T'ai Kung
6th	3rd	6th	12th	9th	Yang Kung

Lunar Month of Birth

CH'ANG SHENG (Birth)

As long as you and your brothers do not live in the same house, you will get on. You will have two or three brothers or cousins.

MU YÜ (Bathing)

You enjoy talking and being with your brothers.

KUAN TAI (Official Belt)

Although you will live with your brothers, you will not communicate with one another.

LIN KUAN (Entering Society)

You and your brothers will encounter dangers and disasters.

TI WANG (Prime)

You and your brothers will all be lucky.

SHUAI KUNG (Decaying Palace)

You and your brothers will separate and meet with disaster and misfortune.

PING KUNG (Sickness Palace)

The youngest brother in your family will be a sybarite and the eldest brother will harbour a spiteful heart.

SZU KUNG (Death Palace)

One brother in your family will be disrespectful to others and will not listen to his brothers.

MU KUNG (Grave Palace)

There will be many brothers in your family and each of them will hold firmly to his own opinions.

CHUEH KUNG (Nothing Palace)

You and your brothers will be separated and one of you will be injured or killed. You will be no help to one another in times of trouble.

T'AI KUNG (Conception Palace)

There will be a rift between you and your brothers and you will not talk things over.

YANG KUNG (Pregnancy Palace)

You will be successful and well known if you leave your brothers and work away from your home town.

Children's Bridges

This section tells you about your children – how many you will have, what their fate might be, and so on.

The Children's Bridges are the twelve bridges over which the spirits of the underworld lead unborn children to their next life. When a child crosses a bridge, a woman becomes pregnant.

To use the chart you need your element (see Table 1) and your lunar month of birth (see the Calendar Tables). Find your element in the headings to the chart and look for your lunar month in the column below. For a man this is the upper row, for a woman the lower one. Opposite your month, in the side headings on the right, you will find the bridge that applies to you. The prediction for that bridge is given in the text below.

Element

Water	Metal	Earth	Fire	Wood		Bridge
10th	1st	4th	1st	7th	M	*First Bridge*
7th	4th	7th	1st	10th	F	
11th	2nd	5th	2nd	8th	M	*Second Bridge*
8th	5th	8th	2nd	11th	F	
12th	3rd	6th	3rd	9th	M	*Third Bridge*
9th	6th	9th	3rd	12th	F	
1st	4th	7th	4th	10th	M	*Fourth Bridge*
10th	7th	10th	4th	1st	F	
2nd	5th	8th	5th	11th	M	*Fifth Bridge*
11th	8th	11th	5th	2nd	F	
3rd	6th	9th	6th	12th	M	*Sixth Bridge*
12th	9th	12th	6th	3rd	F	
4th	7th	10th	7th	1st	M	*Seventh Bridge*
1st	10th	1st	7th	4th	F	
5th	8th	11th	8th	2nd	M	*Eighth Bridge*
2nd	11th	2nd	8th	5th	F	
6th	9th	12th	9th	3rd	M	*Ninth Bridge*
3rd	12th	3rd	9th	6th	F	
7th	10th	1st	10th	4th	M	*Tenth Bridge*
4th	1st	4th	10th	7th	F	
8th	11th	2nd	11th	5th	M	*Eleventh Bridge*
5th	2nd	5th	11th	8th	F	
9th	12th	3rd	12th	6th	M	*Twelfth Bridge*
6th	3rd	6th	12th	9th	F	

Lunar Month of Birth

FIRST BRIDGE

You will have three sons but one will die. If you cultivate kindness you will be healthy and prosperous.

SECOND BRIDGE

You will have six sons, one of whom will emigrate to work. Your last child will be a boy. Be careful of poisonous creatures and people.

THIRD BRIDGE

Your sons and daughters will meet with disasters, so you should try to cultivate virtue and kindness early on. If you do you will have three boys, otherwise you will be left with only one.

FOURTH BRIDGE

If your children are sincere and respectful, some of them will become artists. You will have one boy. If you offer worship properly, when you are old all will be well.

FIFTH BRIDGE

You will have one son, but beware of the malevolent spirit, the Heavenly Dog [an illusory terror used to distract King Chun Ch'i so that he could be cut down from behind], whom you can avoid by worshipping Heaven. If you do so you will have other children, and when you are old you may have two sons.

SIXTH BRIDGE

Your son will be difficult to nourish and troubled by ghosts or evil spirits. You should appoint guardians to care for him alongside his parents, then all will be well.

SEVENTH BRIDGE

You should be sincere and respectful to the Buddha and always burn incense so that your children will be robust. If you do this all will be well in your old age, otherwise you will have a bitter time.

EIGHTH BRIDGE

Your children will be helped by the right people and will become great men and women. Your sons will live far away from you. You will have three sons and good fortune will arise.

NINTH BRIDGE

Your children will be harmed by the Heavenly Dog [see Fifth Bridge above]. Therefore they should worship the Buddha and have guardians appointed to care for them alongside their parents. You will have two sons. Both will bring you good fortune, although one of them may not be your real son.

TENTH BRIDGE

Your life is dominated by a lonely spirit. If your first child is a daughter, there is nothing to fear, as you will also have sons.

ELEVENTH BRIDGE

Your children will come to harm and be difficult to nourish. Therefore you should cultivate kindness and worship the Buddha, and then you need not worry.

TWELFTH BRIDGE

As your children grow, so you will your fears that they will not be good. This is due to three malevolent spirits. Therefore pray and worship the gods, and it will be like throwing seed into the fortune field: all will be well.

Education Stars

The keys in this section reflect your chances of success in study. *Chien* means 'stable': in other words, your family can provide you with a background which fosters study. *Pei* means 'back': in other words, you have turned you back on study and are unwilling to learn. *K'ung* means 'empty': what your teacher says goes in one ear and out the other. *P'o* means 'broken': your family cannot support you and you have no opportunity to study. *Hsiang* means 'facing': you are willing to learn. *Ho* means 'with': you are suited to studying.

To use the chart you need the Earthly Branch for your 'hour' of birth (see Table 1) and your lunar month of birth (see the Calendar Tables). Find your Earthly Branch in the headings to the chart, then look for your lunar month in the column below. Opposite, in the side headings on the right, is the name of your education star. The prediction for that star is given in the text below.

Earthly Branch for 'Hour' of Birth

Hai Mao Wei	Szu Yu Ch'ou	Shen Tzu Chen	Yin Wu Hsü	Education Star
10th	4th	7th	1st	*Chien*
11th	5th	8th	2nd	*Pei*
12th	6th	9th	3rd	*Pei*
1st	7th	10th	4th	*Pei*
2nd	8th	11th	5th	*K'ung*
3rd	9th	12th	6th	*K'ung*
4th	10th	1st	7th	*P'o*
5th	11th	2nd	8th	*Hsiang*
6th	12th	3rd	9th	*Hsiang*
7th	1st	4th	10th	*Hsiang*
8th	2nd	5th	11th	*Ho*
9th	3rd	6th	12th	*Ho*

Lunar Month of Birth

CHIEN (Stable)

You like learning and are a natural student. You will be an accomplished writer. Your prospects are good and you will be famous.

PEI, K'UNG AND P'O (Back, Empty and Broken)

You either have no aptitude for learning, or you have no opportunity to gain an education, or you have the ability but not the interest. When you are old you will regret that you lost the chance to study.

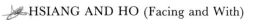

HSIANG AND HO (Facing and With)

You like academic work, especially writing and art, and study hard and well. One day you will be famous.

Schooling and Career Success

Schooling and career success are affected by eight of the twenty-eight constellations (see p. 28): the rat, the fox, the cock, the horse, the dragon, the sheep, the dog and the ox. The fox and the cock have two aspects each.

To use the chart you need the Earthly Branch for your year of birth (see the Calendar Tables) and the Earthly Branch for your 'hour' of birth (see Table 2). Find your Earthly Branch for the year in the side headings to the chart, then look for your Earthly Branch for the 'hour' in the adjacent row. You might find that it is not listed, in which case you are not under the influence of any constellation. At the top of that column you will find the name of the constellation that applies to you. The details of your constellation can be found in the text below.

Ox	Dog	Sheep	Dragon	Cock 2	Fox 2	Horse	Cock 1	Fox 1	Rat	Earthly Branch for Year of Birth
Shen	Hai	Szu	Yin	Shen	Hai	Shen	Szu	Yin	Shen	*Tzu*
Tzu	Mao	Yu	Wu	Tzu	Mao	Tzu	Yu	Wu	Tzu	*Ch'ou*
Ch'en	Wei	Ch'ou	Hsü	Ch'en	Wei	Ch'en	Ch'ou	Hsü	Ch'en	*Yin*
Hai	Yin	Shen	Szu	Hai	Shen	Szu	Yin	Shen	Yin	*Mao*
Mao	Wu	Tzu	Yu	Mao	Tzu	Yu	Wu	Tzu	Wu	*Ch'en*
Wei	Hsü	Ch'en	Ch'ou	Wei	Ch'en	Ch'ou	Hsü	Ch'en	Hsü	*Szu*
Szu	Shen	Yin	Hai	Yin	Szu	Hai	Shen	Hai	Szu	*Wu*
Yu	Tzu	Wu	Mao	Wu	Yu	Mao	Tzu	Mao	Yu	*Wei*
Ch'ou	Ch'en	Hsü	Wei	Hsü	Ch'ou	Wei	Ch'en	Wei	Ch'ou	*Shen*
Yin	Szu	Hai	Shen	Szu	Yin	Yin	Hai	Szu	Hai	*Yu*
Wu	Yu	Mao	Tzu	Yu	Wu	Wu	Mao	Yu	Mao	*Hsü*
Hsü	Ch'ou	Wei	Ch'en	Ch'ou	Hsü	Hsü	Wei	Ch'ou	Wei	*Hai*

Earthly Branch for 'Hour' of Birth

RAT

Education: up to a Master's degree.

Occupation: a senior clerical post.

In Tzu Year (Year of the Rat) you will graduate with your Master's degree.

In Ch'en Year (Year of the Dragon) you will secure the post of an area officer. Your career will blossom and you will reach a senior level.

FOX 1

Education: up to a Bachelor's degree.

Occupation: a clerical post.

In Yin Year (Year of the Tiger) you will start a ten-year course of study and graduate with a Bachelor's degree.

In Ch'ou Year (Year of the Ox) you will start work in the post of area officer.

In Mao Year (Year of the Hare) you will be promoted to a higher post and then all your efforts will bear fruit.

COCK 1

Education: up to at least a Master's degree.

Occupation: a government minister or a managing director.

In the spring of Wei Year (Year of the Sheep) you will graduate.

In the autumn of Yu Year (Year of the Cock) you will start to build up your career and before long you will be well known in your field.

HORSE

Education: up to a Master's degree at least.

Occupation: top management.

In Wu Year (Year of the Horse) you will graduate and then take up your job. You will be a Member of Parliament or a high-level manager in a large organization.

FOX 2

Education: up to a Bachelor's degree.
Occupation: a clerical post.
In Tzu Year (Year of the Rat) you will face some
    difficulties.
In Mao Year (Year of the Rabbit) you will graduate
    and obtain the post of area officer. You will
    have a large fortune.

COCK 2

Education: up to at least a Master's degree.
Occupation: a government minister or a managing
    director.
In Hsu Year (Year of the Dog) you will graduate
    and start to build up your career. Your name will
    soon be renowned and you will reach a position in
    which the public will respect and fear you.

DRAGON

Education: secondary school.
Occupation: junior clerical post.
You will spend a few years in college but will be
    unable to use your education to build up your
    career. You will only have a junior post and will
    seldom receive promotion.

SHEEP

Education: secondary school.
Occupation: skilled worker.
You are clever and a large fortune awaits you. You
    will learn a special skill to build up your career.
    Success will come rather late but your efforts will
    not be wasted.

DOG

Education: secondary school.

Occupation: civil servant.

You will be successful but you will have to work hard.

OX

Education: below secondary school.

Occupation: driver, messenger, tourist guide, sailor, salesman or postman.

You dislike school but like travelling. One day you will choose one of the above jobs.

The Five Elements of Your Career

This section tells you which career field is most suitable for you; in it the five elements are paired with five occupational areas.

To use the chart, you need the Earthly Branch for your 'hour' of birth (see Table 2) and your lunar month of birth (see the Calendar Tables). Find your Earthly Branch in the side headings to the chart, then look for your lunar month in the adjacent row. It may occur more than once or not at all, giving you a number of readings or none. At the top of the column(s) containing your lunar month you will find the combination(s) of element and occupation that apply to you. The predictions for these are given in the text below. Although there are ten combinations in the chart there are only five sets of predictions as a single prediction applies to the same combination of element and occupation irrespective of the order in which the two components are listed. Thus the prediction for Trading Wood is the same as that for Wood Trading, for example.

Occupational Area and Element

Water Prime Minister	Earth Mess- enger	Fire Official	Wood Trading	Metal Palace	Prime Minister Water	Mess- enger Earth	Official Fire	Trading Wood	Palace Metal	Earthly Branch for 'Hour' of Birth
5th	8th	7th	3rd	8th	1st	5th	3rd	4th	2nd	Tzu
8th	1st	10th	9th	1st	8th	8th	4th	7th	4th	Ch'ou
3rd	4th	8th	2nd	4th	2nd	2nd	{1st 8th}	12th	8th	Yin
4th	2nd	1st	4th	2nd	4th	4th	1st	11th	3rd	Mao
9th	2nd	4th	8th	3rd	9th	9th	9th	1st	9th	Ch'en
3rd	9th	2nd	1st	9th	3rd	3rd	1st	3rd	12th	Szu
1st	11th	9th	12th	11th	5th	5th	5th	9th	5th	Wu
1st	5th	3rd	6th	5th	11th	11th	12th	9th	10th	Wei
6th	3rd	11th	5th	12th	6th	6th	3rd	6th	2nd	Shen
12th	6th	5th	11th	6th	12th	12th	6th	1st	6th	Yu
10th	7th	12th	7th	10th	10th	7th	10th	8th	10th	Hsü
7th	10th	6th	6th	7th	7th	10th	7th	12th	7th	Hai

Lunar Month of Birth

PALACE METAL and METAL PALACE

You are suited to a business or occupation related to metal (e.g. blacksmithing, jewellery making, welding, shipbuilding).

TRADING WOOD and WOOD TRADING

You are suited to a business or occupation related to wood (e.g. carpentry, furniture making, forestry, paper making).

OFFICIAL FIRE and FIRE OFFICIAL

You are suited to a business or occupation related to fire (e.g. the oil business, smelting, explosives, chimney sweeping).

MESSENGER EARTH and EARTH MESSENGER

You are suited to a business or occupation related to soil (e.g. china making, civil engineering, agriculture, coalmining).

PRIME MINISTER WATER and WATER PRIME MINISTER

You are suited to a business or occupation related to water (e.g. the water service, sailing, inn keeping, refrigeration).

Career Stars

This section describes in more detail than the preceding one which occupation would best suit you.

To use the chart you need the Heavenly Stem for your day of birth and also your lunar month of birth (see the Calendar Tables). Find your Heavenly Stem in the headings to the chart, then look for your lunar month in the column below. Opposite your lunar month, in the side headings on the right, you will find the occupation that is best for you. Fuller details of this are given in the text below.

Heavenly Stem for Day of Birth

Kuei	Jen	Hsin	Keng	Chi	Mou	Ting	Ping	Yi	Chia	Career
10th	9th	8th	7th	6th	5th	4th	3rd	2nd	1st	*Official*
11th	10th	9th	8th	7th	6th	5th	4th	3rd	2nd	*Butcher*
12th	11th	10th	9th	8th	7th	6th	5th	4th	3rd	*Scholar*
1st	12th	11th	10th	9th	8th	7th	6th	5th	4th	*Blacksmith*
2nd	1st	12th	11th	10th	9th	8th	7th	6th	5th	*Lecturer*
3rd	2nd	1st	12th	11th	10th	9th	8th	7th	6th	*Manager*
4th	3rd	2nd	1st	12th	11th	10th	9th	8th	7th	*Musician*
5th	4th	3rd	2nd	1st	12th	11th	10th	9th	8th	*Herbalist*
6th	5th	4th	3rd	2nd	1st	12th	11th	10th	9th	*Monk*
7th	6th	5th	4th	3rd	2nd	1st	12th	11th	10th	*Tailor*
8th	7th	6th	5th	4th	3rd	2nd	1st	12th	11th	} *Law and Order*
9th	8th	7th	6th	5th	4th	3rd	2nd	1st	12th	*Craftsman*

Lunar Month of Birth

OFFICIAL

You will have great wealth and prosperity. You will be a capable writer with an artistic bent.

BUTCHER

You are too obstinate. The best job for you is that of a butcher or a craftsman. You will never need to worry about money.

SCHOLAR

You will be a skilled writer and will enjoy the arts, at which you will also excel. If you are a woman, you will benefit your husband and always be prosperous.

BLACKSMITH

The best career for you is that of a blacksmith. You should cultivate kindness and virtue, otherwise the members of your family will be separated.

LECTURER

You are best suited to being a lecturer, although you would also do well as an official. Either of these occupations will bring you luck and prosperity. You will never need to worry about your livelihood and there will always be someone to give you help when you need it.

MANAGER

The most appropriate job for you is that of a manger, but you would also be a good butcher. Either job will bring you success and you will never have to worry about money.

MUSICIAN

You are clever and perceptive. You are a talented all-rounder and will have a happy life. Help will be there when you need it and you will always be able to find work.

HERBALIST

You would be good at selling herbs and should live in a herb shop. You would also succeed as a craftsman.

MONK

You will have many conflicts with your family. You are most suited to being a monk but, if this does not appeal, you could develop a career in the arts. You have a promising future and will be famous.

TAILOR

If you have no skill in tailoring you will quarrel with your brothers.

LAW AND ORDER

Your future lies in the sphere of law and order – the police, politics or the armed forces. Administrative work will not suit you. You will have power and fame in your life.

CRAFTSMAN

You are talented and very lucky. The best job for you is that of craftsman. You will be helped by the right person at the right time and your career will flourish.

Travelling Stars

The god of travel is called I-ma and he is accompanied by eleven baleful stars. If you were born under I-ma himself, you will be fortunate when you travel.

To use the chart, you need the Earthly Branch for your 'hour' of birth (see Table 2) and your lunar month of birth (see the Calendar Tables). Find your Earthly Branch in the headings to the chart, then look for your lunar month in the column below. Opposite your month, in the side headings on the right, is the name of your travelling star. In the text below you will find a prediction of how your travelling star will affect your life, particularly in terms of change or stability.

Earthly Branch for 'Hour' of Birth												*Travelling*
Hai	*Hsü*	*Yu*	*Shen*	*Wei*	*Wu*	*Szu*	*Ch'en*	*Mao*	*Yin*	*Ch'ou*	*Tzu*	*Star*
12th	11th	10th	9th	8th	7th	6th	5th	4th	3rd	2nd	1st	*I-ma*
1st	12th	11th	10th	9th	8th	7th	6th	5th	4th	3rd	2nd	*Liu Hai*
2nd	1st	12th	11th	10th	9th	8th	7th	6th	5th	4th	3rd	*Hua Kai*
3rd	2nd	1st	12th	11th	10th	9th	8th	7th	6th	5th	4th	*Chieh Sha*
4th	3rd	2nd	1st	12th	11th	10th	9th	8th	7th	6th	5th	*Tsai Sha*
5th	4th	3rd	2nd	1st	12th	11th	10th	9th	8th	7th	6th	*T'ien Sha*
6th	5th	4th	3rd	2nd	1st	12th	11th	10th	9th	8th	7th	*Ti Sha*
7th	6th	5th	4th	3rd	2nd	1st	12th	11th	10th	9th	8th	*Nien Sha*
8th	7th	6th	5th	4th	3rd	2nd	1st	12th	11th	10th	9th	*Yueh Sha*
9th	8th	7th	6th	5th	4th	3rd	2nd	1st	12th	11th	10th	*Wang Shen*
10th	9th	8th	7th	6th	5th	4th	3rd	2nd	1st	12th	11th	*Chiang Hsing*
11th	10th	9th	8th	7th	6th	5th	4th	3rd	2nd	1st	12th	*P'an An*

Lunar Month of Birth

I-MA

You will be lucky and prosperous and have a great fortune. If you are a woman, you will have splendour, riches and honours. If you are a man, you will own property, land and farms.

LIU HAI

You will not be in harmony with your relatives and will bring bad luck and disaster to your wife and children. You should stay in a monastery and worship the Buddha.

HUA KAI

You will be lucky and have plenty to live on. You are talented in at least three areas of the arts and will be widely respected.

CHIEH SHA

Your parents will die when you are still young. You will not be in harmony with your wife. If you are a man, you will change occupations at least three times. If you are a woman, you will marry more than once.

TSAI SHA

You will encounter much disaster and sickness. Even if you do not suffer from evil forces yourself, your wife and your children will suffer.

T'IEN SHA

You will not be in harmony with your parents or your wife. You will be plagued with disasters or ill health.

TI SHA

You will have many disasters and should take guardians to care for you alongside your parents. You will not be in harmony with your wife and children. You should cultivate kindness and virtue.

NIEN SHA

You will leave your home to work. Your brothers will not give you a hand. You should buy your own house as your family will leave you nothing.

YUEH SHA

You will have a fortune, but will not be in harmony with your wife. You are not a suitable person to live in any house you might inherit. You should buy your own house and then you will be lucky.

WANG SHEN

You will move house at least three times. Your best job will be as a government official. You will not be in harmony with the members of your family. You will buy property outside your home town.

CHIANG HSING

You will be lucky and powerful. In early life you will have great fortune, but when old you will have just enough to live on.

P'AN AN

You will be literary and brilliant in one of the arts. Your future is great.

Wealth Stars

Whether your wealth star suggests you will be rich or poor, if you work hard the god will look favourably on you.

To use the chart, you need the Earthly Branch for your 'hour' of birth (see Table 2) and your lunar month of birth (see the Calendar Tables). Look for your Earthly Branch in the headings to the chart, then find your lunar month in the column below. Opposite your month, in the side headings on the right, is your wealth star. The prediction for that star can be found in the text below. (A 'catty' and a 'tael' are measures of weight.)

Earthly Branch for 'Hour' of Birth

Hai	Hsü	Yu	Shen	Wei	Wu	Szu	Ch'en	Mao	Yin	Ch'ou	Tzu	Wealth Star
2nd	1st	12th	11th	10th	9th	8th	7th	6th	5th	4th	3rd	Chien Lu
3rd	2nd	1st	12th	11th	10th	9th	8th	7th	6th	5th	4th	Ch'u Lu
4th	3rd	2nd	1st	12th	11th	10th	9th	8th	7th	6th	5th	Man Lu
5th	4th	3rd	2nd	1st	12th	11th	10th	9th	8th	7th	6th	P'ing Lu
6th	5th	4th	3rd	2nd	1st	12th	11th	10th	9th	8th	7th	Ting Lu
7th	6th	5th	4th	3rd	2nd	1st	12th	11th	10th	9th	8th	Chih Lu
8th	7th	6th	5th	4th	3rd	2nd	1st	12th	11th	10th	9th	P'o Lu
9th	8th	7th	6th	5th	4th	3rd	2nd	1st	12th	11th	10th	Wei Lu
10th	9th	8th	7th	6th	5th	4th	3rd	2nd	1st	12th	11th	Ch'eng Lu
11th	10th	9th	8th	7th	6th	5th	4th	3rd	2nd	1st	12th	Shou Lu
12th	11th	10th	9th	8th	7th	6th	5th	4th	3rd	2nd	1st	K'ai Lu
1st	12th	11th	10th	9th	8th	7th	6th	5th	4th	3rd	2nd	Pi Lu

Lunar Month of Birth

CHIEN LU

You will have splendour, riches, honours, gold and jewellery. You will have servants and wine and meat right into old age. You will have 1000 catties of rice, ten jars of wine, each holding 18 catties, 2 catties of oil and salt, and 1000 yen.

CH'U LU

You will encounter danger and disaster. You will inherit nothing, but you and your wife will live in happiness and harmony. You will have 250 catties of rice, 5 catties of meat, four jars of wine, 1 catty 4 taels of oil and salt, and 200 coins.

MAN LU

You will have property, land and many cattle. You will have riches and will receive help from the right person. You will have 1500 catties of rice, twelve jars of wine, 60 catties of meat, 2 catties of oil and salt, and 2000 coins.

P'ING LU

You will be prosperous and renowned. You will have several servants, as well as 800 catties of rice, seven jars of wine and 500 catties of meat. You will never have to worry about your livelihood. Wine and meat, more than you need, will be provided.

TING LU

You will have property. You will have a harsh life in your early years, but from middle age onwards you will prosper. You are clever, but impatient. You will have 10 catties of meat, 1000 catties of rice and 300 coins.

CHIH LU

Prosperity and success will be yours. After the first twenty years you will have splendour, riches and honours. You will have 500 catties of rice, two jars of wine, 5 catties of meat, 1 catty 4 taels of oil and salt, and 200 coins.

P'O LU

You will not have much money and will have to work hard to earn your living. Your brothers will be unable to help you and you will not inherit any property. You would do better to work away from your home town. Your life is ordained in Heaven, it is impossible to force anything. The later stage of your life will not be so bad. You will have 100 catties of rice, one jar of wine, 1 catty 4 taels of meat, and 100 coins.

WEI LU

When you are young you will suffer frequent ill health. Your brothers will not be able to help you and the family property and jewellery will have already been spent. However, your children will be able to earn their living. You will have 120 catties of rice, one jar of wine, 5 catties of meat, 10 catties of oil and salt, and 200 coins.

CH'ENG LU

Your life will be lucky and prosperous. You will buy land, property and farms. You and your wife will always live happily. You will have 1000 catties of rice, five jars of wine, 12 catties of meat, 2 catties of oil and salt, and 1000 coins.

SHOU LU

You have great talent and will prosper. Your early years will be unremarkable, but later on you will be attended by good fortune. You will buy cattle and, from the age of thirty-nine or forty, you will have splendour, riches and honours. You will have 1000 catties of rice, five jars of wine, 10 catties of meat, and 1000 coins.

K'AI LU

You will have splendour, riches and honours. You will buy property, land and farms and win fame. You will have 900 catties of rice, one jar of wine, 12 catties of meat, and 50,000 coins.

PI LU

You will have a long life but will not be able to leave your belongings to your children. You will face many troubles. You will have 100 catties of rice, three jars of wine, and 15,000 coins.

Property Stars

It is possible to be wealthy but only to buy property late in life. It is also possible to be less well off, save carefully, and buy property earlier in life.

To use this chart, you need the Earthly Branch for your 'hour' of birth (see Table 2) and your lunar month of birth (see the Calendar Tables). Find your Earthly Branch in the headings to the chart, then look for your lunar month in the column below. You might find that it is not listed, in which case you are not under the influence of any star. Opposite your lunar month, in the side headings on the right, are the stars that apply to you. A key to the stars appears at the foot of the chart and their meanings are explained in the following text.

			Earthly Branch for 'Hour' of Birth									Property Star
Hai	Hsü	Yu	Shen	Wei	Wu	Szu	Ch'en	Mao	Yin	Ch'ou	Tzu	
10th	1st	4th	1st	7th	10th	1st	4th	7th	10th	4th	7th	★ ★ ★
11th	2nd	5th	2nd	8th	11th	2nd	5th	8th	11th	5th	8th	★ ★ ★
12th	3rd	6th	3rd	9th	12th	3rd	6th	9th	12th	6th	9th	★ ★
1st	4th	7th	4th	10th	1st	4th	7th	10th	1st	7th	10th	☆ ☆ ☆
2nd	5th	8th	5th	11th	2nd	5th	8th	11th	2nd	8th	11th	☆
3rd	6th	9th	6th	12th	3rd	6th	9th	12th	3rd	9th	12th	☆ ☆ ☆
4th	7th	10th	7th	1st	4th	7th	10th	1st	4th	10th	1st	☆ ☆
5th	8th	11th	8th	2nd	5th	8th	11th	2nd	5th	11th	2nd	☆ ☆
6th	9th	12th	9th	3rd	6th	9th	12th	3rd	6th	12th	3rd	☆ ☆ ☆
7th	10th	1st	10th	4th	7th	10th	1st	4th	7th	1st	4th	★ ★
8th	11th	2nd	11th	5th	8th	11th	2nd	5th	8th	2nd	5th	★
9th	12th	3rd	12th	6th	9th	12th	3rd	6th	9th	3rd	6th	★ ★ ★

Lunar Month of Birth

KEY

☆ ☆ ☆	Extremely lucky	★ ★ ★	Extremely baleful
☆ ☆	Very lucky	★ ★	Very baleful
☆	Lucky	★	Baleful

☆ ☆ ☆

You will own a farm and inherit a large fortune. Even though the farmhouse will be new, it will be a house of good fortune that brings you wealth.

☆ ☆

You will be able to afford a new house. You will know how to decorate and improve it. Be prepared for a minor illness.

☆

Beware of accidents, especially in May, July and September each year. You will have many opportunities to make money.

★ ★ ★

You are not suited to buying a house on your own. Buy with your partner, or else you will have bad luck and hurt yourself.

★ ★

You will not inherit any property, nor will you be able to afford a new house. Disaster and mourning lie ahead.

★

You will have difficulty buying a house. You will not inherit any property and will move many times before settling down to live peacefully.

Burial Palaces

This section gives the circumstances of your death and funeral and predicts the weather at the time. It was the custom in China for childless couples to adopt children to ensure that their funeral ceremonies would be correctly carried out and that they would be properly venerated and mourned after their death. As with the sections on Marital Harmony and Brothers' Harmony, the palaces follow a cycle of birth, death and rebirth.

To use the chart, you need your element (see Table 1) and the Earthly Branch for your 'hour' of birth (see Table 2). Find your element in the headings to the chart, then look for your Earthly Branch in the column below. Opposite your Earthly Branch, in the side headings on the right, you will find the name of your burial palace. The prediction for your palace appears in the text below. (The ages given in the predictions are according to the Chinese system of reckoning age, so each time an age is mentioned you need to deduct 1 to find the Western equivalent.)

| Element | | | | | Burial |
Water	Metal	Earth	Fire	Wood	Palace
Shen	Szu	Shen	Yin	Hai	*Ch'ang Sheng*
Yu	Wu	Yu	Mao	Tzu	*Mu Yü*
Hsü	Wei	Hsü	Ch'en	Ch'ou	*Kuan Tai*
Hai	Shen	Hai	Szu	Yin	*Lin Kuan*
Tzu	Yu	Tzu	Wu	Mao	*Ti Wang*
Ch'ou	Hsü	Ch'ou	Wei	Ch'en	*Shuai Kung*
Yin	Hai	Yin	Shen	Szu	*Ping Kung*
Mao	Tzu	Mao	Yu	Wu	*Szu Kung*
Ch'en	Ch'ou	Ch'en	Hsü	Wei	*Mu Kung*
Szu	Yin	Szu	Hai	Shen	*Chueh Kung*
Wu	Mao	Wu	Tzu	Yu	*T'ai Kung*
Wei	Ch'en	Wei	Ch'ou	Hsü	*Yang Kung*

Earthly Branch for 'Hour' of Birth

CH'ANG SHENG (Birth)

At sixty-seven you will be ill for two days, then die. The day of your funeral will be sunny. Your grave clothes will be fine and the wood used for the coffin will be yellow. You will have two sons and two daughters to perform your funeral rites. It would not be advisable for those aged forty-five to attend your funeral. There will be four to six monks to carry your coffin to the cemetery. It will be a splendid funeral.

MU YÜ (Bathing)

Your corpse will be damaged and your coffin will be white. Your funeral will take place on a cloudy day. Those aged between seven and nine should not attend your funeral. You will die between the ages of seventy-one and seventy-two. You will have two sons and one daughter to perform your funeral rites and your funeral will be a splendid affair.

KUAN TAI (Official Belt)

From thirty-three to thirty-four you will suffer from ill health and bad luck. Between sixty-three and sixty-four, in or near autumn, you will be ill for two days, then die. You will have a fine coffin. You will have three sons and two daughters to perform your funeral rites and three, five or seven monks to carry your coffin to the cemetery. It will be a splendid funeral.

LIN KUAN (Entering Society)

You will be ill for three days, then die. On the day of your funeral the weather will be changeable. You will have a fine coffin and two sons and two daughters will perform your funeral rites. It will be a splendid funeral.

TI WANG (Prime)

You will be unconscious for five days, then die. On the day of your funeral it will be sunny. You will have five children to perform your funeral rites.

SHUAI KUNG (Decaying Palace)

You will die on a cold, rainy day, but the day of the funeral will be sunny. You will have a fine coffin. You will have two sons and three daughters to perform your funeral rites and five to six monks to carry your coffin to the cemetery. It will be a splendid funeral.

PING KUNG (Sickness Palace)

Your funeral will be held on a very cold day. Your coffin will be slightly damaged. You will have one son and two daughters and some monks to carry your coffin to the cemetery. It will be a splendid funeral.

SZU KUNG (Death Palace)

The day of your funeral will be mild and rainy. As the Lonely Star is approaching you, only two sons will perform your funeral rites. Your coffin will have been made in a hurry. You will not have been on good terms with your relatives so your funeral will be a sorry affair.

MU KUNG (Grave Palace)

Your funeral will be held in the autumn or winter. You will have a fine coffin. Although you will have two sons, only one will be able to perform your funeral rites. You will have been on good terms with your relatives so everyone will come to the funeral, which will be a splendid affair.

CHUEH KUNG (Nothing Palace)

You will go to a relative's party, catch a disease and then die. It will be cold on the day of your funeral. You will have one son, two adopted sons and two old monks to carry your coffin to the cemetery. It will be a splendid funeral.

T'AI KUNG (Conception Palace)

You will suffer from diarrhoea for a while, then die on a sunny day, but it will rain on the day of your funeral. Your coffin will be made in a hurry as the Lonely Star will be approaching you. Although you will have two sons and one daughter to carry your coffin to the cemetery, it will not be a splendid funeral.

YANG KUNG (Pregnancy Palace)

In old age you will still be able to talk easily, even in your last moments. The day you die will be cold and it will rain on the day of the funeral. You will have two sons but one will be a sybarite. All your relatives will go to the funeral, which will be a splendid affair.

Notes

1. Martin Palmer (ed.), *T'ung Shu: The Ancient Chinese Almanac*, Rider, 1986.
2. Cao Xuequin, *The Story of the Stone*, trans. David Hawkes, 2 vols., Penguin Books, 1973, vol. I, p. 47.
3. Holmes Welch, *The Practice of Chinese Buddhism 1900–1950*, Harvard University Press, 1967, p. 121.
4. W. E. Soothill, *The Three Religions of China*, Hodder & Stoughton, 1913.
5. H. C. du Bose, *The Dragon, Image and Demon*, Partridge, London, 1886.
6. See Daniel Overmyer, *Folk Buddhist Religion*, Harvard University Press, 1976, pp. 133 ff.
7. Clifford H. Plopper, *Chinese Religion Seen Through the Proverb*, Shanghai, 1935; Paragon Book Reprint Corp., New York, 1969, p. 97.
8. *The Analects*, Book 2, ch. 5, verse 3 (our translation).
9. See Palmer, op. cit., pp. 197 and 199.
10. From Kenneth Ch'en, *Buddhism in China*, Princeton University Press, 1973, pp. 110–11.
11. See, for example, Mark Elvin, *The Pattern of the Chinese Past*, Stanford University Press, 1973.
12. For a very interesting account of the social and religious disruption of this time, see Richard Hon-chun Shek, 'Religion and Society in Late Ming: Sectarianism and Popular Thought in 16th and 17th Century China', University Microfilms International, USA, 1982.
13. See Shek, op. cit., pp. 61–5, and Ch'en, op. cit., pp. 436–7. The translation is based on that of Shek, with reference to the original Chinese.
14. W. E. Soothill and L. Hodous, *A Dictionary of Chinese Buddhist Terms*, Kegan Paul, Trench, Trubner, 1937; Motilal Banarsidass, Delhi, 1977.

15. Stephen Tang and Martin Palmer, *Chinese Herbal Prescriptions*, Rider, 1986, pp. 19–20.
16. See Henri Doré, *Researches into Chinese Superstitions, 15 vols., Walsh, Shanghai, 1914, vol. IV, pp. 15–21; see also Soothill and Hodous, op. cit., pp. 63–4.*
17. *See Kenneth Ch'en, The Chinese Transformation of Buddhism,* Princeton University Press, 1973, pp. 24–8.
18. See Palmer, *T'ung Shu*, pp. 38 and 39.
19. ibid., Section 23.
20. ibid., p. 46, and Martin Palmer, Kwok Man-ho and Joanne O'Brien, *The Fortune-Teller's I Ching*, Rider, 1986, p. 34.

The Calendar Tables

Much of the material covered below has appeared earlier in the book; it is repeated here in this form to assist the reader to use the Calendar Tables as easily as possible.

The Chinese calendar uses the sexagenary cycle of Heavenly Stems and Earthly Branches for numbering the years, the months and the days (see pp. 23–7). In the pages that follow we have listed the Chinese equivalents for the Western calendar dates from 5 February 1924 to 23 January 2001. To simplify matters, in the main body of the tables we have used codes for the Heavenly Stems and Earthly Branches, and these are shown below.

The tables are divided into years according to the Chinese calendar, and each year is named by a Heavenly Stem and an Earthly Branch from the sexagenary cycle. Thus the first year, which runs from the Western date of 5 February 1924 to 23 January 1925, is Chia Tzu; the next year, from 24 January 1925 to 12 February 1926, is Yi Ch'ou; the next, from 13 February 1926 to 1 February 1927, is Ping Yin; and so on. To find the characters for your year of birth, simply turn to your Western birthday in the tables and look for the heading to the Chinese year in which it appears. For example, someone born on 10 January 1925 comes under the year Chia Tzu.

In the left-hand column of the tables are listed the days and months according to the Western calendar, 10.1 meaning 10 January. The next column gives the corresponding days and months for the Chinese calendar. Thus, in 1925, 10 January becomes 16.12 in the Chinese calendar, that is, the 16th day of the 12th month. Therefore someone born on 10 January 1925 was born on the 16th day of the 12th month in Chia Tzu year.

Note that the relationship between the Western and the Chinese calendars varies from year to year. The 10th of January will not invariably be the 16th day of the 12th month. This is because in the Chinese system the number of days in a year fluctuates between 353 and 355, with an intercalary month every two to three years to keep the calendars in line (see p. 25). Thus in the tables you will see every so often a year with two months which have the same number, the second of which is set in italic – this is the extra month.

The variable number of days in the year is also the reason why the Chinese New Year changes from year to year in relation to the Western calendar, falling anywhere between 21 January and 20 February.

The third column of the tables lists the codes (see below) for the Heavenly Stems and Earthly Branches for the months. In the example already given, 10 January 1925 has the code D2, which gives the Heavenly Stem Ting and the Earthly Branch Ch'ou. These are the characters for the 12th month in Chia Tzu year.

In the fourth column are the codes for the Heavenly Stems and Earthly Branches for the days. For 10 January 1925 the code is A7, which gives the Heavenly Stem Chia and the Earthly Branch Wu. These are the characters for the 16th day of the 12th month in Chia Tzu year.

The characters for the 'hours' are not listed in the Calendar – to do so would have meant including twelve separate entries for each day. The characters for the 'hours' can be found in Table 3 on p. 36.

Finally, in the right-hand column are listed the constellations. There are twenty-eight in all and they change from day to day. For 10 January 1925 the constellation is Pheasant.

Codes for the Heavenly Stems and Earthly Branches

Heavenly Stems		Earthly Branches	
Code	Character	Code	Character
A	Chia	1	Tzu
B	Yi	2	Ch'ou
C	Ping	3	Yin
D	Ting	4	Mao
E	Mou	5	Ch'en
F	Chi	6	Szu
G	Keng	7	Wu
H	Hsin	8	Wei
J*	Jen	9	Shen
K	Kuei	10	Yu
		11	Hsü
		12	Hai

*To avoid possible confusion with the number 1, we have not used the letter I.

CHIA TZU YEAR

Solar date	Lunar date	Month HS/EB	Day HS/EB	Constellation	Solar date	Lunar date	Month HS/EB	Day HS/EB	Constellation
1924					15. 4	12. 3	E5	A1	Serpent
5 2	1. 1	C3	A3	Pig	16. 4	13. 3	E5	B2	Earthworm
6 2	2. 1	C3	B4	Porcupine	17. 4	14. 3	E5	C3	Crocodile
7 2	3. 1	C3	C5	Wolf	18. 4	15. 3	E5	D4	Dragon
8 2	4. 1	C3	D6	Dog	19. 4	16. 3	E5	E5	Badger
9 2	5. 1	C3	E7	Pheasant	20. 4	17. 3	E5	F6	Hare
10. 2	6. 1	C3	F8	Cock	21. 4	18. 3	E5	G7	Fox
11. 2	7. 1	C3	G9	Crow	22. 4	19. 3	E5	H8	Tiger
12. 2	8. 1	C3	H10	Monkey	23. 4	20. 3	E5	J9	Leopard
13. 2	9. 1	C3	J11	Gibbon	24. 4	21. 3	E5	K10	Griffon
14. 2	10. 1	C3	K12	Tapir	25. 4	22. 3	E5	A11	Ox
15. 2	11. 1	C3	A1	Sheep	26. 4	23. 3	E5	B12	Bat
16. 2	12. 1	C3	B2	Deer	27. 4	24. 3	E5	C1	Rat
17. 2	13. 1	C3	C3	Horse	28. 4	25. 3	E5	D2	Swallow
18. 2	14. 1	C3	D4	Stag	29. 4	26. 3	E5	E3	Pig
19. 2	15. 1	C3	E5	Serpent	30. 4	27. 3	E5	F4	Porcupine
20. 2	16. 1	C3	F6	Earthworm	1. 5	28. 3	E5	G5	Wolf
21. 2	17. 1	C3	G7	Crocodile	2. 5	29. 3	E5	H6	Dog
22. 2	18. 1	C3	H8	Dragon	3. 5	30. 3	E5	J7	Pheasant
23. 2	19. 1	C3	J9	Badger	4. 5	1. 4	F6	K8	Cock
24. 2	20. 1	C3	K10	Hare	5. 5	2. 4	F6	A9	Crow
25. 2	21. 1	C3	A11	Fox	6. 5	3. 4	F6	B10	Monkey
26. 2	22. 1	C3	B12	Tiger	7. 5	4. 4	F6	C11	Gibbon
27. 2	23. 1	C3	C1	Leopard	8. 5	5. 4	F6	D12	Tapir
28. 2	24. 1	C3	D2	Griffon	9. 5	6. 4	F6	E1	Sheep
29. 2	25. 1	C3	E3	Ox	10. 5	7. 4	F6	F2	Deer
1. 3	26. 1	C3	F4	Bat	11. 5	8. 4	F6	G3	Horse
2. 3	27. 1	C3	G5	Rat	12. 5	9. 4	F6	H4	Stag
3. 3	28. 1	C3	H6	Swallow	13. 5	10. 4	F6	J5	Serpent
4. 3	29. 1	C3	J7	Pig	14. 5	11. 4	F6	K6	Earthworm
5. 3	1. 2	D4	K8	Porcupine	15. 5	12. 4	F6	A7	Crocodile
6. 3	2. 2	D4	A9	Wolf	16. 5	13. 4	F6	B8	Dragon
7. 3	3. 2	D4	B10	Dog	17. 5	14. 4	F6	C9	Badger
8. 3	4. 2	D4	C11	Pheasant	18. 5	15. 4	F6	D10	Fox
9. 3	5. 2	D4	D12	Cock	19. 5	16. 4	F6	E11	Tiger
10. 3	6. 2	D4	E1	Crow	20. 5	17. 4	F6	F12	Leopard
11. 3	7. 2	D4	F2	Monkey	21. 5	18. 4	F6	G1	Leopard
12. 3	8. 2	D4	G3	Gibbon	22. 5	19. 4	F6	H2	Griffon
13. 3	9. 2	D4	H4	Tapir	23. 5	20. 4	F6	J3	Ox
14. 3	10. 2	D4	J5	Sheep	24. 5	21. 4	F6	K4	Bat
15. 3	11. 2	D4	K6	Deer	25. 5	22. 4	F6	A5	Rat
16. 3	12. 2	D4	A7	Horse	26. 5	23. 4	F6	B6	Swallow
17. 3	13. 2	D4	B8	Stag	27. 5	24. 4	F6	C7	Pig
18. 3	14. 2	D4	C9	Serpent	28. 5	25. 4	F6	D8	Porcupine
19. 3	15. 2	D4	D10	Earthworm	29. 5	26. 4	F6	E9	Wolf
20. 3	16. 2	D4	E11	Crocodile	30. 5	27. 4	F6	F10	Dog
21. 3	17. 2	D4	F12	Dragon	31. 5	28. 4	F6	G11	Pheasant
22. 3	18. 2	D4	G1	Badger	1. 6	29. 4	F6	H12	Cock
23. 3	19. 2	D4	H2	Hare	2. 6	1. 5	G7	J1	Crow
24. 3	20. 2	D4	J3	Fox	3. 6	2. 5	G7	K2	Monkey
25. 3	21. 2	D4	K4	Tiger	4. 6	3. 5	G7	A3	Gibbon
26. 3	22. 2	D4	A5	Leopard	5. 6	4. 5	G7	B4	Tapir
27. 3	23. 2	D4	B6	Griffon	6. 6	5. 5	G7	C5	Sheep
28. 3	24. 2	D4	C7	Ox	7. 6	6. 5	G7	D6	Deer
29. 3	25. 2	D4	D8	Bat	8. 6	7. 5	G7	E7	Horse
30. 3	26. 2	D4	E9	Rat	9. 6	8. 5	G7	F8	Stag
31. 3	27. 2	D4	F10	Swallow	10. 6	9. 5	G7	G9	Serpent
1. 4	28. 2	D4	G11	Pig	11. 6	10. 5	G7	H10	Earthworm
2. 4	29. 2	D4	H12	Porcupine	12. 6	11. 5	G7	J11	Crocodile
3. 4	30. 2	D4	J1	Wolf	13. 6	12. 5	G7	K12	Dragon
4. 4	1. 3	E5	K2	Dog	14. 6	13. 5	G7	A1	Badger
5. 4	2. 3	E5	A3	Pheasant	15. 6	14. 5	G7	B2	Hare
6. 4	3. 3	E5	B4	Cock	16. 6	15. 5	G7	C3	Fox
7. 4	4. 3	E5	C5	Crow	17. 6	16. 5	G7	D4	Tiger
8. 4	5. 3	E5	D6	Monkey	18. 6	17. 5	G7	E5	Leopard
9. 4	6. 3	E5	E7	Gibbon	19. 6	18. 5	G7	F6	Griffon
10. 4	7. 3	E5	F8	Tapir	20. 6	19. 5	G7	G7	Ox
11. 4	8. 3	E5	G9	Sheep	21. 6	20. 5	G7	H8	Bat
12. 4	9. 3	E5	H10	Deer	22. 6	21. 5	G7	J9	Rat
13. 4	10. 3	E5	J11	Horse	23. 6	22. 5	G7	K10	Swallow
14. 4	11. 3	E5	K12	Stag	24. 6	23. 5	G7	A11	Pig

Solar date	Lunar date	Month HS/EB	Day HS/EB	Constellation	Solar date	Lunar date	Month HS/EB	Day HS/EB	Constellation
25. 6	24. 5	G7	B12	Porcupine	6. 9	8. 8	K10	E1	Badger
26. 6	25. 5	G7	C1	Wolf	7. 9	9. 8	K10	F2	Hare
27. 6	26. 5	G7	D2	Dog	8. 9	10. 8	K10	G3	Fox
28. 6	27. 5	G7	E3	Pheasant	9. 9	11. 8	K10	H4	Tiger
29. 6	28. 5	G7	F4	Cock	10. 9	12. 8	K10	J5	Leopard
30. 6	29. 5	G7	G5	Crow	11. 9	13. 8	K10	K6	Griffon
1. 7	30. 5	G7	H6	Monkey	12. 9	14. 8	K10	A7	Ox
2. 7	1. 6	H8	J7	Gibbon	13. 9	15. 8	K10	B8	Bat
3. 7	2. 6	H8	K8	Tapir	14. 9	16. 8	K10	C9	Rat
4. 7	3. 6	H8	A9	Sheep	15. 9	17. 8	K10	D10	Swallow
5. 7	4. 6	H8	B10	Deer	16. 9	18. 8	K10	E11	Pig
6. 7	5. 6	H8	C11	Horse	17. 9	19. 8	K10	F12	Porcupine
7. 7	6. 6	H8	D12	Stag	18. 9	20. 8	K10	G1	Wolf
8. 7	7. 6	H8	E1	Serpent	19. 9	21. 8	K10	H2	Dog
9. 7	8. 6	H8	F2	Earthworm	20. 9	22. 8	K10	J3	Pheasant
10. 7	9. 6	H8	G3	Crocodile	21. 9	23. 8	K10	K4	Cock
11. 7	10. 6	H8	H4	Dragon	22. 9	24. 8	K10	A5	Crow
12. 7	11. 6	H8	J5	Badger	23. 9	25. 8	K10	B6	Monkey
13. 7	12. 6	H8	K6	Hare	24. 9	26. 8	K10	C7	Gibbon
14. 7	13. 6	H8	A7	Fox	25. 9	27. 8	K10	D8	Tapir
15. 7	14. 6	H8	B8	Tiger	26. 9	28. 8	K10	E9	Sheep
16. 7	15. 6	H8	C9	Leopard	27. 9	29. 8	K10	F10	Deer
17. 7	16. 6	H8	D10	Griffon	28. 9	30. 8	K10	G11	Horse
18. 7	17. 6	H8	E11	Ox	29. 9	1. 9	A11	H12	Stag
19. 7	18. 6	H8	F12	Bat	30. 9	2. 9	A11	J1	Serpent
20. 7	19. 6	H8	G1	Rat	1.10	3. 9	A11	K2	Earthworm
21. 7	20. 6	H8	H2	Swallow	2.10	4. 9	A11	A3	Crocodile
22. 7	21. 6	H8	J3	Pig	3.10	5. 9	A11	B4	Dragon
23. 7	22. 6	H8	K4	Porcupine	4.10	6. 9	A11	C5	Badger
24. 7	23. 6	H8	A5	Wolf	5.10	7. 9	A11	D6	Hare
25. 7	24. 6	H8	B6	Dog	6.10	8. 9	A11	E7	Fox
26. 7	25. 6	H8	C7	Pheasant	7.10	9. 9	A11	F8	Tiger
27. 7	26. 6	H8	D8	Cock	8.10	10. 9	A11	G9	Leopard
28. 7	27. 6	H8	E9	Crow	9.10	11. 9	A11	H10	Griffon
29. 7	28. 6	H8	F10	Monkey	10.10	12. 9	A11	J11	Ox
30. 7	29. 6	H8	G11	Gibbon	11.10	13. 9	A11	K12	Bat
31. 7	30. 6	H8	H12	Tapir	12.10	14. 9	A11	A1	Rat
1. 8	1. 7	J9	J1	Sheep	13.10	15. 9	A11	B2	Swallow
2. 8	2. 7	J9	K2	Deer	14.10	16. 9	A11	C3	Pig
3. 8	3. 7	J9	A3	Horse	15.10	17. 9	A11	D4	Porcupine
4. 8	4. 7	J9	B4	Stag	16.10	18. 9	A11	E5	Wolf
5. 8	5. 7	J9	C5	Serpent	17.10	19. 9	A11	F6	Dog
6. 8	6. 7	J9	D6	Earthworm	18.10	20. 9	A11	G7	Pheasant
7. 8	7. 7	J9	E7	Crocodile	19.10	21. 9	A11	H8	Cock
8. 8	8. 7	J9	F8	Dragon	20.10	22. 9	A11	J9	Crow
9. 8	9. 7	J9	G9	Badger	21.10	23. 9	A11	K10	Monkey
10. 8	10. 7	J9	H10	Hare	22.10	24. 9	A11	A11	Gibbon
11. 8	11. 7	J9	J11	Fox	23.10	25. 9	A11	B12	Tapir
12. 8	12. 7	J9	K12	Tiger	24.10	26. 9	A11	C1	Sheep
13. 8	13. 7	J9	A1	Leopard	25.10	27. 9	A11	D2	Deer
14. 8	14. 7	J9	B2	Griffon	26.10	28. 9	A11	E3	Horse
15. 8	15. 7	J9	C3	Ox	27.10	29. 9	A11	F4	Stag
16. 8	16. 7	J9	D4	Bat	28.10	1.10	B12	G5	Serpent
17. 8	17. 7	J9	E5	Rat	29.10	2.10	B12	H6	Earthworm
18. 8	18. 7	J9	F6	Swallow	30.10	3.10	B12	J7	Crocodile
19. 8	19. 7	J9	G7	Pig	31.10	4.10	B12	K8	Dragon
20. 8	20. 7	J9	H8	Porcupine	1.11	5.10	B12	A9	Badger
21. 8	21. 7	J9	J9	Wolf	2.11	6.10	B12	B10	Hare
22. 8	22. 7	J9	K10	Dog	3.11	7.10	B12	C11	Fox
23. 8	23. 7	J9	A11	Pheasant	4.11	8.10	B12	D12	Tiger
24. 8	24. 7	J9	B12	Cock	5.11	9.10	B12	E1	Leopard
25. 8	25. 7	J9	C1	Crow	6.11	10.10	B12	F2	Griffon
26. 8	26. 7	J9	D2	Monkey	7.11	11.10	B12	G3	Ox
27. 8	27. 7	J9	E3	Gibbon	8.11	12.10	B12	H4	Bat
28. 8	28. 7	J9	F4	Tapir	9.11	13.10	B12	J5	Rat
29. 8	29. 7	J9	G5	Sheep	10.11	14.10	B12	K6	Swallow
30. 8	1. 8	K10	H6	Deer	11.11	15.10	B12	A7	Pig
31. 8	2. 8	K10	J7	Horse	12.11	16.10	B12	B8	Porcupine
1. 9	3. 8	K10	K8	Stag	13.11	17.10	B12	C9	Wolf
2. 9	4. 8	K10	A9	Serpent	14.11	18.10	B12	D10	Dog
3. 9	5. 8	K10	B10	Earthworm	15.11	19.10	B12	E11	Pheasant
4. 9	6. 8	K10	C11	Crocodile	16.11	20.10	B12	F12	Cock
5. 9	7. 8	K10	D12	Dragon	17.11	21.10	B12	G1	Crow

Solar date	Lunar date	Month HS/EB	Day HS/EB	Constellation	Solar date	Lunar date	Month HS/EB	Day HS/EB	Constellation
18.11	22.10	B12	H2	Monkey	23.12	27.11	C1	C1	Serpent
19.11	23.10	B12	J3	Gibbon	24.12	28.11	C1	D2	Earthworm
20.11	24.10	B12	K4	Tapir	25.12	29.11	C1	E3	Crocodile
21.11	25.10	B12	A5	Sheep	26.12	1.12	D2	F4	Dragon
22.11	26.10	B12	B6	Deer	27.12	2.12	D2	G5	Badger
23.11	27.10	B12	C7	Horse	28.12	3.12	D2	H6	Hare
24.11	28.10	B12	D8	Stag	29.12	4.12	D2	J7	Fox
25.11	29.10	B12	E9	Serpent	30.12	5.12	D2	K8	Tiger
26.11	30.10	B12	F10	Earthworm	31.12	6.12	D2	A9	Leopard
27.11	1.11	C1	G11	Crocodile					
28.11	2.11	C1	H12	Dragon	**1925**				
29.11	3.11	C1	J1	Badger	1. 1	7.12	D2	B10	Griffon
30.11	4.11	C1	K2	Hare	2. 1	8.12	D2	C11	Ox
1.12	5.11	C1	A3	Fox	3. 1	9.12	D2	D12	Bat
2.12	6.11	C1	B4	Tiger	4. 1	10.12	D2	E1	Rat
3.12	7.11	C1	C5	Leopard	5. 1	11.12	D2	F2	Swallow
4.12	8.11	C1	D6	Griffon	6. 1	12.12	D2	G3	Pig
5.12	9.11	C1	E7	Ox	7. 1	13.12	D2	H4	Porcupine
6.12	10.11	C1	F8	Bat	8. 1	14.12	D2	J5	Wolf
7.12	11.11	C1	G9	Rat	9. 1	15.12	D2	K6	Dog
8.12	12.11	C1	H10	Swallow	10. 1	16.12	D2	A7	Pheasant
9.12	13.11	C1	J11	Pig	11. 1	17.12	D2	B8	Cock
10.12	14.11	C1	K12	Porcupine	12. 1	18.12	D2	C9	Crow
11.12	15.11	C1	A1	Wolf	13. 1	19.12	D2	D10	Monkey
12.12	16.11	C1	B2	Dog	14. 1	20.12	D2	E11	Gibbon
13.12	17.11	C1	C3	Pheasant	15. 1	21.12	D2	F12	Tapir
14.12	18.11	C1	D4	Cock	16. 1	22.12	D2	G1	Sheep
15.12	19.11	C1	E5	Crow	17. 1	23.12	D2	H2	Deer
16.12	20.11	C1	F6	Monkey	18. 1	24.12	D2	J3	Horse
17.12	21.11	C1	G7	Gibbon	19. 1	25.12	D2	K4	Stag
18.12	22.11	C1	H8	Tapir	20. 1	26.12	D2	A5	Serpent
19.12	23.11	C1	J9	Sheep	21. 1	27.12	D2	B6	Earthworm
20.12	24.11	C1	K10	Deer	22. 1	28.12	D2	C7	Crocodile
21.12	25.11	C1	A11	Horse	23. 1	29.12	D2	D8	Dragon
22.12	26.11	C1	B12	Stag					

YI CH'OU YEAR

Solar date	Lunar date	Month HS/EB	Day HS/EB	Constellation	Solar date	Lunar date	Month HS/EB	Day HS/EB	Constellation
24. 1	1. 1	E3	E9	Badger	26. 2	4. 2	F4	H6	Griffon
25. 1	2. 1	E3	F10	Hare	27. 2	5. 2	F4	J7	Ox
26. 1	3. 1	E3	G11	Fox	28. 2	6. 2	F4	K8	Bat
27. 1	4. 1	E3	H12	Tiger	1. 3	7. 2	F4	A9	Rat
28. 1	5. 1	E3	J1	Leopard	2. 3	8. 2	F4	B10	Swallow
29. 1	6. 1	E3	K2	Griffon	3. 3	9. 2	F4	C11	Pig
30. 1	7. 1	E3	A3	Ox	4. 3	10. 2	F4	D12	Porcupine
31. 1	8. 1	E3	B4	Bat	5. 3	11. 2	F4	E1	Wolf
1. 2	9. 1	E3	C5	Rat	6. 3	12. 2	F4	F2	Dog
2. 2	10. 1	E3	D6	Swallow	7. 3	13. 2	F4	G3	Pheasant
3. 2	11. 1	E3	E7	Pig	8. 3	14. 2	F4	H4	Cock
4. 2	12. 1	E3	F8	Porcupine	9. 3	15. 2	F4	J5	Crow
5. 2	13. 1	E3	G9	Wolf	10. 3	16. 2	F4	K6	Monkey
6. 2	14. 1	E3	H10	Dog	11. 3	17. 2	F4	A7	Gibbon
7. 2	15. 1	E3	J11	Pheasant	12. 3	18. 2	F4	B8	Tapir
8. 2	16. 1	E3	K12	Cock	13. 3	19. 2	F4	C9	Sheep
9. 2	17. 1	E3	A1	Crow	14. 3	20. 2	F4	D10	Deer
10. 2	18. 1	E3	B2	Monkey	15. 3	21. 2	F4	E11	Horse
11. 2	19. 1	E3	C3	Gibbon	16. 3	22. 2	F4	F12	Stag
12. 2	20. 1	E3	D4	Tapir	17. 3	23. 2	F4	G1	Serpent
13. 2	21. 1	E3	E5	Sheep	18. 3	24. 2	F4	H2	Earthworm
14. 2	22. 1	E3	F6	Deer	19. 3	25. 2	F4	J3	Crocodile
15. 2	23. 1	E3	G7	Horse	20. 3	26. 2	F4	K4	Dragon
16. 2	24. 1	E3	H8	Stag	21. 3	27. 2	F4	A5	Badger
17. 2	25. 1	E3	J9	Serpent	22. 3	28. 2	F4	B6	Hare
18. 2	26. 1	E3	K10	Earthworm	23. 3	29. 2	F4	C7	Fox
19. 2	27. 1	E3	A11	Crocodile	24. 3	1. 3	G5	D8	Tiger
20. 2	28. 1	E3	B12	Dragon	25. 3	2. 3	G5	E9	Leopard
21. 2	29. 1	E3	C1	Badger	26. 3	3. 3	G5	F10	Griffon
22. 2	30. 1	E3	D2	Hare	27. 3	4. 3	G5	G11	Ox
23. 2	1. 2	F4	E3	Fox	28. 3	5. 3	G5	H12	Bat
24. 2	2. 2	F4	F4	Tiger	29. 3	6. 3	G5	J1	Rat
25. 2	3. 2	F4	G5	Leopard	30. 3	7. 3	G5	K2	Swallow

Solar date	Lunar date	Month HS/EB	Day HS/EB	Constellation
31. 3	8. 3	G5	A3	Pig
1. 4	9. 3	G5	B4	Porcupine
2. 4	10. 3	G5	C5	Wolf
3. 4	11. 3	G5	D6	Dog
4. 4	12. 3	G5	E7	Pheasant
5. 4	13. 3	G5	F8	Cock
6. 4	14. 3	G5	G9	Crow
7. 4	15. 3	G5	H10	Monkey
8. 4	16. 3	G5	J11	Gibbon
9. 4	17. 3	G5	K12	Tapir
10. 4	18. 3	G5	A1	Sheep
11. 4	19. 3	G5	B2	Deer
12. 4	20. 3	G5	C3	Horse
13. 4	21. 3	G5	D4	Stag
14. 4	22. 3	G5	E5	Serpent
15. 4	23. 3	G5	F6	Earthworm
16. 4	24. 3	G5	G7	Crocodile
17. 4	25. 3	G5	H8	Dragon
18. 4	26. 3	G5	J9	Badger
19. 4	27. 3	G5	K10	Hare
20. 4	28. 3	G5	A11	Fox
21. 4	29. 3	G5	B12	Tiger
22. 4	30. 3	G5	C1	Leopard
23. 4	1. 4	H6	D2	Griffon
24. 4	2. 4	H6	E3	Ox
25. 4	3. 4	H6	F4	Bat
26. 4	4. 4	H6	G5	Rat
27. 4	5. 4	H6	H6	Swallow
28. 4	6. 4	H6	J7	Pig
29. 4	7. 4	H6	K8	Porcupine
30. 4	8. 4	H6	A9	Wolf
1. 5	9. 4	H6	B10	Dog
2. 5	10. 4	H6	C11	Pheasant
3. 5	11. 4	H6	D12	Cock
4. 5	12. 4	H6	E1	Crow
5. 5	13. 4	H6	F2	Monkey
6. 5	14. 4	H6	G3	Gibbon
7. 5	15. 4	H6	H4	Tapir
8. 5	16. 4	H6	J5	Sheep
9. 5	17. 4	H6	K6	Deer
10. 5	18. 4	H6	A7	Horse
11. 5	19. 4	H6	B8	Stag
12. 5	20. 4	H6	C9	Serpent
13. 5	21. 4	H6	D10	Earthworm
14. 5	22. 4	H6	E11	Crocodile
15. 5	23. 4	H6	F12	Dragon
16. 5	24. 4	H6	G1	Badger
17. 5	25. 4	H6	H2	Hare
18. 5	26. 4	H6	J3	Fox
19. 5	27. 4	H6	K4	Tiger
20. 5	28. 4	H6	A5	Leopard
21. 5	29. 4	H6	B6	Griffon
22. 5	*1. 4*	*H6*	C7	Ox
23. 5	*2. 4*	*H6*	D8	Bat
24. 5	*3. 4*	*H6*	E9	Rat
25. 5	*4. 4*	*H6*	F10	Swallow
26. 5	*5. 4*	*H6*	G11	Pig
27. 5	*6. 4*	*H6*	H12	Porcupine
28. 5	*7. 4*	*H6*	J1	Wolf
29. 5	*8. 4*	*H6*	K2	Dog
30. 5	*9. 4*	*H6*	A3	Pheasant
31. 5	*10. 4*	*H6*	B4	Cock
1. 6	*11. 4*	*H6*	C5	Crow
2. 6	*12. 4*	*H6*	D6	Monkey
3. 6	*13. 4*	*H6*	E7	Gibbon
4. 6	*14. 4*	*H6*	F8	Tapir
5. 6	*15. 4*	*H6*	G9	Sheep
6. 6	*16. 4*	*H6*	H10	Deer
7. 6	*17. 4*	*H6*	J11	Horse
8. 6	*18. 4*	*H6*	K12	Stag
9. 6	*19. 4*	*H6*	A1	Serpent
10. 6	*20. 4*	*H6*	B2	Earthworm
11. 6	*21. 4*	*H6*	C3	Crocodile
12. 6	*22. 4*	*H6*	D4	Dragon
13. 6	*23. 4*	*H6*	E5	Badger
14. 6	*24. 4*	*H6*	F6	Hare
15. 6	*25. 4*	*H6*	G7	Fox
16. 6	*26. 4*	*H6*	H8	Tiger
17. 6	*27. 4*	*H6*	J9	Leopard
18. 6	*28. 4*	*H6*	K10	Griffon
19. 6	*29. 4*	*H6*	A11	Ox
20. 6	*30. 4*	*H6*	B12	Bat
21. 6	1. 5	J7	C1	Rat
22. 6	2. 5	J7	D2	Swallow
23. 6	3. 5	J7	E3	Pig
24. 6	4. 5	J7	F4	Porcupine
25. 6	5. 5	J7	G5	Wolf
26. 6	6. 5	J7	H6	Dog
27. 6	7. 5	J7	J7	Pheasant
28. 6	8. 5	J7	K8	Cock
29. 6	9. 5	J7	A9	Crow
30. 6	10. 5	J7	B10	Monkey
1. 7	11. 5	J7	C11	Gibbon
2. 7	12. 5	J7	D12	Tapir
3. 7	13. 5	J7	E1	Sheep
4. 7	14. 5	J7	F2	Deer
5. 7	15. 5	J7	G3	Horse
6. 7	16. 5	J7	H4	Stag
7. 7	17. 5	J7	J5	Serpent
8. 7	18. 5	J7	K6	Earthworm
9. 7	19. 5	J7	A7	Crocodile
10. 7	20. 5	J7	B8	Dragon
11. 7	21. 5	J7	C9	Badger
12. 7	22. 5	J7	D10	Hare
13. 7	23. 5	J7	E11	Fox
14. 7	24. 5	J7	F12	Tiger
15. 7	25. 5	J7	G1	Leopard
16. 7	26. 5	J7	H2	Griffon
17. 7	27. 5	J7	J3	Ox
18. 7	28. 5	J7	K4	Bat
19. 7	29. 5	J7	A5	Rat
20. 7	30. 5	J7	B6	Swallow
21. 7	1. 6	K8	C7	Pig
22. 7	2. 6	K8	D8	Porcupine
23. 7	3. 6	K8	E9	Wolf
24. 7	4. 6	K8	F10	Dog
25. 7	5. 6	K8	G11	Pheasant
26. 7	6. 6	K8	H12	Cock
27. 7	7. 6	K8	J1	Crow
28. 7	8. 6	K8	K2	Monkey
29. 7	9. 6	K8	A3	Gibbon
30. 7	10. 6	K8	B4	Tapir
31. 7	11. 6	K8	C5	Sheep
1. 8	12. 6	K8	D6	Deer
2. 8	13. 6	K8	E7	Horse
3. 8	14. 6	K8	F8	Stag
4. 8	15. 6	K8	G9	Serpent
5. 8	16. 6	K8	H10	Earthworm
6. 8	17. 6	K8	J11	Crocodile
7. 8	18. 6	K8	K12	Dragon
8. 8	19. 6	K8	A1	Badger
9. 8	20. 6	K8	B2	Hare
10. 8	21. 6	K8	C3	Fox
11. 8	22. 6	K8	D4	Tiger
12. 8	23. 6	K8	E5	Leopard
13. 8	24. 6	K8	F6	Griffon
14. 8	25. 6	K8	G7	Ox
15. 8	26. 6	K8	H8	Bat
16. 8	27. 6	K8	J9	Rat
17. 8	28. 7	K8	K10	Swallow
18. 8	29. 7	K8	A11	Pig
19. 8	1. 7	A9	B12	Porcupine
20. 8	2. 7	A9	C1	Wolf
21. 8	3. 7	A9	D2	Dog
22. 8	4. 7	A9	E3	Pheasant
23. 8	5. 7	A9	F4	Cock

Solar date	Lunar date	Month HS/EB	Day HS/EB	Constellation	Solar date	Lunar date	Month HS/EB	Day HS/EB	Constellation
24. 8	6. 7	A9	G5	Crow	5.11	19. 9	C11	K6	Griffon
25. 8	7. 7	A9	H6	Monkey	6.11	20. 9	C11	A7	Ox
26. 8	8. 7	A9	J7	Gibbon	7.11	21. 9	C11	B8	Bat
27. 8	9. 7	A9	K8	Tapir	8.11	22. 9	C11	C9	Rat
28. 8	10. 7	A9	A9	Sheep	9.11	23. 9	C11	D10	Swallow
29. 8	11. 7	A9	B10	Deer	10.11	24. 9	C11	E11	Pig
30. 8	12. 7	A9	C11	Horse	11.11	25. 9	C11	F12	Porcupine
31. 8	13. 7	A9	D12	Stag	12.11	26. 9	C11	G1	Wolf
1. 9	14. 7	A9	E1	Serpent	13.11	27. 9	C11	H2	Dog
2. 9	15. 7	A9	F2	Earthworm	14.11	28. 9	C11	J3	Pheasant
3. 9	16. 7	A9	G3	Crocodile	15.11	29. 9	C11	K4	Cock
4. 9	17. 7	A9	H4	Dragon	16.11	1.10	D12	A5	Crow
5. 9	18. 7	A9	J5	Badger	17.11	2.10	D12	B6	Monkey
6. 9	19. 7	A9	K6	Hare	18.11	3.10	D12	C7	Gibbon
7. 9	20. 7	A9	A7	Fox	19.11	4.10	D12	D8	Tapir
8. 9	21. 7	A9	B8	Tiger	20.11	5.10	D12	E9	Sheep
9. 9	22. 7	A9	C9	Leopard	21.11	6.10	D12	F10	Deer
10. 9	23. 7	A9	D10	Griffon	22.11	7.10	D12	G11	Horse
11. 9	24. 7	A9	E11	Ox	23.11	8.10	D12	H12	Stag
12. 9	25. 7	A9	F12	Bat	24.11	9.10	D12	J1	Serpent
13. 9	26. 7	A9	G1	Rat	25.11	10.10	D12	K2	Earthworm
14. 9	27. 7	A9	H2	Swallow	26.11	11.10	D12	A3	Crocodile
15. 9	28. 7	A9	J3	Pig	27.11	12.10	D12	B4	Dragon
16. 9	29. 7	A9	K4	Porcupine	28.11	13.10	D12	C5	Badger
17. 9	30. 7	A9	A5	Wolf	29.11	14.10	D12	D6	Hare
18. 9	1. 8	B10	B6	Dog	30.11	15.10	D12	E7	Fox
19. 9	2. 8	B10	C7	Pheasant	1.12	16.10	D12	F8	Tiger
20. 9	3. 8	B10	D8	Cock	2.12	17.10	D12	G9	Leopard
21. 9	4. 8	B10	E9	Crow	3.12	18.10	D12	H10	Griffon
22. 9	5. 8	B10	F10	Monkey	4.12	19.10	D12	J11	Ox
23. 9	6. 8	B10	G11	Gibbon	5.12	20.10	D12	K12	Bat
24. 9	7. 8	B10	H12	Tapir	6.12	21.10	D12	A1	Rat
25. 9	8. 8	B10	J1	Sheep	7.12	22.10	D12	B2	Swallow
26. 9	9. 8	B10	K2	Deer	8.12	23.10	D12	C3	Pig
27. 9	10. 8	B10	A3	Horse	9.12	24.10	D12	D4	Porcupine
28. 9	11. 8	B10	B4	Stag	10.12	25.10	D12	E5	Wolf
29. 9	12. 8	B10	C5	Serpent	11.12	26.10	D12	F6	Dog
30. 9	13. 8	B10	D6	Earthworm	12.12	27.10	D12	G7	Pheasant
1.10	14. 8	B10	E7	Crocodile	13.12	28.10	D12	H8	Cock
2.10	15. 8	B10	F8	Dragon	14.12	29.10	D12	J9	Crow
3.10	16. 8	B10	G9	Badger	15.12	30.10	D12	K10	Monkey
4.10	17. 8	B10	H10	Hare	16.12	1.11	E1	A11	Gibbon
5.10	18. 8	B10	J11	Fox	17.12	2.11	E1	B12	Tapir
6.10	19. 8	B10	K12	Tiger	18.12	3.11	E1	C1	Sheep
7.10	20. 8	B10	A1	Leopard	19.12	4.11	E1	D2	Deer
8.10	21. 8	B10	B2	Griffon	20.12	5.11	E1	E3	Horse
9.10	22. 8	B10	C3	Ox	21.12	6.11	E1	F4	Stag
10.10	23. 8	B10	D4	Bat	22.12	7.11	E1	G5	Serpent
11.10	24. 8	B10	E5	Rat	23.12	8.11	E1	H6	Earthworm
12.10	25. 8	B10	F6	Swallow	24.12	9.11	E1	J7	Crocodile
13.10	26. 8	B10	G7	Pig	25.12	10.11	E1	K8	Dragon
14.10	27. 8	B10	H8	Porcupine	26.12	11.11	E1	A9	Badger
15.10	28. 8	B10	J9	Wolf	27.12	12.11	E1	B10	Hare
16.10	29. 8	B10	K10	Dog	28.12	13.11	E1	C11	Fox
17.10	30. 8	B10	A11	Pheasant	29.12	14.11	E1	D12	Tiger
18.10	1. 9	C11	B12	Cock	30.12	15.11	E1	E1	Leopard
19.10	2. 9	C11	C1	Crow	31.12	16.11	E1	F2	Griffon
20.10	3. 9	C11	D2	Monkey	**1926**				
21.10	4. 9	C11	E3	Gibbon	1. 1	17.11	E1	G3	Ox
22.10	5. 9	C11	F4	Tapir	2. 1	18.11	E1	H4	Bat
23.10	6. 9	C11	G5	Sheep	3. 1	19.11	E1	J5	Rat
24.10	7. 9	C11	H6	Deer	4. 1	20.11	E1	K6	Swallow
25.10	8. 9	C11	J7	Horse	5. 1	21.11	E1	A7	Pig
26.10	9. 9	C11	K8	Stag	6. 1	22.11	E1	B8	Porcupine
27.10	10. 9	C11	A9	Serpent	7. 1	23.11	E1	C9	Wolf
28.10	11. 9	C11	B10	Earthworm	8. 1	24.11	E1	D10	Dog
29.10	12. 9	C11	C11	Crocodile	9. 1	25.11	E1	E11	Pheasant
30.10	13. 9	C11	D12	Dragon	10. 1	26.11	E1	F12	Cock
31.10	14. 9	C11	E1	Badger	11. 1	27.11	E1	G1	Crow
1.11	15. 9	C11	F2	Hare	12. 1	28.11	E1	H2	Monkey
2.11	16. 9	C11	G3	Fox	13. 1	29.11	E1	J3	Gibbon
3.11	17. 9	C11	H4	Tiger	14. 1	1.12	F2	K4	Tapir
4.11	18. 9	C11	J5	Leopard					

Solar date	Lunar date	Month HS/EB	Day HS/EB	Constellation	Solar date	Lunar date	Month HS/EB	Day HS/EB	Constellation
15. 1	2.12	F2	A5	Sheep	30. 1	17.12	F2	F8	Bat
16. 1	3.12	F2	B6	Deer	31. 1	18.12	F2	G9	Rat
17. 1	4.12	F2	C7	Horse	1. 2	19.12	F2	H10	Swallow
18. 1	5.12	F2	D8	Stag	2. 2	20.12	F2	J11	Pig
19. 1	6.12	F2	E9	Serpent	3. 2	21.12	F2	K12	Porcupine
20. 1	7.12	F2	F10	Earthworm	4. 2	22.12	F2	A1	Wolf
21. 1	8.12	F2	G11	Crocodile	5. 2	23.12	F2	B2	Dog
22. 1	9.12	F2	H12	Dragon	6. 2	24.12	F2	C3	Pheasant
23. 1	10.12	F2	J1	Badger	7. 2	25.12	F2	D4	Cock
24. 1	11.12	F2	K2	Hare	8. 2	26.12	F2	E5	Crow
25. 1	12.12	F2	A3	Fox	9. 2	27.12	F2	F6	Monkey
26. 1	13.12	F2	B4	Tiger	10. 2	28.12	F2	G7	Gibbon
27. 1	14.12	F2	C5	Leopard	11. 2	29.12	F2	H8	Tapir
28. 1	15.12	F2	D6	Griffon	12. 2	30.12	F2	J9	Sheep
29. 1	16.12	F2	E7	Ox					

PING YIN YEAR

Solar date	Lunar date	Month HS/EB	Day HS/EB	Constellation	Solar date	Lunar date	Month HS/EB	Day HS/EB	Constellation
13. 2	1. 1	G3	K10	Deer	7. 4	25. 2	H4	C3	Gibbon
14. 2	2. 1	G3	A11	Horse	8. 4	26. 2	H4	D4	Tapir
15. 2	3. 1	G3	B12	Stag	9. 4	27. 2	H4	E5	Sheep
16. 2	4. 1	G3	C1	Serpent	10. 4	28. 2	H4	F6	Deer
17. 2	5. 1	G3	D2	Earthworm	11. 4	29. 2	H4	G7	Horse
18. 2	6. 1	G3	E3	Crocodile	12. 4	1. 3	J5	H8	Stag
19. 2	7. 1	G3	F4	Dragon	13. 4	2. 3	J5	J9	Serpent
20. 2	8. 1	G3	G5	Badger	14. 4	3. 3	J5	K10	Earthworm
21. 2	9. 1	G3	H6	Hare	15. 4	4. 3	J5	A11	Crocodile
22. 2	10. 1	G3	J7	Fox	16. 4	5. 3	J5	B12	Dragon
23. 2	11. 1	G3	K8	Tiger	17. 4	6. 3	J5	C1	Badger
24. 2	12. 1	G3	A9	Leopard	18. 4	7. 3	J5	D2	Hare
25. 2	13. 1	G3	B10	Griffon	19. 4	8. 3	J5	E3	Fox
26. 2	14. 1	G3	C11	Ox	20. 4	9. 3	J5	F4	Tiger
27. 2	15. 1	G3	D12	Bat	21. 4	10. 3	J5	G5	Leopard
28. 2	16. 1	G3	E1	Rat	22. 4	11. 3	J5	H6	Griffon
1. 3	17. 1	G3	F2	Swallow	23. 4	12. 3	J5	J7	Ox
2. 3	18. 1	G3	G3	Pig	24. 4	13. 3	J5	K8	Bat
3. 3	19. 1	G3	H4	Porcupine	25. 4	14. 3	J5	A9	Rat
4. 3	20. 1	G3	J5	Wolf	26. 4	15. 3	J5	B10	Swallow
5. 3	21. 1	G3	K6	Dog	27. 4	16. 3	J5	C11	Pig
6. 3	22. 1	G3	A7	Pheasant	28. 4	17. 3	J5	D12	Porcupine
7. 3	23. 1	G3	B8	Cock	29. 4	18. 3	J5	E1	Wolf
8. 3	24. 1	G3	C9	Crow	30. 4	19. 3	J5	F2	Dog
9. 3	25. 1	G3	D10	Monkey	1. 5	20. 3	J5	G3	Pheasant
10. 3	26. 1	G3	E11	Gibbon	2. 5	21. 3	J5	H4	Cock
11. 3	27. 1	G3	F12	Tapir	3. 5	22. 3	J5	J5	Crow
12. 3	28. 1	G3	G1	Sheep	4. 5	23. 3	J5	K6	Monkey
13. 3	29. 1	G3	H2	Deer	5. 5	24. 3	J5	A7	Gibbon
14. 3	1. 2	H4	J3	Horse	6. 5	25. 3	J5	B8	Tapir
15. 3	2. 2	H4	K4	Stag	7. 5	26. 3	J5	C9	Sheep
16. 3	3. 2	H4	A5	Serpent	8. 5	27. 3	J5	D10	Deer
17. 3	4. 2	H4	B6	Earthworm	9. 5	28. 3	J5	E11	Horse
18. 3	5. 2	H4	C7	Crocodile	10. 5	29. 3	J5	F12	Stag
19. 3	6. 2	H4	D8	Dragon	11. 5	30. 3	J5	G1	Serpent
20. 3	7. 2	H4	E9	Badger	12. 5	1. 4	K6	H2	Earthworm
21. 3	8. 2	H4	F10	Hare	13. 5	2. 4	K6	J3	Crocodile
22. 3	9. 2	H4	G11	Fox	14. 5	3. 4	K6	K4	Dragon
23. 3	10. 2	H4	H12	Tiger	15. 5	4. 4	K6	A5	Badger
24. 3	11. 2	H4	J1	Leopard	16. 5	5. 4	K6	B6	Hare
25. 3	12. 2	H4	K2	Griffon	17. 5	6. 4	K6	C7	Fox
26. 3	13. 2	H4	A3	Ox	18. 5	7. 4	K6	D8	Tiger
27. 3	14. 2	H4	B4	Bat	19. 5	8. 4	K6	E9	Leopard
28. 3	15. 2	H4	C5	Rat	20. 5	9. 4	K6	F10	Griffon
29. 3	16. 2	H4	D6	Swallow	21. 5	10. 4	K6	G11	Ox
30. 3	17. 2	H4	E7	Pig	22. 5	11. 4	K6	H12	Bat
31. 3	18. 2	H4	F8	Porcupine	23. 5	12. 4	K6	J1	Rat
1. 4	19. 2	H4	G9	Wolf	24. 5	13. 4	K6	K2	Swallow
2. 4	20. 2	H4	H10	Dog	25. 5	14. 4	K6	A3	Pig
3. 4	21. 2	H4	J11	Pheasant	26. 5	15. 4	K6	B4	Porcupine
4. 4	22. 2	H4	K12	Cock	27. 5	16. 4	K6	C5	Wolf
5. 4	23. 2	H4	A1	Crow	28. 5	17. 4	K6	D6	Dog
6. 4	24. 2	H4	B2	Monkey	29. 5	18. 4	K6	E7	Pheasant

Solar date	Lunar date	Month HS/EB	Day HS/EB	Constellation
30. 5	19. 4	K6	F8	Cock
31. 5	20. 4	K6	G9	Crow
1. 6	21. 4	K6	H10	Monkey
2. 6	22. 4	K6	J11	Gibbon
3. 6	23. 4	K6	K12	Tapir
4. 6	24. 4	K6	A1	Sheep
5. 6	25. 4	K6	B2	Deer
6. 6	26. 4	K6	C3	Horse
7. 6	27. 4	K6	D4	Stag
8. 6	28. 4	K6	E5	Serpent
9. 6	29. 4	K6	F6	Earthworm
10. 6	1. 5	A7	G7	Crocodile
11. 6	2. 5	A7	H8	Dragon
12. 6	3. 5	A7	J9	Badger
13. 6	4. 5	A7	K10	Hare
14. 6	5. 5	A7	A11	Fox
15. 6	6. 5	A7	B12	Tiger
16. 6	7. 5	A7	C1	Leopard
17. 6	8. 5	A7	D2	Griffon
18. 6	9. 5	A7	E3	Ox
19. 6	10. 5	A7	F4	Bat
20. 6	11. 5	A7	G5	Rat
21. 6	12. 5	A7	H6	Swallow
22. 6	13. 5	A7	J7	Pig
23. 6	14. 5	A7	K8	Porcupine
24. 6	15. 5	A7	A9	Wolf
25. 6	16. 5	A7	B10	Dog
26. 6	17. 5	A7	C11	Pheasant
27. 6	18. 5	A7	D12	Cock
28. 6	19. 5	A7	E1	Crow
29. 6	20. 5	A7	F2	Monkey
30. 6	21. 5	A7	G3	Gibbon
1. 7	22. 5	A7	H4	Tapir
2. 7	23. 5	A7	J5	Sheep
3. 7	24. 5	A7	K6	Deer
4. 7	25. 5	A7	A7	Horse
5. 7	26. 5	A7	B8	Stag
6. 7	27. 5	A7	C9	Serpent
7. 7	28. 5	A7	D10	Earthworm
8. 7	29. 5	A7	E11	Crocodile
9. 7	30. 5	A7	F12	Dragon
10. 7	1. 6	B8	G1	Badger
11. 7	2. 6	B8	H2	Hare
12. 7	3. 6	B8	J3	Fox
13. 7	4. 6	B8	K4	Tiger
14. 7	5. 6	B8	A5	Leopard
15. 7	6. 6	B8	B6	Griffon
16. 7	7. 6	B8	C7	Ox
17. 7	8. 6	B8	D8	Bat
18. 7	9. 6	B8	E9	Rat
19. 7	10. 6	B8	F10	Swallow
20. 7	11. 6	B8	G11	Pig
21. 7	12. 6	B8	H12	Porcupine
22. 7	13. 6	B8	J1	Wolf
23. 7	14. 6	B8	K2	Dog
24. 7	15. 6	B8	A3	Pheasant
25. 7	16. 6	B8	B4	Cock
26. 7	17. 6	B8	C5	Crow
27. 7	18. 6	B8	D6	Monkey
28. 7	19. 6	B8	E7	Gibbon
29. 7	20. 6	B8	F8	Tapir
30. 7	21. 6	B8	G9	Sheep
31. 7	22. 6	B8	H10	Deer
1. 8	23. 6	B8	J11	Horse
2. 8	24. 6	B8	K12	Stag
3. 8	25. 6	B8	A1	Serpent
4. 8	26. 6	B8	B2	Earthworm
5. 8	27. 6	B8	C3	Crocodile
6. 8	28. 6	B8	D4	Dragon
7. 8	29. 6	B8	E5	Badger
8. 8	1. 7	C9	F6	Hare
9. 8	2. 7	C9	G7	Fox
10. 8	3. 7	C9	H8	Tiger

Solar date	Lunar date	Month HS/EB	Day HS/EB	Constellation
11. 8	4. 7	C9	J9	Leopard
12. 8	5. 7	C9	K10	Griffon
13. 8	6. 7	C9	A11	Ox
14. 8	7. 7	C9	B12	Bat
15. 8	8. 7	C9	C1	Rat
16. 8	9. 7	C9	D2	Swallow
17. 8	10. 7	C9	E3	Pig
18. 8	11. 7	C9	F4	Porcupine
19. 8	12. 7	C9	G5	Wolf
20. 8	13. 7	C9	H6	Dog
21. 8	14. 7	C9	J7	Pheasant
22. 8	15. 7	C9	K8	Cock
23. 8	16. 7	C9	A9	Crow
24. 8	17. 7	C9	B10	Monkey
25. 8	18. 7	C9	C11	Gibbon
26. 8	19. 7	C9	D12	Tapir
27. 8	20. 7	C9	E1	Sheep
28. 8	21. 7	C9	F2	Deer
29. 8	22. 7	C9	G3	Horse
30. 8	23. 7	C9	H4	Stag
31. 8	24. 7	C9	J5	Serpent
1. 9	25. 7	C9	K6	Earthworm
2. 9	26. 7	C9	A7	Crocodile
3. 9	27. 7	C9	B8	Dragon
4. 9	28. 7	C9	C9	Badger
5. 9	29. 7	C9	D10	Hare
6. 9	30. 7	C9	E11	Fox
7. 9	1. 8	D10	F12	Tiger
8. 9	2. 8	D10	G1	Leopard
9. 9	3. 8	D10	H2	Griffon
10. 9	4. 8	D10	J3	Ox
11. 9	5. 8	D10	K4	Bat
12. 9	6. 8	D10	A5	Rat
13. 9	7. 8	D10	B6	Swallow
14. 9	8. 8	D10	C7	Pig
15. 9	9. 8	D10	D8	Porcupine
16. 9	10. 8	D10	E9	Wolf
17. 9	11. 8	D10	F10	Dog
18. 9	12. 8	D10	G11	Pheasant
19. 9	13. 8	D10	H12	Cock
20. 9	14. 8	D10	J1	Crow
21. 9	15. 8	D10	K2	Monkey
22. 9	16. 8	D10	A3	Gibbon
23. 9	17. 8	D10	B4	Tapir
24. 9	18. 8	D10	C5	Sheep
25. 9	19. 8	D10	D6	Deer
26. 9	20. 8	D10	E7	Horse
27. 9	21. 8	D10	F8	Stag
28. 9	22. 8	D10	G9	Serpent
29. 9	23. 8	D10	H10	Earthworm
30. 9	24. 8	D10	J11	Crocodile
1.10	25. 8	D10	K12	Dragon
2.10	26. 8	D10	A1	Badger
3.10	27. 8	D10	B2	Hare
4.10	28. 8	D10	C3	Fox
5.10	29. 8	D10	D4	Tiger
6.10	30. 8	D10	E5	Leopard
7.10	1. 9	E11	F6	Griffon
8.10	2. 9	E11	G7	Ox
9.10	3. 9	E11	H8	Bat
10.10	4. 9	E11	J9	Rat
11.10	5. 9	E11	K10	Swallow
12.10	6. 9	E11	A11	Pig
13.10	7. 9	E11	B12	Porcupine
14.10	8. 9	E11	C1	Wolf
15.10	9. 9	E11	D2	Dog
16.10	10. 9	E11	E3	Pheasant
17.10	11. 9	E11	F4	Cock
18.10	12. 9	E11	G5	Crow
19.10	13. 9	E11	H6	Monkey
20.10	14. 9	E11	J7	Gibbon
21.10	15. 9	E11	K8	Tapir
22.10	16. 9	E11	A9	Sheep

Solar date	Lunar date	Month HS/EB	Day HS/EB	Constellation
23.10	17. 9	E11	B10	Deer
24.10	18. 9	E11	C11	Horse
25.10	19. 9	E11	D12	Stag
26.10	20. 9	E11	E1	Serpent
27.10	21. 9	E11	F2	Earthworm
28.10	22. 9	E11	G3	Crocodile
29.10	23. 9	E11	H4	Dragon
30.10	24. 9	E11	J5	Badger
31.10	25. 9	E11	K6	Hare
1.11	26. 9	E11	A7	Fox
2.11	27. 9	E11	B8	Tiger
3.11	28. 9	E11	C9	Leopard
4.11	29. 9	E11	D10	Griffon
5.11	1.10	F12	E11	Ox
6.11	2.10	F12	F12	Bat
7.11	3.10	F12	G1	Rat
8.11	4.10	F12	H2	Swallow
9.11	5.10	F12	J3	Pig
10.11	6.10	F12	K4	Porcupine
11.11	7.10	F12	A5	Wolf
12.11	8.10	F12	B6	Dog
13.11	9.10	F12	C7	Pheasant
14.11	10.10	F12	D8	Cock
15.11	11.10	F12	E9	Crow
16.11	12.10	F12	F10	Monkey
17.11	13.10	F12	G11	Gibbon
18.11	14.10	F12	H12	Tapir
19.11	15.10	F12	J1	Sheep
20.11	16.10	F12	K2	Deer
21.11	17.10	F12	A3	Horse
22.11	18.10	F12	B4	Stag
23.11	19.10	F12	C5	Serpent
24.11	20.10	F12	D6	Earthworm
25.11	21.10	F12	E7	Crocodile
26.11	22.10	F12	F8	Dragon
27.11	23.10	F12	G9	Badger
28.11	24.10	F12	H10	Hare
29.11	25.10	F12	J11	Fox
30.11	26.10	F12	K12	Tiger
1.12	27.10	F12	A1	Leopard
2.12	28.10	F12	B2	Griffon
3.12	29.10	F12	C3	Ox
4.12	30.10	F12	D4	Bat
5.12	1.11	G1	E5	Rat
6.12	2.11	G1	F6	Swallow
7.12	3.11	G1	G7	Pig
8.12	4.11	G1	H8	Porcupine
9.12	5.11	G1	J9	Wolf
10.12	6.11	G1	K10	Dog
11.12	7.11	G1	A11	Pheasant
12.12	8.11	G1	B12	Cock
13.12	9.11	G1	C1	Crow
14.12	10.11	G1	D2	Monkey
15.12	11.11	G1	E3	Gibbon
16.12	12.11	G1	F4	Tapir
17.12	13.11	G1	G5	Sheep
18.12	14.11	G1	H6	Deer
19.12	15.11	G1	J7	Horse
20.12	16.11	G1	K8	Stag
21.12	17.11	G1	A9	Serpent
22.12	18.11	G1	B10	Earthworm
23.12	19.11	G1	C11	Crocodile
24.12	20.11	G1	D12	Dragon
25.12	21.11	G1	E1	Badger
26.12	22.11	G1	F2	Hare
27.12	23.11	G1	G3	Fox
28.12	24.11	G1	H4	Tiger
29.12	25.11	G1	J5	Leopard
30.12	26.11	G1	K6	Griffon
31.12	27.11	G1	A7	Ox

1927

Solar date	Lunar date	Month HS/EB	Day HS/EB	Constellation
1. 1	28.11	G1	B8	Bat
2. 1	29.11	G1	C9	Rat
3. 1	30.11	G1	D10	Swallow
4. 1	1.12	H2	E11	Pig
5. 1	2.12	H2	F12	Porcupine
6. 1	3.12	H2	G1	Wolf
7. 1	4.12	H2	H2	Dog
8. 1	5.12	H2	J3	Pheasant
9. 1	6.12	H2	K4	Cock
10. 1	7.12	H2	A5	Crow
11. 1	8.12	H2	B6	Monkey
12. 1	9.12	H2	C7	Gibbon
13. 1	10.12	H2	D8	Tapir
14. 1	11.12	H2	E9	Sheep
15. 1	12.12	H2	F10	Deer
16. 1	13.12	H2	G11	Horse
17. 1	14.12	H2	H12	Stag
18. 1	15.12	H2	J1	Serpent
19. 1	16.12	H2	K2	Earthworm
20. 1	17.12	H2	A3	Crocodile
21. 1	18.12	H2	B4	Dragon
22. 1	19.12	H2	C5	Badger
23. 1	20.12	H2	D6	Hare
24. 1	21.12	H2	E7	Fox
25. 1	22.12	H2	F8	Tiger
26. 1	23.12	H2	G9	Leopard
27. 1	24.12	H2	H10	Griffon
28. 1	25.12	H2	J11	Ox
29. 1	26.12	H2	K12	Bat
30. 1	27.12	H2	A1	Rat
31. 1	28.12	H2	B2	Swallow
1. 2	29.12	H2	C3	Pig

TING MAO YEAR

Solar date	Lunar date	Month HS/EB	Day HS/EB	Constellation
2. 2	1. 1	J3	D4	Porcupine
3. 2	2. 1	J3	E5	Wolf
4. 2	3. 1	J3	F6	Dog
5. 2	4. 1	J3	G7	Pheasant
6. 2	5. 1	J3	H8	Cock
7. 2	6. 1	J3	J9	Crow
8. 2	7. 1	J3	K10	Monkey
9. 2	8. 1	J3	A11	Gibbon
10. 2	9. 1	J3	B12	Tapir
11. 2	10. 1	J3	C1	Sheep
12. 2	11. 1	J3	D2	Deer
13. 2	12. 1	J3	E3	Horse
14. 2	13. 1	J3	F4	Stag
15. 2	14. 1	J3	G5	Serpent
16. 2	15. 1	J3	H6	Earthworm
17. 2	16. 1	J3	J7	Crocodile
18. 2	17. 1	J3	K8	Dragon
19. 2	18. 1	J3	A9	Badger
20. 2	19. 1	J3	B10	Hare
21. 2	20. 1	J3	C11	Fox
22. 2	21. 1	J3	D12	Tiger
23. 2	22. 1	J3	E1	Leopard
24. 2	23. 1	J3	F2	Griffon
25. 2	24. 1	J3	G3	Ox
26. 2	25. 1	J3	H4	Bat
27. 2	26. 1	J3	J5	Rat
28. 2	27. 1	J3	K6	Swallow
1. 3	28. 1	J3	A7	Pig
2. 3	29. 1	J3	B8	Porcupine
3. 3	30. 1	J3	C9	Wolf
4. 3	1. 2	K4	D10	Dog
5. 3	2. 2	K4	E11	Pheasant

Solar date	Lunar date	Month HS/EB	Day HS/EB	Constellation	Solar date	Lunar date	Month HS/EB	Day HS/EB	Constellation
6. 3	3. 2	K4	F12	Cock	18. 5	18. 4	B6	J1	Leopard
7. 3	4. 2	K4	G1	Crow	19. 5	19. 4	B6	K2	Griffon
8. 3	5. 2	K4	H2	Monkey	20. 5	20. 4	B6	A3	Ox
9. 3	6. 2	K4	J3	Gibbon	21. 5	21. 4	B6	B4	Bat
10. 3	7. 2	K4	K4	Tapir	22. 5	22. 4	B6	C5	Rat
11. 3	8. 2	K4	A5	Sheep	23. 5	23. 4	B6	D6	Swallow
12. 3	9. 2	K4	B6	Deer	24. 5	24. 4	B6	E7	Pig
13. 3	10. 2	K4	C7	Horse	25. 5	25. 4	B6	F8	Porcupine
14. 3	11. 2	K4	D8	Stag	26. 5	26. 4	B6	G9	Wolf
15. 3	12. 2	K4	E9	Serpent	27. 5	27. 4	B6	H10	Dog
16. 3	13. 2	K4	F10	Earthworm	28. 5	28. 4	B6	J11	Pheasant
17. 3	14. 2	K4	G11	Crocodile	29. 5	29. 4	B6	K12	Cock
18. 3	15. 2	K4	H12	Dragon	30. 5	30. 4	B6	A1	Crow
19. 3	16. 2	K4	J1	Badger	31. 5	1. 5	C7	B2	Monkey
20. 3	17. 2	K4	K2	Hare	1. 6	2. 5	C7	C3	Gibbon
21. 3	18. 2	K4	A3	Fox	2. 6	3. 5	C7	D4	Tapir
22. 3	19. 2	K4	B4	Tiger	3. 6	4. 5	C7	E5	Sheep
23. 3	20. 2	K4	C5	Leopard	4. 6	5. 5	C7	F6	Deer
24. 3	21. 2	K4	D6	Griffon	5. 6	6. 5	C7	G7	Horse
25. 3	22. 2	K4	E7	Ox	6. 6	7. 5	C7	H8	Stag
26. 3	23. 2	K4	F8	Bat	7. 6	8. 5	C7	J9	Serpent
27. 3	24. 2	K4	G9	Rat	8. 6	9. 5	C7	K10	Earthworm
28. 3	25. 2	K4	H10	Swallow	9. 6	10. 5	C7	A11	Crocodile
29. 3	26. 2	K4	J11	Pig	10. 6	11. 5	C7	B12	Dragon
30. 3	27. 2	K4	K12	Porcupine	11. 6	12. 5	C7	C1	Badger
31. 3	28. 2	K4	A1	Wolf	12. 6	13. 5	C7	D2	Hare
1. 4	29. 2	K4	B2	Dog	13. 6	14. 5	C7	E3	Fox
2. 4	1. 3	A5	C3	Pheasant	14. 6	15. 5	C7	F4	Tiger
3. 4	2. 3	A5	D4	Cock	15. 6	16. 5	C7	G5	Leopard
4. 4	3. 3	A5	E5	Crow	16. 6	17. 5	C7	H6	Griffon
5. 4	4. 3	A5	F6	Monkey	17. 6	18. 5	C7	J7	Ox
6. 4	5. 3	A5	G7	Gibbon	18. 6	19. 5	C7	K8	Bat
7. 4	6. 3	A5	H8	Tapir	19. 6	20. 5	C7	A9	Rat
8. 4	7. 3	A5	J9	Sheep	20. 6	21. 5	C7	B10	Swallow
9. 4	8. 3	A5	K10	Deer	21. 6	22. 5	C7	C11	Pig
10. 4	9. 3	A5	A11	Horse	22. 6	23. 5	C7	D12	Porcupine
11. 4	10. 3	A5	B12	Stag	23. 6	24. 5	C7	E1	Wolf
12. 4	11. 3	A5	C1	Serpent	24. 6	25. 5	C7	F2	Dog
13. 4	12. 3	A5	D2	Earthworm	25. 6	26. 5	C7	G3	Pheasant
14. 4	13. 3	A5	E3	Crocodile	26. 6	27. 5	C7	H4	Cock
15. 4	14. 3	A5	F4	Dragon	27. 6	28. 5	C7	J5	Crow
16. 4	15. 3	A5	G5	Badger	28. 6	29. 5	C7	K6	Monkey
17. 4	16. 3	A5	H6	Hare	29. 6	1. 6	D8	A7	Gibbon
18. 4	17. 3	A5	J7	Fox	30. 6	2. 6	D8	B8	Tapir
19. 4	18. 3	A5	K8	Tiger	1. 7	3. 6	D8	C9	Sheep
20. 4	19. 3	A5	A9	Leopard	2. 7	4. 6	D8	D10	Deer
21. 4	20. 3	A5	B10	Griffon	3. 7	5. 6	D8	E11	Horse
22. 4	21. 3	A5	C11	Ox	4. 7	6. 6	D8	F12	Stag
23. 4	22. 3	A5	D12	Bat	5. 7	7. 6	D8	G1	Serpent
24. 4	23. 3	A5	E1	Rat	6. 7	8. 6	D8	H2	Earthworm
25. 4	24. 3	A5	F2	Swallow	7. 7	9. 6	D8	J3	Crocodile
26. 4	25. 3	A5	G3	Pig	8. 7	10. 6	D8	K4	Dragon
27. 4	26. 3	A5	H4	Porcupine	9. 7	11. 6	D8	A5	Badger
28. 4	27. 3	A5	J5	Wolf	10. 7	12. 6	D8	B6	Hare
29. 4	28. 3	A5	K6	Dog	11. 7	13. 6	D8	C7	Fox
30. 4	29. 3	A5	A7	Pheasant	12. 7	14. 6	D8	D8	Tiger
1. 5	1. 4	B6	B8	Cock	13. 7	15. 6	D8	E9	Leopard
2. 5	2. 4	B6	C9	Crow	14. 7	16. 6	D8	F10	Griffon
3. 5	3. 4	B6	D10	Monkey	15. 7	17. 6	D8	G11	Ox
4. 5	4. 4	B6	E11	Gibbon	16. 7	18. 6	D8	H12	Bat
5. 5	5. 4	B6	F12	Tapir	17. 7	19. 6	D8	J1	Rat
6. 5	6. 4	B6	G1	Sheep	18. 7	20. 6	D8	K2	Swallow
7. 5	7. 4	B6	H2	Deer	19. 7	21. 6	D8	A3	Pig
8. 5	8. 4	B6	J3	Horse	20. 7	22. 6	D8	B4	Porcupine
9. 5	9. 4	B6	K4	Stag	21. 7	23. 6	D8	C5	Wolf
10. 5	10. 4	B6	A5	Serpent	22. 7	24. 6	D8	D6	Dog
11. 5	11. 4	B6	B6	Earthworm	23. 7	25. 6	D8	E7	Pheasant
12. 5	12. 4	B6	C7	Crocodile	24. 7	26. 6	D8	F8	Cock
13. 5	13. 4	B6	D8	Dragon	25. 7	27. 6	D8	G9	Crow
14. 5	14. 4	B6	E9	Badger	26. 7	28. 6	D8	H10	Monkey
15. 5	15. 4	B6	F10	Hare	27. 7	29. 6	D8	J11	Gibbon
16. 5	16. 4	B6	G11	Fox	28. 7	30. 6	D8	K12	Tapir
17. 5	17. 4	B6	H12	Tiger	29. 7	1. 7	E9	A1	Sheep

Solar date	Lunar date	Month HS/EB	Day HS/EB	Constellation
30. 7	2. 7	E9	B2	Deer
31. 7	3. 7	E9	C3	Horse
1. 8	4. 7	E9	D4	Stag
2. 8	5. 7	E9	E5	Serpent
3. 8	6. 7	E9	F6	Earthworm
4. 8	7. 7	E9	G7	Crocodile
5. 8	8. 7	E9	H8	Dragon
6. 8	9. 7	E9	J9	Badger
7. 8	10. 7	E9	K10	Hare
8. 8	11. 7	E9	A11	Fox
9. 8	12. 7	E9	B12	Tiger
10. 8	13. 7	E9	C1	Leopard
11. 8	14. 7	E9	D2	Griffon
12. 8	15. 7	E9	E3	Ox
13. 8	16. 7	E9	F4	Bat
14. 8	17. 7	E9	G5	Rat
15. 8	18. 7	E9	H6	Swallow
16. 8	19. 7	E9	J7	Pig
17. 8	20. 7	E9	K8	Porcupine
18. 8	21. 7	E9	A9	Wolf
19. 8	22. 7	E9	B10	Dog
20. 8	23. 7	E9	C11	Pheasant
21. 8	24. 7	E9	D12	Cock
22. 8	25. 7	E9	E1	Crow
23. 8	26. 7	E9	F2	Monkey
24. 8	27. 7	E9	G3	Gibbon
25. 8	28. 7	E9	H4	Tapir
26. 8	29. 7	E9	J5	Sheep
27. 8	1. 8	F10	K6	Deer
28. 8	2. 8	F10	A7	Horse
29. 8	3. 8	F10	B8	Stag
30. 8	4. 8	F10	C9	Serpent
31. 8	5. 8	F10	D10	Earthworm
1. 9	6. 8	F10	E11	Crocodile
2. 9	7. 8	F10	F12	Dragon
3. 9	8. 8	F10	G1	Badger
4. 9	9. 8	F10	H2	Hare
5. 9	10. 8	F10	J3	Fox
6. 9	11. 8	F10	K4	Tiger
7. 9	12. 8	F10	A5	Leopard
8. 9	13. 8	F10	B6	Griffon
9. 9	14. 8	F10	C7	Ox
10. 9	15. 8	F10	D8	Bat
11. 9	16. 8	F10	E9	Rat
12. 9	17. 8	F10	F10	Swallow
13. 9	18. 8	F10	G11	Pig
14. 9	19. 8	F10	H12	Porcupine
15. 9	20. 8	F10	J1	Wolf
16. 9	21. 8	F10	K2	Dog
17. 9	22. 8	F10	A3	Pheasant
18. 9	23. 8	F10	B4	Cock
19. 9	24. 8	F10	C5	Crow
20. 9	25. 8	F10	D6	Monkey
21. 9	26. 8	F10	E7	Gibbon
22. 9	27. 8	F10	F8	Tapir
23. 9	28. 8	F10	G9	Sheep
24. 9	29. 8	F10	H10	Deer
25. 9	30. 8	F10	J11	Horse
26. 9	1. 9	G11	K12	Stag
27. 9	2. 9	G11	A1	Serpent
28. 9	3. 9	G11	B2	Earthworm
29. 9	4. 9	G11	C3	Crocodile
30. 9	5. 9	G11	D4	Dragon
1.10	6. 9	G11	E5	Badger
2.10	7. 9	G11	F6	Hare
3.10	8. 9	G11	G7	Fox
4.10	9. 9	G11	H8	Tiger
5.10	10. 9	G11	J9	Leopard
6.10	11. 9	G11	K10	Griffon
7.10	12. 9	G11	A11	Ox
8.10	13. 9	G11	B12	Bat
9.10	14. 9	G11	C1	Rat
10.10	15. 9	G11	D2	Swallow
11.10	16. 9	G11	E3	Pig
12.10	17. 9	G11	F4	Porcupine
13.10	18. 9	G11	G5	Wolf
14.10	19. 9	G11	H6	Dog
15.10	20. 9	G11	J7	Pheasant
16.10	21. 9	G11	K8	Cock
17.10	22. 9	G11	A9	Crow
18.10	23. 9	G11	B10	Monkey
19.10	24. 9	G11	C11	Gibbon
20.10	25. 9	G11	D12	Tapir
21.10	26. 9	G11	E1	Sheep
22.10	27. 9	G11	F2	Deer
23.10	28. 9	G11	G3	Horse
24.10	29. 9	G11	H4	Stag
25.10	1.10	H12	J5	Serpent
26.10	2.10	H12	K6	Earthworm
27.10	3.10	H12	A7	Crocodile
28.10	4.10	H12	B8	Dragon
29.10	5.10	H12	C9	Badger
30.10	6.10	H12	D10	Hare
31.10	7.10	H12	E11	Fox
1.11	8.10	H12	F12	Tiger
2.11	9.10	H12	G1	Leopard
3.11	10.10	H12	H2	Griffon
4.11	11.10	H12	J3	Ox
5.11	12.10	H12	K4	Bat
6.11	13.10	H12	A5	Rat
7.11	14.10	H12	B6	Swallow
8.11	15.10	H12	C7	Pig
9.11	16.10	H12	D8	Porcupine
10.11	17.10	H12	E9	Wolf
11.11	18.10	H12	F10	Dog
12.11	19.10	H12	G11	Pheasant
13.11	20.10	H12	H12	Cock
14.11	21.10	H12	J1	Crow
15.11	22.10	H12	K2	Monkey
16.11	23.10	H12	A3	Gibbon
17.11	24.10	H12	B4	Tapir
18.11	25.10	H12	C5	Sheep
19.11	26.10	H12	D6	Deer
20.11	27.10	H12	E7	Horse
21.11	28.10	H12	F8	Stag
22.11	29.10	H12	G9	Serpent
23.11	30.10	H12	H10	Earthworm
24.11	1.11	J1	J11	Crocodile
25.11	2.11	J1	K12	Dragon
26.11	3.11	J1	A1	Badger
27.11	4.11	J1	B2	Hare
28.11	5.11	J1	C3	Fox
29.11	6.11	J1	D4	Tiger
30.11	7.11	J1	E5	Leopard
1.12	8.11	J1	F6	Griffon
2.12	9.11	J1	G7	Ox
3.12	10.11	J1	H8	Bat
4.12	11.11	J1	J9	Rat
5.12	12.11	J1	K10	Swallow
6.12	13.11	J1	A11	Pig
7.12	14.11	J1	B12	Porcupine
8.12	15.11	J1	C1	Wolf
9.12	16.11	J1	D2	Dog
10.12	17.11	J1	E3	Pheasant
11.12	18.11	J1	F4	Cock
12.12	19.11	J1	G5	Crow
13.12	20.11	J1	H6	Monkey
14.12	21.11	J1	J7	Gibbon
15.12	22.11	J1	K8	Tapir
16.12	23.11	J1	A9	Sheep
17.12	24.11	J1	B10	Deer
18.12	25.11	J1	C11	Horse
19.12	26.11	J1	D12	Stag
20.12	27.11	J1	E1	Serpent
21.12	28.11	J1	F2	Earthworm
22.12	29.11	J1	G3	Crocodile

Solar date	Lunar date	Month HS/EB	Day HS/EB	Constellation
23.12	30.11	J1	H4	Dragon
24.12	1.12	K2	J5	Badger
25.12	2.12	K2	K6	Hare
26.12	3.12	K2	A7	Fox
27.12	4.12	K2	B8	Tiger
28.12	5.12	K2	C9	Leopard
29.12	6.12	K2	D10	Griffon
30.12	7.12	K2	E11	Ox
31.12	8.12	K2	F12	Bat
1928				
1. 1	9.12	K2	G1	Rat
2. 1	10.12	K2	H2	Swallow
3. 1	11.12	K2	J3	Pig
4. 1	12.12	K2	K4	Porcupine
5. 1	13.12	K2	A5	Wolf
6. 1	14.12	K2	B6	Dog
7. 1	15.12	K2	C7	Pheasant
8. 1	16.12	K2	D8	Cock
9. 1	17.12	K2	E9	Crow
10. 1	18.12	K2	F10	Monkey
11. 1	19.12	K2	G11	Gibbon
12. 1	20.12	K2	H12	Tapir
13. 1	21.12	K2	J1	Sheep
14. 1	22.12	K2	K2	Deer
15. 1	23.12	K2	A3	Horse
16. 1	24.12	K2	B4	Stag
17. 1	25.12	K2	C5	Serpent
18. 1	26.12	K2	D6	Earthworm
19. 1	27.12	K2	E7	Crocodile
20. 1	28.12	K2	F8	Dragon
21. 1	29.12	K2	G9	Badger
22. 1	30.12	K2	H10	Hare

MOU CH'EN YEAR

Solar date	Lunar date	Month HS/EB	Day HS/EB	Constellation
23. 1	1. 1	A3	J11	Fox
24. 1	2. 1	A3	K12	Tiger
25. 1	3. 1	A3	A1	Leopard
26. 1	4. 1	A3	B2	Griffon
27. 1	5. 1	A3	C3	Ox
28. 1	6. 1	A3	D4	Bat
29. 1	7. 1	A3	E5	Rat
30. 1	8. 1	A3	F6	Swallow
31. 1	9. 1	A3	G7	Pig
1. 2	10. 1	A3	H8	Porcupine
2. 2	11. 1	A3	J9	Wolf
3. 2	12. 1	A3	K10	Dog
4. 2	13. 1	A3	A11	Pheasant
5. 2	14. 1	A3	B12	Cock
6. 2	15. 1	A3	C1	Crow
7. 2	16. 1	A3	D2	Monkey
8. 2	17. 1	A3	E3	Gibbon
9. 2	18. 1	A3	F4	Tapir
10. 2	19. 1	A3	G5	Sheep
11. 2	20. 1	A3	H6	Deer
12. 2	21. 1	A3	J7	Horse
13. 2	22. 1	A3	K8	Stag
14. 2	23. 1	A3	A9	Serpent
15. 2	24. 1	A3	B10	Earthworm
16. 2	25. 1	A3	C11	Crocodile
17. 2	26. 1	A3	D12	Dragon
18. 2	27. 1	A3	E1	Badger
19. 2	28. 1	A3	F2	Hare
20. 2	29. 1	A3	G3	Fox
21. 2	1. 2	B4	H4	Tiger
22. 2	2. 2	B4	J5	Leopard
23. 2	3. 2	B4	K6	Griffon
24. 2	4. 2	B4	A7	Ox
25. 2	5. 2	B4	B8	Bat
26. 2	6. 2	B4	C9	Rat
27. 2	7. 2	B4	D10	Swallow
28. 2	8. 2	B4	E11	Pig
29. 2	9. 2	B4	F12	Porcupine
1. 3	10. 2	B4	G1	Wolf
2. 3	11. 2	B4	H2	Dog
3. 3	12. 2	B4	J3	Pheasant
4. 3	13. 2	B4	K4	Cock
5. 3	14. 2	B4	A5	Crow
6. 3	15. 2	B4	B6	Monkey
7. 3	16. 2	B4	C7	Gibbon
8. 3	17. 2	B4	D8	Tapir
9. 3	18. 2	B4	E9	Sheep
10. 3	19. 2	B4	F10	Deer
11. 3	20. 2	B4	G11	Horse
12. 3	21. 2	B4	H12	Stag
13. 3	22. 2	B4	J1	Serpent
14. 3	23. 2	B4	K2	Earthworm
15. 3	24. 2	B4	A3	Crocodile
16. 3	25. 2	B4	B4	Dragon
17. 3	26. 2	B4	C5	Badger
18. 3	27. 2	B4	D6	Hare
19. 3	28. 2	B4	E7	Fox
20. 3	29. 2	B4	F8	Tiger
21. 3	30. 2	B4	G9	Leopard
22. 3	*1. 2*	*B4*	H10	Griffon
23. 3	*2. 2*	*B4*	J11	Ox
24. 3	*3. 2*	*B4*	K12	Bat
25. 3	*4. 2*	*B4*	A1	Rat
26. 3	*5. 2*	*B4*	B2	Swallow
27. 3	*6. 2*	*B4*	C3	Pig
28. 3	*7. 2*	*B4*	D4	Porcupine
29. 3	*8. 2*	*B4*	E5	Wolf
30. 3	*9. 2*	*B4*	F6	Dog
31. 3	*10. 2*	*B4*	G7	Pheasant
1. 4	*11. 2*	*B4*	H8	Cock
2. 4	*12. 2*	*B4*	J9	Crow
3. 4	*13. 2*	*B4*	K10	Monkey
4. 4	*14. 2*	*B4*	A11	Gibbon
5. 4	*15. 2*	*B4*	B12	Tapir
6. 4	*16. 2*	*B4*	C1	Sheep
7. 4	*17. 2*	*B4*	D2	Deer
8. 4	*18. 2*	*B4*	E3	Horse
9. 4	*19. 2*	*B4*	F4	Stag
10. 4	*20. 2*	*B4*	G5	Serpent
11. 4	*21. 2*	*B4*	H6	Earthworm
12. 4	*22. 2*	*B4*	J7	Crocodile
13. 4	*23. 2*	*B4*	K8	Dragon
14. 4	*24. 2*	*B4*	A9	Badger
15. 4	*25. 2*	*B4*	B10	Hare
16. 4	*26. 2*	*B4*	C11	Fox
17. 4	*27. 2*	*B4*	D12	Tiger
18. 4	*28. 2*	*B4*	E1	Leopard
19. 4	*29. 2*	*B4*	F2	Griffon
20. 4	1. 3	C5	G3	Ox
21. 4	2. 3	C5	H4	Bat
22. 4	3. 3	C5	J5	Rat
23. 4	4. 3	C5	K6	Swallow
24. 4	5. 3	C5	A7	Pig
25. 4	6. 3	C5	B8	Porcupine
26. 4	7. 3	C5	C9	Wolf
27. 4	8. 3	C5	D10	Dog
28. 4	9. 3	C5	E11	Pheasant
29. 4	10. 3	C5	F12	Cock
30. 4	11. 3	C5	G1	Crow
1. 5	12. 3	C5	H2	Monkey
2. 5	13. 3	C5	J3	Gibbon
3. 5	14. 3	C5	K4	Tapir

Solar date	Lunar date	Month HS/EB	Day HS/EB	Constellation	Solar date	Lunar date	Month HS/EB	Day HS/EB	Constellation
4. 5	15. 3	C5	A5	Sheep	16. 7	29. 5	E7	D6	Swallow
5. 5	16. 3	C5	B6	Deer	17. 7	1. 6	F8	E7	Pig
6. 5	17. 3	C5	C7	Horse	18. 7	2. 6	F8	F8	Porcupine
7. 5	18. 3	C5	D8	Stag	19. 7	3. 6	F8	G9	Wolf
8. 5	19. 3	C5	E9	Serpent	20. 7	4. 6	F8	H10	Dog
9. 5	20. 3	C5	F10	Earthworm	21. 7	5. 6	F8	J11	Pheasant
10. 5	21. 3	C5	G11	Crocodile	22. 7	6. 6	F8	K12	Cock
11. 5	22. 3	C5	H12	Dragon	23. 7	7. 6	F8	A1	Crow
12. 5	23. 3	C5	J1	Badger	24. 7	8. 6	F8	B2	Monkey
13. 5	24. 3	C5	K2	Hare	25. 7	9. 6	F8	C3	Gibbon
14. 5	25. 3	C5	A3	Fox	26. 7	10. 6	F8	D4	Tapir
15. 5	26. 3	C5	B4	Tiger	27. 7	11. 6	F8	E5	Sheep
16. 5	27. 3	C5	C5	Leopard	28. 7	12. 6	F8	F6	Deer
17. 5	28. 3	C5	D6	Griffon	29. 7	13. 6	F8	G7	Horse
18. 5	29. 3	C5	E7	Ox	30. 7	14. 6	F8	H8	Stag
19. 5	1. 4	D6	F8	Bat	31. 7	15. 6	F8	J9	Serpent
20. 5	2. 4	D6	G9	Rat	1. 8	16. 6	F8	K10	Earthworm
21. 5	3. 4	D6	H10	Swallow	2. 8	17. 6	F8	A11	Crocodile
22. 5	4. 4	D6	J11	Pig	3. 8	18. 6	F8	B12	Dragon
23. 5	5. 4	D6	K12	Porcupine	4. 8	19. 6	F8	C1	Badger
24. 5	6. 4	D6	A1	Wolf	5. 8	20. 6	F8	D2	Hare
25. 5	7. 4	D6	B2	Dog	6. 8	21. 6	F8	E3	Fox
26. 5	8. 4	D6	C3	Pheasant	7. 8	22. 6	F8	F4	Tiger
27. 5	9. 4	D6	D4	Cock	8. 8	23. 6	F8	G5	Leopard
28. 5	10. 4	D6	E5	Crow	9. 8	24. 6	F8	H6	Griffon
29. 5	11. 4	D6	F6	Monkey	10. 8	25. 6	F8	J7	Ox
30. 5	12. 4	D6	G7	Gibbon	11. 8	26. 6	F8	K8	Bat
31. 5	13. 4	D6	H8	Tapir	12. 8	27. 6	F8	A9	Rat
1. 6	14. 4	D6	J9	Sheep	13. 8	28. 6	F8	B10	Swallow
2. 6	15. 4	D6	K10	Deer	14. 8	29. 6	F8	C11	Pig
3. 6	16. 4	D6	A11	Horse	15. 8	1. 7	G9	D12	Porcupine
4. 6	17. 4	D6	B12	Stag	16. 8	2. 7	G9	E1	Wolf
5. 6	18. 4	D6	C1	Serpent	17. 8	3. 7	G9	F2	Dog
6. 6	19. 4	D6	D2	Earthworm	18. 8	4. 7	G9	G3	Pheasant
7. 6	20. 4	D6	E3	Crocodile	19. 8	5. 7	G9	H4	Cock
8. 6	21. 4	D6	F4	Dragon	20. 8	6. 7	G9	J5	Crow
9. 6	22. 4	D6	G5	Badger	21. 8	7. 7	G9	K6	Monkey
10. 6	23. 4	D6	H6	Hare	22. 8	8. 7	G9	A7	Gibbon
11. 6	24. 4	D6	J7	Fox	23. 8	9. 7	G9	B8	Tapir
12. 6	25. 4	D6	K8	Tiger	24. 8	10. 7	G9	C9	Sheep
13. 6	26. 4	D6	A9	Leopard	25. 8	11. 7	G9	D10	Deer
14. 6	27. 4	D6	B10	Griffon	26. 8	12. 7	G9	E11	Horse
15. 6	28. 4	D6	C11	Ox	27. 8	13. 7	G9	F12	Stag
16. 6	29. 4	D6	D12	Bat	28. 8	14. 7	G9	G1	Serpent
17. 6	30. 4	D6	E1	Rat	29. 8	15. 7	G9	H2	Earthworm
18. 6	1. 5	E7	F2	Swallow	30. 8	16. 7	G9	J3	Crocodile
19. 6	2. 5	E7	G3	Pig	31. 8	17. 7	G9	K4	Dragon
20. 6	3. 5	E7	H4	Porcupine	1. 9	18. 7	G9	A5	Badger
21. 6	4. 5	E7	J5	Wolf	2. 9	19. 7	G9	B6	Hare
22. 6	5. 5	E7	K6	Dog	3. 9	20. 7	G9	C7	Fox
23. 6	6. 5	E7	A7	Pheasant	4. 9	21. 7	G9	D8	Tiger
24. 6	7. 5	E7	B8	Cock	5. 9	22. 7	G9	E9	Leopard
25. 6	8. 5	E7	C9	Crow	6. 9	23. 7	G9	F10	Griffon
26. 6	9. 5	E7	D10	Monkey	7. 9	24. 7	G9	G11	Ox
27. 6	10. 5	E7	E11	Gibbon	8. 9	25. 7	G9	H12	Bat
28. 6	11. 5	E7	F12	Tapir	9. 9	26. 7	G9	J1	Rat
29. 6	12. 5	E7	G1	Sheep	10. 9	27. 7	G9	K2	Swallow
30. 6	13. 5	E7	H2	Deer	11. 9	28. 7	G9	A3	Pig
1. 7	14. 5	E7	J3	Horse	12. 9	29. 7	G9	B4	Porcupine
2. 7	15. 5	E7	K4	Stag	13. 9	30. 7	G9	C5	Wolf
3. 7	16. 5	E7	A5	Serpent	14. 9	1. 8	H10	D6	Dog
4. 7	17. 5	E7	B6	Earthworm	15. 9	2. 8	H10	E7	Pheasant
5. 7	18. 5	E7	C7	Crocodile	16. 9	3. 8	H10	F8	Cock
6. 7	19. 5	E7	D8	Dragon	17. 9	4. 8	H10	G9	Crow
7. 7	20. 5	E7	E9	Badger	18. 9	5. 8	H10	H10	Monkey
8. 7	21. 5	E7	F10	Hare	19. 9	6. 8	H10	J11	Gibbon
9. 7	22. 5	E7	G11	Fox	20. 9	7. 8	H10	K12	Tapir
10. 7	23. 5	E7	H12	Tiger	21. 9	8. 8	H10	A1	Sheep
11. 7	24. 5	E7	J1	Leopard	22. 9	9. 8	H10	B2	Deer
12. 7	25. 5	E7	K2	Griffon	23. 9	10. 8	H10	C3	Horse
13. 7	26. 5	E7	A3	Ox	24. 9	11. 8	H10	D4	Stag
14. 7	27. 5	E7	B4	Bat	25. 9	12. 8	H10	E5	Serpent
15. 7	28. 5	E7	C5	Rat	26. 9	13. 8	H10	F6	Earthworm

Solar date	Lunar date	Month HS/EB	Day HS/EB	Constellation	Solar date	Lunar date	Month HS/EB	Day HS/EB	Constellation
27. 9	14. 8	H10	G7	Crocodile	5.12	24.10	K12	F4	Porcupine
28. 9	15. 8	H10	H8	Dragon	6.12	25.10	K12	G5	Wolf
29. 9	16. 8	H10	J9	Badger	7.12	26.10	K12	H6	Dog
30. 9	17. 8	H10	K10	Hare	8.12	27.10	K12	J7	Pheasant
1.10	18. 8	G10	A11	Fox	9.12	28.10	K12	K8	Cock
2.10	19. 8	G10	B12	Tiger	10.12	29.10	K12	A9	Crow
3.10	20. 8	G10	C1	Leopard	11.12	30.10	K12	B10	Monkey
4.10	21. 8	G10	D2	Griffon	12.12	1.11	A1	C11	Gibbon
5.10	22. 8	G10	E3	Ox	13.12	2.11	A1	D12	Tapir
6.10	23. 8	G10	F4	Bat	14.12	3.11	A1	E1	Sheep
7.10	24. 8	G10	G5	Rat	15.12	4.11	A1	F2	Deer
8.10	25. 8	G10	H6	Swallow	16.12	5.11	A1	G3	Horse
9.10	26. 8	G10	J7	Pig	17.12	6.11	A1	H4	Stag
10.10	27. 8	G10	K8	Porcupine	18.12	7.11	A1	J5	Serpent
11.10	28. 8	G10	A9	Wolf	19.12	8.11	A1	K6	Earthworm
12.10	29. 8	G10	B10	Dog	20.12	9.11	A1	A7	Crocodile
13.10	1. 9	J11	C11	Pheasant	21.12	10.11	A1	B8	Dragon
14.10	2. 9	J11	D12	Cock	22.12	11.11	A1	C9	Badger
15.10	3. 9	J11	E1	Crow	23.12	12.11	A1	D10	Hare
16.10	4. 9	J11	F2	Monkey	24.12	13.11	A1	E11	Fox
17.10	5. 9	J11	G3	Gibbon	25.12	14.11	A1	F12	Tiger
18.10	6. 9	J11	H4	Tapir	26.12	15.11	A1	G1	Leopard
19.10	7. 9	J11	J5	Sheep	27.12	16.11	A1	H2	Griffon
20.10	8. 9	J11	K6	Deer	28.12	17.11	A1	J3	Ox
21.10	9. 9	J11	A7	Horse	29.12	18.11	A1	K4	Bat
22.10	10. 9	J11	B8	Stag	30.12	19.11	A1	A5	Rat
23.10	11. 9	J11	C9	Serpent	31.12	20.11	A1	B6	Swallow
24.10	12. 9	J11	D10	Earthworm	**1929**				
25.10	13. 9	J11	E11	Crocodile					
26.10	14. 9	J11	F12	Dragon	1. 1	21.11	A1	C7	Pig
27.10	15. 9	J11	G1	Badger	2. 1	22.11	A1	D8	Porcupine
28.10	16. 9	J11	H2	Hare	3. 1	23.11	A1	E9	Wolf
29.10	17. 9	J11	J3	Fox	4. 1	24.11	A1	F10	Dog
30.10	18. 9	J11	K4	Tiger	5. 1	25.11	A1	G11	Pheasant
31.10	19. 9	J11	A5	Leopard	6. 1	26.11	A1	H12	Cock
1.11	20. 9	J11	B6	Griffon	7. 1	27.11	A1	J1	Crow
2.11	21. 9	J11	C7	Ox	8. 1	28.11	A1	K2	Monkey
3.11	22. 9	J11	D8	Rat	9. 1	29.11	A1	A3	Gibbon
4.11	23. 9	J11	E9	Rat	10. 1	30.11	A1	B4	Tapir
5.11	24. 9	J11	F10	Swallow	11. 1	1.12	B2	C5	Sheep
6.11	25. 9	J11	G11	Pig	12. 1	2.12	B2	D6	Deer
7.11	26. 9	J11	H12	Porcupine	13. 1	3.12	B2	E7	Horse
8.11	27. 9	J11	J1	Wolf	14. 1	4.12	B2	F8	Stag
9.11	28. 9	J11	K2	Dog	15. 1	5.12	B2	G9	Serpent
10.11	29. 9	J11	A3	Pheasant	16. 1	6.12	B2	H10	Earthworm
11.11	30. 9	J11	B4	Cock	17. 1	7.12	B2	J11	Crocodile
12.11	1.10	K12	C5	Crow	18. 1	8.12	B2	K12	Dragon
13.11	2.10	K12	D6	Monkey	19. 1	9.12	B2	A1	Badger
14.11	3.10	K12	E7	Gibbon	20. 1	10.12	B2	B2	Hare
15.11	4.10	K12	F8	Tapir	21. 1	11.12	B2	C3	Fox
16.11	5.10	K12	G9	Sheep	22. 1	12.12	B2	D4	Tiger
17.11	6.10	K12	H10	Deer	23. 1	13.12	B2	E5	Leopard
18.11	7.10	K12	J11	Horse	24. 1	14.12	B2	F6	Griffon
19.11	8.10	K12	K12	Stag	25. 1	15.12	B2	G7	Ox
20.11	9.10	K12	A1	Serpent	26. 1	16.12	B2	H8	Bat
21.11	10.10	K12	B2	Earthworm	27. 1	17.12	B2	J9	Rat
22.11	11.10	K12	C3	Crocodile	28. 1	18.12	B2	K10	Swallow
23.11	12.10	K12	D4	Dragon	29. 1	19.12	B2	A11	Pig
24.11	13.10	K12	E5	Badger	30. 1	20.12	B2	B12	Porcupine
25.11	14.10	K12	F6	Hare	31. 1	21.12	B2	C1	Wolf
26.11	15.10	K12	G7	Fox	1. 2	22.12	B2	D2	Dog
27.11	16.10	K12	H8	Tiger	2. 2	23.12	B2	E3	Pheasant
28.11	17.10	K12	J9	Leopard	3. 2	24.12	B2	F4	Cock
29.11	18.10	K12	K10	Griffon	4. 2	25.12	B2	G5	Crow
30.11	19.10	K12	A11	Ox	5. 2	26.12	B2	H6	Monkey
1.12	20.10	K12	B12	Bat	6. 2	27.12	B2	J7	Gibbon
2.12	21.10	K12	C1	Rat	7. 2	28.12	B2	K8	Tapir
3.12	22.10	K12	D2	Swallow	8. 2	29.12	B2	A9	Sheep
4.12	23.10	K12	E3	Pig	9. 2	30.12	B2	B10	Deer

CHI SZU YEAR

Solar date	Lunar date	Month HS/EB	Day HS/EB	Constellation	Solar date	Lunar date	Month HS/EB	Day HS/EB	Constellation
10. 2	1. 1	C3	C11	Horse	22. 4	13. 3	E5	D10	Swallow
11. 2	2. 1	C3	D12	Stag	23. 4	14. 3	E5	E11	Pig
12. 2	3. 1	C3	E1	Serpent	24. 4	15. 3	E5	F12	Porcupine
13. 2	4. 1	C3	F2	Earthworm	25. 4	16. 3	E5	G1	Wolf
14. 2	5. 1	C3	G3	Crocodile	26. 4	17. 3	E5	H2	Dog
15. 2	6. 1	C3	H4	Dragon	27. 4	18. 3	E5	J3	Pheasant
16. 2	7. 1	C3	J5	Badger	28. 4	19. 3	E5	K4	Cock
17. 2	8. 1	C3	K6	Hare	29. 4	20. 3	E5	A5	Crow
18. 2	9. 1	C3	A7	Fox	30. 4	21. 3	E5	B6	Monkey
19. 2	10. 1	C3	B8	Tiger	1. 5	22. 3	E5	C7	Gibbon
20. 2	11. 1	C3	C9	Leopard	2. 5	23. 3	E5	D8	Tapir
21. 2	12. 1	C3	D10	Griffon	3. 5	24. 3	E5	E9	Sheep
22. 2	13. 1	C3	E11	Ox	4. 5	25. 3	E5	F10	Deer
23. 2	14. 1	C3	F12	Bat	5. 5	26. 3	E5	G11	Horse
24. 2	15. 1	C3	G1	Rat	6. 5	27. 3	E5	H12	Stag
25. 2	16. 1	C3	H2	Swallow	7. 5	28. 3	E5	J1	Serpent
26. 2	17. 1	C3	J3	Pig	8. 5	29. 3	E5	K2	Earthworm
27. 2	18. 1	C3	K4	Porcupine	9. 5	1. 4	F6	A3	Crocodile
28. 2	19. 1	C3	A5	Wolf	10. 5	2. 4	F6	B4	Dragon
1. 3	20. 1	C3	B6	Dog	11. 5	3. 4	F6	C5	Badger
2. 3	21. 1	C3	C7	Pheasant	12. 5	4. 4	F6	D6	Hare
3. 3	22. 1	C3	D8	Cock	13. 5	5. 4	F6	E7	Fox
4. 3	23. 1	C3	E9	Crow	14. 5	6. 4	F6	F8	Tiger
5. 3	24. 1	C3	F10	Monkey	15. 5	7. 4	F6	G9	Leopard
6. 3	25. 1	C3	G11	Gibbon	16. 5	8. 4	F6	H10	Griffon
7. 3	26. 1	C3	H12	Tapir	17. 5	9. 4	F6	J11	Ox
8. 3	27. 1	C3	J1	Sheep	18. 5	10. 4	F6	K12	Bat
9. 3	28. 1	C3	K2	Deer	19. 5	11. 4	F6	A1	Rat
10. 3	29. 1	C3	A3	Horse	20. 5	12. 4	F6	B2	Swallow
11. 3	1. 2	D4	B4	Stag	21. 5	13. 4	F6	C3	Pig
12. 3	2. 2	D4	C5	Serpent	22. 5	14. 4	F6	D4	Porcupine
13. 3	3. 2	D4	D6	Earthworm	23. 5	15. 4	F6	E5	Wolf
14. 3	4. 2	D4	E7	Crocodile	24. 5	16. 4	F6	F6	Dog
15. 3	5. 2	D4	F8	Dragon	25. 5	17. 4	F6	G7	Pheasant
16. 3	6. 2	D4	G9	Badger	26. 5	18. 4	F6	H8	Cock
17. 3	7. 2	D4	H10	Hare	27. 5	19. 4	F6	J9	Crow
18. 3	8. 2	D4	J11	Fox	28. 5	20. 4	F6	K10	Monkey
19. 3	9. 2	D4	K12	Tiger	29. 5	21. 4	F6	A11	Gibbon
20. 3	10. 2	D4	A1	Leopard	30. 5	22. 4	F6	B12	Tapir
21. 3	11. 2	D4	B2	Griffon	31. 5	23. 4	F6	C1	Sheep
22. 3	12. 2	D4	C3	Ox	1. 6	24. 4	F6	D2	Deer
23. 3	13. 2	D4	D4	Bat	2. 6	25. 4	F6	E3	Horse
24. 3	14. 2	D4	E5	Rat	3. 6	26. 4	F6	F4	Stag
25. 3	15. 2	D4	F6	Swallow	4. 6	27. 4	F6	G5	Serpent
26. 3	16. 2	D4	G7	Pig	5. 6	28. 4	F6	H6	Earthworm
27. 3	17. 2	D4	H8	Porcupine	6. 6	29. 4	F6	J7	Crocodile
28. 3	18. 2	D4	J9	Wolf	7. 6	1. 5	G7	K8	Dragon
29. 3	19. 2	D4	K10	Dog	8. 6	2. 5	G7	A9	Badger
30. 3	20. 2	D4	A11	Pheasant	9. 6	3. 5	G7	B10	Hare
31. 3	21. 2	D4	B12	Cock	10. 6	4. 5	G7	C11	Fox
1. 4	22. 2	D4	C1	Crow	11. 6	5. 5	G7	D12	Tiger
2. 4	23. 2	D4	D2	Monkey	12. 6	6. 5	G7	E1	Leopard
3. 4	24. 2	D4	E3	Gibbon	13. 6	7. 5	G7	F2	Griffon
4. 4	25. 2	D4	F4	Tapi	14. 6	8. 5	G7	G3	Ox
5. 4	26. 2	D4	G5	Sheep	15. 6	9. 5	G7	H4	Bat
6. 4	27. 2	D4	H6	Deer	16. 6	10. 5	G7	J5	Rat
7. 4	28. 2	D4	J7	Horse	17. 6	11. 5	G7	K6	Swallow
8. 4	29. 2	D4	K8	Stag	18. 6	12. 5	G7	A7	Pig
9. 4	30. 2	D4	A9	Serpent	19. 6	13. 5	G7	B8	Porcupine
10. 4	1. 3	E5	B10	Earthworm	20. 6	14. 5	G7	C9	Wolf
11. 4	2. 3	E5	C11	Crocodile	21. 6	15. 5	G7	D10	Dog
12. 4	3. 3	E5	D12	Dragon	22. 6	16. 5	G7	E11	Pheasant
13. 4	4. 3	E5	E1	Badger	23. 6	17. 5	G7	F12	Cock
14. 4	5. 3	E5	F2	Hare	24. 6	18. 5	G7	G1	Crow
15. 4	6. 3	E5	G3	Fox	25. 6	19. 5	G7	H2	Monkey
16. 4	7. 3	E5	H4	Tiger	26. 6	20. 5	G7	J3	Gibbon
17. 4	8. 3	E5	J5	Leopard	27. 6	21. 5	G7	K4	Tapir
18. 4	9. 3	E5	K6	Griffon	28. 6	22. 5	G7	A5	Sheep
19. 4	10. 3	E5	A7	Ox	29. 6	23. 5	G7	B6	Deer
20. 4	11. 3	E5	B8	Bat	30. 6	24. 5	G7	C7	Horse
21. 4	12. 3	E5	C9	Rat	1. 7	25. 5	G7	D8	Stag

Solar date	Lunar date	Month HS/EB	Day HS/EB	Constellation
2. 7	26. 5	G7	E9	Serpent
3. 7	27. 5	G7	F10	Earthworm
4. 7	28. 5	G7	G11	Crocodile
5. 7	29. 5	G7	H12	Dragon
6. 7	30. 5	G7	J1	Badger
7. 7	1. 6	H8	K2	Hare
8. 7	2. 6	H8	A3	Fox
9. 7	3. 6	H8	B4	Tiger
10. 7	4. 6	H8	C5	Leopard
11. 7	5. 6	H8	D6	Griffon
12. 7	6. 6	H8	E7	Ox
13. 7	7. 6	H8	F8	Bat
14. 7	8. 6	H8	G9	Rat
15. 7	9. 6	H8	H10	Swallow
16. 7	10. 6	H8	J11	Pig
17. 7	11. 6	H8	K12	Porcupine
18. 7	12. 6	H8	A1	Wolf
19. 7	13. 6	H8	B2	Dog
20. 7	14. 6	H8	C3	Pheasant
21. 7	15. 6	H8	D4	Cock
22. 7	16. 6	H8	E5	Crow
23. 7	17. 6	H8	F6	Monkey
24. 7	18. 6	H8	G7	Gibbon
25. 7	19. 6	H8	H8	Tapir
26. 7	20. 6	H8	J9	Sheep
27. 7	21. 6	H8	K10	Deer
28. 7	22. 6	H8	A11	Horse
29. 7	23. 6	H8	B12	Stag
30. 7	24. 6	H8	C1	Serpent
31. 7	25. 6	H8	D2	Earthworm
1. 8	26. 6	H8	E3	Crocodile
2. 8	27. 6	H8	F4	Dragon
3. 8	28. 6	H8	G5	Badger
4. 8	29. 6	H8	H6	Hare
5. 8	1. 7	J9	J7	Fox
6. 8	2. 7	J9	K8	Tiger
7. 8	3. 7	J9	A9	Leopard
8. 8	4. 7	J9	B10	Griffon
9. 8	5. 7	J9	C11	Ox
10. 8	6. 7	J9	D12	Bat
11. 8	7. 7	J9	E1	Rat
12. 8	8. 7	J9	F2	Swallow
13. 8	9. 7	J9	G3	Pig
14. 8	10. 7	J9	H4	Porcupine
15. 8	11. 7	J9	J5	Wolf
16. 8	12. 7	J9	K6	Dog
17. 8	13. 7	J9	A7	Pheasant
18. 8	14. 7	J9	B8	Cock
19. 8	15. 7	J9	C9	Crow
20. 8	16. 7	J9	D10	Monkey
21. 8	17. 7	J9	E11	Gibbon
22. 8	18. 7	J9	F12	Tapir
23. 8	19. 7	J9	G1	Sheep
24. 8	20. 7	J9	H2	Deer
25. 8	21. 7	J9	J3	Horse
26. 8	22. 7	J9	K4	Stag
27. 8	23. 7	J9	A5	Serpent
28. 8	24. 7	J9	B6	Earthworm
29. 8	25. 7	J9	C7	Crocodile
30. 8	26. 7	J9	D8	Dragon
31. 8	27. 7	J9	E9	Badger
1. 9	28. 7	J9	F10	Hare
2. 9	29. 7	J9	G11	Fox
3. 9	1. 8	K10	H12	Tiger
4. 9	2. 8	K10	J1	Leopard
5. 9	3. 8	K10	K2	Griffon
6. 9	4. 8	K10	A3	Ox
7. 9	5. 8	K10	B4	Bat
8. 9	6. 8	K10	C5	Rat
9. 9	7. 8	K10	D6	Swallow
10. 9	8. 8	K10	E7	Pig
11. 9	9. 8	K10	F8	Porcupine
12. 9	10. 8	K10	G9	Wolf
13. 9	11. 8	K10	H10	Dog
14. 9	12. 8	K10	J11	Pheasant
15. 9	13. 8	K10	K12	Cock
16. 9	14. 8	K10	A1	Crow
17. 9	15. 8	K10	B2	Monkey
18. 9	16. 8	K10	C3	Gibbon
19. 9	17. 8	K10	D4	Tapir
20. 9	18. 8	K10	E5	Sheep
21. 9	19. 8	K10	F6	Deer
22. 9	20. 8	K10	G7	Horse
23. 9	21. 8	K10	H8	Stag
24. 9	22. 8	K10	J9	Serpent
25. 9	23. 8	K10	K10	Earthworm
26. 9	24. 8	K10	A11	Crocodile
27. 9	25. 8	K10	B12	Dragon
28. 9	26. 8	K10	C1	Badger
29. 9	27. 8	K10	D2	Hare
30. 9	28. 8	K10	E3	Fox
1.10	29. 8	K10	F4	Tiger
2.10	30. 8	K10	G5	Leopard
3.10	1. 9	A11	H6	Griffon
4.10	2. 9	A11	J7	Ox
5.10	3. 9	A11	K8	Bat
6.10	4. 9	A11	A9	Rat
7.10	5. 9	A11	B10	Swallow
8.10	6. 9	A11	C11	Pig
9.10	7. 9	A11	D12	Porcupine
10.10	8. 9	A11	E1	Wolf
11.10	9. 9	A11	F2	Dog
12.10	10. 9	A11	G3	Pheasant
13.10	11. 9	A11	H4	Cock
14.10	12. 9	A11	J5	Crow
15.10	13. 9	A11	K6	Monkey
16.10	14. 9	A11	A7	Gibbon
17.10	15. 9	A11	B8	Tapir
18.10	16. 9	A11	C9	Sheep
19.10	17. 9	A11	D10	Deer
20.10	18. 9	A11	E11	Horse
21.10	19. 9	A11	F12	Stag
22.10	20. 9	A11	G1	Serpent
23.10	21. 9	A11	H2	Earthworm
24.10	22. 9	A11	J3	Crocodile
25.10	23. 9	A11	K4	Dragon
26.10	24. 9	A11	A5	Badger
27.10	25. 9	A11	B6	Hare
28.10	26. 9	A11	C7	Fox
29.10	27. 9	A11	D8	Tiger
30.10	28. 9	A11	E9	Leopard
31.10	29. 9	A11	F10	Griffon
1.11	1. 10	B12	G11	Ox
2.11	2.10	B12	H12	Bat
3.11	3.10	B12	J1	Rat
4.11	4.10	B12	K2	Swallow
5.11	5.10	B12	A3	Pig
6.11	6.10	B12	B4	Porcupine
7.11	7.10	B12	C5	Wolf
8.11	8.10	B12	D6	Dog
9.11	9.10	B12	E7	Pheasant
10.11	10.10	B12	F8	Cock
11.11	11.10	B12	G9	Crow
12.11	12.10	B12	H10	Monkey
13.11	13.10	B12	J11	Gibbon
14.11	14.10	B12	K12	Tapir
15.11	15.10	B12	A1	Sheep
16.11	16.10	B12	B2	Deer
17.11	17.10	B12	C3	Horse
18.11	18.10	B12	D4	Stag
19.11	19.10	B12	E5	Serpent
20.11	20.10	B12	F6	Earthworm
21.11	21.10	B12	G7	Crocodile
22.11	22.10	B12	H8	Dragon
23.11	23.10	B12	J9	Badger
24.11	24.10	B12	K10	Hare

Solar date	Lunar date	Month HS/EB	Day HS/EB	Constellation
25.11	25.10	B12	A11	Fox
26.11	26.10	B12	B12	Tiger
27.11	27.10	B12	C1	Leopard
28.11	28.10	B12	D2	Griffon
29.11	29.10	B12	E3	Ox
30.11	30.10	B12	F4	Bat
1.12	1.11	C1	G5	Rat
2.12	2.11	C1	H6	Swallow
3.12	3.11	C1	J7	Pig
4.12	4.11	C1	K8	Porcupine
5.12	5.11	C1	A9	Wolf
6.12	6.11	C1	B10	Dog
7.12	7.11	C1	C11	Pheasant
8.12	8.11	C1	D12	Cock
9.12	9.11	C1	E1	Crow
10.12	10.11	C1	F2	Monkey
11.12	11.11	C1	G3	Gibbon
12.12	12.11	C1	H4	Tapir
13.12	13.11	C1	J5	Sheep
14.12	14.11	C1	K6	Deer
15.12	15.11	C1	A7	Horse
16.12	16.11	C1	B8	Stag
17.12	17.11	C1	C9	Serpent
18.12	18.11	C1	D10	Earthworm
19.12	19.11	C1	E11	Crocodile
20.12	20.11	C1	F12	Dragon
21.12	21.11	C1	G1	Badger
22.12	22.11	C1	H2	Hare
23.12	23.11	C1	J3	Fox
24.12	24.11	C1	K4	Tiger
25.12	25.11	C1	A5	Leopard
26.12	26.11	C1	B6	Griffon
27.12	27.11	C1	C7	Ox
28.12	28.11	C1	D8	Bat
29.12	29.11	C1	E9	Rat
30.12	30.11	C1	F10	Swallow
31.12	1.12	D2	G11	Pig

1930

Solar date	Lunar date	Month HS/EB	Day HS/EB	Constellation
1. 1	2.12	D2	H12	Porcupine
2. 1	3.12	D2	J1	Wolf
3. 1	4.12	D2	K2	Dog
4. 1	5.12	D2	A3	Pheasant
5. 1	6.12	D2	B4	Cock
6. 1	7.12	D2	C5	Crow
7. 1	8.12	D2	D6	Monkey
8. 1	9.12	D2	E7	Gibbon
9. 1	10.12	D2	F8	Tapir
10. 1	11.12	D2	G9	Sheep
11. 1	12.12	D2	H10	Deer
12. 1	13.12	D2	J11	Horse
13. 1	14.12	D2	K12	Stag
14. 1	15.12	D2	A1	Serpent
15. 1	16.12	D2	B2	Earthworm
16. 1	17.12	D2	C3	Crocodile
17. 1	18.12	D2	D4	Dragon
18. 1	19.12	D2	E5	Badger
19. 1	20.12	D2	F6	Hare
20. 1	21.12	D2	G7	Fox
21. 1	22.12	D2	H8	Tiger
22. 1	23.12	D2	J9	Leopard
23. 1	24.12	D2	K10	Griffon
24. 1	25.12	D2	A11	Ox
25. 1	26.12	D2	B12	Bat
26. 1	27.12	D2	C1	Rat
27. 1	28.12	D2	D2	Swallow
28. 1	29.12	D2	E3	Pig
29. 1	30.12	D2	F4	Porcupine

KENG WU YEAR

Solar date	Lunar date	Month HS/EB	Day HS/EB	Constellation
30. 1	1. 1	E3	G5	Wolf
31. 1	2. 1	E3	H6	Dog
1. 2	3. 1	E3	J7	Pheasant
2. 2	4. 1	E3	K8	Cock
3. 2	5. 1	E3	A9	Crow
4. 2	6. 1	E3	B10	Monkey
5. 2	7. 1	E3	C11	Gibbon
6. 2	8. 1	E3	D12	Tapir
7. 2	9. 1	E3	E1	Sheep
8. 2	10. 1	E3	F2	Deer
9. 2	11. 1	E3	G3	Horse
10. 2	12. 1	E3	H4	Stag
11. 2	13. 1	E3	J5	Serpent
12. 2	14. 1	E3	K6	Earthworm
13. 2	15. 1	E3	A7	Crocodile
14. 2	16. 1	E3	B8	Dragon
15. 2	17. 1	E3	C9	Badger
16. 2	18. 1	E3	D10	Hare
17. 2	19. 1	E3	E11	Fox
18. 2	20. 1	E3	F12	Tiger
19. 2	21. 1	E3	G1	Leopard
20. 2	22. 1	E3	H2	Griffon
21. 2	23. 1	E3	J3	Ox
22. 2	24. 1	E3	K4	Bat
23. 2	25. 1	E3	A5	Rat
24. 2	26. 1	E3	B6	Swallow
25. 2	27. 1	E3	C7	Pig
26. 2	28. 1	E3	D8	Porcupine
27. 2	29. 1	E3	E9	Wolf
28. 2	1. 2	F4	F10	Dog
1. 3	2. 2	F4	G11	Pheasant
2. 3	3. 2	F4	H12	Cock
3. 3	4. 2	F4	J1	Crow
4. 3	5. 2	F4	K2	Monkey
5. 3	6. 2	F4	A3	Gibbon
6. 3	7. 2	F4	B4	Tapir
7. 3	8. 2	F4	C5	Sheep
8. 3	9. 2	F4	D6	Deer
9. 3	10. 2	F4	E7	Horse
10. 3	11. 2	F4	F8	Stag
11. 3	12. 2	F4	G9	Serpent
12. 3	13. 2	F4	H10	Earthworm
13. 3	14. 2	F4	J11	Crocodile
14. 3	15. 2	F4	K12	Dragon
15. 3	16. 2	F4	A1	Badger
16. 3	17. 2	F4	B2	Hare
17. 3	18. 2	F4	C3	Fox
18. 3	19. 2	F4	D4	Tiger
19. 3	20. 2	F4	E5	Leopard
20. 3	21. 2	F4	F6	Griffon
21. 3	22. 2	F4	G7	Ox
22. 3	23. 2	F4	H8	Bat
23. 3	24. 2	F4	J9	Rat
24. 3	25. 2	F4	K10	Swallow
25. 3	26. 2	F4	A11	Pig
26. 3	27. 2	F4	B12	Porcupine
27. 3	28. 2	F4	C1	Wolf
28. 3	29. 2	F4	D2	Dog
29. 3	30. 2	F4	E3	Pheasant
30. 3	1. 3	G5	F4	Cock
31. 3	2. 3	G5	G5	Crow
1. 4	3. 3	G5	H6	Monkey
2. 4	4. 3	G5	J7	Gibbon
3. 4	5. 3	G5	K8	Tapir
4. 4	6. 3	G5	A9	Sheep
5. 4	7. 3	G5	B10	Deer
6. 4	8. 3	G5	C11	Horse
7. 4	9. 3	G5	D12	Stag

Solar date	Lunar date	Month HS/EB	Day HS/EB	Constellation	Solar date	Lunar date	Month HS/EB	Day HS/EB	Constellation
8. 4	10. 3	G5	E1	Serpent	20. 6	24. 5	J7	H2	Dog
9. 4	11. 3	G5	F2	Earthworm	21. 6	25. 5	J7	J3	Pheasant
10. 4	12. 3	G5	G3	Crocodile	22. 6	26. 5	J7	K4	Cock
11. 4	13. 3	G5	H4	Dragon	23. 6	27. 5	J7	A5	Crow
12. 4	14. 3	G5	J5	Badger	24. 6	28. 5	J7	B6	Monkey
13. 4	15. 3	G5	K6	Hare	25. 6	29. 5	J7	C7	Gibbon
14. 4	16. 3	G5	A7	Fox	26. 6	1. 6	K8	D8	Tapir
15. 4	17. 3	G5	B8	Tiger	27. 6	2. 6	K8	E9	Sheep
16. 4	18. 3	G5	C9	Leopard	28. 6	3. 6	K8	F10	Deer
17. 4	19. 3	G5	D10	Griffon	29. 6	4. 6	K8	G11	Horse
18. 4	20. 3	G5	E11	Ox	30. 6	5. 6	K8	H12	Stag
19. 4	21. 3	G5	F12	Bat	1. 7	6. 6	K8	J1	Serpent
20. 4	22. 3	G5	G1	Rat	2. 7	7. 6	K8	K2	Earthworm
21. 4	23. 3	G5	H2	Swallow	3. 7	8. 6	K8	A3	Crocodile
22. 4	24. 3	G5	J3	Pig	4. 7	9. 6	K8	B4	Dragon
23. 4	25. 3	G5	K4	Porcupine	5. 7	10. 6	K8	C5	Badger
24. 4	26. 3	G5	A5	Wolf	6. 7	11. 6	K8	D6	Hare
25. 4	27. 3	G5	B6	Dog	7. 7	12. 6	K8	E7	Fox
26. 4	28. 3	G5	C7	Pheasant	8. 7	13. 6	K8	F8	Tiger
27. 4	29. 3	G5	D8	Cock	9. 7	14. 6	K8	G9	Leopard
28. 4	30. 3	G5	E9	Crow	10. 7	15. 6	K8	H10	Griffon
29. 4	1. 4	H6	F10	Monkey	11. 7	16. 6	K8	J11	Ox
30. 4	2. 4	H6	G11	Gibbon	12. 7	17. 6	K8	K12	Bat
1. 5	3. 4	H6	H12	Tapir	13. 7	18. 6	K8	A1	Rat
2. 5	4. 4	H6	J1	Sheep	14. 7	19. 6	K8	B2	Swallow
3. 5	5. 4	H6	K2	Deer	15. 7	20. 6	K8	C3	Pig
4. 5	6. 4	H6	A3	Horse	16. 7	21. 6	K8	D4	Porcupine
5. 5	7. 4	H6	B4	Stag	17. 7	22. 6	K8	E5	Wolf
6. 5	8. 4	H6	C5	Serpent	18. 7	23. 6	K8	F6	Dog
7. 5	9. 4	H6	D6	Earthworm	19. 7	24. 6	K8	G7	Pheasant
8. 5	10. 4	H6	E7	Crocodile	20. 7	25. 6	K8	H8	Cock
9. 5	11. 4	H6	F8	Dragon	21. 7	26. 6	K8	J9	Crow
10. 5	12. 4	H6	G9	Badger	22. 7	27. 6	K8	K10	Monkey
11. 5	13. 4	H6	H10	Hare	23. 7	28. 6	K8	A11	Gibbon
12. 5	14. 4	H6	J11	Fox	24. 7	29. 6	K8	B12	Tapir
13. 5	15. 4	H6	K12	Tiger	25. 7	30. 6	K8	C1	Sheep
14. 5	16. 4	H6	A1	Leopard	26. 7	*1. 6*	*K8*	D2	Deer
15. 5	17. 4	H6	B2	Griffon	27. 7	*2. 6*	*K8*	E3	Horse
16. 5	18. 4	H6	C3	Ox	28. 7	*3. 6*	*K8*	F4	Stag
17. 5	19. 4	H6	D4	Bat	29. 7	*4. 6*	*K8*	G5	Serpent
18. 5	20. 4	H6	E5	Rat	30. 7	*5. 6*	*K8*	H6	Earthworm
19. 5	21. 4	H6	F6	Swallow	31. 7	*6. 6*	*K8*	J7	Crocodile
20. 5	22. 4	H6	G7	Pig	1. 8	*7. 6*	*K8*	K8	Dragon
21. 5	23. 4	H6	H8	Porcupine	2. 8	*8. 6*	*K8*	A9	Badger
22. 5	24. 4	H6	J9	Wolf	3. 8	*9. 6*	*K8*	B10	Hare
23. 5	25. 4	H6	K10	Dog	4. 8	*10. 6*	*K8*	C11	Fox
24. 5	26. 4	H6	A11	Pheasant	5. 8	*11. 6*	*K8*	D12	Tiger
25. 5	27. 4	H6	B12	Cock	6. 8	*12. 6*	*K8*	E1	Leopard
26. 5	28. 4	H6	C1	Crow	7. 8	*13. 6*	*K8*	F2	Griffon
27. 5	29. 4	H6	D2	Monkey	8. 8	*14. 6*	*K8*	G3	Ox
28. 5	1. 5	J7	E3	Gibbon	9. 8	*15. 6*	*K8*	H4	Bat
29. 5	2. 5	J7	F4	Tapir	10. 8	*16. 6*	*K8*	J5	Rat
30. 5	3. 5	J7	G5	Sheep	11. 8	*17. 6*	*K8*	K6	Swallow
31. 5	4. 5	J7	H6	Deer	12. 8	*18. 6*	*K8*	A7	Pig
1. 6	5. 5	J7	J7	Horse	13. 8	*19. 6*	*K8*	B8	Porcupine
2. 6	6. 5	J7	K8	Stag	14. 8	*20. 6*	*K8*	C9	Wolf
3. 6	7. 5	J7	A9	Serpent	15. 8	*21. 6*	*K8*	D10	Dog
4. 6	8. 5	J7	B10	Earthworm	16. 8	*22. 6*	*K8*	E11	Pheasant
5. 6	9. 5	J7	C11	Crocodile	17. 8	*23. 6*	*K8*	F12	Cock
6. 6	10. 5	J7	D12	Dragon	18. 8	*24. 6*	*K8*	G1	Crow
7. 6	11. 5	J7	E1	Badger	19. 8	*25. 6*	*K8*	H2	Monkey
8. 6	12. 5	J7	F2	Hare	20. 8	*26. 6*	*K8*	J3	Gibbon
9. 6	13. 5	J7	G3	Fox	21. 8	*27. 6*	*K8*	K4	Tapir
10. 6	14. 5	J7	H4	Tiger	22. 8	*28. 6*	*K8*	A5	Sheep
11. 6	15. 5	J7	J5	Leopard	23. 8	*29. 6*	*K8*	B6	Deer
12. 6	16. 5	J7	K6	Griffon	24. 8	1. 7	A9	C7	Horse
13. 6	17. 5	J7	A7	Ox	25. 8	2. 7	A9	D8	Stag
14. 6	18. 5	J7	B8	Bat	26. 8	3. 7	A9	E9	Serpent
15. 6	19. 5	J7	C9	Rat	27. 8	4. 7	A9	F10	Earthworm
16. 6	20. 5	J7	D10	Swallow	28. 8	5. 7	A9	G11	Crocodile
17. 6	21. 5	J7	E11	Pig	29. 8	6. 7	A9	H12	Dragon
18. 6	22. 5	J7	F12	Porcupine	30. 8	7. 7	A9	J1	Badger
19. 6	23. 5	J7	G1	Wolf	31. 8	8. 7	A9	K2	Hare

Solar date	Lunar date	Month HS/EB	Day HS/EB	Constellation
1. 9	9. 7	A9	A3	Fox
2. 9	10. 7	A9	B4	Tiger
3. 9	11. 7	A9	C5	Leopard
4. 9	12. 7	A9	D6	Griffon
5. 9	13. 7	A9	E7	Ox
6. 9	14. 7	A9	F8	Bat
7. 9	15. 7	A9	G9	Rat
8. 9	16. 7	A9	H10	Swallow
9. 9	17. 7	A9	J11	Pig
10. 9	18. 7	A9	K12	Porcupine
11. 9	19. 7	A9	A1	Wolf
12. 9	20. 7	A9	B2	Dog
13. 9	21. 7	A9	C3	Pheasant
14. 9	22. 7	A9	D4	Cock
15. 9	23. 7	A9	E5	Crow
16. 9	24. 7	A9	F6	Monkey
17. 9	25. 7	A9	G7	Gibbon
18. 9	26. 7	A9	H8	Tapir
19. 9	27. 7	A9	J9	Sheep
20. 9	28. 7	A9	K10	Deer
21. 9	29. 7	A9	A11	Horse
22. 9	1. 8	B10	B12	Stag
23. 9	2. 8	B10	C1	Serpent
24. 9	3. 8	B10	D2	Earthworm
25. 9	4. 8	B10	E3	Crocodile
26. 9	5. 8	B10	F4	Dragon
27. 9	6. 8	B10	G5	Badger
28. 9	7. 8	B10	H6	Hare
29. 9	8. 8	B10	J7	Fox
30. 9	9. 8	B10	K8	Tiger
1.10	10. 8	B10	A9	Leopard
2.10	11. 8	B10	B10	Griffon
3.10	12. 8	B10	C11	Ox
4.10	13. 8	B10	D12	Bat
5.10	14. 8	B10	E1	Rat
6.10	15. 8	B10	F2	Swallow
7.10	16. 8	B10	G3	Pig
8.10	17. 8	B10	H4	Porcupine
9.10	18. 8	B10	J5	Wolf
10.10	19. 8	B10	K6	Dog
11.10	20. 8	B10	A7	Pheasant
12.10	21. 8	B10	B8	Cock
13.10	22. 8	B10	C9	Crow
14.10	23. 8	B10	D10	Monkey
15.10	24. 8	B10	E11	Gibbon
16.10	25. 8	B10	F12	Tapir
17.10	26. 8	B10	G1	Sheep
18.10	27. 8	B10	H2	Deer
19.10	28. 8	B10	J3	Horse
20.10	29. 8	B10	K4	Stag
21.10	30. 8	B10	A5	Serpent
22.10	1. 9	C11	B6	Earthworm
23.10	2. 9	C11	C7	Crocodile
24.10	3. 9	C11	D8	Dragon
25.10	4. 9	C11	E9	Badger
26.10	5. 9	C11	F10	Hare
27.10	6. 9	C11	G11	Fox
28.10	7. 9	C11	H12	Tiger
29.10	8. 9	C11	J1	Leopard
30.10	9. 9	C11	K2	Griffon
31.10	10. 9	C11	A3	Ox
1.11	11. 9	C11	B4	Bat
2.11	12. 9	C11	C5	Rat
3.11	13. 9	C11	D6	Swallow
4.11	14. 9	C11	E7	Pig
5.11	15. 9	C11	F8	Porcupine
6.11	16. 9	C11	G9	Wolf
7.11	17. 9	C11	H10	Dog
8.11	18. 9	C11	J11	Pheasant
9.11	19. 9	C11	K12	Cock
10.11	20. 9	C11	A1	Crow
11.11	21. 9	C11	B2	Monkey
12.11	22. 9	C11	C3	Gibbon
13.11	23. 9	C11	D4	Tapir
14.11	24. 9	C11	E5	Sheep
15.11	25. 9	C11	F6	Deer
16.11	26. 9	C11	G7	Horse
17.11	27. 9	C11	H8	Stag
18.11	28. 9	C11	J9	Serpent
19.11	29. 9	C11	K10	Earthworm
20.11	1.10	D12	A11	Crocodile
21.11	2.10	D12	B12	Dragon
22.11	3.10	D12	C1	Badger
23.11	4.10	D12	D2	Hare
24.11	5.10	D12	E3	Fox
25.11	6.10	D12	F4	Tiger
26.11	7.10	D12	G5	Leopard
27.11	8.10	D12	H6	Griffon
28.11	9.10	D12	J7	Ox
29.11	10.10	D12	K8	Bat
30.11	11.10	D12	A9	Rat
1.12	12.10	D12	B10	Swallow
2.12	13.10	D12	C11	Pig
3.12	14.10	D12	D12	Porcupine
4.12	15.10	D12	E1	Wolf
5.12	16.10	D12	F2	Dog
6.12	17.10	D12	G3	Pheasant
7.12	18.10	D12	H4	Cock
8.12	19.10	D12	J5	Crow
9.12	20.10	D12	K6	Monkey
10.12	21.10	D12	A7	Gibbon
11.12	22.10	D12	B8	Tapir
12.12	23.10	D12	C9	Sheep
13.12	24.10	D12	D10	Deer
14.12	25.10	D12	E11	Horse
15.12	26.10	D12	F12	Stag
16.12	27.10	D12	G1	Serpent
17.12	28.10	D12	H2	Earthworm
18.12	29.10	D12	J3	Crocodile
19.12	30.10	D12	K4	Dragon
20.12	1.11	E1	A5	Badger
21.12	2.11	E1	B6	Hare
22.12	3.11	E1	C7	Fox
23.12	4.11	E1	D8	Tiger
24.12	5.11	E1	E9	Leopard
25.12	6.11	E1	F10	Griffon
26.12	7.11	E1	G11	Ox
27.12	8.11	E1	H12	Bat
28.12	9.11	E1	J1	Rat
29.12	10.11	E1	K2	Swallow
30.12	11.11	E1	A3	Pig
31.12	12.11	E1	B4	Porcupine

1931

Solar date	Lunar date	Month HS/EB	Day HS/EB	Constellation
1. 1	13.11	E1	C5	Wolf
2. 1	14.11	E1	D6	Dog
3. 1	15.11	E1	E7	Pheasant
4. 1	16.11	E1	F8	Cock
5. 1	17.11	E1	G9	Crow
6. 1	18.11	E1	H10	Monkey
7. 1	19.11	E1	J11	Gibbon
8. 1	20.11	E1	K12	Tapir
9. 1	21.11	E1	A1	Sheep
10. 1	22.11	E1	B2	Deer
11. 1	23.11	E1	C3	Horse
12. 1	24.11	E1	D4	Stag
13. 1	25.11	E1	E5	Serpent
14. 1	26.11	E1	F6	Earthworm
15. 1	27.11	E1	G7	Crocodile
16. 1	28.11	E1	H8	Dragon
17. 1	29.11	E1	J9	Badger
18. 1	30.11	E1	K10	Hare
19. 1	1.12	F2	A11	Fox
20. 1	2.12	F2	B12	Tiger
21. 1	3.12	F2	C1	Leopard
22. 1	4.12	F2	D2	Griffon

Solar date	Lunar date	Month HS/EB	Day HS/EB	Constellation	Solar date	Lunar date	Month HS/EB	Day HS/EB	Constellation
23. 1	5.12	F2	E3	Ox	5. 2	18.12	F2	H4	Tapir
24. 1	6.12	F2	F4	Bat	6. 2	19.12	F2	J5	Sheep
25. 1	7.12	F2	G5	Rat	7. 2	20.12	F2	K6	Deer
26. 1	8.12	F2	H6	Swallow	8. 2	21.12	F2	A7	Horse
27. 1	9.12	F2	J7	Pig	9. 2	22.12	F2	B8	Stag
28. 1	10.12	F2	K8	Porcupine	10. 2	23.12	F2	C9	Serpent
29. 1	11.12	F2	A9	Wolf	11. 2	24.12	F2	D10	Earthworm
30. 1	12.12	F2	B10	Dog	12. 2	25.12	F2	E11	Crocodile
31. 1	13.12	F2	C11	Pheasant	13. 2	26.12	F2	F12	Dragon
1. 2	14.12	F2	D12	Cock	14. 2	27.12	F2	G1	Badger
2. 2	15.12	F2	E1	Crow	15. 2	28.12	F2	H2	Hare
3. 2	16.12	F2	F2	Monkey	16. 2	29.12	F2	J3	Fox
4. 2	17.12	F2	G3	Gibbon					

HSIN WEI YEAR

Solar date	Lunar date	Month HS/EB	Day HS/EB	Constellation	Solar date	Lunar date	Month HS/EB	Day HS/EB	Constellation
17. 2	1. 1	G3	K4	Tiger	13. 4	26. 2	H4	E11	Fox
18. 2	2. 1	G3	A5	Leopard	14. 4	27. 2	H4	F12	Tiger
19. 2	3. 1	G3	B6	Griffon	15. 4	28. 2	H4	G1	Leopard
20. 2	4. 1	G3	C7	Ox	16. 4	29. 2	H4	H2	Griffon
21. 2	5. 1	G3	D8	Bat	17. 4	30. 2	H4	J3	Ox
22. 2	6. 1	G3	E9	Rat	18. 4	1. 3	J5	K4	Bat
23. 2	7. 1	G3	F10	Swallow	19. 4	2. 3	J5	A5	Rat
24. 2	8. 1	G3	G11	Pig	20. 4	3. 3	J5	B6	Swallow
25. 2	9. 1	G3	H12	Porcupine	21. 4	4. 3	J5	C7	Pig
26. 2	10. 1	G3	J1	Wolf	22. 4	5. 3	J5	D8	Porcupine
27. 2	11. 1	G3	K2	Dog	23. 4	6. 3	J5	E9	Wolf
28. 2	12. 1	G3	A3	Pheasant	24. 4	7. 3	J5	F10	Dog
1. 3	13. 1	G3	B4	Cock	25. 4	8. 3	J5	G11	Pheasant
2. 3	14. 1	G3	C5	Crow	26. 4	9. 3	J5	H12	Cock
3. 3	15. 1	G3	D6	Monkey	27. 4	10. 3	J5	J1	Crow
4. 3	16. 1	G3	E7	Gibbon	28. 4	11. 3	J5	K2	Monkey
5. 3	17. 1	G3	F8	Tapir	29. 4	12. 3	J5	A3	Gibbon
6. 3	18. 1	G3	G9	Sheep	30. 4	13. 3	J5	B4	Tapir
7. 3	19. 1	G3	H10	Deer	1. 5	14. 3	J5	C5	Sheep
8. 3	20. 1	G3	J11	Horse	2. 5	15. 3	J5	D6	Deer
9. 3	21. 1	G3	K12	Stag	3. 5	16. 3	J5	E7	Horse
10. 3	22. 1	G3	A1	Serpent	4. 5	17. 3	J5	F8	Stag
11. 3	23. 1	G3	B2	Earthworm	5. 5	18. 3	J5	G9	Serpent
12. 3	24. 1	G3	C3	Crocodile	6. 5	19. 3	J5	H10	Earthworm
13. 3	25. 1	G3	D4	Dragon	7. 5	20. 3	J5	J11	Crocodile
14. 3	26. 1	G3	E5	Badger	8. 5	21. 3	J5	K12	Dragon
15. 3	27. 1	G3	F6	Hare	9. 5	22. 3	J5	A1	Badger
16. 3	28. 1	G3	G7	Fox	10. 5	23. 3	J5	B2	Hare
17. 3	29. 1	G3	H8	Tiger	11. 5	24. 3	J5	C3	Fox
18. 3	30. 1	G3	J9	Leopard	12. 5	25. 3	J5	D4	Tiger
19. 3	1. 2	H4	K10	Griffon	13. 5	26. 3	J5	E5	Leopard
20. 3	2. 2	H4	A11	Ox	14. 5	27. 3	J5	F6	Griffon
21. 3	3. 2	H4	B12	Bat	15. 5	28. 3	J5	G7	Ox
22. 3	4. 2	H4	C1	Rat	16. 5	29. 3	J5	H8	Bat
23. 3	5. 2	H4	D2	Swallow	17. 5	1. 4	K6	J9	Rat
24. 3	6. 2	H4	E3	Pig	18. 5	2. 4	K6	K10	Swallow
25. 3	7. 2	H4	F4	Porcupine	19. 5	3. 4	K6	A11	Pig
26. 3	8. 2	H4	G5	Wolf	20. 5	4. 4	K6	B12	Porcupine
27. 3	9. 2	H4	H6	Dog	21. 5	5. 4	K6	C1	Wolf
28. 3	10. 2	H4	J7	Pheasant	22. 5	6. 4	K6	D2	Dog
29. 3	11. 2	H4	K8	Cock	23. 5	7. 4	K6	E3	Pheasant
30. 3	12. 2	H4	A9	Crow	24. 5	8. 4	K6	F4	Cock
31. 3	13. 2	H4	B10	Monkey	25. 5	9. 4	K6	G5	Crow
1. 4	14. 2	H4	C11	Gibbon	26. 5	10. 4	K6	H6	Monkey
2. 4	15. 2	H4	D12	Tapir	27. 5	11. 4	K6	J7	Gibbon
3. 4	16. 2	H4	E1	Sheep	28. 5	12. 4	K6	K8	Tapir
4. 4	17. 2	H4	F2	Deer	29. 5	13. 4	K6	A9	Sheep
5. 4	18. 2	H4	G3	Horse	30. 5	14. 4	K6	B10	Deer
6. 4	19. 2	H4	H4	Stag	31. 5	15. 4	K6	C11	Horse
7. 4	20. 2	H4	J5	Serpent	1. 6	16. 4	K6	D12	Stag
8. 4	21. 2	H4	K6	Earthworm	2. 6	17. 4	K6	E1	Serpent
9. 4	22. 2	H4	A7	Crocodile	3. 6	18. 4	K6	F2	Earthworm
10. 4	23. 2	H4	B8	Dragon	4. 6	19. 4	K6	G3	Crocodile
11. 4	24. 2	H4	C9	Badger	5. 6	20. 4	K6	H4	Dragon
12. 4	25. 2	H4	D10	Hare	6. 6	21. 4	K6	J5	Badger

Solar date	Lunar date	Month HS/EB	Day HS/EB	Constellation	Solar date	Lunar date	Month HS/EB	Day HS/EB	Constellation
7. 6	22. 4	K6	K6	Hare	19. 8	6. 7	C9	C7	Gibbon
8. 6	23. 4	K6	A7	Fox	20. 8	7. 7	C9	D8	Tapir
9. 6	24. 4	K6	B8	Tiger	21. 8	8. 7	C9	E9	Sheep
10. 6	25. 4	K6	C9	Leopard	22. 8	9. 7	C9	F10	Deer
11. 6	26. 4	K6	D10	Griffon	23. 8	10. 7	C9	G11	Horse
12. 6	27. 4	K6	E11	Ox	24. 8	11. 7	C9	H12	Stag
13. 6	28. 4	K6	F12	Bat	25. 8	12. 7	C9	J1	Serpent
14. 6	29. 4	K6	G1	Rat	26. 8	13. 7	C9	K2	Earthworm
15. 6	30. 4	K6	H2	Swallow	27. 8	14. 7	C9	A3	Crocodile
16. 6	1. 5	A7	J3	Pig	28. 8	15. 7	C9	B4	Dragon
17. 6	2. 5	A7	K4	Porcupine	29. 8	16. 7	C9	C5	Badger
18. 6	3. 5	A7	A5	Wolf	30. 8	17. 7	C9	D6	Hare
19. 6	4. 5	A7	B6	Dog	31. 8	18. 7	C9	E7	Fox
20. 6	5. 5	A7	C7	Pheasant	1. 9	19. 7	C9	F8	Tiger
21. 6	6. 5	A7	D8	Cock	2. 9	20. 7	C9	G9	Leopard
22. 6	7. 5	A7	E9	Crow	3. 9	21. 7	C9	H10	Griffon
23. 6	8. 5	A7	F10	Monkey	4. 9	22. 7	C9	J11	Ox
24. 6	9. 5	A7	G11	Gibbon	5. 9	23. 7	C9	K12	Bat
25. 6	10. 5	A7	H12	Tapir	6. 9	24. 7	C9	A1	Rat
26. 6	11. 5	A7	J1	Sheep	7. 9	25. 7	C9	B2	Swallow
27. 6	12. 5	A7	K2	Deer	8. 9	26. 7	C9	C3	Pig
28. 6	13. 5	A7	A3	Horse	9. 9	27. 7	C9	D4	Porcupine
29. 6	14. 5	A7	B4	Stag	10. 9	28. 7	C9	E5	Wolf
30. 6	15. 5	A7	C5	Serpent	11. 9	29. 7	C9	F6	Dog
1. 7	16. 5	A7	D6	Earthworm	12. 9	1. 8	D10	G7	Pheasant
2. 7	17. 5	A7	E7	Crocodile	13. 9	2. 8	D10	H8	Cock
3. 7	18. 5	A7	F8	Dragon	14. 9	3. 8	D10	J9	Crow
4. 7	19. 5	A7	G9	Badger	15. 9	4. 8	D10	K10	Monkey
5. 7	20. 5	A7	H10	Hare	16. 9	5. 8	D10	A11	Gibbon
6. 7	21. 5	A7	J11	Fox	17. 9	6. 8	D10	B12	Tapir
7. 7	22. 5	A7	K12	Tiger	18. 9	7. 8	D10	C1	Sheep
8. 7	23. 5	A7	A1	Leopard	19. 9	8. 8	D10	D2	Deer
9. 7	24. 5	A7	B2	Griffon	20. 9	9. 8	D10	E3	Horse
10. 7	25. 5	A7	C3	Ox	21. 9	10. 8	D10	F4	Stag
11. 7	26. 5	A7	D4	Bat	22. 9	11. 8	D10	G5	Serpent
12. 7	27. 5	A7	E5	Rat	23. 9	12. 8	D10	H6	Earthworm
13. 7	28. 5	A7	F6	Swallow	24. 9	13. 8	D10	J7	Crocodile
14. 7	29. 5	A7	G7	Pig	25. 9	14. 8	D10	K8	Dragon
15. 7	1. 6	B8	H8	Porcupine	26. 9	15. 8	D10	A9	Badger
16. 7	2. 6	B8	J9	Wolf	27. 9	16. 8	D10	B10	Hare
17. 7	3. 6	B8	K10	Dog	28. 9	17. 8	D10	C11	Fox
18. 7	4. 6	B8	A11	Pheasant	29. 9	18. 8	D10	D12	Tiger
19. 7	5. 6	B8	B12	Cock	30. 9	19. 8	D10	E1	Leopard
20. 7	6. 6	B8	C1	Crow	1.10	20. 8	D10	F2	Griffon
21. 7	7. 6	B8	D2	Monkey	2.10	21. 8	D10	G3	Ox
22. 7	8. 6	B8	E3	Gibbon	3.10	22. 8	D10	H4	Bat
23. 7	9. 6	B8	F4	Tapir	4.10	23. 8	D10	J5	Rat
24. 7	10. 6	B8	G5	Sheep	5.10	24. 8	D10	K6	Swallow
25. 7	11. 6	B8	H6	Deer	6.10	25. 8	D10	A7	Pig
26. 7	12. 6	B8	J7	Horse	7.10	26. 8	D10	B8	Porcupine
27. 7	13. 6	B8	K8	Stag	8.10	27. 8	D10	C9	Wolf
28. 7	14. 6	B8	A9	Serpent	9.10	28. 8	D10	D10	Dog
29. 7	15. 6	B8	B10	Earthworm	10.10	29. 8	D10	E11	Pheasant
30. 7	16. 6	B8	C11	Crocodile	11.10	1. 9	E11	F12	Cock
31. 7	17. 6	B8	D12	Dragon	12.10	2. 9	E11	G1	Crow
1. 8	18. 6	B8	E1	Badger	13.10	3. 9	E11	H2	Monkey
2. 8	19. 6	B8	F2	Hare	14.10	4. 9	E11	J3	Gibbon
3. 8	20. 6	B8	G3	Fox	15.10	5. 9	E11	K4	Tapir
4. 8	21. 6	B8	H4	Tiger	16.10	6. 9	E11	A5	Sheep
5. 8	22. 6	B8	J5	Leopard	17.10	7. 9	E11	B6	Deer
6. 8	23. 6	B8	K6	Griffon	18.10	8. 9	E11	C7	Horse
7. 8	24. 6	B8	A7	Ox	19.10	9. 9	E11	D8	Stag
8. 8	25. 6	B8	B8	Bat	20.10	10. 9	E11	E9	Serpent
9. 8	26. 6	B8	C9	Rat	21.10	11. 9	E11	F10	Earthworm
10. 8	27. 6	B8	D10	Swallow	22.10	12. 9	E11	G11	Crocodile
11. 8	28. 6	B8	E11	Pig	23.10	13. 9	E11	H12	Dragon
12. 8	29. 6	B8	F12	Porcupine	24.10	14. 9	E11	J1	Badger
13. 8	30. 6	B8	G1	Wolf	25.10	15. 9	E11	K2	Hare
14. 8	1. 7	C9	H2	Dog	26.10	16. 9	E11	A3	Fox
15. 8	2. 7	C9	J3	Pheasant	27.10	17. 9	E11	B4	Tiger
16. 8	3. 7	C9	K4	Cock	28.10	18. 9	E11	C5	Leopard
17. 8	4. 7	C9	A5	Crow	29.10	19. 9	E11	D6	Griffon
18. 8	5. 7	C9	B6	Monkey	30.10	20. 9	E11	E7	Ox

Solar date	Lunar date	Month HS/EB	Day HS/EB	Constellation	Solar date	Lunar date	Month HS/EB	Day HS/EB	Constellation
31.10	21. 9	E11	F8	Bat	20.12	12.11	G1	F10	Hare
1.11	22. 9	E11	G9	Rat	21.12	13.11	G1	G11	Fox
2.11	23. 9	E11	H10	Swallow	22.12	14.11	G1	H12	Tiger
3.11	24. 9	E11	J11	Pig	23.12	15.11	G1	J1	Leopard
4.11	25. 9	E11	K12	Porcupine	24.12	16.11	G1	K2	Griffon
5.11	26. 9	E11	A1	Wolf	25.12	17.11	G1	A3	Ox
6.11	27. 9	E11	B2	Dog	26.12	18.11	G1	B4	Bat
7.11	28. 9	E11	C3	Pheasant	27.12	19.11	G1	C5	Rat
8.11	29. 9	E11	D4	Cock	28.12	20.11	G1	D6	Swallow
9.11	30. 9	E11	E5	Crow	29.12	21.11	G1	E7	Pig
10.11	1.10	F12	F6	Monkey	30.12	22.11	G1	F8	Porcupine
11.11	2.10	F12	G7	Gibbon	31.12	23.11	G1	G9	Wolf
12.11	3.10	F12	H8	Tapir					
13.11	4.10	F12	J9	Sheep	**1932**				
14.11	5.10	F12	K10	Deer	1. 1	24.11	G1	H10	Dog
15.11	6.10	F12	A11	Horse	2. 1	25.11	G1	J11	Pheasant
16.11	7.10	F12	B12	Stag	3. 1	26.11	G1	K12	Cock
17.11	8.10	F12	C1	Serpent	4. 1	27.11	G1	A1	Crow
18.11	9.10	F12	D2	Earthworm	5. 1	28.11	G1	B2	Monkey
19.11	10.10	F12	E3	Crocodile	6. 1	29.11	G1	C3	Gibbon
20.11	11.10	F12	F4	Dragon	7. 1	30.11	G1	D4	Tapir
21.11	12.10	F12	G5	Badger	8. 1	1.12	H2	E5	Sheep
22.11	13.10	F12	H6	Hare	9. 1	2.12	H2	F6	Deer
23.11	14.10	F12	J7	Fox	10. 1	3.12	H2	G7	Horse
24.11	15.10	F12	K8	Tiger	11. 1	4.12	H2	H8	Stag
25.11	16.10	F12	A9	Leopard	12. 1	5.12	H2	J9	Serpent
26.11	17.10	F12	B10	Griffon	13. 1	6.12	H2	K10	Earthworm
27.11	18.10	F12	C11	Ox	14. 1	7.12	H2	A11	Crocodile
28.11	19.10	F12	D12	Bat	15. 1	8.12	H2	B12	Dragon
29.11	20.10	F12	E1	Rat	16. 1	9.12	H2	C1	Badger
30.11	21.10	F12	F2	Swallow	17. 1	10.12	H2	D2	Hare
1.12	22.10	F12	G3	Pig	18. 1	11.12	H2	E3	Fox
2.12	23.10	F12	H4	Porcupine	19. 1	12.12	H2	F4	Tiger
3.12	24.10	F12	J5	Wolf	20. 1	13.12	H2	G5	Leopard
4.12	25.10	F12	K6	Dog	21. 1	14.12	H2	H6	Griffon
5.12	26.10	F12	A7	Pheasant	22. 1	15.12	H2	J7	Ox
6.12	27.10	F12	B8	Cock	23. 1	16.12	H2	K8	Bat
7.12	28.10	F12	C9	Crow	24. 1	17.12	H2	A9	Rat
8.12	29.10	F12	D10	Monkey	25. 1	18.12	H2	B10	Swallow
9.12	1.11	G1	E11	Gibbon	26. 1	19.12	H2	C11	Pig
10.12	2.11	G1	F12	Tapir	27. 1	20.12	H2	D12	Porcupine
11.12	3.11	G1	G1	Sheep	28. 1	21.12	H2	E1	Wolf
12.12	4.11	G1	H2	Deer	29. 1	22.12	H2	F2	Dog
13.12	5.11	G1	J3	Horse	30. 1	23.12	H2	G3	Pheasant
14.12	6.11	G1	K4	Stag	31. 1	24.12	H2	H4	Cock
15.12	7.11	G1	A5	Serpent	1. 2	25.12	H2	J5	Crow
16.12	8.11	G1	B6	Earthworm	2. 2	26.12	H2	K6	Monkey
17.12	9.11	G1	C7	Crocodile	3. 2	27.12	H2	A7	Gibbon
18.12	10.11	G1	D8	Dragon	4. 2	28.12	H2	B8	Tapir
19.12	11.11	G1	E9	Badger	5. 2	29.12	H2	C9	Sheep

JEN SHEN YEAR

Solar date	Lunar date	Month HS/EB	Day HS/EB	Constellation	Solar date	Lunar date	Month HS/EB	Day HS/EB	Constellation
6. 2	1. 1	J3	D10	Deer	24. 2	19. 1	J3	B4	Porcupine
7. 2	2. 1	J3	E11	Horse	25. 2	20. 1	J3	C5	Wolf
8. 2	3. 1	J3	F12	Stag	26. 2	21. 1	J3	D6	Dog
9. 2	4. 1	J3	G1	Serpent	27. 2	22. 1	J3	E7	Pheasant
10. 2	5. 1	J3	H2	Earthworm	28. 2	23. 1	J3	F8	Cock
11. 2	6. 1	J3	J3	Crocodile	29. 2	24. 1	J3	G9	Crow
12. 2	7. 1	J3	K4	Dragon	1. 3	25. 1	J3	H10	Monkey
13. 2	8. 1	J3	A5	Badger	2. 3	26. 1	J3	J11	Gibbon
14. 2	9. 1	J3	B6	Hare	3. 3	27. 1	J3	K12	Tapir
15. 2	10. 1	J3	C7	Fox	4. 3	28. 1	J3	A1	Sheep
16. 2	11. 1	J3	D8	Tiger	5. 3	29. 1	J3	B2	Deer
17. 2	12. 1	J3	E9	Leopard	6. 3	30. 1	J3	C3	Horse
18. 2	13. 1	J3	F10	Griffon	7. 3	1. 2	K4	D4	Stag
19. 2	14. 1	J3	G11	Ox	8. 3	2. 2	K4	E5	Serpent
20. 2	15. 1	J3	H12	Bat	9. 3	3. 2	K4	F6	Earthworm
21. 2	16. 1	J3	J1	Rat	10. 3	4. 2	K4	G7	Crocodile
22. 2	17. 1	J3	K2	Swallow	11. 3	5. 2	K4	H8	Dragon
23. 2	18. 1	J3	A3	Pig	12. 3	6. 2	K4	J9	Badger

Solar date	Lunar date	Month HS/EB	Day HS/EB	Constellation	Solar date	Lunar date	Month HS/EB	Day HS/EB	Constellation
13. 3	7. 2	K4	K10	Hare	25. 5	20. 4	B6	C11	Gibbon
14. 3	8. 2	K4	A11	Fox	26. 5	21. 4	B6	D12	Tapir
15. 3	9. 2	K4	B12	Tiger	27. 5	22. 4	B6	E1	Sheep
16. 3	10. 2	K4	C1	Leopard	28. 5	23. 4	B6	F2	Deer
17. 3	11. 2	K4	D2	Griffon	29. 5	24. 4	B6	G3	Horse
18. 3	12. 2	K4	E3	Ox	30. 5	25. 4	B6	H4	Stag
19. 3	13. 2	K4	F4	Bat	31. 5	26. 4	B6	J5	Serpent
20. 3	14. 2	K4	G5	Rat	1. 6	27. 4	B6	K6	Earthworm
21. 3	15. 2	K4	H6	Swallow	2. 6	28. 4	B6	A7	Crocodile
22. 3	16. 2	K4	J7	Pig	3. 6	29. 4	B6	B8	Dragon
23. 3	17. 2	K4	K8	Porcupine	4. 6	1. 5	C7	C9	Badger
24. 3	18. 2	K4	A9	Wolf	5. 6	2. 5	C7	D10	Hare
25. 3	19. 2	K4	B10	Dog	6. 6	3. 5	C7	E11	Fox
26. 3	20. 2	K4	C11	Pheasant	7. 6	4. 5	C7	F12	Tiger
27. 3	21. 2	K4	D12	Cock	8. 6	5. 5	C7	G1	Leopard
28. 3	22. 2	K4	E1	Crow	9. 6	6. 5	C7	H2	Griffon
29. 3	23. 2	K4	F2	Monkey	10. 6	7. 5	C7	J3	Ox
30. 3	24. 2	K4	G3	Gibbon	11. 6	8. 5	C7	K4	Bat
31. 3	25. 2	K4	H4	Tapir	12. 6	9. 5	C7	A5	Rat
1. 4	26. 2	K4	J5	Sheep	13. 6	10. 5	C7	B6	Swallow
2. 4	27. 2	K4	K6	Deer	14. 6	11. 5	C7	C7	Pig
3. 4	28. 2	K4	A7	Horse	15. 6	12. 5	C7	D8	Porcupine
4. 4	29. 2	K4	B8	Stag	16. 6	13. 5	C7	E9	Wolf
5. 4	30. 2	K4	C9	Serpent	17. 6	14. 5	C7	F10	Dog
6. 4	1. 3	A5	D10	Earthworm	18. 6	15. 5	C7	G11	Pheasant
7. 4	2. 3	A5	E11	Crocodile	19. 6	16. 5	C7	H12	Cock
8. 4	3. 3	A5	F12	Dragon	20. 6	17. 5	C7	J1	Crow
9. 4	4. 3	A5	G1	Badger	21. 6	18. 5	C7	K2	Monkey
10. 4	5. 3	A5	H2	Hare	22. 6	19. 5	C7	A3	Gibbon
11. 4	6. 3	A5	J3	Fox	23. 6	20. 5	C7	B4	Tapir
12. 4	7. 3	A5	K4	Tiger	24. 6	21. 5	C7	C5	Sheep
13. 4	8. 3	A5	A5	Leopard	25. 6	22. 5	C7	D6	Deer
14. 4	9. 3	A5	B6	Griffon	26. 6	23. 5	C7	E7	Horse
15. 4	10. 3	A5	C7	Ox	27. 6	24. 5	C7	F8	Stag
16. 4	11. 3	A5	D8	Bat	28. 6	25. 5	C7	G9	Serpent
17. 4	12. 3	A5	E9	Rat	29. 6	26. 5	C7	H10	Earthworm
18. 4	13. 3	A5	F10	Swallow	30. 6	27. 5	C7	J11	Crocodile
19. 4	14. 3	A5	G11	Pig	1. 7	28. 5	C7	K12	Dragon
20. 4	15. 3	A5	H12	Porcupine	2. 7	29. 5	C7	A1	Badger
21. 4	16. 3	A5	J1	Wolf	3. 7	30. 5	C7	B2	Hare
22. 4	17. 3	A5	K2	Dog	4. 7	1. 6	D8	C3	Fox
23. 4	18. 3	A5	A3	Pheasant	5. 7	2. 6	D8	D4	Tiger
24. 4	19. 3	A5	B4	Cock	6. 7	3. 6	D8	E5	Leopard
25. 4	20. 3	A5	C5	Crow	7. 7	4. 6	D8	F6	Griffon
26. 4	21. 3	A5	D6	Monkey	8. 7	5. 6	D8	G7	Ox
27. 4	22. 3	A5	E7	Gibbon	9. 7	6. 6	D8	H8	Bat
28. 4	23. 3	A5	F8	Tapir	10. 7	7. 6	D8	J9	Rat
29. 4	24. 3	A5	G9	Sheep	11. 7	8. 6	D8	K10	Swallow
30. 4	25. 3	A5	H10	Deer	12. 7	9. 6	D8	A11	Pig
1. 5	26. 3	A5	J11	Horse	13. 7	10. 6	D8	B12	Porcupine
2. 5	27. 3	A5	K12	Stag	14. 7	11. 6	D8	C1	Wolf
3. 5	28. 3	A5	A1	Serpent	15. 7	12. 6	D8	D2	Dog
4. 5	29. 3	A5	B2	Earthworm	16. 7	13. 6	D8	E3	Pheasant
5. 5	30. 3	A5	C3	Crocodile	17. 7	14. 6	D8	F4	Cock
6. 5	1. 4	B6	D4	Dragon	18. 7	15. 6	D8	G5	Crow
7. 5	2. 4	B6	E5	Badger	19. 7	16. 6	D8	H6	Monkey
8. 5	3. 4	B6	F6	Hare	20. 7	17. 6	D8	J7	Gibbon
9. 5	4. 4	B6	G7	Fox	21. 7	18. 6	D8	K8	Tapir
10. 5	5. 4	B6	H8	Tiger	22. 7	19. 6	D8	A9	Sheep
11. 5	6. 4	B6	J9	Leopard	23. 7	20. 6	D8	B10	Deer
12. 5	7. 4	B6	K10	Griffon	24. 7	21. 6	D8	C11	Horse
13. 5	8. 4	B6	A11	Ox	25. 7	22. 6	D8	D12	Stag
14. 5	9. 4	B6	B12	Bat	26. 7	23. 6	D8	E1	Serpent
15. 5	10. 4	B6	C1	Rat	27. 7	24. 6	D8	F2	Earthworm
16. 5	11. 4	B6	D2	Swallow	28. 7	25. 6	D8	G3	Crocodile
17. 5	12. 4	B6	E3	Pig	29. 7	26. 6	D8	H4	Dragon
18. 5	13. 4	B6	F4	Porcupine	30. 7	27. 6	D8	J5	Badger
19. 5	14. 4	B6	G5	Wolf	31. 7	28. 6	D8	K6	Hare
20. 5	15. 4	B6	H6	Dog	1. 8	29. 6	D8	A7	Fox
21. 5	16. 4	B6	J7	Pheasant	2. 8	1. 7	E9	B8	Tiger
22. 5	17. 4	B6	K8	Cock	3. 8	2. 7	E9	C9	Leopard
23. 5	18. 4	B6	A9	Crow	4. 8	3. 7	E9	D10	Griffon
24. 5	19. 4	B6	B10	Monkey	5. 8	4. 7	E9	E11	Ox

Solar date	Lunar date	Month HS/EB	Day HS/EB	Constellation	Solar date	Lunar date	Month HS/EB	Day HS/EB	Constellation
6. 8	5. 7	E9	F12	Bat	18.10	19. 9	G11	J1	Serpent
7. 8	6. 7	E9	G1	Rat	19.10	20. 9	G11	K2	Earthworm
8. 8	7. 7	E9	H2	Swallow	20.10	21. 9	G11	A3	Crocodile
9. 8	8. 7	E9	J3	Pig	21.10	22. 9	G11	B4	Dragon
10. 8	9. 7	E9	K4	Porcupine	22.10	23. 9	G11	C5	Badger
11. 8	10. 7	E9	A5	Wolf	23.10	24. 9	G11	D6	Hare
12. 8	11. 7	E9	B6	Dog	24.10	25. 9	G11	E7	Fox
13. 8	12. 7	E9	C7	Pheasant	25.10	26. 9	G11	F8	Tiger
14. 8	13. 7	E9	D8	Cock	26.10	27. 9	G11	G9	Leopard
15. 8	14. 7	E9	E9	Crow	27.10	28. 9	G11	H10	Griffon
16. 8	15. 7	E9	F10	Monkey	28.10	29. 9	G11	J11	Ox
17. 8	16. 7	E9	G11	Gibbon	29.10	1.10	H12	K12	Bat
18. 8	17. 7	E9	H12	Tapir	30.10	2.10	H12	A1	Rat
19. 8	18. 7	E9	J1	Sheep	31.10	3.10	H12	B2	Swallow
20. 8	19. 7	E9	K2	Deer	1.11	4.10	H12	C3	Pig
21. 8	20. 7	E9	A3	Horse	2.11	5.10	H12	D4	Porcupine
22. 8	21. 7	E9	B4	Stag	3.11	6.10	H12	E5	Wolf
23. 8	22. 7	E9	C5	Serpent	4.11	7.10	H12	F6	Dog
24. 8	23. 7	E9	D6	Earthworm	5.11	8.10	H12	G7	Pheasant
25. 8	24. 7	E9	E7	Crocodile	6.11	9.10	H12	H8	Cock
26. 8	25. 7	E9	F8	Dragon	7.11	10.10	H12	J9	Crow
27. 8	26. 7	E9	G9	Badger	8.11	11.10	H12	K10	Monkey
28. 8	27. 7	E9	H10	Hare	9.11	12.10	H12	A11	Gibbon
29. 8	28. 7	E9	J11	Fox	10.11	13.10	H12	B12	Tapir
30. 8	29. 7	E9	K12	Tiger	11.11	14.10	H12	C1	Sheep
31. 8	30. 7	E9	A1	Leopard	12.11	15.10	H12	D2	Deer
1. 9	1. 8	F10	B2	Griffon	13.11	16.10	H12	E3	Horse
2. 9	2. 8	F10	C3	Ox	14.11	17.10	H12	F4	Stag
3. 9	3. 8	F10	D4	Bat	15.11	18.10	H12	G5	Serpent
4. 9	4. 8	F10	E5	Rat	16.11	19.10	H12	H6	Earthworm
5. 9	5. 8	F10	F6	Swallow	17.11	20.10	H12	J7	Crocodile
6. 9	6. 8	F10	G7	Pig	18.11	21.10	H12	K8	Dragon
7. 9	7. 8	F10	H8	Porcupine	19.11	22.10	H12	A9	Badger
8. 9	8. 8	F10	J9	Wolf	20.11	23.10	H12	B10	Hare
9. 9	9. 8	F10	K10	Dog	21.11	24.10	H12	C11	Fox
10. 9	10. 8	F10	A11	Pheasant	22.11	25.10	H12	D12	Tiger
11. 9	11. 8	F10	B12	Cock	23.11	26.10	H12	E1	Leopard
12. 9	12. 8	F10	C1	Crow	24.11	27.10	H12	F2	Griffon
13. 9	13. 8	F10	D2	Monkey	25.11	28.10	H12	G3	Ox
14. 9	14. 8	F10	E3	Gibbon	26.11	29.10	H12	H4	Bat
15. 9	15. 8	F10	F4	Tapir	27.11	30.10	H12	J5	Rat
16. 9	16. 8	F10	G5	Sheep	28.11	1.11	J1	K6	Swallow
17. 9	17. 8	F10	H6	Deer	29.11	2.11	J1	A7	Pig
18. 9	18. 8	F10	J7	Horse	30.11	3.11	J1	B8	Porcupine
19. 9	19. 8	F10	K8	Stag	1.12	4.11	J1	C9	Wolf
20. 9	20. 8	F10	A9	Serpent	2.12	5.11	J1	D10	Dog
21. 9	21. 8	F10	B10	Earthworm	3.12	6.11	J1	E11	Pheasant
22. 9	22. 8	F10	C11	Crocodile	4.12	7.11	J1	F12	Cock
23. 9	23. 8	F10	D12	Dragon	5.12	8.11	J1	G1	Crow
24. 9	24. 8	F10	E1	Badger	6.12	9.11	J1	H2	Monkey
25. 9	25. 8	F10	F2	Hare	7.12	10.11	J1	J3	Gibbon
26. 9	26. 8	F10	G3	Fox	8.12	11.11	J1	K4	Tapir
27. 9	27. 8	F10	H4	Tiger	9.12	12.11	J1	A5	Sheep
28. 9	28. 8	F10	J5	Leopard	10.12	13.11	J1	B6	Deer
29. 9	29. 8	F10	K6	Griffon	11.12	14.11	J1	C7	Horse
30. 9	1. 9	G11	A7	Ox	12.12	15.11	J1	D8	Stag
1.10	2. 9	G11	B8	Bat	13.12	16.11	J1	E9	Serpent
2.10	3. 9	G11	C9	Rat	14.12	17.11	J1	F10	Earthworm
3.10	4. 9	G11	D10	Swallow	15.12	18.11	J1	G11	Crocodile
4.10	5. 9	G11	E11	Pig	16.12	19.11	J1	H12	Dragon
5.10	6. 9	G11	F12	Porcupine	17.12	20.11	J1	J1	Badger
6.10	7. 9	G11	G1	Wolf	18.12	21.11	J1	K2	Hare
7.10	8. 9	G11	H2	Dog	19.12	22.11	J1	A3	Fox
8.10	9. 9	G11	J3	Pheasant	20.12	23.11	J1	B4	Tiger
9.10	10. 9	G11	K4	Cock	21.12	24.11	J1	C5	Leopard
10.10	11. 9	G11	A5	Crow	22.12	25.11	J1	D6	Griffon
11.10	12. 9	G11	B6	Monkey	23.12	26.11	J1	E7	Ox
12.10	13. 9	G11	C7	Gibbon	24.12	27.11	J1	F8	Bat
13.10	14. 9	G11	D8	Tapir	25.12	28.11	J1	G9	Rat
14.10	15. 9	G11	E9	Sheep	26.12	29.11	J1	H10	Swallow
15.10	16. 9	G11	F10	Deer	27.12	1.12	K2	J11	Pig
16.10	17. 9	G11	G11	Horse	28.12	2.12	K2	K12	Porcupine
17.10	18. 9	G11	H12	Stag	29.12	3.12	K2	A1	Wolf

Solar date	Lunar date	Month HS/EB	Day HS/EB	Constellation
30.12	4.12	K2	B2	Dog
31.12	5.12	K2	C3	Pheasant
1933				
1. 1	6.12	K2	D4	Cock
2. 1	7.12	K2	E5	Crow
3. 1	8.12	K2	F6	Monkey
4. 1	9.12	K2	G7	Gibbon
5. 1	10.12	K2	H8	Tapir
6. 1	11.12	K2	J9	Sheep
7. 1	12.12	K2	K10	Deer
8. 1	13.12	K2	A11	Horse
9. 1	14.12	K2	B12	Stag
10. 1	15.12	K2	C1	Serpent
11. 1	16.12	K2	D2	Earthworm
12. 1	17.12	K2	E3	Crocodile
13. 1	18.12	K2	F4	Dragon
14. 1	19.12	K2	G5	Badger
15. 1	20.12	K2	H6	Hare
16. 1	21.12	K2	J7	Fox
17. 1	22.12	K2	K8	Tiger
18. 1	23.12	K2	A9	Leopard
19. 1	24.12	K2	B10	Griffon
20. 1	25.12	K2	C11	Ox
21. 1	26.12	K2	D12	Bat
22. 1	27.12	K2	E1	Rat
23. 1	28.12	K2	F2	Swallow
24. 1	29.12	K2	G3	Pig
25. 1	30.12	K2	H4	Porcupine

KUEI YU YEAR

Solar date	Lunar date	Month HS/EB	Day HS/EB	Constellation
26. 1	1. 1	A3	J5	Wolf
27. 1	2. 1	A3	K6	Dog
28. 1	3. 1	A3	A7	Pheasant
29. 1	4. 1	A3	B8	Cock
30. 1	5. 1	A3	C9	Crow
31. 1	6. 1	A3	D10	Monkey
1. 2	7. 1	A3	E11	Gibbon
2. 2	8. 1	A3	F12	Tapir
3. 2	9. 1	A3	G1	Sheep
4. 2	10. 1	A3	H2	Deer
5. 2	11. 1	A3	J3	Horse
6. 2	12. 1	A3	K4	Stag
7. 2	13. 1	A3	A5	Serpent
8. 2	14. 1	A3	B6	Earthworm
9. 2	15. 1	A3	C7	Crocodile
10. 2	16. 1	A3	D8	Dragon
11. 2	17. 1	A3	E9	Badger
12. 2	18. 1	A3	F10	Hare
13. 2	19. 1	A3	G11	Fox
14. 2	20. 1	A3	H12	Tiger
15. 2	21. 1	A3	J1	Leopard
16. 2	22. 1	A3	K2	Griffon
17. 2	23. 1	A3	A3	Ox
18. 2	24. 1	A3	B4	Bat
19. 2	25. 1	A3	C5	Rat
20. 2	26. 1	A3	D6	Swallow
21. 2	27. 1	A3	E7	Pig
22. 2	28. 1	A3	F8	Porcupine
23. 2	29. 1	A3	G9	Wolf
24. 2	1. 2	B4	H10	Dog
25. 2	2. 2	B4	J11	Pheasant
26. 2	3. 2	B4	K12	Cock
27. 2	4. 2	B4	A1	Crow
28. 2	5. 2	B4	B2	Monkey
1. 3	6. 2	B4	C3	Gibbon
2. 3	7. 2	B4	D4	Tapir
3. 3	8. 2	B4	E5	Sheep
4. 3	9. 2	B4	F6	Deer
5. 3	10. 2	B4	G7	Horse
6. 3	11. 2	B4	H8	Stag
7. 3	12. 2	B4	J9	Serpent
8. 3	13. 2	B4	K10	Earthworm
9. 3	14. 2	B4	A11	Crocodile
10. 3	15. 2	B4	B12	Dragon
11. 3	16. 2	B4	C1	Badger
12. 3	17. 2	B4	D2	Hare
13. 3	18. 2	B4	E3	Fox
14. 3	19. 2	B4	F4	Tiger
15. 3	20. 2	B4	G5	Leopard
16. 3	21. 2	B4	H6	Griffon
17. 3	22. 2	B4	J7	Ox
18. 3	23. 2	B4	K8	Bat
19. 3	24. 2	B4	A9	Rat
20. 3	25. 2	B4	B10	Swallow
21. 3	26. 2	B4	C11	Pig
22. 3	27. 2	B4	D12	Porcupine
23. 3	28. 2	B4	E1	Wolf
24. 3	29. 2	B4	F2	Dog
25. 3	30. 2	B4	G3	Pheasant
26. 3	1. 3	C5	H4	Cock
27. 3	2. 3	C5	J5	Crow
28. 3	3. 3	C5	K6	Monkey
29. 3	4. 3	C5	A7	Gibbon
30. 3	5. 3	C5	B8	Tapir
31. 3	6. 3	C5	C9	Sheep
1. 4	7. 3	C5	D10	Deer
2. 4	8. 3	C5	E11	Horse
3. 4	9. 3	C5	F12	Stag
4. 4	10. 3	C5	G1	Serpent
5. 4	11. 3	C5	H2	Earthworm
6. 4	12. 3	C5	J3	Crocodile
7. 4	13. 3	C5	K4	Dragon
8. 4	14. 3	C5	A5	Badger
9. 4	15. 3	C5	B6	Hare
10. 4	16. 3	C5	C7	Fox
11. 4	17. 3	C5	D8	Tiger
12. 4	18. 3	C5	E9	Leopard
13. 4	19. 3	C5	F10	Griffon
14. 4	20. 3	C5	G11	Ox
15. 4	21. 3	C5	H12	Bat
16. 4	22. 3	C5	J1	Rat
17. 4	23. 3	C5	K2	Swallow
18. 4	24. 3	C5	A3	Pig
19. 4	25. 3	C5	B4	Porcupine
20. 4	26. 3	C5	C5	Wolf
21. 4	27. 3	C5	D6	Dog
22. 4	28. 3	C5	E7*	Pheasant
23. 4	29. 3	C5	F8	Cock
24. 4	30. 3	C5	G9	Crow
25. 4	1. 4	D6	H10	Monkey
26. 4	2. 4	D6	J11	Gibbon
27. 4	3. 4	D6	K12	Tapir
28. 4	4. 4	D6	A1	Sheep
29. 4	5. 4	D6	B2	Deer
30. 4	6. 4	D6	C3	Horse
1. 5	7. 4	D6	D4	Stag
2. 5	8. 4	D6	E5	Serpent
3. 5	9. 4	D6	F6	Earthworm
4. 5	10. 4	D6	G7	Crocodile
5. 5	11. 4	D6	H8	Dragon
6. 5	12. 4	D6	J9	Badger
7. 5	13. 4	D6	K10	Hare
8. 5	14. 4	D6	A11	Fox
9. 5	15. 4	D6	B12	Tiger
10. 5	16. 4	D6	C1	Leopard
11. 5	17. 4	D6	D2	Griffon

Solar date	Lunar date	Month HS/EB	Day HS/EB	Constellation
12. 5	18. 4	D6	E3	Ox
13. 5	19. 4	D6	F4	Bat
14. 5	20. 4	D6	G5	Rat
15. 5	21. 4	D6	H6	Swallow
16. 5	22. 4	D6	J7	Pig
17. 5	23. 4	D6	K8	Porcupine
18. 5	24. 4	D6	A9	Wolf
19. 5	25. 4	D6	B10	Dog
20. 5	26. 4	D6	C11	Pheasant
21. 5	27. 4	D6	D12	Cock
22. 5	28. 4	D6	E1	Crow
23. 5	29. 4	D6	F2	Monkey
24. 5	1. 5	E7	G3	Gibbon
25. 5	2. 5	E7	H4	Tapir
26. 5	3. 5	E7	J5	Sheep
27. 5	4. 5	E7	K6	Deer
28. 5	5. 5	E7	A7	Horse
29. 5	6. 5	E7	B8	Stag
30. 5	7. 5	E7	C9	Serpent
31. 5	8. 5	E7	D10	Earthworm
1. 6	9. 5	E7	E11	Crocodile
2. 6	10. 5	E7	F12	Dragon
3. 5	11. 5	E7	G1	Badger
4. 5	12. 5	E7	H2	Hare
5. 6	13. 5	E7	J3	Fox
6. 6	14. 5	E7	K4	Tiger
7. 6	15. 5	E7	A5	Leopard
8. 6	16. 5	E7	B6	Griffon
9. 6	17. 5	E7	C7	Ox
10. 6	18. 5	E7	D8	Bat
11. 6	19. 5	E7	E9	Rat
12. 6	20. 5	E7	F10	Swallow
13. 6	21. 5	E7	G11	Pig
14. 6	22. 5	E7	H12	Porcupine
15. 6	23. 5	E7	J1	Wolf
16. 6	24. 5	E7	K2	Dog
17. 6	25. 5	E7	A3	Pheasant
18. 6	26. 5	E7	B4	Cock
19. 6	27. 5	E7	C5	Crow
20. 6	28. 5	E7	D6	Monkey
21. 6	29. 5	E7	E7	Gibbon
22. 6	30. 5	E7	F8	Tapir
23. 6	*1. 5*	*E7*	G9	Sheep
24. 6	*2. 5*	*E7*	H10	Deer
25. 6	*3. 5*	*E7*	J11	Horse
26. 6	*4. 5*	*E7*	K12	Stag
27. 6	*5. 5*	*E7*	A1	Serpent
28. 6	*6. 5*	*E7*	B2	Earthworm
29. 6	*7. 5*	*E7*	C3	Crocodile
30. 6	*8. 5*	*E7*	D4	Dragon
1. 7	*9. 5*	*E7*	E5	Badger
2. 7	*10. 5*	*E7*	F6	Hare
3. 7	*11. 5*	*E7*	G7	Fox
4. 7	*12. 5*	*E7*	H8	Tiger
5. 7	*13. 5*	*E7*	J9	Leopard
6. 7	*14. 5*	*E7*	K10	Griffon
7. 7	*15. 5*	*E7*	A11	Ox
8. 7	*16. 5*	*E7*	B12	Bat
9. 7	*17. 5*	*E7*	C1	Rat
10. 7	*18. 5*	*E7*	D2	Swallow
11. 7	*19. 5*	*E7*	E3	Pig
12. 7	*20. 5*	*E7*	F4	Porcupine
13. 7	*21. 5*	*E7*	G5	Wolf
14. 7	*22. 5*	*E7*	H6	Dog
15. 7	*23. 5*	*E7*	J7	Pheasant
16. 7	*24. 5*	*E7*	K8	Cock
17. 7	*25. 5*	*E7*	A9	Crow
18. 7	*26. 5*	*E7*	B10	Monkey
19. 7	*27. 5*	*E7*	C11	Gibbon
20. 7	*28. 5*	*E7*	D12	Tapir
21. 7	*29. 5*	*E7*	E1	Sheep
22. 7	*30. 5*	*E7*	F2	Deer
23. 7	1. 6	F8	G3	Horse
24. 7	2. 6	F8	H4	Stag
25. 7	3. 6	F8	J5	Serpent
26. 7	4. 6	F8	K6	Earthworm
27. 7	5. 6	F8	A7	Crocodile
28. 7	6. 6	F8	B8	Dragon
29. 7	7. 6	F8	C9	Badger
30. 7	8. 6	F8	D10	Hare
31. 7	9. 6	F8	E11	Fox
1. 8	10. 6	F8	F12	Tiger
2. 8	11. 6	F8	G1	Leopard
3. 8	12. 6	F8	H2	Griffon
4. 8	13. 6	F8	J3	Ox
5. 8	14. 6	F8	K4	Bat
6. 8	15. 6	F8	A5	Rat
7. 8	16. 6	F8	B6	Swallow
8. 8	17. 6	F8	C7	Pig
9. 8	18. 6	F8	D8	Porcupine
10. 8	19. 6	F8	E9	Wolf
11. 8	20. 6	F8	F10	Dog
12. 8	21. 6	F8	G11	Pheasant
13. 8	22. 6	F8	H12	Cock
14. 8	23. 6	F8	J1	Crow
15. 8	24. 6	F8	K2	Monkey
16. 8	25. 6	F8	A3	Gibbon
17. 8	26. 6	F8	B4	Tapir
18. 8	27. 6	F8	C5	Sheep
19. 8	28. 6	F8	D6	Deer
20. 8	29. 6	F8	E7	Horse
21. 8	1. 7	G9	F8	Stag
22. 8	2. 7	G9	G9	Serpent
23. 8	3. 7	G9	H10	Earthworm
24. 8	4. 7	G9	J11	Crocodile
25. 8	5. 7	G9	K12	Dragon
26. 8	6. 7	G9	A1	Badger
27. 8	7. 7	G9	B2	Hare
28. 8	8. 7	G9	C3	Fox
29. 8	9. 7	G9	D4	Tiger
30. 8	10. 7	G9	E5	Leopard
31. 8	11. 7	G9	F6	Griffon
1. 9	12. 7	G9	G7	Ox
2. 9	13. 7	G9	H8	Bat
3. 9	14. 7	G9	J9	Rat
4. 9	15. 7	G9	K10	Swallow
5. 9	16. 7	G9	A11	Pig
6. 9	17. 7	G9	B12	Porcupine
7. 9	18. 7	G9	C1	Wolf
8. 9	19. 7	G9	D2	Dog
9. 9	20. 7	G9	E3	Pheasant
10. 9	21. 7	G9	F4	Cock
11. 9	22. 7	G9	G5	Crow
12. 9	23. 7	G9	H6	Monkey
13. 9	24. 7	G9	J7	Gibbon
14. 9	25. 7	G9	K8	Tapir
15. 9	26. 7	G9	A9	Sheep
16. 9	27. 7	G9	B10	Deer
17. 9	28. 7	G9	C11	Horse
18. 9	29. 7	G9	D12	Stag
19. 9	30. 7	G9	E1	Serpent
20. 9	1. 8	H10	F2	Earthworm
21. 9	2. 8	H10	G3	Crocodile
22. 9	3. 8	H10	H4	Dragon
23. 9	4. 8	H10	J5	Badger
24. 9	5. 8	H10	K6	Hare
25. 9	6. 8	H10	A7	Fox
26. 9	7. 8	H10	B8	Tiger
27. 9	8. 8	H10	C9	Leopard
28. 9	9. 8	H10	D10	Griffon
29. 9	10. 8	H10	E11	Ox
30. 9	11. 8	H10	F12	Bat
1.10	12. 8	H10	G1	Rat
2.10	13. 8	H10	H2	Swallow
3.10	14. 8	H10	J3	Pig
4.10	15. 8	H10	K4	Porcupine

Solar date	Lunar date	Month HS/EB	Day HS/EB	Constellation
5.10	16. 8	H10	A5	Wolf
6.10	17. 8	H10	B6	Dog
7.10	18. 8	H10	C7	Pheasant
8.10	19. 8	H10	D8	Cock
9.10	20. 8	H10	E9	Crow
10.10	21. 8	H10	F10	Monkey
11.10	22. 8	H10	G11	Gibbon
12.10	23. 8	H10	H12	Tapir
13.10	24. 8	H10	J1	Sheep
14.10	25. 8	H10	K2	Deer
15.10	26. 8	H10	A3	Horse
16.10	27. 8	H10	B4	Stag
17.10	28. 8	H10	C5	Serpent
18.10	29. 8	H10	D6	Earthworm
19.10	1. 9	J11	E7	Crocodile
20.10	2. 9	J11	F8	Dragon
21.10	3. 9	J11	G9	Badger
22.10	4. 9	J11	H10	Hare
23.10	5. 9	J11	J11	Fox
24.10	6. 9	J11	K12	Tiger
25.10	7. 9	J11	A1	Leopard
26.10	8. 9	J11	B2	Griffon
27.10	9. 9	J11	C3	Ox
28.10	10. 9	J11	D4	Bat
29.10	11. 9	J11	E5	Rat
30.10	12. 9	J11	F6	Swallow
31.10	13. 9	J11	G7	Pig
1.11	14. 9	J11	H8	Porcupine
2.11	15. 9	J11	J9	Wolf
3.11	16. 9	J11	K10	Dog
4.11	17. 9	J11	A11	Pheasant
5.11	18. 9	J11	B12	Cock
6.11	19. 9	J11	C1	Crow
7.11	20. 9	J11	D2	Monkey
8.11	21. 9	J11	E3	Gibbon
9.11	22. 9	J11	F4	Tapir
10.11	23. 9	J11	G5	Sheep
11.11	24. 9	J11	H6	Deer
12.11	25. 9	J11	J7	Horse
13.11	26. 9	J11	K8	Stag
14.11	27. 9	J11	A9	Serpent
15.11	28. 9	J11	B10	Earthworm
16.11	29. 9	J11	C11	Crocodile
17.11	30. 9	J11	D12	Dragon
18.11	1.10	K12	E1	Badger
19.11	2.10	K12	F2	Hare
20.11	3.10	K12	G3	Fox
21.11	4.10	K12	H4	Tiger
22.11	5.10	K12	J5	Leopard
23.11	6.10	K12	K6	Griffon
24.11	7.10	K12	A7	Ox
25.11	8.10	K12	B8	Bat
26.11	9.10	K12	C9	Rat
27.11	10.10	K12	D10	Swallow
28.11	11.10	K12	E11	Pig
29.11	12.10	K12	F12	Porcupine
30.11	13.10	K12	G1	Wolf
1.12	14.10	K12	H2	Dog
2.12	15.10	K12	J3	Pheasant
3.12	16.10	K12	K4	Cock
4.12	17.10	K12	A5	Crow
5.12	18.10	K12	B6	Monkey
6.12	19.10	K12	C7	Gibbon
7.12	20.10	K12	D8	Tapir
8.12	21.10	K12	E9	Sheep
9.12	22.10	K12	F10	Deer
10.12	23.10	K12	G11	Horse

Solar date	Lunar date	Month HS/EB	Day HS/EB	Constellation
11.12	24.10	K12	H12	Stag
12.12	25.10	K12	J1	Serpent
13.12	26.10	K12	K2	Earthworm
14.12	27.10	K12	A3	Crocodile
15.12	28.10	K12	B4	Dragon
16.12	29.10	K12	C5	Badger
17.12	1.11	A1	D6	Hare
18.12	2.11	A1	E7	Fox
19.12	3.11	A1	F8	Tiger
20.12	4.11	A1	G9	Leopard
21.12	5.11	A1	H10	Griffon
22.12	6.11	A1	J11	Ox
23.12	7.11	A1	K12	Bat
24.12	8.11	A1	A1	Rat
25.12	9.11	A1	B2	Swallow
26.12	10.11	A1	C3	Pig
27.12	11.11	A1	D4	Porcupine
28.12	12.11	A1	E5	Wolf
29.12	13.11	A1	F6	Dog
30.12	14.11	A1	G7	Pheasant
31.12	15.11	A1	H8	Cock

1934

Solar date	Lunar date	Month HS/EB	Day HS/EB	Constellation
1. 1	16.11	A1	J9	Crow
2. 1	17.11	A1	K10	Monkey
3. 1	18.11	A1	A11	Gibbon
4. 1	19.11	A1	B12	Tapir
5. 1	20.11	A1	C1	Sheep
6. 1	21.11	A1	D2	Deer
7. 1	22.11	A1	E3	Horse
8. 1	23.11	A1	F4	Stag
9. 1	24.11	A1	G5	Serpent
10. 1	25.11	A1	H6	Earthworm
11. 1	26.11	A1	J7	Crocodile
12. 1	27.11	A1	K8	Dragon
13. 1	28.11	A1	A9	Badger
14. 1	29.11	A1	B10	Hare
15. 1	1.12	B2	C11	Fox
16. 1	2.12	B2	D12	Tiger
17. 1	3.12	B2	E1	Leopard
18. 1	4.12	B2	F2	Griffon
19. 1	5.12	B2	G3	Ox
20. 1	6.12	B2	H4	Bat
21. 1	7.12	B2	J5	Rat
22. 1	8.12	B2	K6	Swallow
23. 1	9.12	B2	A7	Pig
24. 1	10.12	B2	B8	Porcupine
25. 1	11.12	B2	C9	Wolf
26. 1	12.12	B2	D10	Dog
27. 1	13.12	B2	E11	Pheasant
28. 1	14.12	B2	F12	Cock
29. 1	15.12	B2	G1	Crow
30. 1	16.12	B2	H2	Monkey
31. 1	17.12	B2	J3	Gibbon
1. 2	18.12	B2	K4	Tapir
2. 2	19.12	B2	A5	Sheep
3. 2	20.12	B2	B6	Deer
4. 2	21.12	B2	C7	Horse
5. 2	22.12	B2	D8	Stag
6. 2	23.12	B2	E9	Serpent
7. 2	24.12	B2	F10	Earthworm
8. 2	25.12	B2	G11	Crocodile
9. 2	26.12	B2	H12	Dragon
10. 2	27.12	B2	J1	Badger
11. 2	28.12	B2	K2	Hare
12. 2	29.12	B2	A3	Fox
13. 2	30.12	B2	B4	Tiger

CHIA HSÜ YEAR

Solar date	Lunar date	Month HS/EB	Day HS/EB	Constellation	Solar date	Lunar date	Month HS/EB	Day HS/EB	Constellation
14. 2	1. 1	C3	C5	Leopard	26. 4	13. 3	E5	D4	Tapir
15. 2	2. 1	C3	D6	Griffon	27. 4	14. 3	E5	E5	Sheep
16. 2	3. 1	C3	E7	Ox	28. 4	15. 3	E5	F6	Deer
17. 2	4. 1	C3	F8	Bat	29. 4	16. 3	E5	G7	Horse
18. 2	5. 1	C3	G9	Rat	30. 4	17. 3	E5	H8	Stag
19. 2	6. 1	C3	H10	Swallow	1. 5	18. 3	E5	J9	Serpent
20. 2	7. 1	C3	J11	Pig	2. 5	19. 3	E5	K10	Earthworm
21. 2	8. 1	C3	K12	Porcupine	3. 5	20. 3	E5	A11	Crocodile
22. 2	9. 1	C3	A1	Wolf	4. 5	21. 3	E5	B12	Dragon
23. 2	10. 1	C3	B2	Dog	5. 5	22. 3	E5	C1	Badger
24. 2	11. 1	C3	C3	Pheasant	6. 5	23. 3	E5	D2	Hare
25. 2	12. 1	C3	D4	Cock	7. 5	24. 3	E5	E3	Fox
26. 2	13. 1	C3	E5	Crow	8. 5	25. 3	E5	F4	Tiger
27. 2	14. 1	C3	F6	Monkey	9. 5	26. 3	E5	G5	Leopard
28. 2	15. 1	C3	G7	Gibbon	10. 5	27. 3	E5	H6	Griffon
1. 3	16. 1	C3	H8	Tapir	11. 5	28. 3	E5	J7	Ox
2. 3	17. 1	C3	J9	Sheep	12. 5	29. 3	E5	K8	Bat
3. 3	18. 1	C3	K10	Deer	13. 5	1. 4	F6	A9	Rat
4. 3	19. 1	C3	A11	Horse	14. 5	2. 4	F6	B10	Swallow
5. 3	20. 1	C3	B12	Stag	15. 5	3. 4	F6	C11	Pig
6. 3	21. 1	C3	C1	Serpent	16. 5	4. 4	F6	D12	Porcupine
7. 3	22. 1	C3	D2	Earthworm	17. 5	5. 4	F6	E1	Wolf
8. 3	23. 1	C3	E3	Crocodile	18. 5	6. 4	F6	F2	Dog
9. 3	24. 1	C3	F4	Dragon	19. 5	7. 4	F6	G3	Pheasant
10. 3	25. 1	C3	G5	Badger	20. 5	8. 4	F6	H4	Cock
11. 3	26. 1	C3	H6	Hare	21. 5	9. 4	F6	J5	Crow
12. 3	27. 1	C3	J7	Fox	22. 5	10. 4	F6	K6	Monkey
13. 3	28. 1	C3	K8	Tiger	23. 5	11. 4	F6	A7	Gibbon
14. 3	29. 1	C3	A9	Leopard	24. 5	12. 4	F6	B8	Tapir
15. 3	1. 2	D4	B10	Griffon	25. 5	13. 4	F6	C9	Sheep
16. 3	2. 2	D4	C11	Ox	26. 5	14. 4	F6	D10	Deer
17. 3	3. 2	D4	D12	Bat	27. 5	15. 4	F6	E11	Horse
18. 3	4. 2	D4	E1	Rat	28. 5	16. 4	F6	F12	Stag
19. 3	5. 2	D4	F2	Swallow	29. 5	17. 4	F6	G1	Serpent
20. 3	6. 2	D4	G3	Pig	30. 5	18. 4	F6	H2	Earthworm
21. 3	7. 2	D4	H4	Porcupine	31. 5	19. 4	F6	J3	Crocodile
22. 3	8. 2	D4	J5	Wolf	1. 6	20. 4	F6	K4	Dragon
23. 3	9. 2	D4	K6	Dog	2. 6	21. 4	F6	A5	Badger
24. 3	10. 2	D4	A7	Pheasant	3. 6	22. 4	F6	B6	Hare
25. 3	11. 2	D4	B8	Cock	4. 6	23. 4	F6	C7	Fox
26. 3	12. 2	D4	C9	Crow	5. 6	24. 4	F6	D8	Tiger
27. 3	13. 2	D4	D10	Monkey	6. 6	25. 4	F6	E9	Leopard
28. 3	14. 2	D4	E11	Gibbon	7. 6	26. 4	F6	F10	Griffon
29. 3	15. 2	D4	F12	Tapir	8. 6	27. 4	F6	G11	Ox
30. 3	16. 2	D4	G1	Sheep	9. 6	28. 4	F6	H12	Bat
31. 3	17. 2	D4	H2	Deer	10. 6	29. 4	F6	J1	Rat
1. 4	18. 2	D4	J3	Horse	11. 6	30. 4	F6	K2	Swallow
2. 4	19. 2	D4	K4	Stag	12. 6	1. 5	G7	A3	Pig
3. 4	20. 2	D4	A5	Serpent	13. 6	2. 5	G7	B4	Porcupine
4. 4	21. 2	D4	B6	Earthworm	14. 6	3. 5	G7	C5	Wolf
5. 4	22. 2	D4	C7	Crocodile	15. 6	4. 5	G7	D6	Dog
6. 4	23. 2	D4	D8	Dragon	16. 6	5. 5	G7	E7	Pheasant
7. 4	24. 2	D4	E9	Badger	17. 6	6. 5	G7	F8	Cock
8. 4	25. 2	D4	F10	Hare	18. 6	7. 5	G7	G9	Crow
9. 4	26. 2	D4	G11	Fox	19. 6	8. 5	G7	H10	Monkey
10. 4	27. 2	D4	H12	Tiger	20. 6	9. 5	G7	J11	Gibbon
11. 4	28. 2	D4	J1	Leopard	21. 6	10. 5	G7	K12	Tapir
12. 4	29. 2	D4	K2	Griffon	22. 6	11. 5	G7	A1	Sheep
13. 4	30. 2	D4	A3	Ox	23. 6	12. 5	G7	B2	Deer
14. 4	1. 3	E5	B4	Bat	24. 6	13. 5	G7	C3	Horse
15. 4	2. 3	E5	C5	Rat	25. 6	14. 5	G7	D4	Stag
16. 4	3. 3	E5	D6	Swallow	26. 6	15. 5	G7	E5	Serpent
17. 4	4. 3	E5	E7	Pig	27. 6	16. 5	G7	F6	Earthworm
18. 4	5. 3	E5	F8	Porcupine	28. 6	17. 5	G7	G7	Crocodile
19. 4	6. 3	E5	G9	Wolf	29. 6	18. 5	G7	H8	Dragon
20. 4	7. 3	E5	H10	Dog	30. 6	19. 5	G7	J9	Badger
21. 4	8. 3	E5	J11	Pheasant	1. 7	20. 5	G7	K10	Hare
22. 4	9. 3	E5	K12	Cock	2. 7	21. 5	G7	A11	Fox
23. 4	10. 3	E5	A1	Crow	3. 7	22. 5	G7	B12	Tiger
24. 4	11. 3	E5	B2	Monkey	4. 7	23. 5	G7	C1	Leopard
25. 4	12. 3	E5	C3	Gibbon	5. 7	24. 5	G7	D2	Griffon

Solar date	Lunar date	Month HS/EB	Day HS/EB	Constellation
6. 7	25. 5	G7	E3	Ox
7. 7	26. 5	G7	F4	Bat
8. 7	27. 5	G7	G5	Rat
9. 7	28. 5	G7	H6	Swallow
10. 7	29. 5	G7	J7	Pig
11. 7	30. 5	G7	K8	Porcupine
12. 7	1. 6	H8	A9	Wolf
13. 7	2. 6	H8	B10	Dog
14. 7	3. 6	H8	C11	Pheasant
15. 7	4. 6	H8	D12	Cock
16. 7	5. 6	H8	E1	Crow
17. 7	6. 6	H8	F2	Monkey
18. 7	7. 6	H8	G3	Gibbon
19. 7	8. 6	H8	H4	Tapir
20. 7	9. 6	H8	J5	Sheep
21. 7	10. 6	H8	K6	Deer
22. 7	11. 6	H8	A7	Horse
23. 7	12. 6	H8	B8	Stag
24. 7	13. 6	H8	C9	Serpent
25. 7	14. 6	H8	D10	Earthworm
26. 7	15. 6	H8	E11	Crocodile
27. 7	16. 6	H8	F12	Dragon
28. 7	17. 6	H8	G1	Badger
29. 7	18. 6	H8	H2	Hare
30. 7	19. 6	H8	J3	Fox
31. 7	20. 6	H8	K4	Tiger
1. 8	21. 6	H8	A5	Leopard
2. 8	22. 6	H8	B6	Griffon
3. 8	23. 6	H8	C7	Ox
4. 8	24. 6	H8	D8	Bat
5. 8	25. 6	H8	E9	Rat
6. 8	26. 6	H8	F10	Swallow
7. 8	27. 6	H8	G11	Pig
8. 8	28. 6	H8	H12	Porcupine
9. 8	29. 6	H8	J1	Wolf
10. 8	1. 7	J9	K2	Dog
11. 8	2. 7	J9	A3	Pheasant
12. 8	3. 7	J9	B4	Cock
13. 8	4. 7	J9	C5	Crow
14. 8	5. 7	J9	D6	Monkey
15. 8	6. 7	J9	E7	Gibbon
16. 8	7. 7	J9	F8	Tapir
17. 8	8. 7	J9	G9	Sheep
18. 8	9. 7	J9	H10	Deer
19. 8	10. 7	J9	J11	Horse
20. 8	11. 7	J9	K12	Stag
21. 8	12. 7	J9	A1	Serpent
22. 8	13. 7	J9	B2	Earthworm
23. 8	14. 7	J9	C3	Crocodile
24. 8	15. 7	J9	D4	Dragon
25. 8	16. 7	J9	E5	Badger
26. 8	17. 7	J9	F6	Hare
27. 8	18. 7	J9	G7	Fox
28. 8	19. 7	J9	H8	Tiger
29. 8	20. 7	J9	J9	Leopard
30. 8	21. 7	J9	K10	Griffon
31. 8	22. 7	J9	A11	Ox
1. 9	23. 7	J9	B12	Bat
2. 9	24. 7	J9	C1	Rat
3. 9	25. 7	J9	D2	Swallow
4. 9	26. 7	J9	E3	Pig
5. 9	27. 7	J9	F4	Porcupine
6. 9	28. 7	J9	G5	Wolf
7. 9	29. 7	J9	H6	Dog
8. 9	30. 7	J9	J7	Pheasant
9. 9	1. 8	K10	K8	Cock
10. 9	2. 8	K10	A9	Crow
11. 9	3. 8	K10	B10	Monkey
12. 9	4. 8	K10	C11	Gibbon
13. 9	5. 8	K10	D12	Tapir
14. 9	6. 8	K10	E1	Sheep
15. 9	7. 8	K10	F2	Deer
16. 9	8. 8	K10	G3	Horse

Solar date	Lunar date	Month HS/EB	Day HS/EB	Constellation
17. 9	9. 8	K10	H4	Stag
18. 9	10. 8	K10	J5	Serpent
19. 9	11. 8	K10	K6	Earthworm
20. 9	12. 8	K10	A7	Crocodile
21. 9	13. 8	K10	B8	Dragon
22. 9	14. 8	K10	C9	Badger
23. 9	15. 8	K10	D10	Hare
24. 9	16. 8	K10	E11	Fox
25. 9	17. 8	K10	F12	Tiger
26. 9	18. 8	K10	G1	Leopard
27. 9	19. 8	K10	H2	Griffon
28. 9	20. 8	K10	J3	Ox
29. 9	21. 8	K10	K4	Rat
30. 9	22. 8	K10	A5	Swallow
1.10	23. 8	K10	B6	Swallow
2.10	24. 8	K10	C7	Pig
3.10	25. 8	K10	D8	Porcupine
4.10	26. 8	K10	E9	Wolf
5.10	27. 8	K10	F10	Dog
6.10	28. 8	K10	G11	Pheasant
7.10	29. 8	K10	H12	Cock
8.10	1. 9	A11	J1	Crow
9.10	2. 9	A11	K2	Monkey
10.10	3. 9	A11	A3	Gibbon
11.10	4. 9	A11	B4	Tapir
12.10	5. 9	A11	C5	Sheep
13.10	6. 9	A11	D6	Deer
14.10	7. 9	A11	E7	Horse
15.10	8. 9	A11	F8	Stag
16.10	9. 9	A11	G9	Serpent
17.10	10. 9	A11	H10	Earthworm
18.10	11. 9	A11	J11	Crocodile
19.10	12. 9	A11	K12	Dragon
20.10	13. 9	A11	A1	Badger
21.10	14. 9	A11	B2	Hare
22.10	15. 9	A11	C3	Fox
23.10	16. 9	A11	D4	Tiger
24.10	17. 9	A11	E5	Leopard
25.10	18. 9	A11	F6	Griffon
26.10	19. 9	A11	G7	Ox
27.10	20. 9	A11	H8	Bat
28.10	21. 9	A11	J9	Rat
29.10	22. 9	A11	K10	Swallow
30.10	23. 9	A11	A11	Pig
31.10	24. 9	A11	B12	Porcupine
1.11	25. 9	A11	C1	Wolf
2.11	26. 9	A11	D2	Dog
3.11	27. 9	A11	E3	Pheasant
4.11	28. 9	A11	F4	Cock
5.11	29. 9	A11	G5	Crow
6.11	30. 9	A11	H6	Monkey
7.11	1.10	B12	J7	Gibbon
8.11	2.10	B12	K8	Tapir
9.11	3.10	B12	A9	Sheep
10.11	4.10	B12	B10	Deer
11.11	5.10	B12	C11	Horse
12.11	6.10	B12	D12	Stag
13.11	7.10	B12	E1	Serpent
14.11	8.10	B12	F2	Earthworm
15.11	9.10	B12	G3	Crocodile
16.11	10.10	B12	H4	Dragon
17.11	11.10	B12	J5	Badger
18.11	12.10	B12	K6	Hare
19.11	13.10	B12	A7	Fox
20.11	14.10	B12	B8	Tiger
21.11	15.10	B12	C9	Leopard
22.11	16.10	B12	D10	Griffon
23.11	17.10	B12	E11	Ox
24.11	18.10	B12	F12	Bat
25.11	19.10	B12	G1	Rat
26.11	20.10	B12	H2	Swallow
27.11	21.10	B12	J3	Pig
28.11	22.10	B12	K4	Porcupine

Solar date	Lunar date	Month HS/EB	Day HS/EB	Constellation	Solar date	Lunar date	Month HS/EB	Day HS/EB	Constellation
29.11	23.10	B12	A5	Wolf	2. 1	27.11	C1	E3	Gibbon
30.11	24.10	B12	B6	Dog	3. 1	28.11	C1	F4	Tapir
1.12	25.10	B12	C7	Pheasant	4. 1	29.11	C1	G5	Sheep
2.12	26.10	B12	D8	Cock	5. 1	1.12	D2	H6	Deer
3.12	27.10	B12	E9	Crow	6. 1	2.12	D2	J7	Horse
4.12	28.10	B12	F10	Monkey	7. 1	3.12	D2	K8	Stag
5.12	29.10	B12	G11	Gibbon	8. 1	4.12	D2	A9	Serpent
6.12	30.10	B12	H12	Tapir	9. 1	5.12	D2	B10	Earthworm
7.12	1.11	C1	J1	Sheep	10. 1	6.12	D2	C11	Crocodile
8.12	2.11	C1	K2	Deer	11. 1	7.12	D2	D12	Dragon
9.12	3.11	C1	A3	Horse	12. 1	8.12	D2	E1	Badger
10.12	4.11	C1	B4	Stag	13. 1	9.12	D2	F2	Hare
11.12	5.11	C1	C5	Serpent	14. 1	10.12	D2	G3	Fox
12.12	6.11	C1	D6	Earthworm	15. 1	11.12	D2	H4	Tiger
13.12	7.11	C1	E7	Crocodile	16. 1	12.12	D2	J5	Leopard
14.12	8.11	C1	F8	Dragon	17. 1	13.12	D2	K6	Griffon
15.12	9.11	C1	G9	Badger	18. 1	14.12	D2	A7	Ox
16.12	10.11	C1	H10	Hare	19. 1	15.12	D2	B8	Bat
17.12	11.11	C1	J11	Fox	20. 1	16.12	D2	C9	Rat
18.12	12.11	C1	K12	Tiger	21. 1	17.12	D2	D10	Swallow
19.12	13.11	C1	A1	Leopard	22. 1	18.12	D2	E11	Pig
20.12	14.11	C1	B2	Griffon	23. 1	19.12	D2	F12	Porcupine
21.12	15.11	C1	C3	Ox	24. 1	20.12	D2	G1	Wolf
22.12	16.11	C1	D4	Bat	25. 1	21.12	D2	H2	Dog
23.12	17.11	C1	E5	Rat	26. 1	22.12	D2	J3	Pheasant
24.12	18.11	C1	F6	Swallow	27. 1	23.12	D2	K4	Cock
25.12	19.11	C1	G7	Pig	28. 1	24.12	D2	A5	Crow
26.12	20.11	C1	H8	Porcupine	29. 1	25.12	D2	B6	Monkey
27.12	21.11	C1	J9	Wolf	30. 1	26.12	D2	C7	Gibbon
28.12	22.11	C1	K10	Dog	31. 1	27.12	D2	D8	Tapir
29.12	23.11	C1	A11	Pheasant	1. 2	28.12	D2	E9	Sheep
30.12	24.11	C1	B12	Cock	2. 2	29.12	D2	F10	Deer
31.12	25.11	C1	C1	Crow	3. 2	30.12	D2	G11	Horse
1935									
1. 1	26.11	C1	D2	Monkey					

YI HAI YEAR

Solar date	Lunar date	Month HS/EB	Day HS/EB	Constellation	Solar date	Lunar date	Month HS/EB	Day HS/EB	Constellation
4. 2	1. 1	E3	H12	Stag	8. 3	4. 2	F4	K8	Dragon
5. 2	2. 1	E3	J1	Serpent	9. 3	5. 2	F4	A9	Badger
6. 2	3. 1	E3	K2	Earthworm	10. 3	6. 2	F4	B10	Hare
7. 2	4. 1	E3	A3	Crocodile	11. 3	7. 2	F4	C11	Fox
8. 2	5. 1	E3	B4	Dragon	12. 3	8. 2	F4	D12	Tiger
9. 2	6. 1	E3	C5	Badger	13. 3	9. 2	F4	E1	Leopard
10. 2	7. 1	E3	D6	Hare	14. 3	10. 2	F4	F2	Griffon
11. 2	8. 1	E3	E7	Fox	15. 3	11. 2	F4	G3	Ox
12. 2	9. 1	E3	F8	Tiger	16. 3	12. 2	F4	H4	Bat
13. 2	10. 1	E3	G9	Leopard	17. 3	13. 2	F4	J5	Rat
14. 2	11. 1	E3	H10	Griffon	18. 3	14. 2	F4	K6	Swallow
15. 2	12. 1	E3	J11	Ox	19. 3	15. 2	F4	A7	Pig
16. 2	13. 1	E3	K12	Bat	20. 3	16. 2	F4	B8	Porcupine
17. 2	14. 1	E3	A1	Rat	21. 3	17. 2	F4	C9	Wolf
18. 2	15. 1	E3	B2	Swallow	22. 3	18. 2	F4	D10	Dog
19. 2	16. 1	E3	C3	Pig	23. 3	19. 2	F4	E11	Pheasant
20. 2	17. 1	E3	D4	Porcupine	24. 3	20. 2	F4	F12	Cock
21. 2	18. 1	E3	E5	Wolf	25. 3	21. 2	F4	G1	Crow
22. 2	19. 1	E3	F6	Dog	26. 3	22. 2	F4	H2	Monkey
23. 2	20. 1	E3	G7	Pheasant	27. 3	23. 2	F4	J3	Gibbon
24. 2	21. 1	E3	H8	Cock	28. 3	24. 2	F4	K4	Tapir
25. 2	22. 1	E3	J9	Crow	29. 3	25. 2	F4	A5	Sheep
26. 2	23. 1	E3	K10	Monkey	30. 3	26. 2	F4	B6	Deer
27. 2	24. 1	E3	A11	Gibbon	31. 3	27. 2	F4	C7	Horse
28. 2	25. 1	E3	B12	Tapir	1. 4	28. 2	F4	D8	Stag
1. 3	26. 1	E3	C1	Sheep	2. 4	29. 2	F4	E9	Serpent
2. 3	27. 1	E3	D2	Deer	3. 4	1. 3	G5	F10	Earthworm
3. 3	28. 1	E3	E3	Horse	4. 4	2. 3	G5	G11	Crocodile
4. 3	29. 1	E3	F4	Stag	5. 4	3. 3	G5	H12	Dragon
5. 3	1. 2	F4	G5	Serpent	6. 4	4. 3	G5	J1	Badger
6. 3	2. 2	F4	H6	Earthworm	7. 4	5. 3	G5	K2	Hare
7. 3	3. 2	F4	J7	Crocodile	8. 4	6. 3	G5	A3	Fox

Solar date	Lunar date	Month HS/EB	Day HS/EB	Constellation
9. 4	7. 3	G5	B4	Tiger
10. 4	8. 3	G5	C5	Leopard
11. 4	9. 3	G5	D6	Griffon
12. 4	10. 3	G5	E7	Ox
13. 4	11. 3	G5	F8	Bat
14. 4	12. 3	G5	G9	Rat
15. 4	13. 3	G5	H10	Swallow
16. 4	14. 3	G5	J11	Pig
17. 4	15. 3	G5	K12	Porcupine
18. 4	16. 3	G5	A1	Wolf
19. 4	17. 3	G5	B2	Dog
20. 4	18. 3	G5	C3	Pheasant
21. 4	19. 3	G5	D4	Cock
22. 4	20. 3	G5	E5	Crow
23. 4	21. 3	G5	F6	Monkey
24. 4	22. 3	G5	G7	Gibbon
25. 4	23. 3	G5	H8	Tapir
26. 4	24. 3	G5	J9	Sheep
27. 4	25. 3	G5	K10	Deer
28. 4	26. 3	G5	A11	Horse
29. 4	27. 3	G5	B12	Stag
30. 4	28. 3	G5	C1	Serpent
1. 5	29. 3	G5	D2	Earthworm
2. 5	30. 3	G5	E3	Crocodile
3. 5	1. 4	H6	F4	Dragon
4. 5	2. 4	H6	G5	Badger
5. 5	3. 4	H6	H6	Hare
6. 5	4. 4	H6	J7	Fox
7. 5	5. 4	H6	K8	Tiger
8. 5	6. 4	H6	A9	Leopard
9. 5	7. 4	H6	B10	Griffon
10. 5	8. 4	H6	C11	Ox
11. 5	9. 4	H6	D12	Bat
12. 5	10. 4	H6	E1	Rat
13. 5	11. 4	H6	F2	Swallow
14. 5	12. 4	H6	G3	Pig
15. 5	13. 4	H6	H4	Porcupine
16. 5	14. 4	H6	J5	Wolf
17. 5	15. 4	H6	K6	Dog
18. 5	16. 4	H6	A7	Pheasant
19. 5	17. 4	H6	B8	Cock
20. 5	18. 4	H6	C9	Crow
21. 5	19. 4	H6	D10	Monkey
22. 5	20. 4	H6	E11	Gibbon
23. 5	21. 4	H6	F12	Tapir
24. 5	22. 4	H6	G1	Sheep
25. 5	23. 4	H6	H2	Deer
26. 5	24. 4	H6	J3	Horse
27. 5	25. 4	H6	K4	Stag
28. 5	26. 4	H6	A5	Serpent
29. 5	27. 4	H6	B6	Earthworm
30. 5	28. 4	H6	C7	Crocodile
31. 5	29. 4	H6	D8	Dragon
1. 6	1. 5	J7	E9	Badger
2. 6	2. 5	J7	F10	Hare
3. 6	3. 5	J7	G11	Fox
4. 6	4. 5	J7	H12	Tiger
5. 6	5. 5	J7	J1	Leopard
6. 6	6. 5	J7	K2	Griffon
7. 6	7. 5	J7	A3	Ox
8. 6	8. 5	J7	B4	Bat
9. 6	9. 5	J7	C5	Rat
10. 6	10. 5	J7	D6	Swallow
11. 6	11. 5	J7	E7	Pig
12. 6	12. 5	J7	F8	Porcupine
13. 6	13. 5	J7	G9	Wolf
14. 6	14. 5	J7	H10	Dog
15. 6	15. 5	J7	J11	Pheasant
16. 6	16. 5	J7	K12	Cock
17. 6	17. 5	J7	A1	Crow
18. 6	18. 5	J7	B2	Monkey
19. 6	19. 5	J7	C3	Gibbon
20. 6	20. 5	J7	D4	Tapir
21. 6	21. 5	J7	E5	Sheep
22. 6	22. 5	J7	F6	Deer
23. 6	23. 5	J7	G7	Horse
24. 6	24. 5	J7	H8	Stag
25. 6	25. 5	J7	J9	Serpent
26. 6	26. 5	J7	K10	Earthworm
27. 6	27. 5	J7	A11	Crocodile
28. 6	28. 5	J7	B12	Dragon
29. 6	29. 5	J7	C1	Badger
30. 6	30. 5	J7	D2	Hare
1. 7	1. 6	K8	E3	Fox
2. 7	2. 6	K8	F4	Tiger
3. 7	3. 6	K8	G5	Leopard
4. 7	4. 6	K8	H6	Griffon
5. 7	5. 6	K8	J7	Ox
6. 7	6. 6	K8	K8	Bat
7. 7	7. 6	K8	A9	Rat
8. 7	8. 6	K8	B10	Swallow
9. 7	9. 6	K8	C11	Pig
10. 7	10. 6	K8	D12	Porcupine
11. 7	11. 6	K8	E1	Wolf
12. 7	12. 6	K8	F2	Dog
13. 7	13. 6	K8	G3	Pheasant
14. 7	14. 6	K8	H4	Cock
15. 7	15. 6	K8	J5	Crow
16. 7	16. 6	K8	K6	Monkey
17. 7	17. 6	K8	A7	Gibbon
18. 7	18. 6	K8	B8	Tapir
19. 7	19. 6	K8	C9	Sheep
20. 7	20. 6	K8	D10	Deer
21. 7	21. 6	K8	E11	Horse
22. 7	22. 6	K8	F12	Stag
23. 7	23. 6	K8	G1	Serpent
24. 7	24. 6	K8	H2	Earthworm
25. 7	25. 6	K8	J3	Crocodile
26. 7	26. 6	K8	K4	Dragon
27. 7	27. 6	K8	A5	Badger
28. 7	28. 6	K8	B6	Hare
29. 7	29. 6	K8	C7	Fox
30. 7	1. 7	A9	D8	Tiger
31. 7	2. 7	A9	E9	Leopard
1. 8	3. 7	A9	F10	Griffon
2. 8	4. 7	A9	G11	Ox
3. 8	5. 7	A9	H12	Bat
4. 8	6. 7	A9	J1	Rat
5. 8	7. 7	A9	K2	Swallow
6. 8	8. 7	A9	A3	Pig
7. 8	9. 7	A9	B4	Porcupine
8. 8	10. 7	A9	C5	Wolf
9. 8	11. 7	A9	D6	Dog
10. 8	12. 7	A9	E7	Pheasant
11. 8	13. 7	A9	F8	Cock
12. 8	14. 7	A9	G9	Crow
13. 8	15. 7	A9	H10	Monkey
14. 8	16. 7	A9	J11	Gibbon
15. 8	17. 7	A9	K12	Tapir
16. 8	18. 7	A9	A1	Sheep
17. 8	19. 7	A9	B2	Deer
18. 8	20. 7	A9	C3	Horse
19. 8	21. 7	A9	D4	Stag
20. 8	22. 7	A9	E5	Serpent
21. 8	23. 7	A9	F6	Earthworm
22. 8	24. 7	A9	G7	Crocodile
23. 8	25. 7	A9	H8	Dragon
24. 8	26. 7	A9	J9	Badger
25. 8	27. 7	A9	K10	Hare
26. 8	28. 7	A9	A11	Fox
27. 8	29. 7	A9	B12	Tiger
28. 8	30. 7	A9	C1	Leopard
29. 8	1. 8	B10	D2	Griffon
30. 8	2. 8	B10	E3	Ox
31. 8	3. 8	B10	F4	Bat
1. 9	4. 8	B10	G5	Rat

Solar date	Lunar date	Month HS/EB	Day HS/EB	Constellation	Solar date	Lunar date	Month HS/EB	Day HS/EB	Constellation
2. 9	5. 8	B10	H6	Swallow	14.11	19.10	D12	A7	Crocodile
3. 9	6. 8	B10	J7	Pig	15.11	20.10	D12	B8	Dragon
4. 9	7. 8	B10	K8	Porcupine	16.11	21.10	D12	C9	Badger
5. 9	8. 8	B10	A9	Wolf	17.11	22.10	D12	D10	Hare
6. 9	9. 8	B10	B10	Dog	18.11	23.10	D12	E11	Fox
7. 9	10. 8	B10	C11	Pheasant	19.11	24.10	D12	F12	Tiger
8. 9	11. 8	B10	D12	Cock	20.11	25.10	D12	G1	Leopard
9. 9	12. 8	B10	E1	Crow	21.11	26.10	D12	H2	Griffon
10. 9	13. 8	B10	F2	Monkey	22.11	27.10	D12	J3	Ox
11. 9	14. 8	B10	G3	Gibbon	23.11	28.10	D12	K4	Bat
12. 9	15. 8	B10	H4	Tapir	24.11	29.10	D12	A5	Rat
13. 9	16. 8	B10	J5	Sheep	25.11	30.10	D12	B6	Swallow
14. 9	17. 8	B10	K6	Deer	26.11	1.11	E1	C7	Pig
15. 9	18. 8	B10	A7	Horse	27.11	2.11	E1	D8	Porcupine
16. 9	19. 8	B10	B8	Stag	28.11	3.11	E1	E9	Wolf
17. 9	20. 8	B10	C9	Serpent	29.11	4.11	E1	F10	Dog
18. 9	21. 8	B10	D10	Earthworm	30.11	5.11	E1	G11	Pheasant
19. 9	22. 8	B10	E11	Crocodile	1.12	6.11	E1	H12	Cock
20. 9	23. 8	B10	F12	Dragon	2.12	7.11	E1	J1	Crow
21. 9	24. 8	B10	G1	Badger	3.12	8.11	E1	K2	Monkey
22. 9	25. 8	B10	H2	Hare	4.12	9.11	E1	A3	Gibbon
23. 9	26. 8	B10	J3	Fox	5.12	10.11	E1	B4	Tapir
24. 9	27. 8	B10	K4	Tiger	6.12	11.11	E1	C5	Sheep
25. 9	28. 8	B10	A5	Leopard	7.12	12.11	E1	D6	Deer
26. 9	29. 8	B10	B6	Griffon	8.12	13.11	E1	E7	Horse
27. 9	30. 8	B10	C7	Ox	9.12	14.11	E1	F8	Stag
28. 9	1. 9	C11	D8	Bat	10.12	15.11	E1	G9	Serpent
29. 9	2. 9	C11	E9	Rat	11.12	16.11	E1	H10	Earthworm
30. 9	3. 9	C11	F10	Swallow	12.12	17.11	E1	J11	Crocodile
1.10	4. 9	C11	G11	Pig	13.12	18.11	E1	K12	Dragon
2.10	5. 9	C11	H12	Porcupine	14.12	19.11	E1	A1	Badger
3.10	6. 9	C11	J1	Wolf	15.12	20.11	E1	B2	Hare
4.10	7. 9	C11	K2	Dog	16.12	21.11	E1	C3	Fox
5.10	8. 9	C11	A3	Pheasant	17.12	22.11	E1	D4	Tiger
6.10	9. 9	C11	B4	Cock	18.12	23.11	E1	E5	Leopard
7.10	10. 9	C11	C5	Crow	19.12	24.11	E1	F6	Griffon
8.10	11. 9	C11	D6	Monkey	20.12	25.11	E1	G7	Ox
9.10	12. 9	C11	E7	Gibbon	21.12	26.11	E1	H8	Bat
10.10	13. 9	C11	F8	Tapir	22.12	27.11	E1	J9	Rat
11.10	14. 9	C11	G9	Sheep	23.12	28.11	E1	K10	Swallow
12.10	15. 9	C11	H10	Deer	24.12	29.11	E1	A11	Pig
13.10	16. 9	C11	J11	Horse	25.12	30.11	E1	B12	Porcupine
14.10	17. 9	C11	K12	Stag	26.12	1.12	F2	C1	Wolf
15.10	18. 9	C11	A1	Serpent	27.12	2.12	F2	D2	Dog
16.10	19. 9	C11	B2	Earthworm	28.12	3.12	F2	E3	Pheasant
17.10	20. 9	C11	C3	Crocodile	29.12	4.12	F2	F4	Cock
18.10	21. 9	C11	D4	Dragon	30.12	5.12	F2	G5	Crow
19.10	22. 9	C11	E5	Badger	31.12	6.12	F2	H6	Monkey
20.10	23. 9	C11	F6	Hare					
21.10	24. 9	C11	G7	Fox	**1936**				
22.10	25. 9	C11	H8	Tiger	1. 1	7.12	F2	J7	Gibbon
23.10	26. 9	C11	J9	Leopard	2. 1	8.12	F2	K8	Tapir
24.10	27. 9	C11	K10	Griffon	3. 1	9.12	F2	A9	Sheep
25.10	28. 9	C11	A11	Ox	4. 1	10.12	F2	B10	Deer
26.10	29. 9	C11	B12	Bat	5. 1	11.12	F2	C11	Horse
27.10	1.10	D12	C1	Rat	6. 1	12.12	F2	D12	Stag
28.10	2.10	D12	D2	Swallow	7. 1	13.12	F2	E1	Serpent
29.10	3.10	D12	E3	Pig	8. 1	14.12	F2	F2	Earthworm
30.10	4.10	D12	F4	Porcupine	9. 1	15.12	F2	G3	Crocodile
31.10	5.10	D12	G5	Wolf	10. 1	16.12	F2	H4	Dragon
1.11	6.10	D12	H6	Dog	11. 1	17.12	F2	J5	Badger
2.11	7.10	D12	J7	Pheasant	12. 1	18.12	F2	K6	Hare
3.11	8.10	D12	K8	Cock	13. 1	19.12	F2	A7	Fox
4.11	9.10	D12	A9	Crow	14. 1	20.12	F2	B8	Tiger
5.11	10.10	D12	B10	Monkey	15. 1	21.12	F2	C9	Leopard
6.11	11.10	D12	C11	Gibbon	16. 1	22.12	F2	D10	Griffon
7.11	12.10	D12	D12	Tapir	17. 1	23.12	F2	E11	Ox
8.11	13.10	D12	E1	Sheep	18. 1	24.12	F2	F12	Bat
9.11	14.10	D12	F2	Deer	19. 1	25.12	F2	G1	Rat
10.11	15.10	D12	G3	Horse	20. 1	26.12	F2	H2	Swallow
11.11	16.10	D12	H4	Stag	21. 1	27.12	F2	J3	Pig
12.11	17.10	D12	J5	Serpent	22. 1	28.12	F2	K4	Porcupine
13.11	18.10	D12	K6	Earthworm	23. 1	29.12	F2	A5	Wolf

PING TZU YEAR

Solar date	Lunar date	Month HS/EB	Day HS/EB	Constellation
24. 1	1. 1	G3	B6	Dog
25. 1	2. 1	G3	C7	Pheasant
26. 1	3. 1	G3	D8	Cock
27. 1	4. 1	G3	E9	Crow
28. 1	5. 1	G3	F10	Monkey
29. 1	6. 1	G3	G11	Gibbon
30. 1	7. 1	G3	H12	Tapir
31. 1	8. 1	G3	J1	Sheep
1. 2	9. 1	G3	K2	Deer
2. 2	10. 1	G3	A3	Horse
3. 2	11. 1	G3	B4	Stag
4. 2	12. 1	G3	C5	Serpent
5. 2	13. 1	G3	D6	Earthworm
6. 2	14. 1	G3	E7	Crocodile
7. 2	15. 1	G3	F8	Dragon
8. 2	16. 1	G3	G9	Badger
9. 2	17. 1	G3	H10	Hare
10. 2	18. 1	G3	J11	Fox
11. 2	19. 1	G3	K12	Tiger
12. 2	20. 1	G3	A1	Leopard
13. 2	21. 1	G3	B2	Griffon
14. 2	22. 1	G3	C3	Ox
15. 2	23. 1	G3	D4	Bat
16. 2	24. 1	G3	E5	Rat
17. 2	25. 1	G3	F6	Swallow
18. 2	26. 1	G3	G7	Pig
19. 2	27. 1	G3	H8	Porcupine
20. 2	28. 1	G3	J9	Wolf
21. 2	29. 1	G3	K10	Dog
22. 2	30. 1	G3	A11	Pheasant
23. 2	1. 2	H4	B12	Cock
24. 2	2. 2	H4	C1	Crow
25. 2	3. 2	H4	D2	Monkey
26. 2	3. 2	H4	E3	Griffon
27. 2	4. 2	H4	F4	Tapir
28. 2	6. 2	H4	G5	Sheep
29. 2	7. 2	H4	H6	Deer
1. 3	8. 2	H4	J7	Horse
2. 3	9. 2	H4	K8	Stag
3. 3	10. 2	H4	A9	Serpent
4. 3	11. 2	H4	B10	Earthworm
5. 3	12. 2	H4	C11	Crocodile
6. 3	13. 2	H4	D12	Dragon
7. 3	14. 2	H4	E1	Badger
8. 3	15. 2	H4	F2	Hare
9. 3	16. 2	H4	G3	Fox
10. 3	17. 2	H4	H4	Tiger
11. 3	18. 2	H4	J5	Leopard
12. 3	19. 2	H4	K6	Griffon
13. 3	20. 2	H4	A7	Ox
14. 3	21. 2	H4	B8	Bat
15. 3	22. 2	H4	C9	Rat
16. 3	23. 2	H4	D10	Swallow
17. 3	24. 2	H4	E11	Pig
18. 3	25. 2	H4	F12	Porcupine
19. 3	26. 2	H4	G1	Wolf
20. 3	27. 2	H4	H2	Dog
21. 3	28. 2	H4	J3	Pheasant
22. 3	29. 2	H4	K4	Cock
23. 3	1. 3	J5	A5	Crow
24. 3	2. 3	J5	B6	Monkey
25. 3	3. 3	J5	C7	Gibbon
26. 3	4. 3	J5	D8	Tapir
27. 3	5. 3	J5	E9	Sheep
28. 3	6. 3	J5	F10	Deer
29. 3	7. 3	J5	G11	Horse
30. 3	8. 3	J5	H12	Stag
31. 3	9. 3	J5	J1	Serpent
1. 4	10. 3	J5	K2	Earthworm
2. 4	11. 3	J5	A3	Crocodile
3. 4	12. 3	J5	B4	Dragon
4. 4	13. 3	J5	C5	Badger
5. 4	14. 3	J5	D6	Hare
6. 4	15. 3	J5	E7	Fox
7. 4	16. 3	J5	F8	Tiger
8. 4	17. 3	J5	G9	Leopard
9. 4	18. 3	J5	H10	Griffon
10. 4	19. 3	J5	J11	Ox
11. 4	20. 3	J5	K12	Bat
12. 4	21. 3	J5	A1	Rat
13. 4	22. 3	J5	B2	Swallow
14. 4	23. 3	J5	C3	Pig
15. 4	24. 3	J5	D4	Porcupine
16. 4	25. 3	J5	E5	Wolf
17. 4	26. 3	J5	F6	Dog
18. 4	27. 3	J5	G7	Pheasant
19. 4	28. 3	J5	H8	Cock
20. 4	29. 3	J5	J9	Crow
21. 4	1. 3	J5	K10	Monkey
22. 4	2. 3	J5	A11	Gibbon
23. 4	3. 3	J5	B12	Tapir
24. 4	4. 3	J5	C1	Sheep
25. 4	5. 3	J5	D2	Deer
26. 4	6. 3	J5	E3	Horse
27. 4	7. 3	J5	F4	Stag
28. 4	8. 3	J5	G5	Serpent
29. 4	9. 3	J5	H6	Earthworm
30. 4	10. 3	J5	J7	Crocodile
1. 5	11. 3	J5	K8	Dragon
2. 5	12. 3	J5	A9	Badger
3. 5	13. 3	J5	B10	Hare
4. 5	14. 3	J5	C11	Fox
5. 5	15. 3	J5	D12	Tiger
6. 5	16. 3	J5	E1	Leopard
7. 5	17. 3	J5	F2	Griffon
8. 5	18. 3	J5	G3	Ox
9. 5	19. 3	J5	H4	Bat
10. 5	20. 3	J5	J5	Rat
11. 5	21. 3	J5	K6	Swallow
12. 5	22. 3	J5	A7	Pig
13. 5	23. 3	J5	B8	Porcupine
14. 5	24. 3	J5	C9	Wolf
15. 5	25. 3	J5	D10	Dog
16. 5	26. 3	J5	E11	Pheasant
17. 5	27. 3	J5	F12	Cock
18. 5	28. 3	J5	G1	Crow
19. 5	29. 3	J5	H2	Monkey
20. 5	30. 3	J5	J3	Gibbon
21. 5	1. 4	K6	K4	Tapir
22. 5	2. 4	K6	A5	Sheep
23. 5	3. 4	K6	B6	Deer
24. 5	4. 4	K6	C7	Horse
25. 5	5. 4	K6	D8	Stag
26. 5	6. 4	K6	E9	Serpent
27. 5	7. 4	K6	F10	Earthworm
28. 5	8. 4	K6	G11	Crocodile
29. 5	9. 4	K6	H12	Dragon
30. 5	10. 4	K6	J1	Badger
31. 5	11. 4	K6	K2	Hare
1. 6	12. 4	K6	A3	Fox
2. 6	13. 4	K6	B4	Tiger
3. 6	14. 4	K6	C5	Leopard
4. 6	15. 4	K6	D6	Griffon
5. 6	16. 4	K6	E7	Ox
6. 6	17. 4	K6	F8	Bat
7. 6	18. 4	K6	G9	Rat
8. 6	19. 4	K6	H10	Swallow
9. 6	20. 4	K6	J11	Pig
10. 6	21. 4	K6	K12	Porcupine
11. 6	22. 4	K6	A1	Wolf
12. 6	23. 4	K6	B2	Dog
13. 6	24. 4	K6	C3	Pheasant

Solar date	Lunar date	Month HS/EB	Day HS/EB	Constellation
14. 6	25. 4	K6	D4	Cock
15. 6	26. 4	K6	E5	Crow
16. 6	27. 4	K6	F6	Monkey
17. 6	28. 4	K6	G7	Gibbon
18. 6	29. 4	K6	H8	Tapir
19. 6	1. 5	A7	J9	Sheep
20. 6	2. 5	A7	K10	Deer
21. 6	3. 5	A7	A11	Horse
22. 6	4. 5	A7	B12	Stag
23. 6	5. 5	A7	C1	Serpent
24. 6	6. 5	A7	D2	Earthworm
25. 6	7. 5	A7	E3	Crocodile
26. 6	8. 5	A7	F4	Dragon
27. 6	9. 5	A7	G5	Badger
28. 6	10. 5	A7	H6	Hare
29. 6	11. 5	A7	J7	Fox
30. 6	12. 5	A7	K8	Tiger
1. 7	13. 5	A7	A9	Leopard
2. 7	14. 5	A7	B10	Griffon
3. 7	15. 5	A7	C11	Ox
4. 7	16. 5	A7	D12	Bat
5. 7	17. 5	A7	E1	Rat
6. 7	18. 5	A7	F2	Swallow
7. 7	19. 5	A7	G3	Pig
8. 7	20. 5	A7	H4	Porcupine
9. 7	21. 5	A7	J5	Wolf
10. 7	22. 5	A7	K6	Dog
11. 7	23. 5	A7	A7	Pheasant
12. 7	24. 5	A7	B8	Cock
13. 7	25. 5	A7	C9	Crow
14. 7	26. 5	A7	D10	Monkey
15. 7	27. 5	A7	E11	Gibbon
16. 7	28. 5	A7	F12	Tapir
17. 7	29. 5	A7	G1	Sheep
18. 7	1. 6	B8	H2	Deer
19. 7	2. 6	B8	J3	Horse
20. 7	3. 6	B8	K4	Stag
21. 7	4. 6	B8	A5	Serpent
22. 7	5. 6	B8	B6	Earthworm
23. 7	6. 6	B8	C7	Crocodile
24. 7	7. 6	B8	D8	Dragon
25. 7	8. 6	B8	E9	Badger
26. 7	9. 6	B8	F10	Hare
27. 7	10. 6	B8	G11	Fox
28. 7	11. 6	B8	H12	Tiger
29. 7	12. 6	B8	J1	Leopard
30. 7	13. 6	B8	K2	Griffon
31. 7	14. 6	B8	A3	Ox
1. 8	15. 6	B8	B4	Bat
2. 8	16. 6	B8	C5	Rat
3. 8	17. 6	B8	D6	Swallow
4. 8	18. 6	B8	E7	Pig
5. 8	19. 6	B8	F8	Porcupine
6. 8	20. 6	B8	G9	Wolf
7. 8	21. 6	B8	H10	Dog
8. 8	22. 6	B8	J11	Pheasant
9. 8	23. 6	B8	K12	Cock
10. 8	24. 6	B8	A1	Crow
11. 8	25. 6	B8	B2	Monkey
12. 8	26. 6	B8	C3	Gibbon
13. 8	27. 6	B8	D4	Tapir
14. 8	28. 6	B8	E5	Sheep
15. 8	29. 6	B8	F6	Deer
16. 8	30. 6	B8	G7	Horse
17. 8	1. 7	C9	H8	Stag
18. 8	2. 7	C9	J9	Serpent
19. 8	3. 7	C9	K10	Earthworm
20. 8	4. 7	C9	A11	Crocodile
21. 8	5. 7	C9	B12	Dragon
22. 8	6. 7	C9	C1	Badger
23. 8	7. 7	C9	D2	Hare
24. 8	8. 7	C9	E3	Fox
25. 8	9. 7	C9	F4	Tiger
26. 8	10. 7	C9	G5	Leopard
27. 8	11. 7	C9	H6	Griffon
28. 8	12. 7	C9	J7	Ox
29. 8	13. 7	C9	K8	Bat
30. 8	14. 7	C9	A9	Rat
31. 8	15. 7	C9	B10	Swallow
1. 9	16. 7	C9	C11	Pig
2. 9	17. 7	C9	D12	Porcupine
3. 9	18. 7	C9	E1	Wolf
4. 9	19. 7	C9	F2	Dog
5. 9	20. 7	C9	G3	Pheasant
6. 9	21. 7	C9	H4	Cock
7. 9	22. 7	C9	J5	Crow
8. 9	23. 7	C9	K6	Monkey
9. 9	24. 7	C9	A7	Gibbon
10. 9	25. 7	C9	B8	Tapir
11. 9	26. 7	C9	C9	Sheep
12. 9	27. 7	C9	D10	Deer
13. 9	28. 7	C9	E11	Horse
14. 9	29. 7	C9	F12	Stag
15. 9	30. 7	C9	G1	Serpent
16. 9	1. 8	D10	H2	Earthworm
17. 9	2. 8	D10	J3	Crocodile
18. 9	3. 8	D10	K4	Dragon
19. 9	4. 8	D10	A5	Badger
20. 9	5. 8	D10	B6	Hare
21. 9	6. 8	D10	C7	Fox
22. 9	7. 8	D10	D8	Tiger
23. 9	8. 8	D10	E9	Leopard
24. 9	9. 8	D10	F10	Griffon
25. 9	10. 8	D10	G11	Ox
26. 9	11. 8	D10	H12	Bat
27. 9	12. 8	D10	J1	Rat
28. 9	13. 8	D10	K2	Swallow
29. 9	14. 8	D10	A3	Pig
30. 9	15. 8	D10	B4	Porcupine
1.10	16. 8	D10	C5	Wolf
2.10	17. 8	D10	D6	Dog
3.10	18. 8	D10	E7	Pheasant
4.10	19. 8	D10	F8	Cock
5.10	20. 8	D10	G9	Crow
6.10	21. 8	D10	H10	Monkey
7.10	22. 8	D10	J11	Gibbon
8.10	23. 8	D10	K12	Tapir
9.10	24. 8	D10	A1	Sheep
10.10	25. 8	D10	B2	Deer
11.10	26. 8	D10	C3	Horse
12.10	27. 8	D10	D4	Stag
13.10	28. 8	D10	E5	Serpent
14.10	29. 8	D10	F6	Earthworm
15.10	1. 9	E11	G7	Crocodile
16.10	2. 9	E11	H8	Dragon
17.10	3. 9	E11	J9	Badger
18.10	4. 9	E11	K10	Hare
19.10	5. 9	E11	A11	Fox
20.10	6. 9	E11	B12	Tiger
21.10	7. 9	E11	C1	Leopard
22.10	8. 9	E11	D2	Griffon
23.10	9. 9	E11	E3	Ox
24.10	10. 9	E11	F4	Bat
25.10	11. 9	E11	G5	Rat
26.10	12. 9	E11	H6	Swallow
27.10	13. 9	E11	J7	Pig
28.10	14. 9	E11	K8	Porcupine
29.10	15. 9	E11	A9	Wolf
30.10	16. 9	E11	B10	Dog
31.10	17. 9	E11	C11	Pheasant
1.11	18. 9	E11	D12	Cock
2.11	19. 9	E11	E1	Crow
3.11	20. 9	E11	F2	Monkey
4.11	21. 9	E11	G3	Gibbon
5.11	22. 9	E11	H4	Tapir
6.11	23. 9	E11	J5	Sheep

Solar date	Lunar date	Month HS/EB	Day HS/EB	Constellation	Solar date	Lunar date	Month HS/EB	Day HS/EB	Constellation
7.11	24. 9	E11	K6	Deer	26.12	13.11	G1	J7	Pheasant
8.11	25. 9	E11	A7	Horse	27.12	14.11	G1	K8	Cock
9.11	26. 9	E11	B8	Stag	28.12	15.11	G1	A9	Crow
10.11	27. 9	E11	C9	Serpent	29.12	16.11	G1	B10	Monkey
11.11	28. 9	E11	D10	Earthworm	30.12	17.11	G1	C11	Gibbon
12.11	29. 9	E11	E11	Crocodile	31.12	18.11	G1	D12	Tapir
13.11	30. 9	E11	F12	Dragon	**1937**				
14.11	1.10	F12	G1	Badger	1. 1	19.11	G1	E1	Sheep
15.11	2.10	F12	H2	Hare	2. 1	20.11	G1	F2	Deer
16.11	3.10	F12	J3	Fox	3. 1	21.11	G1	G3	Horse
17.11	4.10	F12	K4	Tiger	4. 1	22.11	G1	H4	Stag
18.11	5.10	F12	A5	Leopard	5. 1	23.11	G1	J5	Serpent
19.11	6.10	F12	B6	Griffon	6. 1	24.11	G1	K6	Earthworm
20.11	7.10	F12	C7	Ox	7. 1	25.11	G1	A7	Crocodile
21.11	8.10	F12	D8	Bat	8. 1	26.11	G1	B8	Dragon
22.11	9.10	F12	E9	Rat	9. 1	27.11	G1	C9	Badger
23.11	10.10	F12	F10	Swallow	10. 1	28.11	G1	D10	Hare
24.11	11.10	F12	G11	Pig	11. 1	29.11	G1	E11	Fox
25.11	12.10	F12	H12	Porcupine	12. 1	30.11	G1	F12	Tiger
26.11	13.10	F12	J1	Wolf	13. 1	1.12	H2	G1	Leopard
27.11	14.10	F12	K2	Dog	14. 1	2.12	H2	H2	Griffon
28.11	15.10	F12	A3	Pheasant	15. 1	3.12	H2	J3	Ox
29.11	16.10	F12	B4	Cock	16. 1	4.12	H2	K4	Bat
30.11	17.10	F12	C5	Crow	17. 1	5.12	H2	A5	Rat
1.12	18.10	F12	D6	Monkey	18. 1	6.12	H2	B6	Swallow
2.12	19.10	F12	E7	Gibbon	19. 1	7.12	H2	C7	Pig
3.12	20.10	F12	F8	Tapir	20. 1	8.12	H2	D8	Porcupine
4.12	21.10	F12	G9	Sheep	21. 1	9.12	H2	E9	Wolf
5.12	22.10	F12	H10	Deer	22. 1	10.12	H2	F10	Dog
6.12	23.10	F12	J11	Horse	23. 1	11.12	H2	G11	Pheasant
7.12	24.10	F12	K12	Stag	24. 1	12.12	H2	H12	Cock
8.12	25.10	F12	A1	Serpent	25. 1	13.12	H2	J1	Crow
9.12	26.10	F12	B2	Earthworm	26. 1	14.12	H2	K2	Monkey
10.12	27.10	F12	C3	Crocodile	27. 1	15.12	H2	A3	Gibbon
11.12	28.10	F12	D4	Dragon	28. 1	16.12	H2	B4	Tapir
12.12	29.10	F12	E5	Badger	29. 1	17.12	H2	C5	Sheep
13.12	30.10	F12	F6	Hare	30. 1	18.12	H2	D6	Deer
14.12	1.11	G1	G7	Fox	31. 1	19.12	H2	E7	Horse
15.12	2.11	G1	H8	Tiger	1. 2	20.12	H2	F8	Stag
16.12	3.11	G1	J9	Leopard	2. 2	21.12	H2	G9	Serpent
17.12	4.11	G1	K10	Griffon	3. 2	22.12	H2	H10	Earthworm
18.12	5.11	G1	A11	Ox	4. 2	23.12	H2	J11	Crocodile
19.12	6.11	G1	B12	Bat	5. 2	24.12	H2	K12	Dragon
20.12	7.11	G1	C1	Rat	6. 2	25.12	H2	A1	Badger
21.12	8.11	G1	D2	Swallow	7. 2	26.12	H2	B2	Hare
22.12	9.11	G1	E3	Pig	8. 2	27.12	H2	C3	Fox
23.12	10.11	G1	F4	Porcupine	9. 2	28.12	H2	D4	Tiger
24.12	11.11	G1	G5	Wolf	10. 2	29.12	H2	E5	Leopard
25.12	12.11	G1	H6	Dog					

TING CH'OU YEAR

Solar date	Lunar date	Month HS/EB	Day HS/EB	Constellation	Solar date	Lunar date	Month HS/EB	Day HS/EB	Constellation
11. 2	1. 1	J3	F6	Griffon	2. 3	20. 1	J3	E1	Serpent
12. 2	2. 1	J3	G7	Ox	3. 3	21. 1	J3	F2	Earthworm
13. 2	3. 1	J3	H8	Bat	4. 3	22. 1	J3	G3	Crocodile
14. 2	4. 1	J3	J9	Rat	5. 3	23. 1	J3	H4	Dragon
15. 2	5. 1	J3	K10	Swallow	6. 3	24. 1	J3	J5	Badger
16. 2	6. 1	J3	A11	Pig	7. 3	25. 1	J3	K6	Hare
17. 2	7. 1	J3	B12	Porcupine	8. 3	26. 1	J3	A7	Fox
18. 2	8. 1	J3	C1	Wolf	9. 3	27. 1	J3	B8	Tiger
19. 2	9. 1	J3	D2	Dog	10. 3	28. 1	J3	C9	Leopard
20. 2	10. 1	J3	E3	Pheasant	11. 3	29. 1	J3	D10	Griffon
21. 2	11. 1	J3	F4	Cock	12. 3	30. 1	J3	E11	Ox
22. 2	12. 1	J3	G5	Crow	13. 3	1. 2	K4	F12	Bat
23. 2	13. 1	J3	H6	Monkey	14. 3	2. 2	K4	G1	Rat
24. 2	14. 1	J3	J7	Gibbon	15. 3	3. 2	K4	H2	Swallow
25. 2	15. 1	J3	K8	Tapir	16. 3	4. 2	K4	J3	Pig
26. 2	16. 1	J3	A9	Sheep	17. 3	5. 2	K4	K4	Porcupine
27. 2	17. 1	J3	B10	Deer	18. 3	6. 2	K4	A5	Wolf
28. 2	18. 1	J3	C11	Horse	19. 3	7. 2	K4	B6	Dog
1. 3	19. 1	J3	D12	Stag	20. 3	8. 2	K4	C7	Pheasant

Solar date	Lunar date	Month HS/EB	Day HS/EB	Constellation	Solar date	Lunar date	Month HS/EB	Day HS/EB	Constellation
21. 3	9. 2	K4	D8	Cock	2. 6	24. 4	B6	G9	Leopard
22. 3	10. 2	K4	E9	Crow	3. 6	25. 4	B6	H10	Griffon
23. 3	11. 2	K4	F10	Monkey	4. 6	26. 4	B6	J11	Ox
24. 3	12. 2	K4	G11	Gibbon	5. 6	27. 4	B6	K12	Bat
25. 3	13. 2	K4	H12	Tapir	6. 6	28. 4	B6	A1	Rat
26. 3	14. 2	K4	J1	Sheep	7. 6	29. 4	B6	B2	Swallow
27. 3	15. 2	K4	K2	Deer	8. 6	30. 4	B6	C3	Pig
28. 3	16. 2	K4	A3	Horse	9. 6	1. 5	C7	D4	Porcupine
29. 3	17. 2	K4	B4	Stag	10. 6	2. 5	C7	E5	Wolf
30. 3	18. 2	K4	C5	Serpent	11. 6	3. 5	C7	F6	Dog
31. 3	19. 2	K4	D6	Earthworm	12. 6	4. 5	C7	G7	Pheasant
1. 4	20. 2	K4	E7	Crocodile	13. 6	5. 5	C7	H8	Cock
2. 4	21. 2	K4	F8	Dragon	14. 6	6. 5	C7	J9	Crow
3. 4	22. 2	K4	G9	Badger	15. 6	7. 5	C7	K10	Monkey
4. 4	23. 2	K4	H10	Hare	16. 6	8. 5	C7	A11	Gibbon
5. 4	24. 2	K4	J11	Fox	17. 6	9. 5	C7	B12	Tapir
6. 4	25. 2	K4	K12	Tiger	18. 6	10. 5	C7	C1	Sheep
7. 4	26. 2	K4	A1	Leopard	19. 6	11. 5	C7	D2	Deer
8. 4	27. 2	K4	B2	Griffon	20. 6	12. 5	C7	E3	Horse
9. 4	28. 2	K4	C3	Ox	21. 6	13. 5	C7	F4	Stag
10. 4	29. 2	K4	D4	Bat	22. 6	14. 5	C7	G5	Serpent
11. 4	1. 3	A5	E5	Rat	23. 6	15. 5	C7	H6	Earthworm
12. 4	2. 3	A5	F6	Swallow	24. 6	16. 5	C7	J7	Crocodile
13. 4	3. 3	A5	G7	Pig	25. 6	17. 5	C7	K8	Dragon
14. 4	4. 3	A5	H8	Porcupine	26. 6	18. 5	C7	A9	Badger
15. 4	5. 3	A5	J9	Wolf	27. 6	19. 5	C7	B10	Hare
16. 4	6. 3	A5	K10	Dog	28. 6	20. 5	C7	C11	Fox
17. 4	7. 3	A5	A11	Pheasant	29. 6	21. 5	C7	D12	Tiger
18. 4	8. 3	A5	B12	Cock	30. 6	22. 5	C7	E1	Leopard
19. 4	9. 3	A5	C1	Crow	1. 7	23. 5	C7	F2	Griffon
20. 4	10. 3	A5	D2	Monkey	2. 7	24. 5	C7	G3	Ox
21. 4	11. 3	A5	E3	Gibbon	3. 7	25. 5	C7	H4	Bat
22. 4	12. 3	A5	F4	Tapir	4. 7	26. 5	C7	J5	Rat
23. 4	13. 3	A5	G5	Sheep	5. 7	27. 5	C7	K6	Swallow
24. 4	14. 3	A5	H6	Deer	6. 7	28. 5	C7	A7	Pig
25. 4	15. 3	A5	J7	Horse	7. 7	29. 5	C7	B8	Porcupine
26. 4	16. 3	A5	K8	Stag	8. 7	1. 6	D8	C9	Wolf
27. 4	17. 3	A5	A9	Serpent	9. 7	2. 6	D8	D10	Dog
28. 4	18. 3	A5	B10	Earthworm	10. 7	3. 6	D8	E11	Pheasant
29. 4	19. 3	A5	C11	Crocodile	11. 7	4. 6	D8	F12	Cock
30. 4	20. 3	A5	D12	Dragon	12. 7	5. 6	D8	G1	Crow
1. 5	21. 3	A5	E1	Badger	13. 7	6. 6	D8	H2	Monkey
2. 5	22. 3	A5	F2	Hare	14. 7	7. 6	D8	J3	Gibbon
3. 5	23. 3	A5	G3	Fox	15. 7	8. 6	D8	K4	Tapir
4. 5	24. 3	A5	H4	Tiger	16. 7	9. 6	D8	A5	Sheep
5. 5	25. 3	A5	J5	Leopard	17. 7	10. 6	D8	B6	Deer
6. 5	26. 3	A5	K6	Griffon	18. 7	11. 6	D8	C7	Horse
7. 5	27. 3	A5	A7	Ox	19. 7	12. 6	D8	D8	Stag
8. 5	28. 3	A5	B8	Bat	20. 7	13. 6	D8	E9	Serpent
9. 5	29. 3	A5	C9	Rat	21. 7	14. 6	D8	F10	Earthworm
10. 5	1. 4	B6	D10	Swallow	22. 7	15. 6	D8	G11	Crocodile
11. 5	2. 4	B6	E11	Pig	23. 7	16. 6	D8	H12	Dragon
12. 5	3. 4	B6	F12	Porcupine	24. 7	17. 6	D8	J1	Badger
13. 5	4. 4	B6	G1	Wolf	25. 7	18. 6	D8	K2	Hare
14. 5	5. 4	B6	H2	Dog	26. 7	19. 6	D8	A3	Fox
15. 5	6. 4	B6	J3	Pheasant	27. 7	20. 6	D8	B4	Tiger
16. 5	7. 4	B6	K4	Cock	28. 7	21. 6	D8	C5	Leopard
17. 5	8. 4	B6	A5	Crow	29. 7	22. 6	D8	D6	Griffon
18. 5	9. 4	B6	B6	Monkey	30. 7	23. 6	D8	E7	Ox
19. 5	10. 4	B6	C7	Gibbon	31. 7	24. 6	D8	F8	Bat
20. 5	11. 4	B6	D8	Tapir	1. 8	25. 6	D8	G9	Rat
21. 5	12. 4	B6	E9	Sheep	2. 8	26. 6	D8	H10	Swallow
22. 5	13. 4	B6	F10	Deer	3. 8	27. 6	D8	J11	Pig
23. 5	14. 4	B6	G11	Horse	4. 8	28. 6	D8	K12	Porcupine
24. 5	15. 4	B6	H12	Stag	5. 8	29. 6	D8	A1	Wolf
25. 5	16. 4	B6	J1	Serpent	6. 8	1. 7	E9	B2	Dog
26. 5	17. 4	B6	K2	Earthworm	7. 8	2. 7	E9	C3	Pheasant
27. 5	18. 4	B6	A3	Crocodile	8. 8	3. 7	E9	D4	Cock
28. 5	19. 4	B6	B4	Dragon	9. 8	4. 7	E9	E5	Crow
29. 5	20. 4	B6	C5	Badger	10. 8	5. 7	E9	F6	Monkey
30. 5	21. 4	B6	D6	Hare	11. 8	6. 7	E9	G7	Gibbon
31. 5	22. 4	B6	E7	Fox	12. 8	7. 7	E9	H8	Tapir
1. 6	23. 4	B6	F8	Tiger	13. 8	8. 7	E9	J9	Sheep

Solar date	Lunar date	Month HS/EB	Day HS/EB	Constellation	Solar date	Lunar date	Month HS/EB	Day HS/EB	Constellation
14. 8	9. 7	E9	K10	Deer	26.10	23. 9	G11	C11	Pig
15. 8	10. 7	E9	A11	Horse	27.10	24. 9	G11	D12	Porcupine
16. 8	11. 7	E9	B12	Stag	28.10	25. 9	G11	E1	Wolf
17. 8	12. 7	E9	C1	Serpent	29.10	26. 9	G11	F2	Dog
18. 8	13. 7	E9	D2	Earthworm	30.10	27. 9	G11	G3	Pheasant
19. 8	14. 7	E9	E3	Crocodile	31.10	28. 9	G11	H4	Cock
20. 8	15. 7	E9	F4	Dragon	1.11	29. 9	G11	J5	Crow
21. 8	16. 7	E9	G5	Badger	2.11	30. 9	G11	K6	Monkey
22. 8	17. 7	E9	H6	Hare	3.11	1.10	H12	A7	Gibbon
23. 8	18. 7	E9	J7	Fox	4.11	2.10	H12	B8	Tapir
24. 8	19. 7	E9	K8	Tiger	5.11	3.10	H12	C9	Sheep
25. 8	20. 7	E9	A9	Leopard	6.11	4.10	H12	D10	Deer
26. 8	21. 7	E9	B10	Griffon	7.11	5.10	H12	E11	Horse
27. 8	22. 7	E9	C11	Ox	8.11	6.10	H12	F12	Stag
28. 8	23. 7	E9	D12	Bat	9.11	7.10	H12	G1	Serpent
29. 8	24. 7	E9	E1	Rat	10.11	8.10	H12	H2	Earthworm
30. 8	25. 7	E9	F2	Swallow	11.11	9.10	H12	J3	Crocodile
31. 8	26. 7	E9	G3	Pig	12.11	10.10	H12	K4	Dragon
1. 9	27. 7	E9	H4	Porcupine	13.11	11.10	H12	A5	Badger
2. 9	28. 7	E9	J5	Wolf	14.11	12.10	H12	B6	Hare
3. 9	29. 7	E9	K6	Dog	15.11	13.10	H12	C7	Fox
4. 9	30. 7	E9	A7	Pheasant	16.11	14.10	H12	D8	Tiger
5. 9	1. 8	F10	B8	Cock	17.11	15.10	H12	E9	Leopard
6. 9	2. 8	F10	C9	Crow	18.11	16.10	H12	F10	Griffon
7. 9	3. 8	F10	D10	Monkey	19.11	17.10	H12	G11	Ox
8. 9	4. 8	F10	E11	Gibbon	20.11	18.10	H12	H12	Bat
9. 9	5. 8	F10	F12	Tapir	21.11	19.10	H12	J1	Rat
10. 9	6. 8	F10	G1	Sheep	22.11	20.10	H12	K2	Swallow
11. 9	7. 8	F10	H2	Deer	23.11	21.10	H12	A3	Pig
12. 9	8. 8	F10	J3	Horse	24.11	22.10	H12	B4	Porcupine
13. 9	9. 8	F10	K4	Stag	25.11	23.10	H12	C5	Wolf
14. 9	10. 8	F10	A5	Serpent	26.11	24.10	H12	D6	Dog
15. 9	11. 8	F10	B6	Earthworm	27.11	25.10	H12	E7	Pheasant
16. 9	12. 8	F10	C7	Crocodile	28.11	26.10	H12	F8	Cock
17. 9	13. 8	F10	D8	Dragon	29.11	27.10	H12	G9	Crow
18. 9	14. 8	F10	E9	Badger	30.11	28.10	H12	H10	Monkey
19. 9	15. 8	F10	F10	Hare	1.12	29.10	H12	J11	Gibbon
20. 9	16. 8	F10	G11	Fox	2.12	30.10	H12	K12	Tapir
21. 9	17. 8	F10	H12	Tiger	3.12	1.11	J1	A1	Sheep
22. 9	18. 8	F10	J1	Leopard	4.12	2.11	J1	B2	Deer
23. 9	19. 8	F10	K2	Griffon	5.12	3.11	J1	C3	Horse
24. 9	20. 8	F10	A3	Ox	6.12	4.11	J1	D4	Stag
25. 9	21. 8	F10	B4	Bat	7.12	5.11	J1	E5	Serpent
26. 9	22. 8	F10	C5	Rat	8.12	6.11	J1	F6	Earthworm
27. 9	23. 8	F10	D6	Swallow	9.12	7.11	J1	G7	Crocodile
28. 9	24. 8	F10	E7	Pig	10.12	8.11	J1	H8	Dragon
29. 9	25. 8	F10	F8	Porcupine	11.12	9.11	J1	J9	Badger
30. 9	26. 8	F10	G9	Wolf	12.12	10.11	J1	K10	Hare
1.10	27. 8	F10	H10	Dog	13.12	11.11	J1	A11	Fox
2.10	28. 8	F10	J11	Pheasant	14.12	12.11	J1	B12	Tiger
3.10	29. 8	F10	K12	Cock	15.12	13.11	J1	C1	Leopard
4.10	1. 9	G11	A1	Crow	16.12	14.11	J1	D2	Griffon
5.10	2. 9	G11	B2	Monkey	17.12	15.11	J1	E3	Ox
6.10	3. 9	G11	C3	Gibbon	18.12	16.11	J1	F4	Bat
7.10	4. 9	G11	D4	Tapir	19.12	17.11	J1	G5	Rat
8.10	5. 9	G11	E5	Sheep	20.12	18.11	J1	H6	Swallow
9.10	6. 9	G11	F6	Deer	21.12	19.11	J1	J7	Pig
10.10	7. 9	G11	G7	Horse	22.12	20.11	J1	K8	Porcupine
11.10	8. 9	G11	H8	Stag	23.12	21.11	J1	A9	Wolf
12.10	9. 9	G11	J9	Serpent	24.12	22.11	J1	B10	Dog
13.10	10. 9	G11	K10	Earthworm	25.12	23.11	J1	C11	Pheasant
14.10	11. 9	G11	A11	Crocodile	26.12	24.11	J1	D12	Cock
15.10	12. 9	G11	B12	Dragon	27.12	25.11	J1	E1	Crow
16.10	13. 9	G11	C1	Badger	28.12	26.11	J1	F2	Monkey
17.10	14. 9	G11	D2	Hare	29.12	27.11	J1	G3	Gibbon
18.10	15. 9	G11	E3	Fox	30.12	28.11	J1	H4	Tapir
19.10	16. 9	G11	F4	Tiger	31.12	29.11	J1	J5	Sheep
20.10	17. 9	G11	G5	Leopard	**1938**				
21.10	18. 9	G11	H6	Griffon	1. 1	30.11	J1	K6	Deer
22.10	19. 9	G11	J7	Ox	2. 1	1.12	K2	A7	Horse
23.10	20. 9	G11	K8	Bat	3. 1	2.12	K2	B8	Stag
24.10	21. 9	G11	A9	Rat	4. 1	3.12	K2	C9	Serpent
25.10	22. 9	G11	B10	Swallow					

Solar date	Lunar date	Month HS/EB	Day HS/EB	Constellation	Solar date	Lunar date	Month HS/EB	Day HS/EB	Constellation
5. 1	4.12	K2	D10	Earthworm	18. 1	17.12	K2	G11	Pig
6. 1	5.12	K2	E11	Crocodile	19. 1	18.12	K2	H12	Porcupine
7. 1	6.12	K2	F12	Dragon	20. 1	19.12	K2	J1	Wolf
8. 1	7.12	K2	G1	Badger	21. 1	20.12	K2	K2	Dog
9. 1	8.12	K2	H2	Hare	22. 1	21.12	K2	A3	Pheasant
10. 1	9.12	K2	J3	Fox	23. 1	22.12	K2	B4	Cock
11. 1	10.12	K2	K4	Tiger	24. 1	23.12	K2	C5	Crow
12. 1	11.12	K2	A5	Leopard	25. 1	24.12	K2	D6	Monkey
13. 1	12.12	K2	B6	Griffon	26. 1	25.12	K2	E7	Gibbon
14. 1	13.12	K2	C7	Ox	27. 1	26.12	K2	F8	Tapir
15. 1	14.12	K2	D8	Bat	28. 1	27.12	K2	G9	Sheep
16. 1	15.12	K2	E9	Rat	29. 1	28.12	K2	H10	Deer
17. 1	16.12	K2	F10	Swallow	30. 1	29.12	K2	J11	Horse

MOU YIN YEAR

Solar date	Lunar date	Month HS/EB	Day HS/EB	Constellation	Solar date	Lunar date	Month HS/EB	Day HS/EB	Constellation
31. 1	1. 1	A3	K12	Stag	26. 3	25. 2	B4	D6	Deer
1. 2	2. 1	A3	A1	Serpent	27. 3	26. 2	B4	E7	Horse
2. 2	3. 1	A3	B2	Earthworm	28. 3	27. 2	B4	F8	Stag
3. 2	4. 1	A3	C3	Crocodile	29. 3	28. 2	B4	G9	Serpent
4. 2	5. 1	A3	D4	Dragon	30. 3	29. 2	B4	H10	Earthworm
5. 2	6. 1	A3	E5	Badger	31. 3	30. 2	B4	J11	Crocodile
6. 2	7. 1	A3	F6	Hare	1. 4	1. 3	C5	K12	Dragon
7. 2	8. 1	A3	G7	Fox	2. 4	2. 3	C5	A1	Badger
8. 2	9. 1	A3	H8	Tiger	3. 4	3. 3	C5	B2	Hare
9. 2	10. 1	A3	J9	Leopard	4. 4	4. 3	C5	C3	Fox
10. 2	11. 1	A3	K10	Griffon	5. 4	5. 3	C5	D4	Tiger
11. 2	12. 1	A3	A11	Ox	6. 4	6. 3	C5	E5	Leopard
12. 2	13. 1	A3	B12	Bat	7. 4	7. 3	C5	F6	Griffon
13. 2	14. 1	A3	C1	Rat	8. 4	8. 3	C5	G7	Ox
14. 2	15. 1	A3	D2	Swallow	9. 4	9. 3	C5	H8	Bat
15. 2	16. 1	A3	E3	Pig	10. 4	10. 3	C5	J9	Rat
16. 2	17. 1	A3	F4	Porcupine	11. 4	11. 3	C5	K10	Swallow
17. 2	18. 1	A3	G5	Wolf	12. 4	12. 3	C5	A11	Pig
18. 2	19. 1	A3	H6	Dog	13. 4	13. 3	C5	B12	Porcupine
19. 2	20. 1	A3	J7	Pheasant	14. 4	14. 3	C5	C1	Wolf
20. 2	21. 1	A3	K8	Cock	15. 4	15. 3	C5	D2	Dog
21. 2	22. 1	A3	A9	Crow	16. 4	16. 3	C5	E3	Pheasant
22. 2	23. 1	A3	B10	Monkey	17. 4	17. 3	C5	F4	Cock
23. 2	24. 1	A3	C11	Gibbon	18. 4	18. 3	C5	G5	Crow
24. 2	25. 1	A3	D12	Tapir	19. 4	19. 3	C5	H6	Monkey
25. 2	26. 1	A3	E1	Sheep	20. 4	20. 3	C5	J7	Gibbon
26. 2	27. 1	A3	F2	Deer	21. 4	21. 3	C5	K8	Tapir
27. 2	28. 1	A3	G3	Horse	22. 4	22. 3	C5	A9	Sheep
28. 2	29. 1	A3	H4	Stag	23. 4	23. 3	C5	B10	Deer
1. 3	30. 1	A3	J5	Serpent	24. 4	24. 3	C5	C11	Horse
2. 3	1. 2	B4	K6	Earthworm	25. 4	25. 3	C5	D12	Stag
3. 3	2. 2	B4	A7	Crocodile	26. 4	26. 3	C5	E1	Serpent
4. 3	3. 2	B4	B8	Dragon	27. 4	27. 3	C5	F2	Earthworm
5. 3	4. 2	B4	C9	Badger	28. 4	28. 3	C5	G3	Crocodile
6. 3	5. 2	B4	D10	Hare	29. 4	29. 3	C5	H4	Dragon
7. 3	6. 2	B4	E11	Fox	30. 4	1. 4	D6	J5	Badger
8. 3	7. 2	B4	F12	Tiger	1. 5	2. 4	D6	K6	Hare
9. 3	8. 2	B4	G1	Leopard	2. 5	3. 4	D6	A7	Fox
10. 3	9. 2	B4	H2	Griffon	3. 5	4. 4	D6	B8	Tiger
11. 3	10. 2	B4	J3	Ox	4. 5	5. 4	D6	C9	Leopard
12. 3	11. 2	B4	K4	Bat	5. 5	6. 4	D6	D10	Griffon
13. 3	12. 2	B4	A5	Rat	6. 5	7. 4	D6	E11	Ox
14. 3	13. 2	B4	B6	Swallow	7. 5	8. 4	D6	F12	Bat
15. 3	14. 2	B4	C7	Pig	8. 5	9. 4	D6	G1	Rat
16. 3	15. 2	B4	D8	Porcupine	9. 5	10. 4	D6	H2	Swallow
17. 3	16. 2	B4	E9	Wolf	10. 5	11. 4	D6	J3	Pig
18. 3	17. 2	B4	F10	Dog	11. 5	12. 4	D6	K4	Porcupine
19. 3	18. 2	B4	G11	Pheasant	12. 5	13. 4	D6	A5	Wolf
20. 3	19. 2	B4	H12	Cock	13. 5	14. 4	D6	B6	Dog
21. 3	20. 2	B4	J1	Crow	14. 5	15. 4	D6	C7	Pheasant
22. 3	21. 2	B4	K2	Monkey	15. 5	16. 4	D6	D8	Cock
23. 3	22. 2	B4	A3	Gibbon	16. 5	17. 4	D6	E9	Crow
24. 3	23. 2	B4	B4	Tapir	17. 5	18. 4	D6	F10	Monkey
25. 3	24. 2	B4	C5	Sheep	18. 5	19. 4	D6	G11	Gibbon

Solar date	Lunar date	Month HS/EB	Day HS/EB	Constellation
19. 5	20. 4	D6	H12	Tapir
20. 5	21. 4	D6	J1	Sheep
21. 5	22. 4	D6	K2	Deer
22. 5	23. 4	D6	A3	Horse
23. 5	24. 4	D6	B4	Stag
24. 5	25. 4	D6	C5	Serpent
25. 5	26. 4	D6	D6	Earthworm
26. 5	27. 4	D6	E7	Crocodile
27. 5	28. 4	D6	F8	Dragon
28. 5	29. 4	D6	G9	Badger
29. 5	1. 5	E7	H10	Hare
30. 5	2. 5	E7	J11	Fox
31. 5	3. 5	E7	K12	Tiger
1. 6	4. 5	E7	A1	Leopard
2. 6	5. 5	E7	B2	Griffon
3. 6	6. 5	E7	C3	Ox
4. 6	7. 5	E7	D4	Bat
5. 6	8. 5	E7	E5	Rat
6. 6	9. 5	E7	F6	Swallow
7. 6	10. 5	E7	G7	Pig
8. 6	11. 5	E7	H8	Porcupine
9. 6	12. 5	E7	J9	Wolf
10. 6	13. 5	E7	K10	Dog
11. 6	14. 5	E7	A11	Pheasant
12. 6	15. 5	E7	B12	Cock
13. 6	16. 5	E7	C1	Crow
14. 6	17. 5	E7	D2	Monkey
15. 6	18. 5	E7	E3	Gibbon
16. 6	19. 5	E7	F4	Tapir
17. 6	20. 5	E7	G5	Sheep
18. 6	21. 5	E7	H6	Deer
19. 6	22. 5	E7	J7	Horse
20. 6	23. 5	E7	K8	Stag
21. 6	24. 5	E7	A9	Serpent
22. 6	25. 5	E7	B10	Earthworm
23. 6	26. 5	E7	C11	Crocodile
24. 6	27. 5	E7	D12	Dragon
25. 6	28. 5	E7	E1	Badger
26. 6	29. 5	E7	F2	Hare
27. 6	30. 5	E7	G3	Fox
28. 6	1. 6	F8	H4	Tiger
29. 6	2. 6	F8	J5	Leopard
30. 6	3. 6	F8	K6	Griffon
1. 7	4. 6	F8	A7	Ox
2. 7	5. 6	F8	B8	Bat
3. 7	6. 6	F8	C9	Rat
4. 7	7. 6	F8	D10	Swallow
5. 7	8. 6	F8	E11	Pig
6. 7	9. 6	F8	F12	Porcupine
7. 7	10. 6	F8	G1	Wolf
8. 7	11. 6	F8	H2	Dog
9. 7	12. 6	F8	J3	Pheasant
10. 7	13. 6	F8	K4	Cock
11. 7	14. 6	F8	A5	Crow
12. 7	15. 6	F8	B6	Monkey
13. 7	16. 6	F8	C7	Gibbon
14. 7	17. 6	F8	D8	Tapir
15. 7	18. 6	F8	E9	Sheep
16. 7	19. 6	F8	F10	Deer
17. 7	20. 6	F8	G11	Horse
18. 7	21. 6	F8	H12	Stag
19. 7	22. 6	F8	J1	Serpent
20. 7	23. 6	F8	K2	Earthworm
21. 7	24. 6	F8	A3	Crocodile
22. 7	25. 6	F8	B4	Dragon
23. 7	26. 6	F8	C5	Badger
24. 7	27. 6	F8	D6	Hare
25. 7	28. 6	F8	E7	Fox
26. 7	29. 6	F8	F8	Tiger
27. 7	1. 7	G9	G9	Leopard
28. 7	2. 7	G9	H10	Griffon
29. 7	3. 7	G9	J11	Ox
30. 7	4. 7	G9	K12	Bat
31. 7	5. 7	G9	A1	Rat
1. 8	6. 7	G9	B2	Swallow
2. 8	7. 7	G9	C3	Pig
3. 8	8. 7	G9	D4	Porcupine
4. 8	9. 7	G9	E5	Wolf
5. 8	10. 7	G9	F6	Dog
6. 8	11. 7	G9	G7	Pheasant
7. 8	12. 7	G9	H8	Cock
8. 8	13. 7	G9	J9	Crow
9. 8	14. 7	G9	K10	Monkey
10. 8	15. 7	G9	A11	Gibbon
11. 8	16. 7	G9	B12	Tapir
12. 8	17. 7	G9	C1	Sheep
13. 8	18. 7	G9	D2	Deer
14. 8	19. 7	G9	E3	Horse
15. 8	20. 7	G9	F4	Stag
16. 8	21. 7	G9	G5	Serpent
17. 8	22. 7	G9	H6	Earthworm
18. 8	23. 7	G9	J7	Crocodile
19. 8	24. 7	G9	K8	Dragon
20. 8	25. 7	G9	A9	Badger
21. 8	26. 7	G9	B10	Hare
22. 8	27. 7	G9	C11	Fox
23. 8	28. 7	G9	D12	Tiger
24. 8	29. 7	G9	E1	Leopard
25. 8	*1. 7*	*G9*	F2	Griffon
26. 8	*2. 7*	*G9*	G3	Ox
27. 8	*3. 7*	*G9*	H4	Bat
28. 8	*4. 7*	*G9*	J5	Rat
29. 8	*5. 7*	*G9*	K6	Swallow
30. 8	*6. 7*	*G9*	A7	Pig
31. 8	*7. 7*	*G9*	B8	Porcupine
1. 9	*8. 7*	*G9*	C9	Wolf
2. 9	*9. 7*	*G9*	D10	Dog
3. 9	*10. 7*	*G9*	E11	Pheasant
4. 9	*11. 7*	*G9*	F12	Cock
5. 9	*12. 7*	*G9*	G1	Crow
6. 9	*13. 7*	*G9*	H2	Monkey
7. 9	*14. 7*	*G9*	J3	Gibbon
8. 9	*15. 7*	*G9*	K4	Tapir
9. 9	*16. 7*	*G9*	A5	Sheep
10. 9	*17. 7*	*G9*	B6	Deer
11. 9	*18. 7*	*G9*	C7	Horse
12. 9	*19. 7*	*G9*	D8	Stag
13. 9	*20. 7*	*G9*	E9	Serpent
14. 9	*21. 7*	*G9*	F10	Earthworm
15. 9	*22. 7*	*G9*	G11	Crocodile
16. 9	*23. 7*	*G9*	H12	Dragon
17. 9	*24. 7*	*G9*	J1	Badger
18. 9	*25. 7*	*G9*	K2	Hare
19. 9	*26. 7*	*G9*	A3	Fox
20. 9	*27. 7*	*G9*	B4	Tiger
21. 9	*28. 7*	*G9*	C5	Leopard
22. 9	*29. 7*	*G9*	D6	Griffon
23. 9	*30. 7*	*G9*	E7	Ox
24. 9	1. 8	H10	F8	Bat
25. 9	2. 8	H10	G9	Rat
26. 9	3. 8	H10	H10	Swallow
27. 9	4. 8	H10	J11	Pig
28. 9	5. 8	H10	K12	Porcupine
29. 9	6. 8	H10	A1	Wolf
30. 9	7. 8	H10	B2	Dog
1.10	8. 8	H10	C3	Pheasant
2.10	9. 8	H10	D4	Cock
3.10	10. 8	H10	E5	Crow
4.10	11. 8	H10	F6	Monkey
5.10	12. 8	H10	G7	Gibbon
6.10	13. 8	H10	H8	Tapir
7.10	14. 8	H10	J9	Sheep
8.10	15. 8	H10	K10	Deer
9.10	16. 8	H10	A11	Horse
10.10	17. 8	H10	B12	Stag
11.10	18. 8	H10	C1	Serpent

Solar date	Lunar date	Month HS/EB	Day HS/EB	Constellation	Solar date	Lunar date	Month HS/EB	Day HS/EB	Constellation
12.10	19. 8	H10	D2	Earthworm	17.12	26.10	K12	K8	Bat
13.10	20. 8	H10	E3	Crocodile	18.12	27.10	K12	A9	Rat
14.10	21. 8	H10	F4	Dragon	19.12	28.10	K12	B10	Swallow
15.10	22. 8	H10	G5	Badger	20.12	29.10	K12	C11	Pig
16.10	23. 8	H10	H6	Hare	21.12	30.10	K12	D12	Porcupine
17.10	24. 8	H10	J7	Fox	22.12	1.11	A1	E1	Wolf
18.10	25. 8	H10	K8	Tiger	23.12	2.11	A1	F2	Dog
19.10	26. 8	H10	A9	Leopard	24.12	3.11	A1	G3	Pheasant
20.10	27. 8	H10	B10	Griffon	25.12	4.11	A1	H4	Cock
21.10	28. 8	H10	C11	Ox	26.12	5.11	A1	J5	Crow
22.10	29. 8	H10	D12	Bat	27.12	6.11	A1	K6	Monkey
23.10	1. 9	J11	E1	Rat	28.12	7.11	A1	A7	Gibbon
24.10	2. 9	J11	F2	Swallow	29.12	8.11	A1	B8	Tapir
25.10	3. 9	J11	G3	Pig	30.12	9.11	A1	C9	Sheep
26.10	4. 9	J11	H4	Porcupine	31.12	10.11	A1	D10	Deer
27.10	5. 9	J11	J5	Wolf					
28.10	6. 9	J11	K6	Dog	**1939**				
29.10	7. 9	J11	A7	Pheasant	1. 1	11.11	A1	E11	Horse
30.10	8. 9	J11	B8	Cock	2. 1	12.11	A1	F12	Stag
31.10	9. 9	J11	C9	Crow	3. 1	13.11	A1	G1	Serpent
1.11	10. 9	J11	D10	Monkey	4. 1	14.11	A1	H2	Earthworm
2.11	11. 9	J11	E11	Gibbon	5. 1	15.11	A1	J3	Crocodile
3.11	12. 9	J11	F12	Tapir	6. 1	16.11	A1	K4	Dragon
4.11	13. 9	J11	G1	Sheep	7. 1	17.11	A1	A5	Badger
5.11	14. 9	J11	H2	Deer	8. 1	18.11	A1	B6	Hare
6.11	15. 9	J11	J3	Horse	9. 1	19.11	A1	C7	Fox
7.11	16. 9	J11	K4	Stag	10. 1	20.11	A1	D8	Tiger
8.11	17. 9	J11	A5	Serpent	11. 1	21.11	A1	E9	Leopard
9.11	18. 9	J11	B6	Earthworm	12. 1	22.11	A1	F10	Griffon
10.11	19. 9	J11	C7	Crocodile	13. 1	23.11	A1	G11	Ox
11.11	20. 9	J11	D8	Dragon	14. 1	24.11	A1	H12	Bat
12.11	21. 9	J11	E9	Badger	15. 1	25.11	A1	J1	Rat
13.11	22. 9	J11	F10	Hare	16. 1	26.11	A1	K2	Swallow
14.11	23. 9	J11	G11	Fox	17. 1	27.11	A1	A3	Pig
15.11	24. 9	J11	H12	Tiger	18. 1	28.11	A1	B4	Porcupine
16.11	25. 9	J11	J1	Leopard	19. 1	29.11	A1	C5	Wolf
17.11	26. 9	J11	K2	Griffon	20. 1	1.12	B2	D6	Dog
18.11	27. 9	J11	A3	Ox	21. 1	2.12	B2	E7	Pheasant
19.11	28. 9	J11	B4	Bat	22. 1	3.12	B2	F8	Cock
20.11	29. 9	J11	C5	Rat	23. 1	4.12	B2	G9	Crow
21.11	30. 9	J11	D6	Swallow	24. 1	5.12	B2	H10	Monkey
22.11	1.10	K12	E7	Pig	25. 1	6.12	B2	J11	Gibbon
23.11	2.10	K12	F8	Porcupine	26. 1	7.12	B2	K12	Tapir
24.11	3.10	K12	G9	Wolf	27. 1	8.12	B2	A1	Sheep
25.11	4.10	K12	H10	Dog	28. 1	9.12	B2	B2	Deer
26.11	5.10	K12	J11	Pheasant	29. 1	10.12	B2	C3	Horse
27.11	6.10	K12	K12	Cock	30. 1	11.12	B2	D4	Stag
28.11	7.10	K12	A1	Crow	31. 1	12.12	B2	E5	Serpent
29.11	8.10	K12	B2	Monkey	1. 2	13.12	B2	F6	Earthworm
30.11	9.10	K12	C3	Gibbon	2. 2	14.12	B2	G7	Crocodile
1.12	10.10	K12	D4	Tapir	3. 2	15.12	B2	H8	Dragon
2.12	11.10	K12	E5	Sheep	4. 2	16.12	B2	J9	Badger
3.12	12.10	K12	F6	Deer	5. 2	17.12	B2	K10	Hare
4.12	13.10	K12	G7	Horse	6. 2	18.12	B2	A11	Fox
5.12	14.10	K12	H8	Stag	7. 2	19.12	B2	B12	Tiger
6.12	15.10	K12	J9	Serpent	8. 2	20.12	B2	C1	Leopard
7.12	16.10	K12	K10	Earthworm	9. 2	21.12	B2	D2	Griffon
8.12	17.10	K12	A11	Crocodile	10. 2	22.12	B2	E3	Ox
9.12	18.10	K12	B12	Dragon	11. 2	23.12	B2	F4	Bat
10.12	19.10	K12	C1	Badger	12. 2	24.12	B2	G5	Rat
11.12	20.10	K12	D2	Hare	13. 2	25.12	B2	H6	Swallow
12.12	21.10	K12	E3	Fox	14. 2	26.12	B2	J7	Pig
13.12	22.10	K12	F4	Tiger	15. 2	27.12	B2	K8	Porcupine
14.12	23.10	K12	G5	Leopard	16. 2	28.12	B2	A9	Wolf
15.12	24.10	K12	H6	Griffon	17. 2	29.12	B2	B10	Dog
16.12	25.10	K12	J7	Ox	18. 2	30.12	B2	C11	Pheasant

CHI MAO YEAR

Solar date	Lunar date	Month HS/EB	Day HS/EB	Constellation	Solar date	Lunar date	Month HS/EB	Day HS/EB	Constellation
19. 2	1. 1	C3	D12	Cock	1. 5	12. 3	E5	E11	Fox
20. 2	2. 1	C3	E1	Crow	2. 5	13. 3	E5	F12	Tiger
21. 2	3. 1	C3	F2	Monkey	3. 5	14. 3	E5	G1	Leopard
22. 2	4. 1	C3	G3	Gibbon	4. 5	15. 3	E5	H2	Griffon
23. 2	5. 1	C3	H4	Tapir	5. 5	16. 3	E5	J3	Ox
24. 2	6. 1	C3	J5	Sheep	6. 5	17. 3	E5	K4	Bat
25. 2	7. 1	C3	K6	Deer	7. 5	18. 3	E5	A5	Rat
26. 2	8. 1	C3	A7	Horse	8. 5	19. 3	E5	B6	Swallow
27. 2	9. 1	C3	B8	Stag	9. 5	20. 3	E5	C7	Pig
28. 2	10. 1	C3	C9	Serpent	10. 5	21. 3	E5	D8	Porcupine
1. 3	11. 1	C3	D10	Earthworm	11. 5	22. 3	E5	E9	Wolf
2. 3	12. 1	C3	E11	Crocodile	12. 5	23. 3	E5	F10	Dog
3. 3	13. 1	C3	F12	Dragon	13. 5	24. 3	E5	G11	Pheasant
4. 3	14. 1	C3	G1	Badger	14. 5	25. 3	E5	H12	Cock
5. 3	15. 1	C3	H2	Hare	15. 5	26. 3	E5	J1	Crow
6. 3	16. 1	C3	J3	Fox	16. 5	27. 3	E5	K2	Monkey
7. 3	17. 1	C3	K4	Tiger	17. 5	28. 3	E5	A3	Gibbon
8. 3	18. 1	C3	A5	Leopard	18. 5	29. 3	E5	B4	Tapir
9. 3	19. 1	C3	B6	Griffon	19. 5	1. 4	F6	C5	Sheep
10. 3	20. 1	C3	C7	Ox	20. 5	2. 4	F6	D6	Deer
11. 3	21. 1	C3	D8	Bat	21. 5	3. 4	F6	E7	Horse
12. 3	22. 1	C3	E9	Rat	22. 5	4. 4	F6	F8	Stag
13. 3	23. 1	C3	F10	Swallow	23. 5	5. 4	F6	G9	Serpent
14. 3	24. 1	C3	G11	Pig	24. 5	6. 4	F6	H10	Earthworm
15. 3	25. 1	C3	H12	Porcupine	25. 5	7. 4	F6	J11	Crocodile
16. 3	26. 1	C3	J1	Wolf	26. 5	8. 4	F6	K12	Dragon
17. 3	27. 1	C3	K2	Dog	27. 5	9. 4	F6	A1	Badger
18. 3	28. 1	C3	A3	Pheasant	28. 5	10. 4	F6	B2	Hare
19. 3	29. 1	C3	B4	Cock	29. 5	11. 4	F6	C3	Fox
20. 3	30. 1	C3	C5	Crow	30. 5	12. 4	F6	D4	Tiger
21. 3	1. 2	D4	D6	Monkey	31. 5	13. 4	F6	E5	Leopard
22. 3	2. 2	D4	E7	Gibbon	1. 6	14. 4	F6	F6	Griffon
23. 3	3. 2	D4	F8	Tapir	2. 6	15. 4	F6	G7	Ox
24. 3	4. 2	D4	G9	Sheep	3. 6	16. 4	F6	H8	Bat
25. 3	5. 2	D4	H10	Deer	4. 6	17. 4	F6	J9	Rat
26. 3	6. 2	D4	J11	Horse	5. 6	18. 4	F6	K10	Swallow
27. 3	7. 2	D4	K12	Stag	6. 6	19. 4	F6	A11	Pig
28. 3	8. 2	D4	A1	Serpent	7. 6	20. 4	F6	B12	Porcupine
29. 3	9. 2	D4	B2	Earthworm	8. 6	21. 4	F6	C1	Wolf
30. 3	10. 2	D4	C3	Crocodile	9. 6	22. 4	F6	D2	Dog
31. 3	11. 2	D4	D4	Dragon	10. 6	23. 4	F6	E3	Pheasant
1. 4	12. 2	D4	E5	Badger	11. 6	24. 4	F6	F4	Cock
2. 4	13. 2	D4	F6	Hare	12. 6	25. 4	F6	G5	Crow
3. 4	14. 2	D4	G7	Fox	13. 6	26. 4	F6	H6	Monkey
4. 4	15. 2	D4	H8	Tiger	14. 6	27. 4	F6	J7	Gibbon
5. 4	16. 2	D4	J9	Leopard	15. 6	28. 4	F6	K8	Tapir
6. 4	17. 2	D4	K10	Griffon	16. 6	29. 4	F6	A9	Sheep
7. 4	18. 2	D4	A11	Ox	17. 6	1. 5	G7	B10	Deer
8. 4	19. 2	D4	B12	Bat	18. 6	2. 5	G7	C11	Horse
9. 4	20. 2	D4	C1	Rat	19. 6	3. 5	G7	D12	Stag
10. 4	21. 2	D4	D2	Swallow	20. 6	4. 5	G7	E1	Serpent
11. 4	22. 2	D4	E3	Pig	21. 6	5. 5	G7	F2	Earthworm
12. 4	23. 2	D4	F4	Porcupine	22. 6	6. 5	G7	G3	Crocodile
13. 4	24. 2	D4	G5	Wolf	23. 6	7. 5	G7	H4	Dragon
14. 4	25. 2	D4	H6	Dog	24. 6	8. 5	G7	J5	Badger
15. 4	26. 2	D4	J7	Pheasant	25. 6	9. 5	G7	K6	Hare
16. 4	27. 2	D4	K8	Cock	26. 6	10. 5	G7	A7	Fox
17. 4	28. 2	D4	A9	Crow	27. 6	11. 5	G7	B8	Tiger
18. 4	29. 2	D4	B10	Monkey	28. 6	12. 5	G7	C9	Leopard
19. 4	30. 2	D4	C11	Gibbon	29. 6	13. 5	G7	D10	Griffon
20. 4	1. 3	E5	D12	Tapir	30. 6	14. 5	G7	E11	Ox
21. 4	2. 3	E5	E1	Sheep	1. 7	15. 5	G7	F12	Bat
22. 4	3. 3	E5	F2	Deer	2. 7	16. 5	G7	G1	Rat
23. 4	4. 3	E5	G3	Horse	3. 7	17. 5	G7	H2	Swallow
24. 4	5. 3	E5	H4	Stag	4. 7	18. 5	G7	J3	Pig
25. 4	6. 3	E5	J5	Serpent	5. 7	19. 5	G7	K4	Porcupine
26. 4	7. 3	E5	K6	Earthworm	6. 7	20. 5	G7	A5	Wolf
27. 4	8. 3	E5	A7	Crocodile	7. 7	21. 5	G7	B6	Dog
28. 4	9. 3	E5	B8	Dragon	8. 7	22. 5	G7	C7	Pheasant
29. 4	10. 3	E5	C9	Badger	9. 7	23. 5	G7	D8	Cock
30. 4	11. 3	E5	D10	Hare	10. 7	24. 5	G7	E9	Crow

Solar date	Lunar date	Month HS/EB	Day HS/EB	Constellation	Solar date	Lunar date	Month HS/EB	Day HS/EB	Constellation
11. 7	25. 5	G7	F10	Monkey	22. 9	10. 8	K10	J11	Ox
12. 7	26. 5	G7	G11	Gibbon	23. 9	11. 8	K10	K12	Bat
13. 7	27. 5	G7	H12	Tapir	24. 9	12. 8	K10	A1	Rat
14. 7	28. 5	G7	J1	Sheep	25. 9	13. 8	K10	B2	Swallow
15. 7	29. 5	G7	K2	Deer	26. 9	14. 8	K10	C3	Pig
16. 7	30. 5	G7	A3	Horse	27. 9	15. 8	K10	D4	Porcupine
17. 7	1. 6	H8	B4	Stag	28. 9	16. 8	K10	E5	Wolf
18. 7	2. 6	H8	C5	Serpent	29. 9	17. 8	K10	F6	Dog
19. 7	3. 6	H8	D6	Earthworm	30. 9	18. 8	K10	G7	Pheasant
20. 7	4. 6	H8	E7	Crocodile	1.10	19. 8	K10	H8	Cock
21. 7	5. 6	H8	F8	Dragon	2.10	20. 8	K10	J9	Crow
22. 7	6. 6	H8	G9	Badger	3.10	21. 8	K10	K10	Monkey
23. 7	7. 6	H8	H10	Hare	4.10	22. 8	K10	A11	Gibbon
24. 7	8. 6	H8	J11	Fox	5.10	23. 8	K10	B12	Tapir
25. 7	9. 6	H8	K12	Tiger	6.10	24. 8	K10	C1	Sheep
26. 7	10. 6	H8	A1	Leopard	7.10	25. 8	K10	D2	Deer
27. 7	11. 6	H8	B2	Griffon	8.10	26. 8	K10	E3	Horse
28. 7	12. 6	H8	C3	Ox	9.10	27. 8	K10	F4	Stag
29. 7	13. 6	H8	D4	Bat	10.10	28. 8	K10	G5	Serpent
30. 7	14. 6	H8	E5	Rat	11.10	29. 8	K10	H6	Earthworm
31. 7	15. 6	H8	F6	Swallow	12.10	30. 8	K10	J7	Crocodile
1. 8	16. 6	H8	G7	Pig	13.10	1. 9	A11	K8	Dragon
2. 8	17. 6	H8	H8	Porcupine	14.10	2. 9	A11	A9	Badger
3. 8	18. 6	H8	J9	Wolf	15.10	3. 9	A11	B10	Hare
4. 8	19. 6	H8	K10	Dog	16.10	4. 9	A11	C11	Fox
5. 8	20. 6	H8	A11	Pheasant	17.10	5. 9	A11	D12	Tiger
6. 8	21. 6	H8	B12	Cock	18.10	6. 9	A11	E1	Leopard
7. 8	22. 6	H8	C1	Crow	19.10	7. 9	A11	F2	Griffon
8. 8	23. 6	H8	D2	Monkey	20.10	8. 9	A11	G3	Ox
9. 8	24. 6	H8	E3	Gibbon	21.10	9. 9	A11	H4	Bat
10. 8	25. 6	H8	F4	Tapir	22.10	10. 9	A11	J5	Rat
11. 8	26. 6	H8	G5	Sheep	23.10	11. 9	A11	K6	Swallow
12. 8	27. 6	H8	H6	Deer	24.10	12. 9	A11	A7	Pig
13. 8	28. 6	H8	J7	Horse	25.10	13. 9	A11	B8	Porcupine
14. 8	29. 6	H8	K8	Stag	26.10	14. 9	A11	C9	Wolf
15. 8	1. 7	J9	A9	Serpent	27.10	15. 9	A11	D10	Dog
16. 8	2. 7	J9	B10	Earthworm	28.10	16. 9	A11	E11	Pheasant
17. 8	3. 7	J9	C11	Crocodile	29.10	17. 9	A11	F12	Cock
18. 8	4. 7	J9	D12	Dragon	30.10	18. 9	A11	G1	Crow
19. 8	5. 7	J9	E1	Badger	31.10	19. 9	A11	H2	Monkey
20. 8	6. 7	J9	F2	Hare	1.11	20. 9	A11	J3	Gibbon
21. 8	7. 7	J9	G3	Fox	2.11	21. 9	A11	K4	Tapir
22. 8	8. 7	J9	H4	Tiger	3.11	22. 9	A11	A5	Sheep
23. 8	9. 7	J9	J5	Leopard	4.11	23. 9	A11	B6	Deer
24. 8	10. 7	J9	K6	Griffon	5.11	24. 9	A11	C7	Horse
25. 8	11. 7	J9	A7	Ox	6.11	25. 9	A11	D8	Stag
26. 8	12. 7	J9	B8	Bat	7.11	26. 9	A11	E9	Serpent
27. 8	13. 7	J9	C9	Rat	8.11	27. 9	A11	F10	Earthworm
28. 8	14. 7	J9	D10	Swallow	9.11	28. 9	A11	G11	Crocodile
29. 8	15. 7	J9	E11	Pig	10.11	29. 9	A11	H12	Dragon
30. 8	16. 7	J9	F12	Porcupine	11.11	1.10	B12	J1	Badger
31. 8	17. 7	J9	G1	Wolf	12.11	2.10	B12	K2	Hare
1. 9	18. 7	J9	H2	Dog	13.11	3.10	B12	A3	Fox
2. 9	19. 7	J9	J3	Pheasant	14.11	4.10	B12	B4	Tiger
3. 9	20. 7	J9	K4	Cock	15.11	5.10	B12	C5	Leopard
4. 9	21. 7	J9	A5	Crow	16.11	6.10	B12	D6	Griffon
5. 9	22. 7	J9	B6	Monkey	17.11	7.10	B12	E7	Ox
6. 9	23. 7	J9	C7	Gibbon	18.11	8.10	B12	F8	Bat
7. 9	24. 7	J9	D8	Tapir	19.11	9.10	B12	G9	Rat
8. 9	25. 7	J9	E9	Sheep	20.11	10.10	B12	H10	Swallow
9. 9	26. 7	J9	F10	Deer	21.11	11.10	B12	J11	Pig
10. 9	27. 7	J9	G11	Horse	22.11	12.10	B12	K12	Porcupine
11. 9	28. 7	J9	H12	Stag	23.11	13.10	B12	A1	Wolf
12. 9	29. 7	J9	J1	Serpent	24.11	14.10	B12	B2	Dog
13. 9	1. 8	K10	K2	Earthworm	25.11	15.10	B12	C3	Pheasant
14. 9	2. 8	K10	A3	Crocodile	26.11	16.10	B12	D4	Cock
15. 9	3. 8	K10	B4	Dragon	27.11	17.10	B12	E5	Crow
16. 9	4. 8	K10	C5	Badger	28.11	18.10	B12	F6	Monkey
17. 9	5. 8	K10	D6	Hare	29.11	19.10	B12	G7	Gibbon
18. 9	6. 8	K10	E7	Fox	30.11	20.10	B12	H8	Tapir
19. 9	7. 8	K10	F8	Tiger	1.12	21.10	B12	J9	Sheep
20. 9	8. 8	K10	G9	Leopard	2.12	22.10	B12	K10	Deer
21. 9	9. 8	K10	H10	Griffon	3.12	23.10	B12	A11	Horse

Solar date	Lunar date	Month HS/EB	Day HS/EB	Constellation
4.12	24.10	B12	B12	Stag
5.12	25.10	B12	C1	Serpent
6.12	26.10	B12	D2	Earthworm
7.12	27.10	B12	E3	Crocodile
8.12	28.10	B12	F4	Dragon
9.12	29.10	B12	G5	Badger
10.12	30.10	B12	H6	Hare
11.12	1.11	C1	J7	Fox
12.12	2.11	C1	K8	Tiger
13.12	3.11	C1	A9	Leopard
14.12	4.11	C1	B10	Griffon
15.12	5.11	C1	C11	Ox
16.12	6.11	C1	D12	Bat
17.12	7.11	C1	E1	Rat
18.12	8.11	C1	F2	Swallow
19.12	9.11	C1	G3	Pig
20.12	10.11	C1	H4	Porcupine
21.12	11.11	C1	J5	Wolf
22.12	12.11	C1	K6	Dog
23.12	13.11	C1	A7	Pheasant
24.12	14.11	C1	B8	Cock
25.12	15.11	C1	C9	Crow
26.12	16.11	C1	D10	Monkey
27.12	17.11	C1	E11	Gibbon
28.12	18.11	C1	F12	Tapir
29.12	19.11	C1	G1	Sheep
30.12	20.11	C1	H2	Deer
31.12	21.11	C1	J3	Horse
1940				
1. 1	22.11	C1	K4	Stag
2. 1	23.11	C1	A5	Serpent
3. 1	24.11	C1	B6	Earthworm
4. 1	25.11	C1	C7	Crocodile
5. 1	26.11	C1	D8	Dragon
6. 1	27.11	C1	E9	Badger
7. 1	28.11	C1	F10	Hare
8. 1	29.11	C1	G11	Fox
9. 1	1.12	D2	H12	Tiger
10. 1	2.12	D2	J1	Leopard
11. 1	3.12	D2	K2	Griffon
12. 1	4.12	D2	A3	Ox
13. 1	5.12	D2	B4	Bat
14. 1	6.12	D2	C5	Rat
15. 1	7.12	D2	D6	Swallow
16. 1	8.12	D2	E7	Pig
17. 1	9.12	D2	F8	Porcupine
18. 1	10.12	D2	G9	Wolf
19. 1	11.12	D2	H10	Dog
20. 1	12.12	D2	J11	Pheasant
21. 1	13.12	D2	K12	Cock
22. 1	14.12	D2	A1	Crow
23. 1	15.12	D2	B2	Monkey
24. 1	16.12	D2	C3	Gibbon
25. 1	17.12	D2	D4	Tapir
26. 1	18.12	D2	E5	Sheep
27. 1	19.12	D2	F6	Deer
28. 1	20.12	D2	G7	Horse
29. 1	21.12	D2	H8	Stag
30. 1	22.12	D2	J9	Serpent
31. 1	23.12	D2	K10	Earthworm
1. 2	24.12	D2	A11	Crocodile
2. 2	25.12	D2	B12	Dragon
3. 2	26.12	D2	C1	Badger
4. 2	27.12	D2	D2	Hare
5. 2	28.12	D2	E3	Fox
6. 2	29.12	D2	F4	Tiger
7. 2	30.12	D2	G5	Leopard

KENG CH'EN YEAR

Solar date	Lunar date	Month HS/EB	Day HS/EB	Constellation
8. 2	1. 1	E3	H6	Griffon
9. 2	2. 1	E3	J7	Ox
10. 2	3. 1	E3	K8	Bat
11. 2	4. 1	E3	A9	Rat
12. 2	5. 1	E3	B10	Swallow
13. 2	6. 1	E3	C11	Pig
14. 2	7. 1	E3	D12	Porcupine
15. 2	8. 1	E3	E1	Wolf
16. 2	9. 1	E3	F2	Dog
17. 2	10. 1	E3	G3	Pheasant
18. 2	11. 1	E3	H4	Cock
19. 2	12. 1	E3	J5	Crow
20. 2	13. 1	E3	K6	Monkey
21. 2	14. 1	E3	A7	Gibbon
22. 2	15. 1	E3	B8	Tapir
23. 2	16. 1	E3	C9	Sheep
24. 2	17. 1	E3	D10	Deer
25. 2	18. 1	E3	E11	Horse
26. 2	19. 1	E3	F12	Stag
27. 2	20. 1	E3	G1	Serpent
28. 2	21. 1	E3	H2	Earthworm
29. 2	22. 1	E3	J3	Crocodile
1. 3	23. 1	E3	K4	Dragon
2. 3	24. 1	E3	A5	Badger
3. 3	25. 1	E3	B6	Hare
4. 3	26. 1	E3	C7	Fox
5. 3	27. 1	E3	D8	Tiger
6. 3	28. 1	E3	E9	Leopard
7. 3	29. 1	E3	F10	Griffon
8. 3	30. 1	E3	G11	Ox
9. 3	1. 2	F4	H12	Bat
10. 3	2. 2	F4	J1	Rat
11. 3	3. 2	F4	K2	Swallow
12. 3	4. 2	F4	A3	Pig
13. 3	5. 2	F4	B4	Porcupine
14. 3	6. 2	F4	C5	Wolf
15. 3	7. 2	F4	D6	Dog
16. 3	8. 2	F4	E7	Pheasant
17. 3	9. 2	F4	F8	Cock
18. 3	10. 2	F4	G9	Crow
19. 3	11. 2	F4	H10	Monkey
20. 3	12. 2	F4	J11	Gibbon
21. 3	13. 2	F4	K12	Tapir
22. 3	14. 2	F4	A1	Sheep
23. 3	15. 2	F4	B2	Deer
24. 3	16. 2	F4	C3	Horse
25. 3	17. 2	F4	D4	Stag
26. 3	18. 2	F4	E5	Serpent
27. 3	19. 2	F4	F6	Earthworm
28. 3	20. 2	F4	G7	Crocodile
29. 3	21. 2	F4	H8	Dragon
30. 3	22. 2	F4	J9	Badger
31. 3	23. 2	F4	K10	Hare
1. 4	24. 2	F4	A11	Fox
2. 4	25. 2	F4	B12	Tiger
3. 4	26. 2	F4	C1	Leopard
4. 4	27. 2	F4	D2	Griffon
5. 4	28. 2	F4	E3	Ox
6. 4	29. 2	F4	F4	Bat
7. 4	30. 2	F4	G5	Rat
8. 4	1. 3	G5	H6	Swallow
9. 4	2. 3	G5	J7	Pig
10. 4	3. 3	G5	K8	Porcupine
11. 4	4. 3	G5	A9	Wolf
12. 4	5. 3	G5	B10	Dog
13. 4	6. 3	G5	C11	Pheasant
14. 4	7. 3	G5	D12	Cock
15. 4	8. 3	G5	E1	Crow

Solar date	Lunar date	Month HS/EB	Day HS/EB	Constellation
16. 4	9. 3	G5	F2	Monkey
17. 4	10. 3	G5	G3	Gibbon
18. 4	11. 3	G5	H4	Tapir
19. 4	12. 3	G5	J5	Sheep
20. 4	13. 3	G5	K6	Deer
21. 4	14. 3	G5	A7	Horse
22. 4	15. 3	G5	B8	Stag
23. 4	16. 3	G5	C9	Serpent
24. 4	17. 3	G5	D10	Earthworm
25. 4	18. 3	G5	E11	Crocodile
26. 4	19. 3	G5	F12	Dragon
27. 4	20. 3	G5	G1	Badger
28. 4	21. 3	G5	H2	Hare
29. 4	22. 3	G5	J3	Fox
30. 4	23. 3	G5	K4	Tiger
1. 5	24. 3	G5	A5	Leopard
2. 5	25. 3	G5	B6	Griffon
3. 5	26. 3	G5	C7	Ox
4. 5	27. 3	G5	D8	Bat
5. 5	28. 3	G5	E9	Rat
6. 5	29. 3	G5	F10	Swallow
7. 5	1. 4	H6	G11	Pig
8. 5	2. 4	H6	H12	Porcupine
9. 5	3. 4	H6	J1	Wolf
10. 5	4. 4	H6	K2	Dog
11. 5	5. 4	H6	A3	Pheasant
12. 5	6. 4	H6	B4	Cock
13. 5	7. 4	H6	C5	Crow
14. 5	8. 4	H6	D6	Monkey
15. 5	9. 4	H6	E7	Gibbon
16. 5	10. 4	H6	F8	Tapir
17. 5	11. 4	H6	G9	Sheep
18. 5	12. 4	H6	H10	Deer
19. 5	13. 4	H6	J11	Horse
20. 5	14. 4	H6	K12	Stag
21. 5	15. 4	H6	A1	Serpent
22. 5	16. 4	H6	B2	Earthworm
23. 5	17. 4	H6	C3	Crocodile
24. 5	18. 4	H6	D4	Dragon
25. 5	19. 4	H6	E5	Badger
26. 5	20. 4	H6	F6	Hare
27. 5	21. 4	H6	G7	Fox
28. 5	22. 4	H6	H8	Tiger
29. 5	23. 4	H6	J9	Leopard
30. 5	24. 4	H6	K10	Griffon
31. 5	25. 4	H6	A11	Ox
1. 6	26. 4	H6	B12	Bat
2. 6	27. 4	H6	C1	Rat
3. 6	28. 4	H6	D2	Swallow
4. 6	29. 4	H6	E3	Pig
5. 6	30. 4	H6	F4	Porcupine
6. 6	1. 5	J7	G5	Wolf
7. 6	2. 5	J7	H6	Dog
8. 6	3. 5	J7	J7	Pheasant
9. 6	4. 5	J7	K8	Cock
10. 6	5. 5	J7	A9	Crow
11. 6	6. 5	J7	B10	Monkey
12. 6	7. 5	J7	C11	Gibbon
13. 6	8. 5	J7	D12	Tapir
14. 6	9. 5	J7	E1	Sheep
15. 6	10. 5	J7	F2	Deer
16. 6	11. 5	J7	G3	Horse
17. 6	12. 5	J7	H4	Stag
18. 6	13. 5	J7	J5	Serpent
19. 6	14. 5	J7	K6	Earthworm
20. 6	15. 5	J7	A7	Crocodile
21. 6	16. 5	J7	B8	Dragon
22. 6	17. 5	J7	C9	Badger
23. 6	18. 5	J7	D10	Hare
24. 6	19. 5	J7	E11	Fox
25. 6	20. 5	J7	F12	Tiger
26. 6	21. 5	J7	G1	Leopard
27. 6	22. 5	J7	H2	Griffon

Solar date	Lunar date	Month HS/EB	Day HS/EB	Constellation
28. 6	23. 5	J7	J3	Ox
29. 6	24. 5	J7	K4	Bat
30. 6	25. 5	J7	A5	Rat
1. 7	26. 5	J7	B6	Swallow
2. 7	27. 5	J7	C7	Pig
3. 7	28. 5	J7	D8	Porcupine
4. 7	29. 5	J7	E9	Wolf
5. 7	1. 6	K8	F10	Dog
6. 7	2. 6	K8	G11	Pheasant
7. 7	3. 6	K8	H12	Cock
8. 7	4. 6	K8	J1	Crow
9. 7	5. 6	K8	K2	Monkey
10. 7	6. 6	K8	A3	Gibbon
11. 7	7. 6	K8	B4	Tapir
12. 7	8. 6	K8	C5	Sheep
13. 7	9. 6	K8	D6	Deer
14. 7	10. 6	K8	E7	Horse
15. 7	11. 6	K8	F8	Stag
16. 7	12. 6	K8	G9	Serpent
17. 7	13. 6	K8	H10	Earthworm
18. 7	14. 6	K8	J11	Crocodile
19. 7	15. 6	K8	K12	Dragon
20. 7	16. 6	K8	A1	Badger
21. 7	17. 6	K8	B2	Hare
22. 7	18. 6	K8	C3	Fox
23. 7	19. 6	K8	D4	Tiger
24. 7	20. 6	K8	E5	Leopard
25. 7	21. 6	K8	F6	Griffon
26. 7	22. 6	K8	G7	Ox
27. 7	23. 6	K8	H8	Bat
28. 7	24. 6	K8	J9	Rat
29. 7	25. 6	K8	K10	Swallow
30. 7	26. 6	K8	A11	Pig
31. 7	27. 6	K8	B12	Porcupine
1. 8	28. 6	K8	C1	Wolf
2. 8	29. 6	K8	D2	Dog
3. 8	30. 6	K8	E3	Pheasant
4. 8	1. 7	A9	F4	Cock
5. 8	2. 7	A9	G5	Crow
6. 8	3. 7	A9	H6	Monkey
7. 8	4. 7	A9	J7	Gibbon
8. 8	5. 7	A9	K8	Tapir
9. 8	6. 7	A9	A9	Sheep
10. 8	7. 7	A9	B10	Deer
11. 8	8. 7	A9	C11	Horse
12. 8	9. 7	A9	D12	Stag
13. 8	10. 7	A9	E1	Serpent
14. 8	11. 7	A9	F2	Earthworm
15. 8	12. 7	A9	G3	Crocodile
16. 8	13. 7	A9	H4	Dragon
17. 8	14. 7	A9	J5	Badger
18. 8	15. 7	A9	K6	Hare
19. 8	16. 7	A9	A7	Fox
20. 8	17. 7	A9	B8	Tiger
21. 8	18. 7	A9	C9	Leopard
22. 8	19. 7	A9	D10	Griffon
23. 8	20. 7	A9	E11	Ox
24. 8	21. 7	A9	F12	Bat
25. 8	22. 7	A9	G1	Rat
26. 8	23. 7	A9	H2	Swallow
27. 8	24. 7	A9	J3	Pig
28. 8	25. 7	A9	K4	Porcupine
29. 8	26. 7	A9	A5	Wolf
30. 8	27. 7	A9	B6	Dog
31. 8	28. 7	A9	C7	Pheasant
1. 9	29. 7	A9	D8	Cock
2. 9	1. 8	B10	E9	Crow
3. 9	2. 8	B10	F10	Monkey
4. 9	3. 8	B10	G11	Gibbon
5. 9	4. 8	B10	H12	Tapir
6. 9	5. 8	B10	J1	Sheep
7. 9	6. 8	B10	K2	Deer
8. 9	7. 8	B10	A3	Horse

Solar date	Lunar date	Month HS/EB	Day HS/EB	Constellation
9. 9	8. 8	B10	B4	Stag
10. 9	9. 8	B10	C5	Serpent
11. 9	10. 8	B10	D6	Earthworm
12. 9	11. 8	B10	E7	Crocodile
13. 9	12. 8	B10	F8	Dragon
14. 9	13. 8	B10	G9	Badger
15. 9	14. 8	B10	H10	Hare
16. 9	15. 8	B10	J11	Fox
17. 9	16. 8	B10	K12	Tiger
18. 9	17. 8	B10	A1	Leopard
19. 9	18. 8	B10	B2	Griffon
20. 9	19. 8	B10	C3	Ox
21. 9	20. 8	B10	D4	Bat
22. 9	21. 8	B10	E5	Rat
23. 9	22. 8	B10	F6	Swallow
24. 9	23. 8	B10	G7	Pig
25. 9	24. 8	B10	H8	Porcupine
26. 9	25. 8	B10	J9	Wolf
27. 9	26. 8	B10	K10	Dog
28. 9	27. 8	B10	A11	Pheasant
29. 9	28. 8	B10	B12	Cock
30. 9	29. 8	B10	C1	Crow
1.10	1. 9	C11	D2	Monkey
2.10	2. 9	C11	E3	Gibbon
3.10	3. 9	C11	F4	Tapir
4.10	4. 9	C11	G5	Sheep
5.10	5. 9	C11	H6	Deer
6.10	6. 9	C11	J7	Horse
7.10	7. 9	C11	K8	Stag
8.10	8. 9	C11	A9	Serpent
9.10	9. 9	C11	B10	Earthworm
10.10	10. 9	C11	C11	Crocodile
11.10	11. 9	C11	D12	Dragon
12.10	12. 9	C11	E1	Badger
13.10	13. 9	C11	F2	Hare
14.10	14. 9	C11	G3	Fox
15.10	15. 9	C11	H4	Tiger
16.10	16. 9	C11	J5	Leopard
17.10	17. 9	C11	K6	Griffon
18.10	18. 9	C11	A7	Ox
19.10	19. 9	C11	B8	Bat
20.10	20. 9	C11	C9	Swallow
21.10	21. 9	C11	D10	Swallow
22.10	22. 9	C11	E11	Pig
23.10	23. 9	C11	F12	Porcupine
24.10	24. 9	C11	G1	Wolf
25.10	25. 9	C11	H2	Dog
26.10	26. 9	C11	J3	Pheasant
27.10	27. 9	C11	K4	Cock
28.10	28. 9	C11	A5	Crow
29.10	29. 9	C11	B6	Monkey
30.10	30. 9	C11	C7	Gibbon
31.10	1.10	D12	D8	Tapir
1.11	2.10	D12	E9	Sheep
2.11	3.10	D12	F10	Deer
3.11	4.10	D12	G11	Horse
4.11	5.10	D12	H12	Stag
5.11	6.10	D12	J1	Serpent
6.11	7.10	D12	K2	Earthworm
7.11	8.10	D12	A3	Crocodile
8.11	9.10	D12	B4	Dragon
9.11	10.10	D12	C5	Badger
10.11	11.10	D12	D6	Hare
11.11	12.10	D12	E7	Fox
12.11	13.10	D12	F8	Tiger
13.11	14.10	D12	G9	Leopard
14.11	15.10	D12	H10	Griffon
15.11	16.10	D12	J11	Ox
16.11	17.10	D12	K12	Bat
17.11	18.10	D12	A1	Rat
18.11	19.10	D12	B2	Swallow

Solar date	Lunar date	Month HS/EB	Day HS/EB	Constellation
19.11	20.10	D12	C3	Pig
20.11	21.10	D12	D4	Porcupine
21.11	22.10	D12	E5	Wolf
22.11	23.10	D12	F6	Dog
23.11	24.10	D12	G7	Pheasant
24.11	25.10	D12	H8	Cock
25.11	26.10	D12	J9	Crow
26.11	27.10	D12	K10	Monkey
27.11	28.10	D12	A11	Gibbon
28.11	29.10	D12	B12	Tapir
29.11	1.11	E1	C1	Sheep
30.11	2.11	E1	D2	Deer
1.12	3.11	E1	E3	Horse
2.12	4.11	E1	F4	Stag
3.12	5.11	E1	G5	Serpent
4.12	6.11	E1	H6	Earthworm
5.12	7.11	E1	J7	Crocodile
6.12	8.11	E1	K8	Dragon
7.12	9.11	E1	A9	Badger
8.12	10.11	E1	B10	Hare
9.12	11.11	E1	C11	Fox
10.12	12.11	E1	D12	Tiger
11.12	13.11	E1	E1	Leopard
12.12	14.11	E1	F2	Griffon
13.12	15.11	E1	G3	Ox
14.12	16.11	E1	H4	Bat
15.12	17.11	E1	J5	Rat
16.12	18.11	E1	K6	Swallow
17.12	19.11	E1	A7	Pig
18.12	20.11	E1	B8	Porcupine
19.12	21.11	E1	C9	Wolf
20.12	22.11	E1	D10	Dog
21.12	23.11	E1	E11	Pheasant
22.12	24.11	E1	F12	Cock
23.12	25.11	E1	G1	Crow
24.12	26.11	E1	H2	Monkey
25.12	27.11	E1	J3	Gibbon
26.12	28.11	E1	K4	Tapir
27.12	29.11	E1	A5	Sheep
28.12	30.11	E1	B6	Deer
29.12	1.12	F2	C7	Horse
30.12	2.12	F2	D8	Stag
31.12	3.12	F2	E9	Serpent
1941				
1. 1	4.12	F2	F10	Earthworm
2. 1	5.12	F2	G11	Crocodile
3. 1	6.12	F2	H12	Dragon
4. 1	7.12	F2	J1	Badger
5. 1	8.12	F2	K2	Hare
6. 1	9.12	F2	A3	Fox
7. 1	10.12	F2	B4	Tiger
8. 1	11.12	F2	C5	Leopard
9. 1	12.12	F2	D6	Griffon
10. 1	13.12	F2	E7	Ox
11. 1	14.12	F2	F8	Bat
12. 1	15.12	F2	G9	Rat
13. 1	16.12	F2	H10	Swallow
14. 1	17.12	F2	J11	Pig
15. 1	18.12	F2	K12	Porcupine
16. 1	19.12	F2	A1	Wolf
17. 1	20.12	F2	B2	Dog
18. 1	21.12	F2	C3	Pheasant
19. 1	22.12	F2	D4	Cock
20. 1	23.12	F2	E5	Crow
21. 1	24.12	F2	F6	Monkey
22. 1	25.12	F2	G7	Gibbon
23. 1	26.12	F2	H8	Tapir
24. 1	27.12	F2	J9	Sheep
25. 1	28.12	F2	K10	Deer
26. 1	29.12	F2	A11	Horse

HSIN SZU YEAR

Solar date	Lunar date	Month HS/EB	Day HS/EB	Constellation	Solar date	Lunar date	Month HS/EB	Day HS/EB	Constellation
27. 1	1. 1	G3	B12	Stag	8. 4	12. 3	J5	C11	Pig
28. 1	2. 1	G3	C1	Serpent	9. 4	13. 3	J5	D12	Porcupine
29. 1	3. 1	G3	D2	Earthworm	10. 4	14. 3	J5	E1	Wolf
30. 1	4. 1	G3	E3	Crocodile	11. 4	15. 3	J5	F2	Dog
31. 1	5. 1	G3	F4	Dragon	12. 4	16. 3	J5	G3	Pheasant
1. 2	6. 1	G3	G5	Badger	13. 4	17. 3	J5	H4	Cock
2. 2	7. 1	G3	H6	Hare	14. 4	18. 3	J5	J5	Crow
3. 2	8. 1	G3	J7	Fox	15. 4	19. 3	J5	K6	Monkey
4. 2	9. 1	G3	K8	Tiger	16. 4	20. 3	J5	A7	Gibbon
5. 2	10. 1	G3	A9	Leopard	17. 4	21. 3	J5	B8	Tapir
6. 2	11. 1	G3	B10	Griffon	18. 4	22. 3	J5	C9	Sheep
7. 2	12. 1	G3	C11	Ox	19. 4	23. 3	J5	D10	Deer
8. 2	13. 1	G3	D12	Bat	20. 4	24. 3	J5	E11	Horse
9. 2	14. 1	G3	E1	Rat	21. 4	25. 3	J5	F12	Stag
10. 2	15. 1	G3	F2	Swallow	22. 4	26. 3	J5	G1	Serpent
11. 2	16. 1	G3	G3	Pig	23. 4	27. 3	J5	H2	Earthworm
12. 2	17. 1	G3	H4	Porcupine	24. 4	28. 3	J5	J3	Crocodile
13. 2	18. 1	G3	J5	Wolf	25. 4	29. 3	J5	K4	Dragon
14. 2	19. 1	G3	K6	Dog	26. 4	1. 4	K6	A5	Badger
15. 2	20. 1	G3	A7	Pheasant	27. 4	2. 4	K6	B6	Hare
16. 2	21. 1	G3	B8	Cock	28. 4	3. 4	K6	C7	Fox
17. 2	22. 1	G3	C9	Crow	29. 4	4. 4	K6	D8	Tiger
18. 2	23. 1	G3	D10	Monkey	30. 4	5. 4	K6	E9	Leopard
19. 2	24. 1	G3	E11	Gibbon	1. 5	6. 4	K6	F10	Griffon
20. 2	25. 1	G3	F12	Tapir	2. 5	7. 4	K6	G11	Ox
21. 2	26. 1	G3	G1	Sheep	3. 5	8. 4	K6	H12	Bat
22. 2	27. 1	G3	H2	Deer	4. 5	9. 4	K6	J1	Rat
23. 2	28. 1	G3	J3	Horse	5. 5	10. 4	K6	K2	Swallow
24. 2	29. 1	G3	K4	Stag	6. 5	11. 4	K6	A3	Pig
25. 2	30. 1	G3	A5	Serpent	7. 5	12. 4	K6	B4	Porcupine
26. 2	1. 2	H4	B6	Earthworm	8. 5	13. 4	K6	C5	Wolf
27. 2	2. 2	H4	C7	Crocodile	9. 5	14. 4	K6	D6	Dog
28. 2	3. 2	H4	D8	Dragon	10. 5	15. 4	K6	E7	Pheasant
1. 3	4. 2	H4	E9	Badger	11. 5	16. 4	K6	F8	Cock
2. 3	5. 2	H4	F10	Hare	12. 5	17. 4	K6	G9	Crow
3. 3	6. 2	H4	G11	Fox	13. 5	18. 4	K6	H10	Monkey
4. 3	7. 2	H4	H12	Tiger	14. 5	19. 4	K6	J11	Gibbon
5. 3	8. 2	H4	J1	Leopard	15. 5	20. 4	K6	K12	Tapir
6. 3	9. 2	H4	K2	Griffon	16. 5	21. 4	K6	A1	Sheep
7. 3	10. 2	H4	A3	Ox	17. 5	22. 4	K6	B2	Deer
8. 3	11. 2	H4	B4	Bat	18. 5	23. 4	K6	C3	Horse
9. 3	12. 2	H4	C5	Rat	19. 5	24. 4	K6	D4	Stag
10. 3	13. 2	H4	D6	Swallow	20. 5	25. 4	K6	E5	Serpent
11. 3	14. 2	H4	E7	Pig	21. 5	26. 4	K6	F6	Earthworm
12. 3	15. 2	H4	F8	Porcupine	22. 5	27. 4	K6	G7	Crocodile
13. 3	16. 2	H4	G9	Wolf	23. 5	28. 4	K6	H8	Dragon
14. 3	17. 2	H4	H10	Dog	24. 5	29. 4	K6	J9	Badger
15. 3	18. 2	H4	J11	Pheasant	25. 5	30. 4	K6	K10	Hare
16. 3	19. 2	H4	K12	Cock	26. 5	1. 5	A7	A11	Fox
17. 3	20. 2	H4	A1	Crow	27. 5	2. 5	A7	B12	Tiger
18. 3	21. 2	H4	B2	Monkey	28. 5	3. 5	A7	C1	Leopard
19. 3	22. 2	H4	C3	Gibbon	29. 5	4. 5	A7	D2	Griffon
20. 3	23. 2	H4	D4	Tapir	30. 5	5. 5	A7	E3	Ox
21. 3	24. 2	H4	E5	Sheep	31. 5	6. 5	A7	F4	Bat
22. 3	25. 2	H4	F6	Deer	1. 6	7. 5	A7	G5	Rat
23. 3	26. 2	H4	G7	Horse	2. 6	8. 5	A7	H6	Swallow
24. 3	27. 2	H4	H8	Stag	3. 6	9. 5	A7	J7	Pig
25. 3	28. 2	H4	J9	Serpent	4. 6	10. 5	A7	K8	Porcupine
26. 3	29. 2	H4	K10	Earthworm	5. 6	11. 5	A7	A9	Wolf
27. 3	30. 2	H4	A11	Crocodile	6. 6	12. 5	A7	B10	Dog
28. 3	1. 3	J5	B12	Dragon	7. 6	13. 5	A7	C11	Pheasant
29. 3	2. 3	J5	C1	Badger	8. 6	14. 5	A7	D12	Cock
30. 3	3. 3	J5	D2	Hare	9. 6	15. 5	A7	E1	Crow
31. 3	4. 3	J5	E3	Fox	10. 6	16. 5	A7	F2	Monkey
1. 4	5. 3	J5	F4	Tiger	11. 6	17. 5	A7	G3	Gibbon
2. 4	6. 3	J5	G5	Leopard	12. 6	18. 5	A7	H4	Tapir
3. 4	7. 3	J5	H6	Griffon	13. 6	19. 5	A7	J5	Sheep
4. 4	8. 3	J5	J7	Ox	14. 6	20. 5	A7	K6	Deer
5. 4	9. 3	J5	K8	Bat	15. 6	21. 5	A7	A7	Horse
6. 4	10. 3	J5	A9	Rat	16. 6	22. 5	A7	B8	Stag
7. 4	11. 3	J5	B10	Swallow	17. 6	23. 5	A7	C9	Serpent

Solar date	Lunar date	Month HS/EB	Day HS/EB	Constellation
18. 6	24. 5	A7	D10	Earthworm
19. 6	25. 5	A7	E11	Crocodile
20. 6	26. 5	A7	F12	Dragon
21. 6	27. 5	A7	G1	Badger
22. 6	28. 5	A7	H2	Hare
23. 6	29. 5	A7	J3	Fox
24. 6	30. 5	A7	K4	Tiger
25. 6	1. 6	B8	A5	Leopard
26. 6	2. 6	B8	B6	Griffon
27. 6	3. 6	B8	C7	Ox
28. 6	4. 6	B8	D8	Bat
29. 6	5. 6	B8	E9	Rat
30. 6	6. 6	B8	F10	Swallow
1. 7	7. 6	B8	G11	Pig
2. 7	8. 6	B8	H12	Porcupine
3. 7	9. 6	B8	J1	Wolf
4. 7	10. 6	B8	K2	Dog
5. 7	11. 6	B8	A3	Pheasant
6. 7	12. 6	B8	B4	Cock
7. 7	13. 6	B8	C5	Crow
8. 7	14. 6	B8	D6	Monkey
9. 7	15. 6	B8	E7	Gibbon
10. 7	16. 6	B8	F8	Tapir
11. 7	17. 6	B8	G9	Sheep
12. 7	18. 6	B8	H10	Deer
13. 7	19. 6	B8	J11	Horse
14. 7	20. 6	B8	K12	Stag
15. 7	21. 6	B8	A1	Serpent
16. 7	22. 6	B8	B2	Earthworm
17. 7	23. 6	B8	C3	Crocodile
18. 7	24. 6	B8	D4	Dragon
19. 7	25. 6	B8	E5	Badger
20. 7	26. 6	B8	F6	Hare
21. 7	27. 6	B8	G7	Fox
22. 7	28. 6	B8	H8	Tiger
23. 7	29. 6	B8	J9	Leopard
24. 7	*1. 6*	*B8*	K10	Griffon
25. 7	*2. 6*	*B8*	A11	Ox
26. 7	*3. 6*	*B8*	B12	Bat
27. 7	*4. 6*	*B8*	C1	Rat
28. 7	*5. 6*	*B8*	D2	Swallow
29. 7	*6. 6*	*B8*	E3	Pig
30. 7	*7. 6*	*B8*	F4	Porcupine
31. 7	*8. 6*	*B8*	G5	Wolf
1. 8	*9. 6*	*B8*	H6	Dog
2. 8	*10. 6*	*B8*	J7	Pheasant
3. 8	*11. 6*	*B8*	K8	Cock
4. 8	*12. 6*	*B8*	A9	Crow
5. 8	*13. 6*	*B8*	B10	Monkey
6. 8	*14. 6*	*B8*	C11	Gibbon
7. 8	*15. 6*	*B8*	D12	Tapir
8. 8	*16. 6*	*B8*	E1	Sheep
9. 8	*17. 6*	*B8*	F2	Deer
10. 8	*18. 6*	*B8*	G3	Horse
11. 8	*19. 6*	*B8*	H4	Stag
12. 8	*20. 6*	*B8*	J5	Serpent
13. 8	*21. 6*	*B8*	K6	Earthworm
14. 8	*22. 6*	*B8*	A7	Crocodile
15. 8	*23. 6*	*B8*	B8	Dragon
16. 8	*24. 6*	*B8*	C9	Badger
17. 8	*25. 6*	*B8*	D10	Hare
18. 8	*26. 6*	*B8*	E11	Fox
19. 8	*27. 6*	*B8*	F12	Tiger
20. 8	*28. 6*	*B8*	G1	Leopard
21. 8	*29. 6*	*B8*	H2	Griffon
22. 8	*30. 6*	*B8*	J3	Ox
23. 8	1. 7	C9	K4	Bat
24. 8	2. 7	C9	A5	Rat
25. 8	3. 7	C9	B6	Swallow
26. 8	4. 7	C9	C7	Pig
27. 8	5. 7	C9	D8	Porcupine
28. 8	6. 7	C9	E9	Wolf
29. 8	7. 7	C9	F10	Dog
30. 8	8. 7	C9	G11	Pheasant
31. 8	9. 7	C9	H12	Cock
1. 9	10. 7	C9	J1	Crow
2. 9	11. 7	C9	K2	Monkey
3. 9	12. 7	C9	A3	Gibbon
4. 9	13. 7	C9	B4	Tapir
5. 9	14. 7	C9	C5	Sheep
6. 9	15. 7	C9	D6	Deer
7. 9	16. 7	C9	E7	Horse
8. 9	17. 7	C9	F8	Stag
9. 9	18. 7	C9	G9	Serpent
10. 9	19. 7	C9	H10	Earthworm
11. 9	20. 7	C9	J11	Crocodile
12. 9	21. 7	C9	K12	Dragon
13. 9	22. 7	C9	A1	Badger
14. 9	23. 7	C9	B2	Hare
15. 9	24. 7	C9	C3	Fox
16. 9	25. 7	C9	D4	Tiger
17. 9	26. 7	C9	E5	Leopard
18. 9	27. 7	C9	F6	Griffon
19. 9	28. 7	C9	G7	Ox
20. 9	29. 7	C9	H8	Bat
21. 9	1. 8	D10	J9	Rat
22. 9	2. 8	D10	K10	Swallow
23. 9	3. 8	D10	A11	Pig
24. 9	4. 8	D10	B12	Porcupine
25. 9	5. 8	D10	C1	Wolf
26. 9	6. 8	D10	D2	Dog
27. 9	7. 8	D10	E3	Pheasant
28. 9	8. 8	D10	F4	Cock
29. 9	9. 8	D10	G5	Crow
30. 9	10. 8	D10	H6	Monkey
1.10	11. 8	D10	J7	Gibbon
2.10	12. 8	D10	K8	Tapir
3.10	13. 8	D10	A9	Sheep
4.10	14. 8	D10	B10	Deer
5.10	15. 8	D10	C11	Horse
6.10	16. 8	D10	D12	Stag
7.10	17. 8	D10	E1	Serpent
8.10	18. 8	D10	F2	Earthworm
9.10	19. 8	D10	G3	Crocodile
10.10	20. 8	D10	H4	Dragon
11.10	21. 8	D10	J5	Badger
12.10	22. 8	D10	K6	Hare
13.10	23. 8	D10	A7	Fox
14.10	24. 8	D10	B8	Tiger
15.10	25. 8	D10	C9	Leopard
16.10	26. 8	D10	D10	Griffon
17.10	27. 8	D10	E11	Ox
18.10	28. 8	D10	F12	Bat
19.10	29. 8	D10	G1	Rat
20.10	1. 9	E11	H2	Swallow
21.10	2. 9	E11	J3	Pig
22.10	3. 9	E11	K4	Porcupine
23.10	4. 9	E11	A5	Wolf
24.10	5. 9	E11	B6	Dog
25.10	6. 9	E11	C7	Pheasant
26.10	7. 9	E11	D8	Cock
27.10	8. 9	E11	E9	Crow
28.10	9. 9	E11	F10	Monkey
29.10	10. 9	E11	G11	Gibbon
30.10	11. 9	E11	H12	Tapir
31.10	12. 9	E11	J1	Sheep
1.11	13. 9	E11	K2	Deer
2.11	14. 9	E11	A3	Horse
3.11	15. 9	E11	B4	Stag
4.11	16. 9	E11	C5	Serpent
5.11	17. 9	E11	D6	Earthworm
6.11	18. 9	E11	E7	Crocodile
7.11	19. 9	E11	F8	Dragon
8.11	20. 9	E11	G9	Badger
9.11	21. 9	E11	H10	Hare
10.11	22. 9	E11	J11	Fox

Solar date	Lunar date	Month HS/EB	Day HS/EB	Constellation	Solar date	Lunar date	Month HS/EB	Day HS/EB	Constellation
11.11	23. 9	E11	K12	Tiger	30.12	13.11	G1	J1	Serpent
12.11	24. 9	E11	A1	Leopard	31.12	14.11	G1	K2	Earthworm
13.11	25. 9	E11	B2	Griffon	**1942**				
14.11	26. 9	E11	C3	Ox	1. 1	15.11	G1	A3	Crocodile
15.11	27. 9	E11	D4	Bat	2. 1	16.11	G1	B4	Dragon
16.11	28. 9	E11	E5	Rat	3. 1	17.11	G1	C5	Badger
17.11	29. 9	E11	F6	Swallow	4. 1	18.11	G1	D6	Hare
18.11	30. 9	E11	G7	Pig	5. 1	19.11	G1	E7	Fox
19.11	1.10	F12	H8	Porcupine	6. 1	20.11	G1	F8	Tiger
20.11	2.10	F12	J9	Wolf	7. 1	21.11	G1	G9	Leopard
21.11	3.10	F12	K10	Dog	8. 1	22.11	G1	H10	Griffon
22.11	4.10	F12	A11	Pheasant	9. 1	23.11	G1	J11	Ox
23.11	5.10	F12	B12	Cock	10. 1	24.11	G1	K12	Bat
24.11	6.10	F12	C1	Crow	11. 1	25.11	G1	A1	Rat
25.11	7.10	F12	D2	Monkey	12. 1	26.11	G1	B2	Swallow
26.11	8.10	F12	E3	Gibbon	13. 1	27.11	G1	C3	Pig
27.11	9.10	F12	F4	Tapir	14. 1	28.11	G1	D4	Porcupine
28.11	10.10	F12	G5	Sheep	15. 1	29.11	G1	E5	Wolf
29.11	11.10	F12	H6	Deer	16. 1	30.11	G1	F6	Dog
30.11	12.10	F12	J7	Horse	17. 1	1.12	H2	G7	Pheasant
1.12	13.10	F12	K8	Stag	18. 1	2.12	H2	H8	Cock
2.12	14.10	F12	A9	Serpent	19. 1	3.12	H2	J9	Crow
3.12	15.10	F12	B10	Earthworm	20. 1	4.12	H2	K10	Monkey
4.12	16.10	F12	C11	Crocodile	21. 1	5.12	H2	A11	Gibbon
5.12	17.10	F12	D12	Dragon	22. 1	6.12	H2	B12	Tapir
6.12	18.10	F12	E1	Badger	23. 1	7.12	H2	C1	Sheep
7.12	19.10	F12	F2	Hare	24. 1	8.12	H2	D2	Deer
8.12	20.10	F12	G3	Fox	25. 1	9.12	H2	E3	Horse
9.12	21.10	F12	H4	Tiger	26. 1	10.12	H2	F4	Stag
10.12	22.10	F12	J5	Leopard	27. 1	11.12	H2	G5	Serpent
11.12	23.10	F12	K6	Griffon	28. 1	12.12	H2	H6	Earthworm
12.12	24.10	F12	A7	Ox	29. 1	13.12	H2	J7	Crocodile
13.12	25.10	F12	B8	Bat	30. 1	14.12	H2	K8	Dragon
14.12	26.10	F12	C9	Rat	31. 1	15.12	H2	A9	Badger
15.12	27.10	F12	D10	Swallow	1. 2	16.12	H2	B10	Hare
16.12	28.10	F12	E11	Pig	2. 2	17.12	H2	C11	Fox
17.12	29.10	F12	F12	Porcupine	3. 2	18.12	H2	D12	Tiger
18.12	1.11	G1	G1	Wolf	4. 2	19.12	H2	E1	Leopard
19.12	2.11	G1	H2	Dog	5. 2	20.12	H2	F2	Griffon
20.12	3.11	G1	J3	Pheasant	6. 2	21.12	H2	G3	Ox
21.12	4.11	G1	K4	Cock	7. 2	22.12	H2	H4	Bat
22.12	5.11	G1	A5	Crow	8. 2	23.12	H2	J5	Rat
23.12	6.11	G1	B6	Monkey	9. 2	24.12	H2	K6	Swallow
24.12	7.11	G1	C7	Gibbon	10. 2	25.12	H2	A7	Pig
25.12	8.11	G1	D8	Tapir	11. 2	26.12	H2	B8	Porcupine
26.12	9.11	G1	E9	Sheep	12. 2	27.12	H2	C9	Wolf
27.12	10.11	G1	F10	Deer	13. 2	28.12	H2	D10	Dog
28.12	11.11	G1	G11	Horse	14. 2	29.12	H2	E11	Pheasant
29.12	12.11	G1	H12	Stag					

JEN WU YEAR

Solar date	Lunar date	Month HS/EB	Day HS/EB	Constellation	Solar date	Lunar date	Month HS/EB	Day HS/EB	Constellation
15. 2	1. 1	J3	F12	Cock	6. 3	20. 1	J3	E7	Ox
16. 2	2. 1	J3	G1	Crow	7. 3	21. 1	J3	F8	Bat
17. 2	3. 1	J3	H2	Monkey	8. 3	22. 1	J3	G9	Rat
18. 2	4. 1	J3	J3	Gibbon	9. 3	23. 1	J3	H10	Swallow
19. 2	5. 1	J3	K4	Tapir	10. 3	24. 1	J3	J11	Pig
20. 2	6. 1	J3	A5	Sheep	11. 3	25. 1	J3	K12	Porcupine
21. 2	7. 1	J3	B6	Deer	12. 3	26. 1	J3	A1	Wolf
22. 2	8. 1	J3	C7	Horse	13. 3	27. 1	J3	B2	Dog
23. 2	9. 1	J3	D8	Stag	14. 3	28. 1	J3	C3	Pheasant
24. 2	10. 1	J3	E9	Serpent	15. 3	29. 1	J3	D4	Cock
25. 2	11. 1	J3	F10	Earthworm	16. 3	30. 1	J3	E5	Crow
26. 2	12. 1	J3	G11	Crocodile	17. 3	1. 2	K4	F6	Monkey
27. 2	13. 1	J3	H12	Dragon	18. 3	2. 2	K4	G7	Gibbon
28. 2	14. 1	J3	J1	Badger	19. 3	3. 2	K4	H8	Tapir
1. 3	15. 1	J3	K2	Hare	20. 3	4. 2	K4	J9	Sheep
2. 3	16. 1	J3	A3	Fox	21. 3	5. 2	K4	K10	Deer
3. 3	17. 1	J3	B4	Tiger	22. 3	6. 2	K4	A11	Horse
4. 3	18. 1	J3	C5	Leopard	23. 3	7. 2	K4	B12	Stag
5. 3	19. 1	J3	D6	Griffon	24. 3	8. 2	K4	C1	Serpent

Solar date	Lunar date	Month HS/EB	Day HS/EB	Constellation	Solar date	Lunar date	Month HS/EB	Day HS/EB	Constellation
25. 3	9. 2	K4	D2	Earthworm	6. 6	23. 4	B6	G3	Pheasant
26. 3	10. 2	K4	E3	Crocodile	7. 6	24. 4	B6	H4	Cock
27. 3	11. 2	K4	F4	Dragon	8. 6	25. 4	B6	J5	Crow
28. 3	12. 2	K4	G5	Badger	9. 6	26. 4	B6	K6	Monkey
29. 3	13. 2	K4	H6	Hare	10. 6	27. 4	B6	A7	Gibbon
30. 3	14. 2	K4	J7	Fox	11. 6	28. 4	B6	B8	Tapir
31. 3	15. 2	K4	K8	Tiger	12. 6	29. 4	B6	C9	Sheep
1. 4	16. 2	K4	A9	Leopard	13. 6	30. 4	B6	D10	Deer
2. 4	17. 2	K4	B10	Griffon	14. 6	1. 5	C7	E11	Horse
3. 4	18. 2	K4	C11	Ox	15. 6	2. 5	C7	F12	Stag
4. 4	19. 2	K4	D12	Bat	16. 6	3. 5	C7	G1	Serpent
5. 4	20. 2	K4	E1	Rat	17. 6	4. 5	C7	H2	Earthworm
6. 4	21. 2	K4	F2	Swallow	18. 6	5. 5	C7	J3	Crocodile
7. 4	22. 2	K4	G3	Pig	19. 6	6. 5	C7	K4	Dragon
8. 4	23. 2	K4	H4	Porcupine	20. 6	7. 5	C7	A5	Badger
9. 4	24. 2	K4	J5	Wolf	21. 6	8. 5	C7	B6	Hare
10. 4	25. 2	K4	K6	Dog	22. 6	9. 5	C7	C7	Fox
11. 4	26. 2	K4	A7	Pheasant	23. 6	10. 5	C7	D8	Tiger
12. 4	27. 2	K4	B8	Cock	24. 6	11. 5	C7	E9	Leopard
13. 4	28. 2	K4	C9	Crow	25. 6	12. 5	C7	F10	Griffon
14. 4	29. 2	K4	D10	Monkey	26. 6	13. 5	C7	G11	Ox
15. 4	1. 3	A5	E11	Gibbon	27. 6	14. 5	C7	H12	Bat
16. 4	2. 3	A5	F12	Tapir	28. 6	15. 5	C7	J1	Rat
17. 4	3. 3	A5	G1	Sheep	29. 6	16. 5	C7	K2	Swallow
18. 4	4. 3	A5	H2	Deer	30. 6	17. 5	C7	A3	Pig
19. 4	5. 3	A5	J3	Horse	1. 7	18. 5	C7	B4	Porcupine
20. 4	6. 3	A5	K4	Stag	2. 7	19. 5	C7	C5	Wolf
21. 4	7. 3	A5	A5	Serpent	3. 7	20. 5	C7	D6	Dog
22. 4	8. 3	A5	B6	Earthworm	4. 7	21. 5	C7	E7	Pheasant
23. 4	9. 3	A5	C7	Crocodile	5. 7	22. 5	C7	F8	Cock
24. 4	10. 3	A5	D8	Dragon	6. 7	23. 5	C7	G9	Crow
25. 4	11. 3	A5	E9	Badger	7. 7	24. 5	C7	H10	Monkey
26. 4	12. 3	A5	F10	Hare	8. 7	25. 5	C7	J11	Gibbon
27. 4	13. 3	A5	G11	Fox	9. 7	26. 5	C7	K12	Tapir
28. 4	14. 3	A5	H12	Tiger	10. 7	27. 5	C7	A1	Sheep
29. 4	15. 3	A5	J1	Leopard	11. 7	28. 5	C7	B2	Deer
30. 4	16. 3	A5	K2	Griffon	12. 7	29. 5	C7	C3	Horse
1. 5	17. 3	A5	A3	Ox	13. 7	1. 6	D8	D4	Stag
2. 5	18. 3	A5	B4	Bat	14. 7	2. 6	D8	E5	Serpent
3. 5	19. 3	A5	C5	Rat	15. 7	3. 6	D8	F6	Earthworm
4. 5	20. 3	A5	D6	Swallow	16. 7	4. 6	D8	G7	Crocodile
5. 5	21. 3	A5	E7	Pig	17. 7	5. 6	D8	H8	Dragon
6. 5	22. 3	A5	F8	Porcupine	18. 7	6. 6	D8	J9	Badger
7. 5	23. 3	A5	G9	Wolf	19. 7	7. 6	D8	K10	Hare
8. 5	24. 3	A5	H10	Dog	20. 7	8. 6	D8	A11	Fox
9. 5	25. 3	A5	J11	Pheasant	21. 7	9. 6	D8	B12	Tiger
10. 5	26. 3	A5	K12	Cock	22. 7	10. 6	D8	C1	Leopard
11. 5	27. 3	A5	A1	Crow	23. 7	11. 6	D8	D2	Griffon
12. 5	28. 3	A5	B2	Monkey	24. 7	12. 6	D8	E3	Ox
13. 5	29. 3	A5	C3	Gibbon	25. 7	13. 6	D8	F4	Bat
14. 5	30. 3	A5	D4	Tapir	26. 7	14. 6	D8	G5	Rat
15. 5	1. 4	B6	E5	Sheep	27. 7	15. 6	D8	H6	Swallow
16. 5	2. 4	B6	F6	Deer	28. 7	16. 6	D8	J7	Pig
17. 5	3. 4	B6	G7	Horse	29. 7	17. 6	D8	K8	Porcupine
18. 5	4. 4	B6	H8	Stag	30. 7	18. 6	D8	A9	Wolf
19. 5	5. 4	B6	J9	Serpent	31. 7	19. 6	D8	B10	Dog
20. 5	6. 4	B6	K10	Earthworm	1. 8	20. 6	D8	C11	Pheasant
21. 5	7. 4	B6	A11	Crocodile	2. 8	21. 6	D8	D12	Cock
22. 5	8. 4	B6	B12	Dragon	3. 8	22. 6	D8	E1	Crow
23. 5	9. 4	B6	C1	Badger	4. 8	23. 6	D8	F2	Monkey
24. 5	10. 4	B6	D2	Hare	5. 8	24. 6	D8	G3	Gibbon
25. 5	11. 4	B6	E3	Fox	6. 8	25. 6	D8	H4	Tapir
26. 5	12. 4	B6	F4	Tiger	7. 8	26. 6	D8	J5	Sheep
27. 5	13. 4	B6	G5	Leopard	8. 8	27. 6	D8	K6	Deer
28. 5	14. 4	B6	H6	Griffon	9. 8	28. 6	D8	A7	Horse
29. 5	15. 4	B6	J7	Ox	10. 8	29. 6	D8	B8	Stag
30. 5	16. 4	B6	K8	Bat	11. 8	30. 6	D8	C9	Serpent
31. 5	17. 4	B6	A9	Rat	12. 8	1. 7	E9	D10	Earthworm
1. 6	18. 4	B6	B10	Swallow	13. 8	2. 7	E9	E11	Crocodile
2. 6	19. 4	B6	C11	Pig	14. 8	3. 7	E9	F12	Dragon
3. 6	20. 4	B6	D12	Porcupine	15. 8	4. 7	E9	G1	Badger
4. 6	21. 4	B6	E1	Wolf	16. 8	5. 7	E9	H2	Hare
5. 6	22. 4	B6	F2	Dog	17. 8	6. 7	E9	J3	Fox

Solar date	Lunar date	Month HS/EB	Day HS/EB	Constellation
18. 8	7. 7	E9	K4	Tiger
19. 8	8. 7	E9	A5	Leopard
20. 8	9. 7	E9	B6	Griffon
21. 8	10. 7	E9	C7	Ox
22. 8	11. 7	E9	D8	Bat
23. 8	12. 7	E9	E9	Rat
24. 8	13. 7	E9	F10	Swallow
25. 8	14. 7	E9	G11	Pig
26. 8	15. 7	E9	H12	Porcupine
27. 8	16. 7	E9	J1	Wolf
28. 8	17. 7	E9	K2	Dog
29. 8	18. 7	E9	A3	Pheasant
30. 8	19. 7	E9	B4	Cock
31. 8	20. 7	E9	C5	Crow
1. 9	21. 7	E9	D6	Monkey
2. 9	22. 7	E9	E7	Gibbon
3. 9	23. 7	E9	F8	Tapir
4. 9	24. 7	E9	G9	Sheep
5. 9	25. 7	E9	H10	Deer
6. 9	26. 7	E9	J11	Horse
7. 9	27. 7	E9	K12	Stag
8. 9	28. 7	E9	A1	Serpent
9. 9	29. 7	E9	B2	Earthworm
10. 9	1. 8	F10	C3	Crocodile
11. 9	2. 8	F10	D4	Dragon
12. 9	3. 8	F10	E5	Badger
13. 9	4. 8	F10	F6	Hare
14. 9	5. 8	F10	G7	Fox
15. 9	6. 8	F10	H8	Tiger
16. 9	7. 8	F10	J9	Leopard
17. 9	8. 8	F10	K10	Griffon
18. 9	9. 8	F10	A11	Ox
19. 9	10. 8	F10	B12	Bat
20. 9	11. 8	F10	C1	Rat
21. 9	12. 8	F10	D2	Swallow
22. 9	13. 8	F10	E3	Pig
23. 9	14. 8	F10	F4	Porcupine
24. 9	15. 8	F10	G5	Wolf
25. 9	16. 8	F10	H6	Dog
26. 9	17. 8	F10	J7	Pheasant
27. 9	18. 8	F10	K8	Cock
28. 9	19. 8	F10	A9	Crow
29. 9	20. 8	F10	B10	Monkey
30. 9	21. 8	F10	C11	Gibbon
1.10	22. 8	F10	D12	Tapir
2.10	23. 8	F10	E1	Sheep
3.10	24. 8	F10	F2	Deer
4.10	25. 8	F10	G3	Horse
5.10	26. 8	F10	H4	Stag
6.10	27. 8	F10	J5	Serpent
7.10	28. 8	F10	K6	Earthworm
8.10	29. 8	F10	A7	Crocodile
9.10	30. 8	F10	B8	Dragon
10.10	1. 9	G11	C9	Badger
11.10	2. 9	G11	D10	Hare
12.10	3. 9	G11	E11	Fox
13.10	4. 9	G11	F12	Tiger
14.10	5. 9	G11	G1	Leopard
15.10	6. 9	G11	H2	Griffon
16.10	7. 9	G11	J3	Ox
17.10	8. 9	G11	K4	Bat
18.10	9. 9	G11	A5	Rat
19.10	10. 9	G11	B6	Swallow
20.10	11. 9	G11	C7	Pig
21.10	12. 9	G11	D8	Porcupine
22.10	13. 9	G11	E9	Wolf
23.10	14. 9	G11	F10	Dog
24.10	15. 9	G11	G11	Pheasant
25.10	16. 9	G11	H12	Cock
26.10	17. 9	G11	J1	Crow
27.10	18. 9	G11	K2	Monkey
28.10	19. 9	G11	A3	Gibbon
29.10	20. 9	G11	B4	Tapir
30.10	21. 9	G11	C5	Sheep
31.10	22. 9	G11	D6	Deer
1.11	23. 9	G11	E7	Horse
2.11	24. 9	G11	F8	Stag
3.11	25. 9	G11	G9	Serpent
4.11	26. 9	G11	H10	Earthworm
5.11	27. 9	G11	J11	Crocodile
6.11	28. 9	G11	K12	Dragon
7.11	29. 9	G11	A1	Badger
8.11	1.10	H12	B2	Hare
9.11	2.10	H12	C3	Fox
10.11	3.10	H12	D4	Tiger
11.11	4.10	H12	E5	Leopard
12.11	5.10	H12	F6	Griffon
13.11	6.10	H12	G7	Ox
14.11	7.10	H12	H8	Bat
15.11	8.10	H12	J9	Rat
16.11	9.10	H12	K10	Swallow
17.11	10.10	H12	A11	Pig
18.11	11.10	H12	B12	Porcupine
19.11	12.10	H12	C1	Wolf
20.11	13.10	H12	D2	Dog
21.11	14.10	H12	E3	Pheasant
22.11	15.10	H12	F4	Cock
23.11	16.10	H12	G5	Crow
24.11	17.10	H12	H6	Monkey
25.11	18.10	H12	J7	Gibbon
26.11	19.10	H12	K8	Tapir
27.11	20.10	H12	A9	Sheep
28.11	21.10	H12	B10	Deer
29.11	22.10	H12	C11	Horse
30.11	23.10	H12	D12	Stag
1.12	24.10	H12	E1	Serpent
2.12	25.10	H12	F2	Earthworm
3.12	26.10	H12	G3	Crocodile
4.12	27.10	H12	H4	Dragon
5.12	28.10	H12	J5	Badger
6.12	29.10	H12	K6	Hare
7.12	30.10	H12	A7	Fox
8.12	1.11	J1	B8	Tiger
9.12	2.11	J1	C9	Leopard
10.12	3.11	J1	D10	Griffon
11.12	4.11	J1	E11	Ox
12.12	5.11	J1	F12	Bat
13.12	6.11	J1	G1	Rat
14.12	7.11	J1	H2	Swallow
15.12	8.11	J1	J3	Pig
16.12	9.11	J1	K4	Porcupine
17.12	10.11	J1	A5	Wolf
18.12	11.11	J1	B6	Dog
19.12	12.11	J1	C7	Pheasant
20.12	13.11	J1	D8	Cock
21.12	14.11	J1	E9	Crow
22.12	15.11	J1	F10	Monkey
23.12	16.11	J1	G11	Gibbon
24.12	17.11	J1	H12	Tapir
25.12	18.11	J1	J1	Sheep
26.12	19.11	J1	K2	Deer
27.12	20.11	J1	A3	Horse
28.12	21.11	J1	B4	Stag
29.12	22.11	J1	C5	Serpent
30.12	23.11	J1	D6	Earthworm
31.12	24.11	J1	E7	Crocodile
1943				
1. 1	25.11	J1	F8	Dragon
2. 1	26.11	J1	G9	Badger
3. 1	27.11	J1	H10	Hare
4. 1	28.11	J1	J11	Fox
5. 1	29.11	J1	K12	Tiger
6. 1	1.12	K2	A1	Leopard
7. 1	2.12	K2	B2	Griffon
8. 1	3.12	K2	C3	Ox

Solar date	Lunar date	Month HS/EB	Day HS/EB	Constellation
9. 1	4.12	K2	D4	Bat
10. 1	5.12	K2	E5	Rat
11. 1	6.12	K2	F6	Swallow
12. 1	7.12	K2	G7	Pig
13. 1	8.12	K2	H8	Porcupine
14. 1	9.12	K2	J9	Wolf
15. 1	10.12	K2	K10	Dog
16. 1	11.12	K2	A11	Pheasant
17. 1	12.12	K2	B12	Cock
18. 1	13.12	K2	C1	Crow
19. 1	14.12	K2	D2	Monkey
20. 1	15.12	K2	E3	Gibbon
21. 1	16.12	K2	F4	Tapir
22. 1	17.12	K2	G5	Sheep
23. 1	18.12	K2	H6	Deer
24. 1	19.12	K2	J7	Horse
25. 1	20.12	K2	K8	Stag
26. 1	21.12	K2	A9	Serpent
27. 1	22.12	K2	B10	Earthworm
28. 1	23.12	K2	C11	Crocodile
29. 1	24.12	K2	D12	Dragon
30. 1	25.12	K2	E1	Badger
31. 1	26.12	K2	F2	Hare
1. 2	27.12	K2	G3	Fox
2. 2	28.12	K2	H4	Tiger
3. 2	29.12	K2	J5	Leopard
4. 2	30.12	K2	K6	Griffon

KUEI WEI YEAR

Solar date	Lunar date	Month HS/EB	Day HS/EB	Constellation
5. 2	1. 1	A3	A7	Ox
6. 2	2. 1	A3	B8	Bat
7. 2	3. 1	A3	C9	Rat
8. 2	4. 1	A3	D10	Swallow
9. 2	5. 1	A3	E11	Pig
10. 2	6. 1	A3	F12	Porcupine
11. 2	7. 1	A3	G1	Wolf
12. 2	8. 1	A3	H2	Dog
13. 2	9. 1	A3	J3	Pheasant
14. 2	10. 1	A3	K4	Cock
15. 2	11. 1	A3	A5	Crow
16. 2	12. 1	A3	B6	Monkey
17. 2	13. 1	A3	C7	Gibbon
18. 2	14. 1	A3	D8	Tapir
19. 2	15. 1	A3	E9	Sheep
20. 2	16. 1	A3	F10	Deer
21. 2	17. 1	A3	G11	Horse
22. 2	18. 1	A3	H12	Stag
23. 2	19. 1	A3	J1	Serpent
24. 2	20. 1	A3	K2	Earthworm
25. 2	21. 1	A3	A3	Crocodile
26. 2	22. 1	A3	B4	Dragon
27. 2	23. 1	A3	C5	Badger
28. 2	24. 1	A3	D6	Hare
1. 3	25. 1	A3	E7	Fox
2. 3	26. 1	A3	F8	Tiger
3. 3	27. 1	A3	G9	Leopard
4. 3	28. 1	A3	H10	Griffon
5. 3	29. 1	A3	J11	Ox
6. 3	1. 2	B4	K12	Bat
7. 3	2. 2	B4	A1	Rat
8. 3	3. 2	B4	B2	Swallow
9. 3	4. 2	B4	C3	Pig
10. 3	5. 2	B4	D4	Porcupine
11. 3	6. 2	B4	E5	Wolf
12. 3	7. 2	B4	F6	Dog
13. 3	8. 2	B4	G7	Pheasant
14. 3	9. 2	B4	H8	Cock
15. 3	10. 2	B4	J9	Crow
16. 3	11. 2	B4	K10	Monkey
17. 3	12. 2	B4	A11	Gibbon
18. 3	13. 2	B4	B12	Tapir
19. 3	14. 2	B4	C1	Sheep
20. 3	15. 2	B4	D2	Deer
21. 3	16. 2	B4	E3	Horse
22. 3	17. 2	B4	F4	Stag
23. 3	18. 2	B4	G5	Serpent
24. 3	19. 2	B4	H6	Earthworm
25. 3	20. 2	B4	J7	Crocodile
26. 3	21. 2	B4	K8	Dragon
27. 3	22. 2	B4	A9	Badger
28. 3	23. 2	B4	B10	Hare
29. 3	24. 2	B4	C11	Fox
30. 3	25. 2	B4	D12	Tiger
31. 3	26. 2	B4	E1	Leopard
1. 4	27. 2	B4	F2	Griffon
2. 4	28. 2	B4	G3	Ox
3. 4	29. 2	B4	H4	Bat
4. 4	30. 2	B4	J5	Rat
5. 4	1. 3	C5	K6	Swallow
6. 4	2. 3	C5	A7	Pig
7. 4	3. 3	C5	B8	Porcupine
8. 4	4. 3	C5	C9	Wolf
9. 4	5. 3	C5	D10	Dog
10. 4	6. 3	C5	E11	Pheasant
11. 4	7. 3	C5	F12	Cock
12. 4	8. 3	C5	G1	Crow
13. 4	9. 3	C5	H2	Monkey
14. 4	10. 3	C5	J3	Gibbon
15. 4	11. 3	C5	K4	Tapir
16. 4	12. 3	C5	A5	Sheep
17. 4	13. 3	C5	B6	Deer
18. 4	14. 3	C5	C7	Horse
19. 4	15. 3	C5	D8	Stag
20. 4	16. 3	C5	E9	Serpent
21. 4	17. 3	C5	F10	Earthworm
22. 4	18. 3	C5	G11	Crocodile
23. 4	19. 3	C5	H12	Dragon
24. 4	20. 3	C5	J1	Badger
25. 4	21. 3	C5	K2	Hare
26. 4	22. 3	C5	A3	Fox
27. 4	23. 3	C5	B4	Tiger
28. 4	24. 3	C5	C5	Leopard
29. 4	25. 3	C5	D6	Griffon
30. 4	26. 3	C5	E7	Ox
1. 5	27. 3	C5	F8	Bat
2. 5	28. 3	C5	G9	Rat
3. 5	29. 3	C5	H10	Swallow
4. 5	1. 4	D6	J11	Pig
5. 5	2. 4	D6	K12	Porcupine
6. 5	3. 4	D6	A1	Wolf
7. 5	4. 4	D6	B2	Dog
8. 5	5. 4	D6	C3	Pheasant
9. 5	6. 4	D6	D4	Cock
10. 5	7. 4	D6	E5	Crow
11. 5	8. 4	D6	F6	Monkey
12. 5	9. 4	D6	G7	Gibbon
13. 5	10. 4	D6	H8	Tapir
14. 5	11. 4	D6	J9	Sheep
15. 5	12. 4	D6	K10	Deer
16. 5	13. 4	D6	A11	Horse
17. 5	14. 4	D6	B12	Stag
18. 5	15. 4	D6	C1	Serpent
19. 5	16. 4	D6	D2	Earthworm
20. 5	17. 4	D6	E3	Crocodile
21. 5	18. 4	D6	F4	Dragon
22. 5	19. 4	D6	G5	Badger
23. 5	20. 4	D6	H6	Hare

Solar date	Lunar date	Month HS/EB	Day HS/EB	Constellation	Solar date	Lunar date	Month HS/EB	Day HS/EB	Constellation
24. 5	21. 4	D6	J7	Fox	5. 8	5. 7	G9	B8	Tapir
25. 5	22. 4	D6	K8	Tiger	6. 8	6. 7	G9	C9	Sheep
26. 5	23. 4	D6	A9	Leopard	7. 8	7. 7	G9	D10	Deer
27. 5	24. 4	D6	B10	Griffon	8. 8	8. 7	G9	E11	Horse
28. 5	25. 4	D6	C11	Ox	9. 8	9. 7	G9	F12	Stag
29. 5	26. 4	D6	D12	Bat	10. 8	10. 7	G9	G1	Serpent
30. 5	27. 4	D6	E1	Rat	11. 8	11. 7	G9	H2	Earthworm
31. 5	28. 4	D6	F2	Swallow	12. 8	12. 7	G9	J3	Crocodile
1. 6	29. 4	D6	G3	Pig	13. 8	13. 7	G9	K4	Dragon
2. 6	30. 4	D6	H4	Porcupine	14. 8	14. 7	G9	A5	Badger
3. 6	1. 5	E7	J5	Wolf	15. 8	15. 7	G9	B6	Hare
4. 6	2. 5	E7	K6	Dog	16. 8	16. 7	G9	C7	Fox
5. 6	3. 5	E7	A7	Pheasant	17. 8	17. 7	G9	D8	Tiger
6. 6	4. 5	E7	B8	Cock	18. 8	18. 7	G9	E9	Leopard
7. 6	5. 5	E7	C9	Crow	19. 8	19. 7	G9	F10	Griffon
8. 6	6. 5	E7	D10	Monkey	20. 8	20. 7	G9	G11	Ox
9. 6	7. 5	E7	E11	Gibbon	21. 8	21. 7	G9	H12	Bat
10. 6	8. 5	E7	F12	Tapir	22. 8	22. 7	G9	J1	Rat
11. 6	9. 5	E7	G1	Sheep	23. 8	23. 7	G9	K2	Swallow
12. 6	10. 5	E7	H2	Deer	24. 8	24. 7	G9	A3	Pig
13. 6	11. 5	E7	J3	Horse	25. 8	25. 7	G9	B4	Porcupine
14. 6	12. 5	E7	K4	Stag	26. 8	26. 7	G9	C5	Wolf
15. 6	13. 5	E7	A5	Serpent	27. 8	27. 7	G9	D6	Dog
16. 6	14. 5	E7	B6	Earthworm	28. 8	28. 7	G9	E7	Pheasant
17. 6	15. 5	E7	C7	Crocodile	29. 8	29. 7	G9	F8	Cock
18. 6	16. 5	E7	D8	Dragon	30. 8	30. 7	G9	G9	Crow
19. 6	17. 5	E7	E9	Badger	31. 8	1. 8	H10	H10	Monkey
20. 6	18. 5	E7	F10	Hare	1. 9	2. 8	H10	J11	Gibbon
21. 6	19. 5	E7	G11	Fox	2. 9	3. 8	H10	K12	Tapir
22. 6	20. 5	E7	H12	Tiger	3. 9	4. 8	H10	A1	Sheep
23. 6	21. 5	E7	J1	Leopard	4. 9	5. 8	H10	B2	Deer
24. 6	22. 5	E7	K2	Griffon	5. 9	6. 8	H10	C3	Horse
25. 6	23. 5	E7	A3	Ox	6. 9	7. 8	H10	D4	Stag
26. 6	24. 5	E7	B4	Bat	7. 9	8. 8	H10	E5	Serpent
27. 6	25. 5	E7	C5	Rat	8. 9	9. 8	H10	F6	Earthworm
28. 6	26. 5	E7	D6	Swallow	9. 9	10. 8	H10	G7	Crocodile
29. 6	27. 5	E7	E7	Pig	10. 9	11. 8	H10	H8	Dragon
30. 6	28. 5	E7	F8	Porcupine	11. 9	12. 8	H10	J9	Badger
1. 7	29. 5	E7	G9	Wolf	12. 9	13. 8	H10	K10	Hare
2. 7	1. 6	F8	H10	Dog	13. 9	14. 8	H10	A11	Fox
3. 7	2. 6	F8	J11	Pheasant	14. 9	15. 8	H10	B12	Tiger
4. 7	3. 6	F8	K12	Cock	15. 9	16. 8	H10	C1	Leopard
5. 7	4. 6	F8	A1	Crow	16. 9	17. 8	H10	D2	Griffon
6. 7	5. 6	F8	B2	Monkey	17. 9	18. 8	H10	E3	Ox
7. 7	6. 6	F8	C3	Gibbon	18. 9	19. 8	H10	F4	Bat
8. 7	7. 6	F8	D4	Tapir	19. 9	20. 8	H10	G5	Rat
9. 7	8. 6	F8	E5	Sheep	20. 9	21. 8	H10	H6	Swallow
10. 7	9. 6	F8	F6	Deer	21. 9	22. 8	H10	J7	Pig
11. 7	10. 6	F8	G7	Horse	22. 9	23. 8	H10	K8	Porcupine
12. 7	11. 6	F8	H8	Stag	23. 9	24. 8	H10	A9	Wolf
13. 7	12. 6	F8	J9	Serpent	24. 9	25. 8	H10	B10	Dog
14. 7	13. 6	F8	K10	Earthworm	25. 9	26. 8	H10	C11	Pheasant
15. 7	14. 6	F8	A11	Crocodile	26. 9	27. 8	H10	D12	Cock
16. 7	15. 6	F8	B12	Dragon	27. 9	28. 8	H10	E1	Crow
17. 7	16. 6	F8	C1	Badger	28. 9	29. 8	H10	F2	Monkey
18. 7	17. 6	F8	D2	Hare	29. 9	1. 9	J11	G3	Gibbon
19. 7	18. 6	F8	E3	Fox	30. 9	2. 9	J11	H4	Tapir
20. 7	19. 6	F8	F4	Tiger	1.10	3. 9	J11	J5	Sheep
21. 7	20. 6	F8	G5	Leopard	2.10	4. 9	J11	K6	Deer
22. 7	21. 6	F8	H6	Griffon	3.10	5. 9	J11	A7	Horse
23. 7	22. 6	F8	J7	Ox	4.10	6. 9	J11	B8	Stag
24. 7	23. 6	F8	K8	Bat	5.10	7. 9	J11	C9	Serpent
25. 7	24. 6	F8	A9	Rat	6.10	8. 9	J11	D10	Earthworm
26. 7	25. 6	F8	B10	Swallow	7.10	9. 9	J11	E11	Crocodile
27. 7	26. 6	F8	C11	Pig	8.10	10. 9	J11	F12	Dragon
28. 7	27. 6	F8	D12	Porcupine	9.10	11. 9	J11	G1	Badger
29. 7	28. 6	F8	E1	Wolf	10.10	12. 9	J11	H2	Hare
30. 7	29. 6	F8	F2	Dog	11.10	13. 9	J11	J3	Fox
31. 7	30. 6	F8	G3	Pheasant	12.10	14. 9	J11	K4	Tiger
1. 8	1. 7	G9	H4	Cock	13.10	15. 9	J11	A5	Leopard
2. 8	2. 7	G9	J5	Crow	14.10	16. 9	J11	B6	Griffon
3. 8	3. 7	G9	K6	Monkey	15.10	17. 9	J11	C7	Ox
4. 8	4. 7	G9	A7	Gibbon	16.10	18. 9	J11	D8	Bat

Solar date	Lunar date	Month HS/EB	Day HS/EB	Constellation	Solar date	Lunar date	Month HS/EB	Day HS/EB	Constellation
17.10	19. 9	J11	E9	Rat	7.12	11.11	A1	F12	Tiger
18.10	20. 9	J11	F10	Swallow	8.12	12.11	A1	G1	Leopard
19.10	21. 9	J11	G11	Pig	9.12	13.11	A1	H2	Griffon
20.10	22. 9	J11	H12	Porcupine	10.12	14.11	A1	J3	Ox
21.10	23. 9	J11	J1	Wolf	11.12	15.11	A1	K4	Bat
22.10	24. 9	J11	K2	Dog	12.12	16.11	A1	A5	Rat
23.10	25. 9	J11	A3	Pheasant	13.12	17.11	A1	B6	Swallow
24.10	26. 9	J11	B4	Cock	14.12	18.11	A1	C7	Pig
25.10	27. 9	J11	C5	Crow	15.12	19.11	A1	D8	Porcupine
26.10	28. 9	J11	D6	Monkey	16.12	20.11	A1	E9	Wolf
27.10	29. 9	J11	E7	Gibbon	17.12	21.11	A1	F10	Dog
28.10	30. 9	J11	F8	Tapir	18.12	22.11	A1	G11	Pheasant
29.10	1.10	K12	G9	Sheep	19.12	23.11	A1	H12	Cock
30.10	2.10	K12	H10	Deer	20.12	24.11	A1	J1	Crow
31.10	3.10	K12	J11	Horse	21.12	25.11	A1	K2	Monkey
1.11	4.10	K12	K12	Stag	22.12	26.11	A1	A3	Gibbon
2.11	5.10	K12	A1	Serpent	23.12	27.11	A1	B4	Tapir
3.11	6.10	K12	B2	Earthworm	24.12	28.11	A1	C5	Sheep
4.11	7.10	K12	C3	Crocodile	25.12	29.11	A1	D6	Deer
5.11	8.10	K12	D4	Dragon	26.12	30.11	A1	E7	Horse
6.11	9.10	K12	E5	Badger	27.12	1.12	B2	F8	Stag
7.11	10.10	K12	F6	Hare	28.12	2.12	B2	G9	Serpent
8.11	11.10	K12	G7	Fox	29.12	3.12	B2	H10	Earthworm
9.11	12.10	K12	H8	Tiger	30.12	4.12	B2	J11	Crocodile
10.11	13.10	K12	J9	Leopard	31.12	5.12	B2	K12	Dragon
11.11	14.10	K12	K10	Griffon	**1944**				
12.11	15.10	K12	A11	Ox	1. 1	6.12	B2	A1	Badger
13.11	16.10	K12	B12	Bat	2. 1	7.12	B2	B2	Hare
14.11	17.10	K12	C1	Rat	3. 1	8.12	B2	C3	Fox
15.11	18.10	K12	D2	Swallow	4. 1	9.12	B2	D4	Tiger
16.11	19.10	K12	E3	Pig	5. 1	10.12	B2	E5	Leopard
17.11	20.10	K12	F4	Porcupine	6. 1	11.12	B2	F6	Griffon
18.11	21.10	K12	G5	Wolf	7. 1	12.12	B2	G7	Ox
19.11	22.10	K12	H6	Dog	8. 1	13.12	B2	H8	Bat
20.11	23.10	K12	J7	Pheasant	9. 1	14.12	B2	J9	Rat
21.11	24.10	K12	K8	Cock	10. 1	15.12	B2	K10	Swallow
22.11	25.10	K12	A9	Crow	11. 1	16.12	B2	A11	Pig
23.11	26.10	K12	B10	Monkey	12. 1	17.12	B2	B12	Porcupine
24.11	27.10	K12	C11	Gibbon	13. 1	18.12	B2	C1	Wolf
25.11	28.10	K12	D12	Tapir	14. 1	19.12	B2	D2	Dog
26.11	29.10	K12	E1	Sheep	15. 1	20.12	B2	E3	Pheasant
27.11	1.11	A1	F2	Deer	16. 1	21.12	B2	F4	Cock
28.11	2.11	A1	G3	Horse	17. 1	22.12	B2	G5	Crow
29.11	3.11	A1	H4	Stag	18. 1	23.12	B2	H6	Monkey
30.11	4.11	A1	J5	Serpent	19. 1	24.12	B2	J7	Gibbon
1.12	5.11	A1	K6	Earthworm	20. 1	25.12	B2	K8	Tapir
2.12	6.11	A1	A7	Crocodile	21. 1	26.12	B2	A9	Sheep
3.12	7.11	A1	B8	Dragon	22. 1	27.12	B2	B10	Deer
4.12	8.11	A1	C9	Badger	23. 1	28.12	B2	C11	Horse
5.12	9.11	A1	D10	Hare	24. 1	29.12	B2	D12	Stag
6.12	10.11	A1	E11	Fox					

CHIA SHEN YEAR

Solar date	Lunar date	Month HS/EB	Day HS/EB	Constellation	Solar date	Lunar date	Month HS/EB	Day HS/EB	Constellation
25. 1	1. 1	C3	E1	Serpent	11. 2	18. 1	C3	B6	Dog
26. 1	2. 1	C3	F2	Earthworm	12. 2	19. 1	C3	C7	Pheasant
27. 1	3. 1	C3	G3	Crocodile	13. 2	20. 1	C3	D8	Cock
28. 1	4. 1	C3	H4	Dragon	14. 2	21. 1	C3	E9	Crow
29. 1	5. 1	C3	J5	Badger	15. 2	22. 1	C3	F10	Monkey
30. 1	6. 1	C3	K6	Hare	16. 2	23. 1	C3	G11	Gibbon
31. 1	7. 1	C3	A7	Fox	17. 2	24. 1	C3	H12	Tapir
1. 2	8. 1	C3	B8	Tiger	18. 2	25. 1	C3	J1	Sheep
2. 2	9. 1	C3	C9	Leopard	19. 2	26. 1	C3	K2	Deer
3. 2	10. 1	C3	D10	Griffon	20. 2	27. 1	C3	A3	Horse
4. 2	11. 1	C3	E11	Ox	21. 2	28. 1	C3	B4	Stag
5. 2	12. 1	C3	F12	Bat	22. 2	29. 1	C3	C5	Serpent
6. 2	13. 1	C3	G1	Rat	23. 2	30. 1	C3	D6	Earthworm
7. 2	14. 1	C3	H2	Swallow	24. 2	1. 2	D4	E7	Crocodile
8. 2	15. 1	C3	J3	Pig	25. 2	2. 2	D4	F8	Dragon
9. 2	16. 1	C3	K4	Porcupine	26. 2	3. 2	D4	G9	Badger
10. 2	17. 1	C3	A5	Wolf	27. 2	4. 2	D4	H10	Hare

Solar date	Lunar date	Month HS/EB	Day HS/EB	Constellation	Solar date	Lunar date	Month HS/EB	Day HS/EB	Constellation
28. 2	5. 2	D4	J11	Fox	11. 5	19. 4	F6	B12	Tapir
29. 2	6. 2	D4	K12	Tiger	12. 5	20. 4	F6	C1	Sheep
1. 3	7. 2	D4	A1	Leopard	13. 5	21. 4	F6	D2	Deer
2. 3	8. 2	D4	B2	Griffon	14. 5	22. 4	F6	E3	Horse
3. 3	9. 2	D4	C3	Ox	15. 5	23. 4	F6	F4	Stag
4. 3	10. 2	D4	D4	Bat	16. 5	24. 4	F6	G5	Serpent
5. 3	11. 2	D4	E5	Rat	17. 5	25. 4	F6	H6	Earthworm
6. 3	12. 2	D4	F6	Swallow	18. 5	26. 4	F6	J7	Crocodile
7. 3	13. 2	D4	G7	Pig	19. 5	27. 4	F6	K8	Dragon
8. 3	14. 2	D4	H8	Porcupine	20. 5	28. 4	F6	A9	Badger
9. 3	15. 2	D4	J9	Wolf	21. 5	29. 4	F6	B10	Hare
10. 3	16. 2	D4	K10	Dog	22. 5	1. 4	F6	C11	Fox
11. 3	17. 2	D4	A11	Pheasant	23. 5	2. 4	F6	D12	Tiger
12. 3	18. 2	D4	B12	Cock	24. 5	3. 4	F6	E1	Leopard
13. 3	19. 2	D4	C1	Crow	25. 5	4. 4	F6	F2	Griffon
14. 3	20. 2	D4	D2	Monkey	26. 5	5. 4	F6	G3	Ox
15. 3	21. 2	D4	E3	Gibbon	27. 5	6. 4	F6	H4	Bat
16. 3	22. 2	D4	F4	Tapir	28. 5	7. 4	F6	J5	Rat
17. 3	23. 2	D4	G5	Sheep	29. 5	8. 4	F6	K6	Swallow
18. 3	24. 2	D4	H6	Deer	30. 5	9. 4	F6	A7	Pig
19. 3	25. 2	D4	J7	Horse	31. 5	10. 4	F6	B8	Porcupine
20. 3	26. 2	D4	K8	Stag	1. 6	11. 4	F6	C9	Wolf
21. 3	27. 2	D4	A9	Serpent	2. 6	12. 4	F6	D10	Dog
22. 3	28. 2	D4	B10	Earthworm	3. 6	13. 4	F6	E11	Pheasant
23. 3	29. 2	D4	C11	Crocodile	4. 6	14. 4	F6	F12	Cock
24. 3	1. 3	E5	D12	Dragon	5. 6	15. 4	F6	G1	Crow
25. 3	2. 3	E5	E1	Badger	6. 6	16. 4	F6	H2	Monkey
26. 3	3. 3	E5	F2	Hare	7. 6	17. 4	F6	J3	Gibbon
27. 3	4. 3	E5	G3	Fox	8. 6	18. 4	F6	K4	Tapir
28. 3	5. 3	E5	H4	Tiger	9. 6	19. 4	F6	A5	Sheep
29. 3	6. 3	E5	J5	Leopard	10. 6	20. 4	F6	B6	Deer
30. 3	7. 3	E5	K6	Griffon	11. 6	21. 4	F6	C7	Horse
31. 3	8. 3	E5	A7	Ox	12. 6	22. 4	F6	D8	Stag
1. 4	9. 3	E5	B8	Bat	13. 6	23. 4	F6	E9	Serpent
2. 4	10. 3	E5	C9	Rat	14. 6	24. 4	F6	F10	Earthworm
3. 4	11. 3	E5	D10	Swallow	15. 6	25. 4	F6	G11	Crocodile
4. 4	12. 3	E5	E11	Pig	16. 6	26. 4	F6	H12	Dragon
5. 4	13. 3	E5	F12	Porcupine	17. 6	27. 4	F6	J1	Badger
6. 4	14. 3	E5	G1	Wolf	18. 6	28. 4	F6	K2	Hare
7. 4	15. 3	E5	H2	Dog	19. 6	29. 4	F6	A3	Fox
8. 4	16. 3	E5	J3	Pheasant	20. 6	30. 4	F6	B4	Tiger
9. 4	17. 3	E5	K4	Cock	21. 6	1. 5	G7	C5	Leopard
10. 4	18. 3	E5	A5	Crow	22. 6	2. 5	G7	D6	Griffon
11. 4	19. 3	E5	B6	Monkey	23. 6	3. 5	G7	E7	Ox
12. 4	20. 3	E5	C7	Gibbon	24. 6	4. 5	G7	F8	Bat
13. 4	21. 3	E5	D8	Tapir	25. 6	5. 5	G7	G9	Rat
14. 4	22. 3	E5	E9	Sheep	26. 6	6. 5	G7	H10	Swallow
15. 4	23. 3	E5	F10	Deer	27. 6	7. 5	G7	J11	Pig
16. 4	24. 3	E5	G11	Horse	28. 6	8. 5	G7	K12	Porcupine
17. 4	25. 3	E5	H12	Stag	29. 6	9. 5	G7	A1	Wolf
18. 4	26. 3	E5	J1	Serpent	30. 6	10. 5	G7	B2	Dog
19. 4	27. 3	E5	K2	Earthworm	1. 7	11. 5	G7	C3	Pheasant
20. 4	28. 3	E5	A3	Crocodile	2. 7	12. 5	G7	D4	Cock
21. 4	29. 3	E5	B4	Dragon	3. 7	13. 5	G7	E5	Crow
22. 4	30. 3	E5	C5	Badger	4. 7	14. 5	G7	F6	Monkey
23. 4	1. 4	F6	D6	Hare	5. 7	15. 5	G7	G7	Gibbon
24. 4	2. 4	F6	E7	Fox	6. 7	16. 5	G7	H8	Tapir
25. 4	3. 4	F6	F8	Tiger	7. 7	17. 5	G7	J9	Sheep
26. 4	4. 4	F6	G9	Leopard	8. 7	18. 5	G7	K10	Deer
27. 4	5. 4	F6	H10	Griffon	9. 7	19. 5	G7	A11	Horse
28. 4	6. 4	F6	J11	Ox	10. 7	20. 5	G7	B12	Stag
29. 4	7. 4	F6	K12	Bat	11. 7	21. 5	G7	C1	Serpent
30. 4	8. 4	F6	A1	Rat	12. 7	22. 5	G7	D2	Earthworm
1. 5	9. 4	F6	B2	Swallow	13. 7	23. 5	G7	E3	Crocodile
2. 5	10. 4	F6	C3	Pig	14. 7	24. 5	G7	F4	Dragon
3. 5	11. 4	F6	D4	Porcupine	15. 7	25. 5	G7	G5	Badger
4. 5	12. 4	F6	E5	Wolf	16. 7	26. 5	G7	H6	Hare
5. 5	13. 4	F6	F6	Dog	17. 7	27. 5	G7	J7	Fox
6. 5	14. 4	F6	G7	Pheasant	18. 7	28. 5	G7	K8	Tiger
7. 5	15. 4	F6	H8	Cock	19. 7	29. 5	G7	A9	Leopard
8. 5	16. 4	F6	J9	Crow	20. 7	1. 6	H8	B10	Griffon
9. 5	17. 4	F6	K10	Monkey	21. 7	2. 6	H8	C11	Ox
10. 5	18. 4	F6	A11	Gibbon	22. 7	3. 6	H8	D12	Bat

Solar date	Lunar date	Month HS/EB	Day HS/EB	Constellation
23. 7	4. 6	H8	E1	Rat
24. 7	5. 6	H8	F2	Swallow
25. 7	6. 6	H8	G3	Pig
26. 7	7. 6	H8	H4	Porcupine
27. 7	8. 6	H8	J5	Wolf
28. 7	9. 6	H8	K6	Dog
29. 7	10. 6	H8	A7	Pheasant
30. 7	11. 6	H8	B8	Cock
31. 7	12. 6	H8	C9	Crow
1. 8	13. 6	H8	D10	Monkey
2. 8	14. 6	H8	E11	Gibbon
3. 8	15. 6	H8	F12	Tapir
4. 8	16. 6	H8	G1	Sheep
5. 8	17. 6	H8	H2	Deer
6. 8	18. 6	H8	J3	Horse
7. 8	19. 6	H8	K4	Stag
8. 8	20. 6	H8	A5	Serpent
9. 8	21. 6	H8	B6	Earthworm
10. 8	22. 6	H8	C7	Crocodile
11. 8	23. 6	H8	D8	Dragon
12. 8	24. 6	H8	E9	Badger
13. 8	25. 6	H8	F10	Hare
14. 8	26. 6	H8	G11	Fox
15. 8	27. 6	H8	H12	Tiger
16. 8	28. 6	H8	J1	Leopard
17. 8	29. 6	H8	K2	Griffon
18. 8	30. 6	H8	A3	Ox
19. 8	1. 7	J9	B4	Bat
20. 8	2. 7	J9	C5	Rat
21. 8	3. 7	J9	D6	Swallow
22. 8	4. 7	J9	E7	Pig
23. 8	5. 7	J9	F8	Porcupine
24. 8	6. 7	J9	G9	Wolf
25. 8	7. 7	J9	H10	Dog
26. 8	8. 7	J9	J11	Pheasant
27. 8	9. 7	J9	K12	Cock
28. 8	10. 7	J9	A1	Crow
29. 8	11. 7	J9	B2	Monkey
30. 8	12. 7	J9	C3	Gibbon
31. 8	13. 7	J9	D4	Tapir
1. 9	14. 7	J9	E5	Sheep
2. 9	15. 7	J9	F6	Deer
3. 9	16. 7	J9	G7	Horse
4. 9	17. 7	J9	H8	Stag
5. 9	18. 7	J9	J9	Serpent
6. 9	19. 7	J9	K10	Earthworm
7. 9	20. 7	J9	A11	Crocodile
8. 9	21. 7	J9	B12	Dragon
9. 9	22. 7	J9	C1	Badger
10. 9	23. 7	J9	D2	Hare
11. 9	24. 7	J9	E3	Fox
12. 9	25. 7	J9	F4	Tiger
13. 9	26. 7	J9	G5	Leopard
14. 9	27. 7	J9	H6	Griffon
15. 9	28. 7	J9	J7	Ox
16. 9	29. 7	J9	K8	Bat
17. 9	1. 8	K10	A9	Rat
18. 9	2. 8	K10	B10	Swallow
19. 9	3. 8	K10	C11	Pig
20. 9	4. 8	K10	D12	Porcupine
21. 9	5. 8	K10	E1	Wolf
22. 9	6. 8	K10	F2	Dog
23. 9	7. 8	K10	G3	Pheasant
24. 9	8. 8	K10	H4	Cock
25. 9	9. 8	K10	J5	Crow
26. 9	10. 8	K10	K6	Monkey
27. 9	11. 8	K10	A7	Gibbon
28. 9	12. 8	K10	B8	Tapir
29. 9	13. 8	K10	C9	Sheep
30. 9	14. 8	K10	D10	Deer
1.10	15. 8	K10	E11	Horse
2.10	16. 8	K10	F12	Stag
3.10	17. 8	K10	G1	Serpent

Solar date	Lunar date	Month HS/EB	Day HS/EB	Constellation
4.10	18. 8	K10	H2	Earthworm
5.10	19. 8	K10	J3	Crocodile
6.10	20. 8	K10	K4	Dragon
7.10	21. 8	K10	A5	Badger
8.10	22. 8	K10	B6	Hare
9.10	23. 8	K10	C7	Fox
10.10	24. 8	K10	D8	Tiger
11.10	25. 8	K10	E9	Leopard
12.10	26. 8	K10	F10	Griffon
13.10	27. 8	K10	G11	Ox
14.10	28. 8	K10	H12	Bat
15.10	29. 8	K10	J1	Rat
16.10	30. 8	K10	K2	Swallow
17.10	1. 9	A11	A3	Pig
18.10	2. 9	A11	B4	Porcupine
19.10	3. 9	A11	C5	Wolf
20.10	4. 9	A11	D6	Dog
21.10	5. 9	A11	E7	Pheasant
22.10	6. 9	A11	F8	Cock
23.10	7. 9	A11	G9	Crow
24.10	8. 9	A11	H10	Monkey
25.10	9. 9	A11	J11	Gibbon
26.10	10. 9	A11	K12	Tapir
27.10	11. 9	A11	A1	Sheep
28.10	12. 9	A11	B2	Deer
29.10	13. 9	A11	C3	Horse
30.10	14. 9	A11	D4	Stag
31.10	15. 9	A11	E5	Serpent
1.11	16. 9	A11	F6	Earthworm
2.11	17. 9	A11	G7	Crocodile
3.11	18. 9	A11	H8	Dragon
4.11	19. 9	A11	J9	Badger
5.11	20. 9	A11	K10	Hare
6.11	21. 9	A11	A11	Fox
7.11	22. 9	A11	B12	Tiger
8.11	23. 9	A11	C1	Leopard
9.11	24. 9	A11	D2	Griffon
10.11	25. 9	A11	E3	Ox
11.11	26. 9	A11	F4	Bat
12.11	27. 9	A11	G5	Rat
13.11	28. 9	A11	H6	Swallow
14.11	29. 9	A11	J7	Pig
15.11	30. 9	A11	K8	Porcupine
16.11	1.10	B12	A9	Wolf
17.11	2.10	B12	B10	Dog
18.11	3.10	B12	C11	Pheasant
19.11	4.10	B12	D12	Cock
20.11	5.10	B12	E1	Crow
21.11	6.10	B12	F2	Monkey
22.11	7.10	B12	G3	Gibbon
23.11	8.10	B12	H4	Tapir
24.11	9.10	B12	J5	Sheep
25.11	10.10	B12	K6	Deer
26.11	11.10	B12	A7	Horse
27.11	12.10	B12	B8	Stag
28.11	13.10	B12	C9	Serpent
29.11	14.10	B12	D10	Earthworm
30.11	15.10	B12	E11	Crocodile
1.12	16.10	B12	F12	Dragon
2.12	17.10	B12	G1	Badger
3.12	18.10	B12	H2	Hare
4.12	19.10	B12	J3	Fox
5.12	20.10	B12	K4	Tiger
6.12	21.10	B12	A5	Leopard
7.12	22.10	B12	B6	Griffon
8.12	23.10	B12	C7	Ox
9.12	24.10	B12	D8	Bat
10.12	25.10	B12	E9	Rat
11.12	26.10	B12	F10	Swallow
12.12	27.10	B12	G11	Pig
13.12	28.10	B12	H12	Porcupine
14.12	29.10	B12	J1	Wolf
15.12	1.11	C1	K2	Dog

Solar date	Lunar date	Month HS/EB	Day HS/EB	Constellation	Solar date	Lunar date	Month HS/EB	Day HS/EB	Constellation
16.12	2.11	C1	A3	Pheasant	14. 1	1.12	D2	K8	Cock
17.12	3.11	C1	B4	Cock	15. 1	2.12	D2	A9	Crow
18.12	4.11	C1	C5	Crow	16. 1	3.12	D2	B10	Monkey
19.12	5.11	C1	D6	Monkey	17. 1	4.12	D2	C11	Gibbon
20.12	6.11	C1	E7	Gibbon	18. 1	5.12	D2	D12	Tapir
21.12	7.11	C1	F8	Tapir	19. 1	6.12	D2	E1	Sheep
22.12	8.11	C1	G9	Sheep	20. 1	7.12	D2	F2	Deer
23.12	9.11	C1	H10	Deer	21. 1	8.12	D2	G3	Horse
24.12	10.11	C1	J11	Horse	22. 1	9.12	D2	H4	Stag
25.12	11.11	C1	K12	Stag	23. 1	10.12	D2	J5	Serpent
26.12	12.11	C1	A1	Serpent	24. 1	11.12	D2	K6	Earthworm
27.12	13.11	C1	B2	Earthworm	25. 1	12.12	D2	A7	Crocodile
28.12	14.11	C1	C3	Crocodile	26. 1	13.12	D2	B8	Dragon
29.12	15.11	C1	D4	Dragon	27. 1	14.12	D2	C9	Badger
30.12	16.11	C1	E5	Badger	28. 1	15.12	D2	D10	Hare
31.12	17.11	C1	F6	Hare	29. 1	16.12	D2	E11	Fox
					30. 1	17.12	D2	F12	Tiger
1945					31. 1	18.12	D2	G1	Leopard
1. 1	18.11	C1	G7	Fox	1. 2	19.12	D2	H2	Griffon
2. 1	19.11	C1	H8	Tiger	2. 2	20.12	D2	J3	Ox
3. 1	20.11	C1	J9	Leopard	3. 2	21.12	D2	K4	Bat
4. 1	21.11	C1	K10	Griffon	4. 2	22.12	D2	A5	Rat
5. 1	22.11	C1	A11	Ox	5. 2	23.12	D2	B6	Swallow
6. 1	23.11	C1	B12	Bat	6. 2	24.12	D2	C7	Pig
7. 1	24.11	C1	C1	Rat	7. 2	25.12	D2	D8	Porcupine
8. 1	25.11	C1	D2	Swallow	8. 2	26.12	D2	E9	Wolf
9. 1	26.11	C1	E3	Pig	9. 2	27.12	D2	F10	Dog
10. 1	27.11	C1	F4	Porcupine	10. 2	28.12	D2	G11	Pheasant
11. 1	28.11	C1	G5	Wolf	11. 2	29.12	D2	H12	Cock
12. 1	29.11	C1	H6	Dog	12. 2	30.12	D2	J1	Crow
13. 1	30.11	C1	J7	Pheasant					

YI YU YEAR

Solar date	Lunar date	Month HS/EB	Day HS/EB	Constellation	Solar date	Lunar date	Month HS/EB	Day HS/EB	Constellation
13. 2	1. 1	E3	K2	Monkey	22. 3	9. 2	F4	G3	Crocodile
14. 2	2. 1	E3	A3	Gibbon	23. 3	10. 2	F4	H4	Dragon
15. 2	3. 1	E3	B4	Tapir	24. 3	11. 2	F4	J5	Badger
16. 2	4. 1	E3	C5	Sheep	25. 3	12. 2	F4	K6	Hare
17. 2	5. 1	E3	D6	Deer	26. 3	13. 2	F4	A7	Fox
18. 2	6. 1	E3	E7	Horse	27. 3	14. 2	F4	B8	Tiger
19. 2	7. 1	E3	F8	Stag	28. 3	15. 2	F4	C9	Leopard
20. 2	8. 1	E3	G9	Serpent	29. 3	16. 2	F4	D10	Griffon
21. 2	9. 1	E3	H10	Earthworm	30. 3	17. 2	F4	E11	Ox
22. 2	10. 1	E3	J11	Crocodile	31. 3	18. 2	F4	F12	Bat
23. 2	11. 1	E3	K12	Dragon	1. 4	19. 2	F4	G1	Rat
24. 2	12. 1	E3	A1	Badger	2. 4	20. 2	F4	H2	Swallow
25. 2	13. 1	E3	B2	Hare	3. 4	21. 2	F4	J3	Pig
26. 2	14. 1	E3	C3	Fox	4. 4	22. 2	F4	K4	Porcupine
27. 2	15. 1	E3	D4	Tiger	5. 4	23. 2	F4	A5	Wolf
28. 2	16. 1	E3	E5	Leopard	6. 4	24. 2	F4	B6	Dog
1. 3	17. 1	E3	F6	Griffon	7. 4	25. 2	F4	C7	Pheasant
2. 3	18. 1	E3	G7	Ox	8. 4	26. 2	F4	D8	Cock
3. 3	19. 1	E3	H8	Bat	9. 4	27. 2	F4	E9	Crow
4. 3	20. 1	E3	J9	Rat	10. 4	28. 2	F4	F10	Monkey
5. 3	21. 1	E3	K10	Swallow	11. 4	29. 2	F4	G11	Gibbon
6. 3	22. 1	E3	A11	Pig	12. 4	1. 3	G5	H12	Tapir
7. 3	23. 1	E3	B12	Porcupine	13. 4	2. 3	G5	J1	Sheep
8. 3	24. 1	E3	C1	Wolf	14. 4	3. 3	G5	K2	Deer
9. 3	25. 1	E3	D2	Dog	15. 4	4. 3	G5	A3	Horse
10. 3	26. 1	E3	E3	Pheasant	16. 4	5. 3	G5	B4	Stag
11. 3	27. 1	E3	F4	Cock	17. 4	6. 3	G5	C5	Serpent
12. 3	28. 1	E3	G5	Crow	18. 4	7. 3	G5	D6	Earthworm
13. 3	29. 1	E3	H6	Monkey	19. 4	8. 3	G5	E7	Crocodile
14. 3	1. 2	F4	J7	Gibbon	20. 4	9. 3	G5	F8	Dragon
15. 3	2. 2	F4	K8	Tapir	21. 4	10. 3	G5	G9	Badger
16. 3	3. 2	F4	A9	Sheep	22. 4	11. 3	G5	H10	Hare
17. 3	4. 2	F4	B10	Deer	23. 4	12. 3	G5	J11	Fox
18. 3	5. 2	F4	C11	Horse	24. 4	13. 3	G5	K12	Tiger
19. 3	6. 2	F4	D12	Stag	25. 4	14. 3	G5	A1	Leopard
20. 3	7. 2	F4	E1	Serpent	26. 4	15. 3	G5	B2	Griffon
21. 3	8. 2	F4	F2	Earthworm	27. 4	16. 3	G5	C3	Ox

Solar date	Lunar date	Month HS/EB	Day HS/EB	Constellation	Solar date	Lunar date	Month HS/EB	Day HS/EB	Constellation
28. 4	17. 3	G5	D4	Bat	10. 7	2. 6	K8	G5	Serpent
29. 4	18. 3	G5	E5	Rat	11. 7	3. 6	K8	H6	Earthworm
30. 4	19. 3	G5	F6	Swallow	12. 7	4. 6	K8	J7	Crocodile
1. 5	20. 3	G5	G7	Pig	13. 7	5. 6	K8	K8	Dragon
2. 5	21. 3	G5	H8	Porcupine	14. 7	6. 6	K8	A9	Badger
3. 5	22. 3	G5	J9	Wolf	15. 7	7. 6	K8	B10	Hare
4. 5	23. 3	G5	K10	Dog	16. 7	8. 6	K8	C11	Fox
5. 5	24. 3	G5	A11	Pheasant	17. 7	9. 6	K8	D12	Tiger
6. 5	25. 3	G5	B12	Cock	18. 7	10. 6	K8	E1	Leopard
7. 5	26. 3	G5	C1	Crow	19. 7	11. 6	K8	F2	Griffon
8. 5	27. 3	G5	D2	Monkey	20. 7	12. 6	K8	G3	Ox
9. 5	28. 3	G5	E3	Gibbon	21. 7	13. 6	K8	H4	Bat
10. 5	29. 3	G5	F4	Tapir	22. 7	14. 6	K8	J5	Rat
11. 5	30. 3	G5	G5	Sheep	23. 7	15. 6	K8	K6	Swallow
12. 5	1. 4	H6	H6	Deer	24. 7	16. 6	K8	A7	Pig
13. 5	2. 4	H6	J7	Horse	25. 7	17. 6	K8	B8	Porcupine
14. 5	3. 4	H6	K8	Stag	26. 7	18. 6	K8	C9	Wolf
15. 5	4. 4	H6	A9	Serpent	27. 7	19. 6	K8	D10	Dog
16. 5	5. 4	H6	B10	Earthworm	28. 7	20. 6	K8	E11	Pheasant
17. 5	6. 4	H6	C11	Crocodile	29. 7	21. 6	K8	F12	Cock
18. 5	7. 4	H6	D12	Dragon	30. 7	22. 6	K8	G1	Crow
19. 5	8. 4	H6	E1	Badger	31. 7	23. 6	K8	H2	Monkey
20. 5	9. 4	H6	F2	Hare	1. 8	24. 6	K8	J3	Gibbon
21. 5	10. 4	H6	G3	Fox	2. 8	25. 6	K8	K4	Tapir
22. 5	11. 4	H6	H4	Tiger	3. 8	26. 6	K8	A5	Sheep
23. 5	12. 4	H6	J5	Leopard	4. 8	27. 6	K8	B6	Deer
24. 5	13. 4	H6	K6	Griffon	5. 8	28. 6	K8	C7	Horse
25. 5	14. 4	H6	A7	Ox	6. 8	29. 6	K8	D8	Stag
26. 5	15. 4	H6	B8	Bat	7. 8	30. 6	K8	E9	Serpent
27. 5	16. 4	H6	C9	Rat	8. 8	1. 7	A9	F10	Earthworm
28. 5	17. 4	H6	D10	Swallow	9. 8	2. 7	A9	G11	Crocodile
29. 5	18. 4	H6	E11	Pig	10. 8	3. 7	A9	H12	Dragon
30. 5	19. 4	H6	F12	Porcupine	11. 8	4. 7	A9	J1	Badger
31. 5	20. 4	H6	G1	Wolf	12. 8	5. 7	A9	K2	Hare
1. 6	21. 4	H6	H2	Dog	13. 8	6. 7	A9	A3	Fox
2. 6	22. 4	H6	J3	Pheasant	14. 8	7. 7	A9	B4	Tiger
3. 6	23. 4	H6	K4	Cock	15. 8	8. 7	A9	C5	Leopard
4. 6	24. 4	H6	A5	Crow	16. 8	9. 7	A9	D6	Griffon
5. 6	25. 4	H6	B6	Monkey	17. 8	10. 7	A9	E7	Ox
6. 6	26. 4	H6	C7	Gibbon	18. 8	11. 7	A9	F8	Bat
7. 6	27. 4	H6	D8	Tapir	19. 8	12. 7	A9	G9	Rat
8. 6	28. 4	H6	E9	Sheep	20. 8	13. 7	A9	H10	Swallow
9. 6	29. 4	H6	F10	Deer	21. 8	14. 7	A9	J11	Pig
10. 6	1. 5	J7	G11	Horse	22. 8	15. 7	A9	K12	Porcupine
11. 6	2. 5	J7	H12	Stag	23. 8	16. 7	A9	A1	Wolf
12. 6	3. 5	J7	J1	Serpent	24. 8	17. 7	A9	B2	Dog
13. 6	4. 5	J7	K2	Earthworm	25. 8	18. 7	A9	C3	Pheasant
14. 6	5. 5	J7	A3	Crocodile	26. 8	19. 7	A9	D4	Cock
15. 6	6. 5	J7	B4	Dragon	27. 8	20. 7	A9	E5	Crow
16. 6	7. 5	J7	C5	Badger	28. 8	21. 7	A9	F6	Monkey
17. 6	8. 5	J7	D6	Hare	29. 8	22. 7	A9	G7	Gibbon
18. 6	9. 5	J7	E7	Fox	30. 8	23. 7	A9	H8	Tapir
19. 6	10. 5	J7	F8	Tiger	31. 8	24. 7	A9	J9	Sheep
20. 6	11. 5	J7	G9	Leopard	1. 9	25. 7	A9	K10	Deer
21. 6	12. 5	J7	H10	Griffon	2. 9	26. 7	A9	A11	Horse
22. 6	13. 5	J7	J11	Ox	3. 9	27. 7	A9	B12	Stag
23. 6	14. 5	J7	K12	Bat	4. 9	28. 7	A9	C1	Serpent
24. 6	15. 5	J7	A1	Rat	5. 9	29. 7	A9	D2	Earthworm
25. 6	16. 5	J7	B2	Swallow	6. 9	1. 8	B10	E3	Crocodile
26. 6	17. 5	J7	C3	Pig	7. 9	2. 8	B10	F4	Dragon
27. 6	18. 5	J7	D4	Porcupine	8. 9	3. 8	B10	G5	Badger
28. 6	19. 5	J7	E5	Wolf	9. 9	4. 8	B10	H6	Hare
29. 6	20. 5	J7	F6	Dog	10. 9	5. 8	B10	J7	Fox
30. 6	21. 5	J7	G7	Pheasant	11. 9	6. 8	B10	K8	Tiger
1. 7	22. 5	J7	H8	Cock	12. 9	7. 8	B10	A9	Leopard
2. 7	23. 5	J7	J9	Crow	13. 9	8. 8	B10	B10	Griffon
3. 7	24. 5	J7	K10	Monkey	14. 9	9. 8	B10	C11	Ox
4. 7	25. 5	J7	A11	Gibbon	15. 9	10. 8	B10	D12	Bat
5. 7	26. 5	J7	B12	Tapir	16. 9	11. 8	B10	E1	Rat
6. 7	27. 5	J7	C1	Sheep	17. 9	12. 8	B10	F2	Swallow
7. 7	28. 5	J7	D2	Deer	18. 9	13. 8	B10	G3	Pig
8. 7	29. 5	J7	E3	Horse	19. 9	14. 8	B10	H4	Porcupine
9. 7	1. 6	K8	F4	Stag	20. 9	15. 8	B10	J5	Wolf

Solar date	Lunar date	Month HS/EB	Day HS/EB	Constellation	Solar date	Lunar date	Month HS/EB	Day HS/EB	Constellation
21. 9	16. 8	B10	K6	Dog	28.11	24.10	D12	H2	Earthworm
22. 9	17. 8	B10	A7	Pheasant	29.11	25.10	D12	J3	Crocodile
23. 9	18. 8	B10	B8	Cock	30.11	26.10	D12	K4	Dragon
24. 9	19. 8	B10	C9	Crow	1.12	27.10	D12	A5	Badger
25. 9	20. 8	B10	D10	Monkey	2.12	28.10	D12	B6	Hare
26. 9	21. 8	B10	E11	Gibbon	3.12	29.10	D12	C7	Fox
27. 9	22. 8	B10	F12	Tapir	4.12	30.10	D12	D8	Tiger
28. 9	23. 8	B10	G1	Sheep	5.12	1.11	E1	E9	Leopard
29. 9	24. 8	B10	H2	Deer	6.12	2.11	E1	F10	Griffon
30. 9	25. 8	B10	J3	Horse	7.12	3.11	E1	G11	Ox
1.10	26. 8	B10	K4	Stag	8.12	4.11	E1	H12	Bat
2.10	27. 8	B10	A5	Serpent	9.12	5.11	E1	J1	Rat
3.10	28. 8	B10	B6	Earthworm	10.12	6.11	E1	K2	Swallow
4.10	29. 8	B10	C7	Crocodile	11.12	7.11	E1	A3	Pig
5.10	30. 8	B10	D8	Dragon	12.12	8.11	E1	B4	Porcupine
6.10	1. 9	C11	E9	Badger	13.12	9.11	E1	C5	Wolf
7.10	2. 9	C11	F10	Hare	14.12	10.11	E1	D6	Dog
8.10	3. 9	C11	G11	Fox	15.12	11.11	E1	E7	Pheasant
9.10	4. 9	C11	H12	Tiger	16.12	12.11	E1	F8	Cock
10.10	5. 9	C11	J1	Leopard	17.12	13.11	E1	G9	Crow
11.10	6. 9	C11	K2	Griffon	18.12	14.11	E1	H10	Monkey
12.10	7. 9	C11	A3	Ox	19.12	15.11	E1	J11	Gibbon
13.10	8. 9	C11	B4	Bat	20.12	16.11	E1	K12	Tapir
14.10	9. 9	C11	C5	Rat	21.12	17.11	E1	A1	Sheep
15.10	10. 9	C11	D6	Swallow	22.12	18.11	E1	B2	Deer
16.10	11. 9	C11	E7	Pig	23.12	19.11	E1	C3	Horse
17.10	12. 9	C11	F8	Porcupine	24.12	20.11	E1	D4	Stag
18.10	13. 9	C11	G9	Wolf	25.12	21.11	E1	E5	Serpent
19.10	14. 9	C11	H10	Dog	26.12	22.11	E1	F6	Earthworm
20.10	15. 9	C11	J11	Pheasant	27.12	23.11	E1	G7	Crocodile
21.10	16. 9	C11	K12	Cock	28.12	24.11	E1	H8	Dragon
22.10	17. 9	C11	A1	Crow	29.12	25.11	E1	J9	Badger
23.10	18. 9	C11	B2	Monkey	30.12	26.11	E1	K10	Hare
24.10	19. 9	C11	C3	Gibbon	31.12	27.11	E1	A11	Fox
25.10	20. 9	C11	D4	Tapir	**1946**				
26.10	21. 9	C11	E5	Sheep	1. 1	28.11	E1	B12	Tiger
27.10	22. 9	C11	F6	Deer	2. 1	29.11	E1	C1	Leopard
28.10	23. 9	C11	G7	Horse	3. 1	1.12	F2	D2	Griffon
29.10	24. 9	C11	H8	Stag	4. 1	2.12	F2	E3	Ox
30.10	25. 9	C11	J9	Serpent	5. 1	3.12	F2	F4	Bat
31.10	26. 9	C11	K10	Earthworm	6. 1	4.12	F2	G5	Rat
1.11	27. 9	C11	A11	Crocodile	7. 1	5.12	F2	H6	Swallow
2.11	28. 9	C11	B12	Dragon	8. 1	6.12	F2	J7	Pig
3.11	29. 9	C11	C1	Badger	9. 1	7.12	F2	K8	Porcupine
4.11	30. 9	C11	D2	Hare	10. 1	8.12	F2	A9	Wolf
5.11	1.10	D12	E3	Fox	11. 1	9.12	F2	B10	Dog
6.11	2.10	D12	F4	Tiger	12. 1	10.12	F2	C11	Pheasant
7.11	3.10	D12	G5	Leopard	13. 1	11.12	F2	D12	Cock
8.11	4.10	D12	H6	Griffon	14. 1	12.12	F2	E1	Crow
9.11	5.10	D12	J7	Ox	15. 1	13.12	F2	F2	Monkey
10.11	6.10	D12	K8	Bat	16. 1	14.12	F2	G3	Gibbon
11.11	7.10	D12	A9	Rat	17. 1	15.12	F2	H4	Tapir
12.11	8.10	D12	B10	Swallow	18. 1	16.12	F2	J5	Sheep
13.11	9.10	D12	C11	Pig	19. 1	17.12	F2	K6	Deer
14.11	10.10	D12	D12	Porcupine	20. 1	18.12	F2	A7	Horse
15.11	11.10	D12	E1	Wolf	21. 1	19.12	F2	B8	Stag
16.11	12.10	D12	F2	Dog	22. 1	20.12	F2	C9	Serpent
17.11	13.10	D12	G3	Pheasant	23. 1	21.12	F2	D10	Earthworm
18.11	14.10	D12	H4	Cock	24. 1	22.12	F2	E11	Crocodile
19.11	15.10	D12	J5	Crow	25. 1	23.12	F2	F12	Dragon
20.11	16.10	D12	K6	Monkey	26. 1	24.12	F2	G1	Badger
21.11	17.10	D12	A7	Gibbon	27. 1	25.12	F2	H2	Hare
22.11	18.10	D12	B8	Tapir	28. 1	26.12	F2	J3	Fox
23.11	19.10	D12	C9	Sheep	29. 1	27.12	F2	K4	Tiger
24.11	20.10	D12	D10	Deer	30. 1	28.12	F2	A5	Leopard
25.11	21.10	D12	E11	Horse	31. 1	29.12	F2	B6	Griffon
26.11	22.10	D12	F12	Stag	1. 2	30.12	F2	C7	Ox
27.11	23.10	D12	G1	Serpent					

PING HSÜ YEAR

Solar date	Lunar date	Month HS/EB	Day HS/EB	Constellation	Solar date	Lunar date	Month HS/EB	Day HS/EB	Constellation
2. 2	1. 1	G3	D8	Bat	14. 4	13. 3	J5	E7	Horse
3. 2	2. 1	G3	E9	Rat	15. 4	14. 3	J5	F8	Stag
4. 2	3. 1	G3	F10	Swallow	16. 4	15. 3	J5	G9	Serpent
5. 2	4. 1	G3	G11	Pig	17. 4	16. 3	J5	H10	Earthworm
6. 2	5. 1	G3	H12	Porcupine	18. 4	17. 3	J5	J11	Crocodile
7. 2	6. 1	G3	J1	Wolf	19. 4	18. 3	J5	K12	Dragon
8. 2	7. 1	G3	K2	Dog	20. 4	19. 3	J5	A1	Badger
9. 2	8. 1	G3	A3	Pheasant	21. 4	20. 3	J5	B2	Hare
10. 2	9. 1	G3	B4	Cock	22. 4	21. 3	J5	C3	Fox
11. 2	10. 1	G3	C5	Crow	23. 4	22. 3	J5	D4	Tiger
12. 2	11. 1	G3	D6	Monkey	24. 4	23. 3	J5	E5	Leopard
13. 2	12. 1	G3	E7	Gibbon	25. 4	24. 3	J5	F6	Griffon
14. 2	13. 1	G3	F8	Tapir	26. 4	25. 3	J5	G7	Ox
15. 2	14. 1	G3	G9	Sheep	27. 4	26. 3	J5	H8	Bat
16. 2	15. 1	G3	H10	Deer	28. 4	27. 3	J5	J9	Rat
17. 2	16. 1	G3	J11	Horse	29. 4	28. 3	J5	K10	Swallow
18. 2	17. 1	G3	K12	Stag	30. 4	29. 3	J5	A11	Pig
19. 2	18. 1	G3	A1	Serpent	1. 5	1. 4	K6	B12	Porcupine
20. 2	19. 1	G3	B2	Earthworm	2. 5	2. 4	K6	C1	Wolf
21. 2	20. 1	G3	C3	Crocodile	3. 5	3. 4	K6	D2	Dog
22. 2	21. 1	G3	D4	Dragon	4. 5	4. 4	K6	E3	Pheasant
23. 2	22. 1	G3	E5	Badger	5. 5	5. 4	K6	F4	Cock
24. 2	23. 1	G3	F6	Hare	6. 5	6. 4	K6	G5	Crow
25. 2	24. 1	G3	G7	Fox	7. 5	7. 4	K6	H6	Monkey
26. 2	25. 1	G3	H8	Tiger	8. 5	8. 4	K6	J7	Gibbon
27. 2	26. 1	G3	J9	Leopard	9. 5	9. 4	K6	K8	Tapir
28. 2	27. 1	G3	K10	Griffon	10. 5	10. 4	K6	A9	Sheep
1. 3	28. 1	G3	A11	Ox	11. 5	11. 4	K6	B10	Deer
2. 3	29. 1	G3	B12	Bat	12. 5	12. 4	K6	C11	Horse
3. 3	30. 1	G3	C1	Rat	13. 5	13. 4	K6	D12	Stag
4. 3	1. 2	H4	D2	Swallow	14. 5	14. 4	K6	E1	Serpent
5. 3	2. 2	H4	E3	Pig	15. 5	15. 4	K6	F2	Earthworm
6. 3	3. 2	H4	F4	Porcupine	16. 5	16. 4	K6	G3	Crocodile
7. 3	4. 2	H4	G5	Wolf	17. 5	17. 4	K6	H4	Dragon
8. 3	5. 2	H4	H6	Dog	18. 5	18. 4	K6	J5	Badger
9. 3	6. 2	H4	J7	Pheasant	19. 5	19. 4	K6	K6	Hare
10. 3	7. 2	H4	K8	Cock	20. 5	20. 4	K6	A7	Fox
11. 3	8. 2	H4	A9	Crow	21. 5	21. 4	K6	B8	Tiger
12. 3	9. 2	H4	B10	Monkey	22. 5	22. 4	K6	C9	Leopard
13. 3	10. 2	H4	C11	Gibbon	23. 5	23. 4	K6	D10	Griffon
14. 3	11. 2	H4	D12	Tapir	24. 5	24. 4	K6	E11	Ox
15. 3	12. 2	H4	E1	Sheep	25. 5	25. 4	K6	F12	Bat
16. 3	13. 2	H4	F2	Deer	26. 5	26. 4	K6	G1	Rat
17. 3	14. 2	H4	G3	Horse	27. 5	27. 4	K6	H2	Swallow
18. 3	15. 2	H4	H4	Stag	28. 5	28. 4	K6	J3	Pig
19. 3	16. 2	H4	J5	Serpent	29. 5	29. 4	K6	K4	Porcupine
20. 3	17. 2	H4	K6	Earthworm	30. 5	30. 4	K6	A5	Wolf
21. 3	18. 2	H4	A7	Crocodile	31. 5	1. 5	A7	B6	Dog
22. 3	19. 2	H4	B8	Dragon	1. 6	2. 5	A7	C7	Pheasant
23. 3	20. 2	H4	C9	Badger	2. 6	3. 5	A7	D8	Cock
24. 3	21. 2	H4	D10	Hare	3. 6	4. 5	A7	E9	Crow
25. 3	22. 2	H4	E11	Fox	4. 6	5. 5	A7	F10	Monkey
26. 3	23. 2	H4	F12	Tiger	5. 6	6. 5	A7	G11	Gibbon
27. 3	24. 2	H4	G1	Leopard	6. 6	7. 5	A7	H12	Tapir
28. 3	25. 2	H4	H2	Griffon	7. 6	8. 5	A7	J1	Sheep
29. 3	26. 2	H4	J3	Ox	8. 6	9. 5	A7	K2	Deer
30. 3	27. 2	H4	K4	Bat	9. 6	10. 5	A7	A3	Horse
31. 3	28. 2	H4	A5	Rat	10. 6	11. 5	A7	B4	Stag
1. 4	29. 2	H4	B6	Swallow	11. 6	12. 5	A7	C5	Serpent
2. 4	1. 3	J5	C7	Pig	12. 6	13. 5	A7	D6	Earthworm
3. 4	2. 3	J5	D8	Porcupine	13. 6	14. 5	A7	E7	Crocodile
4. 4	3. 3	J5	E9	Wolf	14. 6	15. 5	A7	F8	Dragon
5. 4	4. 3	J5	F10	Dog	15. 6	16. 5	A7	G9	Badger
6. 4	5. 3	J5	G11	Pheasant	16. 6	17. 5	A7	H10	Hare
7. 4	6. 3	J5	H12	Cock	17. 6	18. 5	A7	J11	Fox
8. 4	7. 3	J5	J1	Crow	18. 6	19. 5	A7	K12	Tiger
9. 4	8. 3	J5	K2	Monkey	19. 6	20. 5	A7	A1	Leopard
10. 4	9. 3	J5	A3	Gibbon	20. 6	21. 5	A7	B2	Griffon
11. 4	10. 3	J5	B4	Tapir	21. 6	22. 5	A7	C3	Ox
12. 4	11. 3	J5	C5	Sheep	22. 6	23. 5	A7	D4	Bat
13. 4	12. 3	J5	D6	Deer	23. 6	24. 5	A7	E5	Rat

Solar date	Lunar date	Month HS/EB	Day HS/EB	Constellation	Solar date	Lunar date	Month HS/EB	Day HS/EB	Constellation
24. 6	25. 5	A7	F6	Swallow	5. 9	10. 8	D10	J7	Crocodile
25. 6	26. 5	A7	G7	Pig	6. 9	11. 8	D10	K8	Dragon
26. 6	27. 5	A7	H8	Porcupine	7. 9	12. 8	D10	A9	Badger
27. 6	28. 5	A7	J9	Wolf	8. 9	13. 8	D10	B10	Hare
28. 6	29. 5	A7	K10	Dog	9. 9	14. 8	D10	C11	Fox
29. 6	1. 6	B8	A11	Pheasant	10. 9	15. 8	D10	D12	Tiger
30. 6	2. 6	B8	B12	Cock	11. 9	16. 8	D10	E1	Leopard
1. 7	3. 6	B8	C1	Crow	12. 9	17. 8	D10	F2	Griffon
2. 7	4. 6	B8	D2	Monkey	13. 9	18. 8	D10	G3	Ox
3. 7	5. 6	B8	E3	Gibbon	14. 9	19. 8	D10	H4	Bat
4. 7	6. 6	B8	F4	Tapir	15. 9	20. 8	D10	J5	Rat
5. 7	7. 6	B8	G5	Sheep	16. 9	21. 8	D10	K6	Swallow
6. 7	8. 6	B8	H6	Deer	17. 9	22. 8	D10	A7	Pig
7. 7	9. 6	B8	J7	Horse	18. 9	23. 8	D10	B8	Porcupine
8. 7	10. 6	B8	K8	Stag	19. 9	24. 8	D10	C9	Wolf
9. 7	11. 6	B8	A9	Serpent	20. 9	25. 8	D10	D10	Dog
10. 7	12. 6	B8	B10	Earthworm	21. 9	26. 8	D10	E11	Pheasant
11. 7	13. 6	B8	C11	Crocodile	22. 9	27. 8	D10	F12	Cock
12. 7	14. 6	B8	D12	Dragon	23. 9	28. 8	D10	G1	Crow
13. 7	15. 6	B8	E1	Badger	24. 9	29. 8	D10	H2	Monkey
14. 7	16. 6	B8	F2	Hare	25. 9	1. 9	E11	J3	Gibbon
15. 7	17. 6	B8	G3	Fox	26. 9	2. 9	E11	K4	Tapir
16. 7	18. 6	B8	H4	Tiger	27. 9	3. 9	E11	A5	Sheep
17. 7	19. 6	B8	J5	Leopard	28. 9	4. 9	E11	B6	Deer
18. 7	20. 6	B8	K6	Griffon	29. 9	5. 9	E11	C7	Horse
19. 7	21. 6	B8	A7	Ox	30. 9	6. 9	E11	D8	Stag
20. 7	22. 6	B8	B8	Bat	1.10	7. 9	E11	E9	Serpent
21. 7	23. 6	B8	C9	Rat	2.10	8. 9	E11	F10	Earthworm
22. 7	24. 6	B8	D10	Swallow	3.10	9. 9	E11	G11	Crocodile
23. 7	25. 6	B8	E11	Pig	4.10	10. 9	E11	H12	Dragon
24. 7	26. 6	B8	F12	Porcupine	5.10	11. 9	E11	J1	Badger
25. 7	27. 6	B8	G1	Wolf	6.10	12. 9	E11	K2	Hare
26. 7	28. 6	B8	H2	Dog	7.10	13. 9	E11	A3	Fox
27. 7	29. 6	B8	J3	Pheasant	8.10	14. 9	E11	B4	Tiger
28. 7	1. 7	C9	K4	Cock	9.10	15. 9	E11	C5	Leopard
29. 7	2. 7	C9	A5	Crow	10.10	16. 9	E11	D6	Griffon
30. 7	3. 7	C9	B6	Monkey	11.10	17. 9	E11	E7	Ox
31. 7	4. 7	C9	C7	Gibbon	12.10	18. 9	E11	F8	Bat
1. 8	5. 7	C9	D8	Tapir	13.10	19. 9	E11	G9	Rat
2. 8	6. 7	C9	E9	Sheep	14.10	20. 9	E11	H10	Swallow
3. 8	7. 7	C9	F10	Deer	15.10	21. 9	E11	J11	Pig
4. 8	8. 7	C9	G11	Horse	16.10	22. 9	E11	K12	Porcupine
5. 8	9. 7	C9	H12	Stag	17.10	23. 9	E11	A1	Wolf
6. 8	10. 7	C9	J1	Serpent	18.10	24. 9	E11	B2	Dog
7. 8	11. 7	C9	K2	Earthworm	19.10	25. 9	E11	C3	Pheasant
8. 8	12. 7	C9	A3	Crocodile	20.10	26. 9	E11	D4	Cock
9. 8	13. 7	C9	B4	Dragon	21.10	27. 9	E11	E5	Crow
10. 8	14. 7	C9	C5	Badger	22.10	28. 9	E11	F6	Monkey
11. 8	15. 7	C9	D6	Hare	23.10	29. 9	E11	G7	Gibbon
12. 8	16. 7	C9	E7	Fox	24.10	30. 9	E11	H8	Tapir
13. 8	17. 7	C9	F8	Tiger	25.10	1.10	F12	J9	Sheep
14. 8	18. 7	C9	G9	Leopard	26.10	2.10	F12	K10	Deer
15. 8	19. 7	C9	H10	Griffon	27.10	3.10	F12	A11	Horse
16. 8	20. 7	C9	J11	Ox	28.10	4.10	F12	B12	Stag
17. 8	21. 7	C9	K12	Bat	29.10	5.10	F12	C1	Serpent
18. 8	22. 7	C9	A1	Rat	30.10	6.10	F12	D2	Earthworm
19. 8	23. 7	C9	B2	Swallow	31.10	7.10	F12	E3	Crocodile
20. 8	24. 7	C9	C3	Pig	1.11	8.10	F12	F4	Dragon
21. 8	25. 7	C9	D4	Porcupine	2.11	9.10	F12	G5	Badger
22. 8	26. 7	C9	E5	Wolf	3.11	10.10	F12	H6	Hare
23. 8	27. 7	C9	F6	Dog	4.11	11.10	F12	J7	Fox
24. 8	28. 7	C9	G7	Pheasant	5.11	12.10	F12	K8	Tiger
25. 8	29. 7	C9	H8	Cock	6.11	13.10	F12	A9	Leopard
26. 8	30. 7	C9	J9	Crow	7.11	14.10	F12	B10	Griffon
27. 8	1. 8	D10	K10	Monkey	8.11	15.10	F12	C11	Ox
28. 8	2. 8	D10	A11	Gibbon	9.11	16.10	F12	D12	Bat
29. 8	3. 8	D10	B12	Tapir	10.11	17.10	F12	E1	Rat
30. 8	4. 8	D10	C1	Sheep	11.11	18.10	F12	F2	Swallow
31. 8	5. 8	D10	D2	Deer	12.11	19.10	F12	G3	Pig
1. 9	6. 8	D10	E3	Horse	13.11	20.10	F12	H4	Porcupine
2. 9	7. 8	D10	F4	Stag	14.11	21.10	F12	J5	Wolf
3. 9	8. 8	D10	G5	Serpent	15.11	22.10	F12	K6	Dog
4. 9	9. 8	D10	H6	Earthworm	16.11	23.10	F12	A7	Pheasant

Solar date	Lunar date	Month HS/EB	Day HS/EB	Constellation
17.11	24.10	F12	B8	Cock
18.11	25.10	F12	C9	Crow
19.11	26.10	F12	D10	Monkey
20.11	27.10	F12	E11	Gibbon
21.11	28.10	F12	F12	Tapir
22.11	29.10	F12	G1	Sheep
23.11	30.10	F12	H2	Deer
24.11	1.11	G1	J3	Horse
25.11	2.11	G1	K4	Stag
26.11	3.11	G1	A5	Serpent
27.11	4.11	G1	B6	Earthworm
28.11	5.11	G1	C7	Crocodile
29.11	6.11	G1	D8	Dragon
30.11	7.11	G1	E9	Badger
1.12	8.11	G1	F10	Hare
2.12	9.11	G1	G11	Fox
3.12	10.11	G1	H12	Tiger
4.12	11.11	G1	J1	Leopard
5.12	12.11	G1	K2	Griffon
6.12	13.11	G1	A3	Ox
7.12	14.11	G1	B4	Bat
8.12	15.11	G1	C5	Rat
9.12	16.11	G1	D6	Swallow
10.12	17.11	G1	E7	Pig
11.12	18.11	G1	F8	Porcupine
12.12	19.11	G1	G9	Wolf
13.12	20.11	G1	H10	Dog
14.12	21.11	G1	J11	Pheasant
15.12	22.11	G1	K12	Cock
16.12	23.11	G1	A1	Crow
17.12	24.11	G1	B2	Monkey
18.12	25.11	G1	C3	Gibbon
19.12	26.11	G1	D4	Tapir
20.12	27.11	G1	E5	Sheep
21.12	28.11	G1	F6	Deer
22.12	29.11	G1	G7	Horse
23.12	1.12	H2	H8	Stag
24.12	2.12	H2	J9	Serpent
25.12	3.12	H2	K10	Earthworm
26.12	4.12	H2	A11	Crocodile
27.12	5.12	H2	B12	Dragon
28.12	6.12	H2	C1	Badger
29.12	7.12	H2	D2	Hare
30.12	8.12	H2	E3	Fox
31.12	9.12	H2	F4	Tiger

1947

Solar date	Lunar date	Month HS/EB	Day HS/EB	Constellation
1. 1	10.12	H2	G5	Leopard
2. 1	11.12	H2	H6	Griffon
3. 1	12.12	H2	J7	Ox
4. 1	13.12	H2	K8	Bat
5. 1	14.12	H2	A9	Rat
6. 1	15.12	H2	B10	Swallow
7. 1	16.12	H2	C11	Pig
8. 1	17.12	H2	D12	Porcupine
9. 1	18.12	H2	E1	Wolf
10. 1	19.12	H2	F2	Dog
11. 1	20.12	H2	G3	Pheasant
12. 1	21.12	H2	H4	Cock
13. 1	22.12	H2	J5	Crow
14. 1	23.12	H2	K6	Monkey
15. 1	24.12	H2	A7	Gibbon
16. 1	25.12	H2	B8	Tapir
17. 1	26.12	H2	C9	Sheep
18. 1	27.12	H2	D10	Deer
19. 1	28.12	H2	E11	Horse
20. 1	29.12	H2	F12	Stag
21. 1	30.12	H2	G1	Serpent

TING HAI YEAR

Solar date	Lunar date	Month HS/EB	Day HS/EB	Constellation
22. 1	1. 1	J3	H2	Earthworm
23. 1	2. 1	J3	J3	Crocodile
24. 1	3. 1	J3	K4	Dragon
25. 1	4. 1	J3	A5	Badger
26. 1	5. 1	J3	B6	Hare
27. 1	6. 1	J3	C7	Fox
28. 1	7. 1	J3	D8	Tiger
29. 1	8. 1	J3	E9	Leopard
30. 1	9. 1	J3	F10	Griffon
31. 1	10. 1	J3	G11	Ox
1. 2	11. 1	J3	H12	Bat
2. 2	12. 1	J3	J1	Rat
3. 2	13. 1	J3	K2	Swallow
4. 2	14. 1	J3	A3	Pig
5. 2	15. 1	J3	B4	Porcupine
6. 2	16. 1	J3	C5	Wolf
7. 2	17. 1	J3	D6	Dog
8. 2	18. 1	J3	E7	Pheasant
9. 2	19. 1	J3	F8	Cock
10. 2	20. 1	J3	G9	Crow
11. 2	21. 1	J3	H10	Monkey
12. 2	22. 1	J3	J11	Gibbon
13. 2	23. 1	J3	K12	Tapir
14. 2	24. 1	J3	A1	Sheep
15. 2	25. 1	J3	B2	Deer
16. 2	26. 1	J3	C3	Horse
17. 2	27. 1	J3	D4	Stag
18. 2	28. 1	J3	E5	Serpent
19. 2	29. 1	J3	F6	Earthworm
20. 2	30. 1	J3	G7	Crocodile
21. 2	1. 2	K4	H8	Dragon
22. 2	2. 2	K4	J9	Badger
23. 2	3. 2	K4	K10	Hare
24. 2	4. 2	K4	A11	Fox
25. 2	5. 2	K4	B12	Tiger
26. 2	6. 2	K4	C1	Leopard
27. 2	7. 2	K4	D2	Griffon
28. 2	8. 2	K4	E3	Ox
1. 3	9. 2	K4	F4	Bat
2. 3	10. 2	K4	G5	Rat
3. 3	11. 2	K4	H6	Swallow
4. 3	12. 2	K4	J7	Pig
5. 3	13. 2	K4	K8	Porcupine
6. 3	14. 2	K4	A9	Wolf
7. 3	15. 2	K4	B10	Dog
8. 3	16. 2	K4	C11	Pheasant
9. 3	17. 2	K4	D12	Cock
10. 3	18. 2	K4	E1	Crow
11. 3	19. 2	K4	F2	Monkey
12. 3	20. 2	K4	G3	Gibbon
13. 3	21. 2	K4	H4	Tapir
14. 3	22. 2	K4	J5	Sheep
15. 3	23. 2	K4	K6	Deer
16. 3	24. 2	K4	A7	Horse
17. 3	25. 2	K4	B8	Stag
18. 3	26. 2	K4	C9	Serpent
19. 3	27. 2	K4	D10	Earthworm
20. 3	28. 2	K4	E11	Crocodile
21. 3	29. 2	K4	F12	Dragon
22. 3	30. 2	K4	G1	Badger
23. 3	1. 2	K4	H2	Hare
24. 3	2. 2	K4	J3	Fox
25. 3	3. 2	K4	K4	Tiger
26. 3	4. 2	K4	A5	Leopard
27. 3	5. 2	K4	B6	Griffon
28. 3	6. 2	K4	C7	Ox
29. 3	7. 2	K4	D8	Bat
30. 3	8. 2	K4	E9	Rat

Solar date	Lunar date	Month HS/EB	Day HS/EB	Constellation	Solar date	Lunar date	Month HS/EB	Day HS/EB	Constellation
31. 3	9. 2	K4	F10	Swallow	12. 6	24. 4	B6	J11	Crocodile
1. 4	10. 2	K4	G11	Pig	13. 6	25. 4	B6	K12	Dragon
2. 4	11. 2	K4	H12	Porcupine	14. 6	26. 4	B6	A1	Badger
3. 4	12. 2	K4	J1	Wolf	15. 6	27. 4	B6	B2	Hare
4. 4	13. 2	K4	K2	Dog	16. 6	28. 4	B6	C3	Fox
5. 4	14. 2	K4	A3	Pheasant	17. 6	29. 4	B6	D4	Tiger
6. 4	15. 2	K4	B4	Cock	18. 6	30. 4	B6	E5	Leopard
7. 4	16. 2	K4	C5	Crow	19. 6	1. 5	C7	F6	Griffon
8. 4	17. 2	K4	D6	Monkey	20. 6	2. 5	C7	G7	Ox
9. 4	18. 2	K4	E7	Gibbon	21. 6	3. 5	C7	H8	Bat
10. 4	19. 2	K4	F8	Tapir	22. 6	4. 5	C7	J9	Rat
11. 4	20. 2	K4	G9	Sheep	23. 6	5. 5	C7	K10	Swallow
12. 4	21. 2	K4	H10	Deer	24. 6	6. 5	C7	A11	Pig
13. 4	22. 2	K4	J11	Horse	25. 6	7. 5	C7	B12	Porcupine
14. 4	23. 2	K4	K12	Stag	26. 6	8. 5	C7	C1	Wolf
15. 4	24. 2	K4	A1	Serpent	27. 6	9. 5	C7	D2	Dog
16. 4	25. 2	K4	B2	Earthworm	28. 6	10. 5	C7	E3	Pheasant
17. 4	26. 2	K4	C3	Crocodile	29. 6	11. 5	C7	F4	Cock
18. 4	27. 2	K4	D4	Dragon	30. 6	12. 5	C7	G5	Crow
19. 4	28. 2	K4	E5	Badger	1. 7	13. 5	C7	H6	Monkey
20. 4	29. 2	K4	F6	Hare	2. 7	14. 5	C7	J7	Gibbon
21. 4	1. 3	A5	G7	Fox	3. 7	15. 5	C7	K8	Tapir
22. 4	2. 3	A5	H8	Tiger	4. 7	16. 5	C7	A9	Sheep
23. 4	3. 3	A5	J9	Leopard	5. 7	17. 5	C7	B10	Deer
24. 4	4. 3	A5	K10	Griffon	6. 7	18. 5	C7	C11	Horse
25. 4	5. 3	A5	A11	Ox	7. 7	19. 5	C7	D12	Stag
26. 4	6. 3	A5	B12	Bat	8. 7	20. 5	C7	E1	Serpent
27. 4	7. 3	A5	C1	Rat	9. 7	21. 5	C7	F2	Earthworm
28. 4	8. 3	A5	D2	Swallow	10. 7	22. 5	C7	G3	Crocodile
29. 4	9. 3	A5	E3	Pig	11. 7	23. 5	C7	H4	Dragon
30. 4	10. 3	A5	F4	Porcupine	12. 7	24. 5	C7	J5	Badger
1. 5	11. 3	A5	G5	Wolf	13. 7	25. 5	C7	K6	Fox
2. 5	12. 3	A5	H6	Dog	14. 7	26. 5	C7	A7	Fox
3. 5	13. 3	A5	J7	Pheasant	15. 7	27. 5	C7	B8	Tiger
4. 5	14. 3	A5	K8	Cock	16. 7	28. 5	C7	C9	Leopard
5. 5	15. 3	A5	A9	Crow	17. 7	29. 5	C7	D10	Griffon
6. 5	16. 3	A5	B10	Monkey	18. 7	1. 6	D8	E11	Ox
7. 5	17. 3	A5	C11	Gibbon	19. 7	2. 6	D8	F12	Bat
8. 5	18. 3	A5	D12	Tapir	20. 7	3. 6	D8	G1	Rat
9. 5	19. 3	A5	E1	Sheep	21. 7	4. 6	D8	H2	Swallow
10. 5	20. 3	A5	F2	Deer	22. 7	5. 6	D8	J3	Pig
11. 5	21. 3	A5	G3	Horse	23. 7	6. 6	D8	K4	Porcupine
12. 5	22. 3	A5	H4	Stag	24. 7	7. 6	D8	A5	Wolf
13. 5	23. 3	A5	J5	Serpent	25. 7	8. 6	D8	B6	Dog
14. 5	24. 3	A5	K6	Earthworm	26. 7	9. 6	D8	C7	Pheasant
15. 5	25. 3	A5	A7	Crocodile	27. 7	10. 6	D8	D8	Cock
16. 5	26. 3	A5	B8	Dragon	28. 7	11. 6	D8	E9	Crow
17. 5	27. 3	A5	C9	Badger	29. 7	12. 6	D8	F10	Monkey
18. 5	28. 3	A5	D10	Hare	30. 7	13. 6	D8	G11	Gibbon
19. 5	29. 3	A5	E11	Fox	31. 7	14. 6	D8	H12	Tapir
20. 5	1. 4	B6	F12	Tiger	1. 8	15. 6	D8	J1	Sheep
21. 5	2. 4	B6	G1	Leopard	2. 8	16. 6	D8	K2	Deer
22. 5	3. 4	B6	H2	Griffon	3. 8	17. 6	D8	A3	Horse
23. 5	4. 4	B6	J3	Ox	4. 8	18. 6	D8	B4	Stag
24. 5	5. 4	B6	K4	Bat	5. 8	19. 6	D8	C5	Serpent
25. 5	6. 4	B6	A5	Rat	6. 8	20. 6	D8	D6	Earthworm
26. 5	7. 4	B6	B6	Swallow	7. 8	21. 6	D8	E7	Crocodile
27. 5	8. 4	B6	C7	Pig	8. 8	22. 6	D8	F8	Dragon
28. 5	9. 4	B6	D8	Porcupine	9. 8	23. 6	D8	G9	Badger
29. 5	10. 4	B6	E9	Wolf	10. 8	24. 6	D8	H10	Hare
30. 5	11. 4	B6	F10	Dog	11. 8	25. 6	D8	J11	Fox
31. 5	12. 4	B6	G11	Pheasant	12. 8	26. 6	D8	K12	Tiger
1. 6	13. 4	B6	H12	Cock	13. 8	27. 6	D8	A1	Leopard
2. 6	14. 4	B6	J1	Crow	14. 8	28. 6	D8	B2	Griffon
3. 6	15. 4	B6	K2	Monkey	15. 8	29. 6	D8	C3	Ox
4. 6	16. 4	B6	A3	Gibbon	16. 8	1. 7	E9	D4	Bat
5. 6	17. 4	B6	B4	Tapir	17. 8	2. 7	E9	E5	Rat
6. 6	18. 4	B6	C5	Sheep	18. 8	3. 7	E9	F6	Swallow
7. 6	19. 4	B6	D6	Deer	19. 8	4. 7	E9	G7	Pig
8. 6	20. 4	B6	E7	Horse	20. 8	5. 7	E9	H8	Porcupine
9. 6	21. 4	B6	F8	Stag	21. 8	6. 7	E9	J9	Wolf
10. 6	22. 4	B6	G9	Serpent	22. 8	7. 7	E9	K10	Dog
11. 6	23. 4	B6	H10	Earthworm	23. 8	8. 7	E9	A11	Pheasant

Solar date	Lunar date	Month HS/EB	Day HS/EB	Constellation
24. 8	9. 7	E9	B12	Cock
25. 8	10. 7	E9	C1	Crow
26. 8	11. 7	E9	D2	Monkey
27. 8	12. 7	E9	E3	Gibbon
28. 8	13. 7	E9	F4	Tapir
29. 8	14. 7	E9	G5	Sheep
30. 8	15. 7	E9	H6	Deer
31. 8	16. 7	E9	J7	Horse
1. 9	17. 7	E9	K8	Stag
2. 9	18. 7	E9	A9	Serpent
3. 9	19. 7	E9	B10	Earthworm
4. 9	20. 7	E9	C11	Crocodile
5. 9	21. 7	E9	D12	Dragon
6. 9	22. 7	E9	E1	Badger
7. 9	23. 7	E9	F2	Hare
8. 9	24. 7	E9	G3	Fox
9. 9	25. 7	E9	H4	Tiger
10. 9	26. 7	E9	J5	Leopard
11. 9	27. 7	E9	K6	Griffon
12. 9	28. 7	E9	A7	Ox
13. 9	29. 7	E9	B8	Bat
14. 9	30. 7	E9	C9	Rat
15. 9	1. 8	F10	D10	Swallow
16. 9	2. 8	F10	E11	Pig
17. 9	3. 8	F10	F12	Porcupine
18. 9	4. 8	F10	G1	Wolf
19. 9	5. 8	F10	H2	Dog
20. 9	6. 8	F10	J3	Pheasant
21. 9	7. 8	F10	K4	Cock
22. 9	8. 8	F10	A5	Crow
23. 9	9. 8	F10	B6	Monkey
24. 9	10. 8	F10	C7	Gibbon
25. 9	11. 8	F10	D8	Tapir
26. 9	12. 8	F10	E9	Sheep
27. 9	13. 8	F10	F10	Deer
28. 9	14. 8	F10	G11	Horse
29. 9	15. 8	F10	H12	Stag
30. 9	16. 8	F10	J1	Serpent
1.10	17. 8	F10	K2	Earthworm
2.10	18. 8	F10	A3	Crocodile
3.10	19. 8	F10	B4	Dragon
4.10	20. 8	F10	C5	Badger
5.10	21. 8	F10	D6	Hare
6.10	22. 8	F10	E7	Fox
7.10	23. 8	F10	F8	Tiger
8.10	24. 8	F10	G9	Leopard
9.10	25. 8	F10	H10	Griffon
10.10	26. 8	F10	J11	Ox
11.10	27. 8	F10	K12	Bat
12.10	28. 8	F10	A1	Rat
13.10	29. 8	F10	B2	Swallow
14.10	1. 9	G11	C3	Pig
15.10	2. 9	G11	D4	Porcupine
16.10	3. 9	G11	E5	Wolf
17.10	4. 9	G11	F6	Dog
18.10	5. 9	G11	G7	Pheasant
19.10	6. 9	G11	H8	Cock
20.10	7. 9	G11	J9	Crow
21.10	8. 9	G11	K10	Monkey
22.10	9. 9	G11	A11	Gibbon
23.10	10. 9	G11	B12	Tapir
24.10	11. 9	G11	C1	Sheep
25.10	12. 9	G11	D2	Deer
26.10	13. 9	G11	E3	Horse
27.10	14. 9	G11	F4	Stag
28.10	15. 9	G11	G5	Serpent
29.10	16. 9	G11	H6	Earthworm
30.10	17. 9	G11	J7	Crocodile
31.10	18. 9	G11	K8	Dragon
1.11	19. 9	G11	A9	Badger
2.11	20. 9	G11	B10	Hare
3.11	21. 9	G11	C11	Fox
4.11	22. 9	G11	D12	Tiger
5.11	23. 9	G11	E1	Leopard
6.11	24. 9	G11	F2	Griffon
7.11	25. 9	G11	G3	Ox
8.11	26. 9	G11	H4	Bat
9.11	27. 9	G11	J5	Rat
10.11	28. 9	G11	K6	Swallow
11.11	29. 9	G11	A7	Pig
12.11	30. 9	G11	B8	Porcupine
13.11	1.10	H12	C9	Wolf
14.11	2.10	H12	D10	Dog
15.11	3.10	H12	E11	Pheasant
16.11	4.10	H12	F12	Cock
17.11	5.10	H12	G1	Crow
18.11	6.10	H12	H2	Monkey
19.11	7.10	H12	J3	Gibbon
20.11	8.10	H12	K4	Tapir
21.11	9.10	H12	A5	Sheep
22.11	10.10	H12	B6	Deer
23.11	11.10	H12	C7	Horse
24.11	12.10	H12	D8	Stag
25.11	13.10	H12	E9	Serpent
26.11	14.10	H12	F10	Earthworm
27.11	15.10	H12	G11	Crocodile
28.11	16.10	H12	H12	Dragon
29.11	17.10	H12	J1	Badger
30.11	18.10	H12	K2	Hare
1.12	19.10	H12	A3	Fox
2.12	20.10	H12	B4	Tiger
3.12	21.10	H12	C5	Leopard
4.12	22.10	H12	D6	Griffon
5.12	23.10	H12	E7	Ox
6.12	24.10	H12	F8	Bat
7.12	25.10	H12	G9	Rat
8.12	26.10	H12	H10	Swallow
9.12	27.10	H12	J11	Pig
10.12	28.10	H12	K12	Porcupine
11.12	29.10	H12	A1	Wolf
12.12	1.11	J1	B2	Dog
13.12	2.11	J1	C3	Pheasant
14.12	3.11	J1	D4	Cock
15.12	4.11	J1	E5	Crow
16.12	5.11	J1	F6	Monkey
17.12	6.11	J1	G7	Gibbon
18.12	7.11	J1	H8	Tapir
19.12	8.11	J1	J9	Sheep
20.12	9.11	J1	K10	Deer
21.12	10.11	J1	A11	Horse
22.12	11.11	J1	B12	Stag
23.12	12.11	J1	C1	Serpent
24.12	13.11	J1	D2	Earthworm
25.12	14.11	J1	E3	Crocodile
26.12	15.11	J1	F4	Dragon
27.12	16.11	J1	G5	Badger
28.12	17.11	J1	H6	Hare
29.12	18.11	J1	J7	Fox
30.12	19.11	J1	K8	Tiger
31.12	20.11	J1	A9	Leopard

1948

Solar date	Lunar date	Month HS/EB	Day HS/EB	Constellation
1. 1	21.11	J1	B10	Griffon
2. 1	22.11	J1	C11	Ox
3. 1	23.11	J1	D12	Bat
4. 1	24.11	J1	E1	Rat
5. 1	25.11	J1	F2	Swallow
6. 1	26.11	J1	G3	Pig
7. 1	27.11	J1	H4	Porcupine
8. 1	28.11	J1	J5	Wolf
9. 1	29.11	J1	K6	Dog
10. 1	30.11	J1	A7	Pheasant
11. 1	1.12	K2	B8	Cock
12. 1	2.12	K2	C9	Crow
13. 1	3.12	K2	D10	Monkey
14. 1	4.12	K2	E11	Gibbon

Solar date	Lunar date	Month HS/EB	Day HS/EB	Constellation
15. 1	5.12	K2	F12	Tapir
16. 1	6.12	K2	G1	Sheep
17. 1	7.12	K2	H2	Deer
18. 1	8.12	K2	J3	Horse
19. 1	9.12	K2	K4	Stag
20. 1	10.12	K2	A5	Serpent
21. 1	11.12	K2	B6	Earthworm
22. 1	12.12	K2	C7	Crocodile
23. 1	13.12	K2	D8	Dragon
24. 1	14.12	K2	E9	Badger
25. 1	15.12	K2	F10	Hare
26. 1	16.12	K2	G11	Fox
27. 1	17.12	K2	H12	Tiger
28. 1	18.12	K2	J1	Leopard
29. 1	19.12	K2	K2	Griffon
30. 1	20.12	K2	A3	Ox
31. 1	21.12	K2	B4	Bat
1. 2	22.12	K2	C5	Rat
2. 2	23.12	K2	D6	Swallow
3. 2	24.12	K2	E7	Pig
4. 2	25.12	K2	F8	Porcupine
5. 2	26.12	K2	G9	Wolf
6. 2	27.12	K2	H10	Dog
7. 2	28.12	K2	J11	Pheasant
8. 2	29.12	K2	K12	Cock
9. 2	30.12	K2	A1	Crow

MOU TZU YEAR

Solar date	Lunar date	Month HS/EB	Day HS/EB	Constellation
10. 2	1. 1	A3	B2	Monkey
11. 2	2. 1	A3	C3	Gibbon
12. 2	3. 1	A3	D4	Tapir
13. 2	4. 1	A3	E5	Sheep
14. 2	5. 1	A3	F6	Deer
15. 2	6. 1	A3	G7	Horse
16. 2	7. 1	A3	H8	Stag
17. 2	8. 1	A3	J9	Serpent
18. 2	9. 1	A3	K10	Earthworm
19. 2	10. 1	A3	A11	Crocodile
20. 2	11. 1	A3	B12	Dragon
21. 2	12. 1	A3	C1	Badger
22. 2	13. 1	A3	D2	Hare
23. 2	14. 1	A3	E3	Fox
24. 2	15. 1	A3	F4	Tiger
25. 2	16. 1	A3	G5	Leopard
26. 2	17. 1	A3	H6	Griffon
27. 2	18. 1	A3	J7	Ox
28. 2	19. 1	A3	K8	Bat
29. 2	20. 1	A3	A9	Rat
1. 3	21. 1	A3	B10	Swallow
2. 3	22. 1	A3	C11	Pig
3. 3	23. 1	A3	D12	Porcupine
4. 3	24. 1	A3	E1	Wolf
5. 3	25. 1	A3	F2	Dog
6. 3	26. 1	A3	G3	Pheasant
7. 3	27. 1	A3	H4	Cock
8. 3	28. 1	A3	J5	Crow
9. 3	29. 1	A3	K6	Monkey
10. 3	30. 1	A3	A7	Gibbon
11. 3	1. 2	B4	B8	Tapir
12. 3	2. 2	B4	C9	Sheep
13. 3	3. 2	B4	D10	Deer
14. 3	4. 2	B4	E11	Horse
15. 3	5. 2	B4	F12	Stag
16. 3	6. 2	B4	G1	Serpent
17. 3	7. 2	B4	H2	Earthworm
18. 3	8. 2	B4	J3	Crocodile
19. 3	9. 2	B4	K4	Dragon
20. 3	10. 2	B4	A5	Badger
21. 3	11. 2	B4	B6	Hare
22. 3	12. 2	B4	C7	Fox
23. 3	13. 2	B4	D8	Tiger
24. 3	14. 2	B4	E9	Leopard
25. 3	15. 2	B4	F10	Griffon
26. 3	16. 2	B4	G11	Ox
27. 3	17. 2	B4	H12	Bat
28. 3	18. 2	B4	J1	Rat
29. 3	19. 2	B4	K2	Swallow
30. 3	20. 2	B4	A3	Pig
31. 3	21. 2	B4	B4	Porcupine
1. 4	22. 2	B4	C5	Wolf
2. 4	23. 2	B4	D6	Dog
3. 4	24. 2	B4	E7	Pheasant
4. 4	25. 2	B4	F8	Cock
5. 4	26. 2	B4	G9	Crow
6. 4	27. 2	B4	H10	Monkey
7. 4	28. 2	B4	J11	Gibbon
8. 4	29. 2	B4	K12	Tapir
9. 4	1. 3	C5	A1	Sheep
10. 4	2. 3	C5	B2	Deer
11. 4	3. 3	C5	C3	Horse
12. 4	4. 3	C5	D4	Stag
13. 4	5. 3	C5	E5	Serpent
14. 4	6. 3	C5	F6	Earthworm
15. 4	7. 3	C5	G7	Crocodile
16. 4	8. 3	C5	H8	Dragon
17. 4	9. 3	C5	J9	Badger
18. 4	10. 3	C5	K10	Hare
19. 4	11. 3	C5	A11	Fox
20. 4	12. 3	C5	B12	Tiger
21. 4	13. 3	C5	C1	Leopard
22. 4	14. 3	C5	D2	Griffon
23. 4	15. 3	C5	E3	Ox
24. 4	16. 3	C5	F4	Bat
25. 4	17. 3	C5	G5	Rat
26. 4	18. 3	C5	H6	Swallow
27. 4	19. 3	C5	J7	Pig
28. 4	20. 3	C5	K8	Porcupine
29. 4	21. 3	C5	A9	Wolf
30. 4	22. 3	C5	B10	Dog
1. 5	23. 3	C5	C11	Pheasant
2. 5	24. 3	C5	D12	Cock
3. 5	25. 3	C5	E1	Crow
4. 5	26. 3	C5	F2	Monkey
5. 5	27. 3	C5	G3	Gibbon
6. 5	28. 3	C5	H4	Tapir
7. 5	29. 3	C5	J5	Sheep
8. 5	30. 3	C5	K6	Deer
9. 5	1. 4	D6	A7	Horse
10. 5	2. 4	D6	B8	Stag
11. 5	3. 4	D6	C9	Serpent
12. 5	4. 4	D6	D10	Earthworm
13. 5	5. 4	D6	E11	Crocodile
14. 5	6. 4	D6	F12	Dragon
15. 5	7. 4	D6	G1	Badger
16. 5	8. 4	D6	H2	Hare
17. 5	9. 4	D6	J3	Fox
18. 5	10. 4	D6	K4	Tiger
19. 5	11. 4	D6	A5	Leopard
20. 5	12. 4	D6	B6	Griffon
21. 5	13. 4	D6	C7	Ox
22. 5	14. 4	D6	D8	Bat
23. 5	15. 4	D6	E9	Rat
24. 5	16. 4	D6	F10	Swallow
25. 5	17. 4	D6	G11	Pig
26. 5	18. 4	D6	H12	Porcupine
27. 5	19. 4	D5	J1	Wolf
28. 5	20. 4	D6	K2	Dog
29. 5	21. 4	D6	A3	Pheasant

Solar date	Lunar date	Month HS/EB	Day HS/EB	Constellation	Solar date	Lunar date	Month HS/EB	Day HS/EB	Constellation
30. 5	22. 4	D6	B4	Cock	11. 8	7. 7	G9	E5	Leopard
31. 5	23. 4	D6	C5	Crow	12. 8	8. 7	G9	F6	Griffon
1. 6	24. 4	D6	D6	Monkey	13. 8	9. 7	G9	G7	Ox
2. 6	25. 4	D6	E7	Gibbon	14. 8	10. 7	G9	H8	Bat
3. 6	26. 4	D6	F8	Tapir	15. 8	11. 7	G9	J9	Rat
4. 6	27. 4	D6	G9	Sheep	16. 8	12. 7	G9	K10	Swallow
5. 6	28. 4	D6	H10	Deer	17. 8	13. 7	G9	A11	Pig
6. 6	29. 4	D6	J11	Horse	18. 8	14. 7	G9	B12	Porcupine
7. 6	1. 5	E7	K12	Stag	19. 8	15. 7	G9	C1	Wolf
8. 6	2. 5	E7	A1	Serpent	20. 8	16. 7	G9	D2	Dog
9. 6	3. 5	E7	B2	Earthworm	21. 8	17. 7	G9	E3	Pheasant
10. 6	4. 5	E7	C3	Crocodile	22. 8	18. 7	G9	F4	Cock
11. 6	5. 5	E7	D4	Dragon	23. 8	19. 7	G9	G5	Crow
12. 6	6. 5	E7	E5	Badger	24. 8	20. 7	G9	H6	Monkey
13. 6	7. 5	E7	F6	Hare	25. 8	21. 7	G9	J7	Gibbon
14. 6	8. 5	E7	G7	Fox	26. 8	22. 7	G9	K8	Tapir
15. 6	9. 5	E7	H8	Tiger	27. 8	23. 7	G9	A9	Sheep
16. 6	10. 5	E7	J9	Leopard	28. 8	24. 7	G9	B10	Deer
17. 6	11. 5	E7	K10	Griffon	29. 8	25. 7	G9	C11	Horse
18. 6	12. 5	E7	A11	Ox	30. 8	26. 7	G9	D12	Stag
19. 6	13. 5	E7	B12	Bat	31. 8	27. 7	G9	E1	Serpent
20. 6	14. 5	E7	C1	Rat	1. 9	28. 7	G9	F2	Earthworm
21. 6	15. 5	E7	D2	Swallow	2. 9	29. 7	G9	G3	Crocodile
22. 6	16. 5	E7	E3	Pig	3. 9	1. 8	H10	H4	Dragon
23. 6	17. 5	E7	F4	Porcupine	4. 9	2. 8	H10	J5	Badger
24. 6	18. 5	E7	G5	Wolf	5. 9	3. 8	H10	K6	Hare
25. 6	19. 5	E7	H6	Dog	6. 9	4. 8	H10	A7	Fox
26. 6	20. 5	E7	J7	Pheasant	7. 9	5. 8	H10	B8	Tiger
27. 6	21. 5	E7	K8	Cock	8. 9	6. 8	H10	C9	Leopard
28. 6	22. 5	E7	A9	Crow	9. 9	7. 8	H10	D10	Griffon
29. 6	23. 5	E7	B10	Monkey	10. 9	8. 8	H10	E11	Ox
30. 6	24. 5	E7	C11	Gibbon	11. 9	9. 8	H10	F12	Bat
1. 7	25. 5	E7	D12	Tapir	12. 9	10. 8	H10	G1	Rat
2. 7	26. 5	E7	E1	Sheep	13. 9	11. 8	H10	H2	Swallow
3. 7	27. 5	E7	F2	Deer	14. 9	12. 8	H10	J3	Pig
4. 7	28. 5	E7	G3	Horse	15. 9	13. 8	H10	K4	Porcupine
5. 7	29. 5	E7	H4	Stag	16. 9	14. 8	H10	A5	Wolf
6. 7	30. 5	E7	J5	Serpent	17. 9	15. 8	H10	B6	Dog
7. 7	1. 6	F8	K6	Earthworm	18. 9	16. 8	H10	C7	Pheasant
8. 7	2. 6	F8	A7	Crocodile	19. 9	17. 8	H10	D8	Cock
9. 7	3. 6	F8	B8	Dragon	20. 9	18. 8	H10	E9	Crow
10. 7	4. 6	F8	C9	Badger	21. 9	19. 8	H10	F10	Monkey
11. 7	5. 6	F8	D10	Hare	22. 9	20. 8	H10	G11	Gibbon
12. 7	6. 6	F8	E11	Fox	23. 9	21. 8	H10	H12	Tapir
13. 7	7. 6	F8	F12	Tiger	24. 9	22. 8	H10	J1	Sheep
14. 7	8. 6	F8	G1	Leopard	25. 9	23. 8	H10	K2	Deer
15. 7	9. 6	F8	H2	Griffon	26. 9	24. 8	H10	A3	Horse
16. 7	10. 6	F8	J3	Ox	27. 9	25. 8	H10	B4	Stag
17. 7	11. 6	F8	K4	Bat	28. 9	26. 8	H10	C5	Serpent
18. 7	12. 6	F8	A5	Rat	29. 9	27. 8	H10	D6	Earthworm
19. 7	13. 6	F8	B6	Swallow	30. 9	28. 8	H10	E7	Crocodile
20. 7	14. 6	F8	C7	Pig	1.10	29. 8	H10	F8	Dragon
21. 7	15. 6	F8	D8	Porcupine	2.10	30. 8	H10	G9	Badger
22. 7	16. 6	F8	E9	Wolf	3.10	1. 9	J11	H10	Hare
23. 7	17. 6	F8	F10	Dog	4.10	2. 9	J11	J11	Fox
24. 7	18. 6	F8	G11	Pheasant	5.10	3. 9	J11	K12	Tiger
25. 7	19. 6	F8	H12	Cock	6.10	4. 9	J11	A1	Leopard
26. 7	20. 6	F8	J1	Crow	7.10	5. 9	J11	B2	Griffon
27. 7	21. 6	F8	K2	Monkey	8.10	6. 9	J11	C3	Ox
28. 7	22. 6	F8	A3	Gibbon	9.10	7. 9	J11	D4	Bat
29. 7	23. 6	F8	B4	Tapir	10.10	8. 9	J11	E5	Rat
30. 7	24. 6	F8	C5	Sheep	11.10	9. 9	J11	F6	Swallow
31. 7	25. 6	F8	D6	Deer	12.10	10. 9	J11	G7	Pig
1. 8	26. 6	F8	E7	Horse	13.10	11. 9	J11	H8	Porcupine
2. 8	27. 6	F8	F8	Stag	14.10	12. 9	J11	J9	Wolf
3. 8	28. 6	F8	G9	Serpent	15.10	13. 9	J11	K10	Dog
4. 8	29. 6	F8	H10	Earthworm	16.10	14. 9	J11	A11	Pheasant
5. 8	1. 7	G9	J11	Crocodile	17.10	15. 9	J11	B12	Cock
6. 8	2. 7	G9	K12	Dragon	18.10	16. 9	J11	C1	Crow
7. 8	3. 7	G9	A1	Badger	19.10	17. 9	J11	D2	Monkey
8. 8	4. 7	G9	B2	Hare	20.10	18. 9	J11	E3	Gibbon
9. 8	5. 7	G9	C3	Fox	21.10	19. 9	J11	F4	Tapir
10. 8	6. 7	G9	D4	Tiger	22.10	20. 9	J11	G5	Sheep

Solar date	Lunar date	Month HS/EB	Day HS/EB	Constellation	Solar date	Lunar date	Month HS/EB	Day HS/EB	Constellation
23.10	21. 9	J11	H6	Deer	12.12	12.11	A1	H8	Cock
24.10	22. 9	J11	J7	Horse	13.12	13.11	A1	J9	Crow
25.10	23. 9	J11	K8	Stag	14.12	14.11	A1	K10	Monkey
26.10	24. 9	J11	A9	Serpent	15.12	15.11	A1	A11	Gibbon
27.10	25. 9	J11	B10	Earthworm	16.12	16.11	A1	B12	Tapir
28.10	26. 9	J11	C11	Crocodile	17.12	17.11	A1	C1	Sheep
29.10	27. 9	J11	D12	Dragon	18.12	18.11	A1	D2	Deer
30.10	28. 9	J11	E1	Badger	19.12	19.11	A1	E3	Horse
31.10	29. 9	J11	F2	Hare	20.12	20.11	A1	F4	Stag
1.11	1.10	K12	G3	Fox	21.12	21.11	A1	G5	Serpent
2.11	2.10	K12	H4	Tiger	22.12	22.11	A1	H6	Earthworm
3.11	3.10	K12	J5	Leopard	23.12	23.11	A1	J7	Crocodile
4.11	4.10	K12	K6	Griffon	24.12	24.11	A1	K8	Dragon
5.11	5.10	K12	A7	Ox	25.12	25.11	A1	A9	Badger
6.11	6.10	K12	B8	Bat	26.12	26.11	A1	B10	Hare
7.11	7.10	K12	C9	Rat	27.12	27.11	A1	C11	Fox
8.11	8.10	K12	D10	Swallow	28.12	28.11	A1	D12	Tiger
9.11	9.10	K12	E11	Pig	29.12	29.11	A1	E1	Leopard
10.11	10.10	K12	F12	Porcupine	30.12	1.12	B2	F2	Griffon
11.11	11.10	K12	G1	Wolf	31.12	2.12	B2	G3	Ox
12.11	12.10	K12	H2	Dog	**1949**				
13.11	13.10	K12	J3	Pheasant	1. 1	3.12	B2	H4	Bat
14.11	14.10	K12	K4	Cock	2. 1	4.12	B2	J5	Rat
15.11	15.10	K12	A5	Crow	3. 1	5.12	B2	K6	Swallow
16.11	16.10	K12	B6	Monkey	4. 1	6.12	B2	A7	Pig
17.11	17.10	K12	C7	Gibbon	5. 1	7.12	B2	B8	Porcupine
18.11	18.10	K12	D8	Tapir	6. 1	8.12	B2	C9	Wolf
19.11	19.10	K12	E9	Sheep	7. 1	9.12	B2	D10	Dog
20.11	20.10	K12	F10	Deer	8. 1	10.12	B2	E11	Pheasant
21.11	21.10	K12	G11	Horse	9. 1	11.12	B2	F12	Cock
22.11	22.10	K12	H12	Stag	10. 1	12.12	B2	G1	Crow
23.11	23.10	K12	J1	Serpent	11. 1	13.12	B2	H2	Monkey
24.11	24.10	K12	K2	Earthworm	12. 1	14.12	B2	J3	Gibbon
25.11	25.10	K12	A3	Crocodile	13. 1	15.12	B2	K4	Tapir
26.11	26.10	K12	B4	Dragon	14. 1	16.12	B2	A5	Sheep
27.11	27.10	K12	C5	Badger	15. 1	17.12	B2	B6	Deer
28.11	28.10	K12	D6	Hare	16. 1	18.12	B2	C7	Horse
29.11	29.10	K12	E7	Fox	17. 1	19.12	B2	D8	Stag
30.11	30.10	K12	F8	Tiger	18. 1	20.12	B2	E9	Serpent
1.12	1.11	A1	G9	Leopard	19. 1	21.12	B2	F10	Earthworm
2.12	2.11	A1	H10	Griffon	20. 1	22.12	B2	G11	Crocodile
3.12	3.11	A1	J11	Ox	21. 1	23.12	B2	H12	Dragon
4.12	4.11	A1	K12	Bat	22. 1	24.12	B2	J1	Badger
5.12	5.11	A1	A1	Rat	23. 1	25.12	B2	K2	Hare
6.12	6.11	A1	B2	Swallow	24. 1	26.12	B2	A3	Fox
7.12	7.11	A1	C3	Pig	25. 1	27.12	B2	B4	Tiger
8.12	8.11	A1	D4	Porcupine	26. 1	28.12	B2	C5	Leopard
9.12	9.11	A1	E5	Wolf	27. 1	29.12	B2	D6	Griffon
10.12	10.11	A1	F6	Dog	28. 1	30.12	B2	E7	Ox
11.12	11.11	A1	G7	Pheasant					

CHI CH'OU YEAR

Solar date	Lunar date	Month HS/EB	Day HS/EB	Constellation	Solar date	Lunar date	Month HS/EB	Day HS/EB	Constellation
29. 1	1. 1	C3	F8	Bat	16. 2	19. 1	C3	D2	Earthworm
30. 1	2. 1	C3	G9	Rat	17. 2	20. 1	C3	E3	Crocodile
31. 1	3. 1	C3	H10	Swallow	18. 2	21. 1	C3	F4	Dragon
1. 2	4. 1	C3	J11	Pig	19. 2	22. 1	C3	G5	Badger
2. 2	5. 1	C3	K12	Porcupine	20. 2	23. 1	C3	H6	Hare
3. 2	6. 1	C3	A1	Wolf	21. 2	24. 1	C3	J7	Fox
4. 2	7. 1	C3	B2	Dog	22. 2	25. 1	C3	K8	Tiger
5. 2	8. 1	C3	C3	Pheasant	23. 2	26. 1	C3	A9	Leopard
6. 2	9. 1	C3	D4	Cock	24. 2	27. 1	C3	B10	Griffon
7. 2	10. 1	C3	E5	Crow	25. 2	28. 1	C3	C11	Ox
8. 2	11. 1	C3	F6	Monkey	26. 2	29. 1	C3	D12	Bat
9. 2	12. 1	C3	G7	Gibbon	27. 2	30. 1	C3	E1	Rat
10. 2	13. 1	C3	H8	Tapir	28. 2	1. 2	D4	F2	Swallow
11. 2	14. 1	C3	J9	Sheep	1. 3	2. 2	D4	G3	Pig
12. 2	15. 1	C3	K10	Deer	2. 3	3. 2	D4	H4	Porcupine
13. 2	16. 1	C3	A11	Horse	3. 3	4. 2	D4	J5	Wolf
14. 2	17. 1	C3	B12	Stag	4. 3	5. 2	D4	K6	Dog
15. 2	18. 1	C3	C1	Serpent	5. 3	6. 2	D4	A7	Pheasant

Solar date	Lunar date	Month HS/EB	Day HS/EB	Constellation
6. 3	7. 2	D4	B8	Cock
7. 3	8. 2	D4	C9	Crow
8. 3	9. 2	D4	D10	Monkey
9. 3	10. 2	D4	E11	Gibbon
10. 3	11. 2	D4	F12	Tapir
11. 3	12. 2	D4	G1	Sheep
12. 3	13. 2	D4	H2	Deer
13. 3	14. 2	D4	J3	Horse
14. 3	15. 2	D4	K4	Stag
15. 3	16. 2	D4	A5	Serpent
16. 3	17. 2	D4	B6	Earthworm
17. 3	18. 2	D4	C7	Crocodile
18. 3	19. 2	D4	D8	Dragon
19. 3	20. 2	D4	E9	Badger
20. 3	21. 2	D4	F10	Hare
21. 3	22. 2	D4	G11	Fox
22. 3	23. 2	D4	H12	Tiger
23. 3	24. 2	D4	J1	Leopard
24. 3	25. 2	D4	K2	Griffon
25. 3	26. 2	D4	A3	Ox
26. 3	27. 2	D4	B4	Bat
27. 3	28. 2	D4	C5	Rat
28. 3	29. 2	D4	D6	Swallow
29. 3	1. 3	E5	E7	Pig
30. 3	2. 3	E5	F8	Porcupine
31. 3	3. 3	E5	G9	Wolf
1. 4	4. 3	E5	H10	Dog
2. 4	5. 3	E5	J11	Pheasant
3. 4	6. 3	E5	K12	Cock
4. 4	7. 3	E5	A1	Crow
5. 4	8. 3	E5	B2	Monkey
6. 4	9. 3	E5	C3	Gibbon
7. 4	10. 3	E5	D4	Tapir
8. 4	11. 3	E5	E5	Sheep
9. 4	12. 3	E5	F6	Deer
10. 4	13. 3	E5	G7	Horse
11. 4	14. 3	E5	H8	Stag
12. 4	15. 3	E5	J9	Serpent
13. 4	16. 3	E5	K10	Earthworm
14. 4	17. 3	E5	A11	Crocodile
15. 4	18. 3	E5	B12	Dragon
16. 4	19. 3	E5	C1	Badger
17. 4	20. 3	E5	D2	Hare
18. 4	21. 3	E5	E3	Fox
19. 4	22. 3	E5	F4	Tiger
20. 4	23. 3	E5	G5	Leopard
21. 4	24. 3	E5	H6	Griffon
22. 4	25. 3	E5	J7	Ox
23. 4	26. 3	E5	K8	Bat
24. 4	27. 3	E5	A9	Rat
25. 4	28. 3	E5	B10	Swallow
26. 4	29. 3	E5	C11	Pig
27. 4	30. 3	E5	D12	Porcupine
28. 4	1. 4	F6	E1	Wolf
29. 4	2. 4	F6	F2	Dog
30. 4	3. 4	F6	G3	Pheasant
1. 5	4. 4	F6	H4	Cock
2. 5	5. 4	F6	J5	Crow
3. 5	6. 4	F6	K6	Monkey
4. 5	7. 4	F6	A7	Gibbon
5. 5	8. 4	F6	B8	Tapir
6. 5	9. 4	F6	C9	Sheep
7. 5	10. 4	F6	D10	Deer
8. 5	11. 4	F6	E11	Horse
9. 5	12. 4	F6	F12	Stag
10. 5	13. 4	F6	G1	Serpent
11. 5	14. 4	F6	H2	Earthworm
12. 5	15. 4	F6	J3	Crocodile
13. 5	16. 4	F6	K4	Dragon
14. 5	17. 4	F6	A5	Badger
15. 5	18. 4	F6	B6	Hare
16. 5	19. 4	F6	C7	Fox
17. 5	20. 4	F6	D8	Tiger
18. 5	21. 4	F6	E9	Leopard
19. 5	22. 4	F6	F10	Griffon
20. 5	23. 4	F6	G11	Ox
21. 5	24. 4	F6	H12	Bat
22. 5	25. 4	F6	J1	Rat
23. 5	26. 4	F6	K2	Swallow
24. 5	27. 4	F6	A3	Pig
25. 5	28. 4	F6	B4	Porcupine
26. 5	29. 4	F6	C5	Wolf
27. 5	30. 4	F6	D6	Dog
28. 5	1. 5	G7	E7	Pheasant
29. 5	2. 5	G7	F8	Cock
30. 5	3. 5	G7	G9	Crow
31. 5	4. 5	G7	H10	Monkey
1. 6	5. 5	G7	J11	Gibbon
2. 6	6. 5	G7	K12	Tapir
3. 6	7. 5	G7	A1	Sheep
4. 6	8. 5	G7	B2	Deer
5. 6	9. 5	G7	C3	Horse
6. 6	10. 5	G7	D4	Stag
7. 6	11. 5	G7	E5	Serpent
8. 6	12. 5	G7	F6	Earthworm
9. 6	13. 5	G7	G7	Crocodile
10. 6	14. 5	G7	H8	Dragon
11. 6	15. 5	G7	J9	Badger
12. 6	16. 5	G7	K10	Hare
13. 6	17. 5	G7	A11	Fox
14. 6	18. 5	G7	B12	Tiger
15. 6	19. 5	G7	C1	Leopard
16. 6	20. 5	G7	D2	Griffon
17. 6	21. 5	G7	E3	Ox
18. 6	22. 5	G7	F4	Bat
19. 6	23. 5	G7	G5	Rat
20. 6	24. 5	G7	H6	Swallow
21. 6	25. 5	G7	J7	Pig
22. 6	26. 5	G7	K8	Porcupine
23. 6	27. 5	G7	A9	Wolf
24. 6	28. 5	G7	B10	Dog
25. 6	29. 5	G7	C11	Pheasant
26. 6	1. 6	H8	D12	Cock
27. 6	2. 6	H8	E1	Crow
28. 6	3. 6	H8	F2	Monkey
29. 6	4. 6	H8	G3	Gibbon
30. 6	5. 6	H8	H4	Tapir
1. 7	6. 6	H8	J5	Sheep
2. 7	7. 6	H8	K6	Deer
3. 7	8. 6	H8	A7	Horse
4. 7	9. 6	H8	B8	Stag
5. 7	10. 6	H8	C9	Serpent
6. 7	11. 6	H8	D10	Earthworm
7. 7	12. 6	H8	E11	Crocodile
8. 7	13. 6	H8	F12	Dragon
9. 7	14. 6	H8	G1	Badger
10. 7	15. 6	H8	H2	Hare
11. 7	16. 6	H8	J3	Fox
12. 7	17. 6	H8	K4	Tiger
13. 7	18. 6	H8	A5	Leopard
14. 7	19. 6	H8	B6	Griffon
15. 7	20. 6	H8	C7	Ox
16. 7	21. 6	H8	D8	Bat
17. 7	22. 6	H8	E9	Rat
18. 7	23. 6	H8	F10	Swallow
19. 7	24. 6	H8	G11	Pig
20. 7	25. 6	H8	H12	Porcupine
21. 7	26. 6	H8	J1	Wolf
22. 7	27. 6	H8	K2	Dog
23. 7	28. 6	H8	A3	Pheasant
24. 7	29. 6	H8	B4	Cock
25. 7	30. 6	H8	C5	Crow
26. 7	1. 7	J9	D6	Monkey
27. 7	2. 7	J9	E7	Gibbon
28. 7	3. 7	J9	F8	Tapir
29. 7	4. 7	J9	G9	Sheep

Solar date	Lunar date	Month HS/EB	Day HS/EB	Constellation	Solar date	Lunar date	Month HS/EB	Day HS/EB	Constellation
30. 7	5. 7	J9	H10	Deer	11.10	20. 8	K10	A11	Pig
31. 7	6. 7	J9	J11	Horse	12.10	21. 8	K10	B12	Porcupine
1. 8	7. 7	J9	K12	Stag	13.10	22. 8	K10	C1	Wolf
2. 8	8. 7	J9	A1	Serpent	14.10	23. 8	K10	D2	Dog
3. 8	9. 7	J9	B2	Earthworm	15.10	24. 8	K10	E3	Pheasant
4. 8	10. 7	J9	C3	Crocodile	16.10	25. 8	K10	F4	Cock
5. 8	11. 7	J9	D4	Dragon	17.10	26. 8	K10	G5	Crow
6. 8	12. 7	J9	E5	Badger	18.10	27. 8	K10	H6	Monkey
7. 8	13. 7	J9	F6	Hare	19.10	28. 8	K10	J7	Gibbon
8. 8	14. 7	J9	G7	Fox	20.10	29. 8	K10	K8	Tapir
9. 8	15. 7	J9	H8	Tiger	21.10	30. 8	K10	A9	Sheep
10. 8	16. 7	J9	J9	Leopard	22.10	1. 9	A11	B10	Deer
11. 8	17. 7	J9	K10	Griffon	23.10	2. 9	A11	C11	Horse
12. 8	18. 7	J9	A11	Ox	24.10	3. 9	A11	D12	Stag
13. 8	19. 7	J9	B12	Bat	25.10	4. 9	A11	E1	Serpent
14. 8	20. 7	J9	C1	Rat	26.10	5. 9	A11	F2	Earthworm
15. 8	21. 7	J9	D2	Swallow	27.10	6. 9	A11	G3	Crocodile
16. 8	22. 7	J9	E3	Pig	28.10	7. 9	A11	H4	Dragon
17. 8	23. 7	J9	F4	Porcupine	29.10	8. 9	A11	J5	Badger
18. 8	24. 7	J9	G5	Wolf	30.10	9. 9	A11	K6	Hare
19. 8	25. 7	J9	H6	Dog	31.10	10. 9	A11	A7	Fox
20. 8	26. 7	J9	J7	Pheasant	1.11	11. 9	A11	B8	Tiger
21. 8	27. 7	J9	K8	Cock	2.11	12. 9	A11	C9	Leopard
22. 8	28. 7	J9	A9	Crow	3.11	13. 9	A11	D10	Griffon
23. 8	29. 7	J9	B10	Monkey	4.11	14. 9	A11	E11	Ox
24. 8	*1. 7*	*J9*	C11	Gibbon	5.11	15. 9	A11	F12	Bat
25. 8	*2. 7*	*J9*	D12	Tapir	6.11	16. 9	A11	G1	Rat
26. 8	*3. 7*	*J9*	E1	Sheep	7.11	17. 9	A11	H2	Swallow
27. 8	*4. 7*	*J9*	F2	Deer	8.11	18. 9	A11	J3	Pig
28. 8	*5. 7*	*J9*	G3	Horse	9.11	19. 9	A11	K4	Porcupine
29. 8	*6. 7*	*J9*	H4	Stag	10.11	20. 9	A11	A5	Wolf
30. 8	*7. 7*	*J9*	J5	Serpent	11.11	21. 9	A11	B6	Dog
31. 8	*8. 7*	*J9*	K6	Earthworm	12.11	22. 9	A11	C7	Pheasant
1. 9	*9. 7*	*J9*	A7	Crocodile	13.11	23. 9	A11	D8	Cock
2. 9	*10. 7*	*J9*	B8	Dragon	14.11	24. 9	A11	E9	Crow
3. 9	*11. 7*	*J9*	C9	Badger	15.11	25. 9	A11	F10	Monkey
4. 9	*12. 7*	*J9*	D10	Hare	16.11	26. 9	A11	G11	Gibbon
5. 9	*13. 7*	*J9*	E11	Fox	17.11	27. 9	A11	H12	Tapir
6. 9	*14. 7*	*J9*	F12	Tiger	18.11	28. 9	A11	J1	Sheep
7. 9	*15. 7*	*J9*	G1	Leopard	19.11	29. 9	A11	K2	Deer
8. 9	*16. 7*	*J9*	H2	Griffon	20.11	1.10	B12	A3	Horse
9. 9	*17. 7*	*J9*	J3	Ox	21.11	2.10	B12	B4	Stag
10. 9	*18. 7*	*J9*	K4	Bat	22.11	3.10	B12	C5	Serpent
11. 9	*19. 7*	*J9*	A5	Rat	23.11	4.10	B12	D6	Earthworm
12. 9	*20. 7*	*J9*	B6	Swallow	24.11	5.10	B12	E7	Crocodile
13. 9	*21. 7*	*J9*	C7	Pig	25.11	6.10	B12	F8	Dragon
14. 9	*22. 7*	*J9*	D8	Porcupine	26.11	7.10	B12	G9	Badger
15. 9	*23. 7*	*J9*	E9	Wolf	27.11	8.10	B12	H10	Hare
16. 9	*24. 7*	*J9*	F10	Dog	28.11	9.10	B12	J11	Fox
17. 9	*25. 7*	*J9*	G11	Pheasant	29.11	10.10	B12	K12	Tiger
18. 9	*26. 7*	*J9*	H12	Cock	30.11	11.10	B12	A1	Leopard
19. 9	*27. 7*	*J9*	J1	Crow	1.12	12.10	B12	B2	Griffon
20. 9	*28. 7*	*J9*	K2	Monkey	2.12	13.10	B12	C3	Ox
21. 9	*29. 7*	*J9*	A3	Gibbon	3.12	14.10	B12	D4	Bat
22. 9	1. 8	K10	B4	Tapir	4.12	15.10	B12	E5	Rat
23. 9	2. 8	K10	C5	Sheep	5.12	16.10	B12	F6	Swallow
24. 9	3. 8	K10	D6	Deer	6.12	17.10	B12	G7	Pig
25. 9	4. 8	K10	E7	Horse	7.12	18.10	B12	H8	Porcupine
26. 9	5. 8	K10	F8	Stag	8.12	19.10	B12	J9	Wolf
27. 9	6. 8	K10	G9	Serpent	9.12	20.10	B12	K10	Dog
28. 9	7. 8	K10	H10	Earthworm	10.12	21.10	B12	A11	Pheasant
29. 9	8. 8	K10	J11	Crocodile	11.12	22.10	B12	B12	Cock
30. 9	9. 8	K10	K12	Dragon	12.12	23.10	B12	C1	Crow
1.10	10. 8	K10	A1	Badger	13.12	24.10	B12	D2	Monkey
2.10	11. 8	K10	B2	Hare	14.12	25.10	B12	E3	Gibbon
3.10	12. 8	K10	C3	Fox	15.12	26.10	B12	F4	Tapir
4.10	13. 8	K10	D4	Tiger	16.12	27.10	B12	G5	Sheep
5.10	14. 8	K10	E5	Leopard	17.12	28.10	B12	H6	Deer
6.10	15. 8	K10	F6	Griffon	18.12	29.10	B12	J7	Horse
7.10	16. 8	K10	G7	Ox	19.12	30.10	B12	K8	Stag
8.10	17. 8	K10	H8	Bat	20.12	1.11	C1	A9	Serpent
9.10	18. 8	K10	J9	Rat	21.12	2.11	C1	B12	Earthworm
10.10	19. 8	K10	K10	Swallow	22.12	3.11	C1	C11	Crocodile

Solar date	Lunar date	Month HS/EB	Day HS/EB	Constellation	Solar date	Lunar date	Month HS/EB	Day HS/EB	Constellation
23.12	4.11	C1	D12	Dragon	19. 1	2.12	D2	A3	Crocodile
24.12	5.11	C1	E1	Badger	20. 1	3.12	D2	B4	Dragon
25.12	6.11	C1	F2	Hare	21. 1	4.12	D2	C5	Badger
26.12	7.11	C1	G3	Fox	22. 1	5.12	D2	D6	Hare
27.12	8.11	C1	H4	Tiger	23. 1	6.12	D2	E7	Fox
28.12	9.11	C1	J5	Leopard	24. 1	7.12	D2	F8	Tiger
29.12	10.11	C1	K6	Griffon	25. 1	8.12	D2	G9	Leopard
30.12	11.11	C1	A7	Ox	26. 1	9.12	D2	H10	Griffon
31.12	12.11	C1	B8	Bat	27. 1	10.12	D2	J11	Ox
1950					28. 1	11.12	D2	K12	Bat
1. 1	13.11	C1	C9	Rat	29. 1	12.12	D2	A1	Rat
2. 1	14.11	C1	D10	Swallow	30. 1	13.12	D2	B2	Swallow
3. 1	15.11	C1	E11	Pig	31. 1	14.12	D2	C3	Pig
4. 1	16.11	C1	F12	Porcupine	1. 2	15.12	D2	D4	Porcupine
5. 1	17.11	C1	G1	Wolf	2. 2	16.12	D2	E5	Wolf
6. 1	18.11	C1	H2	Dog	3. 2	17.12	D2	F6	Dog
7. 1	19.11	C1	J3	Pheasant	4. 2	18.12	D2	G7	Pheasant
8. 1	20.11	C1	K4	Cock	5. 2	19.12	D2	H8	Cock
9. 1	21.11	C1	A5	Crow	6. 2	20.12	D2	J9	Crow
10. 1	22.11	C1	B6	Monkey	7. 2	21.12	D2	K10	Monkey
11. 1	23.11	C1	C7	Gibbon	8. 2	22.12	D2	A11	Gibbon
12. 1	24.11	C1	D8	Tapir	9. 2	23.12	D2	B12	Tapir
13. 1	25.11	C1	E9	Sheep	10. 2	24.12	D2	C1	Sheep
14. 1	26.11	C1	F10	Deer	11. 2	25.12	D2	D2	Deer
15. 1	27.11	C1	G11	Horse	12. 2	26.12	D2	E3	Horse
16. 1	28.11	C1	H12	Stag	13. 2	27.12	D2	F4	Stag
17. 1	29.11	C1	J1	Serpent	14. 2	28.12	D2	G5	Serpent
18. 1	1.12	D2	K2	Earthworm	15. 2	29.12	D2	H6	Earthworm
					16. 2	30.12	D2	J7	Crocodile

KENG YIN YEAR

Solar date	Lunar date	Month HS/EB	Day HS/EB	Constellation	Solar date	Lunar date	Month HS/EB	Day HS/EB	Constellation
17. 2	1. 1	E3	K8	Dragon	28. 3	11. 2	F4	J11	Pig
18. 2	2. 1	E3	A9	Badger	29. 3	12. 2	F4	K12	Porcupine
19. 2	3. 1	E3	B10	Hare	30. 3	13. 2	F4	A1	Wolf
20. 2	4. 1	E3	C11	Fox	31. 3	14. 2	F4	B2	Dog
21. 2	5. 1	E3	D12	Tiger	1. 4	15. 2	F4	C3	Pheasant
22. 2	6. 1	E3	E1	Leopard	2. 4	16. 2	F4	D4	Cock
23. 2	7. 1	E3	F2	Griffon	3. 4	17. 2	F4	E5	Crow
24. 2	8. 1	E3	G3	Ox	4. 4	18. 2	F4	F6	Monkey
25. 2	9. 1	E3	H4	Bat	5. 4	19. 2	F4	G7	Gibbon
26. 2	10. 1	E3	J5	Rat	6. 4	20. 2	F4	H8	Tapir
27. 2	11. 1	E3	K6	Swallow	7. 4	21. 2	F4	J9	Sheep
28. 2	12. 1	E3	A7	Pig	8. 4	22. 2	F4	K10	Deer
1. 3	13. 1	E3	B8	Porcupine	9. 4	23. 2	F4	A11	Horse
2. 3	14. 1	E3	C9	Wolf	10. 4	24. 2	F4	B12	Stag
3. 3	15. 1	E3	D10	Dog	11. 4	25. 2	F4	C1	Serpent
4. 3	16. 1	E3	E11	Pheasant	12. 4	26. 2	F4	D2	Earthworm
5. 3	17. 1	E3	F12	Cock	13. 4	27. 2	F4	E3	Crocodile
6. 3	18. 1	E3	G1	Crow	14. 4	28. 2	F4	F4	Dragon
7. 3	19. 1	E3	H2	Monkey	15. 4	29. 2	F4	G5	Badger
8. 3	20. 1	E3	J3	Gibbon	16. 4	30. 2	F4	H6	Hare
9. 3	21. 1	E3	K4	Tapir	17. 4	1. 3	G5	J7	Fox
10. 3	22. 1	E3	A5	Sheep	18. 4	2. 3	G5	K8	Tiger
11. 3	23. 1	E3	B6	Deer	19. 4	3. 3	G5	A9	Leopard
12. 3	24. 1	E3	C7	Horse	20. 4	4. 3	G5	B10	Griffon
13. 3	25. 1	E3	D8	Stag	21. 4	5. 3	G5	C11	Ox
14. 3	26. 1	E3	E9	Serpent	22. 4	6. 3	G5	D12	Bat
15. 3	27. 1	E3	F10	Earthworm	23. 4	7. 3	G5	E1	Rat
16. 3	28. 1	E3	G11	Crocodile	24. 4	8. 3	G5	F2	Swallow
17. 3	29. 1	E3	H12	Dragon	25. 4	9. 3	G5	G3	Pig
18. 3	1. 2	F4	J1	Badger	26. 4	10. 3	G5	H4	Porcupine
19. 3	2. 2	F4	K2	Hare	27. 4	11. 3	G5	J5	Wolf
20. 3	3. 2	F4	A3	Fox	28. 4	12. 3	G5	K6	Dog
21. 3	4. 2	F4	B4	Tiger	29. 4	13. 3	G5	A7	Pheasant
22. 3	5. 2	F4	C5	Leopard	30. 4	14. 3	G5	B8	Cock
23. 3	6. 2	F4	D6	Griffon	1. 5	15. 3	G5	C9	Crow
24. 3	7. 2	F4	E7	Ox	2. 5	16. 3	G5	D10	Monkey
25. 3	8. 2	F4	F8	Bat	3. 5	17. 3	G5	E11	Gibbon
26. 3	9. 2	F4	G9	Rat	4. 5	18. 3	G5	F12	Tapir
27. 3	10. 2	F4	H10	Swallow	5. 5	19. 3	G5	G1	Sheep

Solar date	Lunar date	Month HS/EB	Day HS/EB	Constellation	Solar date	Lunar date	Month HS/EB	Day HS/EB	Constellation
6. 5	20. 3	G5	H2	Deer	18. 7	4. 6	K8	A3	Pig
7. 5	21. 3	G5	J3	Horse	19. 7	5. 6	K8	B4	Porcupine
8. 5	22. 3	G5	K4	Stag	20. 7	6. 6	K8	C5	Wolf
9. 5	23. 3	G5	A5	Serpent	21. 7	7. 6	K8	D6	Dog
10. 5	24. 3	G5	B6	Earthworm	22. 7	8. 6	K8	E7	Pheasant
11. 5	25. 3	G5	C7	Crocodile	23. 7	9. 6	K8	F8	Cock
12. 5	26. 3	G5	D8	Dragon	24. 7	10. 6	K8	G9	Crow
13. 5	27. 3	G5	E9	Badger	25. 7	11. 6	K8	H10	Monkey
14. 5	28. 3	G5	F10	Hare	26. 7	12. 6	K8	J11	Gibbon
15. 5	29. 3	G5	G11	Fox	27. 7	13. 6	K8	K12	Tapir
16. 5	30. 3	G5	H12	Tiger	28. 7	14. 6	K8	A1	Sheep
17. 5	1. 4	H6	J1	Leopard	29. 7	15. 6	K8	B2	Deer
18. 5	2. 4	H6	K2	Griffon	30. 7	16. 6	K8	C3	Horse
19. 5	3. 4	H6	A3	Ox	31. 7	17. 6	K8	D4	Stag
20. 5	4. 4	H6	B4	Bat	1. 8	18. 6	K8	E5	Serpent
21. 5	5. 4	H6	C5	Rat	2. 8	19. 6	K8	F6	Earthworm
22. 5	6. 4	H6	D6	Swallow	3. 8	20. 6	K8	G7	Crocodile
23. 5	7. 4	H6	E7	Pig	4. 8	21. 6	K8	H8	Dragon
24. 5	8. 4	H6	F8	Porcupine	5. 8	22. 6	K8	J9	Badger
25. 5	9. 4	H6	G9	Wolf	6. 8	23. 6	K8	K10	Hare
26. 5	10. 4	H6	H10	Dog	7. 8	24. 6	K8	A11	Fox
27. 5	11. 4	H6	J11	Pheasant	8. 8	25. 6	K8	B12	Tiger
28. 5	12. 4	H6	K12	Cock	9. 8	26. 6	K8	C1	Leopard
29. 5	13. 4	H6	A1	Crow	10. 8	27. 6	K8	D2	Griffon
30. 5	14. 4	H6	B2	Monkey	11. 8	28. 6	K8	E3	Ox
31. 5	15. 4	H6	C3	Gibbon	12. 8	29. 6	K8	F4	Bat
1. 6	16. 4	H6	D4	Tapir	13. 8	30. 6	K8	G5	Rat
2. 6	17. 4	H6	E5	Sheep	14. 8	1. 7	A9	H6	Swallow
3. 6	18. 4	H6	F6	Deer	15. 8	2. 7	A9	J7	Pig
4. 6	19. 4	H6	G7	Horse	16. 8	3. 7	A9	K8	Porcupine
5. 6	20. 4	H6	H8	Stag	17. 8	4. 7	A9	A9	Wolf
6. 6	21. 4	H6	J9	Serpent	18. 8	5. 7	A9	B10	Dog
7. 6	22. 4	H6	K10	Earthworm	19. 8	6. 7	A9	C11	Pheasant
8. 6	23. 4	H6	A11	Crocodile	20. 8	7. 7	A9	D12	Cock
9. 6	24. 4	H6	B12	Dragon	21. 8	8. 7	A9	E1	Crow
10. 6	25. 4	H6	C1	Badger	22. 8	9. 7	A9	F2	Monkey
11. 6	26. 4	H6	D2	Hare	23. 8	10. 7	A9	G3	Gibbon
12. 6	27. 4	H6	E3	Fox	24. 8	11. 7	A9	H4	Tapir
13. 6	28. 4	H6	F4	Tiger	25. 8	12. 7	A9	J5	Sheep
14. 6	29. 4	H6	G5	Leopard	26. 8	13. 7	A9	K6	Deer
15. 6	1. 5	J7	H6	Griffon	27. 8	14. 7	A9	A7	Horse
16. 6	2. 5	J7	J7	Ox	28. 8	15. 7	A9	B8	Stag
17. 6	3. 5	J7	K8	Bat	29. 8	16. 7	A9	C9	Serpent
18. 6	4. 5	J7	A9	Rat	30. 8	17. 7	A9	D10	Earthworm
19. 6	5. 5	J7	B10	Swallow	31. 8	18. 7	A9	E11	Crocodile
20. 6	6. 5	J7	C11	Pig	1. 9	19. 7	A9	F12	Dragon
21. 6	7. 5	J7	D12	Porcupine	2. 9	20. 7	A9	G1	Badger
22. 6	8. 5	J7	E1	Wolf	3. 9	21. 7	A9	H2	Hare
23. 6	9. 5	J7	F2	Dog	4. 9	22. 7	A9	J3	Fox
24. 6	10. 5	J7	G3	Pheasant	5. 9	23. 7	A9	K4	Tiger
25.• 6	11. 5	J7	H4	Cock	6. 9	24. 7	A9	A5	Leopard
26. 6	12. 5	J7	J5	Crow	7. 9	25. 7	A9	B6	Griffon
27. 6	13. 5	J7	K6	Monkey	8. 9	26. 7	A9	C7	Ox
28. 6	14. 5	J7	A7	Gibbon	9. 9	27. 7	A9	D8	Bat
29. 6	15. 5	J7	B8	Tapir	10. 9	28. 7	A9	E9	Rat
30. 6	16. 5	J7	C9	Sheep	11. 9	29 .7	A9	F10	Swallow
1. 7	17. 5	J7	D10	Deer	12. 9	1. 8	B10	G11	Pig
2. 7	18. 5	J7	E11	Horse	13. 9	2. 8	B10	H12	Porcupine
3. 7	19. 5	J7	F12	Stag	14. 9	3. 8	B10	J1	Wolf
4. 7	20. 5	J7	G1	Serpent	15. 9	4. 8	B10	K2	Dog
5. 7	21. 5	J7	H2	Earthworm	16. 9	5. 8	B10	A3	Pheasant
6. 7	22. 5	J7	J3	Crocodile	17. 9	6. 8	B10	B4	Cock
7. 7	23. 5	J7	K4	Dragon	18. 9	7. 8	B10	C5	Crow
8. 7	24. 5	J7	A5	Badger	19. 9	8. 8	B10	D6	Monkey
9. 7	25. 5	J7	B6	Hare	20. 9	9. 8	B10	E7	Gibbon
10. 7	26. 5	J7	C7	Fox	21. 9	10. 8	B10	F8	Tapir
11. 7	27. 5	J7	D8	Tiger	22. 9	11. 8	B10	G9	Sheep
12. 7	28. 5	J7	E9	Leopard	23. 9	12. 8	B10	H10	Deer
13. 7	29. 5	J7	F10	Griffon	24. 9	13. 8	B10	J11	Horse
14. 7	30. 5	J7	G11	Ox	25. 9	14. 8	B10	K12	Stag
15. 7	1. 6	K8	H12	Bat	26. 9	15. 8	B10	A1	Serpent
16. 7	2. 6	K8	J1	Rat	27. 9	16. 8	B10	B2	Earthworm
17. 7	3. 6	K8	K2	Swallow	28. 9	17. 8	B10	C3	Crocodile

Solar date	Lunar date	Month HS/EB	Day HS/EB	Constellation
29. 9	18. 8	B10	D4	Dragon
30. 9	19. 8	B10	E5	Badger
1.10	20. 8	B10	F6	Hare
2.10	21. 8	B10	G7	Fox
3.10	22. 8	B10	H8	Tiger
4.10	23. 8	B10	J9	Leopard
5.10	24. 8	B10	K10	Griffon
6.10	25. 8	B10	A11	Ox
7.10	26. 8	B10	B12	Batr
8.10	27. 8	B10	C1	Rat
9.10	28. 8	B10	D2	Swallow
10.10	29. 8	B10	E3	Pig
11.10	1. 9	C11	F4	Porcupine
12.10	2. 9	C11	G5	Wolf
13.10	3. 9	C11	H6	Dog
14.10	4. 9	C11	J7	Pheasant
15.10	5. 9	C11	K8	Cock
16.10	6. 9	C11	A9	Crow
17.10	7. 9	C11	B10	Monkey
18.10	8. 9	C11	C11	Gibbon
19.10	9. 9	C11	D12	Tapir
20.10	10. 9	C11	E1	Sheep
21.10	11. 9	C11	F2	Deer
22.10	12.'9	C11	G3	Horse
23.10	13. 9	C11	H4	Stag
24.10	14. 9	C11	J5	Serpent
25.10	15. 9	C11	K6	Earthworm
26.10	16. 9	C11	A7	Crocodile
27.10	17. 9	C11	B8	Dragon
28.10	18. 9	C11	C9	Badger
29.10	19. 9	C11	D10	Hare
30.10	20. 9	C11	E11	Fox
31.10	21. 9	C11	F12	Tiger
1.11	22. 9	C11	G1	Leopard
2.11	23. 9	C11	H2	Griffon
3.11	24. 9	C11	J3	Ox
4.11	25. 9	C11	K4	Bat
5.11	26. 9	C11	A5	Rat
6.11	27. 9	C11	B6	Swallow
7.11	28. 9	C11	C7	Pig
8.11	29. 9	C11	D8	Porcupine
9.11	30. 9	C11	E9	Wolf
10.11	1.10	D12	F10	Dog
11.11	2.10	D12	G11	Pheasant
12.11	3.10	D12	H12	Cock
13.11	4.10	D12	J1	Crow
14.11	5.10	D12	K2	Monkey
15.11	6.10	D12	A3	Gibbon
16.11	7.10	D12	B4	Tapir
17.11	8.10	D12	C5	Sheep
18.11	9.10	D12	D6	Deer
19.11	10.10	D12	E7	Horse
20.11	11.10	D12	F8	Stag
21.11	12.10	D12	G9	Serpent
22.11	13.10	D12	H10	Earthworm
23.11	14.10	D12	J11	Crocodile
24.11	15.10	D12	K12	Dragon
25.11	16.10	D12	A1	Badger
26.11	17.10	D12	B2	Hare
27.11	18.10	D12	C3	Fox
28.11	19.10	D12	D4	Tiger
29.11	20.10	D12	E5	Leopard
30.11	21.10	D12	F6	Griffon
1.12	22.10	D12	G7	Ox
2.12	23.10	D12	H8	Bat
3.12	24.10	D12	J9	Rat

Solar date	Lunar date	Month HS/EB	Day HS/EB	Constellation
4.12	25.10	D12	K10	Swallow
5.12	26.10	D12	A11	Pig
6.12	27.10	D12	B12	Porcupine
7.12	28.10	D12	C1	Wolf
8.12	29.10	D12	D2	Dog
9.12	1.11	E1	E3	Pheasant
10.12	2.11	E1	F4	Cock
11.12	3.11	E1	G5	Crow
12.12	4.11	E1	H6	Monkey
13.12	5.11	E1	J7	Gibbon
14.12	6.11	E1	K8	Tapir
15.12	7.11	E1	A9	Sheep
16.12	8.11	E1	B10	Deer
17.12	9.11	E1	C11	Horse
18.12	10.11	E1	D12	Stag
19.12	11.11	E1	E1	Serpent
20.12	12.11	E1	F2	Earthworm
21.12	13.11	E1	G3	Crocodile
22.12	14.11	E1	H4	Dragon
23.12	15.11	E1	J5	Badger
24.12	16.11	E1	K6	Hare
25.12	17.11	E1	A7	Fox
26.12	18.11	E1	B8	Tiger
27.12	19.11	E1	C9	Leopard
28.12	20.11	E1	D10	Griffon
29.12	21.11	E1	E11	Ox
30.12	22.11	E1	F12	Bat
31.12	23.11	E1	G1	Rat

1951

Solar date	Lunar date	Month HS/EB	Day HS/EB	Constellation
1. 1	23.11	E1	H2	Swallow
2. 1	25.11	E1	J3	Pig
3. 1	26.11	E1	K4	Porcupine
4. 1	27.11	E1	A5	Wolf
5. 1	28.11	E1	B6	Dog
6. 1	29.11	E1	C7	Pheasant
7. 1	30.11	E1	D8	Cock
8. 1	1.12	F2	E9	Crow
9. 1	2.12	F2	F10	Monkey
10. 1	3.12	F2	G11	Gibbon
11. 1	4.12	F2	H12	Tapir
12. 1	5.12	F2	J1	Sheep
13. 1	6.12	F2	K2	Deer
14. 1	7.12	F2	A3	Horse
15. 1	8.12	F2	B4	Stag
16. 1	9.12	F2	C5	Serpent
17. 1	10.12	F2	D6	Earthworm
18. 1	11.12	F2	E7	Crocodile
19. 1	12.12	F2	F8	Dragon
20. 1	13.12	F2	G9	Badger
21. 1	14.12	F2	H10	Hare
22. 1	15.12	F2	J11	Fox
23. 1	16.12	F2	K12	Tiger
24. 1	17.12	F2	A1	Leopard
25. 1	18.12	F2	B2	Griffon
26. 1	19.12	F2	C3	Ox
27. 1	20.12	F2	D4	Bat
28. 1	21.12	F2	E5	Rat
29. 1	22.12	F2	F6	Swallow
30. 1	23.12	F2	G7	Pig
31. 1	24.12	F2	H8	Porcupine
1. 2	25.12	F2	J9	Wolf
2. 2	26.12	F2	K10	Dog
3. 2	27.12	F2	A11	Pheasant
4. 2	28.12	F2	B12	Cock
5. 2	29.12	F2	C1	Crow

HSIN MAO YEAR

Solar date	Lunar date	Month HS/EB	Day HS/EB	Constellation	Solar date	Lunar date	Month HS/EB	Day HS/EB	Constellation
6. 2	1. 1	G3	D2	Monkey	18. 4	13. 3	J5	E1	Leopard
7. 2	2. 1	G3	E3	Gibbon	19. 4	14. 3	J5	F2	Griffon
8. 2	3. 1	G3	F4	Tapir	20. 4	15. 3	J5	G3	Ox
9. 2	4. 1	G3	G5	Sheep	21. 4	16. 3	J5	H4	Bat
10. 2	5. 1	G3	H6	Deer	22. 4	17. 3	J5	J5	Rat
11. 2	6. 1	G3	J7	Horse	23. 4	18. 3	J5	K6	Swallow
12. 2	7. 1	G3	K8	Stag	24. 4	19. 3	J5	A7	Pig
13. 2	8. 1	G3	A9	Serpent	25. 4	20. 3	J5	B8	Porcupine
14. 2	9. 1	G3	B10	Earthworm	26. 4	21. 3	J5	C9	Wolf
15. 2	10. 1	G3	C11	Crocodile	27. 4	22. 3	J5	D10	Dog
16. 2	11. 1	G3	D12	Dragon	28. 4	23. 3	J5	E11	Pheasant
17. 2	12. 1	G3	E1	Badger	29. 4	24. 3	J5	F12	Cock
18. 2	13. 1	G3	F2	Hare	30. 4	25. 3	J5	G1	Crow
19. 2	14. 1	G3	G3	Fox	1. 5	26. 3	J5	H2	Monkey
20. 2	15. 1	G3	H4	Tiger	2. 5	27. 3	J5	J3	Gibbon
21. 2	16. 1	G3	J5	Leopard	3. 5	28. 3	J5	K4	Tapir
22. 2	17. 1	G3	K6	Griffon	4. 5	29. 3	J5	A5	Sheep
23. 2	18. 1	G3	A7	Ox	5. 5	30. 3	J5	B6	Deer
24. 2	19. 1	G3	B8	Bat	6. 5	1. 4	K6	C7	Horse
25. 2	20. 1	G3	C9	Rat	7. 5	2. 4	K6	D8	Stag
26. 2	21. 1	G3	D10	Swallow	8. 5	3. 4	K6	E9	Serpent
27. 2	22. 1	G3	E11	Pig	9. 5	4. 4	K6	F10	Earthworm
28. 2	23. 1	G3	F12	Porcupine	10. 5	5. 4	K6	G11	Crocodile
1. 3	24. 1	G3	G1	Wolf	11. 5	6. 4	K6	H12	Dragon
2. 3	25. 1	G3	H2	Dog	12. 5	7. 4	K6	J1	Badger
3. 3	26. 1	G3	J3	Pheasant	13. 5	8. 4	K6	K2	Hare
4. 3	27. 1	G3	K4	Cock	14. 5	9. 4	K6	A3	Fox
5. 3	28. 1	G3	A5	Crow	15. 5	10. 4	K6	B4	Tiger
6. 3	29. 1	G3	B6	Monkey	16. 5	11. 4	K6	C5	Leopard
7. 3	30. 1	G3	C7	Gibbon	17. 5	12. 4	K6	D6	Griffon
8. 3	1. 2	H4	D8	Tapir	18. 5	13. 4	K6	E7	Ox
9. 3	2. 2	H4	E9	Sheep	19. 5	14. 4	K6	F8	Bat
10. 3	3. 2	H4	F10	Deer	20. 5	15. 4	K6	G9	Rat
11. 3	4. 2	H4	G11	Horse	21. 5	16. 4	K6	H10	Swallow
12. 3	5. 2	H4	H12	Stag	22. 5	17. 4	K6	J11	Pig
13. 3	6. 2	H4	J1	Serpent	23. 5	18. 4	K6	K12	Porcupine
14. 3	7. 2	H4	K2	Earthworm	24. 5	19. 4	K6	A1	Wolf
15. 3	8. 2	H4	A3	Crocodile	25. 5	20. 4	K6	B2	Dog
16. 3	9. 2	H4	B4	Dragon	26. 5	21. 4	K6	C3	Pheasant
17. 3	10. 2	H4	C5	Badger	27. 5	22. 4	K6	D4	Cock
18. 3	11. 2	H4	D6	Hare	28. 5	23. 4	K6	E5	Crow
19. 3	12. 2	H4	E7	Fox	29. 5	24. 4	K6	F6	Monkey
20. 3	13. 2	H4	F8	Tiger	30. 5	25. 4	K6	G7	Gibbon
21. 3	14. 2	H4	G9	Leopard	31. 5	26. 4	K6	H8	Tapir
22. 3	15. 2	H4	H10	Griffon	1. 6	27. 4	K6	J9	Sheep
23. 3	16. 2	H4	J11	Ox	2. 6	28. 4	K6	K10	Deer
24. 3	17. 2	H4	K12	Bat	3. 6	29. 4	K6	A11	Horse
25. 3	18. 2	H4	A1	Rat	4. 6	30. 4	K6	B12	Stag
26. 3	19. 2	H4	B2	Swallow	5. 6	1. 5	A2	C1	Serpent
27. 3	20. 2	H4	C3	Pig	6. 6	2. 5	A7	D2	Earthworm
28. 3	21. 2	H4	D4	Porcupine	7. 6	3. 5	A7	E3	Crocodile
29. 3	22. 2	H4	E5	Wolf	8. 6	4. 5	A7	F4	Dragon
30. 3	23. 2	H4	F6	Dog	9. 6	5. 5	A7	G5	Badger
31. 3	24. 2	H4	G7	Pheasant	10. 6	6. 5	A7	H6	Hare
1. 4	25. 2	H4	H8	Cock	11. 6	7. 5	A7	J7	Fox
2. 4	26. 2	H4	J9	Crow	12. 6	8. 5	A7	K8	Tiger
3. 4	27. 2	H4	K10	Monkey	13. 6	9. 5	A7	A9	Leopard
4. 4	28. 2	H4	A11	Gibbon	14. 6	10. 5	A7	B10	Griffon
5. 4	29. 2	H4	B12	Tapir	15. 6	11. 5	A7	C11	Ox
6. 4	1. 3	J5	C1	Sheep	16. 6	12. 5	A7	D12	Bat
7. 4	2. 3	J5	D2	Deer	17. 6	13. 5	A7	E1	Rat
8. 4	3. 3	J5	E3	Horse	18. 6	14. 5	A7	F2	Swallow
9. 4	4. 3	J5	F4	Stag	19. 6	15. 5	A7	G3	Pig
10. 4	5. 3	J5	G5	Serpent	20. 6	16. 5	A7	H4	Porcupine
11. 4	6. 3	J5	H6	Earthworm	21. 6	17. 5	A7	J5	Wolf
12. 4	7. 3	J5	J7	Crocodile	22. 6	18. 5	A7	K6	Dog
13. 4	8. 3	J5	K8	Dragon	23. 6	19. 5	A7	A7	Pheasant
14. 4	9. 3	J5	A9	Badger	24. 6	20. 5	A7	B8	Cock
15. 4	10. 3	J5	B10	Hare	25. 6	21. 5	A7	C9	Crow
16. 4	11. 3	J5	C11	Fox	26. 6	22. 5	A7	D10	Monkey
17. 4	12. 3	J5	D12	Tiger	27. 6	23. 5	A7	E11	Gibbon

Solar date	Lunar date	Month HS/EB	Day HS/EB	Constellation	Solar date	Lunar date	Month HS/EB	Day HS/EB	Constellation
28. 6	24. 5	A7	F12	Tapir	9. 9	9. 8	D10	J1	Rat
29. 6	25. 5	A7	G1	Sheep	10. 9	10. 8	D10	K2	Swallow
30. 6	26. 5	A7	H2	Deer	11. 9	11. 8	D10	A3	Pig
1. 7	27. 5	A7	J3	Horse	12. 9	12. 8	D10	B4	Porcupine
2. 7	28. 5	A7	K4	Stag	13. 9	13. 8	D10	C5	Wolf
3. 7	29. 5	A7	A5	Serpent	14. 9	14. 8	D10	D6	Dog
4. 7	1. 6	B8	B6	Earthworm	15. 9	15. 8	D10	E7	Pheasant
5. 7	2. 6	B8	C7	Crocodile	16. 9	16. 8	D10	F8	Cock
6. 7	3. 6	B8	D8	Dragon	17. 9	17. 8	D10	G9	Crow
7. 7	4. 6	B8	E9	Badger	18. 9	18. 8	D10	H10	Monkey
8. 7	5. 6	B8	F10	Hare	19. 9	19. 8	D10	J11	Gibbon
9. 7	6. 6	B8	G11	Fox	20. 9	20. 8	D10	K12	Tapir
10. 7	7. 6	B8	H12	Tiger	21. 9	21. 8	D10	A1	Sheep
11. 7	8. 6	B8	J1	Leopard	22. 9	22. 8	D10	B2	Deer
12. 7	9. 6	B8	K2	Griffon	23. 9	23. 8	D10	C3	Horse
13. 7	10. 6	B8	A3	Ox	24. 9	24. 8	D10	D4	Stag
14. 7	11. 6	B8	B4	Bat	25. 9	25. 8	D10	E5	Serpent
15. 7	12. 6	B8	C5	Rat	26. 9	26. 8	D10	F6	Earthworm
16. 7	13. 6	B8	D6	Swallow	27. 9	27. 8	D10	G7	Crocodile
17. 7	14. 6	B8	E7	Pig	28. 9	28. 8	D10	H8	Dragon
18. 7	15. 6	B8	F8	Porcupine	29. 9	29. 8	D10	J9	Badger
19. 7	16. 6	B8	G9	Wolf	30. 9	30. 8	D10	K10	Hare
20. 7	17. 6	B8	H10	Dog	1.10	1. 9	E11	A11	Fox
21. 7	18. 6	B8	J11	Pheasant	2.10	2. 9	E11	B12	Tiger
22. 7	19. 6	B8	K12	Cock	3.10	3. 9	E11	C1	Leopard
23. 7	20. 6	B8	A1	Crow	4.10	4. 9	E11	D2	Griffon
24. 7	21. 6	B8	B2	Monkey	5.10	5. 9	E11	E3	Ox
25. 7	22. 6	B8	C3	Gibbon	6.10	6. 9	E11	F4	Bat
26. 7	23. 6	B8	D4	Tapir	7.10	7. 9	E11	G5	Rat
27. 7	24. 6	B8	E5	Sheep	8.10	8. 9	E11	H6	Swallow
28. 7	25. 6	B8	F6	Deer	9.10	9. 9	E11	J7	Pig
29. 7	26. 6	B8	G7	Horse	10.10	10. 9	E11	K8	Porcupine
30. 7	27. 6	B8	H8	Stag	11.10	11. 9	E11	A9	Wolf
31. 7	28. 6	B8	J9	Serpent	12.10	12. 9	E11	B10	Dog
1. 8	29. 6	B8	K10	Earthworm	13.10	13. 9	E11	C11	Pheasant
2. 8	30. 6	B8	A11	Crocodile	14.10	14. 9	E11	D12	Cock
3. 8	1. 7	C9	B12	Dragon	15.10	15. 9	E11	E1	Crow
4. 8	2. 7	C9	C1	Badger	16.10	16. 9	E11	F2	Monkey
5. 8	3. 7	C9	D2	Hare	17.10	17. 9	E11	G3	Gibbon
6. 8	4. 7	C9	E3	Fox	18.10	18. 9	E11	H4	Tapir
7. 8	5. 7	C9	F4	Tiger	19.10	19. 9	E11	J5	Sheep
8. 8	6. 7	C9	G5	Leopard	20.10	20. 9	E11	K6	Deer
9. 8	7. 7	C9	H6	Griffon	21.10	21. 9	E11	A7	Horse
10. 8	8. 7	C9	J7	Ox	22.10	22. 9	E11	B8	Stag
11. 8	9. 7	C9	K8	Bat	23.10	23. 9	E11	C9	Serpent
12. 8	10. 7	C9	A9	Rat	24.10	24. 9	E11	D10	Earthworm
13. 8	11. 7	C9	B10	Swallow	25.10	25. 9	E11	E11	Crocodile
14. 8	12. 7	C9	C11	Pig	26.10	26. 9	E11	F12	Dragon
15. 8	13. 7	C9	D12	Porcupine	27.10	27. 9	E11	G1	Badger
16. 8	14. 7	C9	E1	Wolf	28.10	28. 9	E11	H2	Hare
17. 8	15. 7	C9	F2	Dog	29.10	29. 9	E11	J3	Fox
18. 8	16. 7	C9	G3	Pheasant	30.10	1.10	F12	K4	Tiger
19. 8	17. 7	C9	H4	Cock	31.10	2.10	F12	A5	Leopard
20. 8	18. 7	C9	J5	Crow	1.11	3.10	F12	B6	Griffon
21. 8	19. 7	C9	K6	Monkey	2.11	4.10	F12	C7	Ox
22. 8	20. 7	C9	A7	Gibbon	3.11	5.10	F12	D8	Bat
23. 8	21. 7	C9	B8	Tapir	4.11	6.10	F12	E9	Rat
24. 8	22. 7	C9	C9	Sheep	5.11	7.10	F12	F10	Swallow
25. 8	23. 7	C9	D10	Deer	6.11	8.10	F12	G11	Pig
26. 8	24. 7	C9	E11	Horse	7.11	9.10	F12	H12	Porcupine
27. 8	25. 7	C9	F12	Stag	8.11	10.10	F12	J1	Wolf
28. 8	26. 7	C9	G1	Serpent	9.11	11.10	F12	K2	Dog
29. 8	27. 7	C9	H2	Earthworm	10.11	12.10	F12	A3	Pheasant
30. 8	28. 7	C9	J3	Crocodile	11.11	13.10	F12	B4	Cock
31. 8	29. 7	C9	K4	Dragon	12.11	14.10	F12	C5	Crow
1. 9	1. 8	D10	A5	Badger	13.11	15.10	F12	D6	Monkey
2. 9	2. 8	D10	B6	Hare	14.11	16.10	F12	E7	Gibbon
3. 9	3. 8	D10	C7	Fox	15.11	17.10	F12	F8	Tapir
4. 9	4. 8	D10	D8	Tiger	16.11	18.10	F12	G9	Sheep
5. 9	5. 8	D10	E9	Leopard	17.11	19.10	F12	H10	Deer
6. 9	6. 8	D10	F10	Griffon	18.11	20.10	F12	J11	Horse
7. 9	7. 8	D10	G11	Ox	19.11	21.10	F12	K12	Stag
8. 9	8. 8	D10	H12	Bat	20.11	22.10	F12	A1	Serpent

Solar date	Lunar date	Month HS/EB	Day HS/EB	Constellation
21.11	23.10	F12	B2	Earthworm
22.11	24.10	F12	C3	Crocodile
23.11	25.10	F12	D4	Dragon
24.11	26.10	F12	E5	Badger
25.11	27.10	F12	F6	Hare
26.11	28.10	F12	G7	Fox
27.11	29.10	F12	H8	Tiger
28.11	30.10	F12	J9	Leopard
29.11	1.11	G1	K10	Griffon
30.11	2.11	G1	A11	Ox
1.12	3.11	G1	B12	Bat
2.12	4.11	G1	C1	Rat
3.12	5.11	G1	D2	Swallow
4.12	6.11	G1	E3	Pig
5.12	7.11	G1	F4	Porcupine
6.12	8.11	G1	G5	Wolf
7.12	9.11	G1	H6	Dog
8.12	10.11	G1	J7	Pheasant
9.12	11.11	G1	K8	Cock
10.12	12.11	G1	A9	Crow
11.12	13.11	G1	B10	Monkey
12.12	14.11	G1	C11	Gibbon
13.12	15.11	G1	D12	Tapir
14.12	16.11	G1	E1	Sheep
15.12	17.11	G1	F2	Deer
16.12	18.11	G1	G3	Horse
17.12	19.11	G1	H4	Stag
18.12	20.11	G1	J5	Serpent
19.12	21.11	G1	K6	Earthworm
20.12	22.11	G1	A7	Crocodile
21.12	23.11	G1	B8	Dragon
22.12	24.11	G1	C9	Badger
23.12	25.11	G1	D10	Hare
24.12	26.11	G1	E11	Fox
25.12	27.11	G1	F12	Tiger
26.12	28.11	G1	G1	Leopard
27.12	29.11	G1	H2	Griffon
28.12	1.12	H2	J3	Ox
29.12	2.12	H2	K4	Bat
30.12	3.12	H2	A5	Rat
31.12	4.12	H2	B6	Swallow
1952				
1. 1	5.12	H2	C7	Pig
2. 1	6.12	H2	D8	Porcupine
3. 1	7.12	H2	E9	Wolf
4. 1	8.12	H2	F10	Dog
5. 1	9.12	H2	G11	Pheasant
6. 1	10.12	H2	H12	Cock
7. 1	11.12	H2	J1	Crow
8. 1	12.12	H2	K2	Monkey
9. 1	13.12	H2	A3	Gibbon
10. 1	14.12	H2	B4	Tapir
11. 1	15.12	H2	C5	Sheep
12. 1	16.12	H2	D6	Deer
13. 1	17.12	H2	E7	Horse
14. 1	18.12	H2	F8	Stag
15. 1	19.12	H2	G9	Serpent
16. 1	20.12	H2	H10	Earthworm
17. 1	21.12	H2	J11	Crocodile
18. 1	22.12	H2	K12	Dragon
19. 1	23.12	H2	A1	Badger
20. 1	24.12	H2	B2	Hare
21. 1	25.12	H2	C3	Fox
22. 1	26.12	H2	D4	Tiger
23. 1	27.12	H2	E5	Leopard
24. 1	28.12	H2	F6	Griffon
25. 2	29.12	H2	G7	Ox
26. 1	30.12	H2	H8	Bat

JEN CH'EN YEAR

Solar date	Lunar date	Month HS/EB	Day HS/EB	Constellation
27. 1	1. 1	J3	J9	Rat
28. 1	2. 1	J3	K10	Swallow
29. 1	3. 1	J3	A11	Pig
30. 1	4. 1	J3	B12	Porcupine
31. 1	5. 1	J3	C1	Wolf
1. 2	6. 1	J3	D2	Dog
2. 2	7. 1	J3	E3	Pheasant
3. 2	8. 1	J3	F4	Cock
4. 2	9. 1	J3	G5	Crow
5. 2	10. 1	J3	H6	Monkey
6. 2	11. 1	J3	J7	Gibbon
7. 2	12. 1	J3	K8	Tapir
8. 2	13. 1	J3	A9	Sheep
9. 2	14. 1	J3	B10	Deer
10. 2	15. 1	J3	C11	Horse
11. 2	16. 1	J3	D12	Stag
12. 2	17. 1	J3	E1	Serpent
13. 2	18. 1	J3	F2	Earthworm
14. 2	19. 1	J3	G3	Crocodile
15. 2	20. 1	J3	H4	Dragon
16. 2	21. 1	J3	J5	Badger
17. 2	22. 1	J3	K6	Hare
18. 2	23. 1	J3	A7	Fox
19. 2	24. 1	J3	B8	Tiger
20. 2	25. 1	J3	C9	Leopard
21. 2	26. 1	J3	D10	Griffon
22. 2	27. 1	J3	E11	Ox
23. 2	28. 1	J3	F12	Bat
24. 2	29. 1	J3	G1	Rat
25. 2	1. 2	K4	H2	Swallow
26. 2	2. 2	K4	J3	Pig
27. 2	3. 2	K4	K4	Porcupine
28. 2	4. 2	K4	A5	Wolf
29. 2	5. 2	K4	B6	Dog
1. 3	6. 2	K4	C7	Pheasant
2. 3	7. 2	K4	D8	Cock
3. 3	8. 2	K4	E9	Crow
4. 3	9. 2	K4	F10	Monkey
5. 3	10. 2	K4	G11	Gibbon
6. 3	11. 2	K4	H12	Tapir
7. 3	12. 2	K4	J1	Sheep
8. 3	13. 2	K4	K2	Deer
9. 3	14. 2	K4	A3	Horse
10. 3	15. 2	K4	B4	Stag
11. 3	16. 2	K4	C5	Serpent
12. 3	17. 2	K4	D6	Earthworm
13. 3	18. 2	K4	E7	Crocodile
14. 3	19. 2	K4	F8	Dragon
15. 3	20. 2	K4	G9	Badger
16. 3	21. 2	K4	H10	Hare
17. 3	22. 2	K4	J11	Fox
18. 3	23. 2	K4	K12	Tiger
19. 3	24. 2	K4	A1	Leopard
20. 3	25. 2	K4	B2	Griffon
21. 3	26. 2	K4	C3	Ox
22. 3	27. 2	K4	D4	Bat
23. 3	28. 2	K4	E5	Rat
24. 3	29. 2	K4	F6	Swallow
25. 3	30. 2	K4	G7	Pig
26. 3	1. 3	A5	H8	Porcupine
27. 3	2. 3	A5	J9	Wolf
28. 3	3. 3	A5	K10	Dog
29. 3	4. 3	A5	A11	Pheasant
30. 3	5. 3	A5	B12	Cock
31. 3	6. 3	A5	C1	Crow
1. 4	7. 3	A5	D2	Monkey

Solar date	Lunar date	Month HS/EB	Day HS/EB	Constellation	Solar date	Lunar date	Month HS/EB	Day HS/EB	Constellation
2. 4	8. 3	A5	E3	Gibbon	14. 6	22. 5	C7	H4	Bat
3. 4	9. 3	A5	F4	Tapir	15. 6	23. 5	C7	J5	Rat
4. 4	10. 3	A5	G5	Sheep	16. 6	24. 5	C7	K6	Swallow
5. 4	11. 3	A5	H6	Deer	17. 6	25. 5	C7	A7	Pig
6. 4	12. 3	A5	J7	Horse	18. 6	26. 5	C7	B8	Porcupine
7. 4	13. 3	A5	K8	Stag	19. 6	27. 5	C7	C9	Wolf
8. 4	14. 3	A5	A9	Serpent	20. 6	28. 5	C7	D10	Dog
9. 4	15. 3	A5	B10	Earthworm	21. 6	29. 5	C7	E11	Pheasant
10. 4	16. 3	A5	C11	Crocodile	22. 6	1. 5	C7	F12	Cock
11. 4	17. 3	A5	D12	Dragon	23. 6	2. 5	C7	G1	Crow
12. 4	18. 3	A5	E1	Badger	24. 6	3. 5	C7	H2	Monkey
13. 4	19. 3	A5	F2	Hare	25. 6	4. 5	C7	J3	Gibbon
14. 4	20. 3	A5	G3	Fox	26. 6	5. 5	C7	K4	Tapir
15. 4	21. 3	A5	H4	Tiger	27. 6	6. 5	C7	A5	Sheep
16. 4	22. 3	A5	J5	Leopard	28. 6	7. 5	C7	B6	Deer
17. 4	23. 3	A5	K6	Griffon	29. 6	8. 5	C7	C7	Horse
18. 4	24. 3	A5	A7	Ox	30. 6	9. 5	C7	D8	Stag
19. 4	25. 3	A5	B8	Bat	1. 7	10. 5	C7	E9	Serpent
20. 4	26. 3	A5	C9	Rat	2. 7	11. 5	C7	F10	Earthworm
21. 4	27. 3	A5	D10	Swallow	3. 7	12. 5	C7	G11	Crocodile
22. 4	28. 3	A5	E11	Pig	4. 7	13. 5	C7	H12	Dragon
23. 4	29. 3	A5	F12	Porcupine	5. 7	14. 5	C7	J1	Badger
24. 4	1. 4	B6	G1	Wolf	6. 7	15. 5	C7	K2	Hare
25. 4	2. 4	B6	H2	Dog	7. 7	16. 5	C7	A3	Fox
26. 4	3. 4	B6	J3	Pheasant	8. 7	17. 5	C7	B4	Tiger
27. 4	4. 4	B6	K4	Cock	9. 7	18. 5	C7	C5	Leopard
28. 4	5. 4	B6	A5	Crow	10. 7	19. 5	C7	D6	Griffon
29. 4	6. 4	B6	B6	Monkey	11. 7	20. 5	C7	E7	Ox
30. 4	7. 4	B6	C7	Gibbon	12. 7	21. 5	C7	F8	Bat
1. 5	8. 4	B6	D8	Tapir	13. 7	22. 5	C7	G9	Rat
2. 5	9. 4	B6	E9	Sheep	14. 7	23. 5	C7	H10	Swallow
3. 5	10. 4	B6	F10	Deer	15. 7	24. 5	C7	J11	Pig
4. 5	11. 4	B6	G11	Horse	16. 7	25. 5	C7	K12	Porcupine
5. 5	12. 4	B6	H12	Stag	17. 7	26. 5	C7	A1	Wolf
6. 5	13. 4	B6	J1	Serpent	18. 7	27. 5	C7	B2	Dog
7. 5	14. 4	B6	K2	Earthworm	19. 7	28. 5	C7	C3	Pheasant
8. 5	15. 4	B6	A3	Crocodile	20. 7	29. 5	C7	D4	Cock
9. 5	16. 4	B6	B4	Dragon	21. 7	30. 5	C7	E5	Crow
10. 5	17. 4	B6	C5	Badger	22. 7	1. 6	D8	F6	Monkey
11. 5	18. 4	B6	D6	Hare	23. 7	2. 6	D8	G7	Gibbon
12. 5	19. 4	B6	E7	Fox	24. 7	3. 6	D8	H8	Tapir
13. 5	20. 4	B6	F8	Tiger	25. 7	4. 6	D8	J9	Sheep
14. 5	21. 4	B6	G9	Leopard	26. 7	5. 6	D8	K10	Deer
15. 5	22. 4	B6	H10	Griffon	27. 7	6. 6	D8	A11	Horse
16. 5	23. 4	B6	J11	Ox	28. 7	7. 6	D8	B12	Stag
17. 5	24. 4	B6	K12	Bat	29. 7	8. 6	D8	C1	Serpent
18. 5	25. 4	B6	A1	Rat	30. 7	9. 6	D8	D2	Earthworm
19. 5	26. 4	B6	B2	Swallow	31. 7	10. 6	D8	E3	Crocodile
20. 5	27. 4	B6	C3	Pig	1. 8	11. 6	D8	F4	Dragon
21. 5	28. 4	B6	D4	Porcupine	2. 8	12. 6	D8	G5	Badger
22. 5	29. 4	B6	E5	Wolf	3. 8	13. 6	D8	H6	Hare
23. 5	30. 4	B6	F6	Dog	4. 8	14. 6	D8	J7	Fox
24. 5	1. 5	C7	G7	Pheasant	5. 8	15. 6	D8	K8	Tiger
25. 5	2. 5	C7	H8	Cock	6. 8	16. 6	D8	A9	Leopard
26. 5	3. 5	C7	J9	Crow	7. 8	17. 6	D8	B10	Griffon
27. 5	4. 5	C7	K10	Monkey	8. 8	18. 6	D8	C11	Ox
28. 5	5. 5	C7	A11	Gibbon	9. 8	19. 6	D8	D12	Bat
29. 5	6. 5	C7	B12	Tapir	10. 8	20. 6	D8	E1	Rat
30. 5	7. 5	C7	C1	Sheep	11. 8	21. 6	D8	F2	Swallow
31. 5	8. 5	C7	D2	Deer	12. 8	22. 6	D8	G3	Pig
1. 6	9. 5	C7	E3	Horse	13. 8	23. 6	D8	H4	Porcupine
2. 6	10. 5	C7	F4	Stag	14. 8	24. 6	D8	J5	Wolf
3. 6	11. 5	C7	G5	Serpent	15. 8	25. 6	D8	K6	Dog
4. 6	12. 5	C7	H6	Earthworm	16. 8	26. 6	D8	A7	Pheasant
5. 6	13. 5	C7	J7	Crocodile	17. 8	27. 6	D8	B8	Cock
6. 6	14. 5	C7	K8	Dragon	18. 8	28. 6	D8	C9	Crow
7. 6	15. 5	C7	A9	Badger	19. 8	29. 6	D8	D10	Monkey
8. 6	16. 5	C7	B10	Hare	20. 8	1. 7	E9	E11	Gibbon
9. 6	17. 5	C7	C11	Fox	21. 8	2. 7	E9	F12	Tapir
10. 6	18. 5	C7	D12	Tiger	22. 8	3. 7	E9	G1	Sheep
11. 6	19. 5	C7	E1	Leopard	23. 8	4. 7	E9	H2	Deer
12. 6	20. 5	C7	F2	Griffon	24. 8	5. 7	E9	J3	Horse
13. 6	21. 5	C7	G3	Ox	25. 8	6. 7	E9	K4	Stag

Solar date	Lunar date	Month HS/EB	Day HS/EB	Constellation	Solar date	Lunar date	Month HS/EB	Day HS/EB	Constellation
26. 8	7. 7	E9	A5	Serpent	7.11	20. 9	G11	D6	Dog
27. 8	8. 7	E9	B6	Earthworm	8.11	21. 9	G11	E7	Pheasant
28. 8	9. 7	E9	C7	Crocodile	9.11	22. 9	G11	F8	Cock
29. 8	10. 7	E9	D8	Dragon	10.11	23. 9	G11	G9	Crow
30. 8	11. 7	E9	E9	Badger	11.11	24. 9	G11	H10	Monkey
31. 8	12. 7	E9	F10	Hare	12.11	25. 9	G11	J11	Gibbon
1. 9	13. 7	E9	G11	Fox	13.11	26. 9	G11	K12	Tapir
2. 9	14. 7	E9	H12	Tiger	14.11	27. 9	G11	A1	Sheep
3. 9	15. 7	E9	J1	Leopard	15.11	28. 9	G11	B2	Deer
4. 9	16. 7	E9	K2	Griffon	16.11	29. 9	G11	C3	Horse
5. 9	17. 7	E9	A3	Ox	17.11	1.10	H12	D4	Stag
6. 9	18. 7	E9	B4	Bat	18.11	2.10	H12	E5	Serpent
7. 9	19. 7	E9	C5	Rat	19.11	3.10	H12	F6	Earthworm
8. 9	20. 7	E9	D6	Swallow	20.11	4.10	H12	G7	Crocodile
9. 9	21. 7	E9	E7	Pig	21.11	5.10	H12	H8	Dragon
10. 9	22. 7	E9	F8	Porcupine	22.11	6.10	H12	J9	Badger
11. 9	23. 7	E9	G9	Wolf	23.11	7.10	H12	K10	Hare
12. 9	24. 7	E9	H10	Dog	24.11	8.10	H12	A11	Fox
13. 9	25. 7	E9	J11	Pheasant	25.11	9.10	H12	B12	Tiger
14. 9	26. 7	E9	K12	Cock	26.11	10.10	H12	C1	Leopard
15. 9	27. 7	E9	A1	Crow	27.11	11.10	H12	D2	Griffon
16. 9	28. 7	E9	B2	Monkey	28.11	12.10	H12	E3	Ox
17. 9	29. 7	E9	C3	Gibbon	29.11	13.10	H12	F4	Bat
18. 9	30. 7	E9	D4	Tapir	30.11	14.10	H12	G5	Rat
19. 9	1. 8	F10	E5	Sheep	1.12	15.10	H12	H6	Swallow
20. 9	2. 8	F10	F6	Deer	2.12	16.10	H12	J7	Pig
21. 9	3. 8	F10	G7	Horse	3.12	17.10	H12	K8	Porcupine
22. 9	4. 8	F10	H8	Stag	4.12	18.10	H12	A9	Wolf
23. 9	5. 8	F10	J9	Serpent	5.12	19.10	H12	B10	Dog
24. 9	6. 8	F10	K10	Earthworm	6.12	20.10	H12	C11	Pheasant
25. 9	7. 8	F10	A11	Crocodile	7.12	21.10	H12	D12	Cock
26. 9	8. 8	F10	B12	Dragon	8.12	22.10	H12	E1	Crow
27. 9	9. 8	F10	C1	Badger	9.12	23.10	H12	F2	Monkey
28. 9	10. 8	F10	D2	Hare	10.12	24.10	H12	G3	Gibbon
29. 9	11. 8	F10	E3	Fox	11.12	25.10	H12	H4	Tapir
30. 9	12. 8	F10	F4	Tiger	12.12	26.10	H12	J5	Sheep
1.10	13. 8	F10	G5	Leopard	13.12	27.10	H12	K6	Deer
2.10	14. 8	F10	H6	Griffon	14.12	28.10	H12	A7	Horse
3.10	15. 8	F10	J7	Ox	15.12	29.10	H12	B8	Stag
4.10	16. 8	F10	K8	Bat	16.12	30.10	H12	C9	Serpent
5.10	17. 8	F10	A9	Rat	17.12	1.11	J1	D10	Earthworm
6.10	18. 8	F10	B10	Swallow	18.12	2.11	J1	E11	Crocodile
7.10	19. 8	F10	C11	Pig	19.12	3.11	J1	F12	Dragon
8.10	20. 8	F10	D12	Porcupine	20.12	4.11	J1	G1	Badger
9.10	21. 8	F10	E1	Wolf	21.12	5.11	J1	H2	Hare
10.10	22. 8	F10	F2	Dog	22.12	6.11	J1	J3	Fox
11.10	23. 8	F10	G3	Pheasant	23.12	7.11	J1	K4	Tiger
12.10	24. 8	F10	H4	Cock	24.12	8.11	J1	A5	Leopard
13.10	25. 8	F10	J5	Crow	25.12	9.11	J1	B6	Griffon
14.10	26. 8	F10	K6	Monkey	26.12	10.11	J1	C7	Ox
15.10	27. 8	F10	A7	Gibbon	27.12	11.11	J1	D8	Bat
16.10	28. 8	F10	B8	Tapir	28.12	12.11	J1	E9	Rat
17.10	29. 8	F10	C9	Sheep	29.12	13.11	J1	F10	Swallow
18.10	30. 8	F10	D10	Deer	30.12	14.11	J1	G11	Pig
19.10	1. 9	G11	E11	Horse	31.12	15.11	J1	H12	Porcupine
20.10	2. 9	G11	F12	Stag					
21.10	3. 9	G11	G1	Serpent	**1953**				
22.10	4. 9	G11	H2	Earthworm	1. 1	16.11	J1	J1	Wolf
23.10	5. 9	G11	J3	Crocodile	2. 1	17.11	J1	K2	Dog
24.10	6. 9	G11	K4	Dragon	3. 1	18.11	J1	A3	Pheasant
25.10	7. 9	G11	A5	Badger	4. 1	19.11	J1	B4	Cock
26.10	8. 9	G11	B6	Hare	5. 1	20.11	J1	C5	Crow
27.10	9. 9	G11	C7	Fox	6. 1	21.11	J1	D6	Monkey
28.10	10. 9	G11	D8	Tiger	7. 1	22.11	J1	E7	Gibbon
29.10	11. 9	G11	E9	Leopard	8. 1	23.11	J1	F8	Tapir
30.10	12. 9	G11	F10	Griffon	9. 1	24.11	J1	G9	Sheep
31.10	13. 9	G11	G11	Ox	10. 1	25.11	J1	H10	Deer
1.11	14. 9	G11	H12	Bat	11. 1	26.11	J1	J11	Horse
2.11	15. 9	G11	J1	Rat	12. 1	27.11	J1	K12	Stag
3.11	16. 9	G11	K2	Swallow	13. 1	28.11	J1	A1	Serpent
4.11	17.19	G11	A3	Pig	14. 1	29.11	J1	B2	Earthworm
5.11	18. 9	G11	B4	Porcupine	15. 1	1.12	K2	C3	Crocodile
6.11	19. 9	G11	C5	Wolf	16. 1	2.12	K2	D4	Dragon

Solar date	Lunar date	Month HS/EB	Day HS/EB	Constellation	Solar date	Lunar date	Month HS/EB	Day HS/EB	Constellation
17. 1	3.12	K2	E5	Badger	31. 1	17.12	K2	J7	Pheasant
18. 1	4.12	K2	F6	Hare	1. 2	18.12	K2	K8	Cock
19. 1	5.12	K2	G7	Fox	2. 2	19.12	K2	A9	Crow
20. 1	6.12	K2	H8	Tiger	3. 2	20.12	K2	B10	Monkey
21. 1	7.12	K2	J9	Leopard	4. 2	21.12	K2	C11	Gibbon
22. 1	8.12	K2	K10	Griffon	5. 2	22.12	K2	D12	Tapir
23. 1	9.12	K2	A11	Ox	6. 2	23.12	K2	E1	Sheep
24. 1	10.12	K2	B12	Batr	7. 2	24.12	K2	F2	Deer
25. 1	11.12	K2	C1	Rat	8. 2	25.12	K2	G3	Horse
26. 1	12.12	K2	D2	Swallow	9. 2	26.12	K2	H4	Stag
27. 1	13.12	K2	E3	Pig	10. 2	27.12	K2	J5	Serpent
28. 1	14.12	K2	F4	Porcupine	11. 2	28.12	K2	K6	Earthworm
29. 1	15.12	K2	G5	Wolf	12. 2	29.12	K2	A7	Crocodile
30. 1	16.12	K2	H6	Dog	13. 2	30.12	K2	B8	Dragon

KUEI SZU YEAR

Solar date	Lunar date	Month HS/EB	Day HS/EB	Constellation	Solar date	Lunar date	Month HS/EB	Day HS/EB	Constellation
14. 2	1. 1	A3	C9	Badger	9. 4	26. 2	B4	G3	Crocodile
15. 2	2. 1	A3	D10	Hare	10. 4	27. 2	B4	H4	Dragon
16. 2	3. 1	A3	E11	Fox	11. 4	28. 2	B4	J5	Badger
17. 2	4. 1	A3	F12	Tiger	12. 4	29. 2	B4	K6	Hare
18. 2	5. 1	A3	G1	Leopard	13. 4	30. 2	B4	A7	Fox
19. 2	6. 1	A3	H2	Griffon	14. 4	1. 3	C5	B8	Tiger
20. 2	7. 1	A3	J3	Ox	15. 4	2. 3	C5	C9	Leopard
21. 2	8. 1	A3	K4	Bat	16. 4	3. 3	C5	D10	Griffon
22. 2	9. 1	A3	A5	Rat	17. 4	4. 3	C5	E11	Ox
23. 2	10. 1	A3	B6	Swallow	18. 4	5. 3	C5	F12	Bat
24. 2	11. 1	A3	C7	Pig	19. 4	6. 3	C5	G1	Rat
25. 2	12. 1	A3	D8	Porcupine	20. 4	7. 3	C5	H2	Swallow
26. 2	13. 1	A3	E9	Wolf	21. 4	8. 3	C5	J3	Pig
27. 2	14. 1	A3	F10	Dog	22. 4	9. 3	C5	K4	Porcupine
28. 2	15. 1	A3	G11	Pheasant	23. 4	10. 3	C5	A5	Wolf
1. 3	16. 1	A3	H12	Cock	24. 4	11. 3	C5	B6	Dog
2. 3	17. 1	A3	J1	Crow	25. 4	12. 3	C5	C7	Pheasant
3. 3	18. 1	A3	K2	Monkey	26. 4	13. 3	C5	D8	Cock
4. 3	19. 1	A3	A3	Gibbon	27. 4	14. 3	C5	E9	Crow
5. 3	20. 1	A3	B4	Tapir	28. 4	15. 3	C5	F10	Monkey
6. 3	21. 1	A3	C5	Sheep	29. 4	16. 3	C5	G11	Gibbon
7. 3	22. 1	A3	D6	Deer	30. 4	17. 3	C5	H12	Tapir
8. 3	23. 1	A3	E7	Horse	1. 5	18. 3	C5	J1	Sheep
9. 3	24. 1	A3	F8	Stag	2. 5	19. 3	C5	K2	Deer
10. 3	25. 1	A3	G9	Serpent	3. 5	20. 3	C5	A3	Horse
11. 3	26. 1	A3	H10	Earthworm	4. 5	21. 3	C5	B4	Stag
12. 3	27. 1	A3	J11	Crocodile	5. 5	22. 3	C5	C5	Serpent
13. 3	28. 1	A3	K12	Dragon	6. 5	23. 3	C5	D6	Earthworm
14. 3	29. 1	A3	A1	Badger	7. 5	24. 3	C5	E7	Crocodile
15. 3	1. 2	B4	B2	Hare	8. 5	25. 3	C5	F8	Dragon
16. 3	2. 2	B4	C3	Fox	9. 5	26. 3	C5	G9	Badger
17. 3	3. 2	B4	D4	Tiger	10. 5	27. 3	C5	H10	Hare
18. 3	4. 2	B4	E5	Leopard	11. 5	28. 3	C5	J11	Fox
19. 3	5. 2	B4	F6	Griffon	12. 5	29. 3	C5	K12	Tiger
20. 3	6. 2	B4	G7	Ox	13. 5	1. 4	D6	A1	Leopard
21. 3	7. 2	B4	H8	Bat	14. 5	2. 4	D6	B2	Griffon
22. 3	8. 2	B4	J9	Rat	15. 5	3. 4	D6	C3	Ox
23. 3	9. 2	B4	K10	Swallow	16. 5	4. 4	D6	D4	Bat
24. 3	10. 2	B4	A11	Pig	17. 5	5. 4	D6	E5	Rat
25. 3	11. 2	B4	B12	Porcupine	18. 5	6. 4	D6	F6	Swallow
26. 3	12. 2	B4	C1	Wolf	19. 5	7. 4	D6	G7	Pig
27. 3	13. 2	B4	D2	Dog	20. 5	8. 4	D6	H8	Porcupine
28. 3	14. 2	B4	E3	Pheasant	21. 5	9. 4	D6	J9	Wolf
29. 3	15. 2	B4	F4	Cock	22. 5	10. 4	D6	K10	Dog
30. 3	16. 2	B4	G5	Crow	23. 5	11. 4	D6	A11	Pheasant
31. 3	17. 2	B4	H6	Monkey	24. 5	12. 4	D6	B12	Cock
1. 4	18. 2	B4	J7	Gibbon	25. 5	13. 4	D6	C1	Crow
2. 4	19. 2	B4	K8	Tapir	26. 5	14. 4	D6	D2	Monkey
3. 4	20. 2	B4	A9	Sheep	27. 5	15. 4	D6	E3	Gibbon
4. 4	21. 2	B4	B10	Deer	28. 5	16. 4	D6	F4	Tapir
5. 4	22. 2	B4	C11	Horse	29. 5	17. 4	D6	G5	Sheep
6. 4	23. 2	B4	D12	Stag	30. 5	18. 4	D6	H6	Deer
7. 4	24. 2	B4	E1	Serpent	31. 5	19. 4	D6	J7	Horse
8. 4	25. 2	B4	F2	Earthworm	1. 6	20. 4	D6	K8	Stag

Solar date	Lunar date	Month HS/EB	Day HS/EB	Constellation	Solar date	Lunar date	Month HS/EB	Day HS/EB	Constellation
2. 6	21. 4	D6	A9	Serpent	14. 8	5. 7	G9	D10	Dog
3. 6	22. 4	D6	B10	Earthworm	15. 8	6. 7	G9	E11	Pheasant
4. 6	23. 4	D6	C11	Crocodile	16. 8	7. 7	G9	F12	Cock
5. 6	24. 4	D6	D12	Drgon	17. 8	8. 7	G9	G1	Crow
6. 6	25. 4	D6	E1	Badger	18. 8	9. 7	G9	H2	Monkey
7. 6	26. 4	D6	F2	Hare	19. 8	10. 7	G9	J3	Gibbon
8. 6	27. 4	D6	G3	Fox	20. 8	11. 7	G9	K4	Tapir
9. 6	28. 4	D6	H4	Tiger	21. 8	12. 7	G9	A5	Sheep
10. 6	29. 4	D6	J5	Leopard	22. 8	13. 7	G9	B6	Deer
11. 6	1. 5	E7	K6	Griffon	23. 8	14. 7	G9	C7	Horse
12. 6	2. 5	E7	A7	Ox	24. 8	15. 7	G9	D8	Stag
13. 6	3. 5	E7	B8	Bat	25. 8	16. 7	G9	E9	Serpent
14. 6	4. 5	E7	C9	Rat	26. 8	17. 7	G9	F10	Earthworm
15. 6	5. 5	E7	D10	Swallow	27. 8	18. 7	G9	G11	Crocodile
16. 6	6. 5	E7	E11	Pig	28. 8	19. 7	G9	H12	Dragon
17. 6	7. 5	E7	F12	Porcupine	29. 8	20. 7	G9	J1	Badger
18. 6	8. 5	E7	G1	Wolf	30. 8	21. 7	G9	K2	Hare
19. 6	9. 5	E7	H2	Dog	31. 8	22. 7	G9	A3	Fox
20. 6	10. 5	E7	J3	Pheasant	1. 9	23. 7	G9	B4	Tiger
21. 6	11. 5	E7	K4	Cock	2. 9	24. 7	G9	C5	Leopard
22. 6	12. 5	E7	A5	Crow	3. 9	25. 7	G9	D6	Griffon
23. 6	13. 5	E7	B6	Monkey	4. 9	26. 7	G9	E7	Ox
24. 6	14. 5	E7	C7	Gibbon	5. 9	27. 7	G9	F8	Bat
25. 6	15. 5	E7	D8	Tapir	6. 9	28. 7	G9	G9	Rat
26. 6	16. 5	E7	E9	Sheep	7. 9	29. 7	G9	H10	Swallow
27. 6	17. 5	E7	F10	Deer	8. 9	1. 8	H10	J11	Pig
28. 6	18. 5	E7	G11	Horse	9. 9	2. 8	H10	K12	Porcupine
29. 6	19. 5	E7	H12	Stag	10. 9	3. 8	H10	A1	Wolf
30. 6	20. 5	E7	J1	Serpent	11. 9	4. 8	H10	B2	Dog
1. 7	21. 5	E7	K2	Earthworm	12. 9	5. 8	H10	C3	Pheasant
2. 7	22. 5	E7	A3	Crocodile	13. 9	6. 8	H10	D4	Cock
3. 7	23. 5	E7	B4	Dragon	14. 9	7. 8	H10	E5	Crow
4. 7	24. 5	E7	C5	Badger	15. 9	8. 8	H10	F6	Monkey
5. 7	25. 5	E7	D6	Hare	16. 9	9. 8	H10	G7	Gibbon
6. 7	26. 5	E7	E7	Fox	17. 9	10. 8	H10	H8	Tapir
7. 7	27. 5	E7	F8	Tiger	18. 9	11. 8	H10	J9	Sheep
8. 7	28. 5	E7	G9	Leopard	19. 9	12. 8	H10	K10	Deer
9. 7	29. 5	E7	H10	Griffon	20. 9	13. 8	H10	A11	Horse
10. 7	30. 5	E7	J11	Ox	21. 9	14. 8	H10	B12	Stag
11. 7	1. 6	F8	K12	Bat	22. 9	15. 8	H10	C1	Serpent
12. 7	2. 6	F8	A1	Rat	23. 9	16. 8	H10	D2	Earthworm
13. 7	3. 6	F8	B2	Swallow	24. 9	17. 8	H10	E3	Crocodile
14. 7	4. 6	F8	C3	Pig	25. 9	18. 8	H10	F4	Dragon
15. 7	5. 6	F8	D4	Porcupine	26. 9	19. 8	H10	G5	Badger
16. 7	6. 6	F8	E5	Wolf	27. 9	20. 8	H10	H6	Hare
17. 7	7. 6	F8	F6	Dog	28. 9	21. 8	H10	J7	Fox
18. 7	8. 6	F8	G7	Pheasant	29. 9	22. 8	H10	K8	Tiger
19. 7	9. 6	F8	H8	Cock	30. 9	23. 8	H10	A9	Leopard
20. 7	10. 6	F8	J9	Crow	1.10	24. 8	H10	B10	Griffon
21. 7	11. 6	F8	K10	Monkey	2.10	25. 8	H10	C11	Ox
22. 7	12. 6	F8	A11	Gibbon	3.10	26. 8	H10	D12	Bat
23. 7	13. 6	F8	B12	Tapir	4.10	27. 8	H10	E1	Rat
24. 7	14. 6	F8	C1	Sheep	5.10	28. 8	H10	F2	Swallow
25. 7	15. 6	F8	D2	Deer	6.10	29. 8	H10	G3	Pig
26. 7	16. 6	F8	E3	Horse	7.10	30. 8	H10	H4	Porcupine
27. 7	17. 6	F8	F4	Stag	8.10	1. 9	J11	J5	Wolf
28. 7	18. 6	F8	G5	Serpent	9.10	2. 9	J11	K6	Dog
29. 7	19. 6	F8	H6	Earthworm	10.10	3. 9	J11	A7	Pheasant
30. 7	20. 6	F8	J7	Crocodile	11.10	4. 9	J11	B8	Cock
31. 7	21. 6	F8	K8	Dragon	12.10	5. 9	J11	C9	Crow
1. 8	22. 6	F8	A9	Badger	13.10	6. 9	J11	D10	Monkey
2. 8	23. 6	F8	B10	Hare	14.10	7. 9	J11	E11	Gibbon
3. 8	24. 6	F8	C11	Fox	15.10	8. 9	J11	F12	Tapir
4. 8	25. 6	F8	D12	Tiger	16.10	9. 9	J11	G1	Sheep
5. 8	26. 6	F8	E1	Leopard	17.10	10. 9	J11	H2	Deer
6. 8	27. 6	F8	F2	Griffon	18.10	11. 9	J11	J3	Horse
7. 8	28. 6	F8	G3	Ox	19.10	12. 9	J11	K4	Stag
8. 8	29. 6	F8	H4	Bat	20.10	13. 9	J11	A5	Serpent
9. 8	30. 6	F8	J5	Rat	21.10	14. 9	J11	B6	Earthworm
10. 8	1. 7	G9	K6	Swallow	22.10	15. 9	J11	C7	Crocodile
11. 8	2. 7	G9	A7	Pig	23.10	16. 9	J11	D8	Dragon
12. 8	3. 7	G9	B8	Porcupine	24.10	17. 9	J11	E9	Badger
13. 8	4. 7	G9	C9	Wolf	25.10	18. 9	J11	F10	Hare

Solar date	Lunar date	Month HS/EB	Day HS/EB	Constellation
26.10	19. 9	J11	G11	Fox
27.10	20. 9	J11	H12	Tiger
28.10	21. 9	J11	J1	Leopard
29.10	22. 9	J11	K2	Griffon
30.10	23. 9	J11	A3	Ox
31.10	24. 9	J11	B4	Bat
1.11	25. 9	J11	C5	Rat
2.11	26. 9	J11	D6	Swallow
3.11	27. 9	J11	E7	Pig
4.11	28. 9	J11	F8	Porcupine
5.11	29. 9	J11	G9	Wolf
6.11	30. 9	J11	H10	Dog
7.11	1.10	K12	J11	Pheasant
8.11	2.10	K12	K12	Cock
9.11	3.10	K12	A1	Crow
10.11	4.10	K12	B2	Monkey
11.11	5.10	K12	C3	Gibbon
12.11	6.10	K12	D4	Tapir
13.11	7.10	K12	E5	Sheep
14.11	8.10	K12	F6	Deer
15.11	9.10	K12	G7	Horse
16.11	10.10	K12	H8	Stag
17.11	11.10	K12	J9	Serpent
18.11	12.10	K12	K10	Earthworm
19.11	13.10	K12	A11	Crocodile
20.11	14.10	K12	B12	Dragon
21.11	15.10	K12	C1	Badger
22.11	16.10	K12	D2	Hare
23.11	17.10	K12	E3	Fox
24.11	18.10	K12	F4	Tiger
25.11	19.10	K12	G5	Leopard
26.11	20.10	K12	H6	Griffon
27.11	21.10	K12	J7	Ox
28.11	22.10	K12	K8	Bat
29.11	23.10	K12	A9	Rat
30.11	24.10	K12	B10	Swallow
1.12	25.10	K12	C11	Pig
2.12	26.10	K12	D12	Porcupine
3.12	27.10	K12	E1	Wolf
4.12	28.10	K12	F2	Dog
5.12	29.10	K12	G3	Pheasant
6.12	1.11	A1	H4	Cock
7.12	2.11	A1	J5	Crow
8.12	3.11	A1	K6	Monkey
9.12	4.11	A1	A7	Gibbon
10.12	5.11	A1	B8	Tapir
11.12	6.11	A1	C9	Sheep
12.12	7.11	A1	D10	Deer
13.12	8.11	A1	E11	Horse
14.12	9.11	A1	F12	Stag
15.12	10.11	A1	G1	Serpent
16.12	11.11	A1	H2	Earthworm
17.12	12.11	A1	J3	Crocodile
18.12	13.11	A1	K4	Dragon
19.12	14.11	A1	A5	Badger
20.12	15.11	A1	B6	Hare
21.12	16.11	A1	C7	Fox
22.12	17.11	A1	D8	Tiger
23.12	18.11	A1	E9	Leopard
24.12	19.11	A1	F10	Griffon
25.12	20.11	A1	G11	Ox
26.12	21.11	A1	H12	Bat
27.12	22.11	A1	J1	Rat
28.12	23.11	A1	K2	Swallow
29.12	24.11	A1	A3	Pig
30.12	25.11	A1	B4	Porcupine
31.12	26.11	A1	C5	Wolf

1954

Solar date	Lunar date	Month HS/EB	Day HS/EB	Constellation
1. 1	27.11	A1	D6	Dog
2. 1	28.11	A1	E7	Pheasant
3. 1	29.11	A1	F8	Cock
4. 1	30.11	A1	G9	Crow
5. 1	1.12	B2	H10	Monkey
6. 1	2.12	B2	J11	Gibbon
7. 1	3.12	B2	K12	Tapir
8. 1	4.12	B2	A1	Sheep
9. 1	5.12	B2	B2	Deer
10. 1	6.12	B2	C3	Horse
11. 1	7.12	B2	D4	Stag
12. 1	8.12	B2	E5	Serpent
13. 1	9.12	B2	F6	Earthworm
14. 1	10.12	B2	G7	Crocodile
15. 1	11.12	B2	H8	Dragon
16. 1	12.12	B2	J9	Badger
17. 1	13.12	B2	K10	Hare
18. 1	14.12	B2	A11	Fox
19. 1	15.12	B2	B12	Tiger
20. 1	16.12	B2	C1	Leopard
21. 1	17.12	B2	D2	Griffon
22. 1	18.12	B2	E3	Ox
23. 1	19.12	B2	F4	Bat
24. 1	20.12	B2	G5	Rat
25. 1	21.12	B2	H6	Swallow
26. 1	22.12	B2	J7	Pig
27. 1	23.12	B2	K8	Porcupine
28. 1	24.12	B2	A9	Wolf
29. 1	25.12	B2	B10	Dog
30. 1	26.12	B2	C11	Pheasant
31. 1	27.12	B2	D12	Cock
1. 2	28.12	B2	E1	Crow
2. 2	29.12	B2	F2	Monkey

CHIA WU YEAR

Solar date	Lunar date	Month HS/EB	Day HS/EB	Constellation
3. 2	1. 1	C3	G3	Gibbon
4. 2	2. 1	C3	H4	Tapir
5. 2	3. 1	C3	J5	Sheep
6. 2	4. 1	C3	K6	Deer
7. 2	5. 1	C3	A7	Horse
8. 2	6. 1	C3	B8	Stag
9. 2	7. 1	C3	C9	Serpent
10. 2	8. 1	C3	D10	Earthworm
11. 2	9. 1	C3	E11	Crocodile
12. 2	10. 1	C3	F12	Dragon
13. 2	11. 1	C3	G1	Badger
14. 2	12. 1	C3	H2	Hare
15. 2	13. 1	C3	J3	Fox
16. 2	14. 1	C3	K4	Tiger
17. 2	15. 1	C3	A5	Leopard
18. 2	16. 1	C3	B6	Griffon
19. 2	17. 1	C3	C7	Ox
20. 2	18. 1	C3	D8	Bat
21. 2	19. 1	C3	E9	Rat
22. 2	20. 1	C3	F10	Swallow
23. 2	21. 1	C3	G11	Pig
24. 2	22. 1	C3	H12	Porcupine
25. 2	23. 1	C3	J1	Wolf
26. 2	24. 1	C3	K2	Dog
27. 2	25. 1	C3	A3	Pheasant
28. 2	26. 1	C3	B4	Cock
1. 3	27. 1	C3	C5	Crow
2. 3	28. 1	C3	D6	Monkey
3. 3	29. 1	C3	E7	Gibbon
4. 3	30. 1	C3	F8	Tapir
5. 3	1. 2	D4	G9	Sheep
6. 3	2. 2	D4	H10	Deer
7. 3	3. 2	D4	J11	Horse
8. 3	4. 2	D4	K12	Stag

Solar date	Lunar date	Month HS/EB	Day HS/EB	Constellation	Solar date	Lunar date	Month HS/EB	Day HS/EB	Constellation
9. 3	5. 2	D4	A1	Serpent	21. 5	19. 4	F6	D2	Dog
10. 3	6. 2	D4	B2	Earthworm	22. 5	20. 4	F6	E3	Pheasant
11. 3	7. 2	D4	C3	Crocodile	23. 5	21. 4	F6	F4	Cock
12. 3	8. 2	D4	D4	Dragon	24. 5	22. 4	F6	G5	Crow
13. 3	9. 2	D4	E5	Badger	25. 5	23. 4	F6	H6	Monkey
14. 3	10. 2	D4	F6	Hare	26. 5	24. 4	F6	J7	Gibbon
15. 3	11. 2	D4	G7	Fox	27. 5	25. 4	F6	K8	Tapir
16. 3	12. 2	D4	H8	Tiger	28. 5	26. 4	F6	A9	Sheep
17. 3	13. 2	D4	J9	Leopard	29. 5	27. 4	F6	B10	Deer
18. 3	14. 2	D4	K10	Griffon	30. 5	28. 4	F6	C11	Horse
19. 3	15. 2	D4	A11	Ox	31. 5	29. 4	F6	D12	Stag
20. 3	16. 2	D4	B12	Bat	1. 6	1. 5	G7	E1	Serpent
21. 3	17. 2	D4	C1	Rat	2. 6	2. 5	G7	F2	Earthworm
22. 3	18. 2	D4	D2	Swallow	3. 6	3. 5	G7	G3	Crocodile
23. 3	19. 2	D4	E3	Pig	4. 6	4. 5	G7	H4	Dragon
24. 3	20. 2	D4	F4	Porcupine	5. 6	5. 5	G7	J5	Badger
25. 3	21. 2	D4	G5	Wolf	6. 6	6. 5	G7	K6	Hare
26. 3	22, 2	D4	H6	Dog	7. 6	7. 5	G7	A7	Fox
27. 3	23. 2	D4	J7	Pheasant	8. 6	8. 5	G7	B8	Tiger
28. 3	24. 2	D4	K8	Cock	9. 6	9. 5	G7	C9	Leopard
29. 3	25. 2	D4	A9	Crow	10. 6	10. 5	G7	D10	Griffon
30. 3	26. 2	D4	B10	Monkey	11. 6	11. 5	G7	E11	Ox
31. 3	27. 2	D4	C11	Gibbon	12. 6	12. 5	G7	F12	Bat
1. 4	28. 2	D4	D12	Tapir	13. 6	13. 5	G7	G1	Rat
2. 4	29. 2	D4	E1	Sheep	14. 6	14. 5	G7	H2	Swallow
3. 4	1. 3	E5	F2	Deer	15. 6	15. 5	G7	J3	Pig
4. 4	2. 3	E5	G3	Horse	16. 6	16. 5	G7	K4	Porcupine
5. 4	3. 3	E5	H4	Stag	17. 6	17. 5	G7	A5	Wolf
6. 4	4. 3	E5	J5	Serpent	18. 6	18. 5	G7	B6	Dog
7. 4	5. 3	E5	K6	Earthworm	19. 6	19. 5	G7	C7	Pheasant
8. 4	6. 3	E5	A7	Crocodile	20. 6	20. 5	G7	D8	Cock
9. 4	7. 3	E5	B8	Dragon	21. 6	21. 5	G7	E9	Crow
10. 4	8. 3	E5	C9	Badger	22. 6	22. 5	G7	F10	Monkey
11. 4	9. 3	E5	D10	Hare	23. 6	23. 5	G7	G11	Gibbon
12. 4	10. 3	E5	E11	Fox	24. 6	24. 5	G7	H12	Tapir
13. 4	11. 3	E5	F12	Tiger	25. 6	25. 5	G7	J1	Sheep
14. 4	12. 3	E5	G1	Leopard	26. 6	26. 5	G7	K2	Deer
15. 4	13. 3	E5	H2	Griffon	27. 6	27. 5	G7	A3	Horse
16. 4	14. 3	E5	J3	Ox	28. 6	28. 5	G7	B4	Stag
17. 4	15. 3	E5	K4	Bat	29. 6	29. 5	G7	C5	Serpent
18. 4	16. 3	E5	A5	Rat	30. 6	1. 6	H8	D6	Earthworm
19. 4	17. 3	E5	B6	Swallow	1. 7	2. 6	H8	E7	Crocodile
20. 4	18. 3	E5	C7	Pig	2. 7	3. 6	H8	F8	Dragon
21. 4	19. 3	E5	D8	Porcupine	3. 7	4. 6	H8	G9	Badger
22. 4	20. 3	E5	E9	Wolf	4. 7	5. 6	H8	H10	Hare
23. 4	21. 3	E5	F10	Dog	5. 7	6. 6	H8	J11	Fox
24. 4	22. 3	E5	G11	Pheasant	6. 7	7. 6	H8	K12	Tiger
25. 4	23. 3	E5	H12	Cock	7. 7	8. 6	H8	A1	Leopard
26. 4	24. 3	E5	J1	Crow	8. 7	9. 6	H8	B2	Griffon
27. 4	25. 3	E5	K2	Monkey	9. 7	10. 6	H8	C3	Ox
28. 4	26. 3	E5	A3	Gibbon	10. 7	11. 6	H8	D4	Bat
29. 4	27. 3	E5	B4	Tapir	11. 7	12. 6	H8	E5	Rat
30. 4	28. 3	E5	C5	Sheep	12. 7	13. 6	H8	F6	Swallow
1. 5	29. 3	E5	D6	Deer	13. 7	14. 6	H8	G7	Pig
2. 5	30. 3	E5	E7	Horse	14. 7	15. 6	H8	H8	Porcupine
3. 5	1. 4	F6	F8	Stag	15. 7	16. 6	H8	J9	Wolf
4. 5	2. 4	F6	G9	Serpent	16. 7	17. 6	H8	K10	Dog
5. 5	3. 4	F6	H10	Earthworm	17. 7	18. 6	H8	A11	Pheasant
6. 5	4. 4	F6	J11	Crocodile	18. 7	19. 6	H8	B12	Cock
7. 5	5. 4	F6	K12	Dragon	19. 7	20. 6	H8	C1	Crow
8. 5	6. 4	F6	A1	Badger	20. 7	21. 6	H8	D2	Monkey
9. 5	7. 4	F6	B2	Hare	21. 7	22. 6	H8	E3	Gibbon
10. 5	8. 4	F6	C3	Fox	22. 7	23. 6	H8	F4	Tapir
11. 5	9. 4	F6	D4	Tiger	23. 7	24. 6	H8	G5	Sheep
12. 5	10. 4	F6	E5	Leopard	24. 7	25. 6	H8	H6	Deer
13. 5	11. 4	F6	F6	Griffon	25. 7	26. 6	H8	J7	Horse
14. 5	12. 4	F6	G7	Ox	26. 7	27. 6	H8	K8	Stag
15. 5	13. 4	F6	H8	Bat	27. 7	28. 6	H8	A9	Serpent
16. 5	14. 4	F6	J9	Rat	28. 7	29. 6	H8	B10	Earthworm
17. 5	15. 4	F6	K10	Swallow	29. 7	30. 6	H8	C11	Crocodile
18. 5	16. 4	F6	A11	Pig	30. 7	1. 7	J9	D12	Dragon
19. 5	17. 4	F6	B12	Porcupine	31. 7	2. 7	J9	E1	Badger
20. 5	18. 4	F6	C1	Wolf	1. 8	3. 7	J9	F2	Hare

Solar date	Lunar date	Month HS/EB	Day HS/EB	Constellation	Solar date	Lunar date	Month HS/EB	Day HS/EB	Constellation
2. 8	4. 7	J9	G3	Fox	14.10	18. 9	A11	K4	Tapir
3. 8	5. 7	J9	H4	Tiger	15.10	19. 9	A11	A5	Sheep
4. 8	6. 7	J9	J5	Leopard	16.10	20. 9	A11	B6	Deer
5. 8	7. 7	J9	K6	Griffon	17.10	21. 9	A11	C7	Horse
6. 8	8. 7	J9	A7	Ox	18.10	22. 9	A11	D8	Stag
7. 8	9. 7	J9	B8	Bat	19.10	23. 9	A11	E9	Serpent
8. 8	10. 7	J9	C9	Rat	20.10	24. 9	A11	F10	Earthworm
9. 8	11. 7	J9	D10	Swallow	21.10	25. 9	A11	G11	Crocodile
10. 8	12. 7	J9	E11	Pig	22.10	26. 9	A11	H12	Dragon
11. 8	13. 7	J9	F12	Porcupine	23.10	27. 9	A11	J1	Badger
12. 8	14. 7	J9	G1	Wolf	24.10	28. 9	A11	K2	Hare
13. 8	15. 7	J9	H2	Dog	25.10	29. 9	A11	A3	Fox
14. 8	16. 7	J9	J3	Pheasant	26.10	30. 9	A11	B4	Tiger
15. 8	17. 7	J9	K4	Cock	27.10	1.10	B12	C5	Leopard
16. 8	18. 7	J9	A5	Crow	28.10	2.10	B12	D6	Griffon
17. 8	19. 7	J9	B6	Monkey	29.10	3.10	B12	E7	Ox
18. 8	20. 7	J9	C7	Gibbon	30.10	4.10	B12	F8	Bat
19. 8	21. 7	J9	D8	Tapir	31.10	5.10	B12	G9	Rat
20. 8	22. 7	J9	E9	Sheep	1.11	6.10	B12	H10	Swallow
21. 8	23. 7	J9	F10	Deer	2.11	7.10	B12	J11	Pig
22. 8	24. 7	J9	G11	Horse	3.11	8.10	B12	K12	Porcupine
23. 8	25. 7	J9	H12	Stag	4.11	9.10	B12	A1	Wolf
24. 8	26. 7	J9	J1	Serpent	5.11	10.10	B12	B2	Dog
25. 8	27. 7	J9	K2	Earthworm	6.11	11.10	B12	C3	Pheasant
26. 8	28. 7	J9	A3	Crocodile	7.11	12.10	B12	D4	Cock
27. 8	29. 7	J9	B4	Dragon	8.11	13.10	B12	E5	Crow
28. 8	1. 8	K10	C5	Badger	9.11	14.10	B12	F6	Monkey
29. 8	2. 8	K10	D6	Hare	10.11	15.10	B12	G7	Gibbon
30. 8	3. 8	K10	E7	Fox	11.11	16.10	B12	H8	Tapir
31. 8	4. 8	K10	F8	Tiger	12.11	17.10	B12	J9	Sheep
1. 9	5. 8	K10	G9	Leopard	13.11	18.10	B12	K10	Deer
2. 9	6. 8	K10	H10	Griffon	14.11	19.10	B12	A11	Horse
3. 9	7. 8	K10	J11	Ox	15.11	20.10	B12	B12	Stag
4. 9	8. 8	K10	K12	Bat	16.11	21.10	B12	C1	Serpent
5. 9	9. 8	K10	A1	Rat	17.11	22.10	B12	D2	Earthworm
6. 9	10. 8	K10	B2	Swallow	18.11	23.10	B12	E3	Crocodile
7. 9	11. 8	K10	C3	Pig	19.11	24.10	B12	F4	Dragon
8. 9	12. 8	K10	D4	Porcupine	20.11	25.10	B12	G5	Badger
9. 9	13. 8	K10	E5	Wolf	21.11	26.10	B12	H6	Hare
10. 9	14. 8	K10	F6	Dog	22.11	27.10	B12	J7	Fox
11. 9	15. 8	K10	G7	Pheasant	23.11	28.10	B12	K8	Tiger
12. 9	16. 8	K10	H8	Cock	24.11	29.10	B12	A9	Leopard
13. 9	17. 8	K10	J9	Crow	25.11	1.11	C1	B10	Griffon
14. 9	18. 8	K10	K10	Monkey	26.11	2.11 .	C1	C11	Ox
15. 9	19. 8	K10	A11	Gibbon	27.11	3.11	C1	D12	Bat
16. 9	20. 8	K10	B12	Tapir	28.11	4.11	C1	E1	Rat
17. 9	21. 8	K10	C1	Sheep	29.11	5.11	C1	F2	Swallow
18. 9	22. 8	K10	D2	Deer	30.11	6.11	C1	G3	Pig
19. 9	23. 8	K10	E3	Horse	1.12	7.11	C1	H4	Porcupine
20. 9	24. 8	K10	F4	Stag	2.12	8.11	C1	J5	Wolf
21. 9	25. 8	K10	G5	Serpent	3.12	9.11	C1	K6	Dog
22. 9	26. 8	K10	H6	Earthworm	4.12	10.11	C1	A7	Pheasant
23. 9	27. 8	K10	J7	Crocodile	5.12	11.11	C1	B8	Cock
24. 9	28. 8	K10	K8	Dragon	6.12	12.11	C1	C9	Crow
25. 9	29. 8	K10	A9	Badger	7.12	13.11	C1	D10	Monkey
26. 9	30. 8	K10	B10	Hare	8.12	14.11	C1	E11	Gibbon
27. 9	1. 9	A11	C11	Fox	9.12	15.11	C1	F12	Tapir
28. 9	2. 9	A11	D12	Tiger	10.12	16.11	C1	G1	Sheep
29. 9	3. 9	A11	E1	Leopard	11.12	17.11	C1	H2	Deer
30. 9	4. 9	A11	F2	Griffon	12.12	18.11	C1	J3	Horse
1.10	5. 9	A11	G3	Ox	13.12	19.11	C1	K4	Stag
2.10	6. 9	A11	H4	Bat	14.12	20.11	C1	A5	Serpent
3.10	7. 9	A11	J5	Rat	15.12	21.11	C1	B6	Earthworm
4.10	8. 9	A11	K6	Swallow	16.12	22.11	C1	C7	Crocodile
5.10	9. 9	A11	A7	Pig	17.12	23.11	C1	D8	Dragon
6.10	10. 9	A11	B8	Porcupine	18.12	24.11	C1	E9	Badger
7.10	11. 9	A11	C9	Wolf	19.12	25.11	C1	F10	Hare
8.10	12. 9	A11	D10	Dog	20.12	26.11	C1	G11	Fox
9.10	13. 9	A11	E11	Pheasant	21.12	27.11	C1	H12	Tiger
10.10	14. 9	A11	F12	Cock	22.12	28.11	C1	J1	Leopard
11.10	15. 9	A11	G1	Crow	23.12	29.11	C1	K2	Griffon
12.10	16. 9	A11	H2	Monkey	24.12	30.11	C1	A3	Ox
13.10	17. 9	A11	J3	Gibbon	25.12	1. 12	D2	B4	Bat

Solar date	Lunar date	Month HS/EB	Day HS/EB	Constellation
26.12	2.12	D2	C5	Rat
27.12	3.12	D2	D6	Swallow
28.12	4.12	D2	E7	Pig
29.12	5.12	D2	F8	Porcupine
30.12	6.12	D2	G9	Wolf
31.12	7.12	D2	H10	Dog
1955				
1. 1	8.12	D2	J11	Pheasant
2. 1	9.12	D2	K12	Cock
3. 1	10.12	D2	A1	Crow
4. 1	11.12	D2	B2	Monkey
5. 1	12.12	D2	C3	Gibbon
6. 1	13.12	D2	D4	Tapir
7. 1	14.12	D2	E5	Sheep
8. 1	15.12	D2	F6	Deer
9. 1	16.12	D2	G7	Horse
10. 1	17.12	D2	H8	Stag
11. 1	18.12	D2	J9	Serpent
12. 1	19.12	D2	K10	Earthworm
13. 1	20.12	D2	A11	Crocodile
14. 1	21.12	D2	B12	Dragon
15. 1	22.12	D2	C1	Badger
16. 1	23.12	D2	D2	Hare
17. 1	24.12	D2	E3	Fox
18. 1	25.12	D2	F4	Tiger
19. 1	26.12	D2	G5	Leopard
20. 1	27.12	D2	H6	Griffon
21. 1	28.12	D2	J7	Ox
22. 1	29.12	D2	K8	Bat
23. 1	30.12	D2	A9	Rat

YI WEI YEAR

Solar date	Lunar date	Month HS/EB	Day HS/EB	Constellation
24. 1	1. 1	E3	B10	Swallow
25. 1	2. 1	E3	C11	Pig
26. 1	3. 1	E3	D12	Porcupine
27. 1	4. 1	E3	E1	Wolf
28. 1	5. 1	E3	F2	Dog
29. 1	6. 1	E3	G3	Pheasant
30. 1	7. 1	E3	H4	Cock
31. 1	8. 1	E3	J5	Crow
1. 2	9. 1	E3	K6	Monkey
2. 2	10. 1	E3	A7	Gibbon
3. 2	11. 1	E3	B8	Tapir
4. 2	12. 1	E3	C9	Sheep
5. 2	13. 1	E3	D10	Deer
6. 2	14. 1	E3	E11	Horse
7. 2	15. 1	E3	F12	Stag
8. 2	16. 1	E3	G1	Serpent
9. 2	17. 1	E3	H2	Earthworm
10. 2	18. 1	E3	J3	Crocodile
11. 2	19. 1	E3	K4	Dragon
12. 2	20. 1	E3	A5	Badger
13. 2	21. 1	E3	B6	Hare
14. 2	22. 1	E3	C7	Fox
15. 2	23. 1	E3	D8	Tiger
16. 2	24. 1	E3	E9	Leopard
17. 2	25. 1	E3	F10	Griffon
18. 2	26. 1	E3	G11	Ox
19. 2	27. 1	E3	H12	Bat
20. 2	28. 1	E3	J1	Rat
21. 2	29. 1	E3	K2	Swallow
22. 2	1. 2	F4	A3	Pig
23. 2	2. 2	F4	B4	Porcupine
24. 2	3. 2	F4	C5	Wolf
25. 2	4. 2	F4	D6	Dog
26. 2	5. 2	F4	E7	Pheasant
27. 2	6. 2	F4	F8	Cock
28. 2	7. 2	F4	G9	Crow
1. 3	8. 2	F4	H10	Monkey
2. 3	9. 2	F4	J11	Gibbon
3. 3	10. 2	F4	K12	Tapir
4. 3	11. 2	F4	A1	Sheep
5. 3	12. 2	F4	B2	Deer
6. 3	13. 2	F4	C3	Horse
7. 3	14. 2	F4	D4	Stag
8. 3	15. 2	F4	E5	Serpent
9. 3	16. 2	F4	F6	Earthworm
10. 3	17. 2	F4	G7	Crocodile
11. 3	18. 2	F4	H8	Dragon
12. 3	19. 2	F4	H8	Badger
13. 3	20. 2	F4	K10	Hare
14. 3	21. 2	F4	A11	Fox
15. 3	22. 2	F4	B12	Tiger
16. 3	23. 2	F4	C1	Leopard
17. 3	24. 2	F4	D2	Griffon
18. 3	25. 2	F4	E3	Ox
19. 3	26. 2	F4	F4	Bat
20. 3	27. 2	F4	G5	Rat
21. 3	28. 2	F4	H6	Swallow
22. 3	29. 2	F4	J7	Pig
23. 3	30. 2	F4	K8	Porcupine
24. 3	1. 3	G5	A9	Wolf
25. 3	2. 3	G5	B10	Dog
26. 3	3. 3	G5	C11	Pheasant
27. 3	4. 3	G5	D12	Cock
28. 3	5. 3	G5	E1	Crow
29. 3	6. 3	G5	F2	Monkey
30. 3	7. 3	G5	G3	Gibbon
31. 3	8. 3	G5	H4	Tapir
1. 4	9. 3	G5	J5	Sheep
2. 4	10. 3	G5	K6	Deer
3. 4	11. 3	G5	A7	Horse
4. 4	12. 3	G5	B8	Stag
5. 4	13. 3	G5	C9	Serpent
6. 4	14. 3	G5	D10	Earthworm
7. 4	15. 3	G5	E11	Crocodile
8. 4	16. 3	G5	F12	Dragon
9. 4	17. 3	G5	G1	Badger
10. 4	18. 3	G5	H2	Hare
11. 4	19. 3	G5	J3	Fox
12. 4	20. 3	G5	K4	Tiger
13. 4	21. 3	G5	A5	Leopard
14. 4	22. 3	G5	B6	Griffon
15. 4	23. 3	G5	C7	Ox
16. 4	24. 3	G5	D8	Bat
17. 4	25. 3	G5	E9	Rat
18. 4	26. 3	G5	F10	Swallow
19. 4	27. 3	G5	G11	Pig
20. 4	28. 3	G5	H12	Porcupine
21. 4	29. 3	G5	J1	Wolf
22. 4	*1. 3*	*G5*	K2	Dog
23. 4	*2. 3*	*G5*	A3	Pheasant
24. 4	*3. 3*	*G5*	B4	Cock
25. 4	*4. 3*	*G5*	C5	Crow
26. 4	*5. 3*	*G5*	D6	Monkey
27. 4	*6. 3*	*G5*	E7	Gibbon
28. 4	*7. 3*	*G5*	F8	Tapir
29. 4	*8. 3*	*G5*	G9	Sheep
30. 4	*9. 3*	*G5*	H10	Deer
1. 5	*10. 3*	*G5*	J11	Horse
2. 5	*11. 3*	*G5*	K12	Stag
3. 5	*12. 3*	*G5*	A1	Serpent
4. 5	*13. 3*	*G5*	B2	Earthworm
5. 5	*14. 3*	*G5*	C3	Crocodile
6. 5	*15. 3*	*G5*	D4	Dragon
7. 5	*16. 3*	*G5*	E5	Badger

Solar date	Lunar date	Month HS/EB	Day HS/EB	Constellation
8. 5	17. 3	G5	F6	Hare
9. 5	18. 3	G5	G7	Fox
10. 5	19. 3	G5	H8	Tiger
11. 5	20. 3	G5	J9	Leopard
12. 5	21. 3	G5	K10	Griffon
13. 5	22. 3	G5	A11	Ox
14. 5	23. 3	G5	B12	Bat
15. 5	24. 3	G5	C1	Rat
16. 5	25. 3	G5	D2	Swallow
17. 5	26. 3	G5	E3	Pig
18. 5	27. 3	G5	F4	Porcupine
19. 5	28. 3	G5	G5	Wolf
20. 5	29. 3	G5	H6	Dog
21. 5	30. 3	G5	J7	Pheasant
22. 5	1. 4	H6	K8	Cock
23. 5	2. 4	H6	A9	Crow
24. 5	3. 4	H6	B10	Monkey
25. 5	4. 4	H6	C11	Gibbon
26. 5	5. 4	H6	D12	Tapir
27. 5	6. 4	H6	E1	Sheep
28. 5	7. 4	H6	F2	Deer
29. 5	8. 4	H6	G3	Horse
30. 5	9. 4	H6	H4	Stag
31. 5	10. 4	H6	J5	Serpent
1. 6	11. 4	H6	K6	Earthworm
2. 6	12. 4	H6	A7	Crocodile
3. 6	13. 4	H6	B8	Dragon
4. 6	14. 4	H6	C9	Badger
5. 6	15. 4	H6	D10	Hare
6. 6	16. 4	H6	E11	Fox
7. 6	17. 4	H6	F12	Tiger
8. 6	18. 4	H6	G1	Leopard
9. 6	19. 4	H6	H2	Griffon
10. 6	20. 4	H6	J3	Ox
11. 6	21. 4	H6	K4	Bat
12. 6	22. 4	H6	A5	Rat
13. 6	23. 4	H6	B6	Swallow
14. 6	24. 4	H6	C7	Pig
15. 6	25. 4	H6	D8	Porcupine
16. 6	26. 4	H6	E9	Wolf
17. 6	27. 4	H6	F10	Dog
18. 6	28. 4	H6	G11	Pheasant
19. 6	29. 4	H6	H12	Cock
20. 6	1. 5	J7	J1	Crow
21. 6	2. 5	J7	K2	Monkey
22. 6	3. 5	J7	A3	Gibbon
23. 6	4. 5	J7	B4	Tapir
24. 6	5. 5	J7	C5	Sheep
25. 6	6. 5	J7	D6	Deer
26. 6	7. 5	J7	E7	Horse
27. 6	8. 5	J7	F8	Stag
28. 6	9. 5	J7	G9	Serpent
29. 6	10. 5	J7	H10	Earthworm
30. 6	11. 5	J7	J11	Crocodile
1. 7	12. 5	J7	K12	Dragon
2. 7	13. 5	J7	A1	Badger
3. 7	14. 5	J7	B2	Hare
4. 7	15. 5	J7	C3	Fox
5. 7	16. 5	J7	D4	Tiger
6. 7	17. 5	J7	E5	Leopard
7. 7	18. 5	J7	F6	Griffon
8. 7	19. 5	J7	G7	Ox
9. 7	20. 5	J7	H8	Bat
10. 7	21. 5	J7	J9	Rat
11. 7	22. 5	J7	K10	Swallow
12. 7	23. 5	J7	A11	Pig
13. 7	24. 5	J7	B12	Porcupine
14. 7	25. 5	J7	C1	Wolf
15. 7	26. 5	J7	D2	Dog
16. 7	27. 5	J7	E3	Pheasant
17. 7	28. 5	J7	F4	Cock
18. 7	29. 5	J7	G5	Crow
19. 7	1. 6	K8	H6	Monkey
20. 7	2. 6	K8	J7	Gibbon
21. 7	3. 6	K8	K8	Tapir
22. 7	4. 6	K8	A9	Sheep
23. 7	5. 6	K8	B10	Deer
24. 7	6. 6	K8	C11	Horse
25. 7	7. 6	K8	D12	Stag
26. 7	8. 6	K8	E1	Serpent
27. 7	9. 6	K8	F2	Earthworm
28. 7	10. 6	K8	G3	Crocodile
29. 7	11. 6	K8	H4	Dragon
30. 7	12. 6	K8	J5	Badger
31. 7	13. 6	K8	K6	Hare
1. 8	14. 6	K8	A7	Fox
2. 8	15. 6	K8	B8	Tiger
3. 8	16. 6	K8	C9	Leopard
4. 8	17. 6	K8	D10	Griffon
5. 8	18. 6	K8	E11	Ox
6. 8	19. 6	K8	F12	Bat
7. 8	20. 6	K8	G1	Rat
8. 8	21. 6	K8	H2	Swallow
9. 8	22. 6	K8	J3	Pig
10. 8	23. 6	K8	K4	Porcupine
11. 8	24. 6	K8	A5	Wolf
12. 8	25. 6	K8	B6	Dog
13. 8	26. 6	K8	C7	Pheasant
14. 8	27. 6	K8	D8	Cock
15. 8	28. 6	K8	E9	Crow
16. 8	29. 6	K8	F10	Monkey
17. 8	30. 6	K8	G11	Gibbon
18. 8	1. 7	A9	H12	Tapir
19. 8	2. 7	A9	J1	Sheep
20. 8	3. 7	A9	K2	Deer
21. 8	4. 7	A9	A3	Horse
22. 8	5. 7	A9	B4	Stag
23. 8	6. 7	A9	C5	Serpent
24. 8	7. 7	A9	D6	Earthworm
25. 8	8. 7	A9	E7	Crocodile
26. 8	9. 7	A9	F8	Dragon
27. 8	10. 7	A9	G9	Badger
28. 8	11. 7	A9	H10	Hare
29. 8	12. 7	A9	J11	Fox
30. 8	13. 7	A9	K12	Tiger
31. 8	14. 7	A9	A1	Leopard
1. 9	15. 7	A9	B2	Griffon
2. 9	16. 7	A9	C3	Ox
3. 9	17. 7	A9	D4	Bat
4. 9	18. 7	A9	E5	Rat
5. 9	19. 7	A9	F6	Swallow
6. 9	20. 7	A9	G7	Pig
7. 9	21. 7	A9	H8	Porcupine
8. 9	22. 7	A9	J9	Wolf
9. 9	23. 7	A9	K10	Dog
10. 9	24. 7	A9	A11	Pheasant
11. 9	25. 7	A9	B12	Cock
12. 9	26. 7	A9	C1	Crow
13. 9	27. 7	A9	D2	Monkey
14. 9	28. 7	A9	E3	Gibbon
15. 9	29. 7	A9	F4	Tapir
16. 9	1. 8	B10	G5	Sheep
17. 9	2. 8	B10	H6	Deer
18. 9	3. 8	B10	J7	Horse
19. 9	4. 8	B10	K8	Stag
20. 9	5. 8	B10	A9	Serpent
21. 9	6. 8	B10	B10	Earthworm
22. 9	7. 8	B10	C11	Crocodile
23. 9	8. 8	B10	D12	Dragon
24. 9	9. 8	B10	E1	Badger
25. 9	10. 8	B10	F2	Hare
26. 9	11. 8	B10	G3	Fox
27. 9	12. 8	B10	H4	Tiger
28. 9	13. 8	B10	J5	Leopard
29. 9	14. 8	B10	K6	Griffon
30. 9	15. 8	B10	A7	Ox

Solar date	Lunar date	Month HS/EB	Day HS/EB	Constellation	Solar date	Lunar date	Month HS/EB	Day HS/EB	Constellation
1.10	16. 8	B10	B8	Bat	8.12	25.10	D12	K4	Tapir
2.10	17. 8	B10	C9	Rat	9.12	26.10	D12	A5	Sheep
3.10	18. 8	B10	D10	Swallow	10.12	27.10	D12	B6	Deer
4.10	19. 8	B10	E11	Pig	11.12	28.10	D12	C7	Horse
5.10	20. 8	B10	F12	Porcupine	12.12	29.10	D12	D8	Stag
6.10	21. 8	B10	G1	Wolf	13.12	30.10	D12	E9	Serpent
7.10	22. 8	B10	H2	Dog	14.12	1.11	E1	F10	Earthworm
8.10	23. 8	B10	J3	Pheasant	15.12	2.11	E1	G11	Crocodile
9.10	24. 8	B10	K4	Cock	16.12	3.11	E1	H12	Dragon
10.10	25. 8	B10	A5	Crow	17.12	4.11	E1	J1	Badger
11.10	26. 8	B10	B6	Monkey	18.12	5.11	E1	K2	Hare
12.10	27. 8	B10	C7	Gibbon	19.12	6.11	E1	A3	Fox
13.10	28. 8	B10	D8	Tapir	20.12	7.11	E1	B4	Tiger
14.10	29. 8	B10	E9	Sheep	21.12	8.11	E1	C5	Leopard
15.10	30. 8	B10	F10	Deer	22.12	9.11	E1	D6	Griffon
16.10	1. 9	C11	G11	Horse	23.12	10.11	E1	E7	Ox
17.10	2. 9	C11	H12	Stag	24.12	11.11	E1	F8	Bat
18.10	3. 9	C11	J1	Serpent	25.12	12.11	E1	G9	Rat
19.10	4. 9	C11	K2	Earthworm	26.12	13.11	E1	H10	Swallow
20.10	5. 9	C11	A3	Crocodile	27.12	14.11	E1	J11	Pig
21.10	6. 9	C11	B4	Dragon	28.12	15.11	E1	K12	Porcupine
22.10	7. 9	C11	C5	Badger	29.12	16.11	E1	A1	Wolf
23.10	8. 9	C11	D6	Hare	30.12	17.11	E1	B2	Dog
24.10	9. 9	C11	E7	Fox	31.12	18.11	E1	C3	Pheasant
25.10	10. 9	C11	F8	Tiger					
26.10	11. 9	C11	G9	Leopard	**1956**				
27.10	12. 9	C11	H10	Griffon	1. 1	19.11	E1	D4	Cock
28.10	13. 9	C11	J11	Ox	2. 1	20.11	E1	E5	Crow
29.10	14. 9	C11	K12	Bat	3. 1	21.11	E1	F6	Monkey
30.10	15. 9	C11	A1	Rat	4. 1	22.11	E1	G7	Gibbon
31.10	16. 9	C11	B2	Swallow	5. 1	23.11	E1	H8	Tapir
1.11	17. 9	C11	C3	Pig	6. 1	24.11	E1	J9	Sheep
2.11	18. 9	C11	D4	Porcupine	7. 1	25.11	E1	K10	Deer
3.11	19. 9	C11	E5	Wolf	8. 1	26.11	E1	A11	Horse
4.11	20. 9	C11	F6	Dog	9. 1	27.11	E1	B12	Stag
5.11	21. 9	C11	G7	Pheasant	10. 1	28.11	E1	C1	Serpent
6.11	22. 9	C11	H8	Cock	11. 1	29.11	E1	D2	Earthworm
7.11	23. 9	C11	J9	Crow	12. 1	30.11	E1	E3	Crocodile
8.11	24. 9	C11	K10	Monkey	13. 1	1.12	F2	F4	Dragon
9.11	25. 9	C11	A11	Gibbon	14. 1	2.12	F2	G5	Badger
10.11	26. 9	C11	B12	Tapir	15. 1	3.12	F2	H6	Hare
11.11	27. 9	C11	C1	Sheep	16. 1	4.12	F2	J7	Fox
12.11	28. 9	C11	D2	Deer	17. 1	5.12	F2	K8	Tiger
13.11	29. 9	C11	E3	Horse	18. 1	6.12	F2	A9	Leopard
14.11	1.10	D12	F4	Stag	19. 1	7.12	F2	B10	Griffon
15.11	2.10	D12	G5	Serpent	20. 1	8.12	F2	C11	Ox
16.11	3.10	D12	H6	Earthworm	21. 1	9.12	F2	D12	Bat
17.11	4.10	D12	J7	Crocodile	22. 1	10.12	F2	E1	Rat
18.11	5.10	D12	K8	Dragon	23. 1	11.12	F2	F2	Swallow
19.11	6.10	D12	A9	Badger	24. 1	12.12	F2	G3	Pig
20.11	7.10	D12	B10	Hare	25. 1	13.12	F2	H4	Porcupine
21.11	8.10	D12	C11	Fox	26. 1	14.12	F2	J5	Wolf
22.11	9.10	D12	D12	Tiger	27. 1	15.12	F2	K6	Dog
23.11	10.10	D12	E1	Leopard	28. 1	16.12	F2	A7	Pheasant
24.11	11.10	D12	F2	Griffon	29. 1	17.12	F2	B8	Cock
25.11	12.10	D12	G3	Ox	30. 1	18.12	F2	C9	Crow
26.11	13.10	D12	H4	Bat	31. 1	19.12	F2	D10	Monkey
27.11	14.10	D12	J5	Rat	1. 2	20.12	F2	E11	Gibbon
28.11	15.10	D12	K6	Swallow	2. 2	21.12	F2	F12	Tapir
29.11	16.10	D12	A7	Pig	3. 2	22.12	F2	G1	Sheep
30.11	17.10	D12	B8	Porcupine	4. 2	23.12	F2	H2	Deer
1.12	18.10	D12	C9	Wolf	5. 2	24.12	F2	J3	Horse
2.12	19.10	D12	D10	Dog	6. 2	25.12	F2	K4	Stag
3.12	20.10	D12	E11	Pheasant	7. 2	26.12	F2	A5	Serpent
4.12	21.10	D12	F12	Cock	8. 2	27.12	F2	B6	Earthworm
5.12	22.10	D12	G1	Crow	9. 2	28.12	F2	C7	Crocodile
6.12	23.10	D12	H2	Monkey	10. 2	29.12	F2	D8	Dragon
7.12	24.10	D12	J3	Gibbon	11. 2	30.12	F2	E9	Badger

PING SHEN YEAR

Solar date	Lunar date	Month HS/EB	Day HS/EB	Constellation	Solar date	Lunar date	Month HS/EB	Day HS/EB	Constellation
12. 2	1. 1	G3	F10	Hare	23. 4	13. 3	J5	G9	Crow
13. 2	2. 1	G3	G11	Fox	24. 4	14. 3	J5	H10	Monkey
14. 2	3. 1	G3	H12	Tiger	25. 4	15. 3	J5	J11	Gibbon
15. 2	4. 1	G3	J1	Leopard	26. 4	16. 3	J5	K12	Tapir
16. 2	5. 1	G3	K2	Griffon	27. 4	17. 3	J5	A1	Sheep
17. 2	6. 1	G3	A3	Ox	28. 4	18. 3	J5	B2	Deer
18. 2	7. 1	G3	B4	Bat	29. 4	19. 3	J5	C3	Horse
19. 2	8. 1	G3	C5	Rat	30. 4	20. 3	J5	D4	Stag
20. 2	9. 1	G3	D6	Swallow	1. 5	21. 3	J5	E5	Serpent
21. 2	10. 1	G3	E7	Pig	2. 5	22. 3	J5	F6	Earthworm
22. 2	11. 1	G3	F8	Porcupine	3. 5	23. 3	J5	G7	Crocodile
23. 2	12. 1	G3	G9	Wolf	4. 5	24. 3	J5	H8	Dragon
24. 2	13. 1	G3	H10	Dog	5. 5	25. 3	J5	J9	Badger
25. 2	14. 1	G3	J11	Pheasant	6. 5	26. 3	J5	K10	Hare
26. 2	15. 1	G3	K12	Cock	7. 5	27. 3	J5	A11	Fox
27. 2	16. 1	G3	A1	Crow	8. 5	28. 3	J5	B12	Tiger
28. 2	17. 1	G3	B2	Monkey	9. 5	29. 3	J5	C1	Leopard
29. 2	18. 1	G3	C3	Gibbon	10. 5	1. 4	K6	D2	Griffon
1. 3	19. 1	G3	D4	Tapir	11. 5	2. 4	K6	E3	Ox
2. 3	20. 1	G3	E5	Sheep	12. 5	3. 4	K6	F4	Bat
3. 3	21. 1	G3	F6	Deer	13. 5	4. 4	K6	G5	Rat
4. 3	22. 1	G3	G7	Horse	14. 5	5. 4	K6	H6	Swallow
5. 3	23. 1	G3	H8	Stag	15. 5	6. 4	K6	J7	Pig
6. 3	24. 1	G3	J9	Serpent	16. 5	7. 4	K6	K8	Porcupine
7. 3	25. 1	G3	K10	Earthworm	17. 5	8. 4	K6	A9	Wolf
8. 3	26. 1	G3	A11	Crocodile	18. 5	9. 4	K6	B10	Dog
9. 3	27. 1	G3	B12	Dragon	19. 5	10. 4	K6	C11	Pheasant
10. 3	28. 1	G3	C1	Badger	20. 5	11. 4	K6	D12	Cock
11. 3	29. 1	G3	D2	Hare	21. 5	12. 4	K6	E1	Crow
12. 3	1. 2	H4	E3	Fox	22. 5	13. 4	K6	F2	Monkey
13. 3	2. 2	H4	F4	Tiger	23. 5	14. 4	K6	G3	Gibbon
14. 3	3. 2	H4	G5	Leopard	24. 5	15. 4	K6	H4	Tapir
15. 3	4. 2	H4	H6	Griffon	25. 5	16. 4	K6	J5	Sheep
16. 3	5. 2	H4	J7	Ox	26. 5	17. 4	K6	K6	Deer
17. 3	6. 2	H4	K8	Bat	27. 5	18. 4	K6	A7	Horse
18. 3	7. 2	H4	A9	Rat	28. 5	19. 4	K6	B8	Stag
19. 3	8. 2	H4	B10	Swallow	29. 5	20. 4	K6	C9	Serpent
20. 3	9. 2	H4	C11	Pig	30. 5	21. 4	K6	D10	Earthworm
21. 3	10. 2	H4	D12	Porcupine	31. 5	22. 4	K6	E11	Crocodile
22. 3	11. 2	H4	E1	Wolf	1. 6	23. 4	K6	F12	Dragon
23. 3	12. 2	H4	F2	Dog	2. 6	24. 4	K6	G1	Badger
24. 3	13. 2	H4	G3	Pheasant	3. 6	25. 4	K6	H2	Hare
25. 3	14. 2	H4	H4	Cock	4. 6	26. 4	K6	J3	Fox
26. 3	15. 2	H4	J5	Crow	5. 6	27. 4	K6	K4	Tiger
27. 3	16. 2	H4	K6	Monkey	6. 6	28. 4	K6	A5	Leopard
28. 3	18. 2	H4	A7	Gibbon	7. 6	29. 4	K6	B6	Griffon
29. 3	18. 2	H4	B8	Tapir	8. 6	30. 4	K6	C7	Ox
30. 3	19. 2	H4	C9	Sheep	9. 6	1. 5	A7	D8	Bat
31. 3	20. 2	H4	D10	Deer	10. 6	2. 5	A7	E9	Rat
1. 4	21. 2	H4	E11	Horse	11. 6	3. 5	A7	F10	Swallow
2. 4	22. 2	H4	F12	Stag	12. 6	4. 5	A7	G11	Pig
3. 4	23. 2	H4	G1	Serpent	13. 6	5. 5	A7	H12	Porcupine
4. 4	24. 2	H4	H2	Earthworm	14. 6	6. 5	A7	J1	Wolf
5. 4	25. 2	H4	J3	Crocodile	15. 6	7. 5	A7	K2	Dog
6. 4	26. 2	H4	K4	Dragon	16. 6	8. 5	A7	A3	Pheasant
7. 4	27. 2	H4	A5	Badger	17. 6	9. 5	A7	B4	Cock
8. 4	28. 2	H4	B6	Hare	18. 6	10. 5	A7	C5	Crow
9. 4	29. 2	H4	C7	Fox	19. 6	11. 5	A7	D6	Monkey
10. 4	30. 2	H4	D8	Tiger	20. 6	12. 5	A7	E7	Gibbon
11. 4	1. 3	J5	E9	Leopard	21. 6	13. 5	A7	F8	Tapir
12. 4	2. 3	J5	F10	Griffon	22. 6	14. 5	A7	G9	Sheep
13. 4	3. 3	J5	G11	Ox	23. 6	15. 5	A7	H10	Deer
14. 4	4. 3	J5	H12	Bat	24. 6	16. 5	A7	J11	Horse
15. 4	5. 3	J5	J1	Rat	25. 6	17. 5	A7	K12	Stag
16. 4	6. 3	J5	K2	Swallow	26. 6	18. 5	A7	A1	Serpent
17. 4	7. 3	J5	A3	Pig	27. 6	19. 5	A7	B2	Earthworm
18. 4	8. 3	J5	B4	Porcupine	28. 6	20. 5	A7	C3	Crocodile
19. 4	9. 3	J5	C5	Wolf	29. 6	21. 5	A7	D4	Dragon
20. 4	10. 3	J5	D6	Dog	30. 6	22. 5	A7	E5	Badger
21. 4	11. 3	J5	E7	Pheasant	1. 7	23. 5	A7	F6	Hare
22. 4	12. 3	J5	F8	Cock	2. 7	24. 5	A7	G7	Fox

Solar date	Lunar date	Month HS/EB	Day HS/EB	Constellation	Solar date	Lunar date	Month HS/EB	Day HS/EB	Constellation
3. 7	25. 5	A7	H8	Tiger	14. 9	10. 8	D10	A9	Sheep
4. 7	26. 5	A7	J9	Leopard	15. 9	11. 8	D10	B10	Deer
5. 7	27. 5	A7	K10	Griffon	16. 9	12. 8	D10	C11	Horse
6. 7	28. 5	A7	A11	Ox	17. 9	13. 8	D10	D12	Stag
7. 7	29. 5	A7	B12	Bat	18. 9	14. 8	D10	E1	Serpent
8. 7	1. 6	B8	C1	Rat	19. 9	15. 8	D10	F2	Earthworm
9. 7	2. 6	B8	D2	Swallow	20. 9	16. 8	D10	G3	Crocodile
10. 7	3. 6	B8	E3	Pig	21. 9	17. 8	D10	H4	Dragon
11. 7	4. 6	B8	F4	Porcupine	22. 9	18. 8	D10	J5	Badger
12. 7	5. 6	B8	G5	Wolf	23. 9	19. 8	D10	K6	Hare
13. 7	6. 6	B8	H6	Dog	24. 9	20. 8	D10	A7	Fox
14. 7	7. 6	B8	J7	Pheasant	25. 9	21. 8	D10	B8	Tiger
15. 7	8. 6	B8	K8	Cock	26. 9	22. 8	D10	C9	Leopard
16. 7	9. 6	B8	A9	Crow	27. 9	23. 8	D10	D10	Griffon
17. 7	10. 6	B8	B10	Monkey	28. 9	24. 8	D10	E11	Ox
18. 7	11. 6	B8	C11	Gibbon	29. 9	25. 8	D10	F12	Bat
19. 7	12. 6	B8	D12	Tapir	30. 9	26. 8	D10	G1	Rat
20. 7	13. 6	B8	E1	Sheep	1.10	27. 8	D10	H2	Swallow
21. 7	14. 6	B8	F2	Deer	2.10	28. 8	D10	J3	Pig
22. 7	15. 6	B8	G3	Horse	3.10	29. 8	D10	K4	Porcupine
23. 7	16. 6	B8	H4	Stag	4.10	1. 9	E11	A5	Wolf
24. 7	17. 6	B8	J5	Serpent	5.10	2. 9	E11	B6	Dog
25. 7	18. 6	B8	K6	Earthworm	6.10	3. 9	E11	C7	Pheasant
26. 7	19. 6	B8	A7	Crocodile	7.10	4. 9	E11	D8	Cock
27. 7	20. 6	B8	B8	Dragon	8.10	5. 9	E11	E9	Crow
28. 7	21. 6	B8	C9	Badger	9.10	6. 9	E11	F10	Monkey
29. 7	22. 6	B8	D10	Hare	10.10	7. 9	E11	G11	Gibbon
30. 7	23. 6	B8	E11	Fox	11.10	8. 9	E11	H12	Tapir
31. 7	24. 6	B8	F12	Tiger	12.10	9. 9	E11	J1	Sheep
1. 8	25. 6	B8	G1	Leopard	13.10	10. 9	E11	K2	Deer
2. 8	26. 6	B8	H2	Griffon	14.10	11. 9	E11	A3	Horse
3. 8	27. 6	B8	J3	Ox	15.10	12. 9	E11	B4	Stag
4. 8	28. 6	B8	K4	Bat	16.10	13. 9	E11	C5	Serpent
5. 8	29. 6	B8	A5	Rat	17.10	14. 9	E11	D6	Earthworm
6. 8	1. 7	C9	B6	Swallow	18.10	15. 9	E11	E7	Crocodile
7. 8	2. 7	C9	C7	Pig	19.10	16. 9	E11	F8	Dragon
8. 8	3. 7	C9	D8	Porcupine	20.10	17. 9	E11	G9	Badger
9. 8	4. 7	C9	E9	Wolf	21.10	18. 9	E11	H10	Hare
10. 8	5. 7	C9	F10	Dog	22.10	19. 9	E11	J11	Fox
11. 8	6. 7	C9	G11	Pheasant	23.10	20. 9	E11	K12	Tiger
12. 8	7. 7	C9	H12	Cock	24.10	21. 9	E11	A1	Leopard
13. 8	8. 7	C9	J1	Crow	25.10	22. 9	E11	B2	Griffon
14. 8	9. 7	C9	K2	Monkey	26.10	23. 9	E11	C3	Ox
15. 8	10. 7	C9	A3	Gibbon	27.10	24. 9	E11	D4	Bat
16. 8	11. 7	C9	B4	Tapir	28.10	25. 9	E11	E5	Rat
17. 8	12. 7	C9	C5	Sheep	29.10	26. 9	E11	F6	Swallow
18. 8	13. 7	C9	D6	Deer	30.10	27. 9	E11	G7	Pig
19. 8	14. 7	C9	E7	Horse	31.10	28. 9	E11	H8	Porcupine
20. 8	15. 7	C9	F8	Stag	1.11	29. 9	E11	J9	Wolf
21. 8	16. 7	C9	G9	Serpent	2.11	30. 9	E11	K10	Dog
22. 8	17. 7	C9	H10	Earthworm	3.11	1.10	F12	A11	Pheasant
23. 8	18. 7	C9	J11	Crocodile	4.11	2.10	F12	B12	Cock
24. 8	19. 7	C9	K12	Dragon	5.11	3.10	F12	C1	Crow
25. 8	20. 7	C9	A1	Badger	6.11	4.10	F12	D2	Monkey
26. 8	21. 7	C9	B2	Hare	7.11	5.10	F12	E3	Gibbon
27. 8	22. 7	C9	C3	Fox	8.11	6.10	F12	F4	Tapir
28. 8	23. 7	C9	D4	Tiger	9.11	7.10	F12	G5	Sheep
29. 8	24. 7	C9	E5	Leopard	10.11	8.10	F12	H6	Deer
30. 8	25. 7	C9	F6	Griffon	11.11	9.10	F12	J7	Horse
31. 8	26. 7	C9	G7	Ox	12.11	10.10	F12	K8	Stag
1. 9	27. 7	C9	H8	Bat	13.11	11.10	F12	A9	Serpent
2. 9	28. 7	C9	J9	Rat	14.11	12.10	F12	B10	Earthworm
3. 9	29. 7	C9	K10	Swallow	15.11	13.10	F12	C11	Crocodile
4. 9	30. 7	C9	A11	Pig	16.11	14.10	F12	D12	Dragon
5. 9	1. 8	D10	B12	Porcupine	17.11	15.10	F12	E1	Badger
6. 9	2. 8	D10	C1	Wolf	18.11	16.10	F12	F2	Hare
7. 9	3. 8	D10	D2	Dog	19.11	17.10	F12	G3	Fox
8. 9	4. 8	D10	E3	Pheasant	20.11	18.10	F12	H4	Tiger
9. 9	5. 8	D10	F4	Cock	21.11	19.10	F12	J5	Leopard
10. 9	6. 8	D10	G5	Crow	22.11	20.10	F12	K6	Griffon
11. 9	7. 8	D10	H6	Monkey	23.11	21.10	F12	A7	Ox
12. 9	8. 8	D10	J7	Gibbon	24.11	22.10	F12	B8	Bat
13. 9	9. 8	D10	K8	Tapir	25.11	23.10	F12	C9	Rat

Solar date	Lunar date	Month HS/EB	Day HS/EB	Constellation	Solar date	Lunar date	Month HS/EB	Day HS/EB	Constellation
26.11	24.10	F12	D10	Swallow	30.12	29.11	G1	H8	Cock
27.11	25.10	F12	E11	Pig	31.12	30.11	G1	J9	Crow
28.11	26.10	F12	F12	Porcupine	**1957**				
29.11	27.10	F12	G1	Wolf	1. 1	1.12	H2	K10	Monkey
30.11	28.10	F12	H2	Dog	2. 1	2.12	H2	A11	Gibbon
1.12	29.10	F12	J3	Pheasant	3. 1	3.12	H2	B12	Tapir
2.12	1.11	G1	K4	Cock	4. 1	4.12	H2	C1	Sheep
3.12	2.11	G1	A5	Crow	5. 1	5.12	H2	D2	Deer
4.12	3.11	G1	B6	Monkey	6. 1	6.12	H2	E3	Horse
5.12	4.11	G1	C7	Gibbon	7. 1	7.12	H2	F4	Stag
6.12	5.11	G1	D8	Tapir	8. 1	8.12	H2	G5	Serpent
7.12	6.11	G1	E9	Sheep	9. 1	9.12	H2	H6	Earthworm
8.12	7.11	G1	F10	Deer	10. 1	10.12	H2	J7	Crocodile
9.12	8.11	G1	G11	Horse	11. 1	11.12	H2	K8	Dragon
10.12	9.11	G1	H12	Stag	12. 1	12.12	H2	A9	Badger
11.12	10.11	G1	J1	Serpent	13. 1	13.12	H2	B10	Hare
12.12	11.11	G1	K2	Earthworm	14. 1	14.12	H2	C11	Fox
13.12	12.11	G1	A3	Crocodile	15. 1	15.12	H2	D12	Tiger
14.12	13.11	G1	B4	Dragon	16. 1	16.12	H2	E1	Leopard
15.12	14.11	G1	C5	Badger	17. 1	17.12	H2	F2	Griffon
16.12	15.11	G1	D6	Hare	18. 1	18.12	H2	G3	Ox
17.12	16.11	G1	E7	Fox	19. 1	19.12	H2	H4	Bat
18.12	17.11	G1	F8	Tiger	20. 1	20.12	H2	J5	Rat
19.12	18.11	G1	G9	Leopard	21. 1	21.12	H2	K6	Swallow
20.12	19.11	G1	H10	Griffon	22. 1	22.12	H2	A7	Pig
21.12	20.11	G1	J11	Ox	23. 1	23.12	H2	B8	Porcupine
22.12	21.11	G1	K12	Bat	24. 1	24.12	H2	C9	Wolf
23.12	22.11	G1	A1	Rat	25. 1	25.12	H2	D10	Dog
24.12	23.11	G1	B2	Swallow	26. 1	26.12	H2	E11	Pheasant
25.12	24.11	G1	C3	Pig	27. 1	27.12	H2	F12	Cock
26.12	25.11	G1	D4	Porcupine	28. 1	28.12	H2	G1	Crow
27.12	26.11	G1	E5	Wolf	29. 1	29.12	H2	H2	Monkey
28.12	27.11	G1	F6	Dog	30. 1	30.12	H2	J3	Gibbon
29.12	28.11	G1	G7	Pheasant					

TING YU YEAR

Solar date	Lunar date	Month HS/EB	Day HS/EB	Constellation	Solar date	Lunar date	Month HS/EB	Day HS/EB	Constellation
31. 1	1. 1	J3	K4	Tapir	6. 3	5. 2	K4	D2	Earthworm
1. 2	2. 1	J3	A5	Sheep	7. 3	6. 2	K4	E3	Crocodile
2. 2	3. 1	J3	B6	Deer	8. 3	7. 2	K4	F4	Dragon
3. 2	4. 1	J3	C7	Horse	9. 3	8. 2	K4	G5	Badger
4. 2	5. 1	J3	D8	Stag	10. 3	9. 2	K4	H6	Hare
5. 2	6. 1	J3	E9	Serpent	11. 3	10. 2	K4	J7	Fox
6. 2	7. 1	J3	F10	Earthworm	12. 3	11. 2	K4	K8	Tiger
7. 2	8. 1	J3	G11	Crocodile	13. 3	12. 2	K4	A9	Leopard
8. 2	9. 1	J3	H12	Dragon	14. 3	13. 2	K4	B10	Griffon
9. 2	10. 1	J3	J1	Badger	15. 3	14. 2	K4	C11	Ox
10. 2	11. 1	J3	K2	Hare	16. 3	15. 2	K4	D12	Bat
11. 2	12. 1	J3	A3	Fox	17. 3	16. 2	K4	E1	Rat
12. 2	13. 1	J3	B4	Tiger	18. 3	17. 2	K4	F2	Swallow
13. 2	14. 1	J3	C5	Leopard	19. 3	18. 2	K4	G3	Pig
14. 2	15. 1	J3	D6	Griffon	20. 3	19. 2	K4	H4	Porcupine
15. 2	16. 1	J3	E7	Ox	21. 3	20. 2	K4	J5	Wolf
16. 2	17. 1	J3	F8	Bat	22. 3	21. 2	K4	K6	Dog
17. 2	18. 1	J3	G9	Rat	13. 3	22. 2	K4	A7	Pheasant
18. 2	19. 1	J3	H10	Swallow	24. 3	23. 2	K4	B8	Cock
19. 2	20. 1	J3	J11	Pig	25. 3	24. 2	K4	C9	Crow
20. 2	21. 1	J3	K12	Porcupine	26. 3	25. 2	K4	D10	Monkey
21. 2	22. 1	J3	A1	Wolf	27. 3	26. 2	K4	E11	Gibbon
22. 2	23. 1	J3	B2	Dog	28. 3	27. 2	K4	F12	Tapir
23. 2	24. 1	J3	C3	Pheasant	29. 3	28. 2	K4	G1	Sheep
24. 2	25. 1	J3	D4	Cock	30. 3	29. 2	K4	H2	Deer
25. 2	26. 1	J3	E5	Crow	31. 3	1. 3	A5	J3	Horse
26. 2	27. 1	J3	F6	Monkey	1. 4	2. 3	A5	K4	Stag
27. 2	28. 1	J3	G7	Gibbon	2. 4	3. 3	A5	A5	Serpent
28. 2	29. 1	J3	H8	Tapir	3. 4	4. 3	A5	B6	Earthworm
1. 3	30. 1	J3	J9	Sheep	4. 4	5. 3	A5	C7	Crocodile
2. 3	1. 2	K4	K10	Deer	5. 4	6. 3	A5	D8	Dragon
3. 3	2. 2	K4	A11	Horse	6. 4	7. 3	A5	E9	Badger
4. 3	3. 2	K4	B12	Stag	7. 4	8. 3	A5	F10	Hare
5. 3	4. 2	K4	C1	Serpent	8. 4	9. 3	A5	G11	Fox

Solar date	Lunar date	Month HS/EB	Day HS/EB	Constellation	Solar date	Lunar date	Month HS/EB	Day HS/EB	Constellation
9. 4	10. 3	A5	H12	Tiger	21. 6	24. 5	C7	A1	Sheep
10. 4	11. 3	A5	J1	Leopard	22. 6	25. 5	C7	B2	Deer
11. 4	12. 3	A5	K2	Griffon	23. 6	26. 5	C7	C3	Horse
12. 4	13. 3	A5	A3	Ox	24. 6	27. 5	C7	D4	Stag
13. 4	14. 3	A5	B4	Bat	25. 6	28. 5	C7	E5	Serpent
14. 4	15. 3	A5	C5	Rat	26. 6	29. 5	C7	F6	Earthworm
15. 4	16. 3	A5	D6	Swallow	27. 6	30. 5	C7	G7	Crocodile
16. 4	17. 3	A5	E7	Pig	28. 6	1. 6	D8	H8	Dragon
17. 4	18. 3	A5	F8	Porcupine	29. 6	2. 6	D8	J9	Badger
18. 4	19. 3	A5	G9	Wolf	30. 6	3. 6	D8	K10	Hare
19. 4	20. 3	A5	H10	Dog	1. 7	4. 6	D8	A11	Fox
20. 4	21. 3	A5	J11	Pheasant	2. 7	5. 6	D8	B12	Tiger
21. 4	22. 3	A5	K12	Cock	3. 7	6. 6	D8	C1	Leopard
22. 4	23. 3	A5	A1	Crow	4. 7	7. 6	D8	D2	Griffon
23. 4	24. 3	A5	B2	Monkey	5. 7	8. 6	D8	E3	Ox
24. 4	25. 3	A5	C3	Gibbon	6. 7	9. 6	D8	F4	Bat
25. 4	26. 3	A5	D4	Tapir	7. 7	10. 6	D8	G5	Rat
26. 4	27. 3	A5	E5	Sheep	8. 7	11. 6	D8	H6	Swallow
27. 4	28. 3	A5	F6	Deer	9. 7	12. 6	D8	J7	Pig
28. 4	29. 3	A5	G7	Horse	10. 7	13. 6	D8	K8	Porcupine
29. 4	30. 3	A5	H8	Stag	11. 7	14. 6	D8	A9	Wolf
30. 4	1. 4	B6	J9	Serpent	12. 7	15. 6	D8	B10	Dog
1. 5	2. 4	B6	K10	Earthworm	13. 7	16. 6	D8	C11	Pheasant
2. 5	3. 4	B6	A11	Crocodile	14. 7	17. 6	D8	D12	Cock
3. 5	4. 4	B6	B12	Dragon	15. 7	18. 6	D8	E1	Crow
4. 5	5. 4	B6	C1	Badger	16. 7	19. 6	D8	F2	Monkey
5. 5	6. 4	B6	D2	Hare	17. 7	20. 6	D8	G3	Gibbon
6. 5	7. 4	B6	E3	Fox	18. 7	21. 6	D8	H4	Tapir
7. 5	8. 4	B6	F4	Tiger	19. 7	22. 6	D8	J5	Sheep
8. 5	9. 4	B6	G5	Leopard	20. 7	23. 6	D8	K6	Deer
9. 5	10. 4	B6	H6	Griffon	21. 7	24. 6	D8	A7	Horse
10. 5	11. 4	B6	J7	Ox	22. 7	25. 6	D8	B8	Stag
11. 5	12. 4	B6	K8	Bat	23. 7	26. 6	D8	C9	Serpent
12. 5	13. 4	B6	A9	Rat	24. 7	27. 6	D8	D10	Earthworm
13. 5	14. 4	B6	B10	Swallow	25. 7	28. 6	D8	E11	Crocodile
14. 5	15. 4	B6	C11	Pig	26. 7	29. 6	D8	F12	Dragon
15. 5	16. 4	B6	D12	Porcupine	27. 7	1. 7	E9	G1	Badger
16. 5	17. 4	B6	E1	Wolf	28. 7	2. 7	E9	H2	Hare
17. 5	18. 4	B6	F2	Dog	29. 7	3. 7	E9	J3	Fox
18. 5	19. 4	B6	G3	Pheasant	30. 7	4. 7	E9	K4	Tiger
19. 5	20. 4	B6	H4	Cock	31. 7	5. 7	E9	A5	Leopard
20. 5	21. 4	B6	J5	Crow	1. 8	6. 7	E9	B6	Griffon
21. 5	22. 4	B6	K6	Monkey	2. 8	7. 7	E9	C7	Ox
22. 5	23. 4	B6	A7	Gibbon	3. 8	8. 7	E9	D8	Bat
23. 5	24. 4	B6	B8	Tapir	4. 8	9. 7	E9	E9	Rat
24. 5	25. 4	B6	C9	Sheep	5. 8	10. 7	E9	F10	Swallow
25. 5	26. 4	B6	D10	Deer	6. 8	11. 7	E9	G11	Pig
26. 5	27. 4	B6	E11	Horse	7. 8	12. 7	E9	H12	Porcupine
27. 5	28. 4	B6	F12	Stag	8. 8	13. 7	E9	J1	Wolf
28. 5	29. 4	B6	G1	Serpent	9. 8	14. 7	E9	K2	Dog
29. 5	1. 5	C7	H2	Earthworm	10. 8	15. 7	E9	A3	Pheasant
30. 5	2. 5	C7	J3	Crocodile	11. 8	16. 7	E9	B4	Cock
31. 5	3. 5	C7	K4	Dragon	12. 8	17. 7	E9	C5	Crow
1. 6	4. 5	C7	A5	Badger	13. 8	18. 7	E9	D6	Monkey
2. 6	5. 5	C7	B6	Hare	14. 8	19. 7	E9	E7	Gibbon
3. 6	6. 5	C7	C7	Fox	15. 8	20. 7	E9	F8	Tapir
4. 6	7. 5	C7	D8	Tiger	16. 8	21. 7	E9	G9	Sheep
5. 6	8. 5	C7	E9	Leopard	17. 8	22. 7	E9	H10	Deer
6. 6	9. 5	C7	F10	Griffon	18. 8	23. 7	E9	J11	Horse
7. 6	10. 5	C7	G11	Ox	19. 8	24. 7	E9	K12	Stag
8. 6	11. 5	C7	H12	Bat	20. 8	25. 7	E9	A1	Serpent
9. 6	12. 5	C7	J1	Rat	21. 8	26. 7	E9	B2	Earthworm
10. 6	13. 5	C7	K2	Swallow	22. 8	27. 7	E9	C3	Crocodile
11. 6	14. 5	C7	A3	Pig	23. 8	28. 7	E9	D4	Dragon
12. 6	15. 5	C7	B4	Porcupine	24. 8	29. 7	E9	E5	Badger
13. 6	16. 5	C7	C5	Wolf	25. 8	1. 8	F10	F6	Hare
14. 6	17. 5	C7	D6	Dog	26. 8	2. 8	F10	G7	Fox
15. 6	18. 5	C7	E7	Pheasant	27. 8	3. 8	F10	H8	Tiger
16. 6	19. 5	C7	F8	Cock	28. 8	4. 8	F10	J9	Leopard
17. 6	20. 5	C7	G9	Crow	29. 8	5. 8	F10	K10	Griffon
18. 6	21. 5	C7	H10	Monkey	30. 8	6. 8	F10	A11	Ox
19. 6	22. 5	C7	J11	Gibbon	31. 8	7. 8	F10	B12	Bat
20. 6	23. 5	C7	K12	Tapir	1. 9	8. 8	F10	C1	Rat

Solar date	Lunar date	Month HS/EB	Day HS/EB	Constellation	Solar date	Lunar date	Month HS/EB	Day HS/EB	Constellation
2. 9	9. 8	F10	D2	Swallow	14.11	23. 9	G11	G3	Crocodile
3. 9	10. 8	F10	E3	Pig	15.11	24. 9	G11	H4	Dragon
4. 9	11. 8	F10	F4	Porcupine	16.11	25. 9	G11	J5	Badger
5. 9	12. 8	F10	G5	Wolf	17.11	26. 9	G11	K6	Hare
6. 9	13. 8	F10	H6	Dog	18.11	27. 9	G11	A7	Fox
7. 9	14. 8	F10	J7	Pheasant	19.11	28. 9	G11	B8	Tiger
8. 9	15. 8	F10	K8	Cock	20.11	29. 9	G11	C9	Leopard
9. 9	16. 8	F10	A9	Crow	21.11	30. 9	G11	D10	Griffon
10. 9	17. 8	F10	B10	Monkey	22.11	1.10	H12	E11	Ox
11. 9	18. 8	F10	C11	Gibbon	23.11	2.10	H12	F12	Bat
12. 9	19. 8	F10	D12	Tapir	24.11	3.10	H12	G1	Rat
13. 9	20. 8	F10	E1	Sheep	25.11	4.10	H12	H2	Swallow
14. 9	21. 8	F10	F2	Deer	26.11	5.10	H12	J3	Pig
15. 9	22. 8	F10	G3	Horse	27.11	6.10	H12	K4	Porcupine
16. 9	23. 8	F10	H4	Stag	28.11	7.10	H12	A5	Wolf
17. 9	24. 8	F10	J5	Serpent	29.11	8.10	H12	B6	Dog
18. 9	25. 8	F10	K6	Earthworm	30.11	9.10	H12	C7	Pheasant
19. 9	26. 8	F10	A7	Crocodile	1.12	10.10	H12	D8	Cock
20. 9	27. 8	F10	B8	Dragon	2.12	11.10	H12	E9	Crow
21. 9	28. 8	F10	C9	Badger	3.12	12.10	H12	F10	Monkey
22. 9	29. 8	F10	D10	Hare	4.12	13.10	H12	G11	Gibbon
23. 9	30. 8	F10	E11	Fox	5.12	14.10	H12	H12	Tapir
24. 9	1. 8	F10	F12	Tiger	6.12	15.10	H12	J1	Sheep
25. 9	2. 8	F10	G1	Leopard	7.12	16.10	H12	K2	Deer
26. 9	3. 8	F10	H2	Griffon	8.12	17.10	H12	A3	Horse
27. 9	4. 8	F10	J3	Ox	9.12	18.10	H12	B4	Stag
28. 9	5. 8	F10	K4	Bat	10.12	19.10	H12	C5	Serpent
29. 9	6. 8	F10	A5	Rat	11.12	20.10	H12	D6	Earthworm
30. 9	7. 8	F10	B6	Swallow	12.12	21.10	H12	E7	Crocodile
1.10	8. 8	F10	C7	Pig	13.12	22.10	H12	F8	Dragon
2.10	9. 8	F10	D8	Porcupine	14.12	23.10	H12	G9	Badger
3.10	10. 8	F10	E9	Wolf	15.12	24.10	H12	H10	Hare
4.10	11. 8	F10	F10	Dog	16.12	25.10	H12	J11	Fox
5.10	12. 8	F10	G11	Pheasant	17.12	26.10	H12	K12	Tiger
6.10	13. 8	F10	H12	Cock	18.12	27.10	H12	A1	Leopard
7.10	14. 8	F10	J1	Crow	19.12	28.10	H12	B2	Griffon
8.10	15. 8	F10	K2	Monkey	20.12	29.10	H12	C3	Ox
9.10	16. 8	F10	A3	Gibbon	21.12	1.11	J1	D4	Bat
10.10	17. 8	F10	B4	Tapir	22.12	2.11	J1	E5	Rat
11.10	18. 8	F10	C5	Sheep	23.12	3.11	J1	F6	Swallow
12.10	19. 8	F10	D6	Deer	24.12	4.11	J1	G7	Pig
13.10	20. 8	F10	E7	Horse	25.12	5.11	J1	H8	Porcupine
14.10	21. 8	F10	F8	Stag	26.12	6.11	J1	J9	Wolf
15.10	22. 8	F10	G9	Serpent	27.12	7.11	J1	K10	Dog
16.10	23. 8	F10	H10	Earthworm	28.12	8.11	J1	A11	Pheasant
17.10	24. 8	F10	J11	Crocodile	29.12	9.11	J1	B12	Cock
18.10	25. 8	F10	K12	Dragon	30.12	10.11	J1	C1	Crow
19.10	26. 8	F10	A1	Badger	31.12	11.11	J1	D2	Monkey
20.10	27. 8	F10	B2	Hare					
21.10	28. 8	F10	C3	Fox	**1958**				
22.10	29. 8	F10	D4	Tiger	1. 1	12.11	J1	E3	Gibbon
23.10	1. 9	G11	E5	Leopard	2. 1	13.11	J1	F4	Tapir
24.10	2. 9	G11	F6	Griffon	3. 1	14.11	J1	G5	Sheep
25.10	3. 9	G11	G7	Ox	4. 1	15.11	J1	H6	Deer
26.10	4. 9	G11	H8	Bat	5. 1	16.11	J1	J7	Horse
27.10	5. 9	G11	J9	Rat	6. 1	17.11	J1	K8	Stag
28.10	6. 9	G11	K10	Swallow	7. 1	18.11	J1	A9	Serpent
29.10	7. 9	G11	A11	Pig	8. 1	19.11	J1	B10	Earthworm
30.10	8. 9	G11	B12	Porcupine	9. 1	20.11	J1	C11	Crocodile
31.10	9. 9	G11	C1	Wolf	10. 1	21.11	J1	D12	Dragon
1.11	10. 9	G11	D2	Dog	11. 1	22.11	J1	E1	Badger
2.11	11. 9	G11	E3	Pheasant	12. 1	23.11	J1	F2	Hare
3.11	12. 9	G11	F4	Cock	13. 1	24.11	J1	G3	Fox
4.11	13. 9	G11	G5	Crow	14. 1	25.11	J1	H4	Tiger
5.11	14. 9	G11	H6	Monkey	15. 1	26.11	J1	J5	Leopard
6.11	15. 9	G11	J7	Gibbon	16. 1	27.11	J1	K6	Griffon
7.11	16. 9	G11	K8	Tapir	17. 1	28.11	J1	A7	Ox
8.11	17. 9	G11	A9	Sheep	18. 1	29.11	J1	B8	Bat
9.11	18. 9	G11	B10	Deer	19. 1	30.11	J1	C9	Rat
10.11	19. 9	G11	C11	Horse	20. 1	1.12	K2	D10	Swallow
11.11	20. 9	G11	D12	Stag	21. 1	2.12	K2	E11	Pig
12.11	21. 9	G11	E1	Serpent	22. 1	3.12	K2	F12	Porcupine
13.11	22. 9	G11	F2	Earthworm	23. 1	4.12	K2	G1	Wolf

Solar date	Lunar date	Month HS/EB	Day HS/EB	Constellation		Solar date	Lunar date	Month HS/EB	Day HS/EB	Constellation
24. 1	5.12	K2	H2	Dog		6. 2	18.12	K2	A3	Crocodile
25. 1	6.12	K2	J3	Pheasant		7. 2	19.12	K2	B4	Dragon
26. 1	7.12	K2	K4	Cock		8. 2	20.12	K2	C5	Badger
27. 1	8.12	K2	A5	Crow		9. 2	21.12	K2	D6	Hare
28. 1	9.12	K2	B6	Monkey		10. 2	22.12	K2	E7	Fox
29. 1	10.12	K2	C7	Gibbon		11. 2	23.12	K2	F8	Tiger
30. 1	11.12	K2	D8	Tapir		12. 2	24.12	K2	G9	Leopard
31. 1	12.12	K2	E9	Sheep		13. 2	25.12	K2	H10	Griffon
1. 2	13.12	K2	F10	Deer		14. 2	26.12	K2	J11	Ox
2. 2	14.12	K2	G11	Horse		15. 2	27.12	K2	K12	Bat
3. 2	15.12	K2	H12	Stag		16. 2	28.12	K2	A1	Rat
4. 2	16.12	K2	J1	Serpent		17. 2	29.12	K2	B2	Swallow
5. 2	17.12	K2	K2	Earthworm						

MOU HSÜ YEAR

Solar date	Lunar date	Month HS/EB	Day HS/EB	Constellation		Solar date	Lunar date	Month HS/EB	Day HS/EB	Constellation
18. 2	1. 1	A3	C3	Pig		14. 4	26. 2	B4	H10	Swallow
19. 2	2. 1	A3	D4	Porcupine		15. 4	27. 2	B4	J11	Pig
20. 2	3. 1	A3	E5	Wolf		16. 4	28. 2	B4	K12	Porcupine
21. 2	4. 1	A3	F6	Dog		17. 4	29. 2	B4	A1	Wolf
22. 2	5. 1	A3	G7	Pheasant		18. 4	30. 2	B4	B2	Dog
23. 2	6. 1	A3	H8	Cock		19. 4	1. 3	C5	C3	Pheasant
24. 2	7. 1	A3	J9	Crow		20. 4	2. 3	C5	D4	Cock
25. 2	8. 1	A3	K10	Monkey		21. 4	3. 3	C5	E5	Crow
26. 2	9. 1	A3	A11	Gibbon		22. 4	4. 3	C5	F6	Monkey
27. 2	10. 1	A3	B12	Tapir		23. 4	5. 3	C5	G7	Gibbon
28. 2	11. 1	A3	C1	Sheep		24. 4	6. 3	C5	H8	Tapir
1. 3	12. 1	A3	D2	Deer		25. 4	7. 3	C5	J9	Sheep
2. 3	13. 1	A3	E3	Horse		26. 4	8. 3	C5	K10	Deer
3. 3	14. 1	A3	F4	Stag		27. 4	9. 3	C5	A11	Horse
4. 3	15. 1	A3	G5	Serpent		28. 4	10. 3	C5	B12	Stag
5. 3	16. 1	A3	H6	Earthworm		29. 4	11. 3	C5	C1	Serpent
6. 3	17. 1	A3	J7	Crocodile		30. 4	12. 3	C5	D2	Earthworm
7. 3	18. 1	A3	K8	Dragon		1. 5	13. 3	C5	E3	Crocodile
8. 3	19. 1	A3	A9	Badger		2. 5	14. 3	C5	F4	Dragon
9. 3	20. 1	A3	B10	Hare		3. 5	15. 3	C5	G5	Badger
10. 3	21. 1	A3	C11	Fox		4. 5	16. 3	C5	H6	Hare
11. 3	22. 1	A3	D12	Tiger		5. 5	17. 3	C5	J7	Fox
12. 3	23. 1	A3	E1	Leopard		6. 5	18. 3	C5	K8	Tiger
13. 3	24. 1	A3	F2	Griffon		7. 5	19. 3	C5	A9	Leopard
14. 3	25. 1	A3	G3	Ox		8. 5	20. 3	C5	B10	Griffon
15. 3	26. 1	A3	H4	Bat		9. 5	21. 3	C5	C11	Ox
16. 3	27. 1	A3	J5	Rat		10. 5	22. 3	C5	D12	Bat
17. 3	28. 1	A3	K6	Swallow		11. 5	23. 3	C5	E1	Rat
18. 3	29. 1	A3	A7	Pig		12. 5	24. 3	C5	F2	Swallow
19. 3	30. 1	A3	B8	Porcupine		13. 5	25. 3	C5	G3	Pig
20. 3	1. 2	B4	C9	Wolf		14. 5	26. 3	C5	H4	Porcupine
21. 3	2. 2	B4	D10	Dog		15. 5	27. 3	C5	J5	Wolf
22. 3	3. 2	B4	E11	Pheasant		16. 5	28. 3	C5	K6	Dog
23. 3	4. 2	B4	F12	Cock		17. 5	29. 3	C5	A7	Pheasant
24. 3	5. 2	B4	G1	Crow		18. 5	30. 3	C5	B8	Cock
25. 3	6. 2	B4	H2	Monkey		19. 5	1. 4	D6	C9	Crow
26. 3	7. 2	B4	J3	Gibbon		20. 5	2. 4	D6	D10	Monkey
27. 3	8. 2	B4	K4	Tapir		21. 5	3. 4	D6	E11	Gibbon
28. 3	9. 2	B4	A5	Sheep		22. 5	4. 4	D6	F12	Tapir
29. 3	10. 2	B4	B6	Deer		23. 5	5. 4	D6	G1	Sheep
30. 3	11. 2	B4	C7	Horse		24. 5	6. 4	D6	H2	Deer
31. 3	12. 2	B4	D8	Stag		25. 5	7. 4	D6	J3	Horse
1. 4	13. 2	B4	E9	Serpent		26. 5	8. 4	D6	K4	Stag
2. 4	14. 2	B4	F10	Earthworm		27. 5	9. 4	D6	A5	Serpent
3. 4	15. 2	B4	G11	Crocodile		28. 5	10. 4	D6	B6	Earthworm
4. 4	16. 2	B4	H12	Dragon		29. 5	11. 4	D6	C7	Crocodile
5. 4	17. 2	B4	J1	Badger		30. 5	12. 4	D6	D8	Dragon
6. 4	18. 2	B4	K2	Hare		31. 5	13. 4	D6	E9	Badger
7. 4	19. 2	B4	A3	Fox		1. 6	14. 4	D6	F10	Hare
8. 4	20. 2	B4	B4	Tiger		2. 6	15. 4	D6	G11	Fox
9. 4	21. 2	B4	C5	Leopard		3. 6	16. 4	D6	H12	Tiger
10. 4	22. 2	B4	D6	Griffon		4. 6	17. 4	D6	J1	Leopard
11. 4	23. 2	B4	E7	Ox		5. 6	18. 4	D6	K2	Griffon
12. 4	24. 2	B4	F8	Bat		6. 6	19. 4	D6	A3	Ox
13. 4	25. 2	B4	G9	Rat		7. 6	20. 4	D6	B4	Bat

Solar date	Lunar date	Month HS/EB	Day HS/EB	Constellation	Solar date	Lunar date	Month HS/EB	Day HS/EB	Constellation
8. 6	21. 4	D6	C5	Rat	20. 8	6. 7	G9	F6	Earthworm
9. 6	22. 4	D6	D6	Swallow	21. 8	7. 7	G9	G7	Crocodile
10. 6	23. 4	D6	E7	Pig	22. 8	8. 7	G9	H8	Dragon
11. 6	24. 4	D6	F8	Porcupine	23. 8	9. 7	G9	J9	Badger
12. 6	25. 4	D6	G9	Wolf	24. 8	10. 7	G9	K10	Hare
13. 6	26. 4	D6	H10	Dog	25. 8	11. 7	G9	A11	Fox
14. 6	27. 4	D6	J11	Pheasant	26. 8	12. 7	G9	B12	Tiger
15. 6	28. 4	D6	K12	Cock	27. 8	13. 7	G9	C1	Leopard
16. 6	29. 4	D6	A1	Crow	28. 8	14. 7	G9	D2	Griffon
17. 6	1. 5	E7	B2	Monkey	29. 8	15. 7	G9	E3	Ox
18. 6	2. 5	E7	C3	Gibbon	30. 8	16. 7	G9	F4	Bat
19. 6	3. 5	E7	D4	Tapir	31. 8	17. 7	G9	G5	Rat
20. 6	4. 5	E7	E5	Sheep	1. 9	18. 7	G9	H6	Swallow
21. 6	5. 5	E7	F6	Deer	2. 9	19. 7	G9	J7	Pig
22. 6	6. 5	E7	G7	Horse	3. 9	20. 7	G9	K8	Porcupine
23. 6	7. 5	E7	H8	Stag	4. 9	21. 7	G9	A9	Wolf
24. 6	8. 5	E7	J9	Serpent	5. 9	22. 7	G9	B10	Dog
25. 6	9. 5	E7	K10	Earthworm	6. 9	23. 7	G9	C11	Pheasant
26. 6	10. 5	E7	A11	Crocodile	7. 9	24. 7	G9	D12	Cock
27. 6	11. 5	E7	B12	Dragon	8. 9	25. 7	G9	E1	Crow
28. 6	12. 5	E7	C1	Badger	9. 9	26. 7	G9	F2	Monkey
29. 6	13. 5	E7	D2	Hare	10. 9	27. 7	G9	G3	Gibbon
30. 6	14. 5	E7	E3	Fox	11. 9	28. 7	G9	H4	Tapir
1. 7	15. 5	E7	F4	Tiger	12. 9	29. 7	G9	J5	Sheep
2. 7	16. 5	E7	G5	Leopard	13. 9	1. 8	H10	K6	Deer
3. 7	17. 5	E7	H6	Griffon	14. 9	2. 8	H10	A7	Horse
4. 7	18. 5	E7	J7	Ox	15. 9	3. 8	H10	B8	Stag
5. 7	19. 5	E7	K8	Bat	16. 9	4. 8	H10	C9	Serpent
6. 7	20. 5	E7	A9	Rat	17. 9	5. 8	H10	D10	Earthworm
7. 7	21. 5	E7	B10	Swallow	18. 9	6. 8	H10	E11	Crocodile
8. 7	22. 5	E7	C11	Pig	19. 9	7. 8	H10	F12	Dragon
9. 7	23. 5	E7	D12	Porcupine	20. 9	8. 8	H10	G1	Badger
10. 7	24. 5	E7	E1	Wolf	21. 9	9. 8	H10	H2	Hare
11. 7	25. 5	E7	F2	Dog	22. 9	10. 8	H10	J3	Fox
12. 7	26. 5	E7	G3	Pheasant	23. 9	11. 8	H10	K4	Tiger
13. 7	27. 5	E7	H4	Cock	24. 9	12. 8	H10	A5	Leopard
14. 7	28. 5	E7	J5	Crow	25. 9	13. 8	H10	B6	Griffon
15. 7	29. 5	E7	K6	Monkey	26. 9	14. 8	H10	C7	Ox
16. 7	30. 5	E7	A7	Gibbon	27. 9	15. 8	H10	D8	Bat
17. 7	1. 6	F8	B8	Tapir	28. 9	16. 8	H10	E9	Rat
18. 7	2. 6	F8	C9	Sheep	29. 9	17. 8	H10	F10	Swallow
19. 7	3. 6	F8	D10	Deer	30. 9	18. 8	H10	G11	Pig
20. 7	4. 6	F8	E11	Horse	1.10	19. 8	H10	H12	Porcupine
21. 7	5. 6	F8	F12	Stag	2.10	20. 8	H10	J1	Wolf
22. 7	6. 6	F8	G1	Serpent	3.10	21. 8	H10	K2	Dog
23. 7	7. 6	F8	H2	Earthworm	4.10	22. 8	H10	A3	Pheasant
24. 7	8. 6	F8	J3	Crocodile	5.10	23. 8	H10	B4	Cock
25. 7	9. 6	F8	K4	Dragon	6.10	24. 8	H10	C5	Crow
26. 7	10. 6	F8	A5	Badger	7.10	25. 8	H10	D6	Monkey
27. 7	11. 6	F8	B6	Hare	8.10	26. 8	H10	E7	Gibbon
28. 7	12. 6	F8	C7	Fox	9.10	27. 8	H10	F8	Tapir
29. 7	13. 6	F8	D8	Tiger	10.10	28. 8	H10	G9	Sheep
30. 7	14. 6	F8	E9	Leopard	11.10	29. 8	H10	H10	Deer
31. 7	15. 6	F8	F10	Griffon	12.10	30. 8	H10	J11	Horse
1. 8	16. 6	F8	G11	Ox	13.10	1. 9	J11	K12	Stag
2. 8	17. 6	F8	H12	Bat	14.10	2. 9	J11	A1	Serpent
3. 8	18. 6	F8	J1	Rat	15.10	3. 9	J11	B2	Earthworm
4. 8	19. 6	F8	K2	Swallow	16.10	4. 9	J11	C3	Crocodile
5. 8	20. 6	F8	A3	Pig	17.10	5. 9	J11	D4	Dragon
6. 8	21. 6	F8	B4	Porcupine	18.10	6. 9	J11	E5	Badger
7. 8	22. 6	F8	C5	Wolf	19.10	7. 9	J11	F6	Hare
8. 8	23. 6	F8	D6	Dog	20.10	8. 9	J11	G7	Fox
9. 8	24. 6	F8	E7	Pheasant	21.10	9. 9	J11	H8	Tiger
10. 8	25. 6	F8	F8	Cock	22.10	10. 9	J11	J9	Leopard
11. 8	26. 6	F8	G9	Crow	23.10	11. 9	J11	K10	Griffon
12. 8	27. 6	F8	H10	Monkey	24.10	12. 9	J11	A11	Ox
13. 8	28. 6	F8	J11	Gibbon	25.10	13. 9	J11	B12	Bat
14. 8	29. 6	F8	K12	Tapir	26.10	14. 9	J11	C1	Rat
15. 8	1. 7	G9	A1	Sheep	27.10	15. 9	J11	D2	Swallow
16. 8	2. 7	G9	B2	Deer	28.10	16. 9	J11	E3	Pig
17. 8	3. 7	G9	C3	Horse	29.10	17. 9	J11	F4	Porcupine
18. 8	4. 7	G9	D4	Stag	30.10	18. 9	J11	G5	Wolf
19. 8	5. 7	G9	E5	Serpent	31.10	19. 9	J11	H6	Dog

Solar date	Lunar date	Month HS/EB	Day HS/EB	Constellation	Solar date	Lunar date	Month HS/EB	Day HS/EB	Constellation
1.11	20. 9	J11	J7	Pheasant	22.12	12.11	A1	K10	Swallow
2.11	21. 9	J11	K8	Cock	23.12	13.11	A1	A11	Pig
3.11	22. 9	J11	A9	Crow	24.12	14.11	A1	B12	Porcupine
4.11	23. 9	J11	B10	Monkey	25.12	15.11	A1	C1	Wolf
5.11	24. 9	J11	C11	Gibbon	26.12	16.11	A1	D2	Dog
6.11	25. 9	J11	D12	Tapir	27.12	17.11	A1	E3	Pheasant
7.11	26. 9	J11	E1	Sheep	28.12	18.11	A1	F4	Cock
8.11	27. 9	J11	F2	Deer	29.12	19.11	A1	G5	Crow
9.11	28. 9	J11	G3	Horse	30.12	20.11	A1	H6	Monkey
10.11	29. 9	J11	H4	Stag	31.12	21.11	A1	J7	Gibbon
11.11	1.10	K12	J5	Serpent					
12.11	2.10	K12	K6	Earthworm	**1959**				
13.11	3.10	K12	A7	Crocodile					
14.11	4.10	K12	B8	Dragon	1. 1	22.11	A1	K8	Tapir
15.11	5.10	K12	C9	Badger	2. 1	23.11	A1	A9	Sheep
16.11	6.10	K12	D10	Hare	3. 1	24.11	A1	B10	Deer
17.11	7.10	K12	E11	Fox	4. 1	25.11	A1	C11	Horse
18.11	8.10	K12	F12	Tiger	5. 1	26.11	A1	D12	Stag
19.11	9.10	K12	G1	Leopard	6. 1	27.11	A1	E1	Serpent
20.11	10.10	K12	H2	Griffon	7. 1	28.11	A1	F2	Earthworm
21.11	11.10	K12	J3	Ox	8. 1	29.11	A1	G3	Crocodile
22.11	12.10	K12	K4	Bat	9. 1	1.12	B2	H4	Dragon
23.11	13.10	K12	A5	Rat	10. 1	2.12	B2	J5	Badger
24.11	14.10	K12	B6	Swallow	11. 1	3.12	B2	K6	Hare
25.11	15.10	K12	C7	Pig	12. 1	4.12	B2	A7	Fox
26.11	16.10	K12	D8	Porcupine	13. 1	5.12	B2	B8	Tiger
27.11	17.10	K12	E9	Wolf	14. 1	6.12	B2	C9	Leopard
28.11	18.10	K12	F10	Dog	15. 1	7.12	B2	D10	Griffon
29.11	19.10	K12	G11	Pheasant	16. 1	8.12	B2	E11	Ox
30.11	20.10	K12	H12	Cock	17. 1	9.12	B2	F12	Bat
1.12	21.10	K12	J1	Crow	18. 1	10.12	B2	G1	Rat
2.12	22.10	K12	K2	Monkey	19. 1	11.12	B2	H2	Swallow
3.12	23.10	K12	A3	Gibbon	20. 1	12.12	B2	J3	Pig
4.12	24.10	K12	B4	Tapir	21. 1	13.12	B2	K4	Porcupine
5.12	25.10	K12	C5	Sheep	22. 1	14.12	B2	A5	Wolf
6.12	26.10	K12	D6	Deer	23. 1	15.12	B2	B6	Dog
7.12	27.10	K12	E7	Horse	24. 1	16.12	B2	C7	Pheasant
8.12	28.10	K12	F8	Stag	25. 1	17.12	B2	D8	Cock
9.12	29.10	K12	G9	Serpent	26. 1	18.12	B2	E9	Crow
10.12	30.10	K12	H10	Earthworm	27. 1	19.12	B2	F10	Monkey
11.12	1.11	A1	J11	Crocodile	28. 1	20.12	B2	G11	Gibbon
12.12	2.11	A1	K12	Dragon	29. 1	21.12	B2	H12	Tapir
13.12	3.11	A1	A1	Badger	30. 1	22.12	B2	J1	Sheep
14.12	4.11	A1	B2	Hare	31. 1	23.12	B2	K2	Deer
15.12	5.11	A1	C3	Fox	1. 2	24.12	B2	A3	Horse
16.12	6.11	A1	D4	Tiger	2. 2	25.12	B2	B4	Stag
17.12	7.11	A1	E5	Leopard	3. 2	26.12	B2	C5	Serpent
18.12	8.11	A1	F6	Griffon	4. 2	27.12	B2	D6	Earthworm
19.12	9.11	A1	G7	Ox	5. 2	28.12	B2	E7	Crocodile
20.12	10.11	A1	H8	Bat	6. 2	29.12	B2	F8	Dragon
21.12	11.11	A1	J9	Rat	7. 2	30.12	B2	G9	Badger

CHI HAI YEAR

Solar date	Lunar date	Month HS/EB	Day HS/EB	Constellation	Solar date	Lunar date	Month HS/EB	Day HS/EB	Constellation
8. 2	1. 1	C3	H10	Hare	25. 2	18. 1	C3	E3	Gibbon
9. 2	2. 1	C3	J11	Fox	26. 2	19. 1	C3	F4	Tapir
10. 2	3. 1	C3	K12	Tiger	27. 2	20. 1	C3	G5	Sheep
11. 2	4. 1	C3	A1	Leopard	28. 2	21. 1	C3	H6	Deer
12. 2	5. 1	C3	B2	Griffon	1. 3	22. 1	C3	J7	Horse
13. 2	6. 1	C3	C3	Ox	2. 3	23. 1	C3	K8	Stag
14. 2	7. 1	C3	D4	Bat	3. 3	24. 1	C3	A9	Serpent
15. 2	8. 1	C3	E5	Rat	4. 3	25. 1	C3	B10	Earthworm
16. 2	9. 1	C3	F6	Swallow	5. 3	26. 1	C3	C11	Crocodile
17. 2	10. 1	C3	G7	Pig	6. 3	27. 1	C3	D12	Dragon
18. 2	11. 1	C3	H8	Porcupine	7. 3	28. 1	C3	E1	Badger
19. 2	12. 1	C3	J9	Wolf	8. 3	29. 1	C3	F2	Hare
20. 2	13. 1	C3	K10	Dog	9. 3	1. 2	D4	G3	Fox
21. 2	14. 1	C3	A11	Pheasant	10. 3	2. 2	D4	H4	Tiger
22. 2	15. 1	C3	B12	Cock	11. 3	3. 2	D4	J5	Leopard
23. 2	16. 1	C3	C1	Crow	12. 3	4. 2	D4	K6	Griffon
24. 2	17. 1	C3	D2	Monkey	13. 3	5. 2	D4	A7	Ox

Solar date	Lunar date	Month HS/EB	Day HS/EB	Constellation
14. 3	6. 2	D4	B8	Bat
15. 3	7. 2	D4	C9	Rat
16. 3	8. 2	D4	D10	Swallow
17. 3	9. 2	D4	E11	Pig
18. 3	10. 2	D4	F12	Porcupine
19. 3	11. 2	D4	G1	Wolf
20. 3	12. 2	D4	H4	Dog
21. 3	13. 2	D4	J3	Pheasant
22. 3	14. 2	D4	K4	Cock
23. 3	15. 2	D4	A5	Crow
24. 3	16. 2	D4	B6	Monkey
25. 3	17. 2	D4	C7	Gibbon
26. 3	18. 2	D4	D8	Tapir
27. 3	19. 2	D4	E9	Sheep
28. 3	20. 2	D4	F10	Deer
29. 3	21. 1	D4	G11	Horse
30. 3	22. 2	D4	H12	Stag
31. 3	23. 2	D4	J1	Serpent
1. 4	24. 2	D4	K2	Earthworm
2. 4	25. 2	D4	A3	Crocodile
3. 4	26. 2	D4	B4	Dragon
4. 4	27. 2	D4	C5	Badger
5. 4	28. 2	D4	D6	Hare
6. 4	29. 2	D4	E7	Fox
7. 4	30. 2	D4	F8	Tiger
8. 4	1. 3	E5	G9	Leopard
9. 4	2. 3	E5	H10	Griffon
10. 4	3. 3	E5	J11	Ox
11. 4	4. 3	E5	K12	Bat
12. 4	5. 3	E5	A1	Rat
13. 4	6. 3	E5	B2	Swallow
14. 4	7. 3	E5	C3	Pig
15. 4	8. 3	E5	D4	Porcupine
16. 4	9. 3	E5	E5	Wolf
17. 4	10. 3	E5	F6	Dog
18. 4	11. 3	E5	G7	Pheasant
19. 4	12. 3	E5	H8	Cock
20. 4	13. 3	E5	J9	Crow
21. 4	14. 3	E5	K10	Monkey
22. 4	15. 3	E5	A11	Gibbon
23. 4	16. 3	E5	B12	Tapir
24. 4	17. 3	E5	C1	Sheep
25. 4	18. 3	E5	D2	Deer
26. 4	19. 3	E5	E3	Horse
27. 4	20. 3	E5	F4	Stag
28. 4	21. 3	E5	G5	Serpent
29. 4	22. 3	E5	H6	Earthworm
30. 4	23. 3	E5	J7	Crocodile
1. 5	24. 3	E5	K8	Dragon
2. 5	25. 3	E5	A9	Badger
3. 5	26. 3	E5	B10	Hare
4. 5	27. 3	E5	C11	Fox
5. 5	28. 3	E5	D12	Tiger
6. 5	29. 3	E5	E1	Leopard
7. 5	30. 3	E5	F2	Griffon
8. 5	1. 4	F6	G3	Ox
9. 5	2. 4	F6	H4	Bat
10. 5	3. 4	F6	J5	Rat
11. 5	4. 4	F6	K6	Swallow
12. 5	5. 4	F6	A7	Pig
13. 5	6. 4	F6	B8	Porcupine
14. 5	7. 4	F6	C9	Wolf
15. 5	8. 4	F6	D10	Dog
16. 5	9. 4	F6	E11	Pheasant
17. 5	10. 4	F6	F12	Cock
18. 5	11. 4	F6	G1	Crow
19. 5	12. 4	F6	H2	Monkey
20. 5	13. 4	F6	J3	Gibbon
21. 5	14. 4	F6	K4	Tapir
22. 5	15. 4	F6	A5	Sheep
23. 5	16. 4	F6	B6	Deer
24. 5	17. 4	F6	C7	Horse
25. 5	18. 4	F6	D8	Stag
26. 5	19. 4	F6	E9	Serpent
27. 5	20. 4	F6	F10	Earthworm
28. 5	21. 4	F6	G11	Crocodile
29. 5	22. 4	F6	H12	Dragon
30. 5	23. 4	F6	J1	Badger
31. 5	24. 4	F6	K2	Hare
1. 6	25. 4	F6	A3	Fox
2. 6	26. 4	F6	B4	Tiger
3. 6	27. 4	F6	C5	Leopard
4. 6	28. 4	F6	D6	Griffon
5. 6	29. 4	F6	E7	Ox
6. 6	1. 5	G7	F8	Bat
7. 6	2. 5	G7	G9	Rat
8. 6	3. 5	G7	H10	Swallow
9. 6	4. 5	G7	J11	Pig
10. 6	5. 5	G7	K12	Porcupine
11. 6	6. 5	G7	A1	Wolf
12. 6	7. 5	G7	B2	Dog
13. 6	8. 5	G7	C3	Pheasant
14. 6	9. 5	G7	D4	Cock
15. 6	10. 5	G7	E5	Crow
16. 6	11. 5	G7	F6	Monkey
17. 6	12. 5	G7	G7	Gibbon
18. 6	13. 5	G7	H8	Tapir
19. 6	14. 5	G7	J9	Sheep
20. 6	15. 5	G7	K10	Deer
21. 6	16. 5	G7	A11	Horse
22. 6	17. 5	G7	B12	Stag
23. 6	18. 5	G7	C1	Serpent
24. 6	19. 5	G7	D2	Earthworm
25. 6	20. 5	G7	E3	Crocodile
26. 6	21. 5	G7	F4	Dragon
27. 6	22. 5	G7	G5	Badger
28. 6	23. 5	G7	H6	Hare
29. 6	24. 5	G7	J7	Fox
30. 6	25. 5	G7	K8	Tiger
1. 7	26. 5	G7	A9	Leopard
2. 7	27. 5	G7	B10	Griffon
3. 7	28. 5	G7	C11	Ox
4. 7	29. 5	G7	D12	Bat
5. 7	30. 5	G7	E1	Rat
6. 7	1. 6	H8	F2	Swallow
7. 7	2. 6	H8	G3	Pig
8. 7	3. 6	H8	H4	Porcupine
9. 7	4. 6	H8	J5	Wolf
10. 7	5. 6	H8	K6	Dog
11. 7	6. 6	H8	A7	Pheasant
12. 7	7. 6	H8	B8	Cock
13. 7	8. 6	H8	C9	Crow
14. 7	9. 6	H8	D10	Monkey
15. 7	10. 6	H8	E11	Gibbon
16. 7	11. 6	H8	F12	Tapir
17. 7	12. 6	H8	G1	Sheep
18. 7	13. 6	H8	H2	Deer
19. 7	14. 6	H8	J3	Horse
20. 7	15. 6	H8	K4	Stag
21. 7	16. 6	H8	A5	Serpent
22. 7	17. 6	H8	B6	Earthworm
23. 7	18. 6	H8	C7	Crocodile
24. 7	19. 6	H8	D8	Dragon
25. 7	20. 6	H8	E9	Badger
26. 7	21. 6	H8	F10	Hare
27. 7	22. 6	H8	G11	Fox
28. 7	23. 6	H8	H12	Tiger
29. 7	24. 6	H8	J1	Leopard
30. 7	25. 6	H8	K2	Griffon
31. 7	26. 6	H8	A3	Ox
1. 8	27. 6	H8	B4	Bat
2. 8	28. 6	H8	C5	Rat
3. 8	29. 6	H8	D6	Swallow
4. 8	1. 7	J9	E7	Pig
5. 8	2. 7	J9	F8	Porcupine
6. 8	3. 7	J9	G9	Wolf

Solar date	Lunar date	Month HS/EB	Day HS/EB	Constellation	Solar date	Lunar date	Month HS/EB	Day HS/EB	Constellation
7. 8	4. 7	J9	H10	Dog	19.10	18. 9	A11	A11	Fox
8. 8	5. 7	J9	J11	Pheasant	20.10	19. 9	A11	B12	Tiger
9. 8	6. 7	J9	K12	Cock	21.10	20. 9	A11	C1	Leopard
10. 8	7. 7	J9	A1	Crow	22.10	21. 9	A11	D2	Griffon
11. 8	8. 7	J9	B2	Monkey	23.10	22. 9	A11	E3	Ox
12. 8	9. 7	J9	C3	Gibbon	24.10	23. 9	A11	F4	Bat
13. 8	10. 7	J9	D4	Tapir	25.10	24. 9	A11	G5	Rat
14. 8	11. 7	J9	E5	Sheep	26.10	25. 9	A11	H6	Swallow
15. 8	12. 7	J9	F6	Deer	27.10	26. 9	A11	J7	Pig
16. 8	13. 7	J9	G7	Horse	28.10	27. 9	A11	K8	Porcupine
17. 8	14. 7	J9	H8	Stag	29.10	28. 9	A11	A9	Wolf
18. 8	15. 7	J9	J9	Serpent	30.10	29. 9	A11	B10	Dog
19. 8	16. 7	J9	K10	Earthworm	31.10	30. 9	A11	C11	Pheasant
20. 8	17. 7	J9	A11	Crocodile	1.11	1.10	B12	D12	Cock
21. 8	18. 7	J9	B12	Dragon	2.11	2.10	B12	E1	Crow
22. 8	19. 7	J9	C1	Badger	3.11	3.10	B12	F2	Monkey
23. 8	20. 7	J9	D2	Hare	4.11	4.10	B12	G3	Gibbon
24. 8	21. 7	J9	E3	Fox	5.11	5.10	B12	H4	Tapir
25. 8	22. 7	J9	F4	Tiger	6.11	6.10	B12	J5	Sheep
26. 8	23. 7	J9	G5	Leopard	7.11	7.10	B12	K6	Deer
27. 8	24. 7	J9	H6	Griffon	8.11	8.10	B12	A7	Horse
28. 8	25. 7	J9	J7	Ox	9.11	9.10	B12	B8	Stag
29. 8	26. 7	J9	K8	Bat	10.11	10.10	B12	C9	Serpent
30. 8	27. 7	J9	A9	Rat	11.11	11.10	B12	D10	Earthworm
31. 8	28. 7	J9	B10	Swallow	12.11	12.10	B12	E11	Crocodile
1. 9	29. 7	J9	C11	Pig	13.11	13.10	B12	F12	Dragon
2. 9	30. 7	J9	D12	Porcupine	14.11	14.10	B12	G1	Badger
3. 9	1. 8	K10	E1	Wolf	15.11	15.10	B12	H2	Hare
4. 9	2. 8	K10	F2	Dog	16.11	16.10	B12	J3	Fox
5. 9	3. 8	K10	G3	Pheasant	17.11	17.10	B12	K4	Tiger
6. 9	4. 8	K10	H4	Cock	18.11	18.10	B12	A5	Leopard
7. 9	5. 8	K10	J5	Crow	19.11	19.10	B12	B6	Griffon
8. 9	6. 8	K10	K6	Monkey	20.11	20.10	B12	C7	Ox
9. 9	7. 8	K10	A7	Gibbon	21.11	21.10	B12	D8	Bat
10. 9	8. 8	K10	B8	Tapir	22.11	22.10	B12	E9	Rat
11. 9	9. 8	K10	C9	Sheep	23.11	23.10	B12	F10	Swallow
12. 9	10. 8	K10	D10	Deer	24.11	24.10	B12	G11	Pig
13. 9	11. 8	K10	E11	Horse	25.11	25.10	B12	H12	Porcupine
14. 9	12. 8	K10	F12	Stag	26.11	26.10	B12	J1	Wolf
15. 9	13. 8	K10	G1	Serpent	27.11	27.10	B12	K2	Dog
16. 9	14. 8	K10	H2	Earthworm	28.11	28.10	B12	A3	Pheasant
17. 9	15. 8	K10	J3	Crocodile	29.11	29.10	B12	B4	Cock
18. 9	16. 8	K10	K4	Dragon	30.11	1.11	C1	C5	Crow
19. 9	17. 8	K10	A5	Badger	1.12	2.11	C1	D6	Monkey
20. 9	18. 8	K10	B6	Hare	2.12	3.11	C1	E7	Gibbon
21. 9	19. 8	K10	C7	Fox	3.12	4.11	C1	F8	Tapir
22. 9	20. 8	K10	D8	Tiger	4.12	5.11	C1	G9	Sheep
23. 9	21. 8	K10	E9	Leopard	5.12	6.11	C1	H10	Deer
24. 9	22. 8	K10	F10	Griffon	6.12	7.11	C1	J11	Horse
25. 9	23. 8	K10	G11	Ox	7.12	8.11	C1	K12	Stag
26. 9	24. 8	K10	H12	Bat	8.12	9.11	C1	A1	Serpent
27. 9	25. 8	K10	J1	Rat	9.12	10.11	C1	B2	Earthworm
28. 9	26. 8	K10	K2	Swallow	10.12	11.11	C1	C3	Crocodile
29. 9	27. 8	K10	A3	Pig	11.12	12.11	C1	D4	Dragon
30. 9	28. 8	K10	B4	Porcupine	12.12	13.11	C1	E5	Badger
1.10	29. 8	K10	C5	Wolf	13.12	14.11	C1	F6	Hare
2.10	1. 9	A11	D6	Dog	14.12	15.11	C1	G7	Fox
3.10	2. 9	A11	E7	Pheasant	15.12	16.11	C1	H8	Tiger
4.10	3. 9	A11	F8	Cock	16.12	17.11	C1	J9	Leopard
5.10	4. 9	A11	G9	Crow	17.12	18.11	C1	K10	Griffon
6.10	5. 9	A11	H10	Monkey	18.12	19.11	C1	A11	Ox
7.10	6. 9	A11	J11	Gibbon	19.12	20.11	C1	B12	Bat
8.10	7. 9	A11	K12	Tapir	20.12	21.11	C1	C1	Rat
9.10	8. 9	A11	A1	Sheep	21.12	22.11	C1	D2	Swallow
10.10	9. 9	A11	B2	Deer	22.12	23.11	C1	E3	Pig
11.10	10. 9	A11	C3	Horse	23.12	24.11	C1	F4	Porcupine
12.10	11. 9	A11	D4	Stag	24.12	25.11	C1	G5	Wolf
13.10	12. 9	A11	E5	Serpent	25.12	26.11	C1	H6	Dog
14.10	13. 9	A11	F6	Earthworm	26.12	27.11	C1	J7	Pheasant
15.10	14. 9	A11	G7	Crocodile	27.12	28.11	C1	K8	Cock
16.10	15. 9	A11	H8	Dragon	28.12	29.11	C1	A9	Crow
17.10	16. 9	A11	J9	Badger	29.12	30.11	C1	B10	Monkey
18.10	17. 9	A11	K10	Hare	30.12	1.12	D2	C11	Gibbon

Solar date	Lunar date	Month HS/EB	Day HS/EB	Constellation
31.12	2.12	D2	D12	Tapir
1960				
1. 1	3.12	D2	E1	Sheep
2. 1	4.12	D2	F2	Deer
3. 1	5.12	D2	G3	Horse
4. 1	6.12	D2	H4	Stag
5. 1	7.12	D2	J5	Serpent
6. 1	8.12	D2	K6	Earthworm
7. 1	9.12	D2	A7	Crocodile
8. 1	10.12	D2	B8	Dragon
9. 1	11.12	D2	C9	Badger
10. 1	12.12	D2	D10	Hare
11. 1	13.12	D2	E11	Fox
12. 1	14.12	D2	F12	Tiger
13. 1	15.12	D2	G1	Leopard
14. 1	16.12	D2	H2	Griffon
15. 1	17.12	D2	J3	Ox
16. 1	18.12	D2	K4	Bat
17. 1	19.12	D2	A5	Rat
18. 1	20.12	D2	B6	Swallow
19. 1	21.12	D2	C7	Pig
20. 1	22.12	D2	D8	Porcupine
21. 1	23.12	D2	E9	Wolf
22. 1	24.12	D2	F10	Dog
23. 1	25.12	D2	G11	Pheasant
24. 1	26.12	D2	H12	Cock
25. 1	27.12	D2	J1	Crow
26. 1	28.12	D2	K2	Monkey
27. 1	29.12	D2	A3	Gibbon

KENG TZU YEAR

Solar date	Lunar date	Month HS/EB	Day HS/EB	Constellation
28. 1	1. 1	E3	B4	Tapir
29. 1	2. 1	E3	C5	Sheep
30. 1	3. 1	E3	D6	Deer
31. 1	4. 1	E3	E7	Horse
1. 2	5. 1	E3	F8	Stag
2. 2	6. 1	E3	G9	Serpent
3. 2	7. 1	E3	H10	Earthworm
4. 2	8. 1	E3	J11	Crocodile
5. 2	9. 1	E3	K12	Dragon
6. 2	10. 1	E3	A1	Badger
7. 2	11. 1	E3	B2	Hare
8. 2	12. 1	E3	C3	Fox
9. 2	13. 1	E3	D4	Tiger
10. 2	14. 1	E3	E5	Laopard
11. 2	15. 1	E3	F6	Griffon
12. 2	16. 1	E3	G7	Ox
13. 1	17. 1	E3	H8	Bat
14. 1	18. 1	E3	J9	Rat
15. 2	19. 1	E3	K10	Swallow
16. 2	20. 1	E3	A11	Pig
17. 2	21. 1	E3	B12	Porcupine
18. 2	22. 1	E3	C1	Wolf
19. 2	23. 1	E3	D2	Dog
20. 2	24. 1	E3	E3	Pheasant
21. 2	25. 1	E3	F4	Cock
22. 2	26. 1	E3	G5	Crow
23. 2	27. 1	E3	H6	Monkey
24. 2	28. 1	E3	J7	Gibbon
25. 2	29. 1	E3	K8	Tapir
26. 2	30. 1	E3	A9	Sheep
27. 2	1. 2	F4	B10	Deer
28. 2	2. 2	F4	C11	Horse
29. 2	3. 2	F4	D12	Stag
1. 3	4. 2	F4	E1	Serpent
2. 3	5. 2	F4	F2	Earthworm
3. 3	6. 2	F4	G3	Crocodile
4. 3	7. 2	F4	H4	Dragon
5. 3	8. 2	F4	J5	Badger
6. 3	9. 2	F4	K6	Hare
7. 3	10. 2	F4	A7	Fox
8. 3	11. 2	F4	B8	Tiger
9. 3	12. 2	F4	C9	Leopard
10. 3	13. 2	F4	D10	Griffon
11. 3	14. 2	F4	E11	Ox
12. 3	15. 2	F4	F12	Bat
13. 3	16. 2	F4	G1	Rat
14. 3	17. 2	F4	H2	Swallow
15. 3	18. 2	F4	J3	Pig
16. 3	19. 2	F4	K4	Porcupine
17. 3	20. 2	F4	A5	Wolf
18. 3	21. 2	F4	B6	Dog
19. 3	22. 2	F4	C7	Pheasant
20. 3	23. 2	F4	D8	Cock
21. 3	24. 2	F4	E9	Crow
22. 3	25. 2	F4	F10	Monkey
23. 3	26. 2	F4	G11	Gibbon
24. 3	27. 2	F4	H12	Tapir
25. 3	28. 2	F4	J1	Sheep
26. 3	29. 2	F4	K2	Deer
27. 3	1. 3	G5	A3	Horse
28. 3	2. 3	G5	B4	Stag
29. 3	3. 3	G5	C5	Serpent
30. 3	4. 3	G5	D6	Earthworm
31. 3	5. 3	G5	E7	Crocodile
1. 4	6. 3	G5	F8	Dragon
2. 4	7. 3	G5	G9	Badger
3. 4	8. 3	G5	H10	Hare
4. 4	9. 3	G5	J11	Fox
5. 4	10. 3	G5	K12	Tiger
6. 4	11. 3	G5	A1	Leopard
7. 4	12. 3	G5	B2	Griffon
8. 4	13. 3	G5	C3	Ox
9. 4	14. 3	G5	D4	Bat
10. 4	15. 3	G5	E5	Rat
11. 4	16. 3	G5	F6	Swallow
12. 4	17. 3	G5	G7	Pig
13. 4	18. 3	G5	H8	Porcupine
14. 4	19. 3	G5	J9	Wolf
15. 4	20. 3	G5	K10	Dog
16. 4	21. 3	G5	A11	Pheasant
17. 4	22. 3	G5	B12	Cock
18. 4	23. 3	G5	C1	Crow
19. 4	24. 3	G5	D2	Monkey
20. 4	25. 3	G5	E3	Gibbon
21. 4	26. 3	G5	F4	Tapir
22. 4	27. 3	G5	G5	Sheep
23. 4	28. 3	G5	H6	Deer
24. 4	29. 3	G5	J7	Horse
25. 4	30. 3	G5	K8	Stag
26. 4	1. 4	H6	A9	Serpent
27. 4	2. 4	H6	B10	Earthworm
28. 4	3. 4	H6	C11	Crocodile
29. 4	4. 4	H6	D12	Dragon
30. 4	5. 4	H6	E1	Badger
1. 5	6. 4	H6	F2	Hare
2. 5	7. 4	H6	G3	Fox
3. 5	8. 4	H6	H4	Tiger
4. 5	9. 4	H6	J5	Leopard
5. 5	10. 4	H6	K6	Griffon
6. 5	11. 4	H6	A7	Ox
7. 5	12. 4	H6	B8	Bat
8. 5	13. 4	H6	C9	Rat
9. 5	14. 4	H6	D10	Swallow
10. 5	15. 4	H6	E11	Pig
11. 5	16. 4	H6	F12	Porcupine
12. 5	17. 4	H6	G1	Wolf

Solar date	Lunar date	Month HS/EB	Day HS/EB	Constellation
13. 5	18. 4	H6	H2	Dog
14. 5	19. 4	H6	J3	Pheasant
15. 5	20. 4	H6	K4	Cock
16. 5	21. 4	H6	A5	Crow
17. 5	22. 4	H6	B6	Monkey
18. 5	23. 4	H6	C7	Gibbon
19. 5	24. 4	H6	D8	Tapir
20. 5	25. 4	H6	E9	Sheep
21. 5	26. 4	H6	F10	Deer
22. 5	27. 4	H6	G11	Horse
23. 5	28. 4	H6	H12	Stag
24. 5	29. 4	H6	J1	Serpent
25. 5	1. 5	J7	K2	Earthworm
26. 5	2. 5	J7	A3	Crocodile
27. 5	3. 5	J7	B4	Dragon
28. 5	4. 5	J7	C5	Badger
29. 5	5. 5	J7	D6	Hare
30. 5	6. 5	J7	E7	Fox
31. 5	7. 5	J7	F8	Tiger
1. 6	8. 5	J7	G9	Leopard
2. 6	9. 5	J7	H10	Griffon
3. 6	10. 5	J7	J11	Ox
4. 6	11. 5	J7	K12	Bat
5. 6	12. 5	J7	A1	Rat
6. 6	13. 5	J7	B2	Swallow
7. 6	14. 5	J7	C3	Pig
8. 6	15. 5	J7	D4	Porcupine
9. 6	16. 5	J7	E5	Wolf
10. 6	17. 5	J7	F6	Dog
11. 6	18. 5	J7	G7	Pheasant
12. 6	19. 5	J7	H8	Cock
13. 6	20. 5	J7	J9	Crow
14. 6	21. 5	J7	K10	Monkey
15. 6	22. 5	J7	A11	Gibbon
16. 6	23. 5	J7	B12	Tapir
17. 6	24. 5	J7	C1	Sheep
18. 6	25. 5	J7	D2	Deer
19. 6	26. 5	J7	E3	Horse
20. 6	27. 5	J7	F4	Stag
21. 6	28. 5	J7	G5	Serpent
22. 6	29. 5	J7	H6	Earthworm
23. 6	30. 5	J7	J7	Crocodile
24. 6	1. 6	K8	K8	Dragon
25. 6	2. 6	K8	A9	Badger
26. 6	3. 6	K8	B10	Hare
27. 6	4. 6	K8	C11	Fox
28. 6	5. 6	K8	D12	Tiger
29. 6	6. 6	K8	E1	Leopard
30. 6	7. 6	K8	F2	Griffon
1. 7	8. 6	K8	G3	Ox
2. 7	9. 6	K8	H4	Bat
3. 7	10. 6	K8	J5	Rat
4. 7	11. 6	K8	K6	Swallow
5. 7	12. 6	K8	A7	Pig
6. 7	13. 6	K8	B8	Porcupine
7. 7	14. 6	K8	C9	Wolf
8. 7	15. 6	K8	D10	Dog
9. 7	16. 6	K8	E11	Pheasant
10. 7	17. 6	K8	F12	Cock
11. 7	18. 6	K8	G1	Crow
12. 7	19. 6	K8	H2	Monkey
13. 7	20. 6	K8	J3	Gibbon
14. 7	21. 6	K8	K4	Tapir
15. 7	22. 6	K8	A5	Sheep
16. 7	23. 6	K8	B6	Deer
17. 7	24. 6	K8	C7	Horse
18. 7	25. 6	K8	D8	Stag
19. 7	26. 6	K8	E9	Serpent
20. 7	27. 6	K8	F10	Earthworm
21. 7	28. 6	K8	G11	Crocodile
22. 7	29. 6	K8	H12	Dragon
23. 7	30. 6	K8	J1	Badger
24. 7	*1. 6*	*K8*	K2	Hare

Solar date	Lunar date	Month HS/EB	Day HS/EB	Constellation
25. 7	*2. 6*	*K8*	A3	Fox
26. 7	*3. 6*	*K8*	B4	Tiger
27. 7	*4. 6*	*K8*	C5	Leopard
28. 7	*5. 6*	*K8*	D6	Griffon
29. 7	*6. 6*	*K8*	E7	Ox
30. 7	*7. 6*	*K8*	F8	Bat
31. 7	*8. 6*	*K8*	G9	Rat
1. 8	*9. 6*	*K8*	H10	Swallow
2. 8	*10. 6*	*K8*	J11	Pig
3. 8	*11. 6*	*K8*	K12	Porcupine
4. 8	*12. 6*	*K8*	A1	Wolf
5. 8	*13. 6*	*K8*	B2	Dog
6. 8	*14. 6*	*K8*	C3	Pheasant
7. 8	*15. 6*	*K8*	D4	Cock
8. 8	*16. 6*	*K8*	E5	Crow
9. 8	*17. 6*	*K8*	F6	Monkey
10. 8	*18. 6*	*K8*	G7	Gibbon
11. 8	*19. 6*	*K8*	H8	Tapir
12. 8	*20. 6*	*K8*	J9	Sheep
13. 8	*21. 6*	*K8*	K10	Deer
14. 8	*22. 6*	*K8*	A11	Horse
15. 8	*23. 6*	*K8*	B12	Stag
16. 8	*24. 6*	*K8*	C1	Serpent
17. 8	*25. 6*	*K8*	D2	Earthworm
18. 8	*26. 6*	*K8*	E3	Crocodile
19. 8	*27. 6*	*K8*	F4	Dragon
20. 8	*28. 6*	*K8*	G5	Badger
21. 8	*29. 6*	*K8*	H6	Hare
22. 8	1. 7	A9	J7	Fox
23. 8	2. 7	A9	K8	Tiger
24. 8	3. 7	A9	A9	Leopard
25. 8	4. 7	A9	B10	Griffon
26. 8	5. 7	A9	C11	Ox
27. 8	6. 7	A9	D12	Bat
28. 8	7. 7	A9	E1	Rat
29. 8	8. 7	A9	F2	Swallow
30. 8	9. 7	A9	G3	Pig
31. 8	10. 7	A9	H4	Porcupine
1. 9	11. 7	A9	J5	Wolf
2. 9	12. 7	A9	K6	Dog
3. 9	13. 7	A9	A7	Pheasant
4. 9	14. 7	A9	B8	Cock
5. 9	15. 7	A9	C9	Crow
6. 9	16. 7	A9	D10	Monkey
7. 9	17. 7	A9	E11	Gibbon
8. 9	18. 7	A9	F12	Tapir
9. 9	19. 7	A9	G1	Sheep
10. 9	20. 7	A9	H2	Deer
11. 9	21. 7	A9	J3	Horse
12. 9	22. 7	A9	K4	Stag
13. 9	23. 7	A9	A5	Serpent
14. 9	24. 7	A9	B6	Earthworm
15. 9	25. 7	A9	C7	Crocodile
16. 9	26. 7	A9	D8	Dragon
17. 9	27. 7	A9	E9	Badger
18. 9	28. 7	A9	F10	Hare
19. 9	29. 7	A9	G11	Fox
20. 9	30. 7	A9	H12	Tiger
21. 9	1. 8	B10	J1	Leopard
22. 9	2. 8	B10	K2	Griffon
23. 9	3. 8	B10	A3	Ox
24. 9	4. 8	B10	B4	Bat
25. 9	5. 8	B10	C5	Rat
26. 9	6. 8	B10	D6	Swallow
27. 9	7. 8	B10	E7	Pig
28. 9	8. 8	B10	F8	Porcupine
29. 9	9. 8	B10	G9	Wolf
30. 9	10. 8	B10	H10	Dog
1.10	11. 8	B10	J11	Pheasant
2.10	12. 8	B10	K12	Cock
3.10	13. 8	B10	A1	Crow
4.10	14. 8	B10	B2	Monkey
5.10	15. 8	B10	C3	Gibbon

Solar date	Lunar date	Month HS/EB	Day HS/EB	Constellation	Solar date	Lunar date	Month HS/EB	Day HS/EB	Constellation
6.10	16. 8	B10	D4	Tapir	12.12	24.10	D12	A11	Fox
7.10	17. 8	B10	E5	Sheep	13.12	25.10	D12	B12	Tiger
8.10	18. 8	B10	F6	Deer	14.12	26.10	D12	C1	Leopard
9.10	19. 8	B10	G7	Horse	15.12	27.10	D12	D2	Griffon
10.10	20. 8	B10	H8	Stag	16.12	28.10	D12	E3	Ox
11.10	21. 8	B10	J9	Serpent	17.12	29.10	D12	F4	Bat
12.10	22. 8	B10	K10	Earthworm	18.12	1.11	E1	G5	Rat
13.10	23. 8	B10	A11	Crocodile	19.12	2.11	E1	H6	Swallow
14.10	24. 8	B10	B12	Dragon	20.12	3.11	E1	J7	Pig
15.10	25. 8	B10	C1	Badger	21.12	4.11	E1	K8	Porcupine
16.10	26. 8	B10	D2	Hare	22.12	5.11	E1	A9	Wolf
17.10	27. 8	B10	E3	Fox	23.12	6.11	E1	B10	Dog
18.10	28. 8	B10	F4	Tiger	24.12	7.11	E1	C11	Pheasant
19.10	29. 8	B10	G5	Leopard	25.12	8.11	E1	D12	Cock
20.10	1. 9	C11	H6	Griffon	26.12	9.11	E1	E1	Crow
21.10	2. 9	C11	J7	Ox	27.12	10.11	E1	F2	Monkey
22.10	3. 9	C11	K8	Bat	28.12	11.11	E1	G3	Gibbon
23.10	4. 9	C11	A9	Rat	29.12	12.11	E1	H4	Tapir
24.10	5. 9	C11	B10	Swallow	30.12	13.11	E1	J5	Sheep
25.10	6. 9	C11	C11	Pig	31.12	14.11	E1	K6	Deer
26.10	7. 9	C11	D12	Porcupine	**1961**				
27.10	8. 9	C11	E1	Wolf	1. 1	15.11	E1	A7	Horse
28.10	9. 9	C11	F2	Dog	2. 1	16.11	E1	B8	Stag
29.10	10. 9	C11	G3	Pheasant	3. 1	17.11	E1	C9	Serpent
30.10	11. 9	C11	H4	Cock	4. 1	18.11	E1	D10	Earthworm
31.10	12. 9	C11	J5	Crow	5. 1	19.11	E1	E11	Crocodile
1.11	13. 9	C11	K6	Monkey	6. 1	20.11	E1	F12	Dragon
2.11	14. 9	C11	A7	Gibbon	7. 1	21.11	E1	G1	Badger
3.11	15. 9	C11	B8	Tapir	8. 1	22.11	E1	H2	Hare
4.11	16. 9	C11	C9	Sheep	9. 1	23.11	E1	J3	Fox
5.11	17. 9	C11	D10	Deer	10. 1	24.11	E1	K4	Tiger
6.11	18. 9	C11	E11	Horse	11. 1	25.11	E1	A5	Leopard
7.11	19. 9	C11	F12	Stag	12. 1	26.11	E1	B6	Griffon
8.11	20. 9	C11	G1	Serpent	13. 1	27.11	E1	C7	Ox
9.11	21. 9	C11	H2	Earthworm	14. 1	28.11	E1	D8	Bat
10.11	22. 9	C11	J3	Crocodile	15. 1	29.11	E1	E9	Rat
11.11	23. 9	C11	K4	Dragon	16. 1	30.11	E1	F10	Swallow
12.11	24. 9	C11	A5	Badger	17. 1	1.12	F2	G11	Pig
13.11	25. 9	C11	B6	Hare	18. 1	2.12	F2	H12	Porcupine
14.11	26. 9	C11	C7	Fox	19. 1	3.12	F2	J1	Wolf
15.11	27. 9	C11	D8	Tiger	20. 1	4.12	F2	K2	Dog
16.11	28. 9	C11	E9	Leopard	21. 1	5.12	F2	A3	Pheasant
17.11	29. 9	C11	F10	Griffon	22. 1	6.12	F2	B4	Cock
18.11	30. 9	C11	G11	Ox	23. 1	7.12	F2	C5	Crow
19.11	1.10	D12	H12	Bat	24. 1	8.12	F2	D6	Monkey
20.11	2.10	D12	J1	Rat	25. 1	9.12	F2	E7	Gibbon
21.11	3.10	D12	K2	Swallow	26. 1	10.12	F2	F8	Tapir
22.11	4.10	D12	A3	Pig	27. 1	11.12	F2	G9	Sheep
23.11	5.10	D12	B4	Porcupine	28. 1	12.12	F2	H10	Deer
24.11	6.10	D12	C5	Wolf	29. 1	13.12	F2	J11	Horse
25.11	7.10	D12	D6	Dog	30. 1	14.12	F2	K12	Stag
26.11	8.10	D12	E7	Pheasant	31. 1	15.12	F2	A1	Serpent
27.11	9.10	D12	F8	Cock	1. 2	16.12	F2	B2	Earthworm
28.11	10.10	D12	G9	Crow	2. 2	17.12	F2	C3	Crocodile
29.11	11.10	D12	H10	Monkey	3. 2	18.12	F2	D4	Dragon
30.11	12.10	D12	J11	Gibbon	4. 2	19.12	F2	E5	Badger
1.12	13.10	D12	K12	Tapir	5. 2	20.12	F2	F6	Hare
2.12	14.10	D12	A1	Sheep	6. 2	21.12	F2	G7	Fox
3.12	15.10	D12	B2	Deer	7. 2	22.12	F2	H8	Tiger
4.12	16.10	D12	C3	Horse	8. 2	23.12	F2	J9	Leopard
5.12	17.10	D12	D4	Stag	9. 2	24.12	F2	K10	Griffon
6.12	18.10	D12	E5	Serpent	10. 2	25.12	F2	A11	Ox
7.12	19.10	D12	F6	Earthworm	11. 2	26.12	F2	B12	Bat
8.12	20.10	D12	G7	Crocodile	12. 2	27.12	F2	C1	Rat
9.12	21.10	D12	H8	Dragon	13. 2	28.12	F2	D2	Swallow
10.12	22.10	D12	J9	Badger	14. 2	29.12	F2	E3	Pig
11.12	23.10	D12	K10	Hare					

HSIN CH'OU YEAR

Solar date	Lunar date	Month HS/EB	Day HS/EB	Constellation	Solar date	Lunar date	Month HS/EB	Day HS/EB	Constellation
15. 2	1. 1	G3	F4	Porcupine	27. 4	13. 3	J5	G3	Crocodile
16. 2	2. 1	G3	G5	Wolf	28. 4	14. 3	J5	H4	Dragon
17. 2	3. 1	G3	H6	Dog	29. 4	15. 3	J5	J5	Badger
18. 2	4. 1	G3	J7	Pheasant	30. 4	16. 3	J5	K6	Hare
19. 2	5. 1	G3	K8	Cock	1. 5	17. 3	J5	A7	Fox
20. 2	6. 1	G3	A9	Crow	2. 5	18. 3	J5	B8	Tiger
21. 2	7. 1	G3	B10	Monkey	3. 5	19. 3	J5	C9	Leopard
22. 2	8. 1	G3	C11	Gibbon	4. 5	20. 3	J5	D10	Griffon
23. 2	9. 1	G3	D12	Tapir	5. 5	21. 3	J5	E11	Ox
24. 2	10. 1	G3	E1	Sheep	6. 5	22. 3	J5	F12	Bat
25. 2	11. 1	G3	F2	Deer	7. 5	23. 3	J5	G1	Rat
26. 2	12. 1	G3	G3	Horse	8. 5	24. 3	J5	H2	Swallow
27. 2	13. 1	G3	H4	Stag	9. 5	25. 3	J5	J3	Pig
28. 2	14. 1	G3	J5	Serpent	10. 5	26. 3	J5	K4	Porcupine
1. 3	15. 1	G3	K6	Earthworm	11. 5	27. 3	J5	A5	Wolf
2. 3	16. 1	G3	A7	Crocodile	12. 5	28. 3	J5	B6	Dog
3. 3	17. 1	G3	B8	Dragon	13. 5	29. 3	J5	C7	Pheasant
4. 3	18. 1	G3	C9	Badger	14. 5	30. 3	J5	D8	Cock
5. 3	19. 1	G3	D10	Hare	15. 5	1. 4	K6	E9	Crow
6. 3	20. 1	G3	E11	Fox	16. 5	2. 4	K6	F10	Monkey
7. 3	21. 1	G3	F12	Tiger	17. 5	3. 4	K6	G11	Gibbon
8. 3	22. 1	G3	G1	Leopard	18. 5	4. 4	K6	H12	Tapir
9. 3	23. 1	G3	H2	Griffon	19. 5	5. 4	K6	J1	Sheep
10. 3	24. 1	G3	J3	Ox	20. 5	6. 4	K6	K2	Deer
11. 3	25. 1	G3	K4	Bat	21. 5	7. 4	K6	A3	Horse
12. 3	26. 1	G3	A5	Rat	22. 5	8. 4	K6	B4	Stag
13. 3	27. 1	G3	B6	Swallow	23. 5	9. 4	K6	C5	Serpent
14. 3	28. 1	G3	C7	Pig	24. 5	10. 4	K6	D6	Earthworm
15. 3	29. 1	G3	D8	Porcupine	25. 5	11. 4	K6	E7	Crocodile
16. 3	30. 1	G3	E9	Wolf	26. 5	12. 4	K6	F8	Dragon
17. 3	1. 2	H4	F10	Dog	27. 5	13. 4	K6	G9	Badger
18. 3	2. 2	H4	G11	Pheasant	28. 5	14. 4	K6	H10	Hare
19. 3	3. 2	H4	H12	Cock	29. 5	15. 4	K6	J11	Fox
20. 3	4. 2	H4	J1	Crow	30. 5	16. 4	K6	K12	Tiger
21. 3	5. 2	H4	K2	Monkey	31. 5	17. 4	K6	A1	Leopard
22. 3	6. 2	H4	A3	Gibbon	1. 6	18. 4	K6	B2	Griffon
23. 3	7. 2	H4	B4	Tapir	2. 6	19. 4	K6	C3	Ox
24. 3	8. 2	H4	C5	Sheep	3. 6	20. 4	K6	D4	Bat
25. 3	9. 2	H4	D6	Deer	4. 6	21. 4	K6	E5	Rat
26. 3	10. 2	H4	E7	Horse	5. 6	22. 4	K6	F6	Swallow
27. 3	11. 2	H4	F8	Stag	6. 6	23. 4	K6	G7	Pig
28. 3	12. 2	H4	G9	Serpent	7. 6	24. 4	K6	H8	Porcupine
29. 3	13. 2	H4	H10	Earthworm	8. 6	25. 4	K6	J9	Wolf
30. 3	14. 2	H4	J11	Crocodile	9. 6	26. 4	K6	K10	Dog
31. 3	15. 2	H4	K12	Dragon	10. 6	27. 4	K6	A11	Pheasant
1. 4	16. 2	H4	A1	Badger	11. 6	28. 4	K6	B12	Cock
2. 4	17. 2	H4	B2	Hare	12. 6	29. 4	K6	C1	Crow
3. 4	18. 2	H4	C3	Fox	13. 6	1. 5	A7	D2	Monkey
4. 4	19. 2	H4	D4	Tiger	14. 6	2. 5	A7	E3	Gibbon
5. 4	20. 2	H4	E5	Leopard	15. 6	3. 5	A7	F4	Tapir
6. 4	21. 2	H4	F6	Griffon	16. 6	4. 5	A7	G5	Sheep
7. 4	22. 2	H4	G7	Ox	17. 6	5. 5	A7	H6	Deer
8. 4	23. 2	H4	H8	Bat	18. 6	6. 5	A7	J7	Horse
9. 4	24. 2	H4	J9	Rat	19. 6	7. 5	A7	K8	Stag
10. 4	25. 2	H4	K10	Swallow	20. 6	8. 5	A7	A9	Serpent
11. 4	26. 2	H4	A11	Pig	21. 6	9. 5	A7	B10	Earthworm
12. 4	27. 2	H4	B12	Porcupine	22. 6	10. 5	A7	C11	Crocodile
13. 4	28. 2	H4	C1	Wolf	23. 6	11. 5	A7	D12	Dragon
14. 4	29. 2	H4	D2	Dog	24. 6	12. 5	A7	E1	Badger
15. 4	1. 3	J5	E3	Pheasant	25. 6	13. 5	A7	F2	Hare
16. 4	2. 3	J5	F4	Cock	26. 6	14. 5	A7	G3	Fox
17. 4	3. 3	J5	G5	Crow	27. 6	15. 5	A7	H4	Tiger
18. 4	4. 3	J5	H6	Monkey	28. 6	16. 5	A7	J5	Leopard
19. 4	5. 3	J5	J7	Gibbon	29. 6	17. 5	A7	K6	Griffon
20. 4	6. 3	J5	K8	Tapir	30. 6	18. 5	A7	A7	Ox
21. 4	7. 3	J5	A9	Sheep	1. 7	19. 5	A7	B8	Bat
22. 4	8. 3	J5	B10	Deer	2. 7	20. 5	A7	C9	Rat
23. 4	9. 3	J5	C11	Horse	3. 7	21. 5	A7	D10	Swallow
24. 4	10. 3	J5	D12	Stag	4. 7	22. 5	A7	E11	Pig
25. 4	11. 3	J5	E1	Serpent	5. 7	23. 5	A7	F12	Porcupine
26. 4	12. 3	J5	F2	Earthworm	6. 7	24. 5	A7	G1	Wolf

Solar date	Lunar date	Month HS/EB	Day HS/EB	Constellation	Solar date	Lunar date	Month HS/EB	Day HS/EB	Constellation
7. 7	25. 5	A7	H2	Dog	18. 9	9. 8	D10	A3	Fox
8. 7	26. 5	A7	J3	Pheasant	19. 9	10. 8	D10	B4	Tiger
9. 7	27. 5	A7	K4	Cock	20. 9	11. 8	D10	C5	Leopard
10. 7	28. 5	A7	A5	Crow	21. 9	12. 8	D10	D6	Griffon
11. 7	29. 5	A7	B6	Monkey	22. 9	13. 8	D10	E7	Ox
12. 7	30. 5	A7	C7	Gibbon	23. 9	14. 8	D10	F8	Bat
13. 7	1. 6	B8	D8	Tapir	24. 9	15. 8	D10	G9	Rat
14. 7	2. 6	B8	E9	Sheep	25. 9	16. 8	D10	H10	Swallow
15. 7	3. 6	B8	F10	Deer	26. 9	17. 8	D10	J11	Pig
16. 7	4. 6	B8	G11	Horse	27. 9	18. 8	D10	K12	Porcupine
17. 7	5. 6	B8	H12	Stag	28. 9	19. 8	D10	A1	Wolf
18. 7	6. 6	B8	J1	Serpent	29. 9	20. 8	D10	B2	Dog
19. 7	7. 6	B8	K2	Earthworm	30. 9	21. 8	D10	C3	Pheasant
20. 7	8. 6	B8	A3	Crocodile	1.10	22. 8	D10	D4	Cock
21. 7	9. 6	B8	B4	Dragon	2.10	23. 8	D10	E5	Crow
22. 7	10. 6	B8	C5	Badger	3.10	24. 8	D10	F6	Monkey
23. 7	11. 6	B8	D6	Hare	4.10	25. 8	D10	G7	Gibbon
24. 7	12. 6	B8	E7	Fox	5.10	26. 8	D10	H8	Tapir
25. 7	13. 6	B8	F8	Tiger	6.10	27. 8	D10	J9	Sheep
26. 7	14. 6	B8	G9	Leopard	7.10	28. 8	D10	K10	Deer
27. 7	15. 6	B8	H10	Griffon	8.10	29. 8	D10	A11	Horse
28. 7	16. 6	B8	J11	Ox	9.10	30. 8	D10	B12	Stag
29. 7	17. 6	B8	K12	Bat	10.10	1. 9	E11	C1	Serpent
30. 7	18. 6	B8	A1	Rat	11.10	2. 9	E11	D2	Earthworm
31. 7	19. 6	B8	B2	Swallow	12.10	3. 9	E11	E3	Crocodile
1. 8	20. 6	B8	C3	Pig	13.10	4. 9	E11	F4	Dragon
2. 8	21. 6	B8	D4	Porcupine	14.10	5. 9	E11	G5	Badger
3. 8	22. 6	B8	E5	Wolf	15.10	6. 9	E11	H6	Hare
4. 8	23. 6	B8	F6	Dog	16.10	7. 9	E11	J7	Fox
5. 8	24. 6	B8	G7	Pheasant	17.10	8. 9	E11	K8	Tiger
6. 8	25. 6	B8	H8	Cock	18.10	9. 9	E11	A9	Leopard
7. 8	26. 6	B8	J9	Crow	19.10	10. 9	E11	B10	Griffon
8. 8	27. 6	B8	K10	Monkey	20.10	11. 9	E11	C11	Ox
9. 8	28. 6	B8	A11	Gibbon	21.10	12. 9	E11	D12	Bat
10. 8	29. 6	B8	B12	Tapir	22.10	13. 9	E11	E1	Rat
11. 8	1. 7	C9	C1	Sheep	23.10	14. 9	E11	F2	Swallow
12. 8	2. 7	C9	D2	Deer	24.10	15. 9	E11	G3	Pig
13. 8	3. 7	C9	E3	Horse	25.10	16. 9	E11	H4	Porcupine
14. 8	4. 7	C9	F4	Stag	26.10	17. 9	E11	J5	Wolf
15. 8	5. 7	C9	G5	Serpent	27.10	18. 9	E11	K6	Dog
16. 8	6. 7	C9	H6	Earthworm	28.10	19. 9	E11	A7	Pheasant
17. 8	7. 7	C9	J7	Crocodile	29.10	20. 9	E11	B8	Cock
18. 8	8. 7	C9	K8	Dragon	30.10	21. 9	E11	C9	Crow
19. 8	9. 7	C9	A9	Badger	31.10	22. 9	E11	D10	Monkey
20. 8	10. 7	C9	B10	Hare	1.11	23. 9	E11	E11	Gibbon
21. 8	11. 7	C9	C11	Fox	2.11	24. 9	E11	F12	Tapir
22. 8	12. 7	C9	D12	Tiger	3.11	25. 9	E11	G1	Sheep
23. 8	13. 7	C9	E1	Leopard	4.11	26. 9	E11	H2	Deer
24. 8	14. 7	C9	F2	Griffon	5.11	27. 9	E11	J3	Horse
25. 8	15. 7	C9	G3	Ox	6.11	28. 9	E11	K4	Stag
26. 8	16. 7	C9	H4	Bat	7.11	29. 9	E11	A5	Serpent
27. 8	17. 7	C9	J5	Rat	8.11	1. 10	F12	B6	Earthworm
28. 8	18. 7	C9	K6	Swallow	9.11	2. 10	F12	C7	Crocodile
29. 8	19. 7	C9	A7	Pig	10.11	3. 10	F12	D8	Dragon
30. 8	20. 7	C9	B8	Porcupine	11.11	4. 10	F12	E9	Badger
31. 8	21. 7	C9	C9	Wolf	12.11	5. 10	F12	F10	Hare
1. 9	22. 7	C9	D10	Dog	13.11	6. 10	F12	G11	Fox
2. 9	23. 7	C9	E11	Pheasant	14.11	7. 10	F12	H12	Tiger
3. 9	24. 7	C9	F12	Cock	15.11	8. 10	F12	J1	Leopard
4. 9	25. 7	C9	G1	Crow	16.11	9. 10	F12	K2	Griffon
5. 9	26. 7	C9	H2	Monkey	17.11	10. 10	F12	A3	Ox
6. 9	27. 7	C9	J3	Gibbon	18.11	11. 10	F12	B4	Bat
7. 9	28. 7	C9	K4	Tapir	19.11	12. 10	F12	C5	Rat
8. 9	29. 7	C9	A5	Sheep	20.11	13. 10	F12	D6	Swallow
9. 9	30. 7	C9	B6	Deer	21.11	14. 10	F12	E7	Pig
10. 9	1. 8	D10	C7	Horse	22.11	15. 10	F12	F8	Porcupine
11. 9	2. 8	D10	D8	Stag	23.11	16. 10	F12	G9	Wolf
12. 9	3. 8	D10	E9	Serpent	24.11	17. 10	F12	H10	Dog
13. 9	4. 8	D10	F10	Earthworm	25.11	18. 10	F12	J11	Pheasant
14. 9	5. 8	D10	G11	Crocodile	26.11	19. 10	F12	K12	Cock
15. 9	6. 8	D10	H12	Dragon	27.11	20. 10	F12	A1	Crow
16. 9	7. 8	D10	J1	Badger	28.11	21. 10	F12	B2	Monkey
17. 9	8. 8	D10	K2	Hare	29.11	22. 10	F12	C3	Gibbon

Solar date	Lunar date	Month HS/EB	Day HS/EB	Constellation	Solar date	Lunar date	Month HS/EB	Day HS/EB	Constellation
30.11	23.10	F12	D4	Tapir	2. 1	26.11	G1	G1	Serpent
1.12	24.10	F12	E5	Sheep	3. 1	27.11	G1	H2	Earthworm
2.12	25.10	F12	F6	Deer	4. 1	28.11	G1	J3	Crocodile
3.12	26.10	F12	G7	Horse	5. 1	29.11	G1	K4	Dragon
4.12	27.10	F12	H8	Stag	6. 1	1.12	H2	A5	Badger
5.12	28.10	F12	J9	Serpent	7. 1	2.12	H2	B6	Hare
6.12	29.10	F12	K10	Earthworm	8. 1	3.12	H2	C7	Fox
7.12	30.10	F12	A11	Crocodile	9. 1	4.12	H2	D8	Tiger
8.12	1.11	G1	B12	Dragon	10. 1	5.12	H2	E9	Leopard
9.12	2.11	G1	C1	Badger	11. 1	5.12	H2	F10	Griffon
10.12	3.11	G1	D2	Hare	12. 1	7.12	H2	G11	Ox
11.12	4.11	G1	E3	Fox	13. 1	8.12	H2	H12	Bat
12.12	5.11	G1	F4	Tiger	14. 1	9.12	H2	J1	Rat
13.12	6.11	G1	G5	Leopard	15. 1	10.12	H2	K2	Swallow
14.12	7.11	G1	H6	Griffon	16. 1	11.12	H2	A3	Pig
15.12	8.11	G1	J7	Ox	17. 1	12.12	H2	B4	Porcupine
16.12	9.11	G1	K8	Bat	18. 1	13.12	H2	C5	Wolf
17.12	10.11	G1	A9	Rat	19. 1	14.12	H2	D6	Dog
18.12	11.11	G1	B10	Swallow	20. 1	15.12	H2	E7	Pheasant
19.12	12.11	G1	C11	Pig	21. 1	16.12	H2	F8	Cock
20.12	13.11	G1	D12	Porcupine	22. 1	17.12	H2	G9	Crow
21.12	14.11	G1	E1	Wolf	23. 1	18.12	H2	H10	Monkey
22.12	15.11	G1	F2	Dog	24. 1	19.12	H2	J11	Gibbon
23.12	16.11	G1	G3	Pheasant	25. 1	20.12	H2	K12	Tapir
24.12	17.11	G1	H4	Cock	26. 1	21.12	H2	A1	Sheep
25.12	18.11	G1	J5	Crow	27. 1	22.12	H2	B2	Deer
26.12	19.11	G1	K6	Monkey	28. 1	23.12	H2	C3	Horse
27.12	20.11	G1	A7	Gibbon	29. 1	24.12	H2	D4	Stag
28.12	21.11	G1	B8	Tapir	30. 1	25.12	H2	E5	Serpent
29.12	22.11	G1	C9	Sheep	31. 1	26.12	H2	F6	Earthworm
30.12	23.11	G1	D10	Deer	1. 2	27.12	H2	G7	Crocodile
31.12	24.11	G1	E11	Horse	2. 2	28.12	H2	H8	Dragon
1962					3. 2	29.12	H2	J9	Badger
1. 1	25.11	G1	F12	Stag	4. 2	30.12	H2	K10	Hare

JEN YIN YEAR

Solar date	Lunar date	Month HS/EB	Day HS/EB	Constellation	Solar date	Lunar date	Month HS/EB	Day HS/EB	Constellation
5. 2	1. 1	J3	A11	Fox	10. 3	5. 2	K4	D8	Bat
6. 2	2. 1	J3	B12	Tiger	11. 3	6. 2	K4	E9	Rat
7. 2	3. 1	J3	C1	Leopard	12. 3	7. 2	K4	F10	Swallow
8. 2	4. 1	J3	D2	Griffon	13. 3	8. 2	K4	G11	Pig
9. 2	5. 1	J3	E3	Ox	14. 3	9. 2	K4	H12	Porcupine
10. 2	6. 1	J3	F4	Bat	15. 3	10. 2	K4	J1	Wolf
11. 2	7. 1	J3	G5	Rat	16. 3	11. 2	K4	K2	Dog
12. 2	8. 1	J3	H6	Swallow	17. 3	12. 2	K4	A3	Pheasant
13. 2	9. 1	J3	J7	Pig	18. 3	13. 2	K4	B4	Cock
14. 2	10. 1	J3	K8	Porcupine	19. 3	14. 2	K4	C5	Crow
15. 2	11. 1	J3	A9	Wolf	20. 3	15. 2	K4	D6	Monkey
16. 2	12. 1	J3	B10	Dog	21. 3	16. 2	K4	E7	Gibbon
17. 2	13. 1	J3	C11	Pheasant	22. 3	17. 2	K4	F8	Tapir
18. 2	14. 1	J3	D12	Cock	23. 3	18. 2	K4	G9	Sheep
19. 2	15. 1	J3	E1	Crow	24. 3	19. 2	K4	H10	Deer
20. 2	16. 1	J3	F2	Monkey	25. 3	20. 2	K4	J11	Horse
21. 2	17. 1	J3	G3	Gibbon	26. 3	21. 2	K4	K12	Stag
22. 2	18. 1	J3	H4	Tapir	27. 3	22. 2	K4	A1	Serpent
23. 2	19. 1	J3	J5	Sheep	28. 3	23. 2	K4	B2	Earthworm
24. 2	20. 1	J3	K6	Deer	29. 3	24. 2	K4	C3	Crocodile
25. 2	21. 1	J3	A7	Horse	30. 3	25. 2	K4	D4	Dragon
26. 2	22. 1	J3	B8	Stag	31. 3	26. 2	K4	E5	Badger
27. 2	23. 1	J3	C9	Serpent	1. 4	27. 2	K4	F6	Hare
28. 2	24. 1	J3	D10	Earthworm	2. 4	28. 2	K4	G7	Fox
1. 3	25. 1	J3	E11	Crocodile	3. 4	29. 2	K4	H8	Tiger
2. 3	26. 1	J3	F12	Dragon	4. 4	30. 2	K4	J9	Leopard
3. 3	27. 1	J3	G1	Badger	5. 4	1. 3	A5	K10	Griffon
4. 3	28. 1	J3	H2	Hare	6. 4	2. 3	A5	A11	Ox
5. 3	29. 1	J3	J3	Fox	7. 4	3. 3	A5	B12	Bat
6. 3	1. 2	K4	K4	Tiger	8. 4	4. 3	A5	C1	Rat
7. 3	2. 2	K4	A5	Leopard	9. 4	5. 3	A5	D2	Swallow
8. 3	3. 2	K4	B6	Griffon	10. 4	6. 3	A5	E3	Pig
9. 3	4. 2	K4	C7	Ox	11. 4	7. 3	A5	F4	Porcupine

Solar date	Lunar date	Month HS/EB	Day HS/EB	Constellation
12. 4	8. 3	A5	G5	Wolf
13. 4	9. 3	A5	H6	Dog
14. 4	10. 3	A5	J7	Pheasant
15. 4	11. 3	A5	K8	Cock
16. 4	12. 3	A5	A9	Crow
17. 4	13. 3	A5	B10	Monkey
18. 4	14. 3	A5	C11	Gibbon
19. 4	15. 3	A5	D12	Tapir
20. 4	16. 3	A5	E1	Sheep
21. 4	17. 3	A5	F2	Deer
22. 4	18. 3	A5	G3	Horse
23. 4	19. 3	A5	H4	Stag
24. 4	20. 3	A5	J5	Serpent
25. 4	21. 3	A5	K6	Earthworm
26. 4	22. 3	A5	A7	Crocodile
27. 4	23. 3	A5	B8	Dragon
28. 4	24. 3	A5	C9	Badger
29. 4	25. 3	A5	D10	Hare
30. 4	26. 3	A5	E11	Fox
1. 5	27. 3	A5	F12	Tiger
2. 5	28. 3	A5	G1	Leopard
3. 5	29. 3	A5	H2	Griffon
4. 5	1. 4	B6	J3	Ox
5. 5	2. 4	B6	K4	Bat
6. 5	3. 4	B6	A5	Rat
7. 5	4. 4	B6	B6	Swallow
8. 5	5. 4	B6	C7	Pig
9. 5	6. 4	B6	D8	Porcupine
10. 5	7. 4	B6	E9	Wolf
11. 5	8. 4	B6	F10	Dog
12. 5	9. 4	B6	G11	Pheasant
13. 5	10. 4	B6	H12	Cock
14. 5	11. 4	B6	J1	Crow
15. 5	12. 4	B6	K2	Monkey
16. 5	13. 4	B6	A3	Gibbon
17. 5	14. 4	B6	B4	Tapir
18. 5	15. 4	B6	C5	Sheep
19. 5	16. 4	B6	D6	Deer
20. 5	17. 4	B6	E7	Horse
21. 5	18. 4	B6	F8	Stag
22. 5	19. 4	B6	G9	Serpent
23. 5	20. 4	B6	H10	Earthworm
24. 5	21. 4	B6	J11	Crocodile
25. 5	22. 4	B6	K12	Dragon
26. 5	23. 4	B6	A1	Badger
27. 5	24. 4	B6	B2	Hare
28. 5	25. 4	B6	C3	Fox
29. 5	26. 4	B6	D4	Tiger
30. 5	27. 4	B6	E5	Leopard
31. 5	28. 4	B6	F6	Griffon
1. 6	29. 4	B6	G7	Ox
2. 6	1. 5	C7	H8	Bat
3. 6	2. 5	C7	J9	Rat
4. 6	3. 5	C7	K10	Swallow
5. 6	4. 5	C7	A11	Pig
6. 6	5. 5	C7	B12	Porcupine
7. 6	6. 5	C7	C1	Wolf
8. 6	7. 5	C7	D2	Dog
9. 6	8. 5	C7	E3	Pheasant
10. 6	9. 5	C7	F4	Cock
11. 6	10. 5	C7	G5	Crow
12. 6	11. 5	C7	H6	Monkey
13. 6	12. 5	C7	J7	Gibbon
14. 6	13. 5	C7	K8	Tapir
15. 6	14. 5	C7	A9	Sheep
16. 6	15. 5	C7	B10	Deer
17. 6	16. 5	C7	C11	Horse
18. 6	17. 5	C7	D12	Stag
19. 6	18. 5	C7	E1	Serpent
20. 6	19. 5	C7	F2	Earthworm
21. 6	20. 5	C7	G3	Crocodile
22. 6	21. 5	C7	H4	Dragon
23. 6	22. 5	C7	J5	Badger
24. 6	23. 5	C7	K6	Hare
25. 6	24. 5	C7	A7	Fox
26. 6	25. 5	C7	B8	Tiger
27. 6	26. 5	C7	C9	Leopard
28. 6	27. 5	C7	D10	Griffon
29. 6	28. 5	C7	E11	Ox
30. 6	29. 5	C7	F12	Bat
1. 7	30. 5	C7	G1	Rat
2. 7	1. 6	D8	H2	Swallow
3. 7	2. 6	D8	J3	Pig
4. 7	3. 6	D8	K4	Porcupine
5. 7	4. 6	D8	A5	Wolf
6. 7	5. 6	D8	B6	Dog
7. 7	6. 6	D8	C7	Pheasant
8. 7	7. 6	D8	D8	Cock
9. 7	8. 6	D8	E9	Crow
10. 7	9. 6	D8	F10	Monkey
11. 7	10. 6	D8	G11	Gibbon
12. 7	11. 6	D8	H12	Tapir
13. 7	12. 6	D8	J1	Sheep
14. 7	13. 6	D8	K2	Deer
15. 7	14. 6	D8	A3	Horse
16. 7	15. 6	D8	B4	Stag
17. 7	16. 6	D8	C5	Serpent
18. 7	17. 6	D8	D6	Earthworm
19. 7	18. 6	D8	E7	Crocodile
20. 7	19. 6	D8	F8	Dragon
21. 7	20. 6	D8	G9	Badger
22. 7	21. 6	D8	H10	Hare
23. 7	22. 6	D8	J11	Fox
24. 7	23. 6	D8	K12	Tiger
25. 7	24. 6	D8	A1	Leopard
26. 7	25. 6	D8	B2	Griffon
27. 7	26. 6	D8	C3	Ox
28. 7	27. 6	D8	D4	Bat
29. 7	28. 6	D8	E5	Rat
30. 7	29. 6	D8	F6	Swallow
31. 7	1. 7	E9	G7	Pig
1. 8	2. 7	E9	H8	Porcupine
2. 8	3. 7	E9	J9	Wolf
3. 8	4. 7	E9	K10	Dog
4. 8	5. 7	E9	A11	Pheasant
5. 8	6: 7	E9	B12	Cock
6. 8	7. 7	E9	C1	Crow
7. 8	8. 7	E9	D2	Monkey
8. 8	9. 7	E9	E3	Gibbon
9. 8	10. 7	E9	F4	Tapir
10. 8	11. 7	E9	G5	Sheep
11. 8	12. 7	E9	H6	Deer
12. 8	13. 7	E9	J7	Horse
13. 8	14. 7	E9	K8	Stag
14. 8	15. 7	E9	A9	Serpent
15. 8	16. 7	E9	B10	Earthworm
16. 8	17. 7	E9	C11	Crocodile
17. 8	18. 7	E9	D12	Dragon
18. 8	19. 7	E9	E1	Badger
19. 8	20. 7	E9	F2	Hare
20. 8	21. 7	E9	G3	Fox
21. 8	22. 7	E9	H4	Tiger
22. 8	23. 7	E9	J5	Leopard
23. 8	24. 7	E9	K6	Griffon
24. 8	25. 7	E9	A7	Ox
25. 8	26. 7	E9	B8	Bat
26. 8	27. 7	E9	C9	Rat
27. 8	28. 7	E9	D10	Swallow
28. 8	29. 7	E9	E11	Pig
29. 8	30. 7	E9	F12	Porcupine
30. 8	1. 8	F10	G1	Wolf
31. 8	2. 8	F10	H2	Dog
1. 9	3. 8	F10	J3	Pheasant
2. 9	4. 8	F10	K4	Cock
3. 9	5. 8	F10	A5	Crow
4. 9	6. 8	F10	B6	Monkey

Solar date	Lunar date	Month HS/EB	Day HS/EB	Constellation	Solar date	Lunar date	Month HS/EB	Day HS/EB	Constellation
5. 9	7. 8	F10	C7	Gibbon	16.11	20.10	H12	E7	Ox
6. 9	8. 8	F10	D8	Tapir	17.11	21.10	H12	F8	Bat
7. 9	9. 8	F10	E9	Sheep	18.11	22.10	H12	G9	Rat
8. 9	10. 8	F10	F10	Deer	19.11	23.10	H12	H10	Swallow
9. 9	11. 8	F10	G11	Horse	20.11	24.10	H12	J11	Pig
10. 9	12. 8	F10	H12	Stag	21.11	25.10	H12	K12	Porcupine
11. 9	13. 8	F10	J1	Serpent	22.11	26.10	H12	A1	Wolf
12. 9	14. 8	F10	K2	Earthworm	23.11	27.10	H12	B2	Dog
13. 9	15. 8	F10	A3	Crocodile	24.11	28.10	H12	C3	Pheasant
14. 9	16. 8	F10	B4	Dragon	25.11	29.10	H12	D4	Cock
15. 9	17. 8	F10	C5	Badger	26.11	30.10	H12	E5	Crow
16. 9	18. 8	F10	D6	Hare	27.11	1.11	J1	F6	Monkey
17. 9	19. 8	F10	E7	Fox	28.11	2.11	J1	G7	Gibbon
18. 9	20. 8	F10	F8	Tiger	29.11	3.11	J1	H8	Tapir
19. 9	21. 8	F10	G9	Leopard	30.11	4.11	J1	J9	Sheep
20. 9	22. 8	F10	H10	Griffon	1.12	5.11	J1	K10	Deer
21. 9	23. 8	F10	J11	Ox	2.12	6.11	J1	A11	Horse
22. 9	24. 8	F10	K12	Bat	3.12	7.11	J1	B12	Stag
23. 9	25. 8	F10	A1	Rat	4.12	8.11	J1	C1	Serpent
24. 9	26. 8	F10	B2	Swallow	5.12	9.11	J1	D2	Earthworm
25. 9	27. 8	F10	C3	Pig	6.12	10.11	J1	E3	Crocodile
26. 9	28. 8	F10	D4	Porcupine	7.12	11.11	J1	F4	Dragon
27. 9	29. 8	F10	E5	Wolf	8.12	12.11	J1	G5	Badger
28. 9	30. 8	F10	F6	Dog	9.12	13.11	J1	H6	Hare
29. 9	1. 9	G11	G7	Pheasant	10.12	14.11	J1	J7	Fox
30. 9	2. 9	G11	H8	Cock	11.12	15.11	J1	K8	Tiger
1.10	3. 9	G11	J9	Crow	12.12	16.11	J1	A9	Leopard
2.10	4. 9	G11	K10	Monkey	13.12	17.11	J1	B10	Griffon
3.10	5. 9	G11	A11	Gibbon	14.12	18.11	J1	C11	Ox
4.10	6. 9	G11	B12	Tapir	15.12	19.11	J1	D12	Bat
5.10	7. 9	G11	C1	Sheep	16.12	20.11	J1	E1	Rat
6.10	8. 9	G11	D2	Deer	17.12	21.11	J1	F2	Swallow
7.10	9. 9	G11	E3	Horse	18.12	22.11	J1	G3	Pig
8.10	10. 9	G11	F4	Stag	19.12	23.11	J1	H4	Porcupine
9.10	11. 9	G11	G5	Serpent	20.12	24.11	J1	J5	Wolf
10.10	12. 9	G11	H6	Earthworm	21.12	25.11	J1	K6	Dog
11.10	13. 9	G11	J7	Crocodile	22.12	26.11	J1	A7	Pheasant
12.10	14. 9	G11	K8	Dragon	23.12	27.11	J1	B8	Cock
13.10	15. 9	G11	A9	Badger	24.12	28.11	J1	C9	Crow
14.10	16. 9	G11	B10	Hare	25.12	29.11	J1	D10	Monkey
15.10	17. 9	G11	C11	Fox	26.12	30.11	J1	E11	Gibbon
16.10	18. 9	G11	D12	Tiger	27.12	1.12	K2	F12	Tapir
17.10	19. 9	G11	E1	Leopard	28.12	2.12	K2	G1	Sheep
18.10	20. 9	G11	F2	Griffon	29.12	3.12	K2	H2	Deer
19.10	21. 9	G11	G3	Ox	30.12	4.12	K2	J3	Horse
20.10	22. 9	G11	H4	Bat	31.12	5.12	K2	K4	Stag
21.10	23. 9	G11	J5	Rat					
22.10	24. 9	G11	K6	Swallow	**1963**				
23.10	25. 9	G11	A7	Pig	1. 1	6.12	K2	A5	Serpent
24.10	26. 9	G11	B8	Porcupine	2. 1	7.12	K2	B6	Earthworm
25.10	27. 9	G11	C9	Wolf	3. 1	8.12	K2	C7	Crocodile
26.10	28. 9	G11	D10	Dog	4. 1	9.12	K2	D8	Dragon
27.10	29. 9	G11	E11	Pheasant	5. 1	10.12	K2	E9	Badger
28.10	1.10	H12	F12	Cock	6. 1	11.12	K2	F10	Hare
29.10	2.10	H12	G1	Crow	7. 1	12.12	K2	G11	Fox
30.10	3.10	H12	H2	Monkey	8. 1	13.12	K2	H12	Tiger
31.10	4.10	H12	J3	Gibbon	9. 1	14.12	K2	J1	Leopard
1.11	5.10	H12	K4	Tapir	10. 1	15.12	K2	K2	Griffon
2.11	6.10	H12	A5	Sheep	11. 1	16.12	K2	A3	Ox
3.11	7.10	H12	B6	Deer	12. 1	17.12	K2	B4	Bat
4.11	8.10	H12	C7	Horse	13. 1	18.12	K2	C5	Rat
5.11	9.10	H12	D8	Stag	14. 1	19.12	K2	D6	Swallow
6.11	10.10	H12	E9	Serpent	15. 1	20.12	K2	E7	Pig
7.11	11.10	H12	F10	Earthworm	16. 1	21.12	K2	F8	Porcupine
8.11	12.10	H12	G11	Crocodile	17. 1	22.12	K2	G9	Wolf
9.11	13.10	H12	H12	Dragon	18. 1	23.12	K2	H10	Dog
10.11	14.10	H12	J1	Badger	19. 1	24.12	K2	J11	Pheasant
11.11	15.10	H12	K2	Hare	20. 1	25.12	K2	K12	Cock
12.11	16.10	H12	A3	Fox	21. 1	26.12	K2	A1	Crow
13.11	17.10	H12	B4	Tiger	22. 1	27.12	K2	B2	Monkey
14.11	18.10	H12	C5	Leopard	23. 1	28.12	K2	C3	Gibbon
15.11	19.10	H12	D6	Griffon	24. 1	29.12	K2	D4	Tapir

KUEI MAO YEAR

Solar date	Lunar date	Month HS/EB	Day HS/EB	Constellation
25. 1	1. 1	A3	E5	Sheep
26. 1	2. 1	A3	F6	Deer
27. 1	3. 1	A3	G7	Horse
28. 1	4. 1	A3	H8	Stag
29. 1	5. 1	A3	J9	Serpent
30. 1	6. 1	A3	K10	Earthworm
31. 1	7. 1	A3	A11	Crocodile
1. 2	8. 1	A3	B12	Dragon
2. 2	9. 1	A3	C1	Badger
3. 2	10. 1	A3	D2	Hare
4. 2	11. 1	A3	E3	Fox
5. 2	12. 1	A3	F4	Tiger
6. 2	13. 1	A3	G5	Leopard
7. 2	14. 1	A3	H6	Griffon
8. 2	15. 1	A3	J7	Ox
9. 2	16. 1	A3	K8	Bat
10. 2	17. 1	A3	A9	Rat
11. 2	18. 1	A3	B10	Swallow
12. 2	19. 1	A3	C11	Pig
13. 2	20. 1	A3	D12	Porcupine
14. 2	21. 1	A3	E1	Wolf
15. 2	22. 1	A3	F2	Dog
16. 2	23. 1	A3	G3	Pheasant
17. 2	24. 1	A3	H4	Cock
18. 2	25. 1	A3	J5	Crow
19. 2	26. 1	A3	K6	Monkey
20. 2	27. 1	A3	A7	Gibbon
21. 2	28. 1	A3	B8	Tapir
22. 2	29. 1	A3	C9	Sheep
23. 2	30. 1	A3	D10	Deer
24. 2	1. 2	B4	E11	Horse
25. 2	2. 2	B4	F12	Stag
26. 2	3. 2	B4	G1	Serpent
27. 2	4. 2	B4	H2	Earthworm
28. 2	5. 2	B4	J3	Crocodile
1. 3	6. 2	B4	K4	Dragon
2. 3	7. 2	B4	A5	Badger
3. 3	8. 2	B4	B6	Hare
4. 3	9. 2	B4	C7	Fox
5. 3	10. 2	B4	D8	Tiger
6. 3	11. 2	B4	E9	Leopard
7. 3	12. 2	B4	F10	Griffon
8. 3	13. 2	B4	G11	Ox
9. 3	14. 2	B4	H12	Bat
10. 3	15. 2	B4	J1	Rat
11. 3	16. 2	B4	K2	Swallow
12. 3	17. 2	B4	A3	Pig
13. 3	18. 2	B4	B4	Porcupine
14. 3	19. 2	B4	C5	Wolf
15. 3	20. 2	B4	D6	Dog
16. 3	21. 2	B4	E7	Pheasant
17. 3	22. 2	B4	F8	Cock
18. 3	23. 2	B4	G9	Crow
19. 3	24. 2	B4	H10	Monkey
20. 3	25. 2	B4	J11	Gibbon
21. 3	26. 2	B4	K12	Tapir
22. 3	27. 2	B4	A1	Sheep
23. 3	28. 2	B4	B2	Deer
24. 3	29. 2	B4	C3	Horse
25. 3	1. 3	C5	D4	Stag
26. 3	2. 3	C5	E5	Serpent
27. 3	3. 3	C5	F6	Earthworm
28. 3	4. 3	C5	G7	Crocodile
29. 3	5. 3	C5	H8	Dragon
30. 3	6. 3	C5	J9	Badger
31. 3	7. 3	C5	K10	Hare
1. 4	8. 3	C5	A11	Fox
2. 4	9. 3	C5	B12	Tiger
3. 4	10. 3	C5	C1	Leopard
4. 4	11. 3	C5	D2	Griffon
5. 4	12. 3	C5	E3	Ox
6. 4	13. 3	C5	F4	Bat
7. 4	14. 3	C5	G5	Rat
8. 4	15. 3	C5	H6	Swallow
9. 4	16. 3	C5	J7	Pig
10. 4	17. 3	C5	K8	Porcupine
11. 4	18. 3	C5	A9	Wolf
12. 4	19. 3	C5	B10	Dog
13. 4	20. 3	C5	C11	Pheasant
14. 4	21. 3	C5	D12	Cock
15. 4	22. 3	C5	E1	Crow
16. 4	23. 3	C5	F2	Monkey
17. 4	24. 3	C5	G3	Gibbon
18. 4	25. 3	C5	H4	Tapir
19. 4	26. 3	C5	J5	Sheep
20. 4	27. 3	C5	K6	Deer
21. 4	28. 3	C5	A7	Horse
22. 4	29. 3	C5	B8	Stag
23. 4	30. 3	C5	C9	Serpent
24. 4	1. 4	D6	D10	Earthworm
25. 4	2. 4	D6	E11	Crocodile
26. 4	3. 4	D6	F12	Dragon
27. 4	4. 4	D6	G1	Badger
28. 4	5. 4	D6	H2	Hare
29. 4	6. 4	D6	J3	Fox
30. 4	7. 4	D6	K4	Tiger
1. 5	8. 4	D6	A5	Leopard
2. 5	9. 4	D6	B6	Griffon
3. 5	10. 4	D6	C7	Ox
4. 5	11. 4	D6	D8	Bat
5. 5	12. 4	D6	E9	Rat
6. 5	13. 4	D6	F10	Swallow
7. 5	14. 4	D6	G11	Pig
8. 5	15. 4	D6	H12	Porcupine
9. 5	16. 4	D6	J1	Wolf
10. 5	17. 4	D6	K2	Dog
11. 5	18. 4	D6	A3	Pheasant
12. 5	19. 4	D6	B4	Cock
13. 5	20. 4	D6	C5	Crow
14. 5	21. 4	D6	D6	Monkey
15. 5	22. 4	D6	E7	Gibbon
16. 5	23. 4	D6	F8	Tapir
17. 5	24. 4	D6	G9	Sheep
18. 5	25. 4	D6	H10	Deer
19. 5	26. 4	D6	J11	Horse
20. 5	27. 4	D6	K12	Stag
21. 5	28. 4	D6	A1	Serpent
22. 5	29. 4	D6	B2	Earthworm
23. 5	*1. 4*	*D6*	C3	Crocodile
24. 5	*2. 4*	*D6*	D4	Dragon
25. 5	*3. 4*	*D6*	E5	Badger
26. 5	*4. 4*	*D6*	F6	Hare
27. 5	*5. 4*	*D6*	G7	Fox
28. 5	*6. 4*	*D6*	H8	Tiger
29. 5	*7. 4*	*D6*	J9	Leopard
30. 5	*8. 4*	*D6*	K10	Griffon
31. 5	*9. 4*	*D6*	A11	Ox
1. 6	*10. 4*	*D6*	B12	Bat
2. 6	*11. 4*	*D6*	C1	Rat
3. 6	*12. 4*	*D6*	D2	Swallow
4. 6	*13. 4*	*D6*	E3	Pig
5. 6	*14. 4*	*D6*	F4	Porcupine
6. 6	*15. 4*	*D6*	G5	Wolf
7. 6	*16. 4*	*D6*	H6	Dog
8. 6	*17. 4*	*D6*	J7	Pheasant
9. 6	*18. 4*	*D6*	K8	Cock
10. 6	*19. 4*	*D6*	A9	Crow
11. 6	*20. 4*	*D6*	B10	Monkey
12. 6	*21. 4*	*D6*	C11	Gibbon
13. 6	*22. 4*	*D6*	D12	Tapir
14. 6	*23. 4*	*D6*	E1	Sheep
15. 6	*24. 4*	*D6*	F2	Deer

Solar date	Lunar date	Month HS/EB	Day HS/EB	Constellation	Solar date	Lunar date	Month HS/EB	Day HS/EB	Constellation
16. 6	25. 4	D6	G3	Horse	28. 8	10. 7	G9	K4	Porcupine
17. 6	26. 4	D6	H4	Stag	29. 8	11. 7	G9	A5	Wolf
18. 6	27. 4	D6	J5	Serpent	30. 8	12. 7	G9	B6	Dog
19. 6	28. 4	D6	K6	Earthworm	31. 8	13. 7	G9	C7	Pheasant
20. 6	29. 4	D6	A7	Crocodile	1. 9	14. 7	G9	D8	Cock
21. 6	1. 5	E7	B8	Dragon	2. 9	15. 7	G9	E9	Crow
22. 6	2. 5	E7	C9	Badger	3. 9	16. 7	G9	F10	Monkey
23. 6	3. 5	E7	D10	Hare	4. 9	17. 7	G9	G11	Gibbon
24. 6	4. 5	E7	E11	Fox	5. 9	18. 7	G9	H12	Tapir
25. 6	5. 5	E7	F12	Tiger	6. 9	19. 7	G9	J1	Sheep
26. 6	6. 5	E7	G1	Leopard	7. 9	20. 7	G9	K2	Deer
27. 6	7. 5	E7	H2	Griffon	8. 9	21. 7	G9	A3	Horse
28. 6	8. 5	E7	J3	Ox	9. 9	22. 7	G9	B4	Stag
29. 6	9. 5	E7	K4	Bat	10. 9	23. 7	G9	C5	Serpent
30. 6	10. 5	E7	A5	Rat	11. 9	24. 7	G9	D6	Earthworm
1. 7	11. 5	E7	B6	Swallow	12. 9	25. 7	G9	E7	Crocodile
2. 7	12. 5	E7	C7	Pig	13. 9	26. 7	G9	F8	Dragon
3. 7	13. 5	E7	D8	Porcupine	14. 9	27. 7	G9	G9	Badger
4. 7	14. 5	E7	E9	Wolf	15. 9	28. 7	G9	H10	Hare
5. 7	15. 5	E7	F10	Dog	16. 9	29. 7	G9	J11	Fox
6. 7	16. 5	E7	G11	Pheasant	17. 9	30. 7	G9	K12	Tiger
7. 7	17. 5	E7	H12	Cock	18. 9	1. 8	H10	A1	Leopard
8. 7	18. 5	E7	J1	Crow	19. 9	2. 8	H10	B2	Griffon
9. 7	19. 5	E7	K2	Monkey	20. 9	3. 8	H10	C3	Ox
10. 7	20. 5	E7	A3	Gibbon	21. 9	4. 8	H10	D4	Bat
11. 7	21. 5	E7	B4	Tapir	22. 9	5. 8	H10	E5	Rat
12. 7	22. 5	E7	C5	Sheep	23. 9	6. 8	H10	F6	Swallow
13. 7	23. 5	E7	D6	Deer	24. 9	7. 8	H10	G7	Pig
14. 7	24. 5	E7	E7	Horse	25. 9	8. 8	H10	H8	Porcupine
15. 7	25. 5	E7	F8	Stag	26. 9	9. 8	H10	J9	Wolf
16. 7	26. 5	E7	G9	Serpent	27. 9	10. 8	H10	K10	Dog
17. 7	27. 5	E7	H10	Earthworm	28. 9	11. 8	H10	A11	Pheasant
18. 7	28. 5	E7	J11	Crocodile	29. 9	12. 8	H10	B12	Cock
19. 7	29. 5	E7	K12	Dragon	30. 9	13. 8	H10	C1	Crow
20. 7	30. 5	E7	A1	Badger	1.10	14. 8	H10	D2	Monkey
21. 7	1. 6	F8	B2	Hare	2.10	15. 8	H10	E3	Gibbon
22. 7	2. 6	F8	C3	Fox	3.10	16. 8	H10	F4	Tapir
23. 7	3. 6	F8	D4	Tiger	4.10	17. 8	H10	G5	Sheep
24. 7	4. 6	F8	E5	Leopard	5.10	18. 8	H10	H6	Deer
25. 7	5. 6	F8	F6	Griffon	6.10	19. 8	H10	J7	Horse
26. 7	6. 6	F8	G7	Ox	7.10	20. 8	H10	K8	Stag
27. 7	7. 6	F8	H8	Bat	8.10	21. 8	H10	A9	Serpent
28. 7	8. 6	F8	J9	Rat	9.10	22. 8	H10	B10	Earthworm
29. 7	9. 6	F8	K10	Swallow	10.10	23. 8	H10	C11	Crocodile
30. 7	10. 6	F8	A11	Pig	11.10	24. 8	H10	D12	Dragon
31. 7	11. 6	F8	B12	Porcupine	12.10	25. 8	H10	E1	Badger
1. 8	12. 6	F8	C1	Wolf	13.10	26. 8	H10	F2	Hare
2. 8	13. 6	F8	D2	Dog	14.10	27. 8	H10	G3	Fox
3. 8	14. 6	F8	E3	Pheasant	15.10	28. 8	H10	H4	Tiger
4. 8	15. 6	F8	F4	Cock	16.10	29. 8	H10	J5	Leopard
5. 8	16. 6	F8	G5	Crow	17.10	1. 9	J11	K6	Griffon
6. 8	17. 6	F8	H6	Monkey	18.10	2. 9	J11	A7	Ox
7. 8	18. 6	F8	J7	Gibbon	19.10	3. 9	J11	B8	Bat
8. 8	19. 6	F8	K8	Tapir	20.20	4. 9	J11	C9	Rat
9. 8	20. 6	F8	A9	Sheep	21.10	5. 9	J11	D10	Swallow
10. 8	21. 6	F8	B10	Deer	22.10	6. 9	J11	E11	Pig
11. 8	22. 6	F8	C11	Horse	23.10	7. 9	J11	F12	Porcupine
12. 8	23. 6	F8	D12	Stag	24.10	8. 9	J11	G1	Wolf
13. 8	24. 6	F8	E1	Serpent	25.10	9. 9	J11	H2	Dog
14. 8	25. 6	F8	F2	Earthworm	26.10	10. 9	J11	J3	Pheasant
15. 8	26. 6	F8	G3	Crocodile	27.10	11. 9	J11	K4	Cock
16. 8	27. 6	F8	H4	Dragon	28.10	12. 9	J11	A5	Crow
17. 8	28. 6	F8	J5	Badger	29.10	13. 9	J11	B6	Monkey
18. 8	29. 6	F8	K6	Hare	30.10	14. 9	J11	C7	Gibbon
19. 8	1. 7	G9	A7	Fox	31.10	15. 9	J11	D8	Tapir
20. 8	2. 7	G9	B8	Tiger	1.11	16. 9	J11	E9	Sheep
21. 8	3. 7	G9	C9	Leopard	2.11	17. 9	J11	F10	Deer
22. 8	4. 7	G9	D10	Griffon	3.11	18. 9	J11	G11	Horse
23. 8	5. 7	G9	E11	Ox	4.11	19. 9	J11	H12	Stag
24. 8	6. 7	G9	F12	Bat	5.11	20. 9	J11	J1	Serpent
25. 8	7. 7	G9	G1	Rat	6.11	21. 9	J11	K2	Earthworm
26. 8	8. 7	G9	H2	Swallow	7.11	22. 9	J11	A3	Crocodile
27. 8	9. 7	G9	J3	Pig	8.11	23. 9	J11	B4	Dragon

Solar date	Lunar date	Month HS/EB	Day HS/EB	Constellation
9.11	24. 9	J11	C5	Badger
10.11	25. 9	J11	D6	Hare
11.11	26. 9	J11	E7	Fox
12.11	27. 9	J11	F8	Tiger
13.11	28. 9	J11	G9	Leopard
14.11	29. 9	J11	H10	Griffon
15.11	30. 9	J11	J11	Ox
16.11	1.10	K12	K12	Bat
17.11	2.10	K12	A1	Rat
18.11	3.10	K12	B2	Swallow
19.11	4.10	K12	C3	Pig
20.11	5.10	K12	D4	Porcupine
21.11	6.10	K12	E5	Wolf
22.11	7.10	K12	F6	Dog
23.11	8.10	K12	G7	Pheasant
24.11	9.10	K12	H8	Cock
25.11	10.10	K12	J9	Crow
26.11	11.10	K12	K10	Monkey
27.11	12.10	K12	A11	Gibbon
28.11	13.10	K12	B12	Tapir
29.11	14.10	K12	C1	Sheep
30.11	15.10	K12	D2	Deer
1.12	16.10	K12	E3	Horse
2.12	17.10	K12	F4	Stag
3.12	18.10	K12	G5	Serpent
4.12	19.10	K12	H6	Earthworm
5.12	20.20	K12	J7	Crocodile
6.12	21.10	K12	K8	Dragon
7.12	22.10	K12	A9	Badger
8.12	23.10	K12	B10	Hare
9.12	24.10	K12	C11	Fox
10.12	25.10	K12	D12	Tiger
11.12	26.10	K12	E1	Leopard
12.12	27.10	K12	F2	Griffon
13.12	28.10	K12	G3	Ox
14.12	29.10	K12	H4	Bat
15.12	30.10	K12	J5	Rat
16.12	1.11	A1	K6	Swallow
17.12	2.11	A1	A7	Pig
18.12	3.11	A1	B8	Porcupine
19.12	4.11	A1	C9	Wolf
20.12	5.11	A1	D10	Dog
21.12	6.11	A1	E11	Pheasant
22.12	7.11	A1	F12	Cock
23.12	8.11	A1	G1	Crow
24.12	9.11	A1	H2	Monkey
25.12	10.11	A1	J3	Gibbon
26.12	11.11	A1	K4	Tapir
27.12	12.11	A1	A5	Sheep
28.12	13.11	A1	B6	Deer
29.12	14.11	A1	C7	Horse
30.12	15.11	A1	D8	Stag
31.12	16.11	A1	E9	Serpent

1964

Solar date	Lunar date	Month HS/EB	Day HS/EB	Constellation
1. 1	17.11	A1	F10	Earthworm
2. 1	18.11	A1	G11	Crocodile
3. 1	19.11	A1	H12	Dragon
4. 1	20.11	A1	J1	Badger
5. 1	21.11	A1	K2	Hare
6. 1	22.11	A1	A3	Fox
7. 1	23.11	A1	B4	Tiger
8. 1	24.11	A1	C5	Leopard
9. 1	25.11	A1	D6	Griffon
10. 1	26.11	A1	E7	Ox
11. 1	27.11	A1	F8	Bat
12. 1	28.11	A1	G9	Rat
13. 1	29.11	A1	H10	Swallow
14. 1	30.11	A1	J11	Pig
15. 1	1.12	B2	K12	Porcupine
16. 1	2.12	B2	A1	Wolf
17. 1	3.12	B2	B2	Dog
18. 1	4.12	B2	C3	Pheasant
19. 1	5.12	B2	D4	Cock
20. 1	6.12	B2	E5	Crow
21. 1	7.12	B2	F6	Monkey
22. 1	8.12	B2	G7	Gibbon
23. 1	9.12	B2	H8	Tapir
24. 1	10.12	B2	J9	Sheep
25. 1	11.12	B2	K10	Deer
26. 1	12.12	B2	A11	Horse
27. 1	13.12	B2	B12	Stag
28. 1	14.12	B2	C1	Serpent
29. 1	15.12	B2	D2	Earthworm
30. 1	16.12	B2	E3	Crocodile
31. 1	17.12	B2	F4	Dragon
1. 2	18.12	B2	G5	Badger
2. 2	19.12	B2	H6	Hare
3. 2	20.12	B2	J7	Fox
4. 2	21.12	B2	K8	Tiger
5. 2	22.12	B2	A9	Leopard
6. 2	23.12	B2	B10	Griffon
7. 2	24.12	B2	C11	Ox
8. 2	25.12	B2	D12	Bat
9. 2	26.12	B2	E1	Rat
10. 2	27.12	B2	F2	Swallow
11. 2	28.12	B2	G3	Pig
12. 2	29.12	B2	H4	Porcupine

CHIA CH'EN YEAR

Solar date	Lunar date	Month HS/EB	Day HS/EB	Constellation
13. 2	1. 1	C3	J5	Wolf
14. 2	2. 1	C3	K6	Dog
15. 2	3. 1	C3	A7	Pheasant
16. 2	4. 1	C3	B8	Cock
17. 2	5. 1	C3	C9	Crow
18. 2	6. 1	C3	D10	Monkey
19. 2	7. 1	C3	E11	Gibbon
20. 2	8. 1	C3	F12	Tapir
21. 2	9. 1	C3	G1	Sheep
22. 2	10. 1	C3	H2	Deer
23. 2	11. 1	C3	J3	Horse
24. 2	12. 1	C3	K4	Stag
25. 2	13. 1	C3	A5	Serpent
26. 2	14. 1	C3	B6	Earthworm
27. 2	15. 1	C3	C7	Crocodile
28. 2	16. 1	C3	D8	Dragon
29. 2	17. 1	C3	E9	Badger
1. 3	18. 1	C3	F10	Hare
2. 3	19. 1	C3	G11	Fox
3. 3	20. 1	C3	H12	Tiger
4. 3	21. 1	C3	J1	Leopard
5. 3	22. 1	C3	K2	Griffon
6. 3	23. 1	C3	A3	Ox
7. 3	24. 1	C3	B4	Bat
8. 3	25. 1	C3	C5	Rat
9. 3	26. 1	C3	D6	Swallow
10. 3	27. 1	C3	E7	Pig
11. 3	28. 1	C3	F8	Porcupine
12. 3	29. 1	C3	G9	Wolf
13. 3	30. 1	C3	H10	Dog
14. 3	1. 2	D4	J11	Pheasant
15. 3	2. 2	D4	K12	Cock
16. 3	3. 2	D4	A1	Crow
17. 3	4. 2	D4	B2	Monkey
18. 3	5. 2	D4	C3	Gibbon
19. 3	6. 2	D4	D4	Tapir
20. 3	7. 2	D4	E5	Sheep
21. 3	8. 2	D4	F6	Deer

Solar date	Lunar date	Month HS/EB	Day HS/EB	Constellation	Solar date	Lunar date	Month HS/EB	Day HS/EB	Constellation
22. 3	9. 2	D4	G7	Horse	3. 6	23. 4	F6	K8	Porcupine
23. 3	10. 2	D4	H8	Stag	4. 6	24. 4	F6	A9	Wolf
24. 3	11. 2	D4	J9	Serpent	5. 6	25. 4	F6	B10	Dog
25. 3	12. 2	D4	K10	Earthworm	6. 6	26. 4	F6	C11	Pheasant
26. 3	13. 2	D4	A11	Crocodile	7. 6	27. 4	F6	D12	Cock
27. 3	14. 2	D4	B12	Dragon	8. 6	28. 4	F6	E1	Crow
28. 3	15. 2	D4	C1	Badger	9. 6	29. 4	F6	F2	Monkey
29. 3	16. 2	D4	D2	Hare	10. 6	1. 5	G7	G3	Gibbon
30. 3	17. 2	D4	E3	Fox	11. 6	2. 5	G7	H4	Tapir
31. 3	18. 2	D4	F4	Tiger	12. 6	3. 5	G7	J5	Sheep
1. 4	19. 2	D4	G5	Leopard	13. 6	4. 5	G7	K6	Deer
2. 4	20. 2	D4	H6	Griffon	14. 6	5. 5	G7	A7	Horse
3. 4	21. 2	D4	J7	Ox	15. 6	6. 5	G7	B8	Stag
4. 4	22. 2	D4	K8	Rat	16. 6	7. 5	G7	C9	Serpent
5. 4	23. 2	D4	A9	Rat	17. 6	8. 5	G7	D10	Earthworm
6. 4	24. 2	D4	B10	Swallow	18. 6	9. 5	G7	E11	Crocodile
7. 4	25. 2	D4	C11	Pig	19. 6	10. 5	G7	F12	Dragon
8. 4	26. 2	D4	D12	Porcupine	20. 6	11. 5	G7	G1	Badger
9. 4	27. 2	D4	E1	Wolf	21. 6	12. 5	G7	H2	Hare
10. 4	28. 2	D4	F2	Dog	22. 6	13. 5	G7	J3	Fox
11. 4	29. 2	D4	G3	Pheasant	23. 6	14. 5	G7	K4	Tiger
12. 4	1. 3	E5	H4	Cock	24. 6	15. 5	G7	A5	Leopard
13. 4	2. 3	E5	J5	Crow	25. 6	16. 5	G7	B6	Griffon
14. 4	3. 3	E5	K6	Monkey	26. 6	17. 5	G7	C7	Ox
15. 4	4. 3	E5	A7	Gibbon	27. 6	18. 5	G7	D8	Bat
16. 4	5. 3	E5	B8	Tapir	28. 6	19. 5	G7	E9	Rat
17. 4	6. 3	E5	C9	Sheep	29. 6	20. 5	G7	F10	Swallow
18. 4	7. 3	E5	D10	Deer	30. 6	21. 5	G7	G11	Pig
19. 4	8. 3	E5	E11	Horse	1. 7	22. 5	G7	H12	Porcupine
20. 4	9. 3	E5	F12	Stag	2. 7	23. 5	G7	J1	Wolf
21. 4	10. 3	E5	G1	Serpent	3. 7	24. 5	G7	K2	Dog
22. 4	11. 3	E5	H2	Earthworm	4. 7	25. 5	G7	A3	Pheasant
23. 4	12. 3	E5	J3	Crocodile	5. 7	26. 5	G7	B4	Cock
24. 4	13. 3	E5	K4	Dragon	6. 7	27. 5	G7	C5	Crow
25. 4	14. 3	E5	A5	Badger	7. 7	28. 5	G7	D6	Monkey
26. 4	15. 3	E5	B6	Hare	8. 7	29. 5	G7	E7	Gibbon
27. 4	16. 3	E5	C7	Fox	9. 7	1. 6	H8	F8	Tapir
28. 4	17. 3	E5	D8	Tiger	10. 7	2. 6	H8	G9	Sheep
29. 4	18. 3	E5	E9	Leopard	11. 7	3. 6	H8	H10	Deer
30. 4	19. 3	E5	F10	Griffon	12. 7	4. 6	H8	J11	Horse
1. 5	20. 3	E5	G11	Ox	13. 7	5. 6	H8	K12	Stag
2. 5	21. 3	E5	H12	Bat	14. 7	6. 6	H8	A1	Serpent
3. 5	22. 3	E5	J1	Rat	15. 7	7. 6	H8	B2	Earthworm
4. 5	23. 3	E5	K2	Swallow	16. 7	8. 6	H8	C3	Crocodile
5. 5	24. 3	E5	A3	Pig	17. 7	9. 6	H8	D4	Dragon
6. 5	25. 3	E5	B4	Porcupine	18. 7	10. 6	H8	E5	Badger
7. 5	26. 3	E5	C5	Wolf	19. 7	11. 6	H8	F6	Hare
8. 5	27. 3	E5	D6	Dog	20. 7	12. 6	H8	G7	Fox
9. 5	28. 3	E5	E7	Pheasant	21. 7	13. 6	H8	H8	Tiger
10. 5	29. 3	E5	F8	Cock	22. 7	14. 6	H8	J9	Leopard
11. 5	30. 3	E5	G9	Crow	23. 7	15. 6	H8	K10	Griffon
12. 5	1. 4	F6	H10	Monkey	24. 7	16. 6	H8	A11	Ox
13. 5	2. 4	F6	J11	Gibbon	25. 7	17. 6	H8	B12	Bat
14. 5	3. 4	F6	K12	Tapir	26. 7	18. 6	H8	C1	Rat
15. 5	4. 4	F6	A1	Sheep	27. 7	19. 6	H8	D2	Swallow
16. 5	5. 4	F6	B2	Deer	28. 7	20. 6	H8	E3	Pig
17. 5	6. 4	F6	C3	Horse	29. 7	21. 6	H8	F4	Porcupine
18. 5	7. 4	F6	D4	Stag	30. 7	22. 6	H8	G5	Wolf
19. 5	8. 4	F6	E5	Serpent	31. 7	23. 6	H8	H6	Dog
20. 5	9. 4	F6	F6	Earthworm	1. 8	24. 6	H8	J7	Pheasant
21. 5	10. 4	F6	G7	Crocodile	2. 8	25. 6	H8	K8	Cock
22. 5	11. 4	F6	H8	Dragon	3. 8	26. 6	H8	A9	Crow
23. 5	12. 4	F6	J9	Badger	4. 8	27. 6	H8	B10	Monkey
24. 5	13. 4	F6	K10	Hare	5. 8	28. 6	H8	C11	Gibbon
25. 5	14. 4	F6	A11	Fox	6. 8	29. 6	H8	D12	Tapir
26. 5	15. 4	F6	B12	Tiger	7. 8	30. 6	H8	E1	Sheep
27. 5	16. 4	F6	C1	Leopard	8. 8	1. 7	J9	F2	Deer
28. 5	17. 4	F6	D2	Griffon	9. 8	2. 7	J9	G3	Horse
29. 5	18. 4	F6	E3	Ox	10. 8	3. 7	J9	H4	Stag
30. 5	19. 4	F6	F4	Bat	11. 8	4. 7	J9	J5	Serpent
31. 5	20. 4	F6	G5	Rat	12. 8	5. 7	J9	K6	Earthworm
1. 6	21. 4	F6	H6	Swallow	13. 8	6. 7	J9	A7	Crocodile
2. 6	22. 4	F6	J7	Pig	14. 8	7. 7	J9	B8	Dragon

Solar date	Lunar date	Month HS/EB	Day HS/EB	Constellation
15. 8	8. 7	J9	C9	Badger
16. 8	9. 7	J9	D10	Hare
17. 8	10. 7	J9	E11	Fox
18. 8	11. 7	J9	F12	Tiger
19. 8	12. 7	J9	G1	Leopard
20. 8	13. 7	J9	H2	Griffon
21. 8	14. 7	J9	J3	Ox
22. 8	15. 7	J9	K4	Bat
23. 8	16. 7	J9	A5	Rat
24. 8	17. 7	J9	B6	Swallow
25. 8	18. 7	J9	C7	Pig
26. 8	19. 7	J9	D8	Porcupine
27. 8	20. 7	J9	E9	Wolf
28. 8	21. 7	J9	F10	Fox
29. 8	22. 7	J9	G11	Pheasant
30. 8	23. 7	J9	H12	Cock
31. 8	24. 7	J9	J1	Crow
1. 9	25. 7	J9	K2	Monkey
2. 9	26. 7	J9	A3	Gibbon
3. 9	27. 7	J9	B4	Tapir
4. 9	28. 7	J9	C5	Sheep
5. 9	29. 7	J9	D6	Deer
6. 9	1. 8	K10	E7	Horse
7. 9	2. 8	K10	F8	Stag
8. 9	3. 8	K10	G9	Serpent
9. 9	4. 8	K10	H10	Earthworm
10. 9	5. 8	K10	J11	Crocodile
11. 9	6. 8	K10	K12	Dragon
12. 9	7. 8	K10	A1	Badger
13. 9	8. 8	K10	B2	Hare
14. 9	9. 8	K10	C3	Fox
15. 9	10. 8	K10	D4	Tiger
16. 9	11. 8	K10	E5	Leopard
17. 9	12. 8	K10	F6	Griffon
18. 9	13. 8	K10	G7	Ox
19. 9	14. 8	K10	H8	Bat
20. 9	15. 8	K10	J9	Rat
21. 9	16. 8	K10	K10	Swallow
22. 9	17. 8	K10	A11	Pig
23. 9	18. 8	K10	B12	Porcupine
24. 9	19. 8	K10	C1	Wolf
25. 9	20. 8	K10	D2	Dog
26. 9	21. 8	K10	E3	Pheasant
27. 9	22. 8	K10	F4	Cock
28. 9	23. 8	K10	G5	Crow
29. 9	24. 8	K10	H6	Monkey
30. 9	25. 8	K10	J7	Gibbon
1.10	26. 8	K10	K8	Tapir
2.10	27. 8	K10	A9	Sheep
3.10	28. 8	K10	B10	Deer
4.10	29. 8	K10	C11	Horse
5.10	30. 8	K10	D12	Stag
6.10	1. 9	A11	E1	Serpent
7.10	2. 9	A11	F2	Earthworm
8.10	3. 9	A11	G3	Crocodile
9.10	4. 9	A11	H4	Dragon
10.10	5. 9	A11	J5	Badger
11.10	6. 9	A11	K6	Hare
12.10	7. 9	A11	A7	Fox
13.10	8. 9	A11	B8	Tiger
14.10	9. 9	A11	C9	Leopard
15.10	10. 9	A11	D10	Griffon
16.10	11. 9	A11	E11	Ox
17.10	12. 9	A11	F12	Bat
18.10	13. 9	A11	G1	Rat
19.10	14. 9	A11	H2	Swallow
20.10	15. 9	A11	J3	Pig
21.10	16. 9	A11	K4	Porcupine
22.10	17. 9	A11	A5	Wolf
23.10	18. 9	A11	B6	Dog
24.10	19. 9	A11	C7	Pheasant
25.10	20. 9	A11	D8	Cock
26.10	21. 9	A11	E9	Crow
27.10	22. 9	A11	F10	Monkey
28.10	23. 9	A11	G11	Gibbon
29.10	24. 9	A11	H12	Tapir
30.10	25. 9	A11	J1	Sheep
31.10	26. 9	A11	K2	Deer
1.11	27. 9	A11	A3	Horse
2.11	28. 9	A11	B4	Stag
3.11	29. 9	A11	C5	Serpent
4.11	1.10	B12	D6	Earthworm
5.11	2.10	B12	E7	Crocodile
6.11	3.10	B12	F8	Dragon
7.11	4.10	B12	G9	Badger
8.11	5.10	B12	H10	Hare
9.11	6.10	B12	J11	Fox
10.11	7.10	B12	K12	Tiger
11.11	8.10	B12	A1	Leopard
12.11	9.10	B12	B2	Griffon
13.11	10.10	B12	C3	Ox
14.11	11.10	B12	D4	Bat
15.11	12.10	B12	E5	Rat
16.11	13.10	B12	F6	Swallow
17.11	14.10	B12	G7	Pig
18.11	15.10	B12	H8	Porcupine
19.11	16.10	B12	J9	Wolf
20.11	17.10	B12	K10	Dog
21.11	18.10	B12	A11	Pheasant
22.11	19.10	B12	B12	Cock
23.11	20.10	B12	C1	Crow
24.11	21.10	B12	D2	Monkey
25.11	22.10	B12	E3	Gibbon
26.11	23.10	B12	F4	Tapir
27.11	24.10	B12	G5	Sheep
28.11	25.10	B12	H6	Deer
29.11	26.10	B12	J7	Horse
30.11	27.10	B12	K8	Stag
1.12	28.10	B12	A9	Serpent
2.12	29.10	B12	B10	Earthworm
3.12	30.10	B12	C11	Crocodile
4.12	1.11	C1	D12	Dragon
5.12	2.11	C1	E1	Badger
6.12	3.11	C1	F2	Hare
7.12	4.11	C1	G3	Fox
8.12	5.11	C1	H4	Tiger
9.12	6.11	C1	J5	Leopard
10.12	7.11	C1	K6	Griffon
11.12	8.11	C1	A7	Ox
12.12	9.11	C1	B8	Bat
13.12	10.11	C1	C9	Rat
14.12	11.11	C1	D10	Swallow
15.12	12.11	C1	E11	Pig
16.12	13.11	C1	F12	Porcupine
17.12	14.11	C1	G1	Wolf
18.12	15.11	C1	H2	Dog
19.12	16.11	C1	J3	Pheasant
20.12	17.11	C1	K4	Cock
21.12	18.11	C1	A5	Crow
22.12	19.11	C1	B6	Monkey
23.12	20.11	C1	C7	Gibbon
24.12	21.11	C1	D8	Tapir
25.12	22.11	C1	E9	Sheep
26.12	23.11	C1	F10	Deer
27.12	24.11	C1	G11	Horse
28.12	25.11	C1	H12	Stag
29.12	26.11	C1	J1	Serpent
30.12	27.11	C1	K2	Earthworm
31.12	28.11	C1	A3	Crocodile

1965

Solar date	Lunar date	Month HS/EB	Day HS/EB	Constellation
1. 1	29.11	C1	B4	Dragon
2. 1	30.11	C1	C5	Badger
3. 1	1.12	D2	D6	Hare
4. 1	2.12	D2	E7	Fox
5. 1	3.12	D2	F8	Tiger

Solar date	Lunar date	Month HS/EB	Day HS/EB	Constellation	Solar date	Lunar date	Month HS/EB	Day HS/EB	Constellation
6. 1	4.12	D2	G9	Leopard	20. 1	18.12	D2	A11	Gibbon
7. 1	5.12	D2	H10	Griffon	21. 1	19.12	D2	B12	Tapir
8. 1	6.12	D2	J11	Ox	22. 1	20.12	D2	C1	Sheep
9. 1	7.12	D2	K12	Bat	23. 1	21.12	D2	D2	Deer
10. 1	8.12	D2	A1	Rat	24. 1	22.12	D2	E3	Horse
11. 1	9.12	D2	B2	Swallow	25. 1	23.12	D2	F4	Stag
12. 1	10.12	D2	C3	Pig	26. 1	24.12	D2	G5	Serpent
13. 1	11.12	D2	D4	Porcupine	27. 1	25.12	D2	H6	Earthworm
14. 1	12.12	D2	E5	Wolf	28. 1	26.12	D2	J7	Crocodile
15. 1	13.12	D2	F6	Dog	29. 1	27.12	D2	K8	Dragon
16. 1	14.12	D2	G7	Pheasant	30. 1	28.12	D2	A9	Badger
17. 1	15.12	D2	H8	Cock	31. 1	29.12	D2	B10	Hare
18. 1	16.12	D2	J9	Crow	1. 2	30.12	D2	C11	Fox
19. 1	17.12	D2	K10	Monkey					

YI SZU YEAR

Solar date	Lunar date	Month HS/EB	Day HS/EB	Constellation	Solar date	Lunar date	Month HS/EB	Day HS/EB	Constellation
2. 2	1. 1	E3	D12	Tiger	28. 3	26. 2	F4	H6	Hare
3. 2	2. 1	E3	E1	Leopard	29. 3	27. 2	F4	J7	Fox
4. 2	3. 1	E3	F2	Griffon	30. 3	28. 2	F4	K8	Tiger
5. 2	4. 1	E3	G3	Ox	31. 3	29. 2	F4	A9	Leopard
6. 2	5. 1	E3	H4	Bat	1. 4	30. 2	F4	B10	Griffon
7. 2	6. 1	E3	J5	Rat	2. 4	1. 3	G5	C11	Ox
8. 2	7. 1	E3	K6	Swallow	3. 4	2. 3	G5	D12	Bat
9. 2	8. 1	E3	A7	Pig	4. 4	3. 3	G5	E1	Rat
10. 2	9. 1	E3	B8	Porcupine	5. 4	4. 3	G5	F2	Swallow
11. 2	10. 1	E3	C9	Wolf	6. 4	5. 3	G5	G3	Pig
12. 2	11. 1	E3	D10	Dog	7. 4	6. 3	G5	H4	Porcupine
13. 2	12. 1	E3	E11	Pheasant	8. 4	7. 3	G5	J5	Wolf
14. 2	13. 1	E3	F12	Cock	9. 4	8. 3	G5	K6	Dog
15. 2	14. 1	E3	G1	Crow	10. 4	9. 3	G5	A7	Pheasant
16. 2	15. 1	E3	H2	Monkey	11. 4	10. 3	F5	B8	Cock
17. 2	16. 1	E3	J3	Gibbon	12. 4	11. 3	G5	C9	Crow
18. 2	17. 1	E3	K4	Tapir	13. 4	12. 3	G5	D10	Monkey
19. 2	18. 1	E3	A5	Sheep	14. 4	13. 3	G5	E11	Gibbon
20. 2	19. 1	E3	B6	Deer	15. 4	14. 3	G5	F12	Tapir
21. 2	20. 1	E3	C7	Horse	16. 4	15. 3	G5	G1	Sheep
22. 2	21. 1	E3	D8	Stag	17. 4	16. 3	G5	H2	Deer
23. 2	22. 1	E3	E9	Serpent	18. 4	17. 3	G5	J3	Horse
24. 2	23. 1	E3	F10	Earthworm	19. 4	18. 3	G5	K4	Stag
25. 2	24. 1	E3	G11	Crocodile	20. 4	19. 3	G5	A5	Serpent
26. 2	25. 1	E3	H12	Dragon	21. 4	20. 3	G5	B6	Earthworm
27. 2	26. 1	E3	J1	Badger	22. 4	21. 3	G5	C7	Crocodile
28. 2	27. 1	E3	K2	Hare	23. 4	22. 3	G5	D8	Dragon
1. 3	28. 1	E3	A3	Fox	24. 4	23. 3	G5	E9	Badger
2. 3	29. 1	E3	B4	Tiger	25. 4	24. 3	G5	F10	Hare
3. 3	1. 2	F4	C5	Leopard	26. 4	25. 3	G5	G11	Fox
4. 3	2. 2	F4	D6	Griffon	27. 4	26. 3	G5	H12	Tiger
5. 3	3. 2	F4	E7	Ox	28. 4	27. 3	G5	J1	Leopard
6. 3	4. 2	F4	F8	Bat	29. 4	28. 3	G5	K2	Griffon
7. 3	5. 2	F4	G9	Rat	30. 4	29. 3	G5	A3	Ox
8. 3	6. 2	F4	H10	Swallow	1. 5	1. 4	H6	B4	Bat
9. 3	7. 2	F4	J11	Pig	2. 5	2. 4	H6	C5	Rat
10. 3	8. 2	F4	K12	Porcupine	3. 5	3. 4	H6	D6	Swallow
11. 3	9. 2	F4	A1	Wolf	4. 5	4. 4	H6	E7	Pig
12. 3	10. 2	F4	B2	Dog	5. 5	5. 4	H6	F8	Porcupine
13. 3	11. 2	F4	C3	Pheasant	6. 5	6. 4	H6	G9	Wolf
14. 3	12. 2	F4	D4	Cock	7. 5	7. 4	H6	H10	Dog
15. 3	13. 2	F4	E5	Crow	8. 5	8. 4	H6	J11	Pheasant
16. 3	14. 2	F4	F6	Monkey	9. 5	9. 4	H6	K12	Cock
17. 3	15. 2	F4	G7	Gibbon	10. 5	10. 4	H6	A1	Crow
18. 3	16. 2	F4	H8	Tapir	11. 5	11. 4	H6	B2	Monkey
19. 3	17. 2	F4	J9	Sheep	12. 5	12. 4	H6	C3	Gibbon
20. 3	18. 2	F4	K10	Deer	13. 5	13. 4	H6	D4	Tapir
21. 3	19. 2	F4	A11	Horse	14. 5	14. 4	H6	E5	Sheep
22. 3	20. 2	F4	B12	Stag	15. 5	15. 4	H6	F6	Deer
23. 3	21. 2	F4	C1	Serpent	16. 5	16. 4	H6	G7	Horse
24. 3	22. 2	F4	D2	Earthworm	17. 5	17. 4	H6	H8	Stag
25. 3	23. 2	F4	E3	Crocodile	18. 5	18. 4	H6	J9	Serpent
26. 3	24. 2	F4	F4	Dragon	19. 5	19. 4	H6	K10	Earthworm
27. 3	25. 2	F4	G5	Badger	20. 5	20. 4	H6	A11	Crocodile

Solar date	Lunar date	Month HS/EB	Day HS/EB	Constellation
21. 5	21. 4	H6	B12	Dragon
22. 5	22. 4	H6	C1	Badger
23. 5	23. 4	H6	D2	Hare
24. 5	24. 4	H6	E3	Fox
25. 5	25. 4	H6	F4	Tiger
26. 5	26. 4	H6	G5	Leopard
27. 5	27. 4	H6	H6	Griffon
28. 5	28. 4	H6	J7	Ox
29. 5	29. 4	H6	K8	Bat
30. 5	30. 4	H6	A9	Rat
31. 5	1. 5	J7	B10	Swallow
1. 6	2. 5	J7	C11	Pig
2. 6	3. 5	J7	D12	Porcupine
3. 6	4. 5	J7	E1	Wolf
4. 6	5. 5	J7	F2	Dog
5. 6	6. 5	J7	G3	Pheasant
6. 6	7. 5	J7	H4	Cock
7. 6	8. 5	J7	J5	Crow
8. 6	9. 5	J7	K6	Monkey
9. 6	10. 5	J7	A7	Gibbon
10. 6	11. 5	J7	B8	Tapir
11. 6	12. 5	J7	C9	Sheep
12. 6	13. 5	J7	D10	Deer
13. 6	14. 5	J7	E11	Horse
14. 6	15. 5	J7	F12	Stag
15. 6	16. 5	J7	G1	Serpent
16. 6	17. 5	J7	H2	Earthworm
17. 6	18. 5	J7	J3	Crocodile
18. 6	19. 5	J7	K4	Dragon
19. 6	20. 5	J7	A5	Badger
20. 6	21. 5	J7	B6	Hare
21. 6	22. 5	J7	C7	Fox
22. 6	23. 5	J7	D8	Tiger
23. 6	24. 5	J7	E9	Leopard
24. 6	25. 5	J7	F10	Griffon
25. 6	26. 5	J7	G11	Ox
26. 6	27. 5	J7	H12	Bat
27. 6	28. 5	J7	J1	Rat
28. 6	29. 5	J7	K2	Swallow
29. 6	1. 6	K8	A3	Pig
30. 6	2. 6	K8	B4	Porcupine
1. 7	3. 6	K8	C5	Wolf
2. 7	4. 6	K8	D6	Dog
3. 7	5. 6	K8	E7	Pheasant
4. 7	6. 6	K8	F8	Cock
5. 7	7. 6	K8	G9	Crow
6. 7	8. 6	K8	H10	Monkey
7. 7	9. 6	K8	J11	Gibbon
8. 7	10. 6	K8	K12	Tapir
9. 7	11. 6	K8	A1	Sheep
10. 7	12. 6	K8	B2	Deer
11. 7	13. 6	K8	C3	Horse
12. 7	14. 6	K8	D4	Stag
13. 7	15. 6	K8	E5	Serpent
14. 7	16. 6	K8	F6	Earthworm
15. 7	17. 6	K8	G7	Crocodile
16. 7	18. 6	K8	H8	Dragon
17. 7	19. 6	K8	J9	Badger
18. 7	20. 6	K8	K10	Hare
19. 7	21. 6	K8	A11	Fox
20. 7	22. 6	K8	B12	Tiger
21. 7	23. 6	K8	C1	Leopard
22. 7	24. 6	K8	D2	Griffon
23. 7	25. 6	K8	E3	Ox
24. 7	26. 6	K8	F4	Bat
25. 7	27. 6	K8	G5	Rat
26. 7	28. 6	K8	H6	Swallow
27. 7	29. 6	K8	J7	Pig
28. 7	1. 7	A9	K8	Porcupine
29. 7	2. 7	A9	A9	Wolf
30. 7	3. 7	A9	B10	Dog
31. 7	4. 7	A9	C11	Pheasant
1. 8	5. 7	A9	D12	Cock
2. 8	6. 7	A9	E1	Crow
3. 8	7. 7	A9	F2	Monkey
4. 8	8. 7	A9	G3	Gibbon
5. 8	9. 7	A9	H4	Tapir
6. 8	10. 7	A9	J5	Sheep
7. 8	11. 7	A9	K6	Deer
8. 8	12. 7	A9	A7	Horse
9. 8	13. 7	A9	B8	Stag
10. 8	14. 7	A9	C9	Serpent
11. 8	15. 7	A9	D10	Earthworm
12. 8	16. 7	A9	E11	Crocodile
13. 8	17. 7	A9	F12	Dragon
14. 8	18. 7	A9	G1	Badger
15. 8	19. 7	A9	H2	Hare
16. 8	20. 7	A9	J3	Fox
17. 8	21. 7	A9	K4	Tiger
18. 8	22. 7	A9	A5	Leopard
19. 8	23. 7	A9	B6	Griffon
20. 8	24. 7	A9	C7	Ox
21. 8	25. 7	A9	D8	Bat
22. 8	26. 7	A9	E9	Rat
23. 8	27. 7	A9	F10	Swallow
24. 8	28. 7	A9	G11	Pig
25. 8	29. 7	A9	H12	Porcupine
26. 8	30. 7	A9	J1	Wolf
27. 8	1. 8	B10	K2	Dog
28. 8	2. 8	B10	A3	Pheasant
29. 8	3. 8	B10	B4	Cock
30. 8	4. 8	B10	C5	Crow
31. 8	5. 8	B10	D6	Monkey
1. 9	6. 8	B10	E7	Gibbon
2. 9	7. 8	B10	F8	Tapir
3. 9	8. 8	B10	G9	Sheep
4. 9	9. 8	B10	H10	Deer
5. 9	10. 8	B10	J11	Horse
6. 9	11. 8	B10	K12	Stag
7. 9	12. 8	B10	A1	Serpent
8. 9	13. 8	B10	B2	Earthworm
9. 9	14. 8	B10	C3	Crocodile
10. 9	15. 8	B10	D4	Dragon
11. 9	16. 8	B10	E5	Badger
12. 9	17. 8	B10	F6	Hare
13. 9	18. 8	B10	G7	Fox
14. 9	19. 8	B10	H8	Tiger
15. 9	20. 8	B10	J9	Leopard
16. 9	21. 8	B10	K10	Griffon
17. 9	22. 8	B10	A11	Ox
18. 9	23. 8	B10	B12	Bat
19. 9	24. 8	B10	C1	Rat
20. 9	25. 8	B10	D2	Swallow
21. 9	26. 8	B10	E3	Pig
22. 9	27. 8	B10	F4	Porcupine
23. 9	28. 8	B10	G5	Wolf
24. 9	29. 8	B10	H6	Dog
25. 9	1. 9	C11	J7	Pheasant
26. 9	2. 9	C11	K8	Cock
27. 9	3. 9	C11	A9	Crow
28. 9	4. 9	C11	B10	Monkey
29. 9	5. 9	C11	C11	Gibbon
30. 9	6. 9	C11	D12	Tapir
1. 10	7. 9	C11	E1	Sheep
2. 10	8. 9	C11	F2	Deer
3. 10	9. 9	C11	G3	Horse
4. 10	10. 9	C11	H4	Stag
5. 10	11. 9	C11	J5	Serpent
6. 10	12. 9	C11	K6	Earthworm
7. 10	13. 9	C11	A7	Crocodile
8. 10	14. 9	C11	B8	Dragon
9. 10	15. 9	C11	C9	Badger
10. 10	16. 9	C11	D10	Hare
11. 10	17. 9	C11	E11	Fox
12. 10	18. 9	C11	F12	Tiger
13. 10	19. 9	C11	G1	Leopard

Solar date	Lunar date	Month HS/EB	Day HS/EB	Constellation
14.10	20. 9	C11	H2	Griffon
15.10	21. 9	C11	J3	Ox
16. 0	22. 9	C11	K4	Bat
17. 0	23. 9	C11	A5	Rat
18.10	24. 9	C11	B6	Swallow
19.10	25. 9	C11	C7	Pig
20.10	26. 9	C11	D8	Porcupine
21.10	27. 9	C11	E9	Wolf
22.10	28. 9	C11	F10	Dog
23.10	29. 9	C11	G11	Pheasant
24.10	1.10	D12	H12	Cock
25.10	2.10	D12	J1	Crow
26.10	3.10	D12	K2	Monkey
27.10	4.10	D12	A3	Gibbon
28.10	5.10	D12	B4	Tapir
29.10	6.10	D12	C5	Sheep
30.10	7.10	D12	D6	Deer
31.10	8.10	D12	E7	Horse
1.11	9.10	D12	F8	Stag
2.11	10.10	D12	G9	Serpent
3.11	11.10	D12	H10	Earthworm
4.11	12.10	D12	J11	Crocodile
5.11	13.10	D12	K12	Dragon
6.11	14.10	D12	A1	Badger
7.11	15.10	D12	B2	Hare
8.11	16.10	D12	C3	Fox
9.11	17.10	D12	D4	Tiger
10.11	18.10	D12	E5	Leopard
11.11	19.10	D12	F6	Griffon
12.11	20.10	D12	G7	Ox
13.11	21.10	D12	H8	Bat
14.11	22.10	D12	J9	Rat
15.11	23.10	D12	K10	Swallow
16.11	24.10	D12	A11	Pig
17.11	25.10	D12	B12	Porcupine
18.11	26.10	D12	C1	Wolf
19.11	27.10	D12	D2	Dog
20.11	28.10	D12	E3	Pheasant
21.11	29.10	D12	F4	Cock
22.11	30.10	D12	G5	Crow
23.11	1.11	E1	H6	Monkey
24.11	2.11	E1	J7	Gibbon
25.11	3.11	E1	K8	Tapir
26.11	4.11	E1	A9	Sheep
27.11	5.11	E1	B10	Deer
28.11	6.11	E1	C11	Horse
29.11	7.11	E1	D12	Stag
30.11	8.11	E1	E1	Serpent
1.12	9.11	E1	F2	Earthworm
2.12	10.11	E1	G3	Crocodile
3.12	11.11	E1	H4	Dragon
4.12	12.11	E1	J5	Badger
5.12	13.11	E1	K6	Hare
6.12	14.11	E1	A7	Fox
7.12	15.11	E1	B8	Tiger
8.12	16.11	E1	C9	Leopard
9.12	17.11	E1	D10	Griffon
10.12	18.11	E1	E11	Ox
11.12	19.11	E1	F12	Bat
12.12	20.11	E1	G1	Rat
13.12	21.11	E1	H2	Swallow
14.12	22.11	E1	J3	Pig
15.11	23.11	E1	K4	Porcupine
16.12	24.11	E1	A5	Wolf
17.12	25.11	E1	B6	Dog
18.11	26.11	E1	C7	Pheasant
19.12	27.11	E1	D8	Cock
20.12	28.11	E1	E9	Crow
21.12	29.11	E1	F10	Monkey
22.12	30.11	E1	G11	Gibbon
23.11	1.12	F2	H12	Tapir
24.12	2.12	F2	J1	Sheep
25.12	3.12	F2	K2	Deer
26.12	4.12	F2	A3	Horse
27.12	5.12	F2	B4	Stag
28.12	6.12	F2	C5	Serpent
29.12	7.12	F2	D6	Earthworm
30.12	8.12	F2	E7	Crocodile
31.12	9.12	F2	F8	Dragon

1966

Solar date	Lunar date	Month HS/EB	Day HS/EB	Constellation
1. 1	10.12	F2	G9	Badger
2. 1	11.12	F2	H10	Hare
3. 1	12.12	F2	J11	Fox
4. 1	13.12	F2	K12	Tiger
5. 1	14.12	F2	A1	Leopard
6. 1	15.12	F2	B2	Griffon
7. 1	16.12	F2	C3	Ox
8. 1	17.12	F2	D4	Bat
9. 1	18.12	F2	E5	Rat
10. 1	19.12	F2	F6	Swallow
11. 1	20.12	F2	G7	Pig
12. 1	21.12	F2	H8	Porcupine
13. 1	22.12	F2	J9	Wolf
14. 1	23.12	F2	K10	Dog
15. 1	24.12	F2	A11	Pheasant
16. 1	25.12	F2	B12	Cock
17. 1	26.12	F2	C1	Crow
18. 1	27.12	F2	D2	Monkey
19. 1	28.12	F2	E3	Gibbon
20. 1	29.12	F2	F4	Tapir

PING WU YEAR

Solar date	Lunar date	Month HS/EB	Day HS/EB	Constellation
21. 1	1. 1	G3	G5	Sheep
22. 1	2. 1	G3	H6	Deer
23. 1	3. 1	G3	J7	Horse
24. 1	4. 1	G3	K8	Stag
25. 1	5. 1	G3	A9	Serpent
26. 1	6. 1	G3	B10	Earthworm
27. 1	7. 1	G3	C11	Crocodile
28. 1	8. 1	G3	D12	Dragon
29. 1	9. 1	G3	E1	Badger
30. 1	10. 1	G3	F2	Hare
31. 1	11. 1	G3	G3	Fox
1. 2	12. 1	G3	H4	Tiger
2. 2	13. 1	G3	J5	Leopard
3. 2	14. 1	G3	K6	Griffon
4. 2	15. 1	G3	A7	Ox
5. 2	16. 1	G3	B8	Bat
6. 2	17. 1	G3	C9	Rat
7. 2	18. 1	G3	D10	Swallow
8. 2	19. 1	G3	E11	Pig
9. 2	20. 1	G3	F12	Porcupine
10. 2	21. 1	G3	G1	Wolf
11. 2	22. 1	G3	H2	Dog
12. 2	23. 1	G3	J3	Pheasant
13. 2	24. 1	G3	K4	Cock
14. 2	25. 1	G3	A5	Crow
15. 2	26. 1	G3	B6	Monkey
16. 2	27. 1	G3	C7	Gibbon
17. 2	28. 1	G3	D8	Tapir
18. 2	29. 1	G3	E9	Sheep
19. 2	30. 1	G3	F10	Deer
20. 2	1. 2	H4	G11	Horse
21. 2	2. 2	H4	H12	Stag
22. 2	3. 2	H4	J1	Serpent
23. 2	4. 2	H4	K2	Earthworm

Solar date	Lunar date	Month HS/EB	Day HS/EB	Constellation
24. 2	5. 2	H4	A3	Crocodile
25. 2	6. 2	H4	B4	Dragon
26. 2	7. 2	H4	C5	Badger
27. 2	8. 2	H4	D6	Hare
28. 2	9. 2	H4	E7	Fox
1. 3	10. 2	H4	F8	Tiger
2. 3	11. 2	H4	G9	Leopard
3. 3	12. 2	H4	H10	Griffon
4. 3	13. 2	H4	J11	Ox
5. 3	14. 2	H4	K12	Bat
6. 3	15. 2	H4	A1	Rat
7. 3	16. 2	H4	B2	Swallow
8. 3	17. 2	H4	C3	Pig
9. 3	18. 2	H4	D4	Porcupine
10. 3	19. 2	H4	E5	Wolf
11. 3	20. 2	H4	F6	Dog
12. 3	21. 2	H4	G7	Pheasant
13. 3	22. 2	H4	H8	Cock
14. 3	23. 2	H4	J9	Crow
15. 3	24. 2	H4	K10	Monkey
16. 3	25. 2	H4	A11	Gibbon
17. 3	26. 2	H4	B12	Tapir
18. 3	27. 2	H4	C1	Sheep
19. 3	28. 2	H4	D2	Deer
20. 3	29. 2	H4	E3	Horse
21. 3	30. 2	H4	F4	Stag
22. 3	1. 3	J5	G5	Serpent
23. 3	2. 3	J5	H6	Earthworm
24. 3	3. 3	J5	J7	Crocodile
25. 3	4. 3	J5	K8	Dragon
26. 3	5. 3	J5	A9	Badger
27. 3	6. 3	J5	B10	Hare
28. 3	7. 3	J5	C11	Fox
29. 3	8. 3	J5	D12	Tiger
30. 3	9. 3	J5	E1	Leopard
31. 3	10. 3	J5	F2	Griffon
1. 4	11. 3	J5	G3	Ox
2. 4	12. 3	J5	H4	Bat
3. 4	13. 3	J5	J5	Rat
4. 4	14. 3	J5	K6	Swallow
5. 4	15. 3	J5	A7	Pig
6. 4	16. 3	J5	B8	Porcupine
7. 4	17. 3	J5	C9	Wolf
8. 4	18. 3	J5	D10	Dog
9. 4	19. 3	J5	E11	Pheasant
10. 4	20. 3	J5	F12	Cock
11. 4	21. 3	J5	G1	Crow
12. 4	22. 3	J5	H2	Monkey
13. 4	23. 3	J5	J3	Gibbon
14. 4	24. 3	J5	K4	Tapir
15. 4	25. 3	J5	A5	Sheep
16. 4	26. 3	J5	B6	Deer
17. 4	27. 3	J5	C7	Horse
18. 4	28. 3	J5	D8	Stag
19. 4	29. 3	J5	E9	Serpent
20. 4	30. 3	J5	F10	Earthworm
21. 4	*1. 3*	*J5*	G11	Crocodile
22. 4	*2. 3*	*J5*	H12	Dragon
23. 4	*3. 3*	*J5*	J1	Badger
24. 4	*4. 3*	*J5*	K2	Hare
25. 4	*5. 3*	*J5*	A3	Fox
26. 4	*6. 3*	*J5*	B4	Tiger
27. 4	*7. 3*	*J5*	C5	Leopard
28. 4	*8. 3*	*J5*	D6	Griffon
29. 4	*9. 3*	*J5*	E7	Ox
30. 4	*10. 3*	*J5*	F8	Bat
1. 5	*11. 3*	*J5*	G9	Rat
2. 5	*12. 3*	*J5*	H10	Swallow
3. 5	*13. 3*	*J5*	J11	Pig
4. 5	*14. 3*	*J5*	K12	Porcupine
5. 5	*15. 3*	*J5*	A1	Wolf
6. 5	*16. 3*	*J5*	B2	Dog
7. 5	*17. 3*	*J5*	C3	Pheasant
8. 5	*18. 3*	*J5*	D4	Cock
9. 5	*19. 3*	*J5*	E5	Crow
10. 5	*20. 3*	*J5*	F6	Monkey
11. 5	*21. 3*	*J5*	G7	Gibbon
12. 5	*22. 3*	*J5*	H8	Tapir
13. 5	*23. 3*	*J5*	J9	Sheep
14. 5	*24. 3*	*J5*	K10	Deer
15. 5	*25. 3*	*J5*	A11	Horse
16. 5	*26. 3*	*J5*	B12	Stag
17. 5	*27. 3*	*J5*	C1	Serpent
18. 5	*28. 3*	*J5*	D2	Earthworm
19. 5	*29. 3*	*J5*	E3	Crocodile
20. 5	1. 4	K6	F4	Dragon
21. 5	2. 4	K6	G5	Badger
22. 5	3. 4	K6	H6	Hare
23. 5	4. 4	K6	J7	Fox
24. 5	5. 4	K6	K8	Tiger
25. 5	6. 4	K6	A9	Leopard
26. 5	7. 4	K6	B10	Griffon
27. 5	8. 4	K6	C11	Ox
28. 5	9. 4	K6	D12	Bat
29. 5	10. 4	K6	E1	Rat
30. 5	11. 4	K6	F2	Swallow
31. 5	12. 4	K6	G3	Pig
1. 6	13. 4	K6	H4	Porcupine
2. 6	14. 4	K6	J5	Wolf
3. 6	15. 4	K6	K6	Dog
4. 6	16. 4	K6	A7	Pheasant
5. 6	17. 4	K6	B8	Cock
6. 6	18. 4	K6	C9	Crow
7. 6	19. 4	K6	D10	Monkey
8. 6	20. 4	K6	E11	Gibbon
9. 6	21. 4	K6	F12	Tapir
10. 6	22. 4	K6	G1	Sheep
11. 6	23. 4	K6	H2	Deer
12. 6	24. 4	K6	J3	Horse
13. 6	25. 4	K6	K4	Stag
14. 6	26. 4	K6	A5	Serpent
15. 6	27. 4	K6	B6	Earthworm
16. 6	28. 4	K6	C7	Crocodile
17. 6	29. 4	K6	D8	Dragon
18. 6	30. 4	K6	E9	Badger
19. 6	1. 5	A7	F10	Hare
20. 6	2. 5	A7	G11	Fox
21. 6	3. 5	A7	H12	Tiger
22. 6	4. 5	A7	J1	Leopard
23. 6	5. 5	A7	K2	Griffon
24. 6	6. 5	A7	A3	Ox
25. 6	7. 5	A7	B4	Bat
26. 6	8. 5	A7	C5	Rat
27. 6	9. 5	A7	D6	Swallow
28. 6	10. 5	A7	E7	Pig
29. 6	11. 5	A7	F8	Porcupine
30. 6	12. 5	A7	G9	Wolf
1. 7	13. 5	A7	H10	Dog
2. 7	14. 5	A7	J11	Pheasant
3. 7	15. 5	A7	K12	Cock
4. 7	16. 5	A7	A1	Crow
5. 7	17. 5	A7	B2	Monkey
6. 7	18. 5	A7	C3	Gibbon
7. 7	19. 5	A7	D4	Tapir
8. 7	20. 5	A7	E5	Sheep
9. 7	21. 5	A7	F6	Deer
10. 7	22. 5	A7	G7	Horse
11. 7	23. 5	A7	H8	Stag
12. 7	24. 5	A7	J9	Serpent
13. 7	25. 5	A7	K10	Earthworm
14. 7	26. 5	A7	A11	Crocodile
15. 7	27. 5	A7	B12	Dragon
16. 7	28. 5	A7	C1	Badger
17. 7	29. 5	A7	D2	Hare
18. 7	1. 6	B8	E3	Fox
19. 7	2. 6	B8	F4	Tiger

Solar date	Lunar date	Month HS/EB	Day HS/EB	Constellation	Solar date	Lunar date	Month HS/EB	Day HS/EB	Constellation
20. 7	3. 6	B8	G5	Leopard	1.10	17. 8	D10	K6	Deer
21. 7	4. 6	B8	H6	Griffon	2.10	18. 8	D10	A7	Horse
22. 7	5. 6	B8	J7	Ox	3.10	19. 8	D10	B8	Stag
23. 7	6. 6	B8	K8	Bat	4.10	20. 8	D10	C9	Serpent
24. 7	7. 6	B8	A9	Rat	5.10	21. 8	D10	D10	Earthworm
25. 7	8. 6	B8	B10	Swallow	6.10	22. 8	D10	E11	Crocodile
26. 7	9. 6	B8	C11	Pig	7.10	23. 8	D10	F12	Dragon
27. 7	10. 6	B8	D12	Porcupine	8.10	24. 8	D10	G1	Badger
28. 7	11. 6	B8	E1	Wolf	9.10	25. 8	D10	H2	Hare
29. 7	12. 6	B8	F2	Dog	10.10	26. 8	D10	J3	Fox
30. 7	13. 6	B8	G3	Pheasant	11.10	27. 8	D10	K4	Tiger
31. 7	14. 6	B8	H4	Cock	12.10	28. 8	D10	A5	Leopard
1. 8	15. 6	B8	J5	Crow	13.10	29. 8	D10	B6	Griffon
2. 8	16. 6	B8	K6	Monkey	14.10	1. 9	E11	C7	Ox
3. 8	17. 6	B8	A7	Gibbon	15.10	2. 9	E11	D8	Bat
4. 8	18. 6	B8	B8	Tapir	16.10	3. 9	E11	E9	Rat
5. 8	19. 6	B8	C9	Sheep	17.10	4. 9	E11	F10	Swallow
6. 8	20. 6	B8	D10	Deer	18.10	5. 9	E11	G11	Pig
7. 8	21. 6	B8	E11	Horse	19.10	6. 9	E11	H12	Porcupine
8. 8	22. 6	B8	F12	Stag	20.10	7. 9	E11	J1	Wolf
9. 8	23. 6	B8	G1	Serpent	21.10	8. 9	E11	K2	Dog
10. 8	24. 6	B8	H2	Earthworm	22.10	9. 9	E11	A3	Pheasant
11. 8	25. 6	B8	J3	Crocodile	23.10	10. 9	E11	B4	Cock
12. 8	26. 6	B8	K4	Dragon	24.10	11. 9	E11	C5	Crow
13. 8	27. 6	B8	A5	Badger	25.10	12. 9	E11	D6	Monkey
14. 8	28. 6	B8	B6	Hare	26.10	13. 9	E11	E7	Gibbon
15. 8	29. 6	B8	C7	Fox	27.10	14. 9	E11	F8	Tapir
16. 8	1. 7	C9	D8	Tiger	28.10	15. 9	E11	G9	Sheep
17. 8	2. 7	C9	E9	Leopard	29.10	16. 9	E11	H10	Deer
18. 8	3. 7	C9	F10	Griffon	30.10	17. 9	E11	J11	Horse
19. 8	4. 7	C9	G11	Ox	31.10	18. 9	E11	K12	Stag
20. 8	5. 7	C9	H12	Bat	1.11	19. 9	E11	A1	Serpent
21. 8	6. 7	C9	J1	Rat	2.11	20. 9	E11	B2	Earthworm
22. 8	7. 7	C9	K2	Swallow	3.11	21. 9	E11	C3	Crocodile
23. 8	8. 7	C9	A3	Pig	4.11	22. 9	E11	D4	Dragon
24. 8	9. 7	C9	B4	Porcupine	5.11	23. 9	E11	E5	Badger
25. 8	10. 7	C9	C5	Wolf	6.11	24. 9	E11	F6	Hare
26. 8	11. 7	C9	D6	Dog	7.11	25. 9	E11	G7	Fox
27. 8	12. 7	C9	E7	Pheasant	8.11	26. 9	E11	H8	Tiger
28. 8	13. 7	C9	F8	Cock	9.11	27. 9	E11	J9	Leopard
29. 8	14. 7	C9	G9	Crow	10.11	28. 9	E11	K10	Griffon
30. 8	15. 7	C9	H10	Monkey	11.11	29. 9	E11	A11	Ox
31. 8	16. 7	C9	J11	Gibbon	12.11	1.10	F12	B12	Bat
1. 9	17. 7	C9	K12	Tapir	13.11	2.10	F12	C1	Rat
2. 9	18. 7	C9	A1	Sheep	14.11	3.10	F12	D2	Swallow
3. 9	19. 7	C9	B2	Deer	15.11	4.10	F12	E3	Pig
4. 9	20. 7	C9	C3	Horse	16.11	5.10	F12	F4	Porcupine
5. 9	21. 7	C9	D4	Stag	17.11	6.10	F12	G5	Wolf
6. 9	22. 7	C9	E5	Serpent	18.11	7.10	F12	H6	Dog
7. 9	23. 7	C9	F6	Earthworm	19.11	8.10	F12	J7	Pheasant
8. 9	24. 7	C9	G7	Crocodile	20.11	9.10	F12	K8	Cock
9. 9	25. 7	C9	H8	Dragon	21.11	10.10	F12	A9	Crow
10. 9	26. 7	C9	J9	Badger	22.11	11.10	F12	B10	Monkey
11. 9	27. 7	C9	K10	Hare	23.11	12.10	F12	C11	Gibbon
12. 9	28. 7	C9	A11	Fox	24.11	13.10	F12	D12	Tapir
13. 9	29. 7	C9	B12	Tiger	25.11	14.10	F12	E1	Sheep
14. 9	30. 7	C9	C1	Leopard	26.11	15.10	F12	F2	Deer
15. 9	1. 8	D10	D2	Griffon	27.11	16.10	F12	G3	Horse
16. 9	2. 8	D10	E3	Ox	28.11	17.10	F12	H4	Stag
17. 9	3. 8	D10	F4	Rat	29.11	18.10	F12	J5	Serpent
18. 9	4. 8	D10	G5	Rat	30.11	19.10	F12	K6	Earthworm
19. 9	5. 8	D10	H6	Swallow	1.12	20.10	F12	A7	Crocodile
20. 9	6. 8	D10	J7	Pig	2.12	21.10	F12	B8	Dragon
21. 9	7. 8	D10	K8	Porcupine	3.12	22.10	F12	C9	Badger
22. 9	8. 8	D10	A9	Wolf	4.12	23.10	F12	D10	Hare
23. 9	9. 8	D10	B10	Dog	5.12	24.10	F12	E11	Fox
24. 9	10. 8	D10	C11	Pheasant	6.12	25.10	F12	F12	Tiger
25. 9	11. 8	D10	D12	Cock	7.12	26.10	F12	G1	Leopard
26. 9	12. 8	D10	E1	Crow	8.12	27.10	F12	H2	Griffon
27. 9	13. 8	D10	F2	Monkey	9.12	28.10	F12	J3	Ox
28. 9	14. 8	D10	G3	Gibbon	10.12	29.10	F12	K4	Bat
29. 9	15. 8	D10	H4	Tapir	11.12	30.10	F12	A5	Rat
30. 9	16. 8	D10	J5	Sheep	12.12	1.11	G1	B6	Swallow

Solar date	Lunar date	Month HS/EB	Day HS/EB	Constellation	Solar date	Lunar date	Month HS/EB	Day HS/EB	Constellation
13.12	2.11	G1	C7	Pig	10. 1	30.11	G1	A11	Pig
14.12	3.11	G1	D8	Porcupine	11. 1	1.12	H2	B12	Porcupine
15.12	4.11	G1	E9	Wolf	12. 1	2.12	H2	C1	Wolf
16.12	5.11	G1	F10	Dog	13. 1	3.12	H2	D2	Dog
17.12	6.11	G1	G11	Pheasant	14. 1	4.12	H2	E3	Pheasant
18.12	7.11	G1	H12	Cock	15. 1	5.12	H2	F4	Cock
19.12	8.11	G1	J1	Crow	16. 1	6.12	H2	G5	Crow
20.12	9.11	G1	K2	Monkey	17. 1	7.12	H2	H6	Monkey
21.12	10.11	G1	A3	Gibbon	18. 1	8.12	H2	J7	Gibbon
22.12	11.11	G1	B4	Tapir	19. 1	9.12	H2	K8	Tapir
23.12	12.11	G1	C5	Sheep	20. 1	10.12	H2	A9	Sheep
24.12	13.11	G1	D6	Deer	21. 1	11.12	H2	B10	Deer
25.12	14.11	G1	E7	Horse	22. 1	12.12	H2	C11	Horse
26.12	15.11	G1	F8	Stag	23. 1	13.12	H2	D12	Stag
27.12	16.11	G1	G9	Serpent	24. 1	14.12	H2	E1	Serpent
28.12	17.11	G1	H10	Earthworm	25. 1	15.12	H2	F2	Earthworm
29.12	18.11	G1	J11	Crocodile	26. 1	16.12	H2	G3	Crocodile
30.12	19.11	G1	K12	Dragon	27. 1	17.12	H2	H4	Dragon
31.12	20.11	G1	A1	Badger	28. 1	18.12	H2	J5	Badger
1967					29. 1	19.12	H2	K6	Hare
1. 1	21.11	G1	B2	Hare	30. 1	20.12	H2	A7	Fox
2. 1	22.11	G1	C3	Fox	31. 1	21.12	H2	B8	Tiger
3. 1	23.11	G1	D4	Tiger	1. 2	22.12	H2	C9	Leopard
4. 1	24.11	G1	E5	Leopard	2. 2	23.12	H2	D10	Griffon
5. 1	25.11	G1	F6	Griffon	3. 2	24.12	H2	E11	Ox
6. 1	26.11	G1	G7	Ox	4. 2	25.12	H2	F12	Bat
7. 1	27.11	G1	H8	Bat	5. 2	26.12	H2	G1	Rat
8. 1	28.11	G1	J9	Rat	6. 2	27.12	H2	H2	Swallow
9. 1	29.11	G1	K10	Swallow	7. 2	28.12	H2	J3	Pig
					8. 2	29.12	H2	K4	Porcupine

TING WEI YEAR

Solar date	Lunar date	Month HS/EB	Day HS/EB	Constellation	Solar date	Lunar date	Month HS/EB	Day HS/EB	Constellation
9. 2	1. 1	J3	A5	Wolf	19. 3	9. 2	K4	J7	Horse
10. 2	2. 1	J3	B6	Dog	20. 3	10. 2	K4	K8	Stag
11. 2	3. 1	J3	C7	Pheasant	21. 3	11. 2	K4	A9	Serpent
12. 2	4. 1	J3	D8	Cock	22. 3	12. 2	K4	B10	Earthworm
13. 2	5. 1	J3	E9	Crow	23. 3	13. 2	K4	C11	Crocodile
14. 2	6. 1	J3	F10	Monkey	24. 3	14. 2	K4	D12	Dragon
15. 2	7. 1	J3	G11	Gibbon	25. 3	15. 2	K4	E1	Badger
16. 2	8. 1	J3	H12	Tapir	26. 3	16. 2	K4	F2	Hare
17. 2	9. 1	J3	J1	Sheep	27. 3	17. 2	K4	G3	Fox
18. 2	10. 1	J3	K2	Deer	28. 3	18. 2	K4	H4	Tiger
19. 2	11. 1	J3	A3	Horse	29. 3	19. 2	K4	J5	Leopard
20. 2	12. 1	J3	B4	Stag	30. 3	20. 2	K4	K6	Griffon
21. 2	13. 1	J3	C5	Serpent	31. 3	21. 2	K4	A7	Ox
22. 2	14. 1	J3	D6	Earthworm	1. 4	22. 2	K4	B8	Bat
23. 2	15. 1	J3	E7	Crocodile	2. 4	23. 2	K4	C9	Rat
24. 2	16. 1	J3	F8	Dragon	3. 4	24. 2	K4	D10	Swallow
25. 2	17. 1	J3	G9	Badger	4. 4	25. 2	K4	E11	Pig
26. 2	18. 1	J3	H10	Hare	5. 4	26. 2	K4	F12	Porcupine
27. 2	19. 1	J3	J11	Fox	6. 4	27. 2	K4	G1	Wolf
28. 2	20. 1	J3	K12	Tiger	7. 4	28. 2	K4	H2	Dog
1. 3	21. 1	J3	A1	Leopard	8. 4	29. 2	K4	J3	Pheasant
2. 3	22. 1	J3	B2	Griffon	9. 4	30. 2	K4	K4	Cock
3. 3	23. 1	J3	C3	Ox	10. 4	1. 3	A5	A5	Crow
4. 3	24. 1	J3	D4	Bat	11. 4	2. 3	A5	B6	Monkey
5. 3	25. 1	J3	E5	Rat	12. 4	3. 3	A5	C7	Gibbon
6. 3	26. 1	J3	F6	Swallow	13. 4	4. 3	A5	D8	Tapir
7. 3	27. 1	J3	G7	Pig	14. 4	5. 3	A5	E9	Sheep
8. 3	28. 1	J3	H8	Porcupine	15. 4	6. 3	A5	F10	Deer
9. 3	29. 1	J3	J9	Wolf	16. 4	7. 3	A5	G11	Horse
10. 3	30. 1	J3	K10	Dog	17. 4	8. 3	A5	H12	Stag
11. 3	1. 2	K4	A11	Pheasant	18. 4	9. 3	A5	J1	Serpent
12. 3	2. 2	K4	B12	Cock	19. 4	10. 3	A5	K2	Earthworm
13. 3	3. 2	K4	C1	Crow	20. 4	11. 3	A5	A3	Crocodile
14. 3	4. 2	K4	D2	Monkey	21. 4	12. 3	A5	B4	Dragon
15. 3	5. 2	K4	E3	Gibbon	22. 4	13. 3	A5	C5	Badger
16. 3	6. 2	K4	F4	Tapir	23. 4	14. 3	A5	D6	Hare
17. 3	7. 2	K4	G5	Sheep	24. 4	15. 3	A5	E7	Fox
18. 3	8. 2	K4	H6	Deer	25. 4	16. 3	A5	F8	Tiger

Solar date	Lunar date	Month HS/EB	Day HS/EB	Constellation
26. 4	17. 3	A5	G9	Leopard
27. 4	18. 3	A5	H10	Griffon
28. 4	19. 3	A5	J11	Ox
29. 4	20. 3	A5	K12	Bat
30. 4	21. 3	A5	A1	Rat
1. 5	22. 3	A5	B2	Swallow
2. 5	23. 3	A5	C3	Pig
3. 5	24. 3	A5	D4	Porcupine
4. 5	25. 3	A5	E5	Wolf
5. 5	26. 3	A5	F6	Dog
6. 5	27. 3	A5	G7	Pheasant
7. 5	28. 3	A5	H8	Cock
8. 5	29. 3	A5	J9	Crow
9. 5	1. 4	B6	K10	Monkey
10. 5	2. 4	B6	A11	Gibbon
11. 5	3. 4	B6	B12	Tapir
12. 5	4. 4	B6	C1	Sheep
13. 5	5. 4	B6	D2	Deer
14. 5	6. 4	B6	E3	Horse
15. 5	7. 4	B6	F4	Stag
16. 5	8. 4	B6	G5	Serpent
17. 5	9. 4	B6	H6	Earthworm
18. 5	10. 4	B6	J7	Crocodile
19. 5	11. 4	B6	K8	Dragon
20. 5	12. 4	B6	A9	Badger
21. 5	13. 4	B6	B10	Hare
22. 5	14. 4	B6	C11	Fox
23. 5	15. 4	B6	D12	Tiger
24. 5	16. 4	B6	F1	Leopard
25. 5	17. 4	B6	F2	Griffon
26. 5	18. 4	B6	G3	Ox
27. 5	19. 4	B6	H4	Bat
28. 5	20. 4	B6	J5	Rat
29. 5	21. 4	B6	K6	Swallow
30. 5	22. 4	B6	A7	Pig
31. 5	23. 4	B6	B8	Porcupine
1. 6	24. 4	B6	C9	Wolf
2. 6	25. 4	B6	D10	Dog
3. 6	26. 4	B6	E11	Pheasant
4. 6	27. 4	B6	F12	Cock
5. 6	28. 4	B6	G1	Crow
6. 6	29. 4	B6	H2	Monkey
7. 6	30. 4	B6	J3	Gibbon
8. 6	1. 5	C7	K4	Tapir
9. 6	2. 5	C7	A5	Sheep
10. 6	3. 5	C7	B6	Deer
11. 6	4. 5	C7	C7	Horse
12. 6	5. 5	C7	D8	Stag
13. 6	6. 5	C7	E9	Serpent
14. 6	7. 5	C7	F10	Earthworm
15. 6	8. 5	C7	G11	Crocodile
16. 6	9. 5	C7	H12	Dragon
17. 6	10. 5	C7	J1	Badger
18. 6	11. 5	C7	K2	Hare
19. 6	12. 5	C7	A3	Fox
20. 6	13. 5	C7	B4	Tiger
21. 6	14. 5	C7	C5	Leopard
22. 6	15. 5	C7	D6	Griffon
12. 6	16. 5	C7	E7	Ox
24. 6	17. 5	C7	F8	Bat
25. 6	18. 5	C7	G9	Rat
26. 6	19. 5	C7	H10	Swallow
27. 6	20. 5	C7	J11	Pig
28. 6	21. 5	C7	K12	Porcupine
29. 6	22. 5	C7	A1	Wolf
30. 6	23. 5	C7	B2	Dog
1. 7	24. 5	C7	C3	Pheasant
2. 7	25. 5	C7	D4	Cock
3. 7	26. 5	C7	E5	Crow
4. 7	27. 5	C7	F6	Monkey
5. 7	28. 5	C7	G7	Gibbon
6. 7	29. 5	C7	H8	Tapir
7. 7	30. 5	C7	J9	Sheep
8. 7	1. 6	D8	K10	Deer
9. 7	2. 6	D8	A11	Horse
10. 7	3. 6	D8	B12	Stag
11. 7	4. 6	D8	C1	Serpent
12. 7	5. 6	D8	D2	Earthworm
13. 7	6. 6	D8	E3	Crocodile
14. 7	7. 6	D8	F4	Dragon
15. 7	8. 6	D8	G5	Badger
16. 7	9. 6	D8	H6	Hare
17. 7	10. 6	D8	J7	Fox
18. 7	11. 6	D8	K8	Tiger
19. 7	12. 6	D8	A9	Leopard
20. 7	13. 6	D8	B10	Griffon
21. 7	14. 6	D8	C11	Ox
22. 7	15. 6	D8	D12	Bat
23. 7	16. 6	D8	E1	Rat
24. 7	17. 6	D8	F2	Swallow
25. 7	18. 6	D8	G3	Pig
26. 7	19. 6	D8	H4	Porcupine
27. 7	20. 6	D8	J5	Wolf
28. 7	21. 6	D8	K6	Dog
29. 7	22. 6	D8	A7	Pheasant
30. 7	23. 6	D8	B8	Cock
31. 7	24. 6	D8	C9	Crow
1. 8	25. 6	D8	D10	Monkey
2. 8	26. 6	D8	E11	Gibbon
3. 8	27. 6	D8	F12	Tapir
4. 8	28. 6	D8	G1	Sheep
5. 8	29. 6	D8	H2	Deer
6. 8	1. 7	E9	J3	Horse
7. 8	2. 7	E9	K4	Stag
8. 8	3. 7	E9	A5	Serpent
9. 8	4. 7	E9	B6	Earthworm
10. 8	5. 7	E9	C7	Crocodile
11. 8	6. 7	E9	D8	Dragon
12. 8	7. 7	E9	E9	Badger
13. 8	8. 7	E9	F10	Hare
14. 8	9. 7	E9	G11	Fox
15. 8	10. 7	E9	H12	Tiger
16. 8	11. 7	E9	J1	Leopard
17. 8	12. 7	E9	K2	Griffon
18. 8	13. 7	E9	A3	Ox
19. 8	14. 7	E9	B4	Bat
20. 8	15. 7	E9	C5	Rat
21. 8	16. 7	E9	D6	Swallow
22. 8	17. 7	E9	E7	Pig
23. 8	18. 7	E9	F8	Porcupine
24. 8	19. 7	E9	G9	Wolf
25. 8	20. 7	E9	H10	Dog
26. 8	21. 7	E9	J11	Pheasant
27. 8	22. 7	E9	K12	Cock
28. 8	23. 7	E9	A1	Crow
29. 8	24. 7	E9	B2	Monkey
30. 8	25. 7	E9	C3	Gibbon
31. 8	26. 7	E9	D4	Tapir
1. 9	27. 7	E9	E5	Sheep
2. 9	28. 7	E9	F6	Deer
3. 9	29. 7	E9	G7	Horse
4. 9	1. 8	F10	H8	Stag
5. 9	2. 8	F10	J9	Serpent
6. 9	3. 8	F10	K10	Earthworm
7. 9	4. 8	F10	A11	Crocodile
8. 9	5. 8	F10	B12	Dragon
9. 9	6. 8	F10	C1	Badger
10. 9	7. 8	F10	D2	Hare
11. 9	8. 8	F10	E3	Fox
12. 9	9. 8	F10	F4	Tiger
13. 9	10. 8	F10	G5	Leopard
14. 9	11. 8	F10	H6	Griffon
15. 9	12. 8	F10	J7	Ox
16. 9	13. 8	F10	K8	Bat
18. 9	15. 8	F10	B10	Swallow
19. 9	16. 8	F10	C11	Pig

Solar date	Lunar date	Month HS/EB	Day HS/EB	Constellation
20. 9	17. 8	F10	D12	Porcupine
21. 9	18. 8	F10	E1	Wolf
22. 9	19. 8	F10	F2	Dog
23. 9	20. 8	F10	G3	Pheasant
24. 9	21. 8	F10	H4	Cock
25. 9	22. 8	F10	J5	Crow
26. 9	23. 8	F10	K6	Monkey
27. 9	24. 8	F10	A7	Gibbon
28. 9	25. 8	F10	B8	Tapir
29. 9	26. 8	F10	C9	Sheep
30. 9	27. 8	F10	D10	Deer
1.10	28. 8	F10	E11	Horse
2.10	29. 8	F10	F12	Stag
3.10	30. 8	F10	G1	Serpent
4.10	1. 9	G11	H2	Earthworm
5.10	2. 9	G11	J3	Crocodile
6.10	3. 9	G11	K4	Dragon
7.10	4. 9	G11	A5	Badger
8.10	5. 9	G11	B6	Hare
9.10	6. 9	G11	C7	Fox
10.10	7. 9	G11	D8	Tiger
11.10	8. 9	G11	E9	Leopard
12.10	9. 9	G11	F10	Griffon
13.10	10. 9	G11	G11	Ox
14.10	11. 9	G11	H12	Bat
15.10	12. 9	G11	J1	Rat
16.10	13. 9	G11	K2	Swallow
17.10	14. 9	G11	A3	Pig
18.10	15. 9	G11	B4	Porcupine
19.10	16. 9	G11	C5	Wolf
20.10	17. 9	G11	D6	Dog
21.10	18. 9	G11	E7	Pheasant
22.10	19. 9	G11	F8	Cock
23.10	20. 9	G11	G9	Crow
24.10	21. 9	G11	H10	Monkey
25.10	22. 9	G11	J11	Gibbon
26.10	23. 9	G11	K12	Tapir
27.10	24. 9	G11	A1	Sheep
28.10	25. 9	G11	B2	Deer
29.10	26. 9	G11	C3	Horse
30.10	27. 9	G11	D4	Stag
31.10	28. 9	G11	E5	Serpent
1.11	29. 9	G11	F6	Earthworm
2.11	1.10	H12	G7	Crocodile
3.11	2.10	H12	H8	Dragon
4.11	3.10	H12	J9	Badger
5.11	4.10	H12	K10	Hare
6.11	5.10	H12	A11	Fox
7.11	6.10	H12	B12	Tiger
8.11	7.10	H12	C1	Leopard
9.11	8.10	H12	D2	Griffon
10.11	9.10	H12	E3	Ox
11.11	10.10	H12	F4	Bat
12.11	11.10	H12	G5	Rat
13.11	12.10	H12	H6	Swallow
14.11	13.10	H12	J7	Pig
15.11	14.10	H12	K8	Porcupine
16.11	15.10	H12	A9	Wolf
17.11	16.10	H12	B10	Dog
18.11	17.10	H12	C11	Pheasant
19.11	18.10	H12	D12	Cock
20.11	19.10	H12	E1	Crow
21.11	20.10	H12	F2	Monkey
22.11	21.10	H12	G3	Gibbon
23.11	22.10	H12	H4	Tapir
24.11	23.10	H12	J5	Sheep
25.11	24.10	H12	K6	Deer

Solar date	Lunar date	Month HS/EB	Day HS/EB	Constellation
26.11	25.10	H12	A7	Horse
27.11	26.10	H12	B8	Stag
28.11	27.10	H12	C9	Serpent
29.11	28.10	H12	D10	Earthworm
30.11	29.10	H12	E11	Crocodile
1.12	30.10	H12	F12	Dragon
2.12	1.11	J1	G1	Badger
3.12	2.11	J1	H2	Hare
4.12	3.11	J1	J3	Fox
5.12	4.11	J1	K4	Tiger
6.12	5.11	J1	A5	Leopard
7.12	6.11	J1	B6	Griffon
8.12	7.11	J1	C7	Ox
9.12	8.11	J1	D8	Bat
10.12	9.11	J1	E9	Rat
11.12	10.11	J1	F10	Swallow
12.12	11.11	J1	G11	Pig
13.12	12.11	J1	H12	Porcupine
14.12	13.11	J1	J1	Wolf
15.12	14.11	J1	K2	Dog
16.12	15.11	J1	A3	Pheasant
17.12	16.11	J1	B4	Cock
18.12	17.11	J1	C5	Crow
19.12	18.11	J1	D6	Monkey
20.12	19.11	J1	E7	Gibbon
21.12	20.11	J1	F8	Tapir
22.12	21.11	J1	G9	Sheep
23.12	22.11	J1	H10	Deer
24.12	23.11	J1	J11	Horse
25.12	24.11	J1	K12	Stag
26.12	25.11	J1	A1	Serpent
27.12	26.11	J1	B2	Earthworm
28.12	27.11	J1	C3	Crocodile
29.12	28.11	J1	D4	Dragon
30.12	29.11	J1	E5	Badger
31.12	1.12	K2	F6	Hare

1968

Solar date	Lunar date	Month HS/EB	Day HS/EB	Constellation
1. 1	2.12	K2	G7	Fox
2. 1	3.12	K2	H8	Tiger
3. 1	4.12	K2	J9	Leopard
4. 1	5.12	K2	K10	Griffon
5. 1	6.12	K2	A11	Ox
6. 1	7.12	K2	B12	Bat
7. 1	8.12	K2	C1	Rat
8. 1	9.12	K2	D2	Swallow
9. 1	10.12	K2	E3	Pig
10. 1	11.12	K2	F4	Porcupine
11. 1	12.12	K2	G5	Wolf
12. 1	13.12	K2	H6	Dog
13. 1	14.12	K2	J7	Pheasant
14. 1	15.12	K2	K8	Cock
15. 1	16.12	K2	A9	Crow
16. 1	17.12	K2	B10	Monkey
17. 1	18.12	K2	C11	Gibbon
18. 1	19.12	K2	D12	Tapir
19. 1	20.12	K2	E1	Sheep
20. 1	21.12	K2	F2	Deer
21. 1	22.12	K2	G3	Horse
22. 1	23.12	K2	H4	Stag
23. 1	24.12	K2	J5	Serpent
24. 1	25.12	K2	K6	Earthworm
25. 1	26.12	K2	A7	Crocodile
26. 1	27.12	K2	B8	Dragon
27. 1	28.12	K2	C9	Badger
28. 1	29.12	K2	D10	Hare
29. 1	30.12	K2	E11	Fox

MOU SHEN YEAR

Solar date	Lunar date	Month HS/EB	Day HS/EB	Constellation	Solar date	Lunar date	Month HS/EB	Day HS/EB	Constellation
30. 1	1. 1	A3	F12	Tiger	10. 4	13. 3	C5	G11	Gibbon
31. 1	2. 1	A3	G1	Leopard	11. 4	14. 3	C5	H12	Tapir
1. 2	3. 1	A3	H2	Griffon	12. 4	15. 3	C5	J1	Sheep
2. 2	4. 1	A3	J3	Ox	13. 4	16. 3	C5	K2	Deer
3. 2	5. 1	A3	K4	Bat	14. 4	17. 3	C5	A3	Horse
4. 2	6. 1	A3	A5	Rat	15. 4	18. 3	C5	B4	Stag
5. 2	7. 1	A3	B6	Swallow	16. 4	19. 3	C5	C5	Serpent
6. 2	8. 1	A3	C7	Pig	17. 4	20. 3	C5	D6	Earthworm
7. 2	9. 1	A3	D8	Porcupine	18. 4	21. 3	C5	E7	Crocodile
8. 2	10. 1	A3	E9	Wolf	19. 4	22. 3	C5	F8	Dragon
9. 2	11. 1	A3	F10	Dog	20. 4	23. 3	C5	G9	Badger
10. 2	12. 1	A3	G11	Pheasant	21. 4	24. 3	C5	H10	Hare
11. 2	13. 1	A3	H12	Cock	22. 4	25. 3	C5	J11	Fox
12. 2	14. 1	A3	J1	Crow	23. 4	26. 3	C5	K12	Tiger
13. 2	15. 1	A3	K2	Monkey	24. 4	27. 3	C5	A1	Leopard
14. 2	16. 1	A3	A3	Gibbon	25. 4	28. 3	C5	B2	Griffon
15. 2	17. 1	A3	B4	Tapir	26. 4	29. 3	C5	C3	Ox
16. 2	18. 1	A3	C5	Sheep	27. 4	1. 4	D6	D4	Bat
17. 2	19. 1	A3	D6	Deer	28. 4	2. 4	D6	E5	Rat
18. 2	20. 1	A3	E7	Horse	29. 4	3. 4	D6	F6	Swallow
19. 2	21. 1	A3	F8	Stag	30. 4	4. 4	D6	G7	Pig
20. 2	22. 1	A3	G9	Serpent	1. 5	5. 4	D6	H8	Porcupine
21. 2	23. 1	A3	H10	Earthworm	2. 5	6. 4	D6	J9	Wolf
22. 2	24. 1	A3	J11	Crocodile	3. 5	7. 4	D6	K10	Dog
23. 2	25. 1	A3	K12	Dragon	4. 5	8. 4	D6	A11	Pheasant
24. 2	26. 1	A3	A1	Badger	5. 5	9. 4	D6	B12	Cock
25. 2	27. 1	A3	B2	Hare	6. 5	10. 4	D6	C1	Crow
26. 2	28. 1	A3	C3	Fox	7. 5	11. 4	D6	D2	Monkey
27. 2	29. 1	A3	D4	Tiger	8. 5	12. 4	D6	E3	Gibbon
28. 2	1. 2	B4	E5	Leopard	9. 5	13. 4	D6	F4	Tapir
29. 2	2. 2	B4	F6	Griffon	10. 5	14. 4	D6	G5	Sheep
1. 3	3. 2	B4	G7	Ox	11. 5	15. 4	D6	H6	Deer
2. 3	4. 2	B4	H8	Bat	12. 5	16. 4	D6	J7	Horse
3. 3	5. 2	B4	J9	Rat	13. 5	17. 4	D6	K8	Stag
4. 3	6. 2	B4	K10	Swallow	14. 5	18. 4	D6	A9	Serpent
5. 3	7. 2	B4	A11	Pig	15. 5	19. 4	D6	B10	Earthworm
6. 3	8. 2	B4	B12	Porcupine	16. 5	20. 4	D6	C11	Crocodile
7. 3	9. 2	B4	C1	Wolf	17. 5	21. 4	D6	D12	Dragon
8. 3	10. 2	B4	D2	Dog	18. 5	22. 4	D6	E1	Badger
9. 3	11. 2	B4	E3	Pheasant	19. 5	23. 4	D6	F2	Hare
10. 3	12. 2	B4	F4	Cock	20. 5	24. 4	D6	G3	Fox
11. 3	13. 2	B4	G5	Crow	21. 5	25. 4	D6	H4	Tiger
12. 3	14. 2	B4	H6	Monkey	22. 5	26. 4	D6	J5	Leopard
13. 3	15. 2	B4	J7	Gibbon	23. 5	27. 4	D6	K6	Griffon
14. 3	16. 2	B4	K8	Tapir	24. 5	28. 4	D6	A7	Ox
15. 3	17. 2	B4	A9	Sheep	25. 5	29. 4	D6	B8	Bat
16. 3	18. 2	B4	B10	Deer	26. 5	30. 4	D6	C9	Rat
17. 3	19. 2	B4	C11	Horse	27. 5	1. 5	E7	D10	Swallow
18. 3	20. 2	B4	D12	Stag	28. 5	2. 5	E7	E11	Pig
19. 3	21. 2	B4	E1	Serpent	29. 5	3. 5	E7	F12	Porcupine
20. 3	22. 2	B4	F2	Earthworm	30. 5	4. 5	E7	G1	Wolf
21. 3	23. 2	B4	G3	Crocodile	31. 5	5. 5	E7	H2	Dog
22. 3	24. 2	B4	H4	Dragon	1. 6	6. 5	E7	J3	Pheasant
23. 3	25. 2	B4	J5	Badger	2. 6	7. 5	E7	K4	Cock
24. 3	26. 2	B4	K6	Hare	3. 6	8. 5	E7	A5	Crow
25. 3	27. 2	B4	A7	Fox	4. 6	9. 5	E7	B6	Monkey
26. 3	28. 2	B4	B8	Tiger	5. 6	10. 5	E7	C7	Gibbon
27. 3	29. 2	B4	C9	Leopard	6. 6	11. 5	E7	D8	Tapir
28. 3	30. 2	B4	D10	Griffon	7. 6	12. 5	E7	E9	Sheep
29. 3	1. 3	C5	E11	Ox	8. 6	13. 5	E7	F10	Deer
30. 3	2. 3	C5	F12	Bat	9. 6	14. 5	E7	G11	Horse
31. 3	3. 3	C5	G1	Rat	10. 6	15. 5	E7	H12	Stag
1. 4	4. 3	C5	H2	Swallow	11. 6	16. 5	E7	J1	Serpent
2. 4	5. 3	C5	J3	Pig	12. 6	17. 5	E7	K2	Earthworm
3. 4	6. 3	C5	K4	Porcupine	13. 6	18. 5	E7	A3	Crocodile
4. 4	7. 3	C5	A5	Wolf	14. 6	19. 5	E7	B4	Dragon
5. 4	8. 3	C5	B6	Dog	15. 6	20. 5	E7	C5	Badger
6. 4	9. 3	C5	C7	Pheasant	16. 6	21. 5	E7	D6	Hare
7. 4	10. 3	C5	D8	Cock	17. 6	22. 5	E7	E7	Fox
8. 4	11. 3	C5	E9	Crow	18. 6	23. 5	E7	F8	Tiger
9. 4	12. 3	C5	F10	Monkey	19. 6	24. 5	E7	G9	Leopard

Solar date	Lunar date	Month HS/EB	Day HS/EB	Constellation
20. 6	25. 5	E7	H10	Griffon
21. 6	26. 5	E7	J11	Ox
22. 6	27. 5	E7	K12	Bat
23. 6	28. 5	E7	A1	Rat
24. 6	29. 5	E7	B2	Swallow
25. 6	30. 5	E7	C3	Pig
26. 6	1. 6	F8	D4	Porcupine
27. 6	2. 6	F8	E5	Wolf
28. 6	3. 6	F8	F6	Dog
29. 6	4. 6	F8	G7	Pheasant
30. 6	5. 6	F8	H8	Cock
1. 7	6. 6	F8	J9	Crow
2. 7	7. 6	F8	K10	Monkey
3. 7	8. 6	F8	A11	Gibbon
4. 7	9. 6	F8	B12	Tapir
5. 7	10. 6	F8	C1	Sheep
6. 7	11. 6	F8	D2	Deer
7. 7	12. 6	F8	E3	Horse
8. 7	13. 6	F8	F4	Stag
9. 7	14. 6	F8	G5	Serpent
10. 7	15. 6	F8	H6	Earthworm
11. 7	16. 6	F8	J7	Crocodile
12. 7	17. 6	F8	K8	Dragon
13. 7	18. 6	F8	A9	Badger
14. 7	19. 6	F8	B10	Hare
15. 7	20. 6	F8	C11	Fox
16. 7	21. 6	F8	D12	Tiger
17. 7	22. 6	F8	E1	Leopard
18. 7	23. 6	F8	F2	Griffon
19. 7	24. 6	F8	G3	Ox
20. 7	25. 6	F8	H4	Bat
21. 7	26. 6	F8	J5	Rat
22. 7	27. 6	F8	K6	Swallow
23. 7	28. 6	F8	A7	Pig
24. 7	29. 6	F8	B8	Porcupine
25. 7	1. 7	G9	C9	Wolf
26. 7	2. 7	G9	D10	Dog
27. 7	3. 7	G9	E11	Pheasant
28. 7	4. 7	G9	F12	Cock
29. 7	5. 7	G9	G1	Crow
30. 7	6. 7	G9	H2	Monkey
31. 7	7. 7	G9	J3	Gibbon
1. 8	8. 7	G9	K4	Tapir
2. 8	9. 7	G9	A5	Sheep
3. 8	10. 7	G9	B6	Deer
4. 8	11. 7	G9	C7	Horse
5. 8	12. 7	G9	D8	Stag
6. 8	13. 7	G9	E9	Serpent
7. 8	14. 7	G9	F10	Earthworm
8. 8	15. 7	G9	G11	Crocodile
9. 8	16. 7	G9	H12	Dragon
10. 8	17. 7	G9	J1	Badger
11. 8	18. 7	G9	K2	Hare
12. 8	19. 7	G9	A3	Fox
13. 8	20. 7	G9	B4	Tiger
14. 8	21. 7	G9	C5	Leopard
15. 8	22. 7	G9	D6	Griffon
16. 8	23. 7	G9	E7	Ox
17. 8	24. 7	G9	F8	Bat
18. 8	25. 7	G9	G9	Rat
19. 8	26. 7	G9	H10	Swallow
20. 8	27. 7	G9	J11	Pig
21. 8	28. 7	G9	K12	Porcupine
22. 8	29. 7	G9	A1	Wolf
23. 8	30. 7	G9	B2	Dog
24. 8	*1. 7*	*G9*	C3	Pheasant
25. 8	*2. 7*	*G9*	D4	Cock
26. 8	*3. 7*	*G9*	E5	Crow
27. 8	*4. 7*	*G9*	F6	Monkey
28. 8	*5. 7*	*G9*	G7	Gibbon
29. 8	*6. 7*	*G9*	H8	Tapir
30. 8	*7. 7*	*G9*	J9	Sheep
31. 8	*8. 7*	*G9*	K10	Deer
1. 9	*9. 7*	*G9*	A11	Horse
2. 9	*10. 7*	*G9*	B12	Stag
3. 9	*11. 7*	*G9*	C1	Serpent
4. 9	*12. 7*	*G9*	D2	Earthworm
5. 9	*13. 7*	*G9*	E3	Crocodile
6. 9	*14. 7*	*G9*	F4	Dragon
7. 9	*15. 7*	*G9*	G5	Badger
8. 9	*16. 7*	*G9*	H6	Hare
9. 9	*17. 7*	*G9*	J7	Fox
10. 9	*18. 7*	*G9*	K8	Tiger
11. 9	*19. 7*	*G9*	A9	Leopard
12. 9	*20. 7*	*G9*	B10	Griffon
13. 9	*21. 7*	*G9*	C11	Ox
14. 9	*22. 7*	*G9*	D12	Bat
15. 9	*23. 7*	*G9*	E1	Rat
16. 9	*24. 7*	*G9*	F2	Swallow
17. 9	*25. 7*	*G9*	G3	Pig
18. 9	*26. 7*	*G9*	H4	Porcupine
19. 9	*27. 7*	*G9*	J5	Wolf
20. 9	*28. 7*	*G9*	K6	Dog
21. 9	*29. 7*	*G9*	A7	Pheasant
22. 9	1. 8	H10	B8	Cock
23. 9	2. 8	H10	C9	Crow
24. 9	3. 8	H10	D10	Monkey
25. 9	4. 8	H10	E11	Gibbon
26. 9	5. 8	H10	F12	Tapir
27. 9	6. 8	H10	G1	Sheep
28. 9	7. 8	H10	H2	Deer
29. 9	8. 8	H10	J3	Horse
30. 9	9. 8	H10	K4	Stag
1.10	10. 8	H10	A5	Serpent
2.10	11. 8	H10	B6	Earthworm
3.10	12. 8	H10	C7	Crocodile
4.10	13. 8	H10	D8	Dragon
5.10	14. 8	H10	E9	Badger
6.10	15. 8	H10	F10	Hare
7.10	16. 8	H10	G11	Fox
8.10	17. 8	H10	H12	Tiger
9.10	18. 8	H10	J1	Leopard
10.10	19. 8	H10	K2	Griffon
11.10	20. 8	H10	A3	Ox
12.10	21. 8	H10	B4	Bat
13.10	22. 8	H10	C5	Rat
14.10	23. 8	H10	D6	Swallow
15.10	24. 8	H10	E7	Pig
16.10	25. 8	H10	F8	Porcupine
17.10	26. 8	H10	G9	Wolf
18.10	27. 8	H10	H10	Dog
19.10	28. 8	H10	J11	Pheasant
20.10	29. 8	H10	K12	Cock
21.10	30. 8	H10	A1	Crow
22.10	1. 9	J11	B2	Monkey
23.10	2. 9	J11	C3	Gibbon
24.10	3. 9	J11	D4	Tapir
25.10	4. 9	J11	E5	Sheep
26.10	5. 9	J11	F6	Deer
27.10	6. 9	J11	G7	Horse
28.10	7. 9	J11	H8	Stag
29.10	8. 9	J11	J9	Serpent
30.10	9. 9	J11	K10	Earthworm
31.10	10. 9	J11	A11	Crocodile
1.11	11. 9	J11	B12	Dragon
2.11	12. 9	J11	C1	Badger
3.11	13. 9	J11	D2	Hare
4.11	14. 9	J11	E3	Fox
5.11	15. 9	J11	F4	Tiger
6.11	16. 9	J11	G5	Leopard
7.11	17. 9	J11	H6	Griffon
8.11	18. 9	J11	J7	Ox
9.11	19. 9	J11	K8	Bat
10.11	20. 9	J11	A9	Rat
11.11	21. 9	J11	B10	Swallow
12.11	22. 9	J11	C11	Pig

Solar date	Lunar date	Month HS/EB	Day HS/EB	Constellation	Solar date	Lunar date	Month HS/EB	Day HS/EB	Constellation
13.11	23. 9	J11	D12	Porcupine	**1969**				
14.11	24. 9	J11	E1	Wolf	1. 1	13.11	A1	C1	Leopard
15.11	25. 9	J11	F2	Dog	2. 1	14.11	A1	D2	Griffon
16.11	26. 9	J11	G3	Pheasant	3. 1	15.11	A1	E3	Ox
17.11	27. 9	J11	H4	Cock	4. 1	16.11	A1	F4	Bat
18.11	28. 9	J11	J5	Crow	5. 1	17.11	A1	G5	Rat
19.11	29. 9	J11	K6	Monkey	6. 1	18.11	A1	H6	Swallow
20.11	1.10	K12	A7	Gibbon	7. 1	19.11	A1	J7	Pig
21.11	2.10	K12	B8	Tapir	8. 1	20.11	A1	K8	Porcupine
22.11	3.10	K12	C9	Sheep	9. 1	21.11	A1	A9	Wolf
23.11	4.10	K12	D10	Deer	10. 1	22.11	A1	B10	Dog
24.11	5.10	K12	E11	Horse	11. 1	23.11	A1	C11	Pheasant
25.11	6.10	K12	F12	Stag	12. 1	24.11	A1	D12	Cock
26.11	7.10	K12	G1	Serpent	13. 1	25.11	A1	E1	Crow
27.11	8.10	K12	H2	Earthworm	14. 1	26.11	A1	F2	Monkey
28.11	9.10	K12	J3	Crocodile	15. 1	27.11	A1	G3	Gibbon
29.11	10.10	K12	K4	Dragon	16. 1	28.11	A1	H4	Tapir
30.11	11.10	K12	A5	Badger	17. 1	29.11	A1	J5	Sheep
1.12	12.10	K12	B6	Hare	18. 1	1.12	B2	K6	Deer
2.12	13.10	K12	C7	Fox	19. 1	2.12	B2	A7	Horse
3.12	14.10	K12	D8	Tiger	20. 1	3.12	B2	B8	Stag
4.12	15.10	K12	E9	Leopard	21. 1	4.12	B2	C9	Serpent
5.12	16.10	K12	F10	Griffon	22. 1	5.12	B2	D10	Earthworm
6.12	17.10	K12	G11	Ox	23. 1	6.12	B2	E11	Crocodile
7.12	18.10	K12	H12	Bat	24. 1	7.12	B2	F12	Dragon
8.12	19.10	K12	J1	Rat	25. 1	8.12	B2	G1	Badger
9.12	20.10	K12	K2	Swallow	26. 1	9.12	B2	H2	Hare
10.12	21.10	K12	A3	Pig	27. 1	10.12	B2	J3	Fox
11.12	22.10	K12	B4	Porcupine	28. 1	11.12	B2	K4	Tiger
12.12	23.10	K12	C5	Wolf	29. 1	12.12	B2	A5	Leopard
13.12	24.10	K12	D6	Dog	30. 1	13.12	B2	B6	Griffon
14.12	25.10	K12	E7	Pheasant	31. 1	14.12	B2	C7	Ox
15.12	26.10	K12	F8	Cock	1. 2	15.12	B2	D8	Bat
16.12	27.10	K12	G9	Crow	2. 2	16.12	B2	E9	Rat
17.12	28.10	K12	H10	Monkey	3. 2	17.12	B2	F10	Swallow
18.12	29.10	K12	J11	Gibbon	4. 2	18.12	B2	G11	Pig
19.12	30.10	K12	K12	Tapir	5. 2	19.12	B2	H12	Porcupine
20.12	1.11	A1	A1	Sheep	6. 2	20.12	B2	J1	Wolf
21.12	2.11	A1	B2	Deer	7. 2	21.12	B2	K2	Dog
22.12	3.11	A1	C3	Horse	8. 2	22.12	B2	A3	Pheasant
23.12	4.11	A1	D4	Stag	9. 2	23.12	B2	B4	Cock
24.12	5.11	A1	E5	Serpent	10. 2	24.12	B2	C5	Crow
25.12	6.11	A1	F6	Earthworm	11. 2	25.12	B2	D6	Monkey
26.12	7.11	A1	G7	Crocodile	12. 2	26.12	B2	E7	Gibbon
27.12	8.11	A1	H8	Dragon	13. 2	27.12	B2	F8	Tapir
28.12	9.11	A1	J9	Badger	14. 2	28.12	B2	G9	Sheep
29.12	10.11	A1	K10	Hare	15. 2	29.12	B2	H10	Deer
30.12	11.11	A1	A11	Fox	16. 2	30.12	B2	J11	Horse
31.12	12.11	A1	B12	Tiger					

CHI YU YEAR

Solar date	Lunar date	Month HS/EB	Day HS/EB	Constellation	Solar date	Lunar date	Month HS/EB	Day HS/EB	Constellation
17. 2	1. 1	C3	K12	Stag	7. 3	19. 1	C3	H6	Dog
18. 2	2. 1	C3	A1	Serpent	8. 3	20. 1	C3	J7	Pheasant
19. 2	3. 1	C3	B2	Earthworm	9. 3	21. 1	C3	K8	Cock
20. 2	4. 1	C3	C3	Crocodile	10. 3	22. 1	C3	A9	Crow
21. 2	5. 1	C3	D4	Dragon	11. 3	23. 1	C3	B10	Monkey
22. 2	6. 1	C3	E5	Badger	12. 3	24. 1	C3	C11	Gibbon
23. 2	7. 1	C3	F6	Hare	13. 3	25. 1	C3	D12	Tapir
24. 2	8. 1	C3	G7	Fox	14. 3	26. 1	C3	E1	Sheep
25. 2	9. 1	C3	H8	Tiger	15. 3	27. 1	C3	F2	Deer
26. 2	10. 1	C3	J9	Leopard	16. 3	28. 1	C3	G3	Horse
27. 2	11. 1	C3	K10	Griffon	17. 3	29. 1	C3	H4	Stag
28. 2	12. 1	C3	A11	Ox	18. 3	1. 2	D4	J5	Serpent
1. 3	13. 1	C3	B12	Bat	19. 3	2. 2	D4	K6	Earthworm
2. 3	14. 1	C3	C1	Rat	20. 3	3. 2	D4	A7	Crocodile
3. 3	15. 1	C3	D2	Swallow	21. 3	4. 2	D4	B8	Dragon
4. 3	16. 1	C3	E3	Pig	22. 3	5. 2	D4	C9	Badger
5. 3	17. 1	C3	F4	Porcupine	23. 3	6. 2	D4	D10	Hare
6. 3	18. 1	C3	G5	Wolf	24. 3	7. 2	D4	E11	Fox

Solar date	Lunar date	Month HS/EB	Day HS/EB	Constellation
25. 3	8. 2	D4	F12	Tiger
26. 3	9. 2	D4	G1	Leopard
27. 3	10. 2	D4	H2	Griffon
28. 3	11. 2	D4	J3	Ox
29. 3	12. 2	D4	K4	Bat
30. 3	13. 2	D4	A5	Rat
31. 3	14. 2	D4	B6	Swallow
1. 4	15. 2	D4	C7	Pig
2. 4	16. 2	D4	D8	Porcupine
3. 4	17. 2	D4	E9	Wolf
4. 4	18. 2	D4	F10	Dog
5. 4	19. 2	D4	G11	Pheasant
6. 4	20. 2	D4	H12	Cock
7. 4	21. 2	D4	J1	Crow
8. 4	22. 2	D4	K2	Monkey
9. 4	23. 2	D4	A3	Gibbon
10. 4	24. 2	D4	B4	Tapir
11. 4	25. 2	D4	C5	Sheep
12. 4	26. 2	D4	D6	Deer
13. 4	27. 2	D4	E7	Horse
14. 4	28. 2	D4	F8	Stag
15. 4	29. 2	D4	G9	Serpent
16. 4	30. 2	D4	H10	Earthworm
17. 4	1. 3	E5	J11	Crocodile
18. 4	2. 3	E5	K12	Dragon
19. 4	3. 3	E5	A1	Badger
20. 4	4. 3	E5	B2	Hare
21. 4	5. 3	E5	C3	Fox
22. 4	6. 3	E5	D4	Tiger
23. 4	7. 3	E5	E5	Leopard
24. 4	8. 3	E5	F6	Griffon
25. 4	9. 3	E5	G7	Ox
26. 4	10. 3	E5	H8	Bat
27. 4	11. 3	E5	J9	Rat
28. 4	12. 3	E5	K10	Swallow
29. 4	13. 3	E5	A11	Pig
30. 4	14. 3	E5	B12	Porcupine
1. 5	15. 3	E5	C1	Wolf
2. 5	16. 3	E5	D2	Dog
3. 5	17. 3	E5	E3	Pheasant
4. 5	18. 3	E5	F4	Cock
5. 5	19. 3	E5	G5	Crow
6. 5	20. 3	E5	H6	Monkey
7. 5	21. 3	E5	J7	Gibbon
8. 5	22. 3	E5	K8	Tapir
9. 5	23. 3	E5	A9	Sheep
10. 5	24. 3	E5	B10	Deer
11. 5	25. 3	E5	C11	Horse
12. 5	26. 3	E5	D12	Stag
13. 5	27. 3	E5	E1	Serpent
14. 5	28. 3	E5	F2	Earthworm
15. 5	29. 3	E5	G3	Crocodile
16. 5	1. 4	F6	H4	Dragon
17. 5	2. 4	F6	J5	Badger
18. 5	3. 4	F6	K6	Hare
19. 5	4. 4	F6	A7	Fox
20. 5	5. 4	F6	B8	Tiger
21. 5	6. 4	F6	C9	Leopard
22. 5	7. 4	F6	D10	Griffon
23. 5	8. 4	F6	E11	Ox
24. 5	9. 4	F6	F12	Bat
25. 5	10. 4	F6	G1	Rat
26. 5	11. 4	F6	H2	Swallow
27. 5	12. 4	F6	J3	Pig
28. 5	13. 4	F6	K4	Porcupine
29. 5	14. 4	F6	A5	Wolf
30. 5	15. 4	F6	B6	Dog
31. 5	16. 4	F6	C7	Pheasant
1. 6	17. 4	F6	D8	Cock
2. 6	18. 4	F6	E9	Crow
3. 6	19. 4	F6	F10	Monkey
4. 6	20. 4	F6	G11	Gibbon
5. 6	21. 4	F6	H12	Tapir

Solar date	Lunar date	Month HS/EB	Day HS/EB	Constellation
6. 6	22. 4	F6	J1	Sheep
7. 6	23. 4	F6	K2	Deer
8. 6	24. 4	F6	A3	Horse
9. 6	25. 4	F6	B4	Stag
10. 6	26. 4	F6	C5	Serpent
11. 6	27. 4	F6	D6	Earthworm
12. 6	28. 4	F6	E7	Crocodile
13. 6	29. 4	F6	F8	Dragon
14. 6	30. 4	F6	G9	Badger
15. 6	1. 5	G7	H10	Hare
16. 6	2. 5	G7	J11	Fox
17. 6	3. 5	G7	K12	Tiger
18. 6	4. 5	G7	A1	Leopard
19. 6	5. 5	G7	B2	Griffon
20. 6	6. 5	G7	C3	Ox
21. 6	7. 5	G7	D4	Bat
22. 6	8. 5	G7	E5	Rat
23. 6	9. 5	G7	F6	Swallow
24. 6	10. 5	G7	G7	Pig
25. 6	11. 5	G7	H8	Porcupine
26. 6	12. 5	G7	J9	Wolf
27. 6	13. 5	G7	K10	Dog
28. 6	14. 5	G7	A11	Pheasant
29. 6	15. 5	G7	B12	Cock
30. 6	16. 5	G7	C1	Crow
1. 7	17. 5	G7	D2	Monkey
2. 7	18. 5	G7	E3	Gibbon
3. 7	19. 5	G7	F4	Tapir
4. 7	20. 5	G7	G5	Sheep
5. 7	21. 5	G7	H6	Deer
6. 7	22. 5	G7	J7	Horse
7. 7	23. 5	G7	K8	Stag
8. 7	24. 5	G7	A9	Serpent
9. 7	25. 5	G7	B10	Earthworm
10. 7	26. 5	G7	C11	Crocodile
11. 7	27. 5	G7	D12	Dragon
12. 7	28. 5	G7	E1	Badger
13. 7	29. 5	G7	F2	Hare
14. 7	1. 6	H8	G3	Fox
15. 7	2. 6	H8	H4	Tiger
16. 7	3. 6	H8	J5	Leopard
17. 7	4. 6	H8	K6	Griffon
18. 7	5. 6	H8	A7	Ox
19. 7	6. 6	H8	B8	Bat
20. 7	7. 6	H8	C9	Rat
21. 7	8. 6	H8	D10	Swallow
22. 7	9. 6	H8	E11	Pig
23. 7	10. 6	H8	F12	Porcupine
24. 7	11. 6	H8	G1	Wolf
25. 7	12. 6	H8	H2	Dog
26. 7	13. 6	H8	J3	Pheasant
27. 7	14. 6	H8	K4	Cock
28. 7	15. 6	H8	A5	Crow
29. 7	16. 6	H8	B6	Monkey
30. 7	17. 6	H8	C7	Gibbon
31. 7	18. 6	H8	D8	Tapir
1. 8	19. 6	H8	E9	Sheep
2. 8	20. 6	H8	F10	Deer
3. 8	21. 6	H8	G11	Horse
4. 8	22. 6	H8	H12	Stag
5. 8	23. 6	H8	J1	Serpent
6. 8	24. 6	H8	K2	Earthworm
7. 8	25. 6	H8	A3	Crocodile
8. 8	26. 6	H8	B4	Dragon
9. 8	27. 6	H8	C5	Badger
10. 8	28. 6	H8	D6	Hare
11. 8	29. 6	H8	E7	Fox
12. 8	30. 6	H8	F8	Tiger
13. 8	1. 7	J9	G9	Leopard
14. 8	2. 7	J9	H10	Griffon
15. 8	3. 7	J9	J11	Ox
16. 8	4. 7	J9	K12	Bat
17. 8	5. 7	J9	A1	Rat

Solar date	Lunar date	Month HS/EB	Day HS/EB	Constellation	Solar date	Lunar date	Month HS/EB	Day HS/EB	Constellation
18. 8	6. 7	J9	B2	Swallow	30.10	20. 9	A11	E3	Crocodile
19. 8	7. 7	J9	C3	Pig	31.10	21. 9	A11	F4	Dragon
20. 8	8. 7	J9	D4	Porcupine	1.11	22. 9	A11	G5	Badger
21. 8	9. 7	J9	E5	Wolf	2.11	23. 9	A11	H6	Hare
22. 8	10. 7	J9	F6	Dog	3.11	24. 9	A11	J7	Fox
23. 8	11. 7	J9	G7	Pheasant	4.11	25. 9	A11	K8	Tiger
24. 8	12. 7	J9	H8	Cock	5.11	26. 9	A11	A9	Leopard
25. 8	13. 7	J9	J9	Crow	6.11	27. 9	A11	B10	Griffon
26. 8	14. 7	J9	K10	Monkey	7.11	28. 9	A11	C11	Ox
27. 8	15. 7	J9	A11	Gibbon	8.11	29. 9	A11	D12	Bat
28. 8	16. 7	J9	B12	Tapir	9.11	30. 9	A11	E1	Rat
29. 8	17. 7	J9	C1	Sheep	10.11	1.10	B12	F2	Swallow
30. 8	18. 7	J9	D2	Deer	11.11	2.10	B12	G3	Pig
31. 8	19. 7	J9	E3	Stag	12.11	2.10	B12	H4	Porcupine
1. 9	20. 7	J9	F4	Stag	13.11	4.10	B12	J5	Wolf
2. 9	21. 7	J9	G5	Serpent	14.11	5.10	B12	K6	Dog
3. 9	22. 7	J9	H6	Earthworm	15.11	6.10	B12	A7	Pheasant
4. 9	23. 7	J9	J7	Crocodile	16.11	7.10	B12	B8	Cock
5. 9	24. 7	J9	K8	Dragon	17.11	8.10	B12	C9	Crow
6. 9	25. 7	J9	A9	Badger	18.11	9.10	B12	D10	Monkey
7. 9	26. 7	J9	B10	Hare	19.11	10.10	B12	E11	Gibbon
8. 9	27. 7	J9	C11	Fox	20.11	11.10	B12	F12	Tapir
9. 9	28. 7	J9	D12	Tiger	21.11	12.10	B12	G1	Sheep
10. 9	29. 7	J9	E1	Leopard	22.11	13.10	B12	H2	Deer
11. 9	30. 7	J9	F2	Griffon	23.11	14.10	B12	J3	Horse
12. 9	1. 8	K10	G3	Ox	24.11	15.10	B12	K4	Stag
13. 9	2. 8	K10	H4	Bat	25.11	16.10	B12	A5	Serpent
14. 9	3. 8	K10	J5	Rat	26.11	17.10	B12	B6	Earthworm
15. 9	4. 8	K10	K6	Swallow	27.11	18.10	B12	C7	Crocodile
16. 9	5. 8	K10	A7	Pig	28.11	19.10	B12	D8	Dragon
17. 9	6. 8	K10	B8	Porcupine	29.11	20.10	B12	E9	Badger
18. 9	7. 8	K10	C9	Wolf	30.11	21.10	B12	F10	Hare
19. 9	8. 8	K10	D10	Dog	1.12	22.10	B12	G11	Fox
20. 9	9. 8	K10	E11	Pheasant	2.12	23.10	B12	H12	Tiger
21. 9	10. 8	K10	F12	Cock	3.12	24.10	B12	J1	Leopard
22. 9	11. 8	K10	G1	Crow	4.12	25.10	B12	K2	Griffon
23. 9	12. 8	K10	H2	Monkey	5.12	26.10	B12	A3	Ox
24. 9	13. 8	K10	J3	Gibbon	6.12	27.10	B12	B4	Bat
25. 9	14. 8	K10	K4	Tapir	7.12	28.10	B12	C5	Rat
26. 9	15. 8	K10	A5	Sheep	8.12	29.10	B12	D6	Swallow
27. 9	16. 8	K10	B6	Deer	9.12	1.11	C1	E7	Pig
28. 9	17. 8	K10	C7	Horse	10.12	2.11	C1	F8	Porcupine
29. 9	18. 8	K10	D8	Stag	11.12	3.11	C1	G9	Wolf
30. 9	19. 8	K10	E9	Serpent	12.12	4.11	C1	H10	Dog
1.10	20. 8	K10	F10	Earthworm	13.12	5.11	C1	J11	Pheasant
2.10	21. 8	K10	G11	Crocodile	14.12	6.11	C1	K12	Cock
3.10	22. 8	K10	H12	Dragon	15.12	7.11	C1	A1	Crow
4.10	23. 8	K10	J1	Badger	16.12	8.11	C1	B2	Monkey
5.10	24. 8	K10	K2	Hare	17.12	9.11	C1	C3	Gibbon
6.10	25. 8	K10	A3	Fox	18.12	10.11	C1	D4	Tapir
7.10	26. 8	K10	B4	Tiger	19.12	11.11	C1	E5	Sheep
8.10	27. 8	K10	C5	Leopard	20.12	12.11	C1	F6	Deer
9.10	28. 8	K10	D6	Griffon	21.12	13.11	C1	G7	Horse
10.10	29. 8	K10	E7	Ox	22.12	14.11	C1	H8	Stag
11.10	1. 9	A11	F8	Bat	23.12	15.11	C1	J9	Serpent
12.10	2. 9	A11	G9	Rat	24.12	16.11	C1	K10	Earthworm
13.10	3. 9	A11	H10	Swallow	25.12	17.11	C1	A11	Crocodile
14.10	4. 9	A11	J11	Pig	26.12	18.11	C1	B12	Dragon
15.10	5. 9	A11	K12	Porcupine	27.12	19.11	C1	C1	Badger
16.10	6. 9	A11	A1	Wolf	28.12	20.11	C1	D2	Hare
17.10	7. 9	A11	B2	Dog	29.12	21.11	C1	E3	Fox
18.10	8. 9	A11	C3	Pheasant	30.12	22.11	C1	F4	Tiger
19.10	9. 9	A11	D4	Cock	31.12	23,11	C1	G5	Leopard
20.10	10. 9	A11	E5	Crow	**1970**				
21.10	11. 9	A11	F6	Monkey	1. 1	24.11	C1	H6	Griffon
22.10	12. 9	A11	G7	Gibbon	2. 1	25.11	C1	J7	Ox
23.10	13. 9	A11	H8	Tapir	3. 1	26.11	C1	K8	Bat
24.10	14. 9	A11	J9	Sheep	4. 1	27.11	C1	A9	Rat
25.10	15. 9	A11	K10	Deer	5. 1	28.11	C1	B10	Swallow
26.10	16. 9	A11	A11	Horse	6. 1	29.11	C1	C11	Pig
27.10	17. 9	A11	B12	Stag	7. 1	30.11	C1	D12	Porcupine
28.10	18. 9	A11	C1	Serpent	8. 1	1.12	D2	E1	Wolf
29.10	19. 9	A11	D2	Earthworm					

Solar date	Lunar date	Month HS/EB	Day HS/EB	Constellation	Solar date	Lunar date	Month HS/EB	Day HS/EB	Constellation
9. 1	2.12	D2	F2	Dog	23. 1	16.12	D2	K4	Dragon
10. 1	3.12	D2	G3	Pheasant	24. 1	17.12	D2	A5	Badger
11. 1	4.12	D2	H4	Cock	25. 1	18.12	D2	B6	Hare
12. 1	5.12	D2	J5	Crow	26. 1	19.12	D2	C7	Fox
13. 1	6.12	D2	K6	Monkey	27. 1	20.12	D2	D8	Tiger
14. 1	7.12	D2	A7	Gibbon	28. 1	21.12	D2	E9	Leopard
15. 1	8.12	D2	B8	Tapir	29. 1	22.12	D2	F10	Griffon
16. 1	9.12	D2	C9	Sheep	30. 1	23.12	D2	G11	Ox
17. 1	10.12	D2	D10	Deer	31. 1	24.12	D2	H12	Bat
18. 1	11.12	D2	E11	Horse	1. 2	25.12	D2	J1	Rat
19. 1	12.12	D2	F12	Stag	2. 2	26.12	D2	K2	Swallow
20. 1	13.12	D2	G1	Serpent	3. 2	27.12	D2	A3	Pig
21. 1	14.12	D2	H2	Earthworm	4. 2	28.12	D2	B4	Porcupine
22. 1	15.12	D2	J3	Crocodile	5. 2	29.12	D2	C5	Wolf

KENG HSÜ YEAR

Solar date	Lunar date	Month HS/EB	Day HS/EB	Constellation	Solar date	Lunar date	Month HS/EB	Day HS/EB	Constellation
6. 2	1. 1	E3	D6	Dog	1. 4	25. 2	F4	H12	Porcupine
7. 2	2. 1	E3	E7	Pheasant	2. 4	26. 2	F4	J1	Wolf
8. 2	3. 1	E3	F8	Cock	3. 4	27. 2	F4	K2	Dog
9. 2	4. 1	E3	G9	Crow	4. 4	28. 2	F4	A3	Pheasant
10. 1	5. 1	E3	H10	Monkey	5. 4	29. 2	F4	B4	Cock
11. 2	6. 1	E3	J11	Gibbon	6. 4	1. 3	G5	C5	Crow
12. 2	7. 1	E3	K12	Tapir	7. 4	2. 3	G5	D6	Monkey
13. 2	8. 1	E3	A1	Sheep	8. 4	3. 3	G5	E7	Gibbon
14. 2	9. 1	E3	B2	Deer	9. 4	4. 3	G5	F8	Tapir
15. 2	10. 1	E3	C3	Horse	10. 4	5. 3	G5	G9	Sheep
16. 2	11. 1	E3	D4	Stag	11. 4	6. 3	G5	H10	Deer
17. 2	12. 1	E3	E5	Serpent	12. 4	7. 3	G5	J11	Horse
18. 2	13. 1	E3	F6	Earthworm	13. 4	8. 3	G5	K12	Stag
19. 2	14. 1	E3	G7	Crocodile	14. 4	9. 3	G5	A1	Serpent
20. 2	15. 1	E3	H8	Dragon	15. 4	10. 3	G5	B2	Earthworm
21. 2	16. 1	E3	J9	Badger	16. 4	11. 3	G5	C3	Crocodile
22. 2	17. 1	E3	K10	Hare	17. 4	12. 3	G5	D4	Dragon
23. 2	18. 1	E3	A11	Fox	18. 4	13. 3	G5	E5	Badger
24. 2	19. 1	E3	B12	Tiger	19. 4	14. 3	G5	F6	Hare
25. 2	20. 1	E3	C1	Leopard	20. 4	15. 3	G5	G7	Fox
26. 2	21. 1	E3	D2	Griffon	21. 4	16. 3	G5	H8	Tiger
27. 2	22. 1	E3	E3	Ox	22. 4	17. 3	G5	J9	Leopard
28. 2	23. 1	E3	F4	Bat	23. 4	18. 3	G5	K10	Griffon
1. 3	24. 1	E3	G5	Rat	24. 4	19. 3	G5	A11	Ox
2. 3	25. 1	E3	H6	Swallow	25. 4	20. 3	G5	B12	Bat
3. 3	26. 1	E3	J7	Pig	26. 4	21. 3	G5	C1	Rat
4. 3	27. 1	E3	K8	Porcupine	27. 4	22. 3	G5	D2	Swallow
5. 3	28. 1	E3	A9	Wolf	28. 4	23. 3	G5	E3	Pig
6. 3	29. 1	E3	B10	Dog	29. 4	24. 3	G5	F4	Porcupine
7. 3	30. 1	E3	C11	Pheasant	30. 4	25. 3	G5	G5	Wolf
8. 3	1. 2	F4	D12	Cock	1. 5	26. 3	G5	H6	Dog
9. 3	2. 2	F4	E1	Crow	2. 5	27. 3	G5	J7	Pheasant
10. 3	3. 2	F4	F2	Monkey	3. 5	28. 3	G5	K8	Cock
11. 3	4. 2	F4	G3	Gibbon	4. 5	29. 3	G5	A9	Crow
12. 3	5. 2	F4	H4	Tapir	5. 5	1. 4	H6	B10	Monkey
13. 3	6. 2	F4	J5	Sheep	6. 5	2. 4	H6	C11	Gibbon
14. 3	7. 2	F4	K6	Deer	7. 5	3. 4	H6	D12	Tapir
15. 3	8. 2	F4	A7	Horse	8. 5	4. 4	H6	E1	Sheep
16. 3	9. 2	F4	B8	Stag	9. 5	5. 4	H6	F2	Deer
17. 3	10. 2	F4	C9	Serpent	10. 5	6. 4	H6	G3	Horse
18. 3	11. 2	F4	D10	Earthworm	11. 5	7. 4	H6	H4	Stag
19. 3	12. 2	F4	E11	Crocodile	12. 5	8. 4	H6	J5	Serpent
20. 3	13. 2	F4	F12	Dragon	13. 5	9. 4	H6	K6	Earthworm
21. 3	14. 2	F4	G1	Badger	14. 5	10. 4	H6	A7	Crocodile
22. 3	15. 2	F4	H2	Hare	15. 5	11. 4	H6	B8	Dragon
23. 3	16. 2	F4	J3	Fox	16. 5	12. 4	H6	C9	Badger
24. 3	17. 2	F4	K4	Tiger	17. 5	13. 4	H6	D10	Hare
25. 3	18. 2	F4	A5	Leopard	18. 5	14. 4	H6	E11	Fox
26. 3	19. 2	F4	B6	Griffon	19. 5	15. 4	H6	F12	Tiger
27. 3	20. 2	F4	C7	Ox	20. 5	16. 4	H6	G1	Leopard
28. 3	21. 2	F4	D8	Bat	21. 5	17. 4	H6	H2	Griffon
29. 3	22. 2	F4	E9	Rat	22. 5	18. 4	H6	J3	Ox
30. 3	23. 2	F4	F10	Swallow	23. 5	19. 4	H6	K4	Bat
31. 3	24. 2	F4	G11	Pig	24. 5	20. 4	H6	A5	Rat

Solar date	Lunar date	Month HS/EB	Day HS/EB	Constellation	Solar date	Lunar date	Month HS/EB	Day HS/EB	Constellation
25. 5	21. 4	H6	B6	Swallow	6. 8	5. 7	A9	E7	Crocodile
26. 5	22. 4	H6	C7	Pig	7. 8	6. 7	A9	F8	Dragon
27. 5	23. 4	H6	D8	Porcupine	8. 8	7. 7	A9	G9	Badger
28. 5	24. 4	H6	E9	Wolf	9. 8	8. 7	A9	H10	Hare
29. 5	25. 4	H6	F10	Dog	10. 8	9. 7	A9	J11	Fox
30. 5	26. 4	H6	G11	Pheasant	11. 8	10. 7	A9	K12	Tiger
31. 5	27. 4	H6	H12	Cock	12. 8	11. 7	A9	A1	Leopard
1. 6	28. 4	H6	J1	Crow	13. 8	12. 7	A9	B2	Griffon
2. 6	29. 4	H6	K2	Monkey	14. 8	13. 7	A9	C3	Ox
3. 6	30. 4	H6	A3	Gibbon	15. 8	14. 7	A9	D4	Bat
4. 6	1. 5	J7	B4	Tapir	16. 8	15. 7	A9	E5	Rat
5. 6	2. 5	J7	C5	Sheep	17. 8	16. 7	A9	F6	Swallow
6. 6	3. 5	J7	D6	Deer	18. 8	17. 7	A9	G7	Pig
7. 6	4. 5	J7	E7	Horse	19. 8	18. 7	A9	H8	Porcupine
8. 6	5. 5	J7	F8	Stag	20. 8	19. 7	A9	J9	Wolf
9. 6	6. 5	J7	G9	Serpent	21. 8	20. 7	A9	K10	Dog
10. 6	7. 5	J7	H10	Earthworm	22. 8	21. 7	A9	A11	Pheasant
11. 6	8. 5	J7	J11	Crocodile	23. 8	22. 7	A9	B12	Cock
12. 6	9. 5	J7	K12	Dragon	24. 8	23. 7	A9	C1	Crow
13. 6	10. 5	J7	A1	Badger	25. 8	24. 7	A9	D2	Monkey
14. 6	11. 5	J7	B2	Hare	26. 8	25. 7	A9	E3	Gibbon
15. 6	12. 5	J7	C3	Fox	27. 8	26. 7	A9	F4	Tapir
16. 6	13. 5	J7	D4	Tiger	28. 8	27. 7	A9	G5	Sheep
17. 6	14. 5	J7	E5	Leopard	29. 8	28. 7	A9	H6	Deer
18. 6	15. 5	J7	F6	Griffon	30. 8	29. 7	A9	J7	Horse
19. 6	16. 5	J7	G7	Ox	31. 8	30. 7	A9	K8	Stag
20. 6	17. 5	J7	H8	Bat	1. 9	1. 8	B10	A9	Serpent
21. 6	18. 5	J7	J9	Rat	2. 9	2. 8	B10	B10	Earthworm
22. 6	19. 5	J7	K10	Swallow	3. 9	3. 8	B10	C11	Crocodile
23. 6	20. 5	J7	A11	Pig	4. 9	4. 8	B10	D12	Dragon
24. 6	21. 5	J7	B12	Porcupine	5. 9	5. 8	B10	E1	Badger
25. 6	22. 5	J7	C1	Wolf	6. 9	6. 8	B10	F2	Hare
26. 6	23. 5	J7	D2	Dog	7. 9	7. 8	B10	G3	Fox
27. 6	24. 5	J7	E3	Pheasant	8. 9	8. 8	B10	H4	Tiger
28. 6	25. 5	J7	F4	Cock	9. 9	9. 8	B10	J5	Leopard
29. 6	26. 5	J7	G5	Crow	10. 9	10. 8	B10	K6	Griffon
30. 6	27. 5	J7	H6	Monkey	11. 9	11. 8	B10	A7	Ox
1. 7	28. 5	J7	J7	Gibbon	12. 9	12. 8	B10	B8	Bat
2. 7	29. 5	J7	K8	Tapir	13. 9	13. 8	B10	C9	Rat
3. 7	1. 6	K8	A9	Sheep	14. 9	14. 8	B10	D10	Swallow
4. 7	2. 6	K8	B10	Deer	15. 9	15. 8	B10	E11	Pig
5. 7	3. 6	K8	C11	Horse	16. 9	16. 8	B10	F12	Porcupine
6. 7	4. 6	K8	D12	Stag	17. 9	17. 8	B10	G1	Wolf
7. 7	5. 6	K8	E1	Serpent	18. 9	18. 8	B10	H2	Dog
8. 7	6. 6	K8	F2	Earthworm	19. 9	19. 8	B10	J3	Pheasant
9. 7	7. 6	K8	G3	Crocodile	20. 9	20. 8	B10	K4	Cock
10. 7	8. 6	K8	H4	Dragon	21. 9	21. 8	B10	A5	Crow
11. 7	9. 6	K8	J5	Badger	22. 9	22. 8	B10	B6	Monkey
12. 7	10. 6	K8	K6	Hare	23. 9	23. 8	B10	C7	Gibbon
13. 7	11. 6	K8	A7	Fox	24. 9	24. 8	B10	D8	Tapir
14. 7	12. 6	K8	B8	Tiger	25. 9	25. 8	B10	E9	Sheep
15. 7	13. 6	K8	C9	Leopard	26. 9	26. 8	B10	F10	Deer
16. 7	14. 6	K8	D10	Griffon	27. 9	27. 8	B10	G11	Horse
17. 7	15. 6	K8	E11	Ox	28. 9	28. 8	B10	H12	Stag
18. 7	16. 6	K8	F12	Bat	29. 9	29. 8	B10	J1	Serpent
19. 7	17. 6	K8	G1	Rat	30. 9	1. 9	C11	K2	Earthworm
20. 7	18. 6	K8	H2	Swallow	1.10	2. 9	C11	A3	Crocodile
21. 7	19. 6	K8	J3	Pig	2.10	3. 9	C11	B4	Dragon
22. 7	20. 6	K8	K4	Porcupine	3.10	4. 9	C11	C5	Badger
23. 7	21. 6	K8	A5	Wolf	4.10	5. 9	C11	D6	Hare
24. 7	22. 6	K8	B6	Dog	5.10	6. 9	C11	E7	Fox
25. 7	23. 6	K8	C7	Pheasant	6.10	7. 9	C11	F8	Tiger
26. 7	24. 6	K8	D8	Cock	7.10	8. 9	C11	G9	Leopard
27. 7	25. 6	K8	E9	Crow	8.10	9. 9	C11	H10	Griffon
28. 7	26. 6	K8	F10	Monkey	9.10	10. 9	C11	J11	Ox
29. 7	27. 6	K8	G11	Gibbon	10.10	11. 9	C11	K12	Bat
30. 7	28. 6	K8	H12	Tapir	11.10	12. 9	C11	A1	Rat
31. 7	29. 6	K8	J1	Sheep	12.10	13. 9	C11	B2	Swallow
1. 8	30. 6	K8	K2	Deer	13.10	14. 9	C11	C3	Pig
2. 8	1. 7	A9	A3	Horse	14.10	15. 9	C11	D4	Porcupine
3. 8	2. 7	A9	B4	Stag	15.10	16. 9	C11	E5	Wolf
4. 8	3. 7	A9	C5	Serpent	16.10	17. 9	C11	F6	Dog
5. 8	4. 7	A9	D6	Earthworm	17.10	18. 9	C11	G7	Pheasant

Solar date	Lunar date	Month HS/EB	Day HS/EB	Constellation
18.10	19. 9	C11	H8	Cock
19.10	20. 9	C11	J9	Crow
20.10	21. 9	C11	K10	Monkey
21.10	22. 9	C11	A11	Gibbon
22.10	23. 9	C11	B12	Tapir
23.10	24. 9	C11	C1	Sheep
24.10	25. 9	C11	D2	Deer
25.10	26. 9	C11	E3	Horse
26.10	27. 9	C11	F4	Stag
27.10	28. 9	C11	G5	Serpent
28.10	29. 9	C11	H6	Earthworm
29.10	30. 9	C11	J7	Crocodile
30.10	1.10	D12	K8	Dragon
31.10	2.10	D12	A9	Badger
1.11	3.10	D12	B10	Hare
2.11	4.10	D12	C11	Fox
3.11	5.10	D12	D12	Tiger
4.11	6.10	D12	E1	Leopard
5.11	7.10	D12	F2	Griffon
6.11	8.10	D12	G3	Ox
7.11	9.10	D12	H4	Bat
8.11	10.10	D12	J5	Rat
9.11	11.10	D12	K6	Swallow
10.11	12.10	D12	A7	Pig
11.11	13.10	D12	B8	Porcupine
12.11	14.10	D12	C9	Wolf
13.11	15.10	D12	D10	Dog
14.11	16.10	D12	E11	Pheasant
15.11	17.10	D12	F12	Cock
16.11	18.10	D12	G1	Crow
17.11	19.10	D12	H2	Monkey
18.11	20.10	D12	J3	Gibbon
19.11	21.10	D12	K4	Tapir
20.11	22.10	D12	A5	Sheep
21.11	23.10	D12	B6	Deer
22.11	24.10	D12	C7	Horse
23.11	25.10	D12	D8	Stag
24.11	26.10	D12	E9	Serpent
25.11	27.10	D12	F10	Earthworm
26.11	28.10	D12	G11	Crocodile
27.11	29.10	D12	H12	Dragon
28.11	30.10	D12	J1	Badger
29.11	1.11	E1	K2	Hare
30.11	2.11	E1	A3	Fox
1.12	3.11	E1	B4	Tiger
2.12	4.11	E1	C5	Leopard
3.12	5.11	E1	D6	Griffon
4.12	6.11	E1	E7	Ox
5.12	7.11	E1	F8	Bat
6.12	8.11	E1	G9	Rat
7.12	9.11	E1	H10	Swallow
8.10	10.11	E1	J11	Pig
9.12	11.11	E1	K12	Porcupine
10.12	12.11	E1	A1	Wolf
11.12	13.11	E1	B2	Dog
12.12	14.11	E1	C3	Pheasant
13.12	15.11	E1	D4	Cock
14.12	16.11	E1	E5	Crow
15.12	17.11	E1	F6	Monkey
16.12	18.11	E1	G7	Gibbon
17.12	19.11	E1	H8	Tapir
18.12	20.11	E1	J9	Sheep
19.12	21.11	E1	K10	Deer
20.12	22.11	E1	A11	Horse
21.12	23.11	E1	B12	Stag
22.12	24.11	E1	C1	Serpent
23.12	25.11	E1	D2	Earthworm
24.12	26.11	E1	E3	Crocodile
25.12	27.11	E1	F4	Dragon
26.12	28.11	E1	G5	Badger
27.12	29.11	E1	H6	Hare
28.12	1.12	F2	J7	Fox
29.12	2.12	F2	K8	Tiger
30.12	3.12	F2	A9	Leopard
31.12	4.12	F2	B10	Griffon

1971

Solar date	Lunar date	Month HS/EB	Day HS/EB	Constellation
1. 1	5.12	F2	C11	Ox
2. 1	6.12	F2	D12	Bat
3. 1	7.12	F2	E1	Rat
4. 1	8.12	F2	F2	Swallow
5. 1	9.12	F2	G3	Pig
6. 1	10.12	F2	H4	Porcupine
7. 1	11.12	F2	J5	Wolf
8. 1	12.12	F2	K6	Dog
9. 1	13.12	F2	A7	Pheasant
10. 1	14.12	F2	B8	Cock
11. 1	15.12	F2	C9	Crow
12. 1	16.12	F2	D10	Monkey
13. 1	17.12	F2	E11	Gibbon
14. 1	18.12	F2	F12	Tapir
15. 1	19.12	F2	G1	Sheep
16. 1	20.12	F2	H2	Deer
17. 1	21.12	F2	J3	Horse
18. 1	22.12	F2	K4	Stag
19. 1	23.12	F2	A5	Serpent
20. 1	24.12	F2	B6	Earthworm
21. 1	25.12	F2	C7	Crocodile
22. 1	26.12	F2	D8	Dragon
23. 1	27.12	F2	E9	Badger
24. 1	28.12	F2	F10	Hare
25. 1	29.12	F2	G11	Fox
26. 1	30.12	F2	H12	Tiger

HSIN HAI YEAR

Solar date	Lunar date	Month HS/EB	Day HS/EB	Constellation
27. 1	1. 1	G3	J1	Leopard
28. 1	2. 1	G3	K2	Griffon
29. 1	3. 1	G3	A3	Ox
30. 1	4. 1	G3	B4	Bat
31. 1	5. 1	G3	C5	Rat
1. 2	6. 1	G3	D6	Swallow
2. 2	7. 1	G3	E7	Pig
3. 2	8. 1	G3	F8	Porcupine
4. 2	9. 1	G3	G9	Wolf
5. 2	10. 1	G3	H10	Dog
6. 2	11. 1	G3	J11	Pheasant
7. 2	12. 1	G3	K12	Cock
8. 2	13. 1	G3	A1	Crow
9. 2	14. 1	G3	B2	Monkey
10. 2	15. 1	G3	C3	Gibbon
11. 2	16. 1	G3	D4	Tapir
12. 2	17. 1	G3	E5	Sheep
13. 2	18. 1	G3	F6	Deer
14. 2	19. 1	G3	G7	Horse
15. 2	20. 1	G3	H8	Stag
16. 2	21. 1	G3	J9	Serpent
17. 2	22. 1	G3	K10	Earthworm
18. 2	23. 1	G3	A11	Crocodile
19. 2	24. 1	G3	B12	Dragon
20. 2	25. 1	G3	C1	Badger
21. 2	26. 1	G3	D2	Hare
22. 2	27. 1	G3	E3	Fox
23. 2	28. 1	G3	F4	Tiger
24. 2	29. 1	G3	G5	Leopard
25. 2	1. 2	H4	H6	Griffon
26. 2	2. 2	H4	J7	Ox
27. 2	3. 2	H4	K8	Bat

Solar date	Lunar date	Month HS/EB	Day HS/EB	Constellation	Solar date	Lunar date	Month HS/EB	Day HS/EB	Constellation
28. 2	4. 2	H4	A9	Rat	12. 5	18. 4	K6	D10	Earthworm
1. 3	5. 2	H4	B10	Swallow	13. 5	19. 4	K6	E11	Crocodile
2. 3	6. 2	H4	C11	Pig	14. 5	20. 4	K6	F12	Dragon
3. 3	7. 2	H4	D12	Porcupine	15. 5	21. 4	K6	G1	Badger
4. 3	8. 2	H4	E1	Wolf	16. 5	22. 4	K6	H2	Hare
5. 3	9. 2	H4	F2	Dog	17. 5	23. 4	K6	J3	Fox
6. 3	10. 2	H4	G3	Pheasant	18. 5	24. 4	K6	K4	Tiger
7. 3	11. 2	H4	H4	Cock	19. 5	25. 4	K6	A5	Leopard
8. 3	12. 2	H4	J5	Crow	20. 5	26. 4	K6	B6	Griffon
9. 3	13. 2	H4	K6	Monkey	21. 5	27. 4	K6	C7	Ox
10. 3	14. 2	H4	A7	Gibbon	22. 5	28. 4	K6	D8	Bat
11. 3	15. 2	H4	B8	Tapir	23. 5	29. 4	K6	E9	Rat
12. 3	16. 2	H4	C9	Sheep	24. 5	1. 5	A7	F10	Swallow
13. 3	17. 2	H4	D10	Deer	25. 5	2. 5	A7	G11	Pig
14. 3	18. 2	H4	E11	Horse	26. 5	3. 5	A7	H12	Porcupine
15. 3	19. 2	H4	F12	Stag	27. 5	4. 5	A7	J1	Wolf
16. 3	20. 2	H4	G1	Serpent	28. 5	5. 5	A7	K2	Dog
17. 3	21. 2	H4	H2	Earthworm	29. 5	6. 5	A7	A3	Pheasant
18. 3	22. 2	H4	J3	Crocodile	30. 5	7. 5	A7	B4	Cock
19. 3	23. 2	H4	K4	Dragon	31. 5	8. 5	A7	C5	Crow
20. 3	24. 2	H4	A5	Badger	1. 6	9. 5	A7	D6	Monkey
21. 3	25. 2	H4	B6	Hare	2. 6	10. 5	A7	E7	Gibbon
22. 3	26. 2	H4	C7	Fox	3. 6	11. 5	A7	F8	Tapir
23. 3	27. 2	H4	D8	Tiger	4. 6	12. 5	A7	G9	Sheep
24. 3	28. 2	H4	E9	Leopard	5. 6	13. 5	A7	H10	Deer
25. 3	29. 2	H4	F10	Griffon	6. 6	14. 5	A7	J11	Horse
26. 3	30. 2	H4	G11	Ox	7. 6	15. 5	A7	K12	Stag
27. 3	1. 3	J5	H12	Bat	8. 6	16. 5	A7	A1	Serpent
28. 3	2. 3	J5	J1	Rat	9. 6	17. 5	A7	B2	Earthworm
29. 3	3. 3	J5	K2	Swallow	10. 6	18. 5	A7	C3	Crocodile
30. 3	4. 3	J5	A3	Pig	11. 6	19. 5	A7	D4	Dragon
31. 3	5. 3	J5	B4	Porcupine	12. 6	20. 5	A7	E5	Badger
1. 4	6. 3	J5	C5	Wolf	13. 6	21. 5	A7	F6	Hare
2. 4	7. 3	J5	D6	Dog	14. 6	22. 5	A7	G7	Fox
3. 4	8. 3	J5	E7	Pheasant	15. 6	23. 5	A7	H8	Tiger
4. 4	9. 3	J5	F8	Cock	16. 6	24. 5	A7	J9	Leopard
5. 4	10. 3	J5	G9	Crow	17. 6	25. 5	A7	K10	Griffon
6. 4	11. 3	J5	H10	Monkey	18. 6	26. 5	A7	A11	Ox
7. 4	12. 3	J5	J11	Gibbon	19. 6	27. 5	A7	B12	Bat
8. 4	13. 3	J5	K12	Tapir	20. 6	28. 5	A7	C1	Rat
9. 4	14. 3	J5	A1	Sheep	21. 6	29. 5	A7	D2	Swallow
10. 4	15. 3	J5	B2	Deer	22. 6	30. 5	A7	E3	Pig
11. 4	16. 3	J5	C3	Horse	23. 6	*1. 5*	*A7*	F4	Porcupine
12. 4	17. 3	J5	D4	Stag	24. 6	*2. 5*	*A7*	G5	Wolf
13. 4	18. 3	J5	E5	Serpent	25. 6	*3. 5*	*A7*	H6	Dog
14. 4	19. 3	J5	F6	Earthworm	26. 6	*4. 5*	*A7*	J7	Pheasant
15. 4	20. 3	J5	G7	Crocodile	27. 6	*5. 5*	*A7*	K8	Cock
16. 4	21. 3	J5	H8	Dragon	28. 6	*6. 5*	*A7*	A9	Crow
17. 4	22. 3	J5	J9	Badger	29. 6	*7. 5*	*A7*	B10	Monkey
18. 4	23. 3	J5	K10	Hare	30. 6	*8. 5*	*A7*	C11	Gibbon
19. 4	24. 3	J5	A11	Fox	1. 7	*9. 5*	*A7*	D12	Tapir
20. 4	25. 3	J5	B12	Tiger	2. 7	*10. 5*	*A7*	E1	Sheep
21. 4	26. 3	J5	C1	Leopard	3. 7	*11. 5*	*A7*	F2	Deer
22. 4	27. 3	J5	D2	Griffon	4. 7	*12. 5*	*A7*	G3	Horse
23. 4	28. 3	J5	E3	Ox	5. 7	*13. 5*	*A7*	H4	Stag
24. 4	29. 3	J5	F4	Bat	6. 7	*14. 5*	*A7*	J5	Serpent
25. 4	1. 4	K6	G5	Rat	7. 7	*15. 5*	*A7*	K6	Earthworm
26. 4	2. 4	K6	H6	Swallow	8. 7	*16. 5*	*A7*	A7	Crocodile
27. 4	3. 4	K6	J7	Pig	9. 7	*17. 5*	*A7*	B8	Dragon
28. 4	4. 4	K6	K8	Porcupine	10. 7	*18. 5*	*A7*	C9	Badger
29. 4	5. 4	K6	A9	Wolf	11. 7	*19. 5*	*A7*	D10	Hare
30. 4	6. 4	K6	B10	Dog	12. 7	*20. 5*	*A7*	E11	Fox
1. 5	7. 4	K6	C11	Pheasant	13. 7	*21. 5*	*A7*	F12	Tiger
2. 5	8. 4	K6	D12	Cock	14. 7	*22. 5*	*A7*	G1	Leopard
3. 5	9. 4	K6	E1	Crow	15. 7	*23. 5*	*A7*	H2	Griffon
4. 5	10. 4	K6	F2	Monkey	16. 7	*24. 5*	*A7*	J3	Ox
5. 5	11. 4	K6	G3	Gibbon	17. 7	*25. 5*	*A7*	K4	Bat
6. 5	12. 4	K6	H4	Tapir	18. 7	*26. 5*	*A7*	A5	Rat
7. 5	13. 4	K6	J5	Sheep	19. 7	*27. 5*	*A7*	B6	Swallow
8. 5	14. 4	K6	K6	Deer	20. 7	*28. 5*	*A7*	C7	Pig
9. 5	15. 4	K6	A7	Horse	21. 7	*29. 5*	*A7*	D8	Porcupine
10. 5	16. 4	K6	B8	Stag	22. 7	1. 6	B8	E9	Wolf
11. 5	17. 4	K6	C9	Serpent	23. 7	2. 6	B8	F10	Dog

Solar date	Lunar date	Month HS/EB	Day HS/EB	Constellation
24. 7	3. 6	B8	G11	Pheasant
25. 7	4. 6	B8	H12	Cock
26. 7	5. 6	B8	J1	Crow
27. 7	6. 6	B8	K2	Monkey
28. 7	7. 6	B8	A3	Gibbon
29. 7	8. 6	B8	B4	Tapir
30. 7	9. 6	B8	C5	Sheep
31. 7	10. 6	B8	D6	Deer
1. 8	11. 6	B8	E7	Horse
2. 8	12. 6	B8	F8	Stag
3. 8	13. 6	B8	G9	Serpent
4. 8	14. 6	B8	H10	Earthworm
5. 8	15. 6	B8	J11	Crocodile
6. 8	16. 6	B8	K12	Dragon
7. 8	17. 6	B8	A1	Badger
8. 8	18. 6	B8	B2	Hare
9. 8	19. 6	B8	C3	Fox
10. 8	20. 6	B8	D4	Tiger
11. 8	21. 6	B8	E5	Leopard
12. 8	22. 6	B8	F6	Griffon
13. 8	23. 6	B8	G7	Ox
14. 8	24. 6	B8	H8	Bat
15. 8	25. 6	B8	J9	Rat
16. 8	26. 6	B8	K10	Swallow
17. 8	27. 6	B8	A11	Pig
18. 8	28. 6	B8	B12	Porcupine
19. 8	29. 6	B8	C1	Wolf
20. 8	30. 6	B8	D2	Dog
21. 8	1. 7	C9	E3	Pheasant
22. 8	2. 7	C9	F4	Cock
23. 8	3. 7	C9	G5	Crow
24. 8	4. 7	C9	H6	Monkey
25. 8	5. 7	C9	J7	Gibbon
26. 8	6. 7	C9	K8	Tapir
27. 8	7. 7	C9	A9	Sheep
28. 8	8. 7	C9	B10	Deer
29. 8	9. 7	C9	C11	Horse
30. 8	10. 7	C9	D12	Stag
31. 8	11. 7	C9	E1	Serpent
1. 9	12. 7	C9	F2	Earthworm
2. 9	13. 7	C9	G3	Crocodile
3. 9	14. 7	C9	H4	Dragon
4. 9	15. 7	C9	J5	Badger
5. 9	16. 7	C9	K6	Hare
6. 9	17. 7	C9	A7	Fox
7. 9	18. 7	C9	B8	Tiger
8. 9	19. 7	C9	C9	Leopard
9. 9	20. 7	C9	D10	Griffon
10. 9	21. 7	C9	E11	Ox
11. 9	22. 7	C9	F12	Bat
12. 9	23. 7	C9	G1	Rat
13. 9	24. 7	C9	H2	Swallow
14. 9	25. 7	C9	J3	Pig
15. 9	26. 7	C9	K4	Porcupine
16. 9	27. 7	C9	A5	Wolf
17. 9	28. 7	C9	B6	Dog
18. 9	29. 7	C9	C7	Pheasant
19. 9	1. 8	D10	D8	Cock
20. 9	2. 8	D10	E9	Crow
21. 9	3. 8	D10	F10	Monkey
22. 9	4. 8	D10	G11	Gibbon
23. 9	5. 8	D10	H12	Tapir
24. 9	6. 8	D10	J1	Sheep
25. 9	7. 8	D10	K2	Deer
26. 9	8. 8	D10	A3	Horse
27. 9	9. 8	D10	B4	Stag
28. 9	10. 8	D10	C5	Serpent
29. 9	11. 8	D10	D6	Earthworm
30. 9	12. 8	D10	E7	Crocodile
1. 0	13. 8	D10	F8	Dragon
2.10	14. 8	D10	G9	Badger
3.10	15. 8	D10	H10	Hare
4.10	16. 8	D10	J11	Fox
5.10	17. 8	D10	K12	Tiger
6.10	18. 8	D10	A1	Leopard
7.10	19. 8	D10	B2	Griffon
8.10	20. 8	D10	C3	Ox
9.10	21. 8	D10	D4	Bat
10.10	22. 8	D10	E5	Rat
11.10	23. 8	D10	F6	Swallow
12.10	24. 8	D10	G7	Pig
13.10	25. 8	D10	H8	Porcupine
14.10	26. 8	D10	J9	Wolf
15.10	27. 8	D10	K10	Dog
16.10	28. 8	D10	A11	Pheasant
17.10	29. 8	D10	B12	Cock
18.10	30. 8	D10	C1	Crow
19.10	1. 9	E11	D2	Monkey
20.10	2. 9	E11	E3	Gibbon
21.10	3. 9	E11	F4	Tapir
22.10	4. 9	E11	G5	Sheep
23.10	5. 9	E11	H6	Deer
24.10	6. 9	E11	J7	Horse
25.10	7. 9	E11	K8	Stag
26.10	8. 9	E11	A9	Serpent
27.10	9. 9	E11	B10	Earthworm
28.10	10. 9	E11	C11	Crocodile
29.10	11. 9	E11	D12	Dragon
20.10	12. 9	E11	E1	Badger
31.10	13. 9	E11	F2	Hare
1.11	14. 9	E11	G3	Fox
2.11	15. 9	E11	H4	Tiger
3.11	16. 9	E11	J5	Leopard
4.11	17. 9	E11	K6	Griffon
5.11	18. 9	E11	A7	Ox
6.11	19. 9	E11	B8	Bat
7.11	20. 9	E11	C9	Rat
8.11	21. 9	E11	D10	Swallow
9.11	22. 9	E11	E11	Pig
10.11	23. 9	E11	F12	Porcupine
11.11	24. 9	E11	G1	Wolf
12.11	25. 9	E11	H2	Dog
13.11	26. 9	E11	J3	Pheasant
14.11	27. 9	E11	K4	Cock
15.11	28. 9	E11	A5	Crow
16.11	29. 9	E11	B6	Monkey
17.11	30. 9	E11	C7	Gibbon
18.11	1. 10	F12	D8	Tapir
19.11	2. 10	F12	E9	Sheep
20.11	3. 10	F12	F10	Deer
21.11	4. 10	F12	G11	Horse
22.11	5. 10	F12	H12	Stag
23.11	6. 10	F12	J1	Serpent
24.11	7. 10	F12	K2	Earthworm
25.11	8. 10	F12	A3	Crocodile
26.11	9. 10	F12	B4	Dragon
27.11	10.10	F12	C5	Badger
28.11	11.10	F12	D6	Hare
29.11	12.10	F12	E7	Fox
30.11	13.10	F12	F8	Tiger
1.12	14.10	F12	G9	Leopard
2.12	15.10	F12	H10	Griffon
3.12	16.10	F12	J11	Ox
4.12	17.10	F12	K12	Bat
5.12	18.10	F12	A1	Rat
6.12	19.10	F12	B2	Swallow
7.12	20.10	F12	C3	Pig
8.12	21.10	F12	D4	Porcupine
9.12	22.10	F12	E5	Wolf
10.12	23.10	F12	F6	Dog
11.12	24.10	F12	G7	Pheasant
12.12	25.10	F12	H8	Cock
13.12	26.10	F12	J9	Crow
14.12	27.10	F12	K10	Monkey
15.12	28.10	F12	A11	Gibbon
16.12	29.10	F12	B12	Tapir

Solar date	Lunar date	Month HS/EB	Day HS/EB	Constellation	Solar date	Lunar date	Month HS/EB	Day HS/EB	Constellation
17.12	30.10	F12	C1	Sheep	15. 1	29.11	G1	B6	Deer
18.12	1.11	G1	D2	Deer	16. 1	1.12	H2	C7	Horse
19.12	2.11	G1	E3	Horse	17. 1	2.12	H2	D8	Stag
20.12	3.11	G1	F4	Stag	18. 1	3.12	H2	E9	Serpent
21.12	4.11	G1	G5	Serpent	19. 1	4.12	H2	F10	Earthworm
22.12	5.11	G1	H6	Earthworm	20. 1	5.12	H2	G11	Crocodile
23.12	6.11	G1	J7	Crocodile	21. 1	6.12	H2	H12	Dragon
24.12	7.11	G1	K8	Dragon	22. 1	7.12	H2	J1	Badger
25.12	8.11	G1	A9	Badger	23. 1	8.12	H2	K2	Hare
26.12	9.11	G1	B10	Hare	24. 1	9.12	H2	A3	Fox
27.12	10.11	G1	C11	Fox	25. 1	10.12	H2	B4	Tiger
28.12	11.11	G1	D12	Tiger	26. 1	11.12	H2	C5	Leopard
29.12	12.11	G1	E1	Leopard	27. 1	12.12	H2	D6	Griffon
30.12	13.11	G1	F2	Griffon	28. 1	13.12	H2	E7	Ox
31.12	14.11	G1	G3	Ox	29. 1	14.12	H2	F8	Bat
1972					30. 1	15.12	H2	G9	Rat
					31. 1	16.12	H2	H10	Swallow
1. 1	15.11	G1	H4	Bat	1. 2	17.12	H2	J11	Pig
2. 1	16.11	G1	J5	Rat	2. 2	18.12	H2	K12	Porcupine
3. 1	17.11	G1	K6	Swallow	3. 2	19.12	H2	A1	Wolf
4. 1	18.11	G1	A7	Pig	4. 2	20.12	H2	B2	Dog
5. 1	19.11	G1	B8	Porcupine	5. 2	21.12	H2	C3	Pheasant
6. 1	20.11	G1	C9	Wolf	6. 2	22.12	H2	D4	Cock
7. 1	21.11	G1	D10	Dog	7. 2	23.12	H2	E5	Crow
8. 1	22.11	G1	E11	Pheasant	8. 2	24.12	H2	F6	Monkey
9. 1	23.11	G1	F12	Cock	9. 2	25.12	H2	G7	Gibbon
10. 1	24.11	G1	G1	Crow	10. 2	26.12	H2	H8	Tapir
11. 1	25.11	G1	H2	Monkey	11. 2	27.12	H2	J9	Sheep
12. 1	26.11	G1	J3	Gibbon	12. 2	28.12	H2	K10	Deer
13. 1	27.11	G1	K4	Tapir	13. 2	29.12	H2	A11	Horse
14. 1	28.11	G1	A5	Sheep	14. 2	30.12	H2	B12	Stag

JEN TZU YEAR

Solar date	Lunar date	Month HS/EB	Day HS/EB	Constellation	Solar date	Lunar date	Month HS/EB	Day HS/EB	Constellation
15. 2	1. 1	J3	C1	Serpent	23. 3	9. 2	K4	K2	Griffon
16. 2	2. 1	J3	D2	Earthworm	24. 3	10. 2	K4	A3	Ox
17. 2	3. 1	J3	E3	Crocodile	25. 3	11. 2	K4	B4	Bat
18. 2	4. 1	J3	F4	Dragon	26. 3	12. 2	K4	C5	Rat
19. 2	5. 1	J3	G5	Badger	27. 3	13. 2	K4	D6	Swallow
20. 2	6. 1	J3	H6	Hare	28. 3	14. 2	K4	E7	Pig
21. 2	7. 1	J3	J7	Fox	29. 3	15. 2	K4	F8	Porcupine
22. 2	8. 1	J3	K8	Tiger	30. 3	16. 2	K4	G9	Wolf
23. 2	9. 1	J3	A9	Leopard	31. 3	17. 2	K4	H10	Dog
24. 2	10. 1	J3	B10	Griffon	1. 4	18. 2	K4	J11	Pheasant
25. 2	11. 1	J3	C11	Ox	2. 4	19. 2	K4	K12	Cock
26. 2	12. 1	J3	D12	Bat	3. 2	20. 2	K4	A1	Crow
27. 2	13. 1	J3	E1	Rat	4. 4	21. 2	K4	B2	Monkey
28. 2	14. 1	J3	F2	Swallow	5. 4	22. 2	K4	C3	Gibbon
29. 2	15. 1	J3	G3	Pig	6. 4	23. 2	K4	D4	Tapir
1. 3	16. 1	J3	H4	Porcupine	7. 4	24. 2	K4	E5	Sheep
2. 3	17. 1	J3	J5	Wolf	8. 4	25. 2	K4	F6	Deer
3. 3	18. 1	J3	K6	Dog	9. 4	26. 2	K4	G7	Horse
4. 3	19. 1	J3	A7	Pheasant	10. 4	27. 2	K4	H8	Stag
5. 3	20. 1	J3	B8	Cock	11. 4	28. 2	K4	J9	Serpent
6. 3	21. 1	J3	C9	Crow	12. 4	29. 2	K4	K10	Earthworm
7. 3	22. 1	J3	D10	Monkey	13. 4	30. 2	K4	A11	Crocodile
8. 3	23. 1	J3	E11	Gibbon	14. 4	1. 3	A5	B12	Dragon
9. 3	24. 1	J3	F12	Tapir	15. 4	2. 3	A5	C1	Badger
10. 3	25. 1	J3	G1	Sheep	16. 4	3. 3	A5	D2	Hare
11. 3	26. 1	J3	H2	Deer	17. 4	4. 3	A5	E3	Fox
12. 3	27. 1	J3	J3	Horse	18. 4	5. 3	A5	F4	Tiger
13. 3	28. 1	J3	K4	Stag	19. 4	6. 3	A5	G5	Leopard
14. 3	29. 1	J3	A5	Serpent	20. 4	7. 3	A5	H6	Griffon
15. 3	1. 2	K4	B6	Earthworm	21. 4	8. 3	A5	J7	Ox
16. 3	2. 2	K4	C7	Crocodile	22. 4	9. 3	A5	K8	Bat
17. 3	3. 2	K4	D8	Dragon	23. 4	10. 3	A5	A9	Rat
18. 3	4. 2	K4	E9	Badger	24. 4	11. 3	A5	B10	Swallow
19. 3	5. 2	K4	F10	Hare	25. 4	12. 3	A5	C11	Pig
20. 3	6. 2	K4	G11	Fox	26. 4	13. 3	A5	D12	Porcupine
21. 3	7. 2	K4	H12	Tiger	27. 4	14. 3	A5	E1	Wolf
22. 3	8. 2	K4	J1	Leopard	28. 4	15. 3	A5	F2	Dog

Solar date	Lunar date	Month HS/EB	Day HS/EB	Constellation
29. 4	16. 3	A5	G3	Pheasant
30. 4	17. 3	A5	H4	Cock
1. 5	18. 3	A5	J5	Crow
2. 5	19. 3	A5	K6	Monkey
3. 5	20. 3	A5	A7	Gibbon
4. 5	21. 3	A5	B8	Tapir
5. 5	22. 3	A5	C9	Sheep
6. 5	23. 3	A5	D10	Deer
7. 5	24. 3	A5	E11	Horse
8. 5	25. 3	A5	F12	Stag
9. 5	26. 3	A5	G1	Serpent
10. 5	27. 3	A5	H2	Earthworm
11. 5	28. 3	A5	J3	Crocodile
12. 5	29. 3	A5	K4	Dragon
13. 5	1. 4	B6	A5	Badger
14. 5	2. 4	B6	B6	Hare
15. 5	3. 4	B6	C7	Fox
16. 5	4. 4	B6	D8	Tiger
17. 5	5. 4	B6	E9	Leopard
18.. 5	6. 4	B6	F10	Griffon
19. 5	7. 4	B6	G11	Ox
20. 5	8. 4	B6	H12	Bat
21. 5	9. 4	B6	J1	Rat
22. 5	10. 4	B6	K2	Swallow
23. 5	11. 4	B6	A3	Pig
24. 5	12. 4	B6	B4	Porcupine
25. 5	13. 4	B6	C5	Wolf
26. 5	14. 4	B6	D6	Dog
27. 5	15. 4	B6	E7	Pheasant
28. 5	16. 4	B6	F8	Cock
29. 5	17. 4	B6	G9	Crow
30. 5	18. 4	B6	H10	Monkey
31. 5	19. 4	B6	J11	Gibbon
1. 6	20. 4	B6	K12	Tapir
2. 6	21. 4	B6	A1	Sheep
3. 6	22. 4	B6	B2	Deer
4. 6	23. 4	B6	C3	Horse
5. 6	24. 4	B6	D4	Stag
6. 6	25. 4	B6	E5	Serpent
7. 6	26. 4	B6	F6	Earthworm
8. 6	27. 4	B6	G7	Crocodile
9. 6	28. 4	B6	H8	Dragon
10. 6	29. 4	B6	J9	Badger
11. 6	1. 5	C7	K10	Hare
12. 6	2. 5	C7	A11	Fox
13. 6	3. 5	C7	B12	Tiger
14. 6	4. 5	C7	C1	Leopard
15. 6	5. 5	C7	D2	Griffon
16. 6	6. 5	C7	E3	Ox
17. 6	7. 5	C7	F4	Bat
18. 6	8. 5	C7	G5	Rat
19. 6	9. 5	C7	H6	Swallow
20. 6	10. 5	C7	J7	Pig
21. 6	11. 5	C7	K8	Porcupine
22. 6	12. 5	C7	A9	Wolf
23. 6	13. 5	C7	B10	Dog
24. 6	14. 5	C7	C11	Pheasant
25. 6	15. 5	C7	D12	Cock
26. 6	16. 5	C7	E1	Crow
27. 6	17. 5	C7	F2	Monkey
28. 6	18. 5	C7	G3	Gibbon
29. 6	19. 5	C7	H4	Tapir
30. 6	20. 5	C7	J5	Sheep
1. 7	21. 5	C7	K6	Deer
2. 7	22. 5	C7	A7	Horse
3. 7	23. 5	C7	B8	Stag
4. 7	24. 5	C7	C9	Serpent
5. 7	25. 5	C7	D10	Earthworm
6. 7	26. 5	C7	E11	Crocodile
7. 7	27. 5	C7	F12	Dragon
8. 7	28. 5	C7	G1	Badger
9. 7	29. 5	C7	H2	Hare
10. 7	30. 5	C7	J3	Fox
11. 7	1. 6	D8	K4	Tiger
12. 7	2. 6	D8	A5	Leopard
13. 7	3. 6	D8	B6	Griffon
14. 7	4. 6	D8	C7	Ox
15. 7	5. 6	D8	D8	Bat
16. 7	6. 6	D8	E9	Rat
17. 7	7. 6	D8	F10	Swallow
18. 7	8. 6	D8	G11	Pig
19. 7	9. 6	D8	H12	Porcupine
20. 7	10. 6	D8	J1	Wolf
21. 7	11. 6	D8	K2	Dog
22. 7	12. 6	D8	A3	Pheasant
23. 7	13. 6	D8	B4	Cock
24. 7	14. 6	D8	C5	Crow
25. 7	15. 6	D8	D6	Monkey
26. 7	16. 6	D8	E7	Gibbon
27. 7	17. 6	D8	F8	Tapir
28. 7	18. 6	D8	G9	Sheep
29. 7	19. 6	D8	H10	Deer
30. 7	20. 6	D8	J11	Horse
31. 7	21. 6	D8	K12	Stag
1. 8	22. 6	D8	A1	Serpent
2. 8	23. 6	D8	B2	Earthworm
3. 8	24. 6	D8	C3	Crocodile
4. 8	25. 6	D8	D4	Dragon
5. 8	26. 6	D8	E5	Badger
6. 8	27. 6	D8	F6	Hare
7. 8	28. 6	D8	G7	Fox
8. 8	29. 6	D8	H8	Tiger
9. 8	1. 7	E9	J9	Leopard
10. 8	2. 7	E9	K10	Griffon
11. 8	3. 7	E9	A11	Ox
12. 8	4. 7	E9	B12	Bat
13. 8	5. 7	E9	C1	Rat
14. 8	6. 7	E9	D2	Swallow
15. 8	7. 7	E9	E3	Pig
16. 8	8. 7	E9	F4	Porcupine
17. 8	9. 7	E9	G5	Wolf
18. 8	10. 7	E9	H6	Dog
19. 8	11. 7	E9	J7	Pheasant
20. 8	12. 7	E9	K8	Cock
21. 8	13. 7	E9	A9	Crow
22. 8	14. 7	E9	B10	Monkey
23. 8	15. 7	E9	C11	Gibbon
24. 8	16. 7	E9	D12	Tapir
25. 8	17. 7	E9	E1	Sheep
26. 8	18. 7	E9	F2	Deer
27. 8	19. 7	E9	G3	Horse
28. 8	20. 7	E9	H4	Stag
29. 8	21. 7	E9	J5	Serpent
30. 8	22. 7	E9	K6	Earthworm
31. 8	23. 7	E9	A7	Crocodile
1. 9	24. 7	E9	B8	Dragon
2. 9	25. 7	E9	C9	Badger
3. 9	26. 7	E9	D10	Hare
4. 9	27. 7	E9	E11	Fox
5. 9	28. 7	E9	F12	Tiger
6. 9	29. 7	E9	G1	Leopard
7. 9	30. 7	E9	H2	Griffon
8. 9	1. 8	F10	J3	Ox
9. 9	2. 8	F10	K4	Bat
10. 9	3. 8	F10	A5	Rat
11. 9	4. 8	F10	B6	Swallow
12. 9	5. 8	F10	C7	Pig
13. 9	6. 8	F10	D8	Porcupine
14. 9	7. 8	F10	E9	Wolf
15. 9	8. 8	F10	F10	Dog
16. 9	9. 8	F10	G11	Pheasant
17. 9	10. 8	F10	H12	Cock
18. 9	11. 8	F10	J1	Crow
19. 9	12. 8	F10	K2	Monkey
20. 9	13. 8	F10	A3	Gibbon
21. 9	14. 8	F10	B4	Tapir

Solar date	Lunar date	Month HS/EB	Day HS/EB	Constellation
22. 9	15. 8	F10	C5	Sheep
23. 9	16. 8	F10	D6	Deer
24. 9	17. 8	F10	E7	Horse
25. 9	18. 8	F10	F8	Stag
26. 9	19. 8	F10	G9	Serpent
27. 9	20. 8	F10	H10	Earthworm
28. 9	21. 8	F10	J11	Crocodile
29. 9	22. 8	F10	K12	Dragon
30. 9	23. 8	F10	A1	Badger
1.10	24. 8	F10	B2	Hare
2.10	25. 8	F10	C3	Fox
3.10	26. 8	F10	D4	Tiger
4.10	27. 8	F10	E5	Leopard
5.10	28. 8	F10	F6	Griffon
6.10	29. 8	F10	G7	Ox
7.10	1. 9	G11	H8	Bat
8.10	2. 9	G11	J9	Rat
9.10	3. 9	G11	K10	Swallow
10.10	4. 9	G11	A11	Pig
11.10	5. 9	G11	B12	Porcupine
12.10	6. 9	G11	C1	Wolf
13.10	7. 9	G11	D2	Dog
14.10	8. 9	G11	E3	Pheasant
15.10	9. 9	G11	F4	Cock
16.10	10. 9	G11	G5	Crow
17.10	11. 9	G11	H6	Monkey
18.10	12. 9	G11	J7	Gibbon
19.10	13. 9	G11	K8	Tapir
20.10	14. 9	G11	A9	Sheep
21.10	15. 9	G11	B10	Deer
22.10	16. 9	G11	C11	Horse
23.10	17. 9	G11	D12	Stag
24.10	18. 9	G11	E1	Serpent
25.10	19. 9	G11	F2	Earthworm
26.10	20. 9	G11	G3	Crocodile
27.10	21. 9	G11	H4	Dragon
28.10	22. 9	G11	J5	Badger
29.10	23. 9	G11	K6	Hare
30.10	24. 9	G11	A7	Fox
31.10	25. 9	G11	B8	Tiger
1.11	26. 9	G11	C9	Leopard
2.11	27. 9	G11	D10	Griffon
3.11	28. 9	G11	E1	Ox
4.11	29. 9	G11	F12	Bat
5.11	30. 9	G11	G1	Rat
6.11	1.10	H12	H2	Swallow
7.11	2.10	H12	J3	Pig
8.11	3.10	H12	K4	Porcupine
9.11	4.10	H12	A5	Wolf
10.11	5.10	H12	B6	Dog
11.11	6.10	H12	C7	Pheasant
12.11	7.10	H12	D8	Cock
13.11	8.10	H12	E9	Crow
14.11	9.10	H12	F10	Monkey
15.11	10.10	H12	G11	Gibbon
16.11	11.10	H12	H12	Tapir
17.11	12.10	H12	J1	Sheep
18.11	13.10	H12	K2	Deer
19.11	14.10	H12	A3	Horse
20.11	15.10	H12	B4	Stag
21.11	16.10	H12	C5	Serpent
22.11	17.10	H12	D6	Earthworm
23.11	18.10	H12	E7	Crocodile
24.11	19.10	H12	F8	Dragon
25.11	20.10	H12	G9	Badger
26.11	21.10	H12	H10	Hare
27.11	22.10	H12	J11	Fox
28.11	23.10	H12	K12	Tiger
29.11	24.10	H12	A1	Leopard
30.11	25.10	H12	B2	Griffon
1.12	26.10	H12	C3	Ox
2.12	27.10	H12	D4	Bat
3.12	28.10	H12	E5	Rat
4.12	29.10	H12	F6	Swallow
5.12	30.10	H12	G7	Pig
6.12	1.11	J1	H8	Porcupine
7.12	2.11	J1	J9	Wolf
8.12	3.11	J1	K10	Dog
9.12	4.11	J1	A11	Pheasant
10.12	5.11	J1	B12	Cock
11.12	6.11	J1	C1	Crow
12.12	7.11	J1	D2	Monkey
13.12	8.11	J1	E3	Gibbon
14.12	9.11	J1	F4	Tapir
15.12	10.11	J1	G5	Sheep
16.12	11.11	J1	H6	Deer
17.12	12.11	J1	J7	Horse
18.12	13.11	J1	K8	Stag
19.12	14.11	J1	A9	Serpent
20.12	15.11	J1	B10	Earthworm
21.12	16.11	J1	C11	Crocodile
22.12	17.11	J1	D12	Dragon
23.12	18.11	J1	E1	Badger
24.12	19.11	J1	F2	Hare
25.12	20.11	J1	G3	Fox
26.12	21.11	J1	H4	Tiger
27.12	22.11	J1	J5	Leopard
28.12	23.11	J1	K6	Griffon
29.12	24.11	J1	A7	Ox
30.12	25.11	J1	B8	Bat
31.12	26.11	J1	C9	Rat

1973

Solar date	Lunar date	Month HS/EB	Day HS/EB	Constellation
1. 1	27.11	J1	D10	Swallow
2. 1	28.11	J1	E11	Pig
3. 1	29.11	J1	F12	Porcupine
4. 1	1.12	K2	G1	Wolf
5. 1	2.12	K2	H2	Dog
6. 1	3.12	K2	J3	Pheasant
7. 1	4.12	K2	K4	Cock
8. 1	5.12	K2	A5	Crow
9. 1	6.12	K2	B6	Monkey
10. 1	7.12	K2	C7	Gibbon
11. 1	8.12	K2	D8	Tapir
12. 1	9.12	K2	E9	Sheep
13. 1	10.12	K2	F10	Deer
14. 1	11.12	K2	G11	Horse
15. 1	12.12	K2	H12	Stag
16. 1	13.12	K2	J1	Serpent
17. 1	14.12	K2	K2	Earthworm
18. 1	15.12	K2	A3	Crocodile
19. 1	16.12	K2	B4	Dragon
20. 1	17.12	K2	C5	Badger
21. 1	18.12	K2	D6	Hare
22. 1	19.12	K2	E7	Fox
23. 1	20.12	K2	F8	Tiger
24. 1	21.12	K2	G9	Leopard
25. 1	22.12	K2	H10	Griffon
26. 1	23.12	K2	J11	Ox
27. 1	24.12	K2	K12	Bat
28. 1	25.12	K2	A1	Rat
29. 1	26.12	K2	B2	Swallow
30. 1	27.12	K2	C3	Pig
31. 1	28.12	K2	D4	Porcupine
1. 2	29.12	K2	E5	Wolf
2. 2	30.12	K2	F6	Dog

KUEI CH'OU YEAR

Solar date	Lunar date	Month HS/EB	Day HS/EB	Constellation	Solar date	Lunar date	Month HS/EB	Day HS/EB	Constellation
3. 2	1. 1	A3	G7	Pheasant	15. 4	13. 3	C5	H6	Hare
4. 2	2. 1	A3	H8	Cock	16. 4	14. 3	C5	J7	Fox
5. 2	3. 1	A3	J9	Crow	17. 4	15. 3	C5	K8	Tiger
6. 2	4. 1	A3	K10	Monkey	18. 4	16. 3	C5	A9	Leopard
7. 2	5. 1	A3	A11	Gibbon	19. 4	17. 3	C5	B10	Griffon
8. 2	6. 1	A3	B12	Tapir	20. 4	18. 3	C5	C11	Ox
9. 2	7. 1	A3	C1	Sheep	21. 4	19. 3	C5	D12	Bat
10. 2	8. 1	A3	D2	Deer	22. 4	20. 3	C5	E1	Rat
11. 2	9. 1	A3	E3	Horse	23. 4	21. 3	C5	F2	Swallow
12. 2	10. 1	A3	F4	Stag	24. 4	22. 3	C5	G3	Pig
13. 2	11. 1	A3	G5	Serpent	25. 4	23. 3	C5	H4	Porcupine
14. 2	12. 1	A3	H6	Earthworm	26. 4	24. 3	C5	J5	Wolf
15. 2	13. 1	A3	J7	Crocodile	27. 4	25. 3	C5	K6	Dog
16. 2	14. 1	A3	K8	Dragon	28. 4	26. 3	C5	A7	Pheasant
17. 2	15. 1	A3	A9	Badger	29. 4	27. 3	C5	B8	Cock
18. 2	16. 1	A3	B10	Hare	30. 4	28. 3	C5	C9	Crow
19. 2	17. 1	A3	C11	Fox	1. 5	29. 3	C5	D10	Monkey
20. 2	18. 1	A3	D12	Tiger	2. 5	30. 3	C5	E11	Gibbon
21. 2	19. 1	A3	E1	Leopard	3. 5	1. 4	D6	F12	Tapir
22. 2	20. 1	A3	F2	Griffon	4. 5	2. 4	D6	G1	Sheep
23. 2	21. 1	A3	G3	Ox	5. 5	3. 4	D6	H2	Deer
24. 2	22. 1	A3	H4	Bat	6. 5	4. 4	D6	J3	Horse
25. 2	23. 1	A3	J5	Rat	7. 5	5. 4	D6	K4	Stag
26. 2	24. 1	A3	K6	Swallow	8. 5	6. 4	D6	A5	Serpent
27. 2	25. 1	A3	A7	Pig	9. 5	7. 4	D6	B6	Earthworm
28. 2	26. 1	A3	B8	Porcupine	10. 5	8. 4	D6	C7	Crocodile
1. 3	27. 1	A3	C9	Wolf	11. 5	9. 4	D6	D8	Dragon
2. 3	28. 1	A3	D10	Dog	12. 5	10. 4	D6	E9	Badger
3. 3	29. 1	A3	E11	Pheasant	13. 5	11. 4	D6	F10	Hare
4. 3	30. 1	A3	F12	Cock	14. 5	12. 4	D6	G11	Fox
5. 3	1. 2	B4	G1	Crow	15. 5	13. 4	D6	H12	Tiger
6. 3	2. 2	B4	H2	Monkey	16. 5	14. 4	D6	J1	Leopard
7. 3	3. 2	B4	J3	Gibbon	17. 5	15. 4	D6	K2	Griffon
8. 3	4. 2	B4	K4	Tapir	18. 5	16. 4	D6	A3	Ox
9. 3	5. 2	B4	A5	Sheep	19. 5	17. 4	D6	B4	Bat
10. 3	6. 2	B4	B6	Deer	20. 5	18. 4	D6	C5	Rat
11. 3	7. 2	B4	C7	Horse	21. 5	19. 4	D6	D6	Swallow
12. 3	8. 2	B4	D8	Stag	22. 5	20. 4	D6	E7	Pig
13. 3	9. 2	B4	E9	Serpent	23. 5	21. 4	D6	F8	Porcupine
14. 3	10. 2	B4	F10	Earthworm	24. 5	22. 4	D6	G9	Wolf
15. 3	11. 2	B4	G11	Crocodile	25. 5	23. 4	D6	H10	Dog
16. 3	12. 2	B4	H12	Dragon	26. 5	24. 4	D6	J11	Pheasant
17. 3	13. 2	B4	J1	Badger	27. 5	25. 4	D6	K12	Cock
18. 3	14. 2	B4	K2	Hare	28. 5	26. 4	D6	A1	Crow
19. 3	15. 2	B4	A3	Fox	29. 5	27. 4	D6	B2	Monkey
20. 3	16. 2	B4	B4	Tiger	30. 5	28. 4	D4	C3	Gibbon
21. 3	17. 2	B4	C5	Leopard	31. 5	29. 4	D4	D4	Tapir
22. 3	18. 2	B4	D6	Griffon	1. 6	1. 5	E7	E5	Sheep
23. 3	19. 2	B4	E7	Ox	2. 6	2. 5	E7	F6	Deer
24. 3	20. 2	B4	F8	Bat	3. 6	3. 5	E7	G7	Horse
25. 3	21. 2	B4	G9	Rat	4. 6	4. 5	E7	H8	Stag
26. 3	22. 2	B4	H10	Swallow	5. 6	5. 5	E7	J9	Serpent
27. 3	23. 2	B4	J11	Pig	6. 6	6. 5	E7	K10	Earthworm
28. 3	24. 2	B4	K12	Porcupine	7. 6	7. 5	E7	A11	Crocodile
29. 3	25. 2	B4	A1	Wolf	8. 6	8. 5	E7	B12	Dragon
30. 3	26. 2	B4	B2	Dog	9. 6	9. 5	E7	C1	Badger
31. 3	27. 2	B4	C3	Pheasant	10. 6	10. 5	E7	D2	Hare
1. 4	28. 2	B4	D4	Cock	11. 6	11. 5	E7	E3	Fox
2. 4	29. 2	B4	E5	Crow	12. 6	12. 5	E7	F4	Tiger
3. 4	1. 3	C5	F6	Monkey	13. 6	13. 5	E7	G5	Leopard
4. 4	2. 3	C5	G7	Gibbon	14. 6	14. 5	E7	H6	Griffon
5. 4	3. 3	C5	H8	Tapir	15. 6	15. 5	E7	J7	Ox
6. 4	4. 3	C5	J9	Sheep	16. 6	16. 5	E7	K8	Bat
7. 4	5. 3	C5	K10	Deer	17. 6	17. 5	E7	A9	Rat
8. 4	6. 3	C5	A11	Horse	18. 6	18. 5	E7	B10	Swallow
9. 4	7. 3	C5	B12	Stag	19. 6	19. 5	E7	C11	Pig
10. 4	8. 3	C5	C1	Serpent	20. 6	20. 5	E7	D12	Porcupine
11. 4	9. 3	C5	D2	Earthworm	21. 6	21. 5	E7	E1	Wolf
12. 4	10. 3	C5	E3	Crocodile	22. 6	22. 5	E7	F2	Dog
13. 4	11. 3	C5	F4	Dragon	23. 6	23. 5	E7	G3	Pheasant
14. 4	12. 3	C5	G5	Badger	24. 6	24. 5	E7	H4	Cock

Solar date	Lunar date	Month HS/EB	Day HS/EB	Constellation
25. 6	25. 5	E7	J5	Crow
26. 6	26. 5	E7	K6	Monkey
27. 6	27. 5	E7	A7	Gibbon
28. 6	28. 5	E7	B8	Tapir
29. 6	29. 5	E7	C9	Sheep
30. 6	1. 6	F8	D10	Deer
1. 7	2. 6	F8	E11	Horse
2. 7	3. 6	F8	F12	Stag
3. 7	4. 6	F8	G1	Serpent
4. 7	5. 6	F8	H2	Earthworm
5. 7	6. 6	F8	J3	Crocodile
6. 7	7. 6	F8	K4	Dragon
7. 7	8. 6	F8	A5	Badger
8. 7	9. 6	F8	B6	Hare
9. 7	10. 6	F8	C7	Fox
10. 7	11. 6	F8	D8	Tiger
11. 7	12. 6	F8	E9	Leopard
12. 7	13. 6	F8	F10	Griffon
13. 7	14. 6	F8	G11	Ox
14. 7	15. 6	F8	H12	Bat
15. 7	16. 6	F8	J1	Rat
16. 7	17. 6	F8	K2	Swallow
17. 7	18. 6	F8	A3	Pig
18. 7	19. 6	F8	B4	Porcupine
19. 7	20. 6	F8	C5	Wolf
20. 7	21. 6	F8	D6	Dog
21. 7	22. 6	F8	E7	Pheasant
22. 7	23. 6	F8	F8	Cock
23. 7	24. 6	F8	G9	Crow
24. 7	25. 6	F8	H10	Monkey
25. 7	26. 6	F8	J11	Gibbon
26. 7	27. 6	F8	K12	Tapir
27. 7	28. 6	F8	A1	Sheep
28. 7	29. 6	F8	B2	Deer
29. 7	30. 6	F8	C3	Horse
30. 7	1. 7	G9	D4	Stag
31. 7	2. 7	G9	E5	Serpent
1. 8	3. 7	G9	F6	Earthworm
2. 8	4. 7	G9	G7	Crocodile
3. 8	5. 7	G9	H8	Dragon
4. 8	6. 7	G9	J9	Badger
5. 8	7. 7	G9	K10	Hare
6. 8	8. 7	G9	A11	Fox
7. 8	9. 7	G9	B12	Tiger
8. 8	10. 7	G9	C1	Leopard
9. 8	11. 7	G9	D2	Griffon
10. 8	12. 7	G9	E3	Ox
11. 8	13. 7	G9	F4	Bat
12. 8	14. 7	G9	G5	Rat
13. 8	15. 7	G9	H6	Swallow
14. 8	16. 7	G9	J7	Pig
15. 8	17. 7	G9	K8	Porcupine
16. 8	18. 7	G9	A9	Wolf
17. 8	19. 7	G9	B10	Dog
18. 8	20. 7	G9	C11	Pheasant
19. 8	21. 7	G9	D12	Cock
20. 8	22. 7	G9	E1	Crow
21. 8	23. 7	G9	F2	Monkey
22. 8	24. 7	G9	G3	Gibbon
23. 8	25. 7	G9	H4	Tapir
24. 8	26. 7	G9	J5	Sheep
25. 8	27. 7	G9	K6	Deer
26. 8	28. 7	G9	A7	Horse
27. 8	29. 7	G9	B8	Stag
28. 8	1. 8	H10	C9	Serpent
29. 8	2. 8	H10	D10	Earthworm
30. 8	3. 8	H10	E11	Crocodile
31. 8	4. 8	H10	F12	Dragon
1. 9	5. 8	H10	G1	Badger
2. 9	6. 8	H10	H2	Hare
3. 9	7. 8	H10	J3	Fox
4. 9	8. 8	H10	K4	Tiger
5. 9	9. 8	H10	A5	Leopard
6. 9	10. 8	H10	B6	Griffon
7. 9	11. 8	H10	C7	Ox
8. 9	12. 8	H10	D8	Bat
9. 9	13. 8	H10	E9	Rat
10. 9	14. 8	H10	F10	Swallow
11. 9	15. 8	H10	G11	Pig
12. 9	16. 8	H10	H12	Porcupine
13. 9	17. 8	H10	J1	Wolf
14. 9	18. 8	H10	K2	Dog
15. 9	19. 8	H10	A3	Pheasant
16. 9	20. 8	H10	B4	Cock
17. 9	21. 8	H10	C5	Crow
18. 9	22. 8	H10	D6	Monkey
19. 9	23. 8	H10	E7	Gibbon
20. 9	24. 8	H10	F8	Tapir
21. 9	25. 8	H10	G9	Sheep
22. 9	26. 8	H10	H10	Deer
23. 9	27. 8	H10	J11	Horse
24. 9	28. 8	H10	K12	Stag
25. 9	29. 8	H10	A1	Serpent
26. 9	1. 9	J11	B2	Earthworm
27. 9	2. 9	J11	C3	Crocodile
28. 9	3. 9	J11	D4	Dragon
29. 9	4. 9	J11	E5	Badger
30. 9	5. 9	J11	F6	Hare
1.10	6. 9	J11	G7	Fox
2.10	7. 9	J11	H8	Tiger
3.10	8. 9	J11	J9	Leopard
4.10	9. 9	J11	K10	Griffon
5.10	10. 9	J11	A11	Ox
6.10	11. 9	J11	B12	Bat
7.10	12. 9	J11	C1	Rat
8.10	13. 9	J11	D2	Swallow
9.10	14. 9	J11	E3	Pig
10.10	15. 9	J11	F4	Porcupine
11. 0	16. 9	J11	G5	Wolf
12.10	17. 9	J11	H6	Dog
13.10	18. 9	J11	J7	Pheasant
14.10	19. 9	J11	K8	Cock
15.10	20. 9	J11	A9	Crow
16.10	21. 9	J11	B10	Monkey
17.10	22. 9	J11	C11	Gibbon
18.10	23. 9	J11	D12	Tapir
19.10	24. 9	J11	E1	Sheep
20.10	25. 9	J11	F2	Deer
21.10	26. 9	J11	G3	Horse
22.10	27. 9	J11	H4	Stag
23.10	28. 9	J11	J5	Serpent
24.10	29. 9	J11	K6	Earthworm
25.10	30. 9	J11	A7	Crocodile
26.10	1.10	K12	B8	Dragon
27.10	2.10	K12	C9	Badger
28.10	3.10	K12	D10	Hare
29.10	4.10	K12	E11	Fox
30.10	5.10	K12	F12	Tiger
31.10	6.10	K12	G1	Leopard
1.11	7.10	K12	H2	Griffon
2.11	8.10	K12	J3	Ox
3.11	9.10	K12	K4	Bat
4.11	10.10	K12	A5	Rat
5.11	11.10	K12	B6	Swallow
6.11	12.10	K12	C7	Pig
7.11	13.10	K12	D8	Porcupine
8.11	14.10	K12	E9	Wolf
9.11	15.10	K12	F10	Dog
10.11	16.10	K12	G11	Pheasant
11.11	17.10	K12	H12	Cock
12.11	18.10	K12	J1	Crow
13.11	19.10	K12	K2	Monkey
14.11	20.10	K12	A3	Gibbon
15.11	21.10	K12	B4	Tapir
16.11	22.10	K12	C5	Sheep
17.11	23.10	K12	D6	Deer

Solar date	Lunar date	Month HS/EB	Day HS/EB	Constellation	Solar date	Lunar date	Month HS/EB	Day HS/EB	Constellation
18.11	24.10	K12	E7	Horse	22.12	28.11	A1	J5	Badger
19.11	25.10	K12	F8	Stag	23.12	29.11	A1	K6	Hare
20.11	26.10	K12	G9	Serpent	24.12	1.12	B2	A7	Fox
21.11	27.10	K12	H10	Earthworm	25.12	2.12	B2	B8	Tiger
22.11	28.10	K12	J11	Crocodile	26.12	3.12	B2	C9	Leopard
23.11	29.10	K12	K12	Dragon	27.12	4.12	B2	D10	Griffon
24.11	30.10	K12	A1	Badger	28.12	5.12	B2	E11	Ox
25.11	1.11	A1	B2	Hare	29.12	6.12	B2	F12	Bat
26.11	2.11	A1	C3	Fox	30.12	7.12	B2	G1	Rat
27.11	3.11	A1	D4	Tiger	31.12	8.12	B2	H2	Swallow
28.11	4.11	A1	E5	Leopard					
29.11	5.11	A1	F6	Griffon	**1974**				
30.11	6.11	A1	G7	Ox	1. 1	9.12	B2	J3	Pig
1.12	7.11	A1	H8	Bat	2. 1	10.12	B2	K4	Porcupine
2.12	8.11	A1	J9	Rat	3. 1	11.12	B2	A5	Wolf
3.12	9.11	A1	K10	Swallow	4. 1	12.12	B2	B6	Dog
4.12	10.11	A1	A11	Pig	5. 1	13.12	B2	C7	Pheasant
5.12	11.11	A1	B12	Porcupine	6. 1	14.12	B2	D8	Cock
6.12	12.11	A1	C1	Wolf	7. 1	15.12	B2	E9	Crow
7.12	13.11	A1	D2	Dog	8. 1	16.12	B2	F10	Monkey
8.12	14.11	A1	E3	Pheasant	9. 1	17.12	B2	G11	Gibbon
9.12	15.11	A1	F4	Cock	10. 1	18.12	B2	H12	Tapir
10.12	16.11	A1	G5	Crow	11. 1	19.12	B2	J1	Sheep
11.12	17.11	A1	H6	Monkey	12. 1	20.12	B2	K2	Deer
12.12	18.11	A1	J7	Gibbon	13. 1	21.12	B2	A3	Horse
13.12	19.11	A1	K8	Tapir	14. 1	22.12	B2	B4	Stag
14.12	20.11	A1	A9	Sheep	15. 1	23.12	B2	C5	Serpent
15.12	21.11	A1	B10	Deer	16. 1	24.12	B2	D6	Earthworm
16.12	22.11	A1	C11	Horse	17. 1	25.12	B2	E7	Crocodile
17.12	23.11	A1	D12	Stag	18. 1	26.12	B2	F8	Dragon
18.12	24.11	A1	E1	Serpent	19. 1	27.12	B2	G9	Badger
19.12	25.11	A1	F2	Earthworm	20. 1	28.12	B2	H10	Hare
20.12	26.11	A1	G3	Crocodile	21. 1	29.12	B2	J11	Fox
21.12	27.11	A1	H4	Dragon	22. 1	30.12	B2	K12	Tiger

CHIA YIN YEAR

Solar date	Lunar date	Month HS/EB	Day HS/EB	Constellation	Solar date	Lunar date	Month HS/EB	Day HS/EB	Constellation
23. 1	1. 1	C3	A1	Leopard	26. 2	5. 2	D4	E11	Pig
24. 1	2. 1	C3	B2	Griffon	27. 2	6. 2	D4	F12	Porcupine
25. 1	3. 1	C3	C3	Ox	28. 2	7. 2	D4	G1	Wolf
26. 1	4. 1	C3	D4	Bat	1. 3	8. 2	D4	H2	Dog
27. 1	5. 1	C3	E5	Rat	2. 3	9. 2	D4	J3	Pheasant
28. 1	6. 1	C3	F6	Swallow	3. 3	10. 2	D4	K4	Cock
29. 1	7. 1	C3	G7	Pig	4. 3	11. 2	D4	A5	Crow
30. 1	8. 1	C3	H8	Porcupine	5. 3	12. 2	D4	B6	Monkey
31. 1	9. 1	C3	J9	Wolf	6. 3	13. 2	D4	C7	Gibbon
1. 2	10. 1	C3	K10	Dog	7. 3	14. 2	D4	D8	Tapir
2. 2	11. 1	C3	A11	Pheasant	8. 3	15. 2	D4	E9	Sheep
3. 2	12. 1	C3	B12	Cock	9. 3	16. 2	D4	F10	Deer
4. 2	13. 1	C3	C1	Crow	10. 3	17. 2	D4	G11	Horse
5. 2	14. 1	C3	D2	Monkey	11. 3	18. 2	D4	H12	Stag
6. 2	15. 1	C3	E3	Gibbon	12. 3	19. 2	D4	J1	Serpent
7. 2	16. 1	C3	F4	Tapir	13. 3	20. 2	D4	K2	Earthworm
8. 2	17. 1	C3	G5	Sheep	14. 3	21. 2	D4	A3	Crocodile
9. 2	18. 1	C3	H6	Deer	15. 3	22. 2	D4	B4	Dragon
10. 2	19. 1	C3	J7	Horse	16. 3	23. 2	D4	C5	Badger
11. 2	20. 1	C3	K8	Stag	17. 3	24. 2	D4	D6	Hare
12. 2	21. 1	C3	A9	Serpent	18. 3	25. 2	D4	E7	Fox
13. 2	22. 1	C3	B10	Earthworm	19. 3	26. 2	D4	F8	Tiger
14. 2	23. 1	C3	C11	Crocodile	20. 3	27. 2	D4	G9	Leopard
15. 2	24. 1	C3	D12	Dragon	21. 3	28. 2	D4	H10	Griffon
16. 2	25. 1	C3	E1	Badger	22. 3	29. 2	D4	J11	Ox
17. 2	26. 1	C3	F2	Hare	23. 3	30. 2	D4	K12	Bat
18. 2	27. 1	C3	G3	Fox	24. 3	1. 3	E5	A1	Rat
19. 2	28. 1	C3	H4	Tiger	25. 3	2. 3	E5	B2	Swallow
20. 2	29. 1	C3	J5	Leopard	26. 3	3. 3	E5	C3	Pig
21. 2	30. 1	C3	K6	Griffon	27. 3	4. 3	E5	D4	Porcupine
22. 2	1. 2	D4	A7	Ox	28. 3	5. 3	E5	E5	Wolf
23. 2	2. 2	D4	B8	Bat	29. 3	6. 3	E5	F6	Dog
24. 2	3. 2	D4	C9	Rat	30. 3	7. 3	E5	G7	Pheasant
25. 2	4. 2	D4	D10	Swallow	31. 3	8. 3	E5	H8	Cock

Solar date	Lunar date	Month HS/EB	Day HS/EB	Constellation	Solar date	Lunar date	Month HS/EB	Day HS/EB	Constellation
1. 4	9. 3	E5	J9	Crow	13. 6	23. 4	F6	B10	Griffon
2. 4	10. 3	E5	K10	Monkey	14. 6	24. 4	F6	C11	Ox
3. 4	11. 3	E5	A11	Gibbon	15. 6	25. 4	F6	D12	Bat
4. 4	12. 3	E5	B12	Tapir	16. 6	26. 4	F6	E1	Rat
5. 4	13. 3	E5	C1	Sheep	17. 6	27. 4	F6	F2	Swallow
6. 4	14. 3	E5	D2	Deer	18. 6	28. 4	F6	G3	Pig
7. 4	15. 3	E5	E3	Horse	19. 6	29. 4	F6	H4	Porcupine
8. 4	16. 3	E5	F4	Stag	20. 6	1. 5	G7	J5	Wolf
9. 4	17. 3	E5	G5	Serpent	21. 6	2. 5	G7	K6	Dog
10. 4	18. 3	E5	H6	Earthworm	22. 6	3. 5	G7	A7	Pheasant
11. 4	19. 3	E5	J7	Crocodile	23. 6	4. 5	G7	B8	Cock
12. 4	20. 3	E5	K8	Dragon	24. 6	5. 5	G7	C9	Crow
13. 4	21. 3	E5	A9	Badger	25. 6	6. 5	G7	D10	Monkey
14. 4	22. 3	E5	B10	Hare	26. 6	7. 5	G7	E11	Gibbon
15. 4	23. 3	E5	C11	Fox	27. 6	8. 5	G7	F12	Tapir
16. 4	24. 3	E5	D12	Tiger	28. 6	9. 5	G7	G1	Sheep
17. 4	25. 3	E5	E1	Leopard	29. 6	10. 5	G7	H2	Deer
18. 4	26. 3	E5	F2	Griffon	30. 6	11. 5	G7	J3	Horse
19. 4	27. 3	E5	G3	Ox	1. 7	12. 5	G7	K4	Stag
20. 4	28. 3	E5	H4	Bat	2. 7	13. 5	G7	A5	Serpent
21. 4	29. 3	E5	J5	Rat	3. 7	14. 5	G7	B6	Earthworm
22. 4	1. 4	F6	K6	Swallow	4. 7	15. 5	G7	C7	Crocodile
23. 4	2. 4	F6	A7	Pig	5. 7	16. 5	G7	D8	Dragon
24. 4	3. 4	F6	B8	Porcupine	6. 7	17. 5	G7	E9	Badger
25. 4	4. 4	F6	C9	Wolf	7. 7	18. 5	G7	F10	Hare
26. 4	5. 4	F6	D10	Dog	8. 7	19. 5	G7	G11	Fox
27. 4	6. 4	F6	E11	Pheasant	9. 7	20. 5	G7	H12	Tiger
28. 4	7. 4	F6	F12	Cock	10. 7	21. 5	G7	J1	Leopard
29. 4	8. 4	F6	G1	Crow	11. 7	22. 5	G7	K2	Griffon
30. 4	9. 4	F6	H2	Monkey	12. 7	23. 5	G7	A3	Ox
1. 5	10. 4	F6	J3	Gibbon	13. 7	24. 5	G7	B4	Bat
2. 5	11. 4	F6	K4	Tapir	14. 7	25. 5	G7	C5	Rat
3. 5	12. 4	F6	A5	Sheep	15. 7	26. 5	G7	D6	Swallow
4. 5	13. 4	F6	B6	Deer	16. 7	27. 5	G7	E7	Pig
5. 5	14. 4	F6	C7	Horse	17. 7	28. 5	G7	F8	Porcupine
6. 5	15. 4	F6	D8	Stag	18. 7	29. 5	G7	G9	Wolf
7. 5	16. 4	F6	E9	Serpent	19. 7	1. 6	H8	H10	Dog
8. 5	17. 4	F6	F10	Earthworm	20. 7	2. 6	H8	J11	Pheasant
9. 5	18. 4	F6	G11	Crocodile	21. 7	3. 6	H8	K12	Cock
10. 5	19. 4	F6	H12	Dragon	22. 7	4. 6	H8	A1	Crow
11. 5	20. 4	F6	J1	Badger	23. 7	5. 6	H8	B2	Monkey
12. 5	21. 4	F6	K2	Hare	24. 7	6. 6	H8	C3	Gibbon
13. 5	22. 4	F6	A3	Fox	25. 7	7. 6	H8	D4	Tapir
14. 5	23. 4	F6	B4	Tiger	26. 7	8. 6	H8	E5	Sheep
15. 5	24. 4	F6	C5	Leopard	27. 7	9. 6	H8	F6	Deer
16. 5	25. 4	F6	D6	Griffon	28. 7	10. 6	H8	F7	Horse
17. 5	26. 4	F6	E7	Ox	29. 7	11. 6	H8	H8	Stag
18. 5	27. 4	F6	F8	Bat	30. 7	12. 6	H8	J9	Serpent
19. 5	28. 4	F6	G9	Rat	31. 7	13. 6	H8	K10	Earthworm
20. 5	29. 4	F6	H10	Swallow	1. 8	14. 6	H8	A11	Crocodile
21. 5	30. 4	F6	J11	Pig	2. 8	15. 6	H8	B12	Dragon
22. 5	*1. 4*	*F6*	K12	Porcupine	3. 8	16. 6	H8	C1	Badger
23. 5	*2. 4*	*F6*	A1	Wolf	4. 8	17. 6	H8	D2	Hare
24. 5	*3. 4*	*F6*	B2	Dog	5. 8	18. 6	H8	E3	Fox
25. 5	*4. 4*	*F6*	C3	Pheasant	6. 8	19. 6	H8	F4	Tiger
26. 5	*5. 4*	*F6*	D4	Cock	7. 8	20. 6	H8	G5	Leopard
27. 5	*6. 4*	*F6*	E5	Crow	8. 8	21. 6	H8	H6	Griffon
28. 5	*7. 4*	*F6*	F6	Monkey	9. 8	22. 6	H8	J7	Ox
29. 5	*8. 4*	*F6*	G7	Gibbon	10. 8	23. 6	H8	K8	Bat
30. 5	*9. 4*	*F6*	H8	Tapir	11. 8	24. 6	H8	A9	Rat
31. 5	*10. 4*	*F6*	J9	Sheep	12. 8	25. 6	H8	B10	Swallow
1. 6	*11. 4*	*F6*	K10	Deer	13. 8	26. 6	H8	C11	Pig
2. 6	*12. 4*	*F6*	A11	Horse	14. 8	27. 6	H8	D12	Porcupine
3. 6	*13. 4*	*F6*	B12	Stag	15. 8	28. 6	H8	E1	Wolf
4. 6	*14. 4*	*F6*	C1	Serpent	16. 8	29. 6	H8	F2	Dog
5. 6	*15. 4*	*F6*	D2	Earthworm	17. 8	30. 6	H8	G3	Pheasant
6. 6	*16. 4*	*F6*	E3	Crocodile	18. 8	1. 7	J9	H4	Cock
7. 6	*17. 4*	*F6*	F4	Dragon	19. 8	2. 7	J9	J5	Crow
8. 6	*18. 4*	*F6*	G5	Badger	20. 8	3. 7	J9	K6	Monkey
9. 6	*19. 4*	*F6*	H6	Hare	21. 8	4. 7	J9	A7	Gibbon
10. 6	*20. 4*	*F6*	J7	Fox	22. 8	5. 7	J9	B8	Tapir
11. 6	*21. 4*	*F6*	K8	Tiger	23. 8	6. 7	J9	C9	Sheep
12. 6	*22. 4*	*F6*	A9	Leopard	24. 8	7. 7	J9	D10	Deer

Solar date	Lunar date	Month HS/EB	Day HS/EB	Constellation	Solar date	Lunar date	Month HS/EB	Day HS/EB	Constellation
25. 8	8. 7	J9	E11	Horse	6.11	23. 9	A11	H12	Porcupine
26. 8	9. 7	J9	F12	Stag	7.11	24. 9	A11	J1	Wolf
27. 8	10. 7	J9	G1	Serpent	8.11	25. 9	A11	K2	Dog
28. 8	11. 7	J9	H2	Earthworm	9.11	26. 9	A11	A3	Pheasant
29. 8	12. 7	J9	J3	Crocodile	10.11	27. 9	A11	B4	Cock
30. 8	13. 7	J9	K4	Dragon	11.11	28. 9	A11	C5	Crow
31. 8	14. 7	J9	A5	Badger	12.11	29. 9	A11	D6	Monkey
1. 9	15. 7	J9	B6	Hare	13.11	30. 9	A11	E7	Gibbon
2. 9	16. 7	J9	C7	Fox	14.11	1.10	B12	F8	Tapir
3. 9	17. 7	J9	D8	Tiger	15.11	2.10	B12	G9	Sheep
4. 9	18. 7	J9	E9	Leopard	16.11	3.10	B12	H10	Deer
5. 9	19. 7	J9	F10	Griffon	17.11	4.10	B12	J11	Horse
6. 9	20. 7	J9	G11	Ox	18.11	5.10	B12	K12	Stag
7. 9	21. 7	J9	H12	Bat	19.11	6.10	B12	A1	Serpent
8. 9	22. 7	J9	J1	Rat	20.11	7.10	B12	B2	Earthworm
9. 9	23. 7	J9	K2	Swallow	21.11	8.10	B12	C3	Crocodile
10. 9	24. 7	J9	A3	Pig	22.11	9.10	B12	D4	Dragon
11. 9	25. 7	J9	B4	Porcupine	23.11	10.10	B12	E5	Badger
12. 9	26. 7	J9	C5	Wolf	24.11	11.10	B12	F6	Hare
13. 9	27. 7	J9	D6	Dog	25.11	12.10	B12	G7	Fox
14. 9	28. 7	J9	E7	Pheasant	26.11	13.10	B12	H8	Tiger
15. 9	29. 7	J9	F8	Cock	27.11	14.10	B12	J9	Leopard
16. 9	1. 8	K10	G9	Crow	28.11	15.10	B12	K10	Griffon
17. 9	2. 8	K10	H10	Monkey	29.11	16.10	B12	A11	Ox
18. 9	3. 8	K10	J11	Gibbon	30.11	17.10	B12	B12	Bat
19. 9	4. 8	K10	K12	Tapir	1.12	18.10	B12	C1	Rat
20. 9	5. 8	K10	A1	Sheep	2.12	19.10	B12	D2	Swallow
21. 9	6. 8	K10	B2	Deer	3.12	20.10	B12	E3	Pig
22. 9	7. 8	K10	C3	Horse	4.12	21.10	B12	F4	Porcupine
23. 9	8. 8	K10	D4	Stag	5.12	22.10	B12	G5	Wolf
24. 9	9. 8	K10	E5	Serpent	6.12	23.10	B12	H6	Dog
25. 9	10. 8	K10	F6	Earthworm	7.12	24.10	B12	J7	Pheasant
26. 9	11. 8	K10	G7	Crocodile	8.12	25.10	B12	K8	Cock
27. 9	12. 8	K10	H8	Dragon	9.12	26.10	B12	A9	Crow
28. 9	13. 8	K10	J9	Badger	10.12	27.10	B12	B10	Monkey
29. 9	14. 8	K10	K10	Hare	11.12	28.10	B12	C11	Gibbon
30. 9	15. 8	K10	A11	Fox	12.12	29.10	B12	D12	Tapir
1.10	16. 8	K10	B12	Tiger	13.12	30.10	B12	E1	Sheep
2.10	17. 8	K10	C1	Leopard	14.12	1.11	C1	F2	Deer
3.10	18. 8	K10	D2	Griffon	15.12	2.11	C1	G3	Horse
4.10	19. 8	K10	E3	Ox	16.12	3.11	C1	H4	Stag
5.10	20. 8	K10	F4	Bat	17.12	4.11	C1	J5	Serpent
6.10	21. 8	K10	G5	Rat	18.12	5.11	C1	K6	Earthworm
7.10	22. 8	K10	H6	Swallow	19.12	6.11	C1	A7	Crocodile
8.10	23. 8	K10	J7	Pig	20.12	7.11	C1	B8	Dragon
9.10	24. 8	K10	K8	Porcupine	21.12	8.11	C1	C9	Badger
10.10	25. 8	K10	A9	Wolf	22.12	9.11	C1	D10	Hare
11.10	26. 8	K10	B10	Dog	23.12	10.11	C1	E11	Fox
12.10	27. 8	K10	C11	Pheasant	24.12	11.11	C1	F12	Tiger
13.10	28. 8	K10	D12	Cock	25.12	12.11	C1	G1	Leopard
14.10	29. 8	K10	E1	Crow	26.12	13.11	C1	H2	Griffon
15.10	1. 9	A11	F2	Monkey	27.12	14.11	C1	J3	Ox
16.10	2. 9	A11	G3	Gibbon	28.12	15.11	C1	K4	Bat
17.10	3. 9	A11	H4	Tapir	29.12	16.11	C1	A5	Rat
18.10	4. 9	A11	J5	Sheep	30.12	17.11	C1	B6	Swallow
19.10	5. 9	A11	K6	Deer	31.12	18.11	C1	C7	Pig
20.10	6. 9	A11	A7	Horse	**1975**				
21.10	7. 9	A11	B8	Stag	1. 1	19.11	C1	D8	Porcupine
22.10	8. 9	A11	C9	Serpent	2. 1	20.11	C1	E9	Wolf
23.10	9. 9	A11	D10	Earthworm	3. 1	21.11	C1	F10	Dog
24.10	10. 9	A11	E11	Crocodile	4. 1	22.11	C1	G11	Pheasant
25.10	11. 9	A11	F12	Dragon	5. 1	23.11	C1	H12	Cock
26.10	12. 9	A11	G1	Badger	6. 1	24.11	C1	J1	Crow
27.10	13. 9	A11	H2	Hare	7. 1	25.11	C1	K2	Monkey
28.10	14. 9	A11	J3	Fox	8. 1	26.11	C1	A3	Gibbon
29.10	15. 9	A11	K4	Tiger	9. 1	27.11	C1	B4	Tapir
30.10	16. 9	A11	A5	Leopard	10. 1	28.11	C1	C5	Sheep
31.10	17. 9	A11	B6	Griffon	11. 1	29.11	C1	D6	Deer
1.11	18. 9	A11	C7	Ox	12. 2	1.12	D2	E7	Horse
2.11	19. 9	A11	D8	Bat	13. 1	2.12	D2	F8	Stag
3.11	20. 9	A11	E9	Rat	14. 1	3.12	D2	G9	Serpent
4.11	21. 9	A11	F10	Swallow	15. 1	4.12	D2	H10	Earthworm
5.11	22. 9	A11	G11	Pig					

Solar date	Lunar date	Month HS/EB	Day HS/EB	Constellation	Solar date	Lunar date	Month HS/EB	Day HS/EB	Constellation
16. 1	5.12	D2	J11	Crocodile	29. 1	18.12	D2	B12	Porcupine
17. 1	6.12	D2	K12	Dragon	30. 1	19.12	D2	C1	Wolf
18. 1	7.12	D2	A1	Badger	31. 1	20.12	D2	D2	Dog
19. 1	8.12	D2	B2	Hare	1. 2	21.12	D2	E3	Pheasant
20. 1	9.12	D2	C3	Fox	2. 2	22.12	D2	F4	Cock
21. 1	10.12	D2	D4	Tiger	3. 2	23.12	D2	G5	Crow
22. 1	11.12	D2	E5	Leopard	4. 2	24.12	D2	H6	Monkey
23. 1	12.12	D2	F6	Griffon	5. 2	25.12	D2	J7	Gibbon
24. 1	13.12	D2	G7	Ox	6. 2	26.12	D2	K8	Tapir
25. 1	14.12	D2	H8	Bat	7. 2	27.12	D2	A9	Sheep
26. 1	15.12	D2	J9	Rat	8. 2	28.12	D2	B10	Deer
27. 1	16.12	D2	K10	Swallow	9. 2	29.12	D2	C11	Horse
28. 1	17.12	D2	A11	Pig	10. 2	30.12	D2	D12	Stag

YI MAO YEAR

Solar date	Lunar date	Month HS/EB	Day HS/EB	Constellation	Solar date	Lunar date	Month HS/EB	Day HS/EB	Constellation
11. 2	1. 1	E3	E1	Serpent	7. 4	26. 2	F4	K8	Stag
12. 2	2. 1	E3	F2	Earthworm	8. 4	27. 2	F4	A9	Serpent
13. 2	3. 1	E3	G3	Crocodile	9. 4	28. 2	F4	B10	Earthworm
14. 2	4. 1	E3	H4	Dragon	10. 4	29. 2	F4	C11	Crocodile
15. 2	5. 1	E3	J5	Badger	11. 4	30. 2	F4	D12	Dragon
16. 2	6. 1	E3	K6	Hare	12. 4	1. 3	G5	E1	Badger
17. 2	7. 1	E3	A7	Fox	13. 4	2. 3	G5	F2	Hare
18. 2	8. 1	E3	B8	Tiger	14. 4	3. 3	G5	G3	Fox
19. 2	9. 1	E3	C9	Leopard	15. 4	4. 3	G5	H4	Tiger
20. 2	10. 1	E3	D10	Griffon	16. 4	5. 3	G5	J5	Leopard
21. 2	11. 1	E3	E11	Ox	17. 4	6. 3	G5	K6	Griffon
22. 2	12. 1	E3	F12	Bat	18. 4	7. 3	G5	A7	Ox
23. 2	13. 1	E3	G1	Rat	19. 4	8. 3	G5	B8	Bat
24. 2	14. 1	E3	H2	Swallow	20. 4	9. 3	G5	C9	Rat
25. 2	15. 1	E3	J3	Pig	21. 4	10. 3	G5	D10	Swallow
26. 2	16. 1	E3	K4	Porcupine	22. 4	11. 3	G5	E11	Pig
27. 2	17. 1	E3	A5	Wolf	23. 4	12. 3	G5	F12	Porcupine
28. 2	18. 1	E3	B6	Dog	24. 4	13. 3	G5	G1	Wolf
1. 3	19. 1	E3	C7	Pheasant	25. 4	14. 3	G5	H2	Dog
2. 3	20. 1	E3	D8	Cock	26. 4	15. 3	G5	J3	Pheasant
3. 3	21. 1	E3	E9	Crow	27. 4	16. 3	G5	K4	Cock
4. 3	22. 1	E3	F10	Monkey	28. 4	17. 3	G5	A5	Crow
5. 3	23. 1	E3	G11	Gibbon	29. 4	18. 3	G5	B6	Monkey
6. 3	24. 1	E3	H12	Tapir	30. 4	19. 3	G5	C7	Gibbon
7. 3	25. 1	E3	J1	Sheep	1. 5	20. 3	G5	D8	Tapir
8. 3	26. 1	E3	K2	Deer	2. 5	21. 3	G5	E9	Sheep
9. 3	27. 1	E3	A3	Horse	3. 5	22. 3	G5	F10	Deer
10. 3	28. 1	E3	B4	Stag	4. 5	23. 3	G5	G11	Horse
11. 3	29. 1	E3	C5	Serpent	5. 5	24. 3	G5	H12	Stag
12. 3	30. 1	E3	D6	Earthworm	6. 5	25. 3	G5	J1	Serpent
13. 3	1. 2	F4	E7	Crocodile	7. 5	26. 3	G5	K2	Earthworm
14. 3	2. 2	F4	F8	Dragon	8. 5	27. 3	G5	A3	Crocodile
15. 3	3. 2	F4	G9	Badger	9. 5	28. 3	G5	B4	Dragon
16. 3	4. 2	F4	H10	Hare	10. 5	29. 3	G5	C5	Badger
17. 3	5. 2	F4	J11	Fox	11. 5	1. 4	H6	D6	Hare
18. 3	6. 2	F4	K12	Tiger	12. 5	2. 4	H6	E7	Fox
19. 3	7. 2	F4	A1	Leopard	13. 5	3. 4	H6	F8	Tiger
20. 3	8. 2	F4	B2	Griffon	14. 5	4. 4	H6	G9	Leopard
21. 3	9. 2	F4	C3	Ox	15. 5	5. 4	H6	H10	Griffon
22. 3	10. 2	F4	D4	Bat	16. 5	6. 4	H6	J11	Ox
23. 3	11. 2	F4	E5	Rat	17. 5	7. 4	H6	K12	Bat
24. 3	12. 2	F4	F6	Swallow	18. 5	8. 4	H6	A1	Rat
25. 3	13. 2	F4	G7	Pig	19. 5	9. 4	H6	B2	Swallow
26. 3	14. 2	F4	H8	Porcupine	20. 5	10. 4	H6	C3	Pig
27. 3	15. 2	F4	J9	Wolf	21. 5	11. 4	H6	D4	Porcupine
28. 3	16. 2	F4	K10	Dog	22. 5	12. 4	H6	E5	Wolf
29. 3	17. 2	F4	A11	Pheasant	23. 5	13. 4	H6	F6	Dog
30. 3	18. 2	F4	B12	Cock	24. 5	14. 4	H6	G7	Pheasant
31. 3	19. 2	F4	C1	Crow	25. 5	15. 4	H6	H8	Cock
1. 4	20. 2	F4	D2	Monkey	26. 5	16. 4	H6	J9	Crow
2. 4	21. 2	F4	E3	Gibbon	27. 5	17. 4	H6	K10	Monkey
3. 4	22. 2	F4	F4	Tapir	28. 5	18. 4	H6	A11	Gibbon
4. 4	23. 2	F4	G5	Sheep	29. 5	19. 4	H6	B12	Tapir
5. 4	24. 2	F4	H6	Deer	30. 5	20. 4	H6	C1	Sheep
6. 4	25. 2	F4	J7	Horse	31. 5	21. 4	H6	D2	Deer

Solar date	Lunar date	Month HS/EB	Day HS/EB	Constellation
1. 6	22. 4	H6	E3	Horse
2. 6	23. 4	H6	F4	Stag
3. 6	24. 4	H6	G5	Serpent
4. 6	25. 4	H6	H6	Earthworm
5. 6	26. 4	H6	J7	Crocodile
6. 6	27. 4	H6	K8	Dragon
7. 6	28. 4	H6	A9	Badger
8. 6	29. 4	H6	B10	Hare
9. 6	30. 4	H6	C11	Fox
10. 6	1. 5	J7	D12	Tiger
11. 6	2. 5	J7	E1	Leopard
12. 6	3. 5	J7	F2	Griffon
13. 6	4. 5	J7	G3	Ox
14. 6	5. 5	J7	H4	Bat
15. 6	6. 5	J7	J5	Rat
16. 6	7. 5	J7	K6	Swallow
17. 6	8. 5	J7	A7	Pig
18. 6	9. 5	J7	B8	Porcupine
19. 6	10. 5	J7	C9	Wolf
20. 6	11. 5	J7	D10	Dog
21. 6	12. 5	J7	E11	Pheasant
22. 6	13. 5	J7	F12	Cock
23. 6	14. 5	J7	G1	Crow
24. 6	15. 5	J7	H2	Monkey
25. 6	16. 5	J7	J3	Gibbon
26. 6	17. 5	J7	K4	Tapir
27. 6	18. 5	J7	A5	Sheep
28. 6	19. 5	J7	B6	Deer
29. 6	20. 5	J7	C7	Horse
30. 6	21. 5	J7	D8	Stag
1. 7	22. 5	J7	E9	Serpent
2. 7	23. 5	J7	F10	Earthworm
3. 7	24. 5	J7	G11	Crocodile
4. 7	25. 5	J7	H12	Dragon
5. 7	26. 5	J7	J1	Badger
6. 7	27. 5	J7	K2	Hare
7. 7	28. 5	J7	A3	Fox
8. 7	29. 5	J7	B4	Tiger
9. 7	1. 6	K8	C5	Leopard
10. 7	2. 6	K8	D6	Griffon
11. 7	3. 6	K8	E7	Ox
12. 7	4. 6	K8	F8	Bat
13. 7	5. 6	K8	G9	Rat
14. 7	6. 6	K8	H10	Swallow
15. 7	7. 6	K8	J11	Pig
16. 7	8. 6	K8	K12	Porcupine
17. 7	9. 6	K8	A1	Wolf
18. 7	10. 6	K8	B2	Dog
19. 7	11. 6	K8	C3	Pheasant
20. 7	12. 6	K8	D4	Cock
21. 7	13. 6	K8	E5	Crow
22. 7	14. 6	K8	F6	Monkey
23. 7	15. 6	K8	G7	Gibbon
24. 7	16. 6	K8	H8	Tapir
25. 7	17. 6	K8	J9	Sheep
26. 7	18. 6	K8	K10	Deer
27. 7	19. 6	K8	A11	Horse
28. 7	20. 6	K8	B12	Stag
29. 7	21. 6	K8	C1	Serpent
30. 7	22. 6	K8	D2	Earthworm
31. 7	23. 6	K8	E3	Crocodile
1. 8	24. 6	K8	F4	Dragon
2. 8	25. 6	K8	G5	Badger
3. 8	26. 6	K8	H6	Hare
4. 8	27. 6	K8	J7	Fox
5. 8	28. 6	K8	K8	Tiger
6. 8	29. 6	K8	A9	Leopard
7. 8	1. 7	A9	B10	Griffon
8. 8	2. 7	A9	C11	Ox
9. 8	3. 7	A9	D12	Bat
10. 8	4. 7	A9	E1	Rat
11. 8	5. 7	A9	F2	Swallow
12. 8	6. 7	A9	G3	Pig
13. 8	7. 7	A9	H4	Porcupine
14. 8	8. 7	A9	J5	Wolf
15. 8	9. 7	A9	K6	Dog
16. 8	10. 7	A9	A7	Pheasant
17. 8	11. 7	A9	B8	Cock
18. 8	12. 7	A9	C9	Crow
19. 8	13. 7	A9	D10	Monkey
20. 8	14. 7	A9	E11	Gibbon
21. 8	15. 7	A9	F12	Tapir
22. 8	16. 7	A9	G1	Sheep
23. 8	17. 7	A9	H2	Deer
24. 8	18. 7	A9	J3	Horse
25. 8	19. 7	A9	K4	Stag
26. 8	20. 7	A9	A5	Serpent
27. 8	21. 7	A9	B6	Earthworm
28. 8	22. 7	A9	C7	Crocodile
29. 8	23. 7	A9	D8	Dragon
30. 8	24. 7	A9	E9	Badger
31. 8	25. 7	A9	F10	Hare
1. 9	26. 7	A9	G11	Fox
2. 9	27. 7	A9	H12	Tiger
3. 9	28. 7	A9	J1	Leopard
4. 9	29. 7	A9	K2	Griffon
5. 9	30. 7	A9	A3	Ox
6. 9	1. 8	B10	B4	Bat
7. 9	2. 8	B10	C5	Rat
8. 9	3. 8	B10	D6	Swallow
9. 9	4. 8	B10	E7	Pig
10. 9	5. 8	B10	F8	Porcupine
11. 9	6. 8	B10	G9	Wolf
12. 9	7. 8	B10	H10	Dog
13. 9	8. 8	B10	J11	Pheasant
14. 9	9. 8	B10	K12	Cock
15. 9	10. 8	B10	A1	Crow
16. 9	11. 8	B10	B2	Monkey
17. 9	12. 8	B10	C3	Gibbon
18. 9	13. 8	B10	D4	Tapir
19. 9	14. 8	B10	E5	Sheep
20. 9	15. 8	B10	F6	Deer
21. 9	16. 8	B10	G7	Horse
22. 9	17. 8	B10	H8	Stag
23. 9	18.18	B10	J9	Serpent
24. 9	19. 8	B10	K10	Earthworm
25. 9	20. 8	B10	A11	Crocodile
26. 9	21. 8	B10	B12	Dragon
27. 9	22. 8	B10	C1	Badger
28. 9	23. 8	B10	D2	Hare
29. 9	24. 8	B10	E3	Fox
30. 9	25. 8	B10	F4	Tiger
1.10	26. 8	B10	G5	Leopard
2.10	27. 8	B10	H6	Griffon
3.10	28. 8	B10	J7	Ox
4.10	29. 8	B10	K8	Bat
5.10	1. 9	C11	A9	Rat
6.10	2. 9	C11	B10	Swallow
7.10	3. 9	C11	C11	Pig
8.10	4. 9	C11	D12	Porcupine
9.10	5. 9	C11	E1	Wolf
10.10	6. 9	C11	F2	Dog
11.10	7. 9	C11	G3	Pheasant
12.10	8. 9	C11	H4	Cock
13.10	9. 9	C11	J5	Crow
14.10	10. 9	C11	K6	Monkey
15.10	11. 9	C11	A7	Gibbon
16.10	12. 9	C11	B8	Tapir
17.10	13. 9	C11	C9	Sheep
18.10	14. 9	C11	D10	Deer
19.10	15. 9	C11	E11	Horse
20.10	16. 9	C11	F12	Stag
21.10	17. 9	C11	G1	Serpent
22.10	18. 9	C11	H2	Earthworm
23.10	19. 9	C11	J3	Crocodile
24.10	20. 9	C11	K4	Dragon

Solar date	Lunar date	Month HS/EB	Day HS/EB	Constellation	Solar date	Lunar date	Month HS/EB	Day HS/EB	Constellation
25.10	21. 9	C11	A5	Badger	14.12	12.11	E1	A7	Horse
26.10	22. 9	C11	B6	Hare	15.12	13.11	E1	B8	Stag
27.10	23. 9	C11	C7	Fox	16.12	14.11	E1	C9	Serpent
28.10	24. 9	C11	D8	Tiger	17.12	15.11	E1	D10	Earthworm
29.10	25. 9	C11	E9	Leopard	18.12	16.11	E1	E11	Crocodile
30.10	26. 9	C11	F10	Griffon	19.12	17.11	E1	F12	Dragon
31.10	27. 9	C11	G11	Ox	20.12	18.11	E1	G1	Badger
1.11	28. 9	C11	H12	Bat	21.12	19.11	E1	H2	Hare
2.11	29. 9	C11	J1	Rat	22.12	20.11	E1	J3	Fox
3.11	1.10	D12	K2	Swallow	23.12	21.11	E1	K4	Tiger
4.11	2.10	D12	A3	Pig	24.12	22.11	E1	A5	Leopard
5.11	3.10	D12	B4	Porcupine	25.12	23.11	E1	B6	Griffon
6.11	4.10	D12	C5	Wolf	26.12	24.11	E1	C7	Ox
7.11	5.10	D12	D6	Dog	27.12	25.11	E1	D8	Bat
8.11	6.10	D12	E7	Pheasant	28.12	26.11	E1	E9	Rat
9.11	7.10	D12	F8	Cock	29.12	27.11	E1	F10	Swallow
10.11	8.10	D12	G9	Crow	30.12	28.11	E1	G11	Pig
11.11	9.10	D12	H10	Monkey	31.12	29.11	E1	H12	Porcupine
12.11	10.10	D12	J11	Gibbon	**1976**				
13.11	11.10	D12	K12	Tapir	1. 1	1.12	F2	J1	Wolf
14.11	12.10	D12	A1	Sheep	2. 1	2.12	F2	K2	Dog
15.11	13.10	D12	B2	Deer	3. 1	3.12	F2	A3	Pheasant
16.11	14.10	D12	C3	Horse	4. 1	4.12	F2	B4	Cock
17.11	15.10	D12	D4	Stag	5. 1	5.12	F2	C5	Crow
18.11	16.10	D12	E5	Serpent	6. 1	6.12	F2	D6	Monkey
19.11	17.10	D12	F6	Earthworm	7. 1	7.12	F2	E7	Gibbon
20.11	18.10	D12	G7	Crocodile	8. 1	8.12	F2	F8	Tapir
21.11	19.10	D12	H8	Dragon	9. 1	9.12	F2	G9	Sheep
22.11	20.10	D12	J9	Badger	10. 1	10.12	F2	H10	Deer
23.11	21.10	D12	K10	Hare	11. 1	11.12	F2	J11	Horse
24.11	22.10	D12	A11	Fox	12. 1	12.12	F2	K12	Stag
25.11	23.10	D12	B12	Tiger	13. 1	13.12	F2	A1	Serpent
26.11	24.10	D12	C1	Leopard	14. 1	14.12	F2	B2	Earthworm
27.11	25.10	D12	D2	Griffon	15. 1	15.12	F2	C3	Crocodile
28.11	26.10	D12	E3	Ox	16. 1	16.12	F2	D4	Dragon
29.11	27.10	D12	F4	Bat	17. 1	17.12	F2	E5	Badger
30.11	28.10	D12	G5	Rat	18. 1	18.12	F2	F6	Hare
1.12	29.10	D12	H6	Swallow	19. 1	19.12	F2	G7	Fox
2.12	30.10	D12	J7	Pig	20. 1	20.12	F2	H8	Tiger
3.12	1.11	E1	K8	Porcupine	21. 1	21.12	F2	J9	Leopard
4.12	2.11	E1	A9	Wolf	22. 1	22.12	F2	K10	Griffon
5.12	3.11	E1	B10	Dog	23. 1	23.12	F2	A11	Ox
6.12	4.11	E1	C11	Pheasant	24. 1	24.12	F2	B12	Bat
7.12	5.11	E1	D12	Cock	25. 1	25.12	F2	C1	Rat
8.12	6.11	E1	E1	Crow	26. 1	26.12	F2	D2	Swallow
9.12	7.11	E1	F2	Monkey	27. 1	27.12	F2	E3	Pig
10.12	8.11	E1	G3	Gibbon	28. 1	28.12	F2	F4	Porcupine
11.12	9.11	E1	H4	Tapir	29. 1	29.12	F2	G5	Wolf
12.12	10.11	E1	J5	Sheep	30. 1	30.12	F2	H6	Dog
13.12	11.11	E1	K6	Deer					

PING CH'EN YEAR

Solar date	Lunar date	Month HS/EB	Day HS/EB	Constellation	Solar date	Lunar date	Month HS/EB	Day HS/EB	Constellation
31. 1	1. 1	G3	J7	Pheasant	18. 2	19. 1	G3	G1	Leopard
1. 2	2. 1	G3	K8	Cock	19. 2	20. 1	G3	H2	Griffon
2. 2	3. 1	G3	A9	Crow	20. 2	21. 1	G3	J3	Ox
3. 2	4. 1	G3	B10	Monkey	21. 2	22. 1	G3	K4	Bat
4. 2	5. 1	G3	C11	Gibbon	22. 2	23. 1	G3	A5	Rat
5. 2	6. 1	G3	D12	Tapir	23. 2	24. 1	G3	B6	Swallow
6. 2	7. 1	G3	E1	Sheep	24. 2	25. 1	G3	C7	Pig
7. 2	8. 1	G3	F2	Deer	25. 2	26. 1	G3	D8	Porcupine
8. 2	9. 1	G3	G3	Horse	26. 2	27. 1	G3	E9	Wolf
9. 2	10. 1	G3	H4	Stag	27. 2	28. 1	G3	F10	Dog
10. 2	11. 1	G3	J5	Serpent	28. 2	29. 1	G3	G11	Pheasant
11. 2	12. 1	G3	K6	Earthworm	29. 2	30. 1	G3	H12	Cock
12. 2	13. 1	G3	A7	Crocodile	1. 3	1. 2	H4	J1	Crow
13. 2	14. 1	G3	B8	Dragon	2. 3	2. 2	H4	K2	Monkey
14. 2	15. 1	G3	C9	Badger	3. 3	3. 2	H4	A3	Gibbon
15. 2	16. 1	G3	D10	Hare	4. 3	4. 2	H4	B4	Tapir
16. 2	17. 1	G3	E11	Fox	5. 3	5. 2	H4	C5	Sheep
17. 2	18. 1	G3	F12	Tiger	6. 3	6. 2	H4	D6	Deer

Solar date	Lunar date	Month HS/EB	Day HS/EB	Constellation
7. 3	7. 2	H4	E7	Horse
8. 3	8. 2	H4	F8	Stag
9. 3	9. 2	H4	G9	Serpent
10. 3	10. 2	H4	H10	Earthworm
11. 3	11. 2	H4	J11	Crocodile
12. 3	12. 2	H4	K12	Dragon
13. 3	13. 2	H4	A1	Badger
14. 3	14. 2	H4	B2	Hare
15. 3	15. 2	H4	C3	Fox
16. 3	16. 2	H4	D4	Tiger
17. 3	17. 2	H4	E5	Leopard
18. 3	18. 2	H4	F6	Griffon
19. 3	19. 2	H4	G7	Ox
20. 3	20. 2	H4	H8	Bat
21. 3	21. 2	H4	J9	Rat
22. 3	22. 2	H4	K10	Swallow
23. 3	23. 2	H4	A11	Pig
24. 3	24. 2	H4	B12	Porcupine
25. 3	25. 2	H4	C1	Wolf
26. 3	26. 2	H4	D2	Dog
27. 3	27. 2	H4	E3	Pheasant
28. 3	28. 2	H4	F4	Cock
29. 3	29. 2	H4	G5	Crow
30. 3	30. 2	H4	H6	Monkey
31. 3	1. 3	J5	J7	Gibbon
1. 4	2. 3	J5	K8	Tapir
2. 4	3. 3	J5	A9	Sheep
3. 4	4. 3	J5	B10	Deer
4. 4	5. 3	J5	C11	Horse
5. 4	6. 3	J5	D12	Stag
6. 4	7. 3	J5	E1	Serpent
7. 4	8. 3	J5	F2	Earthworm
8. 4	9. 3	J5	G3	Crocodile
9. 4	10. 3	J5	H4	Dragon
10. 4	11. 3	J5	J5	Badger
11. 4	12. 3	J5	K6	Hare
12. 4	13. 3	J5	A7	Fox
13. 4	14. 3	J5	B8	Tiger
14. 4	15. 3	J5	C9	Leopard
15. 4	16. 3	J5	D10	Griffon
16. 4	17. 3	J5	E11	Ox
17. 4	18. 3	J5	F12	Bat
18. 4	19. 3	J5	G1	Rat
19. 4	20. 3	J5	H2	Swallow
20. 4	21. 3	J5	J3	Pig
21. 4	22. 3	J5	K4	Porcupine
22. 4	23. 3	J5	A5	Wolf
23. 4	24. 3	J5	B6	Dog
24. 4	25. 3	J5	C7	Pheasant
25. 4	26. 3	J5	D8	Cock
26. 4	27. 3	J5	E9	Crow
27. 4	28. 3	J5	F10	Monkey
28. 4	29. 3	J5	G11	Gibbon
29. 4	1. 4	K6	H12	Tapir
30. 4	2. 4	K6	J1	Sheep
1. 5	3. 4	K6	K2	Deer
2. 5	4. 4	K6	A3	Horse
3. 5	5. 4	K6	B4	Stag
4. 5	6. 4	K6	C5	Serpent
5. 5	7. 4	K6	D6	Earthworm
6. 5	8. 4	K6	E7	Crocodile
7. 5	9. 4	K6	F8	Dragon
8. 5	10. 4	K6	G9	Badger
9. 5	11. 4	K6	H10	Hare
10. 5	12. 4	K6	J11	Fox
11. 5	13. 4	K6	K12	Tiger
12. 5	14. 4	K6	A1	Leopard
13. 5	15. 4	K6	B2	Griffon
14. 5	16. 4	K6	C3	Ox
15. 5	17. 4	K6	D4	Bat
16. 5	18. 4	K6	E5	Rat
17. 5	19. 4	K6	F6	Swallow
18. 5	20. 4	K6	G7	Pig
19. 5	21. 4	K6	H8	Porcupine
20. 5	22. 4	K6	J9	Wolf
21. 5	23. 4	K6	K10	Dog
22. 5	24. 4	K6	A11	Pheasant
23. 5	25. 4	K6	B12	Cock
24. 5	26. 4	K6	C1	Crow
25. 5	27. 4	K6	D2	Monkey
26. 5	28. 4	K6	E3	Gibbon
27. 5	29. 4	K6	F4	Tapir
28. 5	30. 4	K6	G5	Sheep
29. 5	1. 5	A7	H6	Deer
30. 5	2. 5	A7	J7	Horse
31. 5	3. 5	A7	K8	Stag
1. 6	4. 5	A7	A9	Serpent
2. 6	5. 5	A7	B10	Earthworm
3. 6	6. 5	A7	C11	Crocodile
4. 6	7. 5	A7	D12	Dragon
5. 6	8. 5	A7	E1	Badger
6. 6	9. 5	A7	F2	Hare
7. 6	10. 5	A7	G3	Fox
8. 6	11. 5	A7	H4	Tiger
9. 6	12. 5	A7	J5	Leopard
10. 6	13. 5	A7	K6	Griffon
11. 6	14. 5	A7	A7	Ox
12. 6	15. 5	A7	B8	Bat
13. 6	16. 5	A7	C9	Rat
14. 6	17. 5	A7	D10	Swallow
15. 6	18. 5	A7	E11	Pig
16. 6	19. 5	A7	F12	Porcupine
17. 6	20. 5	A7	G1	Wolf
18. 6	21. 5	A7	H2	Dog
19. 6	22. 5	A7	J3	Pheasant
20. 6	23. 5	A7	K4	Cock
21. 6	24. 5	A7	A5	Crow
22. 6	25. 5	A7	B6	Monkey
23. 6	26. 5	A7	C7	Gibbon
24. 6	27. 5	A7	D8	Tapir
25. 6	28. 5	A7	E9	Sheep
26. 6	29. 5	A7	F10	Deer
27. 6	1. 6	B8	G11	Horse
28. 6	2. 6	B8	H12	Stag
29. 6	3. 6	B8	J1	Serpent
30. 6	4. 6	B8	K2	Earthworm
1. 7	5. 6	B8	A3	Crocodile
2. 7	6. 6	B8	B4	Dragon
3. 7	7. 6	B8	C5	Badger
4. 7	8. 6	B8	D6	Hare
5. 7	9. 6	B8	E7	Fox
6. 7	10. 6	B8	F8	Tiger
7. 7	11. 6	B8	G9	Leopard
8. 7	12. 6	B8	H10	Griffon
9. 7	13. 6	B8	J11	Ox
10. 7	14. 6	B8	K12	Bat
11. 7	15. 6	B8	A1	Rat
12. 7	16. 6	B8	B2	Swallow
13. 7	17. 6	B8	C3	Pig
14. 7	18. 6	B8	D4	Porcupine
15. 7	19. 6	B8	E5	Wolf
16. 7	20. 6	B8	F6	Dog
17. 7	21. 6	B8	G7	Pheasant
18. 7	22. 6	B8	H8	Cock
19. 7	23. 6	B8	J9	Crow
20. 7	24. 6	B8	K10	Monkey
21. 7	25. 6	B8	A11	Gibbon
22. 7	26. 6	B8	B12	Tapir
23. 7	27. 6	B8	C1	Sheep
24. 7	28. 6	B8	D2	Deer
25. 7	29. 6	B8	E3	Horse
26. 7	30. 6	B8	F4	Stag
27. 7	1. 7	C9	G5	Serpent
28. 7	2. 7	C9	H6	Earthworm
29. 7	3. 7	C9	J7	Crocodile
30. 7	4. 7	C9	K8	Dragon

Solar date	Lunar date	Month HS/EB	Day HS/EB	Constellation
31. 7	5. 7	C9	A9	Badger
1. 8	6. 7	C9	B10	Hare
2. 8	7. 7	C9	C11	Fox
3. 8	8. 7	C9	D12	Tiger
4. 8	9. 7	C9	E1	Leopard
5. 8	10. 7	C9	F2	Griffon
6. 8	11. 7	C9	G3	Ox
7. 8	12. 7	C9	H4	Bat
8. 8	13. 7	C9	J5	Rat
9. 8	14. 7	C9	K6	Swallow
10. 8	15. 7	C9	A7	Pig
11. 8	16. 7	C9	B8	Porcupine
12. 8	17. 7	C9	C9	Wolf
13. 8	18. 7	C9	D10	Dog
14. 8	19. 7	C9	E11	Pheasant
15. 8	20. 7	C9	F12	Cock
16. 8	21. 7	C9	G1	Crow
17. 8	22. 7	C9	H2	Monkey
18. 8	23. 7	C9	J3	Gibbon
19. 8	24. 7	C9	K4	Tapir
20. 8	25. 7	C9	A5	Sheep
21. 8	26. 7	C9	B6	Deer
22. 8	27. 7	C9	C7	Horse
23. 8	28. 7	C9	D8	Stag
24. 8	29. 7	C9	E9	Serpent
25. 8	1. 8	D10	F10	Earthworm
26. 8	2. 8	D10	G11	Crocodile
27. 8	3. 8	D10	H12	Dragon
28. 8	4. 8	D10	J1	Badger
29. 8	5. 8	D10	K2	Hare
30. 8	6. 8	D10	A3	Fox
31. 8	7. 8	D10	B4	Tiger
1. 9	8. 8	D10	C5	Leopard
2. 9	9. 8	D10	D6	Griffon
3. 9	10. 8	D10	E7	Ox
4. 9	11. 8	D10	F8	Bat
5. 9	12. 8	D10	G9	Rat
6. 9	13. 8	D10	H10	Swallow
7. 9	14. 8	D10	J11	Pig
8. 9	15. 8	D10	K12	Porcupine
9. 9	16. 8	D10	A1	Wolf
10. 9	17. 8	D10	B2	Dog
11. 9	18. 8	D10	C3	Pheasant
12. 9	19. 8	D10	D4	Cock
13. 9	20. 8	D10	E5	Crow
14. 9	21. 8	D10	F6	Monkey
15. 9	22. 8	D10	G7	Gibbon
16. 9	23. 8	D10	H8	Tapir
17. 9	24. 8	D10	J9	Sheep
18. 9	25. 8	D10	K10	Deer
19. 9	26. 8	D10	A11	Horse
20. 9	27. 8	D10	B12	Stag
21. 9	28. 8	D10	C1	Serpent
22. 9	29. 8	D10	D2	Earthworm
23. 9	30. 8	D10	E3	Crocodile
24. 9	*1. 8*	*D10*	F4	Dragon
25. 9	*2. 8*	*D10*	G5	Badger
26. 9	*3. 8*	*D10*	H6	Hare
27. 9	*4. 8*	*D10*	J7	Fox
28. 9	*5. 8*	*D10*	K8	Tiger
29. 9	*6. 8*	*D10*	A9	Leopard
30. 9	*7. 8*	*D10*	B10	Griffon
1. 0	*8. 8*	*D10*	C11	Ox
2.10	*9. 8*	*D10*	D12	Bat
3.10	*10. 8*	*D10*	E1	Rat
4.10	*11. 8*	*D10*	F2	Swallow
5.10	*12. 8*	*D10*	G3	Pig
6.10	*13. 8*	*D10*	H4	Porcupine
7.10	*14. 8*	*D10*	J5	Wolf
8.10	*15. 8*	*D10*	K6	Dog
9.10	*16. 8*	*D10*	A7	Pheasant
10.10	*17. 8*	*D10*	B8	Cock
11.10	*18. 8*	*D10*	C9	Crow
12.10	*19. 8*	*D10*	D10	Monkey
13.10	*20. 8*	*D10*	E11	Gibbon
14.10	*21. 8*	*D10*	F12	Tapir
15.10	*22. 8*	*D10*	G1	Sheep
16. 0	*23. 8*	*D10*	H2	Deer
17. 0	*24. 8*	*D10*	J3	Horse
18.10	*25. 8*	*D10*	K4	Stag
19.10	*26. 8*	*D10*	A5	Serpent
20.10	*27. 8*	*D10*	B6	Earthworm
21.10	*28. 8*	*D10*	C7	Crocodile
22.10	*29. 8*	*D10*	D8	Dragon
23.10	1. 9	E11	E9	Badger
24.10	2. 9	E11	F10	Hare
25.10	3. 9	E11	G11	Fox
26.10	4. 9	E11	H12	Tiger
27.10	5. 9	E11	J1	Leopard
28.10	6. 9	E11	K2	Griffon
29.10	7. 9	E11	A3	Ox
30.10	8. 9	E11	B4	Bat
31.10	9. 9	E11	C5	Rat
1.11	10. 9	E11	D6	Swallow
2.11	11. 9	E11	E7	Pig
3.11	12. 9	E11	F8	Porcupine
4.11	13. 9	E11	G9	Wolf
5.11	14. 9	E11	H10	Dog
6.11	15. 9	E11	J11	Pheasant
7.11	16. 9	E11	K12	Cock
8.11	17. 9	E11	A1	Crow
9.11	18. 9	E11	B2	Monkey
10.11	19. 9	E11	C3	Gibbon
11.11	20. 9	E11	D4	Tapir
12.11	21. 9	E11	E5	Sheep
13.11	22. 9	E11	F6	Deer
14.11	23. 9	E11	G7	Horse
15.11	24. 9	E11	H8	Stag
16.11	25. 9	E11	J9	Serpent
17.11	26. 9	E11	K10	Earthworm
18.11	27. 9	E11	A11	Crocodile
19.11	28. 9	E11	B12	Dragon
20.11	29. 9	E11	C1	Badger
21.11	1.10	F12	D2	Hare
22.11	2.10	F12	E3	Fox
23.11	3.10	F12	F4	Tiger
24.11	4.10	F12	G5	Leopard
25.11	5.10	F12	H6	Griffon
26.11	6.10	F12	J7	Ox
27.11	7.10	F12	K8	Bat
28.11	8.10	F12	A9	Rat
29.11	9.10	F12	B10	Swallow
30.11	10.10	F12	C11	Pig
1.12	11.10	F12	D12	Porcupine
2.12	12.10	F12	E1	Wolf
3.12	13.10	F12	F2	Dog
4.12	14.10	F12	G3	Pheasant
5.12	15.10	F12	H4	Cock
6.12	16.10	F12	J5	Crow
7.12	17.10	F12	K6	Monkey
8.12	18.10	F12	A7	Gibbon
9.12	19.10	F12	B8	Tapir
10.12	20.10	F12	C9	Sheep
11.12	21.10	F12	D10	Deer
12.12	22.10	F12	E11	Horse
13.12	23.10	F12	F12	Stag
14.12	24.10	F12	G1	Serpent
15.12	25.10	F12	H2	Earthworm
16.12	26.10	F12	J3	Crocodile
17.12	27.10	F12	K4	Dragon
18.12	28.10	F12	A5	Badger
19.12	29.10	F12	B6	Hare
20.12	30.10	F12	C7	Fox
21.12	1.11	G1	D8	Tiger
22.12	2.11	G1	E9	Leopard
23.12	3.11	G1	F10	Griffon

Solar date	Lunar date	Month HS/EB	Day HS/EB	Constellation	Solar date	Lunar date	Month HS/EB	Day HS/EB	Constellation
24.12	4.11	G1	G11	Ox	20. 1	2.12	H2	D2	Griffon
25.12	5.11	G1	H12	Bat	21. 1	3.12	H2	E3	Ox
26.12	6.11	G1	J1	Rat	22. 1	4.12	H2	F4	Bat
27.12	7.11	G1	K2	Swallow	23. 1	5.12	H2	G5	Rat
28.12	8.11	G1	A3	Pig	24. 1	6.12	H2	H6	Swallow
29.12	9.11	G1	B4	Porcupine	25. 1	7.12	H2	J7	Pig
30.12	10.11	G1	C5	Wolf	26. 1	8.12	H2	K8	Porcupine
21.12	11.11	G1	D6	Dog	27. 1	9.12	H2	A9	Wolf
					28. 1	10.12	H2	B10	Dog
1977					29. 1	11.12	H2	C11	Pheasant
1. 1	12.11	G1	E7	Pheasant	30. 1	12.12	H2	D12	Cock
2. 1	13.11	G1	F8	Cock	31. 1	13.12	H2	E1	Crow
3. 1	14.11	G1	G9	Crow	1. 2	14.12	H2	F2	Monkey
4. 1	15.11	G1	H10	Monkey	2. 2	15.12	H2	G3	Gibbon
5. 1	16.11	G1	J11	Gibbon	3. 2	16.12	H2	H4	Tapir
6. 1	17.11	G1	K12	Tapir	4. 2	17.12	H2	J5	Sheep
7. 1	18.11	G1	A1	Sheep	5. 2	18.12	H2	K6	Deer
8. 1	19.11	G1	B2	Deer	6. 2	19.12	H2	A7	Horse
9. 1	20.11	G1	C3	Horse	7. 2	10.12	H2	B8	Stag
10. 1	21.11	G1	D4	Stag	8. 2	21.12	H2	C9	Serpent
11. 1	22.11	G1	E5	Serpent	9. 2	22.12	H2	D10	Earthworm
12. 1	23.11	G1	F6	Earthworm	10. 2	23.12	H2	E11	Crocodile
13. 1	24.11	G1	G7	Crocodile	11. 2	24.12	H2	F12	Dragon
14. 1	25.11	G1	H8	Dragon	12. 2	25.12	H2	G1	Badger
15. 1	26.11	G1	J9	Badger	13. 2	26.12	H2	H2	Hare
16. 1	27.11	G1	K10	Hare	14. 2	27.12	H2	J3	Fox
17. 1	28.11	G1	A11	Fox	15. 2	28.12	H2	K4	Tiger
18. 1	29.11	G1	B12	Tiger	16. 2	29.12	H2	A5	Leopard
19. 1	1.12	H2	C1	Leopard	17. 2	30.12	H2	B6	Griffon

TING SZU YEAR

Solar date	Lunar date	Month HS/EB	Day HS/EB	Constellation	Solar date	Lunar date	Month HS/EB	Day HS/EB	Constellation
18. 2	1. 1	J3	C7	Ox	29. 3	10. 2	K4	B10	Monkey
19. 2	2. 1	J3	D8	Bat	30. 3	11. 2	K4	C11	Gibbon
20. 2	3. 1	J3	E9	Rat	31. 3	12. 2	K4	D12	Tapir
21. 2	4. 1	J3	F10	Swallow	1. 4	13. 2	K4	E1	Sheep
22. 2	5. 1	J3	G11	Pig	2. 4	14. 2	K4	F2	Deer
23. 2	6. 1	J3	H12	Porcupine	3. 4	15. 2	K4	G3	Horse
24. 2	7. 1	J3	J1	Wolf	4. 4	16. 2	K4	H4	Stag
25. 2	8. 1	J3	K2	Dog	5. 4	17. 2	K4	J5	Serpent
26. 2	9. 1	J3	A3	Pheasant	6. 4	18. 2	K4	K6	Earthworm
27. 2	10. 1	J3	B4	Cock	7. 4	19. 2	K4	A7	Crocodile
28. 2	11. 1	J3	C5	Crow	8. 4	20. 2	K4	B8	Dragon
1. 3	12. 1	J3	D6	Monkey	9. 4	21. 2	K4	C9	Badger
2. 3	13. 1	J3	E7	Gibbon	10. 4	22. 2	K4	D10	Hare
3. 3	14. 1	J3	F8	Tapir	11. 4	23. 2	K4	E11	Fox
4. 3	15. 1	J3	G9	Sheep	12. 4	24. 2	K4	F12	Tiger
5. 3	16. 1	J3	H10	Deer	13. 4	25. 2	K4	G1	Leopard
6. 3	17. 1	J3	J11	Horse	14. 4	26. 2	K4	H2	Griffon
7. 3	18. 1	J3	K12	Stag	15. 4	27. 2	K4	J3	Ox
8. 3	19. 1	J3	A1	Serpent	16. 4	28. 2	K4	K4	Bat
9. 3	20. 1	J3	B2	Earthworm	17. 4	29. 2	K4	A5	Rat
10. 3	21. 1	J3	C3	Crocodile	18. 4	1. 3	A5	B6	Swallow
11. 3	22. 1	J3	D4	Dragon	19. 4	2. 3	A5	C7	Pig
12. 3	23. 1	J3	E5	Badger	20. 4	3. 3	A5	D8	Porcupine
13. 3	24. 1	J3	F6	Hare	21. 4	4. 3	A5	E9	Wolf
14. 3	25. 1	J3	G7	Fox	22. 4	5. 3	A5	F10	Dog
15. 3	26. 1	J3	H8	Tiger	23. 4	6. 3	A5	G11	Pheasant
16. 3	27. 1	J3	J9	Leopard	24. 4	7. 3	A5	H12	Cock
17. 3	28. 1	J3	K10	Griffon	25. 4	8. 3	A5	J1	Crow
18. 3	29. 1	J3	A11	Ox	26. 4	9. 3	A5	K2	Monkey
19. 3	30. 1	J3	B12	Bat	27. 4	10. 3	A5	A3	Gibbon
20. 3	1. 2	K4	C1	Rat	28. 4	11. 3	A5	B4	Tapir
21. 3	2. 2	K4	D2	Swallow	29. 4	12. 3	A5	C5	Sheep
22. 3	3. 2	K4	E3	Pig	30. 4	13. 3	A5	D6	Deer
23. 3	4. 2	K4	F4	Porcupine	1. 5	14. 3	A5	E7	Horse
24. 3	5. 2	K4	G5	Wolf	2. 5	15. 3	A5	F8	Stag
25. 3	6. 2	K4	H6	Dog	3. 5	16. 3	A5	G9	Serpent
26. 3	7. 2	K4	J7	Pheasant	4. 5	17. 3	A5	H10	Earthworm
27. 3	8. 2	K4	K8	Cock	5. 5	18. 3	A5	J11	Crocodile
28. 3	9. 2	K4	A9	Crow	6. 5	19. 3	A5	K12	Dragon

Solar date	Lunar date	Month HS/EB	Day HS/EB	Constellation
7. 5	20. 3	A5	A1	Badger
8. 5	21. 3	A5	B2	Hare
9. 5	22. 3	A5	C3	Fox
10. 5	23. 3	A5	D4	Tiger
11. 5	24. 3	A5	E5	Leopard
12. 5	25. 3	A5	F6	Griffon
13. 5	26. 3	A5	G7	Ox
14. 5	27. 3	A5	H8	Bat
15. 5	28. 3	A5	J9	Rat
16. 5	29. 3	A5	K10	Swallow
17. 5	30. 3	A5	A11	Pig
18. 5	1. 4	B6	B12	Porcupine
19. 5	2. 4	B6	C1	Wolf
20. 5	3. 4	B6	D2	Dog
21. 5	4. 4	B6	E3	Pheasant
22. 5	5. 4	B6	F4	Cock
23. 5	6. 4	B6	G5	Crow
24. 5	7. 4	B6	H6	Monkey
25. 5	8. 4	B6	J7	Gibbon
26. 5	9. 4	B6	K8	Tapir
27. 5	10. 4	B6	A9	Sheep
28. 5	11. 4	B6	B10	Deer
29. 5	12. 4	B6	C11	Horse
30. 5	13. 4	B6	D12	Stag
31. 5	14. 4	B6	E1	Serpent
1. 6	15. 4	B6	F2	Earthworm
2. 6	16. 4	B6	G3	Crocodile
3. 6	17. 4	B6	H4	Dragon
4. 6	18. 4	B6	J5	Badger
5. 6	19. 4	B6	K6	Hare
6. 6	20. 4	B6	A7	Fox
7. 6	21. 4	B6	B8	Tiger
8. 6	22. 4	B6	C9	Leopard
9. 6	23. 4	B6	D10	Griffon
10. 6	24. 4	B6	E11	Ox
11. 6	25. 4	B6	F12	Bat
12. 6	26. 4	B6	G1	Rat
13. 6	27. 4	B6	H2	Swallow
14. 6	28. 4	B6	J3	Pig
15. 6	29. 4	B6	K4	Porcupine
16. 6	30. 4	B6	A5	Wolf
17. 6	1. 5	C7	B6	Dog
18. 6	2. 5	C7	C7	Pheasant
19. 6	3. 5	C7	D8	Cock
20. 6	4. 5	C7	E9	Crow
21. 6	5. 5	C7	F10	Monkey
22. 6	6. 5	C7	G11	Gibbon
23. 6	7. 5	C7	H12	Tapir
24. 6	8. 5	C7	J1	Sheep
25. 6	9. 5	C7	K2	Deer
26. 6	10. 5	C7	A3	Horse
27. 6	11. 5	C7	B4	Stag
28. 6	12. 5	C7	C5	Serpent
29. 6	13. 5	C7	D6	Earthworm
30. 6	14. 5	C7	E7	Crocodile
1. 7	15. 5	C7	F8	Dragon
2. 7	16. 5	C7	G9	Badger
3. 7	17. 5	C7	H10	Hare
4. 7	18. 5	C7	J11	Fox
5. 7	19. 5	C7	K12	Tiger
6. 7	20. 5	C7	A1	Leopard
7. 7	21. 5	C7	B2	Griffon
8. 7	22. 5	C7	C3	Ox
9. 7	23. 5	C7	D4	Bat
10. 7	24. 5	C7	E5	Rat
11. 7	25. 5	C7	F6	Swallow
12. 7	26. 5	C7	G7	Pig
13. 7	27. 5	C7	H8	Porcupine
14. 7	28. 5	C7	J9	Wolf
15. 7	29. 5	C7	K10	Dog
16. 7	1. 6	D8	A11	Pheasant
17. 7	2. 6	D8	B12	Cock
18. 7	3. 6	D8	C1	Crow
19. 7	4. 6	D8	D2	Monkey
20. 7	5. 6	D8	E3	Gibbon
21. 7	6. 6	D8	F4	Tapir
22. 7	7. 6	D8	G5	Sheep
23. 7	8. 6	D8	H6	Deer
24. 7	9. 6	D8	J7	Horse
25. 7	10. 6	D8	K8	Stag
26. 7	11. 6	D8	A9	Serpent
27. 7	12. 6	D8	B10	Earthworm
28. 7	13. 6	D8	C11	Crocodile
29. 7	14. 6	D8	D12	Dragon
30. 7	15. 6	D8	E1	Badger
31. 7	16. 6	D8	F2	Hare
1. 8	17. 6	D8	G3	Fox
2. 8	18. 6	D8	H4	Tiger
3. 8	19. 6	D8	J5	Leopard
4. 8	20. 6	D8	K6	Griffon
5. 8	21. 6	D8	A7	Ox
6. 8	22. 6	D8	B8	Bat
7. 8	23. 6	D8	C9	Rat
8. 8	24. 6	D8	D10	Swallow
9. 8	25. 6	D8	E11	Pig
10. 8	26. 6	D8	F12	Porcupine
11. 8	27. 6	D8	G1	Wolf
12. 8	28. 6	D8	H2	Dog
13. 8	29. 6	D8	J3	Pheasant
14. 8	30. 6	D8	K4	Cock
15. 8	1. 7	E9	A5	Crow
16. 8	2. 7	E9	B6	Monkey
17. 8	3. 7	E9	C7	Gibbon
18. 8	4. 7	E9	D8	Tapir
19. 8	5. 7	E9	E9	Sheep
20. 8	6. 7	E9	F10	Deer
21. 8	7. 7	E9	G11	Horse
22. 8	8. 7	E9	H12	Stag
23. 8	9. 7	E9	J1	Serpent
24. 8	10. 7	E9	K2	Earthworm
25. 8	11. 7	E9	A3	Crocodile
26. 8	12. 7	E9	B4	Dragon
27. 8	13. 7	E9	C5	Badger
28. 8	14. 7	E9	D6	Hare
29. 8	15. 7	E9	E7	Fox
30. 8	16. 7	E9	F8	Tiger
31. 8	17. 7	E9	G9	Leopard
1. 9	18. 7	E9	H10	Griffon
2. 9	19. 7	E9	J11	Ox
3. 9	20. 7	E9	K12	Bat
4. 9	21. 7	E9	A1	Rat
5. 9	22. 7	E9	B2	Swallow
6. 9	23. 7	E9	C3	Pig
7. 9	24. 7	E9	D4	Porcupine
8. 9	25. 7	E9	E5	Wolf
9. 9	26. 7	E9	F6	Dog
10. 9	27. 7	E9	G7	Pheasant
11. 9	28. 7	E9	H8	Cock
12. 9	29. 7	E9	J9	Crow
13. 9	1. 8	F10	K10	Monkey
14. 9	2. 8	F10	A11	Gibbon
15. 9	3. 8	F10	B12	Tapir
16. 9	4. 8	F10	C1	Sheep
17. 9	5. 8	F10	D2	Deer
18. 9	6. 8	F10	E3	Horse
19. 9	7. 8	F10	F4	Stag
20. 9	8. 8	F10	G5	Serpent
21. 9	9. 8	F10	H6	Earthworm
22. 9	10. 8	F10	J7	Crocodile
23. 9	11. 8	F10	K8	Dragon
24. 9	12. 8	F10	A9	Badger
25. 9	13. 8	F10	B10	Hare
26. 9	14. 8	F10	C11	Fox
27. 9	15. 8	F10	D12	Tiger
28. 9	16. 8	F10	E1	Leopard
29. 9	17. 8	F10	F2	Griffon

Solar date	Lunar date	Month HS/EB	Day HS/EB	Constellation	Solar date	Lunar date	Month HS/EB	Day HS/EB	Constellation
30. 9	18. 8	F10	G3	Ox	6.12	26.10	H12	D10	Monkey
1.10	19. 8	F10	H4	Bat	7.12	27.10	H12	E11	Gibbon
2.10	20. 8	F10	J5	Rat	8.12	28.10	H12	F12	Tapir
3.10	21. 8	F10	K6	Swallow	9.12	29.10	H12	G1	Sheep
4.10	22. 8	F10	A7	Pig	10.12	30.10	H12	H2	Deer
5.10	23. 8	F10	B8	Porcupine	11.12	1.11	J1	J3	Horse
6.10	24. 8	F10	C9	Wolf	12.12	2.11	J1	K4	Stag
7.10	25. 8	F10	D10	Dog	13.12	3.11	J1	A5	Serpent
8.10	26. 8	F10	E11	Pheasant	14.12	4.11	J1	B6	Earthworm
9.10	27. 8	F10	F12	Cock	15.12	5.11	J1	C7	Crocodile
10.10	28. 8	F10	G1	Crow	16.12	6.11	J1	D8	Dragon
11.10	29. 8	F10	H2	Monkey	17.12	7.11	J1	E9	Badger
12.10	30. 8	F10	J3	Gibbon	18.12	8.11	J1	F10	Hare
13.10	1. 9	G11	K4	Tapir	19.12	9.11	J1	G11	Fox
14.10	2. 9	G11	A5	Sheep	20.12	10.11	J1	H12	Tiger
15.10	3. 9	G11	B6	Deer	21.12	11.11	J1	J1	Leopard
16.10	4. 9	G11	C7	Horse	22.12	12.11	J1	K2	Griffon
17.10	5. 9	G11	D8	Stag	23.12	13.11	J1	A3	Ox
19.10	6. 9	G11	E9	Serpent	24.12	14.11	J1	B4	Bat
20.10	8. 9	G11	G11	Crocodile	25.12	15.11	J1	C5	Rat
21.10	9. 9	G11	H12	Dragon	26.12	16.11	J1	D6	Swallow
22.10	10. 9	G11	J1	Badger	27.12	17.11	J1	E7	Pig
23.10	11. 9	G11	K2	Hare	28.12	18.11	J1	F8	Porcupine
24.10	12. 9	G11	A3	Fox	29.12	19.11	J1	G9	Wolf
25.10	13. 9	G11	B4	Tiger	30.12	20.11	J1	H10	Dog
26.10	14. 9	G11	C5	Leopard	31.12	21.11	J1	J11	Pheasant
27.10	15. 9	G11	D6	Griffon					
28.10	16. 9	G11	E7	Ox	**1978**				
29.10	17. 9	G11	F8	Bat	1. 1	22.11	J1	K12	Cock
30.10	18. 9	G11	G9	Rat	2. 1	23.11	J1	A1	Crow
31.10	19. 9	G11	H10	Swallow	3. 1	24.11	J1	B2	Monkey
1.11	20. 9	G11	J11	Pig	4. 1	25.11	J1	C3	Gibbon
2.11	21. 9	G11	K12	Porcupine	5. 1	26.11	J1	D4	Tapir
3.11	22. 9	G11	A1	Wolf	6. 1	27.11	J1	E5	Sheep
4.11	23. 9	G11	B2	Dog	7. 1	28.11	J1	F6	Deer
5.11	24. 9	G11	C3	Pheasant	8. 1	29.11	J1	G7	Horse
6.11	25. 9	G11	D4	Cock	9. 1	1.12	K2	H8	Stag
7.11	26. 9	G11	E5	Crow	10. 1	2.12	K2	J9	Serpent
8.11	27. 9	G11	F6	Monkey	11. 1	3.12	K2	K10	Earthworm
9.11	28. 9	G11	G7	Gibbon	12. 1	4.12	K2	A11	Crocodile
10.11	29. 9	G11	H8	Tapir	13. 1	5.12	K2	B12	Dragon
11.11	1.10	H12	J9	Sheep	14. 1	6.12	K2	C1	Badger
12.11	2.10	H12	K10	Deer	15. 1	7.12	K2	D2	Hare
13.11	3.10	H12	A11	Horse	16. 1	8.12	K2	E3	Fox
14.11	4.10	H12	B12	Stag	17. 1	9.12	K2	F4	Tiger
15.11	5.10	H12	C1	Serpent	18. 1	10.12	K2	G5	Leopard
16.11	6.10	H12	D2	Earthworm	19. 1	11.12	K2	H6	Griffon
17.11	7.10	H12	E3	Crocodile	20. 1	12.12	K2	J7	Ox
18.11	8.10	H12	F4	Dragon	21. 1	13.12	K2	K8	Bat
19.11	9.10	H12	G5	Badger	22. 1	14.12	K2	A9	Rat
20.11	10.10	H12	H6	Hare	23. 1	15.12	K2	B10	Swallow
21.11	11.10	H12	J7	Fox	24. 1	16.12	K2	C11	Pig
22.11	12.10	H12	K8	Tiger	25. 1	17.12	K2	D12	Porcupine
23.11	13.10	H12	A9	Leopard	26. 1	18.12	K2	E1	Wolf
24.11	14.10	H12	H10	Griffon	27. 1	19.12	K2	F2	Dog
25.11	15.10	H12	C11	Ox	28. 1	20.12	K2	G3	Pheasant
26.11	16.10	H12	D12	Bat	29. 1	21.12	K2	H4	Cock
27.11	17.10	H12	E1	Rat	30. 1	22.12	K2	J5	Crow
28.11	18.10	H12	F2	Swallow	31. 1	23.12	K2	K6	Monkey
29.11	19.10	H12	G3	Pig	1. 2	24.12	K2	A7	Gibbon
30.11	20.10	H12	H4	Porcupine	2. 2	25.12	K2	B8	Tapir
1.12	21.10	H12	J5	Wolf	3. 2	26.12	K2	C9	Sheep
2.12	22.10	H12	K6	Dog	4. 2	27.12	K2	D10	Deer
3.12	23.10	H12	A7	Pheasant	5. 2	28.12	K2	E11	Horse
4.12	24.10	H12	B8	Cock	6. 2	29.12	K2	F12	Stag
5.12	25.10	H12	C9	Crow					

MOU WU YEAR

Solar date	Lunar date	Month HS/EB	Day HS/EB	Constellation
7. 2	1. 1	A3	G1	Serpent
8. 2	2. 1	A3	H2	Earthworm
9. 2	3. 1	A3	J3	Crocodile
10. 2	4. 1	A3	K4	Dragon
11. 2	5. 1	A3	A5	Badger
12. 2	6. 1	A3	B6	Hare
13. 2	7. 1	A3	C7	Fox
14. 2	8. 1	A3	D8	Tiger
15. 2	9. 1	A3	E9	Leopard
16. 2	10. 1	A3	F10	Griffon
17. 2	11. 1	A3	G11	Ox
18. 2	12. 1	A3	H12	Bat
19. 2	13. 1	A3	J1	Rat
20. 2	14. 1	A3	K2	Swallow
21. 2	14. 1	A3	A3	Pig
22. 2	16. 1	A3	B4	Porcupine
23. 2	17. 1	A3	C5	Wolf
24. 2	18. 1	A3	D6	Dog
25. 2	19. 1	A3	E7	Pheasant
26. 2	20. 1	A3	F8	Cock
27. 2	21. 1	A3	G9	Crow
28. 2	22. 1	A3	H10	Monkey
1. 3	23. 1	A3	J11	Gibbon
2. 3	24. 1	A3	K12	Tapir
3. 3	25. 1	A3	A1	Sheep
4. 3	26. 1	A3	B2	Deer
5. 3	27. 1	A3	C3	Horse
6. 3	28. 1	A3	D4	Stag
7. 3	29. 1	A3	E5	Serpent
8. 3	30. 1	A3	F6	Earthworm
9. 3	1. 2	B4	G7	Crocodile
10. 3	2. 2	B4	H8	Dragon
11. 3	3. 2	B4	J9	Badger
12. 3	4. 2	B4	K10	Hare
13. 3	5. 2	B4	A11	Fox
14. 3	6. 2	B4	B12	Tiger
15. 3	7. 2	B4	C1	Leopard
16. 3	8. 2	B4	D2	Griffon
17. 3	9. 2	B4	E3	Ox
18. 3	10. 2	B4	F4	Bat
19. 3	11. 2	B4	G5	Rat
20. 3	12. 2	B4	H6	Swallow
21. 3	13. 2	B4	J7	Pig
22. 3	14. 2	B4	K8	Porcupine
23. 3	15. 2	B4	A9	Wolf
24. 3	16. 2	B4	B10	Dog
25. 3	17. 2	B4	C11	Pheasant
26. 3	18. 2	B4	D12	Cock
27. 3	19. 2	B4	E1	Crow
28. 3	20. 2	B4	F2	Monkey
29. 3	21. 2	B4	G3	Gibbon
30. 3	22. 2	B4	H4	Tapir
31. 3	23. 2	B4	J5	Sheep
1. 4	24. 2	B4	K6	Deer
2. 4	25. 2	B4	A7	Horse
3. 4	26. 2	B4	B8	Stag
4. 4	27. 2	B4	C9	Serpent
5. 4	28. 2	B4	D10	Earthworm
6. 4	29. 2	B4	E11	Crocodile
7. 4	1. 3	C5	F12	Dragon
8. 4	2. 3	C5	G1	Badger
9. 4	3. 3	C5	H2	Hare
10. 4	4. 3	C5	J3	Fox
11. 4	5. 3	C5	K4	Tiger
12. 4	6. 3	C5	A5	Leopard
13. 4	7. 3	C5	B6	Griffon
14. 4	8. 3	C5	C7	Ox
15. 4	9. 3	C5	D8	Bat
16. 4	10. 3	C5	E9	Rat
17. 4	11. 3	C5	F10	Swallow
18. 4	12. 3	C5	G11	Pig
19. 4	13. 3	C5	H12	Porcupine
20. 4	14. 3	C5	J1	Wolf
21. 4	15. 3	C5	K2	Dog
22. 4	16. 3	C5	A3	Pheasant
23. 4	17. 3	C5	B4	Cock
24. 4	18. 3	C5	C5	Crow
25. 4	19. 3	C5	D6	Monkey
26. 4	20. 3	C5	E7	Gibbon
27. 4	21. 3	C5	F8	Tapir
28. 4	22. 3	C5	G9	Sheep
29. 4	23. 3	C5	H10	Deer
30. 4	24. 3	C5	J11	Horse
1. 5	25. 3	C5	K12	Stag
2. 5	26. 3	C5	A1	Serpent
3. 5	27. 3	C5	B2	Earthworm
4. 5	28. 3	C5	C3	Crocodile
5. 5	29. 3	C5	D4	Dragon
6. 5	30. 3	C5	E5	Badger
7. 5	1. 4	D6	F6	Hare
8. 5	2. 4	D6	G7	Fox
9. 5	3. 4	D6	H8	Tiger
10. 5	4. 4	D6	J9	Leopard
11. 5	5. 4	D6	K10	Griffon
12. 5	6. 4	D6	A11	Ox
13. 5	7. 4	D6	B12	Bat
14. 5	8. 4	D6	C1	Rat
15. 5	9. 4	D6	D2	Swallow
16. 5	10. 4	D6	E3	Pig
17. 5	11. 4	D6	F4	Porcupine
18. 5	12. 4	D6	G5	Wolf
19. 5	13. 4	D6	H6	Dog
20. 5	14. 4	D6	J7	Pheasant
21. 5	15. 4	D6	K8	Cock
22. 5	16. 4	D6	A9	Crow
23. 5	17. 4	D6	B10	Monkey
24. 5	18. 4	D6	C11	Gibbon
25. 5	19. 4	D6	D12	Tapir
26. 5	20. 4	D6	E1	Sheep
27. 5	21. 4	D6	F2	Deer
28. 5	22. 4	D6	G3	Stag
29. 5	23. 4	D6	H4	Stag
30. 5	24. 4	D6	J5	Serpent
31. 5	25. 4	D6	K6	Earthworm
1. 6	26. 4	D6	A7	Crocodile
2. 6	27. 4	D6	B8	Dragon
3. 6	28. 4	D6	C9	Badger
4. 6	29. 4	D6	D10	Hare
5. 6	30. 4	D6	E11	Fox
6. 6	1. 5	E7	F12	Tiger
7. 6	2. 5	E7	G1	Leopard
8. 6	3. 5	E7	H2	Griffon
9. 6	4. 5	E7	J3	Ox
10. 6	5. 5	E7	K4	Bat
11. 6	6. 5	E7	A5	Rat
12. 6	7. 5	E7	B6	Swallow
13. 6	8. 5	E7	C7	Pig
14. 6	9. 5	E7	D8	Porcupine
15. 6	10. 5	E7	E9	Wolf
16. 6	11. 5	E7	F10	Dog
17. 6	12. 5	E7	G11	Pheasant
18. 6	13. 5	E7	H12	Cock
19. 6	14. 5	E7	J1	Crow
20. 6	15. 5	E7	K2	Monkey
21. 6	16. 5	E7	A3	Gibbon
22. 6	17. 5	E7	B4	Tapir
23. 6	18. 5	E7	C5	Sheep
24. 6	19. 5	E7	D6	Deer
25. 6	20. 5	E7	E7	Horse
26. 6	21. 5	E7	F8	Stag
27. 6	22. 5	E7	G9	Serpent
28. 6	23. 5	E7	H10	Earthworm

Solar date	Lunar date	Month HS/EB	Day HS/EB	Constellation	Solar date	Lunar date	Month HS/EB	Day HS/EB	Constellation
29. 6	24. 5	E7	J11	Crocodile	10. 9	8. 8	H10	B12	Cock
30. 6	25. 5	E7	K12	Dragon	11. 9	9. 8	H10	C1	Crow
1. 7	26. 5	E7	A1	Badger	12. 9	10. 8	H10	D2	Monkey
2. 7	27. 5	E7	B2	Hare	13. 9	11. 8	H10	E3	Gibbon
3. 7	28. 5	E7	C3	Fox	14. 9	12. 8	H10	F4	Tapir
4. 7	29. 5	E7	D4	Tiger	15. 9	13. 8	H10	G5	Sheep
5. 7	1. 6	F8	E5	Leopard	16. 9	14. 8	H10	H6	Deer
6. 7	2. 6	F8	F6	Griffon	17. 9	15. 8	H10	J7	Horse
7. 7	3. 6	F8	G7	Ox	18. 9	16. 8	H10	K8	Stag
8. 7	4. 6	F8	H8	Bat	19. 9	17. 8	H10	A9	Serpent
9. 7	5. 6	F8	J9	Rat	20. 9	18. 8	H10	B10	Earthworm
10. 7	6. 6	F8	K10	Swallow	21. 9	19. 8	H10	C11	Crocodile
11. 7	7. 6	F8	A11	Pig	22. 9	20. 8	H10	D12	Dragon
12. 7	8. 6	F8	B12	Porcupine	23. 9	21. 8	H10	E1	Badger
13. 7	9. 6	F8	C1	Wolf	24. 9	22. 8	H10	F2	Hare
14. 7	10. 6	F8	D2	Dog	25. 9	23. 8	H10	G3	Fox
15. 7	11. 6	F8	E3	Pheasant	26. 9	24. 8	H10	H4	Tiger
16. 7	12. 6	F8	F4	Cock	27. 9	25. 8	H10	J5	Leopard
17. 7	13. 6	F8	G5	Crow	28. 9	26. 8	H10	K6	Griffon
18. 7	14. 6	F8	H6	Monkey	29. 9	27. 8	H10	A7	Ox
19. 7	15. 6	F8	J7	Gibbon	30. 9	28. 8	H10	B8	Bat
20. 7	16. 6	F8	K8	Tapir	1.10	29. 8	H10	C9	Rat
21. 7	17. 6	F8	A9	Sheep	2.10	1. 9	J11	D10	Swallow
22. 7	18. 6	F8	B10	Deer	3.10	2. 9	J11	E11	Pig
23. 7	19. 6	F8	C11	Horse	4.10	3. 9	J11	F12	Porcupine
24. 7	20. 6	F8	D12	Stag	5.10	4. 9	J11	G1	Wolf
25. 7	21. 6	F8	E1	Serpent	6.10	5. 9	J11	H2	Dog
26. 7	22. 6	F8	F2	Earthworm	7.10	6. 9	J11	J3	Pheasant
27. 7	23. 6	F8	G3	Crocodile	8.10	7. 9	J11	K4	Cock
28. 7	24. 6	F8	H4	Dragon	9.10	8. 9	J11	A5	Crow
29. 7	25. 6	F8	J5	Badger	10.10	9. 9	J11	B6	Monkey
30. 7	26. 6	F8	K6	Hare	11.10	10. 9	J11	C7	Gibbon
31. 7	27. 6	F8	A7	Fox	12.10	11. 9	J11	D8	Tapir
1. 8	28. 6	F8	B8	Tiger	13.10	12. 9	J11	E9	Sheep
2. 8	29. 6	F8	C9	Leopard	14.10	13. 9	J11	F10	Deer
3. 8	30. 6	F8	D10	Griffon	15.10	14. 9	J11	G11	Horse
4. 8	1. 7	G9	E11	Ox	16.10	15. 9	J11	H12	Stag
5. 8	2. 7	G9	F12	Bat	17.10	16. 9	J11	J1	Serpent
6. 8	3. 7	G9	G1	Rat	18.10	17. 9	J11	K2	Earthworm
7. 8	4. 7	G9	H2	Swallow	19.10	18. 9	J11	A3	Crocodile
8. 8	5. 7	G9	J3	Pig	20.10	19. 9	J11	B4	Dragon
9. 8	6. 7	G9	K4	Porcupine	21.10	20. 9	J11	C5	Badger
10. 8	7. 7	G9	A5	Wolf	22.10	21. 9	J11	D6	Hare
11. 8	8. 7	G9	B6	Dog	23.10	22. 9	J11	E7	Fox
12. 8	9. 7	G9	C7	Pheasant	24.10	23. 9	J11	F8	Tiger
13. 8	10. 7	G9	D8	Cock	25.10	24. 9	J11	G9	Leopard
14. 8	11. 7	G9	E9	Crow	26.10	25. 9	J11	H10	Griffon
15. 8	12. 7	G9	F10	Monkey	27.10	26. 9	J11	J11	Ox
16. 8	13. 7	G9	G11	Gibbon	28.10	27. 9	J11	K12	Bat
17. 8	14. 7	G9	H12	Tapir	29.10	28. 9	J11	A1	Rat
18. 8	15. 7	G9	J1	Sheep	30.10	29. 9	J11	B2	Swallow
19. 8	16. 7	G9	K2	Deer	31.10	30. 9	J11	C3	Pig
20. 8	17. 7	G9	A3	Horse	1.11	1.10	K12	D4	Porcupine
21. 8	18. 7	G9	B4	Stag	2.11	2.10	K12	E5	Wolf
22. 8	19. 7	G9	C5	Serpent	3.11	3.10	K12	F6	Dog
23. 8	20. 7	G9	D6	Earthworm	4.11	4.10	K12	G7	Pheasant
24. 8	21. 7	G9	E7	Crocodile	5.11	5.10	K12	H8	Cock
25. 8	22. 7	G9	F8	Dragon	6.11	6.10	K12	J9	Crow
26. 8	23. 7	G9	G9	Badger	7.11	7.10	K12	K10	Monkey
27. 8	24. 7	G9	H10	Hare	8.11	8.10	K12	A11	Gibbon
28. 8	25. 7	G9	J11	Fox	9.11	9.10	K12	B12	Tapir
29. 8	26. 7	G9	K12	Tiger	10.11	10.10	K12	C1	Sheep
30. 8	27. 7	G9	A1	Leopard	11.11	11.10	K12	D2	Deer
31. 8	28. 7	G9	B2	Griffon	12.11	12.10	K12	E3	Horse
1. 9	29. 7	G8	C3	Ox	13.11	13.10	K12	F4	Stag
2. 9	30. 7	G9	D4	Bat	14.11	14.10	K12	G5	Serpent
3. 9	1. 8	H10	E5	Rat	15.11	15.10	K12	H6	Earthworm
4. 9	2. 8	H10	F6	Swallow	16.11	16.10	K12	J7	Crocodile
5. 9	3. 8	H10	G7	Pig	17.11	17.10	K12	K8	Dragon
6. 9	4. 8	H10	H8	Porcupine	18.11	18.10	K12	A9	Badger
7. 9	5. 8	H10	J9	Wolf	19.11	19.10	K12	B10	Hare
8. 9	6. 8	H10	K10	Dog	20.11	20.10	K12	C11	Fox
9. 9	7. 8	H10	A11	Pheasant	21.11	21.10	K12	D12	Tiger

Solar date	Lunar date	Month HS/EB	Day HS/EB	Constellation		Solar date	Lunar date	Month HS/EB	Day HS/EB	Constellation
22.11	22.10	K12	E1	Leopard		27.12	28.11	A1	K12	Porcupine
23.11	23.10	K12	F2	Griffon		28.12	29.11	A1	A1	Wolf
24.11	24.10	K12	G3	Ox		29.12	30.11	A1	B2	Dog
25.11	25.10	K12	H4	Bat		30.12	1.12	B2	C3	Pheasant
26.11	26.10	K12	J5	Rat		31.12	2.12	B2	D4	Cock
27.11	27.10	K12	K6	Swallow						
28.11	28.10	K12	A7	Pig		**1979**				
29.11	29.10	K12	B8	Porcupine						
30.11	1.11	A1	C9	Wolf		1. 1	3.12	B2	E5	Crow
1.12	2.11	A1	D10	Dog		2. 1	4.12	B2	F6	Monkey
2.12	3.11	A1	E11	Pheasant		3. 1	5.12	B2	G7	Gibbon
3.12	4.11	A1	F12	Cock		4. 1	6.12	B2	H8	Tapir
4.12	5.11	A1	G1	Crow		5. 1	7.12	B2	J9	Sheep
5.12	6.11	A1	H2	Monkey		6. 1	8.12	B2	K10	Deer
6.12	7.11	A1	J3	Gibbon		7. 1	9.12	B2	A11	Horse
7.12	8.11	A1	K4	Tapir		8. 1	10.12	B2	B12	Stag
8.12	9.11	A1	A5	Sheep		9. 1	11.12	B2	C1	Serpent
9.12	10.11	A1	B6	Deer		10. 1	12.12	B2	D2	Earthworm
10.12	11.11	A1	C7	Horse		11. 1	13.12	B2	E3	Crocodile
11.12	12.11	A1	D8	Stag		12. 1	14.12	B2	F4	Dragon
12.12	13.11	A1	E9	Serpent		13. 1	15.12	B2	G5	Badger
13.12	14.11	A1	F10	Earthworm		14. 1	16.12	B2	H6	Hare
14.12	15.11	A1	G11	Crocodile		15. 1	17.12	B2	J7	Fox
15.12	16.11	A1	H12	Dragon		16. 1	18.12	B2	K8	Tiger
16.12	17.11	A1	J1	Badger		17. 1	19.12	B2	A9	Leopard
17.12	18.11	A1	K2	Hare		18. 1	20.12	B2	B10	Griffon
18.12	19.11	A1	A3	Fox		19. 1	21.12	B2	C11	Ox
19.12	20.11	A1	B4	Tiger		20. 1	22.12	B2	D12	Bat
20.12	21.11	A1	C5	Leopard		21. 1	23.12	B2	E1	Rat
21.12	22.11	A1	D6	Griffon		22. 1	24.12	B2	F2	Swallow
22.12	23.11	A1	E7	Ox		23. 1	25.12	B2	G3	Pig
23.12	24.11	A1	F8	Bat		24. 1	26.12	B2	H4	Porcupine
24.12	25.11	A1	G9	Rat		25. 1	27.12	B2	J5	Wolf
25.12	26.11	A1	H10	Swallow		26. 1	28.12	B2	K6	Dog
26.12	27.11	A1	J11	Pig		27. 1	29.12	B2	A7	Pheasant

CHI WEI YEAR

Solar date	Lunar date	Month HS/EB	Day HS/EB	Constellation		Solar date	Lunar date	Month HS/EB	Day HS/EB	Constellation
28. 1	1. 1	C3	B8	Cock		2. 3	4. 2	D4	E5	Sheep
29. 1	2. 1	C3	C9	Crow		3. 3	5. 2	D4	F6	Deer
30. 1	3. 1	C3	D10	Monkey		4. 3	6. 2	D4	G7	Horse
31. 1	4. 1	C3	E11	Gibbon		5. 3	7. 2	D4	H8	Stag
1. 2	5. 1	C3	F12	Tapir		6. 3	8. 2	D4	J9	Serpent
2. 2	6. 1	C3	G1	Sheep		7. 3	9. 2	D4	K10	Earthworm
3. 2	7. 1	C3	H2	Deer		8. 3	10. 2	D4	A11	Crocodile
4. 2	8. 1	C3	J3	Horse		9. 3	11. 2	D4	B12	Dragon
5. 2	9. 1	C3	K4	Stag		10. 3	12. 2	D4	C1	Badger
6. 2	10. 1	C3	A5	Serpent		11. 3	13. 2	D4	D2	Hare
7. 2	11. 1	C3	B6	Earthworm		12. 3	14. 2	D4	E3	Fox
8. 2	12. 1	C3	C7	Crocodile		13. 3	15. 2	D4	F4	Tiger
9. 2	13. 1	C3	D8	Dragon		14. 3	16. 2	D4	G5	Leopard
10. 2	14. 1	C3	E9	Badger		15. 3	17. 2	D4	H6	Griffon
11. 2	15. 1	C3	F10	Hare		16. 3	18. 2	D4	J7	Ox
12. 2	16. 1	C3	G11	Fox		17. 3	19. 2	D4	K8	Bat
13. 2	17. 1	C3	H12	Tiger		18. 3	20. 2	D4	A9	Rat
14. 2	18. 1	C3	J1	Leopard		19. 3	21. 2	D4	B10	Swallow
15. 2	19. 9	C3	K2	Griffon		20. 3	22. 2	D4	C11	Pig
16. 2	20. 1	C3	A3	Ox		21. 3	23. 2	D4	D12	Porcupine
17. 2	21. 1	C3	B4	Bat		22. 3	24. 2	D4	E1	Wolf
18. 2	22. 1	C3	C5	Rat		23. 3	25. 2	D4	F2	Dog
19. 2	23. 1	C3	D6	Swallow		24. 3	26. 2	D4	G3	Pheasant
20. 2	24. 1	C3	E7	Pig		25. 3	27. 2	D4	H4	Cock
21. 2	25. 1	C3	F8	Porcupine		26. 3	28. 2	D4	J5	Crow
22. 2	26. 1	C3	G9	Wolf		27. 3	29. 2	D4	K6	Monkey
23. 2	27. 1	C3	H10	Dog		28. 3	1. 3	E5	A7	Gibbon
24. 2	28. 1	C3	J11	Pheasant		29. 3	2. 3	E5	B8	Tapir
25. 2	29. 1	C3	K12	Cock		30. 3	3. 3	E5	C9	Sheep
26. 2	30. 1	C3	A1	Crow		31. 3	4. 3	E5	D10	Deer
27. 2	1. 2	D4	B2	Monkey		1. 4	5. 3	E5	E11	Horse
28. 2	2. 2	D4	C3	Gibbon		2. 4	6. 3	E5	F12	Stag
1. 3	3. 2	D4	D4	Tapir		3. 4	7. 3	E5	G1	Serpent

Solar date	Lunar date	Month HS/EB	Day HS/EB	Constellation
4. 4	8. 3	E5	H2	Earthworm
5. 4	9. 3	E5	J3	Crocodile
6. 4	10. 3	E5	K4	Dragon
7. 4	11. 3	E5	A5	Badger
8. 4	12. 3	E5	B6	Hare
9. 4	13. 3	E5	C7	Fox
10. 4	14. 3	E5	D8	Tiger
11. 4	15. 3	E5	E9	Leopard
12. 4	16. 3	E5	F10	Griffon
13. 4	17. 3	E5	G11	Ox
14. 4	18. 3	E5	H12	Rat
15. 4	19. 3	E5	J1	Rat
16. 4	20. 3	E5	K2	Swallow
17. 4	21. 3	E5	A3	Pig
18. 4	22. 3	E5	B4	Porcupine
19. 4	23. 3	E5	C5	Wolf
20. 4	24. 3	E5	D6	Dog
21. 4	25. 3	E5	E7	Pheasant
22. 4	26. 3	E5	F8	Cock
23. 4	27. 3	E5	G9	Crow
24. 4	28. 3	E5	H10	Monkey
25. 4	29. 3	E5	J11	Gibbon
26. 4	1. 4	F6	K12	Tapir
27. 4	2. 4	F6	A1	Sheep
28. 4	3. 4	F6	B2	Deer
29. 4	4. 4	F6	C3	Horse
30. 4	5. 4	F6	D4	Stag
1. 5	6. 4	F6	E5	Serpent
2. 5	7. 4	F6	F6	Earthworm
3. 5	8. 4	F6	G7	Crocodile
4. 5	9. 4	F6	H8	Dragon
5. 5	10. 4	F6	J9	Badger
6. 5	11. 4	F6	K10	Hare
7. 5	12. 4	F6	A11	Fox
8. 5	13. 4	F6	B12	Tiger
9. 5	14. 4	F6	C1	Leopard
10. 5	15. 4	F6	D2	Griffon
11. 5	16. 4	F6	E3	Ox
12. 5	17. 4	F6	F4	Bat
13. 5	18. 4	F6	G5	Rat
14. 5	19. 4	F6	H6	Swallow
15. 5	20. 4	F6	J7	Pig
16. 5	21. 4	F6	K8	Porcupine
17. 5	22. 4	F6	A9	Wolf
18. 5	23. 4	F6	B10	Dog
19. 5	24. 4	F6	C11	Pheasant
20. 5	25. 4	F6	D12	Cock
21. 5	26. 4	F6	E1	Crow
22. 5	27. 4	F6	F2	Monkey
23. 5	28. 4	F6	G3	Gibbon
24. 5	29. 4	F6	H4	Tapir
25. 5	30. 4	F6	J5	Sheep
26. 5	1. 5	G7	K6	Deer
27. 5	2. 5	G7	A7	Horse
28. 5	3. 5	G7	B8	Stag
29. 5	4. 5	G7	C9	Serpent
30. 5	5. 5	G7	D10	Earthworm
31. 5	6. 5	G7	E11	Crocodile
1. 6	7. 5	G7	F12	Dragon
2. 6	8. 5	G7	G1	Badger
3. 6	9. 5	G7	H2	Hare
4. 6	10. 5	G7	J3	Fox
5. 5	11. 5	G7	K4	Tiger
6. 5	12. 5	G7	A5	Leopard
7. 5	13. 5	G7	B6	Griffon
8. 5	14. 5	G7	C7	Ox
9. 5	15. 5	G7	D8	Bat
10. 5	16. 5	G7	E9	Rat
11. 6	17. 5	G7	F10	Swallow
12. 6	18. 5	G7	G11	Pig
13. 6	19. 5	G7	H12	Porcupine
14. 6	20. 5	G7	J1	Wolf
15. 6	21. 5	G7	K2	Dog
16. 6	22. 5	G7	A3	Pheasant
17. 6	23. 5	G7	B4	Cock
18. 6	24. 5	G7	C5	Crow
19. 6	25. 5	G7	D6	Monkey
20. 6	26. 5	G7	E7	Gibbon
21. 6	27. 5	G7	F8	Tapir
22. 6	28. 5	G7	G9	Sheep
23. 6	29. 5	G7	H10	Deer
24. 6	1. 6	H8	J11	Horse
25. 6	2. 6	H8	K12	Stag
26. 6	3. 6	H8	A1	Serpent
27. 6	4. 6	H8	B2	Earthworm
28. 6	5. 6	H8	C3	Crocodile
29. 6	6. 6	H8	D4	Dragon
30. 6	7. 6	H8	E5	Badger
1. 7	8. 6	H8	F6	Hare
2. 7	9. 6	H8	G7	Fox
3. 7	10. 6	H8	H8	Tiger
4. 7	11. 6	H8	J9	Leopard
5. 7	12. 6	H8	K10	Griffon
6. 7	13. 6	H8	A11	Ox
7. 7	14. 6	H8	B12	Bat
8. 7	15. 6	H8	C1	Rat
9. 7	16. 6	H8	D2	Swallow
10. 7	17. 6	H8	E3	Pig
11. 7	18. 6	H8	F4	Porcupine
12. 7	19. 6	H8	G5	Wolf
13. 7	20. 6	H8	H6	Dog
14. 7	21. 6	H8	J7	Pheasant
15. 7	22. 6	H8	K8	Cock
16. 7	23. 6	H8	A9	Crow
17. 7	24. 6	H8	B10	Monkey
18. 7	25. 6	H8	C11	Gibbon
19. 7	26. 6	H8	D12	Tapir
20. 7	27. 6	H8	E1	Sheep
21. 7	28. 6	H8	F2	Deer
22. 7	29. 6	H8	G3	Horse
23. 7	30. 6	H8	H4	Stag
24. 7	*1. 6*	*H8*	J5	Serpent
25. 7	*2. 6*	*H8*	K6	Earthworm
26. 7	*3. 6*	*H8*	A7	Crocodile
27. 7	*4. 6*	*H8*	B8	Dragon
28. 7	*5. 6*	*H8*	C9	Badger
29. 7	*6. 6*	*H8*	D10	Hare
30. 7	*7. 6*	*H8*	E11	Fox
31. 7	*8. 6*	*H8*	F12	Tiger
1. 8	*9. 6*	*H8*	G1	Leopard
2. 8	*10. 6*	*H8*	H2	Griffon
3. 8	*11. 6*	*H8*	J3	Ox
4. 8	*12. 6*	*H8*	K4	Bat
5. 8	*13. 6*	*H8*	A5	Rat
6. 8	*14. 6*	*H8*	B6	Swallow
7. 8	*15. 6*	*H8*	C7	Pig
8. 8	*16. 6*	*H8*	D8	Porcupine
9. 8	*17. 6*	*H8*	E9	Wolf
10. 8	*18. 6*	*H8*	F10	Dog
11. 8	*19. 6*	*H8*	G11	Pheasant
12. 8	*20. 6*	*H8*	H12	Cock
13. 8	*21. 6*	*H8*	J1	Crow
14. 8	*22. 6*	*H8*	K2	Monkey
15. 8	*23. 6*	*H8*	A3	Gibbon
16. 8	*24. 6*	*H8*	B4	Tapir
17. 8	*25. 6*	*H8*	C5	Sheep
18. 8	*26. 6*	*H8*	D6	Deer
19. 8	*27. 6*	*H8*	E7	Horse
20. 8	*28. 6*	*H8*	F8	Stag
21. 8	*29. 6*	*H8*	G9	Serpent
22. 8	*30. 6*	*H8*	H10	Earthworm
23. 8	1. 7	J9	J11	Crocodile
24. 8	2. 7	J9	K12	Dragon
25. 8	3. 7	J9	A1	Badger
26. 8	4. 7	J9	B2	Hare
27. 8	5. 7	J9	C3	Fox

Solar date	Lunar date	Month HS/EB	Day HS/EB	Constellation	Solar date	Lunar date	Month HS/EB	Day HS/EB	Constellation
28. 8	6. 7	J9	D4	Tiger	9.11	20. 9	A11	G5	Sheep
29. 8	7. 7	J9	E5	Leopard	10.11	21. 9	A11	H6	Deer
30. 8	8. 7	J9	F6	Griffon	11.11	22. 9	A11	J7	Horse
31. 8	9. 7	J9	G7	Ox	12.11	23. 9	A11	K8	Stag
1. 9	10. 7	J9	H8	Bat	13.11	24. 9	A11	A9	Serpent
2. 9	11. 7	J9	J9	Rat	14.11	25. 9	A11	B10	Earthworm
3. 9	12. 7	J9	K10	Swallow	15.11	26. 9	A11	C11	Crocodile
4. 9	13. 7	J9	A11	Pig	16.11	27. 9	A11	D12	Dragon
5. 9	14. 7	J9	B12	Porcupine	17.11	28. 9	A11	E1	Badger
6. 9	15. 7	J9	C1	Wolf	18.11	29. 9	A11	F2	Hare
7. 9	16. 7	J9	D2	Dog	19.11	30. 9	A11	G3	Fox
8. 9	17. 7	J9	E3	Pheasant	20.11	1.10	B12	H4	Tiger
9. 9	18. 7	J9	F4	Cock	21.11	2.10	B12	J5	Leopard
10. 9	19. 7	J9	G5	Crow	22.11	3.10	B12	K6	Griffon
11. 9	20. 7	J9	H6	Monkey	23.11	4.10	B12	A7	Ox
12. 9	21. 7	J9	J7	Gibbon	24.11	5.10	B12	B8	Bat
13. 9	22. 7	J9	K8	Tapir	25.11	6.10	B12	C9	Rat
14. 9	23. 7	J9	A9	Sheep	26.11	7.10	B12	D10	Swallow
15. 9	24. 7	J9	B10	Deer	27.11	8.10	B12	E11	Pig
16. 9	25. 7	J9	C11	Horse	28.11	9.10	B12	F12	Porcupine
17. 9	26. 7	J9	D12	Stag	29.11	10.10	B12	G1	Wolf
18. 9	27. 7	J9	E1	Serpent	30.11	11.10	B12	H2	Dog
19. 9	28. 7	J9	F2	Earthworm	1.12	12.10	B12	J3	Pheasant
20. 9	29. 7	J9	G3	Crocodile	2.12	13.10	B12	K4	Cock
21. 9	1. 8	K10	H4	Dragon	3.12	14.10	B12	A5	Crow
22. 9	2. 8	K10	J5	Badger	4.12	15.10	B12	B6	Monkey
23. 9	3. 8	K10	K6	Hare	5.12	16.10	B12	C7	Gibbon
24. 9	4. 8	K10	A7	Fox	6.12	17.10	B12	D8	Tapir
25. 9	5. 8	K10	B8	Tiger	7.12	18.10	B12	E9	Sheep
26. 9	6. 8	K10	C9	Leopard	8.12	19.10	B12	F10	Deer
27. 9	7. 8	K10	D10	Griffon	9.12	20.10	B12	G11	Horse
28. 9	8. 8	K10	E11	Ox	10.12	21.10	B12	H12	Stag
29. 9	9. 8	K10	F12	Bat	11.12	22.10	B12	J1	Serpent
30. 9	10. 8	K10	G1	Rat	12.12	23.10	B12	K2	Earthworm
1.10	11. 8	K10	H2	Swallow	13.12	24.10	B12	A3	Crocodile
2.10	12. 8	K10	J3	Pig	14.12	25.10	B12	B4	Dragon
3.10	13. 8	K10	K4	Porcupine	15.12	26.10	B12	C5	Badger
4.10	14. 8	K10	A5	Wolf	16.12	27.10	B12	D6	Hare
5.10	15. 8	K10	B6	Dog	17.12	28.10	B12	E7	Fox
6.10	16. 8	K10	C7	Pheasant	18.12	29.10	B12	F8	Tiger
7.10	17. 8	K10	D8	Cock	19.12	1.11	C1	G9	Leopard
8.10	18. 8	K10	E9	Crow	20.12	2.11	C1	H10	Griffon
9.10	19. 8	K10	F10	Monkey	21.12	3.11	C1	J11	Ox
10.10	20. 8	K10	G11	Gibbon	22.12	4.11	C1	K12	Bat
11.10	21. 8	K10	H12	Tapir	23.12	5.11	C1	A1	Rat
12.10	22. 8	K10	J1	Sheep	24.12	6.11	C1	B2	Swallow
13.10	23. 8	K10	K2	Deer	25.12	7.11	C1	C3	Pig
14.10	24. 8	K10	A3	Horse	26.12	8.11	C1	D4	Porcupine
15.10	25. 8	K10	B4	Stag	27.12	9.11	C1	E5	Wolf
16.10	26. 8	K10	C5	Serpent	28.12	10.11	C1	F6	Dog
17.10	27. 8	K10	D6	Earthworm	29.12	11.11	C1	G7	Pheasant
18.10	28. 8	K10	E7	Crocodile	30.12	12.11	C1	H8	Cock
19.10	29. 8	K10	F8	Dragon	31.12	13.11	C1	J9	Crow
20.10	30. 8	K10	G9	Badger	**1980**				
21.10	1. 9	A11	H10	Hare	1. 1	14.11	C1	K10	Monkey
22.10	2. 9	A11	J11	Fox	2. 1	15.11	C1	A11	Gibbon
23.10	3. 9	A11	K12	Tiger	3. 1	16.11	C1	B12	Tapir
24.10	4. 9	A11	A1	Leopard	4. 1	17.11	C1	C1	Sheep
25.10	5. 9	A11	B2	Griffon	5. 1	18.11	C1	D2	Deer
26.10	6. 9	A11	C3	Ox	6. 1	19.11	C1	E3	Horse
27.10	7. 9	A11	D4	Bat	7. 1	20.11	C1	F4	Stag
28.10	8. 9	A11	E5	Rat	8. 1	21.11	C1	G5	Serpent
29.10	9. 9	A11	F6	Swallow	9. 1	22.11	C1	H6	Earthworm
30.10	10. 9	A11	G7	Pig	10. 1	23.11	C1	J7	Crocodile
31.10	11. 9	A11	H8	Porcupine	11. 1	24.11	C1	K8	Dragon
1.11	12. 9	A11	J9	Wolf	12. 1	25.11	C1	A9	Badger
2.11	13. 9	A11	K10	Dog	13. 1	26.11	C1	B10	Hare
3.11	14. 9	A11	A11	Pheasant	14. 1	27.11	C1	C11	Fox
4.11	15. 9	A11	B12	Cock	15. 1	28.11	C1	D12	Tiger
5.11	16. 9	A11	C1	Crow	16. 1	29.11	C1	E1	Leopard
6.11	17. 9	A11	D2	Monkey	17. 1	30.11	C1	F2	Griffon
7.11	18. 9	A11	E3	Gibbon	18. 1	1.12	D2	G3	Ox
8.11	19. 9	A11	F4	Tapir					

Solar date	Lunar date	Month HS/EB	Day HS/EB	Constellation	Solar date	Lunar date	Month HS/EB	Day HS/EB	Constellation
19. 1	2.12	D2	H4	Bat	2. 2	16.12	D2	B6	Deer
20. 1	3.12	D2	J5	Rat	3. 2	17.12	D2	C7	Horse
21. 1	4.12	D2	K6	Swallow	4. 2	18.12	D2	D8	Stag
22. 1	5.12	D2	A7	Pig	5. 2	19.12	D2	E9	Serpent
23. 1	6.12	D2	B8	Porcupine	6. 2	20.12	D2	F10	Earthworm
24. 1	7.12	D2	C9	Wolf	7. 2	21.12	D2	G11	Crocodile
25. 1	8.12	D2	D10	Dog	8. 2	22.12	D2	H12	Dragon
26. 1	9.12	D2	E11	Pheasant	9. 2	23.12	D2	J1	Badger
27. 1	10.12	D2	F12	Cock	10. 2	24.12	D2	K2	Hare
28. 1	11.12	D2	G1	Crow	11. 2	25.12	D2	A3	Fox
29. 1	12.12	D2	H2	Monkey	12. 2	26.12	D2	B4	Tiger
30. 1	13.12	D2	J3	Gibbon	13. 2	27.12	D2	C5	Leopard
31. 1	14.12	D2	K4	Tapir	14. 2	28.12	D2	D6	Griffon
1. 2	15.12	D2	A5	Sheep	15. 2	29.12	D2	E7	Ox

KENG SHEN YEAR

Solar date	Lunar date	Month HS/EB	Day HS/EB	Constellation	Solar date	Lunar date	Month HS/EB	Day HS/EB	Constellation
16. 2	1. 1	E3	F8	Bat	10. 4	25. 2	F4	K2	Griffon
17. 2	2. 1	E3	G9	Rat	11. 4	26. 2	F4	A3	Ox
18. 2	3. 1	E3	H10	Swallow	12. 4	27. 2	F4	B4	Bat
19. 2	4. 1	E3	J11	Pig	13. 4	28. 2	F4	C5	Rat
20. 2	5. 1	E3	K12	Porcupine	14. 4	29. 2	F4	D6	Swallow
21. 2	6. 1	E3	A1	Wolf	15. 4	1. 3	G5	E7	Pig
22. 2	7. 1	E3	B2	Dog	16. 4	2. 3	G5	F8	Porcupine
23. 2	8. 1	E3	C3	Pheasant	17. 4	3. 3	G5	G9	Wolf
24. 2	9. 1	E3	D4	Cock	18. 4	4. 3	G5	H10	Dog
25. 2	10. 1	E3	E5	Crow	19. 4	5. 3	G5	J11	Pheasant
26. 2	11. 1	E3	F6	Monkey	20. 4	6. 3	G5	K12	Cock
27. 2	12. 1	E3	G7	Gibbon	21. 4	7. 3	G5	A1	Crow
28. 2	13. 1	E3	H8	Tapir	22. 4	8. 3	G5	B2	Monkey
29. 2	14. 1	E3	J9	Sheep	23. 4	9. 3	G5	C3	Gibbon
1. 3	15. 1	E3	K10	Deer	24. 4	10. 3	G5	D4	Tapir
2. 3	16. 1	E3	A11	Horse	25. 4	11. 3	G5	E5	Sheep
3. 3	17. 1	E3	B12	Stag	26. 4	12. 3	G5	F6	Deer
4. 3	18. 1	E3	C1	Serpent	27. 4	13. 3	G5	G7	Horse
5. 3	19. 1	E3	D2	Earthworm	28. 4	14. 3	G5	H8	Stag
6. 3	20. 1	E3	E3	Crocodile	29. 4	15. 3	G5	J9	Serpent
7. 3	21. 1	E3	F4	Dragon	30. 4	16. 3	G5	K10	Earthworm
8. 3	22. 1	E3	G5	Badger	1. 5	17. 3	G5	A11	Crocodile
9. 3	23. 1	E3	H6	Hare	2. 5	18. 3	G5	B12	Dragon
10. 3	24. 1	E3	J7	Fox	3. 5	19. 3	G5	C1	Badger
11. 3	25. 1	E3	K8	Tiger	4. 5	20. 3	G5	D2	Hare
12. 3	26. 1	E3	A9	Leopard	5. 5	21. 3	G5	E3	Fox
13. 3	27. 1	E3	B10	Griffon	6. 5	22. 3	G5	F4	Tiger
14. 3	28. 1	E3	C11	Ox	7. 5	23. 3	G5	G5	Leopard
15. 3	29. 1	E3	D12	Bat	8. 5	24. 3	G5	H6	Griffon
16. 3	30. 1	E3	E1	Rat	9. 5	25. 3	G5	J7	Ox
17. 3	1. 2	F4	F2	Swallow	10. 5	26. 3	G5	K8	Bat
18. 3	2. 2	F4	G3	Pig	11. 5	27. 3	G5	A9	Rat
19. 3	3. 2	F4	H4	Porcupine	12. 5	28. 3	G5	B10	Swallow
20. 3	4. 2	F4	J5	Wolf	13. 5	29. 3	G5	C11	Pig
21. 3	5. 2	F4	K6	Dog	14. 5	1. 4	H6	D12	Porcupine
22. 3	6. 2	F4	A7	Pheasant	15. 5	2. 4	H6	E1	Wolf
23. 3	7. 2	F4	B8	Cock	16. 5	3. 4	H6	F2	Dog
24. 3	8. 2	F4	C9	Crow	17. 5	4. 4	H6	G3	Pheasant
25. 3	9. 2	F4	D10	Monkey	18. 5	5. 4	H6	H4	Cock
26. 3	10. 2	F4	E11	Gibbon	19. 5	6. 4	H6	J5	Crow
27. 3	11. 2	F4	F12	Tapir	20. 5	7. 4	H6	K6	Monkey
28. 3	12. 2	F4	G1	Sheep	21. 5	8. 4	H6	A7	Gibbon
29. 3	13. 2	F4	H2	Deer	22. 5	9. 4	H6	B8	Tapir
30. 3	14. 2	F4	J3	Horse	23. 5	10. 4	H6	C9	Sheep
31. 3	15. 2	F4	K4	Stag	24. 5	11. 4	H6	D10	Deer
1. 4	16. 2	F4	A5	Serpent	25. 5	12. 4	H6	E11	Horse
2. 4	17. 2	F4	B6	Earthworm	26. 5	13. 4	H6	F12	Stag
3. 4	18. 2	F4	C7	Crocodile	27. 5	14. 4	H6	G1	Serpent
4. 4	19. 2	F4	D8	Dragon	28. 5	15. 4	H6	H2	Earthworm
5. 4	20. 2	F4	E9	Badger	29. 5	16. 4	H6	J3	Crocodile
6. 4	21. 2	F4	F10	Hare	30. 5	17. 4	H6	K4	Dragon
7. 4	22. 2	F4	G11	Fox	31. 5	18. 4	H6	A5	Badger
8. 4	23. 2	F4	H12	Tiger	1. 6	19. 4	H6	B6	Hare
9. 4	24. 2	F4	J1	Leopard	2. 6	20. 4	H6	C7	Fox

Solar date	Lunar date	Month HS/EB	Day HS/EB	Constellation
3. 6	21. 4	H6	D8	Tiger
4. 6	22. 4	H6	E9	Leopard
5. 6	23. 4	H6	F10	Griffon
6. 6	24. 4	H6	G11	Ox
7. 6	25. 4	H6	H12	Bat
8. 6	26. 4	H6	J1	Rat
9. 6	27. 4	H6	K2	Swallow
10. 6	28. 4	H6	A3	Pig
11. 6	29. 4	H6	B4	Porcupine
12. 6	30. 4	H6	C5	Wolf
13. 6	1. 5	J7	D6	Dog
14. 6	2. 5	J7	E7	Pheasant
15. 6	3. 5	J7	F8	Cock
16. 6	4. 5	J7	G9	Crow
17. 6	5. 5	J7	H10	Monkey
18. 6	6. 5	J7	J11	Gibbon
19. 6	7. 5	J7	K12	Tapir
20. 6	8. 5	J7	A1	Sheep
21. 6	9. 5	J7	B2	Deer
22. 6	10. 5	J7	C3	Horse
23. 6	11. 5	J7	D4	Stag
24. 6	12. 5	J7	E5	Serpent
25. 6	13. 5	J7	F6	Earthworm
26. 6	14. 5	J7	G7	Crocodile
27. 6	15. 5	J7	H8	Dragon
28. 6	16. 5	J7	J9	Badger
29. 6	17. 5	J7	K10	Hare
30. 6	18. 5	J7	A11	Fox
1. 7	19. 5	J7	B12	Tiger
2. 7	20. 5	J7	C1	Leopard
3. 7	21. 5	J7	D2	Griffon
4. 7	22. 5	J7	E3	Ox
5. 7	23. 5	J7	F4	Bat
6. 7	24. 5	J7	G5	Rat
7. 7	25. 5	J7	H6	Swallow
8. 7	26. 5	J7	J7	Pig
9. 7	27. 5	J7	K8	Porcupine
10. 7	28. 5	J7	A9	Wolf
11. 7	29. 5	J7	B10	Dog
12. 7	1. 6	K8	C11	Pheasant
13. 7	2. 6	K8	D12	Cock
14. 7	3. 6	K8	E1	Crow
15. 7	4. 6	K8	F2	Monkey
16. 7	5. 6	K8	G3	Gibbon
17. 7	6. 6	K8	H4	Tapir
18. 7	7. 6	K8	J5	Sheep
19. 7	8. 6	K8	K6	Deer
20. 7	9. 6	K8	A7	Horse
21. 7	10. 6	K8	B8	Stag
22. 7	11. 6	K8	C9	Serpent
23. 7	12. 6	K8	D10	Earthworm
24. 7	13. 6	K8	E11	Crocodile
25. 7	14. 6	K8	F12	Dragon
26. 7	15. 6	K8	G1	Badger
27. 7	16. 6	K8	H2	Hare
28. 7	17. 6	K8	J3	Fox
29. 7	18. 6	K8	K4	Tiger
30. 7	19. 6	K8	A5	Leopard
31. 7	20. 6	K8	B6	Griffon
1. 8	21. 6	K8	C7	Ox
2. 8	22. 6	K8	D8	Bat
3. 8	23. 6	K8	E9	Rat
4. 8	24. 6	K8	F10	Swallow
5. 8	25. 6	K8	G11	Pig
6. 8	26. 6	K8	H12	Porcupine
7. 8	27. 6	K8	J1	Wolf
8. 8	28. 6	K8	K2	Dog
9. 8	29. 6	K8	A3	Pheasant
10. 8	30. 6	K8	B4	Cock
11. 8	1. 7	A9	C5	Crow
12. 8	2. 7	A9	D6	Monkey
13. 8	3. 7	A9	E7	Gibbon
14. 8	4. 7	A9	F8	Tapir

Solar date	Lunar date	Month HS/EB	Day HS/EB	Constellation
15. 8	5. 7	A9	G9	Sheep
16. 8	6. 7	A9	H10	Deer
17. 8	7. 7	A9	J11	Horse
18. 8	8. 7	A9	K12	Stag
19. 8	9. 7	A9	A1	Serpent
20. 8	10. 7	A9	B2	Earthworm
21. 8	11. 7	A9	C3	Crocodile
22. 8	12. 7	A9	D4	Dragon
23. 8	13. 7	A9	E5	Badger
24. 8	14. 7	A9	F6	Hare
25. 8	15. 7	A9	G7	Fox
26. 8	16. 7	A9	H8	Tiger
27. 8	17. 7	A9	J9	Leopard
28. 8	18. 7	A9	K10	Griffon
29. 8	19. 7	A9	A11	Ox
30. 8	20. 7	A9	B12	Bat
31. 8	21. 7	A9	C1	Rat
1. 9	22. 7	A9	D2	Swallow
2. 9	23. 7	A9	E3	Pig
3. 9	24. 7	A9	F4	Porcupine
4. 9	25. 7	A9	G5	Wolf
5. 9	26. 7	A9	H6	Dog
6. 9	27. 7	A9	J7	Pheasant
7. 9	28. 7	A9	K8	Cock
8. 9	29. 7	A9	A9	Crow
9. 9	1. 8	B10	B10	Monkey
10. 9	2. 8	B10	C11	Gibbon
11. 9	3. 8	B10	D12	Tapir
12. 9	4. 8	B10	E1	Sheep
13. 9	5. 8	B10	F2	Deer
14. 9	6. 8	B10	G3	Horse
15. 9	7. 8	B10	H4	Stag
16. 9	8. 8	B10	J5	Serpent
17. 9	9. 8	B10	K6	Earthworm
18. 9	10. 8	B10	A7	Crocodile
19. 9	11. 8	B10	B8	Dragon
20. 9	12. 8	B10	C9	Badger
21. 9	13. 8	B10	D10	Hare
22. 9	14. 8	B10	E11	Fox
23. 9	15. 8	B10	F12	Tiger
24. 9	16. 8	B10	G1	Leopard
25. 9	17. 8	B10	H2	Griffon
26. 9	18. 8	B10	J3	Ox
27. 9	19. 8	B10	K4	Bat
28. 9	20. 8	B10	A5	Rat
29. 9	21. 8	B10	B6	Swallow
30. 9	22. 8	B10	C7	Pig
1.10	23. 8	B10	D8	Porcupine
2.10	24. 8	B10	E9	Wolf
3.10	25. 8	B10	F10	Dog
4.10	26. 8	B10	G11	Pheasant
5.10	27. 8	B10	H12	Cock
6.10	28. 8	B10	J1	Crow
7.10	29. 8	B10	K2	Monkey
8.10	30. 8	B10	A3	Gibbon
9.10	1. 9	C11	B4	Tapir
10.10	2. 9	C11	C5	Sheep
11.10	3. 9	C11	D6	Deer
12.10	4. 9	C11	E7	Horse
13.10	5. 9	C11	F8	Stag
14.10	6. 9	C11	G9	Serpent
15.10	7. 9	C11	H10	Earthworm
16.10	8. 9	C11	J11	Crocodile
17.10	9. 9	C11	K12	Dragon
18.10	10. 9	C11	A1	Badger
19.10	11. 9	C11	B2	Hare
20.10	12. 9	C11	C3	Fox
21.10	13. 9	C11	D4	Tiger
22.10	14. 9	C11	E5	Leopard
23.10	15. 9	C11	F6	Griffon
24.10	16. 9	C11	G7	Ox
25.10	17. 9	C11	H8	Bat
26.10	18. 9	C11	J9	Rat

Solar date	Lunar date	Month HS/EB	Day HS/EB	Constellation
27.10	19. 9	C11	K10	Swallow
28.10	20. 9	C11	A11	Pig
29.10	21. 9	C11	B12	Porcupine
30.10	22. 9	C11	C1	Wolf
31.10	23. 9	C11	D2	Dog
1.11	24. 9	C11	E3	Pheasant
2.11	25. 9	C11	F4	Cock
3.11	26. 9	C11	G5	Crow
4.11	27. 9	C11	H6	Monkey
5.11	28. 9	C11	J7	Gibbon
6.11	29. 9	C11	K8	Tapir
7.11	30. 9	C11	A9	Sheep
8.11	1.10	D12	B10	Deer
9.11	2.10	D12	C11	Horse
10.11	3.10	D12	D12	Stag
11.11	4.10	D12	E1	Serpent
12.11	5.10	D12	F2	Earthworm
13.11	6.10	D12	G3	Crocodile
14.11	7.10	D12	H4	Dragon
15.11	8.10	D12	J5	Badger
16.11	9.10	D12	K6	Hare
17.11	10.10	D12	A7	Fox
18.11	11.10	D12	B8	Tiger
19.11	12.10	D12	C9	Leopard
20.11	13.10	D12	D10	Griffon
21.11	14.10	D12	E11	Ox
22.11	15.10	D12	F12	Bat
23.11	16.10	D12	G1	Rat
24.11	17.10	D12	H2	Swallow
25.11	18.10	D12	J3	Pig
26.11	19.10	D12	K4	Porcupine
27.11	20.10	D12	A5	Wolf
28.11	21.10	D12	B6	Dog
29.11	22.10	D12	C7	Pheasant
30.11	23.10	D12	D8	Cock
1.12	24.10	D12	E9	Crow
2.12	25.10	D12	F10	Monkey
3.12	26.10	D12	G11	Gibbon
4.12	27.10	D12	H12	Tapir
5.12	28.10	D12	J1	Sheep
6.12	29.10	D12	K2	Deer
7.12	1.11	E1	A3	Horse
8.12	2.11	E1	B4	Stag
9.12	3.11	E1	C5	Serpent
10.12	4.11	E1	D6	Earthworm
11.12	5.11	E1	E7	Crocodile
12.12	6.11	E1	F8	Dragon
13.12	7.11	E1	G9	Badger
14.12	8.11	E1	H10	Hare
15.12	9.11	E1	J11	Fox
16.12	10.11	E1	K12	Tiger
17.12	11.11	E1	A1	Leopard

Solar date	Lunar date	Month HS/EB	Day HS/EB	Constellation
18.12	12.11	E1	B2	Griffon
19.12	13.11	E1	C3	Ox
20.12	14.11	E1	D4	Bat
21.12	15.11	E1	E5	Rat
22.12	16.11	E1	F6	Swallow
23.12	17.11	E1	G7	Pig
24.12	18.11	E1	H8	Porcupine
25.12	19.11	E1	J9	Wolf
26.12	20.11	E1	K10	Dog
27.12	21.11	E1	A11	Pheasant
28.12	22.11	E1	B12	Cock
29.12	23.11	E1	C1	Crow
30.12	24.11	E1	D2	Monkey
31.12	25.11	E1	E3	Gibbon

1981

Solar date	Lunar date	Month HS/EB	Day HS/EB	Constellation
1. 1	26.11	E1	F4	Tapir
2. 1	27.11	E1	G5	Sheep
3. 1	28.11	E1	H6	Deer
4. 1	29.11	E1	J7	Horse
5. 1	30.11	E1	K8	Stag
6. 1	1.12	F2	A9	Serpent
7. 1	2.12	F2	B10	Earthworm
8. 1	3.12	F2	C11	Crocodile
9. 1	4.12	F2	D12	Dragon
10. 1	5.12	F2	E1	Badger
11. 1	6.12	F2	F2	Hare
12. 1	7.12	F2	G3	Fox
13. 1	8.12	F2	H4	Tiger
14. 1	9.12	F2	J5	Leopard
15. 1	10.12	F2	K6	Griffon
16. 1	11.12	F2	A7	Ox
17. 1	12.12	F2	B8	Bat
18. 1	13.12	F2	C9	Rat
19. 1	14.12	F2	D10	Swallow
20. 1	15.12	F2	E11	Pig
21. 1	16.12	F2	F12	Porcupine
22. 1	17.12	F2	G1	Wolf
23. 1	18.12	F2	H2	Dog
24. 1	19.12	F2	J3	Pheasant
25. 1	20.12	F2	K4	Cock
26. 1	21.12	F2	A5	Crow
27. 1	22.12	F2	B6	Monkey
28. 1	23.12	F2	C7	Gibbon
29. 1	24.12	F2	D8	Tapir
30. 1	25.12	F2	E9	Sheep
31. 1	26.12	F2	F10	Deer
1. 2	27.12	F2	G11	Horse
2. 2	28.12	F2	H12	Stag
3. 2	29.12	F2	J1	Serpent
4. 2	30.12	F2	K2	Earthworm

HSIN YU YEAR

Solar date	Lunar date	Month HS/EB	Day HS/EB	Constellation
5. 2	1. 1	G3	A3	Crocodile
6. 2	2. 1	G3	B4	Dragon
7. 2	3. 1	G3	C5	Badger
8. 2	4. 1	G3	D6	Hare
9. 2	5. 1	G3	E7	Fox
10. 2	6. 1	G3	F8	Tiger
11. 2	7. 1	G3	G9	Leopard
12. 2	8. 1	G3	H10	Griffon
13. 2	9. 1	G3	J11	Ox
14. 2	10. 1	G3	K12	Bat
15. 2	11. 1	G3	A1	Rat
16. 2	12. 1	G3	B2	Swallow
17. 2	13. 1	G3	C3	Pig
18. 2	14. 1	G3	D4	Porcupine
19. 2	15. 1	G3	E5	Wolf
20. 2	16. 1	G3	F6	Dog

Solar date	Lunar date	Month HS/EB	Day HS/EB	Constellation
21. 2	17. 1	G3	G7	Pheasant
22. 2	18. 1	G3	H8	Cock
23. 2	19. 1	G3	J9	Crow
24. 2	20. 1	G3	K10	Monkey
25. 2	21. 1	G3	A11	Gibbon
26. 2	22. 1	G3	B12	Tapir
27. 2	23. 1	G3	C1	Sheep
28. 2	24. 1	G3	D2	Deer
1. 3	25. 1	G3	E3	Horse
2. 3	26. 1	G3	F4	Stag
3. 3	27. 1	G3	G5	Serpent
4. 3	28. 1	G3	H6	Earthworm
5. 3	29. 1	G3	J7	Crocodile
6. 3	1. 2	H4	K8	Dragon
7. 3	2. 2	H4	A9	Badger
8. 3	3. 2	H4	B10	Hare

Solar date	Lunar date	Month HS/EB	Day HS/EB	Constellation	Solar date	Lunar date	Month HS/EB	Day HS/EB	Constellation
9. 3	4. 2	H4	C11	Fox	21. 5	18. 4	K6	F12	Tapir
10. 3	5. 2	H4	D12	Tiger	22. 5	19. 4	K6	G1	Sheep
11. 3	6. 2	H4	E1	Leopard	23. 5	20. 4	K6	H2	Deer
12. 3	7. 2	H4	F2	Griffon	24. 5	21. 4	K6	J3	Horse
13. 3	8. 2	H4	G3	Ox	25. 5	22. 4	K6	K4	Stag
14. 3	9. 2	H4	H4	Bat	26. 5	23. 4	K6	A5	Serpent
15. 3	10. 2	H4	J5	Rat	27. 5	24. 4	K6	B6	Earthworm
16. 3	11. 2	H4	K6	Swallow	28. 5	25. 4	K6	C7	Crocodile
17. 3	12. 2	H4	A7	Pig	29. 5	26. 4	K6	D8	Dragon
18. 3	13. 2	H4	B8	Porcupine	30. 5	27. 4	K6	E9	Badger
19. 3	14. 2	H4	C9	Wolf	31. 5	28. 4	K6	F10	Hare
20. 3	15. 2	H4	D10	Dog	1. 6	29. 4	K6	G11	Fox
21. 3	16. 2	H4	E11	Pheasant	2. 6	1. 4	A7	H12	Tiger
22. 3	17. 2	H4	F12	Cock	3. 6	2. 4	A7	J1	Leopard
23. 3	18. 2	H4	G1	Crow	4. 6	3. 4	A7	K2	Griffon
24. 3	19. 2	H4	H2	Monkey	5. 6	4. 4	A7	A3	Ox
25. 3	20. 2	H4	J3	Gibbon	6. 6	5. 4	A7	B4	Bat
26. 3	21. 2	H4	K4	Tapir	7. 6	6. 4	A7	C5	Rat
27. 3	22. 2	H4	A5	Sheep	8. 6	7. 4	A7	D6	Swallow
28. 3	23. 2	H4	B6	Deer	9. 6	8. 4	A7	E7	Pig
29. 3	24. 2	H4	C7	Horse	10. 6	9. 4	A7	F8	Porcupine
30. 3	25. 2	H4	D8	Stag	11. 6	10. 4	A7	G9	Wolf
31. 3	26. 2	H4	E9	Serpent	12. 6	11. 4	A7	H10	Dog
1. 4	27. 2	H4	F10	Earthworm	13. 6	12. 4	A7	J11	Pheasant
2. 4	28. 2	H4	G11	Crocodile	14. 6	13. 4	A7	K12	Cock
3. 4	29. 2	H4	H12	Dragon	15. 6	14. 4	A7	A1	Crow
4. 4	30. 2	H4	J1	Badger	16. 6	15. 5	A7	B2	Monkey
5. 4	1. 3	J5	K2	Hare	17. 6	16. 5	A7	C3	Gibbon
6. 4	2. 3	J5	A3	Fox	18. 6	17. 5	A7	D4	Tapir
7. 4	3. 3	J5	B4	Tiger	19. 6	18. 5	A7	E5	Sheep
8. 4	4. 3	J5	C5	Leopard	20. 6	19. 5	A7	F6	Deer
9. 4	5. 3	J5	D6	Griffon	21. 6	20. 5	A7	G7	Horse
10. 4	6. 3	J5	E7	Ox	22. 6	21. 5	A7	H8	Stag
11. 4	7. 3	J5	F8	Bat	23. 6	22. 5	A7	J9	Serpent
12. 4	8. 3	J5	G9	Rat	24. 6	23. 5	A7	K10	Earthworm
13. 4	9. 3	J5	H10	Swallow	25. 6	24. 5	A7	A11	Crocodile
14. 4	10. 3	J5	J11	Pig	26. 6	25. 5	A7	B12	Dragon
15. 4	11. 3	J5	K12	Porcupine	27. 6	26. 5	A7	C1	Badger
16. 4	12. 3	J5	A1	Wolf	28. 6	27. 5	A7	D2	Hare
17. 4	13. 3	J5	B2	Dog	29. 6	28. 5	A7	E3	Fox
18. 4	14. 3	J5	C3	Pheasant	30. 6	29. 5	A7	F4	Tiger
19. 4	15. 3	J5	D4	Cock	1. 7	30. 5	A7	G5	Leopard
20. 4	16. 3	J5	E5	Crow	2. 7	1. 6	B8	H6	Griffon
21. 4	17. 3	J5	F6	Monkey	3. 7	2. 6	B8	J7	Ox
22. 4	18. 3	J5	G7	Gibbon	4. 7	3. 6	B8	K8	Bat
23. 4	19. 3	J5	H8	Tapir	5. 7	4. 6	B8	A9	Rat
24. 4	20. 3	J5	J9	Sheep	6. 7	5. 6	B8	B10	Swallow
25. 4	21. 3	J5	K10	Deer	7. 7	6. 6	B8	C11	Pig
26. 4	22. 3	J5	A11	Horse	8. 7	7. 6	B8	D12	Porcupine
27. 4	23. 3	J5	B12	Stag	9. 7	8. 6	B8	E1	Wolf
28. 4	24. 3	J5	C1	Serpent	10. 7	9. 6	B8	F2	Dog
29. 4	25. 3	J5	D2	Earthworm	11. 7	10. 6	B8	G3	Pheasant
30. 4	26. 3	J5	E3	Crocodile	12. 7	11. 6	B8	H4	Cock
1. 5	27. 3	J5	F4	Dragon	13. 7	12. 6	B8	J5	Crow
2. 5	28. 3	J5	G5	Badger	14. 7	13. 6	B8	K6	Monkey
3. 5	29. 3	J5	H6	Hare	15. 7	14. 6	B8	A7	Gibbon
4. 5	1. 4	K6	J7	Fox	16. 7	15. 6	B8	B8	Tapir
5. 5	2. 4	K6	K8	Tiger	17. 7	16. 6	B8	C9	Sheep
6. 5	3. 4	K6	A9	Leopard	18. 7	17. 6	B8	D10	Deer
7. 5	4. 4	K6	B10	Griffon	19. 7	18. 6	B8	E11	Horse
8. 5	5. 4	K6	C11	Ox	20. 7	19. 6	B8	F12	Stag
9. 5	6. 4	K6	D12	Bat	21. 7	20. 6	B8	G1	Serpent
10. 5	7. 4	K6	E1	Rat	22. 7	21. 6	B8	H2	Earthworm
11. 5	8. 4	K6	F2	Swallow	23. 7	22. 6	B8	J3	Crocodile
12. 5	9. 4	K6	G3	Pig	24. 7	23. 6	B8	K4	Dragon
13. 5	10. 4	K6	H4	Porcupine	25. 7	24. 6	B8	A5	Badger
14. 5	11. 4	K6	J5	Wolf	26. 7	25. 6	B8	B6	Hare
15. 5	12. 4	K6	K6	Dog	27. 7	26. 6	B8	C7	Fox
16. 5	13. 4	K6	A7	Pheasant	28. 7	27. 6	B8	D8	Tiger
17. 5	14. 4	K6	B8	Cock	29. 7	28. 6	B8	E9	Leopard
18. 5	15. 4	K6	C9	Crow	30. 7	29. 6	B8	F10	Griffon
19. 5	16. 4	K6	D10	Monkey	31. 7	1. 7	C9	G11	Ox
20. 5	17. 4	K6	E11	Gibbon	1. 8	2. 7	C9	H12	Bat

Solar date	Lunar date	Month HS/EB	Day HS/EB	Constellation
2. 8	3. 7	C9	J1	Rat
3. 8	4. 7	C9	K2	Swallow
4. 8	5. 7	C9	A3	Pig
5. 8	6. 7	C9	B4	Porcupine
6. 8	7. 7	C9	C5	Wolf
7. 8	8. 7	C9	D6	Dog
8. 8	9. 7	C9	E7	Pheasant
9. 8	10. 7	C9	F8	Cock
10. 8	11. 7	C9	G9	Crow
11. 8	12. 7	C9	H10	Monkey
12. 8	13. 7	C9	J11	Gibbon
13. 8	14. 7	C9	K12	Tapir
14. 8	15. 7	C9	A1	Sheep
15. 8	16. 7	C9	B2	Deer
16. 8	17. 7	C9	C3	Horse
17. 8	18. 7	C9	D4	Stag
18. 8	19. 7	C9	E5	Serpent
19. 8	20. 7	C9	F6	Earthworm
20. 8	21. 7	C9	G7	Crocodile
21. 8	22. 7	C9	H8	Dragon
22. 8	23. 7	C9	J9	Badger
23. 8	24. 7	C9	K10	Hare
24. 8	25. 7	C9	A11	Fox
25. 8	26. 7	C9	B12	Tiger
26. 8	27. 7	C9	C1	Leopard
27. 8	28. 7	C9	D2	Griffon
28. 8	29. 7	C9	E3	Ox
29. 8	1. 8	D10	F4	Bat
30. 8	2. 8	D10	G5	Rat
31. 8	3. 8	D10	H6	Swallow
1. 9	4. 8	D10	J7	Pig
2. 9	5. 8	D10	K8	Porcupine
3. 9	6. 8	D10	A9	Wolf
4. 9	7. 8	D10	B10	Dog
5. 9	8. 8	D10	C11	Pheasant
6. 9	9. 8	D10	D12	Cock
7. 9	10. 8	D10	E1	Crow
8. 9	11. 8	D10	F2	Monkey
9. 9	12. 8	D10	G3	Gibbon
10. 9	13. 8	D10	H4	Tapir
11. 9	14. 8	D10	J5	Sheep
12. 9	15. 8	D10	K6	Deer
13. 9	16. 8	D10	A7	Horse
14. 9	17. 8	D10	B8	Stag
15. 9	18. 8	D10	C9	Serpent
16. 9	19. 8	D10	D10	Earthworm
17. 9	20. 8	D10	E11	Crocodile
18. 9	21. 8	D10	F12	Dragon
19. 9	22. 8	D10	G1	Badger
20. 9	23. 8	D10	H2	Hare
21. 9	24. 8	D10	J3	Fox
22. 9	25. 8	D10	K4	Tiger
23. 9	26. 8	D10	A5	Leopard
24. 9	27. 8	D10	B6	Griffon
25. 9	28. 8	D10	C7	Ox
26. 9	29. 8	D10	D8	Bat
27. 9	30. 8	D10	E9	Rat
28. 9	1. 9	E11	F10	Swallow
29. 9	2. 9	E11	G11	Pig
30. 9	3. 9	E11	H12	Porcupine
1.10	4. 9	E11	J1	Wolf
2.10	5. 9	E11	K2	Dog
3.10	6. 9	E11	A3	Pheasant
4. 0	7. 9	E11	B4	Cock
5.10	8. 9	E11	C5	Crow
6.10	9. 9	E11	D6	Monkey
7.10	10. 9	E11	E7	Gibbon
8.10	11. 9	E11	F8	Tapir
9.10	12. 9	E11	G9	Sheep
10.10	13. 9	E11	H10	Deer
11.10	14. 9	E11	J11	Horse
12.10	15. 9	E11	K12	Stag
13.10	16. 9	E11	A1	Serpent
14.10	17. 9	E11	B2	Earthworm
15.10	18. 9	E11	C3	Crocodile
16.10	19. 9	E11	D4	Dragon
17.10	20. 9	E11	E5	Badger
18.10	21. 9	E11	F6	Hare
19.10	22. 9	E11	G7	Fox
20.10	23. 9	E11	H8	Tiger
21.10	24. 9	E11	J9	Leopard
22.10	25. 9	E11	K10	Griffon
23.10	26. 9	E11	A11	Ox
24.10	27. 9	E11	B12	Bat
25.10	28. 9	E11	C1	Rat
26.10	29. 9	E11	D2	Swallow
27.10	30. 9	E11	E3	Pig
28.10	1.10	F12	F4	Porcupine
29.10	2.10	F12	G5	Wolf
30.10	3.10	F12	H6	Dog
31.10	4.10	F12	J7	Pheasant
1.11	5.10	F12	K8	Cock
2.11	6.10	F12	A9	Crow
3.11	7.10	F12	B10	Monkey
4.11	8.10	F12	C11	Gibbon
5.11	9.10	F12	D12	Tapir
6.11	10.10	F12	E1	Sheep
7.11	11.10	F12	F2	Deer
8.11	12.10	F12	G3	Horse
9.11	13.10	F12	H4	Stag
10.11	14.10	F12	J5	Serpent
11.11	15.10	F12	K6	Earthworm
12.11	16.10	F12	A7	Crocodile
13.11	17.10	F12	B8	Dragon
14.11	18.10	F12	C9	Badger
15.11	19.10	F12	D10	Hare
16.11	20.10	F12	E11	Fox
17.11	21.10	F12	F12	Tiger
18.11	22.10	F12	G1	Leopard
19.11	23.10	F12	H2	Griffon
20.11	24.10	F12	J3	Ox
21.11	25.10	F12	K4	Bat
22.11	26.10	F12	A5	Rat
23.11	27.10	F12	B6	Swallow
24.11	28.10	F12	C7	Pig
25.11	29.10	F12	D8	Porcupine
26.11	1.11	G1	E9	Wolf
27.11	2.11	G1	F10	Dog
28.11	3.11	G1	G11	Pheasant
29.11	4.11	G1	H12	Cock
30.11	5.11	G1	J1	Crow
1.12	6.11	G1	K2	Monkey
2.12	7.11	G1	A3	Gibbon
3.12	8.11	G1	B4	Tapir
4.12	9.11	G1	C5	Sheep
5.12	10.11	G1	D6	Deer
6.12	11.11	G1	E7	Horse
7.12	12.11	G1	F8	Stag
8.12	13.11	G1	G9	Serpent
9.12	14.11	G1	H10	Earthworm
10.12	15.11	G1	J11	Crocodile
11.12	16.11	G1	K12	Dragon
12.12	17.11	G1	A1	Badger
13.12	18.11	G1	B2	Hare
14.12	19.11	G1	C3	Fox
15.12	20.11	G1	D4	Tiger
16.12	21.11	G1	E5	Leopard
17.12	22.11	G1	F6	Griffon
18.12	23.11	G1	G7	Ox
19.12	24.11	G1	H8	Bat
20.12	25.11	G1	J9	Rat
21.12	26.11	G1	K10	Swallow
22.12	27.11	G1	A11	Pig
23.12	28.11	G1	B12	Porcupine
24.12	29.11	G1	C1	Wolf
25.12	30.11	G1	D2	Dog

Solar date	Lunar date	Month HS/EB	Day HS/EB	Constellation
26.12	1.12	H2	E3	Pheasant
27.12	2.12	H2	F4	Cock
28.12	3.12	H2	G5	Crow
29.12	4.12	H2	H6	Monkey
30.12	5.12	H2	J7	Gibbon
31.12	6.12	H2	K8	Tapir
1982				
1. 1	7.12	H2	A9	Sheep
2. 1	8.12	H2	B10	Deer
3. 1	9.12	H2	C11	Horse
4. 1	10.12	H2	D12	Stag
5. 1	11.12	H2	E1	Serpent
6. 1	12.12	H2	F2	Earthworm
7. 1	13.12	H2	G3	Crocodile
8. 1	14.12	H2	H4	Dragon
9. 1	15.12	H2	J5	Badger
10. 1	16.12	H2	K6	Hare
11. 1	17.12	H2	A7	Fox
12. 1	18.12	H2	B8	Tiger
13. 1	19.12	H2	C9	Leopard
14. 1	20.12	H2	D10	Griffon
15. 1	21.12	H2	E11	Ox
16. 1	22.12	H2	F12	Bat
17. 1	23.12	H2	G1	Rat
18. 1	24.12	H2	H2	Swallow
19. 1	25.12	H2	J3	Pig
20. 1	26.12	H2	K4	Porcupine
21. 1	27.12	H2	A5	Wolf
22. 1	28.12	H2	B6	Dog
23. 1	29.12	H2	C7	Pheasant
24. 1	30.12	H2	D8	Cock

JEN HSÜ YEAR

Solar date	Lunar date	Month HS/EB	Day HS/EB	Constellation
25. 1	1. 1	J3	E9	Crow
26. 1	2. 1	J3	F10	Monkey
27. 1	3. 1	J3	G11	Gibbon
28. 1	4. 1	J3	H12	Tapir
29. 1	5. 1	J3	J1	Sheep
30. 1	6. 1	J3	K2	Deer
31. 1	7. 1	J3	A3	Horse
1. 2	8. 1	J3	B4	Stag
2. 2	9. 1	J3	C5	Serpent
3. 2	10. 1	J3	D6	Earthworm
4. 2	11. 1	J3	E7	Crocodile
5. 2	12. 1	J3	F8	Dragon
6. 2	13. 1	J3	G9	Badger
7. 2	14. 1	J3	H10	Hare
8. 2	15. 1	J3	J11	Fox
9. 2	16. 1	J3	K12	Tiger
10. 2	17. 1	J3	A1	Leopard
11. 2	18. 1	J3	B2	Griffon
12. 2	19. 1	J3	C3	Ox
13. 2	20. 1	J3	D4	Bat
14. 2	21. 1	J3	E5	Rat
15. 2	22. 1	J3	F6	Swallow
16. 2	23. 1	J3	G7	Pig
17. 2	24. 1	J3	H8	Porcupine
18. 2	25. 1	J3	J9	Wolf
19. 2	26. 1	J3	K10	Dog
20. 2	27. 1	J3	A11	Pheasant
21. 2	28. 1	J3	B12	Cock
22. 2	29. 1	J3	C1	Crow
23. 2	30. 1	J3	D2	Monkey
24. 2	1. 2	K4	E3	Gibbon
25. 2	2. 2	K4	F4	Tapir
26. 2	3. 2	K4	G5	Sheep
27. 2	4. 2	K4	H6	Deer
28. 2	5. 2	K4	J7	Horse
1. 3	6. 2	K4	K8	Stag
2. 3	7. 2	K4	A9	Serpent
3. 3	8. 2	K4	B10	Earthworm
4. 3	9. 2	K4	C11	Crocodile
5. 3	10. 2	K4	D12	Dragon
6. 3	11. 2	K4	E1	Badger
7. 3	12. 2	K4	F2	Hare
8. 3	13. 2	K4	G3	Fox
9. 3	14. 2	K4	H4	Tiger
10. 3	15. 2	K4	J5	Leopard
11. 3	16. 2	K4	K6	Griffon
12. 3	17. 2	K4	A7	Ox
13. 3	18. 2	K4	B8	Bat
14. 3	19. 2	K4	C9	Rat
15. 3	20. 2	K4	D10	Swallow
16. 3	21. 2	K4	E11	Pig
17. 3	22. 2	K4	F12	Porcupine
18. 3	23. 2	K4	G1	Wolf
19. 3	24. 2	K4	H2	Dog
20. 3	25. 2	K4	J3	Pheasant
21. 3	26. 2	K4	K4	Cock
22. 3	27. 2	K4	A5	Crow
23. 3	28. 2	K4	B6	Monkey
24. 3	29. 2	K4	C7	Gibbon
25. 3	1. 3	A5	D8	Tapir
26. 3	2. 3	A5	E9	Sheep
27. 3	3. 3	A5	F10	Deer
28. 3	4. 3	A5	G11	Horse
29. 3	5. 3	A5	H12	Stag
30. 3	6. 3	A5	J1	Serpent
31. 3	7. 3	A5	K2	Earthworm
1. 4	8. 3	A5	A3	Crocodile
2. 4	9. 3	A5	B4	Dragon
3. 4	10. 3	A5	C5	Badger
4. 4	11. 3	A5	D6	Hare
5. 4	12. 3	A5	E7	Fox
6. 4	13. 3	A5	F8	Tiger
7. 4	14. 3	A5	G9	Leopard
8. 4	15. 3	A5	H10	Griffon
9. 4	16. 3	A5	J11	Ox
10. 4	17. 3	A5	K12	Bat
11. 4	18. 3	A5	A1	Rat
12. 4	19. 3	A5	B2	Swallow
13. 4	20. 3	A5	C3	Pig
14. 4	21. 3	A5	D4	Porcupine
15. 4	22. 3	A5	E5	Wolf
16. 4	23. 3	A5	F6	Dog
17. 4	24. 3	A5	G7	Pheasant
18. 4	25. 3	A5	H8	Cock
19. 4	26. 3	A5	J9	Crow
20. 4	27. 3	A5	K10	Monkey
21. 4	28. 3	A5	A11	Gibbon
22. 4	29. 3	A5	B12	Tapir
23. 4	30. 3	A5	C1	Sheep
24. 4	1. 4	B6	D2	Deer
25. 4	2. 4	B6	E3	Horse
26. 4	3. 4	B6	F4	Stag
27. 4	4. 4	B6	G5	Serpent
28. 4	5. 4	B6	H6	Earthworm
29. 4	6. 4	B6	J7	Crocodile
30. 4	7. 4	B6	K8	Dragon
1. 5	8. 4	B6	A9	Badger
2. 5	9. 4	B6	B10	Hare
3. 5	10. 4	B6	C11	Fox
4. 5	11. 4	B6	D12	Tiger
5. 5	12. 4	B6	E1	Leopard
6. 5	13. 4	B6	F2	Griffon
7. 5	14. 4	B6	G3	Ox
8. 5	15. 4	B6	H4	Bat

Solar date	Lunar date	Month HS/EB	Day HS/EB	Constellation
9. 5	16. 4	B6	J5	Rat
10. 5	17. 4	B6	K6	Swallow
11. 5	18. 4	B6	A7	Pig
12. 5	19. 4	B6	B8	Porcupine
13. 5	20. 4	B6	C9	Wolf
14. 5	21. 4	B6	D10	Dog
15. 5	22. 4	B6	E11	Pheasant
16. 5	23. 4	B6	F12	Cock
17. 5	24. 4	B6	G1	Crow
18. 5	25. 4	B6	H2	Monkey
19. 5	26. 4	B6	J3	Gibbon
20. 5	27. 4	B6	K4	Tapir
21. 5	28. 4	B6	A5	Sheep
22. 5	29. 4	B6	B6	Deer
23. 5	*1. 5*	*B6*	C7	Horse
24. 5	*2. 4*	*B6*	D8	Stag
25. 5	*3. 4*	*B6*	E9	Serpent
26. 5	*4. 4*	*B6*	F10	Earthworm
27. 5	*5. 4*	*B6*	G11	Crocodile
28. 5	*6. 4*	*B6*	H12	Dragon
29. 5	*7. 4*	*B6*	J1	Badger
30. 5	*8. 4*	*B6*	K2	Hare
31. 5	*9. 4*	*B6*	A3	Fox
1. 6	*10. 4*	*B6*	B4	Tiger
2. 6	*11. 4*	*B6*	C5	Leopard
3. 6	*12. 4*	*B6*	D6	Griffon
4. 6	*13. 4*	*B6*	E7	Ox
5. 6	*14. 4*	*B6*	F8	Bat
6. 6	*15. 4*	*B6*	G9	Rat
7. 6	*16. 4*	*B6*	H10	Swallow
8. 6	*17. 4*	*B6*	J11	Pig
9. 6	*18. 4*	*B6*	K12	Porcupine
10. 6	*19. 4*	*B6*	A1	Wolf
11. 6	*20. 4*	*B6*	B2	Dog
12. 6	*21. 4*	*B6*	C3	Pheasant
13. 6	*22. 4*	*B6*	D4	Cock
14. 6	*23. 4*	*B6*	E5	Crow
15. 6	*24. 4*	*B6*	F6	Monkey
16. 6	*25. 4*	*B6*	G7	Gibbon
17. 6	*26. 4*	*B6*	H8	Tapir
18. 6	*27. 4*	*B6*	J9	Sheep
19. 6	*28. 4*	*B6*	K10	Deer
20. 6	*29. 4*	*B6*	A11	Horse
21. 6	1. 5	C7	B12	Stag
22. 6	2. 5	C7	C1	Serpent
23. 6	3. 5	C7	D2	Earthworm
24. 6	4. 5	C7	E3	Crocodile
25. 6	5. 5	C7	F4	Dragon
26. 6	6. 5	C7	G5	Badger
27. 6	7. 5	C7	H6	Hare
28. 6	8. 5	C7	J7	Fox
29. 6	9. 5	C7	K8	Tiger
30. 6	10. 5	C7	A9	Leopard
1. 7	11. 5	C7	B10	Griffon
2. 7	12. 5	C7	C11	Ox
3. 7	13. 5	C7	D12	Bat
4. 7	14. 5	C7	E1	Rat
5. 7	15. 5	C7	F2	Swallow
6. 7	16. 5	C7	G3	Pig
7. 7	17. 5	C7	H4	Porcupine
8. 7	18. 5	C7	J5	Wolf
9. 7	19. 5	C7	K6	Dog
10. 7	20. 5	C7	A7	Pheasant
11. 7	21. 5	C7	B8	Cock
12. 7	22. 5	C7	C9	Crow
13. 7	23. 5	C7	D10	Monkey
14. 7	24. 5	C7	E11	Gibbon
15. 7	25. 5	C7	F12	Tapir
16. 7	26. 5	C7	G1	Sheep
17. 7	27. 5	C7	H2	Deer
18. 7	28. 5	C7	J3	Horse
19. 7	29. 5	C7	K4	Stag
20. 7	30. 5	C7	A5	Serpent
21. 7	1. 6	D8	B6	Earthworm
22. 7	2. 6	D8	C7	Crocodile
23. 7	3. 6	D8	D8	Dragon
24. 7	4. 6	D8	E9	Badger
25. 7	5. 6	D8	F10	Hare
26. 7	6. 6	D8	G11	Fox
27. 7	7. 6	D8	H12	Tiger
28. 7	8. 6	D8	J1	Leopard
29. 7	9. 6	D8	K2	Griffon
30. 7	10. 6	D8	A3	Ox
31. 7	11. 6	D8	B4	Bat
1. 8	12. 6	D8	C5	Rat
2. 8	13. 6	D8	D6	Swallow
3. 8	14. 6	D8	E7	Pig
4. 8	15. 6	D8	F8	Porcupine
5. 8	16. 6	D8	G9	Wolf
6. 8	17. 6	D8	H10	Dog
7. 8	18. 6	D8	J11	Pheasant
8. 8	19. 6	D8	K12	Cock
9. 8	20. 6	D8	A1	Crow
10. 8	21. 6	D8	B2	Monkey
11. 8	22. 6	D8	C3	Gibbon
12. 8	23. 6	D8	D4	Tapir
13. 8	24. 6	D8	E5	Sheep
14. 8	25. 6	D8	F6	Deer
15. 8	26. 6	D8	G7	Horse
16. 8	27. 6	D8	H8	Stag
17. 8	28. 6	D8	J9	Serpent
18. 8	29. 6	D8	K10	Earthworm
19. 8	1. 7	E9	A11	Crocodile
20. 8	2. 7	E9	B12	Dragon
21. 8	3. 7	E9	C1	Badger
22. 8	4. 7	E9	D2	Hare
23. 8	5. 7	E9	E3	Fox
24. 8	6. 7	E9	F4	Tiger
25. 8	7. 7	E9	G4	Leopard
26. 8	8. 7	E9	H6	Griffon
27. 8	9. 7	E9	J7	Ox
28. 8	10. 7	E9	K8	Bat
29. 8	11. 7	E9	A9	Rat
30. 8	12. 7	E9	B10	Swallow
31. 8	13. 7	E9	C11	Pig
1. 9	14. 7	E9	D12	Porcupine
2. 9	15. 7	E9	E1	Wolf
3. 9	16. 7	E9	F2	Dog
4. 9	17. 7	E9	G3	Pheasant
5. 9	18. 7	E9	H4	Cock
6. 9	19. 7	E9	J5	Crow
7. 9	20. 7	E9	K6	Monkey
8. 9	21. 7	E9	A7	Gibbon
9. 9	22. 7	E9	B8	Tapir
10. 9	23. 7	E9	C9	Sheep
11. 9	24. 7	E9	D10	Deer
12. 9	25. 7	E9	E11	Horse
13. 9	26. 7	E9	F12	Stag
14. 9	27. 7	E9	G1	Serpent
15. 9	28. 7	E9	H2	Earthworm
16. 9	29. 7	E9	J3	Crocodile
17. 9	1. 8	F10	K4	Dragon
18. 9	2. 8	F10	A5	Badger
19. 9	3. 8	F10	B6	Hare
20. 9	4. 8	F10	C7	Fox
21. 9	5. 8	F10	D8	Tiger
22. 9	6. 8	F10	E9	Leopard
23. 9	7. 8	F10	F10	Griffon
24. 9	8. 8	F10	G11	Ox
25. 9	9. 8	F10	H12	Bat
26. 9	10. 8	F10	J1	Rat
27. 9	11. 8	F10	K2	Swallow
28. 9	12. 8	F10	A3	Pig
29. 9	13. 8	F10	B4	Porcupine
30. 9	14. 8	F10	C5	Wolf
1.10	15. 8	F10	D6	Dog

Solar date	Lunar date	Month HS/EB	Day HS/EB	Constellation	Solar date	Lunar date	Month HS/EB	Day HS/EB	Constellation
2.10	16. 8	F10	E7	Pheasant	9.12	25.10	H12	C3	Crocodile
3.10	17. 8	F10	F8	Cock	10.12	26.10	H12	D4	Dragon
4.10	18. 8	F10	G9	Crow	11.12	27.10	H12	E5	Badger
5.10	19. 8	F10	H10	Monkey	12.12	28.10	H12	F6	Hare
6.10	20. 8	F10	J11	Gibbon	13.12	29.10	H12	G7	Fox
7.10	21. 8	F10	K12	Tapir	14.12	30.10	H12	H8	Tiger
8.10	22. 8	F10	A1	Sheep	15.12	1.11	J1	J9	Leopard
9.10	23. 8	F10	B2	Deer	16.12	2.11	J1	K10	Griffon
10.10	24. 8	F10	C3	Horse	17.12	3.11	J1	A11	Ox
11.10	25. 8	F10	D4	Stag	18.12	4.11	J1	B12	Bat
12.10	26. 8	F10	E5	Serpent	19.12	5.11	J1	C1	Rat
13.10	27. 8	F10	F6	Earthworm	20.12	6.11	J1	D2	Swallow
14.10	28. 8	F10	G7	Crocodile	21.12	7.11	J1	E3	Pig
15.10	29. 8	F10	H8	Dragon	22.12	8.11	J1	F4	Porcupine
16.10	30. 8	F10	J9	Badger	23.12	9.11	J1	G5	Wolf
17.10	1. 9	G11	K10	Hare	24.12	10.11	J1	H6	Dog
18.10	2. 9	G11	A11	Fox	25.12	11.11	J1	J7	Pheasant
19.10	3. 9	G11	B12	Tiger	26.12	12.11	J1	K8	Cock
20.10	4. 9	G11	C1	Leopard	27.12	13.11	J1	A9	Crow
21.10	5. 9	G11	D2	Griffon	28.12	14.11	J1	B10	Monkey
22.10	6. 9	G11	E3	Ox	29.12	15.11	J1	C11	Gibbon
23.10	7. 9	G11	F4	Bat	30.12	16.11	J1	D12	Tapir
24.10	8. 9	G11	G5	Rat	31.12	17.11	J1	E1	Sheep
25.10	9. 9	G11	H6	Swallow					
26.10	10. 9	G11	J7	Pig	**1983**				
27.10	11. 9	G11	K8	Porcupine	1. 1	18.11	J1	F2	Deer
28.10	12. 9	G11	A9	Wolf	2. 1	19.11	J1	G3	Horse
29.10	13. 9	G11	B10	Dog	3. 1	20.11	J1	H4	Stag
30.10	14. 9	G11	C11	Pheasant	4. 1	21.11	J1	J5	Serpent
31.10	15. 9	G11	D12	Cock	5. 1	22.11	J1	K6	Earthworm
1.11	16. 9	G11	E1	Crow	6. 1	23.11	J1	A7	Crocodile
2.11	17. 9	G11	F2	Monkey	7. 1	24.11	J1	B8	Dragon
3.11	18. 9	G11	G3	Gibbon	8. 1	25.11	J1	C9	Badger
4.11	19. 0	G11	H4	Tapir	9. 1	26.11	J1	D10	Hare
5.11	20. 9	G11	J5	Sheep	10. 1	27.11	J1	E11	Fox
6.11	21. 9	G11	K6	Deer	11. 1	28.11	J1	F12	Tiger
7.11	22. 9	G11	A7	Horse	12. 1	29.11	J1	G1	Leopard
8.11	23. 9	G11	B8	Stag	13. 1	30.11	J1	H2	Griffon
9.11	24. 9	G11	C9	Serpent	14. 1	1.12	K2	J3	Ox
10.11	25. 9	G11	D10	Earthworm	15. 1	2.12	K2	K4	Bat
11.11	26. 9	G11	E11	Crocodile	16. 1	3.12	K2	A5	Rat
12.11	27. 9	G11	F12	Dragon	17. 1	4.12	K2	B6	Swallow
13.11	28. 9	G11	G1	Badger	18. 1	5.12	K2	C7	Pig
14.11	29. 9	G11	H2	Hare	19. 1	6.12	K2	D8	Porcupine
15.11	1.10	H12	J3	Fox	20. 1	7.12	K2	E9	Wolf
16.11	2.10	H12	K4	Tiger	21. 1	8.12	K2	F10	Dog
17.11	3.10	H12	A5	Leopard	22. 1	9.12	K2	G11	Pheasant
18.11	4.10	H12	B6	Griffon	23. 1	10.12	K2	H12	Cock
19.11	5.10	H12	C7	Ox	24. 1	11.12	K2	J1	Crow
20.11	6.10	H12	D8	Bat	25. 1	12.12	K2	K2	Monkey
21.11	7.10	H12	E9	Rat	26. 1	13.12	K2	A3	Gibbon
22.11	8.10	H12	F10	Swallow	27. 1	14.12	K2	B4	Tapir
23.11	9.10	H12	G11	Pig	28. 1	15.12	K2	C5	Sheep
24.11	10.10	H12	H12	Porcupine	29. 1	16.12	K2	D6	Deer
25.11	11.10	H12	J1	Wolf	30. 1	17.12	K2	E7	Horse
26.11	12.10	H12	K2	Dog	31. 1	18.12	K2	F8	Stag
27.11	13.10	H12	A3	Pheasant	1. 2	19.12	K2	G9	Serpent
28.11	14.10	H12	B4	Cock	2. 2	20.12	K2	H10	Earthworm
29.11	15.10	H12	C5	Crow	3. 2	21.12	K2	J11	Crocodile
30.11	16.10	H12	D6	Monkey	4. 2	22.12	K2	K12	Dragon
1.12	17.10	H12	E7	Gibbon	5. 2	23.12	K2	A1	Badger
2.12	18.10	H12	F8	Tapir	6. 2	24.12	K2	B2	Hare
3.12	19.10	H12	G9	Sheep	7. 2	25.12	K2	C3	Fox
4.12	20.10	H12	H10	Deer	8. 2	26.12	K2	D4	Tiger
5.12	21.10	H12	J11	Horse	9. 2	27.12	K2	E5	Laopard
6.12	22.10	H12	K12	Stag	10. 2	28.12	K2	F6	Griffon
7.12	23.10	H12	A1	Serpent	11. 2	29.12	K2	G7	Ox
8.12	24.10	H12	B2	Earthworm	12. 2	30.12	K2	H8	Bat

KUEI HAI YEAR

Solar date	Lunar date	Month HS/EB	Day HS/EB	Constellation	Solar date	Lunar date	Month HS/EB	Day HS/EB	Constellation
13. 2	1. 1	A3	J9	Rat	25. 4	13. 3	C5	K8	Stag
14. 2	2. 1	A3	K10	Swallow	26. 4	14. 3	C5	A9	Serpent
15. 2	3. 1	A3	A11	Pig	27. 4	15. 3	C5	B10	Earthworm
16. 2	4. 1	A3	B12	Porcupine	28. 4	16. 3	C5	C11	Crocodile
17. 2	5. 1	A3	C1	Wolf	29. 4	17. 3	C5	D12	Dragon
18. 2	6. 1	A3	D2	Dog	30. 4	18. 3	C5	E1	Badger
19. 2	7. 1	A3	E3	Pheasant	1. 5	19. 3	C5	F2	Hare
20. 2	8. 1	A3	F4	Cock	2. 5	20. 3	C5	G3	Fox
21. 2	9. 1	A3	G5	Crow	3. 5	21. 3	C5	H4	Tiger
22. 2	10. 1	A3	H6	Monkey	4. 5	22. 3	C5	J5	Leopard
23. 2	11. 1	A3	J7	Gibbon	5. 5	23. 3	C5	K6	Griffon
24. 2	12. 1	A3	K8	Tapir	6. 5	24. 3	C5	A7	Ox
25. 2	13. 1	A3	A9	Sheep	7. 5	25. 3	C5	B8	Bat
26. 2	14. 1	A3	B10	Deer	8. 5	26. 3	C5	C9	Rat
27. 2	15. 1	A3	C11	Horse	9. 5	27. 3	C5	D10	Swallow
28. 2	16. 1	A3	D12	Stag	10. 5	28. 3	C5	E11	Pig
1. 3	17. 1	A3	E1	Serpent	11. 5	29. 3	C5	F12	Porcupine
2. 3	18. 1	A3	F2	Earthworm	12. 5	30. 3	C5	G1	Wolf
3. 3	19. 1	A3	G3	Crocodile	13. 5	1. 4	D6	H2	Dog
4. 3	20. 1	A3	H4	Dragon	14. 5	2. 4	D6	J3	Pheasant
5. 3	21. 1	A3	J5	Badger	15. 5	3. 4	D6	K4	Cock
6. 3	22. 1	A3	K6	Hare	16. 5	4. 4	D6	A5	Crow
7. 3	23. 1	A3	A7	Fox	17. 5	5. 4	D6	B6	Monkey
8. 3	24. 1	A3	B8	Tiger	18. 5	6. 4	D6	C7	Gibbon
9. 3	25. 1	A3	C9	Leopard	19. 5	7. 4	D6	D8	Tapir
10. 3	26. 1	A3	D10	Griffon	20. 5	8. 4	D6	E9	Sheep
11. 3	27. 1	A3	E11	Ox	21. 5	9. 4	D6	F10	Deer
12. 3	28. 1	A3	F12	Bat	22. 5	10. 4	D6	G11	Horse
13. 3	29. 1	A3	G1	Rat	23. 5	11. 4	D6	H12	Stag
14. 3	30. 1	A3	H2	Swallow	24. 5	12. 4	D6	J1	Serpent
15. 3	1. 2	B4	J3	Pig	25. 5	13. 4	D6	K2	Earthworm
16. 3	2. 2	B4	K4	Porcupine	26. 5	14. 4	D6	A3	Crocodile
17. 3	3. 2	B4	A5	Wolf	27. 5	15. 4	D6	B4	Dragon
18. 3	4. 2	B4	B6	Dog	28. 5	16. 4	D6	C5	Badger
19. 3	5. 2	B4	C7	Pheasant	29. 5	17. 4	D6	D6	Hare
20. 3	6. 2	B4	D8	Cock	30. 5	18. 4	D6	E7	Fox
21. 3	7. 2	B4	E9	Crow	31. 5	19. 4	D6	F8	Tiger
22. 3	8. 2	B4	F10	Monkey	1. 6	20. 4	D6	G9	Leopard
23. 3	9. 2	B4	G11	Gibbon	2. 6	21. 4	D6	H10	Griffon
24. 3	10. 2	B4	H12	Tapir	3. 6	22. 4	D6	J11	Ox
25. 3	11. 2	B4	J1	Sheep	4. 6	23. 4	D6	K12	Bat
26. 3	12. 2	B4	K2	Deer	5. 6	24. 4	D6	A1	Rat
27. 3	13. 2	B4	A3	Horse	6. 6	25. 4	D6	B2	Swallow
28. 3	14. 2	B4	B4	Stag	7. 6	26. 4	D6	C3	Pig
29. 3	15. 2	B4	C5	Serpent	8. 6	27. 4	D6	D4	Porcupine
30. 3	16. 2	B4	D6	Earthworm	9. 6	28. 4	D6	E5	Wolf
31. 3	17. 2	B4	E7	Crocodile	10. 6	29. 4	D6	F6	Dog
1. 4	18. 2	B4	F8	Dragon	11. 6	1. 5	E7	G7	Pheasant
2. 4	19. 2	B4	G9	Badger	12. 6	2. 5	E7	H8	Cock
3. 4	20. 2	B4	H10	Hare	13. 6	3. 5	E7	J9	Crow
4. 4	21. 2	B4	J11	Fox	14. 6	4. 5	E7	K10	Monkey
5. 4	22. 2	B4	K12	Tiger	15. 6	5. 5	E7	A11	Gibbon
6. 4	23. 2	B4	A1	Leopard	16. 6	6. 5	E7	B12	Tapir
7. 4	24. 2	B4	B2	Griffon	17. 6	7. 5	E7	C1	Sheep
8. 4	25. 2	B4	C3	Ox	18. 6	8. 5	E7	D2	Deer
9. 4	26. 2	B4	D4	Bat	19. 6	9. 5	E7	E3	Horse
10. 4	27. 2	B4	E5	Rat	20. 6	10. 5	E7	F4	Stag
11. 4	28. 2	B4	F6	Swallow	21. 6	11. 5	E7	G5	Serpent
12. 4	29. 2	B4	G7	Pig	22. 6	12. 5	E7	H6	Earthworm
13. 4	1. 3	C5	H8	Porcupine	23. 6	13. 5	E7	J7	Crocodile
14. 4	2. 3	C5	J9	Wolf	24. 6	14. 5	E7	K8	Dragon
15. 4	3. 3	C5	K10	Dog	25. 6	15. 5	E7	A9	Badger
16. 4	4. 3	C5	A11	Pheasant	26. 6	16. 5	E7	B10	Hare
17. 4	5. 3	C5	B12	Cock	27. 6	17. 5	E7	C11	Fox
18. 4	6. 3	C5	C1	Crow	28. 6	18. 5	E7	D12	Tiger
19. 4	7. 3	C5	D2	Monkey	29. 6	19. 5	E7	E1	Leopard
20. 4	8. 3	C5	E3	Gibbon	30. 6	20. 5	E7	F2	Griffon
21. 4	9. 3	C5	F4	Tapir	1. 7	21. 5	E7	G3	Ox
22. 4	10. 3	C5	G5	Sheep	2. 7	22. 5	E7	H4	Bat
23. 4	11. 3	C5	H6	Deer	3. 7	23. 5	E7	J5	Rat
24. 4	12. 3	C5	J7	Horse	4. 7	24. 5	E7	K6	Swallow

Solar date	Lunar date	Month HS/EB	Day HS/EB	Constellation	Solar date	Lunar date	Month HS/EB	Day HS/EB	Constellation
5. 7	25. 5	E7	H7	Pig	16. 9	10. 8	H10	D8	Dragon
6. 7	26. 5	E7	B8	Porcupine	17. 9	11. 8	H10	E9	Badger
7. 7	27. 5	E7	C9	Wolf	18. 9	12. 8	H10	F10	Hare
8. 7	28. 5	E7	D10	Dog	19. 9	13. 8	H10	G11	Fox
9. 7	29. 5	E7	E11	Pheasant	20. 9	14. 8	H10	H12	Tiger
10. 7	1. 6	F8	F12	Cock	21. 9	15. 8	H10	J1	Leopard
11. 7	2. 6	F8	G1	Crow	22. 9	16. 8	H10	K2	Griffon
12. 7	3. 6	F8	H2	Monkey	23. 9	17. 8	H10	A3	Ox
13. 7	4. 6	F8	J3	Gibbon	24. 9	18. 8	H10	B4	Bat
14. 7	5. 6	F8	K4	Tapir	25. 9	19. 8	H10	C5	Rat
15. 7	6. 6	F8	A5	Sheep	26. 9	20. 8	H10	D6	Swallow
16. 7	7. 6	F8	B6	Deer	27. 9	21. 8	H10	E7	Pig
17. 7	8. 6	F8	C7	Horse	28. 9	22. 8	H10	F8	Porcupine
18. 7	9. 6	F8	D8	Stag	29. 9	23. 8	H10	G9	Wolf
19. 7	10. 6	F8	E9	Serpent	30. 9	24. 8	H10	H10	Dog
20. 7	11. 6	F8	F10	Earthworm	1.10	25. 8	H10	J11	Pheasant
21. 7	12. 6	F8	G11	Crocodile	2.10	26. 8	H10	K12	Cock
22. 7	13. 6	F8	H12	Dragon	3.10	27. 8	H10	A1	Crow
23. 7	14. 6	F8	J1	Badger	4.10	28. 8	H10	B2	Monkey
24. 7	15. 6	F8	K2	Hare	5.10	29. 8	H10	C3	Gibbon
25. 7	16. 6	F8	A3	Fox	6.10	1. 9	J11	D4	Tapir
26. 7	17. 6	F8	B4	Tiger	7.10	2. 9	J11	E5	Sheep
27. 7	18. 6	F8	C5	Leopard	8.10	3. 9	J11	F6	Deer
28. 7	19. 6	F8	D6	Griffon	9.10	4. 9	J11	G7	Horse
29. 7	20. 6	F8	E7	Ox	10.10	5. 9	J11	H8	Stag
30. 7	21. 6	F8	F8	Bat	11.10	6. 9	J11	J9	Serpent
31. 7	22. 6	F8	G9	Rat	12.10	7. 9	J11	K10	Earthworm
1. 8	23. 6	F8	H10	Swallow	13.10	8. 9	J11	A11	Crocodile
2. 8	24. 6	F8	J11	Pig	14.10	9. 9	J11	B12	Dragon
3. 8	25. 6	F8	K12	Porcupine	15.10	10. 9	J11	C1	Badger
4. 8	26. 6	F8	A1	Wolf	16.10	11. 9	J11	D2	Hare
5. 8	27. 6	F8	B2	Dog	17.10	12. 9	J11	E3	Fox
6. 8	28. 6	F8	C3	Pheasant	18.10	13. 9	J11	F4	Tiger
7. 8	29. 6	F8	D4	Cock	19.10	14. 9	J11	G5	Leopard
8. 8	30. 6	F8	E5	Crow	20.10	15. 9	J11	H6	Griffon
9. 8	1. 7	G9	F6	Monkey	21.10	16. 9	J11	J7	Ox
10. 8	2. 7	G9	G7	Gibbon	22.10	17. 9	J11	K8	Bat
11. 8	3. 7	G9	H8	Tapir	23.10	18. 9	J11	A9	Rat
12. 8	4. 7	G9	J9	Sheep	24.10	19. 9	J11	B10	Swallow
13. 8	5. 7	G9	K10	Deer	25.10	20. 9	J11	C11	Pig
14. 8	6. 7	G9	A11	Horse	26.10	21. 9	J11	D12	Porcupine
15. 8	7. 7	G9	B12	Stag	27.10	22. 9	J11	E1	Wolf
16. 8	8. 7	G9	C1	Serpent	28.10	23. 9	J11	F2	Dog
17. 8	9. 7	G9	D2	Earthworm	29.10	24. 9	J11	G3	Pheasant
18. 8	10. 7	G9	E3	Crocodile	30.10	25. 9	J11	H4	Cock
19. 8	11. 7	G9	F4	Dragon	31.10	26. 9	J11	J5	Crow
20. 8	12. 7	G9	G5	Badger	1.11	27. 9	J11	K6	Monkey
21. 8	13. 7	G9	H6	Hare	2.11	28. 9	J11	A7	Gibbon
22. 8	14. 7	G9	J7	Fox	3.11	29. 9	J11	B8	Tapir
23. 8	15. 7	G9	K8	Tiger	4.11	30. 9	J11	C9	Sheep
24. 8	16. 7	G9	A9	Leopard	5.11	1.10	K12	D10	Deer
25. 8	17. 7	G9	B10	Griffon	6.11	2.10	K12	E11	Horse
26. 8	18. 7	G9	C11	Ox	7.11	3.10	K12	F12	Stag
27. 8	19. 7	G9	D12	Bat	8.11	4.10	K12	G1	Serpent
28. 8	20. 7	G9	E1	Rat	9.11	5.10	K12	H2	Earthworm
29. 8	21. 7	G9	F2	Swallow	10.11	6.10	K12	J3	Crocodile
30. 8	22. 7	G9	G3	Pig	11.11	7.10	K12	K4	Dragon
31. 8	23. 7	G9	H4	Porcupine	12.11	8.10	K12	A5	Badger
1. 9	24. 7	G9	J5	Wolf	13.11	9.10	K12	B6	Hare
2. 9	25. 7	G9	K6	Dog	14.11	10.10	K12	C7	Fox
3. 9	26. 7	G9	A7	Pheasant	15.11	11.10	K12	D8	Tiger
4. 9	27. 7	G9	B8	Cock	16.11	12.10	K12	E9	Leopard
5. 9	28. 7	G9	C9	Crow	17.11	13.10	K12	F10	Griffon
6. 9	29. 7	G9	D10	Monkey	18.11	14.10	K12	G11	Ox
7. 9	1. 8	H10	E11	Gibbon	19.11	15.10	K12	H12	Bat
8. 9	2. 8	H10	F12	Tapir	20.11	16.10	K12	J1	Rat
9. 9	3. 8	H10	G1	Sheep	21.11	17.10	K12	K2	Swallow
10. 9	4. 8	H10	H2	Deer	22.11	18.10	K12	A3	Pig
11. 9	5. 8	H10	J3	Horse	23.11	19.10	K12	B4	Porcupine
12. 9	6. 8	H10	K4	Stag	24.11	20.10	K12	C5	Wolf
13. 9	7. 8	H10	A5	Serpent	25.11	21.10	K12	D6	Dog
14. 9	8. 8	H10	B6	Earthworm	26.11	22.10	K12	E7	Pheasant
15. 9	9. 8	H10	C7	Crocodile	27.11	23.10	K12	F8	Cock

Solar date	Lunar date	Month HS/EB	Day HS/EB	Constellation
28.11	24.10	K12	G9	Crow
29.11	25.10	K12	H10	Monkey
30.11	26.10	K12	J11	Gibbon
1.12	27.10	K12	K12	Tapir
2.12	28.10	K12	A1	Sheep
3.12	29.10	K12	B2	Deer
4.12	1.11	A1	C3	Horse
5.12	2.11	A1	D4	Stag
6.12	3.11	A1	E5	Serpent
7.12	4.11	A1	F6	Earthworm
8.12	5.11	A1	G7	Crocodile
9.12	6.11	A1	H8	Dragon
10.12	7.11	A1	J9	Badger
11.12	8.11	A1	K10	Hare
12.12	9.11	A1	A11	Fox
13.12	10.11	A1	B12	Tiger
14.12	11.11	A1	C1	Leopard
15.12	12.11	A1	D2	Griffon
16.12	13.11	A1	E3	Ox
17.12	14.11	A1	F4	Bat
18.12	15.11	A1	G5	Rat
19.12	16.11	A1	H6	Swallow
20.12	17.11	A1	J7	Pig
21.12	18.11	A1	K8	Porcupine
22.12	19.11	A1	A9	Wolf
23.12	20.11	A1	B10	Dog
24.12	21.11	A1	C11	Pheasant
25.12	22.11	A1	D12	Cock
26.12	23.11	A1	E1	Crow
27.12	24.11	A1	F2	Monkey
28.12	25.11	A1	G3	Gibbon
29.12	26.11	A1	H4	Tapir
30.12	27.11	A1	J5	Sheep
31.12	28.11	A1	K6	Deer

1984

Solar date	Lunar date	Month HS/EB	Day HS/EB	Constellation
1. 1	29.11	A1	A7	Horse
2. 1	30.11	A1	B8	Stag
3. 1	1.12	B2	C9	Serpent
4. 1	2.12	B2	D10	Earthworm
5. 1	3.12	B2	E11	Crocodile
6. 1	4.12	B2	F12	Dragon
7. 1	5.12	B2	G1	Badger
8. 1	6.12	B2	H2	Hare
9. 1	7.12	B2	J3	Fox
10. 1	8.12	B2	K4	Tiger
11. 1	9.12	B2	A5	Leopard
12. 2	10.12	B2	B6	Griffon
13. 1	11.12	B2	C7	Ox
14. 1	12.12	B2	D8	Bat
15. 1	13.12	B2	E9	Rat
16. 1	14.12	B2	F10	Swallow
17. 1	15.12	B2	G11	Pig
18. 1	16.12	B2	H12	Porcupine
19. 1	17.12	B2	J1	Wolf
20. 1	18.12	B2	K2	Dog
21. 1	19.12	B2	A3	Pheasant
22. 1	20.12	B2	B4	Cock
23. 1	21.12	B2	C5	Crow
24. 1	22.12	B2	D6	Monkey
25. 1	23.12	B2	E7	Gibbon
26. 1	24.12	B2	F8	Tapir
27. 1	25.12	B2	G9	Sheep
28. 1	26.12	B2	H10	Deer
29. 1	27.12	B2	J11	Horse
30. 1	28.12	B2	K12	Stag
31. 1	29.12	B2	A1	Serpent
1. 2	30.12	B2	B2	Earthworm

CHIA TZU YEAR

Solar date	Lunar date	Month HS/EB	Day HS/EB	Constellation
2. 2	1.12	C3	C3	Crocodile
3. 2	2.12	C3	D4	Dragon
4. 2	3.12	C3	E5	Badger
5. 2	4.12	C3	F6	Hare
6. 2	5.12	C3	G7	Fox
7. 2	6.12	C3	H8	Tiger
8. 2	7.12	C3	J9	Leopard
9. 2	8.12	C3	K10	Griffon
10. 2	9.12	C3	A11	Ox
11. 2	10.12	C3	B12	Bat
12. 2	11.12	C3	C1	Rat
13. 2	12.12	C3	D2	Swallow
14. 2	13.12	C3	E3	Pig
15. 2	14. 1	C3	F4	Porcupine
16. 2	15. 1	C3	G5	Wolf
17. 2	16. 1	C3	H6	Dog
18. 2	17. 1	C3	J7	Pheasant
19. 2	18. 1	C3	K8	Cock
20. 2	19. 1	C3	A9	Crow
21. 2	20. 1	C3	B10	Monkey
22. 2	21. 1	C3	C11	Gibbon
23. 2	22. 1	C3	D12	Tapir
24. 2	23. 1	C3	E1	Sheep
25. 2	24. 1	C3	F2	Deer
26. 2	25. 1	C3	G3	Horse
27. 2	26. 1	C3	H4	Stag
28. 2	27. 1	C3	J5	Serpent
29. 2	28. 1	C3	K6	Earthworm
1. 3	29. 1	C3	A7	Crocodile
2. 3	30. 1	C3	B8	Dragon
3. 3	1. 1	D4	C9	Badger
4. 3	2. 1	D4	D10	Hare
5. 3	3. 1	D4	E11	Fox
6. 3	4. 1	D4	F12	Tiger
7. 3	5. 1	D4	G1	Leopard
8. 3	6. 1	D4	H2	Griffon
9. 3	7. 1	D4	J3	Ox
10. 3	8. 1	D4	K4	Bat
11. 3	9. 1	D4	A5	Rat
12. 3	10. 1	D4	B6	Swallow
13. 3	11. 1	D4	C7	Pig
14. 3	12. 1	D4	D8	Porcupine
15. 3	13. 1	D4	E9	Wolf
16. 3	14. 2	D4	F10	Dog
17. 3	15. 2	D4	G11	Pheasant
18. 3	16. 2	D4	H12	Cock
19. 3	17. 2	D4	J1	Crow
20. 3	18. 2	D4	K2	Monkey
21. 3	19. 2	D4	A3	Gibbon
22. 3	20. 2	D4	B4	Tapir
23. 3	21. 2	D4	C5	Sheep
24. 3	22. 2	D4	D6	Deer
25. 3	23. 2	D4	E7	Horse
26. 3	24. 2	D4	F8	Stag
27. 3	25. 2	D4	G9	Serpent
28. 3	26. 2	D4	H10	Earthworm
29. 3	27. 2	D4	J11	Crocodile
30. 3	28. 2	D4	K12	Dragon
31. 3	29. 2	D4	A1	Badger
1. 4	1. 2	E5	B2	Hare
2. 4	2. 2	E5	C3	Fox
3. 4	3. 2	E5	D4	Tiger
4. 4	4. 2	E5	E5	Leopard
5. 4	5. 2	E5	F6	Griffon
6. 4	6. 2	E5	G7	Ox
7. 4	7. 2	E5	H8	Bat
8. 4	8. 2	E5	J9	Rat
9. 4	9. 2	E5	K10	Swallow

Solar date	Lunar date	Month HS/EB	Day HS/EB	Constellation	Solar date	Lunar date	Month HS/EB	Day HS/EB	Constellation
10. 4	10. 2	E5	A11	Pig	22. 6	23. 5	G7	D12	Dragon
11. 4	11. 2	E5	B12	Porcupine	23. 6	24. 5	G7	E1	Badger
12. 4	12. 2	E5	C1	Wolf	24. 6	25. 5	G7	F2	Hare
13. 4	13. 2	E5	D2	Dog	25. 6	26. 5	G7	G3	Fox
14. 4	14. 3	E5	E3	Pheasant	26. 6	27. 5	G7	H4	Tiger
15. 4	15. 3	E5	F4	Cock	27. 6	28. 5	G7	J5	Leopard
16. 4	16. 3	E5	G5	Crow	28. 6	29. 5	G7	K6	Griffon
17. 4	17. 3	E5	H6	Monkey	29. 6	1. 6	H8	A7	Ox
18. 4	18. 3	E5	J7	Gibbon	30. 6	2. 6	H8	B8	Bat
19. 4	19. 3	E5	K8	Tapir	1. 7	3. 6	H8	C9	Rat
20. 4	20. 3	E5	A9	Sheep	2. 7	4. 6	H8	D10	Swallow
21. 4	21. 3	E5	B10	Deer	3. 7	5. 6	H8	E11	Pig
22. 4	22. 3	E5	C11	Horse	4. 7	6. 6	H8	F12	Porcupine
23. 4	23. 3	E5	D12	Stag	5. 7	7. 6	H8	G1	Wolf
24. 4	24. 3	E5	E1	Serpent	6. 7	8. 6	H8	H2	Dog
25. 4	25. 3	E5	F2	Earthworm	7. 7	9. 6	H8	J3	Pheasant
26. 4	26. 3	E5	G3	Crocodile	8. 7	10. 6	H8	K4	Cock
27. 4	27. 3	E5	H4	Dragon	9. 7	11. 6	H8	A5	Crow
28. 4	28. 3	E5	J5	Badger	10. 7	12. 6	H8	B6	Monkey
29. 4	29. 3	E5	K6	Hare	11. 7	13. 6	H8	C7	Gibbon
30. 4	30. 3	E5	A7	Fox	12. 7	14. 6	H8	D8	Tapir
1. 5	1. 4	F6	B8	Tiger	13. 7	15. 6	H8	E9	Sheep
2. 5	2. 4	F6	C9	Leopard	14. 7	16. 6	H8	F10	Deer
3. 5	3. 4	F6	D10	Griffon	15. 7	17. 6	H8	G11	Horse
4. 5	4. 4	F6	E11	Ox	16. 7	18. 6	H8	H12	Stag
5. 5	5. 4	F6	F12	Bat	17. 7	19. 6	H8	J1	Serpent
6. 5	6. 4	F6	G1	Rat	18. 7	20. 6	H8	K2	Earthworm
7. 5	7. 4	F6	H2	Swallow	19. 7	21. 6	H8	A3	Crocodile
8. 5	8. 4	F6	J3	Pig	20. 7	22. 6	H8	B4	Dragon
9. 5	9. 4	F6	K4	Porcupine	21. 7	23. 6	H8	C5	Badger
10. 5	10. 4	F6	A5	Wolf	22. 7	24. 6	H8	D6	Hare
11. 5	11. 4	F6	B6	Dog	23. 7	25. 6	H8	E7	Fox
12. 5	12. 4	F6	C7	Pheasant	24. 7	26. 6	H8	F8	Tiger
13. 5	13. 4	F6	D8	Cock	25. 7	27. 6	H8	G9	Leopard
14. 5	14. 4	F6	E9	Crow	26. 7	28. 6	H8	H10	Griffon
15. 5	15. 4	F6	F10	Monkey	27. 7	29. 6	H8	J11	Ox
16. 5	16. 4	F6	G11	Gibbon	28. 7	1. 7	J9	K12	Bat
17. 5	17. 4	F6	H12	Tapir	29. 7	2. 7	J9	A1	Rat
18. 5	18. 4	F6	J1	Sheep	30. 7	3. 7	J9	B2	Swallow
19. 5	19. 4	F6	K2	Deer	31. 7	4. 7	J9	C3	Pig
20. 5	20. 4	F6	A3	Horse	1. 8	5. 7	J9	D4	Porcupine
21. 5	21. 4	F6	B4	Stag	2. 8	6. 7	J9	E5	Wolf
22. 5	22. 4	F6	C5	Serpent	3. 8	7. 7	J9	F6	Dog
23. 5	23. 4	F6	D6	Earthworm	4. 8	8. 7	J9	G7	Pheasant
24. 5	24. 4	F6	E7	Crocodile	5. 8	9. 7	J9	H8	Cock
25. 5	25. 4	F6	F8	Dragon	6. 8	10. 7	J9	J9	Crow
26. 5	26. 4	F6	G9	Badger	7. 8	11. 7	J9	K10	Monkey
27. 5	27. 4	F6	H10	Hare	8. 8	12. 7	J9	A11	Gibbon
28. 5	28. 4	F6	J11	Fox	9. 8	13. 7	J9	B12	Tapir
29. 5	29. 4	F6	K12	Tiger	10. 8	14. 7	J9	C1	Sheep
30. 5	30. 4	F6	A1	Leopard	11. 8	15. 7	J9	D2	Deer
31. 5	1. 5	G7	B2	Griffon	12. 8	16. 7	J9	E3	Horse
1. 6	2. 5	G7	C3	Ox	13. 8	17. 7	J9	F4	Stag
2. 6	3. 5	G7	D4	Bat	14. 8	18. 7	J9	G5	Serpent
3. 6	4. 5	G7	E5	Rat	15. 8	19. 7	J9	H6	Earthworm
4. 6	5. 5	G7	F6	Swallow	16. 8	20. 7	J9	J7	Crocodile
5. 6	6. 5	G7	G7	Pig	17. 8	21. 7	J9	K8	Dragon
6. 6	7. 5	G7	H8	Porcupine	18. 8	22. 7	J9	A9	Badger
7. 6	8. 5	G7	J9	Wolf	19. 8	23. 7	J9	B10	Hare
8. 6	9. 5	G7	K10	Dog	20. 8	24. 7	J9	C11	Fox
9. 6	10. 5	G7	A11	Pheasant	21. 8	25. 7	J9	D12	Tiger
10. 6	11. 5	G7	B12	Cock	22. 8	26. 7	J9	E1	Leopard
11. 6	12. 5	G7	C1	Crow	23. 8	27. 7	J9	F2	Griffon
12. 6	13. 5	G7	D2	Monkey	24. 8	28. 7	J9	G3	Ox
13. 6	14. 5	G7	E3	Gibbon	25. 8	29. 7	J9	H4	Bat
14. 6	15. 5	G7	F4	Tapir	26. 8	30. 7	J9	J5	Rat
15. 6	16. 5	G7	G5	Sheep	27. 8	1. 8	K10	K6	Swallow
16. 6	17. 5	G7	H6	Deer	28. 8	2. 8	K10	A7	Pig
17. 6	18. 5	G7	J7	Horse	29. 8	3. 8	K10	B8	Porcupine
18. 6	19. 5	G7	K8	Stag	30. 8	4. 8	K10	C9	Wolf
19. 6	20. 5	G7	A9	Serpent	31. 8	5. 8	K10	D10	Dog
20. 6	21. 5	G7	B10	Earthworm	1. 9	6. 8	K10	E11	Pheasant
21. 6	22. 5	G7	C11	Crocodile	2. 9	7. 8	K10	F12	Cock

Solar date	Lunar date	Month HS/EB	Day HS/EB	Constellation	Solar date	Lunar date	Month HS/EB	Day HS/EB	Constellation
3. 9	8. 8	K10	G1	Crow	15.11	23.10	B12	K2	Griffon
4. 9	9. 8	K10	H2	Monkey	16.11	24.10	B12	A3	Ox
5. 9	10. 8	K10	J3	Gibbon	17.11	25.10	B12	B4	Bat
6. 9	11. 8	K10	K4	Tapir	18.11	26.10	B12	C5	Rat
7. 9	12. 8	K10	A5	Sheep	19.11	27.10	B12	D6	Swallow
8. 9	13. 8	K10	B6	Deer	20.11	28.10	B12	E7	Pig
9. 9	14. 8	K10	C7	Horse	21.11	29.10	B12	F8	Porcupine
10. 9	15. 8	K10	D8	Stag	22.11	30.10	B12	G9	Wolf
11. 9	16. 8	K10	E9	Serpent	23.11	*1.10*	*B12*	H10	Dog
12. 9	17. 8	K10	F10	Earthworm	24.11	*2.10*	*B12*	J11	Pheasant
13. 9	18. 8	K10	G11	Crocodile	25.11	*3.10*	*B12*	K12	Cock
14. 9	19. 8	K10	H12	Dragon	26.11	*4.10*	*B12*	A1	Crow
15. 9	20. 8	K10	J1	Badger	27.11	*5.10*	*B12*	B2	Monkey
16. 9	21. 8	K10	K2	Hare	28.11	*6.10*	*B12*	C3	Gibbon
17. 9	22. 8	K10	A3	Fox	29.11	*7.10*	*B12*	D4	Tapir
18. 9	23. 8	K10	B4	Tiger	30.11	*8.10*	*B12*	E5	Sheep
19. 9	24. 8	K10	C5	Leopard	1.12	*9.10*	*B12*	F6	Deer
20. 9	25. 8	K10	D6	Griffon	2.12	*10.10*	*B12*	G7	Horse
21. 9	26. 8	K10	E7	Ox	3.12	*11.10*	*B12*	H8	Stag
22. 9	27. 8	K10	F8	Bat	4.12	*12.10*	*B12*	J9	Serpent
23. 9	28. 8	K10	G9	Rat	5.12	*13.10*	*B12*	K10	Earthworm
24. 9	29. 8	K10	H10	Swallow	6.12	*14.10*	*B12*	A11	Crocodile
25. 9	1. 9	A11	J11	Pig	7.12	*15.10*	*B12*	B12	Dragon
26. 9	2. 9	A11	K12	Porcupine	8.12	*16.10*	*B12*	C1	Badger
27. 9	3. 9	A11	A1	Wolf	9.12	*17.10*	*B12*	D2	Hare
28. 9	4. 9	A11	B2	Dog	10.12	*18.10*	*B12*	E3	Fox
29. 9	5. 9	A11	C3	Pheasant	11.12	*19.10*	*B12*	F4	Tiger
30. 9	6. 9	A11	D4	Cock	12.12	*20.10*	*B12*	G5	Leopard
1.10	7. 9	A11	E5	Crow	13.12	*21.10*	*B12*	H6	Griffon
2.10	8. 9	A11	F6	Monkey	14.12	*22.10*	*B12*	J7	Ox
3.10	9. 9	A11	G7	Gibbon	15.12	*23.10*	*B12*	K8	Bat
4.10	10. 9	A11	H8	Tapir	16.12	*24.10*	*B12*	A9	Rat
5.10	11. 9	A11	J9	Sheep	17.12	*25.10*	*B12*	B10	Swallow
6.10	12. 9	A11	K10	Deer	18.12	*26.10*	*B12*	C11	Pig
7.10	13. 9	A11	A11	Horse	19.12	*27.10*	*B12*	D12	Porcupine
8.10	14. 9	A11	B12	Stag	20.12	*28.10*	*B12*	E1	Wolf
9.10	15. 9	A11	C1	Serpent	21.12	*29.10*	*B12*	F2	Dog
10.10	16. 9	A11	D2	Earthworm	22.12	1.11	C1	G3	Pheasant
11.10	17. 9	A11	E3	Crocodile	23.12	2.11	C1	H4	Cock
12.10	18. 9	A11	F4	Dragon	24.12	3.11	C1	J5	Crow
13.10	19. 9	A11	G5	Badger	25.12	4.11	C1	K6	Monkey
14.10	20. 9	A11	H6	Hare	26.12	5.11	C1	A7	Gibbon
15.10	21. 9	A11	J7	Fox	27.12	6.11	C1	B8	Tapir
16.10	22. 9	A11	K8	Tiger	28.12	7.11	C1	C9	Sheep
17.10	23. 9	A11	A9	Leopard	29.12	8.11	C1	D10	Deer
18.10	24. 9	A11	B10	Griffon	30.12	9.11	C1	E11	Horse
19.10	25. 9	A11	C11	Ox	31.12	10.11	C1	F12	Stag
20.10	26. 9	A11	D12	Bat					
21.10	27. 9	A11	E1	Rat	**1985**				
22.10	28. 9	A11	F2	Swallow	1. 1	11.11	C1	G1	Serpent
23.10	29. 9	A11	G3	Pig	2. 1	12.11	C1	H2	Earthworm
24.10	1.10	B12	H4	Porcupine	3. 1	13.11	C1	J3	Crocodile
25.10	2.10	B12	J5	Wolf	4. 1	14.11	C1	K4	Dragon
26.10	3.10	B12	K6	Dog	5. 1	15.11	C1	A5	Badger
27.10	4.10	B12	A7	Pheasant	6. 1	16.11	C1	B6	Hare
28.10	5.10	B12	B8	Cock	7. 1	17.11	C1	C7	Fox
29.10	6.10	B12	C9	Crow	8. 1	18.11	C1	D8	Tiger
30.10	7.10	B12	D10	Monkey	9. 1	19.11	C1	E9	Leopard
31.10	8.10	B12	E11	Gibbon	10. 1	20.11	C1	F10	Griffon
1.11	9.10	B12	F12	Tapir	11. 1	21.11	C1	G11	Ox
2.11	10.10	B12	G1	Sheep	12. 1	22.11	C1	H12	Bat
3.11	11.10	B12	H2	Deer	13. 1	23.11	C1	J1	Rat
4.11	12.10	B12	J3	Horse	14. 1	24.11	C1	K2	Swallow
5.11	13.10	B12	K4	Stag	15. 1	25.11	C1	A3	Pig
6.11	14.10	B12	A5	Serpent	16. 1	26.11	C1	B4	Porcupine
7.11	15.10	B12	B6	Earthworm	17. 1	27.11	C1	C5	Wolf
8.11	16.10	B12	C7	Crocodile	18. 1	28.11	C1	D6	Dog
9.11	17.10	B12	D8	Dragon	19. 1	29.11	C1	E7	Pheasant
10.11	18.10	B12	E9	Badger	20. 1	30.11	C1	F8	Cock
11.11	19.10	B12	F10	Hare	21. 1	1.12	D2	G9	Crow
12.11	20.10	B12	G11	Fox	22. 1	2.12	D2	H10	Monkey
13.11	21.10	B12	H12	Tiger	23. 1	3.12	D2	J11	Gibbon
14.11	22.10	B12	J1	Leopard	24. 1	4.12	D2	K12	Tapir

Solar date	Lunar date	Month HS/EB	Day HS/EB	Constellation	Solar date	Lunar date	Month HS/EB	Day HS/EB	Constellation
25. 1	5.12	D2	A1	Sheep	7. 2	18.12	D2	D2	Griffon
26. 1	6.12	D2	B2	Deer	8. 2	19.12	D2	E3	Ox
27. 1	7.12	D2	C3	Horse	9. 2	20.12	D2	F4	Bat
28. 1	8.12	D2	D4	Stag	10. 2	21.12	D2	G5	Rat
29. 1	9.12	D2	E5	Serpent	11. 2	22.12	D2	H6	Swallow
30. 1	10.12	D2	F6	Earthworm	12. 2	23.12	D2	J7	Pig
31. 1	11.12	D2	G7	Crocodile	13. 2	24.12	D2	K8	Porcupine
1. 2	12.12	D2	H8	Dragon	14. 2	25.12	D2	A9	Wolf
2. 2	13.12	D2	J9	Badger	15. 2	26.12	D2	B10	Dog
3. 2	14.12	D2	K10	Hare	16. 2	27.12	D2	C11	Pheasant
4. 2	15.12	D2	A11	Fox	17. 2	28.12	D2	D12	Cock
5. 2	16.12	D2	B12	Tiger	18. 2	29.12	D2	E1	Crow
6. 2	17.12	D2	C1	Leopard	19. 2	30.12	D2	F2	Monkey

YI CH'OU YEAR

Solar date	Lunar date	Month HS/EB	Day HS/EB	Constellation	Solar date	Lunar date	Month HS/EB	Day HS/EB	Constellation
20. 2	1. 1	E3	G3	Gibbon	16. 4	27. 2	F4	B10	Monkey
21. 2	2. 1	E3	H4	Tapir	17. 4	28. 2	F4	C11	Gibbon
22. 2	3. 1	E3	J5	Sheep	18. 4	29. 2	F4	D12	Tapir
23. 2	4. 1	E3	K6	Deer	19. 4	30. 2	F4	E1	Sheep
24. 2	5. 1	E3	A7	Horse	20. 4	1. 3	G5	F2	Deer
25. 2	6. 1	E3	B8	Stag	21. 4	2. 3	G5	G3	Horse
26. 2	7. 1	E3	C9	Serpent	22. 4	3. 3	G5	H4	Stag
27. 2	8. 1	E3	D10	Earthworm	23. 4	4. 3	G5	J5	Serpent
28. 2	9. 1	E3	E11	Crocodile	24. 4	5. 3	G5	K6	Earthworm
1. 3	10. 1	E3	F12	Dragon	25. 4	6. 3	G5	A7	Crocodile
2. 3	11. 1	E3	G1	Badger	26. 4	7. 3	G5	B8	Dragon
3. 3	12. 1	E3	H2	Hare	27. 4	8. 3	G5	C9	Badger
4. 3	13. 1	E3	J3	Fox	28. 4	9. 3	G5	D10	Hare
5. 3	14. 1	E3	K4	Tiger	29. 4	10. 3	G5	E11	Fox
6. 3	15. 1	E3	A5	Leopard	30. 4	11. 3	G5	F12	Tiger
7. 3	16. 1	E3	B6	Griffon	1. 5	12. 3	G5	G1	Leopard
8. 3	17. 1	E3	C7	Ox	2. 5	13. 3	G5	H2	Griffon
9. 3	18. 1	E3	D8	Bat	3. 5	14. 3	G5	J3	Ox
10. 3	19. 1	E3	E9	Rat	4. 5	15. 3	G5	K4	Bat
11. 3	20. 1	E3	F10	Swallow	5. 5	16. 3	G5	A5	Rat
12. 3	21. 1	E3	G11	Pig	6. 5	17. 3	G5	B6	Swallow
13. 3	22. 1	E3	H12	Porcupine	7. 5	18. 3	G5	C7	Pig
14. 3	23. 1	E3	J1	Wolf	8. 5	19. 3	G5	D8	Porcupine
15. 3	24. 1	E3	K2	Dog	9. 5	20. 3	G5	E9	Wolf
16. 3	25. 1	E3	A3	Pheasant	10. 5	21. 3	G5	F10	Dog
17. 3	26. 1	E3	B4	Cock	11. 5	22. 3	G5	G11	Pheasant
18. 3	27. 1	E3	C5	Crow	12. 5	23. 3	G5	H12	Cock
19. 3	28. 1	E3	D6	Monkey	13. 5	24. 3	G5	J1	Crow
20. 3	29. 1	E3	E7	Gibbon	14. 5	25. 3	G5	K2	Monkey
21. 3	1. 2	F4	F8	Tapir	15. 5	26. 3	G5	A3	Gibbon
22. 3	2. 2	F4	G9	Sheep	16. 5	27. 3	G5	B4	Tapir
23. 3	3. 2	F4	H10	Deer	17. 5	28. 3	G5	C5	Sheep
24. 3	4. 2	F4	J11	Horse	18. 5	29. 3	G5	D6	Deer
25. 3	5. 2	F4	K12	Stag	19. 5	30. 3	G5	E7	Horse
26. 3	6. 2	F4	A1	Serpent	20. 5	1. 4	H6	F8	Stag
27. 3	7. 2	F4	B2	Earthworm	21. 5	2. 4	H6	G9	Serpent
28. 3	8. 2	F4	C3	Crocodile	22. 5	3. 4	H6	H10	Earthworm
29. 3	9. 2	F4	D4	Dragon	23. 5	4. 4	H6	J11	Crocodile
30. 3	10. 2	F4	E5	Badger	24. 5	5. 4	H6	K12	Dragon
31. 3	11. 2	F4	F6	Hare	25. 5	6. 4	H6	A1	Badger
1. 4	12. 2	F4	G7	Fox	26. 5	7. 4	H6	B2	Hare
2. 4	13. 2	F4	H8	Tiger	27. 5	8. 4	H6	C3	Fox
3. 4	14. 2	F4	J9	Leopard	28. 5	9. 4	H6	D4	Tiger
4. 4	15. 2	F4	K10	Griffon	29. 5	10. 4	H6	E5	Leopard
5. 4	16. 2	F4	A11	Ox	30. 5	11. 4	H6	F6	Griffon
6. 4	17. 2	F4	B12	Bat	31. 5	12. 4	H6	G7	Ox
7. 4	18. 2	F4	C1	Rat	1. 6	13. 4	H6	H8	Bat
8. 4	19. 2	F4	D2	Swallow	2. 6	14. 4	H6	J9	Rat
9. 4	20. 2	F4	E3	Pig	3. 6	15. 4	H6	K10	Swallow
10. 4	21. 2	F4	F4	Porcupine	4. 6	16. 4	H6	A11	Pig
11. 4	22. 2	F4	G5	Wolf	5. 6	17. 4	H6	B12	Porcupine
12. 4	23. 2	F4	H6	Dog	6. 6	18. 4	H6	C1	Wolf
13. 4	24. 2	F4	J7	Pheasant	7. 6	19. 4	H6	D2	Dog
14. 4	25. 2	F4	K8	Cock	8. 6	20. 4	H6	E3	Pheasant
15. 4	26. 2	F4	A9	Crow	9. 6	21. 4	H6	F4	Cock

Solar date	Lunar date	Month HS/EB	Day HS/EB	Constellation	Solar date	Lunar date	Month HS/EB	Day HS/EB	Constellation
10. 6	22. 4	H6	G5	Crow	22. 8	7. 7	A9	K6	Griffon
11. 6	23. 4	H6	H6	Monkey	23. 8	8. 7	A9	A7	Ox
12. 6	24. 4	H6	J7	Gibbon	24. 8	9. 7	A9	B8	Bat
13. 6	25. 4	H6	K8	Tapir	25. 8	10. 7	A9	C9	Rat
14. 6	26. 4	H6	A9	Sheep	26. 8	11. 7	A9	D10	Swallow
15. 6	27. 4	H6	B10	Deer	27. 8	12. 7	A9	E11	Pig
16. 6	28. 4	H6	C11	Horse	28. 8	13. 7	A9	F12	Porcupine
17. 6	29. 4	H6	D12	Stag	29. 8	14. 7	A9	G1	Wolf
18. 6	1. 5	J7	E1	Serpent	30. 8	15. 7	A9	H2	Dog
19. 6	2. 5	J7	F2	Earthworm	31. 8	16. 7	A9	J3	Pheasant
20. 6	3. 5	J7	G3	Crocodile	1. 9	17. 7	A9	K4	Cock
21. 6	4. 5	J7	H4	Dragon	2. 9	18. 7	A9	A5	Crow
22. 6	5. 5	J7	J5	Badger	3. 9	19. 7	A9	B6	Monkey
23. 6	6. 5	J7	K6	Hare	4. 9	20. 7	A9	C7	Gibbon
24. 6	7. 5	J7	A7	Fox	5. 9	21. 7	A9	D8	Tapir
25. 6	8. 5	J7	B8	Tiger	6. 9	22. 7	A9	E9	Sheep
26. 6	9. 5	J7	C9	Leopard	7. 9	23. 7	A9	F10	Deer
27. 6	10. 5	J7	D10	Griffon	8. 9	24. 7	A9	G11	Horse
28. 6	11. 5	J7	E11	Ox	9. 9	25. 7	A9	H12	Stag
29. 6	12. 5	J7	F12	Bat	10. 9	26. 7	A9	J1	Serpent
30. 6	13. 5	J7	G1	Rat	11. 9	27. 7	A9	K2	Earthworm
1. 7	14. 5	J7	H2	Swallow	12. 9	28. 7	A9	A3	Crocodile
2. 7	15. 5	J7	J3	Pig	13. 9	29. 7	A9	B4	Dragon
3. 7	16. 5	J7	K4	Porcupine	14. 9	30. 7	A9	C5	Badger
4. 7	17. 5	J7	A5	Wolf	15. 9	1. 8	B10	D6	Hare
5. 7	18. 5	J7	B6	Dog	16. 9	2. 8	B10	E7	Fox
6. 7	19. 5	J7	C7	Pheasant	17. 9	3. 8	B10	F8	Tiger
7. 7	20. 5	J7	D8	Cock	18. 9	4. 8	B10	G9	Leopard
8. 7	21. 5	J7	E9	Crow	19. 9	5. 8	B10	H10	Griffon
9. 7	22. 5	J7	F10	Monkey	20. 9	6. 8	B10	J11	Ox
10. 7	23. 5	J7	G11	Gibbon	21. 9	7. 8	B10	K12	Bat
11. 7	24. 5	J7	H12	Tapir	22. 9	8. 8	B10	A1	Rat
12. 7	25. 5	J7	J1	Sheep	23. 9	9. 8	B10	B2	Swallow
13. 7	26. 5	J7	K2	Deer	24. 9	10. 8	B10	C3	Pig
14. 7	27. 5	J7	A3	Horse	25. 9	11. 8	B10	D4	Porcupine
15. 7	28. 5	J7	B4	Stag	26. 9	12. 8	B10	E5	Wolf
16. 7	29. 5	J7	C5	Serpent	27. 9	13. 8	B10	F6	Dog
17. 7	30. 5	J7	D6	Earthworm	28. 9	14. 8	B10	G7	Pheasant
18. 7	1. 6	K8	E7	Crocodile	29. 9	15. 8	B10	H8	Cock
19. 7	2. 6	K8	F8	Dragon	30. 9	16. 8	B10	J9	Crow
20. 7	3. 6	K8	G9	Badger	1.10	17. 8	B10	K10	Monkey
21. 7	4. 6	K8	H10	Hare	2.10	18. 8	B10	A11	Gibbon
22. 7	5. 6	K8	J11	Fox	3.10	19. 8	B10	B12	Tapir
23. 7	6. 6	K8	K12	Tiger	4.10	20. 8	B10	C1	Sheep
24. 7	7. 6	K8	A1	Leopard	5.10	21. 8	B10	D2	Deer
25. 7	8. 6	K8	B2	Griffon	6.10	22. 8	B10	E3	Horse
26. 7	9. 6	K8	C3	Ox	7.10	23. 8	B10	F4	Stag
27. 7	10. 6	K8	D4	Bat	8.10	24. 8	B10	G5	Serpent
28. 7	11. 6	K8	E5	Rat	9.10	25. 8	B10	H6	Earthworm
29. 7	12. 6	K8	F6	Swallow	10.10	26. 8	B10	J7	Crocodile
30. 7	13. 6	K8	G7	Pig	11.10	27. 8	B10	K8	Dragon
31. 7	14. 6	K8	H8	Porcupine	12.10	28. 8	B10	A9	Badger
1. 8	15. 6	K8	J9	Wolf	13.10	29. 8	B10	B10	Hare
2. 8	16. 6	K8	K10	Dog	14.10	1. 9	C11	C11	Fox
3. 8	17. 6	K8	A11	Pheasant	15.10	2. 9	C11	D12	Tiger
4. 8	18. 6	K8	B12	Cock	16.10	3. 9	C11	E1	Leopard
5. 8	19. 6	K8	C1	Crow	17.10	4. 9	C11	F2	Griffon
6. 8	20. 6	K8	D2	Monkey	18.10	5. 9	C11	G3	Ox
7. 8	21. 6	K8	E3	Gibbon	19.10	6. 9	C11	H4	Bat
8. 8	22. 6	K8	F4	Tapir	20.10	7. 9	C11	J5	Rat
9. 8	23. 6	K8	G5	Sheep	21.10	8. 9	C11	K6	Swallow
10. 8	24. 6	K8	H6	Deer	22.10	9. 9	C11	A7	Pig
11. 8	25. 6	K8	J7	Horse	23.10	10. 9	C11	B8	Porcupine
12. 8	26. 6	K8	K8	Stag	24.10	11. 9	C11	C9	Wolf
13. 8	27. 6	K8	A9	Serpent	25.10	12. 9	C11	D10	Dog
14. 8	28. 6	K8	B10	Earthworm	26.10	13. 9	C11	E11	Pheasant
15. 8	29. 6	K8	C11	Crocodile	27.10	14. 9	C11	F12	Cock
16. 8	1. 7	A9	D12	Dragon	28.10	15. 9	C11	G1	Crow
17. 8	2. 7	A9	E1	Badger	29.10	16. 9	C11	H2	Monkey
18. 8	3. 7	A9	F2	Hare	30.10	17. 9	C11	J3	Gibbon
19. 8	4. 7	A9	G3	Fox	31.10	18. 9	C11	K4	Tapir
20. 8	5. 7	A9	H4	Tiger	1.11	19. 9	C11	A5	Sheep
21. 8	6. 7	A9	J5	Leopard	2.11	20. 9	C11	B6	Deer

Solar date	Lunar date	Month HS/EB	Day HS/EB	Constellation	Solar date	Lunar date	Month HS/EB	Day HS/EB	Constellation
3.11	21. 9	C11	C7	Horse	23.12	12.11	E1	C9	Crow
4.11	22. 9	C11	D8	Stag	24.12	13.11	E1	D10	Monkey
5.11	23. 9	C11	E9	Serpent	25.12	14.11	E1	E11	Gibbon
6.11	24. 9	C11	F10	Earthworm	26.12	15.11	E1	F12	Tapir
7.11	25. 9	C11	G11	Crocodile	27.12	16.11	E1	G1	Sheep
8.11	26. 9	C11	H12	Dragon	28.12	17.11	E1	H2	Deer
9.11	27. 9	C11	J1	Badger	29.12	18.11	E1	J3	Horse
10.11	28. 9	C11	K2	Hare	30.12	19.11	E1	K4	Stag
11.11	29. 9	C11	A3	Fox	31.12	20.11	E1	A5	Serpent
12.11	1.10	D12	B4	Tiger	**1986**				
13.11	2.10	D12	C5	Leopard	1. 1	21.11	E1	B6	Earthworm
14.11	3.10	D12	D6	Griffon	2. 1	22.11	E1	C7	Crocodile
15.11	4.10	D12	E7	Ox	3. 1	23.11	E1	D8	Dragon
16.11	5.10	D12	F8	Bat	4. 1	24.11	E1	E9	Badger
17.11	6.10	D12	G9	Rat	5. 1	25.11	E1	F10	Hare
18.11	7.10	D12	H10	Swallow	6. 1	26.11	E1	G11	Fox
19.11	8.10	D12	J11	Pig	7. 1	27.11	E1	H12	Tiger
20.11	9.10	D12	K12	Porcupine	8. 1	28.11	E1	J1	Leopard
21.11	10.10	D12	A1	Wolf	9. 1	29.11	E1	K2	Griffon
22.11	11.10	D12	B2	Dog	10. 1	1.12	F2	A3	Ox
23.11	12.10	D12	C3	Pheasant	11. 1	2.12	F2	B4	Bat
24.11	13.10	D12	D4	Cock	12. 1	3.12	F2	C5	Rat
25.11	14.10	D12	E5	Crow	13. 1	4.12	F2	D6	Swallow
26.11	15.10	D12	F6	Monkey	14. 1	5.12	F2	E7	Pig
27.11	16.10	D12	G7	Gibbon	15. 1	6.12	F2	F8	Porcupine
28.11	17.10	D12	H8	Tapir	16. 1	7.12	F2	G9	Wolf
29.11	18.10	D12	J9	Sheep	17. 1	8.12	F2	H10	Dog
30.11	19.10	D12	K10	Deer	18. 1	9.12	F2	J11	Pheasant
1.12	20.10	D12	A11	Horse	19. 1	10.12	F2	K12	Cock
2.12	21.10	D12	B12	Stag	20. 1	11.12	F2	A1	Crow
3.12	22.10	D12	C1	Serpent	21. 1	12.12	F2	B2	Monkey
4.12	23.10	D12	D2	Earthworm	22. 1	13.12	F2	C3	Gibbon
5.12	24.10	D12	E3	Crocodile	23. 1	14.12	F2	D4	Tapir
6.12	25.10	D12	F4	Dragon	24. 1	15.12	F2	E5	Sheep
7.12	26.10	D12	G5	Badger	25. 1	16.12	F2	F6	Deer
8.12	27.10	D12	H6	Hare	26. 1	17.12	F2	G7	Horse
9.12	28.10	D12	J7	Fox	27. 1	18.12	F2	H8	Stag
10.12	29.10	D12	K8	Tiger	28. 1	19.12	F2	J9	Serpent
11.12	30.10	D12	A9	Leopard	29. 1	20.12	F2	K10	Earthworm
12.12	1.11	E1	B10	Griffon	30. 1	21.12	F2	A11	Crocodile
13.12	2.11	E1	C11	Ox	31. 1	22.12	F2	B12	Dragon
14.12	3.11	E1	D12	Bat	1. 2	23.12	F2	C1	Badger
15.12	4.11	E1	E1	Rat	2. 2	24.12	F2	D2	Hare
16.12	5.11	E1	F2	Swallow	3. 2	25.12	F2	E3	Fox
17.12	6.11	E1	G3	Pig	4. 2	26.12	F2	F4	Tiger
18.12	7.11	E1	H4	Porcupine	5. 2	27.12	F2	G5	Leopard
19.12	8.11	E1	J5	Wolf	6. 2	28.12	F2	H6	Griffon
20.12	9.11	E1	K6	Dog	7. 2	29.12	F2	J7	Ox
21.12	10.11	E1	A7	Pheasant	8. 2	30.12	F2	K8	Bat
22.12	11.11	E1	B8	Cock					

PING YIN YEAR

Solar date	Lunar date	Month HS/EB	Day HS/EB	Constellation	Solar date	Lunar date	Month HS/EB	Day HS/EB	Constellation
9. 2	1. 1	G3	A9	Rat	26. 2	18. 1	G3	H2	Earthworm
10. 2	2. 1	G3	B10	Swallow	27. 2	19. 1	G3	J3	Crocodile
11. 2	3. 1	G3	C1	Pig	28. 2	20. 1	G3	K4	Dragon
12. 2	4. 1	G3	D12	Porcupine	1. 3	21. 1	G3	A5	Badger
13. 2	5. 1	G3	E1	Wolf	2. 3	22. 1	G3	B6	Hare
14. 2	6. 1	G3	F2	Dog	3. 3	23. 1	G3	C7	Fox
15. 2	7. 1	G3	G3	Pheasant	4. 3	24. 1	G3	D8	Tiger
16. 2	8. 1	G3	H4	Cock	5. 3	25. 1	G3	E9	Leopard
17. 2	9. 1	G3	J5	Crow	6. 3	26. 1	G3	F10	Griffon
18. 2	10. 1	G3	K6	Monkey	7. 3	27. 1	G3	G11	Ox
19. 2	11. 1	G3	A7	Gibbon	8. 3	28. 1	G3	H12	Bat
20. 2	12. 1	G3	B8	Tapir	9. 3	29. 1	G3	J1	Rat
21. 2	13. 1	G3	C9	Sheep	10. 3	1. 2	H4	K2	Swallow
22. 2	14. 1	G3	D10	Deer	11. 3	2. 2	H4	A3	Pig
23. 2	15. 1	G3	E11	Horse	12. 3	3. 2	H4	B4	Porcupine
24. 2	16. 1	G3	F12	Stag	13. 3	4. 2	H4	C5	Wolf
25. 2	17. 1	G3	G1	Serpent	14. 3	5. 2	H4	D6	Dog

Solar date	Lunar date	Month HS/EB	Day HS/EB	Constellation	Solar date	Lunar date	Month HS/EB	Day HS/EB	Constellation
15. 3	6. 2	H4	E7	Pheasant	27. 5	19. 4	K6	H8	Tiger
16. 3	7. 2	H4	F8	Cock	28. 5	20. 4	K6	J9	Leopard
17. 3	8. 2	H4	G9	Crow	29. 5	21. 4	K6	K10	Griffon
18. 3	9. 2	H4	H10	Monkey	30. 5	22. 4	K6	A11	Ox
19. 3	10. 2	H4	J11	Gibbon	31. 5	23. 4	K6	B12	Bat
20. 3	11. 2	H4	K12	Tapir	1. 6	24. 4	K6	C1	Rat
21. 3	12. 2	H4	A1	Sheep	2. 6	25. 4	K6	D2	Swallow
22. 3	13. 2	H4	B2	Deer	3. 6	26. 4	K6	E3	Pig
23. 3	14. 2	H4	C3	Horse	4. 6	27. 4	K6	F4	Porcupine
24. 3	15. 2	H4	D4	Stag	5. 6	28. 4	K6	G5	Wolf
25. 3	16. 2	H4	E5	Serpent	6. 6	29. 4	K6	H6	Dog
26. 3	17. 2	H4	F6	Earthworm	7. 6	1. 5	A7	J7	Pheasant
27. 3	18. 2	H4	G7	Crocodile	8. 6	2. 5	A7	K8	Cock
28. 3	19. 2	H4	H8	Dragon	9. 6	3. 5	A7	A9	Crow
29. 3	20. 2	H4	J9	Badger	10. 6	4. 5	A7	B10	Monkey
30. 3	21. 2	H4	K10	Hare	11. 6	5. 5	A7	C11	Gibbon
31. 3	22. 2	H4	A11	Fox	12. 6	6. 5	A7	D12	Tapir
1. 4	23. 2	H4	B12	Leopard	13. 6	7. 5	A7	E1	Sheep
2. 4	24. 2	H4	C1	Leopard	14. 6	8. 5	A7	F2	Deer
3. 4	25. 2	H4	D2	Griffon	15. 6	9. 5	A7	G3	Horse
4. 4	26. 2	H4	E3	Ox	16. 6	10. 5	A7	H4	Stag
5. 4	27. 2	H4	F4	Bat	17. 6	11. 5	A7	J5	Serpent
6. 4	28. 2	H4	G5	Rat	18. 6	12. 5	A7	K6	Earthworm
7. 4	29. 2	H4	H6	Swallow	19. 6	13. 5	A7	A7	Crocodile
8. 4	30. 2	H4	J7	Pig	20. 6	14. 5	A7	B8	Dragon
9. 4	1. 3	J5	K8	Porcupine	21. 6	15. 5	A7	C9	Badger
10. 4	2. 3	J5	A9	Wolf	22. 6	16. 5	A7	D10	Hare
11. 4	3. 3	J5	B10	Dog	23. 6	17. 5	A7	E11	Fox
12. 4	4. 3	J5	C11	Pheasant	24. 6	18. 5	A7	F12	Tiger
13. 4	5. 3	J5	D12	Cock	25. 6	19. 5	A7	G1	Leopard
14. 4	6. 3	J5	E1	Crow	26. 6	20. 5	A7	H2	Griffon
15. 4	7. 3	J5	F2	Monkey	27. 6	21. 5	A7	J3	Ox
16. 4	8. 3	J5	G3	Gibbon	28. 6	22. 5	A7	K4	Bat
17. 4	9. 3	J5	H4	Tapir	29. 6	23. 5	A7	A5	Rat
18. 4	10. 3	J5	J5	Sheep	30. 6	24. 5	A7	B6	Swallow
19. 4	11. 3	J5	K6	Deer	1. 7	25. 5	A7	C7	Pig
20. 4	12. 3	J5	A7	Horse	2. 7	26. 5	A7	D8	Porcupine
21. 4	13. 3	J5	B8	Stag	3. 7	27. 5	A7	E9	Wolf
22. 4	14. 3	J5	C9	Serpent	4. 7	28. 5	A7	F10	Dog
23. 4	15. 3	J5	D10	Earthworm	5. 7	29. 5	A7	G11	Pheasant
24. 4	16. 3	J5	E11	Crocodile	6. 7	30. 5	A7	H12	Cock
25. 4	17. 3	J5	F12	Dragon	7. 7	1. 6	B8	J1	Crow
26. 4	18. 3	J5	G1	Badger	8. 7	2. 6	B8	K2	Monkey
27. 4	19. 3	J5	H2	Hare	9. 7	3. 6	B8	A3	Gibbon
28. 4	20. 3	J5	J3	Fox	10. 7	4. 6	B8	B4	Tapir
29. 4	21. 3	J5	K4	Tiger	11. 7	5. 6	B8	C5	Sheep
30. 4	22. 3	J5	A5	Leopard	12. 7	6. 6	B8	D6	Deer
1. 5	23. 3	J5	B6	Griffon	13. 7	7. 6	B8	E7	Horse
2. 5	24. 3	J5	C7	Ox	14. 7	8. 6	B8	F8	Stag
3. 5	25. 3	J5	D8	Bat	15. 7	9. 6	B8	G9	Serpent
4. 5	26. 3	J5	E9	Rat	16. 7	10. 6	B8	H10	Earthworm
5. 5	27. 3	J5	F10	Swallow	17. 7	11. 6	B8	J11	Crocodile
6. 5	28. 3	J5	G11	Pig	18. 7	12. 6	B8	K12	Dragon
7. 5	29. 3	J5	H12	Porcupine	19. 7	13. 6	B8	A1	Badger
8. 5	30. 3	J5	J1	Wolf	20. 7	14. 6	B8	B2	Hare
9. 5	1. 4	K6	K2	Dog	21. 7	15. 6	B8	C3	Fox
10. 5	2. 4	K6	A3	Pheasant	22. 7	16. 6	B8	D4	Tiger
11. 5	3. 4	K6	B4	Cock	23. 7	17. 6	B8	E5	Leopard
12. 5	4. 4	K6	C5	Crow	24. 7	18. 6	B8	F6	Griffon
13. 5	5. 4	K6	D6	Monkey	25. 7	19. 6	B8	G7	Ox
14. 5	6. 4	K6	E7	Gibbon	26. 7	20. 6	B8	H8	Bat
15. 5	7. 4	K6	F8	Tapir	27. 7	21. 6	B8	J9	Rat
16. 5	8. 4	K6	G9	Sheep	28. 7	22. 6	B8	K10	Swallow
17. 5	9. 4	K6	H10	Deer	29. 7	23. 6	B8	A11	Pig
18. 5	10. 4	K6	J11	Horse	30. 7	24. 6	B8	B12	Porcupine
19. 5	11. 4	K6	K12	Stag	31. 7	25. 6	B8	C1	Wolf
20. 5	12. 4	K6	A1	Serpent	1. 8	26. 6	B8	D2	Dog
21. 5	13. 4	K6	B2	Earthworm	2. 8	27. 6	B8	E3	Pheasant
22. 5	14. 4	K6	C3	Crocodile	3. 8	28. 6	B8	F4	Cock
23. 5	15. 4	K6	D4	Dragon	4. 8	29. 6	B8	G5	Crow
24. 5	16. 4	K6	E5	Badger	5. 8	30. 6	B8	H6	Monkey
25. 5	17. 4	K6	F6	Hare	6. 8	1. 7	C9	J7	Gibbon
26. 5	18. 4	K6	G7	Fox	7. 8	2. 7	C9	K8	Tapir

Solar date	Lunar date	Month HS/EB	Day HS/EB	Constellation
8. 8	3. 7	C9	A9	Sheep
9. 8	4. 7	C9	B10	Deer
10. 8	5. 7	C9	C11	Horse
11. 8	6. 7	C9	D12	Stag
12. 8	7. 7	C9	E1	Serpent
13. 8	8. 7	C9	F2	Earthworm
14. 8	9. 7	C9	G3	Crocodile
15. 8	10. 7	C9	H4	Dragon
16. 8	11. 7	C9	J5	Badger
17. 8	12. 7	C9	K6	Hare
18. 8	13. 7	C9	A7	Fox
19. 8	14. 7	C9	B8	Tiger
20. 8	15. 7	C9	C9	Leopard
21. 8	16. 7	C9	D10	Griffon
22. 8	17. 7	C9	E11	Ox
23. 8	18. 7	C9	F12	Bat
24. 8	19. 7	C9	G1	Rat
25. 8	20. 7	C9	H2	Swallow
26. 8	21. 7	C9	J3	Pig
27. 8	22. 7	C9	K4	Porcupine
28. 8	23. 7	C9	A5	Wolf
29. 8	24. 7	C9	B6	Dog
30. 8	25. 7	C9	C7	Pheasant
31. 8	26. 7	C9	D8	Cock
1. 9	27. 7	C9	E9	Crow
2. 9	28. 7	C9	F10	Monkey
3. 9	29. 7	C9	G11	Gibbon
4. 9	1. 8	D10	H12	Tapir
5. 9	2. 8	D10	J1	Sheep
6. 9	3. 8	D10	K2	Deer
7. 9	4. 8	D10	A3	Horse
8. 9	5. 8	D10	B4	Stag
9. 9	6. 8	D10	C5	Serpent
10. 9	7. 8	D10	D6	Earthworm
11. 9	8. 8	D10	E7	Crocodile
12. 9	9. 8	D10	F8	Dragon
13. 9	10. 8	D10	G9	Badger
14. 9	11. 8	D10	H10	Hare
15. 9	12. 8	D10	J11	Fox
16. 9	13. 8	D10	K12	Tiger
17. 9	14. 8	D10	A1	Leopard
18. 9	15. 8	D10	B2	Griffon
19. 9	16. 8	D10	C3	Ox
20. 9	17. 8	D10	D4	Bat
21. 9	18. 8	D10	E5	Rat
22. 9	19. 8	D10	F6	Swallow
23. 9	20. 8	D10	G7	Pig
24. 9	21. 8	D10	H8	Porcupine
25. 9	22. 8	D10	J9	Wolf
26. 9	23. 8	D10	K10	Dog
27. 9	24. 8	D10	A11	Pheasant
28. 9	25. 8	D10	B12	Cock
29. 9	26. 8	D10	C1	Crow
30. 9	27. 8	D10	D2	Monkey
1.10	28. 8	D10	E3	Gibbon
2.10	29. 8	D10	F4	Tapir
3.10	30. 8	D10	G5	Sheep
4.10	1. 9	E11	H6	Deer
5.10	2. 9	E11	J7	Horse
6.10	3. 9	E11	K8	Stag
7.10	4. 9	E11	A9	Serpent
8.10	5. 9	E11	B10	Earthworm
9.10	6. 9	E11	C11	Crocodile
10.10	7. 9	E11	D12	Dragon
11.10	8. 9	E11	E1	Badger
12.10	9. 9	E11	F2	Hare
13.10	10. 9	E11	G3	Fox
14.10	11. 9	E11	H4	Tiger
15.10	12. 9	E11	J5	Leopard
16.10	13. 9	E11	K6	Griffon
17.10	14. 9	E11	A7	Ox
18.10	15. 9	E11	B8	Bat
19.10	16. 9	E11	C9	Rat

Solar date	Lunar date	Month HS/EB	Day HS/EB	Constellation
20.10	17. 9	E11	D10	Swallow
21.10	18. 9	E11	E11	Pig
22.10	19. 9	E11	F12	Porcupine
23.10	20. 9	E11	G1	Wolf
24.10	21. 9	E11	H2	Dog
25.10	22. 9	E11	J3	Pheasant
26.10	23. 9	E11	K4	Cock
27.10	24. 9	E11	A5	Crow
28.10	25. 9	E11	B6	Monkey
29.10	26. 9	E11	C7	Gibbon
30.10	27. 9	E11	D8	Tapir
31.10	28. 9	E11	E9	Sheep
1.11	29. 9	E11	F10	Deer
2.11	1.10	F12	G11	Horse
3.11	2.10	F12	H12	Stag
4.11	3.10	F12	J1	Serpent
5.11	4.10	F12	K2	Earthworm
6.11	5.10	F12	A3	Crocodile
7.11	6.10	F12	B4	Dragon
8.11	7.10	F12	C5	Badger
9.11	8.10	F12	D6	Hare
10.11	9.10	F12	E7	Fox
11.11	10.10	F12	F8	Tiger
12.11	11.10	F12	G9	Leopard
13.11	12.10	F12	H10	Griffon
14.11	13.10	F12	J11	Ox
15.11	14.10	F12	K12	Bat
16.11	15.10	F12	A1	Rat
17.11	16.10	F12	B2	Swallow
18.11	17.10	F12	C3	Pig
19.11	18.10	F12	D4	Porcupine
20.11	19.10	F12	E5	Wolf
21.11	20.10	F12	F6	Dog
22.11	21.10	F12	G7	Pheasant
23.11	22.10	F12	H8	Cock
24.11	23.10	F12	J9	Crow
25.11	24.10	F12	K10	Monkey
26.11	25.10	F12	A11	Gibbon
27.11	26.10	F12	B12	Tapir
28.11	27.10	F12	C1	Sheep
29.11	28.10	F12	D2	Deer
30.11	29.10	F12	E3	Horse
1.12	30.10	F12	F4	Stag
2.12	1.11	G1	G5	Serpent
3.12	2.11	G1	H6	Earthworm
4.12	3.11	G1	J7	Crocodile
5.12	4.11	G1	K8	Dragon
6.12	5.11	G1	A9	Badger
7.12	6.11	G1	B10	Hare
8.12	7.11	G1	C11	Fox
9.12	8.11	G1	D12	Tiger
10.12	9.11	G1	E1	Leopard
11.12	10.11	G1	F2	Griffon
12.12	11.11	G1	G3	Ox
13.12	12.11	G1	H4	Bat
14.12	13.11	G1	J5	Rat
15.12	14.11	G1	K6	Swallow
16.12	15.11	G1	A7	Pig
17.12	16.11	G1	B8	Porcupine
18.12	17.11	G1	C9	Wolf
19.12	18.11	G1	D10	Dog
20.12	19.11	G1	E11	Pheasant
21.12	20.11	G1	F12	Cock
22.12	21.11	G1	G1	Crow
23.12	22.11	G1	H2	Monkey
24.12	23.11	G1	J3	Gibbon
25.12	24.11	G1	K4	Tapir
26.12	25.11	G1	A5	Sheep
27.12	26.11	G1	B6	Deer
28.12	27.11	G1	C7	Horse
29.12	28.11	G1	D8	Stag
30.12	29.11	G1	E9	Serpent
31.12	1.12	H2	F10	Earthworm

Solar date	Lunar date	Month HS/EB	Day HS/EB	Constellation	Solar date	Lunar date	Month HS/EB	Day HS/EB	Constellation
1987					14. 1	15.12	H2	K12	Porcupine
					15. 1	16.12	H2	A1	Wolf
1. 1	2.12	H2	G11	Crocodile	16. 1	17.12	H2	B2	Dog
2. 1	3.12	H2	H12	Dragon	17. 1	18.12	H2	C3	Pheasant
3. 1	4.12	H2	J1	Badger	18. 1	19.12	H2	D4	Cock
4. 1	5.12	H2	K2	Hare	19. 1	20.12	H2	E5	Crow
5. 1	6.12	H2	A3	Fox	20. 1	21.12	H2	F6	Monkey
6. 1	7.12	H2	B4	Tiger	21. 1	22.12	H2	G7	Gibbon
7. 1	8.12	H2	C5	Leopard	22. 1	23.12	H2	H8	Tapir
8. 1	9.12	H2	D6	Griffon	23. 1	24.12	H2	J9	Sheep
9. 1	10.12	H2	E7	Ox	24. 1	25.12	H2	K10	Deer
10. 1	11.12	H2	F8	Bat	25. 1	26.12	H2	A11	Horse
11. 1	12.12	H2	G9	Rat	26. 1	27.12	H2	B12	Stag
12. 1	13.12	H2	H10	Swallow	27. 1	28.12	H2	C1	Serpent
13. 1	14.12	H2	J11	Pig	28. 1	29.12	H2	D2	Earthworm

TING MAO YEAR

Solar date	Lunar date	Month HS/EB	Day HS/EB	Constellation	Solar date	Lunar date	Month HS/EB	Day HS/EB	Constellation
29. 1	1. 1	J3	E3	Crocodile	23. 3	24. 2	K4	H8	Stag
30. 1	2. 1	J3	F4	Dragon	24. 3	25. 2	K4	J9	Serpent
31. 1	3. 1	J3	G5	Badger	25. 3	26. 2	K4	K10	Earthworm
1. 2	4. 1	J3	H6	Hare	26. 3	27. 2	K4	A11	Crocodile
2. 2	5. 1	J3	J7	Fox	27. 3	28. 2	K4	B12	Dragon
3. 2	6. 1	J3	K8	Tiger	28. 3	29. 2	K4	C1	Badger
4. 2	7. 1	J3	A9	Leopard	29. 3	1. 3	A5	D2	Hare
5. 2	8. 1	J3	B10	Griffon	30. 3	2. 3	A5	E3	Fox
6. 2	9. 1	J3	C11	Ox	31. 3	3. 3	A5	F4	Tiger
7. 2	10. 1	J3	D12	Bat	1. 4	4. 3	A5	G5	Leopard
8. 2	11. 1	J3	E1	Rat	2. 4	5. 3	A5	H6	Griffon
9. 2	12. 1	J3	F2	Swallow	3. 4	6. 3	A5	J7	Ox
10. 2	13. 1	J3	G3	Pig	4. 4	7. 3	A5	K8	Bat
11. 2	14. 1	J3	H4	Porcupine	5. 4	8. 3	A5	A9	Rat
12. 2	15. 1	J3	J5	Wolf	6. 4	9. 3	A5	B10	Swallow
13. 2	16. 1	J3	K6	Dog	7. 4	10. 3	A5	C11	Pig
14. 2	17. 1	J3	A7	Pheasant	8. 4	11. 3	A5	D12	Porcupine
15. 2	18. 1	J3	B8	Cock	9. 4	12. 3	A5	E1	Wolf
16. 2	19. 1	J3	C9	Crow	10. 4	13. 3	A5	F2	Dog
17. 2	20. 1	J3	D10	Monkey	11. 4	14. 3	A5	G3	Pheasant
18. 2	21. 1	J3	E11	Gibbon	12. 4	15. 3	A5	H4	Cock
19. 2	22. 1	J3	F12	Tapir	13. 4	16. 3	A5	J5	Crow
20. 2	23. 1	J3	G1	Sheep	14. 4	17. 3	A5	K6	Monkey
21. 2	24. 1	J3	H2	Deer	15. 4	18. 3	A5	A7	Gibbon
22. 2	25. 1	J3	J3	Horse	16. 4	19. 3	A5	B8	Tapir
23. 2	26. 1	J3	K4	Stag	17. 4	20. 3	A5	C9	Sheep
24. 2	27. 1	J3	A5	Serpent	18. 4	21. 3	A5	D10	Deer
25. 2	28. 1	J3	B6	Earthworm	19. 4	22. 3	A5	E11	Horse
26. 2	29. 1	J3	C7	Crocodile	20. 4	23. 3	A5	F12	Stag
27. 2	30. 1	J3	D8	Dragon	21. 4	24. 3	A5	G1	Serpent
28. 2	1. 2	K4	E9	Badger	22. 4	25. 3	A5	H2	Earthworm
1. 3	2. 2	K4	F10	Hare	23. 4	26. 3	A5	J3	Crocodile
2. 3	3. 2	K4	G11	Fox	24. 4	27. 3	A5	K4	Dragon
3. 3	4. 2	K4	H12	Tiger	25. 4	28. 3	A5	A5	Badger
4. 3	5. 2	K4	J1	Leopard	26. 4	29. 3	A5	B6	Hare
5. 3	6. 2	K4	K2	Griffon	27. 4	30. 3	A5	C7	Fox
6. 3	7. 2	K4	A3	Ox	28. 4	1. 4	B6	D8	Tiger
7. 3	8. 2	K4	B4	Bat	29. 4	2. 4	B6	E9	Leopard
8. 3	9. 2	K4	C5	Rat	30. 4	3. 4	B6	F10	Griffon
9. 3	10. 2	K4	D6	Swallow	1. 5	4. 4	B6	G11	Ox
10. 3	11. 2	K4	E7	Pig	2. 5	5. 4	B6	H12	Bat
11. 3	12. 2	K4	F8	Porcupine	3. 5	6. 4	B6	J1	Rat
12. 3	13. 2	K4	G9	Wolf	4. 5	7. 4	B6	K2	Swallow
13. 3	14. 2	K4	H10	Dog	5. 5	8. 4	B6	A3	Pig
14. 3	15. 2	K4	J11	Pheasant	6. 5	9. 4	B6	B4	Porcupine
15. 3	16. 2	K4	K12	Cock	7. 5	10. 4	B6	C5	Wolf
16. 3	17. 2	K4	A1	Crow	8. 5	11. 4	B6	D6	Dog
17. 3	18. 2	K4	B2	Monkey	9. 5	12. 4	B6	E7	Pheasant
18. 3	19. 2	K4	C3	Gibbon	10. 5	13. 4	B6	F8	Cock
19. 3	20. 2	K4	D4	Tapir	11. 5	14. 4	B6	G9	Crow
20. 3	21. 2	K4	E5	Sheep	12. 5	15. 4	B6	H10	Monkey
21. 3	22. 2	K4	F6	Deer	13. 5	16. 4	B6	J11	Gibbon
22. 3	23. 2	K4	G7	Horse	14. 5	17. 4	B6	K12	Tapir

Solar date	Lunar date	Month HS/EB	Day HS/EB	Constellation
15. 5	18. 4	B6	A1	Sheep
16. 5	19. 4	B6	B2	Deer
17. 5	20. 4	B6	C3	Horse
18. 5	21. 4	B6	D4	Stag
19. 5	22. 4	B6	E5	Serpent
20. 5	23. 4	B6	F6	Earthworm
21. 5	24. 4	B6	G7	Crocodile
22. 5	25. 4	B6	H8	Dragon
23. 5	26. 4	B6	J9	Badger
24. 5	27. 4	B6	K10	Hare
25. 5	28. 4	B6	A11	Fox
26. 5	29. 4	B6	B12	Tiger
27. 5	1. 5	C7	C1	Leopard
28. 5	2. 5	C7	D2	Griffon
29. 5	3. 5	C7	E3	Ox
30. 5	4. 5	C7	F4	Bat
31. 5	5. 5	C7	G5	Rat
1. 6	6. 5	C7	H6	Swallow
2. 6	7. 5	C7	J7	Pig
3. 6	8. 5	C7	K8	Porcupine
4. 6	9. 5	C7	A9	Wolf
5. 6	10. 5	C7	B10	Dog
6. 6	11. 5	C7	C11	Pheasant
7. 6	12. 5	C7	D12	Cock
8. 6	13. 5	C7	E1	Crow
9. 6	14. 5	C7	F2	Monkey
10. 6	15. 5	C7	G3	Gibbon
11. 6	16. 5	C7	H4	Tapir
12. 6	17. 5	C7	J5	Sheep
13. 6	18. 5	C7	K6	Deer
14. 6	19. 5	C7	A7	Horse
15. 6	20. 5	C7	B8	Stag
16. 6	21. 5	C7	C9	Serpent
17. 6	22. 5	C7	D10	Earthworm
18. 6	23. 5	C7	E11	Crocodile
19. 6	24. 5	C7	F12	Dragon
20. 6	25. 5	C7	G1	Badger
21. 6	26. 5	C7	H2	Hare
22. 6	27. 5	C7	J3	Fox
23. 6	28. 5	C7	K4	Tiger
24. 6	29. 5	C7	A5	Leopard
25. 6	30. 5	C7	B6	Griffon
26. 6	1. 6	D8	C7	Ox
27. 6	2. 6	D8	D8	Bat
28. 6	3. 6	D8	E9	Rat
29. 6	4. 6	D8	F10	Swallow
30. 6	5. 6	D8	G11	Pig
1. 7	6. 6	D8	H12	Porcupine
2. 7	7. 6	D8	J1	Wolf
3. 7	8. 6	D8	K2	Dog
4. 7	9. 6	D8	A3	Pheasant
5. 7	10. 6	D8	B4	Cock
6. 7	11. 6	D8	C5	Crow
7. 7	12. 6	D8	D6	Monkey
8. 7	13. 6	D8	E7	Gibbon
9. 7	14. 6	D8	F8	Tapir
10. 7	15. 6	D8	G9	Sheep
11. 7	16. 6	D8	H10	Deer
12. 7	17. 6	D8	J11	Horse
13. 7	18. 6	D8	K12	Stag
14. 7	19. 6	D8	A1	Serpent
15. 7	20. 6	D8	B2	Earthworm
16. 7	21. 6	D8	C3	Crocodile
17. 7	22. 6	D8	D4	Dragon
18. 7	23. 6	D8	E5	Badger
19. 7	24. 6	D8	F6	Hare
20. 7	25. 6	D8	G7	Fox
21. 7	26. 6	D8	H8	Tiger
22. 7	27. 6	D8	J9	Leopard
23. 7	28. 6	D8	K10	Griffon
24. 7	29. 6	D8	A11	Ox
25. 7	30. 6	D8	B12	Bat
26. 7	*1. 6*	*D8*	C1	Rat
27. 7	*2. 6*	D8	D2	Swallow
28. 7	*3. 6*	D8	E3	Pig
29. 7	*4. 6*	D8	F4	Porcupine
30. 7	*5. 6*	D8	G5	Wolf
31. 7	*6. 6*	D8	H6	Dog
1. 8	*7. 6*	D8	J7	Pheasant
2. 8	*8. 6*	D8	K8	Cock
3. 8	*9. 6*	D8	A9	Crow
4. 8	*10. 6*	D8	B10	Monkey
5. 8	*11. 6*	D8	C11	Gibbon
6. 8	*12. 6*	D8	D12	Tapir
7. 8	*13. 6*	D8	E1	Sheep
8. 8	*14. 6*	D8	F2	Deer
9. 8	*15. 6*	D8	G3	Horse
10. 8	*16. 6*	D8	H4	Stag
11. 8	*17. 6*	D8	J5	Serpent
12. 8	*18. 6*	D8	K6	Earthworm
13. 8	*19. 6*	D8	A7	Crocodile
14. 8	*20. 6*	D8	B8	Dragon
15. 8	*21. 6*	D8	C9	Badger
16. 8	*22. 6*	D8	D10	Hare
17. 8	*23. 6*	D8	E11	Fox
18. 8	*24. 6*	D8	F12	Tiger
19. 8	*25. 6*	D8	G1	Leopard
20. 8	*26. 6*	D8	H2	Griffon
21. 8	*27. 6*	D8	J3	Ox
22. 8	*28. 6*	D8	K4	Bat
23. 8	*29. 6*	D8	A5	Rat
24. 8	1. 7	E9	B6	Swallow
25. 8	2. 7	E9	C7	Pig
26. 8	3. 7	E9	D8	Porcupine
27. 8	4. 7	E9	E9	Wolf
28. 8	5. 7	E9	F10	Dog
29. 8	6. 7	E9	G11	Pheasant
30. 8	7. 7	E9	H12	Cock
31. 8	8. 7	E9	J1	Crow
1. 9	9. 7	E9	K2	Monkey
2. 9	10. 7	E9	A3	Gibbon
3. 9	11. 7	E9	B4	Tapir
4. 9	12. 7	E9	C5	Sheep
5. 9	13. 7	E9	D6	Deer
6. 9	14. 7	E9	E7	Horse
7. 9	15. 7	E9	F8	Stag
8. 9	16. 7	E9	G9	Serpent
9. 9	17. 7	E9	H10	Earthworm
10. 9	18. 7	E9	J11	Crocodile
11. 9	19. 7	E9	K12	Dragon
12. 9	20. 7	E9	A1	Badger
13. 9	21. 7	E9	B2	Hare
14. 9	22. 7	E9	C3	Fox
15. 9	23. 7	E9	D4	Tiger
16. 9	24. 7	E9	E5	Leopard
17. 9	25. 7	E9	F6	Griffon
18. 9	26. 7	E9	G7	Ox
19. 9	27. 7	E9	H8	Bat
20. 9	28. 7	E9	J9	Rat
21. 9	29. 7	E9	K10	Swallow
22. 9	30. 7	E9	A11	Pig
23. 9	1. 8	F10	B12	Porcupine
24. 9	2. 8	F10	C1	Wolf
25. 9	3. 8	F10	D2	Dog
26. 9	4. 8	F10	E3	Pheasant
27. 9	5. 8	F10	F4	Cock
28. 9	6. 8	F10	G5	Crow
29. 9	7. 8	F10	H6	Monkey
30. 9	8. 8	F10	J7	Gibbon
1.10	9. 8	F10	K8	Tapir
2.10	10. 8	F10	A9	Sheep
3.10	11. 8	F10	B10	Deer
4.10	12. 8	F10	C11	Horse
5.10	13. 8	F10	D12	Stag
6.10	14. 8	F10	E1	Serpent
7.10	15. 8	F10	F2	Earthworm

Solar date	Lunar date	Month HS/EB	Day HS/EB	Constellation	Solar date	Lunar date	Month HS/EB	Day HS/EB	Constellation
8.10	16. 8	F10	G3	Crocodile	14.12	24.10	H12	D10	Swallow
9.10	17. 8	F10	H4	Dragon	15.12	25.10	H12	E11	Pig
10.10	18. 8	F10	J5	Badger	16.12	26.10	H12	F12	Porcupine
11.10	19. 8	F10	K6	Hare	17.12	27.10	H12	G1	Wolf
12.10	20. 8	F10	A7	Fox	18.12	28.10	H12	H2	Dog
13.10	21. 8	F10	B8	Tiger	19.12	29.10	H12	J3	Pheasant
14.10	22. 8	F10	C9	Leopard	20.12	30.10	H12	K4	Cock
15.10	23. 8	F10	D10	Griffon	21.12	1.11	J1	A5	Crow
16.10	24. 8	F10	E11	Ox	22.12	2.11	J1	B6	Monkey
17.10	25. 8	F10	F12	Bat	23.12	3.11	J1	C7	Gibbon
18.10	26. 8	F10	G1	Rat	24.12	4.11	J1	D8	Tapir
19.10	27. 8	F10	H2	Swallow	25.12	5.11	J1	E9	Sheep
20.10	28. 8	F10	J3	Pig	26.12	6.11	J1	F10	Deer
21.10	29. 8	F10	K4	Porcupine	27.12	7.11	J1	G11	Horse
22.10	30. 8	F10	A5	Wolf	28.12	8.11	J1	H12	Stag
23.10	1. 9	G11	B6	Dog	29.12	9.11	J1	J1	Serpent
24.10	2. 9	G11	C7	Pheasant	30.12	10.11	J1	K2	Earthworm
25.10	3. 9	G11	D8	Cock	31.12	11.11	J1	A3	Crocodile
26.10	4. 9	G11	E9	Crow					
27.10	5. 9	G11	F10	Monkey	**1988**				
28.10	6. 9	G11	G11	Gibbon	1. 1	12.11	J1	B4	Dragon
29.10	7. 9	G11	H12	Tapir	2. 1	13.11	J1	C5	Badger
30.10	8. 9	G11	J1	Sheep	3. 1	14.11	J1	D6	Hare
31.10	9. 9	G11	K2	Deer	4. 1	15.11	J1	E7	Fox
1.11	10. 9	G11	A3	Horse	5. 1	16.11	J1	F8	Tiger
2.11	11. 9	G11	B4	Stag	6. 1	17.11	J1	G9	Leopard
3.11	12. 9	G11	C5	Serpent	7. 1	18.11	J1	H10	Griffon
4.11	13. 9	G11	D6	Earthworm	8. 1	19.11	J1	J11	Ox
5.11	14. 9	G11	E7	Crocodile	9. 1	20.11	J1	K12	Bat
6.11	15. 9	G11	F8	Dragon	10. 1	21.11	J1	A1	Rat
7.11	16. 9	G11	G9	Badger	11. 1	22.11	J1	B2	Swallow
8.11	17. 9	G11	H10	Hare	12. 1	23.11	J1	C3	Pig
9.11	18. 9	G11	J11	Fox	13. 1	24.11	J1	D4	Porcupine
10.11	19. 9	G11	K12	Tiger	14. 1	25.11	J1	E5	Wolf
11.11	20. 9	G11	A1	Leopard	15. 1	26.11	J1	F6	Dog
12.11	21. 9	G11	B2	Griffon	16. 1	27.11	J1	G7	Pheasant
13.11	22. 9	G11	C3	Ox	17. 1	28.11	J1	H8	Cock
14.11	23. 9	G11	D4	Bat	18. 1	29.11	J1	J9	Crow
15.11	24. 9	G11	E5	Rat	19. 1	1.12	K2	K10	Monkey
16.11	25. 9	G11	F6	Swallow	20. 1	2.12	K2	A11	Gibbon
17.11	26. 9	G11	G7	Pig	21. 1	3.12	K2	B12	Tapir
18.11	27. 9	G11	H8	Porcupine	22. 1	4.12	K2	C1	Sheep
19.11	28. 9	G11	J9	Wolf	23. 1	5.12	K2	D2	Deer
20.11	29. 9	G11	K10	Dog	24. 1	6.12	K2	E3	Horse
21.11	1.10	H12	A11	Pheasant	25. 1	7.12	K2	F4	Stag
22.11	2.10	H12	B12	Cock	26. 1	8.12	K2	G5	Serpent
23.11	3.10	H12	C1	Crow	27. 1	9.12	K2	H6	Earthworm
24.11	4.10	H12	D2	Monkey	28. 1	10.12	K2	J7	Crocodile
25.11	5.10	H12	E3	Gibbon	29. 1	11.12	K2	K8	Dragon
26.11	6.10	H12	F4	Tapir	30. 1	12.12	K2	A9	Badger
27.11	7.10	H12	G5	Sheep	31. 1	13.12	K2	B10	Hare
28.11	8.10	H12	H6	Deer	1. 2	14.12	K2	C11	Fox
29.11	9.10	H12	J7	Horse	2. 2	15.12	K2	D12	Tiger
30.11	10.10	H12	K8	Stag	3. 2	16.12	K2	E1	Leopard
1.12	11.10	H12	A9	Serpent	4. 2	17.12	K2	F2	Griffon
2.12	12.10	H12	B10	Earthworm	5. 2	18.12	K2	G3	Ox
3.12	13.10	H12	C11	Crocodile	6. 2	19.12	K2	H4	Bat
4.12	14.10	H12	D12	Dragon	7. 2	20.12	K2	J5	Rat
5.12	15.10	H12	E1	Badger	8. 2	21.12	K2	K6	Swallow
6.12	16.10	H12	F2	Hare	9. 2	22.12	K2	A7	Pig
7.12	17.10	H12	G3	Fox	10. 2	23.12	K2	B8	Porcupine
8.12	18.10	H12	H4	Tiger	11. 2	24.12	K2	C9	Wolf
9.12	19.10	H12	J5	Leopard	12. 2	25.12	K2	D10	Dog
10.12	20.10	H12	K6	Griffon	13. 2	26.12	K2	E11	Pheasant
11.12	21.10	H12	A7	Ox	14. 2	27.12	K2	F12	Cock
12.12	22.10	H12	B8	Bat	15. 2	28.12	K2	G1	Crow
13.12	23.10	H12	C9	Rat	16. 2	29.12	K2	H2	Monkey

MOU CH'EN YEAR

Solar date	Lunar date	Month HS/EB	Day HS/EB	Constellation	Solar date	Lunar date	Month HS/EB	Day HS/EB	Constellation
17. 2	1. 1	A3	J3	Gibbon	28. 4	13. 3	C5	K2	Griffon
18. 2	2. 1	A3	K4	Tapir	29. 4	14. 3	C5	A3	Ox
19. 2	3. 1	A3	A5	Sheep	30. 4	15. 3	C5	B4	Bat
20. 2	4. 1	A3	B6	Deer	1. 5	16. 3	C5	C5	Rat
21. 2	5. 1	A3	C7	Horse	2. 5	17. 3	C5	D6	Swallow
22. 2	6. 1	A3	D8	Stag	3. 5	18. 3	C5	E7	Pig
23. 2	7. 1	A3	E9	Serpent	4. 5	19. 3	C5	F8	Porcupine
24. 2	8. 1	A3	F10	Earthworm	5. 5	20. 3	C5	G9	Wolf
25. 2	9. 1	A3	G11	Crocodile	6. 5	21. 3	C5	H10	Dog
26. 2	10. 1	A3	H12	Dragon	7. 5	22. 3	C5	J11	Pheasant
27. 2	11. 1	A3	J1	Badger	8. 5	23. 3	C5	K12	Cock
28. 2	12. 1	A3	K2	Hare	9. 5	24. 3	C5	A1	Crow
29. 2	13. 1	A3	A3	Fox	10. 5	25. 3	C5	B2	Monkey
1. 3	14. 1	A3	B4	Tiger	11. 5	26. 3	C5	C3	Gibbon
2. 3	15. 1	A3	C5	Leopard	12. 5	27. 3	C5	D4	Tapir
3. 3	16. 1	A3	D6	Griffon	13. 5	28. 3	C5	E5	Sheep
4. 3	17. 1	A3	E7	Ox	14. 5	29. 3	C5	F6	Deer
5. 3	18. 1	A3	F8	Bat	15. 5	30. 3	C5	G7	Horse
6. 3	19. 1	A3	G9	Rat	16. 5	1. 4	D6	H8	Stag
7. 3	20. 1	A3	H10	Swallow	17. 5	2. 4	D6	J9	Serpent
8. 3	21. 1	A3	J11	Pig	18. 5	3. 4	D6	K10	Earthworm
9. 3	22. 1	A3	K12	Porcupine	19. 5	4. 4	D6	A11	Crocodile
10. 3	23. 1	A3	A1	Wolf	20. 5	5. 4	D6	B12	Dragon
11. 3	24. 1	A3	B2	Dog	21. 5	6. 4	D6	C1	Badger
12. 3	25. 1	A3	C3	Pheasant	22. 5	7. 4	D6	D2	Hare
13. 3	26. 1	A3	D4	Cock	23. 5	8. 4	D6	E3	Fox
14. 3	27. 1	A3	E5	Crow	24. 5	9. 4	D6	F4	Tiger
15. 3	28. 1	A3	F6	Monkey	25. 5	10. 4	D6	G5	Leopard
16. 3	29. 1	A3	G7	Gibbon	26. 5	11. 4	D6	H6	Griffon
17. 3	30. 1	A3	H8	Tapir	27. 5	12. 4	D6	J7	Ox
18. 3	1. 2	B4	J9	Sheep	28. 5	13. 4	D6	K8	Bat
19. 3	2. 2	B4	K10	Deer	29. 5	14. 4	D6	A9	Rat
20. 3	3. 2	B4	A11	Horse	30. 5	15. 4	D6	B10	Swallow
21. 3	4. 2	B4	B12	Stag	31. 5	16. 4	D6	C11	Pig
22. 3	5. 2	B4	C1	Serpent	1. 6	17. 4	D6	D12	Porcupine
23. 3	6. 2	B4	D2	Earthworm	2. 6	18. 4	D6	E1	Wolf
24. 3	7. 2	B4	E3	Crocodile	3. 6	19. 4	D6	F2	Dog
25. 3	8. 2	B4	F4	Dragon	4. 6	20. 4	D6	G3	Pheasant
26. 3	9. 2	B4	G5	Badger	5. 6	21. 4	D6	H4	Cock
27. 3	10. 2	B4	H6	Hare	6. 6	22. 4	D6	J5	Crow
28. 3	11. 2	B4	J7	Fox	7. 6	23. 4	D6	K6	Monkey
29. 3	12. 2	B4	K8	Tiger	8. 6	24. 4	D6	A7	Gibbon
30. 3	13. 2	B4	A9	Leopard	9. 6	25. 4	D6	B8	Tapir
31. 3	14. 2	B4	B10	Griffon	10. 6	26. 4	D6	C9	Sheep
1. 4	15. 2	B4	C11	Ox	11. 6	27. 4	D6	D10	Deer
2. 4	16. 2	B4	D12	Bat	12. 6	28. 4	D6	E11	Horse
3. 4	17. 2	B4	E1	Rat	13. 6	29. 4	D6	F12	Stag
4. 4	18. 2	B4	F2	Swallow	14. 6	1. 5	E7	G1	Serpent
5. 4	19. 2	B4	G3	Pig	15. 6	2. 5	E7	H2	Earthworm
6. 4	20. 2	B4	H4	Porcupine	16. 6	3. 5	E7	J3	Crocodile
7. 4	21. 2	B4	J5	Wolf	17. 6	4. 5	E7	K4	Dragon
8. 4	22. 2	B4	K6	Dog	18. 6	5. 5	E7	A5	Badger
9. 4	23. 2	B4	A7	Pheasant	19. 6	6. 5	E7	B6	Hare
10. 4	24. 2	B4	B8	Cock	20. 6	7. 5	E7	C7	Fox
11. 4	25. 2	B4	C9	Crow	21. 6	8. 5	E7	D8	Tiger
12. 4	26. 2	B4	D10	Monkey	22. 6	9. 5	E7	E9	Leopard
13. 4	27. 2	B4	E11	Gibbon	23. 6	10. 5	E7	F10	Griffon
14. 4	28. 2	B4	F12	Tapir	24. 6	11. 5	E7	G11	Ox
15. 4	29. 2	B4	G1	Sheep	25. 6	12. 5	E7	H12	Bat
16. 4	1. 3	C5	H2	Deer	26. 6	13. 5	E7	J1	Rat
17. 4	2. 3	C5	J3	Horse	27. 6	14. 5	E7	K2	Swallow
18. 4	3. 3	C5	K4	Stag	28. 6	15. 5	E7	A3	Pig
19. 4	4. 3	C5	A5	Serpent	29. 6	16. 5	E7	B4	Porcupine
20. 4	5. 3	C5	B6	Earthworm	30. 6	17. 5	E7	C5	Wolf
21. 4	6. 3	C5	C7	Crocodile	1. 7	18. 5	E7	D6	Dog
22. 4	7. 3	C5	D8	Dragon	2. 7	19. 5	E7	E7	Pheasant
23. 4	8. 3	C5	E9	Badger	3. 7	20. 5	E7	F8	Cock
24. 4	9. 3	C5	F10	Hare	4. 7	21. 5	E7	G9	Crow
25. 4	10. 3	C5	G11	Fox	5. 7	22. 5	E7	H10	Monkey
26. 4	11. 3	C5	H12	Tiger	6. 7	23. 5	E7	J11	Gibbon
27. 4	12. 3	C5	J1	Leopard	7. 7	24. 5	E7	K12	Tapir

Solar date	Lunar date	Month HS/EB	Day HS/EB	Constellation	Solar date	Lunar date	Month HS/EB	Day HS/EB	Constellation
8. 7	25. 5	E7	A1	Sheep	19. 9	9. 8	H10	D2	Swallow
9. 7	26. 5	E7	B2	Deer	20. 9	10. 8	H10	E3	Pig
10. 7	27. 5	E7	C3	Horse	21. 9	11. 8	H10	F4	Porcupine
11. 7	28. 5	E7	D4	Stag	22. 9	12. 8	H10	G5	Wolf
12. 7	29. 5	E7	E5	Serpent	23. 9	13. 8	H10	H6	Dog
13. 7	30. 5	E7	F6	Earthworm	24. 9	14. 8	H10	J7	Pheasant
14. 7	1. 6	F8	G7	Crocodile	25. 9	15. 8	H10	K8	Cock
15. 7	2. 6	F8	H8	Dragon	26. 9	16. 8	H10	A9	Crow
16. 7	3. 6	F8	J9	Badger	27. 9	17. 8	H10	B10	Monkey
17. 7	4. 6	F8	K10	Hare	28. 9	18.18	H10	C11	Gibbon
18. 7	5. 6	F8	A11	Fox	29. 9	19. 8	H10	D12	Tapir
19. 7	6. 6	F8	B12	Tiger	30. 9	20. 8	H10	E1	Sheep
20. 7	7. 6	F8	C1	Leopard	1.10	21. 8	H10	F2	Deer
21. 7	8. 6	F8	D2	Griffon	2.10	22. 8	H10	G3	Horse
22. 7	9. 6	F8	E3	Ox	3.10	23. 8	H10	H4	Stag
23. 7	10. 6	F8	F4	Bat	4.10	24. 8	H10	J5	Serpent
24. 7	11. 6	F8	G5	Rat	5.10	25. 8	H10	K6	Earthworm
25. 7	12. 6	F8	H6	Swallow	6.10	26. 8	H10	A7	Crocodile
26. 7	13. 6	F8	J7	Pig	7.10	27. 8	H10	B8	Dragon
27. 7	14. 6	F8	K8	Porcupine	8.10	28. 8	H10	C9	Badger
28. 7	15. 6	F8	A9	Wolf	9.10	29. 8	H10	D10	Hare
29. 7	16. 6	F8	B10	Dog	10.10	30. 8	H10	E11	Fox
30. 7	17. 6	F8	C11	Pheasant	11.10	1. 9	J11	F12	Tiger
31. 7	18. 6	F8	D12	Cock	12.10	2. 9	J11	G1	Leopard
1. 8	19. 6	F8	E1	Crow	13.10	3. 9	J11	H2	Griffon
2. 8	20. 6	F8	F2	Monkey	14.10	4. 9	J11	J3	Ox
3. 8	21. 6	F8	G3	Gibbon	15.10	5. 9	J11	K4	Bat
4. 8	22. 6	F8	H4	Tapir	16.10	6. 9	J11	A5	Rat
5. 8	23. 6	F8	J5	Sheep	17.10	7. 9	J11	B6	Swallow
6. 8	24. 6	F8	K6	Deer	18.10	8. 9	J11	C7	Pig
7. 8	25. 6	F8	A7	Horse	19.10	9. 9	J11	D8	Porcupine
8. 8	26. 6	F8	B8	Stag	20.10	10. 9	J11	E9	Wolf
9. 8	27. 6	F8	C9	Serpent	21.10	11. 9	J11	F10	Dog
10. 8	28. 6	F8	D10	Earthworm	22.10	12. 9	J11	G11	Pheasant
11. 8	29. 6	F8	E11	Crocodile	23.10	13. 9	J11	H12	Cock
12. 8	1. 7	G9	F12	Dragon	24.10	14. 9	J11	J1	Crow
13. 8	2. 7	G9	G1	Badger	25.10	15. 9	J11	K2	Monkey
14. 8	3. 7	G9	H2	Hare	26.10	16. 9	J11	A3	Gibbon
15. 8	4. 7	G9	J3	Fox	27.10	17. 9	J11	B4	Tapir
16. 8	5. 7	G9	K4	Tiger	28.10	18. 9	J11	C5	Sheep
17. 8	6. 7	G9	A5	Leopard	29.10	19. 9	J11	D6	Deer
18. 8	7. 7	G9	B6	Griffon	30.10	20. 9	J11	E7	Horse
19. 8	8. 7	G9	C7	Ox	31.10	21. 9	J11	F8	Stag
20. 8	9. 7	G9	D8	Bat	1.11	22. 9	J11	G9	Serpent
21. 8	10. 7	G9	E9	Rat	2.11	23. 9	J11	H10	Earthworm
22. 8	11. 7	G9	F10	Swallow	3.11	24. 9	J11	J11	Crocodile
23. 8	12. 7	G9	G11	Pig	4.11	25. 9	J11	K12	Dragon
24. 8	13. 7	G9	H12	Porcupine	5.11	26. 9	J11	A1	Badger
25. 8	14. 7	G9	J1	Wolf	6.11	27. 9	J11	B2	Hare
26. 8	15. 7	G9	K2	Dog	7.11	28. 9	J11	C3	Fox
27. 8	16. 7	G9	A3	Pheasant	8.11	29. 9	J11	D4	Tiger
28. 8	17. 7	G9	B4	Cock	9.11	1. 10	K12	E5	Leopard
29. 8	18. 7	G9	C5	Crow	10.11	2. 10	K12	F6	Griffon
30. 8	19. 7	G9	D6	Monkey	11.11	3. 10	K12	G7	Ox
31. 8	20. 7	G9	E7	Gibbon	12.11	4. 10	K12	H8	Bat
1. 9	21. 7	G9	F8	Tapir	13.11	5. 10	K12	J9	Rat
2. 9	22. 7	G9	G9	Sheep	14.11	6. 10	K12	K10	Swallow
3. 9	23. 7	G9	H10	Deer	15.11	7. 10	K12	A11	Pig
4. 9	24. 7	G9	J11	Horse	16.11	8. 10	K12	B12	Porcupine
5. 9	25. 7	G9	K12	Stag	17.11	9. 10	K12	C1	Wolf
6. 9	26. 7	G9	A1	Serpent	18.11	10.10	K12	D2	Dog
7. 9	27. 7	G9	B2	Earthworm	19.11	11.10	K12	E3	Pheasant
8. 9	28. 7	G9	C3	Crocodile	20.11	12.10	K12	F4	Cock
9. 9	29. 7	G9	D4	Dragon	21.11	13.10	K12	G5	Crow
10. 9	30. 7	G9	E5	Badger	22.11	14.10	K12	H6	Monkey
11. 9	1. 8	H10	F6	Hare	23.11	15.10	K12	J7	Gibbon
12. 9	2. 8	H10	G7	Fox	24.11	16.10	K12	K8	Tapir
13. 9	3. 8	H10	H8	Tiger	25.11	17.10	K12	A9	Sheep
14. 9	4. 8	H10	J9	Leopard	26.11	18.10	K12	B10	Deer
15. 9	5. 8	H10	K10	Griffon	27.11	19.10	K12	C11	Horse
16. 9	6. 8	H10	A11	Ox	28.11	20.10	K12	D12	Stag
17. 9	7. 8	H10	B12	Bat	29.11	21.10	K12	E1	Serpent
18. 9	8. 8	H10	C1	Rat	30.11	22.10	K12	F2	Earthworm

Solar date	Lunar date	Month HS/EB	Day HS/EB	Constellation
1.12	23.10	K12	G3	Crocodile
2.12	24.10	K12	H4	Dragon
3.12	25.10	K12	J5	Badger
4.12	26.10	K12	K6	Hare
5.12	27.10	K12	A7	Fox
6.12	28.10	K12	B8	Tiger
7.12	29.10	K12	C9	Leopard
8.12	30.10	K12	D10	Griffon
9.12	1.11	A1	E11	Ox
10.12	2.11	A1	F12	Bat
11.12	3.11	A1	G1	Rat
12.12	4.11	A1	H2	Swallow
13.12	5.11	A1	J3	Pig
14.12	6.11	A1	K4	Porcupine
15.12	7.11	A1	A5	Wolf
16.12	8.11	A1	B6	Dog
17.12	9.11	A1	C7	Pheasant
18.12	10.11	A1	D8	Cock
19.12	11.11	A1	E9	Crow
20.12	12.11	A1	F10	Monkey
21.12	13.11	A1	G11	Gibbon
22.12	14.11	A1	H12	Tapir
23.12	15.11	A1	J1	Sheep
24.12	16.11	A1	K2	Deer
25.12	17.11	A1	A3	Horse
26.12	18.11	A1	B4	Stag
27.12	19.11	A1	C5	Serpent
28.12	20.11	A1	D6	Earthworm
29.12	21.11	A1	E7	Crocodile
30.12	22.11	A1	F8	Dragon
31.12	23.11	A1	G9	Badger
1989				
1. 1	24.11	A1	H10	Hare
2. 1	25.11	A1	J11	Fox
3. 1	26.11	A1	K12	Tiger
4. 1	27.11	A1	A1	Leopard
5. 1	28.11	A1	B2	Griffon
6. 1	29.11	A1	C3	Ox
7. 1	30.11	A1	D4	Bat
8. 1	1.12	B2	E5	Rat
9. 1	2.12	B2	F6	Swallow
10. 1	3.12	B2	G7	Pig
11. 1	4.12	B2	H8	Porcupine
12. 1	5.12	B2	J9	Wolf
13. 1	6.12	B2	K10	Dog
14. 1	7.12	B2	A11	Pheasant
15. 1	8.12	B2	B12	Cock
16. 1	9.12	B2	C1	Crow
18. 1	10.12	B2	D2	Monkey
18. 1	11.12	B2	E3	Gibbon
19. 1	12.12	B2	F4	Tapir
20. 1	13.12	B2	G5	Sheep
21. 1	14.12	B2	H6	Deer
22. 1	15.12	B2	J7	Horse
23. 1	16.12	B2	K8	Stag
24. 1	17.12	B2	A9	Serpent
25. 1	18.12	B2	B10	Earthworm
26. 1	19.12	B2	C11	Crocodile
27. 1	20.12	B2	D12	Dragon
28. 1	21.12	B2	E1	Badger
29. 1	22.12	B2	F2	Hare
30. 1	23.12	B2	G3	Fox
31. 1	24.12	B2	H4	Tiger
1. 2	25.12	B2	J5	Leopard
2. 2	26.12	B2	K6	Griffon
3. 2	27.12	B2	A7	Ox
4. 2	28.12	B2	B8	Bat
5. 2	29.12	B2	C9	Rat

CHI SZU YEAR

Solar date	Lunar date	Month HS/EB	Day HS/EB	Constellation
6. 2	1. 1	C3	D10	Swallow
7. 2	2. 1	C3	E11	Pig
8. 2	3. 1	C3	F12	Porcupine
9. 2	4. 1	C3	G1	Wolf
10. 2	5. 1	C3	H2	Dog
11. 2	6. 1	C3	J3	Pheasant
12. 2	7. 1	C3	K4	Cock
13. 2	8. 1	C3	A5	Crow
14. 2	9. 1	C3	B6	Monkey
15. 2	10. 1	C3	C7	Gibbon
16. 2	11. 1	C3	D8	Tapir
17. 2	12. 1	C3	E9	Sheep
18. 2	13. 1	C3	F10	Deer
19. 2	14. 1	C3	G11	Horse
20. 2	15. 1	C3	H12	Stag
21. 2	16. 1	C3	J1	Serpent
22. 2	17. 1	C3	K2	Earthworm
23. 2	18. 1	C3	A3	Crocodile
24. 2	19. 1	C3	B4	Dragon
25. 2	20. 1	C3	C5	Badger
26. 2	21. 1	C3	D6	Hare
27. 2	22. 1	C3	E7	Fox
28. 2	23. 1	C3	F8	Tiger
1. 3	24. 1	C3	G9	Leopard
2. 3	25. 1	C3	H10	Griffon
3. 3	26. 1	C3	J11	Ox
4. 3	27. 1	C3	K12	Bat
5. 3	28. 1	C3	A1	Rat
6. 3	29. 1	C3	B2	Swallow
7. 3	30. 1	C3	C3	Pig
8. 3	1. 2	D4	D4	Porcupine
9. 3	2. 2	D4	E5	Wolf
10. 3	3. 2	D4	F6	Dog
11. 3	4. 2	D4	G7	Pheasant
12. 3	5. 2	D4	H8	Cock
13. 3	6. 2	D4	J9	Crow
14. 3	7. 2	D4	K10	Monkey
15. 3	8. 2	D4	A11	Gibbon
16. 3	9. 2	D4	B12	Tapir
17. 3	10. 2	D4	C1	Sheep
18. 3	11. 2	D4	D2	Deer
19. 3	12. 2	D4	E3	Horse
20. 3	13. 2	D4	F4	Stag
21. 3	14. 2	D4	G5	Serpent
22. 3	15. 2	D4	H6	Earthworm
23. 3	16. 2	D4	J7	Crocodile
24. 3	17. 2	D4	K8	Dragon
25. 3	18. 2	D4	A9	Badger
26. 3	19. 2	D4	B10	Hare
27. 3	20. 2	D4	C11	Fox
28. 3	21. 2	D4	D12	Tiger
29. 3	22. 2	D4	E1	Leopard
30. 3	23. 2	D4	F2	Griffon
31. 3	24. 2	D4	G3	Ox
1. 4	25. 2	D4	H4	Bat
2. 4	26. 2	D4	J5	Rat
3. 4	27. 2	D4	K6	Swallow
4. 4	28. 2	D4	A7	Pig
5. 4	29. 2	D4	B8	Porcupine
6. 4	1. 3	E5	C9	Wolf
7. 4	2. 3	E5	D10	Dog
8. 4	3. 3	E5	E11	Pheasant
9. 4	4. 3	E5	F12	Cock
10. 4	5. 3	E5	G1	Crow
11. 4	6. 3	E5	H2	Monkey
12. 4	7. 3	E5	J3	Gibbon

Solar date	Lunar date	Month HS/EB	Day HS/EB	Constellation
13. 4	8. 3	E5	K4	Tapir
14. 4	9. 3	E5	A5	Sheep
15. 4	10. 3	E5	B6	Deer
16. 4	11. 3	E5	C7	Horse
17. 4	12. 3	E5	D8	Stag
18. 4	13. 3	E5	E9	Serpent
19. 4	14. 3	E5	F10	Earthworm
20. 4	15. 3	E5	G11	Crocodile
21. 4	16. 3	E5	H12	Dragon
22. 4	17. 3	E5	J1	Badger
23. 4	18. 3	E5	K2	Hare
24. 4	19. 3	E5	A3	Fox
25. 4	20. 3	E5	B4	Tiger
26. 4	21. 3	E5	C5	Leopard
27. 4	22. 3	E5	D6	Griffon
28. 4	23. 3	E5	E7	Ox
29. 4	24. 3	E5	F8	Rat
30. 4	25. 3	E5	G9	Rat
1. 5	26. 3	E5	H10	Swallow
2. 5	27. 3	E5	J11	Pig
3. 5	28. 3	E5	K12	Porcupine
4. 5	29. 3	E5	A1	Wolf
5. 5	1. 4	F6	B2	Dog
6. 5	2. 4	F6	C3	Pheasant
7. 5	3. 4	F6	D4	Cock
8. 5	4. 4	F6	E5	Crow
9. 5	5. 4	F6	F6	Monkey
10. 5	6. 4	F6	G7	Gibbon
11. 5	7. 4	F6	H8	Tapir
12. 5	8. 4	F6	J9	Sheep
13. 5	9. 4	F6	K10	Deer
14. 5	10. 4	F6	A11	Horse
15. 5	11. 4	F6	B12	Stag
16. 5	12. 4	F6	C1	Serpent
17. 5	13. 4	F6	D2	Earthworm
18. 5	14. 4	F6	E3	Crocodile
19. 5	15. 4	F6	F4	Dragon
20. 5	16. 4	F6	G5	Badger
21. 5	17. 4	F6	H6	Hare
22. 5	18. 4	F6	J7	Fox
23. 5	19. 4	F6	K8	Tiger
24. 5	20. 4	F6	A9	Leopard
25. 5	21. 4	F6	B10	Griffon
26. 5	22. 4	F6	C11	Ox
27. 5	23. 4	F6	D12	Bat
28. 5	24. 4	F6	E1	Rat
29. 5	25. 4	F6	F2	Swallow
30. 5	26. 4	F6	G3	Pig
31. 5	27. 4	F6	H4	Porcupine
1. 6	28. 4	F6	J5	Wolf
2. 6	29. 4	F6	K6	Dog
3. 6	30. 4	F6	A7	Pheasant
4. 6	1. 5	G7	B8	Cock
5. 6	2. 5	G7	C9	Crow
6. 6	3. 5	G7	D10	Monkey
7. 6	4. 5	G7	E11	Gibbon
8. 6	5. 5	G7	F12	Tapir
9. 6	6. 5	G7	G1	Sheep
10. 6	7. 5	G7	H2	Deer
11. 6	8. 5	G7	J3	Horse
12. 6	9. 5	G7	K4	Stag
13. 6	10. 5	G7	A5	Serpent
14. 6	11. 5	G7	B6	Earthworm
15. 6	12. 5	G7	C7	Crocodile
16. 6	13. 5	G7	D8	Dragon
17. 6	14. 5	G7	E9	Badger
18. 6	15. 5	G7	F10	Hare
19. 6	16. 5	G7	G11	Fox
20. 6	17. 5	G7	H12	Tiger
21. 6	18. 5	G7	J1	Leopard
22. 6	19. 5	G7	K2	Griffon
23. 6	20. 5	G7	A3	Ox
24. 6	21. 5	G7	B4	Bat

Solar date	Lunar date	Month HS/EB	Day HS/EB	Constellation
25. 6	22. 5	G7	C5	Rat
26. 6	23. 5	G7	D6	Swallow
27. 6	24. 5	G7	E7	Pig
28. 6	25. 5	G7	F8	Porcupine
29. 6	26. 5	G7	G9	Wolf
30. 6	27. 5	G7	H10	Dog
1. 7	28. 5	G7	J11	Pheasant
2. 7	29. 5	G7	K12	Cock
3. 7	1. 6	H8	A1	Crow
4. 7	2. 6	H8	B2	Monkey
5. 7	3. 6	H8	C3	Gibbon
6. 7	4. 6	H8	D4	Tapir
7. 7	5. 6	H8	E5	Sheep
8. 7	6. 6	H8	F6	Deer
9. 7	7. 6	H8	G7	Horse
10. 7	8. 6	H8	H8	Stag
11. 7	9. 6	H8	J9	Serpent
12. 7	10. 6	H8	K10	Earthworm
13. 7	11. 6	H8	A11	Crocodile
14. 7	12. 6	H8	B12	Dragon
15. 7	13. 6	H8	C1	Badger
16. 7	14. 6	H8	D2	Hare
17. 7	15. 6	H8	E3	Fox
18. 7	16. 6	H8	F4	Tiger
19. 7	17. 6	H8	G5	Leopard
20. 7	18. 6	H8	H6	Griffon
21. 7	19. 6	H8	J7	Ox
22. 7	20. 6	H8	K8	Bat
23. 7	21. 6	H8	A9	Rat
24. 7	22. 6	H8	B10	Swallow
25. 7	23. 6	H8	C11	Pig
26. 7	24. 6	H8	D12	Porcupine
27. 7	25. 6	H8	E1	Wolf
28. 7	26. 6	H8	F2	Dog
29. 7	27. 6	H8	G3	Pheasant
30. 7	28. 6	H8	H4	Cock
31. 7	29. 6	H8	J5	Crow
1. 8	1. 7	J9	K6	Monkey
2. 8	2. 7	J9	A7	Gibbon
3. 8	3. 7	J9	B8	Tapir
4. 8	4. 7	J9	C9	Sheep
5. 8	5. 7	J9	D10	Deer
6. 8	6. 7	J9	E11	Horse
7. 8	7. 7	J9	F12	Stag
8. 8	8. 7	J9	G1	Serpent
9. 8	9. 7	J9	H2	Earthworm
10. 8	10. 7	J9	J3	Crocodile
11. 8	11. 7	J9	K4	Dragon
12. 8	12. 7	J9	A5	Badger
13. 8	13. 7	J9	B6	Hare
14. 8	14. 7	J9	C7	Fox
15. 8	15. 7	J9	D8	Tiger
16. 8	16. 7	J9	E9	Leopard
17. 8	17. 7	J9	F10	Griffon
18. 8	18. 7	J9	G11	Ox
19. 8	19. 7	J9	H12	Bat
20. 8	20. 7	J9	J1	Rat
21. 8	21. 7	J9	K2	Swallow
22. 8	22. 7	J9	A3	Pig
23. 8	23. 7	J9	B4	Porcupine
24. 8	24. 7	J9	C5	Wolf
25. 8	25. 7	J9	D6	Dog
26. 8	26. 7	J9	E7	Pheasant
27. 8	27. 7	J9	F8	Cock
28. 8	28. 7	J9	G9	Crow
29. 8	29. 7	J9	H10	Monkey
30. 8	30. 7	J9	J11	Gibbon
31. 8	1. 8	K10	K12	Tapir
1. 9	2. 8	K10	A1	Sheep
2. 9	3. 8	K10	B2	Deer
3. 9	4. 8	K10	C3	Horse
4. 9	5. 8	K10	D4	Stag
5. 9	6. 8	K10	E5	Serpent

Solar date	Lunar date	Month HS/EB	Day HS/EB	Constellation	Solar date	Lunar date	Month HS/EB	Day HS/EB	Constellation
6. 9	7. 8	K10	F6	Earthworm	18.11	21.10	B12	J7	Pheasant
7. 9	8. 8	K10	G7	Crocodile	19.11	22.10	B12	K8	Cock
8. 9	9. 8	K10	H8	Dragon	20.11	23.10	B12	A9	Crow
9. 9	10. 8	K10	J9	Badger	21.11	24.10	B12	B10	Monkey
10. 9	11. 8	K10	K10	Hare	22.11	25.10	B12	C11	Gibbon
11. 9	12. 8	K10	A11	Fox	23.11	26.10	B12	D12	Tapir
12. 9	13. 8	K10	B12	Tiger	24.11	27.10	B12	E1	Sheep
13. 9	14. 8	K10	C1	Leopard	25.11	28.10	B12	F2	Deer
14. 9	15. 8	K10	D2	.Griffon	26.11	29.10	B12	G3	Horse
15. 9	16. 8	K10	E3	Ox	27.11	30.10	B12	H4	Stag
16. 9	17. 8	K10	F4	Bat	28.11	1.11	C1	J5	Serpent
17. 9	18. 8	K10	G5	Rat	29.11	2.11	C1	K6	Earthworm
18. 9	19. 8	K10	H6	Swallow	30.11	3.11	C1	A7	Crocodile
19. 9	20. 8	K10	J7	Pig	1.12	4.11	C1	B8	Dragon
20. 9	21. 8	K10	K8	Porcupine	2.12	5.11	C1	C9	Badger
21. 9	22. 8	K10	A9	Wolf	3.12	6.11	C1	D10	Hare
22. 9	23. 8	K10	B10	Dog	4.12	7.11	C1	E11	Fox
23. 9	24. 8	K10	C11	Pheasant	5.12	8.11	C1	F12	Tiger
24. 9	25. 8	K10	D12	Cock	6.12	9.11	C1	G1	Leopard
25. 9	26. 8	K10	E1	Crow	7.12	10.11	C1	H2	Griffon
26. 9	27. 8	K10	F2	Monkey	8.12	11.11	C1	J3	Ox
27. 9	28. 8	K10	G3	Gibbon	9.12	12.11	C1	K4	Bat
28. 9	29. 8	K10	H4	Tapir	10.12	13.11	C1	A5	Rat
29. 9	30. 8	K10	J5	Sheep	11.12	14.11	C1	B6	Swallow
30. 9	1. 9	A11	K6	Deer	12.12	15.11	C1	C7	Pig
1.10	2. 9	A11	A7	Horse	13.12	16.11	C1	D8	Porcupine
2.10	3. 9	A11	B8	Stag	14.12	17.11	C1	E9	Wolf
3.10	4. 9	A11	C9	Serpent	15.12	18.11	C1	F10	Dog
4.10	5. 9	A11	D10	Earthworm	16.12	19.11	C1	G11	Pheasant
5.10	6. 9	A11	E11	Crocodile	17.12	20.11	C1	H12	Cock
6.10	7. 9	A11	F12	Dragon	18.12	21.11	C1	J1	Crow
7.10	8. 9	A11	G1	Badger	19.12	22.11	C1	K2	Monkey
8.10	9. 9	A11	H2	Hare	20.12	23.11	C1	A3	Gibbon
9.10	10. 9	A11	J3	Fox	21.12	24.11	C1	B4	Tapir
10.10	11. 9	A11	K4	Tiger	22.12	25.11	C1	C5	Sheep
11.10	12. 9	A11	A5	Leopard	23.12	26.11	C1	D6	Deer
12.10	13. 9	A11	B6	Griffon	24.12	27.11	C1	E7	Horse
13.10	14. 9	A11	C7	Ox	25.12	28.11	C1	F8	Stag
14.10	15. 9	A11	D8	Bat	26.12	29.11	C1	G9	Serpent
15.10	16. 9	A11	E9	Rat	27.12	30.11	C1	H10	Earthworm
16.10	17. 9	A11	F10	Swallow	28.12	1.12	D2	J11	Crocodile
17.10	18. 9	A11	G11	Pig	29.12	2.12	D2	K12	Dragon
18.10	19. 9	A11	H12	Porcupine	30.12	3.12	D2	A1	Badger
19.10	20. 9	A11	J1	Wolf	31.12	4.12	D2	B2	Hare
20.10	21. 9	A11	K2	Dog					
21.10	22. 9	A11	A3	Pheasant	**1990**				
22.10	23. 9	A11	B4	Cock	1. 1	5.12	D2	C3	Fox
23.10	24. 9	A11	C5	Crow	2. 1	6.12	D2	D4	Tiger
24.10	25. 9	A11	D6	Monkey	3. 1	7.12	D2	E5	Leopard
25.10	26. 9	A11	E7	Gibbon	4. 1	8.12	D2	F6	Griffon
26.10	27. 9	A11	F8	Tapir	5. 1	9.12	D2	G7	Ox
27.10	28. 9	A11	G9	Sheep	6. 1	10.12	D2	H8	Bat
28.10	29. 9	A11	H10	Deer	7. 1	11.12	D2	J9	Rat
29.10	1.10	B12	J11	Horse	8. 1	12.12	D2	K10	Swallow
30.10	2.10	B12	K12	Stag	9. 1	13.12	D2	A11	Pig
31.10	3.10	B12	A1	Serpent	10. 1	14.12	D2	B12	Porcupine
1.11	4.10	B12	B2	Earthworm	11. 1	15.12	D2	C1	Wolf
2.11	5.10	B12	C3	Crocodile	12. 1	16.12	D2	D2	Dog
3.11	6.10	B12	D4	Dragon	13. 1	17.12	D2	E3	Pheasant
4.11	7.10	B12	E5	Badger	14. 1	18.12	D2	F4	Cock
5.11	8.10	B12	F6	Hare	15. 1	19.12	D2	G5	Crow
6.11	9.10	B12	G7	Fox	16. 1	20.12	D2	H6	Monkey
7.11	10.10	B12	H8	Tiger	17. 1	21.12	D2	J7	Gibbon
8.11	11.10	B12	J9	Leopard	18. 1	22.12	D2	K8	Tapir
9.11	12.10	B12	K10	Griffon	19. 1	23.12	D2	A9	Sheep
10.11	13.10	B12	A11	Ox	20. 1	24.12	D2	B10	Deer
11.11	14.10	B12	B12	Bat	21. 1	25.12	D2	C11	Horse
12.11	15.10	B12	C1	Rat	22. 1	26.12	D2	D12	Stag
13.11	16.10	B12	D2	Swallow	23. 1	27.12	D2	E1	Serpent
14.11	17.10	B12	E3	Pig	24. 1	28.12	D2	F2	Earthworm
15.11	18.10	B12	F4	Porcupine	25. 1	29.12	D2	G3	Crocodile
16.11	19.10	B12	G5	Wolf	26. 1	30.12	D2	H4	Dragon
17.11	20.10	B12	H6	Dog					

KENG WU YEAR

Solar date	Lunar date	Month HS/EB	Day HS/EB	Constellation	Solar date	Lunar date	Month HS/EB	Day HS/EB	Constellation
27. 1	1. 1	E3	J5	Badger	8. 4	13. 3	G5	K4	Cock
28. 1	2. 1	E3	K6	Hare	9. 4	14. 3	G5	A5	Crow
29. 1	3. 1	E3	A7	Fox	10. 4	15. 3	G5	B6	Monkey
30. 1	4. 1	E3	B8	Tiger	11. 4	16. 3	G5	C7	Gibbon
31. 1	5. 1	E3	C9	Leopard	12. 4	17. 3	G5	D8	Tapir
1. 2	6. 1	E3	D10	Griffon	13. 4	18. 3	G5	E9	Sheep
2. 2	7. 1	E3	D11	Ox	14. 4	19. 3	G5	F10	Deer
3. 2	8. 1	E3	F12	Bat	15. 4	20. 3	G5	G11	Horse
4. 2	9. 1	E3	G1	Rat	16. 4	21. 3	G5	H12	Stag
5. 2	10. 1	E3	H2	Swallow	17. 4	22. 3	G5	J1	Serpent
6. 2	11. 1	E3	J3	Pig	18. 4	23. 3	G5	K2	Earthworm
7. 2	12. 1	E3	K4	Porcupine	19. 4	24. 3	G5	A3	Crocodile
8. 2	13. 1	E3	A5	Wolf	20. 4	25. 3	G5	B4	Dragon
9. 2	14. 1	E3	B6	Dog	21. 4	26. 3	G5	C5	Badger
10. 2	15. 1	E3	C7	Pheasant	22. 4	27. 3	G5	D6	Hare
11. 2	16. 1	E3	D8	Cock	23. 4	28. 3	G5	E7	Fox
12. 2	17. 1	E3	E9	Crow	24. 4	29. 3	G5	F8	Tiger
13. 2	18. 1	E3	F10	Monkey	25. 4	1. 4	H6	G9	Leopard
14. 2	19. 1	E3	G11	Gibbon	26. 4	2. 4	H6	H10	Griffon
15. 2	20. 1	E3	H12	Tapir	27. 4	3. 4	H6	J11	Ox
16. 2	21. 1	E3	J1	Sheep	28. 4	4. 4	H6	K12	Bat
17. 2	22. 1	E3	K2	Deer	29. 4	5. 4	H6	A1	Rat
18. 2	23. 1	E3	A3	Horse	30. 4	6. 4	H6	B2	Swallow
19. 2	24. 1	E3	B4	Stag	1. 5	7. 4	H6	C3	Pig
20. 2	25. 1	E3	C5	Serpent	2. 5	8. 4	H6	D4	Porcupine
21. 2	26. 1	E3	D6	Earthworm	3. 5	9. 4	H6	E5	Wolf
22. 2	27. 1	E3	E7	Crocodile	4. 5	10. 4	H6	F6	Dog
23. 2	28. 1	E3	F8	Dragon	5. 5	11. 4	H6	G7	Pheasant
24. 2	29. 1	E3	G9	Badger	6. 5	12. 4	H6	H8	Cock
25. 2	1. 2	F4	H10	Hare	7. 5	13. 4	H6	J9	Crow
26. 2	2. 2	F4	J11	Fox	8. 5	14. 4	H6	K10	Monkey
27. 2	3. 2	F4	K12	Tiger	9. 5	15. 4	H6	A11	Gibbon
28. 2	4. 2	F4	A1	Leopard	10. 5	16. 4	H6	B12	Tapir
1. 3	5. 2	F4	B2	Griffon	11. 5	17. 4	H6	C1	Sheep
2. 3	6. 2	F4	C3	Ox	12. 5	18. 4	H6	D2	Deer
3. 3	7. 2	F4	D4	Bat	13. 5	19. 4	H6	E3	Horse
4. 3	8. 2	F4	E5	Rat	14. 5	20. 4	H6	F4	Stag
5. 3	9. 2	F4	F6	Swallow	15. 5	21. 4	H6	G5	Serpent
6. 3	10. 2	F4	G7	Pig	16. 5	22. 4	H6	H6	Earthworm
7. 3	11. 2	F4	H8	Porcupine	17. 5	23. 4	H6	J7	Crocodile
8. 3	12. 2	F4	J9	Wolf	18. 5	24. 4	H6	K8	Dragon
9. 3	13. 2	F4	K10	Dog	19. 5	25. 4	H6	A9	Badger
10. 3	14. 2	F4	A11	Pheasant	20. 5	26. 4	H6	B10	Hare
11. 3	15. 2	F4	B12	Cock	21. 5	27. 4	H6	C11	Fox
12. 3	16. 2	F4	C1	Crow	22. 5	28. 4	H6	D12	Tiger
13. 3	17. 2	F4	D2	Monkey	23. 5	29. 4	H6	E1	Leopard
14. 3	18. 2	F4	E3	Gibbon	24. 5	1. 5	J7	F2	Griffon
15. 3	19. 2	F4	F4	Tapir	25. 5	2. 5	J7	G3	Ox
16. 3	20. 2	F4	G5	Sheep	26. 5	3. 5	J7	H4	Bat
17. 3	21. 2	F4	H6	Deer	27. 5	4. 5	J7	J5	Rat
18. 3	22. 2	F4	J7	Horse	28. 5	5. 5	J7	K6	Swallow
19. 3	23. 2	F4	K8	Stag	29. 5	6. 5	J7	A7	Pig
20. 3	24. 2	F4	A9	Serpent	30. 5	7. 5	J7	B8	Porcupine
21. 3	25. 2	F4	B10	Earthworm	31. 5	8. 5	J7	C9	Wolf
22. 3	26. 2	F4	C11	Crocodile	1. 6	9. 5	J7	D10	Dog
23. 3	27. 2	F4	D12	Dragon	2. 6	10. 5	J7	E11	Pheasant
24. 3	28. 2	F4	E1	Badger	3. 6	11. 5	J7	F12	Cock
25. 3	29. 2	F4	F2	Hare	4. 6	12. 5	J7	G1	Crow
26. 3	30. 2	F4	G3	Fox	5. 6	13. 5	J7	H2	Monkey
27. 3	1. 3	G5	H4	Tiger	6. 6	14. 5	J7	J3	Gibbon
28. 3	2. 3	G5	J5	Leopard	7. 6	15. 5	J7	K4	Tapir
29. 3	3. 3	G5	K6	Griffon	8. 6	16. 5	J7	A5	Sheep
30. 3	4. 3	G5	A7	Ox	9. 6	17. 5	J7	B6	Deer
31. 3	5. 3	G5	B8	Bat	10. 6	18. 5	J7	C7	Horse
1. 4	6. 3	G5	C9	Rat	11. 6	19. 5	J7	D8	Stag
2. 4	7. 3	G5	D10	Swallow	12.16	20. 5	J7	E9	Serpent
3. 4	8. 3	G5	E11	Pig	13. 6	21. 5	J7	F10	Earthworm
4. 4	9. 3	G5	F12	Porcupine	14. 6	22. 5	J7	G11	Crocodile
5. 4	10. 3	G5	G1	Wolf	15. 6	23. 5	J7	H12	Dragon
6. 4	11. 3	G5	H2	Dog	16. 6	24. 5	J7	J1	Badger
7. 4	12. 3	G5	J3	Pheasant	17. 6	25. 5	J7	K2	Hare

Solar date	Lunar date	Month HS/EB	Day HS/EB	Constellation	Solar date	Lunar date	Month HS/EB	Day HS/EB	Constellation
18. 6	26. 5	J7	A3	Fox	30. 8	11. 7	A9	D4	Tapir
19. 6	27. 5	J7	B4	Tiger	31. 8	12. 7	A9	E5	Sheep
20. 6	28. 5	J7	C5	Leopard	1. 9	13. 7	A9	F6	Deer
21. 6	29. 5	J7	D6	Griffon	2. 9	14. 7	A9	G7	Horse
22. 6	30. 5	J7	E7	Ox	3. 9	15. 7	A9	H8	Stag
23. 6	1. 5	J7	F8	Bat	4. 9	16. 7	A9	J9	Serpent
24. 6	2. 5	J7	G9	Rat	5. 9	17. 7	A9	K10	Earthworm
25. 6	3. 5	J7	H10	Swallow	6. 9	18. 7	A9	A11	Crocodile
26. 6	4. 5	J7	J11	Pig	7. 9	19. 7	A9	B12	Dragon
27. 6	5. 5	J7	K12	Porcupine	8. 9	20. 7	A9	C1	Badger
28. 6	6. 5	J7	A1	Wolf	9. 9	21. 7	A9	D2	Hare
29. 6	7. 5	J7	B2	Dog	10. 9	22. 7	A9	E3	Fox
30. 6	8. 5	J7	C3	Pheasant	11. 9	23. 7	A9	F4	Tiger
1. 7	9. 5	J7	D4	Cock	12. 9	24. 7	A9	G5	Leopard
2. 7	10. 5	J7	E5	Crow	13. 9	25. 7	A9	H6	Griffon
3. 7	11. 5	J7	F6	Monkey	14. 9	26. 7	A9	J7	Ox
4. 7	12. 5	J7	G7	Gibbon	15. 9	27. 7	A9	K8	Bat
5. 7	13. 5	J7	H8	Tapir	16. 9	28. 7	A9	A9	Rat
6. 7	14. 5	J7	J9	Sheep	17. 9	29. 7	A9	B10	Swallow
7. 7	15. 5	J7	K10	Deer	18. 9	30. 7	A9	C11	Pig
8. 7	16. 5	J7	A11	Horse	19. 9	1. 8	B10	D12	Porcupine
9. 7	17. 5	J7	B12	Stag	20. 9	2. 8	B10	E1	Wolf
10. 7	18. 5	J7	C1	Serpent	21. 9	3. 8	B10	F2	Dog
11. 7	19. 5	J7	D2	Earthworm	22. 9	4. 8	B10	G3	Pheasant
12. 7	20. 5	J7	E3	Crocodile	23. 9	5. 8	B10	H4	Cock
13. 7	21. 5	J7	F4	Dragon	24. 9	6. 8	B10	J5	Crow
14. 7	22. 5	J7	G5	Badger	25. 9	7. 8	B10	K6	Monkey
15. 7	23. 5	J7	H6	Hare	26. 9	8. 8	B10	A7	Gibbon
16. 7	24. 5	J7	J7	Fox	27. 9	9. 8	B10	B8	Tapir
17. 7	25. 5	J7	K8	Tiger	28. 9	10. 8	B10	C9	Sheep
18. 7	26. 5	J7	A9	Leopard	29. 9	11. 8	B10	D10	Deer
19. 7	27. 5	J7	B10	Griffon	30. 9	12. 8	B10	E11	Horse
20. 7	28. 5	J7	C11	Ox	1.10	13. 8	B10	F12	Stag
21. 7	29. 5	J7	D12	Bat	2.10	14. 8	B10	G1	Serpent
22. 7	1. 6	K8	E1	Rat	3.10	15. 8	B10	H2	Earthworm
23. 7	2. 6	K8	F2	Swallow	4.10	16. 8	B10	J3	Crocodile
24. 7	3. 6	K8	G3	Pig	5.10	17. 8	B10	K4	Dragon
25. 7	4. 6	K8	H4	Porcupine	6.10	18. 8	B10	A5	Badger
26. 7	5. 6	K8	J5	Wolf	7.10	19. 8	B10	B6	Hare
27. 7	6. 6	K8	K6	Dog	8.10	20. 8	B10	C7	Fox
28. 7	7. 6	K8	A7	Pheasant	9.10	21. 8	B10	D8	Tiger
29. 7	8. 6	K8	B8	Cock	10.10	22. 8	B10	E9	Leopard
30. 7	9. 6	K8	C9	Crow	11.10	23. 8	B10	F10	Griffon
31. 7	10. 6	K8	D10	Monkey	12.10	24. 8	B10	G11	Ox
1. 8	11. 6	K8	E11	Gibbon	13.10	25. 8	B10	H12	Bat
2. 8	12. 6	K8	F12	Tapir	14.10	26. 8	B10	J1	Rat
3. 8	13. 6	K8	G1	Sheep	15.10	27. 8	B10	K2	Swallow
4. 8	14. 6	K8	H2	Deer	16.10	28. 8	B10	A3	Pig
5. 8	15. 6	K8	J3	Horse	17.10	29. 8	B10	B4	Porcupine
6. 8	16. 6	K8	K4	Stag	18.10	1. 9	C11	C5	Wolf
7. 8	17. 6	K8	A5	Serpent	19.10	2. 9	C11	D6	Dog
8. 8	18. 6	K8	B6	Earthworm	20.10	3. 9	C11	E7	Pheasant
9. 8	19. 6	K8	C7	Crocodile	21.10	4. 9	C11	F8	Cock
10. 8	20. 6	K8	D8	Dragon	22.10	5. 9	C11	G9	Crow
11. 8	21. 6	K8	E9	Badger	23.10	6. 9	C11	H10	Monkey
12. 8	22. 6	K8	F10	Hare	24.10	7. 9	C11	J11	Gibbon
13. 8	23. 6	K8	G11	Fox	25.10	8. 9	C11	K12	Tapir
14. 8	24. 6	K8	H12	Tiger	26.10	9. 9	C11	A1	Sheep
15. 8	25. 6	K8	J1	Leopard	27.10	10. 9	C11	B2	Deer
16. 8	26. 6	K8	K2	Griffon	28.10	11. 9	C11	C3	Horse
17. 8	27. 6	K8	A3	Ox	29.10	12. 9	C11	D4	Stag
18. 8	28. 6	K8	B4	Bat	30.10	13. 9	C11	E5	Serpent
19. 8	29. 6	K8	C5	Rat	31.10	14. 9	C11	F6	Earthworm
20. 8	1. 7	A9	D6	Swallow	1.11	15. 9	C11	G7	Crocodile
21. 8	2. 7	A9	E7	Pig	2.11	16. 9	C11	H8	Dragon
22. 8	3. 7	A9	F8	Porcupine	3.11	17. 9	C11	J9	Badger
23. 8	4. 7	A9	G9	Wolf	4.11	18. 9	C11	K10	Hare
24. 8	5. 7	A9	H10	Dog	5.11	19. 9	C11	A11	Fox
25. 8	6. 7	A9	J11	Pheasant	6.11	20. 9	C11	B12	Tiger
26. 8	7. 7	A9	K12	Cock	7.11	21. 9	C11	C1	Leopard
27. 8	8. 7	A9	A1	Crow	8.11	22. 9	C11	D2	Griffon
28. 8	9. 7	A9	B2	Monkey	9.11	23. 9	C11	E3	Ox
29. 8	10. 7	A9	C3	Gibbon	10.11	24. 9	C11	F4	Bat

Solar date	Lunar date	Month HS/EB	Day HS/EB	Constellation
11.11	25. 9	C11	G5	Rat
12.11	26. 9	C11	H6	Swallow
13.11	27. 9	C11	J7	Pig
14.11	28. 9	C11	K8	Porcupine
15.11	29. 9	C11	A9	Wolf
16.11	30. 9	C11	B10	Dog
17.11	1.10	D12	C11	Pheasant
18.11	2.10	D12	D12	Cock
19.11	3.10	D12	E1	Crow
20.11	4.10	D12	F2	Monkey
21.11	5.10	D12	G3	Gibbon
22.11	6.10	D12	H4	Tapir
23.11	7.10	D12	J5	Sheep
24.11	8.10	D12	K6	Deer
25.11	9.10	D12	A7	Horse
26.11	10.10	D12	B8	Stag
27.11	11.10	D12	C9	Serpent
28.11	12.10	D12	D10	Earthworm
29.11	13.10	D12	E11	Crocodile
30.11	14.10	D12	F12	Dragon
1.12	15.10	D12	G1	Badger
2.12	16.10	D12	H2	Hare
3.12	17.10	D12	J3	Fox
4.12	18.10	D12	K4	Tiger
5.12	19.10	D12	A5	Leopard
6.12	20.10	D12	B6	Griffon
7.12	21.10	D12	C7	Ox
8.12	22.10	D12	D8	Bat
9.12	23.10	D12	E9	Rat
10.12	24.10	D12	F10	Swallow
11.12	25.10	D12	G11	Pig
12.12	26.10	D12	H12	Porcupine
13.12	27.10	D12	J1	Wolf
14.12	28.10	D12	K2	Dog
15.12	29.10	D12	A3	Pheasant
16.12	30.10	D12	B4	Cock
17.12	1.11	E1	C5	Crow
18.12	2.11	E1	D6	Monkey
19.12	3.11	E1	E7	Gibbon
20.12	4.11	E1	F8	Tapir
21.12	5.11	E1	G9	Sheep
22.12	6.11	E1	H10	Deer
23.12	7.11	E1	J11	Horse
24.12	8.11	E1	K12	Stag
25.12	9.11	E1	A1	Serpent
26.12	10.11	E1	B2	Earthworm
27.12	11.11	E1	C3	Crocodile
28.12	12.11	E1	D4	Dragon
29.12	13.11	E1	E5	Badger
30.12	14.11	E1	F6	Hare
31.12	15.11	E1	G7	Fox

1991

Solar date	Lunar date	Month HS/EB	Day HS/EB	Constellation
1. 1	16.11	E1	H8	Tiger
2. 1	17.11	E1	J9	Leopard
3. 1	18.11	E1	K10	Griffon
4. 1	19.11	E1	A11	Ox
5. 1	20.11	E1	B12	Bat
6. 1	21.11	E1	C1	Rat
7. 1	22.11	E1	D2	Swallow
8. 1	23.11	E1	E3	Pig
9. 1	24.11	E1	F4	Porcupine
10. 1	25.11	E1	G5	Wolf
11. 1	26.11	E1	H6	Dog
12. 1	27.11	E1	J7	Pheasant
13. 1	28.11	E1	K8	Cock
14. 1	29.11	E1	A9	Crow
15. 1	30.11	E1	B10	Monkey
16. 1	1.12	F2	C11	Gibbon
17. 1	2.12	F2	D12	Tapir
18. 1	3.12	F2	E1	Sheep
19. 1	4.12	F2	F2	Deer
20. 1	5.12	F2	G3	Horse
21. 1	6.12	F2	H4	Stag
22. 1	7.12	F2	J5	Serpent
23. 1	8.12	F2	K6	Earthworm
24. 1	9.12	F2	A7	Crocodile
25. 1	10.12	F2	B8	Dragon
26. 1	11.12	F2	C9	Badger
27. 1	12.12	F2	D10	Hare
28. 1	13.12	F2	E11	Fox
29. 1	14.12	F2	F12	Tiger
30. 1	15.12	F2	G1	Leopard
31. 1	16.12	F2	H2	Griffon
1. 2	17.12	F2	J3	Ox
2. 2	18.12	F2	K4	Bat
3. 2	19.12	F2	A5	Rat
4. 2	20.12	F2	B6	Swallow
5. 2	21.12	F2	C7	Pig
6. 2	22.12	F2	D8	Porcupine
7. 2	23.12	F2	E9	Wolf
8. 2	24.12	F2	F10	Dog
9. 2	25.12	F2	G11	Pheasant
10. 2	26.12	F2	H12	Cock
11. 2	27.12	F2	J1	Crow
12. 2	28.12	F2	K2	Monkey
13. 2	29.12	F2	A3	Gibbon
14. 2	30.12	F2	B4	Tapir

HSIN WEI YEAR

Solar date	Lunar date	Month HS/EB	Day HS/EB	Constellation
15. 2	1. 1	G3	C5	Sheep
16. 2	2. 1	G3	D6	Deer
17. 2	3. 1	G3	E7	Horse
18. 2	4. 1	G3	F8	Stag
19. 2	5. 1	G3	G9	Serpent
20. 2	6. 1	G3	H10	Earthworm
21. 2	7. 1	G3	J11	Crocodile
22. 2	8. 1	G3	K12	Dragon
23. 2	9. 1	G3	A1	Badger
24. 2	10. 1	G3	B2	Hare
25. 2	11. 1	G3	C3	Fox
26. 2	12. 1	G3	D4	Tiger
27. 2	13. 1	G3	E5	Leopard
28. 2	14. 1	G3	F6	Griffon
1. 3	15. 1	G3	G7	Ox
2. 3	16. 1	G3	H8	Bat
3. 3	17. 1	G3	J9	Rat
4. 3	18. 1	G3	K10	Swallow
5. 3	19. 1	G3	A11	Pig
6. 3	20. 1	G3	B12	Porcupine
7. 3	21. 1	G3	C1	Wolf
8. 3	22. 1	G3	D2	Dog
9. 3	23. 1	G3	E3	Pheasant
10. 3	24. 1	G3	F4	Cock
11. 3	25. 1	G3	G5	Crow
12. 3	26. 1	G3	H6	Monkey
13. 3	27. 1	G3	J7	Gibbon
14. 3	28. 1	G3	K8	Tapir
15. 3	29. 1	G3	A9	Sheep
16. 3	1. 2	H4	B10	Deer
17. 3	2. 2	H4	C11	Horse
18. 3	3. 2	H4	D12	Stag
19. 3	4. 2	H4	E1	Serpent
20. 3	5. 2	H4	F2	Earthworm
21. 3	6. 2	H4	G3	Crocodile
22. 3	7. 2	H4	H4	Dragon
23. 3	8. 2	H4	J5	Badger
24. 3	9. 2	H4	K6	Hare

Solar date	Lunar date	Month HS/EB	Day HS/EB	Constellation	Solar date	Lunar date	Month HS/EB	Day HS/EB	Constellation
25. 3	10. 2	H4	A7	Fox	6. 6	24. 4	K6	D8	Tapir
26. 3	11. 2	H4	B8	Tiger	7. 6	25. 4	K6	E9	Sheep
27. 3	12. 2	H4	C9	Leopard	8. 6	26. 4	K6	F10	Deer
28. 3	13. 2	H4	D10	Griffon	9. 6	27. 4	K6	G11	Horse
29. 3	14. 2	H4	E11	Ox	10. 6	28. 4	K6	H12	Stag
30. 3	15. 2	H4	F12	Bat	11. 6	29. 4	K6	J1	Serpent
31. 3	16. 2	H4	G1	Rat	12. 6	1. 5	A7	K2	Earthworm
1. 4	17. 2	H4	H2	Swallow	13. 6	2. 5	A7	A3	Crocodile
2. 4	18. 2	H4	J3	Pig	14. 6	3. 5	A7	B4	Dragon
3. 4	19. 2	H4	K4	Porcupine	15. 6	4. 5	A7	C5	Badger
4. 4	20. 2	H4	A5	Wolf	16. 6	5. 5	A7	D6	Hare
5. 4	21. 2	H4	B6	Dog	17. 6	6. 5	A7	E7	Fox
6. 4	22. 2	H4	C7	Pheasant	18. 6	7. 5	A7	F8	Tiger
7. 4	23. 2	H4	D8	Cock	19. 6	8. 5	A7	G9	Leopard
8. 4	24. 2	H4	E9	Crow	20. 6	9. 5	A7	H10	Griffon
9. 4	25. 2	H4	F10	Monkey	21. 6	10. 5	A7	J11	Ox
10. 4	26. 2	H4	G11	Gibbon	22. 6	11. 5	A7	K12	Bat
11. 4	27. 2	H4	H12	Tapir	23. 6	12. 5	A7	A1	Rat
12. 4	28. 2	H4	J1	Sheep	24. 6	13. 5	A7	B2	Swallow
13. 4	29. 2	H4	K2	Deer	25. 6	14. 5	A7	C3	Pig
14. 4	30. 2	H4	A3	Horse	26. 6	15. 5	A7	D4	Porcupine
15. 4	1. 3	J5	B4	Stag	27. 6	16. 5	A7	E5	Wolf
16. 4	2. 3	J5	C5	Serpent	28. 6	17. 5	A7	F6	Dog
17. 4	3. 3	J5	D6	Earthworm	29. 6	18. 5	A7	G7	Pheasant
18. 4	4. 3	J5	E7	Crocodile	30. 6	19. 5	A7	H8	Cock
19. 4	5. 3	J5	F8	Dragon	1. 7	20. 5	A7	J9	Crow
20. 4	6. 3	J5	G9	Badger	2. 7	21. 5	A7	K10	Monkey
21. 4	7. 3	J5	H10	Hare	3. 7	22. 5	A7	A11	Gibbon
22. 4	8. 3	J5	J11	Fox	4. 7	23. 5	A7	B12	Tapir
23. 4	9. 3	J5	K12	Tiger	5. 7	24. 5	A7	C1	Sheep
24. 4	10. 3	J5	A1	Leopard	6. 7	25. 5	A7	D2	Deer
25. 4	11. 3	J5	B2	Griffon	7. 7	26. 5	A7	E3	Horse
26. 4	12. 3	J5	C3	Ox	8. 7	27. 5	A7	F4	Stag
27. 4	13. 3	J5	D4	Bat	9. 7	28. 5	A7	G5	Serpent
28. 4	14. 3	J5	E5	Rat	10. 7	29. 5	A7	H6	Earthworm
29. 4	15. 3	J5	F6	Swallow	11. 7	30. 5	A7	J7	Crocodile
30. 4	16. 3	J5	G7	Pig	12. 7	1. 6	B8	K8	Dragon
1. 5	17. 3	J5	H8	Porcupine	13. 7	2. 6	B8	A9	Badger
2. 5	18. 3	J5	J9	Wolf	14. 7	3. 6	B8	B10	Hare
3. 5	19. 3	J5	K10	Dog	15. 7	4. 6	B8	C11	Fox
4. 5	20. 3	J5	A11	Pheasant	16. 7	5. 6	B8	D12	Tiger
5. 5	21. 3	J5	B12	Cock	17. 7	6. 6	B8	E1	Leopard
6. 5	22. 3	J5	C1	Crow	18. 7	7. 6	B8	F2	Griffon
7. 5	23. 3	J5	D2	Monkey	19. 7	8. 6	B8	G3	Ox
8. 5	24. 3	J5	E3	Gibbon	20. 7	9. 6	B8	H4	Bat
9. 5	25. 3	J5	F4	Tapir	21. 7	10. 6	B8	J5	Rat
10. 5	26. 3	J5	G5	Sheep	22. 7	11. 6	B8	K6	Swallow
11. 5	27. 3	J5	H6	Deer	23. 7	12. 6	B8	A7	Pig
12. 5	28. 3	J5	J7	Horse	24. 7	13. 6	B8	B8	Porcupine
13. 5	29. 3	J5	K8	Stag	25. 7	14. 6	B8	C9	Wolf
14. 5	1. 4	K6	A9	Serpent	26. 7	15. 6	B8	D10	Dog
15. 5	2. 4	K6	B10	Earthworm	27. 7	16. 6	B8	E11	Pheasant
16. 5	3. 4	K6	C11	Crocodile	28. 7	17. 6	B8	F12	Cock
17. 5	4. 4	K6	D12	Dragon	29. 7	18. 6	B8	G1	Crow
18. 5	5. 4	K6	E1	Badger	30. 7	19. 6	B8	H2	Monkey
19. 5	6. 4	K6	F2	Hare	31. 7	20. 6	B8	J3	Gibbon
20. 5	7. 4	K6	G3	Fox	1. 8	21. 6	B8	K4	Tapir
21. 5	8. 4	K6	H4	Tiger	2. 8	22. 6	B8	A5	Sheep
22. 5	9. 4	K6	J5	Leopard	3. 8	23. 6	B8	B6	Deer
23. 5	10. 4	K6	K6	Griffon	4. 8	24. 6	B8	C7	Horse
24. 5	11. 4	K6	A7	Ox	5. 8	25. 6	B8	D8	Stag
25. 5	12. 4	K6	B8	Bat	6. 8	26. 6	B8	E9	Serpent
26. 5	13. 4	K6	C9	Rat	7. 8	27. 6	B8	F10	Earthworm
27. 5	14. 4	K6	D10	Swallow	8. 8	28. 6	B8	G11	Crocodile
28. 5	15. 4	K6	E11	Pig	9. 8	29. 6	B8	H12	Dragon
29. 5	16. 4	K6	F12	Porcupine	10. 8	1. 7	C9	J1	Badger
30. 5	17. 4	K6	G1	Wolf	11. 8	2. 7	C9	K2	Hare
31. 5	18. 4	K6	H2	Dog	12. 8	3. 7	C9	A3	Fox
1. 6	19. 4	K6	J3	Pheasant	13. 8	4. 7	C9	B4	Tiger
2. 6	20. 4	K6	K4	Cock	14. 8	5. 7	C9	C5	Leopard
3. 6	21. 4	K6	A5	Crow	15. 8	6. 7	C9	D6	Griffon
4. 6	22. 4	K6	B6	Monkey	16. 8	7. 7	C9	E7	Ox
5. 6	23. 4	K6	C7	Gibbon	17. 8	8. 7	C9	F8	Bat

Solar date	Lunar date	Month HS/EB	Day HS/EB	Constellation
18. 8	9. 7	C9	G9	Rat
19. 8	10. 7	C9	H10	Swallow
20. 8	11. 7	C9	J11	Pig
21. 8	12. 7	C9	K12	Porcupine
22. 8	13. 7	C9	A1	Wolf
23. 8	14. 7	C9	B2	Dog
24. 8	15. 7	C9	C3	Pheasant
25. 8	16. 7	C9	D4	Cock
26. 8	17. 7	C9	E5	Crow
27. 8	18. 7	C9	F6	Monkey
28. 8	19. 7	C9	G7	Gibbon
29. 8	20. 7	C9	H8	Tapir
30. 8	21. 7	C9	J9	Sheep
31. 8	22. 7	C9	K10	Deer
1. 9	23. 7	C9	A11	Horse
2. 9	24. 7	C9	B12	Stag
3. 9	25. 7	C9	C1	Serpent
4. 9	26. 7	C9	D2	Earthworm
5. 9	27. 7	C9	E3	Crocodile
6. 9	28. 7	C9	F4	Dragon
7. 9	29. 7	C9	G5	Badger
8. 9	1. 8	D10	H6	Hare
9. 9	2. 8	D10	J7	Fox
10. 9	3. 8	D10	K8	Tiger
11. 9	4. 8	D10	A9	Leopard
12. 9	5. 8	D10	B10	Griffon
13. 9	6. 8	D10	C11	Ox
14. 9	7. 8	D10	D12	Bat
15. 9	8. 8	D10	E1	Rat
16. 9	9. 8	D10	F2	Swallow
17. 9	10. 8	D10	G3	Pig
18. 9	11. 8	D10	H4	Porcupine
19. 9	12. 8	D10	J5	Wolf
20. 9	13. 8	D10	K6	Dog
21. 9	14. 8	D10	A7	Pheasant
22. 9	15. 8	D10	B8	Cock
23. 9	16. 8	D10	C9	Crow
24. 9	17. 8	D10	D10	Monkey
25. 9	18. 8	D10	E11	Gibbon
26. 9	19. 8	D10	F12	Tapir
27. 9	20. 8	D10	G1	Sheep
28. 9	21. 8	D10	H2	Deer
29. 9	22. 8	D10	J3	Horse
30. 9	23. 8	D10	K4	Stag
1.10	24. 8	D10	A5	Serpent
2.10	25. 8	D10	B6	Earthworm
3.10	26. 8	D10	C7	Crocodile
4.10	27. 8	D10	D8	Dragon
5.10	28. 8	D10	E9	Badger
6.10	29. 8	D10	F10	Hare
7.10	30. 8	D10	G11	Fox
8.10	1. 9	E11	H12	Tiger
9.10	2. 9	E11	J1	Leopard
10.10	3. 9	E11	K2	Griffon
11.10	4. 9	E11	A3	Ox
12.10	5. 9	E11	B4	Bat
13.10	6. 9	E11	C5	Rat
14.10	7. 9	E11	D6	Swallow
15.10	8. 9	E11	E7	Pig
16.10	9. 9	E11	F8	Porcupine
17.10	10. 9	E11	G9	Wolf
18.10	11. 9	E11	H10	Dog
19.10	12. 9	E11	J11	Pheasant
20.10	13. 9	E11	K12	Cock
21.10	14. 9	E11	A1	Crow
22.10	15. 9	E11	B2	Monkey
23.10	16. 9	E11	C3	Gibbon
24.10	17. 9	E11	D4	Tapir
25.10	18. 9	E11	E5	Sheep
26.10	19. 9	E11	F6	Deer
27.10	20. 9	E11	G7	Horse
28.10	21. 9	E11	H8	Stag
29.10	22. 9	E11	J9	Serpent
30.10	23. 9	E11	K10	Earthworm
31.10	24. 9	E11	A11	Crocodile
1.11	25. 9	E11	B12	Dragon
2.11	26. 9	E11	C1	Badger
3.11	27. 9	E11	D2	Hare
4.11	28. 9	E11	E3	Fox
5.11	29. 9	E11	F4	Tiger
6.11	1.10	F12	G5	Leopard
7.11	2.10	F12	H6	Griffon
8.11	3.10	F12	J7	Ox
9.11	4.10	F12	K8	Bat
10.11	5.10	F12	A9	Rat
11.11	6.10	F12	B10	Swallow
12.11	7.10	F12	C11	Pig
13.11	8.10	F12	D12	Porcupine
14.11	9.10	F12	E1	Wolf
15.11	10. 9	F12	F2	Dog
16.11	11. 9	F12	G3	Pheasant
17.11	12. 9	F12	H4	Cock
18.11	13. 9	F12	J5	Crow
19.11	14. 9	F12	K6	Monkey
20.11	15.10	F12	A7	Gibbon
21.11	16.10	F12	B8	Tapir
22.11	17.10	F12	C9	Sheep
23.11	18.10	F12	D10	Deer
24.11	19.10	F12	E11	Horse
25.11	20.10	F12	F12	Stag
26.11	21.10	F12	G1	Serpent
27.11	22.10	F12	H2	Earthworm
28.11	23.10	F12	J3	Crocodile
29.11	24.10	F12	K4	Dragon
30.11	25.10	F12	A5	Badger
1.12	26.10	F12	B6	Hare
2.12	27.10	F12	C7	Fox
3.12	28.10	F12	D8	Tiger
4.12	29.10	F12	E9	Leopard
5.12	30.10	F12	F10	Griffon
6.12	1.10	G1	G11	Ox
7.12	2.10	G1	H12	Bat
8.12	3.10	G1	J1	Rat
9.12	4.10	G1	K2	Swallow
10.12	5.10	G1	A3	Pig
11.12	6.10	G1	B4	Porcupine
12.12	7.10	G1	C5	Wolf
13.12	8.10	G1	D6	Dog
14.12	9.10	G1	E7	Pheasant
15.12	10.10	G1	F8	Cock
16.12	11.10	G1	G9	Crow
17.12	12.10	G1	H10	Monkey
18.12	13.10	G1	J11	Gibbon
19.12	14.10	G1	K12	Tapir
20.12	15.11	G1	A1	Sheep
21.12	16.11	G1	B2	Deer
22.12	17.11	G1	C3	Horse
23.12	18.11	G1	D4	Stag
24.12	19.11	G1	E5	Serpent
25.12	20.11	G1	F6	Earthworm
26.12	21.11	G1	G7	Crocodile
27.12	22.11	G1	H8	Dragon
28.12	23.11	G1	J9	Badger
29.12	24.11	G1	K10	Hare
30.12	25.11	G1	A11	Fox
31.12	26.11	G1	B12	Tiger
1992				
1. 1	27.11	G1	C1	Leopard
2. 1	28.11	G1	D2	Griffon
3. 1	29.11	G1	E3	Ox
4. 1	30.11	G1	F4	Bat
5. 1	1.11	H2	G5	Rat
6. 1	2.11	H2	H6	Swallow
7. 1	3.11	H2	J7	Pig
8. 1	4.11	H2	K8	Porcupine

Solar date	Lunar date	Month HS/EB	Day HS/EB	Constellation	Solar date	Lunar date	Month HS/EB	Day HS/EB	Constellation
9. 1	5.11	H2	A9	Wolf	22. 1	18.12	H2	D10	Earthworm
10. 1	6.11	H2	B10	Dog	23. 1	19.12	H2	E11	Crocodile
11. 1	7.11	H2	C11	Pheasant	24. 1	20.12	H2	F12	Dragon
12. 1	8.11	H2	D12	Cock	25. 1	21.12	H2	G1	Badger
13. 1	9.11	H2	E1	Crow	26. 1	22.12	H2	H2	Hare
14. 1	10.11	H2	F2	Monkey	27. 1	23.12	H2	J3	Fox
15. 1	11.11	H2	G3	Gibbon	28. 1	24.12	H2	K4	Tiger
16. 1	12.11	H2	H4	Tapir	29. 1	25.12	H2	A5	Leopard
17. 1	13.11	H2	J5	Sheep	30. 1	26.12	H2	B6	Griffon
18. 1	14.12	H2	K6	Deer	31. 1	27.12	H2	C7	Ox
19. 1	15.12	H2	A7	Horse	1. 2	28.12	H2	D8	Bat
20. 1	16.12	H2	B8	Stag	2. 2	29.12	H2	E9	Rat
21. 1	17.12	H2	C9	Serpent	3. 2	30.12	H2	F10	Swallow

JEN SHEN YEAR

Solar date	Lunar date	Month HS/EB	Day HS/EB	Constellation	Solar date	Lunar date	Month HS/EB	Day HS/EB	Constellation
4. 2	1. 1	J3	G11	Pig	30. 3	27. 2	K4	B6	Swallow
5. 2	2. 1	J3	H12	Porcupine	31. 3	28. 2	K4	C7	Pig
6. 2	3. 1	J3	J1	Wolf	1. 4	29. 2	K4	D8	Porcupine
7. 2	4. 1	J3	K2	Dog	2. 4	30. 2	K4	E9	Wolf
8. 2	5. 1	J3	A3	Pheasant	3. 4	1. 3	A5	F10	Dog
9. 2	6. 1	J3	B4	Cock	4. 4	2. 3	A5	G11	Pheasant
10. 2	7. 1	J3	C5	Crow	5. 4	3. 3	A5	H12	Cock
11. 2	8. 1	J3	D6	Monkey	6. 4	4. 3	A5	J1	Crow
12. 2	9. 1	J3	E7	Gibbon	7. 4	5. 3	A5	K2	Monkey
13. 2	10. 1	J3	F8	Tapir	8. 4	6. 3	A5	A3	Gibbon
14. 2	11. 1	J3	G9	Sheep	9. 4	7. 3	A5	B4	Tapir
15. 2	12. 1	J3	H10	Deer	10. 4	8. 3	A5	C5	Sheep
16. 2	13. 1	J3	J11	Horse	11. 4	9. 3	A5	D6	Deer
17. 2	14. 1	J3	K12	Stag	12. 4	10. 3	A5	E7	Horse
18. 2	15. 1	J3	A1	Serpent	13. 4	11. 3	A5	F8	Stag
19. 2	16. 1	J3	B2	Earthworm	14. 4	12. 3	A5	G9	Serpent
20. 2	17. 1	J3	C3	Crocodile	15. 4	13. 3	A5	H10	Earthworm
21. 2	18. 1	J3	D4	Dragon	16. 4	14. 3	A5	J11	Crocodile
22. 2	19. 1	J3	E5	Badger	17. 4	15. 3	A5	K12	Dragon
23. 2	20. 1	J3	F6	Hare	18. 4	16. 3	A5	A1	Badger
24. 2	21. 1	J3	G7	Fox	19. 4	17. 3	A5	B2	Hare
25. 2	22. 1	J3	H8	Tiger	20. 4	18. 3	A5	C3	Fox
26. 2	23. 1	J3	J9	Leopard	21. 4	19. 3	A5	D4	Tiger
27. 2	24. 1	J3	K10	Griffon	22. 4	20. 3	A5	E5	Leopard
28. 2	25. 1	J3	A11	Ox	23. 4	21. 3	A5	F6	Griffon
29. 2	26. 1	J3	B12	Bat	24. 4	22. 3	A5	G7	Ox
1. 3	27. 1	J3	C1	Rat	25. 4	23. 3	A5	H8	Bat
2. 3	28. 1	J3	D2	Swallow	26. 4	24. 3	A5	J9	Rat
3. 3	29. 1	J3	E3	Pig	27. 4	25. 3	A5	K10	Swallow
4. 3	1. 2	K4	F4	Porcupine	28. 4	26. 3	A5	A11	Pig
5. 3	2. 2	K4	G5	Wolf	29. 4	27. 3	A5	B12	Porcupine
6. 3	3. 2	K4	H6	Dog	30. 4	28. 3	A5	C1	Wolf
7. 3	4. 2	K4	J7	Pheasant	1. 5	29. 3	A5	D2	Dog
8. 3	5. 2	K4	K8	Cock	2. 5	30. 3	A5	E3	Pheasant
9. 3	6. 2	K4	A9	Crow	3. 5	1. 4	B6	F4	Cock
10. 3	7. 2	K4	B10	Monkey	4. 5	2. 4	B6	G5	Crow
11. 3	8. 2	K4	C11	Gibbon	5. 5	3. 4	B6	H6	Monkey
12. 3	9. 2	K4	D12	Tapir	6. 5	4. 4	B6	J7	Gibbon
13. 3	10. 2	K4	E1	Sheep	7. 5	5. 4	B6	K8	Tapir
14. 3	11. 2	K4	F2	Deer	8. 5	6. 4	B6	A9	Sheep
15. 3	12. 2	K4	G3	Horse	9. 5	7. 4	B6	B10	Deer
16. 3	13. 2	K4	H4	Stag	10. 5	8. 4	B6	C11	Horse
17. 3	14. 2	K4	J5	Serpent	11. 5	9. 4	B6	D12	Stag
18. 3	15. 2	K4	K6	Earthworm	12. 5	10. 4	B6	E1	Serpent
19. 3	16. 2	K4	A7	Crocodile	13. 5	11. 4	B6	F2	Earthworm
20. 3	17. 2	K4	B8	Dragon	14. 5	12. 4	B6	G3	Crocodile
21. 3	18. 2	K4	C9	Badger	15. 5	13. 4	B6	H4	Dragon
22. 3	19. 2	K4	D10	Hare	16. 5	14. 4	B6	J5	Badger
23. 3	20. 2	K4	E11	Fox	17. 5	15. 4	B6	K6	Hare
24. 3	21. 2	K4	F12	Tiger	18. 5	16. 4	B6	A7	Fox
25. 3	22. 2	K4	G1	Leopard	19. 5	17. 4	B6	B8	Tiger
26. 3	23. 2	K4	H2	Griffon	20. 5	18. 4	B6	C9	Leopard
27. 3	24. 2	K4	J3	Ox	21. 5	19. 4	B6	D10	Griffon
28. 3	25. 2	K4	K4	Bat	22. 5	20. 4	B6	E11	Ox
29. 3	26. 2	K4	A5	Rat	23. 5	21. 4	B6	F12	Bat

Solar date	Lunar date	Month HS/EB	Day HS/EB	Constellation	Solar date	Lunar date	Month HS/EB	Day HS/EB	Constellation
24. 5	22. 4	B6	G1	Rat	5. 8	7. 7	E9	K2	Earthworm
25. 5	23. 4	B6	H2	Swallow	6. 8	8. 7	E9	A3	Crocodile
26. 5	24. 4	B6	J3	Pig	7. 8	9. 7	E9	B4	Dragon
27. 5	25. 4	B6	K4	Porcupine	8. 8	10. 7	E9	C5	Badger
28. 5	26. 4	B6	A5	Wolf	9. 8	11. 7	E9	D6	Hare
29. 5	27. 4	B6	B6	Dog	10. 8	12. 7	E9	E7	Fox
30. 5	28. 4	B6	C7	Pheasant	11. 8	13. 7	E9	F8	Tiger
31. 5	29. 4	B6	D8	Cock	12. 8	14. 7	E9	G9	Leopard
1. 6	1. 5	C7	E9	Crow	13. 8	15. 7	E9	H10	Griffon
2. 6	2. 5	C7	F10	Monkey	14. 8	16. 7	E9	J11	Ox
3. 6	3. 5	C7	G11	Gibbon	15. 8	17. 7	E9	K12	Bat
4. 6	4. 5	C7	H12	Tapir	16. 8	18. 7	E9	A1	Rat
5. 6	5. 5	C7	J1	Sheep	17. 8	19. 7	E9	B2	Swallow
6. 6	6. 5	C7	K2	Deer	18. 8	20. 7	E9	C3	Pig
7. 6	7. 5	C7	A3	Horse	19. 8	21. 7	E9	D4	Porcupine
8. 6	8. 5	C7	B4	Stage	20. 8	22. 7	E9	E5	Wolf
9. 6	9. 5	C7	C5	Serpent	21. 8	23. 7	E9	F6	Dog
10. 6	10. 5	C7	D6	Earthworm	22. 8	24. 7	E9	G7	Pheasant
11. 6	11. 5	C7	E7	Crocodile	23. 8	25. 7	E9	H8	Cock
12. 6	12. 5	C7	F8	Dragon	24. 8	26. 7	E9	J9	Crow
13. 6	13. 5	C7	G9	Badger	25. 8	27. 7	E9	K10	Monkey
14. 6	14. 5	C7	H10	Hare	26. 8	28. 7	E9	A11	Gibbon
15. 6	15. 5	C7	J11	Fox	27. 8	29. 7	E9	B12	Tapir
16. 6	16. 5	C7	K12	Tiger	28. 8	1. 8	F10	C1	Sheep
17. 6	17. 5	C7	A1	Leopard	29. 8	2. 8	F10	D2	Deer
18. 6	18. 5	C7	B2	Griffon	30. 8	3. 8	F10	E3	Horse
19. 6	19. 5	C7	C3	Ox	31. 8	4. 8	F10	F4	Stag
20. 6	20. 5	C7	D4	Bat	1. 9	5. 8	F10	G5	Serpent
21. 6	21. 5	C7	E5	Rat	2. 9	6. 8	F10	H6	Earthworm
22. 6	22. 5	C7	F6	Swallow	3. 9	7. 8	F10	J7	Crocodile
23. 6	23. 5	C7	G7	Pig	4. 9	8. 8	F10	K8	Dragon
24. 6	24. 5	C7	H8	Porcupine	5. 9	9. 8	F10	A9	Badger
25. 6	25. 5	C7	J9	Wolf	6. 9	10. 8	F10	B10	Hare
26. 6	26. 5	C7	K10	Dog	7. 9	11. 8	F10	C11	Fox
27. 6	27. 5	C7	A11	Pheasant	8. 9	12. 8	F10	D12	Tiger
28. 6	28. 5	C7	B12	Cock	9. 9	13. 8	F10	E1	Leopard
29. 6	29. 5	C7	C1	Crow	10. 9	14. 8	F10	F2	Griffon
30. 6	1. 6	D8	D2	Monkey	11. 9	15. 8	F10	G3	Ox
1. 7	2. 6	D8	E3	Gibbon	12. 9	16. 8	F10	H4	Bat
2. 7	3. 6	D8	F4	Tapir	13. 9	17. 8	F10	J5	Rat
3. 7	4. 6	D8	G5	Sheep	14. 9	18. 8	F10	K6	Swallow
4. 7	5. 6	D8	H6	Deer	15. 9	19. 8	F10	A7	Pig
5. 7	6. 6	D8	J7	Horse	16. 9	20. 8	F10	B8	Porcupine
6. 7	7. 6	D8	K8	Stag	17. 9	21. 8	F10	C9	Wolf
7. 7	8. 6	D8	A9	Serpent	18. 9	22. 8	F10	D10	Dog
8. 7	9. 6	D8	B10	Earthworm	19. 9	23. 8	F10	E11	Pheasant
9. 7	10. 6	D8	C11	Crocodile	20. 9	24. 8	F10	F12	Cock
10. 7	11. 6	D8	D12	Dragon	21. 9	25. 8	F10	G1	Crow
11. 7	12. 6	D8	E1	Badger	22. 9	26. 8	F10	H2	Monkey
12. 7	13. 6	D8	F2	Hare	23. 9	27. 8	F10	J3	Gibbon
13. 7	14. 6	D8	G3	Fox	24. 9	28. 8	F10	K4	Tapir
14. 7	15. 6	D8	H4	Tiger	25. 9	29. 8	F10	A5	Sheep
15. 7	16. 6	D8	J5	Leopard	26. 9	1. 9	G11	B6	Deer
16. 7	17. 6	D8	K6	Griffon	27. 9	2. 9	G11	C7	Horse
17. 7	18. 6	D8	A7	Ox	28. 9	3. 9	G11	D8	Stag
18. 7	19. 6	D8	B8	Bat	29. 9	4. 9	G11	E9	Serpent
19. 7	20. 6	D8	C9	Rat	30. 9	5. 9	G11	F10	Earthworm
20. 7	21. 6	D8	D10	Swallow	1.10	6. 9	G11	G11	Crocodile
21. 7	22. 6	D8	E11	Pig	2.10	7. 9	G11	H12	Dragon
22. 7	23. 6	D8	F12	Porcupine	3.10	8. 9	G11	J1	Badger
23. 7	24. 6	D8	G1	Wolf	4.10	9. 9	G11	K2	Hare
24. 7	25. 6	D8	H2	Dog	5.10	10. 9	G11	A3	Fox
25. 7	26. 6	D8	J3	Pheasant	6.10	11. 9	G11	B4	Tiger
26. 7	27. 6	D8	K4	Cock	7.10	12. 9	G11	C5	Leopard
27. 7	28. 6	D8	A5	Crow	8.10	13. 9	G11	D6	Griffon
28. 7	29. 6	D8	B6	Monkey	9.10	14. 9	G11	E7	Ox
29. 7	30. 6	D8	C7	Gibbon	10.10	15. 9	G11	F8	Bat
30. 7	1. 7	E9	D8	Tapir	11.10	16. 9	G11	G9	Rat
31. 7	2. 7	E9	E9	Sheep	12.10	17. 9	G11	H10	Swallow
1. 8	3. 7	E9	F10	Deer	13.10	18. 9	G11	J11	Pig
2. 8	4. 7	E9	G11	Horse	14.10	19. 9	G11	K12	Porcupine
3. 8	5. 7	E9	H12	Stag	15.10	20. 9	G11	A1	Wolf
4. 8	6. 7	E9	J1	Serpent	16.10	21. 9	G11	B2	Dog

Solar date	Lunar date	Month HS/EB	Day HS/EB	Constellation	Solar date	Lunar date	Month HS/EB	Day HS/EB	Constellation
17.10	22. 9	G11	C3	Pheasant	6.12	13.11	J1	C5	Rat
18.10	23. 9	G11	D4	Cock	7.12	14.11	J1	D6	Swallow
19.10	24. 9	G11	E5	Crow	8.12	15.11	J1	E7	Pig
20.10	25. 9	G11	F6	Monkey	9.12	16.11	J1	F8	Porcupine
21.10	26. 9	G11	G7	Gibbon	10.12	17.11	J1	G9	Wolf
22.10	27. 9	G11	H8	Tapir	11.12	18.11	J1	H10	Dog
23.10	28. 9	G11	J9	Sheep	12.12	19.11	J1	J11	Pheasant
24.10	29. 9	G11	K10	Deer	13.12	20.11	J1	K12	Cock
25.10	30. 9	G11	A11	Horse	14.12	21.11	J1	A1	Crow
26.10	1.10	H12	B12	Stag	15.12	22.11	J1	B2	Monkey
27.10	2.10	H12	C1	Serpent	16.12	23.11	J1	C3	Gibbon
28.10	3.10	H12	D2	Earthworm	17.12	24.11	J1	D4	Tapir
29.10	4.10	H12	E3	Crocodile	18.12	25.11	J1	E5	Sheep
30.10	5.10	H12	F4	Dragon	19.12	26.11	J1	F6	Deer
31.10	6.10	H12	G5	Badger	20.12	27.11	J1	G7	Horse
1.11	7.10	H12	H6	Hare	21.12	28.11	J1	H8	Stag
2.11	8.10	H12	J7	Fox	22.12	29.11	J1	J9	Serpent
3.11	9.10	H12	K8	Tiger	23.12	30.11	J1	K10	Earthworm
4.11	10.10	H12	A9	Leopard	24.12	1.12	K2	A1	Crocodile
5.11	11.10	H12	B10	Griffon	25.12	2.12	K2	B12	Dragon
6.11	12.10	H12	C11	Ox	26.12	3.12	K2	C1	Badger
7.11	13.10	H12	D12	Bat	27.12	4.12	K2	D2	Hare
8.11	14.10	H12	E1	Rat	28.12	5.12	K2	E3	Fox
9.11	15.10	H12	F2	Swallow	29.12	6.12	K2	F4	Tiger
10.11	16.10	H12	G3	Pig	30.12	7.12	K2	G5	Leopard
11.11	17.10	H12	H4	Porcupine	31.12	8.12	K2	H6	Griffon
12.11	18.10	H12	J5	Wolf					
13.11	19.10	H12	K6	Dog	**1993**				
14.11	20.10	H12	A7	Pheasant	1. 1	9.12	K2	J7	Ox
15.11	21.10	H12	B8	Cock	2. 1	10.12	K2	K8	Bat
16.11	22.10	H12	C9	Crow	3. 1	11.12	K2	A9	Rat
17.11	23.10	H12	D10	Monkey	4. 1	12.12	K2	B10	Swallow
18.11	24.10	H12	E11	Gibbon	5. 1	13.12	K2	C11	Pig
19.11	25.10	H12	F12	Tapir	6. 1	14.12	K2	D12	Porcupine
20.11	26.10	H12	G1	Sheep	7. 1	15.12	K2	E1	Wolf
21.11	27.10	H12	H2	Deer	8. 1	16.12	K2	F2	Dog
22.11	28.10	H12	J3	Horse	9. 1	17.12	K2	G3	Pheasant
23.11	29.10	H12	K4	Stag	10. 1	18.12	K2	H4	Cock
24.11	1.11	J1	A5	Serpent	11. 1	19.12	K2	J5	Crow
25.11	2.11	J1	B6	Earthworm	12. 1	20.12	K2	K6	Monkey
26.11	3.11	J1	C7	Crocodile	13. 1	21.12	K2	A7	Gibbon
27.11	4.11	J1	D8	Dragon	14. 1	22.12	K2	B8	Tapir
28.11	5.11	J1	E9	Badger	15. 1	23.12	K2	C9	Sheep
29.11	6.11	J1	F10	Hare	16. 1	24.12	K2	D10	Deer
30.11	7.11	J1	G11	Fox	17. 1	25.12	K2	E11	Horse
1.12	8.11	J1	H12	Tiger	18. 1	26.12	K2	F12	Stag
2.12	9.11	J1	J1	Leopard	19. 1	27.12	K2	G1	Serpent
3.12	10.11	J1	K2	Griffon	20. 1	28.12	K2	H2	Earthworm
4.12	11.11	J1	A3	Ox	21. 1	29.12	K2	J3	Crocodile
5.12	12.11	J1	B4	Bat	22. 1	30.12	K2	K4	Dragon

KUEI YU YEAR

Solar date	Lunar date	Month HS/EB	Day HS/EB	Constellation	Solar date	Lunar date	Month HS/EB	Day HS/EB	Constellation
23. 1	1. 1	A3	A5	Badger	10. 2	19. 1	A3	J11	Gibbon
24. 1	2. 1	A3	B6	Hare	11. 2	20. 1	A3	K12	Tapir
25. 1	3. 1	A3	C7	Fox	12. 2	21. 1	A3	A1	Sheep
26. 1	4. 1	A3	D8	Tiger	13. 2	22. 1	A3	B2	Deer
27. 1	5. 1	A3	E9	Leopard	14. 2	23. 1	A3	C3	Horse
28. 1	6. 1	A3	F10	Griffon	15. 2	24. 1	A3	D4	Stag
29. 1	7. 1	A3	G11	Ox	16. 2	25. 1	A3	E5	Serpent
30. 1	8. 1	A3	H12	Bat	17. 2	26. 1	A3	F6	Earthworm
31. 1	9. 1	A3	J1	Rat	18. 2	27. 1	A3	G7	Crocodile
1. 2	10. 1	A3	K2	Swallow	19. 2	28. 1	A3	H8	Dragon
2. 2	11. 1	A3	A3	Pig	20. 2	29. 1	A3	J9	Badger
3. 2	12. 1	A3	B4	Porcupine	21. 2	1. 2	B4	K10	Hare
4. 2	13. 1	A3	C5	Wolf	22. 2	2. 2	B4	A11	Fox
5. 2	14. 1	A3	D6	Dog	23. 2	3. 2	B4	B12	Tiger
6. 2	15. 1	A3	E7	Pheasant	24. 2	4. 2	B4	C1	Leopard
7. 2	16. 1	A3	F8	Cock	25. 2	5. 2	B4	D2	Griffon
8. 2	17. 1	A3	G9	Crow	26. 2	6. 2	B4	E3	Ox
9. 2	18. 1	A3	H10	Monkey	27. 2	7. 2	B4	F4	Bat

Solar date	Lunar date	Month HS/EB	Day HS/EB	Constellation
28. 2	8. 2	B4	G5	Rat
1. 3	9. 2	B4	H6	Swallow
2. 3	10. 2	B4	J7	Pig
3. 3	11. 2	B4	K8	Porcupine
4. 3	12. 2	B4	A9	Wolf
5. 3	13. 2	B4	B10	Dog
6. 3	14. 2	B4	C11	Pheasant
7. 3	15. 2	B4	D12	Cock
8. 3	16. 2	B4	E1	Crow
9. 3	17. 2	B4	F2	Monkey
10. 3	18. 2	B4	G3	Gibbon
11. 3	19. 2	B4	H4	Tapir
12. 3	20. 2	B4	J5	Sheep
13. 3	21. 2	B4	K6	Deer
14. 3	22. 2	B4	A7	Horse
15. 3	23. 2	B4	B8	Stag
16. 3	24. 2	B4	C9	Serpent
17. 3	25. 2	B4	D10	Earthworm
18. 3	26. 2	B4	E11	Crocodile
19. 3	27. 2	B4	F12	Dragon
20. 3	28. 2	B4	G1	Badger
21. 3	29. 2	B4	H2	Hare
22. 3	30. 2	B4	J3	Fox
23. 3	1. 3	C5	K4	Tiger
24. 3	2. 3	C5	A5	Leopard
25. 3	3. 3	C5	B6	Griffon
26. 3	4. 3	C5	C7	Ox
27. 3	5. 3	C5	D8	Bat
28. 3	6. 3	C5	E9	Rat
29. 3	7. 3	C5	F10	Swallow
30. 3	8. 3	C5	G11	Pig
31. 3	9. 3	C5	H12	Porcupine
1. 4	10. 3	C5	J1	Wolf
2. 4	11. 3	C5	K2	Dog
3. 4	12. 3	C5	A3	Pheasant
4. 4	13. 3	C5	B4	Cock
5. 4	14. 3	C5	C5	Crow
6. 4	15. 3	C5	D6	Monkey
7. 4	16. 3	C5	E7	Gibbon
8. 4	17. 3	C5	F8	Tapir
9. 4	18. 3	C5	G9	Sheep
10. 4	19. 3	C5	H10	Deer
11. 4	20. 3	C5	J11	Horse
12. 4	21. 3	C5	K12	Stag
13. 4	22. 3	C5	A1	Serpent
14. 4	23. 3	C5	B2	Earthworm
15. 4	24. 3	C5	C3	Crocodile
16. 4	25. 3	C5	D4	Dragon
17. 4	26. 3	C5	E5	Badger
18. 4	27. 3	C5	F6	Hare
19. 4	28. 3	C5	G7	Fox
20. 4	29. 3	C5	H8	Tiger
21. 4	30. 3	C5	J9	Leopard
22. 4	*1. 3*	*C5*	K10	Griffon
23. 4	*2. 3*	*C5*	A11	Ox
24. 4	*3. 3*	*C5*	B12	Bat
25. 4	*4. 3*	*C5*	C1	Rat
26. 4	*5. 3*	*C5*	D2	Swallow
27. 4	*6. 3*	*C5*	E3	Pig
28. 4	*7. 3*	*C5*	F4	Porcupine
29. 4	*8. 3*	*C5*	G5	Wolf
30. 4	*9. 3*	*C5*	H6	Dog
1. 5	*10. 3*	*C5*	J7	Pheasant
2. 5	*11. 3*	*C5*	K8	Cock
3. 5	*12. 3*	*C5*	A9	Crow
4. 5	*13. 3*	*C5*	B10	Monkey
5. 5	*14. 3*	*C5*	C11	Gibbon
6. 5	*15. 3*	*C5*	D12	Tapir
7. 5	*16. 3*	*C5*	E1	Sheep
8. 5	*17. 3*	*C5*	F2	Deer
9. 5	*18. 3*	*C5*	G3	Horse
10. 5	*19. 3*	*C5*	H4	Stag
11. 5	*20. 3*	*C5*	J5	Serpent
12. 5	*21. 3*	*C5*	K6	Earthworm
13. 5	*22. 3*	*C5*	A7	Crocodile
14. 5	*23. 3*	*C5*	B8	Dragon
15. 5	*24. 3*	*C5*	C9	Badger
16. 5	*25. 3*	*C5*	D10	Hare
17. 5	*26. 3*	*C5*	E11	Fox
18. 5	*27. 3*	*C5*	F12	Tiger
19. 5	*28. 3*	*C5*	G1	Leopard
20. 5	*29. 3*	*C5*	H2	Griffon
21. 5	1. 4	D6	J3	Ox
22. 5	2. 4	D6	K4	Bat
23. 5	3. 4	D6	A5	Rat
24. 5	4. 4	D6	B6	Swallow
25. 5	5. 4	D6	C7	Pig
26. 5	6. 4	D6	D8	Porcupine
27. 5	7. 4	D6	E9	Wolf
28. 5	8. 4	D6	F10	Dog
29. 5	9. 4	D6	G11	Pheasant
30. 5	10. 4	D6	H12	Cock
31. 5	11. 4	D6	J1	Crow
1. 6	12. 4	D6	K2	Monkey
2. 6	13. 4	D6	A3	Gibbon
3. 6	14. 4	D6	B4	Tapir
4. 6	15. 4	D6	C5	Sheep
5. 6	16. 4	D6	D6	Deer
6. 6	17. 4	D6	E7	Horse
7. 6	18. 4	D6	F8	Stag
8. 6	19. 4	D6	G9	Serpent
9. 6	20. 4	D6	H10	Earthworm
10. 6	21. 4	D6	J11	Crocodile
11. 6	22. 4	D6	K12	Dragon
12. 6	23. 4	D6	A1	Badger
13. 6	24. 4	D6	B2	Hare
14. 6	25. 4	D6	C3	Fox
15. 6	26. 4	D6	D4	Tiger
16. 6	27. 4	D6	E5	Leopard
17. 6	28. 4	D6	F6	Griffon
18. 6	29. 4	D6	G7	Ox
19. 6	30. 4	D6	H8	Bat
20. 6	1. 5	E7	J9	Rat
21. 6	2. 5	E7	K10	Swallow
22. 6	3. 5	E7	A11	Pig
23. 6	4. 5	E7	B12	Porcupine
24. 6	5. 5	E7	C1	Wolf
25. 6	6. 5	E7	D2	Dog
26. 6	7. 5	E7	E3	Pheasant
27. 6	8. 5	E7	F4	Cock
28. 6	9. 5	E7	G5	Crow
29. 6	10. 5	E7	H6	Monkey
30. 6	11. 5	E7	J7	Gibbon
1. 7	12. 5	E7	K8	Tapir
2. 7	13. 5	E7	A9	Sheep
3. 7	14. 5	E7	B10	Deer
4. 7	15. 5	E7	C11	Horse
5. 7	16. 5	E7	D12	Stag
6. 7	17. 5	E7	E1	Serpent
7. 7	18. 5	E7	F2	Earthworm
8. 7	19. 5	E7	G3	Crocodile
9. 7	20. 5	E7	H4	Dragon
10. 7	21. 5	E7	J5	Badger
11. 7	22. 5	E7	K6	Hare
12. 7	23. 5	E7	A7	Fox
13. 7	24. 5	E7	B8	Tiger
14. 7	25. 5	E7	C9	Leopard
15. 7	26. 5	E7	D10	Griffon
16. 7	27. 5	E7	E11	Ox
17. 7	28. 5	E7	F12	Bat
18. 7	29. 5	E7	G1	Rat
19. 7	1. 6	F8	H2	Swallow
20. 7	2. 6	F8	J3	Pig
21. 7	3. 6	F8	K4	Porcupine
22. 7	4. 6	F8	A5	Wolf
23. 7	5. 6	F8	B6	Dog

Solar date	Lunar date	Month HS/EB	Day HS/EB	Constellation	Solar date	Lunar date	Month HS/EB	Day HS/EB	Constellation
24. 7	6. 6	F8	C7	Pheasant	5.10	20. 8	H10	F8	Tiger
25. 7	7. 6	F8	D8	Cock	6.10	21. 8	H10	G9	Leopard
26. 7	8. 6	F8	E9	Crow	7.10	22. 8	H10	H10	Griffon
27. 7	9. 6	F8	F10	Monkey	8.10	23. 8	H10	J11	Ox
28. 7	10. 6	F8	G11	Gibbon	9.10	24. 8	H10	K12	Bat
29. 7	11. 6	F8	H12	Tapir	10.10	25. 8	H10	A1	Rat
30. 7	12. 6	F8	J1	Sheep	11.10	26. 8	H10	B2	Swallow
31. 7	13. 6	F8	K2	Deer	12.10	27. 8	H10	C3	Pig
1. 8	14. 6	F8	A3	Horse	13.10	28. 8	H10	D4	Porcupine
2. 8	15. 6	F8	B4	Stag	14.10	29. 8	H10	E5	Wolf
3. 8	16. 6	F8	C5	Serpent	15.10	1. 9	J11	F6	Dog
4. 8	17. 6	F8	D6	Earthworm	16.10	2. 9	J11	G7	Pheasant
5. 8	18. 6	F8	E7	Crocodile	17.10	3. 9	J11	H8	Cock
6. 8	19. 6	F8	F8	Dragon	18.10	4. 9	J11	J9	Crow
7. 8	20. 6	F8	G9	Badger	19.10	5. 9	J11	K10	Monkey
8. 8	21. 6	F8	H10	Hare	20.10	6. 9	J11	A11	Gibbon
9. 8	22. 6	F8	J11	Fox	21.10	7. 9	J11	B12	Tapir
10. 8	23. 6	F8	K12	Tiger	22.10	8. 9	J11	C1	Sheep
11. 8	24. 6	F8	A1	Leopard	23.10	9. 9	J11	D2	Deer
12. 8	25. 6	F8	B2	Griffon	24.10	10. 9	J11	E3	Horse
13. 8	26. 6	F8	C3	Ox	25.10	11. 9	J11	F4	Stag
14. 8	27. 6	F8	D4	Bat	26.10	12. 9	J11	G5	Serpent
15. 8	28. 6	F8	E5	Rat	27.10	13. 9	J11	H6	Earthworm
16. 8	29. 6	F8	F6	Swallow	28.10	14. 9	J11	J7	Crocodile
17. 8	30. 6	F8	G7	Pig	29.10	15. 9	J11	K8	Dragon
18. 8	1. 7	G9	H8	Porcupine	30.10	16. 9	J11	A9	Badger
19. 8	2. 7	G9	J9	Wolf	31.10	17. 9	J11	B10	Hare
20. 8	3. 7	G9	K10	Dog	1.11	18. 9	J11	C11	Fox
21. 8	4. 7	G9	A11	Pheasant	2.11	19. 9	J11	D12	Tiger
22. 8	5. 7	G9	B12	Cock	3.11	20. 9	J11	E1	Leopard
23. 8	6. 7	G9	C1	Crow	4.11	21. 9	J11	F2	Griffon
24. 8	7. 7	G9	D2	Monkey	5.11	22. 9	J11	G3	Ox
25. 8	8. 7	G9	E3	Gibbon	6.11	23. 9	J11	H4	Bat
26. 8	9. 7	G9	F4	Tapir	7.11	24. 9	J11	J5	Rat
27. 8	10. 7	G9	G5	Sheep	8.11	25. 9	J11	K6	Swallow
28. 8	11. 7	G9	H6	Deer	9.11	26. 9	J11	A7	Pig
29. 8	12. 7	G9	J7	Horse	10.11	27. 9	J11	B8	Porcupine
30. 8	13. 7	G9	K8	Stag	11.11	28. 9	J11	C9	Wolf
31. 8	14. 7	G9	A9	Serpent	12.11	29. 9	J11	D10	Dog
1. 9	15. 7	G9	B10	Earthworm	13.11	30. 9	J11	E11	Pheasant
2. 9	16. 7	G9	C11	Crocodile	14.11	1.10	K12	F12	Cock
3. 9	17. 7	G9	D12	Dragon	15.11	2.10	K12	G1	Crow
4. 9	18. 7	G9	E1	Badger	16.11	3.10	K12	H2	Monkey
5. 9	19. 7	G9	F2	Hare	17.11	4.10	K12	J3	Gibbon
6. 9	20. 7	G9	G3	Fox	18.11	5.10	K12	K4	Tapir
7. 9	21. 7	G9	H4	Tiger	19.11	6.10	K12	A5	Sheep
8. 9	22. 7	G9	J5	Leopard	20.11	7.10	K12	B6	Deer
9. 9	23. 7	G9	K6	Griffon	21.11	8.10	K12	C7	Horse
10. 9	24. 7	G9	A7	Ox	22.11	9.10	K12	D8	Stag
11. 9	25. 7	G9	B8	Bat	23.11	10.10	K12	E9	Serpent
12. 9	26. 7	G9	C9	Rat	24.11	11.10	K12	F10	Earthworm
13. 9	27. 7	G9	D10	Swallow	25.11	12.10	K12	G11	Crocodile
14. 9	28. 7	G9	E11	Pig	26.11	13.10	K12	H12	Dragon
15. 9	29. 7	G9	F12	Porcupine	27.11	14.10	K12	J1	Badger
16. 9	1. 8	H10	G1	Wolf	28.11	15.10	K12	K2	Hare
17. 9	2. 8	H10	H2	Dog	29.11	16.10	K12	A3	Fox
18. 9	3. 8	H10	J3	Pheasant	30.11	17.10	K12	B4	Tiger
19. 9	4. 8	H10	K4	Cock	1.12	18.10	K12	C5	Leopard
20. 9	5. 8	H10	A5	Crow	2.12	19.10	K12	D6	Griffon
21. 9	6. 8	H10	B6	Monkey	3.12	20.10	K12	E7	Ox
22. 9	7. 8	H10	C7	Gibbon	4.12	21.10	K12	F8	Bat
23. 9	8. 8	H10	D8	Tapir	5.12	22.10	K12	G9	Rat
24. 9	9. 8	H10	E9	Sheep	6.12	23.10	K12	H10	Swallow
25. 9	10. 8	H10	F10	Deer	7.12	24.10	K12	J11	Pig
26. 9	11. 8	H10	G11	Horse	8.12	25.10	K12	K12	Porcupine
27. 9	12. 8	H10	H12	Stag	9.12	26.10	K12	A1	Wolf
28. 9	13. 8	H10	J1	Serpent	10.12	27.10	K12	B2	Dog
29. 9	14. 8	H10	K2	Earthworm	11.12	28.10	K12	C3	Pheasant
30. 9	15. 8	H10	A3	Crocodile	12.12	29.10	K12	D4	Cock
1.10	16. 8	H10	B4	Dragon	13.12	1.11	A1	E5	Crow
2.10	17. 8	H10	C5	Badger	14.12	2.11	A1	F6	Monkey
3.10	18. 8	H10	D6	Hare	15.12	3.11	A1	G7	Gibbon
4.10	19. 8	H10	E7	Fox	16.12	4.11	A1	H8	Tapir

Solar date	Lunar date	Month HS/EB	Day HS/EB	Constellation
17.12	5.11	A1	J9	Sheep
18.12	6.11	A1	K10	Deer
19.12	7.11	A1	A11	Horse
20.12	8.11	A1	B12	Stag
21.12	9.11	A1	C1	Serpent
22.12	10.11	A1	D2	Earthworm
23.12	11.11	A1	E3	Crocodile
24.12	12.11	A1	F4	Dragon
25.12	13.11	A1	G5	Badger
26.12	14.11	A1	H6	Hare
27.12	15.11	A1	J7	Fox
28.12	16.11	A1	K8	Tiger
29.12	17.11	A1	A9	Leopard
30.12	18.11	A1	B10	Griffon
31.12	19.11	A1	C11	Ox
1994				
1. 1	20.11	A1	D12	Bat
2. 1	21.11	A1	E1	Rat
3. 1	22.11	A1	F2	Swallow
4. 1	23.11	A1	G3	Pig
5. 1	24.11	A1	H4	Porcupine
6. 1	25.11	A1	J5	Wolf
7. 1	26.11	A1	K6	Dog
8. 1	27.11	A1	A7	Pheasant
9. 1	28.11	A1	B8	Cock
10. 1	29.11	A1	C9	Crow
11. 1	30.11	A1	D10	Monkey
12. 1	1.12	B2	E11	Gibbon
13. 1	2.12	B2	F12	Tapir
14. 1	3.12	B2	G1	Sheep
15. 1	4.12	B2	H2	Deer
16. 1	5.12	B2	J3	Horse
17. 1	6.12	B2	K4	Stag
18. 1	7.12	B2	A5	Serpent
19. 1	8.12	B2	B6	Earthworm
20. 1	9.12	B2	C7	Crocodile
21. 1	10.12	B2	D8	Dragon
22. 1	11.12	B2	E9	Badger
23. 1	12.12	B2	F10	Hare
24. 1	13.12	B2	G11	Fox
25. 1	14.12	B2	H12	Tiger
26. 1	15.12	B2	J1	Leopard
27. 1	16.12	B2	K2	Griffon
28. 1	17.12	B2	A3	Ox
29. 1	18.12	B2	B4	Bat
30. 1	19.12	B2	C5	Rat
31. 1	20.12	B2	D6	Swallow
1. 2	21.12	B2	E7	Pig
2. 2	22.12	B2	F8	Porcupine
3. 2	23.12	B2	G9	Wolf
4. 2	24.12	B2	H10	Dog
5. 2	25.12	B2	J11	Pheasant
6. 2	26.12	B2	K12	Cock
7. 2	27.12	B2	A1	Crow
8. 2	28.12	B2	B2	Monkey
9. 2	29.12	B2	C3	Gibbon

CHIA HSÜ YEAR

Solar date	Lunar date	Month HS/EB	Day HS/EB	Constellation
10. 2	1. 1	C3	D4	Tapir
11. 2	2. 1	C3	E5	Sheep
12. 2	3. 1	C3	F6	Deer
13. 2	4. 1	C3	G7	Horse
14. 2	5. 1	C3	H8	Stag
15. 2	6. 1	C3	J9	Serpent
16. 2	7. 1	C3	K10	Earthworm
17. 2	8. 1	C3	A11	Crocodile
18. 2	9. 1	C3	B12	Dragon
19. 2	10. 1	C3	C1	Badger
20. 2	11. 1	C3	D2	Hare
21. 2	12. 1	C3	E3	Fox
22. 2	13. 1	C3	F4	Tiger
23. 2	14. 1	C3	G5	Leopard
24. 2	15. 1	C3	H6	Griffon
25. 2	16. 1	C3	J7	Ox
26. 2	17. 1	C3	K8	Bat
27. 2	18. 1	C3	A9	Rat
28. 2	19. 1	C3	B10	Swallow
1. 3	20. 1	C3	C11	Pig
2. 3	21. 1	C3	D12	Porcupine
3. 3	22. 1	C3	E1	Wolf
4. 3	23. 1	C3	F2	Dog
5. 3	24. 1	C3	G3	Pheasant
6. 3	25. 1	C3	H4	Cock
7. 3	26. 1	C3	J5	Crow
8. 3	27. 1	C3	K6	Monkey
9. 3	28. 1	C3	A7	Gibbon
10. 3	29. 1	C3	B8	Tapir
11. 3	30. 1	C3	C9	Sheep
12. 3	1. 2	D4	D10	Deer
13. 3	2. 2	D4	E11	Horse
14. 3	3. 2	D4	F12	Stag
15. 3	4. 2	D4	G1	Serpent
16. 3	5. 2	D4	H2	Earthworm
17. 3	6. 2	D4	J3	Crocodile
18. 3	7. 2	D4	K4	Dragon
19. 3	8. 2	D4	A5	Badger
20. 3	9. 2	D4	B6	Hare
21. 3	10. 2	D4	C7	Fox
22. 3	11. 2	D4	D8	Tiger
23. 3	12. 2	D4	E9	Leopard
24. 3	13. 2	D4	F10	Griffon
25. 3	14. 2	D4	G11	Ox
26. 3	15. 2	D4	H12	Bat
27. 3	16. 2	D4	J1	Rat
28. 3	17. 2	D4	K2	Swallow
29. 3	18. 2	D4	A3	Pig
30. 3	19. 2	D4	B4	Porcupine
31. 3	20. 2	D4	C5	Wolf
1. 4	21. 2	D4	D6	Dog
2. 4	22. 2	D4	E7	Pheasant
3. 4	23. 2	D4	F8	Cock
4. 4	24. 2	D4	G9	Crow
5. 4	25. 2	D4	H10	Monkey
6. 4	26. 2	D4	J11	Gibbon
7. 4	27. 2	D4	K12	Tapir
8. 4	28. 2	D4	A1	Sheep
9. 4	29. 2	D4	B2	Deer
10. 4	30. 2	D4	C3	Horse
11. 4	1. 3	E5	D4	Stag
12. 4	2. 3	E5	E5	Serpent
13. 4	3. 3	E5	F6	Earthworm
14. 4	4. 3	E5	G7	Crocodile
15. 4	5. 3	E5	H8	Dragon
16. 4	6. 3	E5	J9	Badger
17. 4	7. 3	E5	K10	Hare
18. 4	8. 3	E5	A11	Fox
19. 4	9. 3	E5	B12	Tiger
20. 4	10. 3	E5	C1	Leopard
21. 4	11. 3	E5	D2	Griffon
22. 4	12. 3	E5	E3	Ox
23. 4	13. 3	E5	F4	Bat
24. 4	14. 3	E5	G5	Rat
25. 4	15. 3	E5	H6	Swallow
26. 4	16. 3	E5	J7	Pig
27. 4	17. 3	E5	K8	Porcupine
28. 4	18. 3	E5	A9	Wolf

Solar date	Lunar date	Month HS/EB	Day HS/EB	Constellation	Solar date	Lunar date	Month HS/EB	Day HS/EB	Constellation
29. 4	19. 3	E5	B10	Dog	11. 7	3. 6	H8	E11	Fox
30. 4	20. 3	E5	C11	Pheasant	12. 7	4. 6	H8	F12	Tiger
1. 5	21. 3	E5	D12	Cock	13. 7	5. 6	H8	G1	Leopard
2. 5	22. 3	E5	E1	Crow	14. 7	6. 6	H8	H2	Griffon
3. 5	23. 3	E5	F2	Monkey	15. 7	7. 6	H8	J3	Ox
4. 5	24. 3	E5	G3	Gibbon	16. 7	8. 6	H8	K4	Bat
5. 5	25. 3	E5	H4	Tapir	17. 7	9. 6	H8	A5	Rat
6. 5	26. 3	E5	J5	Sheep	18. 7	10. 6	H8	B6	Swallow
7. 5	27. 3	E5	K6	Deer	19. 7	11. 6	H8	C7	Pig
8. 5	28. 3	E5	A7	Horse	20. 7	12. 6	H8	D8	Porcupine
9. 5	29. 3	E5	B8	Stag	21. 7	13. 6	H8	E9	Wolf
10. 5	30. 3	E5	C9	Serpent	22. 7	14. 6	H8	F10	Dog
11. 5	1. 4	F6	D10	Earthworm	23. 7	15. 6	H8	G11	Pheasant
12. 5	2. 4	F6	E11	Crocodile	24. 7	16. 6	H8	H12	Cock
13. 5	3. 4	F6	F12	Dragon	25. 7	17. 6	H8	J1	Crow
14. 5	4. 4	F6	G1	Badger	26. 7	18. 6	H8	K2	Monkey
15. 5	5. 4	F6	H2	Hare	27. 7	19. 6	H8	A3	Gibbon
16. 5	6. 4	F6	J3	Fox	28. 7	20. 6	H8	B4	Tapir
17. 5	7. 4	F6	K4	Tiger	29. 7	21. 6	H8	C5	Sheep
18. 5	8. 4	F6	A5	Leopard	30. 7	22. 6	H8	D6	Deer
19. 5	9. 4	F6	B6	Griffon	31. 7	23. 6	H8	E7	Horse
20. 5	10. 4	F6	C7	Ox	1. 8	24. 6	H8	F8	Stag
21. 5	11. 4	F6	D8	Bat	2. 8	25. 6	H8	G9	Serpent
22. 5	12. 4	F6	E9	Rat	3. 8	26. 6	H8	H10	Earthworm
23. 5	13. 4	F6	F10	Swallow	4. 8	27. 6	H8	J11	Crocodile
24. 5	14. 4	F6	G11	Pig	5. 8	28. 6	H8	K12	Dragon
25. 5	15. 4	F6	H12	Porcupine	6. 8	29. 6	H8	A1	Badger
26. 5	16. 4	F6	J1	Wolf	7. 8	1. 7	J9	B2	Hare
27. 5	17. 4	F6	K2	Dog	8. 8	2. 7	J9	C3	Fox
28. 5	18. 4	F6	A3	Pheasant	9. 8	3. 7	J9	D4	Tiger
29. 5	19. 4	F6	B4	Cock	10. 8	4. 7	J9	E5	Leopard
30. 5	20. 4	F6	C5	Crow	11. 8	5. 7	J9	F6	Griffon
31. 5	21. 4	F6	D6	Monkey	12. 8	6. 7	J9	G7	Ox
1. 6	22. 4	F6	E7	Gibbon	13. 8	7. 7	J9	H8	Bat
2. 6	23. 4	F6	F8	Tapir	14. 8	8. 7	J9	J9	Rat
3. 6	24. 4	F6	G9	Sheep	15. 8	9. 7	J9	K10	Swallow
4. 6	25. 4	F6	H10	Deer	16. 8	10. 7	J9	A11	Pig
5. 6	26. 4	F6	J11	Horse	17. 8	11. 7	J9	B12	Porcupine
6. 6	27. 4	F6	K12	Stag	18. 8	12. 7	J9	C1	Wolf
7. 6	28. 4	F6	A1	Serpent	19. 8	13. 7	J9	D2	Dog
8. 6	29. 4	F6	B2	Earthworm	20. 8	14. 7	J9	E3	Pheasant
9. 6	1. 5	G7	C3	Crocodile	21. 8	15. 7	J9	F4	Cock
10. 6	2. 5	G7	D4	Dragon	22. 8	16. 7	J9	G5	Crow
11. 6	3. 5	G7	E5	Badger	23. 8	17. 7	J9	H6	Monkey
12. 6	4. 5	G7	F6	Hare	24. 8	18. 7	J9	J7	Gibbon
13. 6	5. 5	G7	G7	Fox	25. 8	19. 7	J9	K8	Tapir
14. 6	6. 5	G7	H8	Tiger	26. 8	20. 7	J9	A9	Sheep
15. 6	7. 5	G7	J9	Leopard	27. 8	21. 7	J9	B10	Deer
16. 6	8. 5	G7	K10	Griffon	28. 8	22. 7	J9	C11	Horse
17. 6	9. 5	G7	A11	Ox	29. 8	23. 7	J9	D12	Stag
18. 6	10. 5	G7	B12	Bat	30. 8	24. 7	J9	E1	Serpent
19. 6	11. 5	G7	C1	Rat	31. 8	25. 7	J9	F2	Earthworm
20. 6	12. 5	G7	D2	Swallow	1. 9	26. 7	J9	G3	Crocodile
21. 6	13. 5	G7	E3	Pig	2. 9	27. 7	J9	H4	Dragon
22. 6	14. 5	G7	F4	Porcupine	3. 9	28. 7	J9	J5	Badger
23. 6	15. 5	G7	G5	Wolf	4. 9	29. 7	J9	K6	Hare
24. 6	16. 5	G7	H6	Dog	5. 9	30. 7	J9	A7	Fox
25. 6	17. 5	G7	J7	Pheasant	6. 9	1. 8	K10	B8	Tiger
26. 6	18. 5	G7	K8	Cock	7. 9	2. 8	K10	C9	Leopard
27. 6	19. 5	G7	A9	Crow	8. 9	3. 8	K10	D10	Griffon
28. 6	20. 5	G7	B10	Monkey	9. 9	4. 8	K10	E11	Ox
29. 6	21. 5	G7	C11	Gibbon	10. 9	5. 8	K10	F12	Bat
30. 6	22. 5	G7	D12	Tapir	11. 9	6. 8	K10	G1	Rat
1. 7	23. 5	G7	E1	Sheep	12. 9	7. 8	K10	H2	Swallow
2. 7	24. 5	G7	F2	Deer	13. 9	8. 8	K10	J3	Pig
3. 7	25. 5	G7	G3	Horse	14. 9	9. 8	K10	K4	Porcupine
4. 7	26. 5	G7	H4	Stag	15. 9	10. 8	K10	A5	Wolf
5. 7	27. 5	G7	J5	Serpent	16. 9	11. 8	K10	B6	Dog
6. 7	28. 5	G7	K6	Earthworm	17. 9	12. 8	K10	C7	Pheasant
7. 7	29. 5	G7	A7	Crocodile	18. 9	13. 8	K10	D8	Cock
8. 7	30. 5	G7	B8	Dragon	19. 9	14. 8	K10	E9	Crow
9. 7	1. 6	H8	C9	Badger	20. 9	15. 8	K10	F10	Monkey
10. 7	2. 6	H8	D10	Hare	21. 9	16. 8	K10	G11	Gibbon

Solar date	Lunar date	Month HS/EB	Day HS/EB	Constellation
22. 9	17. 8	K10	H12	Tapir
23. 9	18. 8	K10	J1	Sheep
24. 9	19. 8	K10	K2	Deer
25. 9	20. 8	K10	A3	Horse
26. 9	21. 8	K10	B4	Stag
27. 9	22. 8	K10	C5	Serpent
28. 9	23. 8	K10	D6	Earthworm
29. 9	24. 8	K10	E7	Crocodile
30. 9	25. 8	K10	F8	Dragon
1.10	26. 8	K10	G9	Badger
2.10	27. 8	K10	H10	Hare
3.10	28. 8	K10	J11	Fox
4.10	29. 8	K10	K12	Tiger
5.10	1. 9	A11	A1	Leopard
6.10	2. 9	A11	B2	Griffon
7.10	3. 9	A11	C3	Ox
8.10	4. 9	A11	D4	Bat
9.10	5. 9	A11	E5	Rat
10.10	6. 9	A11	F6	Swallow
11.10	7. 9	A11	G7	Pig
12.10	8. 9	A11	H8	Porcupine
13.10	9. 9	A11	J9	Wolf
14.10	10. 9	A11	K10	Dog
15.10	11. 9	A11	A11	Pheasant
16.10	12. 9	A11	B12	Cock
17.10	13. 9	A11	C1	Crow
18.10	14. 9	A11	D2	Monkey
19.10	15. 9	A11	E3	Gibbon
20.10	16. 9	A11	F4	Tapir
21.10	17. 9	A11	G5	Sheep
22.10	18. 9	A11	H6	Deer
23.10	19. 9	A11	J7	Horse
24.10	20. 9	A11	K8	Stag
25.10	21. 9	A11	A9	Serpent
26.10	22. 9	A11	B10	Earthworm
27.10	23. 9	A11	C11	Crocodile
28.10	24. 9	A11	D12	Dragon
29.10	25. 9	A11	E1	Badger
30.10	26. 9	A11	F2	Hare
31.10	27. 9	A11	G3	Fox
1.11	28. 9	A11	H4	Tiger
2.11	29. 9	A11	J5	Leopard
3.11	1.10	B12	K6	Griffon
4.11	2.10	B12	A7	Ox
5.11	3.10	B12	B8	Bat
6.11	4.10	B12	C9	Rat
7.11	5.10	B12	D10	Swallow
8.11	6.10	B12	E11	Pig
9.11	7.10	B12	F12	Porcupine
10.11	8.10	B12	G1	Wolf
11.11	9.10	B12	H2	Dog
12.11	10.10	B12	J3	Pheasant
13.11	11.10	B12	K4	Cock
14.11	12.10	B12	A5	Crow
15.11	13.10	B12	B6	Monkey
16.11	14.10	B12	C7	Gibbon
17.11	15.10	B12	D8	Tapir
18.11	16.10	B12	E9	Sheep
19.11	17.10	B12	F10	Deer
20.11	18.10	B12	G11	Horse
21.11	19.10	B12	H12	Stag
22.11	20.10	B12	J1	Serpent
23.11	21.10	B12	K2	Earthworm
24.11	22.10	B12	A3	Crocodile
25.11	23.10	B12	B4	Dragon
26.11	24.10	B12	C5	Badger
27.11	25.10	B12	D6	Hare

Solar date	Lunar date	Month HS/EB	Day HS/EB	Constellation
28.11	26.10	B12	E7	Fox
29.11	27.10	B12	F8	Tiger
30.11	28.10	B12	G9	Leopard
1.12	29.10	B12	H10	Griffon
2.12	30.10	B12	J11	Ox
3.12	1.11	C1	K12	Rat
4.12	2.11	C1	A1	Bat
5.12	3.11	C1	B2	Swallow
6.12	4.11	C1	C3	Pig
7.12	5.11	C1	D4	Porcupine
8.12	6.11	C1	E5	Wolf
9.12	7.11	C1	F6	Dog
10.12	8.11	C1	G7	Pheasant
11.12	9.11	C1	H8	Cock
12.12	10.11	C1	J9	Crow
13.12	11.11	C1	K10	Monkey
14.12	12.11	C1	A11	Gibbon
15.12	13.11	C1	B12	Tapir
16.12	14.11	C1	C1	Sheep
17.12	15.11	C1	D2	Deer
18.12	16.11	C1	E3	Horse
19.12	17.11	C1	F4	Stag
20.12	18.11	C1	G5	Serpent
21.12	19.11	C1	H6	Earthworm
22.12	20.11	C1	J7	Crocodile
23.12	21.11	C1	K8	Dragon
24.12	22.11	C1	A9	Badger
25.12	23.11	C1	B10	Hare
26.12	24.11	C1	C11	Fox
27.12	25.11	C1	D12	Tiger
28.12	26.11	C1	E1	Leopard
29.12	27.11	C1	F2	Griffon
30.12	28.11	C1	G3	Ox
31.12	29.11	C1	H4	Bat

1995

Solar date	Lunar date	Month HS/EB	Day HS/EB	Constellation
1. 1	1.12	D2	J5	Rat
2. 1	2.12	D2	K6	Swallow
3. 1	3.12	D2	A7	Pig
4. 1	4.12	D2	B8	Porcupine
5. 1	5.12	D2	C9	Wolf
6. 1	6.12	D2	D10	Dog
7. 1	7.12	D2	E11	Pheasant
8. 1	8.12	D2	F12	Cock
9. 1	9.12	D2	G1	Crow
10. 1	10.12	D2	H2	Monkey
11. 1	11.12	D2	J3	Gibbon
12. 1	12.12	D2	K4	Tapir
13. 1	13.12	D2	A5	Sheep
14. 1	14.12	D2	B6	Deer
15. 1	15.12	D2	C7	Horse
16. 1	16.12	D2	D8	Stag
17. 1	17.12	D2	E9	Serpent
18. 1	18.12	D2	F10	Earthworm
19. 1	19.12	D2	G11	Crocodile
20. 1	20.12	D2	H12	Dragon
21. 1	21.12	D2	J1	Badger
22. 1	22.12	D2	K2	Hare
23. 1	23.12	D2	A3	Fox
24. 1	24.12	D2	B4	Tiger
25. 1	25.12	D2	C5	Leopard
26. 1	26.12	D2	D6	Griffon
27. 1	27.12	D2	E7	Ox
28. 1	28.12	D2	F8	Bat
29. 1	29.12	D2	G9	Rat
30. 1	30.12	D2	H10	Swallow

YI HAI YEAR

Solar date	Lunar date	Month HS/EB	Day HS/EB	Constellation	Solar date	Lunar date	Month HS/EB	Day HS/EB	Constellation
31. 1	1. 1	E3	J11	Pig	12. 4	13. 3	G5	K10	Earthworm
1. 2	2. 1	E3	K12	Porcupine	13. 4	14. 3	G5	A11	Crocodile
2. 2	3. 1	E3	A1	Wolf	14. 4	15. 3	G5	B12	Dragon
3. 2	4. 1	E3	B2	Dog	15. 4	16. 3	G5	C1	Badger
4. 2	5. 1	E3	C3	Pheasant	16. 4	17. 3	G5	D2	Hare
5. 2	6. 1	E3	D4	Cock	17. 4	18. 3	G5	E3	Fox
6. 2	7. 1	E3	E5	Crow	18. 4	19. 3	G5	F4	Tiger
7. 2	8. 1	E3	F6	Monkey	19. 4	20. 3	G5	G5	Leopard
8. 2	9. 1	E3	G7	Gibbon	20. 4	21. 3	G5	H6	Griffon
9. 2	10. 1	E3	H8	Tapir	21. 4	22. 3	G5	J7	Ox
10. 2	11. 1	E3	J9	Sheep	22. 4	23. 3	G5	K8	Bat
11. 2	12. 1	E3	K10	Deer	23. 4	24. 3	G5	A9	Rat
12. 2	13. 1	E3	A11	Horse	24. 4	25. 3	G5	B10	Swallow
13. 2	14. 1	E3	B12	Stag	25. 4	26. 3	G5	C11	Pig
14. 2	15. 1	E3	C1	Serpent	26. 4	27. 3	G5	D12	Porcupine
15. 2	16. 1	E3	D2	Earthworm	27. 4	28. 3	G5	E1	Wolf
16. 2	17. 1	E3	E3	Crocodile	28. 4	29. 3	G5	F2	Dog
17. 2	18. 1	E3	F4	Dragon	29. 4	30. 3	G5	G3	Pheasant
18. 2	19. 1	E3	G5	Badger	30. 4	1. 4	H6	H4	Cock
19. 2	20. 1	E3	H6	Hare	1. 5	2. 4	H6	J5	Crow
20. 2	21. 1	E3	J7	Fox	2. 5	3. 4	H6	K6	Monkey
21. 2	22. 1	E3	K8	Tiger	3. 5	4. 4	H6	A7	Gibbon
22. 2	23. 1	E3	A9	Leopard	4. 5	5. 4	H6	B8	Tapir
23. 2	24. 1	E3	B10	Griffon	5. 5	6. 4	H6	C9	Sheep
24. 2	25. 1	E3	C11	Ox	6. 5	7. 4	H6	D10	Deer
25. 2	26. 1	E3	D12	Bat	7. 5	8. 4	H6	E11	Horse
26. 2	27. 1	E3	E1	Rat	8. 5	9. 4	H6	F12	Stag
27. 2	28. 1	E3	F2	Swallow	9. 5	10. 4	H6	G1	Serpent
28. 2	29. 1	E3	G3	Pig	10. 5	11. 4	H6	H2	Earthworm
1. 3	1. 2	F4	H4	Porcupine	11. 5	12. 4	H6	J3	Crocodile
2. 3	2. 2	F4	J5	Wolf	12. 5	13. 4	H6	K4	Dragon
3. 3	3. 2	F4	K6	Dog	13. 5	14. 4	H6	A5	Badger
4. 3	4. 2	F4	A7	Pheasant	14. 5	15. 4	H6	B6	Hare
5. 3	5. 2	F4	B8	Cock	15. 5	16. 4	H6	C7	Fox
6. 3	6. 2	F4	C9	Crow	16. 5	17. 4	H6	D8	Tiger
7. 3	7. 2	F4	D10	Monkey	17. 5	18. 4	H6	E9	Leopard
8. 3	8. 2	F4	E11	Gibbon	18. 5	19. 4	H6	F10	Griffon
9. 3	9. 2	F4	F12	Tapir	19. 5	20. 4	H6	G11	Ox
10. 3	10. 2	F4	G1	Sheep	20. 5	21. 4	H6	H12	Bat
11. 3	11. 2	F4	H2	Deer	21. 5	22. 4	H6	J1	Rat
12. 3	12. 2	F4	J3	Horse	22. 5	23. 4	H6	K2	Swallow
13. 3	13. 2	F4	K4	Stag	23. 5	24. 4	H6	A3	Pig
14. 3	14. 2	F4	A5	Serpent	24. 5	25. 4	H6	B4	Porcupine
15. 3	15. 2	F4	B6	Earthworm	25. 5	26. 4	H6	C5	Wolf
16. 3	16. 2	F4	C7	Crocodile	26. 5	27. 4	H6	D6	Dog
17. 3	17. 2	F4	D8	Dragon	27. 5	28. 4	H6	E7	Pheasant
18. 3	18. 2	F4	E9	Badger	28. 5	29. 4	H6	F8	Cock
19. 3	19. 2	F4	F10	Hare	29. 5	1. 5	J7	G9	Cock
20. 3	20. 2	F4	G11	Fox	30. 5	2. 5	J7	H10	Monkey
21. 3	21. 2	F4	H12	Tiger	31. 5	3. 5	J7	J11	Gibbon
22. 3	22. 2	F4	J1	Leopard	1. 6	4. 5	J7	K12	Tapir
23. 3	23. 2	F4	K2	Griffon	2. 6	5. 5	J7	A1	Sheep
24. 3	24. 2	F4	A3	Ox	3. 6	6. 5	J7	B2	Deer
25. 3	25. 2	F4	B4	Bat	4. 6	7. 5	J7	C3	Horse
26. 3	26. 2	F4	C5	Rat	5. 6	8. 5	J7	D4	Stag
27. 3	27. 2	F4	D6	Swallow	6. 6	9. 5	J7	E5	Serpent
28. 3	29. 2	F4	E7	Pig	7. 6	10. 5	J7	F6	Earthworm
29. 3	29. 2	F4	F8	Porcupine	8. 6	11. 5	J7	G7	Crocodile
30. 3	30. 2	F4	G9	Wolf	9. 6	12. 5	J7	H8	Dragon
31. 3	1. 3	G5	H10	Dog	10. 6	13. 5	J7	J9	Badger
1. 4	2. 3	G5	J11	Pheasant	11. 6	14. 5	J7	K10	Hare
2. 4	3. 3	G5	K12	Cock	12. 6	15. 5	J7	A11	Fox
3. 4	4. 3	G5	A1	Crow	13. 6	16. 5	J7	B12	Tiger
4. 4	5. 3	G5	B2	Monkey	14. 6	17. 5	J7	C1	Leopard
5. 4	6. 3	G5	C3	Gibbon	15. 6	18. 5	J7	D2	Griffon
6. 4	7. 3	G5	D4	Tapir	16. 6	19. 5	J7	E3	Ox
7. 4	8. 3	G5	E5	Sheep	17. 6	20. 5	J7	F4	Bat
8. 4	9. 3	G5	F6	Deer	18. 6	21. 5	J7	G5	Rat
9. 4	10. 3	G5	G7	Horse	19. 6	22. 5	J7	H6	Swallow
10. 4	11. 3	G5	H8	Stag	20. 6	23. 5	J7	J7	Pig
11. 4	12. 3	G5	J9	Serpent	21. 6	24. 5	J7	K8	Porcupine

Solar date	Lunar date	Month HS/EB	Day HS/EB	Constellation
22. 6	25. 5	J7	A9	Wolf
23. 6	26. 5	J7	B10	Dog
24. 6	27. 5	J7	C11	Pheasant
25. 6	28. 5	J7	D12	Cock
26. 6	29. 5	J7	E1	Crow
27. 6	30. 5	J7	F2	Monkey
28. 6	1. 6	K8	G3	Gibbon
29. 6	2. 6	K8	H4	Tapir
30. 6	3. 6	K8	J5	Sheep
1. 7	4. 6	K8	K6	Deer
2. 7	5. 6	K8	A7	Horse
3. 7	6. 6	K8	B8	Stag
4. 7	7. 6	K8	C9	Serpent
5. 7	8. 6	K8	D10	Earthworm
6. 7	9. 6	K8	E11	Crocodile
7. 7	10. 6	K8	F12	Dragon
8. 7	11. 6	K8	G1	Badger
9. 7	12. 6	K8	H2	Hare
10. 7	13. 6	K8	J3	Fox
11. 7	14. 6	K8	K4	Tiger
12. 7	15. 6	K8	A5	Leopard
13. 7	16. 6	K8	B6	Griffon
14. 7	17. 6	K8	C7	Ox
15. 7	18. 6	K8	D8	Bat
16. 7	19. 6	K8	E9	Rat
17. 7	20. 6	K8	E10	Swallow
18. 7	21. 6	K8	G11	Pig
19. 7	22. 6	K8	H12	Porcupine
20. 7	23. 6	K8	J1	Wolf
21. 7	24. 6	K8	K2	Dog
22. 7	25. 6	K8	A3	Pheasant
23. 7	26. 6	K8	B4	Cock
24. 7	27. 6	K8	C5	Crow
25. 7	28. 6	K8	D6	Monkey
26. 7	29. 6	K8	E7	Gibbon
27. 7	1. 7	A9	F8	Tapir
28. 7	2. 7	A9	G9	Sheep
29. 7	3. 7	A9	H10	Deer
30. 7	4. 7	A9	J11	Horse
31. 7	5. 7	A9	K12	Stag
1. 8	6. 7	A9	A1	Serpent
2. 8	7. 7	A9	B2	Earthworm
3. 8	8. 7	A9	C3	Crocodile
4. 8	9. 7	A9	D4	Dragon
5. 8	10. 7	A9	E5	Badger
6. 8	11. 7	A9	F6	Hare
7. 8	12. 7	A9	G7	Fox
8. 8	13. 7	A9	H8	Tiger
9. 8	14. 7	A9	J9	Leopard
10. 8	15. 7	A9	K10	Griffon
11. 8	16. 7	A9	A11	Ox
12. 8	17. 7	A9	B12	Bat
13. 8	18. 7	A9	C1	Rat
14. 8	19. 7	A9	D2	Swallow
15. 8	20. 7	A9	E3	Pig
16. 8	21. 7	A9	F4	Porcupine
17. 8	22. 7	A9	G5	Wolf
18. 8	23. 7	A9	H6	Dog
19. 8	24. 7	A9	J7	Pheasant
20. 8	25. 7	A9	K8	Cock
21. 8	26. 7	A9	A9	Crow
22. 8	27. 7	A9	B10	Monkey
23. 8	28. 7	A9	C11	Gibbon
24. 8	29. 7	A9	D12	Tapir
25. 8	30. 7	A9	E1	Sheep
26. 8	1. 8	B10	F2	Deer
27. 8	2. 8	B10	G3	Horse
28. 8	3. 8	B10	H4	Stag
29. 8	4. 8	B10	J5	Serpent
30. 8	5. 8	B10	K6	Earthworm
31. 8	6. 8	B10	A7	Crocodile
1. 9	7. 8	B10	B8	Dragon
2. 9	8. 8	B10	C9	Badger
3. 9	9. 8	B10	D10	Hare
4. 9	10. 8	B10	E11	Fox
5. 9	11. 8	B10	F12	Tiger
6. 9	12. 8	B10	G1	Leopard
7. 9	13. 8	B10	H2	Griffon
8. 9	14. 8	B10	J3	Ox
9. 9	15. 8	B10	K4	Bat
10. 9	16. 8	B10	A5	Rat
11. 9	17. 8	B10	B6	Swallow
12. 9	18. 8	B10	C7	Pig
13. 9	19. 8	B10	D8	Porcupine
14. 9	20. 8	B10	E9	Wolf
15. 9	21. 8	B10	F10	Dog
16. 9	22. 8	B10	G11	Pheasant
17. 9	23. 8	B10	H12	Cock
18. 9	24. 8	B10	J1	Crow
19. 9	25. 8	B10	K2	Monkey
20. 9	26. 8	B10	A3	Gibbon
21. 9	27. 8	B10	B4	Tapir
22. 9	28. 8	B10	C5	Sheep
23. 9	29. 8	B10	D6	Deer
24. 9	30. 8	B10	E7	Horse
25. 9	*1. 8*	*B10*	F8	Stag
26. 9	*2. 8*	*B10*	G9	Serpent
27. 9	*3. 8*	*B10*	H10	Earthworm
28. 9	*4. 8*	*B10*	J11	Crocodile
29. 9	*5. 8*	*B10*	K12	Dragon
30. 9	*6. 8*	*B10*	A1	Badger
1.10	*7. 8*	*B10*	B2	Hare
2.10	*8. 8*	*B10*	C3	Fox
3.10	*9. 8*	*B10*	D4	Tiger
4.10	*10. 9*	*B10*	E5	Leopard
5.10	*11. 8*	*B10*	F6	Griffon
6.10	*12. 8*	*B10*	G7	Ox
7.10	*13. 8*	*B10*	H8	Bat
8.10	*14. 8*	*B10*	J9	Rat
9.10	*15. 8*	*B10*	K10	Swallow
10.10	*16. 8*	*B10*	A11	Pig
11.10	*17. 8*	*B10*	B12	Porcupine
12.10	*18. 8*	*B10*	C1	Wolf
13.10	*19. 8*	*B10*	D2	Dog
14.10	*20. 8*	*B10*	E3	Pheasant
15.10	*21. 8*	*B10*	F4	Cock
16.10	*22. 8*	*B10*	G5	Crow
17.10	*23. 8*	*B10*	H6	Monkey
18.10	*24. 8*	*B10*	J7	Gibbon
19.10	*25. 8*	*B10*	K8	Tapir
20.10	*26. 8*	*B10*	A9	Sheep
21.10	*27. 8*	*B10*	B10	Deer
22.10	*28. 8*	*B10*	C11	Horse
23.10	*29. 8*	*B10*	D12	Stag
24.10	1. 9	C11	E1	Serpent
25.10	2. 9	C11	F2	Earthworm
26.10	3. 9	C11	G3	Crocodile
27.10	4. 9	C1	H4	Dragon
28.10	5. 9	C11	J5	Badger
29.10	6. 9	C11	K6	Hare
30.10	7. 9	C11	A7	Fox
31.10	8. 9	C11	B8	Tiger
1.11	9. 9	C11	C9	Leopard
2.11	10. 9	C11	D10	Griffon
3.11	11. 9	C11	E11	Ox
4.11	12. 9	C11	F12	Bat
5.11	13. 9	C11	G1	Rat
6.11	14. 9	C11	H2	Swallow
7.11	15. 9	C11	J3	Pig
8.11	16. 9	C11	K4	Porcupine
9.11	17. 9	C11	A5	Wolf
10.11	18. 9	C11	B6	Dog
11.11	19. 9	C11	C7	Pheasant
12.11	20. 9	C11	D8	Cock
13.11	21. 9	C11	E9	Crow
14.11	22. 9	C11	F10	Monkey

Solar date	Lunar date	Month HS/EB	Day HS/EB	Constellation
15.11	23. 9	C11	G11	Gibbon
16.11	24. 9	C11	H12	Tapir
17.11	25. 9	C11	J1	Sheep
18.11	26. 9	C11	K2	Deer
19.11	27. 9	C11	A3	Horse
20.11	28. 9	C11	B4	Stag
21.11	29. 9	C11	C5	Serpent
22.11	1.10	D12	D6	Earthworm
23.11	2.10	D12	E7	Crocodile
24.11	3.10	D12	F8	Dragon
25.11	4.10	D12	G9	Badger
26.11	5.10	D12	H10	Hare
27.11	6.10	D12	J11	Fox
28.11	7.10	D12	K12	Tiger
29.11	8.10	D12	A1	Leopard
30.11	9.10	D12	B2	Griffon
1.12	10.10	D12	C3	Ox
2.12	11.10	D12	D4	Bat
3.12	12.10	D12	E5	Rat
4.12	13.10	D12	F6	Swallow
5.12	14.10	D12	G7	Pig
6.12	15.10	D12	H8	Porcupine
7.12	16.10	D12	J9	Wolf
8.12	17.10	D12	K10	Dog
9.12	18.10	D12	A11	Pheasant
10.12	19.10	D12	B12	Cock
11.12	20.10	D12	C1	Crow
12.12	21.10	D12	D2	Monkey
13.12	22.10	D12	E3	Gibbon
14.12	23.10	D12	F4	Tapir
15.12	24.10	D12	G5	Sheep
16.12	25.10	D12	H6	Deer
17.12	26.10	D12	J7	Horse
18.12	27.10	D12	K8	Stag
19.12	28.10	D12	A9	Serpent
20.12	29.10	D12	B10	Earthworm
21.12	30.10	D12	C11	Crocodile
22.12	1.11	E1	D12	Dragon
23.12	2.11	E1	E1	Badger
24.12	3.11	E1	F2	Hare
25.12	4.11	E1	G3	Fox
26.12	5.11	E1	H4	Tiger
27.12	6.11	E1	J5	Leopard
28.12	7.11	E1	K6	Griffon
29.12	8.11	E1	A7	Ox
30.12	9.11	E1	B8	Bat
31.12	10.11	E1	C9	Rat
1996				
1. 1	11.11	E1	D10	Swallow
2. 1	12.11	E1	E11	Pig
3. 1	13.11	E1	F12	Porcupine
4. 1	14.11	E1	G1	Wolf
5. 1	15.11	E1	H2	Dog
6. 1	16.11	E1	J3	Pheasant
7. 1	17.11	E1	K4	Cock
8. 1	18.11	E1	A5	Crow
9. 1	19.11	E1	B6	Monkey
10. 1	20.11	E1	C7	Gibbon
11. 1	21.11	E1	D8	Tapir
12. 1	22.11	E1	E9	Sheep
13. 1	23.11	E1	F10	Deer
14. 1	24.11	E1	G11	Horse
15. 1	25.11	E1	H12	Stag
16. 1	26.11	E1	J1	Serpent
17. 1	27.11	E1	K2	Earthworm
18. 1	28.11	E1	A3	Crocodile
19. 1	29.11	E1	B4	Dragon
20. 1	1.12	F2	C5	Badger
21. 1	2.12	F2	D6	Hare
22. 1	3.12	F2	E7	Fox
23. 1	4.12	F2	F8	Tiger
24. 1	5.12	F2	G9	Leopard
25. 1	6.12	F2	H10	Griffon
26. 1	7.12	F2	J11	Ox
27. 1	8.12	F2	K12	Bat
28. 1	9.12	F2	A1	Rat
29. 1	10.12	F2	B2	Swallow
30. 1	11.12	F2	C3	Pig
31. 1	12.12	F2	D4	Porcupine
1. 2	13.12	F2	E5	Wolf
2. 2	14.12	F2	F6	Dog
3. 2	15.12	F2	G7	Pheasant
4. 2	16.12	f2	H8	Cock
5. 2	17.12	F2	J9	Crow
6. 2	18.12	F2	K10	Monkey
7. 2	19.12	F2	A11	Gibbon
8. 2	20.12	F2	B12	Tapir
9. 2	21.12	F2	C1	Sheep
10. 2	22.12	F2	D2	Deer
11. 2	23.12	F2	E3	Horse
12. 2	24.12	F2	F4	Stag
13. 2	25.12	F2	G5	Serpent
14. 2	26.12	F2	H6	Earthworm
15. 2	27.12	F2	J7	Crocodile
16. 2	28.12	F2	K8	Dragon
17. 2	29.12	F2	A9	Badger
18. 2	30.12	F2	B10	Hare

PING TZU YEAR

Solar date	Lunar date	Month HS/EB	Day HS/EB	Constellation
19. 2	1. 1	G3	C11	Fox
20. 2	2. 1	G3	D12	Tiger
21. 2	3. 1	G3	E1	Leopard
22. 2	4. 1	G3	F2	Griffon
23. 2	5. 1	G3	G3	Ox
24. 2	6. 1	G3	H4	Bat
25. 2	7. 1	G3	J5	Rat
26. 2	8. 1	G3	K6	Swallow
27. 2	9. 1	G3	A7	Pig
28. 2	10. 1	G3	B8	Porcupine
29. 2	11. 1	G3	C9	Wolf
1. 3	12. 1	G3	D10	Dog
2. 3	13. 1	G3	E11	Pheasant
3. 3	14. 1	G3	F12	Cock
4. 3	15. 1	G3	G1	Crow
5. 3	16. 1	G3	H2	Monkey
6. 3	17. 1	G3	J3	Gibbon
7. 3	18. 1	G3	K4	Tapir
8. 3	19. 1	G3	A5	Sheep
9. 3	20. 1	G3	B6	Deer
10. 3	21. 1	G3	C7	Horse
11. 3	22. 1	G3	D8	Stag
12. 3	23. 1	G3	E9	Serpent
13. 3	24. 1	G3	F10	Earthworm
14. 3	25. 1	G3	G11	Crocodile
15. 3	26. 1	G3	H12	Dragon
16. 3	27. 1	G3	J1	Badger
17. 3	28. 1	G3	K2	Hare
18. 3	29. 1	G3	A3	Fox
19. 3	1. 2	H4	B4	Tiger
20. 3	2. 2	H4	C5	Leopard
21. 3	3. 2	H4	D6	Griffon
22. 3	4. 2	H4	E7	Ox
23. 3	5. 2	H4	F8	Bat
24. 3	6. 2	H4	G9	Rat
25. 3	7. 2	H4	H10	Swallow

Solar date	Lunar date	Month HS/EB	Day HS/EB	Constellation
26. 3	8. 2	H4	J11	Pig
27. 3	9. 2	H4	K12	Porcupine
28. 3	10. 2	H4	A1	Wolf
29. 3	11. 2	H4	B2	Dog
30. 3	12. 2	H4	C3	Pheasant
31. 3	13. 2	H4	D4	Cock
1. 4	14. 2	H4	E5	Crow
2. 4	15. 2	H4	F6	Monkey
3. 4	16. 2	H4	G7	Gibbon
4. 4	17. 2	H4	H8	Tapir
5. 2	18. 2	H4	J9	Sheep
6. 4	19. 2	H4	K10	Deer
7. 4	21. 2	H4	A11	Horse
8. 4	21. 2	H4	B12	Stag
9. 4	22. 2	H4	C1	Serpent
10. 4	23. 2	H4	D2	Earthworm
11. 4	24. 2	H4	E3	Crocodile
12. 4	25. 2	H4	F4	Dragon
13. 4	26. 2	H4	G5	Badger
14. 4	27. 2	H4	H6	Hare
15. 4	28. 2	H4	J7	Fox
16. 4	29. 2	H4	K8	Tiger
17. 4	30. 2	H4	A9	Leopard
18. 4	1. 3	J5	B10	Griffon
19. 4	2. 3	J5	C11	Ox
20. 4	3. 3	J5	D12	Bat
21. 4	4. 3	J5	E1	Rat
22. 4	5. 3	J5	F2	Swallow
23. 4	6. 3	J5	G3	Pig
24. 4	7. 3	J5	H4	Porcupine
25. 4	8. 3	J5	J5	Wolf
26. 4	9. 3	J5	K6	Dog
27. 4	10. 3	J5	A7	Pheasant
28. 4	11. 3	J5	B8	Cock
29. 4	12. 3	J5	C9	Crow
30. 4	13. 3	J5	D10	Monkey
1. 5	14. 3	J5	E11	Gibbon
2. 5	15. 3	J5	F12	Tapir
3. 5	16. 3	J5	G1	Sheep
4. 5	17. 3	J5	H2	Deer
5. 5	18. 3	J5	J3	Horse
6. 5	19. 3	J5	K4	Stag
7. 5	20. 3	J5	A5	Serpent
8. 5	21. 3	J5	B6	Earthworm
9. 5	22. 3	J5	C7	Crocodile
10. 5	23. 3	J5	D8	Dragon
11. 5	24. 3	J5	E9	Badger
12. 5	25. 3	J5	F10	Hare
13. 5	26. 3	J5	G11	Fox
14. 5	27. 3	J5	H12	Tiger
15. 5	28. 3	J5	J1	Leopard
16. 5	29. 3	J5	K2	Griffon
17. 5	1. 4	K6	A3	Ox
18. 5	2. 4	K6	B4	Bat
19. 5	3. 4	K6	C5	Rat
20. 5	4. 4	K6	D6	Swallow
21. 5	5. 4	K6	E7	Pig
22. 5	6. 4	K6	F8	Porcupine
23. 5	7. 4	K6	G9	Wolf
24. 5	8. 4	K6	H10	Dog
25. 5	9. 4	K6	J11	Pheasant
26. 5	10. 4	K6	K12	Cock
27. 5	11. 4	K6	A1	Crow
28. 5	12. 4	K6	B2	Monkey
29. 5	13. 4	K6	C3	Gibbon
30. 5	14. 4	K6	D4	Tapir
31. 5	15. 4	K6	E5	Sheep
1. 6	16. 4	K6	F6	Deer
2. 6	17. 4	K6	G7	Horse
3. 6	18. 4	K6	H8	Stag
4. 6	19. 4	K6	J9	Serpent
5. 6	20. 4	K6	K10	Earthworm
6. 6	21. 4	K6	A11	Crocodile
7. 6	22. 4	K6	B12	Dragon
8. 6	23. 4	K6	C1	Badger
9. 6	24. 4	K6	D2	Hare
10. 6	25. 4	K6	E3	Fox
11. 6	26. 4	K6	F4	Tiger
12. 6	27. 4	K6	G5	Leopard
13. 6	28. 4	K6	H6	Griffon
14. 6	29. 4	K6	J7	Ox
15. 6	30. 4	K6	K8	Bat
16. 6	1. 5	A7	A9	Rat
17. 6	2. 5	A7	B10	Swallow
18. 6	3. 5	A7	C11	Pig
19. 6	4. 5	A7	D12	Porcupine
20. 6	5. 5	A7	E1	Wolf
21. 6	6. 5	A7	F2	Dog
22. 6	7. 5	A7	G3	Pheasant
23. 6	8. 5	A7	H4	Cock
24. 6	9. 5	A7	J5	Crow
25. 6	10. 5	A7	K6	Monkey
26. 6	11. 5	A7	A7	Gibbon
27. 6	12. 5	A7	B8	Tapir
28. 6	13. 5	A7	C9	Sheep
29. 6	14. 5	A7	D10	Deer
30. 6	15. 5	A7	E11	Horse
1. 7	16; 5	A7	F12	Stag
2. 7	17. 5	A7	G1	Serpent
3. 7	18. 5	A7	H2	Earthworm
4. 7	19. 5	A7	J3	Crocodile
5. 7	20. 5	A7	K4	Dragon
6. 7	21. 5	A7	A5	Badger
7. 7	22. 5	A7	B6	Hare
8. 7	23. 5	A7	C7	Fox
9. 7	24. 5	A7	D8	Tiger
10. 7	25. 5	A7	E9	Leopard
11. 7	26. 5	A7	F10	Griffon
12. 7	27. 5	A7	G11	Ox
13. 7	28. 5	A7	H12	Bat
14. 7	29. 5	A7	J1	Rat
15. 7	30. 5	A7	K2	Swallow
16. 7	1. 6	B8	A3	Pig
17. 7	2. 6	B8	B4	Porcupine
18. 7	3. 6	B8	C5	Wolf
19. 7	4. 6	B8	D6	Dog
20. 7	5. 6	B8	E7	Pheasant
21. 7	6. 6	B8	F8	Cock
22. 7	7. 6	B8	G9	Crow
23. 7	8. 6	B8	H10	Monkey
24. 7	9. 6	B8	J11	Gibbon
25. 7	10. 6	B8	K12	Tapir
26. 7	11. 6	B8	A1	Sheep
27. 7	12. 6	B8	B2	Deer
28. 7	13. 6	B8	C3	Horse
29. 7	14. 6	B8	D4	Stag
30. 7	15. 6	B8	E5	Serpent
31. 7	16. 6	B8	F6	Earthworm
1. 8	17. 6	B8	G7	Crocodile
2. 8	18. 6	B8	H8	Dragon
3. 8	19. 6	B8	J9	Badger
4. 8	20. 6	B8	K10	Hare
5. 8	21. 6	B8	A11	Fox
6. 8	22. 6	B8	B12	Tiger
7. 8	23. 6	B8	C1	Leopard
8. 8	24. 6	B8	D2	Griffon
9. 8	25. 6	B8	E3	Ox
10. 8	26. 6	B8	F4	Bat
11. 8	27. 6	B8	G5	Rat
12. 8	28. 6	B8	H6	Swallow
13. 8	29. 6	B8	J7	Pig
14. 8	1. 7	C9	K8	Porcupine
15. 8	2. 7	C9	A9	Wolf
16. 8	3. 7	C9	B10	Dog
17. 8	4. 7	C9	C11	Pheasant
18. 8	5. 7	C9	D12	Cock

Solar date	Lunar date	Month HS/EB	Day HS/EB	Constellation	Solar date	Lunar date	Month HS/EB	Day HS/EB	Constellation
19. 8	6. 7	C9	E1	Crow	31.10	20. 9	E11	H2	Griffon
20. 8	7. 7	C9	F2	Monkey	1.11	21. 9	E11	J3	Ox
21. 8	8. 7	C9	G3	Gibbon	2.11	22. 9	E11	K4	Bat
22. 8	9. 7	C9	H4	Tapir	3.11	23. 9	E11	A5	Rat
23. 8	10. 7	C9	J5	Sheep	4.11	24. 9	E11	B6	Swallow
24. 8	11. 7	C9	K6	Deer	5.11	25. 9	E11	C7	Pig
25. 8	12. 7	C9	A7	Horse	6.11	26. 9	E11	D8	Porcupine
26. 8	13. 7	C9	B8	Stag	7.11	27. 9	E11	E9	Wolf
27. 8	14. 7	C9	C9	Serpent	8.11	28. 9	E11	F10	Dog
28. 8	15. 7	C9	D10	Earthworm	9.11	29. 9	E11	G11	Pheasant
29. 8	16. 7	C9	E11	Crocodile	10.11	30. 9	E11	H12	Cock
30. 8	17. 7	C9	F12	Dragon	11.11	1.10	F12	J1	Crow
31. 8	18. 7	C9	G1	Badger	12.11	2.10	F12	K2	Monkey
1. 9	19. 7	C9	H2	Hare	13.11	3.10	F12	A3	Gibbon
2. 9	20. 7	C9	J3	Fox	14.11	4.10	F12	B4	Tapir
3. 9	21. 7	C9	K4	Tiger	15.11	5.10	F12	C5	Sheep
4. 9	22. 7	C9	A5	Leopard	16.11	6.10	F12	D6	Deer
5. 9	23. 7	C9	B6	Griffon	17.11	7.10	F12	E7	Horse
6. 9	24. 7	C9	C7	Ox	18.11	8.10	F12	F8	Stag
7. 9	25. 7	C9	D8	Bat	19.11	9.10	F12	G9	Serpent
8. 9	26. 7	C9	E9	Rat	20.11	10.10	F12	H10	Earthworm
9. 9	27. 7	C9	F10	Swallow	21.11	11.10	F12	J11	Crocodile
10. 9	28. 7	C9	G11	Pig	22.11	12.10	F12	K12	Dragon
11. 9	29. 7	C9	H12	Porcupine	23.11	13.10	F12	A1	Badger
12. 9	30. 7	C9	J1	Wolf	24.11	14.10	F12	B2	Hare
13. 9	1. 8	D10	K2	Dog	25.11	15.10	F12	C3	Fox
14. 9	2. 8	D10	A3	Pheasant	26.11	16.10	F12	D4	Tiger
15. 9	3. 8	D10	B4	Cock	27.11	17.10	F12	E5	Leopard
16. 9	4. 8	D10	C5	Crow	28.11	18.10	F12	F6	Griffon
17. 9	5. 8	D10	D6	Monkey	29.11	19.10	F12	G7	Ox
18. 9	6. 8	D10	E7	Gibbon	30.11	20.10	F12	H8	Bat
19. 9	7. 8	D10	F8	Tapir	1.12	21.10	F12	J9	Rat
20. 9	8. 8	D10	G9	Sheep	2.12	22.10	F12	K10	Swallow
21. 9	9. 8	D10	H10	Deer	3.12	23.10	F12	A11	Pig
22. 9	10. 8	D10	J11	Horse	4.12	24.10	F12	B12	Porcupine
23. 9	11. 8	D10	K12	Stag	5.12	25.10	F12	C1	Wolf
24. 9	12. 8	D10	A1	Serpent	6.12	26.10	F12	D2	Dog
25. 9	13. 8	D10	B2	Earthworm	7.12	27.10	F12	E3	Pheasant
26. 9	14. 8	D10	C3	Crocodile	8.12	28.10	F12	F4	Cock
27. 9	15. 8	D10	D4	Dragon	9.12	29.10	F12	G5	Crow
28. 9	16. 8	D10	E5	Badger	10.12	30.10	F12	H6	Monkey
29. 9	17. 8	D10	F6	Hare	11.12	1.11	G1	J7	Gibbon
30. 9	18. 8	D10	G7	Fox	12.12	2.11	G1	K8	Tapir
1.10	19. 8	D10	H8	Tiger	13.12	3.11	G1	A9	Sheep
2.10	20. 8	D10	J9	Leopard	14.12	4.11	G1	B10	Deer
3.10	21. 8	D10	K10	Griffon	15.12	5.11	G1	C11	Horse
4.10	22. 8	D10	A11	Ox	16.12	6.11	G1	D12	Stag
5.10	23. 8	D10	B12	Bat	17.12	7.11	G1	E1	Serpent
6.10	24. 8	D10	C1	Rat	18.12	8.11	G1	F2	Earthworm
7.10	25. 8	D10	D2	Swallow	19.12	9.11	G1	G3	Crocodile
8.10	26. 8	D10	E3	Pig	20.12	10.11	G1	H4	Dragon
9.10	27. 8	D10	F4	Porcupine	21.12	11.11	G1	J5	Badger
10.10	28. 8	D10	G5	Wolf	22.12	12.11	G1	K6	Hare
11. 0	29. 8	D10	H6	Dog	23.12	13.11	G1	A7	Fox
12.10	1. 9	E11	J7	Pheasant	24.12	14.11	G1	B8	Tiger
13.10	2. 9	E11	K8	Cock	25.12	15.11	G1	C9	Leopard
14.10	3. 9	E11	A9	Crow	26.12	16.11	G1	D10	Griffon
15.10	4. 9	E11	B10	Monkey	27.12	17.11	G1	E11	Ox
16.10	5. 9	E11	C11	Gibbon	28.12	18.11	G1	F12	Bat
17.10	6. 9	E11	D12	Tapir	29.12	19.11	G1	G1	Rat
18.10	7. 9	E11	E1	Sheep	30.12	20.11	G1	H2	Swallow
19.10	8. 9	E11	F2	Deer	31.12	21.11	G1	J3	Pig
20.10	9. 9	E11	G3	Horse					
21.10	10. 9	E11	H4	Stag	**1997**				
22.10	11. 9	E11	J5	Serpent	1. 1	22.11	G1	K4	Porcupine
23.10	12. 9	E11	K6	Earthworm	2. 1	23.11	G1	A5	Wolf
24.10	13. 9	E11	A7	Crocodile	3. 1	24.11	G1	B6	Dog
25.10	14. 9	E11	B8	Dragon	4. 1	25.11	G1	C7	Pheasant
26.10	15. 9	E11	C9	Badger	5. 1	26.11	G1	D8	Cock
27.10	16. 9	E11	D10	Hare	6. 1	27.11	G1	E9	Crow
28.10	17. 9	E11	E11	Fox	7. 1	28.11	G1	F10	Monkey
29.10	18. 9	E11	F12	Tiger	8. 1	29.11	G1	G11	Gibbon
30.10	19. 9	E11	G1	Leopard	9. 1	1.12	H2	H12	Tapir

Solar date	Lunar date	Month HS/EB	Day HS/EB	Constellation	Solar date	Lunar date	Month HS/EB	Day HS/EB	Constellation
10. 1	2.12	H2	J1	Sheep	24. 1	16.12	H2	C3	Ox
11. 1	3.12	H2	K2	Deer	25. 1	17.12	H2	D4	Bat
12. 1	4.12	H2	A3	Horse	26. 1	18.12	H2	E5	Rat
13. 1	5.12	H2	B4	Stag	27. 1	19.12	H2	F6	Swallow
14. 1	6.12	H2	C5	Serpent	28. 1	20.12	H2	G7	Pig
15. 1	7.12	H2	D6	Earthworm	29. 1	21.12	H2	H8	Porcupine
16. 1	8.12	H2	E7	Crocodile	30. 1	22.12	H2	J9	Wolf
17. 1	9.12	H2	F8	Dragon	31. 1	23.12	H2	K10	Dog
18. 1	10.12	H2	G9	Badger	1. 2	24.12	H2	A11	Pheasant
19. 1	11.12	H2	H10	Hare	2. 2	25.12	H2	B12	Cock
20. 1	12.12	H2	J11	Fox	3. 2	26.12	H2	C1	Crow
21. 1	13.12	H2	K12	Tiger	4. 2	27.12	H2	D2	Monkey
22. 1	14.12	H2	A1	Leopard	5. 2	28.12	H2	E3	Gibbon
23. 1	15.12	H2	B2	Griffon	6. 2	29.12	H2	F4	Tapir

TING CH'OU YEAR

Solar date	Lunar date	Month HS/EB	Day HS/EB	Constellation	Solar date	Lunar date	Month HS/EB	Day HS/EB	Constellation
7. 2	1. 1	J3	G5	Sheep	2. 4	25. 2	K4	A11	Gibbon
8. 2	2. 1	J3	H6	Deer	3. 4	26. 2	K4	B12	Tapir
9. 2	3. 1	J3	J7	Horse	4. 4	27. 2	K4	C1	Sheep
10. 2	4. 1	J3	K8	Stag	5. 4	28. 2	K4	D2	Deer
11. 2	5. 1	J3	A9	Serpent	6. 4	29. 2	K4	E3	Horse
12. 2	6. 1	J3	B10	Earthworm	7. 4	1. 3	A5	F4	Stag
13. 2	7. 1	J3	C11	Crocodile	8. 4	2. 3	A5	G5	Serpent
14. 2	8. 1	J3	D12	Dragon	9. 4	3. 3	A5	H6	Earthworm
15. 2	9. 1	J3	E1	Badger	10. 4	4. 3	A5	J7	Crocodile
16. 2	10. 1	J3	F2	Hare	11. 4	5. 3	A5	K8	Dragon
17. 2	11. 1	J3	G3	Fox	12. 4	6. 3	A5	A9	Badger
18. 2	12. 1	J3	H4	Tiger	13. 4	7. 3	A5	B10	Hare
19. 2	13. 1	J3	J5	Leopard	14. 4	8. 3	A5	C11	Fox
20. 2	14. 1	J3	K6	Griffon	15. 4	9. 3	A5	D12	Tiger
21. 2	15. 1	J3	A7	Ox	16. 4	10. 3	A5	E1	Leopard
22. 2	16. 1	J3	B8	Bat	17. 4	11. 3	A5	F2	Griffon
23. 2	17. 1	J3	C9	Rat	18. 4	12. 3	A5	G3	Ox
24. 2	18. 1	J3	D10	Swallow	19. 4	13. 3	A5	H4	Bat
25. 2	19. 1	J3	E11	Pig	20. 4	14. 3	A5	J5	Rat
26. 2	20. 1	J3	F12	Porcupine	21. 4	15. 3	A5	K6	Swallow
27. 2	21. 1	J3	G1	Wolf	22. 4	16. 3	A5	A7	Pig
28. 2	22. 1	J3	H2	Dog	23. 4	17. 3	A5	B8	Porcupine
1. 3	23. 1	J3	J3	Pheasant	24. 4	18. 3	A5	C9	Wolf
2. 3	24. 1	J3	K4	Cock	25. 4	19. 3	A5	D10	Dog
3. 3	25. 1	J3	A5	Crow	26. 4	20. 3	A5	E11	Pheasant
4. 3	26. 1	J3	B6	Monkey	27. 4	21. 3	A5	F12	Cock
5. 3	27. 1	J3	C7	Gibbon	28. 4	22. 3	A5	G1	Crow
6. 3	28. 1	J3	D8	Tapir	29. 4	23. 3	A5	H2	Monkey
7. 3	29. 1	J3	E9	Sheep	30. 4	24. 3	A5	J3	Gibbon
8. 3	30. 1	J3	F10	Deer	1. 5	25. 3	A5	K4	Tapir
9. 3	1. 2	K4	G11	Horse	2. 5	26. 3	A5	A5	Sheep
10. 3	2. 2	K4	H12	Stag	3. 5	27. 3	A5	B6	Deer
11. 3	3. 2	K4	J1	Serpent	4. 5	28. 3	A5	C7	Horse
12. 3	4. 2	K4	K2	Earthworm	5. 5	29. 3	A5	D8	Stag
13. 3	5. 2	K4	A3	Crocodile	6. 5	30. 3	A5	E9	Serpent
14. 3	6. 2	K4	B4	Dragon	7. 5	1. 4	B6	F10	Earthworm
15. 3	7. 2	K4	C5	Badger	8. 5	2. 4	B6	G11	Crocodile
16. 3	8. 2	K4	D6	Hare	9. 5	3. 4	B6	H12	Dragon
17. 3	9. 2	K4	E7	Fox	10. 5	4. 4	B6	J1	Badger
18. 3	10. 2	K4	F8	Tiger	11. 5	5. 4	B6	K2	Hare
19. 3	11. 2	K4	G9	Leopard	12. 5	6. 4	B6	A3	Fox
20. 3	12. 2	K4	H10	Griffon	13. 5	7. 4	B6	B4	Tiger
21. 3	13. 2	K4	J11	Ox	14. 5	8. 4	B6	C5	Leopard
22. 3	14. 2	K4	K12	Bat	15. 5	9. 4	B6	D6	Griffon
23. 3	15. 2	K4	A1	Rat	16. 5	10. 4	B6	E7	Ox
24. 3	16. 2	K4	B2	Swallow	17. 5	11. 4	B6	F8	Bat
25. 3	17. 2	K4	C3	Pig	18. 5	12. 4	B6	G9	Rat
26. 3	18. 2	K4	D4	Porcupine	19. 5	13. 4	B6	H10	Swallow
27. 3	19. 2	K4	E5	Wolf	20. 5	14. 4	B6	J11	Pig
28. 3	20. 2	K4	F6	Dog	21. 5	15. 4	B6	K12	Porcupine
29. 3	21. 2	K4	G7	Pheasant	22. 5	16. 4	B6	A1	Wolf
30. 3	22. 2	K4	H8	Cock	23. 5	17. 4	B6	B2	Dog
31. 3	23. 2	K4	J9	Crow	24. 5	18. 4	B6	C3	Pheasant
1. 4	24. 2	K4	K10	Monkey	25. 5	19. 4	B6	D4	Cock

Solar date	Lunar date	Month HS/EB	Day HS/EB	Constellation	Solar date	Lunar date	Month HS/EB	Day HS/EB	Constellation
26. 5	20. 4	B6	E5	Crow	7. 8	5. 7	E9	H6	Griffon
27. 5	21. 4	B6	F6	Monkey	8. 8	6. 7	E9	J7	Ox
28. 5	22. 4	B6	G7	Gibbon	9. 8	7. 7	E9	K8	Bat
29. 5	23. 4	B6	H8	Tapir	10. 8	8. 7	E9	A9	Rat
30. 5	24. 4	B6	J9	Sheep	11. 8	9. 7	E9	B10	Swallow
31. 5	25. 4	B6	K10	Deer	12. 8	10. 7	E9	C11	Pig
1. 6	26. 4	B6	A11	Horse	13. 8	11. 7	E9	D12	Porcupine
2. 6	27. 4	B6	B12	Stag	14. 8	12. 7	E9	E1	Wolf
3. 6	28. 4	B6	C1	Serpent	15. 8	13. 7	E9	F2	Dog
4. 6	29. 4	B6	D2	Earthworm	16. 8	14. 7	E9	G3	Pheasant
5. 6	1. 5	C7	E3	Crocodile	17. 8	15. 7	E9	H4	Cock
6. 6	2. 5	C7	F4	Dragon	18. 8	16. 7	E9	J5	Crow
7. 6	3. 5	C7	G5	Badger	19. 8	17. 7	E9	K6	Monkey
8. 6	4. 5	C7	H6	Hare	20. 8	18. 7	E9	A7	Gibbon
9. 6	5. 5	C7	J7	Fox	21. 8	19. 7	E9	B8	Tapir
10. 6	6. 5	C7	K8	Tiger	22. 8	20. 7	E9	C9	Sheep
11. 6	7. 5	C7	A9	Leopard	23. 8	21. 7	E9	D10	Deer
12. 6	8. 5	C7	B10	Griffon	24. 8	22. 7	E9	E11	Horse
13. 6	9. 5	C7	C11	Ox	25. 8	23. 7	E9	F12	Stag
14. 6	10. 5	C7	D12	Bat	26. 8	24. 7	E9	G1	Serpent
15. 6	11. 5	C7	E1	Rat	27. 8	25. 7	E9	H2	Earthworm
16. 6	12. 5	C7	F2	Swallow	28. 8	26. 7	E9	J3	Crocodile
17. 6	13. 5	C7	G3	Pig	29. 8	27. 7	E9	K4	Dragon
18. 6	14. 5	C7	H4	Porcupine	30. 8	28. 7	E9	A5	Badger
19. 6	15. 5	C7	J5	Wolf	31. 8	29. 7	E9	B6	Hare
20. 6	16. 5	C7	K6	Dog	1. 9	30. 7	E9	C7	Fox
21. 6	17. 5	C7	A7	Pheasant	2. 9	1. 8	F10	D8	Tiger
22. 6	18. 5	C7	B8	Cock	3. 9	2. 8	F10	E9	Leopard
23. 6	19. 5	C7	C9	Crow	4. 9	3. 8	F10	F10	Griffon
24. 6	20. 5	C7	D10	Monkey	5. 9	4. 8	F10	G11	Ox
25. 6	21. 5	C7	E11	Gibbon	6. 9	5. 8	F10	H12	Bat
26. 6	22. 5	C7	F12	Tapir	7. 9	6. 8	F10	J1	Rat
27. 6	23. 5	C7	G1	Sheep	8. 9	7. 8	F10	K2	Swallow
28. 6	24. 5	C7	H2	Deer	9. 9	8. 8	F10	A3	Pig
29. 6	25. 5	C7	J3	Horse	10. 9	9. 8	F10	B4	Porcupine
30. 6	26. 5	C7	K4	Stag	11. 9	10. 8	F10	C5	Wolf
1. 7	27. 5	C7	A5	Serpent	12. 9	11. 8	F10	D6	Dog
2. 7	28. 5	C7	B6	Earthworm	13. 9	12. 8	F10	E7	Pheasant
3. 7	29. 5	C7	C7	Crocodile	14. 9	13. 8	F10	F8	Cock
4. 7	30. 5	C7	D8	Dragon	15. 9	14. 8	F10	G9	Crow
5. 7	1. 6	D8	E9	Badger	16. 9	15. 8	F10	H10	Monkey
6. 7	2. 6	D8	F10	Hare	17. 9	16. 8	F10	J11	Gibbon
7. 7	3. 6	D8	G11	Fox	18. 9	17. 8	F10	K12	Tapir
8. 7	4. 6	D8	H12	Tiger	19. 9	18. 8	F10	A1	Sheep
9. 7	5. 6	D8	J1	Leopard	20. 9	19. 8	F10	B2	Deer
10. 7	6. 6	D8	K2	Griffon	21. 9	20. 8	F10	C3	Horse
11. 7	7. 6	D8	A3	Ox	22. 9	21. 8	F10	D4	Stag
12. 7	8. 6	D8	B4	Bat	23. 9	22. 8	F10	E5	Serpent
13. 7	9. 6	D8	C5	Rat	24. 9	23. 8	F10	F6	Earthworm
14. 7	10. 6	D8	D6	Swallow	25. 9	24. 8	F10	G7	Crocodile
15. 7	11. 6	D8	E7	Pig	26. 9	25. 8	F10	H8	Dragon
16. 7	12. 6	D8	F8	Porcupine	27. 9	26. 8	F10	J9	Badger
17. 7	13. 6	D8	G9	Wolf	28. 9	27. 8	F10	K10	Hare
18. 7	14. 6	D8	H10	Dog	29. 9	28. 8	F10	A11	Fox
19. 7	15. 6	D8	J11	Pheasant	30. 9	29. 8	F10	B12	Tiger
20. 7	16. 6	D8	K12	Cock	1.10	30. 8	F10	C1	Leopard
21. 7	17. 6	D8	A1	Crow	2.10	1. 9	G11	D2	Griffon
22. 7	18. 6	D8	B2	Monkey	3.10	2. 9	G11	E3	Ox
23. 7	19. 6	D8	C3	Gibbon	4.10	3. 9	G11	F4	Bat
24. 7	20. 6	D8	D4	Tapir	5.10	4. 9	G11	G5	Rat
25. 7	21. 6	D8	E5	Sheep	6.10	5. 9	G11	H6	Swallow
26. 7	22. 6	D8	F6	Deer	7.10	6. 9	G11	J7	Pig
27. 7	23. 6	D8	G7	Horse	8.10	7. 9	G11	K8	Porcupine
28. 7	24. 6	D8	H8	Stag	9.10	8. 9	G11	A9	Wolf
29. 7	25. 6	D8	J9	Serpent	10.10	9. 9	G11	B10	Dog
30. 7	26. 6	D8	K10	Earthworm	11.10	10. 9	G11	C11	Pheasant
31. 7	27. 6	D8	A11	Crocodile	12.10	11. 9	G11	D12	Cock
1. 8	28. 6	D8	B12	Dragon	13.10	12. 9	G11	E1	Crow
2. 8	29. 6	D8	C1	Badger	14.10	13. 9	G11	F2	Monkey
3. 8	1. 7	E9	D2	Hare	15.10	14. 9	G11	G3	Gibbon
4. 8	2. 7	E9	E3	Fox	16.10	15. 9	G11	H4	Tapir
5. 8	3. 7	E9	F4	Tiger	17.10	16. 9	G11	J5	Sheep
6. 8	4. 7	E9	G5	Leopard	18.10	17. 9	G11	K6	Deer

Solar date	Lunar date	Month HS/EB	Day HS/EB	Constellation	Solar date	Lunar date	Month HS/EB	Day HS/EB	Constellation
19.10	18. 9	G11	A7	Horse	10.12	11.11	J1	C11	Gibbon
20.10	19. 9	G11	B8	Stag	11.12	12.11	J1	D12	Tapir
21.10	20. 9	G11	C9	Serpent	12.12	13.11	J1	E1	Sheep
22.10	21. 9	G11	D10	Earthworm	13.12	14.11	J1	F2	Deer
23.10	22. 9	G11	E11	Crocodile	14.12	15.11	J1	G3	Horse
24.10	23. 9	G11	F12	Dragon	15.12	16.11	J1	H4	Stag
25.10	24. 9	G11	G1	Badger	16.12	17.11	J1	J5	Serpent
26.10	25. 9	G11	H2	Hare	17.12	18.11	J1	K6	Earthworm
27.10	26. 9	G11	J3	Fox	18.12	19.11	J1	A7	Crocodile
28.10	27. 9	G11	K4	Tiger	19.12	20.11	J1	B8	Dragon
29.10	28. 9	G11	A5	Leopard	20.12	21.11	J1	C9	Badger
30.10	29. 9	G11	B6	Griffon	21.12	22.11	J1	D10	Hare
31.10	1.10	H12	C7	Ox	22.12	23.11	J1	E11	Fox
1.11	2.10	H12	D8	Rat	23.12	24.11	J1	F12	Tiger
2.11	3.10	H12	E9	Rat	24.12	25.11	J1	G1	Leopard
3.11	4.10	H12	F10	Swallow	25.12	26.11	J1	H2	Griffon
4.11	5.10	H12	G11	Pig	26.12	27.11	J1	J3	Ox
5.11	6.10	H12	H12	Porcupine	27.12	28.11	J1	K4	Bat
6.11	7.10	H12	J1	Wolf	28.12	29.11	J1	A5	Rat
7.11	8.10	H12	K2	Dog	29.12	30.11	J1	B6	Swallow
8.11	9.10	H12	A3	Pheasant	30.12	1.12	K2	C7	Pig
9.11	10.10	H12	B4	Cock	31.12	2.12	K2	D8	Porcupine
10.11	11.10	H12	C5	Crow					
11.11	12.10	H12	D6	Monkey					
12.11	13.10	H12	E7	Gibbon	**1998**				
13.11	14.10	H12	F8	Tapir	1. 1	3.12	K2	E9	Wolf
14.11	15.10	H12	G9	Sheep	2. 1	4.12	K2	F10	Dog
15.11	16.10	H12	H10	Deer	3. 1	5.12	K2	G11	Pheasant
16.11	17.10	H12	J11	Horse	4. 1	6.12	K2	H12	Cock
17.11	18.10	H12	K12	Stag	5. 1	7.12	K2	J1	Crow
18.11	19.10	H12	A1	Serpent	6. 1	8.12	K2	K2	Monkey
19.11	20.10	H12	B2	Earthworm	7. 1	9.12	K2	A3	Gibbon
20.11	21.10	H12	C3	Crocodile	8. 1	10.12	K2	B4	Tapir
21.11	22.10	H12	D4	Dragon	9. 1	11.12	K2	C5	Sheep
22.11	23.10	H12	E5	Badger	10. 1	12.12	K2	D6	Deer
23.11	24.10	H12	F6	Hare	11. 1	13.12	K2	E7	Horse
24.11	25.10	H12	G7	Fox	12. 1	14.12	K2	F8	Stag
25.11	26.10	H12	H8	Tiger	13. 1	15.12	K2	G9	Serpent
26.11	27.10	H12	J9	Leopard	14. 1	16.12	K2	H10	Earthworm
27.11	28.10	H12	K10	Griffon	15. 1	17.12	K2	J11	Crocodile
28.11	29.10	H12	A11	Ox	16. 1	18.12	K2	K12	Dragon
29.11	30.10	H12	B12	Bat	17. 1	19.12	K2	A1	Badger
30.11	1.11	J1	C1	Rat	18. 1	20.12	K2	B2	Hare
1.12	2.11	J1	D2	Swallow	19. 1	21.12	K2	C3	Fox
2.12	3.11	J1	E3	Pig	20. 1	22.12	K2	D4	Tiger
3.12	4.11	J1	F4	Porcupine	21. 1	23.12	K2	E5	Leopard
4.12	5.11	J1	G5	Wolf	22. 1	24.12	K2	F6	Griffon
5.12	6.11	J1	H6	Dog	23. 1	25.12	K2	G7	Ox
6.12	7.11	J1	J7	Pheasant	24. 1	26.12	K2	H8	Bat
7.12	8.11	J1	K8	Cock	25. 1	27.12	K2	J9	Rat
8.12	9.11	J1	A9	Crow	26. 1	28.12	K2	K10	Swallow
9.12	10.11	J1	B10	Monkey	27. 1	29.12	K2	A11	Pig

MOU YIN YEAR

Solar date	Lunar date	Month HS/EB	Day HS/EB	Constellation	Solar date	Lunar date	Month HS/EB	Day HS/EB	Constellation
28. 1	1. 1	A3	B12	Porcupine	13. 2	17. 1	A3	H4	Dragon
29. 1	2. 1	A3	C1	Wolf	14. 2	18. 1	A3	J5	Badger
30. 1	3. 1	A3	D2	Dog	15. 2	19. 1	A3	K6	Hare
31. 1	4. 1	A3	E3	Pheasant	16. 2	20. 1	A3	A7	Fox
1. 2	5. 1	A3	F4	Cock	17. 2	21. 1	A3	B8	Tiger
2. 2	6. 1	A3	G5	Crow	18. 2	22. 1	A3	C9	Leopard
3. 2	7. 1	A3	H6	Monkey	19. 2	23. 1	A3	D10	Griffon
4. 2	8. 1	A3	J7	Gibbon	20. 2	24. 1	A3	E11	Ox
5. 2	9. 1	A3	K8	Tapir	21. 2	25. 1	A3	F12	Bat
6. 2	10. 1	A3	A9	Sheep	22. 2	26. 1	A3	G1	Rat
7. 2	11. 1	A3	B10	Deer	23. 2	27. 1	A3	H2	Swallow
8. 2	12. 1	A3	C11	Horse	24. 2	28. 1	A3	J3	Pig
9. 2	13. 1	A3	D12	Stag	25. 2	29. 1	A3	K4	Porcupine
10. 2	14. 1	A3	E1	Serpent	26. 2	30. 1	A3	A5	Wolf
11. 2	15. 1	A3	F2	Earthworm	27. 2	1. 2	B4	B6	Dog
12. 2	16. 1	A3	G3	Crocodile	28. 2	2. 2	B4	C7	Pheasant

Solar date	Lunar date	Month HS/EB	Day HS/EB	Constellation
1. 3	3. 2	B4	D8	Cock
2. 3	4. 2	B4	E9	Crow
3. 3	5. 2	B4	F10	Monkey
4. 3	6. 2	B4	G11	Gibbon
5. 3	7. 2	B4	H12	Tapir
6. 3	8. 2	B4	J1	Sheep
7. 3	9. 2	B4	K2	Deer
8. 3	10. 2	B4	A3	Horse
9. 3	11. 2	B4	B4	Stag
10. 3	12. 2	B4	C5	Serpent
11. 3	13. 2	B4	D6	Earthworm
12. 3	14. 2	B4	E7	Crocodile
13. 3	15. 2	B4	F8	Dragon
14. 3	16. 2	B4	G9	Badger
15. 3	17. 2	B4	H10	Hare
16. 3	18. 2	B4	J11	Fox
17. 3	19. 2	B4	K12	Tiger
18. 3	20. 2	B4	A1	Leopard
19. 3	21. 2	B4	B2	Griffon
20. 3	22. 2	B4	C3	Ox
21. 3	23. 2	B4	D4	Bat
22. 3	24. 2	B4	E5	Rat
23. 3	25. 2	B4	F6	Swallow
24. 3	26. 2	B4	G7	Pig
25. 3	27. 2	B4	H8	Porcupine
26. 3	28. 2	B4	J9	Wolf
27. 3	29. 2	B4	K10	Dog
28. 3	1. 3	C5	A11	Pheasant
29. 3	2. 3	C5	B12	Cock
30. 3	3. 3	C5	C1	Crow
31. 3	4. 3	C5	D2	Monkey
1. 4	5. 3	C5	E3	Gibbon
2. 4	6. 3	C5	F4	Tapir
3. 4	7. 3	C5	G5	Sheep
4. 4	8. 3	C5	H6	Deer
5. 4	9. 3	C5	J7	Horse
6. 4	10. 3	C5	K8	Stag
7. 4	11. 3	C5	A9	Serpent
8. 4	12. 3	C5	B10	Earthworm
9. 4	13. 3	C5	C11	Crocodile
10. 4	14. 3	C5	D12	Dragon
11. 4	15. 3	C5	E1	Badger
12. 4	16. 3	C5	F2	Hare
13. 4	17. 3	C5	G3	Fox
14. 4	18. 3	C5	H4	Tiger
15. 4	19. 3	C5	J5	Leopard
16. 4	20. 3	C5	K6	Griffon
17. 4	21. 3	C5	A7	Ox
18. 4	22. 3	C5	B8	Bat
19. 4	23. 3	C5	C9	Rat
20. 4	24. 3	C5	D10	Swallow
21. 4	25. 3	C5	E11	Pig
22. 4	26. 3	C5	F12	Porcupine
23. 4	27. 3	C5	G1	Wolf
24. 4	28. 3	C5	H2	Dog
25. 4	29. 3	C5	J3	Pheasant
26. 4	1. 4	D6	K4	Cock
27. 4	2. 4	D6	A5	Crow
28. 4	3. 4	D6	B6	Monkey
29. 4	4. 4	D6	C7	Gibbon
30. 4	5. 4	D6	D8	Tapir
1. 5	6. 4	D6	E9	Sheep
2. 5	7. 4	D6	F10	Deer
3. 5	8. 4	D6	G11	Horse
4. 5	9. 4	D6	H12	Stag
5. 5	10. 4	D6	J1	Serpent
6. 5	11. 4	D6	K2	Earthworm
7. 5	12. 4	D6	A3	Crocodile
8. 5	13. 4	D6	B4	Dragon
9. 5	14. 4	D6	C5	Badger
10. 5	15. 4	D6	D6	Hare
11. 5	16. 4	D6	E7	Fox
12. 5	17. 4	D6	F8	Tiger
13. 5	18. 4	D6	G9	Leopard
14. 5	19. 4	D6	H10	Griffon
15. 5	20. 4	D6	J11	Ox
16. 5	21. 4	D6	K12	Bat
17. 5	22. 4	D6	A1	Rat
18. 5	23. 4	D6	B2	Swallow
19. 5	24. 4	D6	C3	Pig
20. 5	25. 4	D6	D4	Porcupine
21. 5	26. 4	D6	E5	Wolf
22. 5	27. 4	D6	F6	Dog
23. 5	28. 4	D6	G7	Pheasant
24. 5	29. 4	D6	H8	Cock
25. 5	30. 4	D6	J9	Crow
26. 5	1. 5	E7	K10	Monkey
27. 5	2. 5	E7	A11	Gibbon
28. 5	3. 5	E7	B12	Tapir
29. 5	4. 5	E7	C1	Sheep
30. 5	5. 5	E7	D2	Deer
31. 5	6. 5	E7	E3	Horse
1. 6	7. 5	E7	F4	Stag
2. 6	8. 5	E7	G5	Serpent
3. 6	9. 5	E7	H6	Earthworm
4. 6	10. 5	E7	J7	Crocodile
5. 6	11. 5	E7	K8	Dragon
6. 6	12. 5	E7	A9	Badger
7. 6	13. 5	E7	B10	Hare
8. 6	14. 5	E7	C11	Fox
9. 6	15. 5	E7	D12	Tiger
10. 6	16. 5	E7	E1	Leopard
11. 6	17. 5	E7	F2	Griffon
12. 6	18. 5	E7	G3	Ox
13. 6	19. 5	E7	H4	Bat
14. 6	20. 5	E7	J5	Rat
15. 6	21. 5	E7	K6	Swallow
16. 6	22. 5	E7	A7	Pig
17. 6	23. 5	E7	B8	Porcupine
18. 6	24. 5	E7	C9	Wolf
19. 6	25. 5	E7	D10	Dog
20. 6	26. 5	E7	E11	Pheasant
21. 6	27. 5	E7	F12	Cock
22. 6	28. 5	E7	G1	Crow
23. 6	29. 5	E7	H2	Monkey
24. 6	*1. 5*	*E7*	J3	Gibbon
25. 6	*2. 5*	*E7*	K4	Tapir
26. 6	*3. 5*	*E7*	A5	Sheep
27. 6	*4. 5*	*E7*	B6	Deer
28. 6	*5. 5*	*E7*	C7	Horse
29. 6	*6. 5*	*E7*	D8	Stag
30. 6	*7. 5*	*E7*	E9	Serpent
1. 7	*8. 5*	*E7*	F10	Earthworm
2. 7	*9. 5*	*E7*	G11	Crocodile
3. 7	*10. 5*	*E7*	H12	Dragon
4. 7	*11. 5*	*E7*	J1	Badger
5. 7	*12. 5*	*E7*	K2	Hare
6. 7	*13. 5*	*E7*	A3	Fox
7. 7	*14. 5*	*E7*	B4	Tiger
8. 7	*15. 5*	*E7*	C5	Leopard
9. 7	*16. 5*	*E7*	D6	Griffon
10. 7	*17. 5*	*E7*	E7	Ox
11. 7	*18. 5*	*E7*	F8	Bat
12. 7	*19. 5*	*E7*	G9	Rat
13. 7	*20. 5*	*E7*	H10	Swallow
14. 7	*21. 5*	*E7*	J11	Pig
15. 7	*22. 5*	*E7*	K12	Porcupine
16. 7	*23. 5*	*E7*	A1	Wolf
17. 7	*24. 5*	*E7*	B2	Dog
18. 7	*25. 5*	*E7*	C3	Pheasant
19. 7	*26. 5*	*E7*	D4	Cock
20. 7	*27. 5*	*E7*	E5	Crow
21. 7	*28. 5*	*E7*	F6	Monkey
22. 7	*29. 5*	*E7*	G7	Gibbon
23. 7	1. 6	F8	H8	Tapir
24. 7	2. 6	F8	J9	Sheep

Solar date	Lunar date	Month HS/EB	Day HS/EB	Constellation	Solar date	Lunar date	Month HS/EB	Day HS/EB	Constellation
25. 7	3. 6	F8	K10	Deer	6.10	16. 8	H10	C11	Pig
26. 7	4. 6	F8	A11	Horse	7.10	17. 8	H10	D12	Porcupine
27. 7	5. 6	F8	B12	STag	8.10	18. 8	H10	E1	Wolf
28. 7	6. 6	F8	C1	Serpent	9.10	19. 8	H10	F2	Dog
29. 7	7. 6	F8	D2	Earthworm	10.10	20. 8	H10	G3	Pheasant
30. 7	8. 6	F8	E3	Crocodile	11.10	21. 8	H10	H4	Cock
31. 7	9. 6	F8	F4	Dragon	12.10	22. 8	H10	J5	Crow
1. 8	10. 6	F8	G5	Badger	13.10	23. 8	H10	K6	Monkey
2. 8	11. 6	F8	H6	Hare	14.10	24. 8	H10	A7	Gibbon
3. 8	12. 6	F8	J7	Fox	15.10	25. 8	H10	B8	Tapir
4. 8	13. 6	F8	K8	Tiger	16.10	26. 8	H10	C9	Sheep
5. 8	14. 6	F8	A9	Leopard	17.10	27. 8	H10	D10	Deer
6. 8	15. 6	F8	B10	Griffon	18.10	28. 8	H10	E11	Horse
7. 8	16. 6	F8	C11	Ox	19.10	29. 8	H10	F12	Stag
8. 8	17. 6	F8	D12	Bat	20.10	1. 9	J11	G1	Serpent
9. 8	18. 6	F8	E1	Rat	21.10	2. 9	J11	H2	Earthworm
10. 8	19. 6	F8	F2	Swallow	22.10	3. 9	J11	J3	Crocodile
11. 8	20. 6	F8	G3	Pig	23.10	4. 9	J11	K4	Dragon
12. 8	21. 6	F8	H4	Porcupine	24.10	5. 9	J11	A5	Badger
13. 8	22. 6	F8	J5	Wolf	25.10	6. 9	J11	B6	Hare
14. 8	23. 6	F8	K6	Dog	26.10	7. 9	J11	C7	Fox
15. 8	24. 6	F8	A7	Pheasant	27.10	8. 9	J11	D8	Tiger
16. 8	25. 6	F8	B8	Cock	28.10	9. 9	J11	E9	Leopard
17. 8	26. 6	F8	C9	Crow	29.10	10. 9	J11	F10	Griffon
18. 8	27. 6	F8	D10	Monkey	30.10	11. 9	J11	G11	Ox
19. 8	28. 6	F8	E11	Gibbon	31.10	12. 9	J11	H12	Bat
20. 8	29. 6	F8	F12	Tapir	1.11	13. 9	J11	J1	Rat
21. 8	30. 6	F8	G1	Sheep	2.11	14. 9	J11	K2	Swallow
22. 8	1. 7	G9	H2	Deer	3.11	15. 9	J11	A3	Pig
23. 8	2. 7	G9	J3	Horse	4.11	16. 9	J11	B4	Porcupine
24. 8	3. 7	G9	K4	Stag	5.11	17. 9	J11	C5	Wolf
25. 8	4. 7	G9	A5	Serpent	6.11	18. 9	J11	D6	Dog
26. 8	5. 7	G9	B6	Earthworm	7.11	19. 9	J11	E7	Pheasant
27. 8	6. 7	G9	C7	Crocodile	8.11	20. 9	J11	F8	Cock
28. 8	7. 7	G9	D8	Dragon	9.11	21. 9	J11	G9	Crow
29. 8	8. 7	G9	E9	Badger	10.11	22. 9	J11	H10	Monkey
30. 8	9. 7	G9	F10	Hare	11.11	23. 9	J11	J11	Gibbon
31. 8	10. 7	G9	G11	Fox	12.11	24. 9	J11	K12	Tapir
1. 9	11. 7	G9	H12	Tiger	13.11	25. 9	J11	A1	Sheep
2. 9	12. 7	G9	J1	Leopard	14.11	26. 9	J11	B2	Deer
3. 9	13. 7	G9	K2	Griffon	15.11	27. 9	J11	C3	Horse
4. 9	14. 7	G9	A3	Ox	16.11	28. 9	J11	D4	Stag
5. 9	15. 7	G9	B4	Bat	17.11	29. 9	J11	E5	Serpent
6. 9	16. 7	G9	C5	Rat	18.11	30. 9	J11	F6	Earthworm
7. 9	17. 7	G0	D6	Swallow	19.11	1. 10	K12	G7	Crocodile
8. 9	18. 7	G9	E7	Pig	20.11	2.10	K12	H8	Dragon
9. 9	19. 7	G9	F8	Porcupine	21.11	3.10	K12	J9	Badger
10. 9	20. 7	G9	G9	Wolf	22.11	4.10	K12	K10	Hare
11. 9	21. 7	G9	H10	Dog	23.11	5.10	K12	A11	Fox
12. 9	22. 7	G9	J11	Pheasant	24.11	6.10	K12	B12	Tiger
13. 9	23. 7	G9	K12	Cock	25.11	7.10	K12	C1	Leopard
14. 9	24. 7	G9	A1	Crow	26.11	8.10	K12	D2	Griffon
15. 9	25. 7	G9	B2	Monkey	27.11	9.10	K12	E3	Ox
16. 9	26. 7	G9	C3	Gibbon	28.11	10.10	K12	F4	Bat
17. 9	27. 7	G9	D4	Tapir	29.11	11.10	K12	G5	Rat
18. 9	28. 7	G9	E5	Sheep	30.11	12.10	K12	H6	Swallow
19. 9	29. 7	G9	F6	Deer	1.12	13.10	K12	J7	Pig
20. 9	30. 7	G9	G7	Horse	2.12	14.10	K12	K8	Porcupine
21. 9	1. 8	H10	H8	Stag	3.12	15.10	K12	A9	Wolf
22. 9	2. 8	H10	J9	Serpent	4.12	16.10	K12	B10	Dog
23. 9	3. 8	H10	K10	Earthworm	5.12	17.10	K12	C11	Pheasant
24. 9	4. 8	H10	A11	Crocodile	6.12	18.10	K12	D12	Cock
25. 9	5. 8	H10	B12	Dragon	7.12	19.10	K12	E1	Crow
26. 9	6. 8	H10	C1	Badger	8.12	20.10	K12	F2	Monkey
27. 9	7. 8	H10	D2	Hare	9.12	21.10	K12	G3	Gibbon
28. 9	8. 8	H10	E3	Fox	10.12	22.10	K12	H4	Tapir
29. 9	9. 8	H10	F4	Tiger	11.12	23.10	K12	J5	Sheep
30. 9	10. 8	H10	G5	Leopard	12.12	24.10	K12	K6	Deer
1.10	11. 8	H10	H6	Griffon	13.12	25.10	K12	A7	Horse
2.10	12. 8	H10	J7	Ox	14.12	26.10	K12	B8	Stag
3.10	13. 8	H10	K8	Bat	15.12	27.10	K12	C9	Serpent
4.10	14. 8	H10	A9	Rat	16.12	28.10	K12	D10	Earthworm
5.10	15. 8	H10	B10	Swallow	17.12	29.10	K12	E11	Crocodile

Solar date	Lunar date	Month HS/EB	Day HS/EB	Constellation
18.12	30.10	K12	F12	Dragon
19.12	1.11	A1	G1	Badger
20.12	2.11	A1	H2	Hare
21.12	3.11	A1	J3	Fox
22.12	4.11	A1	K4	Tiger
23.12	5.11	A1	A5	Leopard
24.12	6.11	A1	B6	Griffon
25.12	7.11	A1	C7	Ox
26.12	8.11	A1	D8	Bat
27.12	9.11	A1	E9	Rat
28.12	10.11	A1	F10	Swallow
29.12	11.11	A1	G11	Pig
30.12	12.11	A1	H12	Porcupine
31.12	13.11	A1	J1	Wolf
1999				
1. 1	14.11	A1	K2	Dog
2. 1	15.11	A1	A3	Pheasant
3. 1	16.11	A1	B4	Cock
4. 1	17.11	A1	C5	Crow
5. 1	18.11	A1	D6	Monkey
6. 1	19.11	A1	E7	Gibbon
7. 1	20.11	A1	F8	Tapir
8. 1	21.11	A1	G9	Sheep
9. 1	22.11	A1	H10	Deer
10. 1	23.11	A1	J11	Horse
11. 1	24.11	A1	K12	Stag
12. 1	25.11	A1	A1	Serpent
13. 1	26.11	A1	B2	Earthworm
14. 1	27.11	A1	C3	Crocodile
15. 1	28.11	A1	D4	Dragon
16. 1	29.11	A1	E5	Badger
17. 1	1.12	B2	F6	Hare
18. 1	2.12	B2	G7	Fox
19. 1	3.12	B2	H8	Tiger
20. 1	4.12	B2	J9	Leopard
21. 1	5.12	B2	K10	Griffon
22. 1	6.12	B2	A11	Ox
23. 1	7.12	B2	B12	Bat
24. 1	8.12	B2	C1	Rat
25. 1	9.12	B2	D2	Swallow
26. 1	10.12	B2	E3	Pig
27. 1	11.12	B2	F4	Porcupine
28. 1	12.12	B2	G5	Wolf
29. 1	13.12	B2	H6	Dog
30. 1	14.12	B2	J7	Pheasant
31. 1	15.12	B2	K8	Cock
1. 2	16.12	B2	A9	Crow
2. 2	17.12	B2	B10	Monkey
3. 2	18.12	B2	C11	Gibbon
4. 2	19.12	B2	D12	Tapir
5. 2	20.12	B2	E1	Sheep
6. 2	21.12	B2	F2	Deer
7. 2	22.12	B2	G3	Horse
8. 2	23.12	B2	H4	Stag
9. 2	24.12	B2	J5	Serpent
10. 2	25.12	B2	K6	Earthworm
11. 2	26.12	B2	A7	Crocodile
12. 2	27.12	B2	B8	Dragon
13. 2	28.12	B2	C9	Badger
14. 2	29.12	B2	D10	Hare
15. 2	30.12	B2	E11	Fox

CHI MAO YEAR

Solar date	Lunar date	Month HS/EB	Day HS/EB	Constellation
16. 2	1. 1	C3	F12	Tiger
17. 2	2. 1	C3	G1	Leopard
18. 2	3. 1	C3	H2	Griffon
19. 2	4. 1	C3	J3	Ox
20. 2	5. 1	C3	K4	Bat
21. 2	6. 1	C3	A5	Rat
22. 2	7. 1	C3	B6	Swallow
23. 2	8. 1	C3	C7	Pig
24. 2	9. 1	C3	D8	Porcupine
25. 2	10. 1	C3	E9	Wolf
26. 2	11. 1	C3	F10	Dog
27. 2	12. 1	C3	G11	Pheasant
28. 2	13. 1	C3	H12	Cock
1. 3	14. 1	C3	J1	Crow
2. 3	15. 1	C3	K2	Monkey
3. 3	16. 1	C3	A3	Gibbon
4. 3	17. 1	C3	B4	Tapir
5. 3	18. 1	C3	C5	Sheep
6. 3	19. 1	C3	D6	Deer
7. 3	20. 1	C3	E7	Horse
8. 3	21. 1	C3	F8	Stag
9. 3	22. 1	C3	G9	Serpent
10. 3	23. 1	C3	H10	Earthworm
11. 3	24. 1	C3	J11	Crocodile
12. 3	25. 1	C3	K12	Dragon
13. 3	26. 1	C3	A1	Badger
14. 3	27. 1	C3	B2	Hare
15. 3	28. 1	C3	C3	Fox
16. 3	29. 1	C3	D4	Tiger
17. 3	30. 1	C3	E5	Leopard
18. 3	1. 2	D4	F6	Griffon
19. 3	2. 2	D4	G7	Ox
20. 3	3. 2	D4	H8	Bat
21. 3	4. 2	D4	J9	Rat
22. 3	5. 2	D4	K10	Swallow
23. 3	6. 2	D4	A11	Pig
24. 3	7. 2	D4	B12	Porcupine
25. 3	8. 2	D4	C1	Wolf
26. 3	9. 2	D4	D2	Dog
27. 3	10. 2	D4	E3	Pheasant
28. 3	11. 2	D4	F4	Cock
29. 3	12. 2	D4	G5	Crow
30. 3	13. 2	D4	H6	Monkey
31. 3	14. 2	D4	J7	Gibbon
1. 4	15. 2	D4	K8	Tapir
2. 4	16. 2	D4	A9	Sheep
3. 4	17. 2	D4	B10	Deer
4. 4	18. 2	D4	C11	Horse
5. 4	19. 2	D4	D12	Stag
6. 4	20. 2	D4	E1	Serpent
7. 4	21. 2	D4	F2	Earthworm
8. 4	22. 2	D4	G3	Crocodile
9. 4	23. 2	D4	H4	Dragon
10. 4	24. 2	D4	J5	Badger
11. 4	25. 2	D4	K6	Hare
12. 4	26. 2	D4	A7	Fox
13. 4	27. 2	D4	B8	Tiger
14. 4	28. 2	D4	C9	Leopard
15. 4	29. 2	D4	D10	Griffon
16. 4	1. 3	E5	E11	Ox
17. 4	2. 3	E5	F12	Bat
18. 4	3. 3	E5	G1	Rat
19. 4	4. 3	E5	H2	Swallow
20. 4	5. 3	E5	J3	Pig
21. 4	6. 3	E5	K4	Porcupine
22. 4	7. 3	E5	A5	Wolf
23. 4	8. 3	E5	B6	Dog
24. 4	9. 3	E5	C7	Pheasant
25. 4	10. 3	E5	D8	Cock
26. 4	11. 3	E5	E9	Crow
27. 4	12. 3	E5	F10	Monkey
28. 4	13. 3	E5	G11	Gibbon
29. 4	14. 3	E5	H12	Tapir
30. 4	15. 3	E5	J1	Sheep

Solar date	Lunar date	Month HS/EB	Day HS/EB	Constellation	Solar date	Lunar date	Month HS/EB	Day HS/EB	Constellation
1. 5	16. 3	E5	K2	Deer	13. 7	1. 6	H8	C3	Pig
2. 5	17. 3	E5	A3	Horse	14. 7	2. 6	H8	D4	Porcupine
3. 5	18. 3	E5	B4	Stag	15. 7	3. 6	H8	E5	Wolf
4. 5	19. 3	E5	C5	Serpent	16. 7	4. 6	H8	F6	Dog
5. 5	20. 3	E5	D6	Earthworm	17. 7	5. 6	H8	G7	Pheasant
6. 5	21. 3	E5	E7	Crocodile	18. 7	6. 6	H8	H8	Cock
7. 5	22. 3	E5	F8	Dragon	19. 7	7. 6	H8	J9	Crow
8. 5	23. 3	E5	G9	Badger	20. 7	8. 6	H8	K10	Monkey
9. 5	24. 3	E5	H10	Hare	21. 7	9. 6	H8	A11	Gibbon
10. 5	25. 3	E5	J11	Fox	22. 7	10. 6	H8	B12	Tapir
11. 5	26. 3	E5	K12	Tiger	23. 7	11. 6	H8	C1	Sheep
12. 5	27. 3	E5	A1	Leopard	24. 7	12. 6	H8	D2	Deer
13. 5	28. 3	E5	B2	Griffon	25. 7	13. 6	H8	E3	Horse
14. 5	29. 3	E5	C3	Ox	26. 7	14. 6	H8	F4	Stag
15. 5	1. 4	F6	D4	Bat	27. 7	15. 6	H8	G5	Serpent
16. 5	2. 4	F6	E5	Rat	28. 7	16. 6	H8	H6	Earthworm
17. 5	3. 4	F6	F6	Swallow	29. 7	17. 6	H8	J7	Crocodile
18. 5	4. 4	F6	G7	Pig	30. 7	18. 6	H8	K8	Dragon
19. 5	5. 4	F6	H8	Porcupine	31. 7	19. 6	H8	A9	Badger
20. 5	6. 4	F6	J9	Wolf	1. 8	20. 6	H8	B10	Hare
21. 5	7. 4	F6	K10	Dog	2. 8	21. 6	H8	C11	Fox
22. 5	8. 4	F6	A11	Pheasant	3. 8	22. 6	H8	D12	Tiger
23. 5	9. 4	F6	B12	Cock	4. 8	23. 6	H8	E1	Leopard
24. 5	10. 4	F6	C1	Crow	5. 8	24. 6	H8	F2	Griffon
25. 5	11. 4	F6	D2	Monkey	6. 8	25. 6	H8	G3	Ox
26. 5	12. 4	F6	E3	Gibbon	7. 8	26. 6	H8	H4	Bat
27. 5	13. 4	F6	F4	Tapir	8. 8	27. 6	H8	J5	Rat
28. 5	14. 4	F6	G5	Sheep	9. 8	28. 6	H8	K6	Swallow
29. 5	15. 4	F6	H6	Deer	10. 8	29. 6	H8	A7	Pig
30. 5	16. 4	F6	J7	Horse	11. 8	1. 7	J9	B8	Porcupine
31. 5	17. 4	F6	K8	Stag	12. 8	2. 7	J9	C9	Wolf
1. 6	18. 4	F6	A9	Serpent	13. 8	3. 7	J9	D10	Dog
2. 6	19. 4	F6	B10	Earthworm	14. 8	4. 7	J9	E11	Pheasant
3. 6	20. 4	F6	C11	Crocodile	15. 8	5. 7	J9	F12	Cock
4. 6	21. 4	F6	D12	Dragon	16. 8	6. 7	J9	G1	Crow
5. 6	22. 4	F6	E1	Badger	17. 8	7. 7	J9	H2	Monkey
6. 6	23. 4	F6	F2	Hare	18. 8	8. 7	J9	J3	Gibbon
7. 6	24. 4	F6	G3	Fox	19. 8	9. 7	J9	K4	Tapir
8. 6	25. 4	F6	H4	Tiger	20. 8	10. 7	J9	A5	Sheep
9. 6	26. 4	F6	J5	Leopard	21. 8	11. 7	J9	B6	Deer
10. 6	27. 4	F6	K6	Griffon	22. 8	12. 7	J9	C7	Horse
11. 6	28. 4	F6	A7	Ox	23. 8	13. 7	J9	D8	Stag
12. 6	29. 4	F6	B8	Bat	24. 8	14. 7	J9	E9	Serpent
13. 6	30. 4	F6	C9	Rat	25. 8	15. 7	J9	F10	Earthworm
14. 6	1. 5	G7	D10	Swallow	26. 8	16. 7	J9	G11	Crocodile
15. 6	2. 5	G7	E11	Pig	27. 8	17. 7	J9	H12	Dragon
16. 6	3. 5	G7	F12	Porcupine	28. 8	18. 7	J9	J1	Badger
17. 6	4. 5	G7	G1	Wolf	29. 8	19. 7	J9	K2	Hare
18. 6	5. 5	G7	H2	Dog	30. 8	20. 7	J9	A3	Fox
19. 6	6. 5	G7	J3	Pheasant	31. 8	21. 7	J9	B4	Tiger
20. 6	7. 5	G7	K4	Cock	1. 9	22. 7	J9	C5	Leopard
21. 6	8. 5	G7	A5	Crow	2. 9	23. 7	J9	D6	Griffon
22. 6	9. 5	G7	B6	Monkey	3. 9	24. 7	J9	E7	Ox
23. 6	10. 5	G7	C7	Gibbon	4. 9	25. 7	J9	F8	Bat
24. 6	11. 5	G7	D8	Tapir	5. 9	26. 7	J9	G9	Rat
25. 6	12. 5	G7	E9	Sheep	6. 9	27. 7	J9	H10	Swallow
26. 6	13. 5	G7	F10	Deer	7. 9	28. 7	J9	J11	Pig
27. 6	14. 5	G7	G11	Horse	8. 9	29. 7	J9	K12	Porcupine
28. 6	15. 5	G7	H12	Stag	9. 9	30. 7	J9	A1	Wolf
29. 6	16. 5	G7	J1	Serpent	10. 9	1. 8	K10	B2	Dog
30. 6	17. 5	G7	K2	Earthworm	11. 9	2. 8	K10	C3	Pheasant
1. 7	18. 5	G7	A3	Crocodile	12. 9	3. 8	K10	D4	Cock
2. 7	19. 5	G7	B4	Dragon	13. 9	4. 8	K10	E5	Crow
3. 7	20. 5	G7	C5	Badger	14. 9	5. 8	K10	F6	Monkey
4. 7	21. 5	G7	D6	Hare	15. 9	6. 8	K10	G7	Gibbon
5. 7	22. 5	G7	E7	Fox	16. 9	7. 8	K10	H8	Tapir
6. 7	23. 5	G7	F8	Tiger	17. 9	8. 8	K10	J9	Sheep
7. 7	24. 5	G7	G9	Leopard	18. 9	9. 8	K10	K10	Deer
8. 7	25. 5	G7	H10	Griffon	19. 9	10. 8	K10	A11	Horse
9. 7	26. 5	G7	J11	Ox	20. 9	11. 8	K10	B12	Stag
10. 7	27. 5	G7	K12	Bat	21. 9	12. 8	K10	C1	Serpent
11. 7	28. 5	G7	A1	Rat	22. 9	13. 8	K10	D2	Earthworm
12. 7	29. 5	G7	B2	Swallow	23. 9	14. 8	K10	E3	Crocodile

Solar date	Lunar date	Month HS/EB	Day HS/EB	Constellation
24. 9	15. 8	K10	F4	Dragon
25. 9	16. 8	K10	G5	Badger
26. 9	17. 8	K10	H6	Hare
27. 9	18. 8	K10	J7	Fox
28. 9	19. 8	K10	K8	Tiger
29. 9	20. 8	K10	A9	Leopard
30. 9	21. 8	K10	B10	Griffon
1.10	22. 8	K10	C11	Ox
2.10	23. 8	K10	D12	Bat
3.10	24. 8	K10	E1	Rat
4.10	25. 8	K10	F2	Swallow
5.10	26. 8	K10	G3	Pig
6.10	27. 8	K10	H4	Porcupine
7.10	28. 8	K10	J5	Wolf
8.10	29. 8	K10	K6	Dog
9.10	1. 9	A11	A7	Pheasant
10.10	2. 9	A11	B8	Cock
11.10	3. 9	A11	C9	Crow
12.10	4. 9	A11	D10	Monkey
13.10	5. 9	A11	E11	Gibbon
14.10	6. 9	A11	F12	Tapir
15.10	7. 9	A11	G1	Sheep
16.10	8. 9	A11	H2	Deer
17.10	9. 9	A11	J3	Horse
18.10	10. 9	A11	K4	Stag
19.10	11. 9	A11	A5	Serpent
20.10	12. 9	A11	B6	Earthworm
21.10	13. 9	A11	C7	Crocodile
22.10	14. 9	A11	D8	Dragon
23.10	15. 9	A11	E9	Badger
24.10	16. 9	A11	F10	Hare
25.10	17. 9	A11	G11	Fox
26.10	18. 9	A11	H12	Tiger
27.10	19. 9	A11	J1	Leopard
28.10	20. 9	A11	K2	Griffon
29.10	21. 9	A11	A3	Ox
30.10	22. 9	A11	B4	Bat
31.10	23. 9	A11	C5	Rat
1.11	24. 9	A11	D6	Swallow
2.11	25. 9	A11	E7	Pig
3.11	26. 9	A11	F8	Porcupine
4.11	27. 9	A11	G9	Wolf
5.11	28. 9	A11	H10	Dog
6.11	29. 9	A11	J11	Pheasant
7.11	30. 9	A11	K12	Cock
8.11	1.10	B12	A1	Crow
9.11	2.10	B12	B2	Monkey
10.11	3.10	B12	C3	Gibbon
11.11	4.10	B12	D4	Tapir
12.11	5.10	B12	E5	Sheep
13.11	6.10	B12	F6	Deer
14.11	7.10	B12	G7	Horse
15.11	8.10	B12	H8	Stag
16.11	9.10	B12	J9	Serpent
17.11	10.10	B12	K10	Earthworm
18.11	11.10	B12	A11	Crocodile
19.11	12.10	B12	B12	Dragon
20.11	13.10	B12	C1	Badger
21.11	14.10	B12	D2	Hare
22.11	15.10	B12	E3	Fox
23.11	16.10	B12	F4	Tiger
24.11	17.10	B12	G5	Leopard
25.11	18.10	B12	H6	Griffon
26.11	19.10	B12	J7	Ox
27.11	20.10	B12	K8	Bat
28.11	21.10	B12	A9	Rat
29.11	22.10	B12	B10	Swallow
30.11	23.10	B12	C11	Pig
1.12	24.10	B12	D12	Porcupine
2.12	25.10	B12	E1	Wolf
3.12	26.10	B12	F2	Dog
4.12	27.10	B12	G3	Pheasant
5.12	28.10	B12	H4	Cock
6.12	29.10	B12	J5	Crow
7.12	30.10	B12	K6	Monkey
8.12	1.11	C1	A7	Gibbon
9.12	2.11	C1	B8	Tapir
10.12	3.11	C1	C9	Sheep
11.12	4.11	C1	E10	Deer
12.12	5.11	C1	E11	Horse
13.12	6.11	C1	F12	Stag
14.12	7.11	C1	G1	Serpent
15.12	8.11	C1	H2	Earthworm
16.12	9.11	C1	J3	Crocodile
17.12	10.11	C1	K4	Dragon
18.12	11.11	C1	A5	Badger
19.12	12.11	C1	B6	Hare
20.12	13.11	C1	C7	Fox
21.12	14.11	C1	D8	Tiger
22.12	15.11	C1	E9	Leopard
23.12	16.11	C1	F10	Griffon
24.12	17.11	C1	G11	Ox
25.12	18.11	C1	H12	Bat
26.12	19.11	C1	J1	Rat
27.12	20.11	C1	K2	Swallow
28.12	21.11	C1	A3	Pig
29.12	22.11	C1	B4	Porcupine
30.12	23.11	C1	C5	Wolf
31.12	24.11	C1	D6	Dog

2000

Solar date	Lunar date	Month HS/EB	Day HS/EB	Constellation
1. 1	25.11	C1	E7	Pheasant
2. 1	26.11	C1	F8	Cock
3. 1	27.11	C1	G9	Crow
4. 1	28.11	C1	H10	Monkey
5. 1	29.11	C1	J11	Gibbon
6. 1	30.11	C1	K12	Tapir
7. 1	1.12	D2	A1	Sheep
8. 1	2.12	D2	B2	Deer
9. 1	3.12	D2	C3	Horse
10. 1	4.12	D2	D4	Stag
11. 1	5.12	D2	E5	Serpent
12. 1	6.12	D2	F6	Earthworm
13. 1	7.12	D2	G7	Crocodile
14. 1	8.12	D2	H8	Dragon
15. 1	9.12	D2	J9	Badger
16. 1	10.12	D2	K10	Hare
17. 1	11.12	D2	A11	Fox
18. 1	12.12	D2	B12	Tiger
19. 1	13.12	D2	C1	Leopard
20. 1	14.12	D2	D2	Griffon
21. 1	15.12	D2	E3	Ox
22. 1	16.12	D2	F4	Bat
23. 1	17.12	D2	G5	Rat
24. 1	18.12	D2	H6	Swallow
25. 1	19.12	D2	J7	Pig
26. 1	20.12	D2	K8	Porcupine
27. 1	21.12	D2	A9	Wolf
28. 1	22.12	D2	B10	Dog
29. 1	23.12	D2	C11	Pheasant
30. 1	24.12	D2	D12	Cock
31. 1	25.12	D2	E1	Crow
1. 2	26.12	D2	F2	Monkey
2. 2	27.12	D2	G3	Gibbon
3. 2	28.12	D2	H4	Tapir
4. 2	29.12	D2	J5	Sheep

KENG CH'EN YEAR

Solar date	Lunar date	Month HS/EB	Day HS/EB	Constellation
5. 2	1. 1	E3	K6	Deer
6. 2	2. 1	E3	A7	Horse
7. 2	3. 1	E3	B8	Stag
8. 2	4. 1	E3	C9	Serpent
9. 2	5. 1	E3	D10	Earthworm
10. 2	6. 1	E3	E11	Crocodile
11. 2	7. 1	E3	F12	Dragon
12. 2	8. 1	E3	G1	Badger
13. 2	9. 1	E3	H2	Hare
14. 2	10. 1	E3	J3	Fox
15. 2	11. 1	E3	K4	Tiger
16. 2	12. 1	E3	A5	Leopard
17. 2	13. 1	E3	B6	Griffon
18. 2	14. 1	E3	C7	Ox
19. 2	15. 1	E3	D8	Bat
20. 2	16. 1	E3	E9	Rat
21. 2	17. 1	E3	F10	Swallow
22. 2	18. 1	E3	G11	Pig
23. 2	19. 1	E3	H12	Porcupine
24. 2	20. 1	E3	J1	Wolf
25. 2	21. 1	E3	K2	Dog
26. 2	22. 1	E3	A3	Pheasant
27. 2	23. 1	E3	B4	Cock
28. 2	24. 1	E3	C5	Crow
29. 2	25. 1	E3	D6	Monkey
1. 3	26. 1	E3	E7	Gibbon
2. 3	27. 1	E3	F8	Tapir
3. 3	28. 1	E3	G9	Sheep
4. 3	29. 1	E3	H10	Deer
5. 3	30. 1	E3	J11	Horse
6. 3	1. 2	F4	K12	Stag
7. 3	2. 2	F4	A1	Serpent
8. 3	3. 2	F4	B2	Earthworm
9. 3	4. 2	F4	C3	Crocodile
10. 3	5. 2	F4	D4	Dragon
11. 3	6. 2	F4	E5	Badger
12. 3	7. 2	F4	F6	Hare
13. 3	8. 2	F4	G7	Fox
14. 3	9. 2	F4	H8	Tiger
15. 3	10. 2	F4	J9	Leopard
16. 3	11. 2	F4	K10	Griffon
17. 3	12. 2	F4	A11	Ox
18. 3	13. 2	F4	B12	Bat
19. 3	14. 2	F4	C1	Rat
20. 3	15. 2	F4	D2	Swallow
21. 3	16. 2	F4	E3	Pig
22. 3	17. 2	F4	F4	Porcupine
23. 3	18. 2	F4	G5	Wolf
24. 3	19. 2	F4	H6	Dog
25. 3	20. 2	F4	J7	Pheasant
26. 3	21. 2	F4	K8	Cock
27. 3	22. 2	F4	A9	Crow
28. 3	23. 2	F4	B10	Monkey
29. 3	24. 2	F4	C11	Gibbon
30. 3	25. 2	F4	D12	Tapir
31. 3	26. 2	F4	E1	Sheep
1. 4	27. 2	F4	F2	Deer
2. 4	28. 2	F4	G3	Horse
3. 4	29. 2	F4	H4	Stag
4. 4	30. 2	F4	J5	Serpent
5. 4	1. 3	G5	K6	Earthworm
6. 4	2. 3	G5	A7	Crocodile
7. 4	3. 3	G5	B8	Dragon
8. 4	4. 3	G5	C9	Badger
9. 4	5. 3	G5	D10	Hare
10. 4	6. 3	G5	E11	Fox
11. 4	7. 3	G5	F12	Tiger
12. 4	8. 3	G5	G1	Leopard
13. 4	9. 3	G5	H2	Griffon
14. 4	10. 3	G5	J3	Ox
15. 4	11. 3	G5	K4	Bat
16. 4	12. 3	G5	A5	Rat
17. 4	13. 3	G5	B6	Swallow
18. 4	14. 3	G5	C7	Pig
19. 4	15. 3	G5	D8	Porcupine
20. 4	16. 3	G5	E9	Wolf
21. 4	17. 3	G5	F10	Dog
22. 4	18. 3	G5	G11	Pheasant
23. 4	19. 3	G5	H12	Cock
24. 4	20. 3	G5	J1	Crow
25. 4	21. 3	G5	K2	Monkey
26. 4	22. 3	G5	A3	Gibbon
27. 4	23. 3	G5	B4	Tapir
28. 4	24. 3	G5	C5	Sheep
29. 4	25. 3	G5	D6	Deer
30. 4	26. 3	G5	E7	Horse
1. 5	27. 3	G5	F8	Stag
2. 5	28. 3	G5	G9	Serpent
3. 5	29. 3	G5	H10	Earthworm
4. 5	1. 4	H6	J11	Crocodile
5. 5	2. 4	H6	K12	Dragon
6. 5	3. 4	H6	A1	Badger
7. 5	4. 4	H6	B2	Hare
8. 5	5. 4	H6	C3	Fox
9. 5	6. 4	H6	D4	Tiger
10. 5	7. 4	H6	E5	Leopard
11. 5	8. 4	H6	F6	Griffon
12. 5	9. 4	H6	G7	Ox
13. 5	10. 4	H6	H8	Bat
14. 5	11. 4	H6	J9	Rat
15. 5	12. 4	H6	K10	Swallow
16. 5	13. 4	H6	A11	Pig
17. 5	14. 4	H6	B12	Porcupine
18. 5	15. 4	H6	C1	Wolf
19. 5	16. 4	H6	D2	Dog
20. 5	17. 4	H6	E3	Pheasant
21. 5	18. 4	H6	F4	Cock
22. 5	19. 4	H6	G5	Crow
23. 5	20. 4	H6	H6	Monkey
24. 5	21. 4	H6	J7	Gibbon
25. 5	22. 4	H6	K8	Tapir
26. 5	23. 4	H6	A9	Sheep
27. 5	24. 4	H6	B10	Deer
28. 5	25. 4	H6	C11	Horse
29. 5	26. 4	H6	D12	Stag
30. 5	27. 4	H6	E1	Serpent
31. 5	28. 4	H6	F2	Earthworm
1. 6	29. 4	H6	G3	Crocodile
2. 6	1. 5	J7	H4	Dragon
3. 6	2. 5	J7	J5	Badger
4. 6	3. 5	J7	K6	Hare
5. 6	4. 5	J7	A7	Fox
6. 6	5. 5	J7	B8	Tiger
7. 6	6. 5	J7	C9	Leopard
8. 6	7. 5	J7	D10	Griffon
9. 6	8. 5	J7	E11	Ox
10. 6	9. 5	J7	F12	Bat
11. 6	10. 5	J7	G1	Rat
12. 6	11. 5	J7	H2	Swallow
13. 6	12. 5	J7	J3	Pig
14. 6	13. 5	J7	K4	Porcupine
15. 6	14. 5	J7	A5	Wolf
16. 6	15. 5	J7	B6	Dog
17. 6	16. 5	J7	C7	Pheasant
18. 6	17. 5	J7	D8	Cock
19. 6	18. 5	J7	E9	Crow
20. 6	19. 5	J7	F10	Monkey
21. 6	20. 5	J7	G11	Gibbon
22. 6	21. 5	J7	H12	Tapir
23. 6	22. 5	J7	J1	Sheep
24. 6	23. 5	J7	K2	Deer
25. 6	24. 5	J7	A3	Horse

Solar date	Lunar date	Month HS/EB	Day HS/EB	Constellation	Solar date	Lunar date	Month HS/EB	Day HS/EB	Constellation
26. 6	25. 5	J7	B4	Stag	7. 9	10. 8	B10	E5	Wolf
27. 6	26. 5	J7	C5	Serpent	8. 9	11. 8	B10	F6	Dog
28. 6	27. 5	J7	D6	Earthworm	9. 9	12. 8	B10	G7	Pheasant
29. 6	28. 5	J7	E7	Crocodile	10. 9	13. 8	B10	H8	Cock
30. 6	29. 5	J7	F8	Dragon	11. 9	14. 8	B10	J9	Crow
1. 7	30. 5	J7	G9	Badger	12. 9	15. 8	B10	K10	Monkey
2. 7	1. 6	K8	H10	Hare	13. 9	16. 8	B10	A11	Gibbon
3. 7	2. 6	K8	J11	Fox	14. 9	17. 8	B10	B12	Tapir
4. 7	3. 6	K8	K12	Tiger	15. 9	18. 8	B10	C1	Sheep
5. 7	4. 6	K8	A1	Leopard	16. 9	19. 8	B10	D2	Deer
6. 7	5. 6	K8	B2	Griffon	17. 9	20. 8	B10	E3	Horse
7. 7	6. 6	K8	C3	Ox	18. 9	21. 8	B10	F4	Stag
8. 7	7. 6	K8	D4	Bat	19. 9	22. 8	B10	G5	Serpent
9. 7	8. 6	K8	E5	Rat	20. 9	23. 8	B10	H6	Earthworm
10. 7	9. 6	K8	F6	Swallow	21. 9	24. 8	B10	J7	Crocodile
11. 7	10. 6	K8	G7	Pig	22. 9	25. 8	B10	K8	Dragon
12. 7	11. 6	K8	H8	Porcupine	23. 9	26. 8	B10	A9	Badger
13. 7	12. 6	K8	J9	Wolf	24. 9	27. 8	B10	B10	Hare
14. 7	13. 6	K8	K10	Dog	25. 9	28. 8	B10	C11	Fox
15. 7	14. 6	K8	A11	Pheasant	26. 9	29. 8	B10	D12	Tiger
16. 7	15. 6	K8	B12	Cock	27. 9	30. 8	B10	E1	Leopard
17. 7	16. 6	K8	C1	Crow	28. 9	1. 9	C11	F2	Griffon
18. 7	17. 6	K8	D2	Monkey	29. 9	2. 9	C11	G3	Ox
19. 7	18. 6	K8	E3	Gibbon	30. 9	3. 9	C11	H4	Bat
20. 7	19. 6	K8	F4	Tapir	1.10	4. 9	C11	J5	Rat
21. 7	20. 6	K8	G5	Sheep	2.10	5. 9	C11	K6	Swallow
22. 7	21. 6	K8	H6	Deer	3.10	6. 9	C11	A7	Pig
23. 7	22. 6	K8	J7	Horse	4.10	7. 9	C11	B8	Porcupine
24. 7	23. 6	K8	K8	Stag	5.10	8. 9	C11	C9	Wolf
25. 7	24. 6	K8	A9	Serpent	6.10	9. 9	C11	D10	Dog
26. 7	25. 6	K8	B10	Earthworm	7.10	10. 9	C11	E11	Pheasant
27. 7	26. 6	K8	C11	Crocodile	8.10	11. 9	C11	F12	Cock
28. 7	27. 6	K8	D12	Dragon	9.10	12. 9	C11	G1	Crow
29. 7	28. 6	K8	E1	Badger	10.10	13. 9	C11	H2	Monkey
30. 7	29. 6	K8	F2	Hare	11.10	14. 9	C11	J3	Gibbon
31. 7	1. 7	A9	G3	Fox	12.10	15. 9	C11	K4	Tapir
1. 8	2. 7	A9	H4	Tiger	13.10	16. 9	C11	A5	Sheep
2. 8	3. 7	A9	J5	Leopard	14.10	17. 9	C11	B6	Deer
3. 8	4. 7	A9	K6	Griffon	15.10	18. 9	C11	C7	Horse
4. 8	5. 7	A9	A7	Ox	16.10	19. 9	C11	D8	Stag
5. 8	6. 7	A9	B8	Bat	17.10	20. 9	C11	E9	Serpent
6. 8	7. 7	A9	C9	Rat	18.10	21. 9	C11	F10	Earthworm
7. 8	8. 7	A9	D10	Swallow	19.10	22. 9	C11	G11	Crocodile
8. 8	9. 7	A9	E11	Pig	20.10	23. 9	C11	H12	Dragon
9. 8	10. 7	A9	F12	Porcupine	21.10	24. 9	C11	J1	Badger
10. 8	11. 7	A9	G1	Wolf	22.10	25. 9	C11	K2	Hare
11. 8	12. 7	A9	H2	Dog	23.10	26. 9	C11	A3	Fox
12. 8	13. 7	A9	J3	Pheasant	24.10	27. 9	C11	B4	Tiger
13. 8	14. 7	A9	K4	Cock	25.10	28. 9	C11	C5	Leopard
14. 8	15. 7	A9	A5	Crow	26.10	29. 9	C11	D6	Griffon
15. 8	16. 7	A9	B6	Monkey	27.10	1.10	D12	E7	Ox
16. 8	17. 7	A9	C7	Gibbon	28.10	2.10	D12	F8	Bat
17. 8	18. 7	A9	D8	Tapir	29.10	3.10	D12	G9	Rat
18. 8	19. 7	A9	E9	Sheep	30.10	4.10	D12	H10	Swallow
19. 8	20. 7	A9	F10	Deer	31.10	5.10	D12	J11	Pig
20. 8	21. 7	A9	G11	Horse	1.11	6.10	D12	K12	Porcupine
21. 8	22. 7	A9	H12	Stag	2.11	7.10	D12	A1	Wolf
22. 8	23. 7	A9	J1	Serpent	3.11	8.10	D12	B2	Dog
23. 8	24. 7	A9	K2	Earthworm	4.11	9.10	D12	C3	Pheasant
24. 8	25. 7	A9	A3	Crocodile	5.11	10.10	D12	D4	Cock
25. 8	26. 7	A9	B4	Dragon	6.11	11.10	D12	E5	Crow
26. 8	27. 7	A9	C5	Badger	7.11	12.10	D12	F6	Monkey
27. 8	28. 7	A9	D6	Hare	8.11	13.10	D12	G7	Gibbon
28. 8	29. 7	A9	E7	Fox	9.11	14.10	D12	H8	Tapir
29. 8	1. 8	B10	F8	Tiger	10.11	15.10	D12	J9	Sheep
30. 8	2. 8	B10	G9	Leopard	11.11	16.10	D12	K10	Deer
31. 8	3. 8	B10	H10	Griffon	12.11	17.10	D12	A11	Horse
1. 9	4. 8	B10	J11	Ox	13.11	18.10	D12	B12	Stag
2. 9	5. 8	B10	K12	Bat	14.11	19.10	D12	C1	Serpent
3. 9	6. 8	B10	A1	Rat	15.11	20.10	D12	D2	Earthworm
4. 9	7. 8	B10	B2	Swallow	16.11	21.10	D12	E3	Crocodile
5. 9	8. 8	B10	C3	Pig	17.11	22.10	D12	F4	Dragon
6. 9	9. 8	B10	D4	Porcupine	18.11	23.10	D12	G5	Badger

Solar date	Lunar date	Month HS/EB	Day HS/EB	Constellation		Solar date	Lunar date	Month HS/EB	Day HS/EB	Constellation
19.11	24.10	D12	H6	Hare		23.12	28.11	E1	B4	Bat
20.11	25.10	D12	J7	Fox		24.12	29.11	E1	C5	Rat
21.11	26.10	D12	K8	Tiger		25.12	30.11	E1	D6	Swallow
22.11	27.10	D12	A9	Leopard		26.12	1.12	F2	E7	Pig
23.11	28.10	D12	B10	Griffon		27.12	2.12	F2	F8	Porcupine
24.11	29.10	D12	C11	Ox		28.12	3.12	F2	G9	Wolf
25.11	30.10	D12	D12	Bat		29.12	4.12	F2	H10	Dog
26.11	1.11	E1	E1	Rat		30.12	5.12	F2	J11	Pheasant
27.11	2.11	E1	F2	Swallow		31.12	6.12	F2	K12	Cock
28.11	3.11	E1	G3	Pig						
29.11	4.11	E1	H4	Porcupine		**2001**				
30.11	5.11	E1	J5	Wolf		1. 1	7.12	F2	A1	Crow
1.12	6.11	E1	K6	Dog		2. 1	8.12	F2	B2	Monkey
2.12	7.11	E1	A7	Pheasant		3. 1	9.12	F2	C3	Gibbon
3.12	8.11	E1	B8	Cock		4. 1	10.12	F2	D4	Tapir
4.12	9.11	E1	C9	Crow		5. 1	11.12	F2	E5	Sheep
5.12	10.11	E1	D10	Monkey		6. 1	12.12	F2	F6	Deer
6.12	11.11	E1	E11	Gibbon		7. 1	13.12	F2	G7	Horse
7.12	12.11	E1	F12	Tapir		8. 1	14.12	F2	H8	Stag
8.12	13.11	E1	G1	Sheep		9. 1	15.12	F2	J9	Serpent
9.12	14.11	E1	H2	Deer		10. 1	16.12	F2	K10	Earthworm
10.12	15.11	E1	J3	Horse		11. 1	17.12	F2	A11	Crocodile
11.12	16.11	E1	K4	Stag		12. 1	18.12	F2	B12	Dragon
12.12	17.11	E1	A5	Serpent		13. 1	19.12	F2	C1	Badger
13.12	18.11	E1	B6	Earthworm		14. 1	20.12	F2	D2	Hare
14.12	19.11	E1	C7	Crocodile		15. 1	21.12	F2	E3	Fox
15.12	20.11	E1	D8	Dragon		16. 1	22.12	F2	F4	Tiger
16.12	21.11	E1	E9	Badger		17. 1	23.12	F2	G5	Leopard
17.12	22.11	E1	F10	Hare		18. 1	24.12	F2	H6	Griffon
18.12	23.11	E1	G11	Fox		19. 1	25.12	F2	J7	Ox
19.12	24.11	E1	H12	Tiger		20. 1	26.12	F2	K8	Bat
20.12	25.11	E1	J1	Leopard		21. 1	27.12	F2	A9	Rat
21.12	26.11	E1	K2	Griffon		22. 1	28.12	F2	B10	Swallow
22.12	27.11	E1	A3	Ox		23. 1	29.12	F2	C11	Pig